Aruba Certified Switching Professional (ACSP)
OFFICIAL CERTIFICATION STUDY GUIDE
(EXAM HPE6-A73)

First Edition

Richard Deal and Peter Debruyne

HPE Press
660 4th Street, #802
San Francisco, CA 94107

Aruba Certified Switching Professional (ACSP)
Official Certification Study Guide (Exam HPE6-A73)
Richard Deal and Peter Debruyne

Published by:

Hewlett Packard Enterprise Press
660 4th Street, #802
San Francisco, CA 94107

ISBN: **978-1-7346275-8-9**

Printed in Mexico

WARNING AND DISCLAIMER

This book provides information about the topics covered in the Aruba Certified Switching Professional (ACSP) certification exam (HPE6-A73). Every effort has been made to make this book as complete and as accurate as possible, but no warranty or fitness is implied.

The information is provided on an "as is" basis. The author, and Hewlett Packard Enterprise Press, shall have neither liability nor responsibility to any person or entity with respect to any loss or damages arising from the information contained in this book or from the use of the discs or programs that may accompany it.

The opinions expressed in this book belong to the author and are not necessarily those of Hewlett Packard Enterprise Press.

FEEDBACK INFORMATION

At HPE Press, our goal is to create in-depth reference books of the best quality and value. Each book is crafted with care and precision, undergoing rigorous development that involves the expertise of members from the professional technical community.

Readers' feedback is a continuation of the process. If you have any comments regarding how we could improve the quality of this book, or otherwise alter it to better suit your needs, you can contact us through email at hpepress@epac.com. Please make sure to include the book title and ISBN in your message.

We appreciate your feedback.

Publisher: Hewlett Packard Enterprise Press

HPE Press Program Manager: Michael Bishop

About the Authors

Richard Deal is an independent consultant who designs wireless and wired networks and provides network management services for small companies. He has created and developed many networking courses and instructs IT professionals on the best ways to design and implement Aruba's wired and wireless network solutions. Richard has authored countless books on various networking topics.

Peter Debruyne was co-developer of the Implementing ArubaOS-CX Switching course. He is an Aruba Certified Edge Expert (ACCX, ACMX, and ACDX) and ACSP certified. Peter is an Aruba Certified Instructor and resides in Belgium.

Introduction

This book guides you through Aruba wired network solutions involving ArubaOS-CX switching products and features and helps you prepare for the Aruba Certified Switching Professional exam (HPE6-A73). You will learn the following:

- Implementing ArubaOS-CX switches, redundancy technologies, NetEdit switch management, link aggregation techniques, network analytics, and switch virtualization with HPE's Virtual Switching Extension (VSX)
- Configuring dynamic routing with Open Shortest Path First (OSPF), Border Gateway Protocol (BGP), Virtual Routing Forwarding (VRF), and policy-based routing (PBR)
- Implementing IP multicast routing involving IGMP and PIM
- Optimizing networks by incorporating Quality of Service (QoS) priorities and device groups
- Protecting the network using access control lists (ACLs) and traffic classifier policies
- Securing access with 802.1X, MAC authentication, captive portal, dynamic segmentation with user-based tunneling (UBT), and local and downloadable user roles

Aruba Education Services

Aruba Education Services offers comprehensive training and certification programs from fundamental to advanced levels across the Aruba product line.

To learn more about Aruba certifications and training, please visit: https://www.arubanetworks.com/support-services/training-services/

Audience

This book is designed for individuals wanting to continue their journey in understanding the various Aruba products and using best practice design guidelines to implement campus wired solutions involving ArubaOS-CX switches and CX features. The audience includes network technicians, network engineers, network architects, and network presales individuals.

Assumed Knowledge

This is an intermediate-level guide that will leverage ArubaOS-CX switches and features to implement a campus-sized wired solution. It is assumed that you have a knowledge of basic switching technologies that is covered in the Configuring ArubaOS-CX Fundamentals (CXF) course.

Minimum Qualifications

Typical candidates for this certification are IT associates who want to learn about the ArubaOS-CX switching products and the features and protocols used to help implement a campus-switched network. It is assumed that you have the equivalent networking and switching knowledge covered in the Configuring ArubaOS-CX Fundamentals (CXF) course.

Relevant Certifications

The Aruba Certified Switching Professional (ACSP) certification validates that you have the intermediate knowledge and skills required to implement Aruba campus wired solutions involving ArubaOS-CX switches, CX switching features, and various standards-based protocols.

Preparing for Exam HPE6-A73

This self-study guide does not guarantee that you will have all the knowledge you need to pass the exam. It is expected that you will also draw on real-world experience and would benefit from completing the hands-on lab activities provided in the instructor-led training. However, the labs taught in the official course are provided for you here in this book assuming you have the correct hardware and software to perform the labs. This book covers the same material as the actual course. Therefore, to pass the certification exam, you should be intimately familiar with the material presented here. Aruba recommends reading the book and performing the labs three times before attempting the exam. Please note that successful completion of this book, corresponding course, or additional study materials alone does not ensure you will pass the HPE6-A73 exam.

Recommended Training

Recommended training to prepare for each exam is accessible from the ACDA exam page. For more information, please visit: http://www.arubanetworks.com/support-services/training-services/certified-switching-professional/.

Obtain Hands-on Experience

You are not required to take the recommended, supported courses, and completion of training does not guarantee that you will pass the exam. Aruba strongly recommends a combination of training, thorough review of courseware and additional study references, and sufficient on-the-job experience prior to taking an exam.

Exam Registration

To register for an exam, please follow the links provided at: http://www.arubanetworks.com/support-services/training-services/certified-switching-professional/.

CONTENTS

1 Introduction to Aruba Switching

OBJECTIVES

After completing this chapter, you should be able to:

✓ Compare and contrast the different AOS-CX switching models

✓ Describe the important features of the AOS-CX switching product line

Overview

This chapter introduces the AOS-CX products and features that are covered in this guide. AOS-CX switches and operating system was designed for both data center and campus networks. The AOS-CX switch hardware enhancements like HPE's ASICs, with over 20 years of design and development experience, Virtual Output Queuing (VOQ) for dealing with head-of-line blocking, deep packet buffers, always-on POE on the 6300 and 6400 switches, and many other hardware features are needed for both campus and data center networks. The operating system was designed from scratch. It has all your typical features needed in campus and data center networks; however, it has a lot of enhanced features that lead the industry, including enhanced API functionality, network analytics that go beyond what is available with SNMP and sFlow, highly resilient virtual switching with VSX, dynamic segmentation for securely controlling access and forwarding of traffic, and many other features that you will see throughout this guide. The future of switching with HPE is AOS-CX and this guide will provide an intermediate-level coverage for implementing campus wired solutions.

Note

Data center designs and features are covered in other Aruba-related courses. This guide focuses on campus solutions.

AOS-CX Switch Overview

In this first section, you will be provided with a brief introduction of the AOS-CX switching product line.

AOS-CX: Heart of Aruba'sCore, Aggregation, and Access

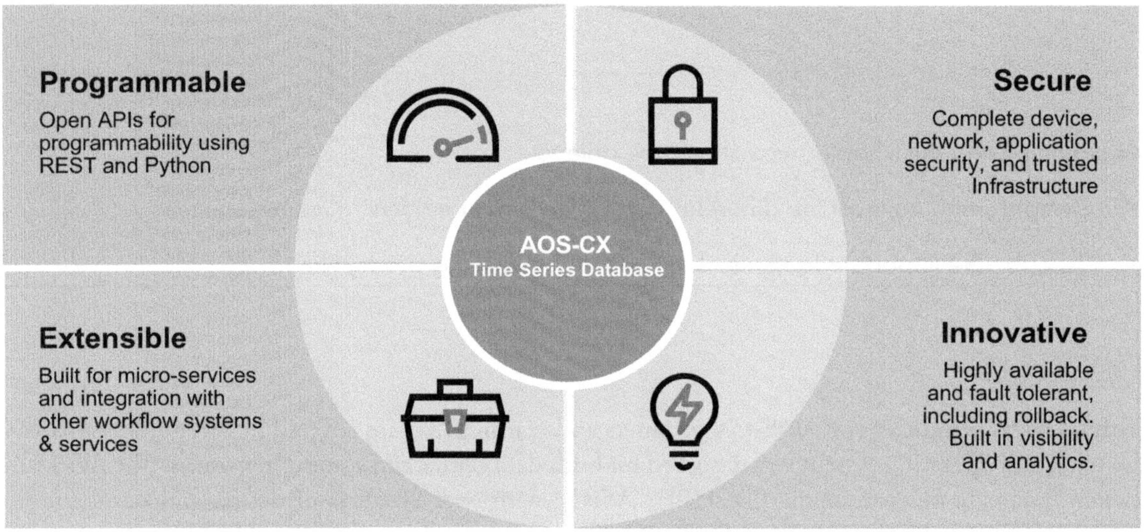

Figure 1-1 AOS-CX: Heart of Aruba'sCore, Aggregation, and Access

The AOS-CX software forms the heart of Aruba's strategy for campus core and aggregation switching, as shown in Figure 1-1. Its programmable nature rests on open REST APIs, which enable external applications to securely view and configure all components of the system. Developers can use Python, a familiar scripting language, to script interaction with the REST API as well as to create Network Analytics Engine (NAE) agents for system monitoring and troubleshooting. AOS-CX is extensible. It is built to support micro-services and, with its open API, to integrate with other workflow systems and services.

The AOS-CX takes an innovative approach to high availability and fault-tolerance. The software architecture supports resiliency; for example, a process that fails can roll back to a good state using the stateful database. AOS-CX has even been honored by the industry for its innovation. CRN awarded the 8400 switch 'Product of the Year 2017' in large part due to NAE. NAE takes the guess-work out of troubleshooting and optimization and will be a game-changer for many customers.

Finally, the AOS-CX is secure and forms the bedrock for a trusted infrastructure. In addition to standard security features such as access control lists (ACLs), the AOS-CX supports a trusted boot process. The software will not boot unless every hardware component checks out as authentic and free from malware and rootkits.

Note

Configuration version roll back may cause issues when going between major AOS-CX software versions.

What Does AOS-CX Mean to Customers?

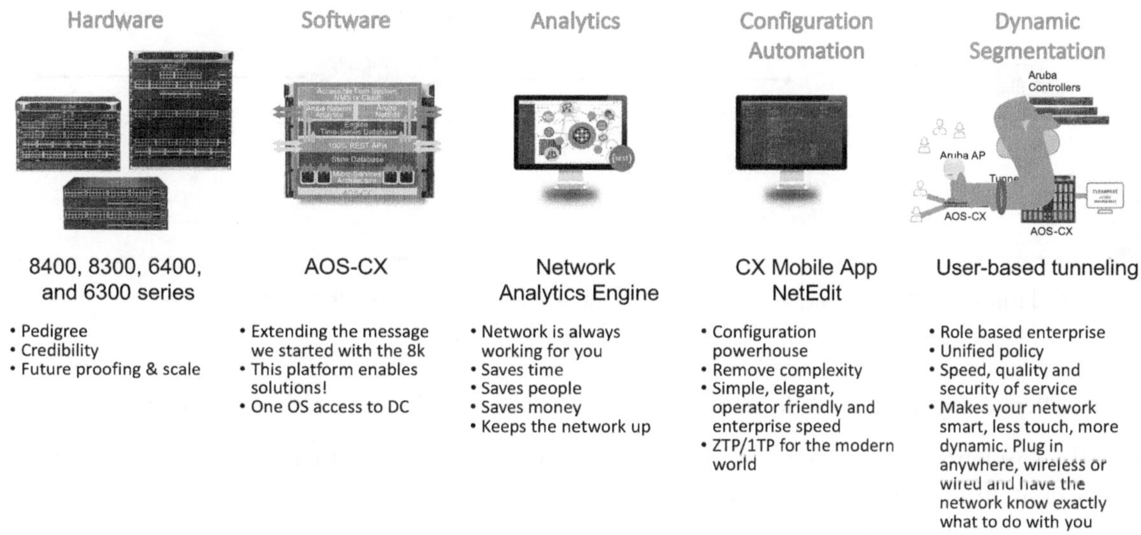

Figure 1-2 What Does AOS-CX Mean to Customers?

By deploying the AOS-CX switches in a campus or data center network, customers get all the benefits of an advanced operating system and the HPE Gen7 ASIC family (Figure 1-2). They get a combination of:

- Proven technologies including dynamic segmentation, which unifies wired and wireless access, enhances and simplifies policy enforcement, and protects IOT and other critical devices
- New hardware that brings together Gen 7 HPE ASICs with Virtual Output Queuing, Smart Rate ports, and up to Class 6 PoE
- The AOS-CX operating system with its modern architecture enables a seamless REST interface, with support for the exclusive Network Analytics Engine
- A set of advanced tools that cover:
    - Enhanced deployment (zero-touch or one-touch) via the CX mobile app
    - Advanced configuration management with NetEdit

End-to-End AOS-CX Architecture

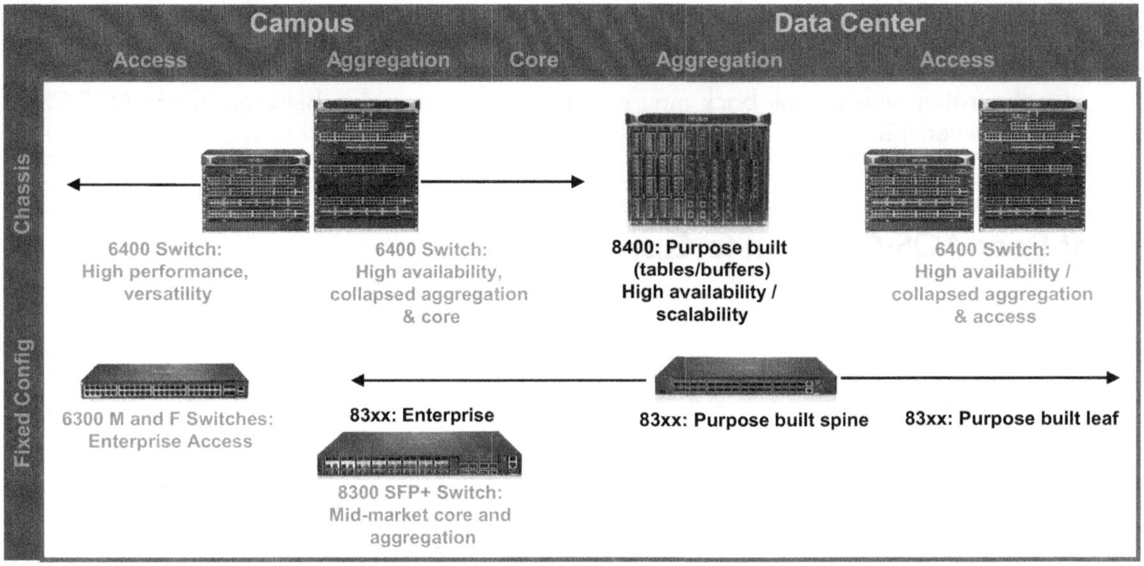

Figure 1-3 End-to-End AOS-CX Architecture: Securely Connects Users and Devices to Applications and Data

Aruba offers many different series of switches with various capabilities, as shown in Figure 1-3:

- The 8400 provides line rate 10GbE/40GbE/100GbE connectivity in a compact 8-slot chassis. It is built to provide high availability and resiliency in every part of the hardware, supporting 99.999% availability.
- The 8300 series provides 2.5Tbps to 6.4Tbps for switching and 1,905-2,000 Mpps for forwarding. All switching and routing are wire-speed to meet the demands of bandwidth-intensive applications today and in the future.
- The 8000 switches run AOS-CX with a modular architecture that allows individual process re-startability and upgrades. REST APIs and Python scripting enable fine-grained programmability of the switch functions.
- The 6400 provides industry-leading line rate 10GbE/25GbE/50GbE port density, very low latency, and scalability for support of full Internet routes.
- The Aruba 6400 is a chassis-based modular switch designed for campus networks. It offers different options in terms of Ethernet port speeds including Smart Rate (multi-rate gigabit Ethernet), power supplies, and PoE. The product family includes a 5-slot and a 10-slot chassis.
- The Aruba 6400 runs the AOS-CX operating system. It offers advanced Layer 2 and Layer 3 features including VXLAN, VSX and OSPF, BGP, as well as Aruba mobility integration features.

- The Aruba 6300 will be defined as a next-generation premium edge campus switch stackable. Aruba 6300 will be a stackable full Layer 3 switch capable of running AOS-CX with associated NAE features and capabilities. Aruba 6300 with two variants: 6300F (fixed uplinks, fixed power supplies, fixed fans) and the 6300M (dual modular power supplies and modular field replaceable fan tray).

In addition of their own capabilities, the new 6300 and 6400 switch series can be integrated with the existing AOS-CX portfolio to provide an end-to-end solution with specialized hardware in each role and for each size and feature requirement.

The benefits of having a single operating system across the entire network are many:

- Ease of maintenance
- Configuration consistency: same CLI and WebUI
- Shorter/flatter learning curve

But even more important, because the end-to-end solution is AOS-CX, the benefits are even greater:

- CX Mobile App for one-touch provisioning
- Using a phone or tablet a technician can easily onboard a switch into NetEdit by filling a few simple forms
- NetEdit for configuration orchestration and auditing
- VRF all the way to the access layer
- Simple IP segmentation, to provide segregated routing domains for different types of traffic including IOT, VOIP, and specific applications
- VXLAN/EVPN (except for the 8320 all platforms will provide full support in the near future)
- VSF and VSX in the right parts of the network
- Full/native REST API
- Network Analytics Engine
- Network administrator can decide "which agents are needed where"

And finally, all these benefits are available for enterprise networks of all types and sizes.

8400: Highly Available and Resilient Aggregation and Core

The Aruba 8400 is targeted for large campus networks (Figure 1-4). It is built to provide high availability and resiliency in every part of the hardware, supporting 99.999% availability. The front of this modular switch houses eight slots for interface modules or line cards (LC). Options for LCs include 32-port 10GbE modules, 8-port 40GbE modules, and 6-port 100GbE modules—all amply supported by the 1.2Tbps capabilities of the LC slot. Refer to the most recent datasheet for the latest list of supported modules and precise specifications.

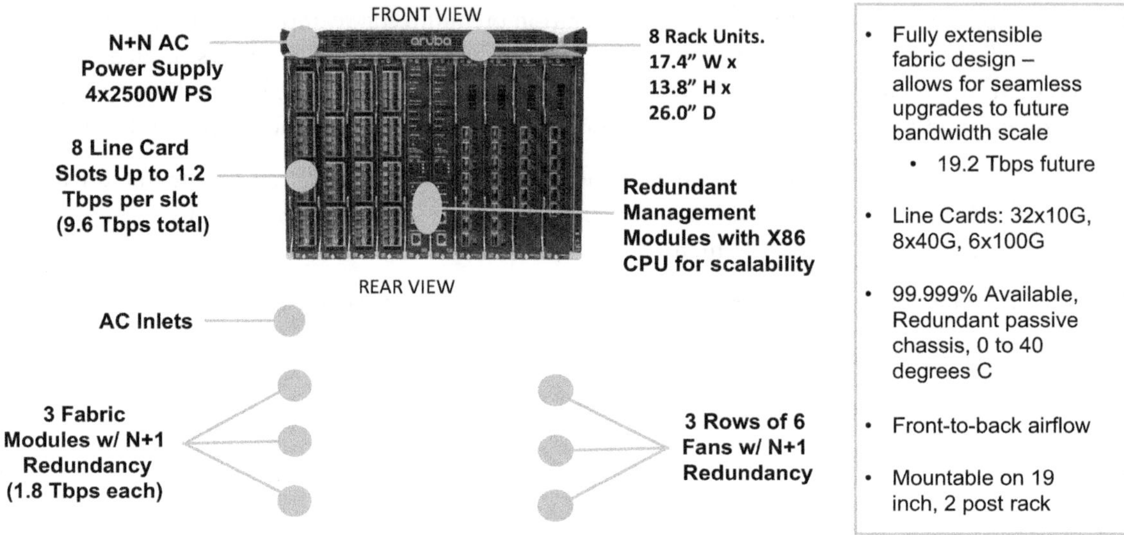

Figure 1-4 8400: Highly Available and Resilient Aggregation and Core

The 8400 also supports redundant management modules (MMs), built on an X86 CPU for scalability. Each management module provides a micro-USB slot and an RJ45 console port, as well as an Ethernet port for out-of-band management (OOBM).

The rear of the 8400 has slots for multiple fabric modules, supporting 1.8Tbps each. The fabric modules deliver high throughput between line cards and N+1 redundancy. On the rear of the chassis are three rows of six fans, again providing N+1 redundancy, and a front-to-back airflow.

To further bolster availability, the 8400 supports up to four power supplies. If customers select high-line voltage supplies (200V to 240V), each supply delivers 2500W. Two power supplies can power a fully loaded chassis, three supplies provide N+1 redundancy, and four supplies provide N+N redundancy. Low-line voltage (110V-120V) supplies are also available and can be appropriate for customers with less full chassis or no redundancy requirements.

8325 Overview

The Aruba 8325 Series is designed to bring the benefits of AOS-CX software to the data center (Figure 1-5). As of the publication of this guide, the series consists of two models. The 8325 32C switch provides 32 40/100 GbE ports. The 8325-48Y8C offers 48 flexible 1/10/25 GbE ports and eight 40/100 GbE ports. The switches support full line rate for all of these high-speed ports with a maximum 6.4Tbps non-blocking architecture and 3.3Bpps forwarding. (Of course, the capacity is also limited by the bandwidth on the ports as well.) The 8325 series provides a very large MAC address table of 98,304.

The switches deliver hardware redundancy with redundant, hot-swappable PSUs and fans.

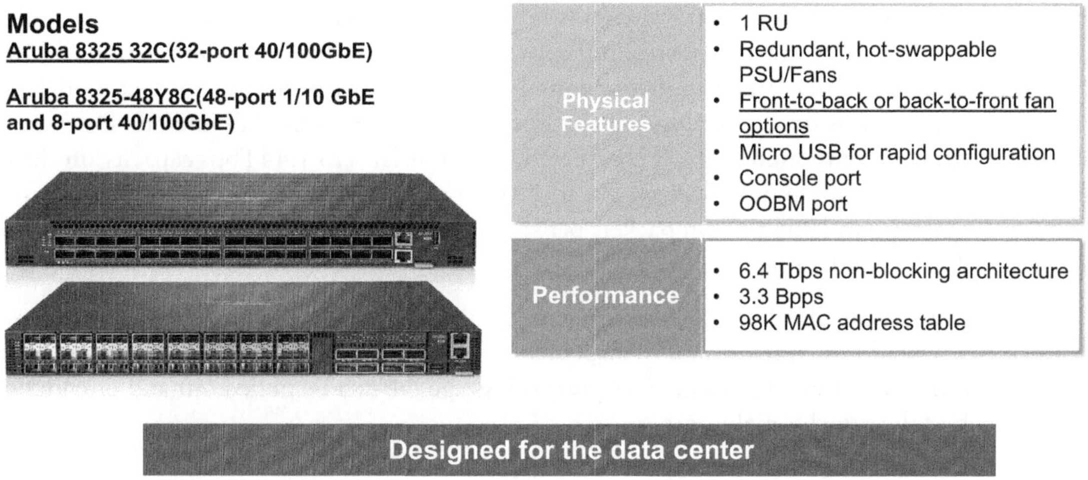

Figure 1-5 8325 Overview

To work within the data center hot-aisle/cold-aisle design, the switches support deployment with either front-to-back or back-to-front airflow. Note the airflow option is two different models of the switch.

They also offer similar management features to other AOS-CX switches, including a USB slot, console port, and OOBM port, as shown in Figure 1-6.

8320 Overview

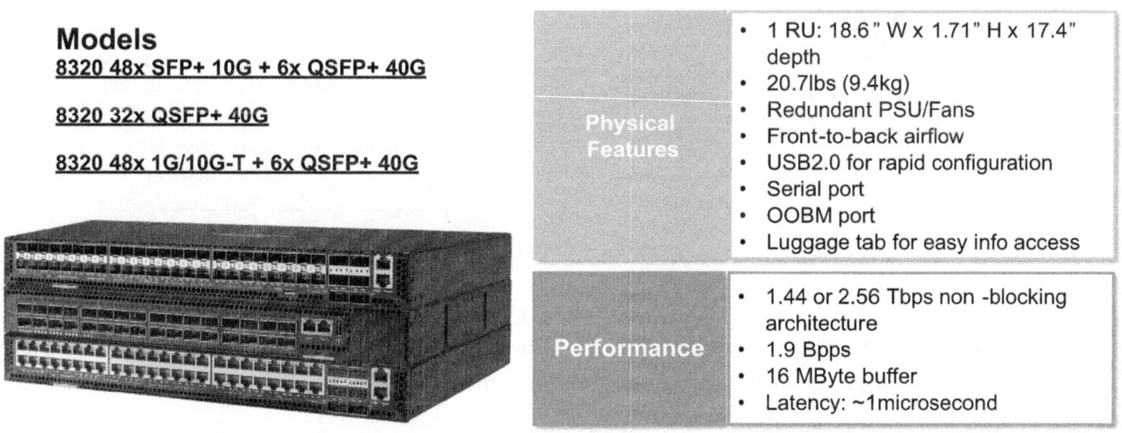

Figure 1-6 8320 Overview

The Aruba 8320 series of fixed-port switches is intended for the core aggregation layer or mid-sized campus cores. The series includes several different modules with different combinations of 10GbE and 40GbE ports. For the 10GbE ports, one model supports fiber ports and another model copper ports. The switches feature a non-blocking architecture that delivers the full line rate for every port. When inbound and outbound traffic is considered, that translates to 1.44Tbps capacity on the models with a mix of 10GbE and 40GbE ports and 2.56Tbps on the model with 32 40GbE ports. The switches support up to 1905 million packets per second (Mpps). They have a large 16MB buffer and deliver low latency under one microsecond.

The 8320 switches are also built for resiliency. They offer redundant power supplies and fans. The front of the switches provides several management features, including a USB2.0 slot, a serial port, and an Ethernet out-of-band management port. A luggage tab can be pulled out and provides information such as the switch serial number.

6400 Series

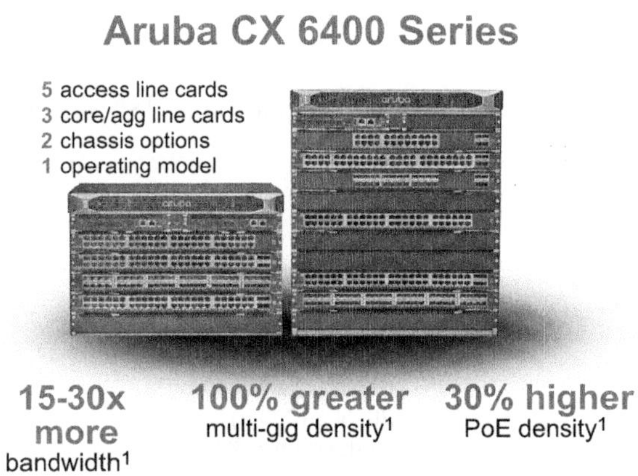

Flexibility and scale:
From 1G PoE access to 28T core

Data center class performance:
Data center class non-blocking, distributed architecture and no oversubscription

Built for Wi-Fi 6:
Up to 480 ports of Smart Rate and 60W always-on PoE

Future ready:
Up to 2.8T per slot and 20 Bpps, 1G to 100G interfaces

High availability:
Live upgrades with VSX, redundant hot-swappable power and fans

Real-time insights:
Embedded analytics from NAE for rapid troubleshooting

Figure 1-7 6400 Series

The first is the AOS-CX 6400 series (Figure 1-7). This family consists of two chassis. There is a 5 slot and a 10 slot chassis and they can support very high-density port counts, with flexibility and scale, giving Aruba a significant competitive advantage.

Aruba built the AOS-CX 6400 products using a lot of internal intellectual property with custom-built ASICs and the AOS-CX operating system. With a non-blocking distributed architecture, with no oversubscription, this greatly simplifies networking. This means network admins do not have to plan around what they are plugging into which port on what slot because the switches support a complete non-blocking fabric.

The port counts vary in terms of the types of connectivity offered with up to 60 watts always-on PoE. You can support all the Wi-Fi 6 and IoT devices that are coming out. The 6400 also supports high-density Smart Rate with 1/2.5/5 gig ports.

It also provides line cards that have 24 ports of 10GbE, both in Gigabit Ethernet, as well as SFP+. There is also a 48-port 25 gig card as well as a 12-port 40/100 gig card. This is a big breadth of different connectivity options, allowing this platform to be used all the way from the access in the campus to the core and also in the data center in some cases. That's a great value proposition for some customers who can simplify their design and standardize on a single platform across their entire network.

For high availability (HA), the AOS-CX 6400 supports VSX live upgrades and also has redundant management cards, fans, power supplies, etc.

Aruba is also extending the Aruba Network Analytics Engine (NAE) onto these platforms. If you are already familiar with 8400 and 8325, that is a key differentiator in terms of providing visibility and telemetry to help with troubleshooting.

6300 Platforms

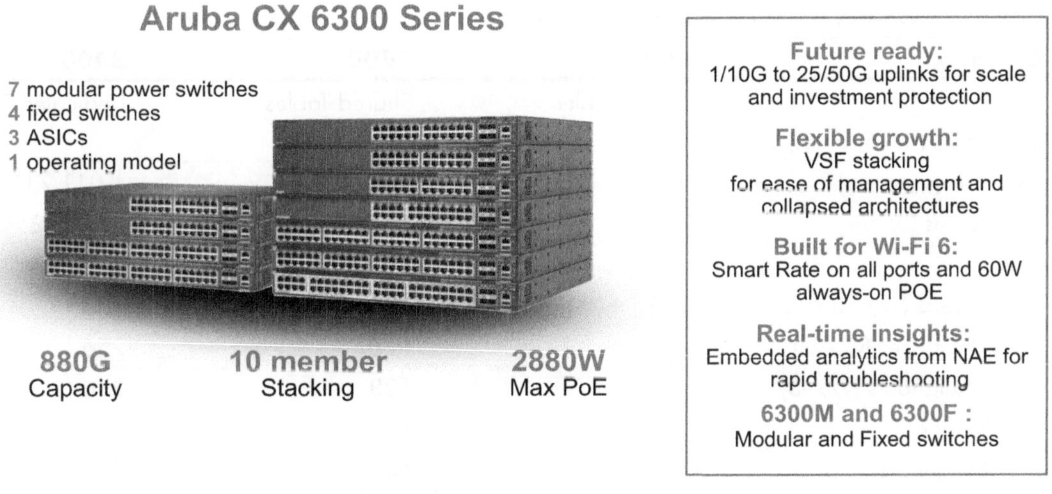

Figure 1-8 6300 Platforms

The second newest AOS-CX hardware platform is the 6300 series, as shown in Figure 1-8, which is essentially built on the same architecture as the 6400. It is a stackable form factor—you can stack up to 10 switches in a single stack which is perfect for different-sized wiring closets. The AOS-CX 6300 also supports a variety of different port types, such as PoE (up to 60 watts), Smart Rate—there are actually 11 different models in this family. Several are fixed and several are modular—the modular ones support modular power supplies and modular fans. These are great for people looking for additional power redundancy. The fixed models are ideal for smaller spaces or areas where that redundancy is not as big of an issue.

It also supports ten-unit VSF stacking. There is a 24-port 10GbE SFP+ model as well, which you can use in the aggregation layer. This means you can do a collapsed access aggregation with just this family of products where you are using stacking to simplify management and deployment.

The AOS-CX 6300 switch series will also support real-time analytics, NAE, as mentioned for the 6400.

There are 11 different SKUs in the Aruba 6300 switch series family, seven modular (6300M) and four fixed (6300F) with two airflow of front to back and left to back respectively. Each switch provides a different number/type of interfaces/ports but they all share the same operating system AOS-CX.

With fixed SKUs there are no hot-swappable power supplies and fans; everything is fixed. Modular SKUs have hot-swappable power supplies and fans. Aruba 6300M SKUs support fan direction front to back (same as 2930M) and two PSU slots (PSU sharable with 3810/2930M).

AOS-CX Switch Capabilities

Tables1-1 and 1-2 provide the comparison for scale among all the AOS-CX platforms for the AOS-CX 10.04 software release.

Table 1-1 AOS-CX Switch Capabilities Part 1

Category	6300	6400	8400
HW Tables (ARP/ND, v4/v6 routes)	Shared Tables	Shared Tables	Dedicated Tables
IPv4 Routes (system)	64,000	64,000	1,011,712
IPv6 Routes (system)	32,000	64,000	524,288
VRFs	64	64	64
OSPF Areas (v2/v3)	128	128	256
OSPF Interfaces (v2/v3)	128	128	256
OSPF Neighbors (v2/v3)	128	128	256
BFD Session	128	128	256
BGP Neighbors	64	64	256
ARP	32,000[4]	32,000[4]	756,000[1]
MAC	32,000[4]	32,000[4]	768,000[1]
ND	32,000[4]	32,000[4]	524,000[2]

Table 1-2 AOS-CX Switch Capabilities Part 2

Category	8325 L3-agg profile	8320 L3-agg profile	8320 L3-core profile
HW Tables (ARP/ND, v4/v6 routes)	Shared Tables	Shared Tables	Dedicated Tables
IPv4 Routes (system)	28,658	12,288	130,993
IPv6 Routes (system)	12,289	7,168	32,768
VRFs	64	64	64
OSPF Areas (v2/v3)	256	256	256
OSPF Interfaces (v2/v3)	256	256	256
OSPF Neighbors (v2/v3)	256	256	256
BFD Session	256	256	256
BGP Neighbors	256	256	256
ARP	120,000[3]	120,000[3]	14,000
MAC	98,304[3]	98,304[3]	32,768
ND	52,000	52,000	7,000

As a large campus core switch, the Aruba 8400 can scale to support a great number of MAC addresses, routes, ARP entries, and other such entries. The scalability depends on an intersection of the hardware and software capabilities. It is important to notice that 6300 and 6400 provide exactly the same scale capability as expected as this is the same ASIC used on 6300 than on 6400. Notice as well that scale for IPv6 is the same than for IPv4 on those new platforms. 8400 remains the only platform with very large-scale numbers. For 8320, 8325, and 8400 the scale numbers are the same in 10.04 than in 10.03.

You can configure an Aruba 8300 switch to operate in one of two modes, depending on how you intend to deploy the switch. The mode affects the limits for various types of entries, allocating memory differently based on where the memory is needed. Mobile First mode is designed for when the switch connects to Mobility Controllers (MCs) that support a great many wireless devices. This mode allocates the greater part of the memory to MAC addresses and ARP addresses, enabling the switch to act as default gateway for large VLANs with many devices. Route mode allocates less memory to MAC and ARP addresses and more to IPv4 and IPv6 routes. Use this mode when the switch needs to learn more routes, but is default gateway for smaller subnets.

1. Number of IPv4 Devices/Clients limited to 81,000 for ARP Resolution – 8400 Egress MAC Table Limit
2. Number of IPv6 Devices/Clients limited to 55,000 for ND Resolution – 8400 FEC Table Limit
3. Number of Devices/Clients limited to 43,000 (8320)/47,000(8325) for ARP/ND Resolution – Egress MAC Table Limit
4. Restrictions are currently the same for the AOS-CX 6300 and 6400 switches

Features

This section introduces some of the important features of the AOS-CX operating system and switches.

Fully Open and Programmatic Software Architecture

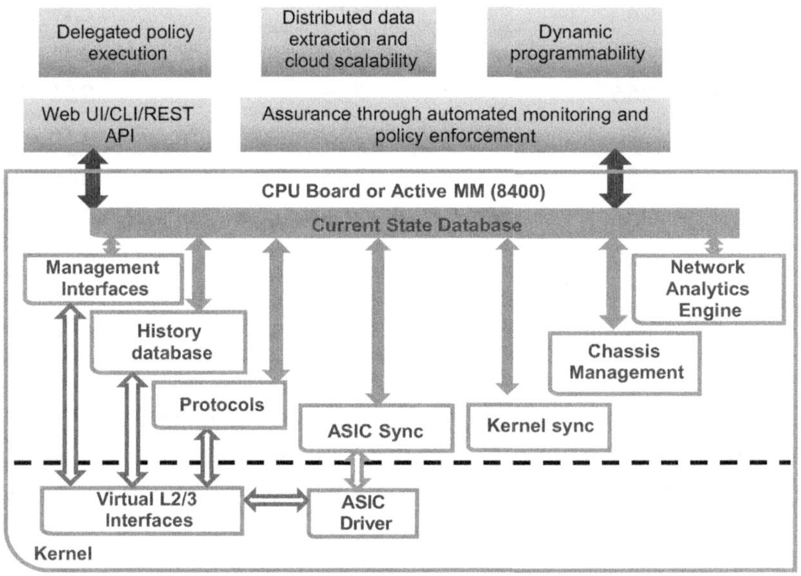

Figure 1-9 Fully Open and Programmatic Software Architecture

AOS-CX is architected to support full programmability through a Representational State Transfer (REST) API, as shown in Figure 1-9. The REST API defines every configurable component as a resource at a specific URI available at the switch management IP address.

Data related to the resource has a predictable, programming friendly structure. For example, an application can contact the URI for an Ethernet interface and receive structured data about the interface's status, configuration, and statistics. By having applications subscribe for information in this way, customers can implement distributed or centralized analytics. Applications can also send correctly structured data back to the resource to update it—in that example, to re-configure the interface.

In other words, AOS-CX switches are fully programmable by external applications of the customer's choice. In this way, they enable network automation, as well as assurance through automatic monitoring and policy enforcement. By scripting their own NAE agents and creating scripts that interact with the agents, customers can implement root cause analytics in order to proactively discover issues, find their cause, and remediate them.

Customers can program applications to execute policies in the network. They can easily extract data and more quickly scale their solution.

AOS-CX Switch Virtualization Solutions: VSX

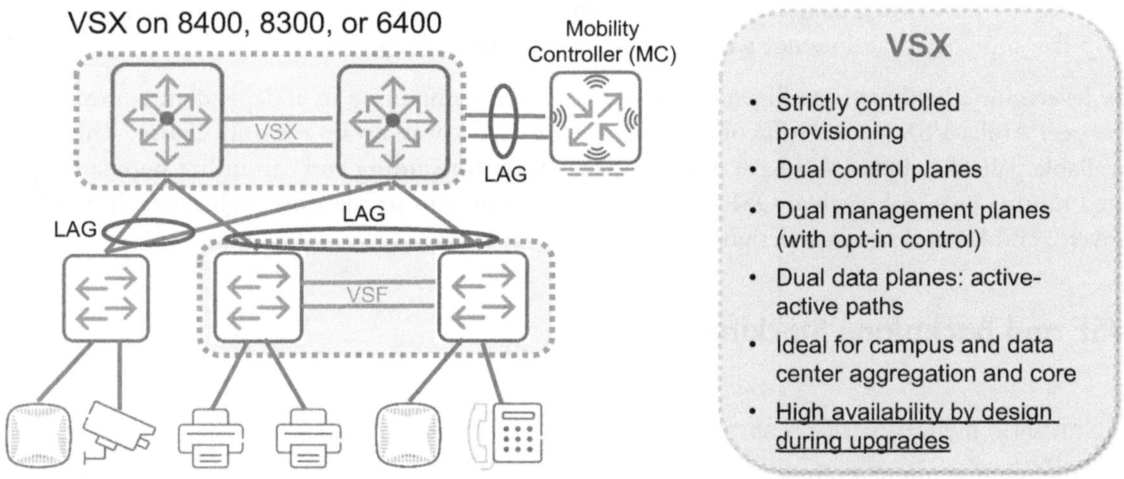

Figure 1-10 AOS-CX Switch Virtualization Solutions: VSX

VSX is designed for use at the aggregation and core layers of a campus network (Figure 1-10). On the other hand, VSF is primarily used at the access layer of a campus network. This difference in design leads to several differences in how the features work. VSF and backplane stacking are configured with a plug-and-play approach in which a switch (at default settings) that connects to another switch automatically becomes one.

VSX, on the other hand, is strictly controlled and requires administrators to manually set the feature up on both switches. VSX maintains a dual control plane and dual management plane. This dual management plane allows for synchronization, but administrators can opt to synchronize specific features.

The two switches in a VSX fabric efficiently use both of the switches' control planes, management planes, and data planes while seeming in many ways to function as one device to other devices in the network. They support an active-active path for Layer 2 traffic, Layer 3 unicast traffic, and Layer 3 multicast traffic. In other words, both switches in the fabric actively switch and route traffic.

VSX maintains the AOS-CX behavior with ports disabled and operating at Layer 3 by default. Finally, VSX is designed to deliver high availability during software upgrades. The upgrade occurs with near zero downtime and with continuous packet forwarding.

High availability and redundancy are delivered by enabling VSX on two switches. Each switch then maintains its independent control, yet stays synchronized with the other for important L2 information like MAC and ARP addresses.

From a link aggregation perspective, neighboring devices see the VSX switch pair as a single switch. If you note the diagram in Figure 1-10, the Mobility Controller, the stand-alone switch, and the VSF stack see the VSX switch pair, when configured for LACP, as a single switch. This enables a redundant loop-free topology that does not require spanning tree protocol (STP).

By leveraging distributed intelligence with each switch maintaining its independent control plane, the peer Aruba VSX chassis will continue to operate as if it was always the only chassis. This highly available pair of switches will have Active-Active packet forwarding and can utilize popular distributed routing protocols such as OSFP and BGP to provide industry-leading high availability in both Layer 2 and Layer 3 network designs.

VSF and Backplane Stacking

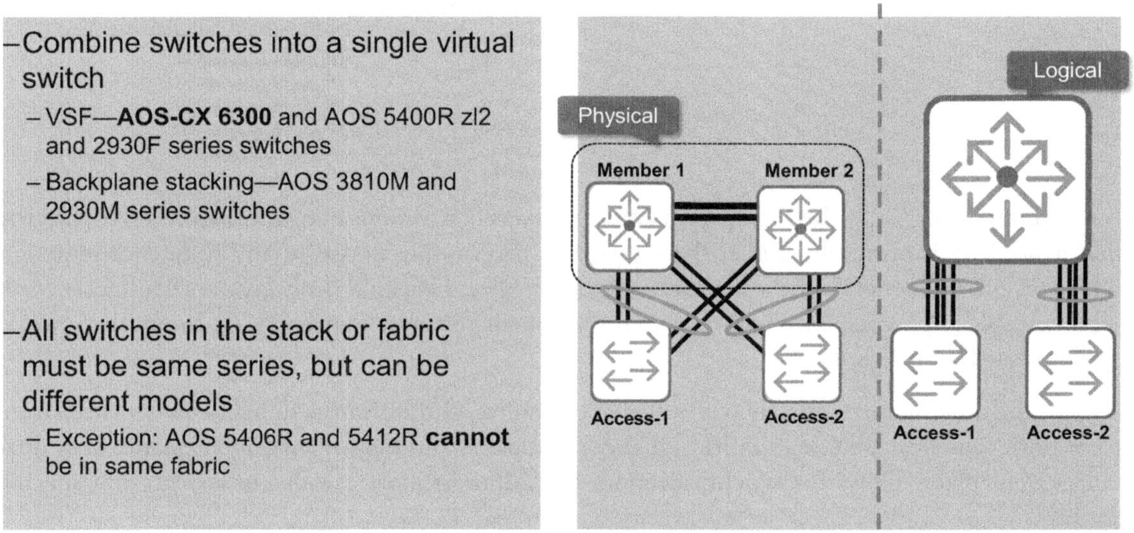

Figure 1-11 VSF and Backplane Stacking

VSF and backplane stacking are Aruba technologies that allow you to combine multiple switches into a single virtual switch (Figure 1-11). You can then manage the combined switches as a single entity. You can also treat switches as a single entity from the viewpoint of designing Layer 2 and 3 protocols. This provides significant advantages as you design a wired network.

The new AOS-CX 6300 series supports VSF. The older AOS 5400R zl2 and 2930F series switches also support VSF. The older AOS 3810M and 2930M switches support backplane stacking.

A VSF fabric must consist of switches that are the same series, such as two Aruba 5406R switches or two or more Aruba 2930F switches. For the 2930F series, you can combine different models in the same fabric. For example, you can combine a 2930F-48G PoE+ switch with a 2930F-48G switch. The latter is also true of the AOS-CX 6300 series of switches.

You cannot combine 5406R and 5412R switches in the same VSF fabric. The two switches can support different interface modules, although Aruba recommends that you install the same modules in both switches for consistency.

VSF and backplane stacking are implemented in different ways. For one thing, VSF is a front-plane stacking technology, meaning that you can connect the switches in the VSF fabric using regular wired switch ports. Backplane stacking, in contrast, is not implemented through wired ports; you must purchase a stacking module and stacking cable to implement this technology.

With VSF fabrics, you will need to plan the VSF links to ensure there is adequate bandwidth to handle the traffic that members exchange. For backplane stacking, all the members are connected through dedicated, high-bandwidth stacking links (40 GbE).

Since VSF members are connected via wired ports, VSF fabrics support long distances between members. However, the distance between backplane stacking members is limited to a maximum of three meters (you can order .5, 1, or 3-meter cable). For this reason, backplane stacking is intended for deployment between members that are relatively close together such as in the same closet.

These two technologies also differ in how they handle traffic forwarding. Within a VSF fabric, deep-level queuing and forwarding are implemented at a member level. With backplane stacking, queuing and forwarding are implemented.

NetEdit

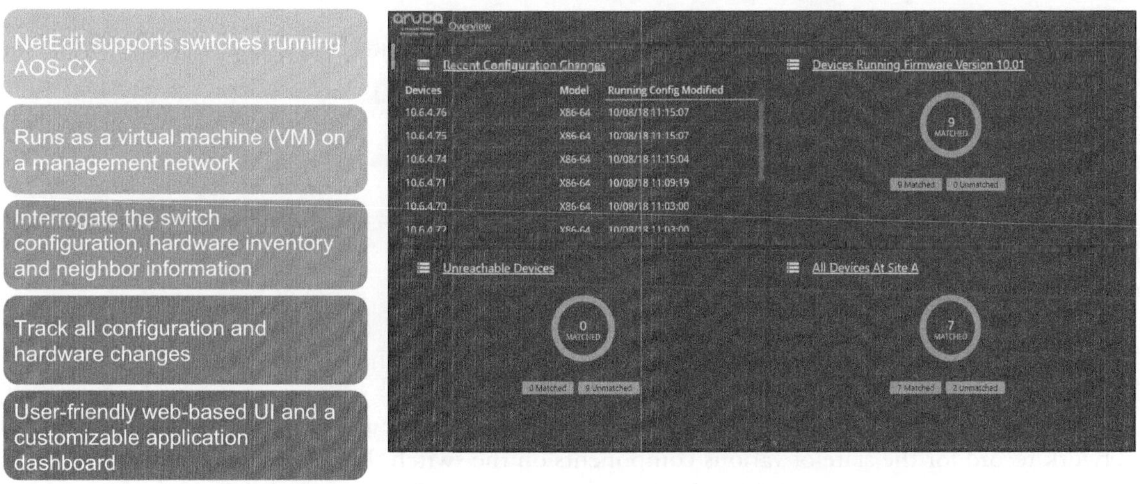

Figure 1-12 NetEdit

NetEdit supports switches running AOS-CX (Figure 1-12). NetEdit runs as an Open Virtualization Application (OVA) virtual machine (for example, VMware's ESXi, KVM, Hyper-V, etc.) on a server. When NetEdit is made aware of a new switch, it will interrogate the switch configuration, hardware inventory, and neighbor information. NetEdit ensures a complete history of all devices, tracking all configuration and hardware changes.

A user-friendly web-based UI allows network admins to interpret the status of network devices easily. The customizable application dashboard provides quick visibility into information and metrics that matter most to you.

NetEdit provides automation for network configuration such as search, plan, edit, validation, deployment, and audit. It provides intelligent assistance and continuous validation to help ensure that device configurations are consistent, compliant, and error free.

You can use NetEdit without retraining by leveraging your existing knowledge and experience with switch configurations. This enables you to automate switch configuration change workflows without having to have programming knowledge.

Network Analysis Engine (NAE) and the Time-Series Database

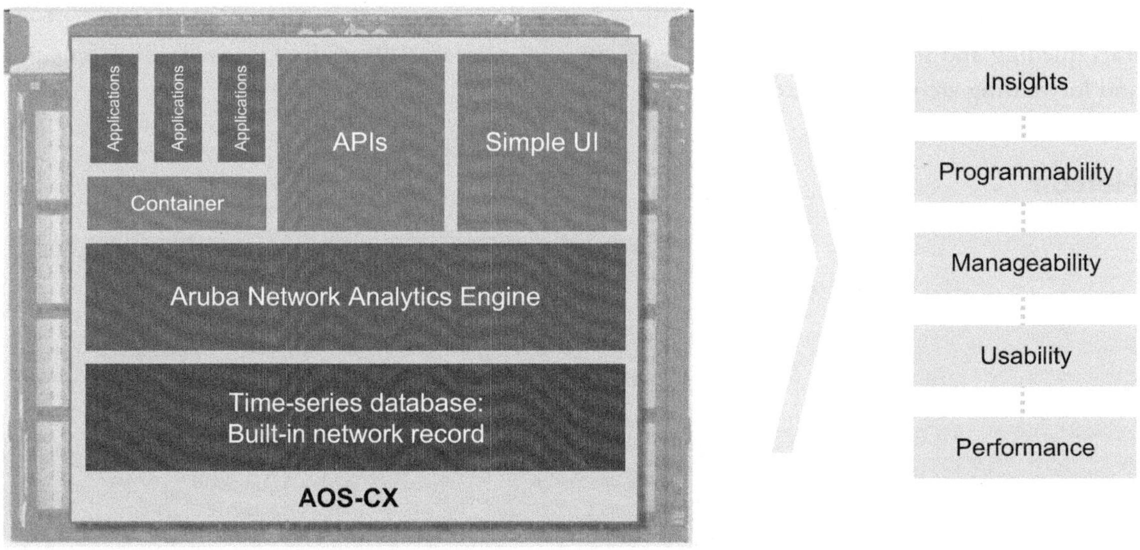

Figure 1-13 Network Analysis Engine (NAE) and the Time-SeriesDatabase

The AOS-CX includes the time-series database, as shown in Figure 1-13, which establishes a built-in network record for the state of various components on the switch. NAE agent monitors the current state of one or more attributes in the Configuration and State Database and then writes the state to a Time-Series Database for an ongoing record. They can establish baselines of normal states and detect significant deviations from those. When they detect issues, they can trigger alerts and actions and collect further data. Customers can create scripts to obtain information about NAE agents from the REST API.

Together, these components create a switch that delivers critical insights that can make the company more secure and competitive. Also, you can program the switch to act on those insights, permitting customers to transform their operations with automated workflows and business application integration.

Dynamic Segmentation

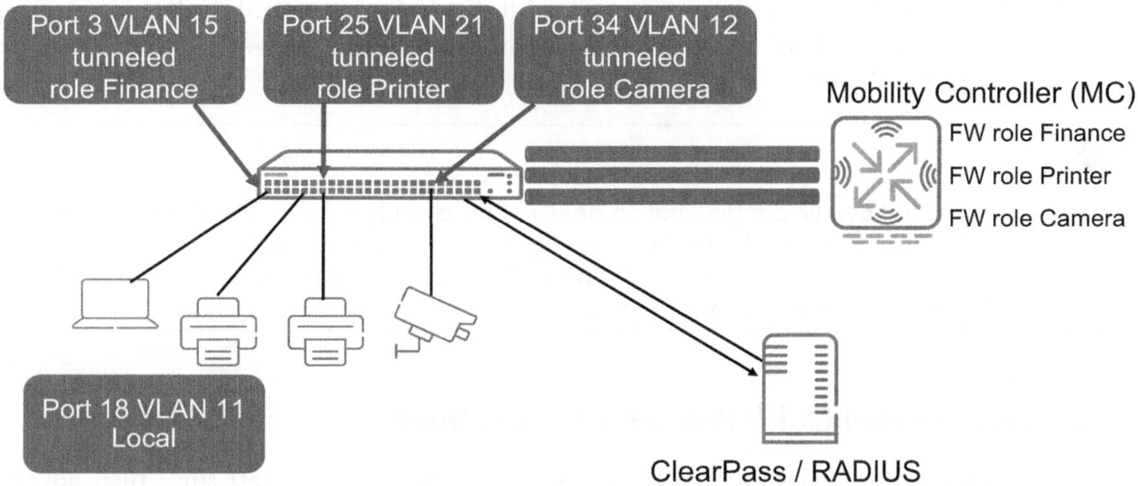

Figure 1-14 Dynamic Segmentation

All modern desktops, laptops, tablets, and smartphones support robust security mechanisms like 802.1X/EAP. However, many devices still lack these security mechanisms. This includes specialty devices, and some devices that rely on Power over Ethernet (PoE), such as security cameras, payment card readers, and medical devices (Figure 1-14).

This lack of endpoint security can pose a serious risk to your infrastructure. A switch with dynamic segmentation can authenticate these devices using ClearPass, and tunnel the client traffic. This enables you to centralize firewall and secure policy services at the Aruba mobility controller. You can continue to use these devices without compromising network security.

ClearPass profiles each device, deems appropriate endpoints as "acceptable", and sends accept messages to the controller. The messages include tunnel information, assigned VLAN, and secondary role. ClearPass can also indicate if a device should remain local. The switch forwards these devices, as normal, and does not use the tunneled node feature. ClearPass can leverage device profiling information, like wired versus wireless, the operating system of the device, and the type of device when assigning policies. This allows you to implement colorless ports on your switches.

A colorless port is basically a port with default characteristics that are then dynamically changed based on the characteristics of the device and the authentication details of the device. The greatest impact/benefit of colorless ports is that you no longer have to statically pre-configure access ports to any VLANs or policies (QoS/ACL). Dynamic segmentation easily allows you to implement colorless ports using roles, which is a feature that has been available for a very long time on Aruba Mobility Controllers. Dynamic segmentation forwarding solutions include:

- Local switching: local forwarding of traffic.
- UBT (User-Based Tunnel): each user is assigned their own role
- PBT (Port-Based Tunnel): each port (as well as all the devices connected to the same port) is assigned the same role (PBT is not currently supported in AOS-CX 10.04 but there are plans to add it in a future release)

Note

Please note that dynamic segmentation does not necessarily mean that traffic is tunneled to the Mobility Controller. With dynamic segmentation, you can define policies where some devices' traffic is tunneled to a Mobility Controller and where other devices' traffic is locally switched by the AOS-CX switch.

Always-on PoE and Quick PoE for the 6300/6400

Campus customers have been using PoE switches (IEEE 802.3af, 802.3at) since their advent; however there is a growing customer need to have PoE power maintained across planned and unplanned software upgrades, with maintaining PoE power with planned upgrades having immediate importance. This feature is known to many of our customers as Persistent PoE (Aruba renamed it to Always-On PoE). This feature ensures that the end device does not power cycle on switch reboot. This is needed especially for some IoT devices which may behave in an erratic fashion on reboot (for example, Zigbee devices, other customer-specific IoT devices) or take a long time to reboot after power is withdrawn due to a switch upgrade.

There is also a use case where with advent of IoT devices, especially PoE powered lighting, where there is a need to provide power immediately to the end device after a power outage. Quick PoE which is also known as Fast PoE, this specific feature can power PDs the moment power is plugged in without waiting for the Operating System to boot up.

Aruba 6300 QuickPoE (Not Part of First Release)

Quick PoE provides power to PDs as quickly as possible, where the switch is booting after power to the switch was lost power. The typical use case for this would be a power outage.This applies to PoE Chassis only. Aruba 6300 Module SKUs are to be released with IEEE802.3bt or 4-pair PoE enabled. The Fixed SKUs are 2-pair PoE but mainboard is HW design to support 4-pair PoE controller and should be 4-pair (60W per port) ready.

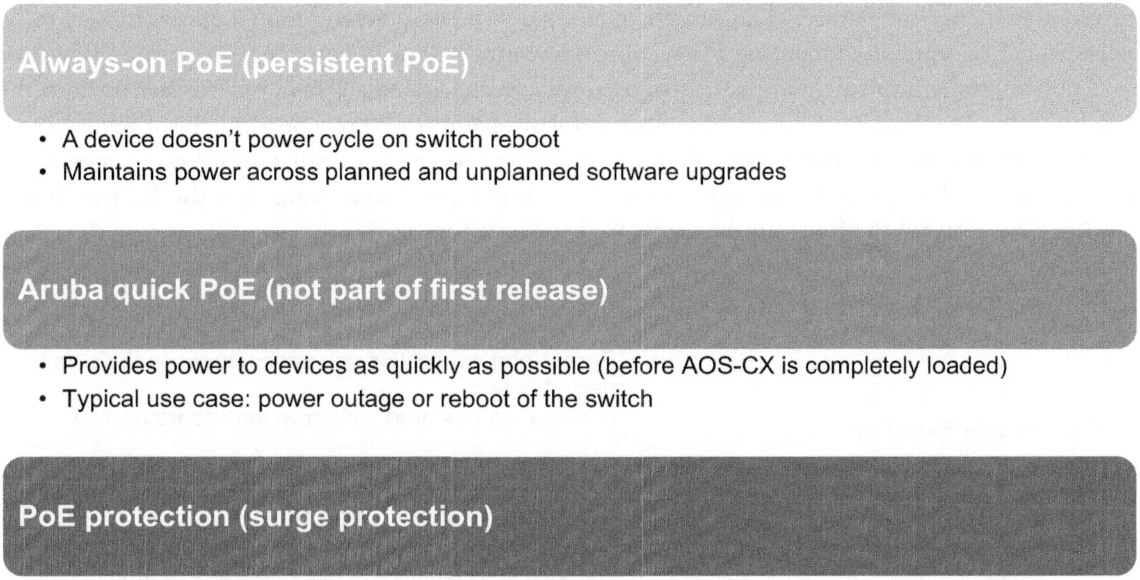

Figure 1-15 Always-on PoE and Quick PoE for the 6300/6400

PoE protection (surge protection)

- **D2—Shockley Diode (100V)**: This Shockley diode is to block a negative Surge on the Line side. When there is a negative Surge, current will flow from PSU to RJ Line side. With this series Shockley diode Microsemi recommended blocks that current and thus protects the PSE chip and downstream devices.
- **AR85—1 M ohms resistor**: With the series Shockley diode on the negative line side, when the PSE is off, there is no discharge path for the charged 100Meter cable. This 1M resistor will then provide the discharge path from neg54 line to Pos54 and finally to PSU Earth Ground through the bleeder resistor in the PSU or system side.
- **Negative surge protection**: D3 is mean to handle any positive 54V surge. In operation, D73 will supply current to the PSE chip Vmain. But when there is a positive surge, the voltage is going to be reverse bias and thus damaging the PSE chip. With the D73, this will protect the reverse current (Figure 1-15).

Virtual Output Queuing (VOQ)

Before understanding virtual output queuing (VOQ), let us understand why it is needed. Head-of-line blocking (HOL blocking) is a performance-limiting phenomenon that occurs when a line of packets is held up by the first packet.

AOS-CX switching platforms utilize VOQ where the majority of the buffering within the switch is on the ingress port. While the physical buffer is on the input, it represents packets queued on the output side (hence the name virtual output queuing). VOQ is a technique that allows buffers to be balanced across sources contending for a congested output port. It ensures fairness and allows for QoS policies to be implemented in a distributed forwarding system. When a packet arrives into the Ingress Traffic Manager, a VOQ credit request is forwarded to the egress port processor requesting a transmission slot on the output port. Packets are queued on ingress until a VOQ grant message is returned (from the Egress Traffic Manager on the output port) indicating that the Ingress Traffic Manager can forward the frame to the egress packet processor.

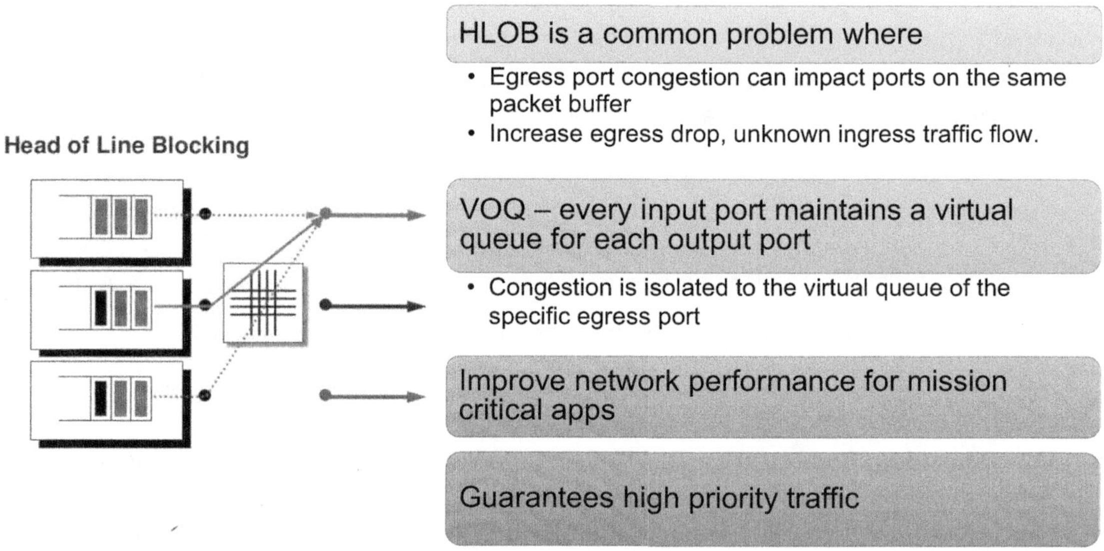

Figure 1-16 Virtual Output Queuing (VOQ)

Note

VOQ is just as important on modular chassis switches like the 8400 and 6400 as it is on the 83xx and 6300s (Figure 1-16).

VOQ in the 6400 Switches

Figure1-17 shows VOQ for the 6400 switches. Note that VOQ is supported on *all* the AOS-CX switches.

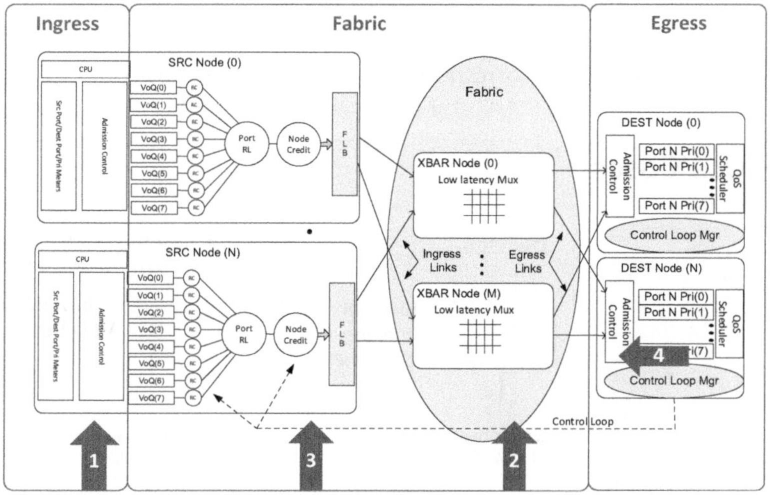

- **SRC Node** : ingress module
- **DEST Node** : egress module
- **FLB**: Fabric load balancing
- **Control loop** : Used by the DEST node to communicate to the ingress module how much they can transmit across the fabric to them
- **Data transmission** : SRC nodes selects packets to transmit based on QoS priorities

Figure 1-17 VOQ in the 6400 Switches

Overview

In a VOQ architecture, the egress side selects which traffic will cross the fabric. In the 6400 Switch Series, the block is called the Traffic Regulator. It sends small messages across the fabric to tell ingress VOQs how much they are to send into the fabric. It is configured to keep just enough packets in egress queues to keep the port fully busy given the port speed. Regarding how VOQs are selected, the port's schedule profile is also a factor. For example, with DWRR, heavier weighted queues get more selections.

Ingress

Once a frame has been processed by the ingress pipeline information like egress port(s) and queue, drop eligibility (color) are available. The Ingress Admission Control puts the frame's descriptor record in the respective VOQ—the frame itself is in the packet buffer.

Fabric

The process starts at the Control Loop Manager in the egress line card (destination node)

- Along with the Admission Control Process, monitors all egress queues in the module, including congestion
- Depending on the queue's available space, sends "credit" messages to the ingress line cards (source node).

The Fabric Load Balancer in the source node transmits the frames with most credits across the fabrics. Packets with the same credit level are selected using a source/destination node hashing algorithm. In multi-ASIC fabrics packets do not have a pre-assigned dedicated path.

Egress

The Egress Admission Control places frames in their corresponding queue for transmission.

Virtual Output Queuing – Use Cases

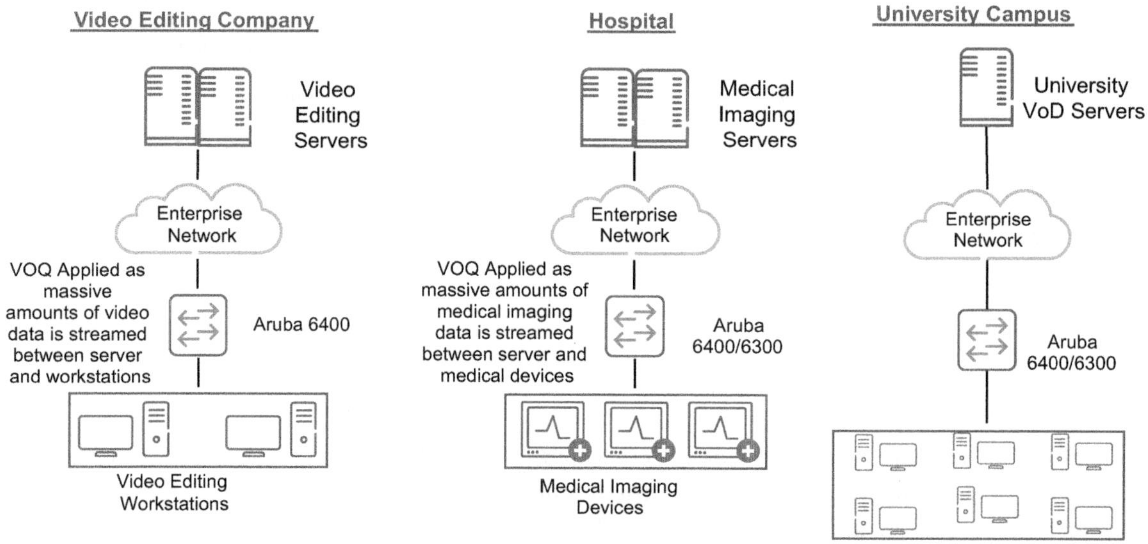

Figure 1-18 Virtual Output Queuing – Use Cases

Here are three use cases for Virtual Output Queuing, as shown in Figure 1-18:

- In the case of a video editing company, many employees would be using video editing workstations to send and receive massive amounts of video traffic, which would congest the network if enough traffic is sent simultaneously with multiple users editing. In the case of congestion, traffic would be queued in the virtual output queues on the 6400, ensuring that the video traffic is sent and received by the correct workstation.
- A hospital may have sophisticated medical imaging equipment which would send massive amounts of imaging data back and forth from the imaging department to the servers handling the data. If it is a busy night in the emergency room, there could be severe congestion with multiple imaging machines in use, which could impede the network. Virtual output queuing would come in to ensure patients' images are sent correctly and not dropped due to a busy network.
- In a university campus, if many students are live streaming video from the university on-demand servers, this could cause congestion at the switch fabrics if other line cards are also streaming traffic or sending large amounts of file transfers.

Lab 1: Base Configuration

In this lab, you will factory reset the switches and apply a basic configuration to them, including access for out-of-band management (OOBM).

Lab Course Topology

This is the lab topology used in the guide (Figure 1-19). Not all labs will use all the equipment shown in the topology.

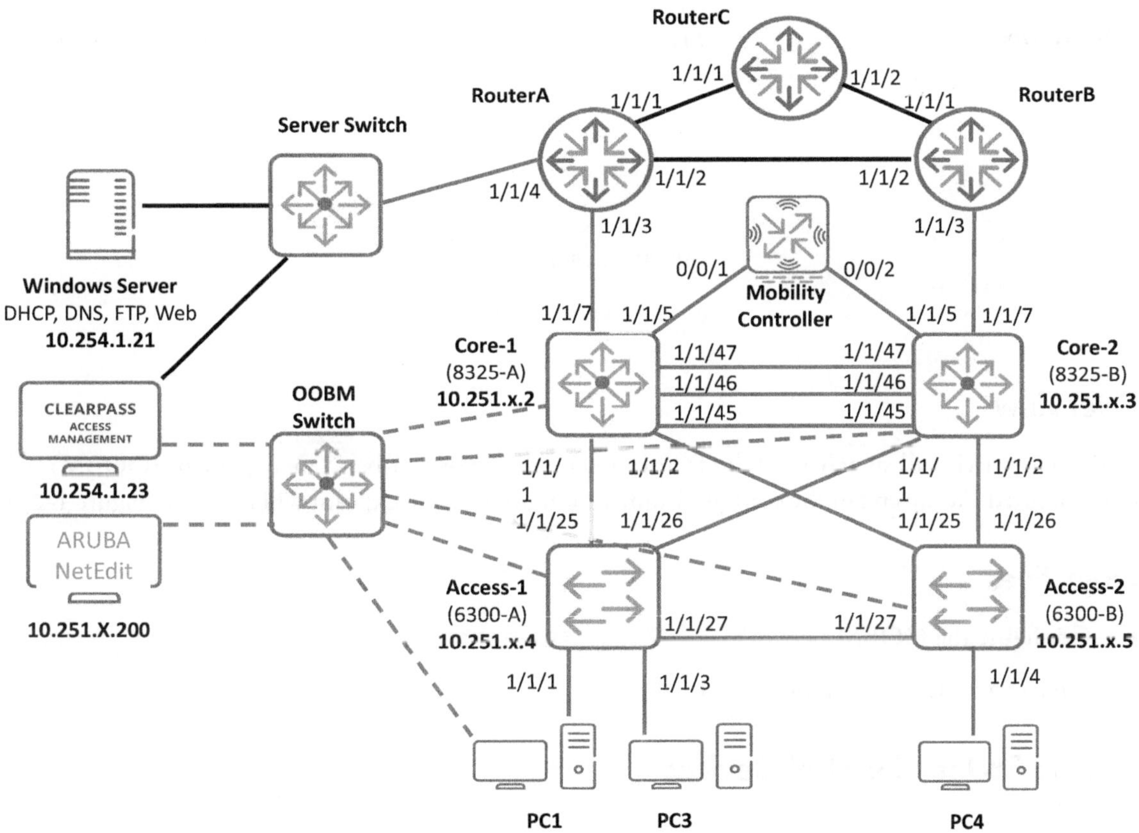

Figure 1-19 Lab Course Topology

Lab 1 Diagram

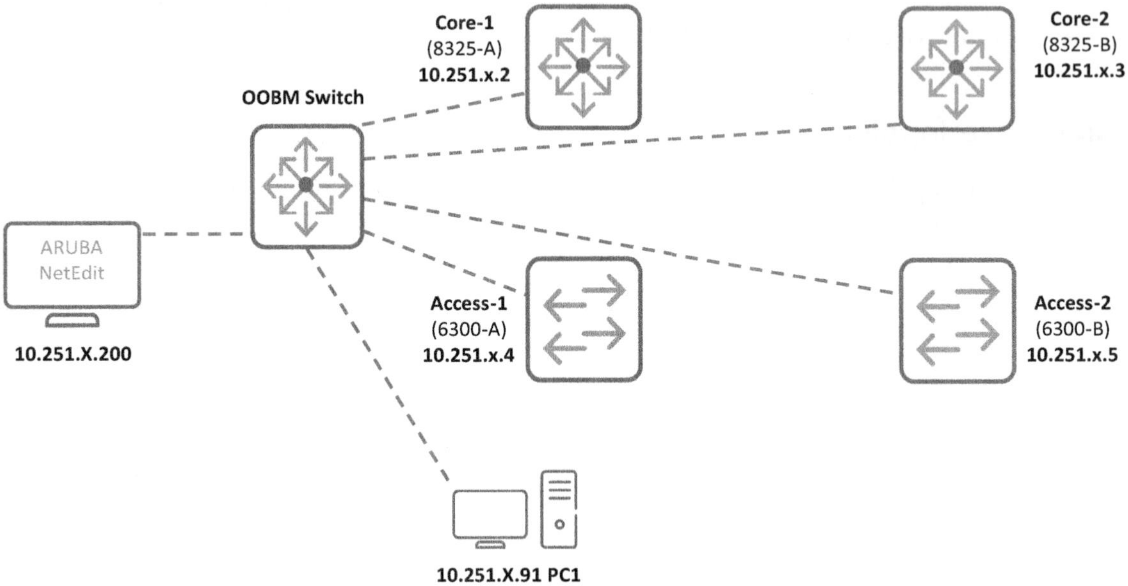

Figure 1-20 Lab 1 Diagram

Overview

In this lab activity all switches will be factory reset and the out-of-band management (OOBM) will be configured. At the end of the configuration, a configuration checkpoint will be made (Figure 1-20).

Objectives

- Configure the OOBM network
- Prepare a basic configuration checkpoint

Task 1: Factory Reset of Devices

Objectives

- Factory reset
- Remove all checkpoints

Note that in case AOS-CX is completely factory-default, the switch will prompt to change the admin password at first login. This will also happen after the 'erase all zeroize' procedure. This procedure will not only clear the startup configuration, but it will also clear any other custom files, such as configuration checkpoints.

Steps

1. Open a console connection to the 6300A. Log in using admin, no password.

Note

The initial hostname may be different from the output below; this depends on the remote lab setup.

```
6300 login: admin
Password:

Last login: 2019-12-08 05:26:49 from the console
User "admin" has logged in 2 times in the past 30 days
6300 #
```

Note

In case the switch prompts to change the password at this point, it is already factory-default, so there is no need to perform the 'erase all zeroize' of the next step. Move on to the next switch, the password will be set in the next task.

2. Clear all configuration files and snapshots.

```
6300# erase all zeroize
This will securely erase all customer data and reset the switch
to factory-defaults. This will initiate a reboot and render the
switch unavailable until the zeroization is complete.
This should take several minutes to one hour to complete.
Continue (y/n)? y
The system is going down for zeroization.
P52-6300A-Table12#
```

3. Open a console connection to the 6300B switch. Log in using admin, no password. Clear all configuration files and snapshots (skip this step if the switch would prompt to change the admin password).

```
6300# erase all zeroize
This will securely erase all customer data and reset the switch
to factory-defaults. This will initiate a reboot and render the
switch unavailable until the zeroization is complete.
This should take several minutes to one hour to complete.
Continue (y/n)? y
The system is going down for zeroization.
P52-6300B-Table12#
```

4. Open a console to 8325A and repeat the factory reset process.

Note

If the switch shows a new password prompt, the switch is already at factory-default, so you can move on to the next step.

5. Open a console to 8325B and repeat the factory reset process.

Note

If the switch shows a new password prompt, the switch is already at factory-default, so you can move on to the next step.

Task 2: Configure the OOBM for Access1

Objectives

- Initial password
- Make a checkpoint of the factory-default configuration
- Disable all interfaces to prevent remote lab network loops
- Configure the OOBM management IP address
- Make the base configuration checkpoint

Steps

1. Switch to the console connection of the 6300A. Log in using admin, no password. Since the switch is factory-default, the software will show a prompt to change the admin password. Set the admin password to **aruba123**.

```
6300 login: admin
Password:

Please configure the 'admin' user account password.
Enter new password: *****
Confirm new password: *****
6300#
```

Note

If you entered a different password, the password can be changed with these commands:

```
6300# configure terminal
6300(config)# user admin password plaintext aruba123
6300(config)# end
```

2. Make a checkpoint named 'icx-factory-default'. This checkpoint is not used in the future labs, but will allow you to switch back to the factory-default state without the 'erase all zeroize' command and reboot.

```
6300 # copy running-config checkpoint icx-factory-default
```

3. Enter the configuration mode and configure the hostname and OOBM IP.

   Ask your instructor for your TABLE number (your kit/student number).

Note

Change "x" to your table number.

```
6300# configure terminal
6300(config)# hostname ICX-Tx-Access1
ICX-Tx-Access1(config)# interface mgmt
ICX-Tx-Access1(config-if-mgmt)# ip static 10.251.x.4/24
ICX-Tx-Access1(config-if-mgmt)# default-gateway 10.251.x.254
ICX-Tx-Access1(config-if-mgmt)# exit
```

Example

If the above would be applied to Table12, this would be the result:

```
6300# configure terminal
6300(config)# hostname ICX-Tx-Access1
ICX-Tx-Access1(config)# interface mgmt
ICX-Tx-Access1(config-if-mgmt)# ip static 10.251.12.4/24
ICX-Tx-Access1(config-if-mgmt)# default-gateway 10.251.12.254
ICX-Tx-Access1(config-if-mgmt)# exit
```

4. Disable all switch ports. Since the remote lab contains several redundant links between all the switches, all interfaces are disabled initially. You will enable the interfaces as needed in later labs.

```
ICX-Tx-Access1(config)# interface 1/1/1-1/1/28
ICX-Tx-Access1(config-if-<1/1/1-1/1/28>)# shutdown
ICX-Tx-Access1(config-if-<1/1/1-1/1/28>)# exit
ICX-Tx-Access1(config)# end
```

5. Verify access on the OOBM network with a ping to the ClearPass host (10.254.1.23).

```
ICX-Tx-Access1# ping 10.254.1.23 vrf mgmt
PING 10.254.1.23 (10.254.1.23) 100(128) bytes of data.
108 bytes from 10.254.1.23: icmp_seq=1 ttl=62 time=1.14 ms
108 bytes from 10.254.1.23: icmp_seq=2 ttl=62 time=0.875 ms
108 bytes from 10.254.1.23: icmp_seq=3 ttl=62 time=0.930 ms
108 bytes from 10.254.1.23: icmp_seq=4 ttl=62 time=1.04 ms
108 bytes from 10.254.1.23: icmp_seq=5 ttl=62 time=1.09 ms

--- 10.254.1.23 ping statistics ---
5 packets transmitted, 5 received, 0% packet loss, time 4057ms
rtt min/avg/max/mdev = 0.875/1.017/1.147/0.108 ms
```

Note

If the ping was not successful, review your settings.

6. You have now completed the base config and verified connectivity. This configuration will be saved as the base configuration checkpoint for future labs. List current checkpoints. Only 'icx-factory-default' snapshot should be in the list after the zeroize factory reset.

Note

There may be an automatic snapshot if 5 minutes have passed since your last configuration change. This is the checkpoint post-configuration feature that is enabled by default.

```
ICX-Tx-Access1# show checkpoint list
icx-factory-default
```

7. Make a checkpoint of the current configuration as ACSP-lab-base.

```
ICX-Tx-Access1# copy running-config checkpoint icx-lab01-base
Configuration changes will take time to process, please be patient.
ICX-Tx-Access1#
```

8. Verify the checkpoint is now in the list (another checkpoint may have been created by the system already; this can be ignored).

```
ICX-Tx-Access1# show checkpoint list
CPC20191215142246
icx-lab01-base
icx-factory-default
ICX-Tx-Access1#
```

9. Verify the contents of the checkpoint.

```
ICX-Tx-Access1# show checkpoint icx-lab01-base
Checkpoint configuration:
!
<output omitted>
```

Note

If you made a mistake you can remove the checkpoint with the command:

```
erase checkpoint <NAME>
```

Note

If you need to see the configuration changes between two checkpoints or between a checkpoint and the running-configuration, the 'checkpoint diff' command can be used. Examples:

```
IAS-Tx-Access2# checkpoint diff icx-factory-defaulticx-lab01-base
IAS-Tx-Access2# checkpoint diff icx-lab01-base running-
configuration
```

Task 3: Configure the OOBM for Access2/Core1/Core2

Objectives

- Apply the initial configuration to the Access2, Core1, and Core2 switches

Steps

6300B Base Config

1. Switch to the console connection of the 6300B.
2. Log in with admin and no password.
3. Configure the admin password as **aruba123**.

```
Please configure the 'admin' user account password.
Enter new password: *********
Confirm new password: *********
```

4. Enter these configuration commands.

```
6300# copy running-config checkpoint icx-factory-default
Configuration changes will take time to process, please be patient.
6300# configure terminal
6300(config)# hostname ICX-Tx-Access2
ICX-Tx-Access2(config)# interface mgmt
ICX-Tx-Access2(config-if-mgmt)# ip static 10.251.x.5/24
ICX-Tx-Access2(config-if-mgmt)# default-gateway 10.251.x.254
ICX-Tx-Access2(config-if-mgmt)# exit
ICX-Tx-Access2(config)# interface 1/1/1-1/1/28
ICX-Tx-Access2(config-if-<1/1/1-1/1/28>)# shutdown
ICX-Tx-Access2(config-if-<1/1/1-1/1/28>)# exit
ICX-Tx-Access2(config)# end
```

5. Verify access to the ClearPass host on the management network.

```
ICX-Tx-Access2# ping 10.254.1.23 vrf mgmt
PING 10.254.1.23 (10.254.1.23) 100(128) bytes of data.
108 bytes from 10.254.1.23: icmp_seq=1 ttl=62 time=1.27 ms
108 bytes from 10.254.1.23: icmp_seq=2 ttl=62 time=1.20 ms
108 bytes from 10.254.1.23: icmp_seq=3 ttl=62 time=1.18 ms
108 bytes from 10.254.1.23: icmp_seq=4 ttl=62 time=1.05 ms
108 bytes from 10.254.1.23: icmp_seq=5 ttl=62 time=1.14 ms

--- 10.254.1.23 ping statistics ---
5 packets transmitted, 5 received, 0% packet loss, time 4004ms
rtt min/avg/max/mdev = 1.057/1.173/1.278/0.072 ms
```

6. Save the configuration checkpoint 'icx-lab01-base'.

```
ICX-Tx-Access2# copy running-config checkpoint icx-lab01-base
Configuration changes will take time to process, please be patient.
```

8325A Base Config

7. Switch to the console connection of the 8325A. Log in with admin and no password.
8. Configure the admin password as **aruba123**.

```
Please configure the 'admin' user account password.
Enter new password: *********
Confirm new password: *********
```

9. Enter these configuration commands.

Note
The command 'system interface-group 1 speed 10g' provides the switch with the instruction of handling port speed for this group of ports.

Note

On the 8xxx platforms:

- all ports are L3 routed ports and shutdown by default
- the HTTPS server is disabled on the in-band network (vrf 'default') by default
- the REST API access is read-only by default.

The command instructions below will enable HTTPS on the 'default' VRF (the default global routing table) and allow read-write access to the REST API.

```
8325# copy running-config checkpoint icx-factory-default
Configuration changes will take time to process, please be patient.
8325# configure terminal
8325(config)# hostname ICX-Tx-Core1
ICX-Tx-Core1(config)# interface mgmt
ICX-Tx-Core1(config-if-mgmt)# ip static 10.251.x.2/24
ICX-Tx-Core1(config-if-mgmt)# default-gateway 10.251.x.254
ICX-Tx-Core1(config-if-mgmt)# exit
ICX-Tx-Core1(config)# https-server rest access-mode read-write
ICX-Tx-Core1(config)# https-server vrf default
ICX-Tx-Core1(config)# system interface-group 1 speed 10g
Changing the group speed will disable all member interfaces that
do not match the new speed.

Continue (y/n)? y
ICX-Tx-Core2(config)# end
```

10. Test access to the ClearPass server on the management network.

```
ICX-Tx-Core1# ping 10.254.1.23 vrf mgmt
```

11. Save a configuration checkpoint name 'icx-lab01-base'.

```
ICX-Tx-Core1# copy running-config checkpoint icx-lab01-base
Configuration changes will take time to process, please be patient.
```

8325B Base Config

12. Switch to the console connection of the 8325B.

13. Log in with admin and no password.

14. Configure the admin password as **aruba123**.

```
Please configure the 'admin' user account password.
Enter new password: *********
Confirm new password: *********
```

15. Enter these configuration commands:

```
8325# copy running-config checkpoint icx-factory-default
Configuration changes will take time to process, please be patient.
8325# configure terminal
8325(config)# hostname ICX-Tx-Core2
ICX-Tx-Core2(config)# interface mgmt
ICX-Tx-Core2(config-if-mgmt)# ip static 10.251.x.3/24
ICX-Tx-Core2(config-if-mgmt)# default-gateway 10.251.x.254
ICX-Tx-Core2(config-if-mgmt)# exit
ICX-Tx-Core2(config)# https-server rest access-mode read-write
ICX-Tx-Core2(config)# https-server vrf default
ICX-Tx-Core2(config)# system interface-group 1 speed 10g
Changing the group speed will disable all member interfaces that
do not match the new speed.

Continue (y/n)? y
ICX-Tx-Core2(config)# end
```

16. Test access to the ClearPass server on the management network.

```
ICX-Tx-Core2# ping 10.254.1.23 vrf mgmt
```

17. Save a configuration checkpoint name 'icx-lab01-base'.

```
ICX-Tx-Core2# copy running-config checkpoint icx-lab01-base
Configuration changes will take time to process, please be patient.
```

Learning Check

Here are some questions that will help you review the information covered in this chapter. Please refer to the Appendix to verify your answers.

1. Which AOS-CX platforms support always-on PoE?
   a. 6300 and 6400
   b. 6300, 6400, and 8320
   c. 6300, 6400, 8320 and 8325
   d. All AOS-CX switches
2. Which AOS-CX feature supports the time-series database to capture important statistics over a period of time and to take actions on the captured data?
   a. NetEdit
   b. Dynamic segmentation
   c. NAE
   d. VSX
3. Which AOS-CX feature supports dual management plane functions with zero-down time during management upgrades?
   a. Backplane stacking
   b. VSF
   c. VSX
   d. VSF and VSX

Summary

Congratulations! You have completed the introduction to AOS-CX switches and features. You now understand how hardware and software components of AOS-CX 8400, 8325, 8320, 6400, and 6300 switches work together to provide high availability and high performance for the network.

You also explored the AOS-CX software and learned how its modular architecture and current state database provide extensibility, visibility, and resiliency. You learned how management modules on 8400 switches synchronize, and how all AOS-CX switches handle packet processing in the software. You were also introduced to some of the more innovative features in the switches, including NAE and an open API that supports programmability.

2 NetEdit

OBJECTIVES

After completing this chapter, you should be able to:

✓ Using the NetEdit tool to coordinate network configuration with conformance checking and validation.

✓ Using the CX mobile app for quick deployment and updating AOS-CX switches.

Overview

In this chapter, you will learn how Aruba NetEdit empowers IT teams to orchestrate multiple switch configurations with intelligent capabilities including search, edit, validation, deployment, and audit. Also, you will become familiar with updates to the AOS-CX mobile app for quick deploy provision and update switches.

NetEdit 2.0 Overview

This section provides an overview of what common management problems customers experience and how NetEdit can be used to deal with some of them. NetEdit provides automation of search, edit, validation, deployment, and audit for network configurations. It provides intelligent assistance and continuous validation to help ensure that device configurations are consistent, compliant, and error free. NetEdit can be used without retraining, by leveraging your existing knowledge and experience with switch configuration. This enables you to automate switch configuration change workflows without programming.

State of the Network

NetEdit arms IT teams with the power to smoothly coordinate end-to-end service rollouts, automate rapid network-wide changes, and ensure policy conformance after network updates. This intelligent assistance and continuous validation help assure that network-wide configurations are consistent and compliant (Figure 2-1).

Figure 2-1 State of the Network

Top 10 Causes of Outages

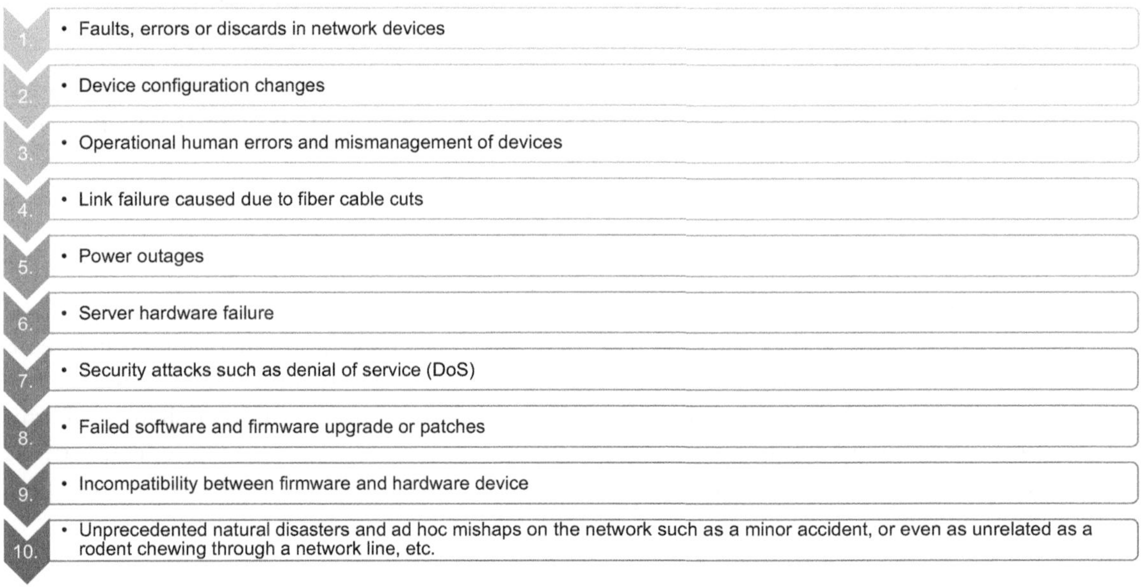

Figure 2-2 Top 10 Causes of Outages

Based on a NetworkWorld survey, most causes of network outages or performance issue are caused by the frequency of network changes. From the list of top 10 causes of outages, as shown in Figure 2-2, Aruba NetEdit remediates device configuration changes (#2) and operational human errors and mismanagement of devices (#3) from the list.

1. Faults, errors, or discards in network devices
2. Device configuration changes
3. Operational human errors and mismanagement of devices
4. Link failure caused due to fiber cable cuts
5. Power outages
6. Server hardware failure
7. Security attacks such as denial of service (DoS)
8. Failed software and firmware upgrade or patches
9. Incompatibility between firmware and hardware device
10. Unprecedented natural disasters and ad hoc mishaps on the network such as a minor accident, or even as unrelated as a rodent chewing through a network line, etc.

Here is the NetworkWorld survey link: https://www.networkworld.com/article/3142838/infrastructure/top-reasons-for-network-downtime.html.

Network Changes and Remediation

Figure 2-3 Network Changes and Remediation

According to NetworkWorld, 69% of admins still use the CLI to verify changes and roll back changes (Figure 2-3). This means there is a constant device to device verification. Using this process, they could forget to run a command, and it is not easy to roll back once a change has been pushed.

Network administrators face numerous challenges that include device proliferation brought on by IoT and BYOD, as well as the need to provide reliable, secure mobile access to any user, anywhere. The high rate of change to support evolving business requirements is another issue. Non-stop adds, moves, and changes can overwhelm what are often short-staffed IT teams, which increases the risk of operator error and, subsequently, performance issues or downtime. In response to these challenges, Aruba NetEdit empowers IT teams to orchestrate the configuration of multiple switches with automation and analytics to ensure deployments are consistent, conformant, and free of errors. The automation workflows allow for changes without the overhead of programming by providing operators with a user-friendly, CLI-like interface. This arms IT teams with the power to smoothly coordinate end-to-end service rollouts, rapidly initiate network-wide changes, and ensure policy conformance after network updates. With embedded analytics delivered from the Aruba Network Analytics Engine (NAE), this intelligent assistance and continuous validation assure that network-wide configuration changes are consistent and compliant, ultimately improving the overall health and security of the network.

Why Cannot I Just Use APIs?

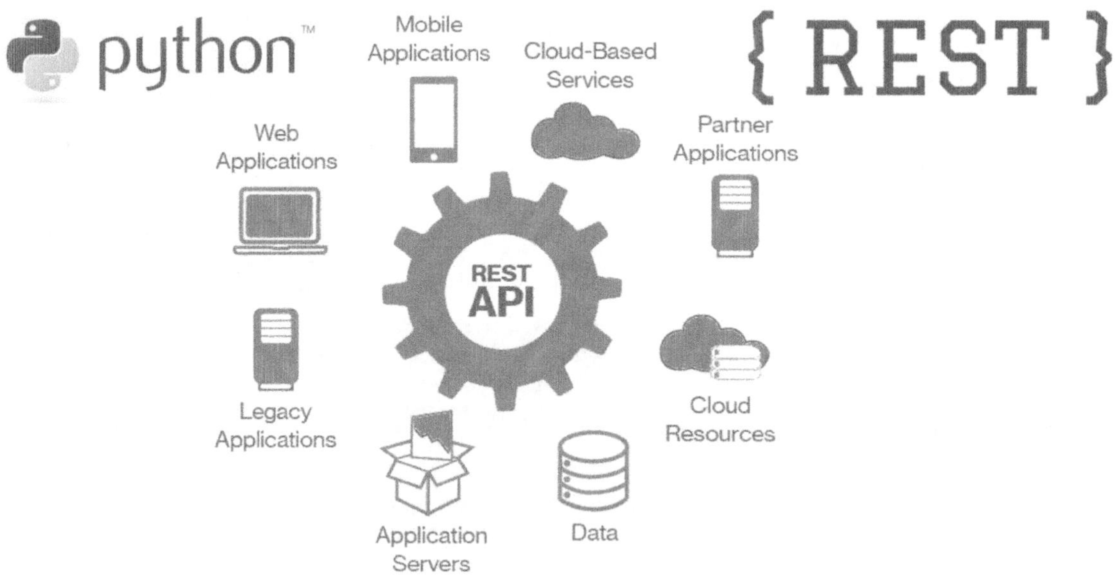

Figure 2-4 Why Cannot I Just Use APIs?

By all means, if you have the skill set to use APIs then use them. However, there are network admins that do not have these skill sets but would like to get some advantages of scripting/API without the overhead of programming, and that is where NetEdit can assist (Figure 2-4).

How NetEdit Works

NetEdit allows operators to get the power of orchestration without the knowledge of API's and we bring this capability to the campus because of the AOS-CX operating system, which NetEdit is leveraging to configure devices.

NetEdit arms IT teams with the power to smoothly coordinate end-to-end service rollouts, automate rapid network-wide changes, and ensure policy conformance after network updates. This intelligent assistance and continuous validation help assure that network-wide configurations are consistent and compliant (Figure 2-5).

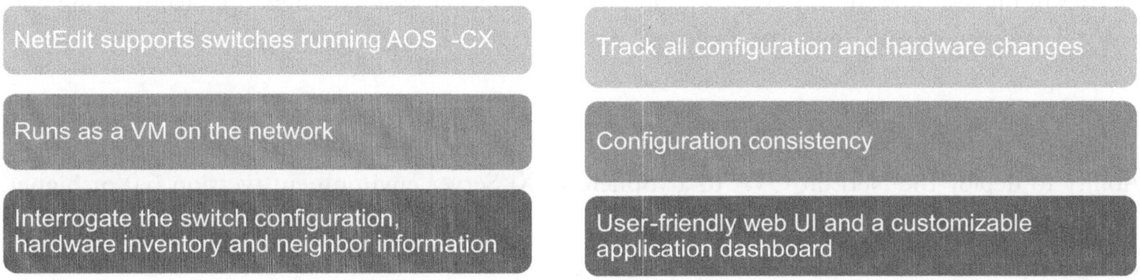

Figure 2-5 How NetEdit Works

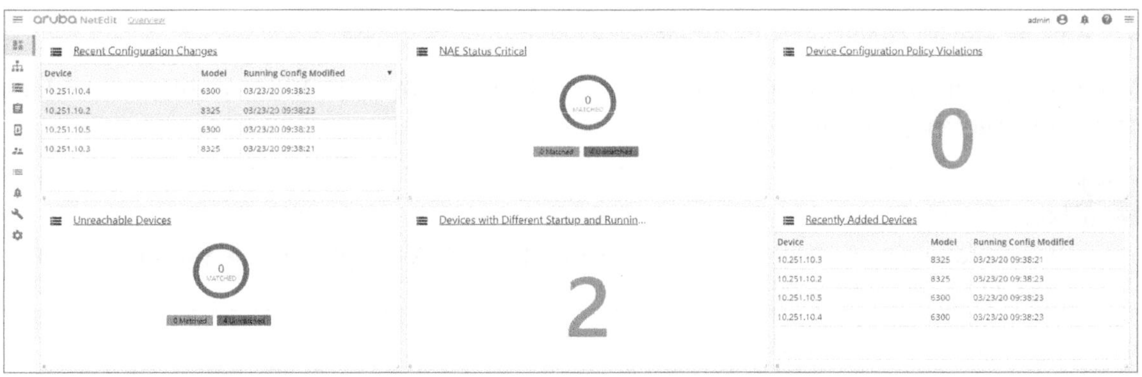

Figure 2-6 NetEdit Dashboard

NetEdit supports all switches running AOS-CX. NetEdit runs as an Open Virtualization Application (OVA) virtual machine (for example, VMware's ESXi, KVM, Hyper-V, etc.) on a server. When NetEdit is made aware of a new switch, it will interrogate the switch configuration, hardware inventory, and neighbor information. NetEdit ensures a complete history of all devices, tracking all configuration and hardware changes (Figure 2-6).

A user-friendly web-based UI allows network admins to interpret the status of network devices easily. The customizable application dashboard provides quick visibility into information and metrics that matter most to you.

To start, operators simply enter their appropriate subnets within NetEdit's web-based user interface. NetEdit then automatically discovers and imports configuration files for each Aruba CX switch. When NetEdit is made aware of a new switch, it will interrogate the switch configuration, hardware inventory, and neighbor information. The admin interface allows operators to easily interpret the status of each network device. A customizable application dashboard provides quick visibility into metrics of highest interest. The Network tab provides a deeper view into network health, along with red/yellow/green statuses for every deployed switch.

NetEdit Server Requirements

Ability to deploy the NetEdit OVA to a vSphere ESXi Server environment (version 6.0 or higher) with:

- 6 CPUs
- 32 GB RAM
- 115 GB disk space (initial size 2.5 GB when thin provisioned)
- A network with connectivity to the target switches to be managed

Minimally, you need a Chrome v75 or Firefox v69 web browser or later. Other web browser products are not officially supported by NetEdit.

Note

These are minimum values. For more detail about OVA installation, please refer to the *NetEdit Installation Guide*.

Note

Aruba does *not* provide OS security updates to the NetEdit VM. To continue to benefit from important security updates offered by Debian, please run the following items periodically:

sudo apt update
sudo apt upgrade

Key Features

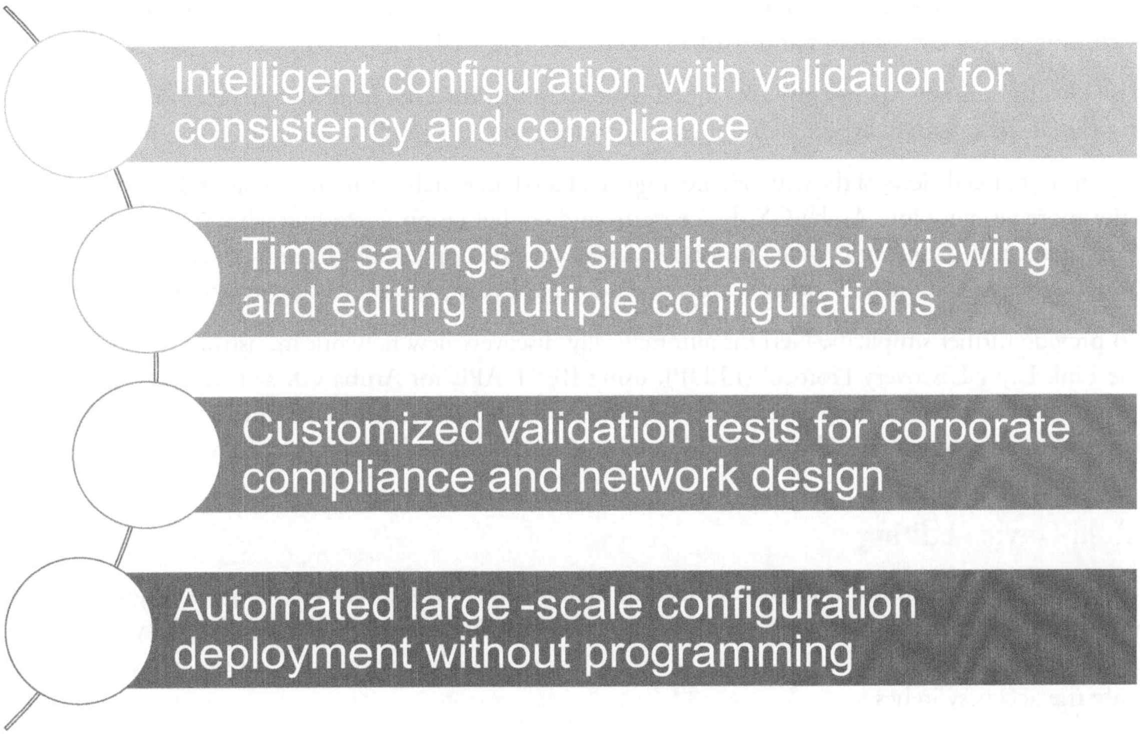

Figure 2-7 Key Features

NetEdit provides automation for network configuration such as search, plan, edit, validation, deployment, and audit. It provides intelligent assistance and continuous validation to help ensure that device configurations are consistent, compliant, and error free (Figure 2-7). You can use NetEdit without retraining by leveraging your existing knowledge and experience with switch configurations. NetEdit provides automation and analytics across the lifecycle of a switch, greatly simplifying common management tasks to elevate the experience for network operators. The following capabilities enable error-free deployments.

Dynamic Network Topology

The Network tab within the interface provides a holistic view of an organization's network topology, including Aruba CX switches and Aruba access points, as well as third-party switches.

The Health Summary panel provides a real-time snapshot into the health of Aruba switches, including the devices that are experiencing inconsistencies and errors, such as security policy violations.

Dynamic, tailored views of the network are triggered based on which layers an operator selects. These layers offer more visibility into Aruba CX device status and configuration, including what is contributing to a performance or compliance issue. Supported layers include application, client service, device, routing, bridging, segmentation, and "other" (which includes all NAE agents not designated to a specific layer).

To provide further simplicity, NetEdit automatically discovers new network infrastructure devices using the Link Layer Discovery Protocol (LLDP), using REST APIs for Aruba CX switches, and SNMP for Aruba wireless and third-party devices. Newly connected switches will appear automatically in the Network tab. les you to automate switch configuration change workflows without programming.

Multi-Device Editing

To keep pace with network changes, NetEdit enables operators to easily change configurations on multiple devices at once using complete details of each configuration file. For example, you can centrally define the NTP or the RADIUS server address for all relevant switches, or set an ACL entry on only the access switches.

NetEdit also taps into an operator's existing knowledge of CLI, so no retraining or new skills are required. Predictive assistance, such as command completion, syntax highlighting, and validation, dramatically reduces the time it takes to enter commands.

To bring even more efficiency to change windows, network teams can also implement common configurations, such as switch-to-switch virtual extensible LANs (VXLANs), by using only a few prompt-driven commands.

One-Click Deployments with Auto-Verification

Using NetEdit, you can stage a deployment (or a rollback) on multiple switches, and validate the correct operation of switches after changes. For instance, you can determine whether a change is working properly before deploying it more widely, or you can quickly back out changes if there is a problem.

Upon deployment, NetEdit automatically collects network and services state information before and after a change, and intelligently displays the difference. This lets you decide whether to keep or roll back the change within your allocated window.

Continuous Validation

Further simplification is provided through the ability to continuously monitor and ensure conformance for both corporate and regulatory policies. Validation checks can be performed on all configuration changes, including those made outside of NetEdit, such as using the switch's CLI or through Ansible.

For example, it is simple to verify that all management IP addresses are on the management subnetwork, or that all routers running OSPF are logging adjacency changes. Validation tests can easily be customized and extended based on your existing knowledge of configuration commands.

Full Audit Trail

NetEdit records all hardware and software versions, as well as other configuration changes. You can then search through and view all changes, or groups of changes. This allows you to track changes to the hardware, software, and configurations using an automated versioning feature, regardless of whether changes are made in NetEdit or through other means. You can also perform these rollbacks selectively, based upon factors such as the location of the switches or the dates of the changes.

Monitoring and Troubleshooting

Integration with the Aruba Network Analytics Engine (NAE) gives operators real-time access to advanced network analytics and built-in automation for troubleshooting, enabling faster detection and resolution of network-impacting issues.

NAE natively gathers telemetry on the switch via agents that are based on Python scripts. The operator can proactively set rules to monitor and collect specific traffic or events of interest. Examples include monitoring of CPU utilization that exceeds a desired threshold, a configuration mismatch, or an OSPF reachability problem.

NetEdit subscribes to the status of the NAE agent, collecting data when an issue of interest occurs. Integrations with tools like ServiceNow, TOPdesk, and Slack then provide for fast notifications, prompting operators to take corrective action.

Upon clicking into NetEdit, the Network tab highlights the devices that match the notification criteria. From here, operators can quickly drill into the impacted device or service and begin troubleshooting by using full diagnostic details that are correlated with the time the event occurred.

In this manner, NetEdit and NAE significantly reduce the number of manual tasks that typically burden operators when troubleshooting. It also produces less load on the network, so performance is not impacted in the process of collecting network-wide telemetry.

Note

Configuration version rollback may cause issues when going between major AOS-CX software versions.

Automatic Imports from the Aruba CX Mobile App

To provide further simplicity, Aruba offers a mobile app that enables operators to install Aruba CX switches on iOS and Android devices. Switches that are connected to the network via the Aruba CX mobile app are automatically imported into NetEdit for policy conformance verification.

Health Layers: Monitoring and Troubleshooting

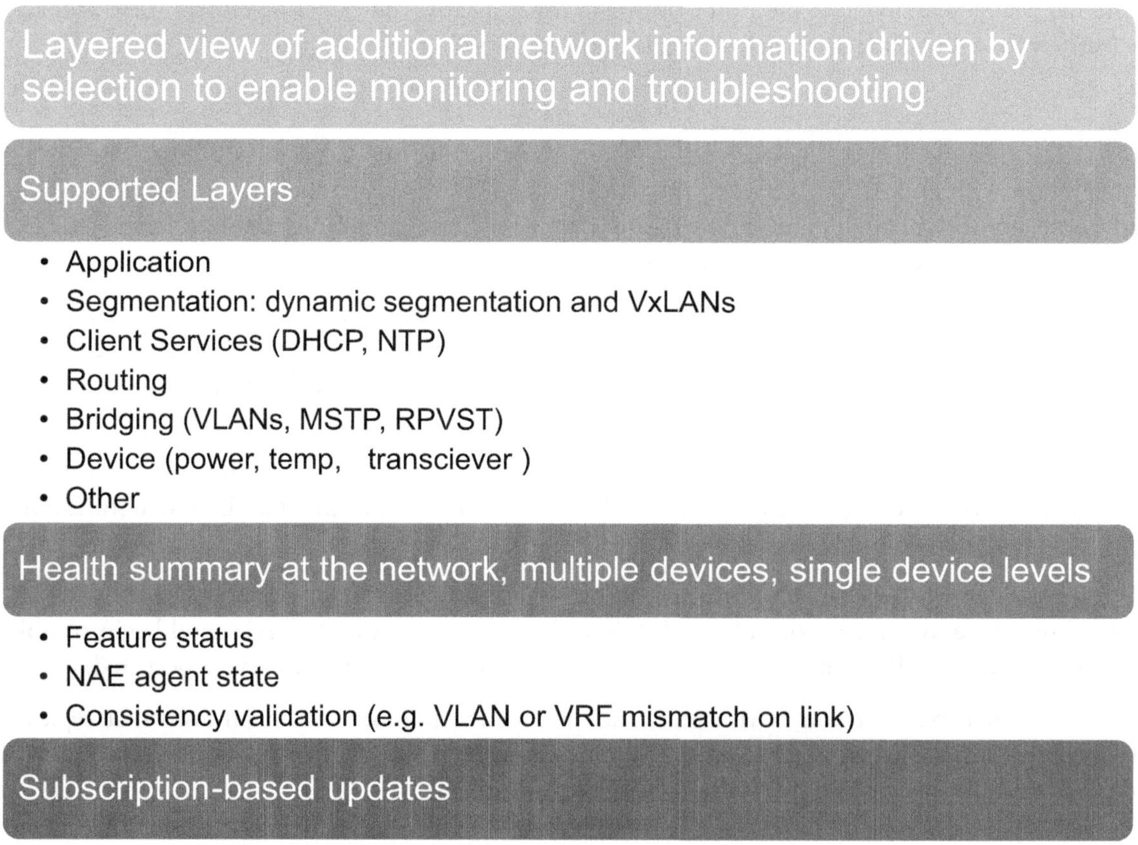

Figure 2-8 Health Layers: Monitoring and Troubleshooting

Topology Health Layers include the following, as shown in Figures 2-8–2-10:

- Application
- Client Service
- Segmentation
- Routing
- Bridging
- Device

NetEdit also supports Aruba Network Analytics Engine (NAE) status aggregation of data.

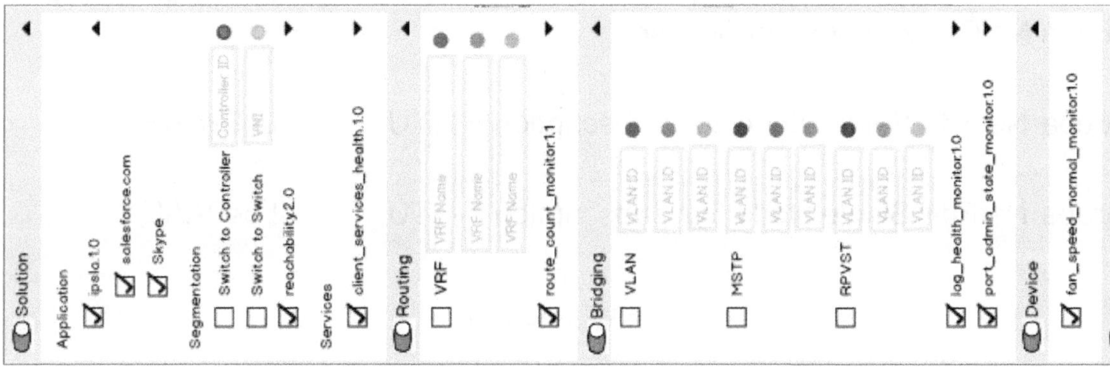

Figure 2-9 Health Layers: Monitoring and Troubleshooting

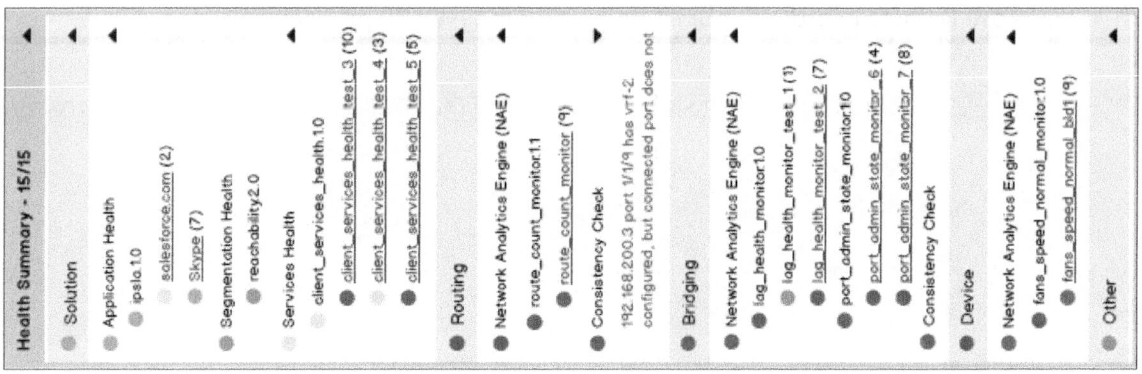

Figure 2-10 Health Layers: Monitoring and Troubleshooting (cont.)

Initial Setup

This section introduces you to what you need prepare on your AOS-CX switches in order for NetEdit to successfully integrate with them as well as how NetEdit can discover devices.

Licensing

NetEdit is currently available on a trial basis for up to 25 nodes. There are also licensing options for one-year and three-year subscriptions (Figure 2-11). Also, when implementing virtual switching, each physical switch in the stack will need a separate NetEdit license.

Description	Part Number
Aruba NetEdit 25 node trial license	N/A
Aruba NetEdit Single Node 1yr Subscription E-STU	JL639AAE
Aruba NetEdit Single Node 3yr Subscription E-STU	JL640AAE

Figure 2-11 Licensing

Note

Aruba does not officially offer support for the trial version of NetEdit. Customers need to purchase licenses in order to obtain support for the NetEdit product.

Minimum AOS-CX Device Configuration for NetEdit

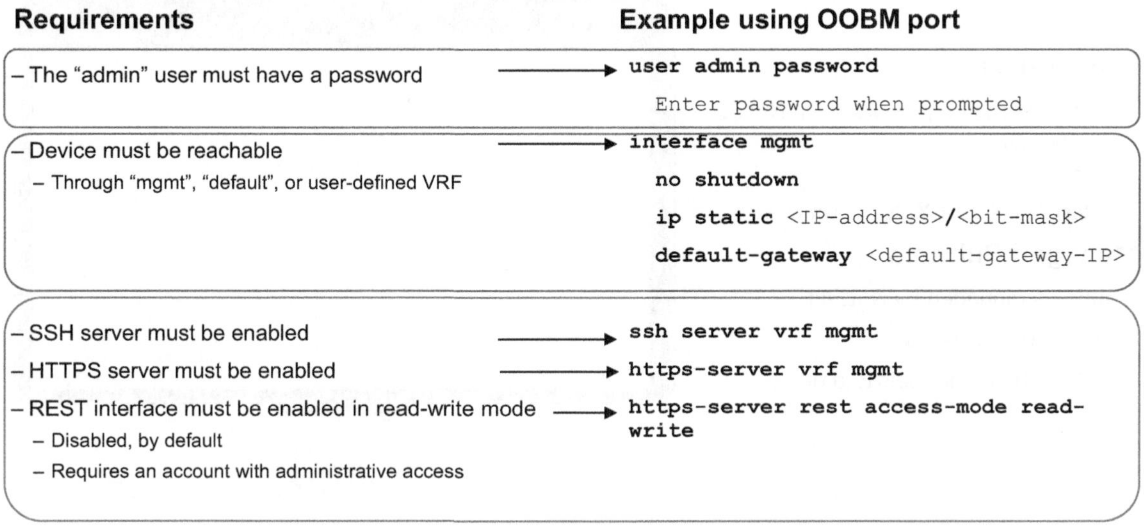

Figure 2-12 Minimum AOS-CX Device Configuration for NetEdit

For successful communication between Aruba NetEdit and the AOS-CX switch, you need to complete a few minimum configuration requirements on the AOS-CX switch (Figure 2-12).

The REST interface is disabled by default and, like HTTPS, must be enabled. Likewise, access requires a switch account with administrative access.

Note

These commands are covered in the Aruba associate-level switching course.

NetEdit Discovering Devices: Credential/Subnet Management

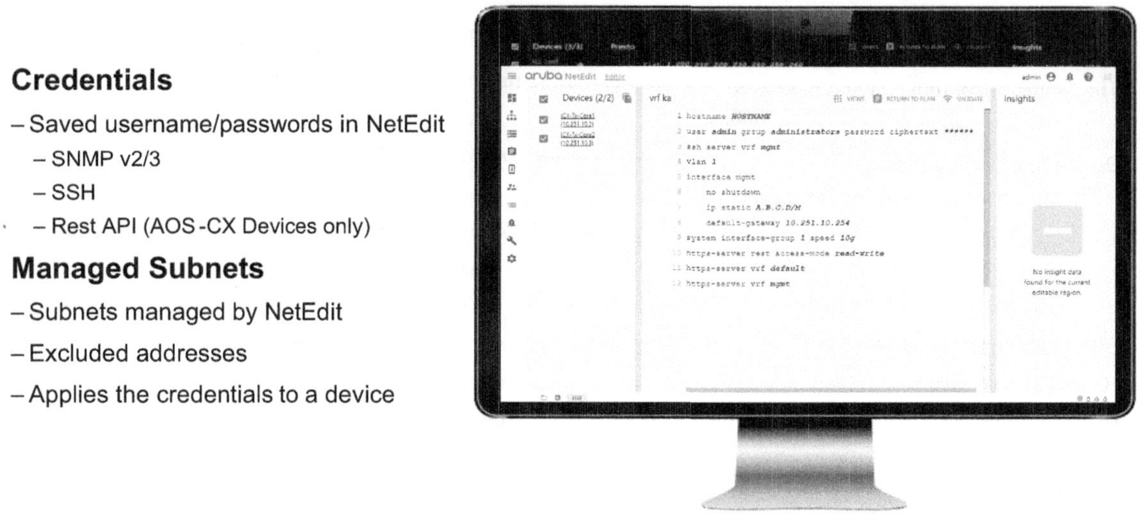

Figure 2-13 NetEdit Discovering Devices: Credential/Subnet Management

NetEdit has two sets of usernames and passwords: one for Linux access and one for NetEdit access. When you log into NetEdit for the first time, you enter a username of admin and a blank password. You are then prompted to change the password, which must minimally be eight characters in length.

In NetEdit 2.0 there is no longer the batch adding and adding single devices. NetEdit now allows for users to save Credentials within NetEdit and discover devices within a subnet (Figure 2-13).

NetEdit will now also discover and display third-party devices that are using the standard MIBs. Using SNMP with NetEdit, administrators can also enter SSH credentials for third-party devices.

The managed subnets are what is used to determine what devices fall under the NetEdit management umbrella, admins can make this umbrella as large or narrow as they would like, and they also have the ability Exclude addresses as well.

NetEdit Discovering Devices: Discovery In-Depth

How do all the pieces fit together? First specify a credential set. Then define a subnet that requires to be discovered and the credential set to be used. Then define one seed device in the subnet that will then discover other devices based on LLDP.

The discovery process follows the steps shown in Figure 2-14:

1. Seed devices are fingerprinted and scanned.
2. Seed devices gather neighbor device info including management IP, LLDP/CDP.

3. NetEdit Checks if the Device is under the managed subnet and not excluded.
4. NetEdit Checks for existing MAC addresses (LLDP change event updates the topology).
5. Device scanning will occur on periodic intervals every 5 minutes.

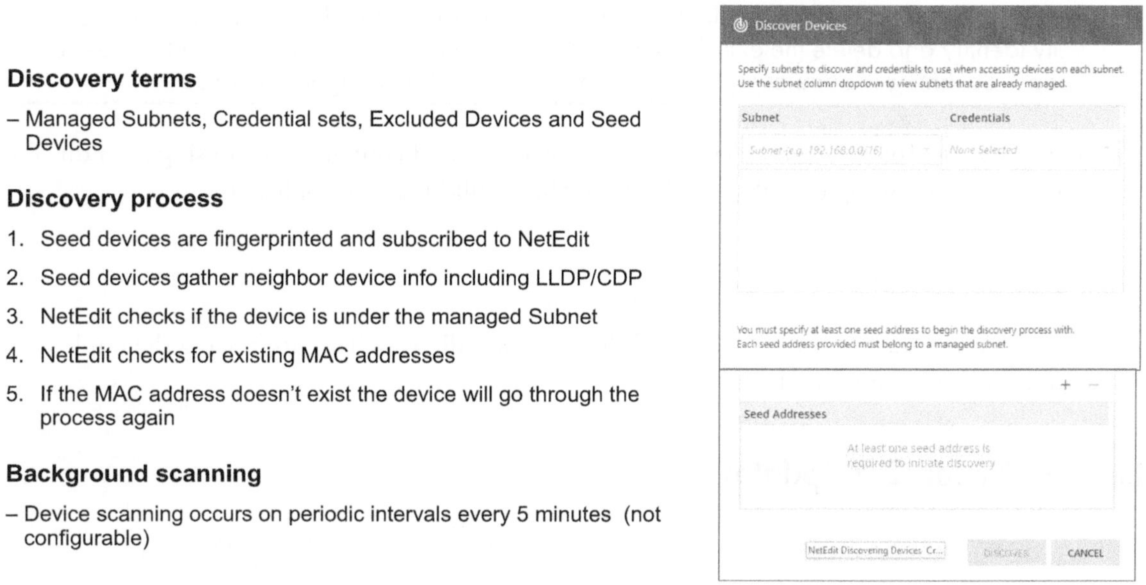

Figure 2-14 NetEdit Discovering Devices: Discovery In-Depth

Specify the subnets NetEdit should use to discover devices. Where connectivity between subnets exists, the discovery process can find all the connected subnets from a single starting point called a seed device. If there are subnets NetEdit should discover that are not connected, provide a seed device to use as a starting point in each separate group of connected subnets.

- Use the top portion of the Discover Devices dialog to enter subnets in CIDR format. Each subnet must be associated with credentials that specify the REST and/or SNMP credentials that NetEdit should use to read data from the devices in that subnet.
- Use the bottom portion of the Discover Devices dialog to enter seed device IP addresses. One seed is needed from each group of connected subnets. If all subnets are connected, then a single seed will suffice as long as the appropriate credentials were specified for each subnet so that NetEdit can traverse all the connecting devices. Multiple seeds may be specified too, but are not required.

Note

When discovery is initiated using a router attached to multiple subnets as a seed device, each IP address of the router that is a subnet that NetEdit should discover may appear as a separate device in NetEdit. Specifying multiple IP addresses from such a router as seeds will definitely cause such "duplicate" devices to appear in NetEdit. If this happens, manually identify and delete the extraneous "duplicate" devices from NetEdit using the Devices page. Scanning is done every 5 minutes and this is not a configurable value.

You should now be able to see the devices on your network and configure them using NetEdit. For more information on using NetEdit, see the online help build into the application.

Key Capabilities

This section introduces some of the key capabilities of NetEdit as well as introducing the implementation of device configuration plans.

NetEdit Version 2.0 Updates

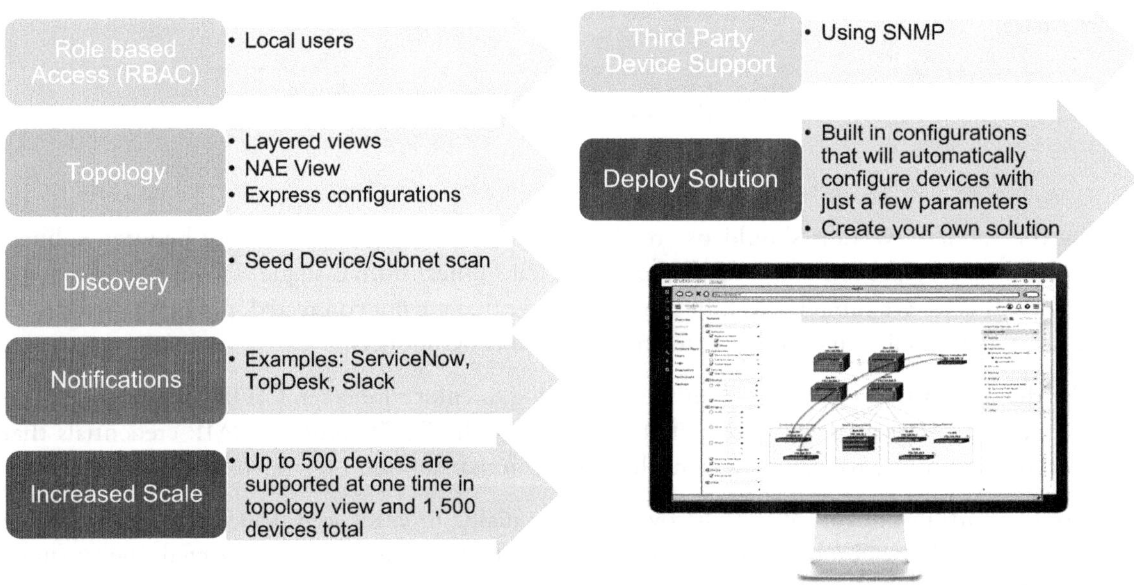

Figure 2-15 NetEdit Version 2.0 Updates

Network View

New in NetEdit 2.0 is a network view (topology page), as shown in Figure 2-16, where you can see the interconnections of both AOS-CX and non-AOS-CX devices that NetEdit learned. Please note that the information on the screen is searchable.

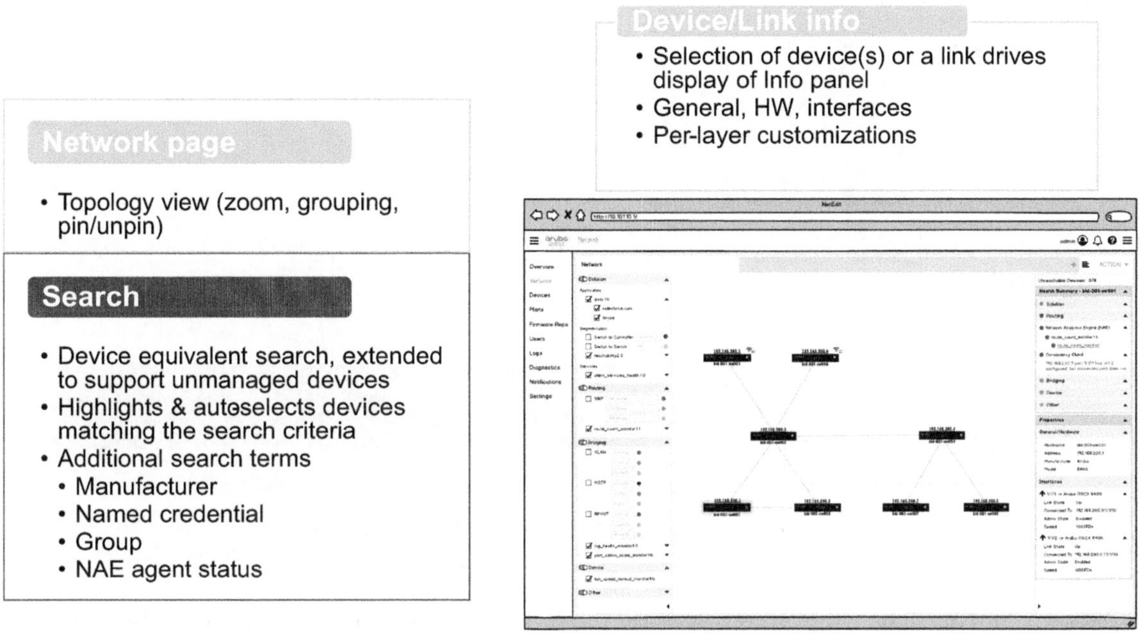

Figure 2-16 Network View

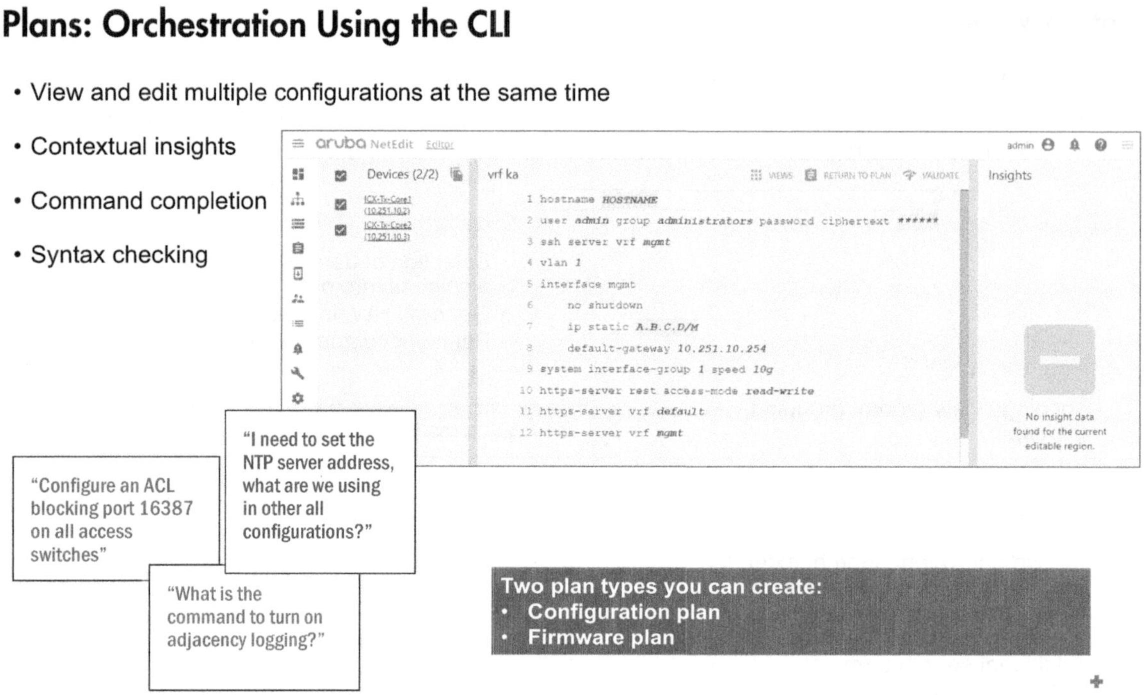

Figure 2-17 Plans: Orchestration Using the CLI

A *plan* is a concept designed to allow users and the NetEdit application to create a container to group devices and allow subsequent execution of operations on the device group. These include edit, deploy, commit, or rollback device configuration or deploy firmware versions. There are seven different plan types. Users can define the *configuration plan* and *firmware plan*, while the NetEdit application defines the remaining plan types (Figure 2-17).

Plans: Configuration Workflow

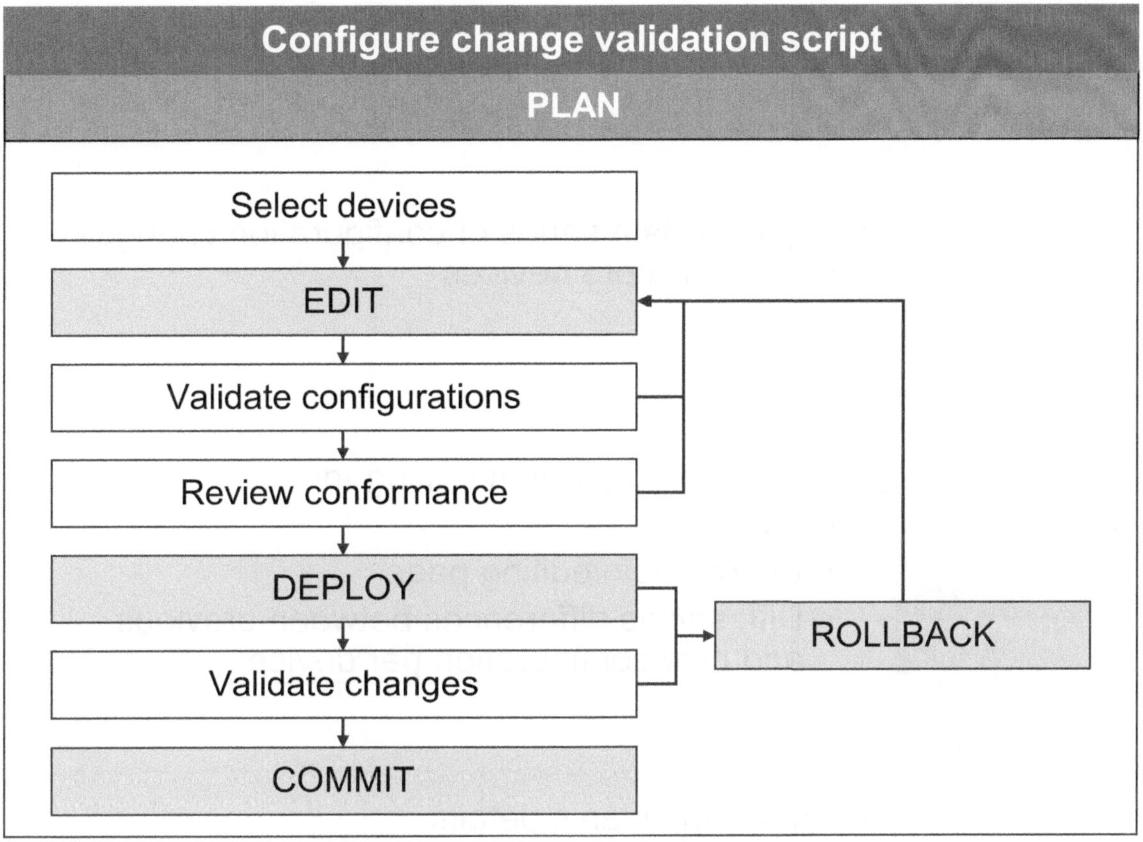

Figure 2-18 Plans: Configuration Workflow

The configuration plan is one of the core features of NetEdit. It allows a user to create configuration plans and edit either running or startup configurations for a set of devices.

The Edit feature lets you change multiple configurations at once using complete knowledge of each configuration file. Using *Edit*, you can take advantage of contextual insights that are automatically displayed. For example, you can use Edit to set the NTP or the RADIUS server address for all relevant switches or to set an ACL entry on all access switches. The Edit feature also includes command completion, syntax highlighting, and validation.

Using the *Deploy* feature, you can stage a deployment (or a rollback) on multiple switches, and validate the correct operation of switches after changes. For instance, you can determine whether a change is working properly before deploying it more widely, or you can quickly remove changes if there is a problem. Deploy automatically collects network and services state information before and after a change, and intelligently displays the difference. This lets you decide whether to keep (*Commit*) or rollback the change within your allocated change window (Figure 2-18).

Configuration Plans

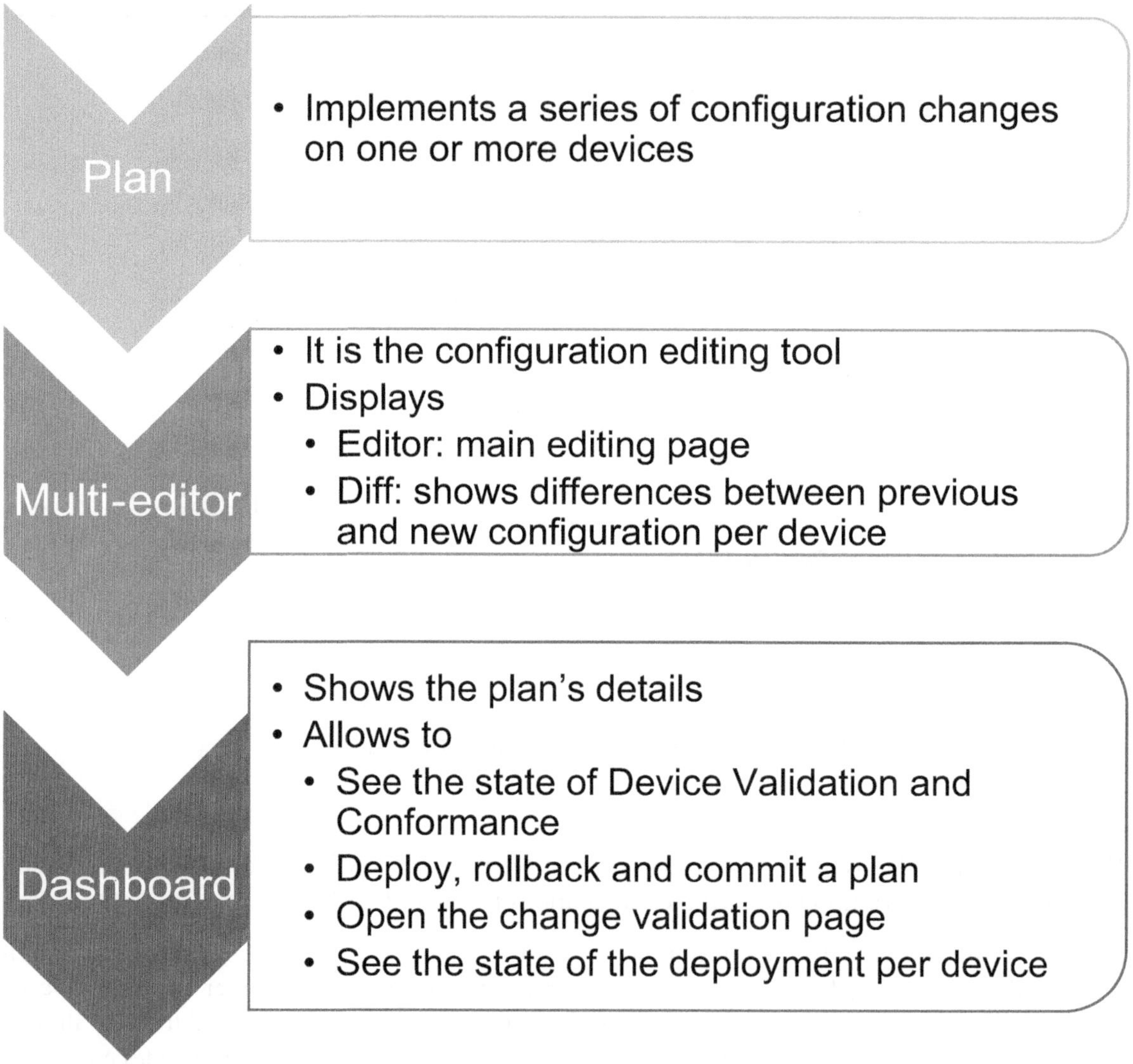

Figure 2-19 Configuration Plans

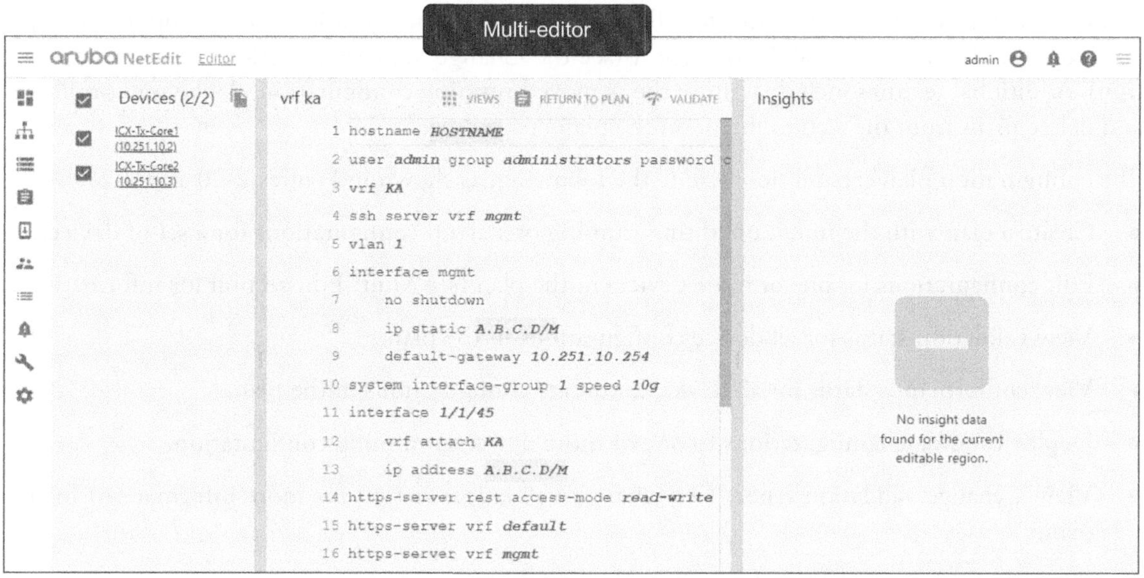

Figure 2-20 Configuration Plans

The configuration plan allows you to create a plan with the intent of editing the running configuration or startup configuration for a set of devices. This plan allows you to edit configurations for one or more devices in the plan. You can also view the validation status for all device configurations in the plan. This plan will deploy candidate configurations to one or more devices running the configuration (Figure 2-19).

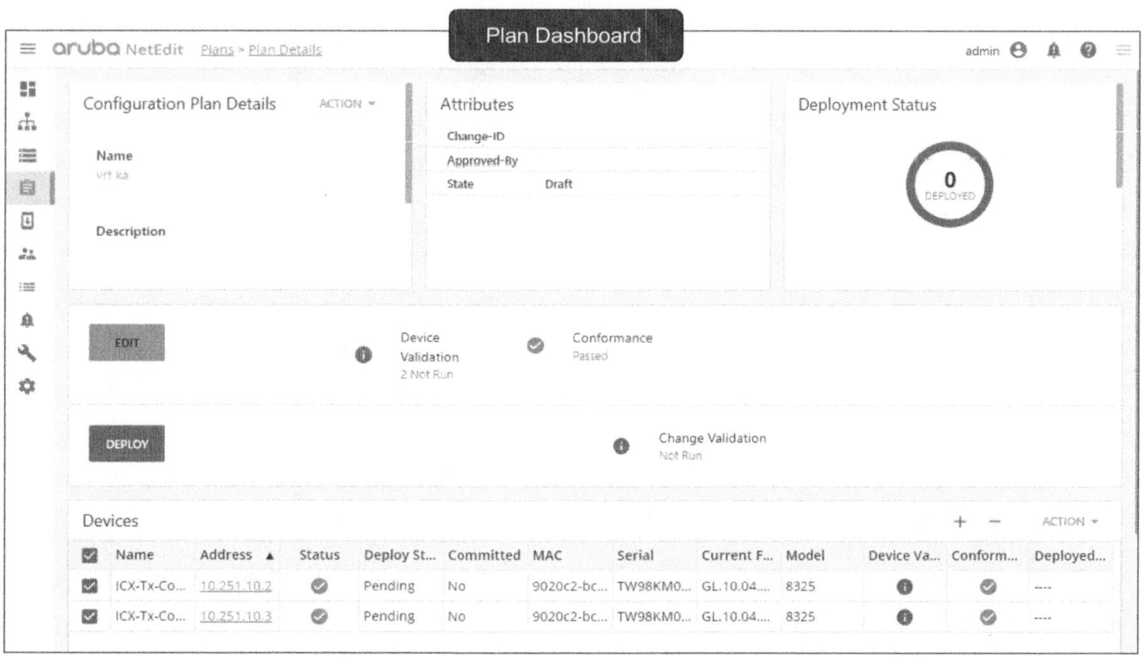

Figure 2-21 Configuration Plans

You can view the conformance status for all device candidate configurations in a configuration plan. You can also view a change validation report (see the Change Validation section for more information). Additional features include writing the deployed running configuration, deployment rollback, and delete plans from the Action menu on the plan's page.

The configuration plan capabilities include the following, as shown in Figures 2-20 and 2-21:

- Create a plan with the intent of editing running or startup configurations for a set of devices.
- Edit configurations for one or more devices in the plan (see Multi-Edit section for information).
- View validation status for all device configurations in the plan.
- View conformance status for all device candidate configurations in the plan.
- Deploy candidate configurations to one or more device(s) running configuration.
- View a change validation report (see Change Validation section for more information) for the plan.
- Write (Commit) the deployed running configuration to startup.
- Rollback (that is, Undo) the deployment as long as the device(s) running configuration is what was deployed from the plan and as long as the commit operation (write to startup) has not been executed from within the plan.
- Plans can be deleted from the Action menu in the plans page.

Search: Analyze Configurations and Plans

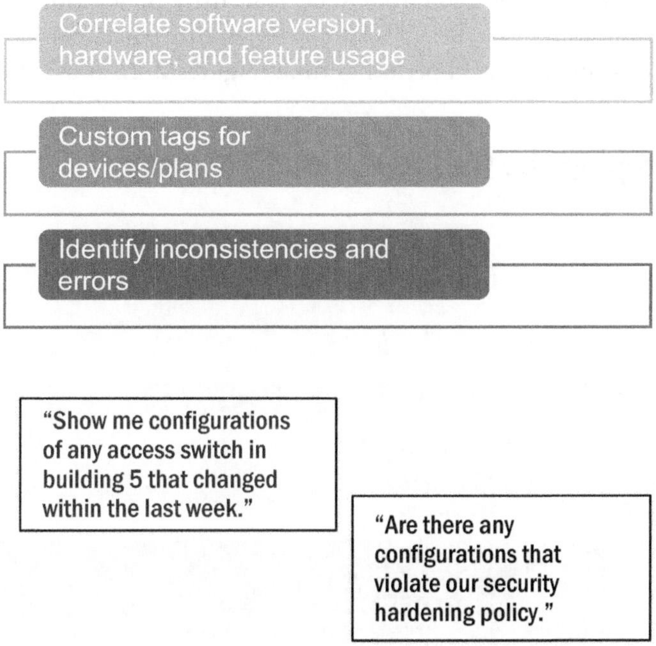

Figure 2-22 Search: Analyze Configurations and Plans

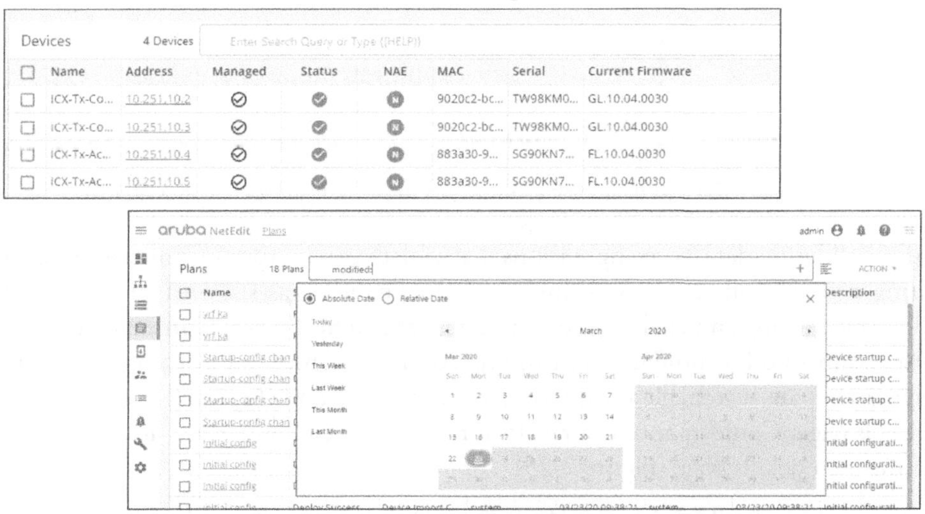

Figure 2-23 Search: Analyze Configurations and Plans

By using the search feature, you can quickly search all switch configurations (including hardware and software versions) to find the group of switches that require configuration changes or investigation. You can also identify inconsistencies and errors, such as security policy violations. For example, you can identify configurations of all switches of a specific type, in a particular location, where the configuration has changed within a selected period of time (Figures 2-22 and 2-23).

Conformance: Keeping the Configuration Consistent

Figure 2-24 Conformance: Keeping the Configuration Consistent

Conformance validation detects configurations that violate your corporate policies or network design by comparing switch configurations against conformance tests, as shown in Figure 2-24. You can define policies by creating and enabling conformance tests in **Settings > Conformance**. The tests run continuously against both candidate and running configurations. Conformance test results for running configurations are searchable on the device search page and displayed on both the dashboard and plan details page. Conformance test results for candidate configurations are displayed in the editor and on the plan details page (Figure 2-25).

The Audit feature records all hardware and software versions, as well as other configuration changes. You can then search and view all changes, or groups of changes. This allows you to track all changes to hardware, software, and configurations (whether made through NetEdit or directly on the switch) with automated versioning. If necessary, you can immediately rollback to any previous configuration. You can perform these rollbacks selectively, based upon factors such as the location of the switches or the date of the changes.

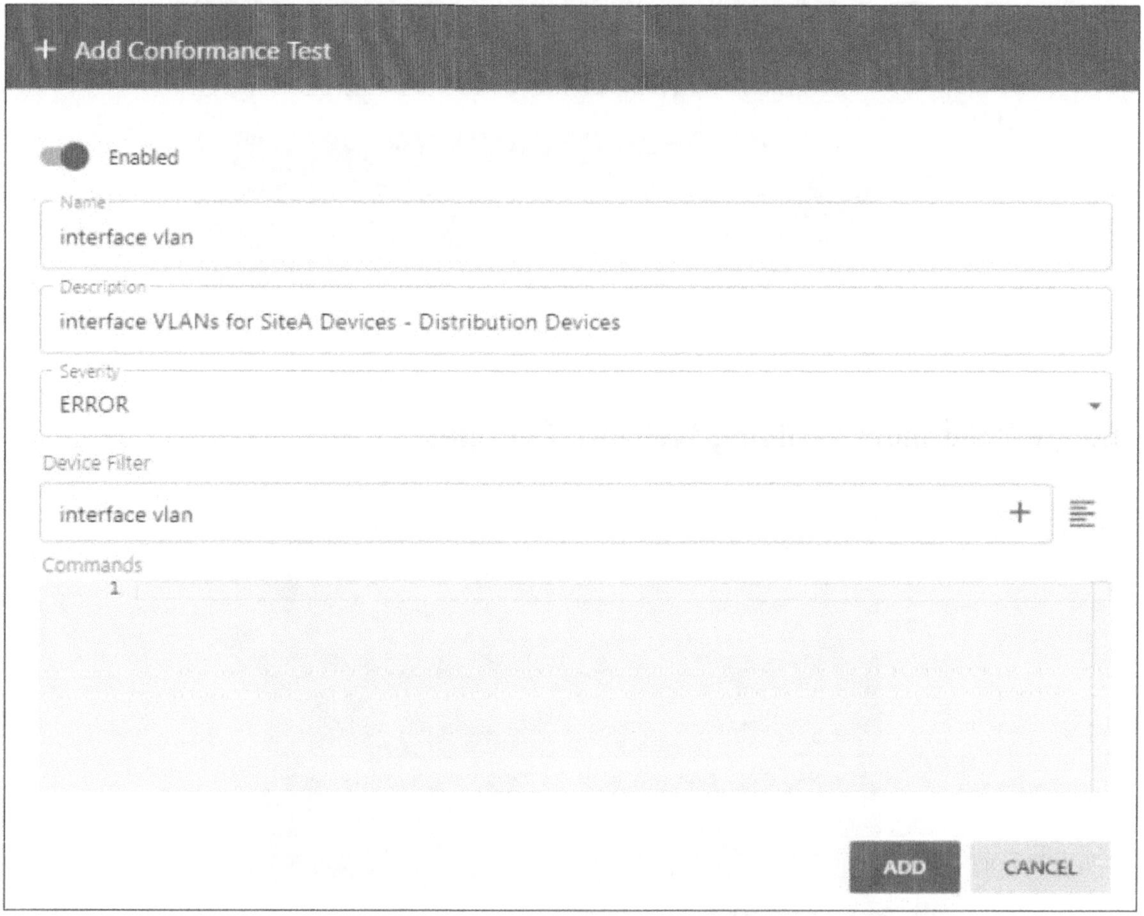

Figure 2-25 Conformance: Keeping the Configuration Consistent

Conformance Validation

Conformance tests run continuously against managed devices. When conformance validation detects a violation in the current running and startup configurations of a device, it will flag the device and you can identify it through a dashboard tile that displays the conformance violating devices (Figure 2-26).

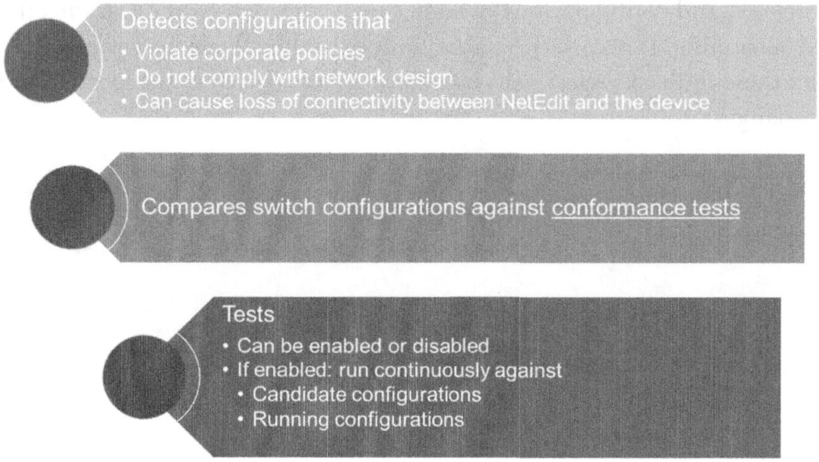

Figure 2-26 Conformance Validation

Change Validation: Verifying Network Changes

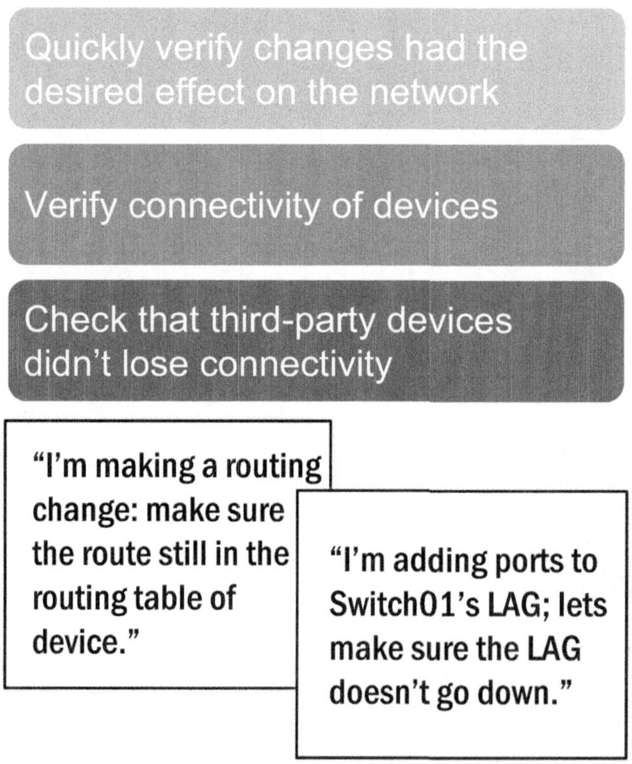

Figure 2-27 Change Validation: Verifying Network Changes

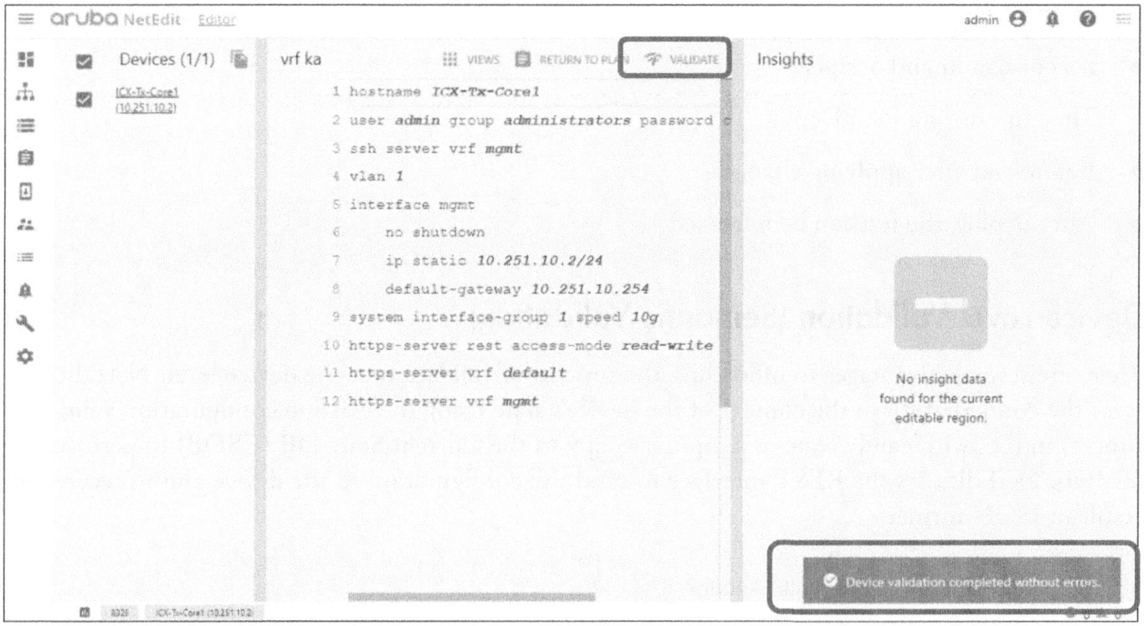

Figure 2-28 Change Validation: Verifying Network Changes

You can use Change Validation to determine whether a deployed configuration change has produced the desired result. This is accomplished by automatically collecting network state information, before and after deployment of a change, and presenting this information in a side-by-side difference formatted report. Network state is gathered using the SSH protocol.

To view the change validation settings or state for a plan, select Change Validation in the plan details page. The parameters are shown before the state is gathered. You can refresh the state information after deployment by selecting the REFRESH button. This is necessary when the network state stabilizes over time, and the difference report will be updated. You can verify expected changes in network state, or detect unexpected by reviewing this report (Figures 2-27 and 2-28).

Configuring Change Validation

The configuration consists of three parts—the **devices/resources** from which to collect state information; the **command scripts** that display the state information; and a **mapping** of the command scripts to the set of devices/resources where those commands will be executed.

Command Scripts:

- Series of **show** commands
- Can be created and updated

Command Mappings:

- Sets of Command Scripts
- They run during Plan Deploy
- Before and after applying changes
- After deploy, the test can be refreshed

Device-Level Validation (Semantic Validation)

There are several advantages to offloading the process of validation at the device level. NetEdit analyzes the configuration in the context of the device's state using the existing configuration validation process in the switch and creates a temporary copy in the Current State DB (CSDB) to perform the analysis. NetEdit uses the REST interface to send the configuration to the device and to receive the result in JSON format.

- Can be triggered from the multi -editor

  - If not, it is executed as the 1st step of the deployment
- It is performed on each device
- Analyzes the configuration in the context of the device's state
- Uses the REST interface to send the configuration to the device and to receive the result (errors)
  - JSON format
- The device uses a temporary copy in the Configuration State DB (CSDB) to perform the analysis

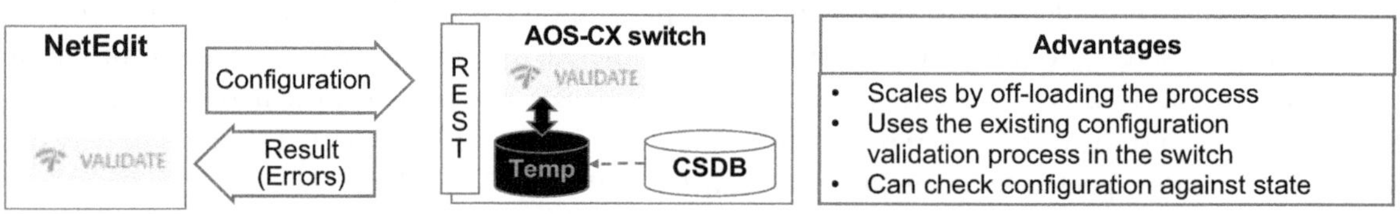

Figure 2-29 Device-Level Validation (Semantic Validation)

Validation Processes

Using **Validate**, you can continuously monitor and ensure conformance to corporate policies. You can perform validation checks on all configuration changes, including those made directly on the switch (that is, outside of NetEdit). For example, you can verify that all management IP addresses are on the management subnetwork, or that all routers running OSPF are logging adjacency changes.

You can easily customize validation tests and extend based on your existing knowledge of configuration commands (Figures 2-29 and 2-30).

Syntax validation

- When: while typing
- What: command syntax including in-line help

Semantics validation

- When: VALIDATE button (in multi-editor) or before DEPLOY
- What: configuration consistency

Conformance validation

- When: while editing
- What: compliance with conformance rules: corporate policies, minimum connectivity requirements, etc.

Consistency validation

- When: while editing
- What: example —same VLANs on two or more switches

Change validation

- When: during DEPLOY (before and after configuration deployment)
- What: compares device state before and after changes are applied (using **show** commands)

Figure 2-30 Validation Processes

AOS-CX Mobile App

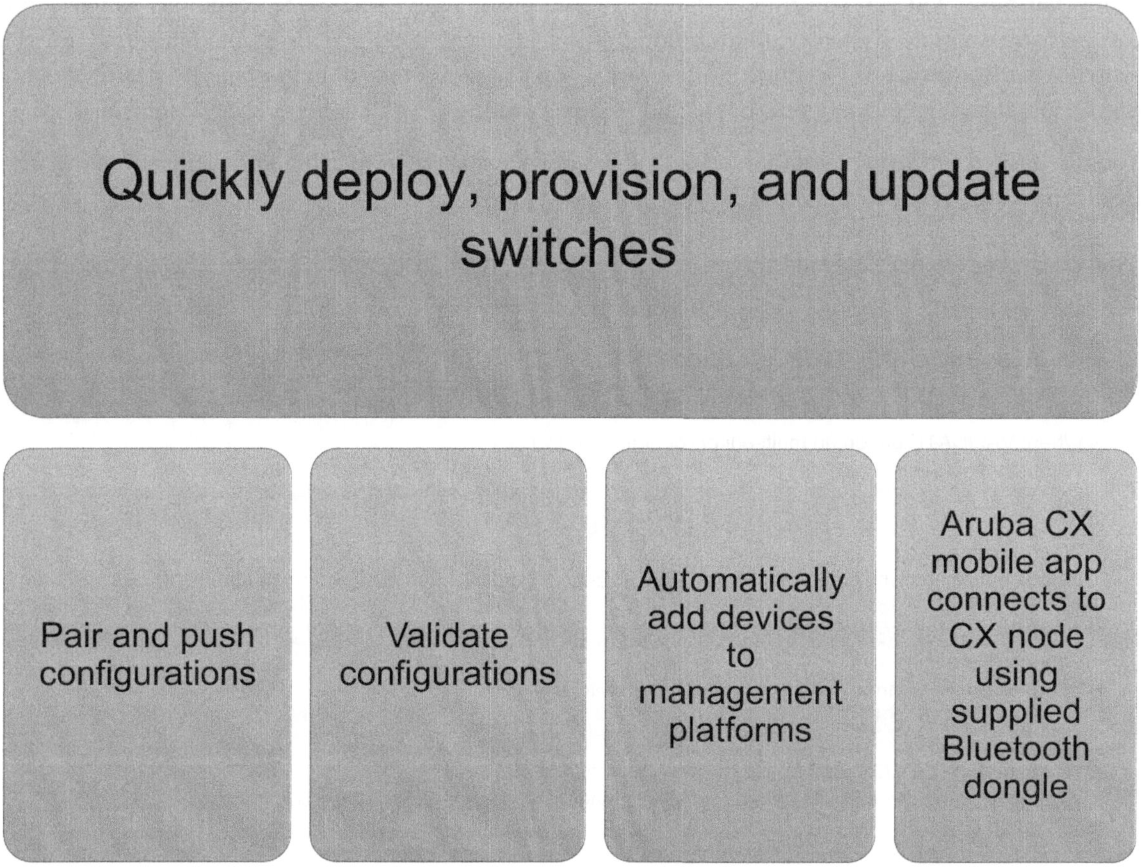

Figure 2-31 AOS-CX Mobile App Overview

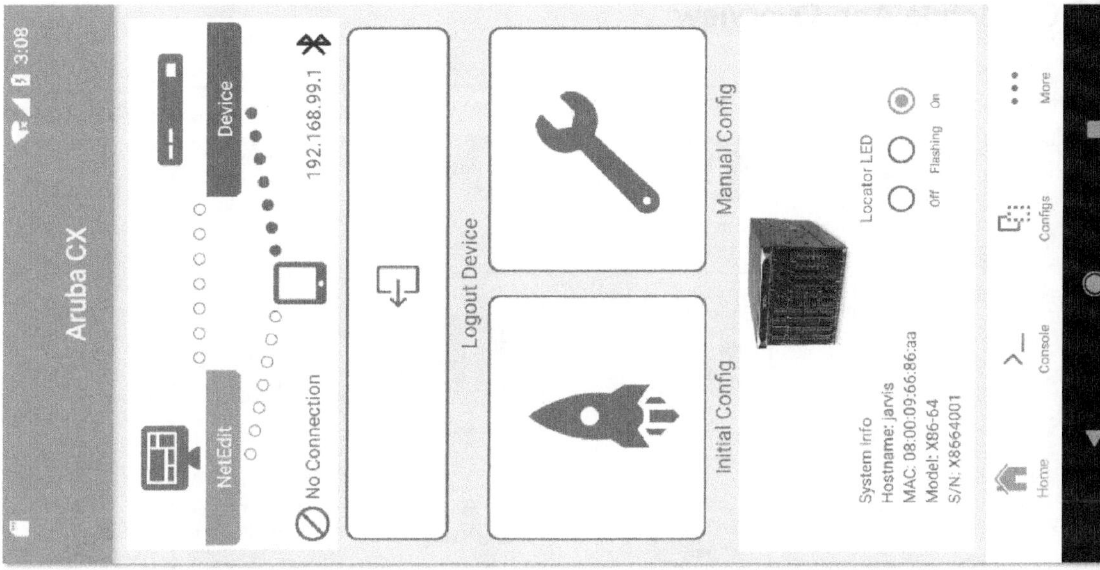

Figure 2-32 AOS-CX Mobile App Overview

Installing switches into an enterprise network just got a whole lot easier. The Aruba CX mobile app accelerates day zero configuration and deployment of Aruba switches by offering easy to configure virtualized stacking and a fast and simple way to monitor PoE usage. Switch configuration and installation at scale can be complicated and time consuming, and it also presents security risks. The AOS-CX mobile app was created to address these complexities and simplify deployment and management tasks. Connecting AOS-CX switches to the network leverages automation to provide a modern approach and the tools needed for today's always-on networking. With the AOS-CX mobile app, technicians can validate that switches were configured and installed correctly—and walk away assured they were successfully deployed—without relying on network admin teams for confirmation. The Aruba CX mobile app integrates with Aruba NetEdit, a powerful management and automation platform for intelligent configuration management, continuous conformance validation, and overall network health (Figures 2-31–2-33).

AOS-CX Mobile App Overview

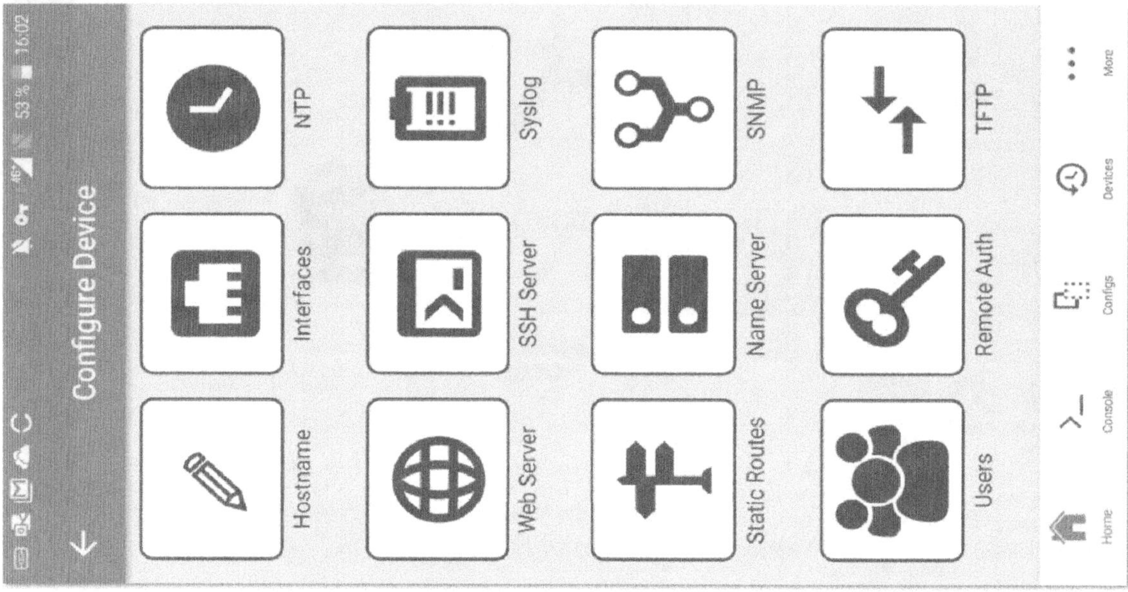

Figure 2-33 AOS-CX Mobile App Overview

The CX mobile app is the go-to application to provision a CX device. The Aruba CX mobile app connects to the CX node using supplied Bluetooth dongle.

Key Features

The Aruba CX mobile app enables you to use your iOS or Android device via Bluetooth or Wi-Fi to configure and manage Aruba AOS-CX switches. Capabilities include:

- Configuration of basic operational settings eliminates having to connect a terminal emulator and cable to the console port.
- Built-in configuration templates or ability to customize and use your own.
- Workflow enables IT to easily view and change the configuration of individual switch features or settings.
- IT can easily manage the running configuration and startup configuration of switches, and perform the following tasks:
  - Transfer files between the switch and your mobile device.
  - Share configuration files from your mobile device.
  - Copy the running configuration to the startup configuration.
  - Access the switch CLI.

  - Check the PoE budget and utilization on switches from the CX mobile app home screen to see available capacity as new PoE devices are added.
- Auto-detection of potential stack members and stack links makes it go from independent switches to a virtualized stack with just a few taps.
- Update Tile feature allows a switch with an http server connection to easily download the latest firmware.
- Integration with Aruba NetEdit provides intelligent configuration management, continuous conformance validation, and overall network health.
- Aruba NetEdit Technician feature lets you limit access to only adding switches, eliminating the possibility of other network changes.

Mobile App Requirements

The minimum supported requirements are:

- Android—5.0 Lollipop and greater
  - Some Android phones do not support simultaneously Bluetooth IP stack and Wi-Fi IP stack. Example: OnePlus3, Sony, etc. With such devices, the NetEdit device import is not possible as part of the Initial Config upload process.
- iPhone—iOS 12
- 8400, 8320, 8325 running at least 10.02.0001 and 6300/6400 running at least 10.04
- Bluetooth 4.0 dongle
- On Android, Internet Sharing has to be enabled while pairing the AOS-CX switch with the phone (otherwise device will not get an IP address over Bluetooth).

Initial Config

Initial Config Menu actions use REST API call to AOS-CX and to NetEdit server. The CX mobile app uses the DryRun API to validate configuration before configuration deployment to the actual running configuration (like NetEdit). This provides access to the Template Selection and the capability to deploy initial configuration even without having access to NetEdit server.

AOS-CX Mobile App Version 2.0 Updates

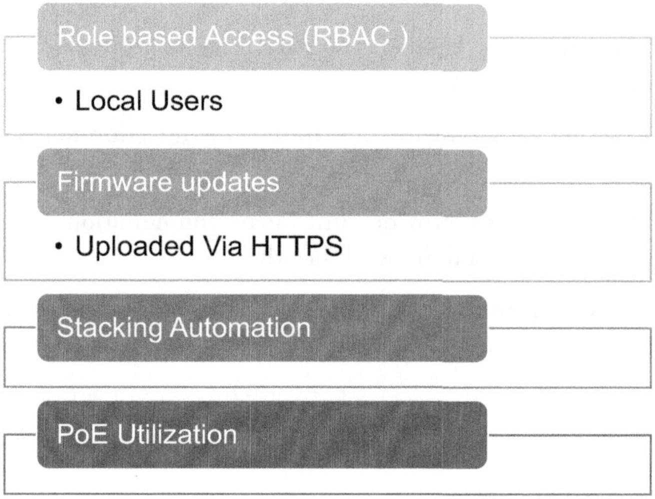

Figure 2-34 AOS-CX Mobile App Version 2.0 Updates

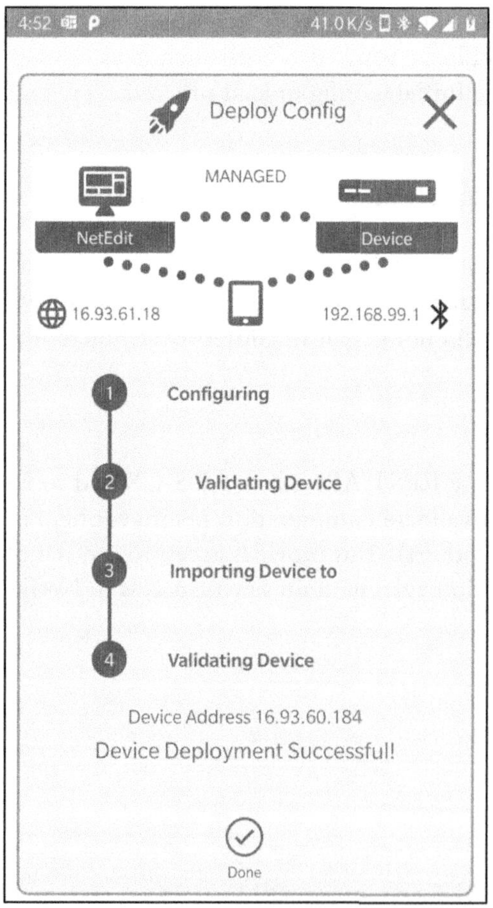

Figure 2-35 AOS-CX Mobile App Version 2.0 Updates

The CX mobile app is the go-to application to provision a CX device. Version 2.0 will allow an operator to stack switches; see PoE utilization, and upgrade devices via HTTPS (Figures 2-34 and 2-35).

Note

See the *Aruba CX Mobile App User Guide* for more information about using the app to manage/monitor a switch(es).

Lab 2: NetEdit

This section covers the NetEdit lab.

Lab Diagram

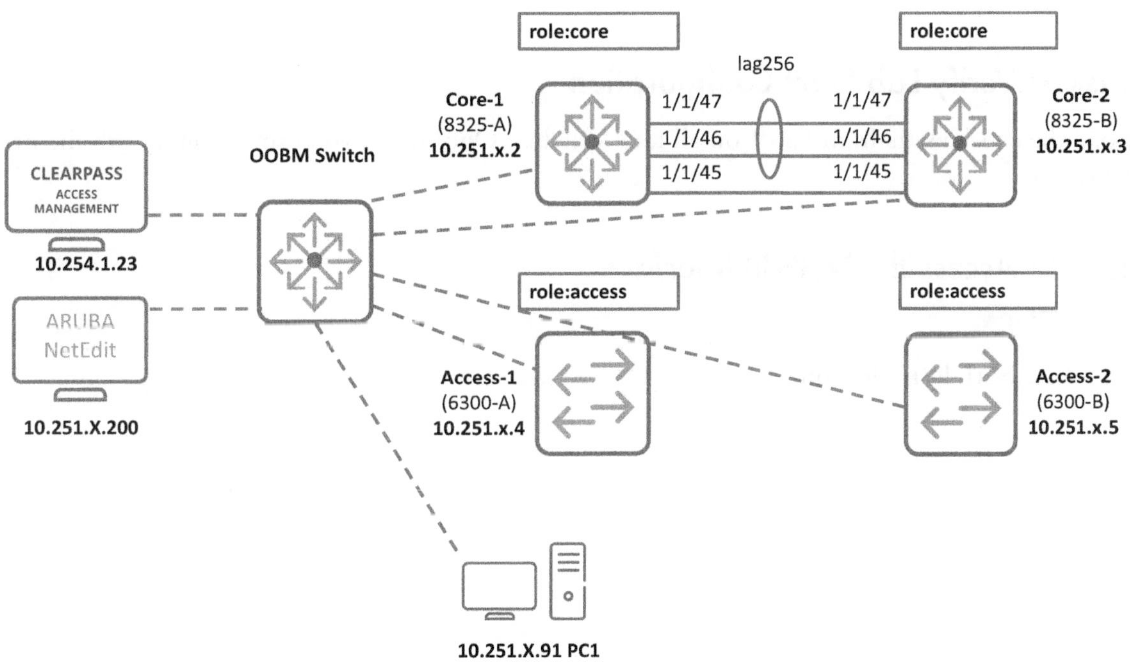

Figure 2-36 Lab Diagram

Overview

In this lab activity, as shown in Figure 2-38, NetEdit will be used to manage and monitor the switches. First the switches will be discovered. Next a configuration plan will be pushed to the switches.

To verify if a configuration change has the expected result, it is possible to define validation rules in NetEdit. This feature will be explored in the lab.

The lab will show how devices in NetEdit can be logically grouped using attributes.

NetEdit supports conformance rules, so an administrator can have automated configuration checks and alerts if a configuration is not compliant.

Objectives

- Learn how to use the NetEdit interface
- Perform device discovery using NetEdit
- Learn how to use a plan to deploy configurations to the switches
- Understand and configure plan validation rules
- Understand device grouping using attributes
- Configure device conformance rules

Task 1: Verify Lab Start Configuration

Load the checkpoints from Lab 1 on all four switches. Once done, you can continue with the next task.

Task 2: Access the NetEdit Interface

Objectives

- Basic NetEdit navigation

Steps

1. Open a session to PC1 (Management PC—OOBM). On the management station, open a web browser (Firefox for example) and navigate to the NetEdit host (**10.251.x.200**). This connection is made via the OOBM network. Log in using a username of **admin** and no password.

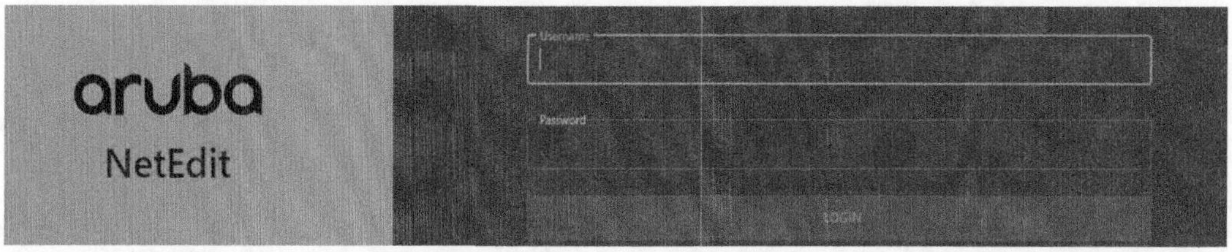

2. After the installation, the first time the admin user connects, a new admin password must be set. Set the password to **aruba123**. The NetEdit overview screen will now be displayed.

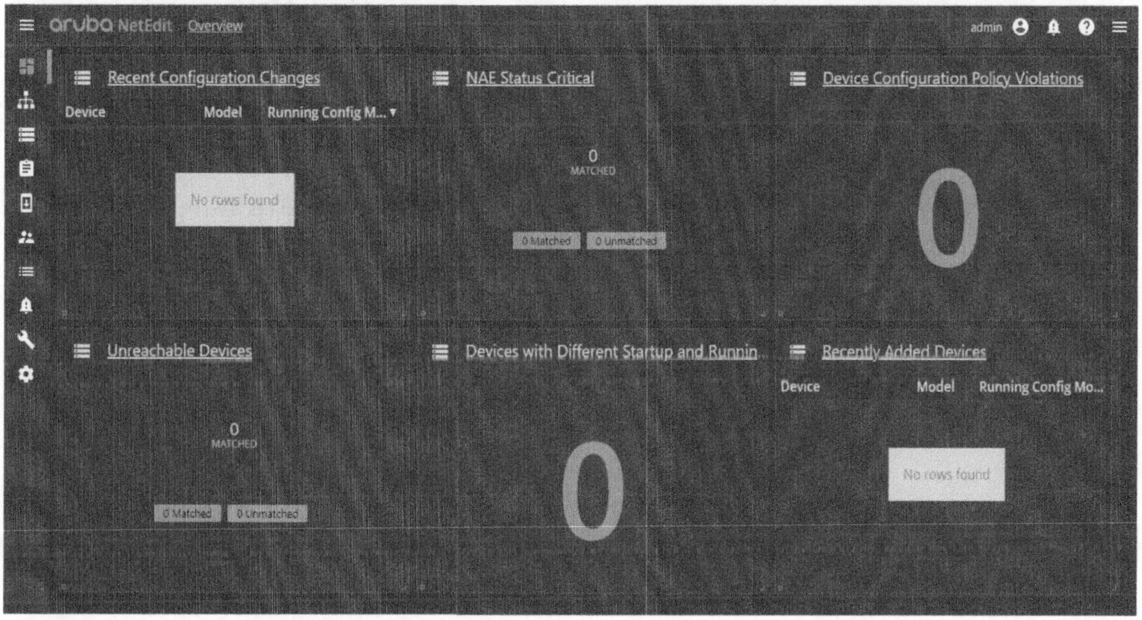

3. The display settings can be changed under **Settings > Appearance**. In the training guide screenshots, the theme has been set to **LIGHT**. You can use your own preferences during the labs.

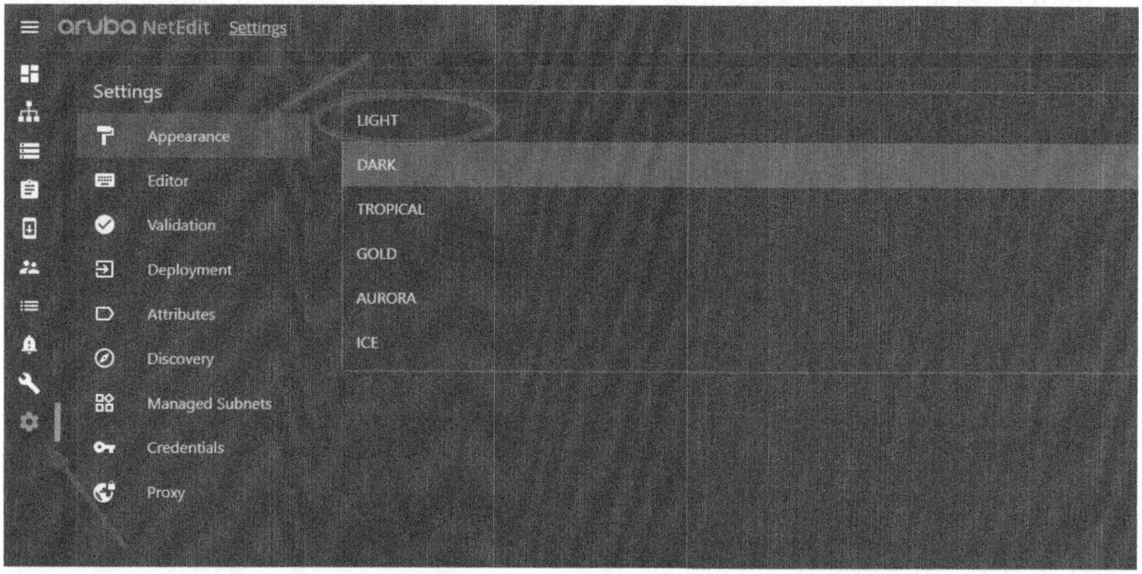

4. Check the current version of NetEdit. Navigate to the **help** icon on the right-top.

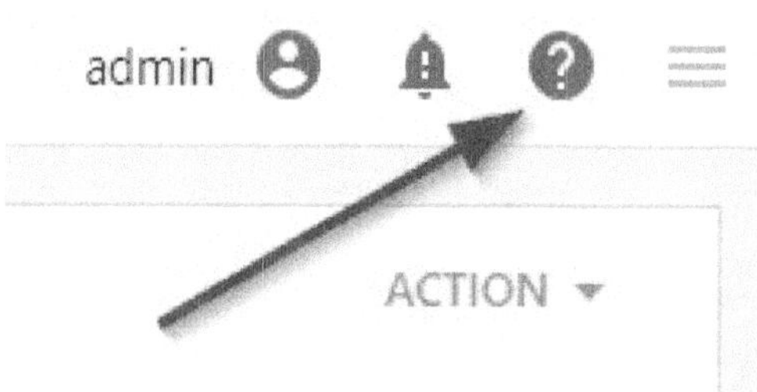

5. Select the **About** option. Review the current version of NetEdit.

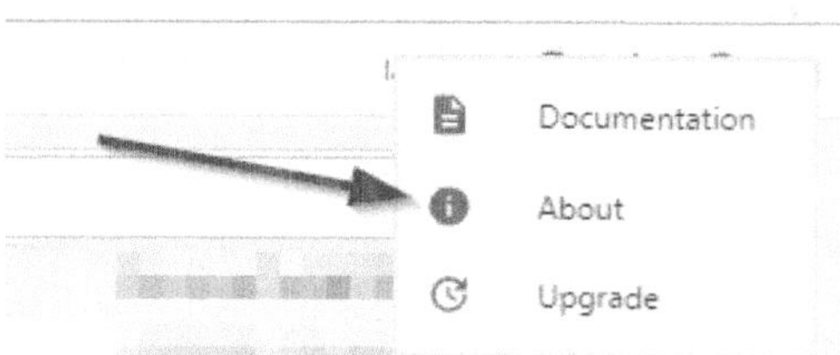

Question: Why is a license needed for NetEdit?

Answer: A subscription license should be installed as of the first switch (node) that NetEdit needs to manage or monitor. This is recommended for every production node in order to be able to get support for NetEdit. There is a trial version of NetEdit that can handle a maximum of 25 nodes, but there is no support for that version.

6. Close the About screen; open the **Help > Documentation** link. The complete NetEdit documentation is included in the product on this link; consult this link when you need more information about NetEdit. Close the documentation webpage by closing the tab in the browser.

Task 3: Device Discovery and Device Information

Objectives

- Discover the switches of your own table
- Set access credentials
- Perform discovery
- Use a seed device address
- Review device details

Steps

NetEdit Device Credentials

1. First, NetEdit must be configured with the correct credentials, so it can access the devices using the REST API. Navigate to **Settings > Credentials**.

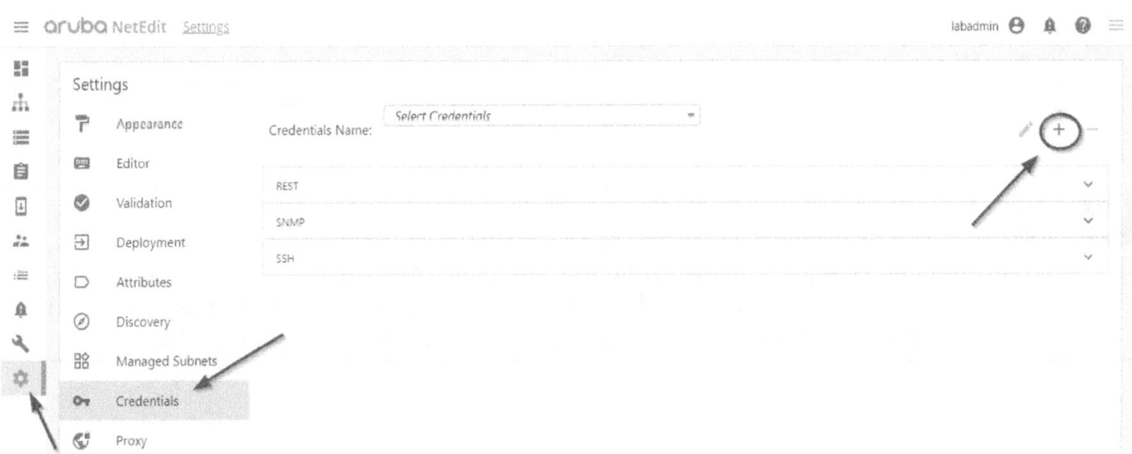

2. Multiple credentials can be used in a network, so NetEdit can be configured with multiple sets of credentials. Add a new set of credentials using these settings.

- Name: **icx-lab**
- REST: **admin/aruba123**
- SSH: **admin/aruba123**
- Click **Create** to save the new credentials.

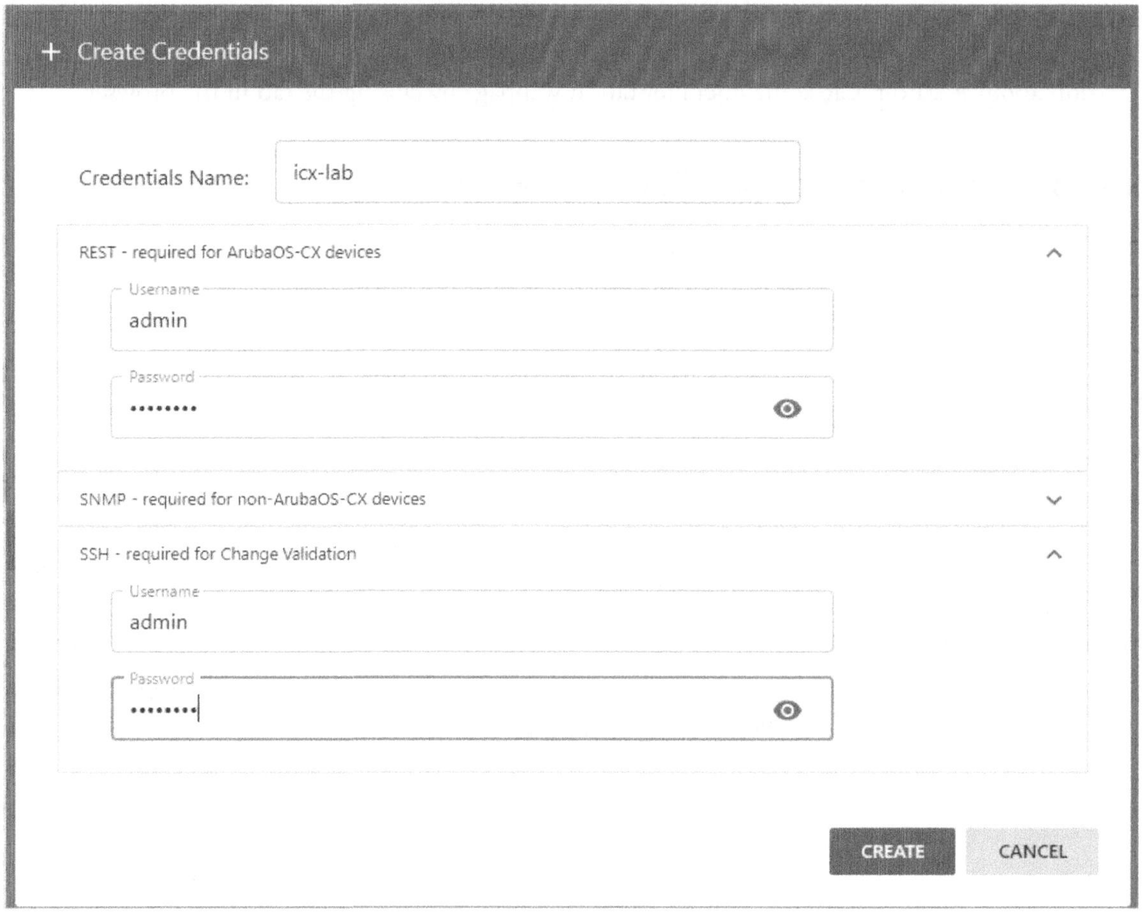

Note

All configuration changes will be made using the REST API. NetEdit can also collect validation information, such as output of 'show' commands, or perform another command, such as 'ping' to some host. These validation commands are executed over SSH.

3. Once the credentials have been added, they should be visible in the credential dropdown list.

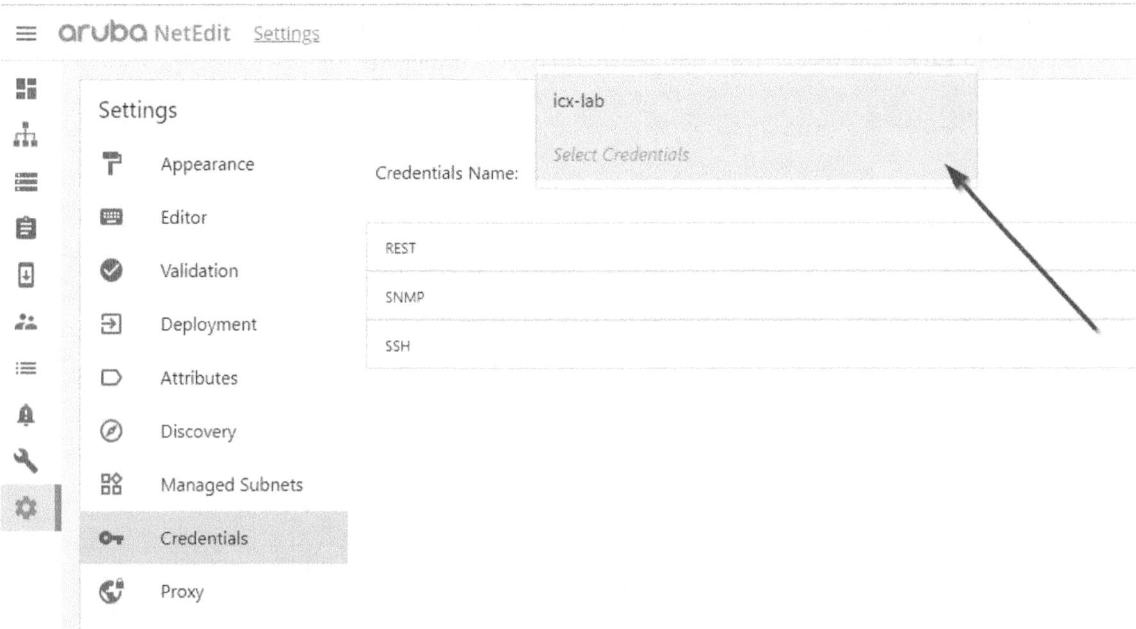

4. If a mistake was made and credentials need to be changed, the 'pen' icon on the right-top can be used.

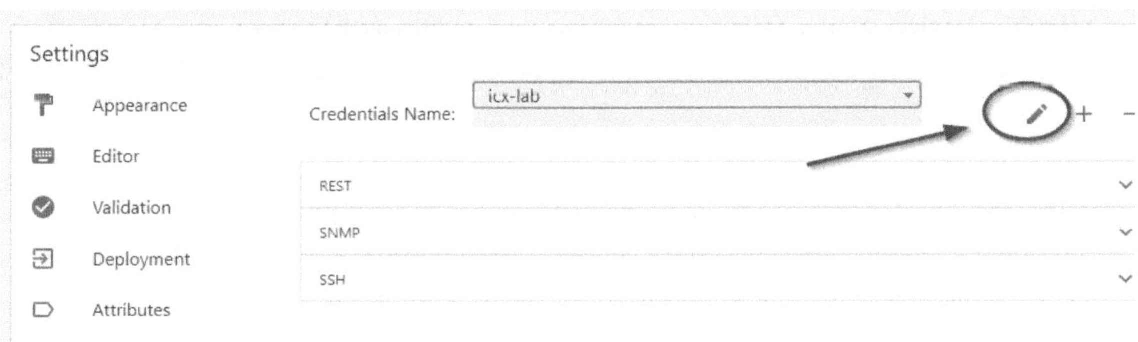

NetEdit Logging

1. Any changes made by an administrator in NetEdit will be recorded in the NetEdit log system. Navigate to **Logs** and review the changes that have been logged.

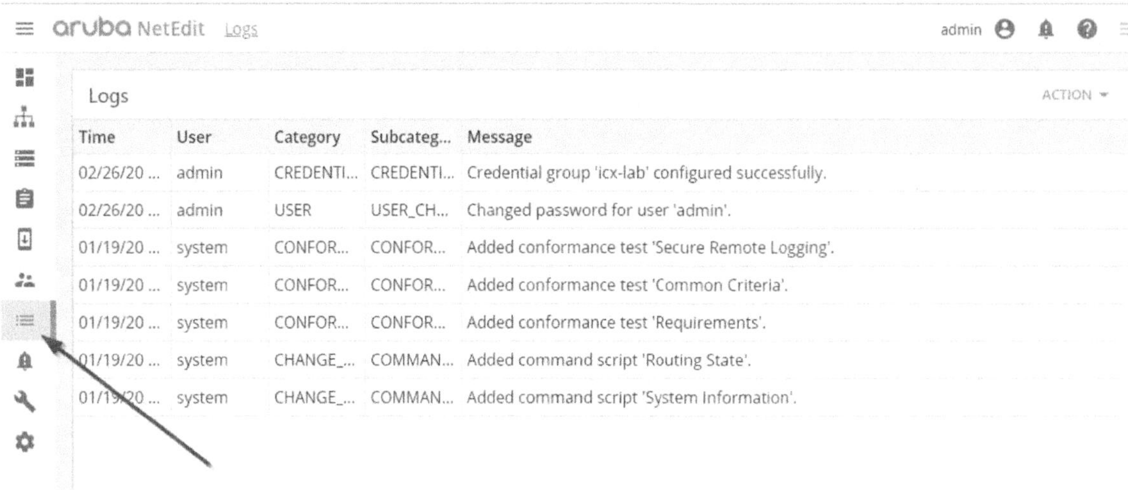

Device Discovery

In this section, the switches will be discovered and added into NetEdit.

1. Select the **Devices** section, from the **Action** menu select **Discover Devices**.

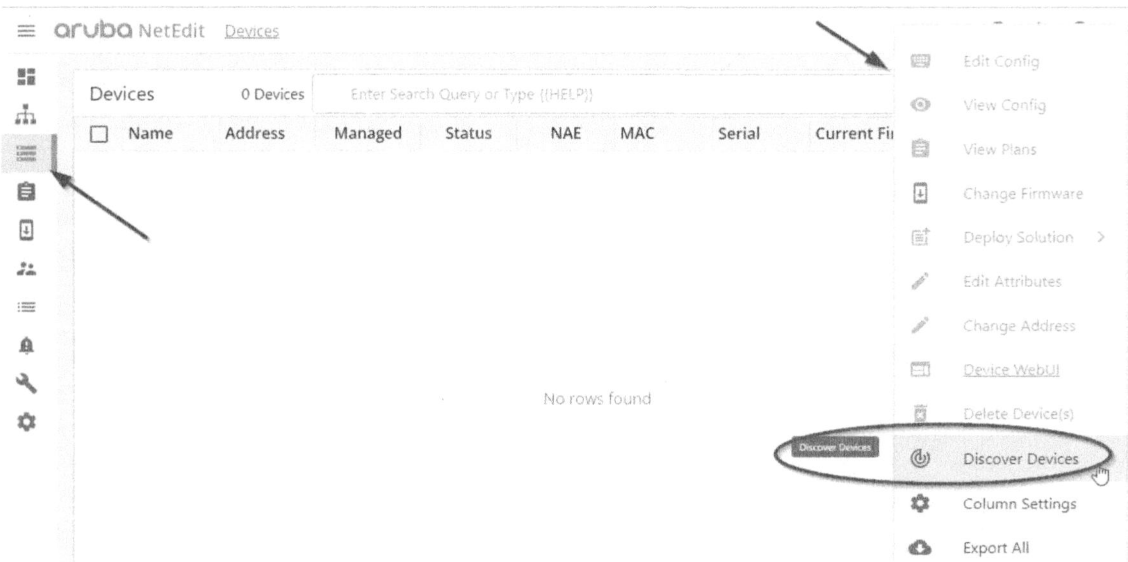

2. Add the management subnet of your table (**10.251.x.0/24**), and select the credentials that were previously defined. In the seed address table, add the OOBM IP addresses of the switches of your table. You may need to scroll down to see the "seed address" list.

Note
In the current state of the lab, the switches do not have an 'in-band' connection, so they cannot discover other switches using LLDP yet. In a network where the switches do have in-band connection, NetEdit would automatically add newly discovered LLDP devices that have an IP address on the configured Subnet.

- Core1: 10.251.x.2
- Core2: 10.251.x.3
- Access1: 10.251.x.4
- Access2: 10.251.x.5
- Select the checkbox for each Seed Address and click **Discover** to start the discovery.

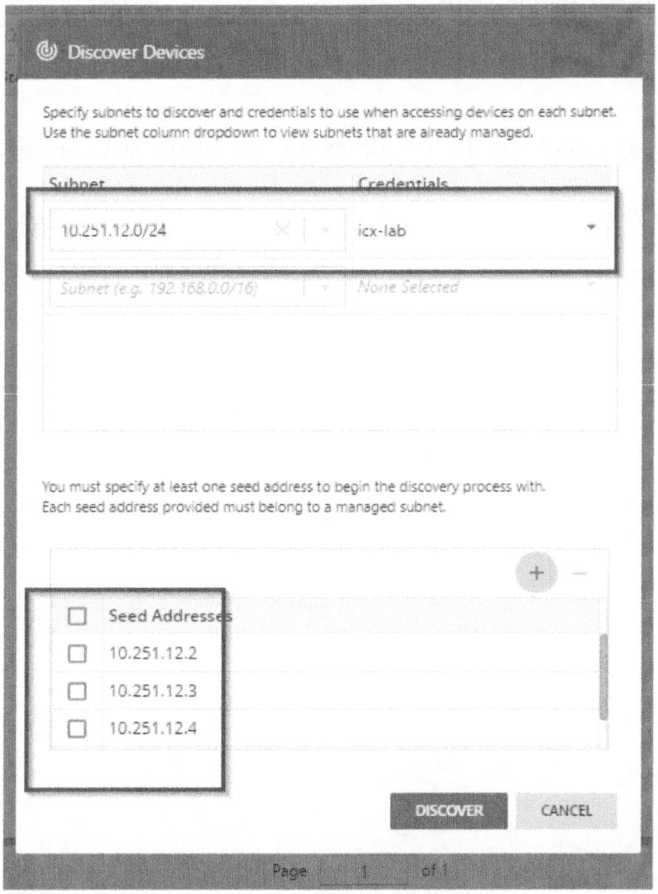

3. Wait a few moments, the four switches should appear in the list.

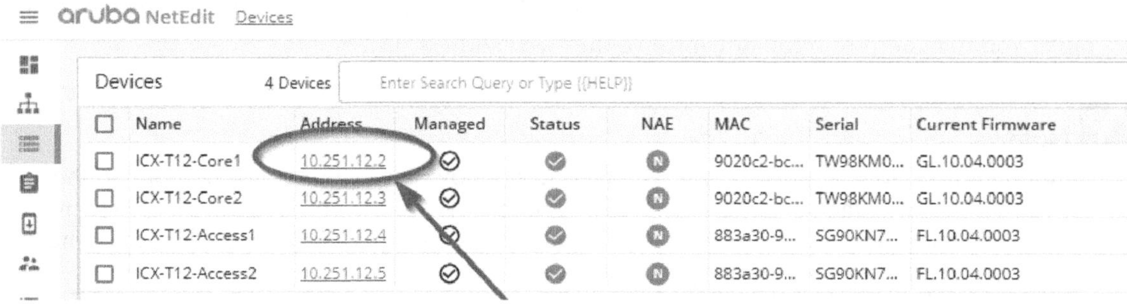

Important

Make sure all four switches are added to NetEdit at this point. In case a device cannot be added, check:

- IP address of the OOBM interface on the devices (interface mgmt)
- admin password
- REST API access was enabled for the 8325 switches
- Refer to Lab 1 for the steps.

Device Details

1. On the **Devices** page, click on the IP address of one of the switches to see the details of the device.

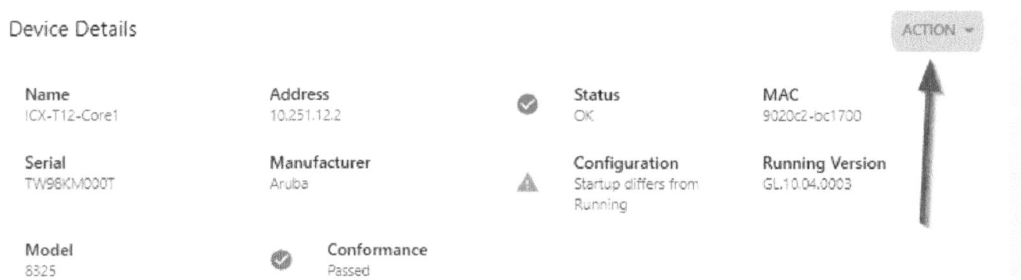

2. In the details screen, the MAC and serial of the device are listed. The **Action** menu provides the administrator with access to the "running" and "startup" configuration, "firmware" and "hardware" information and the option to reboot the device.

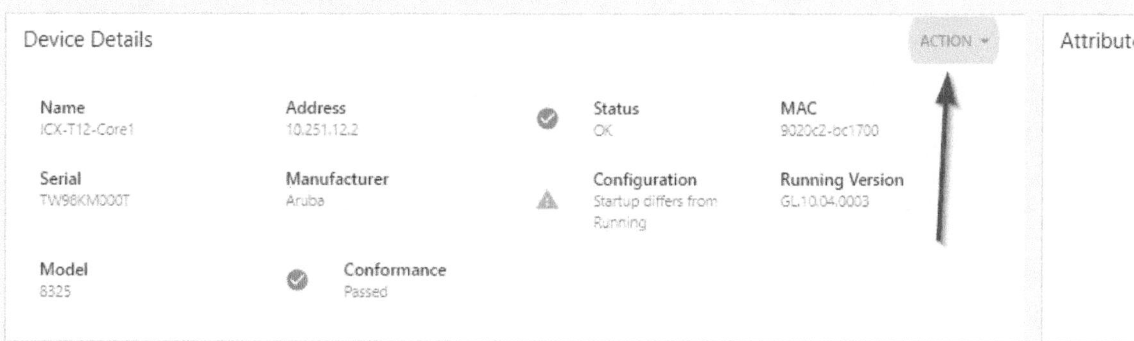

Task 4: Configuration Management Using Plans

Objectives

- Understand how a configuration plan works
- Deploy a new configuration
- Verify the new configuration
- Push configuration changes to multiple devices

Steps

First Configuration Plan

A configuration plan allows the administrator to send configuration changes to one or more AOS-CX switches. In these steps, a new VRF will be created on both Core switches, a port will be assigned, and an IP address will be set. This VRF configuration will be used in the upcoming VSX lab as the 'keep-alive' link between the VSX core switches.

1. On the management PC, login to NetEdit using the admin account. Navigate to **Devices**, select the **Core1** and **Core2**, and right-click to select **Edit Config**.

Note

Many lab activities show how **multiple** devices can be configured together. In case the administrator needs to edit a **single** device, simply select one device in the list and use the 'Edit Config' option.

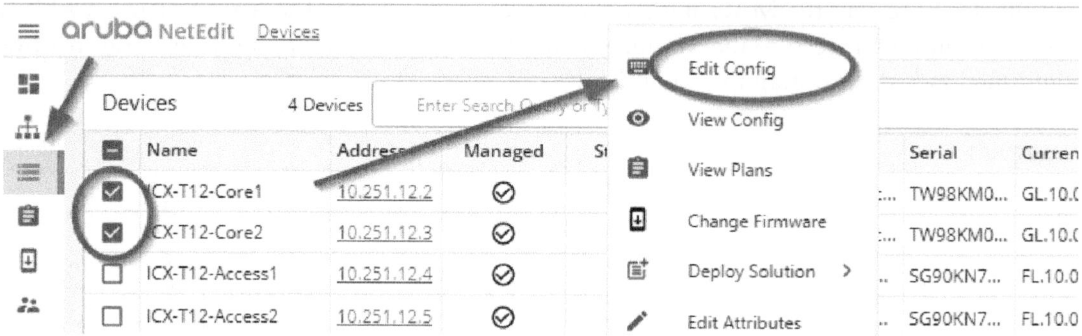
aruba NetEdit
Devices
Devices
4 Devices
Enter Search Query or Ty
Name
Address
Managed
Serial
Curren
ICX-T12-Core1
10.251.12.2
ICX-T12-Core2
10.251.12.3
ICX-T12-Access1
10.251.12.4
ICX-T12-Access2
10.251.12.5
Edit Config
View Config
View Plans
Change Firmware
Deploy Solution
Edit Attributes
TW98KM0...
TW98KM0...
SG90KN7...
SG90KN7...
GL.10.(
GL.10.(
FL.10.0
FL.10.0

2. Provide a meaningful name for the plan, for example **'vrf ka'**. Click **Create** to define the plan. ('ka' stands for keep-alive.)

3. NetEdit will now show the **merged** 'running configuration' of the devices. Any lines that exist on all selected devices will show normally. Any lines that have unique values will include some '**PARAMETER**' placeholder in **UPPERCASE**. Move the mouse over the management IP address parameter, shown as **A.B.C.D/M**. NetEdit will show the configured IP addresses per device.

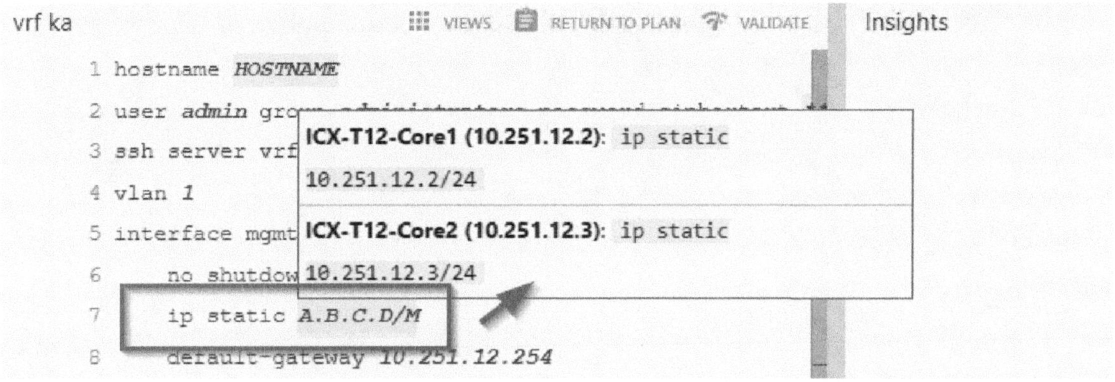

4. The same applies to the **HOSTNAME** parameter. Now right-click on the **'HOSTNAME'** parameter; this window shows the actual hostname configuration for each device and allows the administrator to change the values.

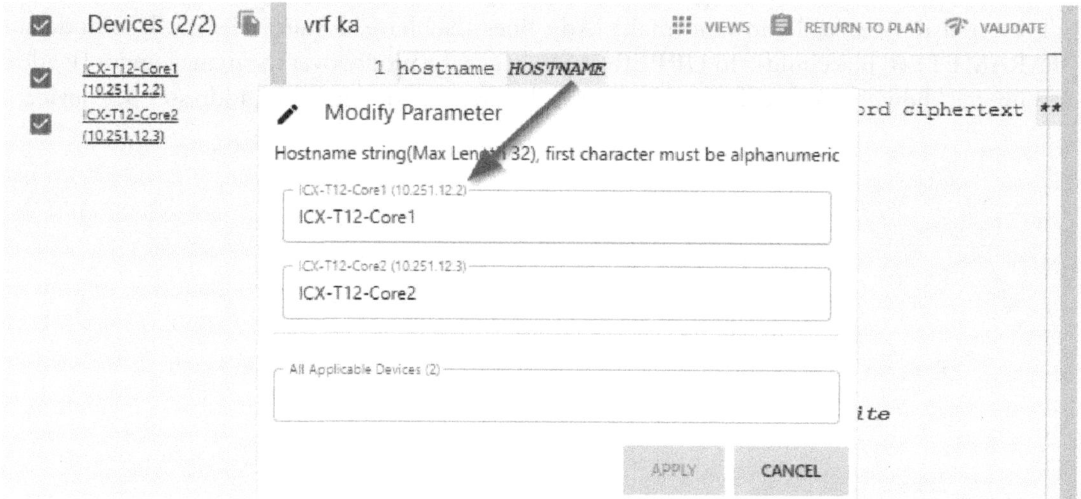

5. Click **Cancel** to close the 'Modify Parameter' window.

Add Configuration Entry

1. Click at the end of the configuration and press **Enter** to get a new line. Start typing '**v**' and notice how the context-sensitive help shows the available options. Next type '**r**' (so '**vr**'). Use <TAB> to complete the word to **vrf**.

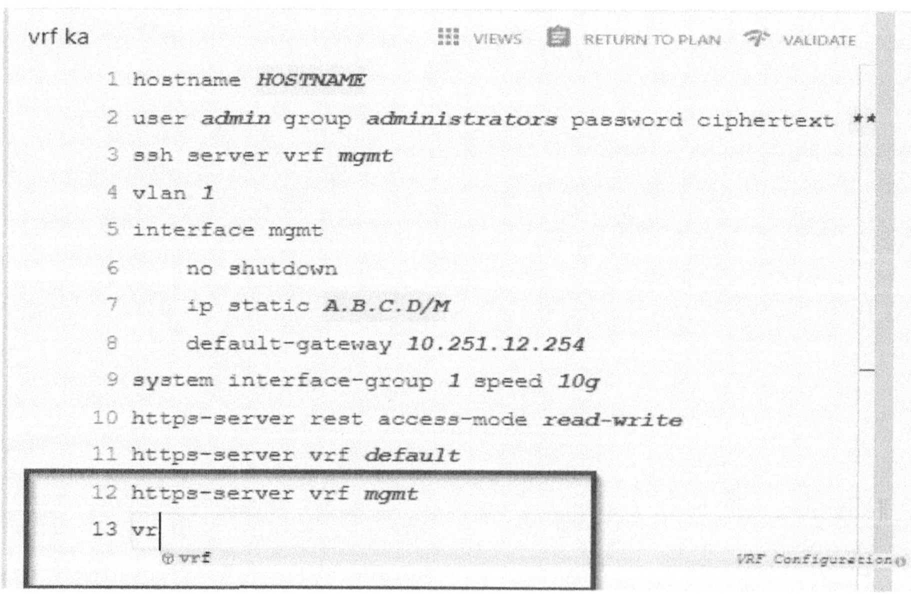

2. Next press <SPACE> and notice the available options for the **vrf** command.

3. Enter 'KA' and use <ENTER> to submit the command. Notice how NetEdit will automatically move the line to the correct location in the configuration.

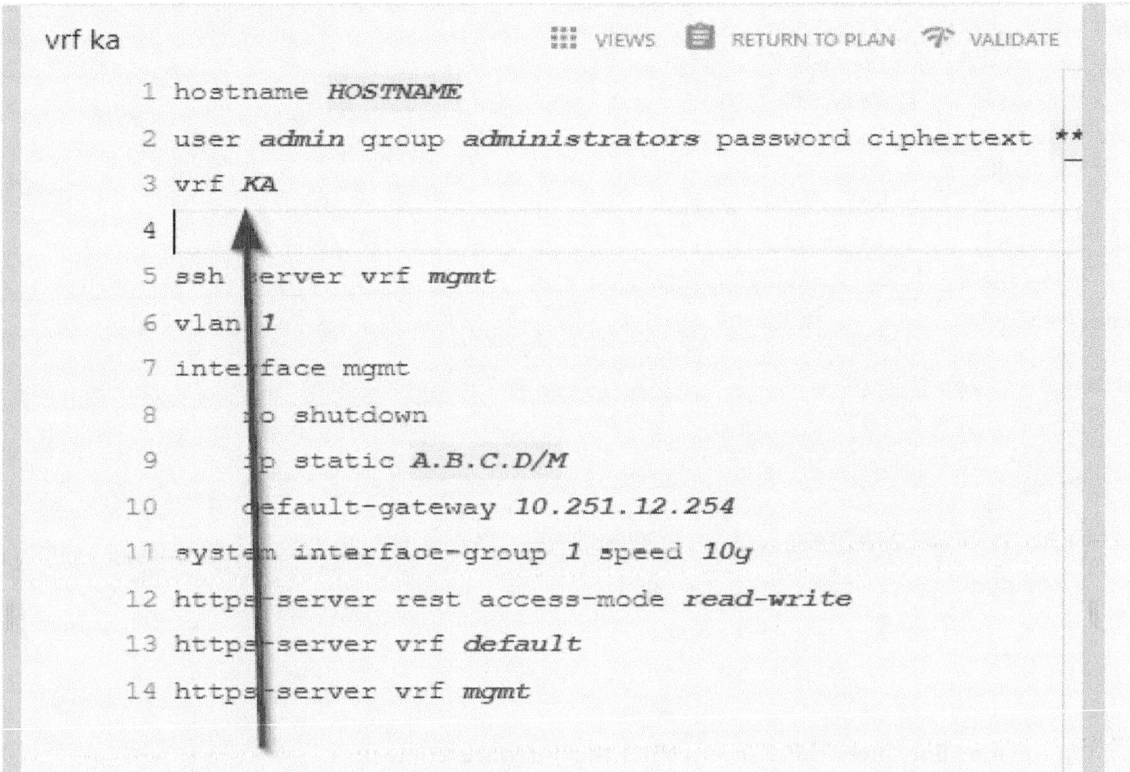

Add Interface Configuration

1. At the end of the configuration, add a line for 'interface 1/1/45' (int<TAB> 1/1/45). Press <ENTER> so NetEdit moves the line to the correct place in the configuration.

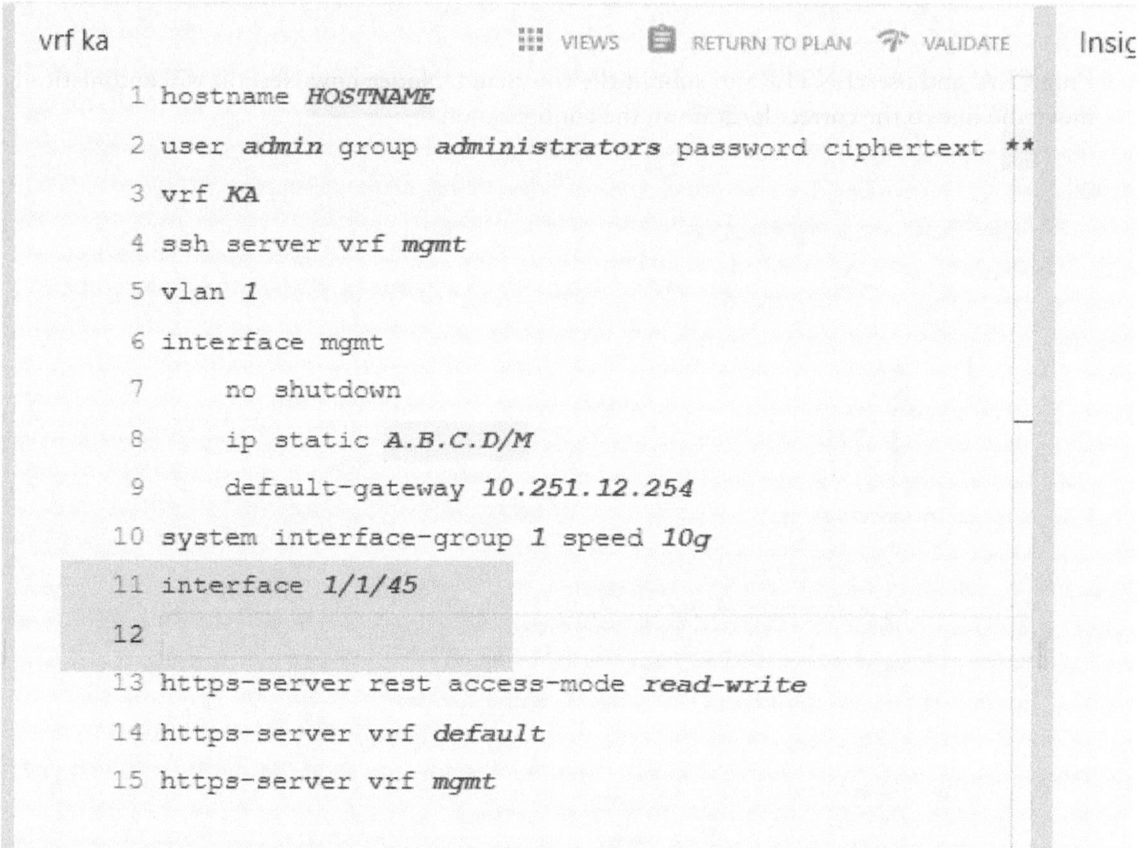

2. On the next line, press <SPACE> to enter the 'interface' context.

Important

The <SPACE> is important here to tell NetEdit that the next command is not a global command, but should be under the interface context. A switch CLI would put you in the 'interface' context, while in the NetEdit CLI you are still at the 'global' level.

---

a. Enter the command '**vrf attach KA';** press <ENTER>.

b. Enter the command **'no shutdown';** press <ENTER>.

c. Enter the command '**ip address 192.168.0.0/31**'; press <ENTER>.

```
system interface-group 1 speed 10g
interface 1/1/45
    vrf attach KA
    no shutdown
    ip address 192.168.0.0/31

https-server rest access-mode read-write
```

Note

AOS-CX allows you to configure /31 as the subnet mask for an IP interface. For point-to-point connections (only 2 hosts on the subnet), this is convenient, since you are not wasting the network and broadcast address.

3. Move the mouse over the '192.168.0.0/31' IP address; right-click to open the 'Modify Parameter' window. Change the **'Core2'** IP to **192.168.0.1/31**, that is the second IP address in this /31 subnet. Click on **Apply** to submit the change.

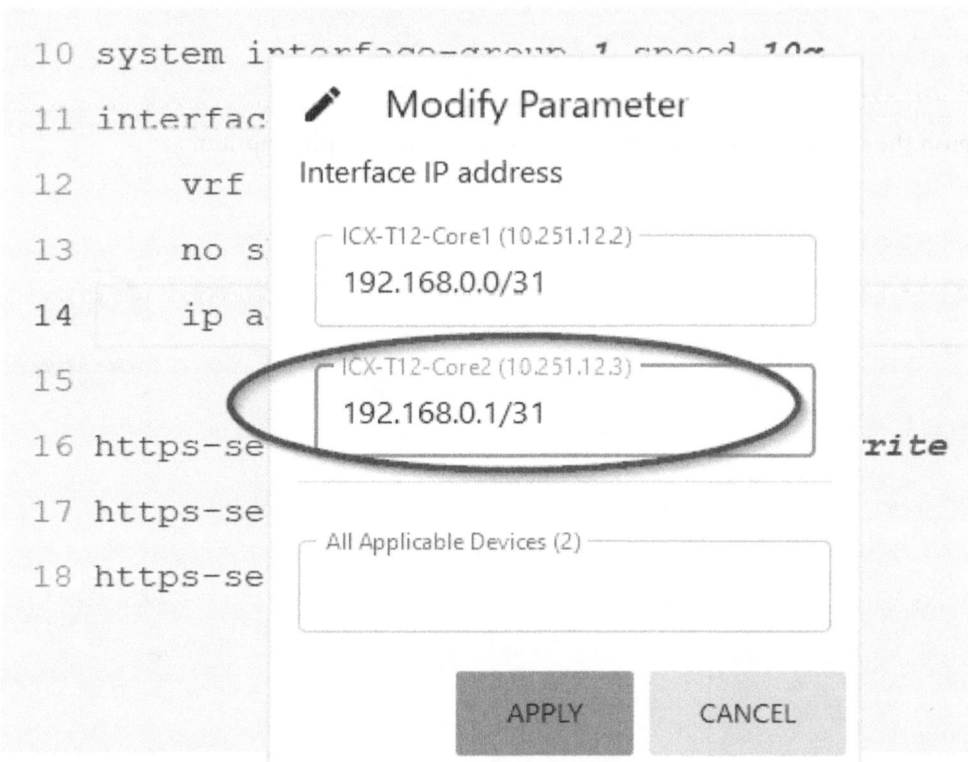

4. Notice how the IP address parameter is now shown as A.B.C.D/M. This is sufficient for the first change; select the **Return to Plan** option to return back to the plan details screen.

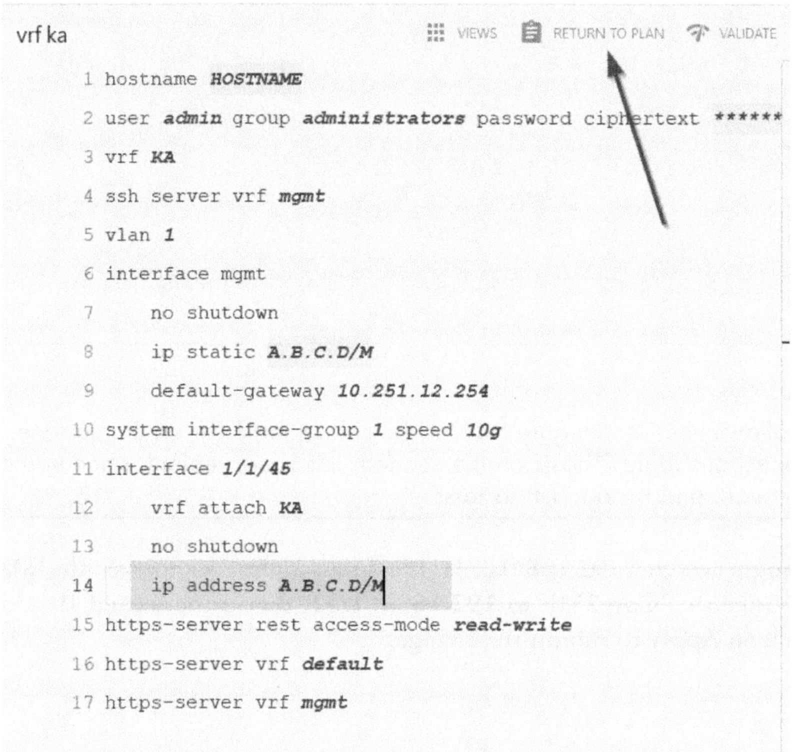

5. To push the configuration change to the device, use the **Deploy** option.

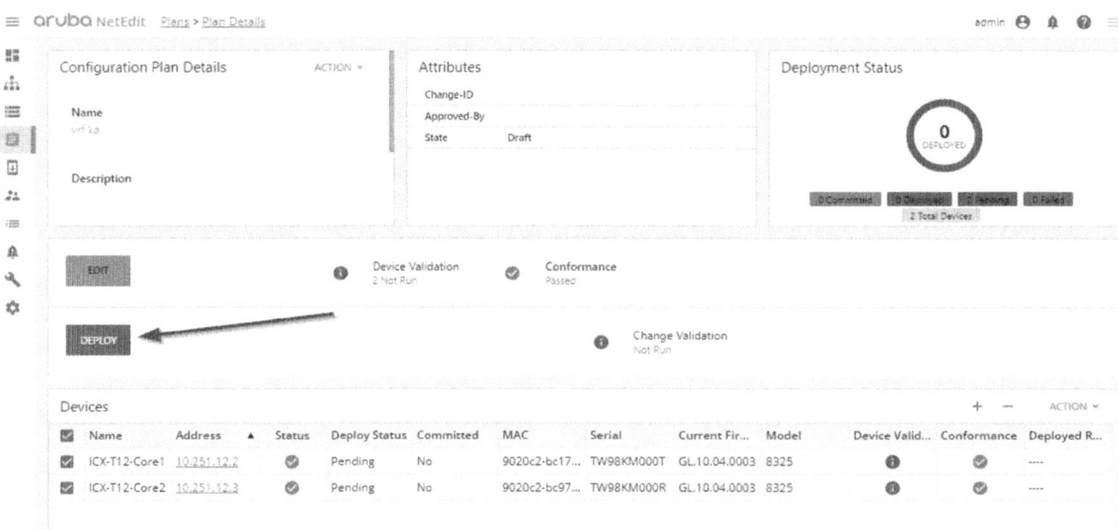

6. Confirm the action dialog with the **Deploy** button.

   Question: What happens when the plan is being deployed?

   Answer: The proposed changes are validated with device, after successful validation, this configuration will be activated. It will be in the running configuration of the device.

7. After a few moments, NetEdit will show the 'Commit' and 'Rollback' options. This allows you to either save the configuration changes or undo these changes by reverting to the previous configuration. Verify the changes by clicking the **Change Validation** option.

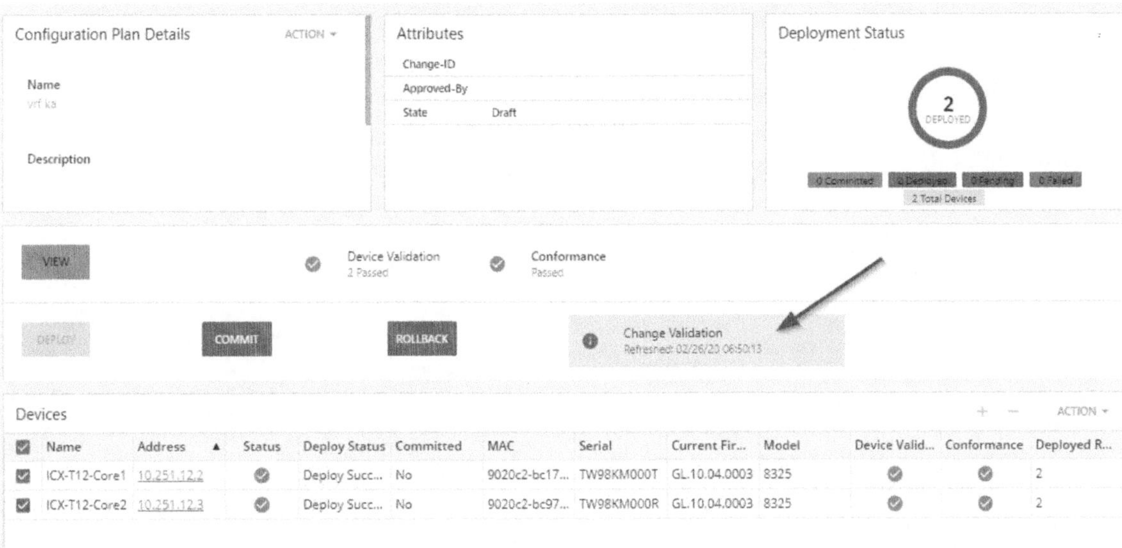

8. Click on the '>' icon for the line ICX-Tx-Core1 … 'show running-config' to see the details. On the left side, the output before the change is shown; on the right side, the output after the change is shown; this should show the configuration changes. Scroll down in the configuration, verify that the vrf KA has been defined, and port 1/1/45 has an IP address.

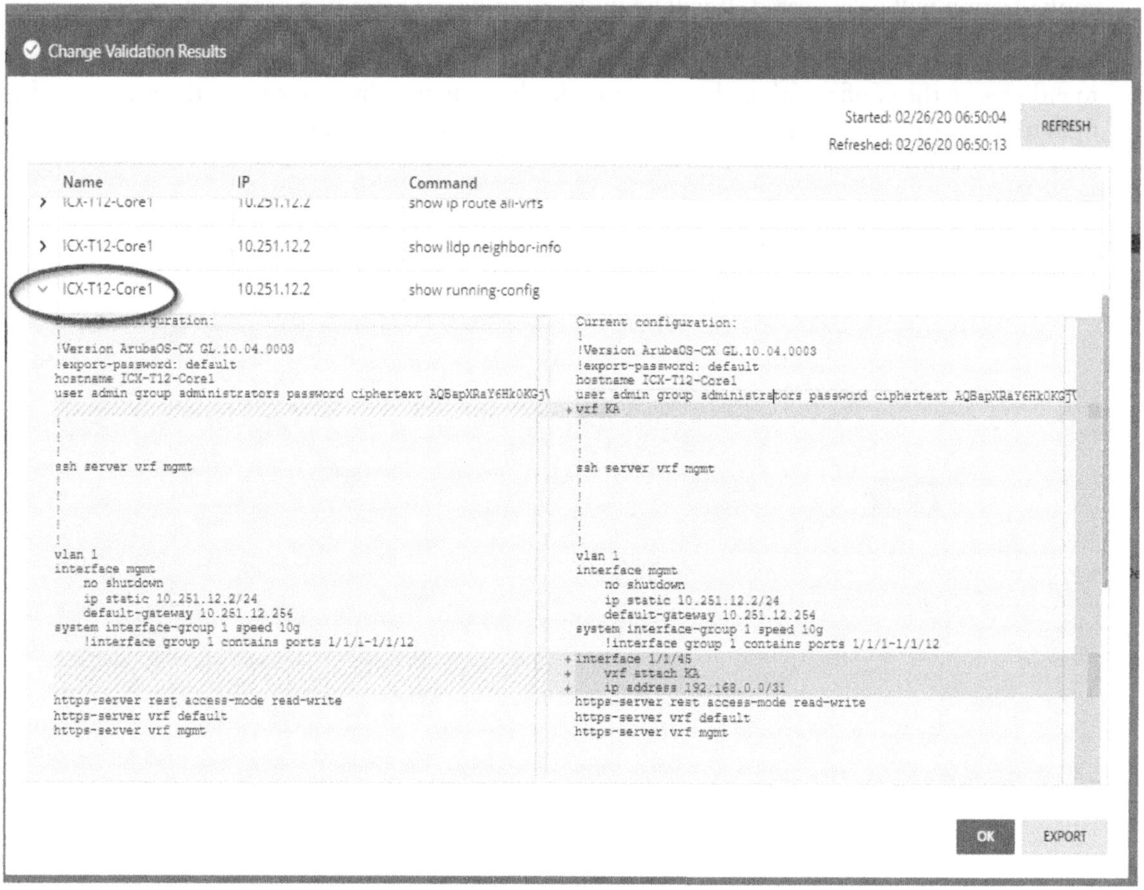

Verify Deployment and Commit the Configuration

1. Click **OK** to return to the management station, in NetEdit, click the **Commit** button to save the configuration on the device.

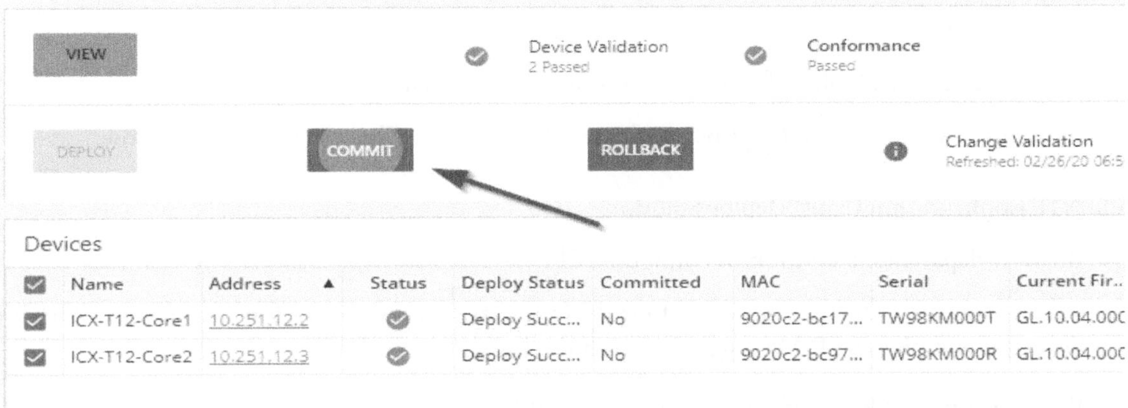

2. NetEdit will prompt a confirmation message, confirm by pressing the **Commit** button.

3. On the Core1 terminal, review the startup config to verify that the NetEdit configuration was actually pushed to the startup configuration of the switch.

```
show startup config
```

Add DNS Configuration using 'Deploy Solution'

This option of NetEdit provides a wizard-like experience to configure essential settings on the devices, such as DNS or NTP. In these steps, the NTP and DNS will be configured on *all four switches*.

1. Open NetEdit, navigate to **Devices**. Select all four devices, from the **Action** menu, select **Deploy Solution** and pick **DNS Management** from the list.

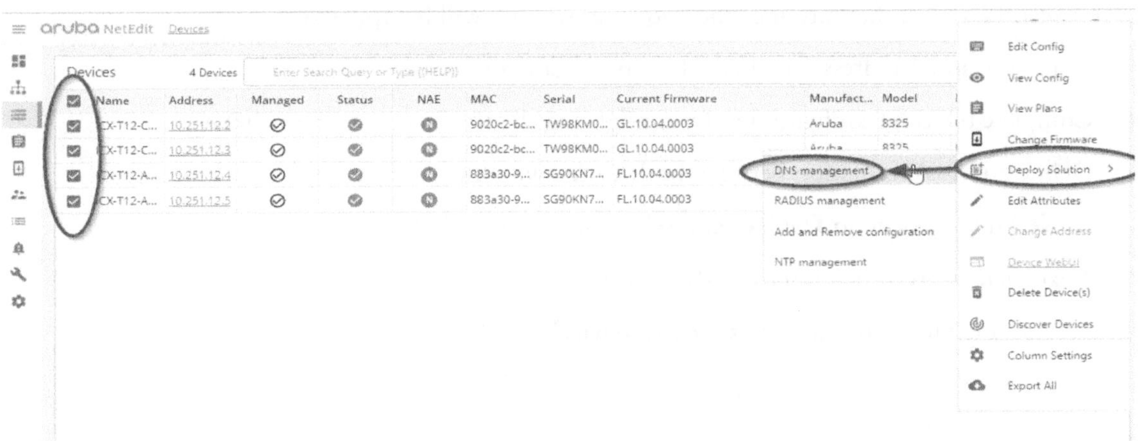

2. In the **Deploy Solution screen**, enter these settings:
   - DNS server IPs: 10.254.1.21
   - Domain List: (leave blank > no value)
   - VRF: mgmt
3. Click **Create**. It will take a few moments to prepare the plan.
4. In the next window, click **Deploy**, confirm with **Yes**. Click **Close** to close the window.

Add NTP Configuration Using 'Deploy Solution'

Use the next deployment solution to configure NTP.

1. Under **NetEdit >Devices**, select all four devices. Navigate to the **Action** menu, select **Deploy Solution** and pick **NTP Management** from the list.
2. In the **Deploy Solution screen**, enter these settings:
   - Preferred Servers: **10.253.1.15**
   - Additional NTP servers: **10.253.1.15**
   - Burst mode: **iburst**
   - VRF: **mgmt**
   - Leave all other settings default. Click **Create**.
3. In the next screen, click **Deploy**; confirm with **Yes**. After a few moments, the deployment should complete. Close the window by selecting the **Close** button.

Second Configuration Plan—Multiple Devices

In this section, the configuration of the two core switches will be updated.

- Configure an IP address on VLAN 1 on both Core switches.
- Complete the time configuration by configuring the time zone on the switches.
- Define a Link Aggregation between both Core Switches.

1. In NetEdit, navigate to **Devices** and select both Core switches.
2. Next click on **Action** and select **Edit Config**.
3. Provide a name for the config: **'core interswitch link'** and click **Create**.

Configure the VLAN 1 IP address for both Core switches.

1. At the end of the config, press <ENTER> to get a new line, define the VLAN 1 L3 interface, and press <ENTER>. NetEdit will automatically move the 'interface VLAN 1' to the right place in the configuration.

```
interface vlan 1
```

2. Press <SPACE> to enter the interface context and assign the IP address of Core1. The IP for Core2 will be set in the next step.

```
ip address 10.x.1.2/24
```

Note

Make sure to include a SPACE at the beginning of the line after the 'interface vlan 1' to be within the interface context. Make sure to press <ENTER> after entering the IP address. The IP address should become highlighted in blue, which indicates NetEdit has recognized it as an IP address and gives you the multi-edit 'right-click' option.

---

3. Right-click on the VLAN 1 IP address to access the 'Modify Parameter' window. Assign IP address **10.x.1.3/24** to the **'Core2'**. Click **Apply** to confirm.

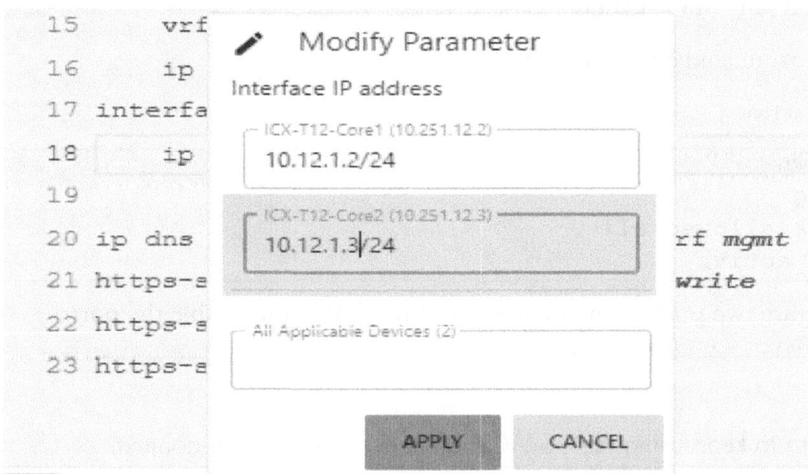

4. Move the mouse over the A.B.C.D/M parameter of VLAN 1 to verify the IP address of both Core switches.

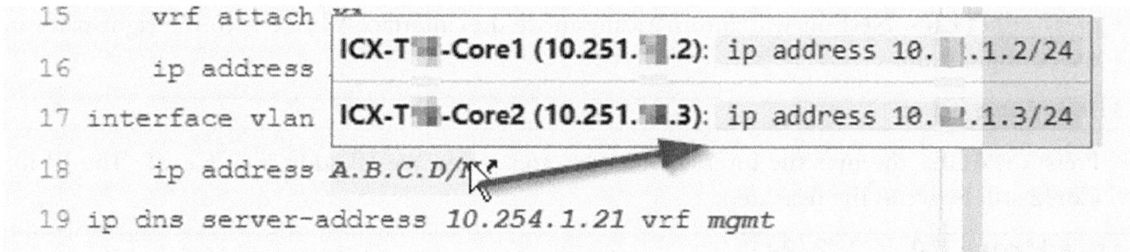

Define a Link Aggregation with Two Interfaces Between the Two Core Switches

1. At the end of the configuration, insert a new line for '**interface lag 256**'. Press <ENTER> after the line so NetEdit can move it to the correct location.

```
interface lag 256
```

2. Press <SPACE> to enter the LAG context, make the LAG:
   - enabled (**no shutdown**)
   - switched port (**no routing**)
   - VLAN trunk and allow all VLANs
   - LACP active

```
no shutdown
no routing
vlan trunk allowed all
lacp mode active
```

3. Next configure two ports as member ports of the LAG, and enable the ports.

Note
Make sure to keep using the <SPACE> to enter the interface context.

```
interface 1/1/46
    no shutdown
    lag 256
interface 1/1/47
    no shutdown
    lag 256
```

4. At the top of the screen, click **Validate** at the top right to check if all of the commands entered are correct. If the validation failed, review and correct your input.

5. Return to the Plan using the **Return to Plan** button.
6. In the Plan Details screen, use **Deploy** to push the changes to the 2 Core switches. Click on **Deploy** to confirm. Once the deployment has completed, click **Commit** to save the configuration on the devices, confirm by clicking **Commit** again.

Third Configuration Plan—All Devices

In these steps, you will push some final management settings to all four devices.

1. In NetEdit, navigate to **Devices** and select all four devices (**Core1/Core2/Access1/Access2**).
2. From the **Action** menu, select **Edit Config**. For the plan name, enter '**management**'. Then click **Create**.

Note

At this point, the configurations of the core and access switches contain several differences. In the plan editor, lines that are unique to some devices will be marked with the hostnames of those devices to handle this.

---

3. Add these lines to the configuration. This will apply the correct time zone for the remote lab and it will increase the admin session timeout to 12 hours.

```
clock timezone us/eastern
cli-session
   timeout 43200
```

4. Select **Return to plan**, click **Deploy,** and confirm with **Deploy**. Once the plan completes the deployment, click **Commit** and confirm by clicking **Commit** again.

Task 5: Configuration Plan Validation

Objectives

- Understand plan validation
- Review plan validation settings
- Define new validation settings

Steps

In the previous task some configuration changes were pushed to the switches and these changes could be manually verified on the switch cli (optional step at the end of the previous task).In this task, the same validation checks will be included in NetEdit. This means NetEdit will be connecting to the devices using SSH and will collect the output of the defined validation commands.

Review Default Plan Validation

1. Open NetEdit, navigate to **Plans**, open the plan called '**core interswitch link**' (click this name). Click the link **Change Validation** to see the default validation steps.

2. The list of commands will be shown here. For each command, NetEdit will collect the data **before** and **after** the configuration change has been made (**Deploy**). When any changes are found, the entry will be marked in green. In this lab, the 'show bgp all-vrf all summary' command will have no changes, so these remain 'black'. The 'show interface brief' will be marked green.

3. Expand the ICX-Tx-Core1—'show interface brief' section. The left side will show the before state, on the right side, the state after the configuration change will be shown.

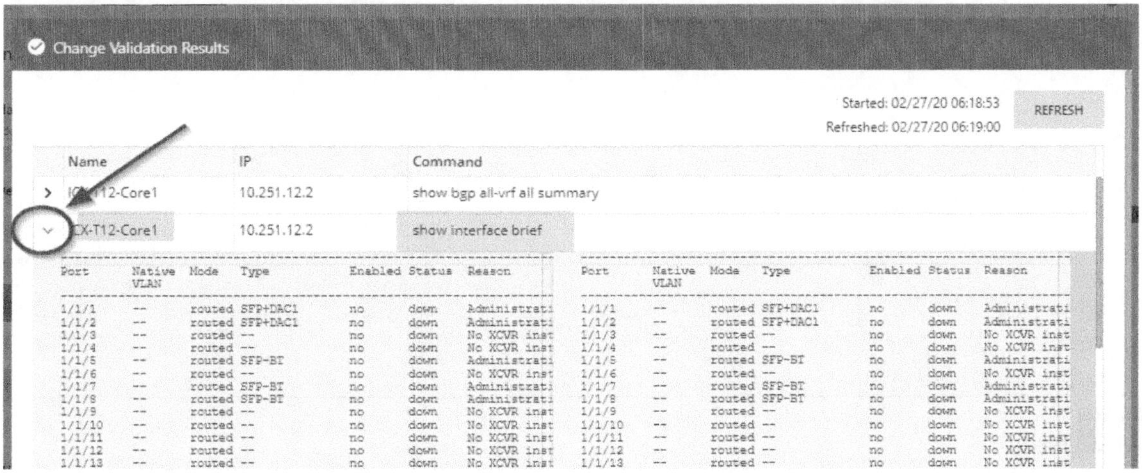

4. Scroll down to check the state of the interfaces. You should see the two interfaces coming UP, and the new VLAN 1 and LAG interface.

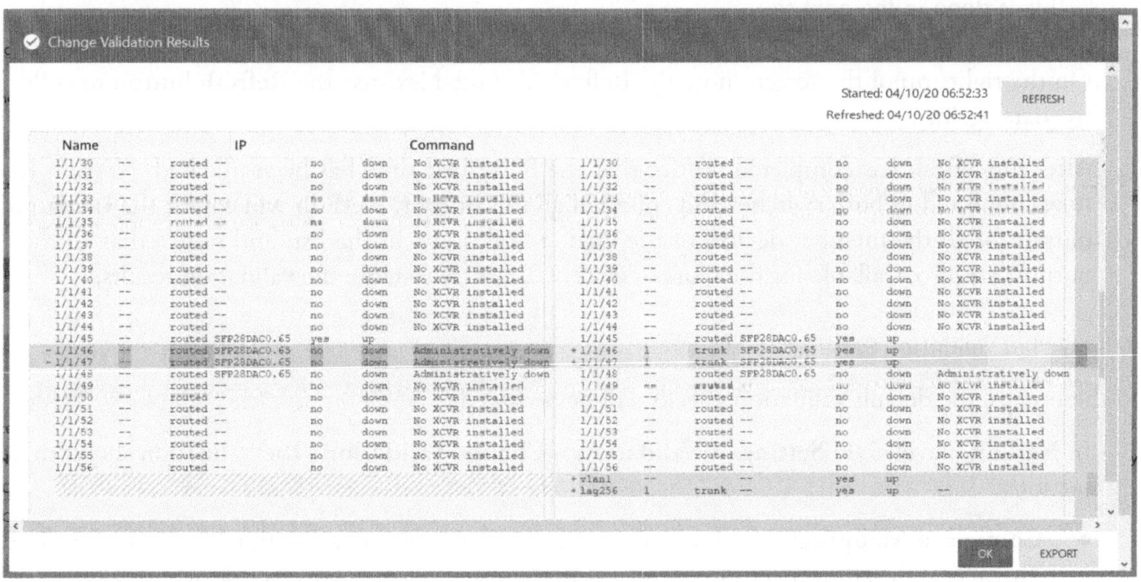

5. Review the LLDP neighbors by clicking on **show lldp neighbor-info** link.

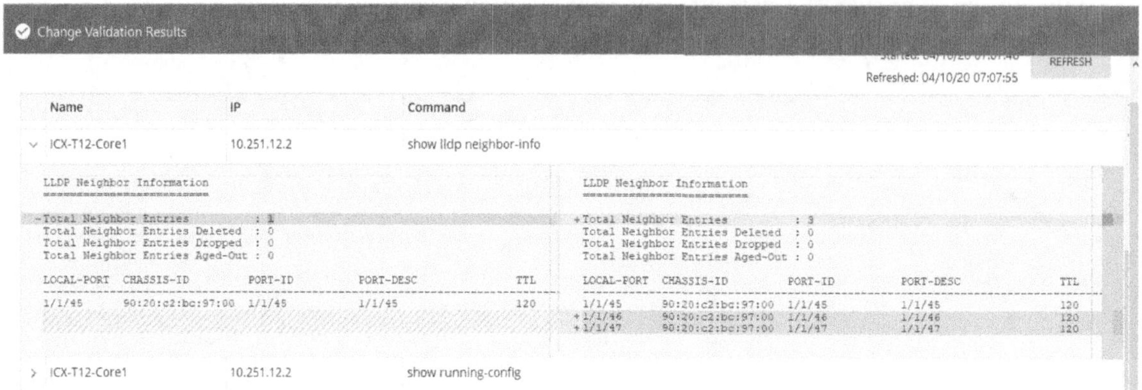

Note

The 'after' output is collected a few seconds after the configuration change was done. Sometimes, a protocol will need more time to show useful output. In case the LLDP neighbors would not be in the list yet, it is possible to manually refresh the 'after' output state. This is done in the next step.

---

6. On the right-top of the screen, note the Refreshed time. Next use the **Refresh** button to collect the data again.

7. After the refresh has completed, notice that the Refreshed time has been updated. NetEdit has now connected to both switches and collected all this output. NetEdit will collect the validation output for all the member devices of the Plan. Scroll down in the list, and notice that all these outputs are also available for the Core2 device. Click **OK** to close the validation results.

Review Plan Validation Settings

In these steps, the default validation checks will be reviewed.

1. In NetEdit, navigate to **Settings > Validation > Change Validation**. The Validation shows three sections:

   - **Command Mapping**: Enables execution of a set of 'Command Scripts' to a set of devices. This allows the administrator to send a command set to a limited set of devices. For example, routing commands should only be sent to the core devices.

   - **Command Scripts**: In this section the actual 'show' commands are defined. This section does not define on which devices the commands will be executed.

   - **Resources**: This allows integration with devices that are not managed by NetEdit.

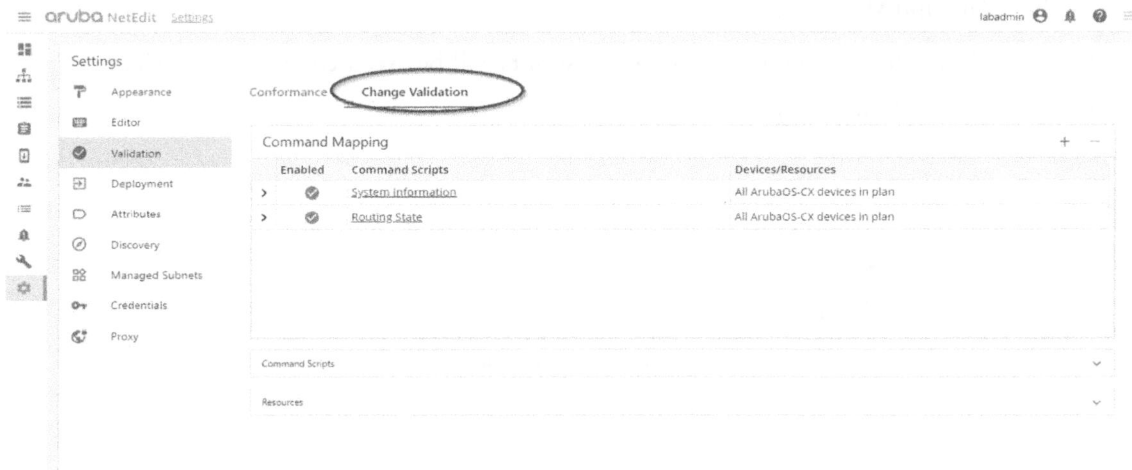

2. Expand **Command Scripts** and click **System Information**.

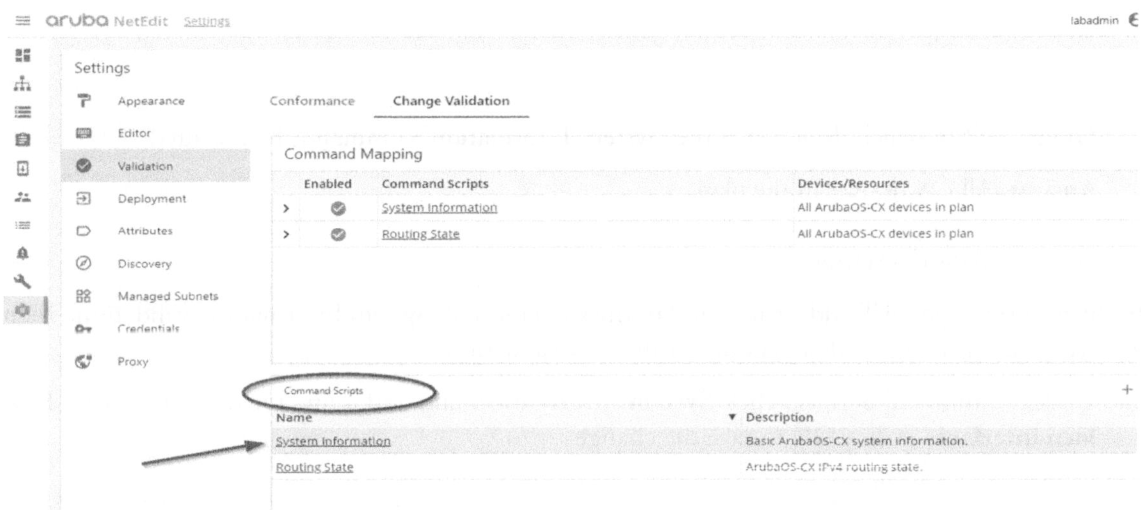

3. Review the **Commands** under System Information. Click **OK** to close the screen.

Review the Command Mappings

The Command Mapping shows which command scripts will be executed by which devices.

1. Review the default mappings.

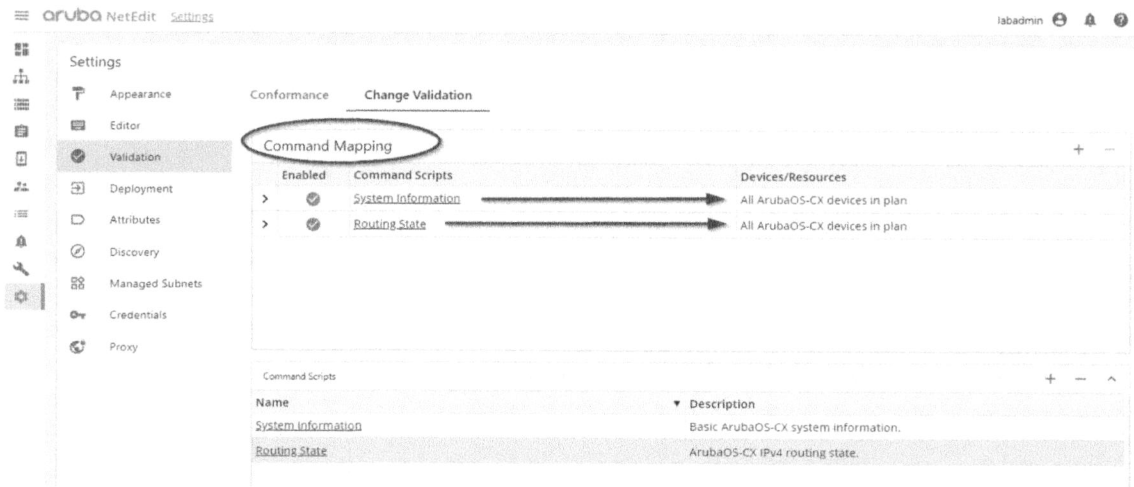

Question: On which devices will the 'System Information' commands be executed?

Answer: All CX devices in the plan.

Define New Validation Settings

In the next steps, you will add a command to the validation of 'System Information' validation. Then you will make a change with a plan to test the new validation.

1. Under 'Command Scripts', click **System information** and add a line for the command '**show lacp interfaces**'. Click **OK** to save the change.

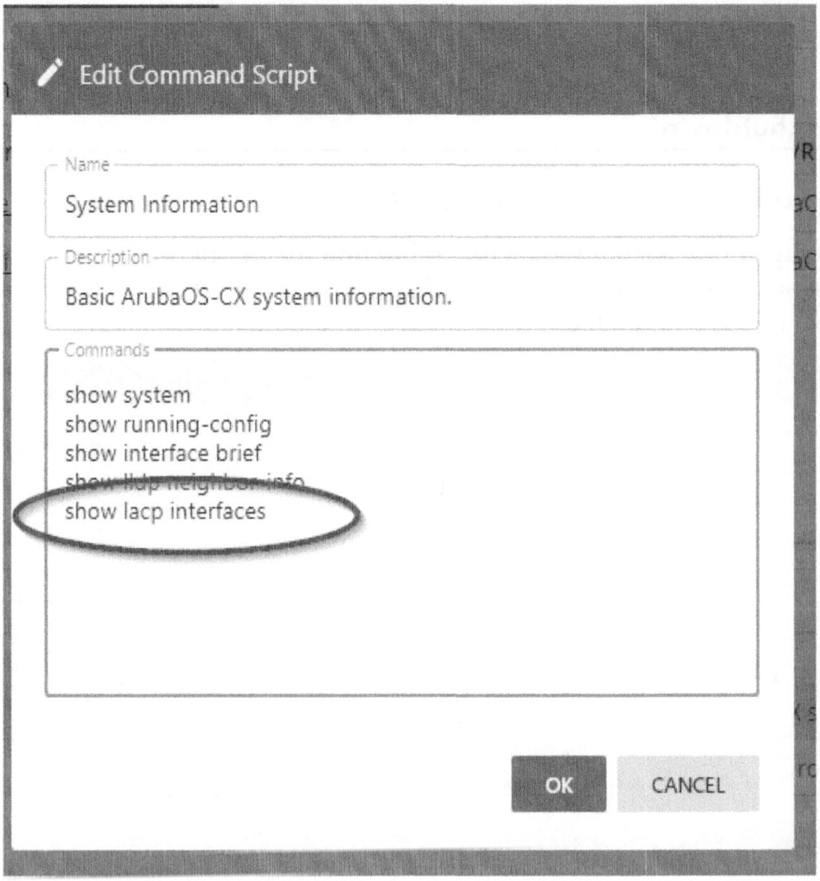

Test the New Validation

Note

The new validation command will only take effect on **new** configuration plans. So, opening the Validation of an existing plan and using Refresh will not include this new command.

1. In NetEdit, navigate to devices, select Core1 (only Core1 in this example), right-click, and select **Edit Config**. For the Plan name, enter **'test validation**. Click **Create** to continue.
2. Shutdown interface 1/1/46: remove **'no'** from the **'no shutdown'** line of the respective interface.

```
interface 1/1/46
    shutdown
```

Note

Make sure to remove the word 'no' from the 'no shutdown' line from the NetEdit configuration, resulting in just '**shutdown**'.

3. Select **Return to plan**, select **Deploy**, and confirm with **Deploy**.
4. Check the Validation results by clicking on the **Change Validation** button, the new command '**show lacp interfaces**' should now be included. Verify that the interface 1/1/46 is shown as '**down**'. Click **OK** to close the Results window.

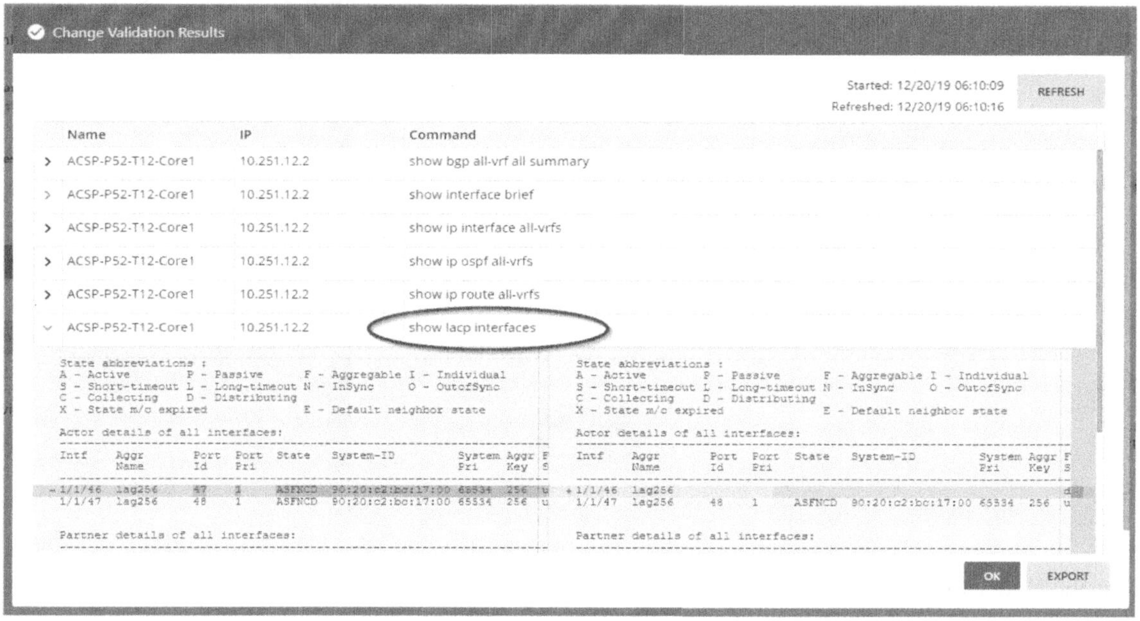

5. Revert the change with the **Rollback** option: confirm by clicking **Rollback**.

Important

In the next steps you will make a checkpoint that will be used for the rest of the labs, it is important to have a valid LAG state in that saved checkpoint.

Save New Configuration Checkpoint

1. Open a terminal connection to ***each*** switch (**Core1/Core2/Access1/Access2**). Save a new configuration checkpoint on ***each*** switch. Call the checkpoint "**icx-lab02-netedit**".

Task 6: Organizing Devices Using Attributes

Objectives

- Define new attributes based on role, location
- Review attributes under device details
- Use attributes in queries and save a query
- Filtered validation

NetEdit allows the administrator to group devices based on features or location. The administrator can define attributes on the devices and assign values to these attributes. These attributes can then be used in:

- Device views and plan configuration
- Configuration validation

By default, devices do not have any attributes defined. It is also possible to assign attributes to a plan. For a plan, NetEdit has predefined attributes for Change Management, such as:

- Change-ID
- Approved-By
- State

Steps

Define New Attributes Based on Role or Location

1. Open NetEdit and navigate to **Settings > Attributes**. Select **Device**, and then select the '+' sign to add a new Attribute.

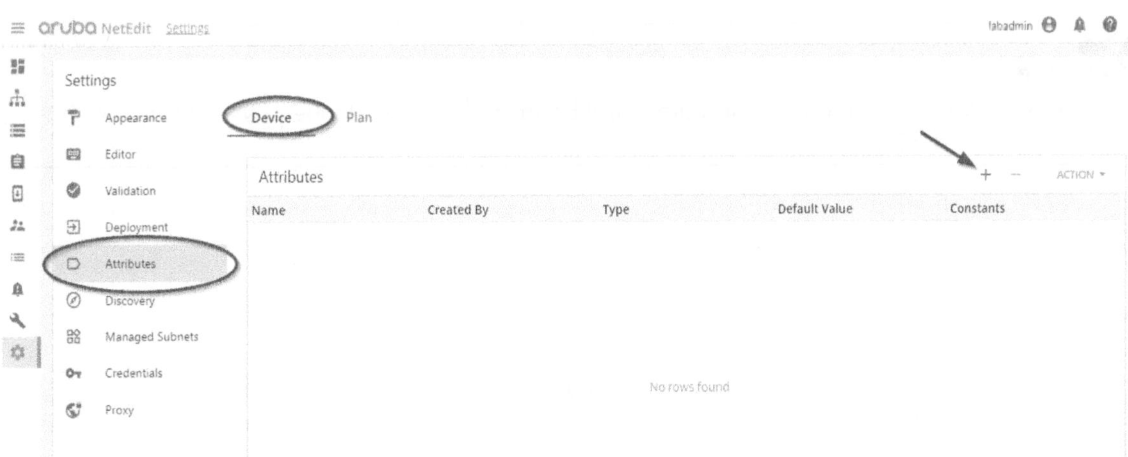

2. Enter the values listed below and click **Create**.
   - Name: **role**
   - Type: **LIST**
   - List Values: **core, access, undefined**

Note

In a similar way, a location attribute could be added to indicate the physical site information of the device.

Assign Attributes to Devices

1. Navigate to **Devices**, select the two core switches, and from the **Action** menu, select **Edit Attributes**.

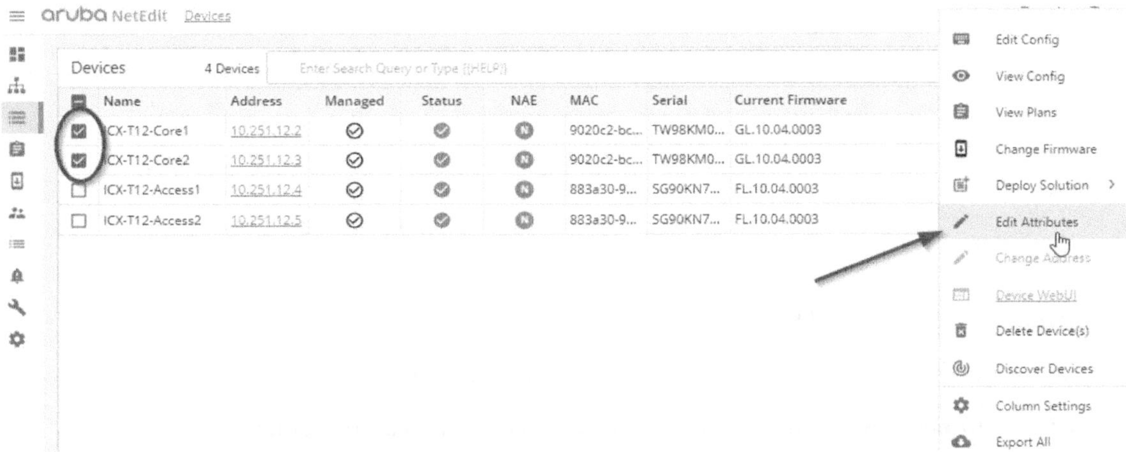

2. Select the **'role'** attribute and set it to **'core'**. Then click **Save**.

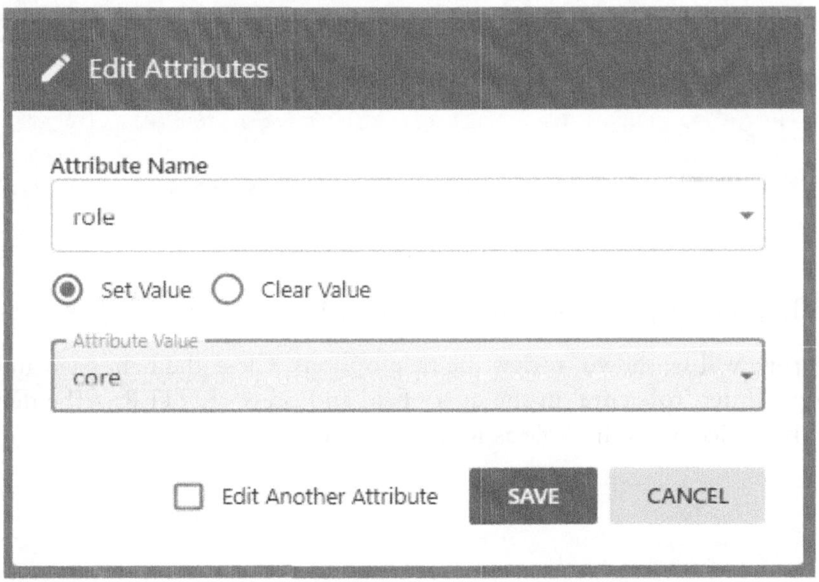

3. Once the attribute has been saved, uncheck the core switches and select both Access switches. Repeat the steps to add the 'role' attribute to the two Access switches. Set the value for 'role' to 'access' and click **Save**.

4. In the device list, open the switch **Core1** by clicking its IP address (10.251.X.2). In the device details, the new attribute will be shown.

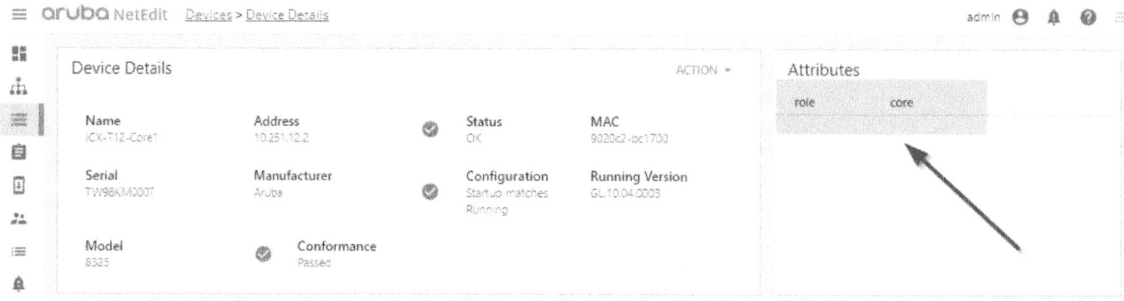

Use Attributes in Queries and Save a Query

These attributes can now be used to filter the devices in the device list.

1. Navigate to **Devices**. At the top of the screen, a query filter can be applied.

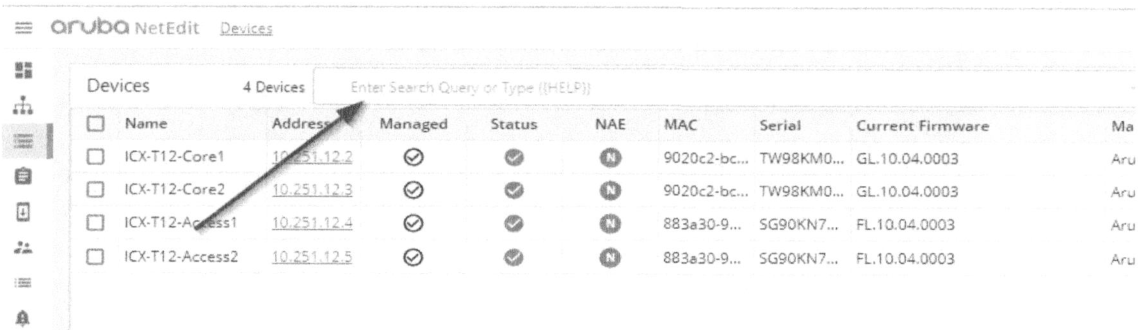

2. Enter **{{HELP}}** in the query field and press **<ENTER>**.

   A help webpage will be shown, review the help options. Close the help page and return to the NetEdit page. Enter **'role:core'** in the query field and press <ENTER>. The device list should only show the devices with that role assigned to them ("core").

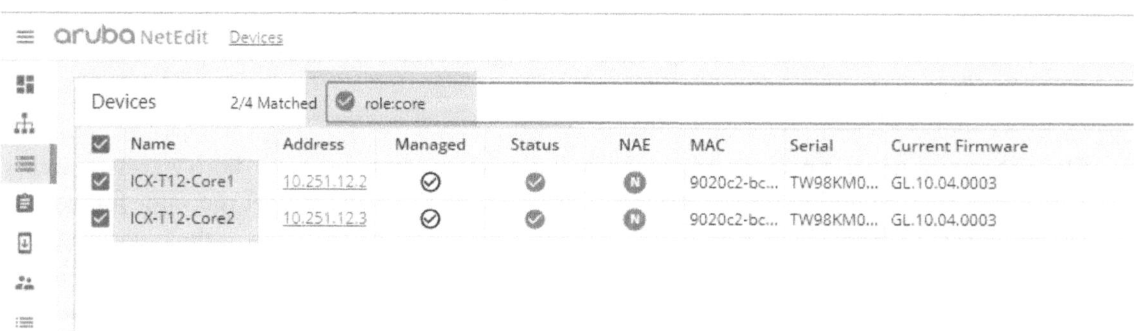

3. Since the administrator may be using the same filter frequently, the query can be saved for future use. On the right side of the filter, click the '+' sign to add a saved query.

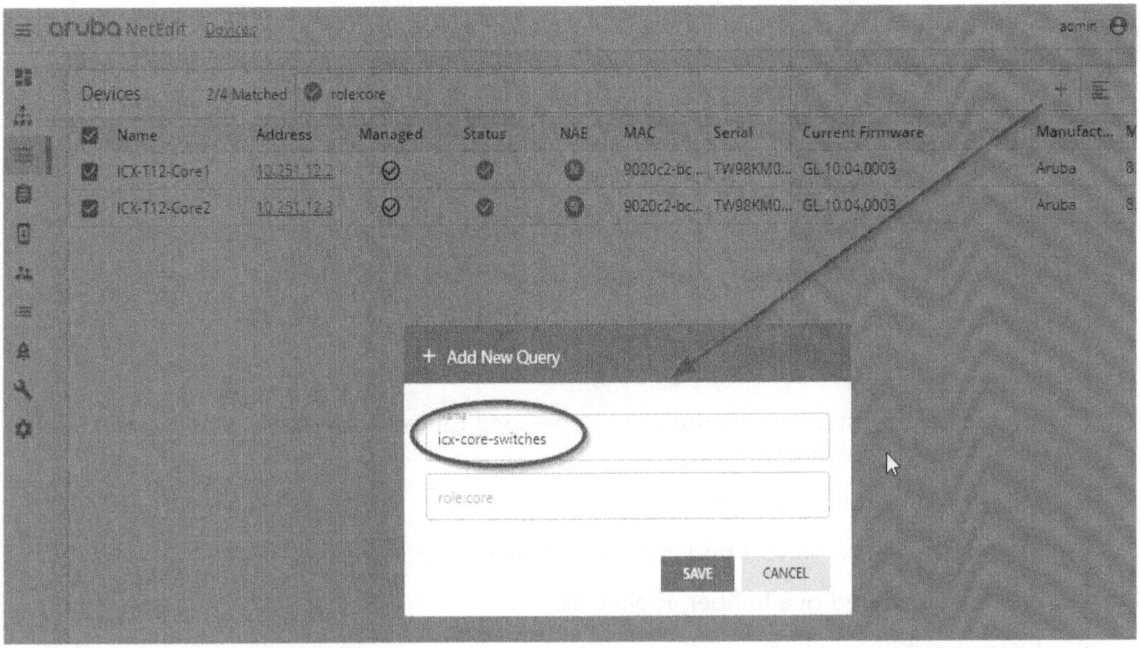

4. Enter **'icx-core-switches'** for the query name. The query will be copied from your currently active query filter, in this example **role:core**. Click **Save** to save the query.
5. Change the 'Search Query' field to **'role:access'**. Verify the two access switches are shown. Save the query as **'icx-access-switches'**.

Using the Saved Filters

1. On the right-side of the filter, select the **Menu** icon to see the saved query filters.

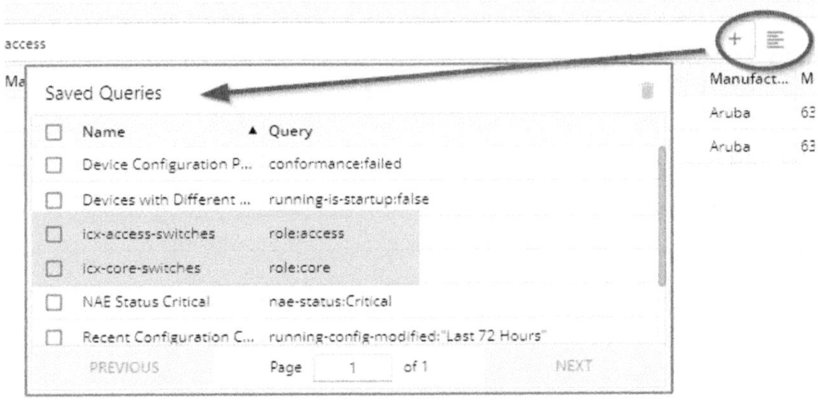

2. Double-click on the '**icx-core-switches**'. This should activate the filter and show the 2 core switches.

Note
The device queries can be used to restrict validation tests to a subset of devices.

Learning Check

1. Aruba NetEdit supports switches running AOS-CX and ArubaOS.
   a. True
   b. False
2. From the following list of most causes of outages and performance issue, you can use NetEdit to remediate which of the two?
   a. Device configuration changes
   b. Operational human errors and mismanagement of devices
   c. Link failure caused due to fiber cable cuts
   d. Server hardware failure
   e. Security attacks such as denial of service (DoS)
3. The configuration plan is one of the core features of NetEdit. It allows a user to create configuration plans, to edit either running or startup configurations for a set of devices.
   a. True
   b. False
4. Which of the following are key capabilities of Aruba NetEdit?
   a. Audit
   b. Conformance validation
   c. Search
   d. Programming
   e. Security Validation
   f. Change Validation
   g. Plan

Summary

Congratulations! In this chapter, you were introduced to managing single and multiple switch configurations with NetEdit, leveraging its intelligent capabilities including search, plan, edit, validation, deployment, and audit. You also became familiar with using the AOS-CX mobile app for quick deploy provisioning and updating of the AOS-CX switches.

3 Network Analytics Engine

OBJECTIVES

After completing this chapter, you should be able to:

- ✓ Explain how the AOS-CX NAE helps you to monitor and troubleshoot
- ✓ Analyze NAE data in the Web UI
- ✓ Install scripts from ASE and create agents based on the scripts
- ✓ Implement sFlow and port mirroring

Overview

This chapter teaches you all about the AOS-CX Network Analytics Engine (NAE). By the time that you have completed this chapter, you will be able to explain how the AOS-CX NAE helps you to monitor and troubleshoot. You will be able to analyze NAE data in the Web UI. You will be able to install scripts from the Aruba Solutions Exchange (ASE) and create agents based on the scripts.

NAE Overview

The Aruba Network Analytics Engine (NAE) is a first-of-its-kind built-in framework for network assurance and remediation. Combining the full automation and deep visibility capabilities of the AOS-CX operating system, this unique framework enables monitoring, collecting network data, evaluating conditions, and taking corrective actions through simple scripting agents.

Introduction to Network Automation with AOS-CX

This NAE engine is integrated with the AOS-CX system configuration and time-series databases, enabling you to examine historical trends and predict future problems due to scale, security, and performance bottlenecks. With that information, you can create software modules that automatically detect such issues and take appropriate actions (Figure 3-1).

With the faster network insights and automation provided by the Aruba Network Analytics Engine, you can reduce the time spent on manual tasks and address current and future demands driven by Mobility and IoT.

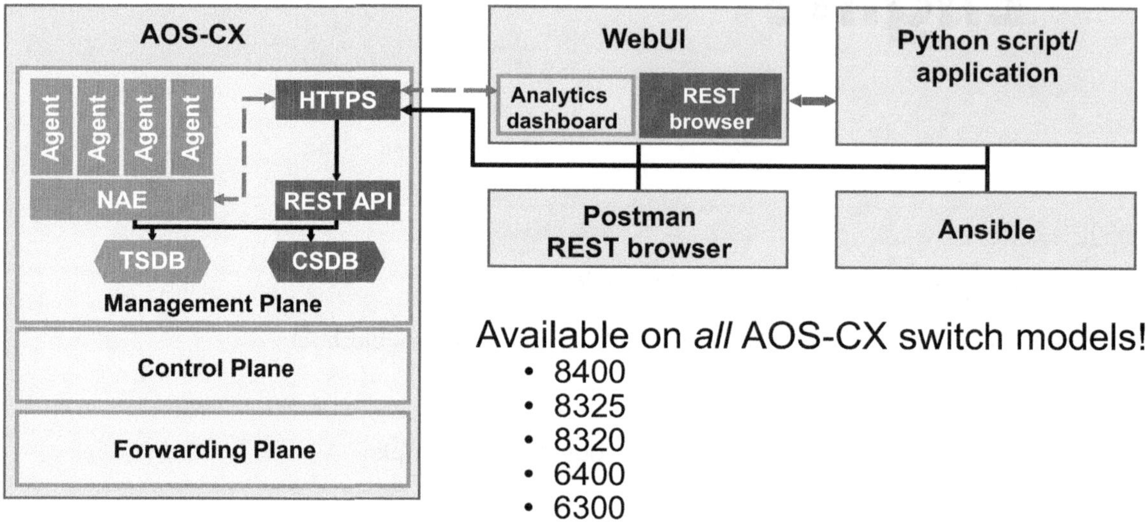

Figure 3-1 Introduction to Network Automation with AOS-CX

The Network Analytics Engine (NAE) in AOS-CX uses python-based agents, developed by Aruba and the Aruba community, to help companies better monitor and troubleshoot their network environment through an automated process. Agents monitor the state, settings, and statistics around specific system components within the current state database. For example, an agent can monitor the number of bytes transmitted on an interface or the switch's operating temperature. The agent then writes the ongoing results to the time-series database for ongoing analysis.

Admins can interact with the NAE through the Web UI's analytics dashboard. They can also automate the NAE through the REST API using tools such as Postman, Ansible, or another choice. They can also create or obtain Python scripts for new agents and load the agents on the switch using the Web UI or the REST API.

AOS-CX REST API

Switches running the AOS-CX software are fully programmable with a REST (REpresentational State Transfer) API, allowing easy integration with other devices both on premises and in the cloud. This programmability—combined with the Aruba Network Analytics Engine—accelerates network administrator understanding of and response to network issues.

The AOS-CX REST API enables programmatic access to the AOS-CX configuration and state database at the heart of the switch. By using a structured model, changes to the content and formatting of the CLI output do not affect the programs you write. And because the configuration is stored in a structured database instead of a text file, rolling back changes is easier than ever, thus dramatically reducing a risk of downtime and performance issues.

The AOS-CX REST API is a web service that performs operations on switch resources using HTTPS POST, GET, PUT, and DELETE methods.

A switch resource is indicated by its Uniform Resource Identifier (URI). A URI can be made up of several components, including the host name or IP address, port number, the path, and an optional query string. The AOS-CX operating system includes the AOS-CX REST API Reference, which is a web interface based on the Swagger UI. The AOS-CX REST API Reference provides the reference documentation for the REST API, including resources URIs, models, methods, and errors.

Python and the REST API for Scripts

Network Analytics Engine scripts are written in Python, and the Network Analytics Engine provides a built-in Python interpreter that is used when validating scripts and creating agents from scripts.

Python is the go-to language for network engineers:

- Python is high-level and human-readable.
- Python is popular with an active development community.
- There are many libraries (code written for you that you can use in your programs) available.

Python and the REST API to the AOS-CX database provide powerful tools to support network automation. By using Python and the REST API, you can move far beyond CLI scripting in network automation.

In the past, a network engineer might use Perl scripts to automate show and configure CLI commands. This scheme provided some automation, but it was inefficient because it still used the CLI to interact with the switch. CLI inputs and outputs are in an unstructured, human-readable format. You must use text processing based on specific CLI output to extract the information you want.

For example, you would have to write code to detect a MAC address in the large continuous string of text that is the CLI output. The CLI output might have many things to make it human-readable, such as table formatting, column headings, introductory text, and so forth, and the way MAC addresses are presented can vary by CLI, operating system version, and sometimes even by individual command output.

In contrast, by using programmatic APIs such as the AOS-CX REST API, you can get the information you are looking for in a predictable and structured way. For example, you can ask for and get just the MAC address.

NAE: AI for Networking

Using NAE, the intelligent AOS-CX switch provides a foundation for security, DevOps/operation automation, supportability, capacity planning, and monitoring/root cause analysis solutions (Figure 3-2).

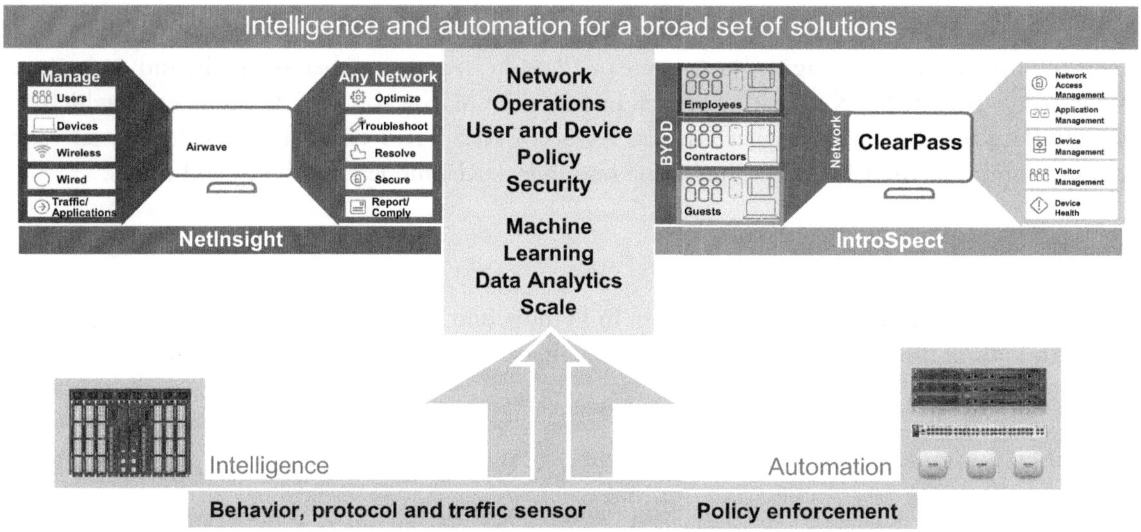

Figure 3-2 NAE: AI for Networking

Agents create baselines for specific components of the system and monitor excessive deviations from those baselines, as well as other aspects of the system. When pre-defined conditions occur, including excessive deviation from a baseline, NAE can take automatic actions to help alert administrators or even mitigate the problem.

NAE can also feed information to external management solutions using REST calls. These solutions include AirWave and ClearPass, as well as third-party ticketing IT service solutions such as ServiceNow and TOPdesk.

Root Cause Analytics

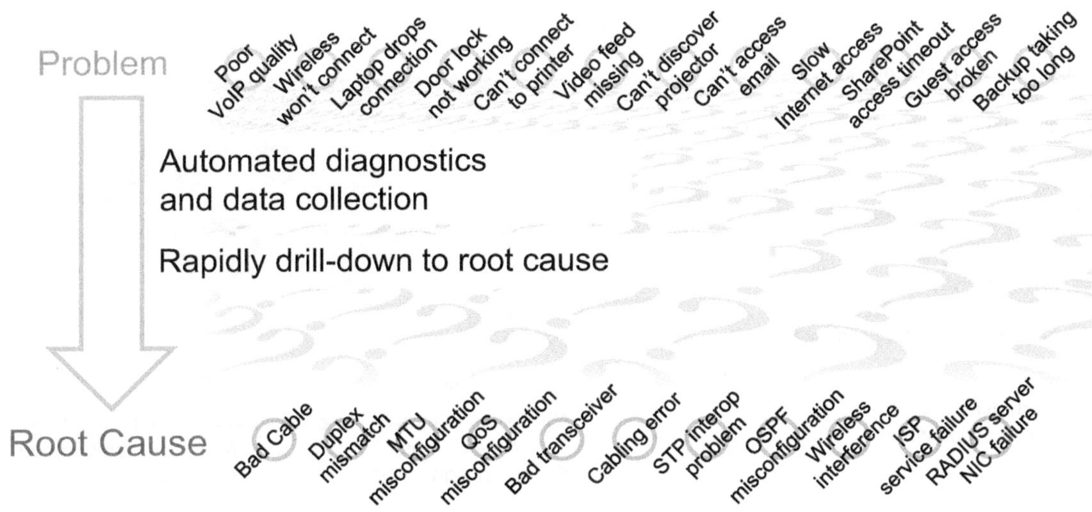

Figure 3-3 Root Cause Analytics

The Aruba NAE is a first-of-its-kind, built-in framework for network assurance and remediation. Combining the full automation and deep visibility capabilities of the AOS-CX operating system, this unique framework enables monitoring, collecting network data, evaluating conditions, and taking corrective actions through simple scripting agents.

This engine is integrated with the AOS-CX system configuration and time series databases, enabling you to examine historical trends and predict future problems due to scale, security, and performance bottlenecks. With that information, you can create software modules that automatically detect such issues and take appropriate actions. With the faster network insights and automation provided by the Aruba Network Analytics Engine, you can reduce the time spent on manual tasks and address current and future demands driven by Mobility and IoT.

IT staff often spend 70% or more of their time troubleshooting network issues. Staff members are confronted with symptoms such as poor VoIP quality or slow Internet access, for example. They must take this symptom and somehow connect it to a bad cable, a misconfigured QoS setting, for poor DNS performance, for example. Searching for the root cause of issues manually is time-consuming and frustrating. NAE uses rule-based, real-time monitoring to track issues as they occur and send alerts. It helps to automate diagnostics and data collection, correlating all data with time using the time-series database, so that staff can quickly find the information that they need to arrive at the root cause of issues (Figure 3-3).

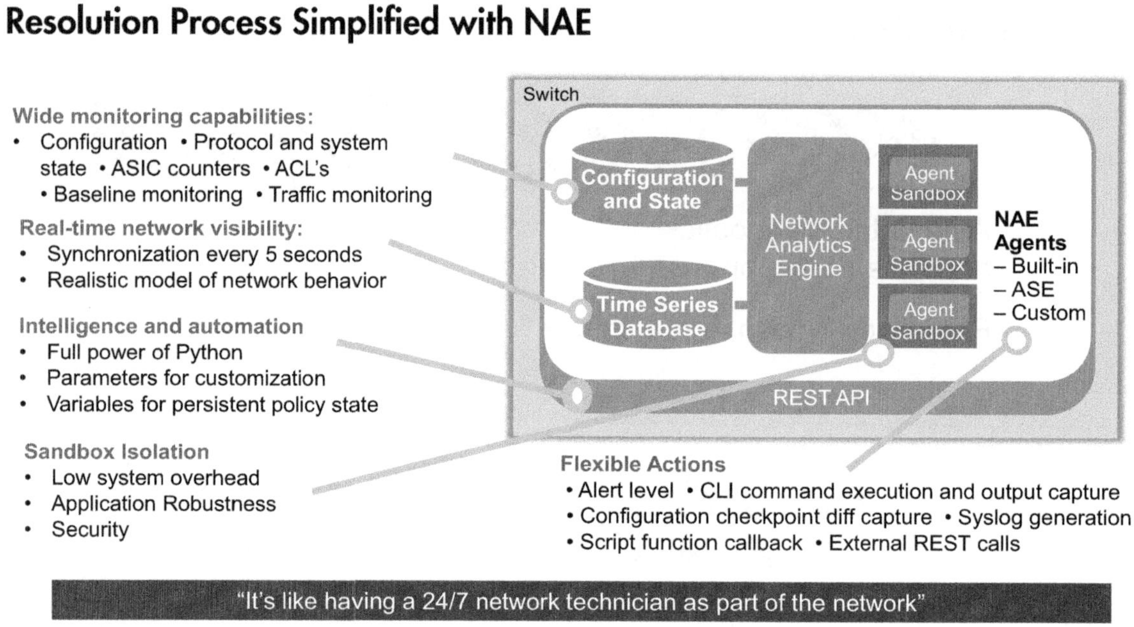

Figure 3-4 Resolution Process Simplified with NAE

Networking today faces complexities in scales that are unlike those of the past. Every new user brings several new devices, and networks are expected to handle the multitude of users all wanting to bring their own device. However, when one of the devices among the crowd faces an issue, the IT help desk has to spring into action to resolve the problem.

A typical troubleshooting and resolution process includes many steps, which can take a long time to complete. First admins need to become aware of a problem, which often means waiting until users have experienced a problem and begin complaining. Next admins try to go from user complaints, which can be vague, to more precise assessments of what the issue is and what impact it is having on services. From there, it is a laborious process to gather all the required information to formulate hypotheses as to the root cause. Only after much initial work, slogging through configs and log files, can the admins make and test hypothesis and, if appropriate, deploy a change and verify that change has had the intended effect.

The NAE simplifies this process in several ways (Figure 3-4). NAE agents can continuously monitor many different aspects of the system. They will begin to detect issues *before* they cause problems for users. NAE agents also help to collect all relevant information at the moment that an issue is occurring. Relevant information may include what has changed on the system, output from CLI show commands, log files, configuration outputs, and tests such as traceroute, ping, and packet captures. The agent can trigger an alert so that admins know more quickly that a problem needs addressing. And now admins do not need to sift through mountains of information and try to find when the issue occurred. Instead the correct information is at their fingertips, making it much simpler for them to find the root cause and fix the issue.

NAE simplifies monitoring and troubleshooting, making it *INCREDIBLY EASY.* This is done through the use of two databases that work together. The first database is the configuration and State DB, which monitors any value you want to look at (including switch configurations, protocol and system state, ASIC statistics, ACL's, and much more). Then those statistics are mapped to the Time-Series DB.

The Time-Series Database monitors any value you want to look at in the Configuration and State Database That gives the user the ability to pull values, and statuses. Plus, because these correlate to a Time Series, gives realistic or real-time model of the network behavior. NAE is built on top of REST API. NAE Agents give visual representation of values and provide automation function.

Configuration and State Database

The AOS-CX operating system is a modular, database-centric operating system. Every aspect of the switch configuration and state information is modeled in the AOS-CX switch database and is accessible through the REST API.

Developers can access a specific configuration, statistic, or status result for any aspect of the switch through its REST URI. Switches that are members of a stack are treated as a single switch. For example:

- The following URI accesses the link state information about interface 1/1/5: /rest/v1/system/ports/1%2F1%2F5?attributes=link_state
- The following URI accesses the link state of all interfaces on the switch: /rest/v1/system/interfaces/*?attributes=link_state
- The following URI accesses the number of received packets on interface 1/1/5: /rest/v1/system/interfaces/1%2F1%2F5?attributes=statistics.rx_packets
- The following URI accesses the link state information about interface 2/1/5 (stack member 2, slot 1, port 5): /rest/v1/system/ports/2%2F1%2F5?attributes=link_state

Time-Series Database

The Aruba Network Analytics Engine includes a built-in time-series database. Time-series data about the resources monitored by agents are automatically collected and presented in graphs in the switch Web UI. The database makes the data seamlessly available to agents that use rules that evaluate network conditions over time.

Old time-series data is removed automatically either as the storage space on the switch is used, or as the maximum number of days of data is reached. The amount of storage space consumed at any given time depends on the number of switch resources being monitored at that time. Each monitored resource creates one time series. Each time series consumes approximately 240 KB of storage for each day.

When creating a script, software developers do not interact with this database directly. Use of the database is automatically handled by the Monitor and Rule functions.

Sandboxes for Agent Actions

When an agent performs an action, the action is performed in a "sandbox" that is created when the action starts and removed when the action completes. The sandbox is in the default VRF, so it does not have access to the management network.

A sandbox is an isolated, tightly controlled environment in which programs can be run. Sandboxes restrict what a program can do, giving it the appropriate permissions and computing resources without allowing it access to the entire computing environment.

This design has the following benefits:

- Agents coexist and are prevented from using an excessive amount of CPU resources.
- Agents can benefit from the high-availability features of AOS-CX. During a switch failover event, the daemon that handles the sandbox can recover its state information and continue operations as before.
- Agents are prevented from accessing sensitive information—such as certificate files—in the switch operating system.

Aruba NAE Areas of Focus

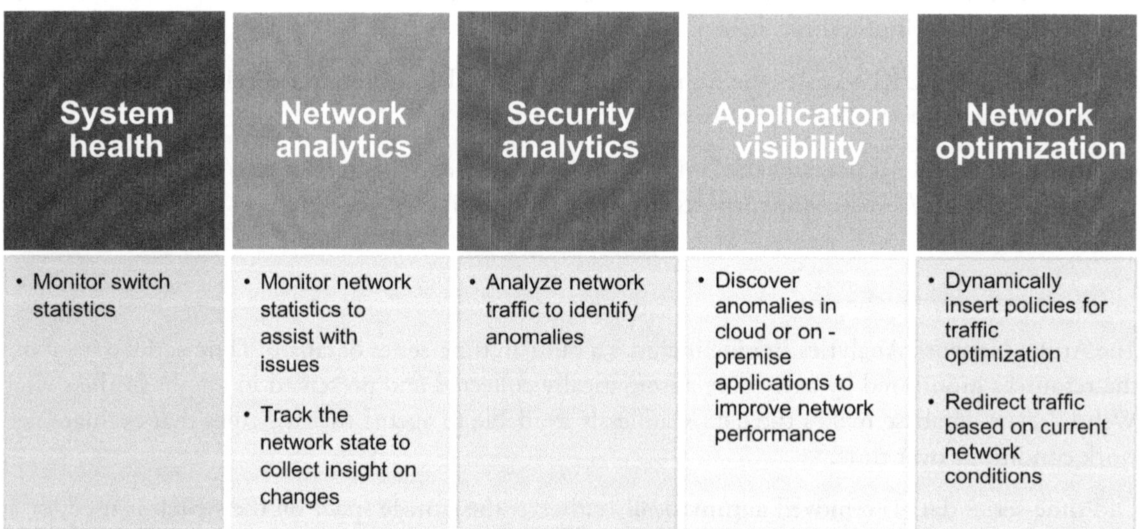

Figure 3-5 Aruba NAE Areas of Focus

With AOS-CX, Aruba's got a system that's designed to add new capabilities; and with NAE, Aruba goes beyond troubleshooting to system health, where you can monitor system statistics for root cause assistance on system issues (Figure 3-5). By using NAE, additional details can be gathered for system health issues like CPU utilization. Network analytics allows you to monitor network statistics to assist with Layer-1, Layer-2, and Layer-3 issues, track the state of OSPF neighbors, STP links, and etcetera, and collect insight information on network changes.

Security analytics is especially interesting, as you can develop agents to analyze network traffic passing through the core and learn about anomalies like east-west traffic flows (perhaps traffic patterns that should not be taking place, like camera going out to a different network segment in the IoT VRF). Application visibility allows you can leverage counters to match traffic going to applications in the cloud or data center to discover anomalies in application performance, cloud, or on-prem. Network optimization allows you to use knowledge of the network and its performance to dynamically insert policies for optimization and take action such as Redirecting destination routes based on link status.

NAE Agents

This section introduces agents and scripts used to implement NAE.

What Does an NAE Agent Do?

An NAE agent is the fundamental component of the AOS-CX NAE, as shown in Figure 3-6. Every agent includes one or more monitors, which track data about a specific attribute on the switch in the current state database. What is an attribute? It can be any state or statistic defined within the AOS-CX REST API. For example, it could be the number of transmitted bytes on a particular interface. Or it could be CPU utilization on a management module. This gives you great flexibility in terms of collecting the data that is relevant for your environment.

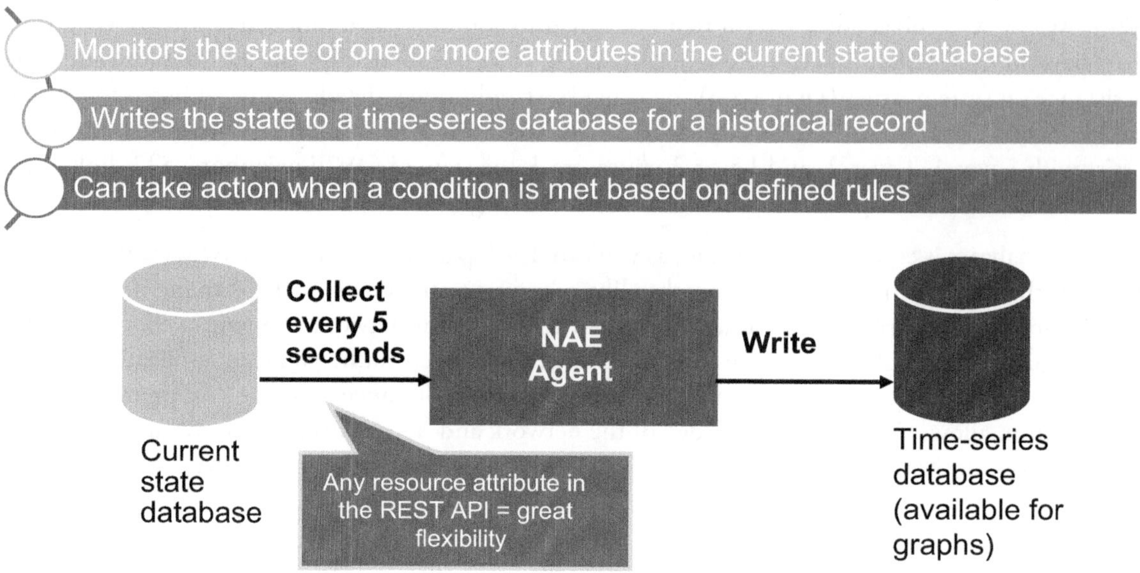

Figure 3-6 What Does an NAE Agent Do?

The agent collects the data every five seconds and writes the data to the time-series database on the switch's hard disk in order to create an ongoing record of the resource's state. You can see a graph of the monitored resource state over time in the AOS-CX Web UI.

If programmed with the appropriate rules, the NAE agent can take action when a particular condition is met. For example, if the agent is monitoring CPU utilization, it can set an alert when the utilization rises above a specific percentage.

Relationship Between NAE Scripts and Agents

Each NAE agent is defined by a Python script that is loaded on the AOS-CX switch. The script defines the agent, including which attributes it monitors and rules for any actions that the agent might take. The script might also define parameters, which are user configurable settings. For example, instead of specifying that an agent monitors transmitted bytes per second (Bps) on a specific interface, the script might specify that the agent monitors transmitted Bps on a variable interface parameter. Then users can choose the interface that they want when they create agents. Scripts can also use parameters to define values in the conditions for rules and in many other ways; it simply depends on how the script is written (Figure 3-7).

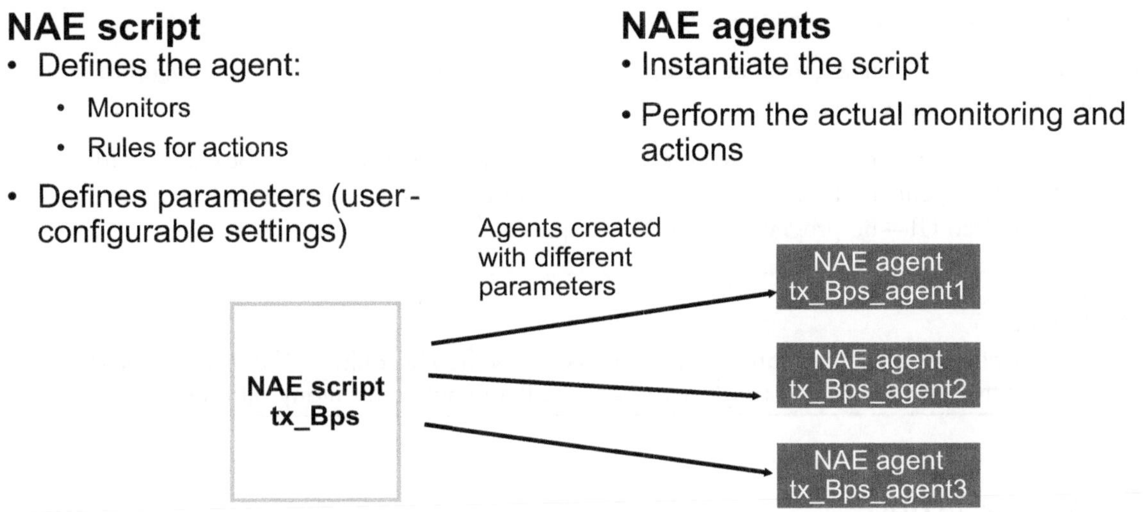

Figure 3-7 Relationship Between NAE Scripts and Agents

Note

An Aruba Network Analytics Engine agent is a specifically configured executable instance of an NAE script on a switch. When the agent is enabled, it performs the tasks defined by the script. Agents have administrator rights.

An NAE script has no effect until it has an agent associated with it. The NAE agent instantiates the script and actually begins monitoring the attribute and taking actions. When you create an agent, you define the values that you want for the parameters. You can create different agents from the same script using different parameters. For example, if one script parameter indicates the interface to monitor, you could create multiple agents, each monitoring a different interface.

Examples of tasks a script can define include the following:

- Monitoring average CPU usage and sending a system log message when the CPU usage is greater than 70% for 5 minutes.
- Monitoring the connection state of a particular BGP neighbor and executing a CLI command when the connection state transitions from UP to DOWN.

An Aruba Network Analytics Engine agent is a specifically configured executable instance of an NAE script on a switch. When the agent is enabled, it performs the tasks defined by the script. Agents have administrator rights. For scripts that provide configuration parameters, different agents can be configured to use specific parameter values when performing the tasks defined by the script. For example, a script that monitors the connection state of a particular BGP neighbor can define a parameter to specify which BGP neighbor to monitor. From that script, you can do the following:

- You can create an agent to monitor a specific BGP neighbor by specifying that BGP neighbor as the value of the parameter.

- You can create multiple agents—one for each BGP neighbor you want to monitor.
- When a new BGP neighbor is added, you can create an agent to monitor that neighbor without having to change the script itself.

Some parameters that are integers—such as a CPU utilization threshold—can be changed for a given agent after that agent has been created. Network administrators can change such parameters easily through the Web UI—no programming skill is required.

Note

A script is used to create an agent, which is a specifically configured executable instance of a script on a switch. A single script can be the template for many different agents.

Sources for Scripts

There are three sources for an agent script:

- Built-in (system-created)
- Aruba Solutions Exchange (ASE)
- User-created

A script can be system created, which means that it is included with the factory-default switch software. When you update the switch software, it updates the system-defined agents as well. You cannot delete these agents.

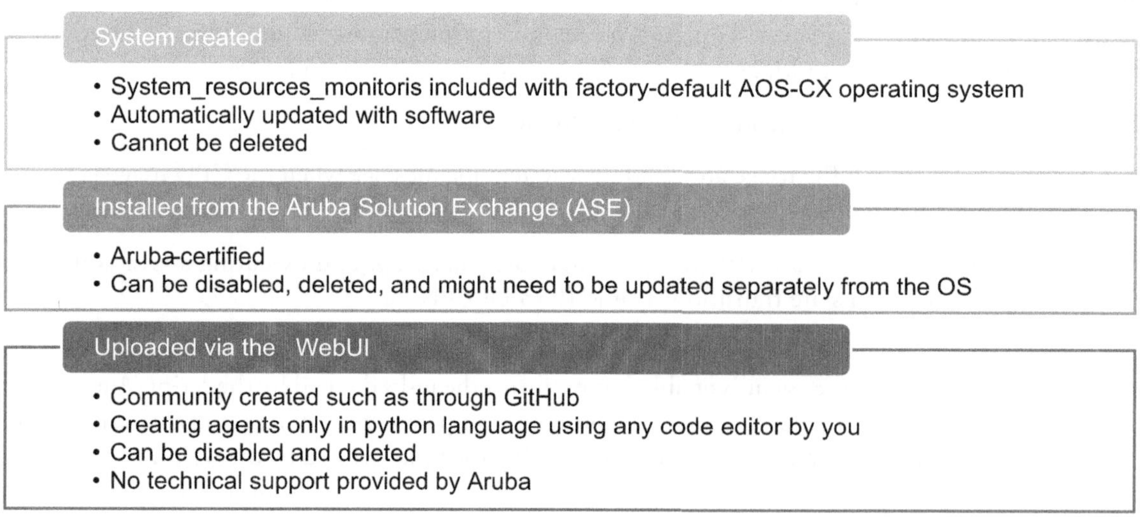

Figure 3-8 Sources for Scripts

Built-In Scripts

Built-in scripts and agents are installed on the switch before the switch is shipped from the factory. All scripts and agents have information about their origin associated with them. Built-in scripts and agents have an origin of "system" and are marked System Created in the Web UI (Figure 3-8).

Built-in scripts and agents cannot be deleted. You can enable, disable, and change the configuration of built- in agents:

- Built-in scripts are not displayed.
- Built-in agents are displayed only if one of more parameters has been changed and saved.

If you create an additional agent from a built-in script, that agent is considered a user-created agent, which can be deleted.

The current software release includes a single built-in script and agent that monitors several system resources:

- Built-in script: system_resource_monitor
- Built-in agent: system_resource_monitor.default

Aruba-Certified Scripts

You can also obtain agent scripts from community sources and load them on your switch. Some scripts, listed as Aruba-certified scripts, Aruba writes and validates do what they are advertised. Community members can create and upload other scripts as well. You should use these scripts at your own risk. You should always evaluate a script before loading it on the switch to ensure that the actions executed are what you expect. You can disable and remove these agents after loading them if you want. Before you complete a software upgrade, you may need to remove an old version of the agent and then, after the upgrade, upload a new one.

Note

Aruba-certified Network Analytics Engine scripts are written and tested by Aruba.

Create Your Own Scripts

Finally, you can create agents on your own with Python script. These agents are managed like the ones that you install from a community source. You can disable, remove, and update them separately from the software.

System-Created Agent

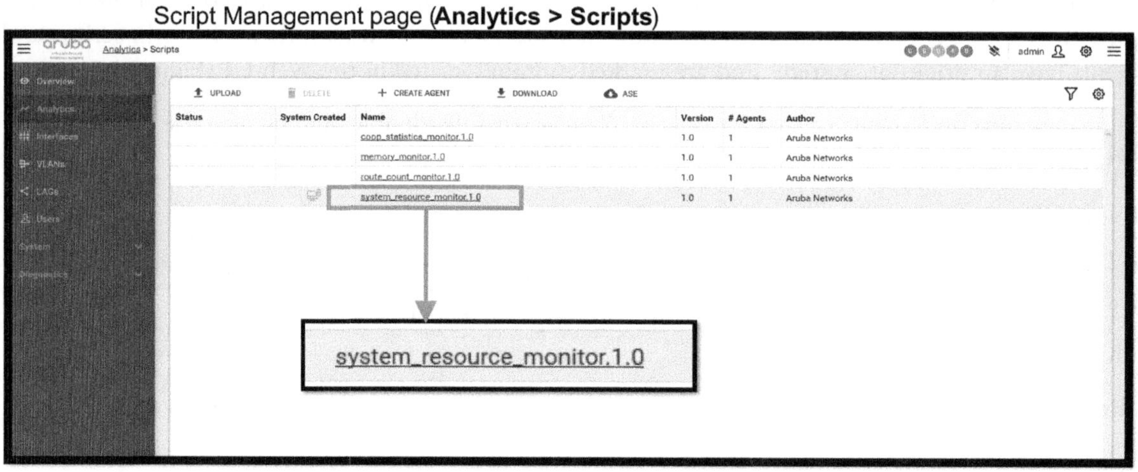

Figure 3-9 System-Created Agent

The AOS-CX Web UI provides access to information related to Aruba Network Analytics Engine agents, scripts, and alerts on the switch, including time-series data graphs and other information generated by the enabled agents.

From the AOS-CX Web UI, select **Analytics** in the navigation pane to view information in the Analytics Dashboard. You can display time-series graph panels for up to nine agents on the dashboard. However, many more agents can be enabled on a switch.

From the Analytics Dashboard, you can open Analytics detail pages. Analytics detail pages allow you to enable, disable, create, delete, or edit agents, upload scripts, and view detailed data about monitored resources. Administrator rights are required for actions that modify an agent.

The Script Management page in the Web UI shows all of the scripts loaded on the switch and the agents associated with them (Figure 3-9). Look in the System Created column to find the system-created script.

AOS-CX supports a single system-created script, which by default has an agent associated with it. This agent monitors CPU and memory utilization over short, medium, or long time periods. It triggers alerts and log messages when utilization passes a particular threshold. The alert severity depends on whether the high usage continues over a short, medium, or long period.

NAE Communities

The primary source for additional NAE scripts is the Aruba Solutions Exchange (ASE). You can access this portal at https://ase.arubanetworks.com/. From there you can browse agents and search for particular types of agents. If you want to view the agent script or download the agent, you must log in with your user account in the Aruba SSO system. You can also access ASE directly through the AOS-CX switch UI, as long as your browser has Internet connectivity. In this case, you do not need to log in.

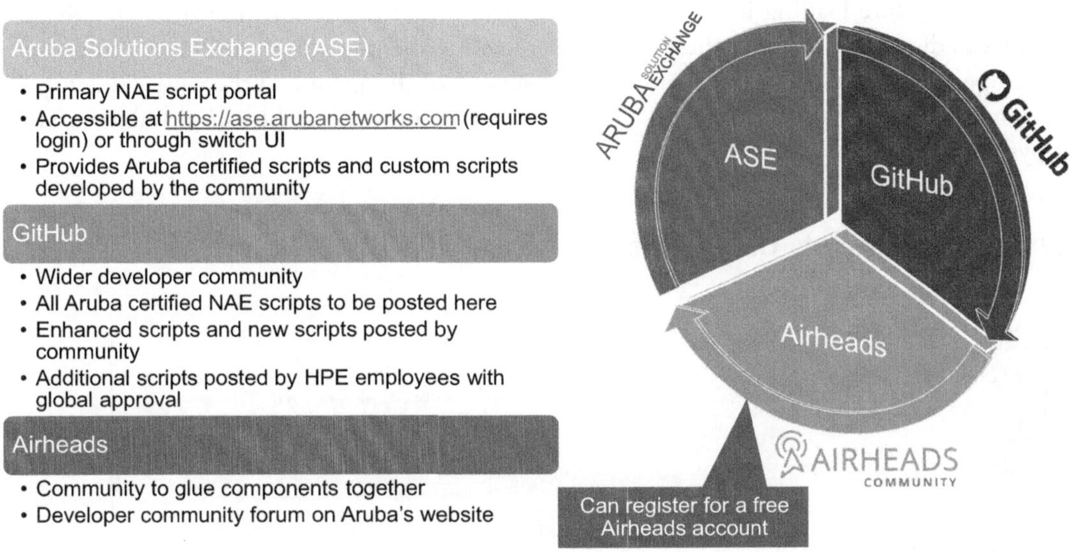

Figure 3-10 NAE Communities

GitHub is a wide-ranging developer community with custom scripts for many different applications. Aruba will post all Aruba-certified NAE scripts here as well as to ASE. The GitHub community can enhance these scripts and create new scripts for sharing within the community. HPE employees can also post NAE scripts to GitHub provided that they pass global approval, which consists of approval from the Open Source Review Board (OSRB) and the legal department (Figure 3-10).

The Airheads community provides a place for members or participants to search for information, read and post about topics of interest, and learn from each other. Guests (unregistered visitors) can browse or search the community for information. Members (registered users) can post messages or comments, track discussions, and get email notifications on posting activity and other community actions. The Airheads community is the glue that holds together all the components of the NAE solutions. Airhead community members can share their expertise and tips and point each other toward relevant agents. There is now a Developer Community forum under the technology category in the Airheads with discussion forums dedicated to automation and NAE questions and support. Aruba is committed to expanding the NAE value with extensive research and development (R&D) investment in building NAE scripts and supporting the community. Within the Airheads community, there is a Developer Community group that is specific to APIs, programming, and automation. The Developer Community is the recommended place to post questions about the Aruba Network Analytics Engine

(NAE). See the Developer community at: https://community.arubanetworks.com/t5/Developer-Community/bd-p/DeveloperCommunity. See the Airheads community at http://community.arubanetworks.com/.

With developer communities such as GitHub, members can create and upload other scripts as well. These are not Aruba supported and you should use these scripts at your own risk. You should always evaluate a script before loading it on the switch to ensure that the actions executed are what you expect. You can disable and remove these agents after loading them if you want. Before you complete a software upgrade, you may need to remove an old version of the agent and then, after the upgrade, upload a new one. AOS-CX scripts on GitHub can be found here: https://github.com/aruba/aos-cx-python.

Obtaining NAE Scripts Using ASE

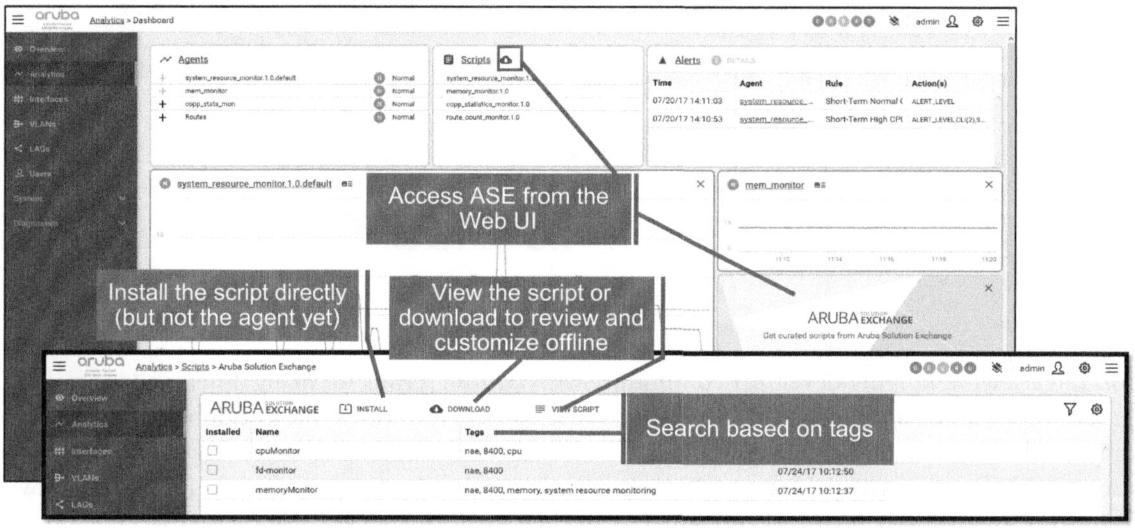

Figure 3-11 Obtaining NAE Scripts Using ASE

Aruba Solution Exchange (ASE) is a utility that allows users to dynamically create configurations for many Aruba products. The exchange offers a set of solutions certified by Aruba for specific use cases. The collective knowledge of the Aruba community powers the Solution Exchange. All users are encouraged to create solutions, modify existing ones, and suggest ideas for new solutions.

Access to the Aruba Solution Exchange is available at: https://ase.arubanetworks.com/.

No login is required to browse the exchange or look at information about solutions. Downloading solutions or viewing solution source code is free for anyone with a valid user account with the Aruba SSO authentication system. If you do not have an existing account, register for a free Airheads Social account at: http://community.arubanetworks.com. For more information about using the Aruba Solution Exchange, see https://ase.arubanetworks.com/docs.

To access ASE from the AOS-CX switch Web UI, navigate to the Analytics dashboard and select the ASE section. Or you can select the download icon in the Scripts section. First, you will connect to the exchange. You can browse through the exchange using tags to narrow your search. Examples of tags include the name of the resource that you want to monitor. Scripts might be specific to a particular switch model or might be usable for any switch. Use the "nae-aruba-certified" designated scripts for Aruba-certified scripts (Figure 3-11).

If you decide that you are interested in an agent, you can select its check box and View Script to see the script or Download to view and possibly customize the script offline. You can also select Install to immediately install the script on your switch.

Note

On the Aruba Solution Exchange, Aruba-certified scripts have the following tag: *nae-aruba-certified.*

Creating and Editing Agents for Existing Scripts

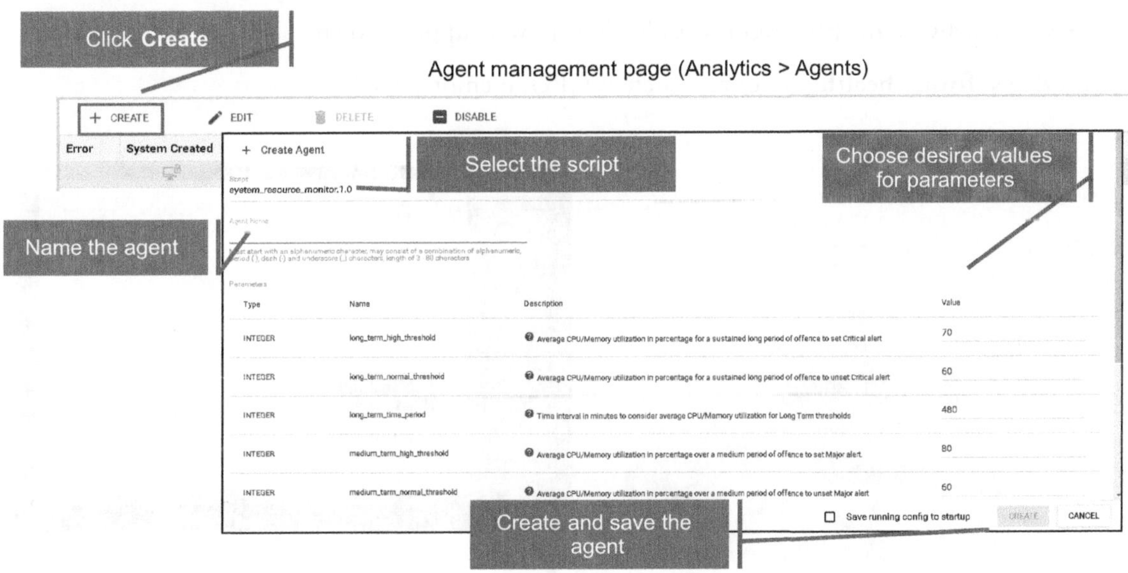

Figure 3-12 Creating and Editing Agents for Existing Scripts

When you install a new script, it does not yet have an agent associated with it. To create an agent based on a script, first access the Agent Management page by selecting Agents in the Analytics Dashboard. Then select **Create** (you can also select Create Agent in the Script Management page). A window appears where you can choose the script on which you want to base the agent. Then define the agent name. Finally, customize the parameters and save it (Figure 3-12).

You can also select an agent in the Agent Management page and select **Edit** to adjust the parameters on an existing agent.

NAE Updates for 10.04

New scripts available in AOS-CX 10.04 include the following categories, as shown in Figure 3-13:

- **Application health**—visibility into the health/performance of a specific application. Helping figure out if the problem of the slowness lies on the network, the application, or the link to that server.
- **Dynamic segmentation health**—a monitor of the wireless overlay traffic, and others
- **Client services health**—RADIUS authentication, DHCP, and DNS services
- **L3 network health**—OSPF initially
- **L1/L2 network health**—interfaces and LAGs
- **L1/L2 network health**—mainly STP at first, LLDP with neighbor statuses, and etc.) Bonus* Bridging Health (may initially be focused on STP)
- **Device hardware health**—resources like fans, power supply, and etc.
- **Device software health**—resources such as CPU, memory, and etc.

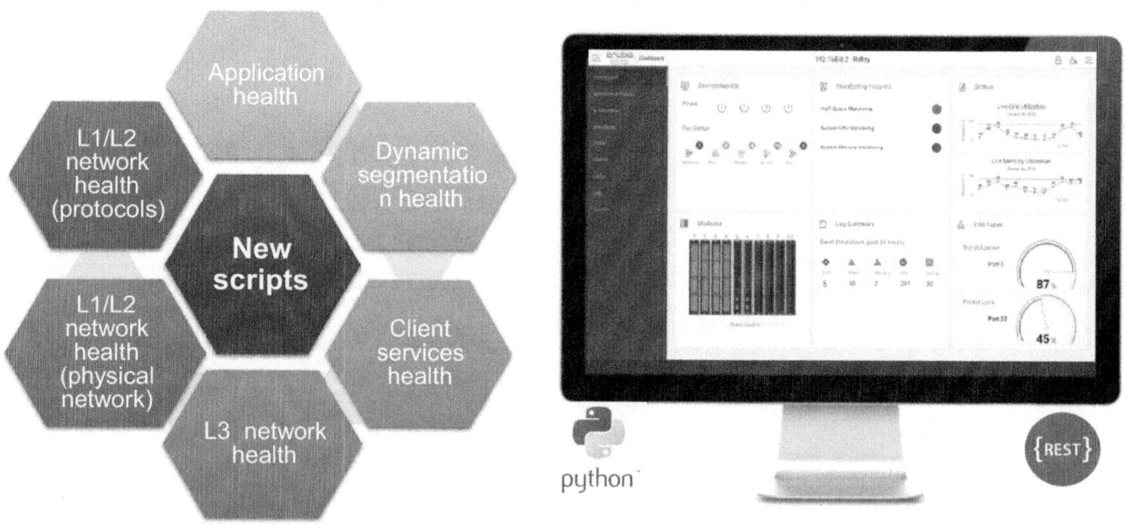

Figure 3-13 NAE Updates for 10.04

NAE Agent Actions

Now that you have learned how to obtain agents, you can examine some of the actions that they can take in more detail. The AOS-CX NAE supports several action types. The agent can send an alert with a critical, major, or minor level. These alerts are visible at a glance in the Analytics dashboard, helping admins find issues quickly. The agent can also remove the alert and return to the normal level.

Action Options

An agent can also execute CLI commands or shell commands. You should be very careful with using shell commands in an agent because mistakes can damage the switch functionality and render the switch unusable. In addition, an agent can make REST API calls to itself or remote devices and applications. This allows for interaction with all of the Aruba portfolio of applications and devices, which have their own REST interfaces. Through REST calls, the NAE can also integrate with third-party applications, including ticket generation systems like ServiceNow and TOPdesk.

An action can also send log messages to a system log or remote Syslog server, indicating information about the condition that has occurred. Finally, an action can generate a custom report with multiple pieces of relevant information about the condition.

For more complex scenarios, a rule can combine multiple actions. Note that AOS-CX uses a safe sandbox environment to execute actions, which prevents agents from using excessive CPU or obtaining access to sensitive files such as certificates. The sandbox has access to the default VRF, not the management one. If actions need access to the Internet to execute properly, make sure that the default VRF has such access (Figure 3-14).

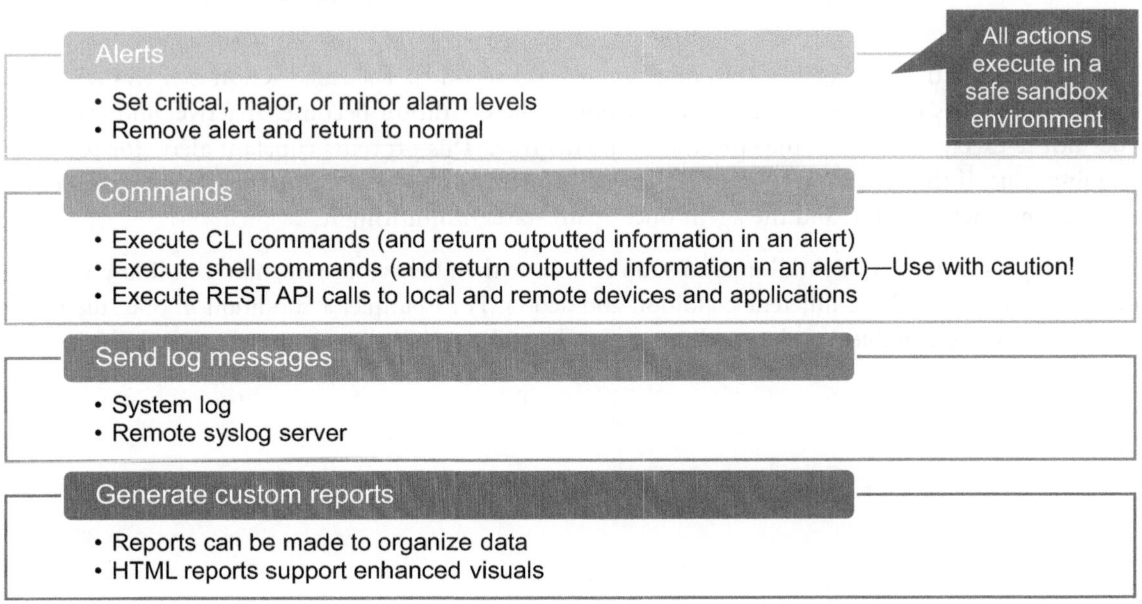

Figure 3-14 Action Options

How Actions are Triggered (Clear Condition Not Met)

Sometimes you only want an agent to track information in the time-series database and produce a graph. However, often, you also want the agent to take automatic action based on the information obtained by the monitor (Figure 3-15). You define these actions with one or more rules. A rule must have a condition, which defines a particular state for the monitored value. At any given moment, the state is either true or false. Generally, the state being true indicates a potential issue that admins should know about. For example, an agent monitors transmitted Bps on an Ethernet interface. A condition in a rule might be that the monitored value is greater than 500 million Bps.

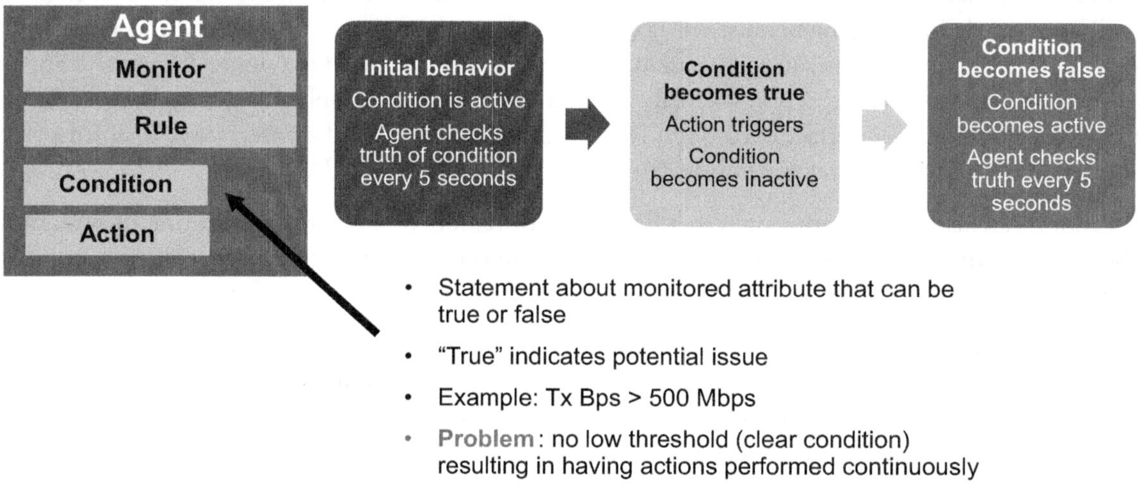

Figure 3-15 How Actions are Triggered (Clear Condition Not Met)

The agent checks the state against the condition every 5 seconds. The rule's action executes when the condition changes from false to true. At that point, the condition becomes inactive, and the agent does not re-execute actions if the condition remains true. This prevents constant alerts for the same ongoing issue. If the condition becomes false again (for example, the Tx Bps drops lower), the condition becomes active again, and the agent once again starts monitoring it.

This example shows just one rule, but agents can customize their behavior to nuanced conditions by using multiple rules, each with a different condition and action. For example, a condition in one rule might indicate a less severe problem and a condition in another rule might indicate a more severe problem.

How Actions Are Triggered (Clear Condition Met)

In some cases, a condition might toggle frequently between true and false. For example, the condition is more than 500 million Bps transmitted on an interface. The interface might transmit 600 million Bps and change the condition from false to true. Then it transmits 490 million Bps and transitions from true to false. Then it transmits 510 million Bps and triggers the action again (Figure 3-16).

To avoid this problem, you can define a clear condition, which must be met to free the main condition. The "clear" condition is a low threshold that the monitored attribute must fall below before the condition triggers the action again. The clear condition becomes active when the condition first transitions from false to true, and the agent begins checking the state of the clear condition every five seconds. Even if the condition becomes false again, the clear condition remains active, and the condition inactive, as long as the clear condition is also false. Only when the clear condition becomes true does the condition transition to active. For example, the clear condition could be transmission of less than 300 million Bps. Now the rate must fall below that (transition to true) before the original condition can become active again. You can optionally define a clear action, which also executes when the clear condition changes from false to true.

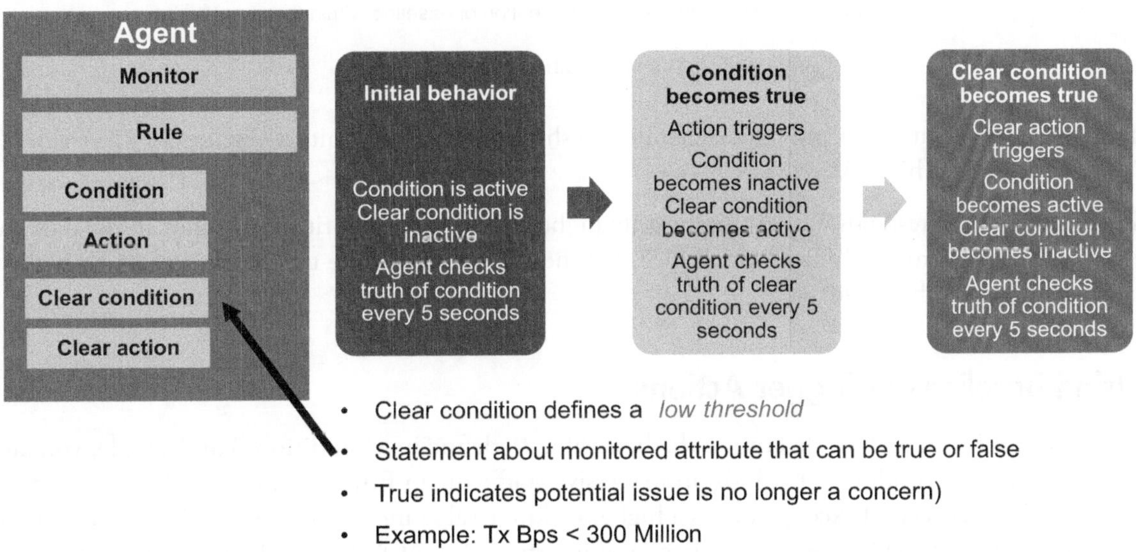

Figure 3-16 How Actions Are Triggered (Clear Condition Met)

Feature: Baselining

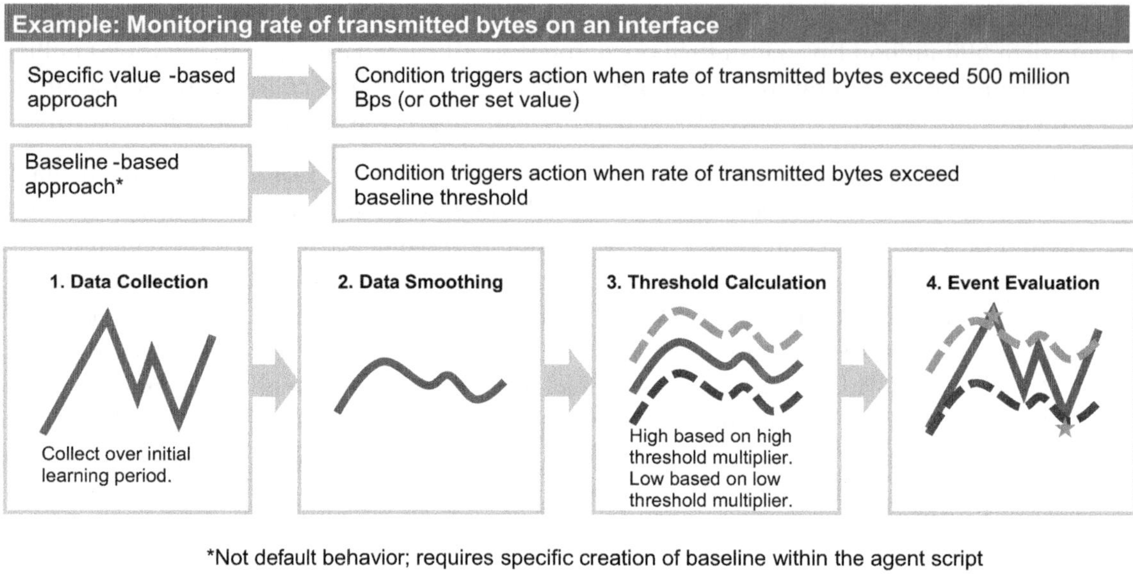

Figure 3-17 Feature: Baselining

Baselining is a feature that provides dynamic thresholds for NAE monitors (Figure 3-17). Artificial intelligence (AI)? This is AI!

In this case, the thresholds are set significantly higher because the algorithm includes all the data in its continuous learning window, which included the time in which the traffic rate was much higher than the previous threshold.

Using Baselines to Trigger Actions

Often, it can be difficult to determine the best value to define in a condition. For example, you are trying to define a condition that indicates excessive traffic on an Ethernet interface. Is a rate of 500 million bytes per second excessive, or is a higher or lower value more appropriate? The answer often depends on the particular network, switch, and interface. The AOS-CX NAE can help to automate and remove the guesswork for defining conditions through the use of baselines. The agent can construct a baseline of normal values for the monitored resource attribute. A condition then triggers if the value deviates too much from the baseline. It is important that you understand, though, that agents do not create baselines by default; whoever creates the agent must specifically script the agent to create the baseline.

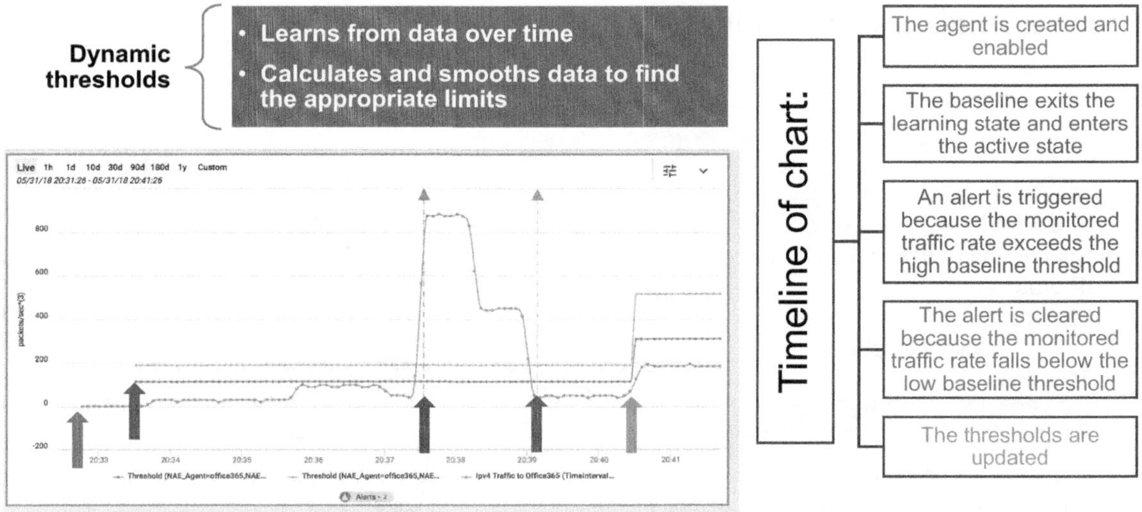

Figure 3-18 Using Baselines to Trigger Actions

When so configured, the agent constructs the baseline by collecting data over an initial learning period, which is configurable. The initial learning period should be long enough that all representative patterns are included. For example, it should be at least a day and maybe as much as a week. The agent then uses an algorithm to smooth the data and create the baseline. The agent next uses a configurable threshold multiplier to determine the high threshold, which indicates when a condition using the baseline changes to true and triggers an associated action. The larger the multiplier, the more deviation allowed and the smaller the multiplier, the less deviation allowed. The low multiplier lets the agent construct a low threshold, which indicates when the condition is cleared and a clear action triggered. You could create several conditions with different multipliers that trigger different actions; the condition with the larger multiplier should have a more significant action because it indicates a greater deviation from normal (Figure 3-18).

In addition to the initial learning period, the agent also uses a continuous learning period to continue to recalibrate the baseline. This lets the agent respond to gradual changes that create a new normal. However, data from a continuous learning period that includes an anomaly that triggered a condition is discarded. This lets the agent detect the anomalies, but not use them to change the baseline.

Feature: Analytics Data Collector

Figure 3-19 Feature: Analytics Data Collector

You can set up agents with scripts that monitor traffic with specific filtering criteria, as shown in Figure 3-19, including:

- Source and/or destination IP addresses (IPv4 or IPv6)
- IP protocol
- Physical switch port
- Layer-4 application port
- TCP flags

Here are some examples:

- A specific private server
- Subnets of web addresses, such as Twitter traffic
- Application traffic usage of cloud services, such as Office365

Viewing NAE Information

You will now look at how you can view the information that NAE agents collect in the AOS-CX Web UI.

Analytics Dashboard

When you enter the Web UI, you see a main dashboard. The Analytics section in this dashboard refers to the NAE functions. It shows how many critical, major, or minor alerts are active. If you want more detailed information, you should view the Analytics Dashboard. You can access this dashboard in two ways: click the Analytics section in the main dashboard or select Analytics in the sidebar (Figure 3-20).

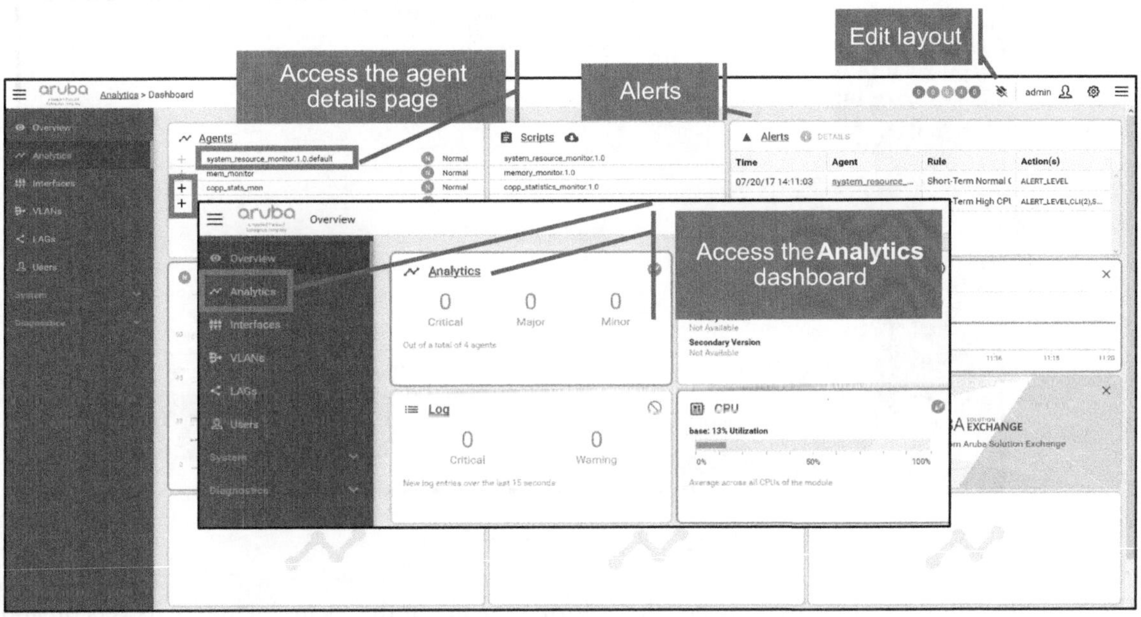

Figure 3-20 Analytics Dashboard

On the Analytics dashboard, the Agents section lists all of the agents on NAE and indicates whether they are operating normally.

- The dashboard also shows one graph for each of the NAE agents that has been added to it.
- You can click the plus icons in the Agents section to add the graph for another agent.
- The Scripts section shows the Python scripts associated with those agents.
- Look to the Alerts section to see more details on any minor, major, or critical alerts that the NAE agents have generated.

You can select the name of these sections to move to a page with details. For example, click the Agents link to see the Agent Management. Or you can select an individual agent to move to that agent's detail page.

You can also change the layout for the dashboard. Click this icon at the top of the bar and choose, Unlock Page Layout. Each section in the dashboard is then outlined with dashed lines. You can click a section and move it around. When you are done editing, you can click the icon again to lock the page layout.

NAE Agent Details

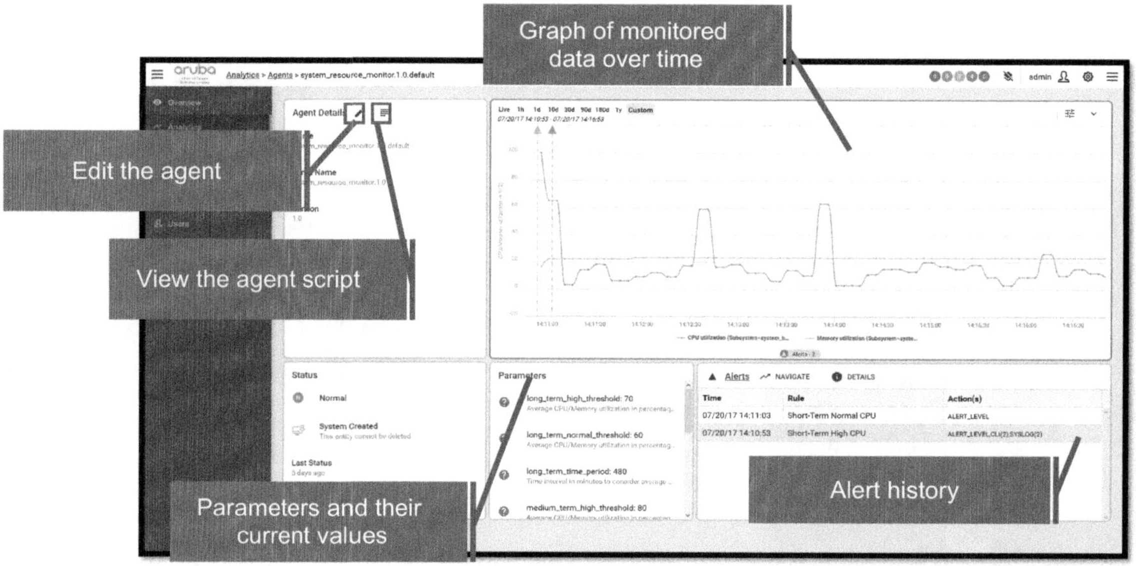

Figure 3-21 NAE Agent Details

The Agent Details page provides more detailed information about the agent, including its version and status. If the agent has multiple monitors, this page shows all of the graphs associated with those monitors. The parameters section shows agent settings that you can configure. You can also click icons to edit the agent or look at its script (Figure 3-21).

Check the alerts section to see information about the alerts this agent generates so that you can take the proper steps to resolve them. You can click a particular alert and then select Details to see a window with Alert details.

Viewing Graphs

Data collected by an Analytics agent is displayed in the Web UI in one or more time-series graphs. An agent has at least one graph. An agent can have multiple graphs as specified in the script, but only one graph represents the agent on the Analytics dashboard. The graph that represents the agent on the Analytics dashboard is specified in the script.

If the Analytics dashboard does not include a graph for an agent, you can add the graph that represents that agent from Analytics dashboard. Graphs on the Analytics dashboard represent a live view only. The graph customization toolbar is not available from the Analytics dashboard.

Here you see a closer view of a graph in an Agent Details page. This graph has multiple lines, one for each monitor within the agent. For example, one line shows the CPU usage averaged over short time periods, one shows CPU usage averaged over long time periods, one shows memory averaged over short time periods, and so on. The legend at the bottom of the graph shows what each line indicates. You can click any of the names in the legend to remove that line from the graph or to re-add it. In this way, you can focus on the information that you want (Figure 3-22).

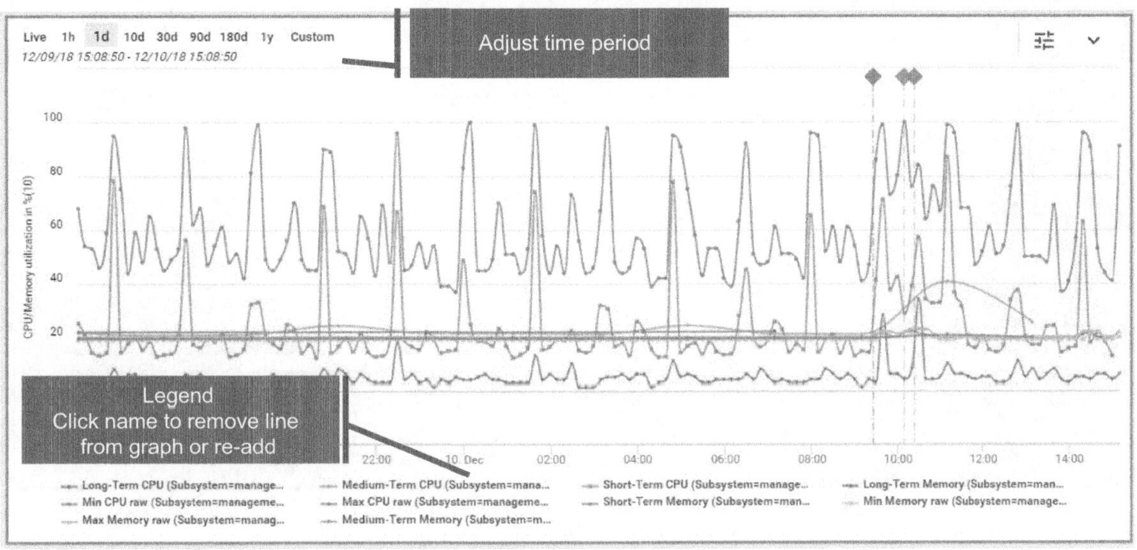

Figure 3-22 Viewing Graphs

Configuration checkpoints and alert indicators are overlaid on the graph. Configuration checkpoints are shown as purple diamonds. Alert indicators can include the following:

- A red or yellow triangle for an alert
- A green triangle for a return to normal
- A blue triangle for an alert on several resources being monitored

You can also change the graph to show different time periods such as the last hour or day up to the last year. Or you can specify a custom time period.

NAE Alert Details

The Alert Details window shows details about when and why the alert occurred, as well as the alert level. You can view a history of the actions taken in association with the condition that triggered this alert. In this example, these actions include syslog messages and CLI commands. You can also collect any information that those actions generated. Select **Output** to see the output from the CLI commands. If the alert generated a custom report, you can click and view that report.

You can also use the REST API to obtain information about NAE and NAE agents. Refer to the documentation and reference interface for more details (Figures 3-23 and 3-24).

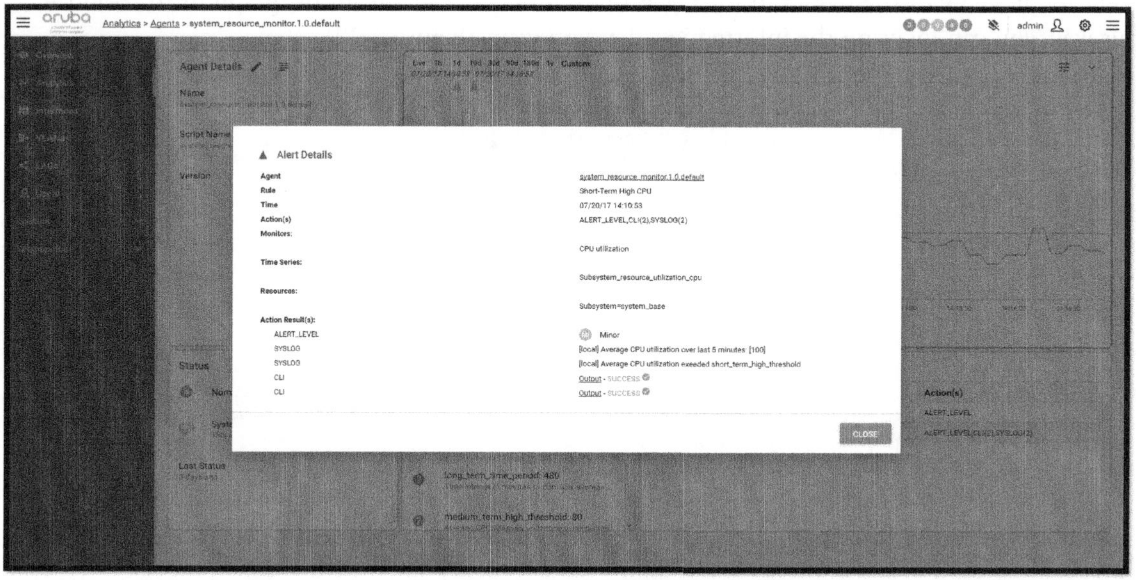

Figure 3-23 NAE Alert Details

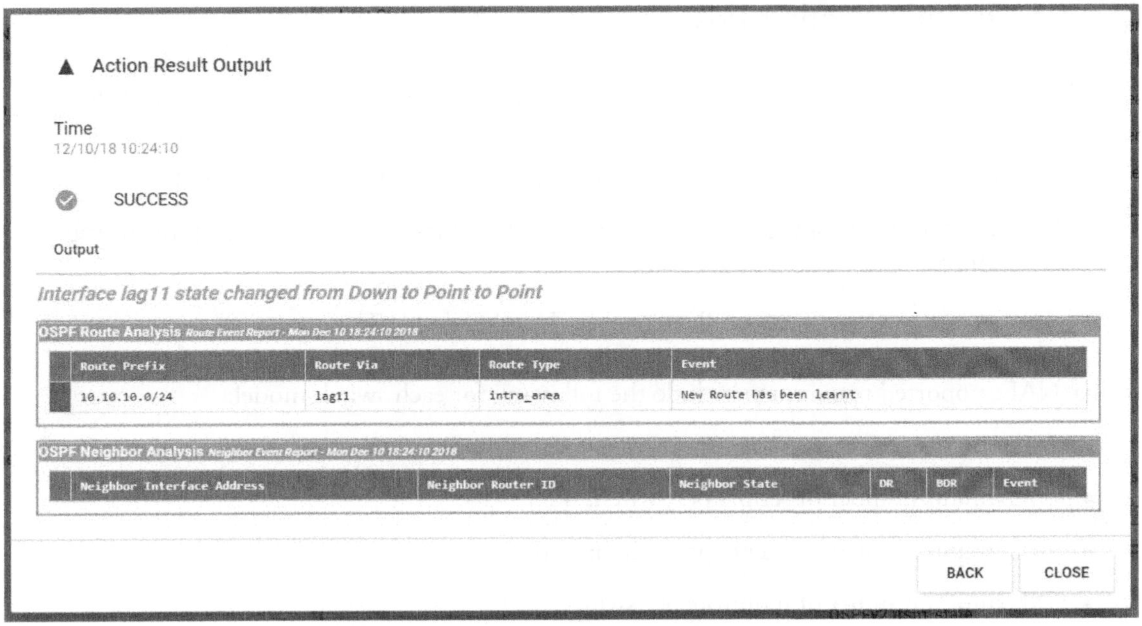

Figure 3-24 NAE Alert Details (cont.)

CLI Verification

You can see which scripts and agents are available from the CLI with the **show nae-script** and **show nae-agent** commands (Figure 3-25).

```
switch# show nae-script
----------------------------------------------------------------------
Script Name                            Version   Origin    Status
----------------------------------------------------------------------
fan_monitor                            1.0       system    VALIDATED
interface_link_flap_monitor            1.0       system    VALIDATED
interface_link_state_monitor           1.0       system    VALIDATED
interface_tx_rx_stats_monitor          1.0       system    VALIDATED
lag_imbalance_monitor                  1.0       system    VALIDATED
lag_status_monitor                     1.0       system    VALIDATED
power_supply_monitor                   1.0       system    VALIDATED
stp_bpdu_tcn_rate_monitor              1.0       system    VALIDATED
system_resource_monitor_mm1.default    1.0       system    VALIDATED
system_resource_monitor_mm2.default    1.0       system    VALIDATED
temp_sensor_monitor                    1.0       system    VALIDATED
```

```
switch# show nae-agent
------------------------------------------------------------------------------------------------------------------------
Agent Name                          Script Name                         Version  Origin  Disabled  Status   Error
------------------------------------------------------------------------------------------------------------------------
com.arubanetworks.monitor.agent     com.arubanetworks.monitor           1.0      user    true      UNKNOWN  NONE
com.arubanetworks.wildcard.vlan.agent com.arubanetworks.wildcard.vlan   1.0      user    false     UNKNOWN  ERROR
system_resource_monitor.default     system_resource_monitor             1.0      system  false     NORMAL   NONE
```

Figure 3-25 CLI Verification

Common Troubleshooting Tips

–Each switch model has limits in regarding to the number of scripts and agents supported

–An AOS -CX software update might require updates to scripts as well

–Make sure your desktop time and the switch's time is synched from the same NTP server

Figure 3-26 Common Troubleshooting Tips

Aruba' NAE supported maximums include the following for each switch model:

- Aruba 8400 switch series:
  - Maximum number of scripts per switch: 50
  - Maximum number of agents per switch: 100
  - Maximum number of monitors per switch: 300
  - Maximum script file size: 256 KB
- Aruba 8320 and Aruba 8325 switch series:
  - Maximum number of scripts per switch: 25
  - Maximum number of agents per switch: 50
  - Maximum number of monitors per switch: 150
  - Maximum script file size: 256 KB
  - Number of days of time-series data to store: 400
  - Amount of switch storage allocated to time-series data: 9 GB
- Aruba 6300 and Aruba 6400 switch series:
  - Maximum number of scripts per switch: 10
  - Maximum number of agents per switch: 10
  - Maximum number of monitors per switch: 130
  - Maximum script file size: 256 KB
  - Number of days of time-series data to store: 45
  - Amount of switch storage allocated to time-series data: 3.1 GB

Note

The NAE limitations defined above can change based on the AOS-CX software version running on the switch. The above limitations are for AOS-CX 10.04.

To monitor the scripts in use, execute the **show capacities-status nae** command:

```
switch# show capacities-status nae
System Capacities Status: Filter NAE
Capacities Status Name                                       Value Maximum
---------------------------------------------------------------------------
Number of configured NAE agents currently active in the system    125
Number of configured NAE monitors currently active in the system  7 50
Number of configured NAE scripts currently active in the system   1 12
```

When you attempt to create an agent, the agent appears in the Agents panel with a red triangle error symbol and status of Unknown. The error message is the following: *The NAE Agent is not created. Please check hpe-policd logs for DB constraint violation errors.* Attempting to create the agent resulted in creating more monitors than the NAE supports on the switch. To view the maximum number of monitors supported on the switch, see the Analytics panel on the Overview page of the Web UI. You can also use the CLI with the **show capacities-status nae** command.

Managing NAE Scripts Across Switch Software Updates

After you update the switch software to a new release or install an older software release on the switch, some Aruba Network Analytics Engine (NAE) scripts might not be valid. A script might not be valid because the script uses a URI or API function that is not valid on that software release. The existing scripts might generate errors, and the NAE data might not be valid until you upload the new scripts and clear the NAE data.

1. For each script that is not marked System Created in the Web UI, locate the version of the script that supports the software release running on the switch.
    a. For Aruba-certified NAE scripts, the Aruba Solutions Exchange (ASE) includes tags that indicate the minimum and maximum supported software release.
    b. When you select the ASE download button in the Web UI, the Web UI displays only the Aruba-certified NAE scripts that are supported on the software release running on the switch.
    c. For scripts that are not Aruba-certified NAE scripts downloaded from the ASE, see the information provided by the script author about which script version is supported.
2. Follow the instructions for updating a script. The steps to update a script depend on the switch software release version that was running when the script was installed.

3. On the Analytics Dashboard, locate and close any time-series graph panels for the default agent from the previous software release.

The default agent is created from the built-in script. The name of the agent is based on the name of the built-in script. Built-in scripts and agents have an origin of "system" and are marked System Created in the Web UI. Built-in scripts and their agents are updated automatically. However, sometimes the time-series graph panel for the previous default agent is not closed during the update. After the software update, instead of graphed data, such panels show an error message beginning with: "Agent data not found".

High Switch CPU and Memory Usage are Affecting Switch Performance

A switch that has Network Analytics Engine (NAE) agents installed is experiencing high CPU usage, high memory usage, or both, and overall performance is affected. The cause is that the NAE is attempting to monitor too many switch resources. For example, a script uses wildcard characters in a URI to monitor all interfaces, ACLs, or VLANs, and the switch has hundreds or thousands of those items.

Verify that the resources associated with the NAE are consuming the memory and CPU resources by entering the following commands in the switch CLI:

- **show system resource-utilization daemon hpe-tsdbd**
- **show system resource-utilization daemon hpe-policyd**
- **show system resource-utilization daemon Prometheus**

Switch Time and Browser Time are Not in Sync

The Web UI displays a yellow caution triangle in the top banner and an error dialog box with the following title: *Switch time and browser time are not in sync.*

The content of the dialog box indicates how many seconds the switch time is ahead of or behind the browser time, and states that the information displayed in the Web UI might not be accurate. In addition, time-series graphs on the Analytics page might be missing expected data, might have data shown with inaccurate times, or might display incorrect data.

Things you can do to fix this issue:

- Try clearing or resetting the web client browser cache.
- Ensure that the web client from which you are viewing the Web UI is set to a time zone based on UTC. For example, if your workstation is set to Eastern Standard Time (EST), and you want to use Pacific Standard Time (PST), change the time by setting the time zone instead of by manually resetting the time.

- Ensure that the switch is set to use NTP or to a time zone based on UTC time. NTP synchronizes the time of day among a set of distributed time servers and clients to correlate events when receiving system logs and other time-specific events from multiple network devices. All NTP communications use Coordinated Universal Time (UTC). To show the NTP status, use the **show ntp status** command. After you configure the switch, clear the NAE data by entering the **clear nae-data** command from the manager context.
- If the switch is set to use NTP and there has been a significant clock change, clear the NAE data by using the **clear nae-data** command.

Note

See the *Network Analytics Engine Guide* for more details on using and troubleshooting the NAE feature (Figure 3-26).

Basic Traffic Monitoring

You will now learn about a few more ways to monitor traffic on AOS-CX switches.

sFlow

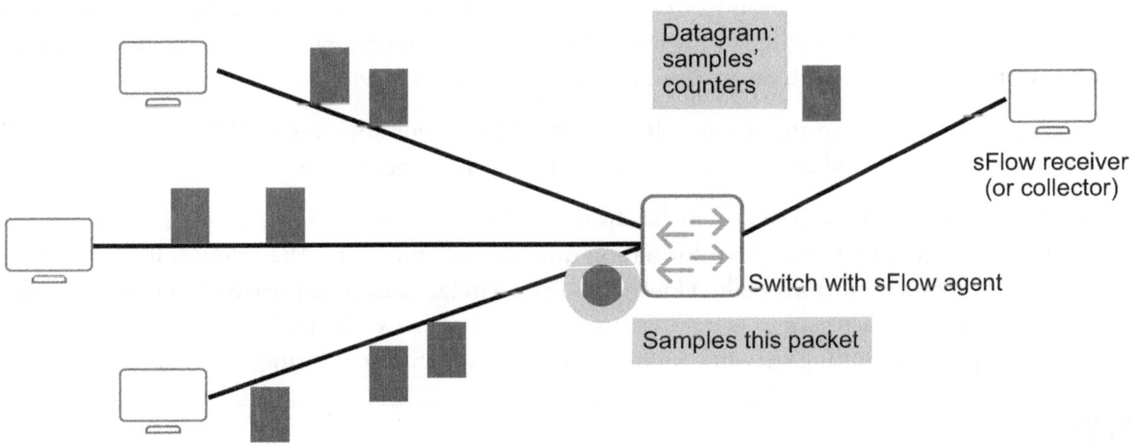

Figure 3-27 sFlow

AOS-CX switches support sFlow, an industry-standard technology that uses statistical sampling to enable network monitoring (Figure 3-27). sFlow relies on two components:

- sFlow agents
- sFlow collector (which is also sometimes called a receiver)

sFlow agents run on network devices—such as switches, routers, and access points—gathering information about the packets transmitted on these devices and sending that information to the sFlow collector for analysis. Specifically, agents can send traffic samples and polling counters.

For traffic samples, the sFlow standard defines all the packets that a network device receives on one interface and are forwarded to another interface as a "flow." Using a statistically accurate algorithm, the sFlow agent examines on average one of every *n*th packet, where *n* is the number of packets. The samples are taken "on average" because sFlow employs some randomness to avoid sampling packets at precise intervals that might coincide with certain traffic patterns.

An sFlow agent packages sampled information into small datagrams, which include Layer-2 through 7 information, such as:

- Source and destination interface
- Sampled packet header
- Length of sampled packet
- Forwarding decision that the switch made for this packet

An sFlow agent can also use counter polling to gather traffic statistics. It polls data sources at specified intervals, adds this information to the sFlow datagrams, and sends them to a specified sFlow collector. On the AOS-CX switches, the data sources are ports (Ethernet interfaces).

The agents can include information from several packets into a single datagram. Because traffic samples are compact and agents sample only a small percentage of traffic, sFlow does not require a large amount of network bandwidth or processing power on network devices.

To forward the datagram to the sFlow collector, the sFlow agent appends a UDP header and an IP header to the datagram and encapsulates the packet in an Ethernet frame.

AOS-CX switches implement sFlow in hardware—which is typically how sFlow is implemented. This allows the switch to deliver the information quickly and efficiently. The sFlow collector analyzes the packaged information from each sFlow agent on a wireless and wired network. From this information, the sFlow collector can create a statistical model of network traffic that can be used for a variety of purposes, including network traffic management, security auditing, or troubleshooting.

Note

For more information about sFlow, visit **http://sflow.org**.

Configuring sFlow on AOS-CX Switches

To configure sFlow on AOS-CX switches, first, you need to enable it globally or on an interface:

```
switch(config)# sflow
```

-or-

```
switch(config)# interface <interface-ID>
switch(config-if)# sflow
```

Optionally you can define the source address on the switch that the switch should use when sending sFlow data to a receiver/collector:

```
switch(config)# sflow <local-IP-address>
```

Next, you must configure the IP address of the sFlow receiver.

```
switch(config)# sflow collector <IP-address> [udp <port-num>] [vrf
<VRF-name>]
```

If you do not include the port in the command, the AOS-CX switch will use the default UDP destination port, 6343.

You can also specify polling and packet sampling rate with the following two commands:

```
switch(config)# sflow polling <polling-interval>
switch(config)# sflow sampling <rate>
```

The default interval is 30 seconds and can span from 10 to 3,600 seconds. The default sampling rate is 1 in every 4,096 packets for a flow. A warning message is displayed when the sampling rate is set to less than 4,096 and proceeds only after user confirmation.

To verify your configuration, use the **show sflow** command:

```
switch# show sflow
sFlow Global           Configuration
-----------------------------------------
sFlow              enabled
Collector IP/Port/Vrf  10.0.0.2/6343/default
             10.0.0.3/6400/default
Agent Address       10.0.0.1
Sampling Rate       1024
```

```
Polling Interval        30
Header Size             128
Max Datagram Size       1400

sFlow Status
-----------------------------------------
Running - Yes

sFlow Statistics
-----------------------------------------
Number of Samples       200
- Agent address is not configured.
```

Note

sFlow and NAE are two different tools that you can use on your AOS-CX switch. sFlow can be used to share information easily with third-party monitoring products, like H3C IMC's Network Traffic Analyzer (NTA) module, which supports protocols like sFlow (open standard), NetFlow (Cisco-proprietary), and NetStream (H3C-proprietary). NAE information is RESTful based and thus can be shared with a multitude of systems that support a RESTful API infrastructure. You can use either one of these, or both of these, depending on what type of external solution you need to share information with!

Local Packet Capturing

Option 1: Local mirroring to the CPU (referred to as *destination CPU*)

1. Redirect packets to the CPU with a mirror session
2. Examine the packets in the captured file
3. Optionally copy the file to a remote desktop

Option 2 : examine packets in real time with tcpdump (**diagutilities tcpdump**)

WARNING: You can overload the switch if care is not taken to limit the amount of traffic mirrored to the CPU

Figure 3-28 Local Packet Capturing

There are two options for looking at packets locally on the AOS-CX switches via the CLI, as shown in Figure 3-28:

- Local mirroring
- **tcpdump**

Option 1

```
Switch(config)# mirror session <session-ID>
Switch(config-mirror)# source interface <port-ID-or-LAG-ID>
Switch(config-mirror)# destination cpu
```

The source interface you specify can be a physical port or a LAG. You can configure one or more mirror sessions to use the CPU (the switch itself). You can create up to four mirror sessions (1-4).

Use the **show mirror** command to verify your configuration.

By default, you do not see any information, even though the traffic being captured is "seen" by the CPU. To start examining the traffic, configure the following:

```
switch# diagnostics
switch# diagnostic utilities tshark [file]
```

Inspecting traffic mirrored to the CPU until Ctrl-C is entered

```
^C Ending traffic inspection.
```

If you specify the **file** parameter, the switch captures packets from a mirror-to-CPU session, and saves the most recent 32MB to PCAP file which can then be copied and analyzed. When capturing a mirror-to-CPU session to a file, packets will not be dumped to the console. Otherwise you are looking at a summary of the captured packets.

If you chose the file option, the file is stored in flash. To delete it, execute this:

```
switch# diagnostics
switch# diagnostic utilities tshark delete
```

To copy the file from the switch to a remote computer, use this command:

```
switch# copy tshark-pcap <remote-URL> [vrf <VRF-name>]
```

You can use TFTP or SFTP for the copy.

Note

AOS-CX only supports one packet capture file. If you start a new diagnostic session, the old file is overwritten by a new one.

Also, you must enter **diagnostics** mode with the **diagnostics** command before using the **diag** command.

Option 2

Your section option is to look at a summary of the packets, in real-time, using Linux's tcpdump utility. Note that you do not have access to the Linux CLI, but the AOS-CX switch utilizes this utility from the AOS-CX CLI. This is accomplished using the **diag utilities tcpdump** command. Here's an example:

```
switch# diagnostics
switch# diag utilities tcpdump ethernet-type 35020 count 1 verbosity
level4 vrf default
1  10:50:07.281354 LLDP, length 109
        Chassis ID TLV (1), length 7
          Subtype MAC address (4): 90:20:c2:bc:97:00 (oui Unknown)
          0x0000:  0490 20c2 bc97 00
        Port ID TLV (2), length 7
          Subtype Interface Name (5): 1/1/46
          0x0000:  0531 2f31 2f34 36
        Time to Live TLV (3), length 2: TTL 120s
          0x0000:  0078
        System Name TLV (5), length 18: ACSP-P52-T12-Core2
          0x0000:  4143 5350 2d50 3532 2d54 3132 2d43 6f72
          0x0010:  6532
        System Description TLV (6), length 27
          Aruba JL635A  GL.10.04.0010
          0x0000:  4172 7562 6120 4a4c 3633 3541 2020 474c
          0x0010:  2e31 302e 3034 2e30 3031 30
        System Capabilities TLV (7), length 4
          System  Capabilities [Bridge, Router] (0x0014)
          Enabled Capabilities [Bridge, Router] (0x0014)
          0x0000:  0014 0014
        Management Address TLV (8), length 12
          Management Address length 5, AFI IPv4 (1): 10.251.12.3
          Unknown Interface Numbering (1): 0
          0x0000:  0501 0afb 0c03 0100 0000 0000
        Port Description TLV (4), length 6: 1/1/46
          0x0000:  312f 312f 3436
        Organization specific TLV (127), length 6: OUI Ethernet bridged
(0x0080c2)
          Port VLAN Id Subtype (1)
            port vlan id (PVID): 1
          0x0000:  0080 c201 0001
        End TLV (0), length 0
1 packet captured
4 packets received by filter
0 packets dropped by kernel
```

> ⚠ **Warning**
>
> Any packet capturing, without the proper filtering, and displaying it to the CLI of the switch can be very CPU-intensive and affect the operation of the switch. Care should be taken when using the **diag utilities tcpdump** command.

Local Traffic Mirroring

Traffic mirroring allows a switch to copy frames that arrive or are sent from a particular port or VLAN and forward them to another port. You can use port mirroring to monitor network traffic to detect threats, troubleshoot problems, or manage the network. For example, you might want to send certain traffic to a security appliance such as an Intrusion Detection System (IDS) device, which can examine the traffic and detect possible threats. Or, you may want to send traffic to a network protocol analyzer, which you can use to examine the traffic and troubleshoot a network problem.

The simplest form of traffic mirroring is local mirroring, in which the switch mirroring the packets sends the copies out a local port.

The mirroring feature (when mirroring received traffic) and the sFlow sampling feature both require the receive (rx) capability of a given port. If both features are configured and enabled to use the receive capability on the same port, only one of the features can perform its task. This interaction does not affect transmit (tx) mirroring because sFlow does not use the transmit (tx) capability of a port.

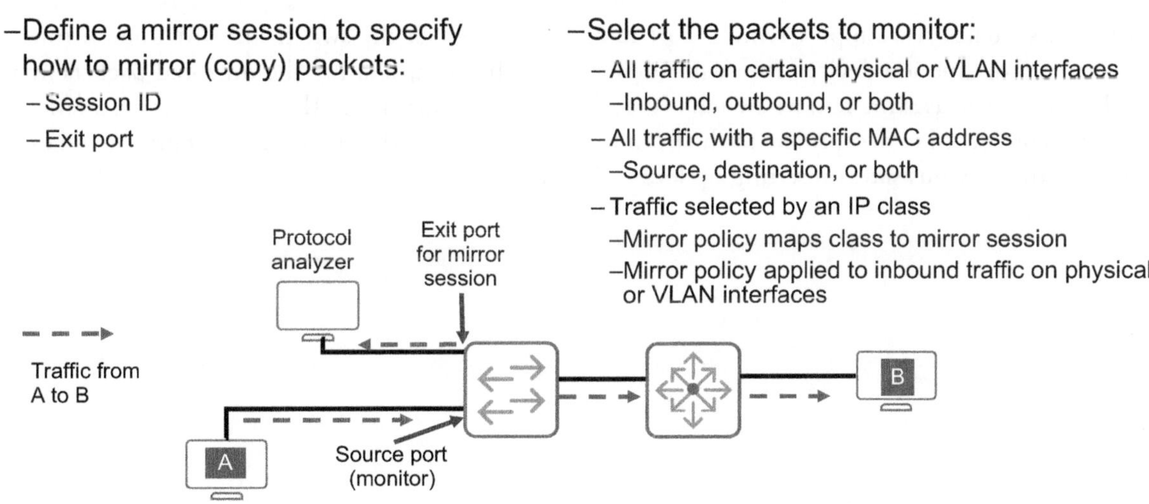

Figure 3-29 Local Traffic Mirroring

To configure local traffic mirroring on AOS-CX switches, you first enter the mirror command, followed by the session number, and then specify the exit port in the interface context (Figure 3-29). The source and exit port can be a single physical interface or a link aggregation for local mirroring:

```
switch(config)# mirror session <session-ID>
switch(config-mirror)# source interface <port-ID-or-LAG-ID> {rx | tx |
both}
switch(config-mirror)# destination interface <port-ID-or-LAG-ID>
```

You can configure one or more mirror sessions to use the same exit port. Or you can specify different exit ports in different sessions to send mirrored traffic to different destination device or on different links to the same destination device. In the latter case, you would want to make sure to set up different sources for each mirroring session. You can create up to four mirror sessions (1-4). Use the **show mirror** command to verify your configuration.

Remote Traffic Mirroring: ERSPAN

ERSPAN is an acronym that stands for *encapsulated remote switched port analyzer*. ERSPAN mirrors traffic on one or more source ports and forwards the mirrored traffic to a destination on a remote device. The traffic is encapsulated in generic routing encapsulation (GRE) and is, therefore, routable across a layer-3 network between the source switch and the destination device, like a packet sniffer, for example Wireshark.

AOS-CX switches also support remote port mirroring, in which the switch forwards the mirrored packets to a destination device. The switch achieves this by encapsulating the mirrored packets in a GRE header that uses the remote switch's IP address as the destination. The remote, or destination, switch is configured to decapsulate traffic from this GRE tunnel and to forward the traffic out an exit port (see the previous slide on setting up local mirroring).

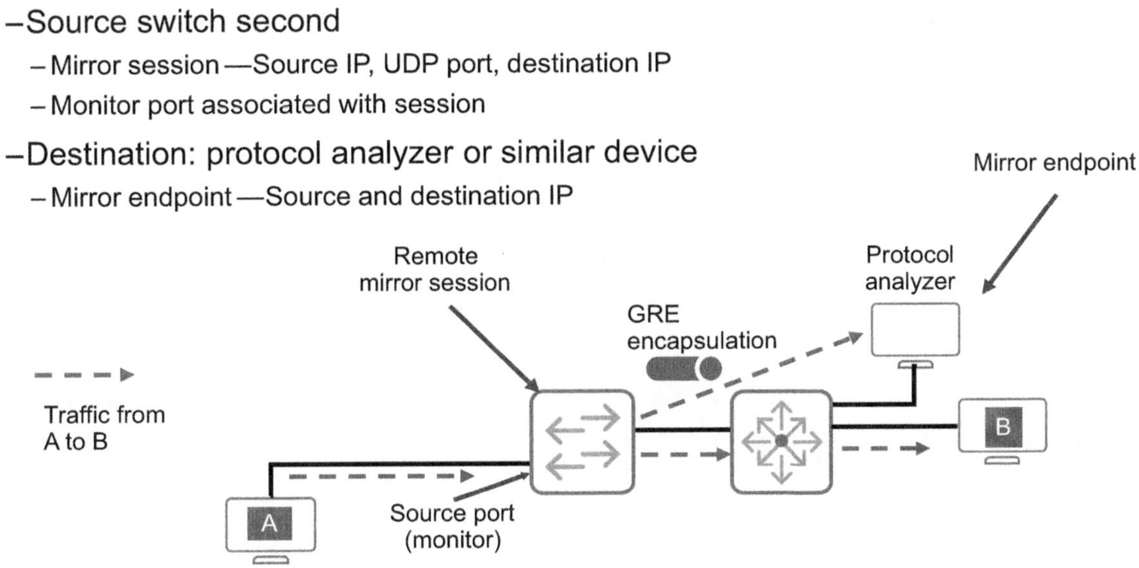

Figure 3-30 Remote Traffic Mirroring: ERSPAN

This command specifies the tunnel to where all mirrored traffic for the session will be transmitted. Only one tunnel destination is allowed per session (Figure 3-30).

```
Switch(config)# mirror session <session-ID> {rx | tx | both}
Switch(config-mirror)# source interface <port-ID-or-LAG-ID>
Switch(config-mirror)# destination tunnel <destination-IP-address>
source <source-IP-address> [dscp <dscp-code>] [vrf <VRF-name>]
```

You may configure multiple mirror sessions with the same source/destination IP address pair; however, only one of those sessions sharing the same source/destination IP address pair can be enabled at a given time.

ERSPAN is not supported leaving the switch by the OOB port. If VRF management is configured for an ERSPAN session, the session will be in "mirror_err_tunnel_oob_port_not_supported" operation status.

ERSPAN is not supported leaving the switch encapsulated within another tunnel (for example, GRE IPv4). When the path to the destination IP address will leave via a tunnel, the session will be in "tunnel_route_resolution_not_populated" operation status.

Note

AOS switches support mirroring to other AOS switches. AOS-CX switches, however, do not support this feature. Instead, the remote mirroring must be to a device that supports it, like Wireshark.

ERSPAN Output

Wireshark example

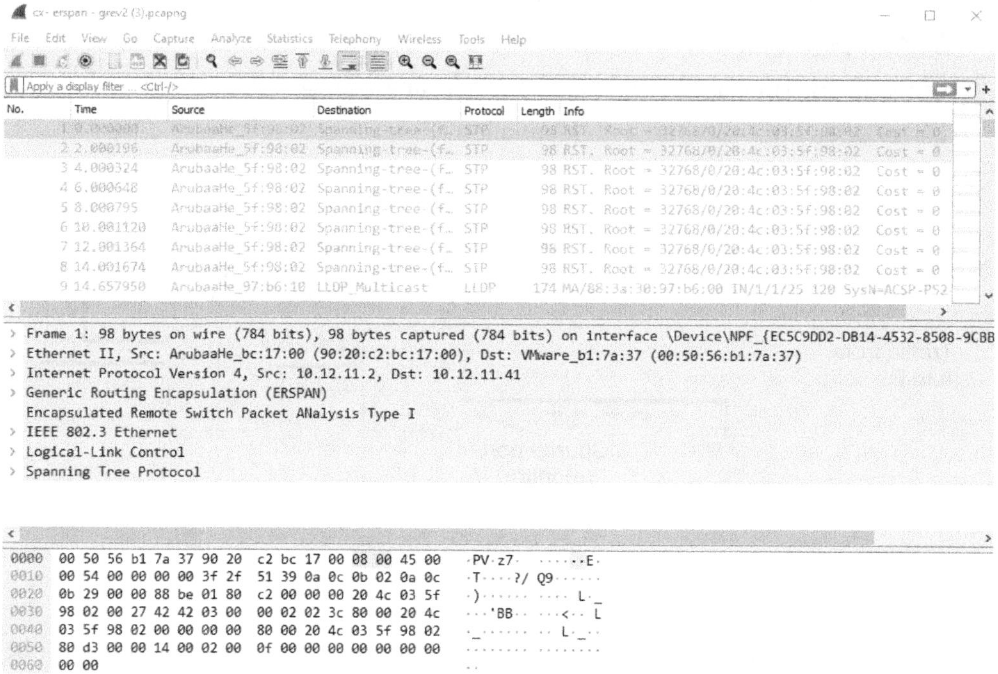

Figure 3-31 ERSPAN Output

Here's an example where a remote mirroring session was set up on an AOS-CX switch to forward packets to Wireshark on a remote desktop. As you can see from the highlighted part of the graphic, the remote desktop is receiving the encapsulated (tunneled traffic) denoted by the ERSPAN packets (Figure 3-31).

Lab 3: Network Analytics Engine

In this lab you will learn how to install a script and set up and run an agent (Figure 3-32).

Lab Diagram

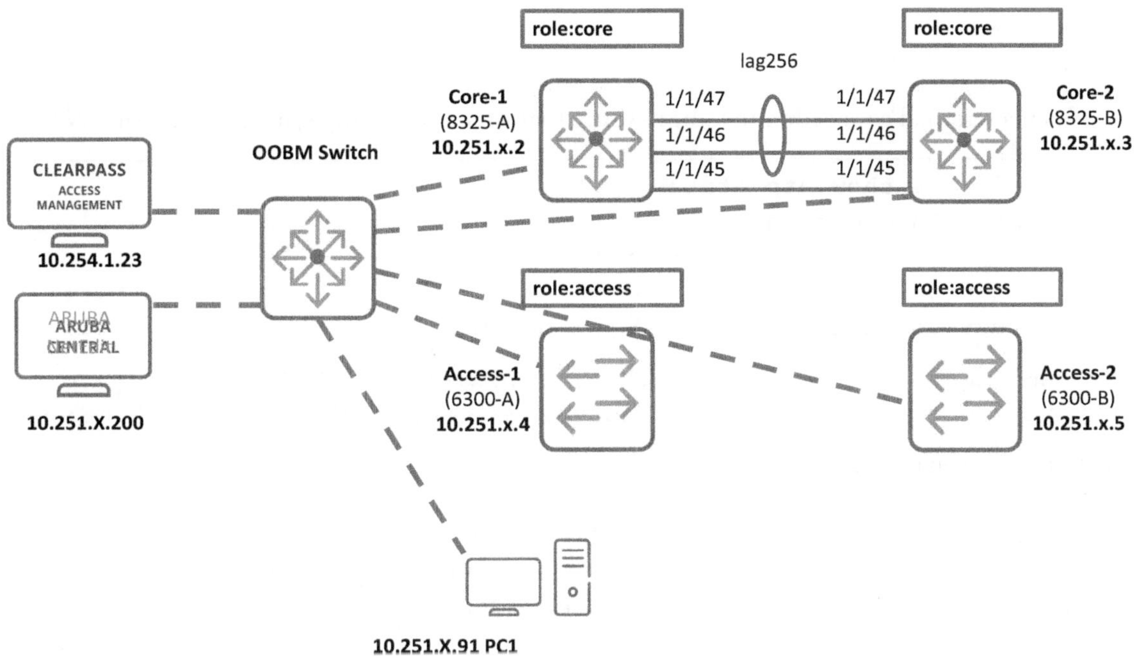

Figure 3-32 Lab Diagram

Overview

In this lab activity, the AOS-CX Network Analytics Engine feature will be explored. First there is a review of the built-in NAE agent. Next a new script will be added and an agent will be configured (Figure 3-32). There is also a task to add another NAE script that integrates with a ping monitor module of the switch. The last task is to review how the NAE script and agent settings are stored in the switch's configuration.

Objectives

- Understand the difference between NAE scripts and agents
- Learn how to configure NAE agent parameters
- Understand NAE agent alerts and graphs
- Understand how NAE scripts and agents are stored in the switch configuration

Task 1: Prepare the Setup

Objectives

- Verify devices are ready for the NAE lab activity
- Must have completed lab 02—NetEdit configuration

Steps

1. Open a terminal connection to Core1. Verify that time is currently synchronized using NTP.

```
ICX-Tx-Core1# show ntp status
NTP Status Information
NTP                           : Enabled
NTP Authentication            : Disabled
NTP Server Connections        : Using the mgmt VRF

System time                   : Thu Feb 13 09:18:46 EST 2020
NTP uptime                    : 2 days, 23 hours, 28 minutes, 30 seconds

NTP Synchronization Information
NTP Server                    : 10.253.1.15 at stratum 2
Poll interval                 : 1024 seconds
Time accuracy                 : Within -0.000247 seconds
Reference time                : Thu Feb 13 2020 8:59:02.459 as per US/
Eastern
```

2. Examine the actual time.

```
ICX-Tx-Core1# show clock
Thu Feb 13 09:16:08 EST 2020
System is configured for timezone : US/Eastern
```

3. On PC1 (Management PC - OOBM), verify the time in a command prompt (cmd.exe). Enter the command **time** and just press <ENTER> when prompted to enter a new time. The time difference should be within seconds. The NAE web UI is using the client browser time to get the time for thelive' graphs, so therefore it is important to have correct time on the PC client and the switch.

```
C:\Users\student> time
The current time is:  9:16:13.51
Enter the new time:
```

Task 2: Review the Built-in NAE Script and Agent

Objectives

- Get experience implementing an NAE script and agent
- Review the built-in System Monitor NAE agent
- Understand the meaning of parameters for an agent
- Review the alerts and alert actions generated by an agent

Steps

1. Open a session to PC1 (Management PC—OOBM). On PC1, open a web browser to the Core1 OOBM IP: **https://10.251.x.2**, where x is your table number. Log into the web interface with **admin/aruba123** credentials. The Overview page will be displayed.

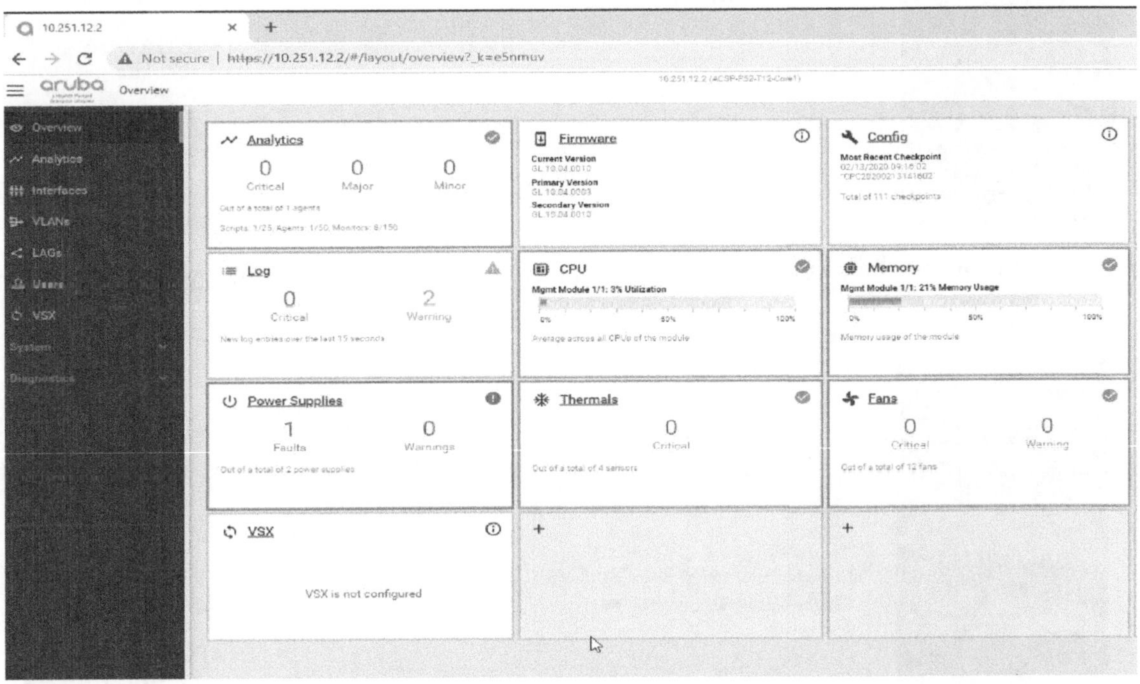

2. Navigate to the Analytics page by selecting **Analytics** in the left navigation pane. This will display the 'Agents' and the 'Scripts'. Scripts are the actual code that can be executed by NAE, while an Agent is an instance of the script. A script that is installed on the switch does not do anything by itself. An agent must be created based on the script to start the actual monitoring. One script may be instantiated multiple times, that would depend on the script:

- Some scripts may monitor all interfaces of the switch, so only 1 instance (agent) would make sense.
- Another script may only monitor 1 interface, where the interface that needs to be monitored would need to be entered by the administrator. This interface name would be a parameter on an agent. When the administrator would want to monitor 2 interfaces, 2 agents would be created based on this script. 1 agent with interface 1, the other agent with interface 2.

3. Click the **Scripts** link.

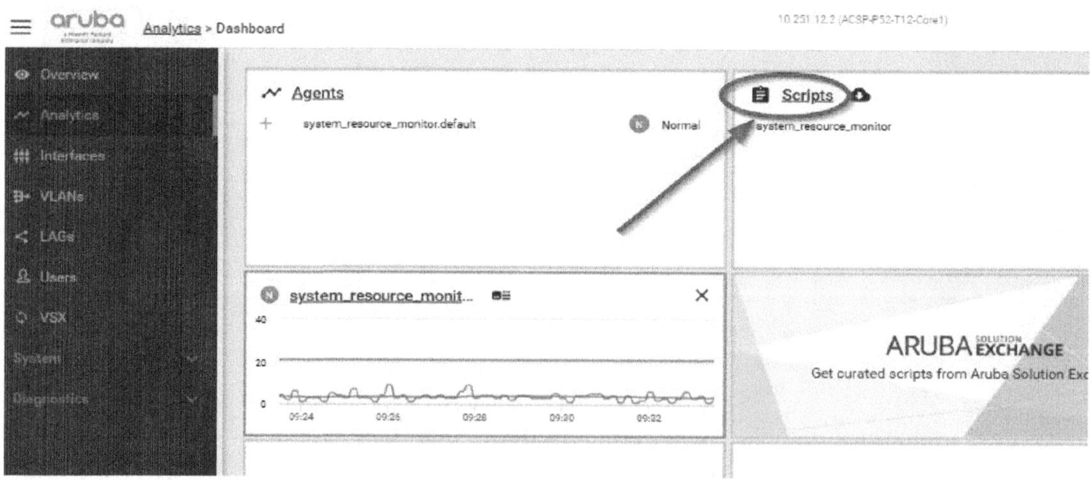

4. There is one built-in script, that is called the 'system_resource_monitor'. This is system-created and therefore cannot be deleted.

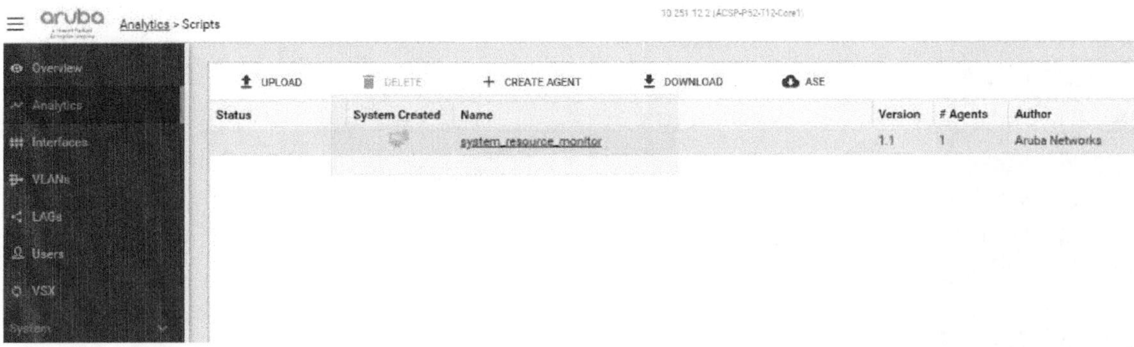

Example Script Details

1. Click the name of the script (**system_resource_monitor**) to see the details of the script. A script on the switch can also be downloaded to an administrator PC from this screen. The download is optional; it is not required in this lab activity.

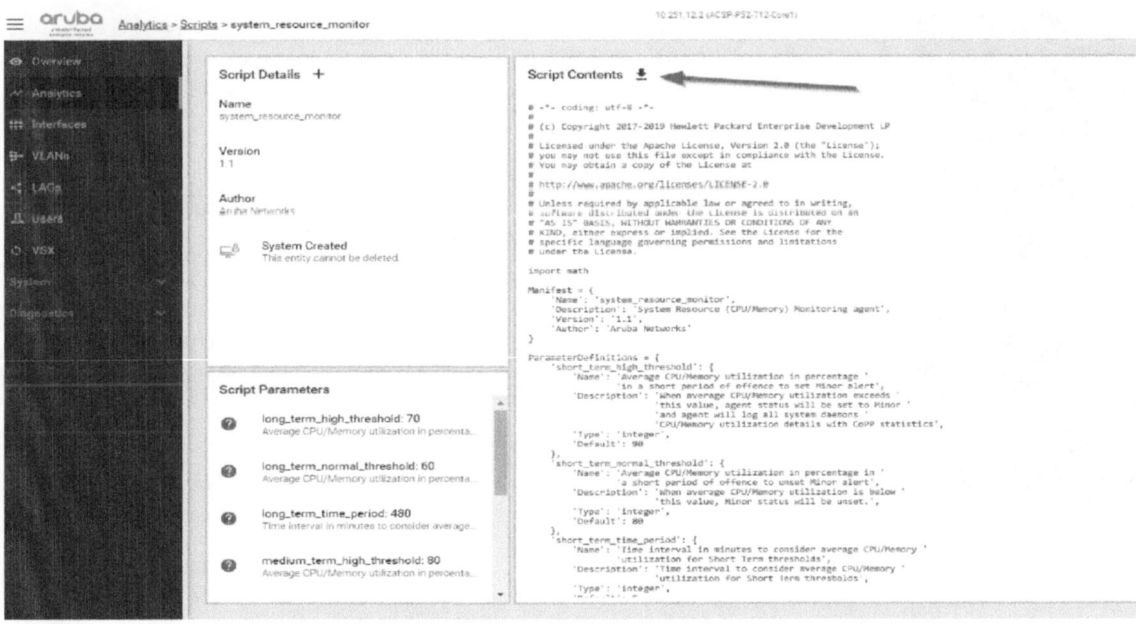

Note

The development of the scripts themselves is beyond the scope of this training. Please consult the product documentation if you want to learn more about the scripts and the syntax.

---

2. Navigate back to **Analytics** to see the Dashboard screen.

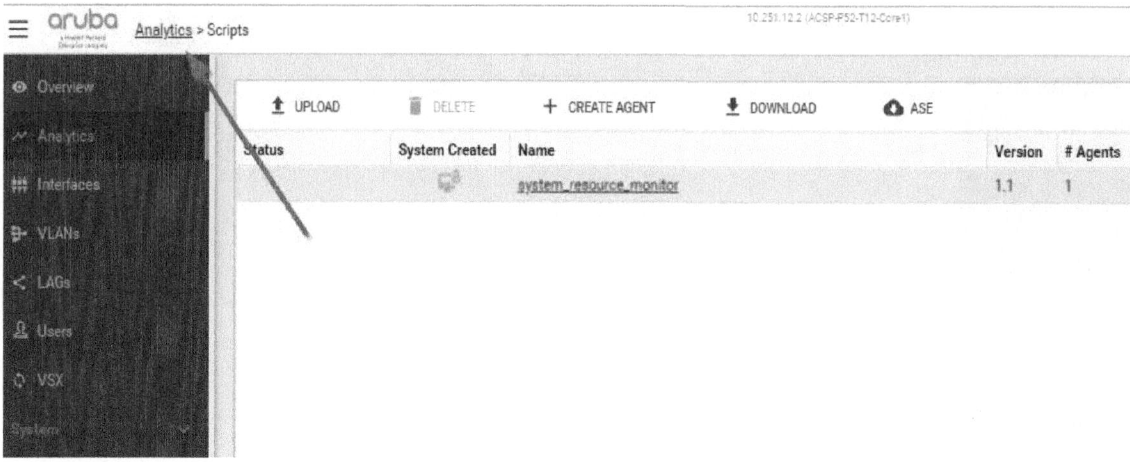

3. Click the **Agents** link to open the Agents window.

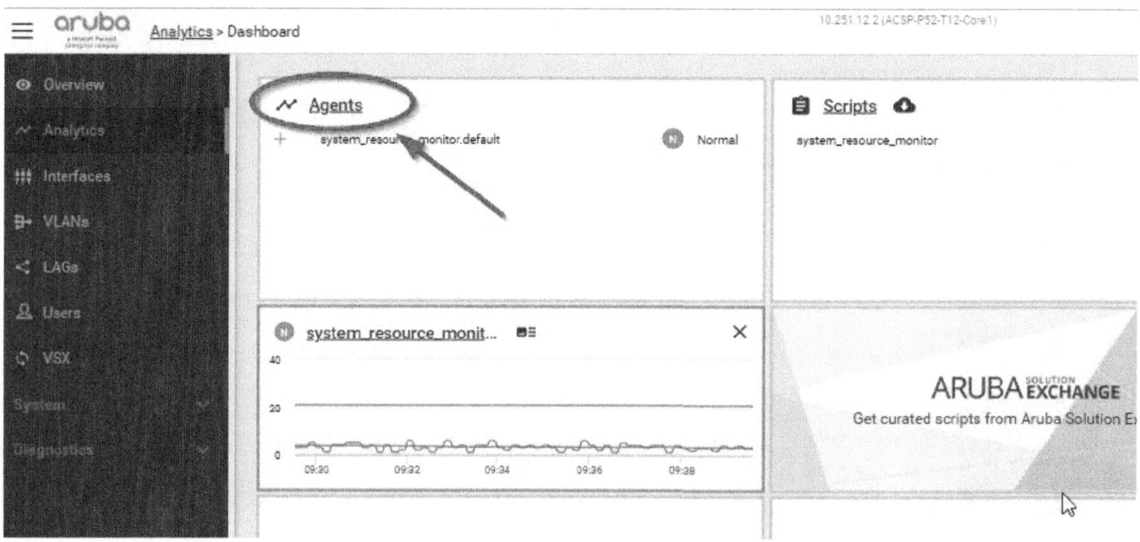

4. This will list the default agent that is running on the switch. The agents are the actual running instances of a script. In this case, there is a default agent that will be monitoring the system resources. This happens out of the box.

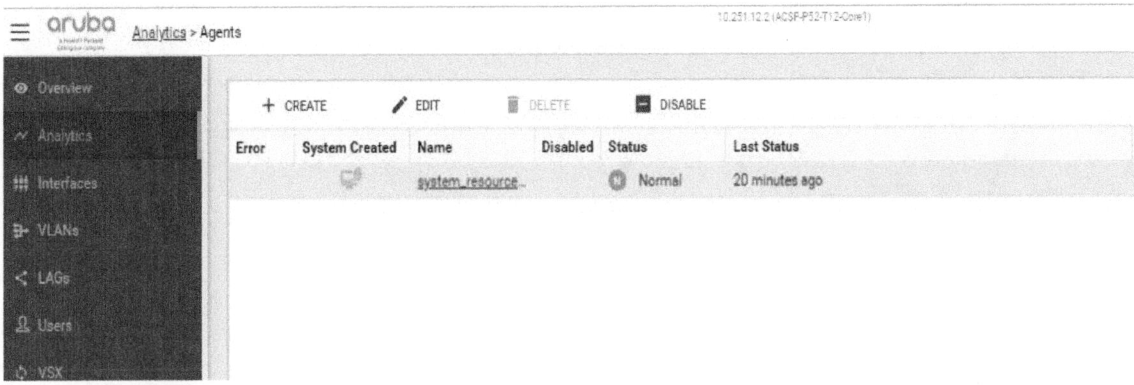

5. Click on the name of the Agent (**system_resource_monitor**) to see its details. The default screen will show:

- the agent details (script that is used for this agent)
- the status
- the parameters that have been set for this agent
- the graph, if applicable
- the alerts, if applicable

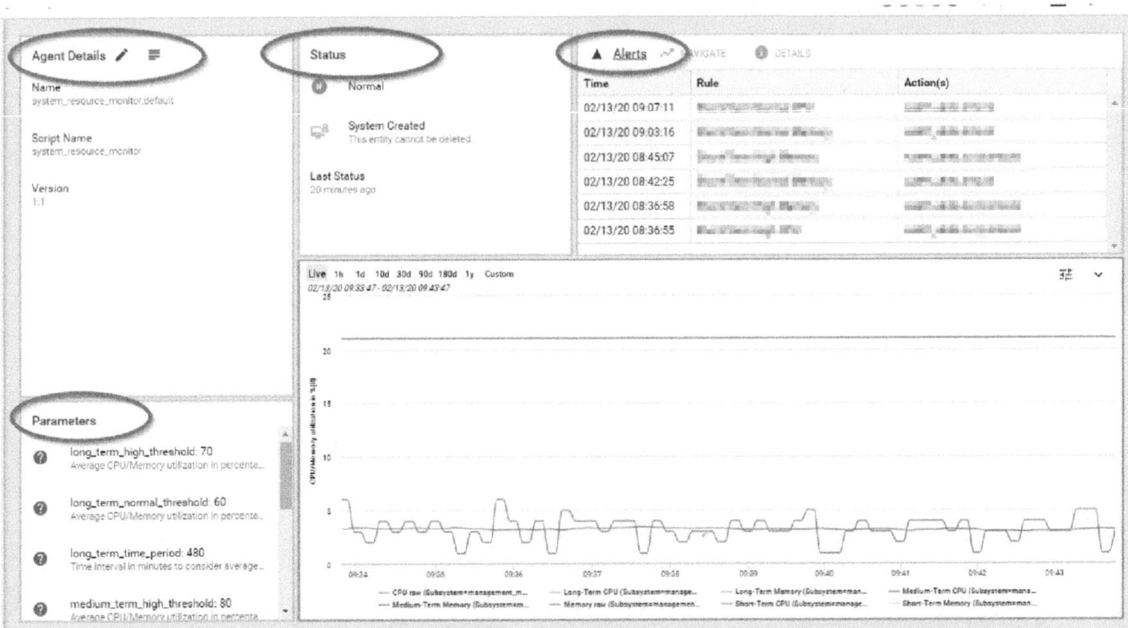

Graph Management

1. The switch has a local database that can store historical data for the agent. In the graph, the administrator can check the history of the agent. Click the '1h', '1d', and 'live' links to explore the differences.

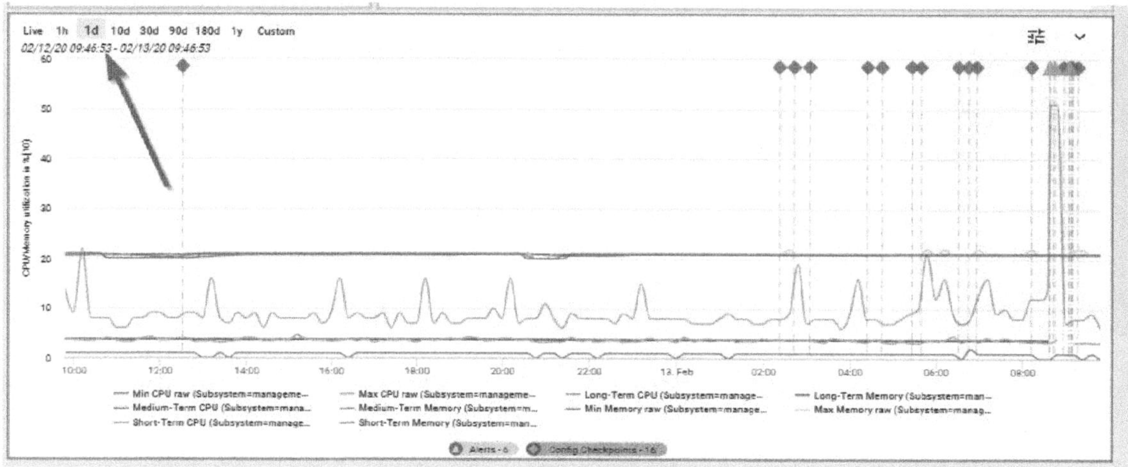

2. The admin can also apply a custom zoom by selecting a time range with the mouse (click and drag).

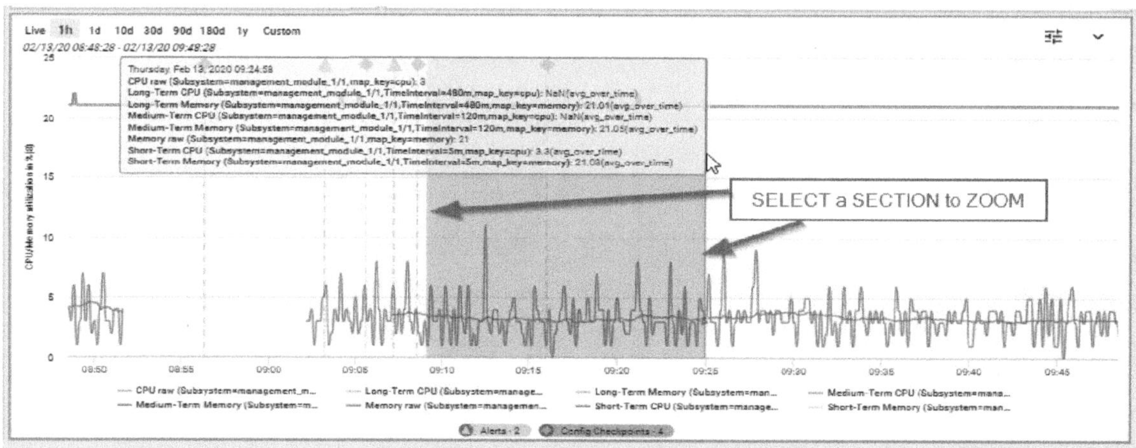

3. The administrator can choose to disable certain lines on the graph by clicking them at the bottom.

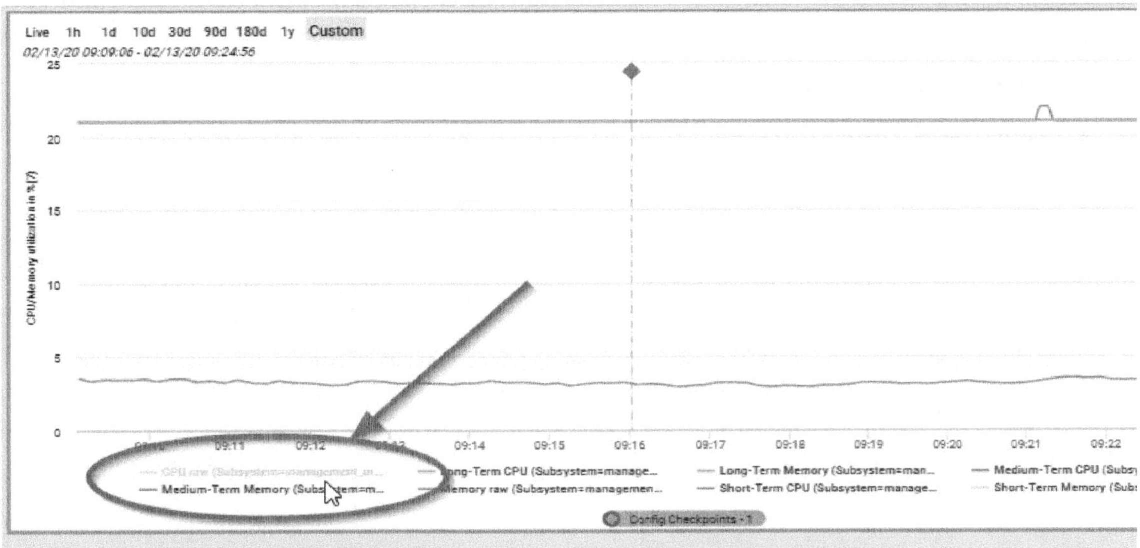

Alerts

Agents can monitor various options in the system. When the agent is configured to compare a value with some threshold, the agent can generate an alert when the threshold is exceeded. The moment an alert is generated, the agent can simply display the alert, but it can also send out a syslog message, or it can run some CLI commands and capture the output. These actions are defined in the script.

To see an example alert, the default parameters that control the threshold of the built-in system monitor will be changed to extreme low values, so that will trigger an alert.

1. In the **Agent Details** pane, click the **pen** icon to edit the Agent settings.

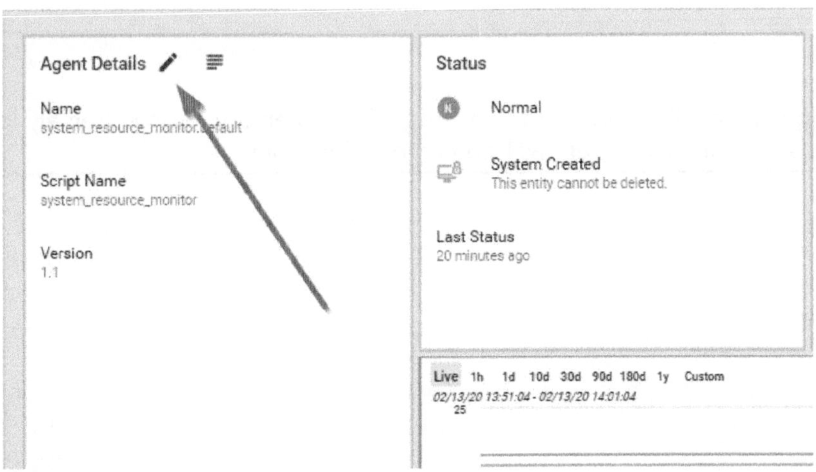

2. It is possible to enable or disable the agent. It is also possible to review or update the agent parameters. Update these parameters for the Average CPU/Memory Utilization, expressed as a percentage:

    - short_term_high_threshold: **2**
    - short_term_normal_threshold: **1**

Note

By setting the high_threshold for the average CPU/Memory to an extremely low number, the NAE system monitor agent will go into an Alert state.

3. Click **Save** to save the settings. Next click **Close** to close the pop-up window.

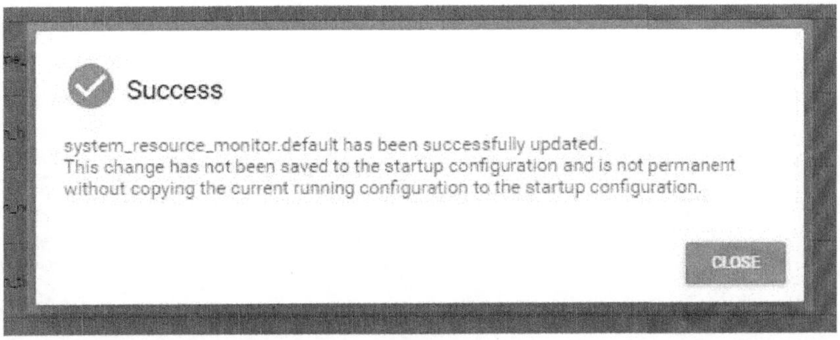

4. In about 10 seconds, a minor alert should be generated. The alert will be displayed at the top of the screen in the top right corner, in the agent details' Status pane to the right of the Agent Details pane, and in the graph bar (make sure **Live** is selected in the graph), displayed as an orange line with an orange triangle. (Note that the color of the alert in the graph corresponds to the alert level; in this example, since the alert categorized as *minor*, the color is orange).

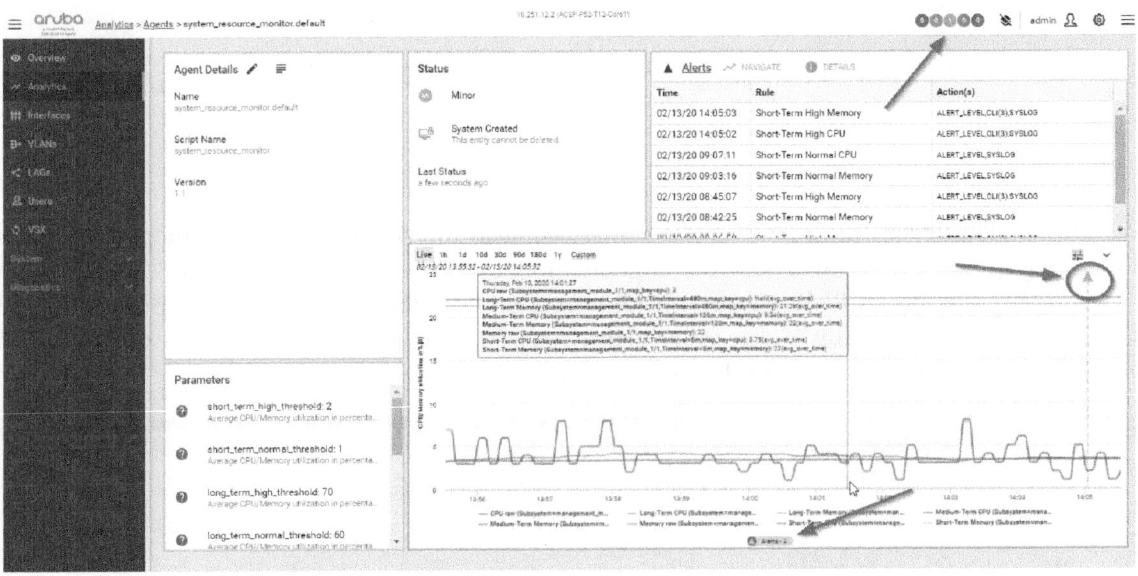

5. Open the details of the alert. This can be done either by clicking on the 'triangle' in the graph or by clicking on the alert in the alert list, and then clicking **DETAILS**.

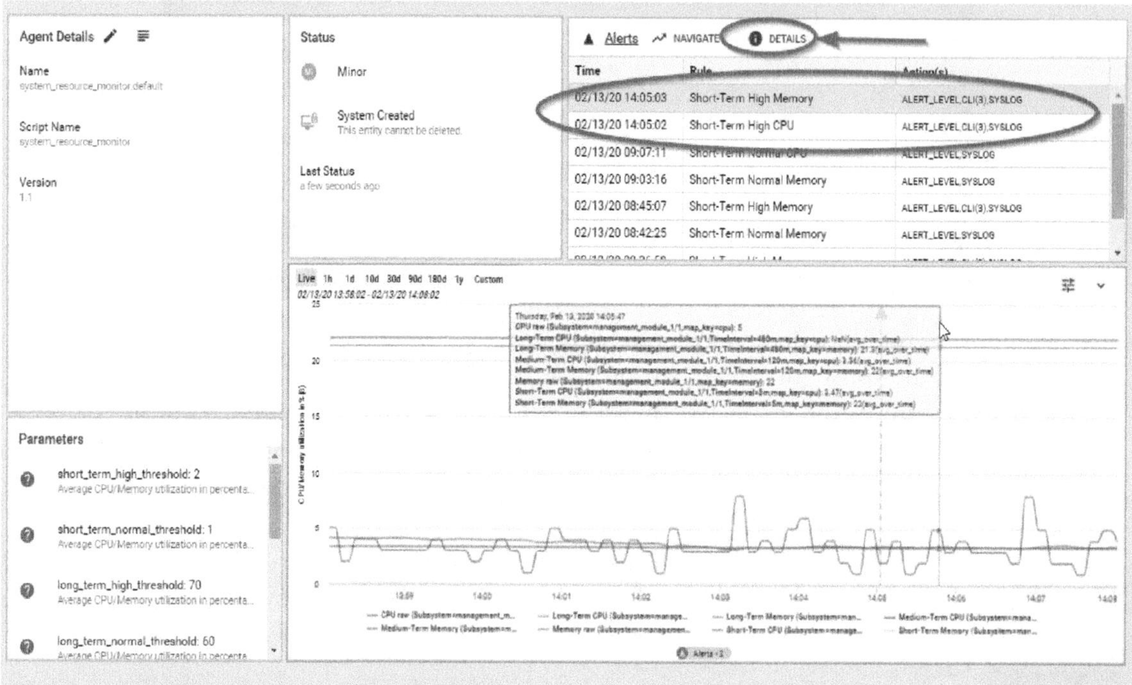

6. In the alert details, the administrator can see detailed information about the monitor that has triggered the alert: in this case, either high memory or high CPU utilization will be indicated. In this script, an alert will also capture CLI information from the switch, where this output is saved as part of the alert. This is very convenient, since it allows the administrator to see additional information about the state of the switch at that point in time.

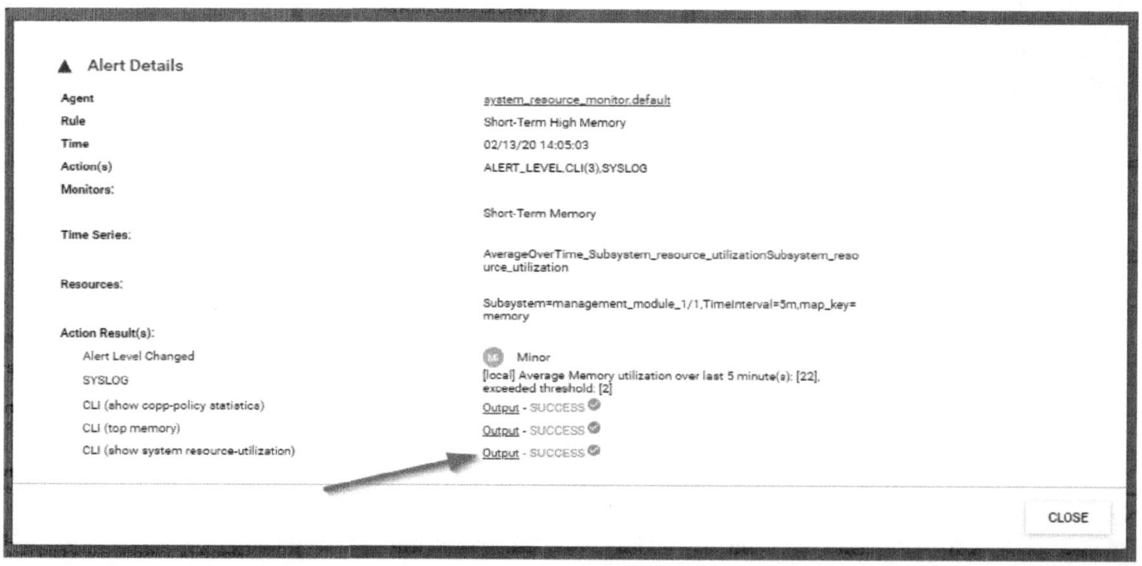

7. Click on the various 'output' links to see the details; this example shows the 'show system resource-utilization' output (click **Back** to return to the Alert Details window). Close the CLI details and the alert.

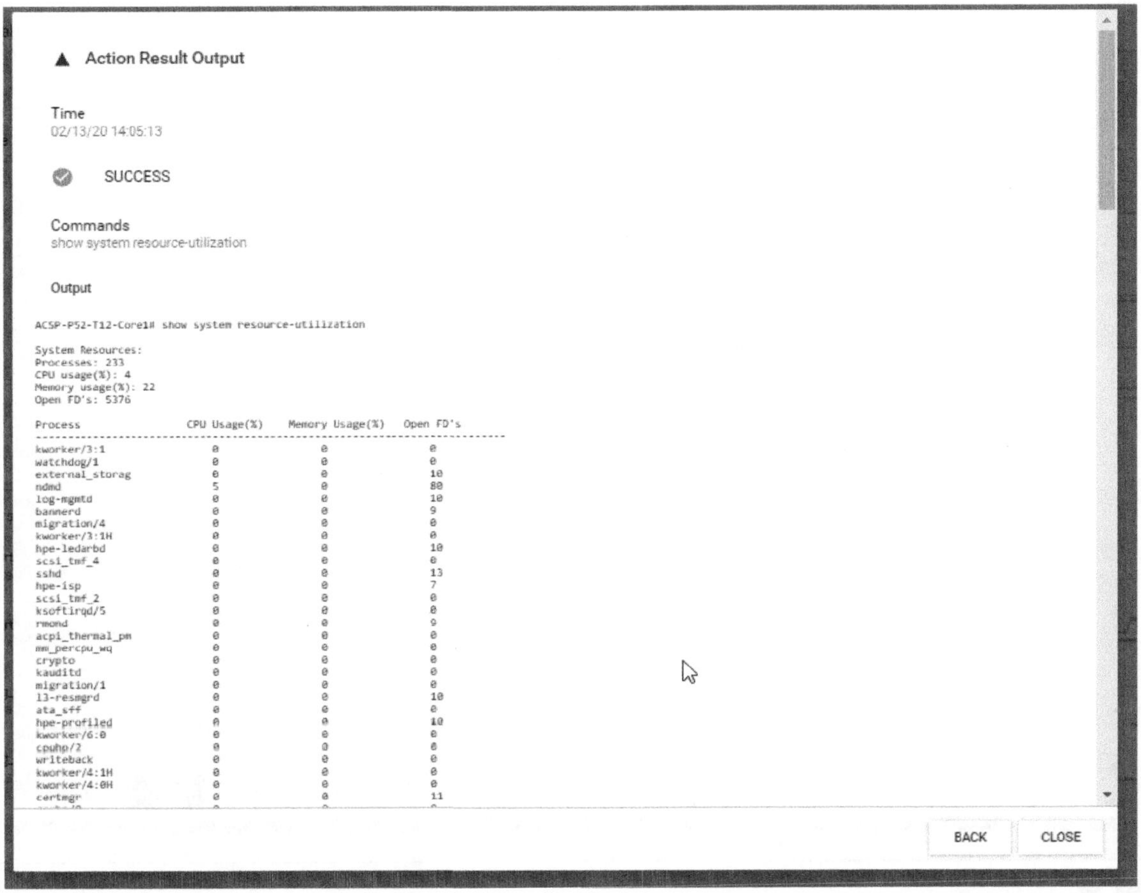

8. Edit the **pen** icon for Agent Details again, and assign high custom values, so the alert can be cleared again. Then click **Save** and **Close** to confirm.

- short_term_high_threshold: **91**
- short_term_normal_threshold: **81**

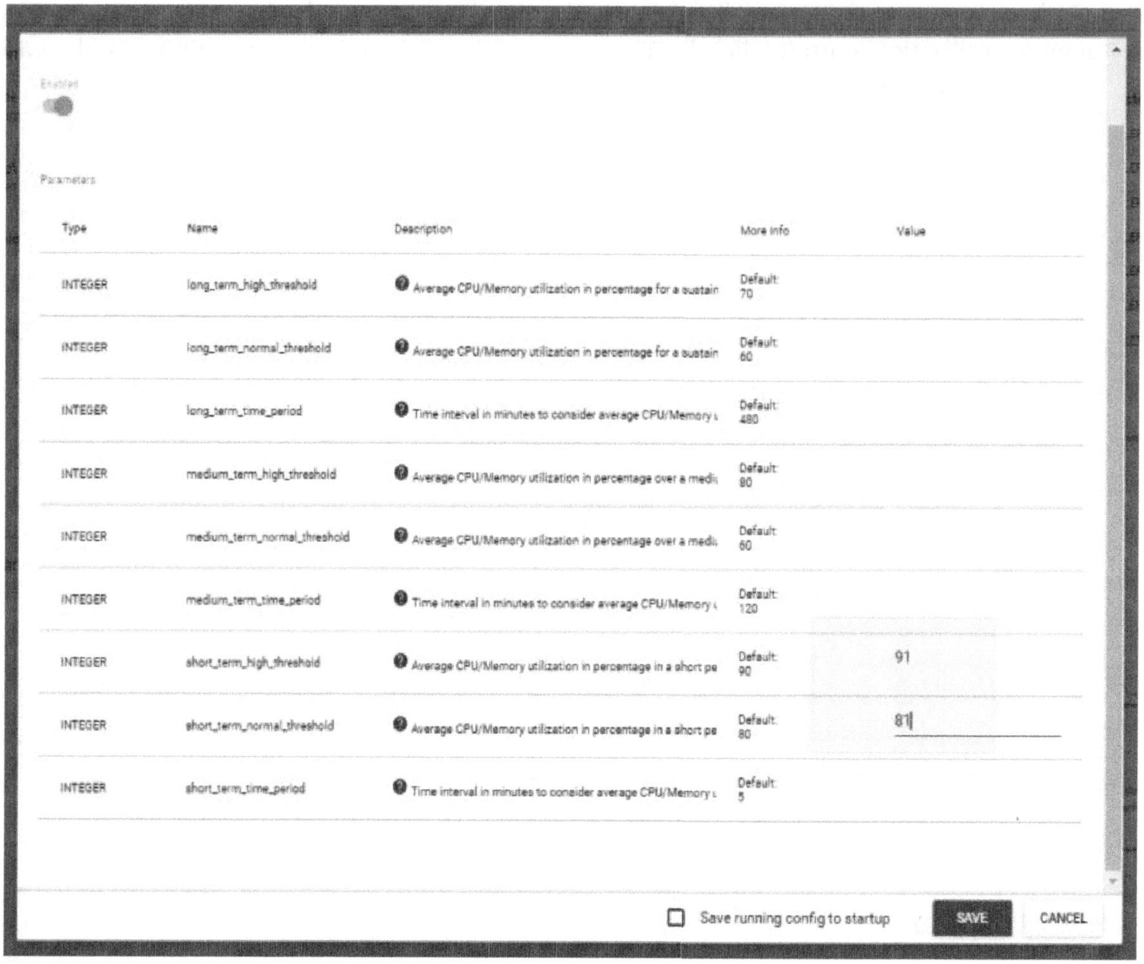

Note

It may take a few minutes for the alert to clear again (where the Status returns to a *normal* state). There is no need to wait for this.

Task 3: Add a New NAE Script and Agent

In this task, a new script and agent will be added to Core1 to monitor link state changes on the switch.

Steps

In the NetEdit lab activity, a keep-alive IP link was previously defined between the Core1 and the Core2 switches using port 1/1/45. This link will be monitored using NAE.First review or adjust this configuration between the Core1 and the Core2 switches.

Core1

1. Open a terminal on Core1 and enter Configuration mode. Review the configuration of port 1/1/45.

```
ICX-Tx-Core1(config)# show run int 1/1/45
interface 1/1/45
    no shutdown
    vrf attach KA
    ip address 192.168.0.0/31
    exit
```

2. Verify reachability to Core2 using the KA VRF.

```
ICX-Tx-Core1(config)# do ping 192.168.0.1 vrf KA
PING 192.168.0.1 (192.168.0.1) 100(128) bytes of data.
108 bytes from 192.168.0.1: icmp_seq=1 ttl=64 time=0.133 ms
108 bytes from 192.168.0.1: icmp_seq=2 ttl=64 time=0.150 ms
108 bytes from 192.168.0.1: icmp_seq=3 ttl=64 time=0.184 ms
108 bytes from 192.168.0.1: icmp_seq=4 ttl=64 time=0.227 ms
108 bytes from 192.168.0.1: icmp_seq=5 ttl=64 time=0.242 ms

--- 192.168.0.1 ping statistics ---
5 packets transmitted, 5 received, 0% packet loss, time 4117ms
rtt min/avg/max/mdev = 0.133/0.187/0.242/0.043 ms
```

Core2

3. **Optional step**: In case the ping did not work, review/update the Core2 configuration.

```
vrf KA
interface 1/1/45
    no shutdown
    vrf attach KA
    ip address 192.168.0.1/31
```

Install the New Script

1. Using PC1, in the switch web UI, navigate to **Analytics > Scripts**.
    1. Click the **Upload** link to install a new script.

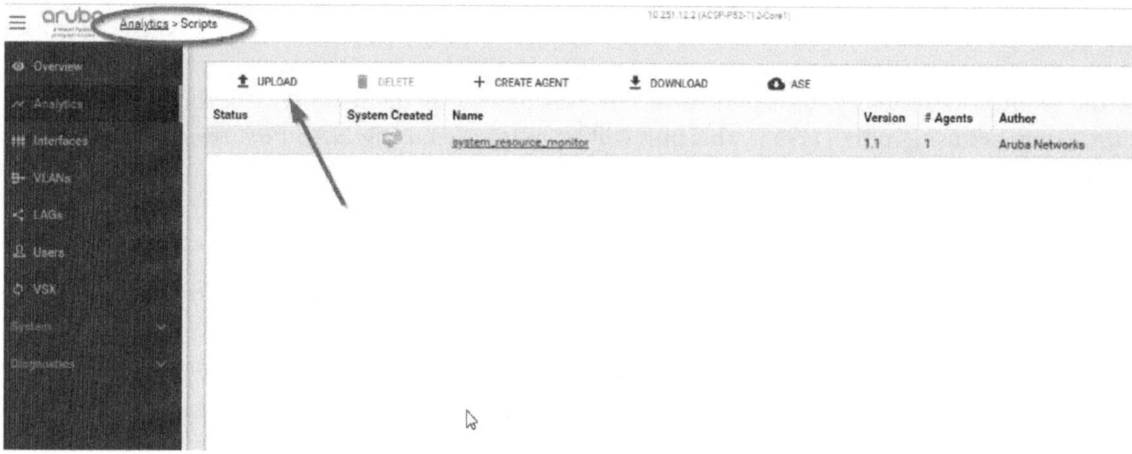

2. Open the **ICX-Files** folder on the desktop, open the **nae** sub-folder and select the '**interface_link_state_monitor.1.0.py**' script, then click **Next**.

3. Review the script manifest data and click **Upload**.

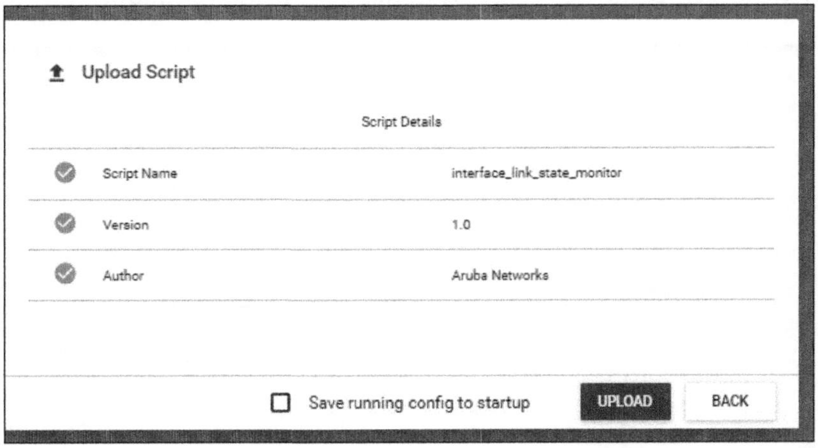

4. Click **Close** for the confirmation; the script will be shown in the list.

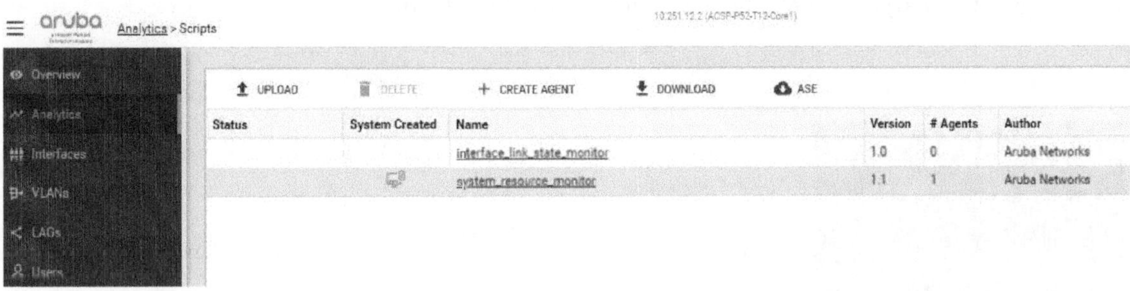

Create an Agent Based on the New Script

5. Navigate to **Analytics > Agents** and define a new agent by clicking **Create**.

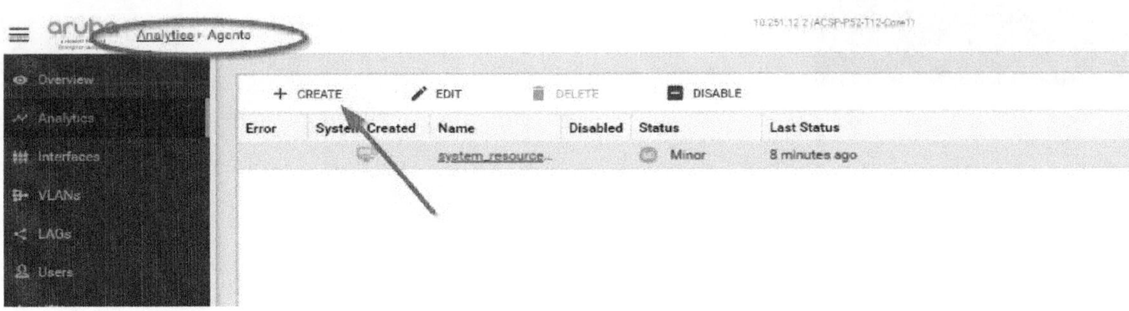

6. Select the '**interface_link_state_monitor**' from the list, and enter an agent name **iface-link-state-mon.** Then click **Create**. Click **Close** in the confirmation window.

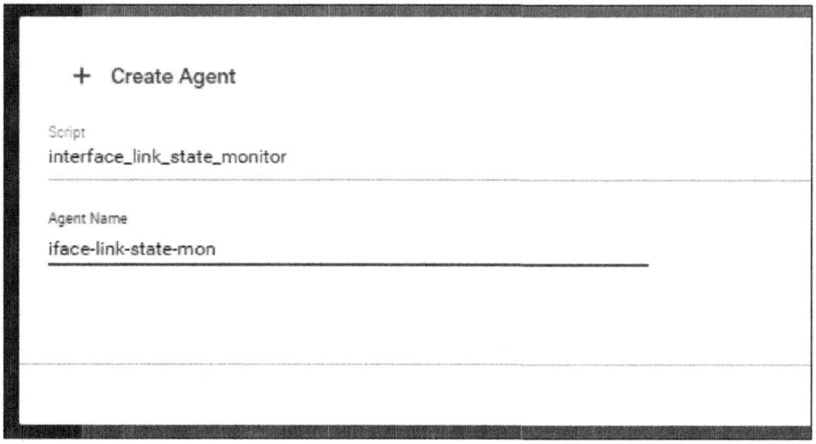

7. Navigate to **Analytics** to see the new Agent in the Dashboard.

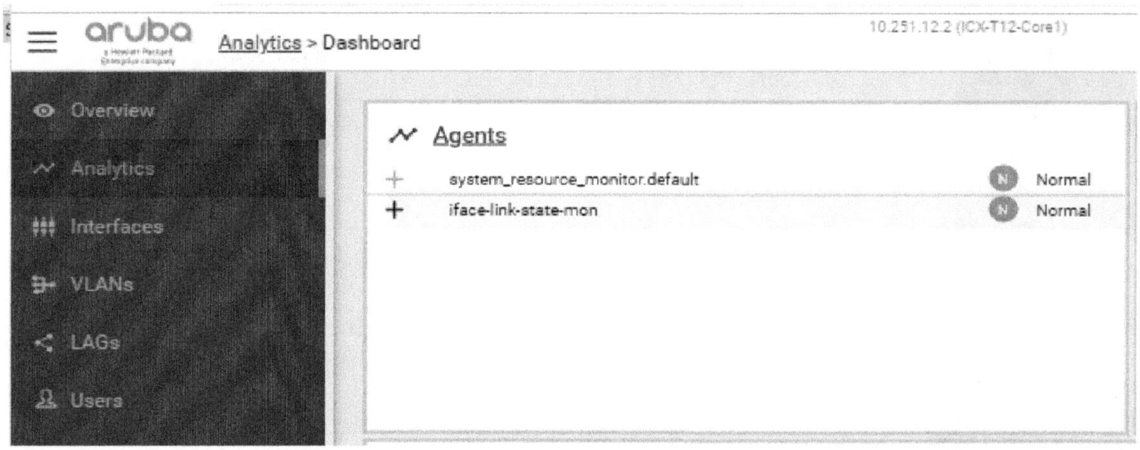

8. Select the name of the agent to see the details.

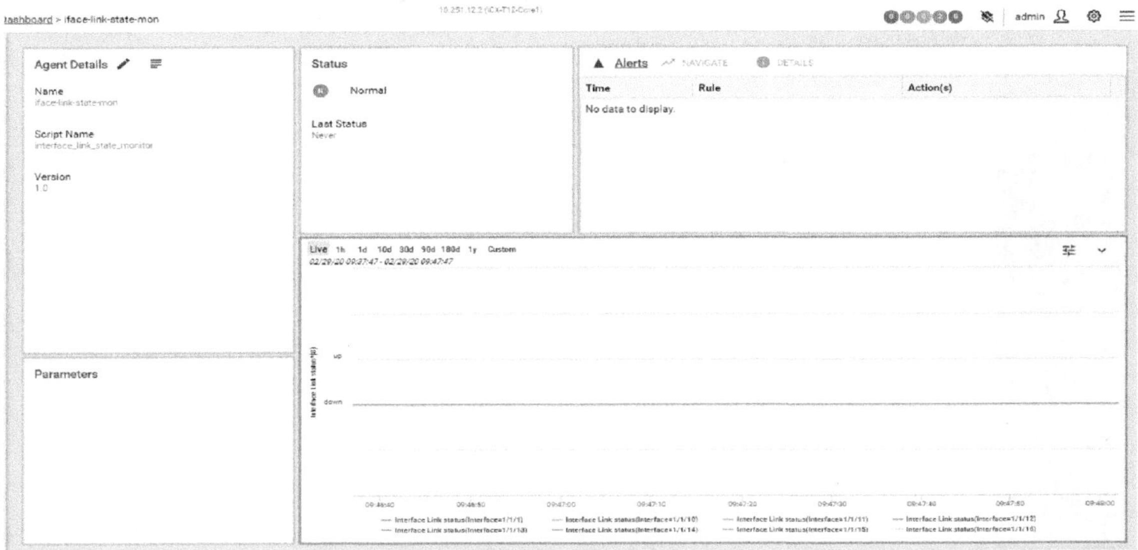

> **Note**
> This script does not have any parameters; it simply monitors all the interface transition from up to down.

Test the Link State Agent

1. On the Core1 switch, disable interface 1/1/45 and save the configuration.

```
ICX-Tx-Core1(config-if)# interface 1/1/45
ICX-Tx-Core1(config-if)# shutdown
```

2. A few moments later, save the configuration.

```
ICX-Tx-Core1(config-if)# write mem
```

3. Return to the switch Analytics Dashboard. The triangle will indicate the moment the alert was detected. The 'diamond' will indicate that a new configuration was saved.

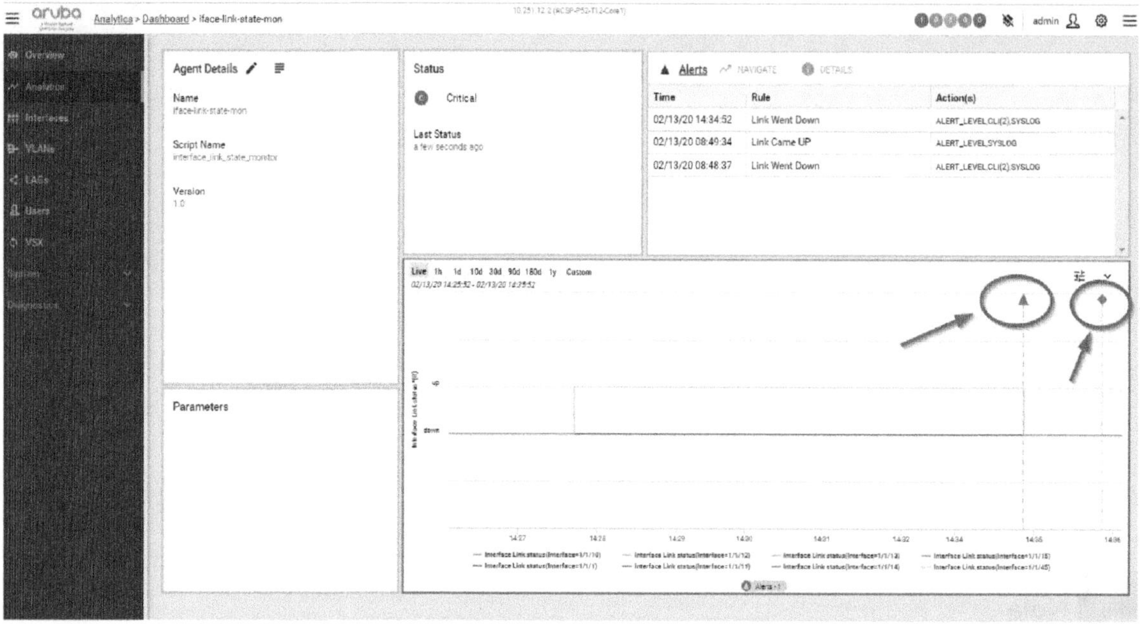

4. Click the **red triangle** in the graph to see the alert details. Review the captured CLI details by clicking the **Output** hyperlinks.

5. Example CLI details.

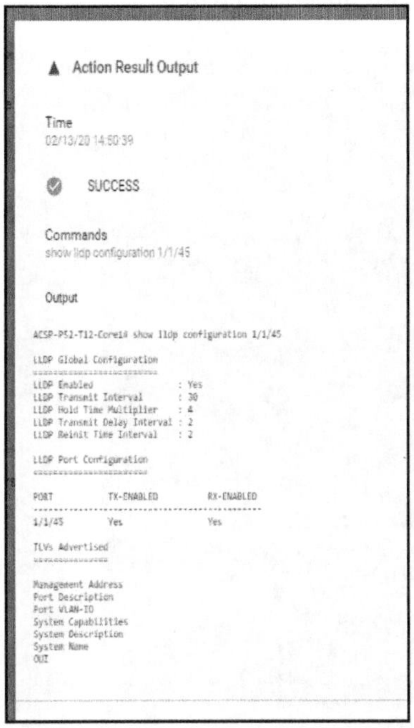

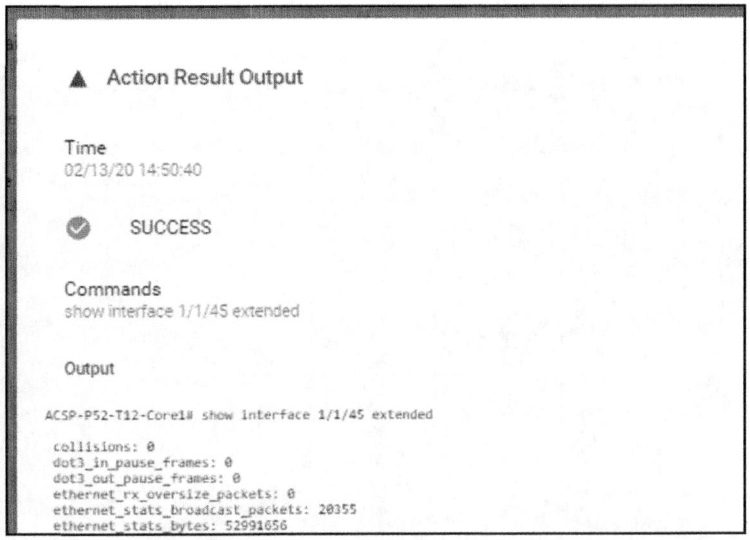

6. Click the **purple diamond** icon in the graph to see the details of the configuration change. This can make it easy for an administrator to correlate an alert to a configuration change.

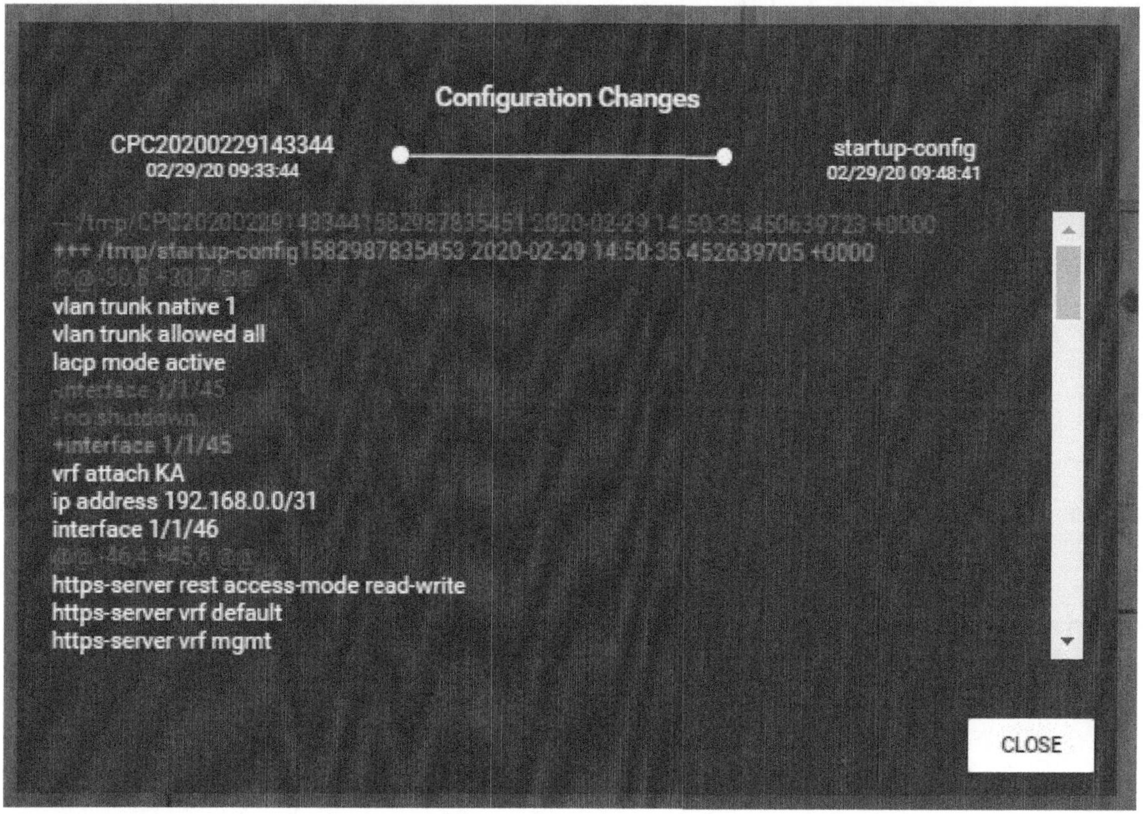

Restore the Interface

1. On the Core1 switch, enable interface 1/1/45 and save the configuration.

```
ICX-Tx-Core1(config)# int 1/1/45
ICX-Tx-Core1(config-if)# no shutdown
ICX-Tx-Core1(config-if)# write mem
```

2. Verify that the agent state is back to normal in the Analytics Dashboard. The Status window pane should show a green icon and display "Normal". In the Alerts section you should see an even listed that the link is now up ("Link Came Up"). In the graph, you should see a green arrow indicating the interface status change. Also, the graph will display a bright blue line indicating that the status is up (examine the graph key for the interfaces at the bottom of the graph).

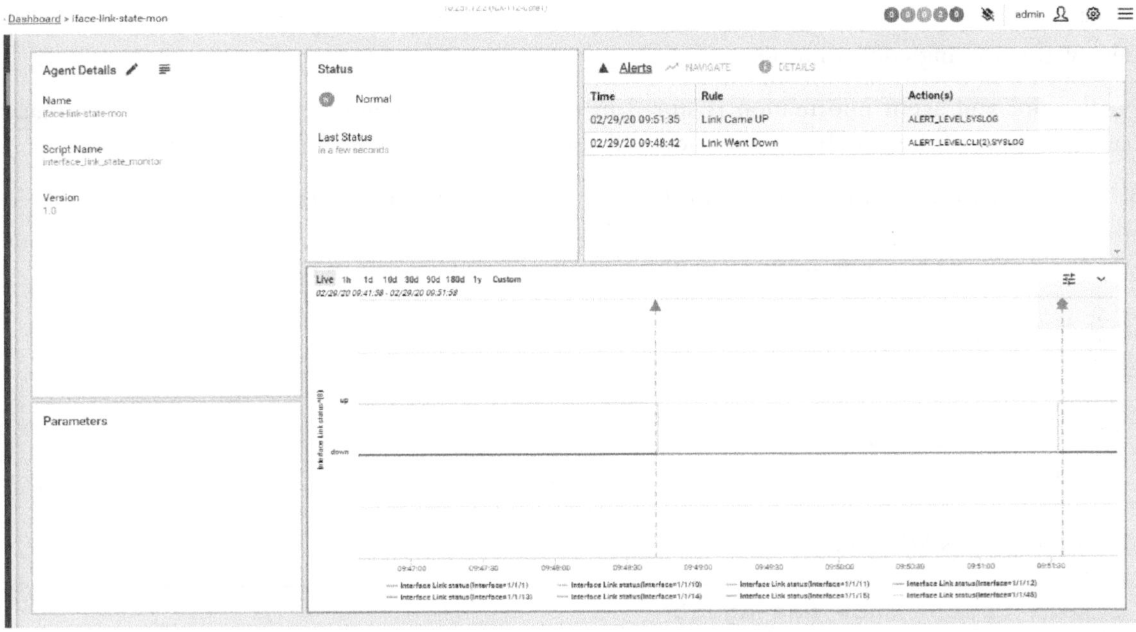

3. In the Agent Details pane, select the **pen** icon to edit the Agent. Move the slider to the off state to disable the agent. Click **Save** to save the settings; click **Close** for the confirmation.

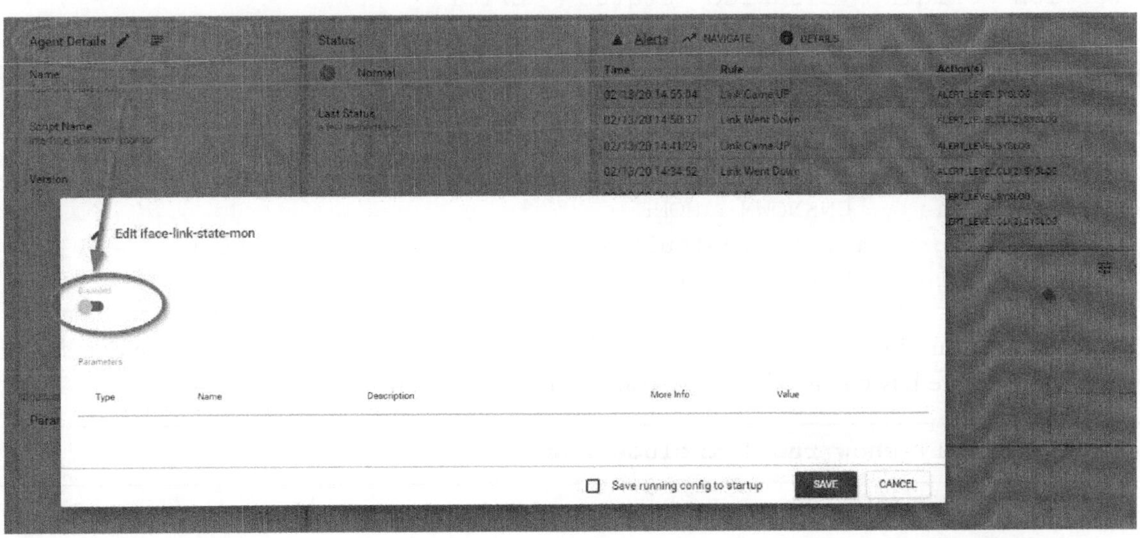

Task 4: Review the NAE agent in the switch configuration file

Objectives

In this task, the NAE script and agent settings will be reviewed in the switch configuration.

Steps

Review the running-configuration

NAE script and agent information is stored in the switch's configuration file. This ensures that a backup/restore of the switch configuration will also maintain the configured monitoring solution.

1. Open a terminal connection to Core1 and review the installed scripts.

```
ICX-Tx-Core1# show nae-script
---------------------------------------------------------------
Script Name                       Version   Origin    Status
---------------------------------------------------------------
connectivity_monitor              1.1       user      VALIDATED
interface_link_state_monitor      1.0       user      VALIDATED
system_resource_monitor           1.1       system    VALIDATED
```

2. Review the NAE agents.

```
ICX-Tx-Core1# show nae-agent
------------------------------------------------------------------
-------------------------------------------------------
Agent Name                           Script Name
Version  Origin   Disabled  Status   Error
------------------------------------------------------------------
-------------------------------------------------------
connectivity-ping-core2            connectivity_monitor          1.1
user     false    NORMAL    NONE
iface-link-state-mon               interface_link_state_monitor  1.0
user     true     UNKNOWN   NONE
system_resource_monitor.default    system_resource_monitor       1.1
system   false    NORMAL    NONE
```

3. Review the running-configuration for lines that 'include' the string 'nae'. The script and the agent parameters are Base64 encoded in the configuration file.

```
ICX-Tx-Core1# show run | include nae
```

4. Here is an example extract.

```
...
nae-script interface_link_state_monitor false
Iy0qLSBjb2Rpbmc6IHV0Zi04IC0qLQ0KIw0KI0NvcHlyaWdodCAoYykgMjAxNyBIZXdsZXR0IFBh
Y2thcmQgRW50ZXJwcmlzZSBEZXZlbG9wbWVudCBMUA0KIw0KI0xpY2Vuc2VkIHVuZGVyIHRoZSBB
cGFjaGUg-
TGljZW5zZSwgVmVyc2lvbiAyLjAgKHRoZSAiTGljZW5zZSIpOw0KI3lvdSBtYXkgbm90IHVzZSB0
aGlzIGZpbGUg-
ZXhjZXB0IGluIGNvbXBsaWFuY2Ugd2l0aCB0aGUgTGljZW5zZS4NCiNZb3UgbWF5IG9idGFpbiBh
IG-
NvcHkgb2YgdGhlIExpY2Vuc2UgYXQNCiMNCiNodHRwOi8vd3d3LmFwYWNoZS5vcmcvbGljZW5zZX
MvTEl-
DRU5TRS0yLjANCiMNCiNVbmxlc3MgcmVxdWlyZWQgYnkgYXBwbGljYWJsZSBsYXcgb3IgYWdyZWV
kIHRvIGluIHdyaXRpbmcsDQojc29mdHdhc
...
```

5. The administrator can simply review the original script text with a Base64 decode of the script. Below is an online example **https://www.base64decode.org/**.

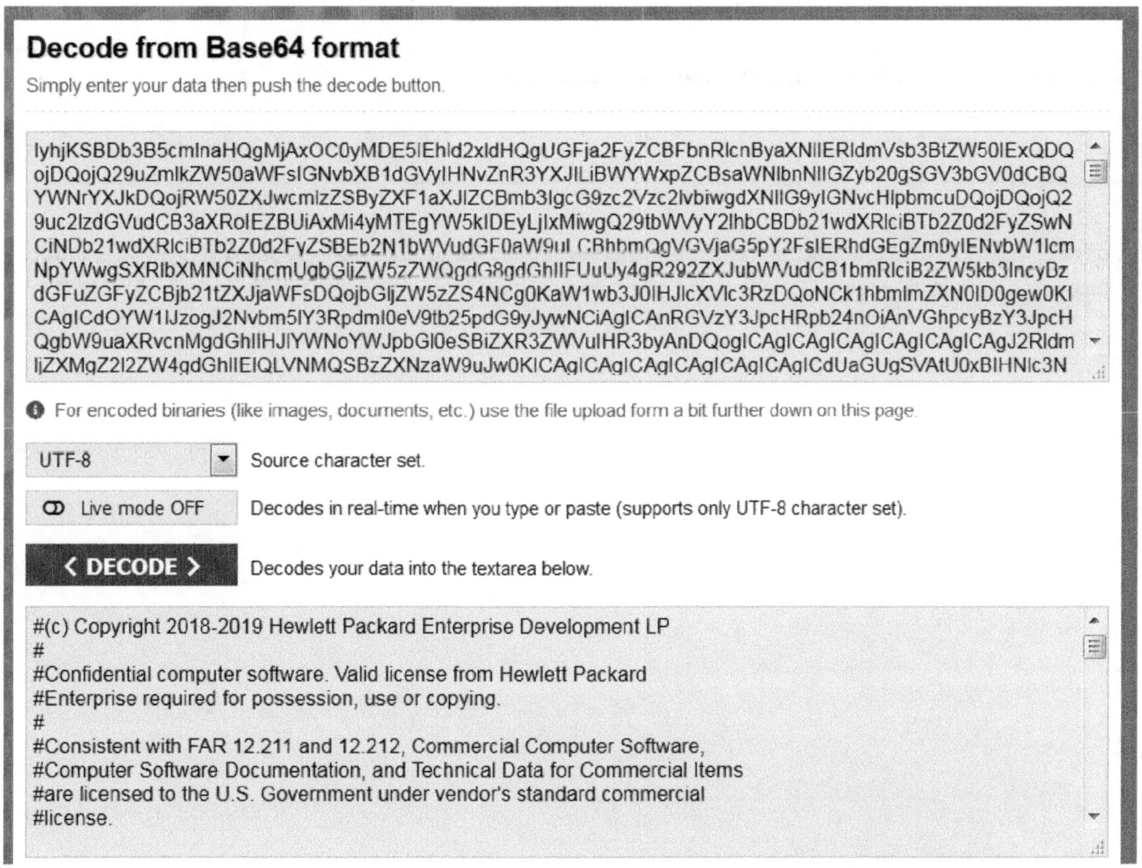

Note

This is informational only: there is no need to actually decode your script in this lab.

6. Each of the created agents based on the script, the agent state (false in the first line), and the parameters (Base64 encoded) are also stored in the configuration file.

```
nae-agent connectivity_monitor connectivity-ping-core2 false ip-
sla_session_name:cGluZy1jb3JlMg==

nae-agent interface_link_state_monitor iface-link-state-mon true

nae-agent system_resource_monitor system_resource_monitor.default false
short_term_high_threshold:OTE= short_term_normal_threshold:ODE=
```

Review the Switch NAE Capacities

1. The switch can handle several scripts and agents. To review the currently active amount of scripts and agents versus the platform limits, use the **show capacities-status nae** command.

```
ICX-Tx-Core1# show capacities-status nae
System Capacities Status: Filter NAE
Capacities Status Name                                          Value Maximum
-----------------------------------------------------------------------------
Number of configured NAE agents currently active in the system    3       50
Number of configured NAE monitors currently active in the system 12      150
Number of configured NAE scripts currently active in the system   3       25
```

Learning Check

1. What are Aruba-certified scripts?
   a. System-created scripts only
   b. Scripts authored by Aruba and posted to ASE and GitHub
   c. Scripts customized by partners and customers
   d. Scripts created by third parties but installed by Aruba in the factory software
2. What lets you view the results of actions taken by the NAE agent?
   a. Main Analytics Dashboard
   b. Graphs on the Agent Details page
   c. NAE Alert Details window
   d. Agent Management page
3. You are not seeing expected NAE data in your web browser. What should you examine?
   a. The time on the switch and your desktop
   b. NAE has been enabled from the CLI
   c. The script is digitally signed
   d. The script is written in SQL

Summary

Congratulations! You have completed the Network Analytics Engine chapter. You can now install new script from ASE and other sources and create agents based on that script. You understand how NAE agents collect information and how they can also take actions based on the information. You can also view the information collected by NAE in the Web UI and use it to gain valuable insights into your network functionality.

You also learned about basic monitoring capabilities, including sFlow and traffic mirroring.

4 VSX

OBJECTIVES

After completing this chapter, you should be able to:

- ✓ Compare and contrast virtual switching technologies
- ✓ Understand how Aruba's VSX technology helps you simplify your network architecture, operations, and management while providing a resiliency and scalability
- ✓ Understand how VSX meets high availability needs for customers
- ✓ Implement best practices for VSX

Overview

This chapter focuses on high availability technologies that help you simplify your network architecture, operations, and management while providing a resiliency and scalability. You will learn how to use Virtual Switching Extension (VSX) and the benefits of using VSX to virtualization the aggregation/core of the campus network. VSX provides advanced capabilities beyond what was previously available with the VSX-LAG feature. You will learn how VSX meets high availability needs of the customers to provide redundancy, resiliency, performance, and simplicity.

Virtual Switching Technologies

This section introduces the virtual switching technologies that Aruba has designed for the ArubaOS and AOS-CX switches.

VSF and Backplane Stacking

Virtual Switching Framework (VSF) and backplane stacking are Aruba technologies that allow you to combine multiple switches into a single virtual switch. You can then manage the combined switches as a single entity. You can also treat switches as a single entity from the viewpoint of designing Layer 2 and 3 protocols. This provides significant advantages as you design a wired network (Figure 4-1).

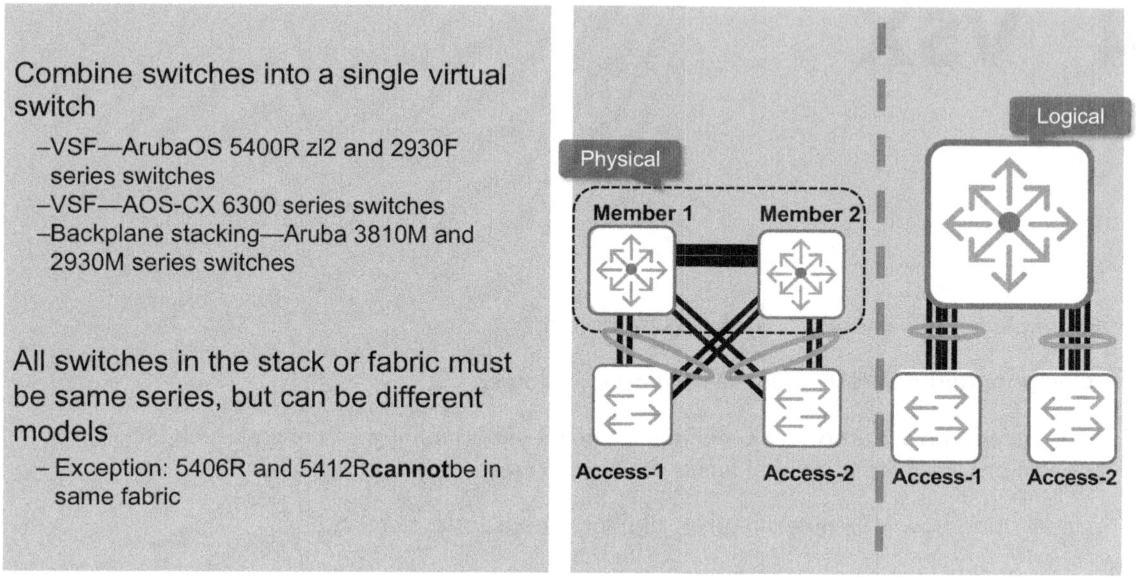

Figure 4-1 VSF and Backplane Stacking

ArubaOS 5400R zl2 and 2930F series switches and AOS-CX 6300 series switches support VSF. ArubaOS 3810M and 2930M switches support backplane stacking.

A VSF fabric must consist of switches that are the same series, such as two Aruba 5406R switches or two Aruba 2930F switches. For the 2930F series, you can combine different models in the same fabric. For example, you can combine a 2930F-48G PoE+ switch with a 2930F-48G switch.

You cannot combine 5406R and 5412R switches in the same VSF fabric. The two switches can support different interface modules, although Aruba recommends that you install the same modules in both switches for consistency.

VSF Versus Backplane Stacking

–Front-plane stacking—using 1/10/40 GbE links	–Stacking module and special cables required
–Need to plan adequate bandwidth on VSF links	–Dedicated, high-bandwidth stacking links
–Long distances supported between members (same limitations as any 1/10/40 GbE link)	–Less distance supported between members (up to 3m)
–Deep-level queuing and forwarding at a member level	–Deep-level queuing and forwarding at a stack level

Figure 4-2 VSF Versus Backplane Stacking

VSF and backplane stacking are implemented in different ways (Figure 4-2). For one thing, VSF is a front-plane stacking technology, meaning that you can connect the switches in the VSF fabric using regular wired switch ports. Backplane stacking, in contrast, is not implemented through wired ports; you must purchase a stacking module and stacking cable to implement this technology.

With VSF fabrics, you will need to plan the VSF links to ensure there is adequate bandwidth to handle the traffic that members exchange. For backplane stacking, all the members are connected through dedicated, high-bandwidth stacking links (40 GbE).

Since VSF members are connected via wired ports, VSF fabrics support long distances between members. However, the distance between backplane stacking members is limited to a maximum of three meters (you can order .5-, 1-, or 3-meter cable). For this reason, backplane stacking is intended for deployment between members that are relatively close together such as in the same closet.

These two technologies also differ in how they handle traffic forwarding. Within a VSF fabric, deep-level queuing and forwarding are implemented at a member level. With backplane stacking, queuing and forwarding are implemented at a stack level. In other words, members can forward traffic on their own, but all traffic has a stacking module for processing, enabling the stack to operate even more deeply as a single entity.

AOS-CX VSX

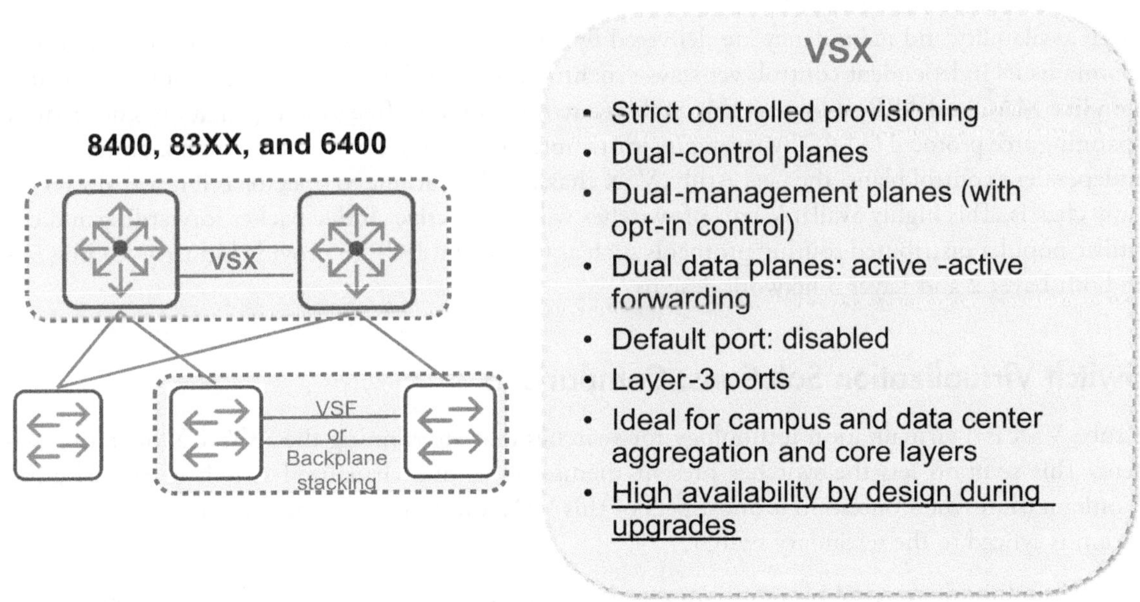

Figure 4-3 AOS-CX VSX

VSX is designed for use at the aggregation layer and sometimes the core of a campus network (Figure 4-3). On the other hand, VSF and backplane stacking is primarily used at the access layer of a campus network. This difference in design leads to several differences in how the features work. VSF and backplane stacking are configured with a plug-and-play approach in which a switch (at default settings) that connects to another switch automatically becomes one.

VSX, on the other hand, is strictly controlled and requires administrators to manually set the feature up on both switches. VSX maintains a dual control plane and dual management plane. This dual management plane allows for synchronization, but administrators can opt to synchronize specific features.

The two switches in a VSX fabric efficiently use both of the switches' control planes, management planes, and data planes while seeming in many ways to function as one device to other devices in the network. They support an active-active path for Layer 2 traffic, Layer 3 unicast traffic, and Layer 3 multicast traffic. In other words, both switches in the fabric actively switch and route traffic. VSX maintains the AOS-CX behavior with ports disabled and operating at Layer 3 by default.

Finally, VSX is designed to deliver high availability during software upgrades. The upgrade occurs with near zero downtime and with continuous packet forwarding.

VSX is available for the 8400, 8325, 8320, and 6400 series of AOS-CX switches. However, with the 6400 series, you cannot mix the two chassis types. A 6405+6405 or 6410+6410 is supported, but a pairing of 6405+6410 is not supported.

High availability and redundancy are delivered by enabling VSX on two switches. Each switch then maintains its independent control, yet stays synchronized with the other for important L2 information like MAC and ARP addresses. This enables a redundant loop-free topology that does not require spanning tree protocol (STP). By leveraging distributed intelligence with each switch maintaining its independent control plane, the peer Aruba VSX chassis will continue to operate as if it was always the only chassis. This highly available pair of switches will have Active-Active packet forwarding and can utilize popular distributed routing protocols such as OSFP and BGP to provide industry-leading HA in both Layer 2 and Layer 3 network designs.

Switch Virtualization Solutions: Comparison

Aruba VSX is a virtualization technology for switches that are running the AOS-CX operating system. This solution lets the switches present themselves as one virtualized switch in critical areas. Configuration synchronization is one aspect of this VSX solution where the primary switch configuration is synced to the secondary switch.

VSX virtualizes the control plane of two switches to function as one device at Layer 2 and as independent devices at Layer 3. From a datapath perspective, each device does an independent forwarding lookup to decide how to handle the traffic. Some of the forwarding databases, such as the MAC forwarding database and neighbor tables, are synchronized between the two devices using a proprietary VSX control plane. Some of the forwarding databases are built independently by each switch.

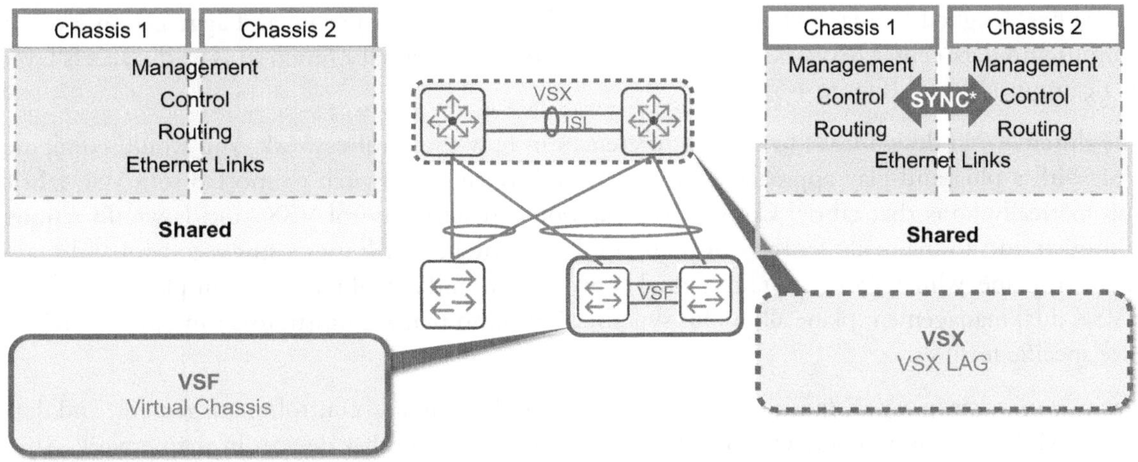

Figure 4-4 Switch Virtualization Solutions: Comparison

Virtual Switching Framework (VSF) is an ArubaOS and AOS-CX technology that allows multiple switches of the same model to act as a single virtual device. VSF helps to provide fast failover, scalability, manageability, and high availability.

A VSF fabric has one active management plane and one active control plane, which the management module in the commander switch provides. The VSF commander proxies the control plane to the standby member. Both members of the fabric participate in the forwarding plane. Interface modules from both members are combined as if over one large switch connected by the VSF link (Figure 4-4).

VSF versus VSX

	VSF	VSX
Virtualization	Chassis	VSX LAG (multi-chassis LAG)
Control plane	Single	Dual
Management plane	Single	Dual (with ***opt-in*** control)
Data plane	Single	Dual (active-active forwarding)
Default port state	Enabled	Disabled
Port usage	Layer 2 default	Layer 3 default
Usage	Campus access layer	Campus and data center aggregation and core
OS upgrades	All switches runs same OS version: possible down time	versions: zero down time

Figure 4-5 VSF versus VSX

Aruba has designed Virtual Switching Extension (VSX) for use at the core and aggregation layer of campus and data center networks. On the other hand, VSF's primary function is at the access layer of a campus network (Figure 4-5).

The difference in design leads to several differences in how the features work. You would configure VSF with a plug-and-play approach where, at default settings, a switch connected to a VSF fabric automatically joins that fabric. Conversely, you would strictly control VSX, and it would require administrators to manually set the feature up on both switches. VSF uses a single control and management plane, which VSX maintains a dual control plane and a dual management plane. However, a VSX dual management plane allows for synchronization so that administrators can opt to synchronize specific features.

The two switches in a VSX fabric efficiently use both of the switches' control, management, and data planes while seeming in many ways to function as one device to other devices in the network. They support an active-active path for Layer 2 traffic, Layer 3 unicast traffic, and Layer 3 multicast traffic. In other words, both switches in the fabric actively switch and route traffic.

VSF, as a technology for access layer switches, keeps Ethernet ports enabled by default and operating at Layer 2. However, VSX maintains the AOS-CX behavior with ports disabled and operating at Layer 3 by default. Finally, Aruba has designed VSX to deliver high availability during software upgrades. The upgrade occurs with near zero downtime and with continuous packet forwarding.

VSX Overview

This section provides a brief overview of AOS-CX's VSX technology.

What Makes for a Good High Availability Solution?

Requirement	Solution capabilities
Redundancy *"What if X breaks and Y fails?"*	1. **HW redundancy** – management modules, fabric, power, fans 2. **SW redundancy** – dual vs single control planes
Resiliency *"What if W sputters and Z hiccoughs?"*	3. **Link virtualization** – virtualize multiple links to one logical link aggregation 4. **Process resiliency** – self-restart to last known good state
Performance *"How long is failover? In what scenarios?"*	5. **Low-latency link failovers** – minimize duration of traffic outage 6. **Fast upgrade time** – minimize time-at-risk during upgrade
Simplicity *"How complex, with what chance for error?"*	7. **Easy to configure** – # entities to configure, # CLI commands 8. **Low risk of error** – config sync & consistency checks

Figure 4-6 What Makes for a Good High Availability Solution?

AOS-CX switches, particularly when deployed with VSX, meet customers' high availability needs by providing redundancy, resiliency, performance, and simplicity (Figure 4-6). Redundancy consists of having at least two of every required component so that the system can continue functioning if one component fails. AOS-CX switches support redundancy at the hardware level with support for multiple management modules, fabric modules, power modules, and fans.

At the software level, VSX maintains two control planes, one in each switch, to ensure redundancy. Resiliency builds on redundancy by allowing the system to take advantage of redundant components. AOS-CX switches in a VSX fabric support link virtualization. This feature enables multiple redundant links, including ones on different members of the VSX fabric, to operate as one logical link, called a link aggregation (LAG). AOS-CX switches also support process resiliency; if a process encounters an error, the system can self-restart to the last known good state.

A good high availability solution should also provide good performance with fast failover in all scenarios. VSX minimizes the duration of traffic outages by providing low-latency link failovers. If one link in the LAG fails, traffic instantly fails over to other links. VSX supports live upgrades so the VSX fabric remains active as one member and then the next upgrades. In addition, the AOS-CX switches have a fast upgrade time, which minimizes the time that the network is at risk, with just one up member during the upgrade process.

Finally, a highly available solution must be simple to configure to lower the chances that operator error introduces unplanned downtime. It is easy to configure VSX on AOS-CX switches with simple CLI commands. VSX also supports configuration synchronization and consistency checks between the members of the fabric to lower the risk of error.

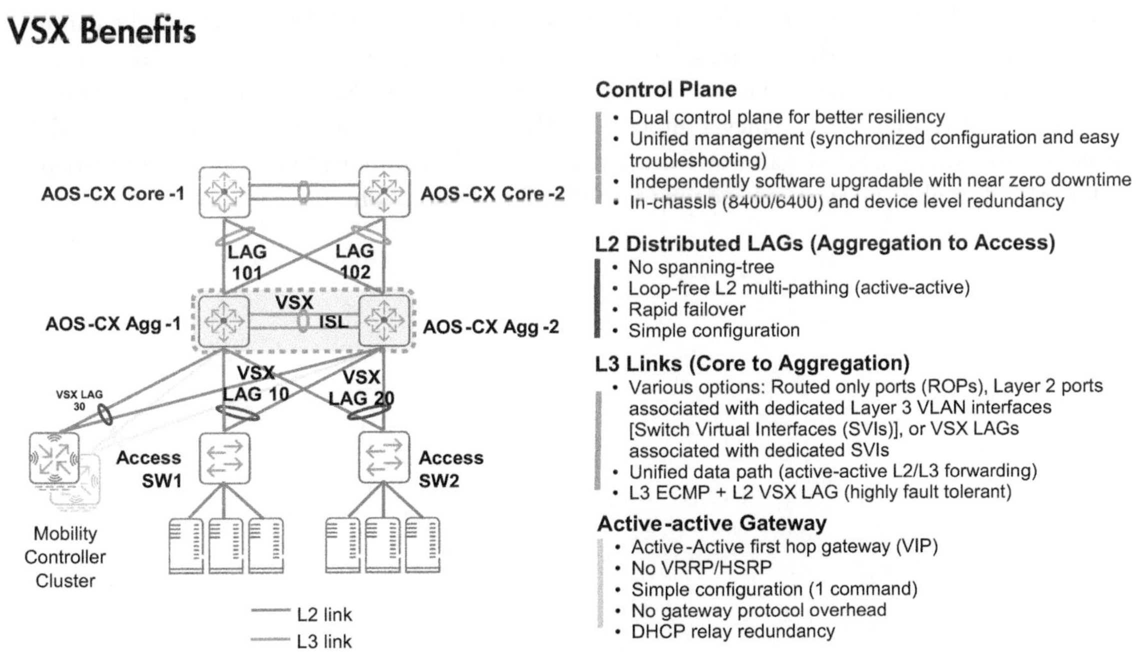

Figure 4-7 VSX Benefits

Figure 4-7 shows an example of an Aruba-recommended topology in which you deploy VSX at the aggregation layer.

While you can deploy VSX at the core if the topology requires, you may prefer to keep redundant core switches entirely independent. A dual control plane provides the best resiliency and software upgrades with near zero downtime. At the same time, VSX permits unified management on the features that administrators choose to synchronize.

The VSX pair uses link aggregations (LAGs) with links on both VSX switches to connect to access layer switches. This type of LAG is called a multi-chassis, distributed, or VSX LAG. These VSX LAGs operate at Layer 2 because the access layer switches do not route, and the aggregation layer VSX pair acts as the default gateway for the access VLANs. The Layer 2 LAGs eliminate the need for Multiple Spanning Tree Protocol (MSTP) or Rapid Per-VLAN Spanning Tree (RPVST) on the redundant links. They provide a loop-free path that permits the use of all the links in the aggregation (active-active design). Configuring a LAG-based topology is simple, and if a link fails, failover occurs very quickly.

The VSX pair has Layer 3 links to the core. Each VSX switch can connect independently to each core switch on a routed-only port (ROP) or on a Layer 2 port associated with Layer 3 VLAN interfaces (also known as Switch Virtual Interfaces—SVIs) dedicated to that port. Alternatively, both VSX switches could connect to each core switch together on a VSX LAG. This LAG would operate at Layer 2 and associate with one or more VSIs. Whichever option you select, VSX can support active-active Layer 3 routing through Equal Cost Multipath (ECMP) and an efficient path for unicast traffic. With the final option, the combination of Layer 3 ECMP and the VSX LAG creates a highly fault-tolerant system.

Remember that the VSX pair acts as the default gateway for the access VLANs. To do so, the pair uses the active-gateway feature. This feature allows each switch in the pair to act as an active default gateway for the VLAN using a shared virtual IP address (VIP) and virtual MAC address. It eliminates the need for Virtual Router Redundancy Protocol (VRRP) or Hot Standby Router Protocol (HSRP). Simple to configure, the active-gateway feature relies on VSX operations so it does not add any protocol overhead. It also supports redundancy for DHCP relay functions.

Data Plane Virtualization: VSX Link Aggregation

Data plane virtualization supports VSX LAGs. It makes the two switches in the VSX pair appear as a single device to the device on the other side of the link aggregation. In this example, those are both downstream access layer switches and upstream core switches (Figure 4-8).

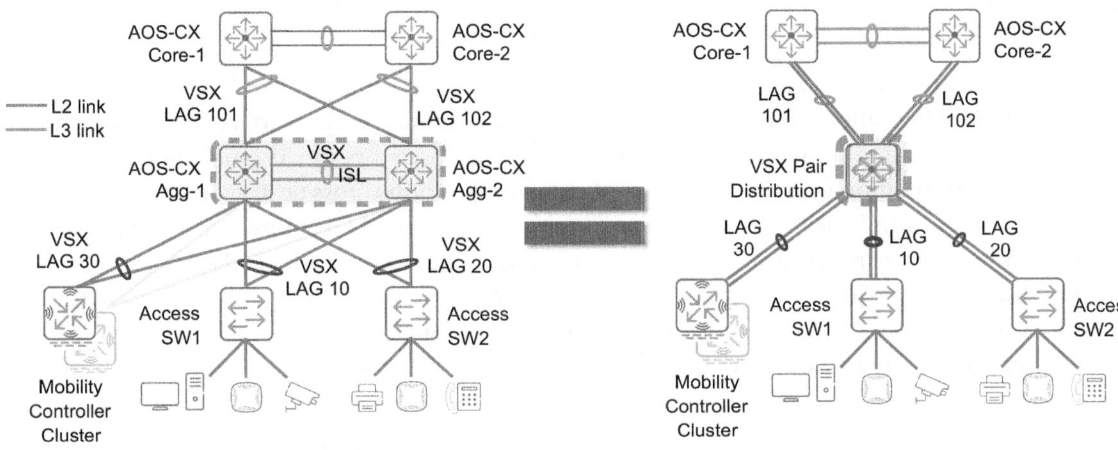

Figure 4-8 Data Plane Virtualization: VSX Link Aggregation

Management Plane Synchronization

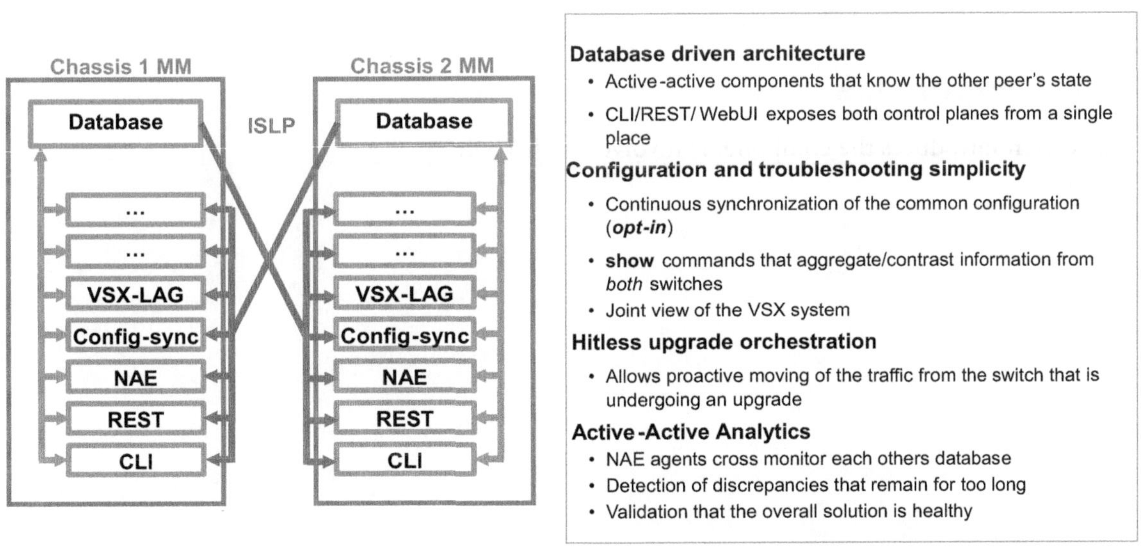

Figure 4-9 Management Plane Synchronization

While VSX uses a dual management plane, the management plane supports synchronization (Figure 4-9). This synchronization is made possible partially through AOS-CX's innovative database-centric design. The peers within the VSX pair can synchronize portions of their database so that each peer can be active in forwarding traffic while also knowing the state of the peer. VSX also supports management simplicity by enabling the CLI, REST interface, and web user interface (UI) to easily expose both control planes to admins and business applications. In addition to simplifying management, this design enables analytics across the redundant pair.

Administrators can choose to synchronize specific components, such as an interface or VLAN, across the VSX pair. Configuration for that component is then continuously synchronized, making the pair easier to configure and minimizing misconfigurations. Administrators can also use **show**-commands that aggregate information from several pieces of the configuration across both switches and compare them, allowing the admins to quickly pick out mismatched settings. Admins can also add the **vsx-peer** option to many commands in order to view information about both the local switch and the peer, providing a simple joint view of the VSX system. VSX synchronization also helps to orchestrate hitless live upgrades. When one member needs to undergo an upgrade, the other member knows, and the pair can proactively move traffic away from the member that needs to be upgraded toward the other member.

While each switch in the VSX pair maintains its own NAE agent, which stores sensor values locally, NAE is aware of VSX. The agent on each member can connect to the other member's database and cross monitor it to detect discrepancies. For example, each NAE agent monitors the number of objects in the primary and secondary members' databases. If synchronization is working correctly, the number of objects should be identical. An alert can trigger if, for example, there are 20%more objects in the primary database than the secondary database for at least 5 minutes. Active-active analytics helps to validate that the overall solution is healthy.

VSX Components

This section introduces the components involved with VSX.

VSX Components Overview

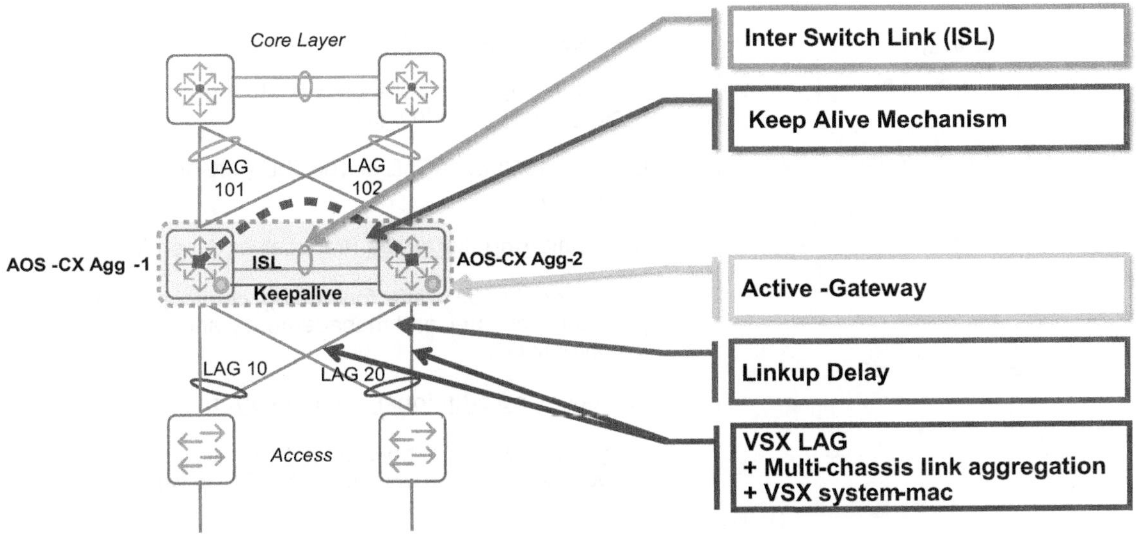

Figure 4-10 VSX Components Overview

VSX supports a link-aggregation technique, in which two or more links across two switches aggregate together to form a LAG that will act as a single logical interface. While the IEEE standard 802.3ad is limited to aggregating links on a single switch or device, the VSX feature uses a proprietary technology to overcome this limitation. VSX supports link aggregation for links spanning across multiple switches in the same VSX stack. An inner switch link (ISL) connects the two switches.

Also, VSX provides node-level redundancy in a network for when one of the switches fails. You need to configure the downstream device as an 802.3ad LAG interface. Even though you connect the LAG to two separate devices, they visualize as a single device. The downstream devices can be any device that supports LACP (802.3ad). In VSX, one device acts as primary and the other device as secondary. If you enable config-sync, the configuration on the primary device will sync to the secondary (Figure 4-10).

When you enable config-sync, the configuration on the primary device syncs to the secondary. This does not sync the entire configuration, just the elements manually enabled VSX-sync items.

VSX Inter-Switch Link (ISL)

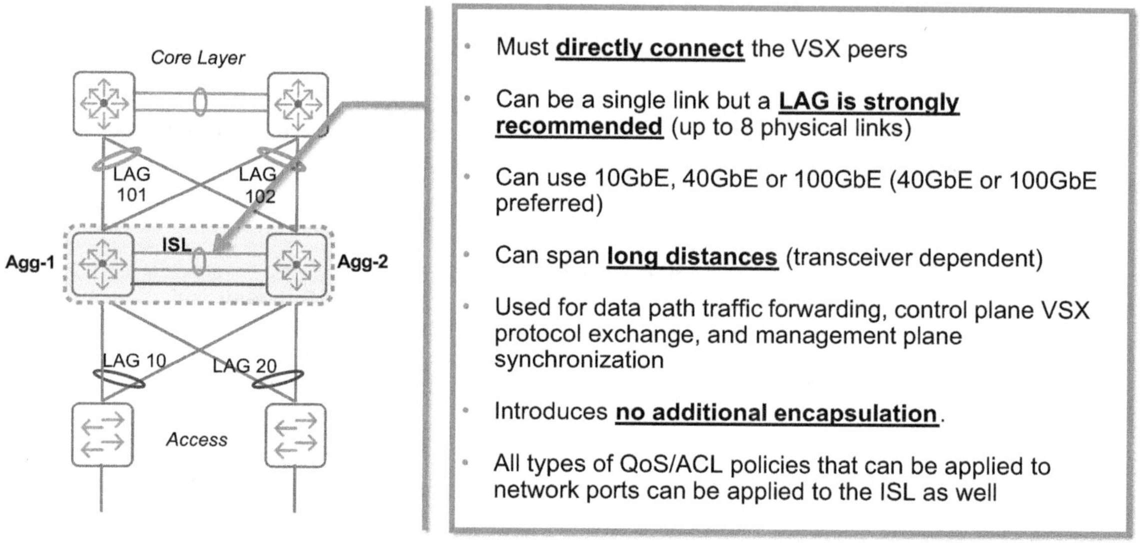

Figure 4-11 VSX Inter-Switch Link (ISL)

An Inter-Switch Link (ISL) is a Layer 2 interface between two VSX peer switches (Figure 4-11). You must configure each VSX switch with an ISL that directly connects to its peer VSX switch. The ISL is used both as a datapath, to forward production traffic, and as a control path, to exchange VSX protocol messages and synchronize the management planes. While the ISL can consist of a single physical link, Aruba recommends a link aggregation, which can have up to 8 physical links, for resiliency. Each link in the LAG must have the same speed as the other links, which could be 10Gbps, 40Gbps, or 100Gbps. Typically, you should use multiple 40Gbps or 100Gbps links in order to ensure adequate bandwidth for the datapath. The ISL uses front-plane ports on the member switches and can use any media. If you select fiber media, the ISL can span long distances with the maximum distance depending on factors such as the fiber type and transceiver type.

The ISL interface is by default a member of all VLANs on the device. You can change ISL membership through the CLI, but you must ensure that any VLAN that is carried on a VSX LAG is also carried on the ISL. In the datapath, traffic is forwarded natively with no additional encapsulation, unlike with VSF. Also note that you can control the ISL with QoS and ACL policies much as you do other interfaces on the switch. Of course, you would want to be careful that the ACL does not block any necessary traffic. The ISL also preserves DSCP remarking. For example, you could configure a VSX LAG might to remark traffic with a specific DSCP. In some cases, the local switch will not be able to transmit the traffic on its own link in the LAG because the link has failed, so it transmits the traffic on the ISL instead. The packet keeps the DSCP value that it would have had if transmitted over the LAG locally. However, the ISL interfaces on the other peer must be configured to trust the DSCP settings on ingress frames.

VSX Inter-Switch Link Protocol (ISLP)

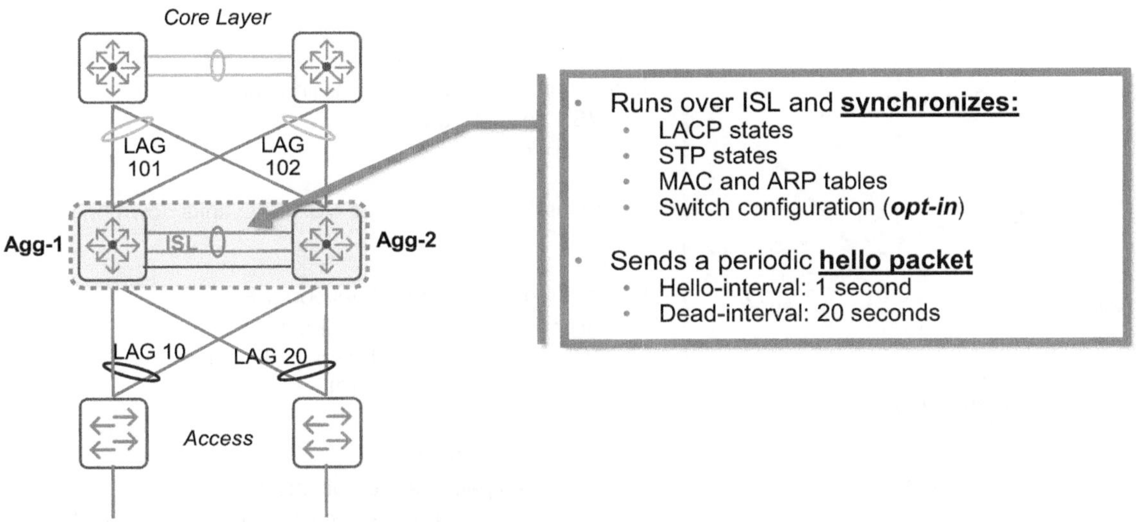

Figure 4-12 VSX Inter-Switch Link Protocol (ISLP)

The Inter-Switch Link Protocol (ISLP) runs over the ISL (Figure 4-12). When you first configure the VSX pair, ISLP synchronizes the switches. Then, on an ongoing basis, ISLP also synchronizes LACP states, MSTP States, MAC tables, and ARP tables, in addition to configuration information. With release 10.2, VSX also supports interoperability with Multiple Spanning Tree Protocol (MSTP) (although it does not provide interoperability with RPVST+).

ISLP runs at Layer 2. In other words, it uses Ethernet frames, but these frames encapsulate ISLP packets, not IP.

ISLP also helps peers to detect each other's status. They periodically exchange a hello packet at a default interval of 1 second. The dead-interval, which is 20 seconds by default, determines when a switch decides that its peer is no longer available on the ISL and initiates split detection. While the dead-interval might seem long, keep in mind that each VSX peer maintains its own control plane. If one peer goes down, all of its links in VSX LAGs go down. Traffic instantly fails over to the links to the other peer, which is already actively forwarding and routing traffic and can continue to do so without interruption. In addition, in most cases, the peers will determine that they need to initiate split detection when the ISL link is down. The ISL link is considered down when all physical links in the ISL are down for the period of the hold time, which is 0 seconds by default.

ISLP uses version control and provides backward compatibility regarding VSX synchronization capabilities. Processes used for VSX include vsxd for VSX LAGs, vsx-synchd for synchronization, and vsx-mgmtd to synchronize REST, NAE, and configuration settings across the pair.

Keepalive: Protection from ISL Failure

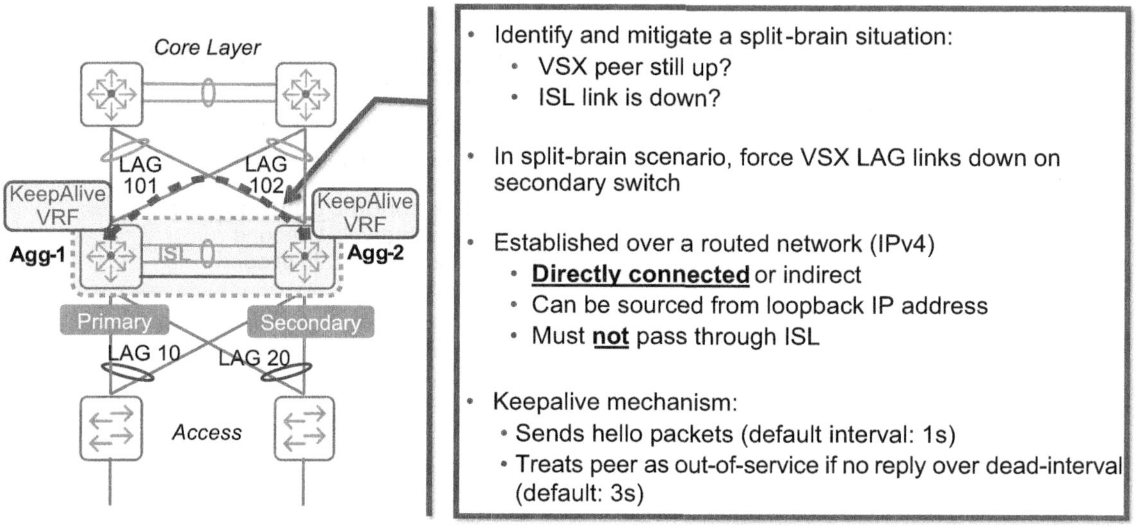

Figure 4-13 Keepalive: Protection from ISL Failure

You should configure each VSX switch with a keepalive connection to the other switch. If the ISL goes down, each VSX peer uses the keepalive communications to identify whether the peer is still up, although unavailable over the ISL—in other words, the VSX pair has a split brain. If the keepalive communications do indicate that the peer is still up, the primary VSX switch keeps its VSX LAG links up, and the secondary VSX switch forces its VSX LAG links down. The primary switch was selected when VSX established based on a user-configured role setting. If you configure the switches with the same role the lowest MAC address acts as a tie-breaker (Figure 4-13).

Peers exchange keepalives over a routed network; the path can consist of a direct Layer 3 link or an indirect link through the upstream Layer 3 network. You can set the source for keepalive packets to a loopback interface for stability. In either case, though, make sure that keepalives do not pass through the ISL.

Keepalive packets are UDP based. By default, they use port 7678, but the UDP port is configurable. By default, keepalive hello packets are sent every one second, but you can configure the interval to a value from 1 to 5 seconds. The keepalive dead-interval is 3 seconds, but has a configurable range of 2 to 20 seconds. If a device does not receive a keepalive packet from its peer within the dead-interval, it treats the peer device as out-of-service and does not implement the split-brain protection mechanisms.

You have two options for establishing the keepalive links. The most crucial rule is that the keepalive communications must *not* pass through the ISL.

- In a directly connected option the keepalive link consists of a directly connected ROP on each peer or a directly connected route LAG. Aruba recommends this type of configuration.
- Alternatively, you can use the through routed path option. Keepalives pass through the upstream Layer 3 network; Aruba does not recommend passing the keepalives through the downstream network. The indirect option is cost-optimized because it requires fewer links.

You can choose an ROP, routed LAG, SVI, or loopback interface for the keepalive source. A loopback interface provides the most stability because the peers can always reach each other's loopback interfaces if even one Layer 3 path is available between each other. If you tie the keepalives to a particular physical interface or SVI, that interface might go down. Remember to advertise the source loopback interface in the dynamic routing protocol.

Note
For additional hardening, Aruba recommends assigning keepalive source interface to its *own* VRF.

Best Practices

- –When initially setting up the VSX topology, make sure both switches initially run the same software version
- –Use a direct Layer-3 connection for the keepalive connection
- –Leave the timers at their default values
- –Use **vsx-sync** to synchronize configurations
  - – Unless it is noted not to do so with the best practices
- –ISL LAG: use at ***least*** 2x40G or faster links
- –Define the VSX system-MAC and do ***not*** let it default to the built-in system-MAC

Figure 4-14 Best Practices

MAC Addressing

One of the main VSX best practices is to set the VSX system-mac and not leave it blank with default HW system-mac being used (Figure 4-14). By doing so, the VSX system-mac is independent from the physical hardware MAC address and in case of hardware replacement of the VSX primary, the new switch can be configured with the same configuration than the previous primary unit with no impact on the VSX secondary as the cluster ID remains unchanged. With such practice, VSX primary HW replacement is hitless for the VSX secondary. (Otherwise the VSX secondary would have to join a new cluster ID, ID from VSX primary, and would turn-off temporary its VSX LAG ports.)

Please use locally administered unicast MAC addresses when assigning system-mac or active-gateway virtual MAC addresses. There are 4 ranges reserved for private use for unicast (with second least significant bit of the first octet of the unicast address set to 1). x is any Hexadecimal value.

- x2-xx-xx-xx-xx-xx
- x6-xx-xx-xx-xx-xx
- xA-xx-xx-xx-xx-xx
- xE-xx-xx-xx-xx-xx

In this example, 02:01:00:00:01:00 is used or system-mac and 12:01:00:00:01:00 is used for active-gateway Virtual MAC.

Here is an example proposal to have unique values being used in the administrative domain in Table 4-1, where XX is reflecting the Unique Cluster ID in the function, and Y is the Virtual MAC ID (0 to 15):

Table 4-1 VSX and MAC Addressing

Function	System-MAC	Active-Gateway Virtual MAC
Access/TOR Layer	02:00:00:00:XX:00	12:00:00:00:XX:0Y
Aggregation	02:01:00:00:XX:00	12:01:00:00:XX:0Y
Core/Spine	02:02:00:00:XX:00	12:02:00:00:XX:0Y

The scope of this VMAC is purely link-local. Consequently, the same Virtual MAC address value can be used on any L3 VLAN interface (SVI).

If some servers or systems have dual-attachment to two different SVIs, and the system administrator would like to see distinct MAC addresses for the next-hops over these separate interfaces, then 16 VMACs are available. For dual-stack IPv4 and IPv6, 16 VMACs can be used for IPv4 and the same VMACs can be used for IPv6. It is however a best practice to use only 8 VMACs for IPv4 and 8 different VMACs for IPV6.

Note

Any other allocation rules can be chosen according to administrative rules in place by the network operational team. Multicast or broadcast MAC addresses must not be used for system-mac.

Firmware/Software Version

Please install the same version on both CX Switches that will create the VSX cluster. It is better to avoid any version mismatch during the creation of the cluster, as a warning would appear.

ISL LAG

It is assumed that 2x40G or 2x50G or 2x100G direct fibers/DACs are already interconnecting AGG-1 and AGG-2.

The best practice for ISL bandwidth is at least 2x40G (QSFP+) or 2x50G (SFP56) or 2x100G (QSFP28). It is technically possible to use 2x10G or 2x25G; however, it is recommended to plan for any uplink failure and associated impact on the bandwidth requirement for the ISL. If the uplinks from AGG-1 fail, traffic from AGG-1 will be redirected to AGG-2 over the ISL before reaching the upstream layer. This is perfectly fine as long as there is enough bandwidth remaining for the ISL protocol and the control-plane communication. It is recommended to size the ISL bandwidth to be equal to, at least, the sum of uplinks bandwidth of one VSX switch. The best practice rule is to size the ISL bandwidth according to the failure domain target.

The best practice for ISL physical ports is to select at least two ports of the same speed (2x40G or 2x50G or 2x100G), and, in case of a chassis, to select these ports from different Line Cards.

The best practice for LAG numbering is to use the last available LAG ID (that is, 256 in AOS-CX10.04) for the ISL, so that LAG ID=1 is used for connecting the Access Switch#1 on port 1/1/1, so that LAG 2 is used to connect the second Access Switch on port 1/1/2, and so on…

The best practice for VLAN trunking on the ISL LAG is to permit ALL VLANs, for simpler configuration. Specifying a restrictive list of VLAN IDs is entirely valid if the network admin wants more control.

The best practice for LACP timers on the ISL LAG is to keep the default long timer (30seconds for LACP rate slow).

The best practice for hashing algorithm on the LAG is to keep the default l3-src-dst (alternative being l2-src-dst).

The best practice for MTU is to configure on all devices the appropriate size to support features such as Dynamic Segmentation as well as other protocols/functions which require MTUs larger than 1500 bytes. Care should be taken to ensure that the IP path from access devices (switches or APs) can provide an MTU of at least 1564 bytes to the mobility controllers. Similarly, for datacenter server connectivity, largest MTU will ensure server jumbo frame traffic over ISL. Recommendation: Ethernet MTU = 9198 bytes.

The best practice for ACL is to not set any access-list on the ISL LAG in order to avoid designing complex and unnecessary ACL entries. The ISL can be seen as a virtual data back-plane and security filtering is processed before and/or after crossing the ISL.

The best practice for QoS trust mode on the ISL LAG is to rely on the **qos trust dscp** that is globally configured on the Aggregation switches. If not configured globally (which is not the recommendation), **qos trust dscp** has to be set on the ISL LAG.

VSX Keepalives

The best practice for the keepalive connection is to use a direct L3 circuit, which can be a low-speed port (1G transceiver is enough, 1GBASE-T works as well) between both VSX nodes. This circuit does not have to be directly connected and the path can include active L2 and L3 equipment. Although this requires an additional dedicated port, it brings simplicity of configuration and operations. In Appendix D of the VSX Best Practice Guide document, VSX keepalive over upstream Layer 3 routing domain is documented as an alternative for network admins who want to protect from a fiber path cut that would impact ISL and keepalive simultaneously; or when the associated cost of a dedicated port is too high (100G). In case of a chassis (6400 or 8400), if possible, it is recommended to use a port from a different Line Card than the ones used for the ISL ports.

The best practice for keepalive routing is to use a dedicated VRF. This is entirely optional and the default VRF can be used as well, typically for the single VRF model with UDP keepalive over the upstream L3 domain. Having a dedicated VRF for Keepalive simplifies the operations and prevents any impact from routing change on the default VRF.

The best practice for the keepalive subnet is to use a /31 subnet as only two nodes will communicate together.

VSX Cluster Creation

The best practice for system-mac is to set the system-mac manually on the VSX primary switch. Please refer to the above section for system-mac values. Here, 02:01:00:00:01:00 is used. The main advantage to set VSX system-mac (and not to leave it blank with default HW system-mac being used) is to be independent from the physical hardware MAC address. In case of hardware replacement of the VSX primary, the new switch can be configured exactly with the same configuration than the previous unit, and there will be no impact on the secondary which will remain in the same cluster ID. HW replacement is hitless for the VSX secondary.

The best practice for inter-switch-link timers (dead-interval, hello-interval, hold-time, peer-detect-interval) is to keep the default timers (that is, no specific configuration).

The best practice for role (primary or secondary) is to have a meaningful relationship with the switch hostname/identification. Example: AGG-1 is VSX primary and AGG-2 is VSX secondary.

- Best practice for **vsx-sync** includes **vsx-global**. Thanks to this **vsx-sync** feature group parameter, the VSX management-plane will synchronize the following VSX settings: inter-switch-link hello-interval, dead-interval, hold-time, peer-detect-interval, keepalive udp-port, hello-interval, keepalive dead-interval, system-mac, split-recovery, linkup-delay timer.
- VSX automatically tags the native VLAN configured on the LAG used for ISL.

VSX Split-Recovery

The best practice for VSX split-recovery is to keep the default split-recovery enabled (no configuration change). This best practice might be revisited in case of VSX and VXLAN. (VXLAN is beyond the scope of this guide.)

VLAN Configuration

The best practice for VLANs configuration is to configure the VLANs on the VSX primary with the **vsx-sync** attribute and let the VSX config-sync automatically synchronize the VLANs on the VSX secondary. Here, VLAN 10, 20 to 30 are the endpoint VLANs.

Downstream VSX-LAG Configuration

In this section, for simplicity, it is assumed that the connected access switch is already configured with uplinks link-aggregation and trunked VLANs. The best practice for VSX LAG is to create the multi-chassis lag interface on the VSX primary with all settings and then create the mirrored lag interface on the VSX secondary. LAG interface settings (including description) will be synchronized automatically. Only "no shut" in the lag interface context has to be performed on the VSX secondary. Once the multi-chassis lag interface is created, it can be assigned to the physical port.

The best practice for allowed VLANs is to exclude the native VLAN 1 from being propagated. This is a very robust method to avoid Layer 2 storm propagation due to potential loop initiated on an access switch. In case of access switch zero-touch provisioning use case, this trunking exclusion is performed after the ZTP process.

The best practice for LAG numbering is to use LAG ID=1 for connecting the Access Switch#1 on port 1/1/1, LAG 2 used to connect a second Access Switch on port 1/1/2, and so on...

The best practice for LACP timers on the VSX LAG is to keep the default long timer (30 seconds = LACP rate slow).

The best practice for MTU is to configure on all devices the appropriate size to support features such as Dynamic Segmentation or server jumbo frame. Care should be taken to ensure that the IP path from the access devices (switches or APs) can provide an MTU of at least 1564 bytes to the mobility controllers and that the server jumbo packet of 9000 bytes can be encapsulated. Flexibility should be anticipated to perform VXLAN encapsulation from the access switch (9000+50) or VXLAN encapsulation from the aggregation layer MTU+50. So, the recommended Ethernet MTU is 9100 bytes for the downstream VSX LAG to the access layer and an MTU of 9000 bytes for endpoints or servers. The SVI IP MTU should match the MTU size on the aggregation layer, so the recommended IP MTU is 9100 bytes.

The best practice for hashing algorithm on the VSX LAG is to keep the default l3-src-dst (alternative being l2-src-dst). This option has an effect only if at least 2 ports per VSX node are members of the same VSX LAG.

Note

Most of the time the VSX LAG includes only two links: one link from the primary and one link from the secondary. Consequently, hashing algorithm selection has no effect on the traffic path as it is forwarded to the local port of the VSX LAG on the switch receiving the traffic.

The **show lacp interfaces multi-chassis** command is very useful to get a complete status of the local LACP partnership as well as the VSX peer partnership details. Actor = local node, Partner = LACP neighbor (the access switch), Remote Actor = the VSX peer, Remote Partner = LACP neighbor of the VSX peer. Note that the port id of the VSX secondary is equal to 1000+ID_of_the_primary (in the example 1001). ALFNCD LACP state-flags should appear on all entries.

The best practice for LACP fallback feature is to enable it on the VSX LAGs for the following use cases: PXE boot, access switch ZTP, server NIC driver migration from active/standby to LACP. When applied to the VSX primary, LACP fallback is automatically synced on the VSX secondary.

MSTP Configuration

The best practices on aggregation layer switches include:

- Do not use loop-protect (MSTP used instead).
- Use the default common instance 0: MST0.
- Lower the spanning-tree priority to 4 to make VSX aggregation the STP root bridge (easier for support).
- Use root-guard on all downlinks to prevent any access switches from becoming Root Bridge.
- Keep the default **port-type admin-network**.
- Let VSX secondary synchronized by the vsx-sync process.

The best practices on access layer switches include:

- Use loop-protect for all endpoint access ports (not configured on uplinks). Set the re-enable timer to 1hour.
- Keep the default common instance 0: MST0.
- Keep the default spanning-tree priority of 8.
- All endpoint access ports are admin-edge, should not receive any BPDU (BDPU guard), should not trigger any topology change notification (TCN guard).
- Use loop-protection on all endpoint access ports as an extra-protection mechanism (in case of MSTP BPDUs are filtered by insertion of unmanaged switches which create a loop).
- Use loop-guard on all uplinks to prevent any flood due to failure of BPDU reception (fiber strand cut).

VSX LAG ACL Configuration

If any ACL is used, the best practice is to have ACLs synchronized on secondary through **vsx-sync**. Any ACL applied on a VSX LAG on the VSX primary will get applied on the VSX secondary as well.

VSX LAG QoS Configuration

QoS Marking being performed on the access layer, the aggregation switch is configured in the global context with **qos trust dscp**. No further configuration is needed as this was already set in previously.

SVI (VLAN Layer 3 [L3} Interface) Configuration

The best practice for SVI active-gateway is to set the active-gateway Virtual IP and Virtual MAC on the VSX primary and get the value synchronized on the VSX secondary with **vsx-sync** command.

The best practice for active-gateway VMAC is to use the same VMAC for all IPv4 SVIs. The scope of this VMAC is purely link-local. If some servers or systems have dual-attachment to two different SVIs, and the system administrator would like to see distinct MAC addresses for the next-hops over these separate interfaces, then 16 VMACs are available. For dual-stack IPv4 and IPv6, 16 VMACs can be used for IPv4 and the same VMACs can be used for IPv6. It is however a best practice to use only 8 VMACs for IPv4 and 8 different VMACs for IPV6.

If multinetting is used, set one VIP per secondary subnet and disable **ip icmp redirect**.

The best practice for IP MTU is to configure on all SVIs the matching size of the L2 MTU: IP MTU recommended value = 9100. This parameter must be identical and manually set on both VSX nodes.

The best practice for DHCP relay is to configure the **ip helper-address** on the VSX primary and let **vsx-sync** configuring the same on the VSX secondary.

OSPF Configuration

It is a best practice to create a dedicated transit VLAN between the VSX primary and the VSX secondary to exchange routes information for subnets that are not attached to both VSX nodes (ex: loopback addresses of each VSX node). This dedicated transit VLAN (here VLAN 2) provides better control and will not carry user data traffic in nominal situation or very limited in case of east-west traffic between single-attached endpoints.

There are two strategies to inject endpoint subnets into the routing table: either through OSPF or through BGP.

- **OSPF**: Most of the campus deployments use OSPF to exchange route information for end-devices. This is simple and can scale very well with appropriate usage of areas.
- **BGP**: A lot of new DC deployments use BGP as a routing protocol due to the usage of EVPN-based VXLANs. Such a design is coming in the Campus as well. Also, for more complex and granular routing engineering, BGP communities and route-map can offer a level of control that OSPF cannot provide.

There are two options to inject end-user subnets into OSPF database: using the **ospf** command on the SVI (VLAN L3 interface), or redistributing the connected into OSPF with route-map control.

The best practice is to use the **ospf** command on SVI as offering a simpler configuration, like for the area the subnets belongs to. This principle is selected as the OSPF best practice in the following described configuration. More details on OSPF best practices can be found in the Aruba IP *Routing Configuration Guide.*

The best practice for point-to-point interconnectivity subnet is to use a /31 subnet.

The best practice for OSPF configuration is to use **vsx-sync ospf** synchronization option and have OSPF parameters automatically synced on the VSX secondary. As shown on the configuration step, very few elements have to be configured on the secondary. Pay attention that to get such a benefit, the interface ID should be mirrored; that is, if interface 1/1/49 is used for uplink on the VSX primary, it is strongly recommended to use the same ID 1/1/49 on the VSX secondary, otherwise OSPF synchronization will not synchronize the proper interface.

The best practice for OSPF cost is to have VSX primary <-> VSX secondary cost lower than Core-1 <-> Core-2 cost, as it is frequent that the ISL bandwidth is higher than the inter core devices bandwidth. In case of single-attachment subnet on one of the VSX node and non-meshed topology, the traffic from core would be sent to the VSX peer closest to the attached destination, avoiding consuming inter-core bandwidth.

The same concept applies for south-to north traffic pattern. In the below example, OSPF cost for Transit VLAN over ISL is set to 50, and 1000 for Core devices. OSPF cost is synchronized from the VSX primary to the VSX secondary, so the importance to use mirrored interface ID.

BGP Configuration

Please read the Aruba *IP Routing Configuration Guide* for detailed information.

Note

VSX provides capability to synchronize the full BGP configuration between the VSX primary and the VSX secondary. Most of the BGP configuration of the VSX secondary is the same than on the VSX primary. Except the configuration for iBGP peering between the VSX nodes inside the cluster, or for remote eBGP upstream peers with neighbor IP address being the physical IP address of the L3 point-to-point circuit (ex: here 1/1/50 with 10.0.0.6/31 remote IP address). In such a case, the specific neighbor parameters are excluded from the VSX configuration synchronization with the following command on the VSX primary only: **neighbor** <IP_adress> **vsx-sync-exclude**.

Multicast Configuration

Please read the Aruba *Multicast Configuration Guide* for detailed information. For multicast on VSX cluster, the best practice is to configure PIM Dual-DR or active/active under the PIM router command. With active-active command, the proxy-DR will also learn the multicast routes, and will allow fast recovery time if the actual DR fails.

Configuring VRF Transit VLANs

The best practice for upstream routing domain connectivity is to create one transit VLAN per VRF per upstream VSX LAG. Consequently, according to the proposed topology, for VRF1, VLAN 101 is created and configured on upstream VSX LAG connecting CORE-1 (VSX LAG 101), VLAN 102 is created on upstream VSX LAG connecting CORE-2 (VSX LAG 102). Similarly, VLAN 201 and 202 are proposed for VRF2 and VLAN 301/302 for VRF3.

Note

For simplicity and readability, only two VRFs are documented: VRF1 and VRF2. VRF3 is not included in the configuration to alleviate the document. Configuration for VRF3 or any additional VRFs is similar to VRF1 and VRF2.

These transit VLANs 101/102 and 201/202 will also serve for VSX intra-cluster routing (unlike the single VRF scenario where a dedicated Transit VLAN (VLAN 2) was created for Transit point-to-point routing between VSX nodes.

Upstream VSX LAG Configuration (VSX LAG 101/102)

In this section, for simplicity, it is assumed that the Core equipment is already configured with link-aggregation and trunked Transit VLANs.

The best practice for upstream VSX LAG is to create the multi-chassis lag interface on the VSX primary with all settings and then create the mirrored lag interface on the VSX secondary. LAG interface settings (including description) will be synchronized automatically. Only "no shut" in the lag interface has to be performed on the VSX secondary. Once multi-chassis lag interface is created it is assigned to the physical port.

The best practice for allowed VLANs is to exclude the native VLAN 1 from being propagated and to allow only the transit VLANs corresponding to the facing Core device: that is, VSX LAG.101 permitting VLAN 101 and 201, VSX LAG 102 permitting VLAN 102 and 202.

The best practice example for LAG numbering is to use LAG ID=101 for connecting the Core-1, LAG ID=102 for connecting Core-2. Any other numbering practice is possible as long as it does not introduce confusion with the downstream VSX LAGs.

The best practice for LACP timers on the VSX LAG is to keep the default long timer (30seconds for LACP rate slow). The best practice for MTU on these upstream VSX LAGs is to configure the maximum value (9198 bytes) like for ISL.

The best practice for hashing algorithm on the VSX LAG is to keep the default l3-src-dst (alternative being l2-src-dst), and would have an effect only if at least 2 ports per VSX node are members of the same VSX LAG.

VSX Linkup-Delay Timer Exclusion

The best practice for VSX LAG exclusion for linkup-delay timer is to exclude the upstream VSX LAGs that are used for Transit VLANs (in the topology above, VSX LAG 101 and VSX LAG 102). By excluding these upstream VSX LAGs, the routing protocols can establish peering over upstream Transit VLANs as soon as the upstream ports (to L3 Core-1 and Core-2) are UP, without waiting for the linkup-delay timer to complete. The benefit is that routes from L3 core are already learned when ASIC is ready to forward traffic to downstream.

Note

For more information about an overview of VSX, best practices, and its configuration, see the *VSX Configuration Best Practices* guide. This has additional best practices based on using a multiple VRF routing model and connecting an access layer VSX cluster to an aggregation VSX cluster. You will also find useful information on maintaining and troubleshooting a VSX topology. And lastly, there are copious configuration examples included in the guide.

Example Configuration for the Primary Switch

1. ISL interface:

```
switch(config)# interface lag 128
switch(config-lag-if)# no shutdown
switch(config-lag-if)# no routing
switch(config-lag-if)# vlan trunk native 1
switch(config-lag-if)# vlan trunk allow x,y,x
switch(config-lag-if)# lacp mode active
switch(config)# interface 1/4/28
switch(config-if)# no shutdown
switch(config-if)# lag 128
switch(config)# interface 1/4/32
switch(config-if)# no shutdown
switch(config-if)# lag 128
```

2. Set up the keepalive interface:

```
switch(config)# interface 1/1/5
switch(config-if)# ip address 192.168.100.1/24
```

3. Set up VSX:

```
switch(config)# vsx
switch(config-vsx)# role primary
switch(config-vsx)# system-mac 02:01:00:00:aa:bb
switch(config-vsx)# inter-switch-link lag 128
```

4. Creating a multi-chassis interface:

```
switch(config)# interface lag 1 multi-chassis
switch(config-lag-if)# no shutdown
switch(config-lag-if)# no routing
switch(config-lag-if)# vlan trunk native 1
switch(config-lag-if)# vlan trunk allowed 11
switch(config-lag-if)# lacp mode active
switch(config)# interface 1/1/1
switch(config-if)# no shutdown
switch(config-if)# lag 1
```

Figure 4-15 Example Configuration for the Primary Switch

Figure 4-15 introduces the configuration of VSX on the primary switch in the pair. First, you need to set up the ISL link. This is defined as a normal Layer 2 LAG. When a native VLAN is defined (as shown this example), the switch automatically executes the **vlan trunk allowed all** command to ensure that the default VLAN is allowed on the trunk. In this example, LAG 128 is being used as the ISL.

The same list of VLANs that are trunked over the VSX LAGs must be configured on the primary and secondary VSX switches in the global configuration. The list of VLANs can be synced to the secondary switch if the **vsx-sync** command is used in the VLAN context. Also verify that the VLAN set is also permitted on the ISL on the primary and secondary VSX switches. To configure VLAN trunking on the ISL, enter the **vlan trunk allowed** [<VLAN-LIST> | **all**] command. If a native VLAN is defined, the switch automatically runs the **vlan trunk allowed all** command to ensure that the default VLAN is allowed on the trunk. To allow only specific VLANs on the trunk, enter the **vlan trunk allowed** <VLAN-LIST> command, for example: **vlan trunk allowed 2,3,4**.

Then activate the LAG on the physical interface(s) between the two switches. Remember that to follow best practices, you should minimally use 2 links in the LAG.

Next, define the Layer 3 interface that will be used for sending keepalives between the two switches. This can be a direct link between the switches. Each switch will need unique IP addressing.

After defining the keepalive interface, you need to set up VSX. Enter the VSX context and define the role: **primary** or **secondary**. Next, specify the LAG that will be used for the ISL link. In the above example, this is LAG 128.

That is all that is necessary to initially set up VSX. For detailed information on configuring, tuning, and troubleshooting VSX, see the *Virtual Switching Extension (VSX) Guide.*

To set up a multi-chassis LAG between this VSX cluster and another device, define a new LAG, but specify the **multi-chassis** parameter: this parameter tells the VSX cluster that there is at least one link on each switch connecting to a neighboring device, like a switch.

VSX Synchronization

This section introduces what information is synchronized between a VSX pair, as well as the synchronization process itself.

Periodic Synchronization

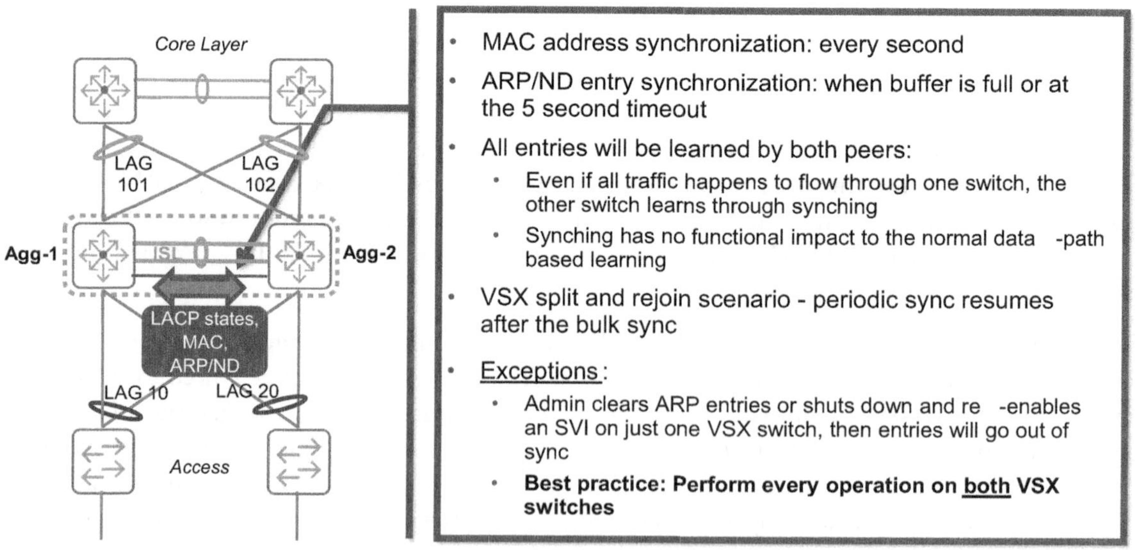

Figure 4-16 Periodic Synchronization

Every second, each VSX switch synchronizes its learned MAC addresses with its VSX peer using ISLP (Figure 4-16). Each VSX switch also buffers and sends its new neighbor ARP/ND entries to the VSX peer every time its buffer is full (64 entries) or when it hits a timeout of 5 seconds. In a VSX scenario where all traffic from the core to the access layer flows through one VSX switch only, the other VSX switch still learns the necessary ARP/ND entries from its VSX peer. VSX has no functional impact on the VSX switches' normal datapath-based learning. If a VSX split occurs and the switches then rejoin together, the switches perform a bulk sync; after that, periodic syncs resume.

Inter-VRF Route Leaking (IVRL) leaks neighbor entries from a source VRF to a destination VRF. This process creates two neighbor entries, one learned through the datapath in the source VRF and one that was induced in the destination VRF. The VSX switches do *not* sync the induced entries either during the initial ARP sync or the periodic syncs. Instead, each switch learns the ARP entries in the source VRF (either through the normal datapath process or through the ARP sync). The local IVRL process then induces the entries into the destination VRF on each VSX switch individually.

Keep one caveat about ARP synching in mind: if an admin clears ARP entries or enables and disables a VLAN interface on one VSX switch, but not on the other, ARP entries will go out of sync between the two switches. The admin must perform such operations on *both* VSX switches so that both devices will re-learn entries and sync up.

Initial Sync and Linkup Delay

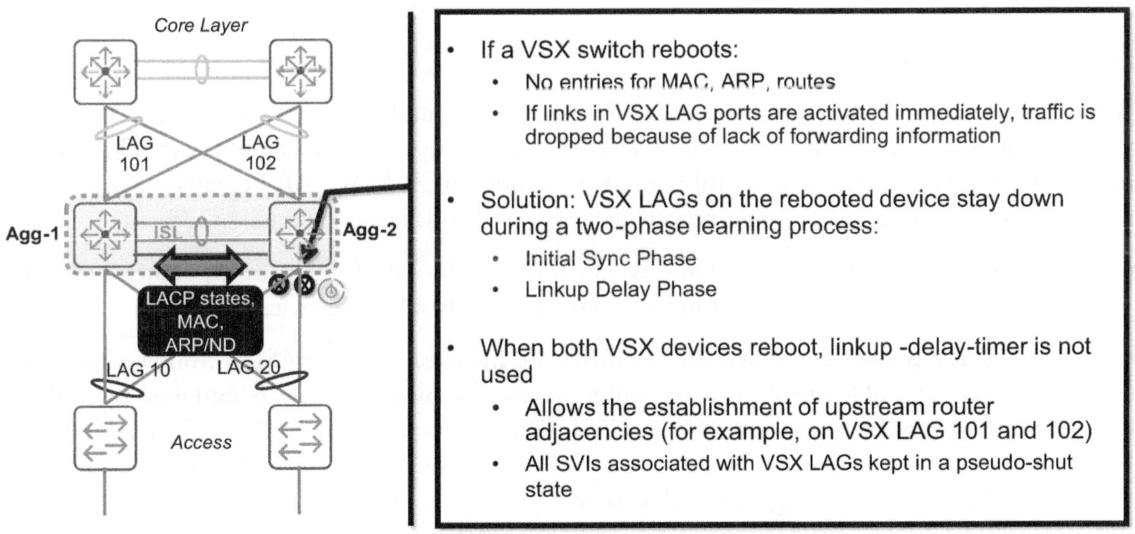

Figure 4-17 Initial Sync and Linkup Delay

Each VSX node synchronizes every second the following with its VSX peer through ISLP:

- Learned MAC addresses
- LACP states
- MSTP states

In a VSX scenario, if all traffic from core to access flows through one switch only, the other device will also learn about ARP/ND from its VSX peer. There is no functional impact to the normal datapath-based learning. A VSX split and rejoin scenario, such as periodic synchronization, resumes after the bulk synchronization. The IVRL-induced neighbor entries are not synced either through the initial ARP synchronization or periodic synchronization. The local IVRL will induce the learning on each side, triggered by either a local datapath ARP learned or the ongoing sync-based ARP learned in the source VRF (Figure 4-17).

Important

If you enter one or more of the following commands on one VSX switch, but not on the other VSX switch, the ARP entries on both switches will become unsynchronized.
- Clear ARP
- Interface VLAN
- Shutdown for a VLAN
- No shutdown for a VLAN

VSX Switch Reboot

After a VSX switch reboots, it has no entries for ARP, MAC, and routes. If downstream VSX LAG ports activate before all this information is relearned, traffic drops. To avoid a traffic drop, VSX LAGs on the rebooted switch stay down until the restoration of LACP, MAC, ARP databases, and MSTP states, if MSTP is used. The learning process for the VSX LAGs has two phases:

- **Initial sync phase**: The LACP states, MAC address table, ARP table, and potentially MSTP states download from the forwarding switch to the freshly rebooted switch.
- **Linkup-delay phase**: The downloaded entries are installed into the ASIC. Router adjacencies with core nodes and learned upstream routes are also established. You can configure the linkup-delay phase with the *linkup-delay-timer <DELAY-TIMER>* command. The default value is 180 seconds. Set the linkup-delay timer to the maximum value of 600 seconds for a network with many MAC addresses, a large ARP table, or a large routing table.

When both VSX switches reboot, the linkup-delay timer is not used because both switches have to relearn the LACP states, MAC address table, and ARP table. To get upstream router adjacencies established during the linkup delay, you have to exclude the upstream LAGs from the scope of the linkup delay. Run the *linkup-delay-timer exclude lag-list <LAG-LIST>* for identifying the LAGs for exclusion.

Initial Sync and Linkup-Delay Phases

When you reboot a VSX switch, during the startup it has no entries for MAC addresses, ARP, or routes. If the switch activates its downstream VSX LAG ports before it relearns all of this information, it will drop the traffic. To avoid a traffic drop, VSX LAGs on the rebooted device will stay down until the LACP, MSTP, MAC, and ARP databases are restored.

The learning process has two phases: Initial Sync and Linkup-Delay phase. The Initial Sync phase is the download phase, in which the rebooted node learns all the LACP, MAC, and ARP database entries from its VSX peer through ISLP. The Initial Sync timer is not configurable. It is the required time to download database information from the peer. The Linkup-Delay phase should last for as long as is required to install the downloaded entries to the ASIC, to establish router adjacencies with core devices, and to learn upstream routes. During this phase, links are forced down. The Linkup-Delay timer's default value is 180 seconds. Depending on the network size, ARP table size, and routing table size, the timer may need to be set to a higher value (the maximum value is 600 seconds).

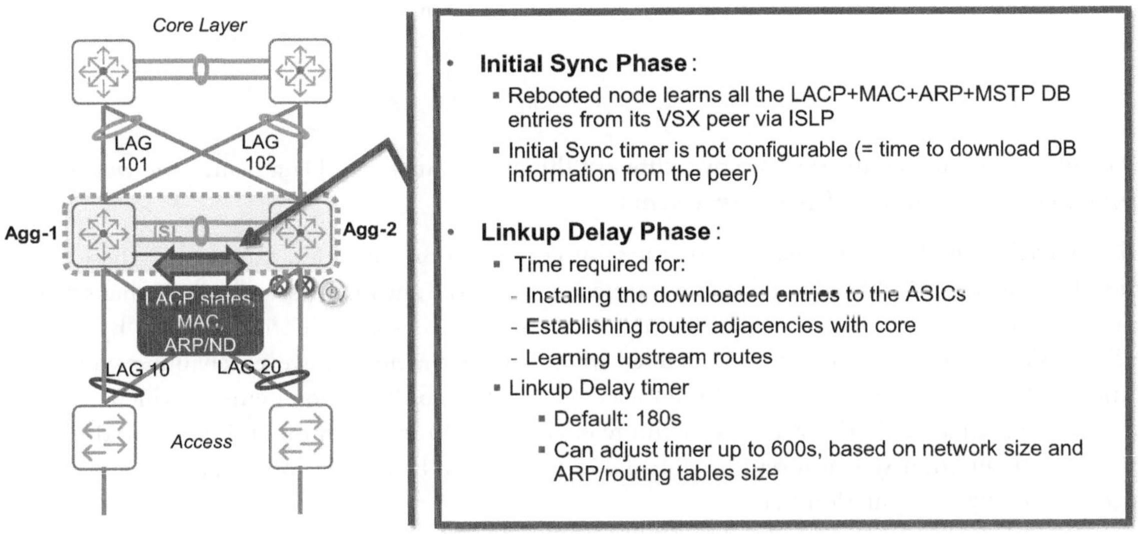

Figure 4-18 Initial Sync and Linkup-Delay Phases

If both VSX devices reboot, the linkup-delay timer is not used. In order to establish upstream router adjacencies during Linkup Delay, the upstream LAG (for example, LAG 101) has to be excluded from the scope of the Linkup Delay. Until linkup-delay timer expires, all SVIs associated with VSX LAGs are kept in a pseudo-shut state (Figure 4-18).

Configuration Synchronization: vsx-sync Attribute

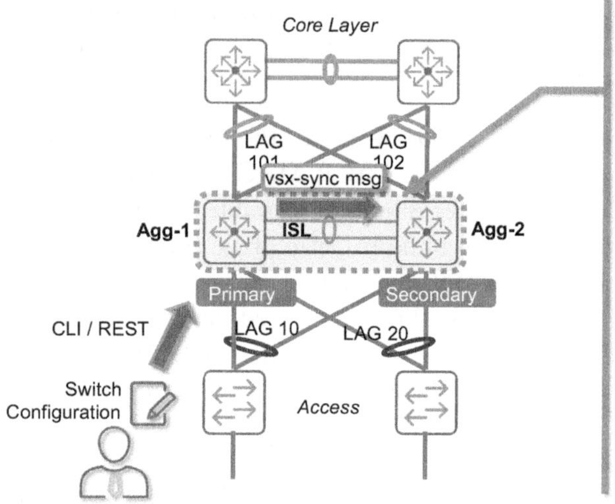

- **vsx-sync** set on primary switch only
- Most configurations same across the VSX pair
  - Exceptions: IP addresses, router IDs, hostnames, etc.
  - Global VSX configuration synchronization available
- These features support synchronization:
  - Individual features (**vsx-sync**): VLANs, ACLs, object-group Class, QoS, Policies, rate-limits, active-gateway, PBR
  - Group features (**vsx-sync**): aaa, copp_policy, dns, vsxlag_interfaces, qos_global, sflow, snmp, ssh, static_routes, time

Figure 4-19 Configuration Synchronization

Data plane sync and config sync are two different things (Figure 4-19). Data plane sync was covered earlier. Let us dive into config-sync (**vsx-sync**).

The two VSX switches should have nearly the same configuration with a few exceptions. These exceptions include host IP addresses on Layer 3 interfaces, router IDs, hostnames, and a few other settings. Configuration synchronization makes it simpler for admins to ensure identical configs. By default, VSX configuration synchronization is enabled when VSX is enabled. However, enabling synchronization globally has no effect until the admin selects individual configuration items on which to enable synchronization as well. The **vsx-sync** attribute enables synchronization on an item. An admin can disable configuration synchronization globally, in which case he can no longer apply the **vsx-sync** attribute to any configuration items.

You must set the **vsx-sync** attribute on the desired items from the VSX primary switch. The primary switch automatically pushes the configuration in question to the secondary switch. If the secondary switch is not available at the time of the primary device configuration, the configuration will be pushed to the secondary switch after the switch comes up. If a certain configuration synchronization operation fails, the CLI status commands will indicate the failure. The admin must manually fix the inconsistency. There is no fail-safe mechanism that disables VSX if configuration synchronization fails.

You are allowed to configure the **vsx-sync** option on secondary switch if config-sync is disabled or if the ISL is down.

The **vsx-synch** attribute is designed with this "opt-in" model due to customers' and partners' preference that they be able to control exactly which features are synched.

vsx-sync

1. Most of the VSX node configuration is the same across the switch pair (exceptions: IP addresses, Router IDs, hostname, and a few others).
2. With VSX enabled, the VSX configuration synchronization process is enabled by default. (However, nothing is synchronized yet.)
   Synchronization can be disabled globally.
3. **vsx-sync** is the CLI attribute that specifies what is to be synced.
4. In nominal condition, **vsx-sync** can be set only on the Primary switch. **vsx-sync** is allowed on Secondary if config-sync is disabled or if ISL link is down.
5. With VSX config-sync feature enabled, the configuration item, set with the **vsx-sync** attribute on the Primary switch, is automatically pushed to the Secondary switch.
6. If the Secondary switch is not available at the time of the Primary device configuration, the configuration will be pushed to the Secondary after it comes up.
7. If a certain configuration synchronization operation failed, it will be indicated in the CLI status commands and the user needs to manually fix the inconsistency.
8. There is no fail-safe mechanism that disables VSX if configuration synchronization fails. (not expected).
9. The following individual features support synchronization (**vsx-sync** tag):
   a. VLANs, ACLs, object-group
   b. Class, QoS, Policies, rate-limits
   c. active-gateway, PBR
10. The following group features support synchronization (**vsx-sync** tag):
    a. At vsx-sync level:aaa, copp_policy, dns, vsxlag_interfaces, qos_global, sflow, snmp, ssh, static_routes, time

---

Note

You can use the **vsx-sync** parameter from the CLI or NetEdit to ensure that the configurations are "synced" between the VSX peers.

Configuration Synchronization: Synchronization Behavior

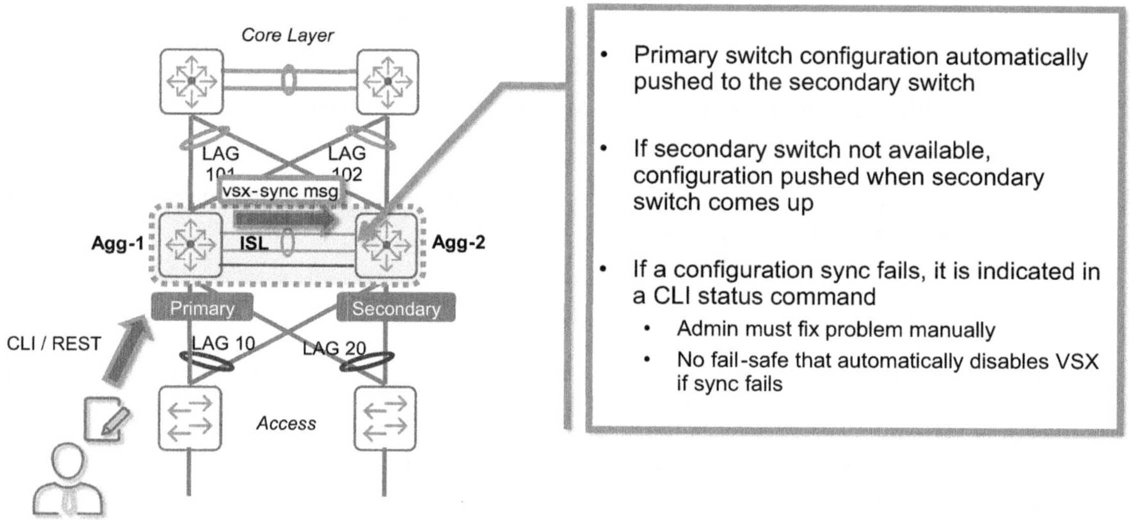

Figure 4-20 Configuration Synchronization: Synchronization Behavior

When the switches are configured for synchronization, the following behaviors, as shown in Figure 4-20, are in effect:

- Primary switch config automatically pushed to secondary switch
- If secondary switch not available, config pushed when secondary switch comes up
- If config sync fails, you will see it indicated in a CLI status command:
  - Admin must fix manually
  - No failsafe that disables VSX if sync fails

Configuration Overlap and Protection

–If a configuration element is set on the Secondary without being synced/pushed from the Primary:

– There is no problem and this is a valid scenario

–However, if on the Primary, the same configuration item is now vsx-synced:

– Primary **overrides** the configuration element on the Secondary that was set previously

–If **vsx-sync** command is removed from the configuration element on the Primary:

– The configuration item will stay on the Secondary (without the **vsx-sync** keyword)

Figure 4-21 Configuration Overlap and Protection

It is perfectly valid for an administrator to configure a setting manually on the secondary switch without that setting being synched from the primary switch. However, if **vsx-sync** is now enabled for this feature on the primary switch, the setting on the primary switch overrides the previous setting on the secondary switch (Figure 4-21). For example, you could add VLAN 10 on the secondary switch with description "employees." You then add VLAN 10 with no description on the primary switch and enable **vsx-sync**. The secondary switch now has VLAN 10, but with no description.

Firmware Upgrade

- Software versions on VSX switches can be mismatched
- vsx-syncd process:
  - Stops any synchronization attempt
  - Performs on-going check to determine if it can sync
  - Detects when peers are on same software version
  - Restarts on-going sync

Figure 4-22 Firmware Upgrade

During a firmware upgrade, software versions will temporarily mismatch on the VSX peers (Figure 4-22). Therefore, the vsx-syncd process, which is still running, stops any synchronization attempts. It then performs an ongoing check to determine if it can sync. Once both VSX peers are running the same firmware, this ongoing check sees that it can restore the synchronization. The vsx-syncd process then continues the ongoing sync. The database connection between the peers works if the firmware versions are the same.

With 10.2, VSX also supports graceful upgrade for routing features. When a member is about to be updated, it takes action such as withdrawing itself from route advertisements so traffic is shifted away from it during the upgrade process.

Troubleshooting Synchronization: vsx-peer Extension of show Commands

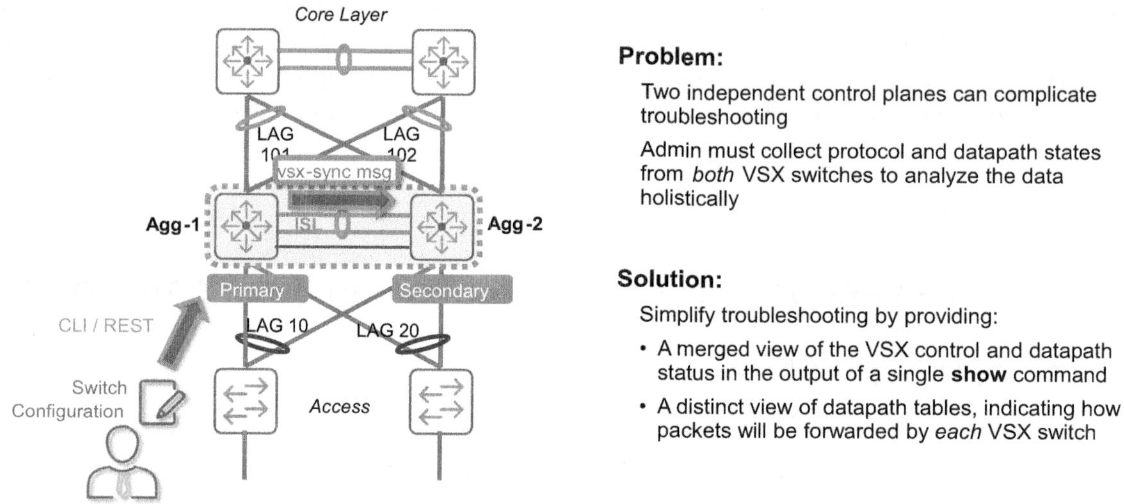

Figure 4-23 Troubleshooting Synchronization: vsx-peer Extension of show Commands

While independent control planes and management planes for the VSX switches help to provide greater availability, they can complicate troubleshooting. The network admin must collect protocol and datapath states from both VSX switches to analyze the issue holistically. To make troubleshooting easier, the AOS-CX CLI offers a **vsx-peer** option for many show commands. When an admin enters a show command with this option, the output merges data from both the local switch and its VSX peer in a single output, making it easier for admins to collect information and troubleshoot. The output also shows the distinct datapath tables on each switch, indicating how each switch will forward packets, which again helps admins to pinpoint issues (Figure 4-23).

The **vsx-peer** option for **show** commands is not available during a firmware upgrade process.

Traffic Forwarding

This section introduces how a VSX cluster processes and forwards traffic.

VSX LAG

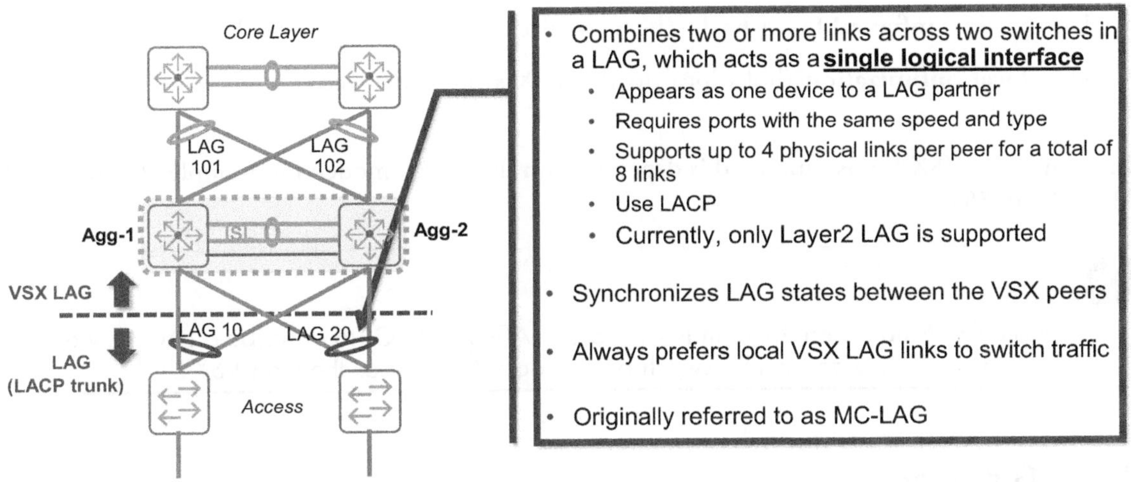

Figure 4-24 VSX LAG

A VSX LAG is a link-aggregation technique in which two or more links across two switches aggregate together to form a LAG (Figure 4-24). A LAG acts as a single logical interface. The two switches appear as a single peer ID to the partner device upstream or downstream that forms the LAG with the VSX pair. Ports must have the same speed. You cannot add one spare port (unused) that has lower speed than the current ports. The LAG can include up to four physical links per peer for eight links max per VSX LAG. As of the publication of this guide, VSX LAGs are Layer 2 only, and VSX LAGs must be LACP-based. A non-LACP or static VSX LAG is not supported.

The two switches in the VSX pair synchronize their LAG states using ISLP. Users can configure a lag-hash scheme, which dictates how the switches load-share traffic across the links in the LAG. (Note: The 8400 provides L4-based hashing, but the 8320 does not.) VSX LAGS are locally optimized, meaning if a switch with local links is in a LAG then it constrains the LAG hash-scheme to look at only local links, and it will only forward traffic over the ISL for transmission on the peer links in the LAG if local links of a VSX LAG are down.

- Combines two or more links across **two** switches in a LAG, which acts as a **single logical interface**.
- Presents the two VSX switches as a **single peer ID** to the partner device on the other side of the VSX LAG.
- Requires ports with the **same speed** (no unused spares with lower speeds).
- Supports up to 4 physical links per peer for **eight (8) links max per VSX LAG**.
- Currently is **Layer 2 only**.

- Is always **LACP-based**.
- Uses ISLP to **synchronize LAG states** between the VSX peers.
- Uses a **user-configurable lag-hash** scheme to load-share traffic across the LAG links.
- Uses **local optimization** (links local to the VSX switch that needs to forward traffic always preferred).

The number of VSX LAGs supported is dependent on the switch model: for example, 255 on 8400, 53 on 8320, 55 on 8325.

Note

Originally, Aruba used the term multi-chassis LAG (MC-LAG) to describe a LAG between an external device and a VSX switch pair. Today, Aruba uses the term *VSX LAG*.

Active-Gateway

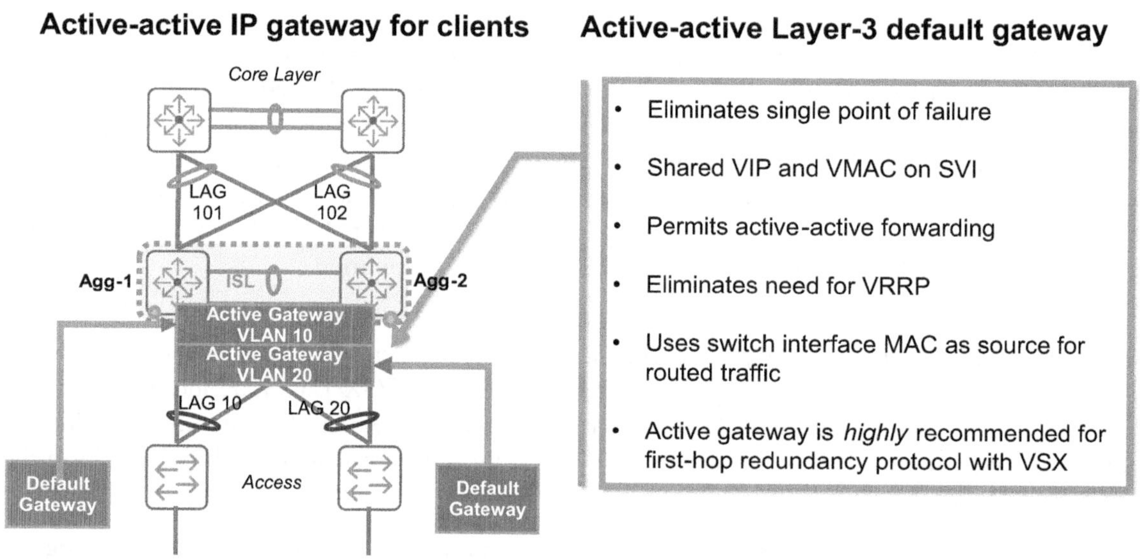

Figure 4-25 Active-Gateway

Active-gateway is a first-hop redundancy protocol that eliminates a single point of failure for default gateway services on an access network. The active-gateway feature improves the reliability and performance of the host network by enabling a virtual router to act as the default gateway for that network (Figure 4-25).

To configure this feature, you simply configure with a shared virtual IP address (VIP) and a shared virtual MAC address (VMAC) on an SVI on both VSX switches. The VIP/VMAC serves as the default gateway for each access VLAN. Which peer in the VSX pair receives a particular piece of traffic from an access VLAN depends on which link in the LAG the downstream access switch's LAG has selected. Whichever peer receives the traffic routes it across to the Layer 3 domain.

When you use active-gateway on a VLAN, the VLAN has no need for VRRP; the features are mutually exclusive. As with VRRP, routed traffic from the VSX peer is sourced from the switch interface MAC, not the VMAC address. Every three minutes (non-configurable), each active-gateway broadcasts a hello packet from the VMAC to avoid VMAC aging on the access switches. The hello from both peers transmits on the same VSX LAG, so no issues occur with the same MAC address appear on different ports. The hello is a non-IP Ethernet packet using HP EtherType, 080009 Hewlett-Packard, and a destination reserved multicast address.

The VSX pair supports up to 16 different VMACs, which are not shareable between IPv4 and IPv6. For example, the pair could use eight VMACs for IPv4 simultaneously with eight VMACs for IPv6.

You should understand some key differences between VRRP and the active-gateway feature. VRRP requires multiple configuration options, including the VRID on the VLAN, the roles on each VRID, the virtual IP address on each VRID, the advertisement timer configurations, and so on. Active-gateway only requires a single line of configuration per VLAN interface: the configuration of the virtual IP/MAC. VRRP and active-gateway also differ in terms of how they forward traffic. VRRP uses an active-standby data plane with only the VRRP master routing traffic. With active-gateway, both devices forward traffic.

1. Eliminates single point of failure for default gateway services
2. Configured by setting a shared virtual IP address (VIP) and a shared virtual MAC address (VMAC) on a SVI on both switches
    - VIP/VMAC = Default gateway for the access VLAN
3. Permits active-active forwarding
    - VSX LAG hash determines which VSX switch receives particular traffic from access layer
    - Whichever VSX switch receives traffic routes it
4. Eliminates need for VRRP
5. Uses switch interface MAC (not VMAC) as source for routed traffic
    - Periodic broadcast hello packet ensures access switches learn VMAC and do not age it out
6. AOS-CX 10.01 limitation:
    - 512 IPv4 + 512 IPv6 active-gateways
    - 16 different VMACs per VSX pair, not shareable between IPv4 and IPv6
    - Example: 8 VMACs for IPv4 simultaneously with max 8 VMACs for IPv6.

7. Key differences between VRRP and active-gateway:

- *Configuration*:

  VRRP: VRIDs configuration per VLAN, roles per VRID, VRRP advertisement timer configuration, etcetera.

  Active-gateway: Single line configuration; Virtual IP/MAC set on the SVI

- *Data plane*:

  VRRP: Active-standby (only VRRP Master routes traffic)

  Active-gateway: Both devices route and forward traffic.

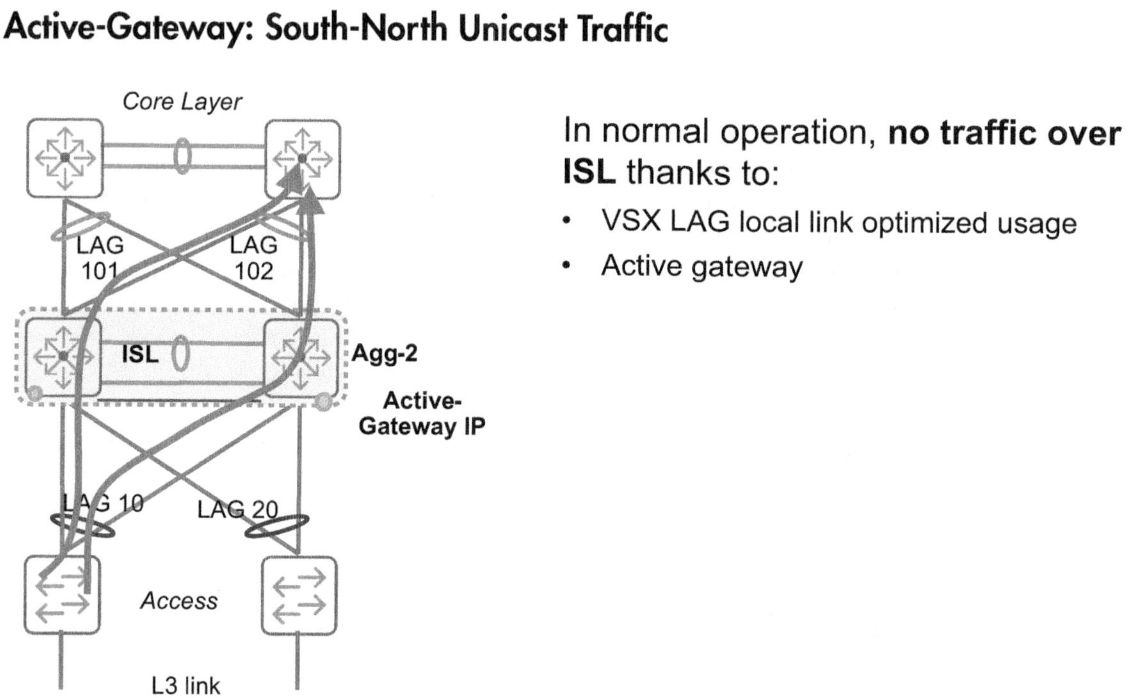

Figure 4-26 Active-Gateway: South-North Unicast Traffic

As long as you configure VSX LAGs with links on each peer, the normal operation unicast traffic sent between the access layer and the core (south-north) uses all access-to-aggregation links and does *not* flow over the ISL. From a Layer 2 perspective, VSX LAGs span two switches and operate in active-active mode. Traffic between the access layer and aggregation layer switches can be forwarded to any of the active links. There are no loops and no need for spanning tree protocol or blocked ports (Figure 4-26).

From a datapath perspective, local link optimized usage ensures that when a VSX switch receives traffic, it always uses its local LAG links to forward the traffic to its destination. The VSX switch only uses the ISL link if the local LAG links are down. An active-gateway ensures that the first VSX switch that receives traffic from the access layer can route the traffic across to the Layer 3 domain.

VSX LAG and Upstream Unicast Routing

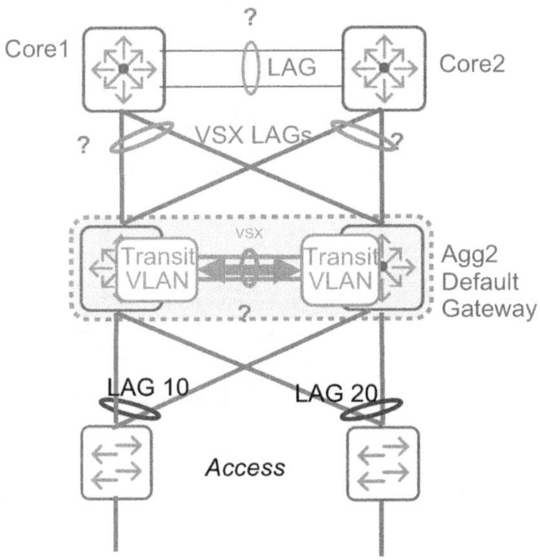

- Constraints?
  - L2 or L3 links with upstream core nodes?
  - Static, OSPF, BGP?
  - Single VRF / Multiple VRF?
  - Sizing/limitations?
  - Best practice for high availability
- Both VSX switches run **independent** control planes
  - Separate OSPF/BGP processes
  - Unique router IDs
- In the data path, they function as a single router and support **active-active forwarding**

Figure 4-27 VSX LAG and Upstream Unicast Routing

You will now turn your attention to how the VSX pair operates on the connections to the upstream core switches, which are generally routed connections. Remember that each VSX peer runs an independent control plane with its own OSPF or BGP processes. Therefore, each VSX peer appears as a different router with its own router ID to the core switches. However, as far as the data path is concerned, the VSX peers function as a single router and support active-active forwarding. This is possible because a core switch that uses ECMP to learn routes to the subnets behind the VSX pair through *both* VSX peers and because the VSX pair supports a feature called "active forwarding," about which you will learn more later. Also remember that VSX LAGs can only operate at Layer 2 (Figure 4-27).

Keeping these principles in mind, you can consider the options that you have for designing the upstream VSX LAGs and unicast routing. You could choose to connect with routed ports or Layer 2 ports associated with Layer 3 VLAN interfaces. Or you can use Layer 2 VSX LAGs, which are associated with Layer 3 VLAN interfaces. For routing, you could choose static routing, OSPF, or BGP. You could use a single VRF or multiple VRFs, depending on the requirements of the scenario. Your choices will be informed by sizing limitations and by best practices for high availability.

Upstream Connectivity: Routed Only Port (ROP)

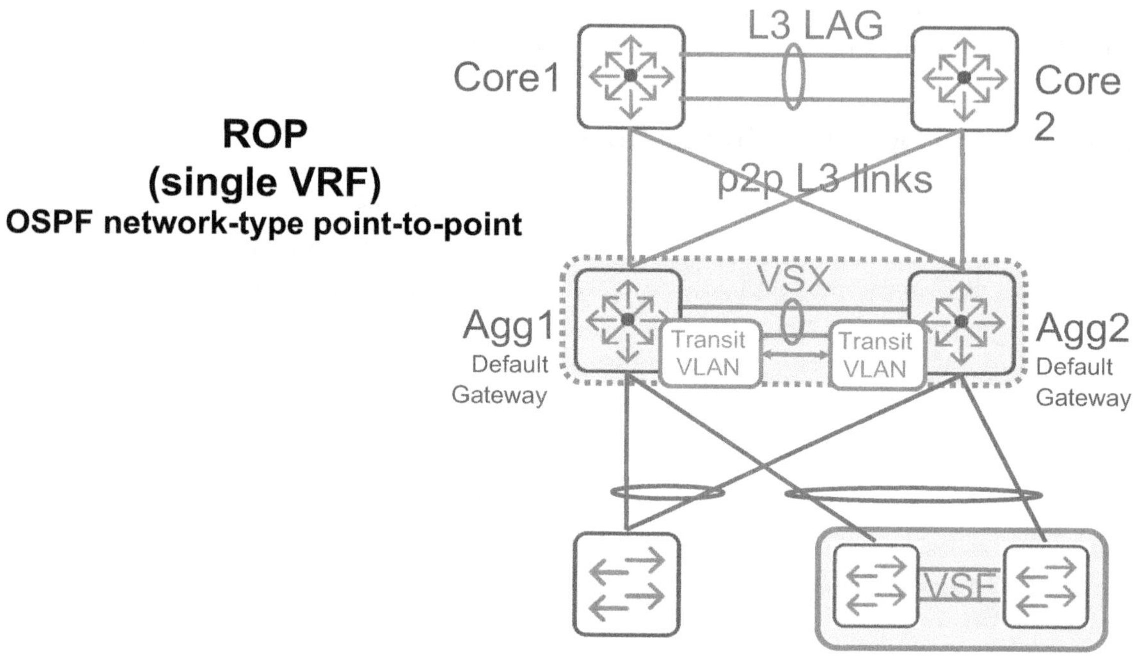

Figure 4-28 Upstream Connectivity: Routed Only Port (ROP)

There are several options for links between the aggregation VSX pair and the core: one involves a single VRF implementation while the other options involve multiple VRFs.

The first option uses ROPs. It could also use routed LAGs, but those routed LAGs would only have links on the local switch; they cannot be multi-chassis. Each VSX switch has its own routed link or LAG to each core switch, and each of these four links is its own /30 or /31 subnet. In OSPF, this would be a point-to-point network. This simple VLAN-free configuration is best suited for a network that runs on a single VRF domain. If the network had multiple VRFs, each VRF would need its own ROP, which is less feasible (Figure 4-28).

The other options are beyond the scope of this guide.

VSX and Upstream Routing

The following chart summarizes the supported scenarios for the upstream connections between a VSX pair and the core. When you have a single VRF, ROPs provide the simplest option. However, Layer 2 ports associated with dedicated SVIs, as well as Layer 2 VSX LAGs associated with dedicated SVIs, work as well.

All of these options work with static routing, OSPF, or BGP (Figure 4-29).

	Single VRF		
	L3 port (ROP)	L2 port (SVI)	VSX LAG (SVI)
Static	Yes (simplest)	yes	yes
OSPF	Yes (simplest)	yes	yes
BGP	Yes (simplest)	yes	yes

Figure 4-29 VSX and Upstream Routing

Split-Brain Condition

This section introduces how a pair of VSX switches determine how an ISL link failure is detected and how the switches deal with the issue, given that they have the same virtual IP and MAC addresses for data forwarding processes.

Split-Brain Scenario

- VSX LAGs on secondary are disabled to prevent "split-brain"
- When ISL is restored, there is no reboot of secondary node
- Secondary VSX LAGs are brought up after linkup-delay timer

	Keepalive-Established	Keepalive-Init
ISL "In-Sync"	Forwarding OK Protection OK	Forwarding OK Protection NO
ISL "Out-of-Sync"	STATE • ISL is down • Peer is UP ISSUE • VSX tables will get out of sync ACTION • On secondary: stop forwarding over VSX-LAGs	STATE • Peer is DOWN ISSUE • Forwarding at 50% capacity ACTION • Keep forwarding

Figure 4-30 Split-Brain Scenario

Figure 4-30 shows a situation in which the ISL between the two VSX switches is down. Both switches are still active, but the switches cannot exchange information, which causes the switches to become out of sync. This situation is called a split brain, and it occurs if the keepalive function is not enabled. The keepalive function prevents split-brain issues by providing an out-of-band mechanism to detect if the link between the VSX switch is down or if the VSX switches are not working. The keepalive functionality brings down the link between Agg2 and Access Switches. The traffic is forced to go from access switches to Agg-1 only.

The table shows what happens with various ISL and keepalive statuses on the VSX pair. As long as the ISL is up and the peers are in sync, the VSX pair can forward traffic normally. If the keepalive connection is established, the system is protected from a split-brain situation. If the keepalive connection is not established, but the ISL is working correctly, the VSX pair can forward traffic normally, but the system is at risk. If the ISL goes down and the peers are out of sync, but the keepalive is established, the peers realize that the other peer is still up. They know that they are at risk of becoming out of sync, so the secondary switch shuts down its VSX LAGs. If the ISL goes down and the keepalive connection cannot establish, the switch assumes that its peer is down and that the system is functional but forwarding at 50% capacity. It keeps forwarding even if it is the secondary peer. It is important that you form the keepalive connection correctly so that this assumption is correct.

ISL Failure: SVI Impact

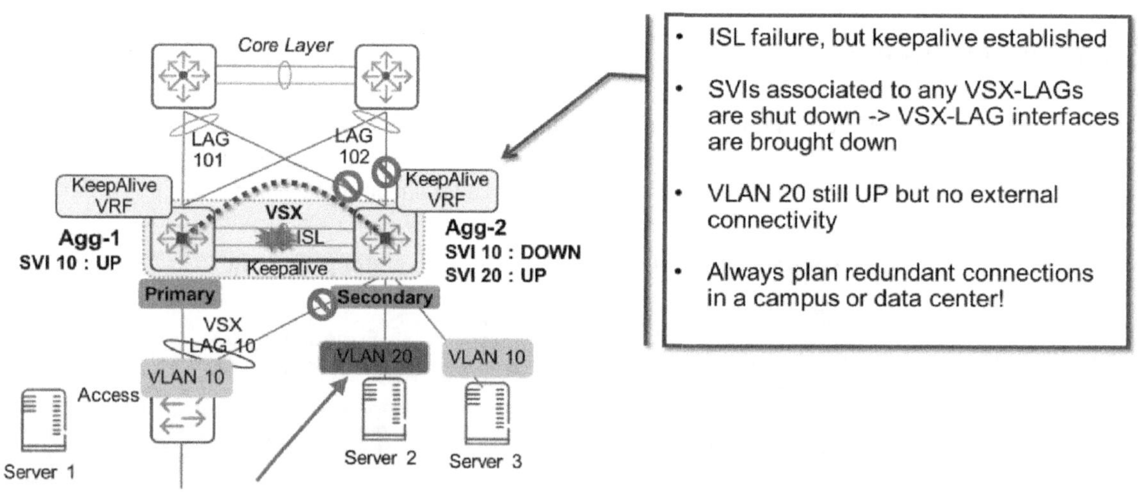

Figure 4-31 ISL Failure: SVI Impact

An ISL cut has no effect on the state (up/down) of VLAN and associated SVI that are not part of any VSX LAG but part of at least one orphan port (beside the ISL LAG, which is not a VSX LAG) (Figure 4-31).

During ISL Cut (Before Initial Sync)

As long as the secondary VSX node has a port that is a member of a VSX LAG, the associated SVI of the VLAN—transported by said VSX LAG—has the VSX secondary node turned to OFF/SHUT, whether or not there are orphan port(s) carrying that given VLAN.

During Linkup-Delay Timer (After Initial Sync)

As long as the secondary VSX node has a port that is a member of a VSX LAG, the associated SVI of the VLAN—transported by said VSX LAG—is kept OFF/SHUT on the VSX secondary node, whether there is an orphan port(s) carrying that given VLAN or not. The associated SVI of the VLAN transported by a VSX LAG restores ON/UP on the VSX secondary node, only if the following conditions are met:

- You have used the command **linkup-delay timer exclude lag** to exclude the said VSX LAG, and...
- The VSX LAG is not part of the exclusion set allowed for a given VLAN.

In the topology above, after an ISL failure, ports and SVI associated to a VSX LAG automatically turned off (shutdown), ports and SVIs not related to and VSX LAG still operating. In this case, server 2 and VLAN 20 are still operating, but since there are no external uplinks and routes, server 2 is isolated. The server's 3 port remains UP, but VLAN 10 SVI shutdown due to ISL failure, as a best practice, always plan for redundant connections at the data center.

Lab 4: Configuring VSX

Overview

In this lab activity, VSX will be configured between the two core switches in the lab setup.VSX has similar benefits as VSF; however, VSX also offers better high availability required in core and data center environments. VSX binds two ArubaOS-CX switches of the same model type to operate as one device for Layer 2. VSX also operates as independent nodes for Layer 3.

Objectives

- Configure VSX
- Understand the VSX configuration synchronization feature
- Configure VSX to peer devices using VSX LAG
- Understand and configure VSX Active-Gateway (first hop redundancy)

- Configure DHCP relay
- Configure and understand split-system protection

Important

The checkpoint of this lab activity will be used as the base configuration for many other lab activities. Make sure to verify your steps and pay attention on which device you are working on as you perform the lab.

Before beginning the lab, load the following checkpoint on each of the four switches (Figure 4-32) (Access1, Access2, Core1, and Core2): **icx-lab02-netedit**.

Task 1: VSX Basic Setup

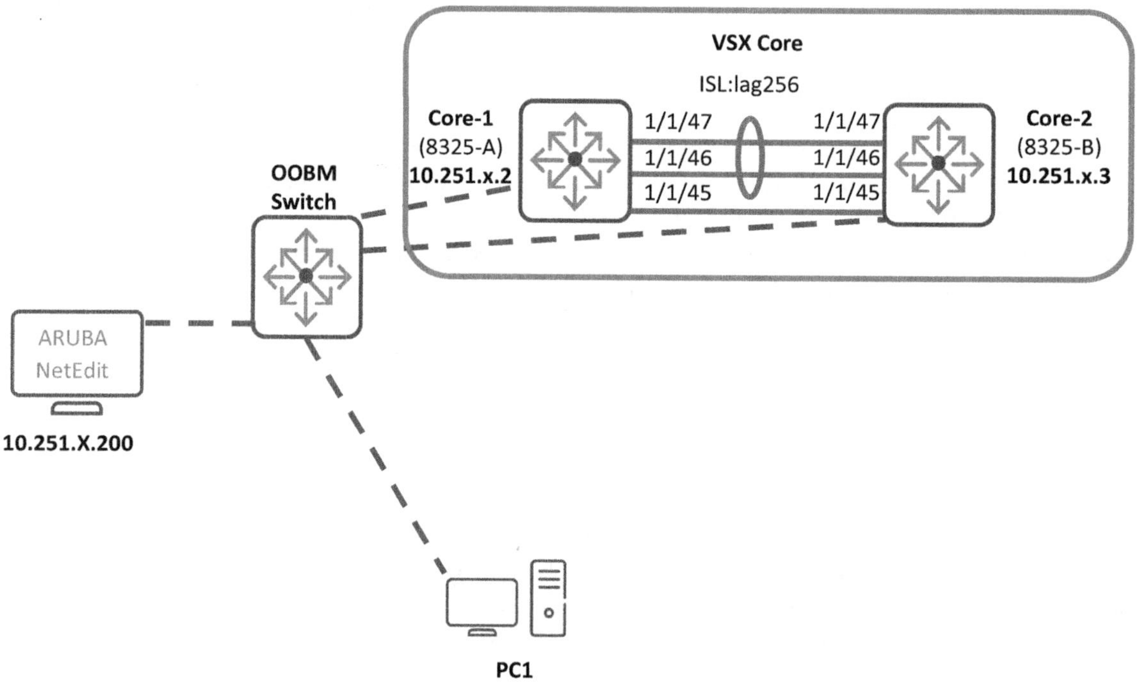

Figure 4-32 Task 1: VSX Basic Setup

Objectives

- Configure a link aggregation that will be used as the Inter Switch Link (ISL)
- Configure the keepalive link
- Set up the ISL link

- Configure the VSX roles
- Verify the status of the VSX cluster

Steps

1. Open a terminal session to Core1 and enter Configuration mode. Take note of the current version.

```
ICX-Tx-Core1(config)# show version
```

2. Review the LAG256 to Core2. This LAG was defined in the NetEdit lab activity.Some best practice guidelines include:
   - Use the last LAG number supported by the switch. In this case, number 256.
   - Allow all the VLANs on the ISL.
   - Enable LACP, use the standard LACP timers (30 seconds).

```
ICX-Tx-Core1# show running-config interface lag256
interface lag 256
   no shutdown
   no routing
vlan trunk native 1
vlan trunk allowed all
lacp mode active
   exit
```

3. Enable support for jumbo frames on the ISL ports. This will be required when using dynamic segmentation.

```
ICX-Tx-Core1# configure terminal
ICX-Tx-Core1(config)# interface 1/1/46-1/1/47
ICX-Tx-Core1(config-if-<1/1/46-1/1/47>)# mtu 9198
ICX-Tx-Core1(config-if-<1/1/46-1/1/47>)# exit
```

4. Review the physical ports of the LAG256 and verify jumbo frame support is enabled.

```
ICX-Tx-Core1(config)# show run int 1/1/46
interface 1/1/46
  no shutdown
  mtu 9198
  lag 256
  exit
```

```
ICX-Tx-Core1(config)# show run int 1/1/47
interface 1/1/47
  no shutdown
  mtu 9198
  lag 256
  exit
```

5. Open a console to Core2 and enter Configuration mode. Check the version; make sure this is the same version as Core1.

```
ICX-Tx-Core2(config)# show version
```

6. Enable jumbo frame support on the ISL ports 1/1/46 and 1/1/47.

```
ICX-Tx-Core2# configure terminal
ICX-Tx-Core2(config)# interface 1/1/46-1/1/47
ICX-Tx-Core2(config-if-<1/1/46-1/1/47>)# mtu 9198
ICX-Tx-Core2(config-if-<1/1/46-1/1/47>)# exit
```

7. On Core1, review the status of the LAG between the Core1 and Core2 switches.

```
ICX-Tx-Core1(config)# show lacp interfaces
State abbreviations :
A - Active        P - Passive       F - Aggregable I - Individual
S - Short-timeout L - Long-timeout N - InSync     O - OutofSync
C - Collecting    D - Distributing
X - State m/c expired               E - Default neighbor state

Actor details of all interfaces:
------------------------------------------------------------------------------
IntfAggrPort  Port  State   System-ID          System Aggr Forwarding
      Name        Id    PriPriKey  State
------------------------------------------------------------------------------
1/1/46  lag256     47    1      ALFNCD  90:20:c2:bc:17:00 65534  256  up
1/1/47  lag256     48    1      ALFNCD  90:20:c2:bc:17:00 65534  256  up

Partner details of all interfaces:
------------------------------------------------------------------------------
IntfAggrPort  Port  State   System-ID          System Aggr
      Name        Id    PriPri    Key
------------------------------------------------------------------------------
1/1/46  lag256     47    1      ALFNCD  90:20:c2:bc:97:00 65534  256
1/1/47  lag256     48    1      ALFNCD  90:20:c2:bc:97:00 65534  256
```

Review the VSX Keepalive Link

The keepalive link is used to handle a split-brain scenario. This means that all the links between the VSX members are down, while both switches are still up. VSX will make an IP connectivity check with its peer. Since this IP check has nothing to do with the rest of the IP network, it is recommended to put this IP link in a dedicated VRF, a separate routing table.

1. On Core1, verify the connectivity to Core2 for this VRF. This VRF and IP have been defined in the NetEdit lab activity.

```
ICX-Tx-Core1(config)# do ping 192.168.0.1 vrf KA
PING 192.168.0.1 (192.168.0.1) 100(128) bytes of data.
108 bytes from 192.168.0.1: icmp_seq=1 ttl=64 time=0.202 ms
108 bytes from 192.168.0.1: icmp_seq=2 ttl=64 time=0.171 ms
108 bytes from 192.168.0.1: icmp_seq=3 ttl=64 time=0.175 ms
108 bytes from 192.168.0.1: icmp_seq=4 ttl=64 time=0.157 ms
108 bytes from 192.168.0.1: icmp_seq=5 ttl=64 time=0.226 ms
--- 192.168.0.1 ping statistics ---
5 packets transmitted, 5 received, 0% packet loss, time 4099ms
rtt min/avg/max/mdev = 0.157/0.186/0.226/0.026 ms
ICX-Tx-Core1(config)#
```

Note

The /31 subnet mask can be used on the AOS-CX devices on point-to-point connections that only have 2 hosts. Thanks to the /31 support, there is no waste of the network and broadcast addresses of the subnet.

Configure the VSX roles

Some best practice guidelines:

- On the VSX primary switch, set the system-mac manually. This will ensure that in case this switch needs to be replaced due to hardware failure, the new switch can be configured with the same system-mac as the original switch. By default, the hardware system MAC is used, which would result in a different system MAC address after a hardware change.
- Use the default values for the ISL link timers.
- Make sure the role is meaningful based on the hostname. For example, the primary role on the system with hostname core1, the secondary role on the system with hostname core2.
- Enable the VSX-global sync. This will keep many parts of the switch configuration automatically synchronized between the switches.

1. On Core1, configure the following. Replace xx with your table # (Table 1 use '01', Table 12 use '12').

```
ICX-Tx-Core1(config)# vsx
ICX-Tx-Core1(config-vsx)# system-mac 02:01:00:00:xx:00
ICX-Tx-Core1(config-vsx)# inter-switch-link lag 256
ICX-Tx-Core1(config-vsx)# role primary
ICX-Tx-Core1(config-vsx)# vsx-sync vsx-global
ICX-Tx-Core1(config-vsx)# exit
```

2. On Core2, configure the following:

```
ICX-Tx-Core2(config)# vsx
ICX-Tx-Core2(config-vsx)# inter-switch-link lag 256
ICX-Tx-Core2(config-vsx)# role secondary
ICX-Tx-Core2(config-vsx)# exit
```

3. On Core1, now review the VSX status.

```
ICX-Tx-Core1(config)# show vsx status
VSX Operational State
---------------------
  ISL channel               :  In-Sync
  ISL mgmt channel          :  operational
  Config Sync Status        :  in-sync
  NAE                       : peer_reachable
  HTTPS Server              : peer_reachable

Attribute           Local               Peer
------------        --------            --------
ISL link            lag256              lag256
ISL version         2                   2
System MAC          02:01:00:00:xx:00   02:01:00:00:xx:00
Platform            8325                8325
Software Version    GL.10.04.0030       GL.10.04.0030
Device Role         primary             secondary

ICX-Tx-Core1(config)#
```

4. Compare the running configuration between Core1 and Core2. Notice that Core2 has received the '**vsx-sync**' command automatically, as well as the 'system-mac' command.

```
ICX-Tx-Core1(config)# show running-config | begin 5 vsx
vsx
    system-mac 02:01:00:00:xx:00
    inter-switch-link lag 256
    role primary
vsx-sync vsx-global
ipdns server-address 10.254.1.21 vrfmgmt
https-server rest access-mode read-write
https-server vrfmgmt
ICX-Tx-Core1(config)#
```

```
ICX-Tx-Core2(config)# show running-config | begin 5 vsx
vsx
system-mac 02:01:00:00:xx:00
    inter-switch-link lag 256
    role secondary
vsx-sync vsx-global
ipdns server-address 10.254.1.21 vrfmgmt
https-server rest access-mode read-write
https-server vrfmgmt
ICX-Tx-Core2(config)#
```

5. On Core1, review the VSX section of the running configuration.

```
ICX-Tx-Core1(config)# show running-config vsx
vsx
    system-mac 02:01:00:00:xx:00
    inter-switch-link lag 256
    role primary
interface lag 256
   no shutdown
   no routing
vlan trunk native 1 tag
vlan trunk allowed all
lacp mode active
interface 1/1/46
   no shutdown
   lag 256
interface 1/1/47
   no shutdown
   lag 256
```

Note

Notice in the above output that the interface that is used for the ISL will automatically set the native VLAN to 'native tagged' state. This means that there is no untagged traffic passing on the ISL.One of the benefits of having the native VLAN tagged is that any 802.1p CoS value would be preserved on the ISL.

6. Review the running configuration on Core2.

```
ICX-Tx-Core2(config)# show running-config vsx
vsx
    system-mac 02:01:00:00:xx:00
    inter-switch-link lag 256
    role secondary
interface lag 256
   no shutdown
   no routing
vlan trunk native 1 tag
vlan trunk allowed all
lacp mode active
interface 1/1/47
   no shutdown
   lag 256
interface 1/1/46
   no shutdown
   lag 256
```

7. Next, review the configuration that is synchronized between the two core switches.

```
ICX-Tx-Core1(config)# show running-config vsx-sync
Current vsx-sync configuration:
!
!Version ArubaOS-CX GL.10.04.0030
!export-password: default
vsx
    system-mac 02:01:00:00:xx:00
vsx-sync vsx-global
```

```
ICX-Tx-Core2(config)# show running-config vsx-sync
Current vsx-sync configuration:
!
!Version ArubaOS-CX GL.10.04.0030
!export-password: default
vsx
    system-mac 02:01:00:00:xx:00
vsx-sync vsx-global
ICX-Tx-Core2(config)#
```

Enable the Keepalive Link

Enable VSX with the keepalive link. This is the detection of split brain, in case all the links of the ISL would be down. The split brain will be tested in a later task.

1. Configure the keepalive link; make sure to check the source and destination IP.

```
ICX-Tx-Core1(config)# vsx
ICX-Tx-Core1(config-vsx)# keepalive peer 192.168.0.1 source 192.168.0.0
vrf KA
ICX-Tx-Core1(config-vsx)# exit
```

2. Set the keepalive link; make sure to inverse the source and destination IP.

```
ICX-Tx-Core2(config)# vsx
ICX-Tx-Core2(config-vsx)# keepalive peer 192.168.0.0 source 192.168.0.1
vrf KA
ICX-Tx-Core2(config-vsx)# exit
```

3. On the core1, verify the VSX status.

```
ICX-Tx-Core1(config)# show vsx brief
ISL State                              : In Sync
Device State                           : Peer-Established
Keepalive State                        :Keepalive-Init
Device Role                            : primary
Number of Multi-chassis LAG interfaces : 0
ICX-Tx-Core1(config)#
```

Note

The above output was taken right after enabling the Keepalive link, showing the Keepalive State as 'Keepalive-init'. A few seconds later, the state will transition to 'Keepalive-Established', so you may see that state already in your output.

4. Review the same output on the console of Core2.

```
ICX-Tx-Core2(config)# show vsx brief
ISL State                              : In-Sync
Device State                           : Peer-Established
Keepalive State                        : Keepalive-Established
Device Role                            : secondary
Number of Multi-chassis LAG interfaces : 0
ICX-Tx-Core2(config)#
```

5. When an administrator is connected to Core1, they may be needed to review some command output on the VSX peer device (Core2). Instead of having to connect to the peer device, many commands have the 'vsx-peer' command option. This indicates to the CLI that the command should be executed on the peer device, so the output of the command comes effectively from the peer device, but there is no need to log in to the peer device.

6. On the Core1, run the same command, but add the 'vsx-peer' option. Compare this output with the previous output that was shown on the console of the Core2 device. The command output should be the same.

```
ICX-Tx-Core1(config)# show vsx brief vsx-peer
ISL State                              : In-Sync
Device State                           : Peer-Established
Keepalive State                        : Keepalive-Established
Device Role                            :secondary
Number of Multi-chassis LAG interfaces : 0
```

7. On Core1, test this feature again with the 'show lldp neighbor 1/1/46' command. When the command is executed using vsx-peer, the output will come from Core2, so Core1 will be listed as an LLDP peer.

```
show lldp neighbor-info 1/1/46
show lldp neighbor-info 1/1/46vsx-peer
```

8. On Core1, verify that the keepalive link is properly connected.

```
ICX-Tx-Core1(config)# show vsx status keepalive
Keepalive State            : Keepalive-Established
Last Established           : Mon Dec 23 16:15:34 2019
Last Failed                : Mon Dec 23 16:13:27 2019
Peer System Id             : 02:01:00:00:xx:00
Peer Device Role           :secondary

Keepalive Counters
Keepalive Packets Tx       : 385
Keepalive Packets Rx       : 255
Keepalive Timeouts         : 0
Keepalive Packets Dropped  : 0
ICX-Tx-Core1(config)#
```

9. On Core1, execute the same command for the VSX peer (Core2). Note the Peer device role and the counters in the 2 command outputs.

```
ICX-Tx-Core1(config)# show vsx status keepalive vsx-peer
Keepalive State           : Keepalive-Established
Last Established          : Mon Dec 23 16:16:16 2019
Last Failed               :
Peer System Id            : 02:01:00:00:xx:00
Peer Device Role          :primary

Keepalive Counters
Keepalive Packets Tx      : 360
Keepalive Packets Rx      : 360
Keepalive Timeouts        : 0
Keepalive Packets Dropped : 0
```

Task 2: VSX Configuration Synchronization

Objectives

- Review default configuration synchronization behavior on both VSX switches
- Enable configuration synchronization
- Verify VSX operation
- Review out of sync status

Steps

In these steps, the current status of the configuration sync will be reviewed. Only a limited set of configurations ('vsx-global sync') are synchronized between the VSX peers at this point. This introduces potential configuration risks, since an administrator should remember to define a VLAN (or most other settings) on **both** VSX peers. In the next steps, this default behavior will be demonstrated. Afterward, the VSX configuration synchronization feature will be used to automatically synchronize the configuration between the VSX peers.

In the configuration, there are:

- **Global** configuration settings: global ACL, time configuration, etc. Synchronization of these settings can be enabled under the VSX global context.
- **Context** configuration settings: VLANs Synchronization of these settings must be enabled per context.

The lab will introduce a global and a context configuration change.

1. On the Core1, verify that the config sync process is active.

```
ICX-Tx-Core1(config)# show vsx status config-sync
Admin state                  : Enabled
Operational State            : Operational
Error State                  : None
Recommended remediation : N/A
Current time                 : Mon Dec 23 16:28:42 2019
Last sync time               : Sun Dec 22 21:21:10 2019
ICX-Tx-Core1(config)#
```

Global Configuration Change

As an example, a new admin user called 'demo' will be defined on the Core1. Since there is no configuration synchronization at this point, the user will not exist on Core2.The admin users are part of the **'aaa'** vsx-sync feature, that will be enabled in the next section.

1. On Core1, define a new admin user.

```
ICX-Tx-Core1(config)# user demo group administrators password plaintextdemo
```

2. Review the running configuration.

```
ICX-Tx-Core1(config)# show running-config | include user
user admin group administrators password ciphertext
AQBapV8rLxVdvc31eF2hwggG6NdJ/p/bqXrRlSsdibXBcJ5SYgAAAI9vpWqHUNb5frqUOqkMd
razRA-
VY0tNdl36lkRQVKggG5ldaN9iEzCWFKQz1b7fMpNMt8xX0nal2et4T8N1aXuXnvJFKH+X1BPs
7BSiKboKXGiEW4/sy/Sv6EGz5yshSNuoB
user demo group administrators password ciphertext
AQBapazfG0p4r497EJ3fcdfaSHIeRNhPeHHvMVYX9r8YpjulYgAAAHGn29l4MqabnQyJ0tQpa
nbi+eao6jzb/tfgRDXefU5s+4U5qDInY5fTjoGUNSxQjTHNeUpgWQ9cbCCXxirTU9eKfbWbU3
jS45B9GGwlM5nySfAopiFDLebNg+S3yEW8o2fy
ICX-Tx-Core1(config)#
```

3. Review the running configuration of the vsx-peer (**Core2**), the user demo should not exist. This was an example of a global configuration change.

```
ICX-Tx-Core1(config)# show running-config vsx-peer | include user
user admin group administrators password ciphertext
ICX-Tx-Core1(config)#
```

Context Configuration Change

Next you will define a new VLAN on Core1 and verify the status on Core2.

1. On Core1, define VLAN 11.

```
ICX-Tx-Core1(config)# vlan 11
ICX-Tx-Core1(config-vlan-11)# exit
```

2. Verify the VLAN list.

```
ICX-Tx-Core1(config)# show vlan
---------------------------------------------------------------------------
VLAN  Name                            Status  Reason  Type      Interfaces
---------------------------------------------------------------------------
1     DEFAULT_VLAN_1                  up      ok      default   lag256
11    VLAN11                          up      ok      static    lag256
```

3. Next, verify the VLAN list on the vsx-peer Core2. This demonstrates that each switch has a local configuration, and, by default, a configuration change on Core1 is not automatically pushed to Core2.

```
ICX-Tx-Core1(config)# show vlan vsx-peer
---------------------------------------------------------------------------
VLAN  Name                            Status  Reason  Type      Interfaces
---------------------------------------------------------------------------
1     DEFAULT_VLAN_1                  up      ok      default   lag256
```

Enable Global Configuration Synchronization for Other Features

The administrator must 'opt-in' for the global features that should be synchronized by the VSX members.

1. On the Core1, review the current VSX configuration.

```
ICX-Tx-Core1(config)# show running-config vsx-sync
Current vsx-sync configuration:
!
!Version ArubaOS-CX GL.10.04.0030
!export-password: default
vsx
    system-mac 02:01:00:00:xx:00
vsx-sync vsx-global
```

2. Next enable some VSX sync features. For this lab exercise, the 'aaa' option is required, since that includes the admin users.

```
ICX-Tx-Core1(config)# vsx
ICX-Tx-Core1(config-vsx)# vsx-sync aaa bfd-global bgp dhcp-relay
mclag-interfaces
ICX-Tx-Core1(config-vsx)# vsx-sync ospf qos-global route-map
ICX-Tx-Core1(config-vsx)# exit
```

Verify Synchronization Operation for Global Features

1. Review the updated output of the VSX sync command.

```
ICX-Tx-Core1(config)# show run vsx-sync
Current vsx-sync configuration:
!
!Version ArubaOS-CX GL.10.04.0030
!export-password: default
user admin group administrators password ciphertext
AQBapXRaY6HkOKGjVzqZjewoYg94PjoFJCPdL8qqusr+/7b/YgAAADi/osVJXNfAMvTortdok
cXfSSG1/9RzFDtehOzaNeea8iMUWOtNNv1SVTufQwLeVHXnk2Crpat4r29ENMWQJ76/Z1cngF
VibQV4M7bELYq8+GJCgZfKHoTgj1NOKjqCb5EO
user demo group administrators password ciphertext
AQBapWf0qG1No/HM5fQb3+D0teB4f9bvCrhVtqExP0xflB1wYgAAAGmR1x0axs0A5LVMSvTMm
JAl1Pr494ilg4ZcSzOCZGXVRDvfXlIgo9+kVA9rAWc42ONmXLE1Q4+0wF3vGiW1Tj1I8ht4VU
rCF4iKIhf+BVc+wQl/lcAcgN+qdHDQZ006CFvb
!
!
vsx
    system-mac 02:01:00:00:xx:00
vsx-sync aaa bfd-global bgpdhcp-relay mclag-interfaces ospfqos-global
route-map vsx-global
```

2. Run the command again with the 'vsx-peer' option. The config of the local Core1 and remote Core2 should be the same now, so the user 'demo' exists in both switch configurations.

```
ICX-Tx-Core1(config)# show running-config vsx-sync vsx-peer
Current vsx-sync configuration:
!
!Version ArubaOS-CX GL.10.04.0030
!export-password: default
user admin group administrators password ciphertext
user demo group administrators password ciphertext
!
```

```
!
vsx
    system-mac 02:01:00:00:xx:00
vsx-sync aaa bfd-global bgpdhcp-relay mclag-interfaces ospfqos-global
route-map vsx-global
```

3. Cleanup: On Core1, remove the ***demo*** user account. This demonstrates the global feature synchronization.

```
ICX-Tx-Core1(config)# no user demo
User demo's home directory and active sessions will be deleted.
Do you want to continue (y/n)? y

ICX-Tx-Core1(config)#
```

Synchronization for Context Features

For a context feature, such as a VLAN, the synchronization must be enabled within the context.

1. On the Core1, enter the VLAN 11 context and enable the VSX sync option for this VLAN.

```
ICX-Tx-Core1(config)# vlan 11
ICX-Tx-Core1(config-vlan-11)# vsx-sync
ICX-Tx-Core1(config-vlan-11)# exit
ICX-Tx-Core1(config)#
```

2. Review the VLAN list of the VSX Peer device.

```
ICX Tx Core1(config)# show vlan vsx-peer
-----------------------------------------------------------------------------
VLAN  Name                        Status  Reason  Type      Interfaces
-----------------------------------------------------------------------------
1     DEFAULT_VLAN_1              up      ok      default   lag256
11    VLAN11                      up      ok      static    lag256
```

3. Enable VLAN 12 and VLAN 13, these will be used in later labs.

```
ICX-Tx-Core1(config)# vlan 12,13
ICX-Tx-Core1(config-vlan-<12,13>)# vsx-sync
ICX-Tx-Core1(config-vlan-<12,13>)# exit
```

4. Verify the VLANs exist on the VSX peer.

```
ICX-Tx-Core1(config)# show vlan vsx-peer
---------------------------------------------------------------------------
VLAN  Name                          Status  Reason   Type      Interfaces
---------------------------------------------------------------------------
1     DEFAULT_VLAN_1                up      ok       default   lag256
11    VLAN11                        up      ok       static    lag256
12    VLAN12                        up      ok       static    lag256
13    VLAN13                        up      ok       static    lag256
```

Review the Sync Process Rules

At this point, the lab has demonstrated that the VSX configuration synchronization feature can help the administrator to perform an action only once on the primary switch, and the synchronization will handle the configuration change on the secondary switch.

There are some rules for the synchronization process:

- For any feature that IS ENABLED for synchronization:
  - Configuration changes MUST be made on the primary switch.
  - If any change is made on the secondary switch, the change will be overwritten by the VSX sync with the primary switch configuration. Therefore, the secondary switch SHOULD NOT be used for those configuration changes.
- For any feature that IS NOT ENABLED for synchronization:
  - Changes can be made on either switch and will only exist in the local configuration of each switch.
- Synchronization status changes:
  - When synchronization is turned off for a feature, each switch maintains the current configuration for that feature in the local configuration. Disabling the configuration sync will not remove that configuration on the secondary node.
  - When both switches have local configuration changes for a feature, and the feature is enabled for synchronization, the version of the primary switch will be leading. The secondary switch will lose any local configuration changes related to this feature.
  - If the sync process is 'out of sync', due to an ISL failure or a member reboot, the system will automatically update all the settings for the enabled features the first time they come back online. Since this is a complete feature sync, any new, modified, or removed configurations are automatically synchronized as well. Any changes applied locally on the secondary node would be lost at this point.

Task 3: VSX Layer 2—VSX Link Aggregation (VSX LAG)

This task will cover the redundant Layer 2 connectivity to a VSX system. Since both VSX members have their own management and control planes, the default behavior would use each system's own unique MAC address for Layer 2 protocols.

Since VSX wants to present itself as a single Layer 2 device to the peer devices, the VSX LAG feature can be used so both VSX members will present themselves with the same MAC address for Layer 2 protocols such as LACP and STP.

A VSX member can still have a local LAG, using only local ports. Any LAG that spans ports of both members of the VSX system, the administrator must define this LAG as a VSX LAG. In this task, two VSX LAGs will be defined: one to Access1 and one to Access2 (Figure 4-33).

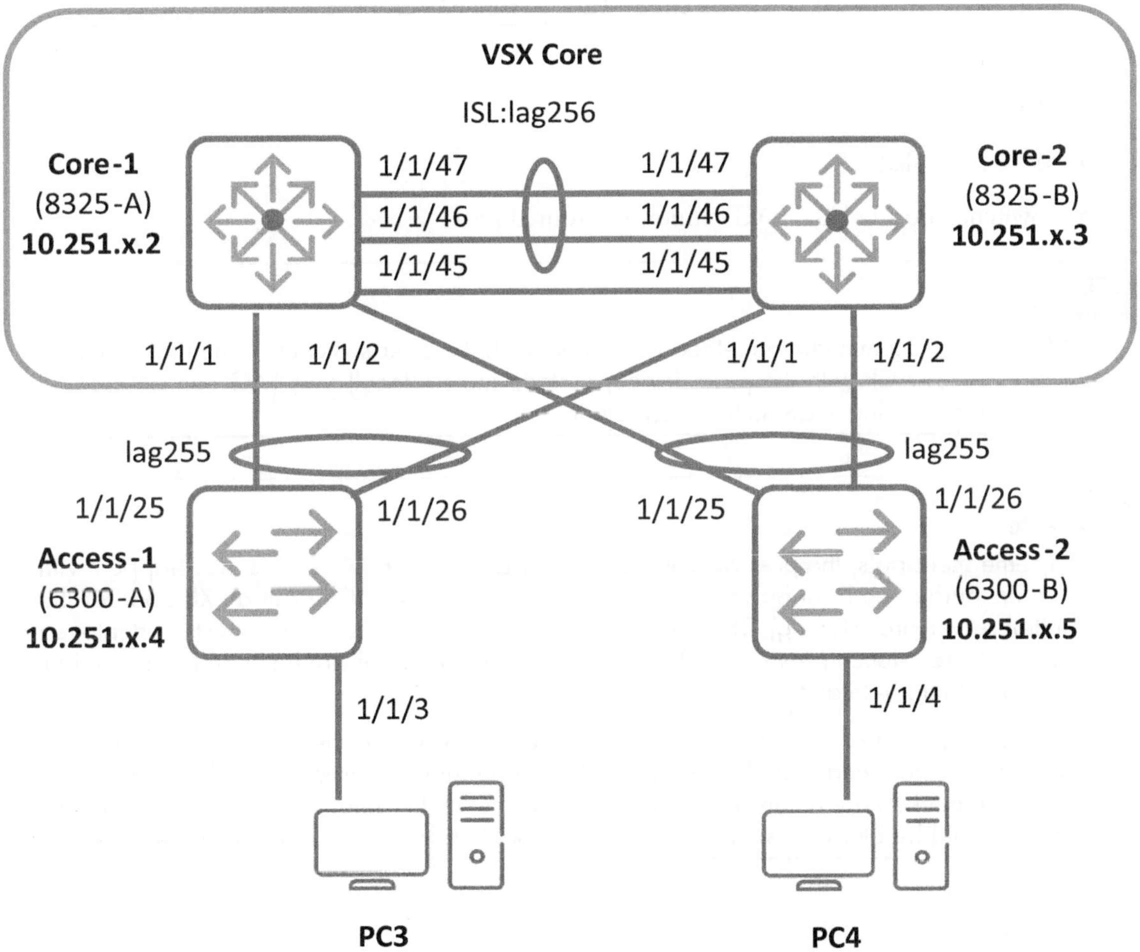

Figure 4-33 Task 3: VSX Layer2—VSX Link Aggregation (VSX LAG)

Objectives

- Set up a VSX LAG with config sync
- Configure peer switches (Access1 and Access2)
- Verify connectivity
- Configure a VSX LAG to the Aruba Mobility Controller

Steps

1. Open a console connection to Core1. Enter configuration mode and define a new LAG of type multi-chassis. This is the VSX LAG.

```
ICX-Tx-Core1(config)# interface lag 1 multi-chassis
```

2. By default, a VSX LAG is:
   - Shutdown
   - LACP enabled
   - Switched port (a VSX LAG cannot be a routed port)

Note

LACP is the recommended method to connect with the peer switches. When it is not possible to use LACP with the peer device, a static (no protocol) VSX LAG can be created using 'interface lag <id> multi-chassis static'.

Note

In some scenario's, the peer device may not always support LACP. This may happen with servers during the boot process (when the server admin wants to use a PXE boot for the initial server provisioning). This may also occur when the peer switch must be deployed with ZTP (zero-touch provisioning), since the peer switch does not have an LACP configuration at factory-default.

For these use cases, it is possible to configure AOS-CX with the LACP fallback feature. With this feature enabled, the switch will keep one interface in a forwarding state when no LACP packets are received from the peer device. In the default LACP mode, both interfaces would be blocked, so the peer device would not be able to reach the network.

3. Review this default state by reviewing the current configuration for the current context.

```
ICX-Tx-Core1(config-lag-if)# show run current-context
interface lag 1 multi-chassis
    no routing
vlan access 1
lacp mode active
```

4. Make the VSX LAG a VLAN trunk and permit VLANs 1 and 11-13.

```
ICX-Tx-Core1(config-lag-if)# vlan trunk allowed 1,11-13
```

Note

In the above command, 11-13 is a range, so VLAN 12 will be included as well.

5. Set a description on the LAG.

```
ICX-Tx-Core1(config-lag-if)# description access1
```

6. Enable the port.

```
ICX-Tx-Core1(config-lag-if)# no shutdown
```

7. Review the configuration changes.

```
ICX-Tx-Core1(config-lag-if)# show run current-context
interface lag 1 multi-chassis
    description access1
    no shutdown
    no routing
vlan trunk native 1
vlan trunk allowed 1,11-13
lacp mode active
ICX-Tx-Core1(config-lag-if)# exit
```

8. Open a console connection to Core2. Define a new VSX LAG with LAG id 1 of type multi-chassis.

```
ICX-Tx-Core2(config)# interface lag 1 multi-chassis
```

9. Review the current configuration.

```
ICX-Tx-Core2(config-lag-if)# show run current-context
interface lag 1 multi-chassis
    description access1
    no routing
vlan trunk native 1
vlan trunk allowed 1,11-13
lacp mode active
```

Question: Why is the VSX LAG already a VLAN trunk and why are the VLANs allowed?

Answer: Due to the global vsx config-sync 'mclag-interfaces'

10. Even though the VLAN configuration has been synchronized, the interface must still be enabled per member. Enable the interface.

```
ICX-Tx-Core2(config-lag-if)# no shutdown
```

11. Review the configuration.

```
ICX-Tx-Core2(config-lag-if)# show run current-context
interface lag 1 multi-chassis
    no shutdown
    description access1
    no routing
vlan trunk native 1
vlan trunk allowed 1,11-13
lacp mode active
ICX-Tx-Core2(config-lag-if)# exit
```

12. On the Core1, assign interface 1/1/1 to the LAG 1: this is the LAG that was created in the previous steps.

- Description: **Access1**
- MTU: 9100
- LAG: **1**
- Status: enabled (**no shut down**)

```
ICX-Tx-Core1(config)# int 1/1/1
ICX-Tx-Core1(config-if)# description access1
ICX-Tx-Core1(config-if)# lag 1
ICX-Tx-Core1(config-if)# mtu 9100
ICX-Tx-Core1(config-if)# no shutdown
ICX-Tx-Core1(config-if)# exit
```

13. On the Core2, repeat the commands of the previous step for interface 1/1/1.

```
ICX-Tx-Core2(config)# interface 1/1/1
ICX-Tx-Core2(config-if)# description access1
ICX-Tx-Core2(config-if)# lag 1
ICX-Tx-Core2(config-if)# mtu 9100
ICX-Tx-Core2(config-if)# no shutdown
ICX-Tx-Core2(config-if)# exit
```

Configure the Link Aggregation to Access2

In these steps, the VSX LAG from the two Core switches to Access2 will be defined.

1. Configure the following on ***both*** Core1 ***and*** Core2:

```
interface lag 2 multi-chassis
    description access2
    no shutdown
    no routing
    vlan trunk native 1
    vlan trunk allowed 1,11-13
    lacp mode active
interface 1/1/2
    description access2
    no shutdown
    mtu 9100
    lag 2
```

Access1 and Access2 LAG to the VSX Core

Both Access1 and Access2 need the uplink LAG defined. Since both access switches will be using the same uplink ports, NetEdit will be used to push the same configuration to both Access switches. Both access switches will be using the same LAG ID as the upstream LAG to connect to the Core switches. This makes it easy to identify the LAG. In these labs, the LAG ID 255 will be used for this LAG.

1. Configure the following on ***both*** Access1 ***and*** Access2.

```
vlan 11-13
interface lag 255
    description core
    no routing
    vlan trunk allowed all
    lacp mode active
    no shutdown
    exit
```

```
interface 1/1/25,1/1/26
    lag 255
    mtu 9100
    no shutdown
    exit
```

Task 4: VSX Layer 3—Active-Gateway

In a VSX system, active-gateway provides redundant default gateway functionality for the end-hosts. The default gateway of the end-host is automatically handled by both the VSX systems. This functionality is similar to VRRP, but VRRP only operates in an active/standby mode, using a keepalive between the active and the standby system to detect the state. To keep the ARP entry of the default gateway valid in case of a VRRP failover, VRRP uses a common MAC address between the VRRP hosts. In case of VRRP, this is based on the VRRP VRID.

The active-gateway feature is also using a virtual MAC address to ensure the ARP entry on the end-hosts is stable. However, the virtual MAC is set by the administrator, it is not controlled by some other ID. The virtual MAC can be reused over multiple VLANs, since the MAC address is only used within the VLAN.

In the VSX setup, the virtual MAC and active-gateway IP is programmed in the hardware tables of both VSX switches, so this results in an active/active setup. Since the peer switches are typically connected with a Multi-Chassis Link Aggregation (VSX LAG), the peer switch load-distribution decides if traffic is sent to VSX member 1 or member 2. Whatever switch receives the traffic first, will be the switch that handles the traffic. Therefore, it does not matter whether VSX member 1 or member 2 receives the traffic first, either of them can route the traffic.

In case of a link-failure, the peer switch will switch the traffic over the other link, so the other VSX member will route all the traffic. Each VSX member still has a local IP address, next to the active-gateway IP address. The same active-gateway IP address and active-gateway MAC address must be configured on both VSX members (Figure 4-34).

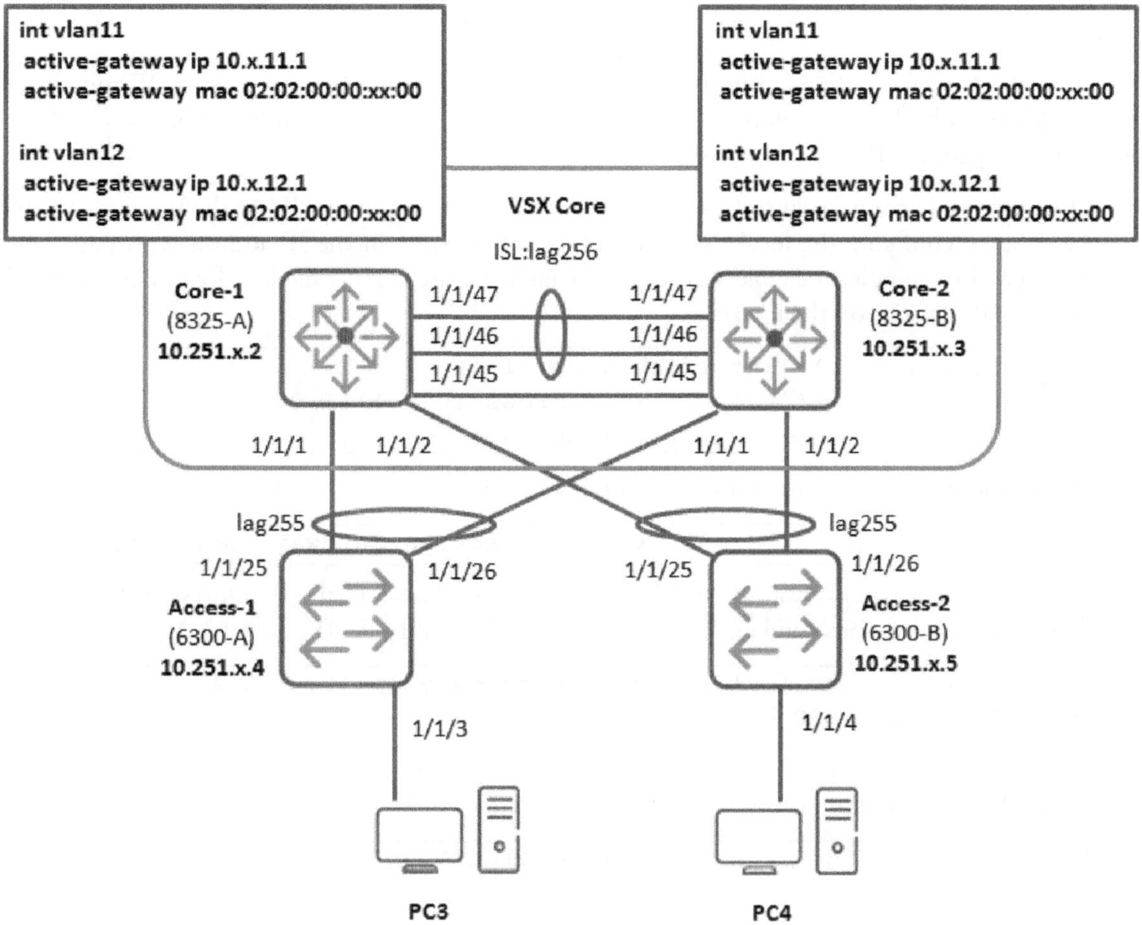

Figure 4-34 Task 4: VSX Layer 3—Active-Gateway

Objectives

- Understand the Active-Gateway principle
- Configuration of the Active-Gateway
- Verify the Active-Gateway configuration
- Verify the Active-Gateway operation on a client
- Set up Active-Gateway in VLAN 1 to the Mobility Controller
- Configure IP helper on the VSX Core

Steps

For each VLAN connected to end-hosts, the administrator must set an active-gateway IP and virtual MAC address on both VSX members. This will be the IP address that must be set on the end-hosts as the default gateway IP.

1. Open a console connection to Core1, enter the configuration mode. Enter the interface VLAN 11 context; configure the local switch IP address. Replace x in the IP address with your table number (for example, for table 1, use '1', for table 12 use '12'). Enable L3 counters; this will provide IP statistics on the interface.

```
ICX-Tx-Core1(config)# interface vlan 11
ICX-Tx-Core1(config-if-vlan)# ip address 10.x.11.2/24
ICX-Tx-Core1(config-if-vlan)# l3-counters
```

2. Enable the VSX-sync feature for this L3 VLAN interface.

```
ICX-Tx-Core1(config-if-vlan)# vsx-sync active-gateways policies
```

3. Configure the active-gateway IP and MAC address. Replace x in the IP address and the MAC address with your table number. For example, table 1 should use '01', for table 12 use '12'.

```
ICX-Tx-Core1(config-if-vlan)# active-gateway ip 10.x.11.1
mac02:02:00:00:xx:00
ICX-Tx-Core1(config-if-vlan)# exit
```

4. Verify the configuration. Output example:

```
ICX-Tx-Core1(config)# show interface vlan11
Interface vlan11 is up
 Admin state is up
 Link transitions: 0
 Description:
 Hardware: Ethernet, MAC Address: 90:20:c2:bc:17:00
IPv4 address 10.x.11.2/24
    active-gateway ip mac 02:02:00:00:xx:00
    active-gateway ip 10.x.11.1
Rx
       L3:
            0 packets, 0 bytes
Tx
       L3:
            0 packets, 0 bytes
```

5. Open a console connection to Core2; enter the configuration mode. Enter the interface VLAN 11 context, configure the Core2 switch IP address, and enable L3 counters.

```
ICX-Tx-Core2(config)# interfacevlan 11
ICX-Tx-Core2(config-if-vlan)# ip address 10.x.11.3/24
ICX-Tx-Core2(config-if-vlan)# l3-counters
```

6. Review the current configuration of the VLAN 11 interface. Verify that VSX-sync has completed the active-gateway configuration synchronization on Core2.

```
ICX-Tx-Core2(config-if-vlan)# show run current-context
interface vlan11
vsx-sync active-gateways policies
ip address 10.12.11.3/24
    active-gateway ip mac 02:02:00:00:12:00
    active-gateway ip 10.12.11.1
l3-counters
```

7. Verify the operational status. Example output from table 12:

```
ICX-Tx-Core2(config-if-vlan)# show interface vlan11
Interface vlan11 is up
 Admin state is up
 Link transitions: 0
 Description:
 Hardware: Ethernet, MAC Address: 90:20:c2:bc:97:00
 IPv4 address 10.x.11.3/24
active-gateway ip mac 02:02:00:00:xx:00
    active-gateway ip 10.x.11.1
 Rx
       L3:
            0 packets, 0 bytes
 Tx
       L3:
            0 packets, 0 bytes
```

VLAN 12 Active-Gateway

1. Configure VLAN12 on Core1. Replace x in the IP address and the MAC address with your table number. For example, table 1 should use '01', for table 12 use '12' for xx in the MAC address.

```
ICX-Tx-Core1(config)# interface vlan 12
ICX-Tx-Core1(config-if-vlan)# ip address 10.x.12.2/24
ICX-Tx-Core1(config-if-vlan)# l3-counters
ICX-Tx-Core1(config-if-vlan)# vsx-sync active-gateways policies
ICX-Tx-Core1(config-if-vlan)# active-gateway ip 10.x.12.1 mac
02:02:00:00:xx:00
ICX-Tx-Core1(config-if-vlan)# exit
```

2. Configure VLAN12 on Core2.

```
ICX-Tx-Core2(config)# interface vlan 12
ICX-Tx-Core2(config-if-vlan)# ip address 10.x.12.3/24
ICX-Tx-Core2(config-if-vlan)# l3-counters
ICX-Tx-Core2(config-if-vlan)# exit
```

VLAN 1 Active-Gateway

Set up VLAN 1 active-gateway. This will be used for communication to the Aruba mobility controller and ensure the mobility controller has a redundant default gateway.

1. On Core1, configure the VLAN1 active-gateway.

```
ICX-Tx-Core1(config)# interface vlan1
ICX-Tx-Core1(config-if-vlan)# vsx-sync active-gateways policies
ICX-Tx-Core1(config-if-vlan)# active-gateway ip mac 02:02:00:00:xx:00
ICX-Tx-Core1(config-if-vlan)# active-gateway ip 10.x.1.1
ICX-Tx-Core1(config-if-vlan)# exit
```

Note

Core2 has been configured with an IP address already, the vsx-sync will ensure the active-gateway configuration is set on Core2 as well.

Configure DHCP Relay on VSX Core

In this lab environment, DHCP scopes have been configured on the MC. On the VSX Core, the DHCP relay, also known as '**ip helper-address**', will be configured to point to the MC as the DHCP server (Figure 4-35).

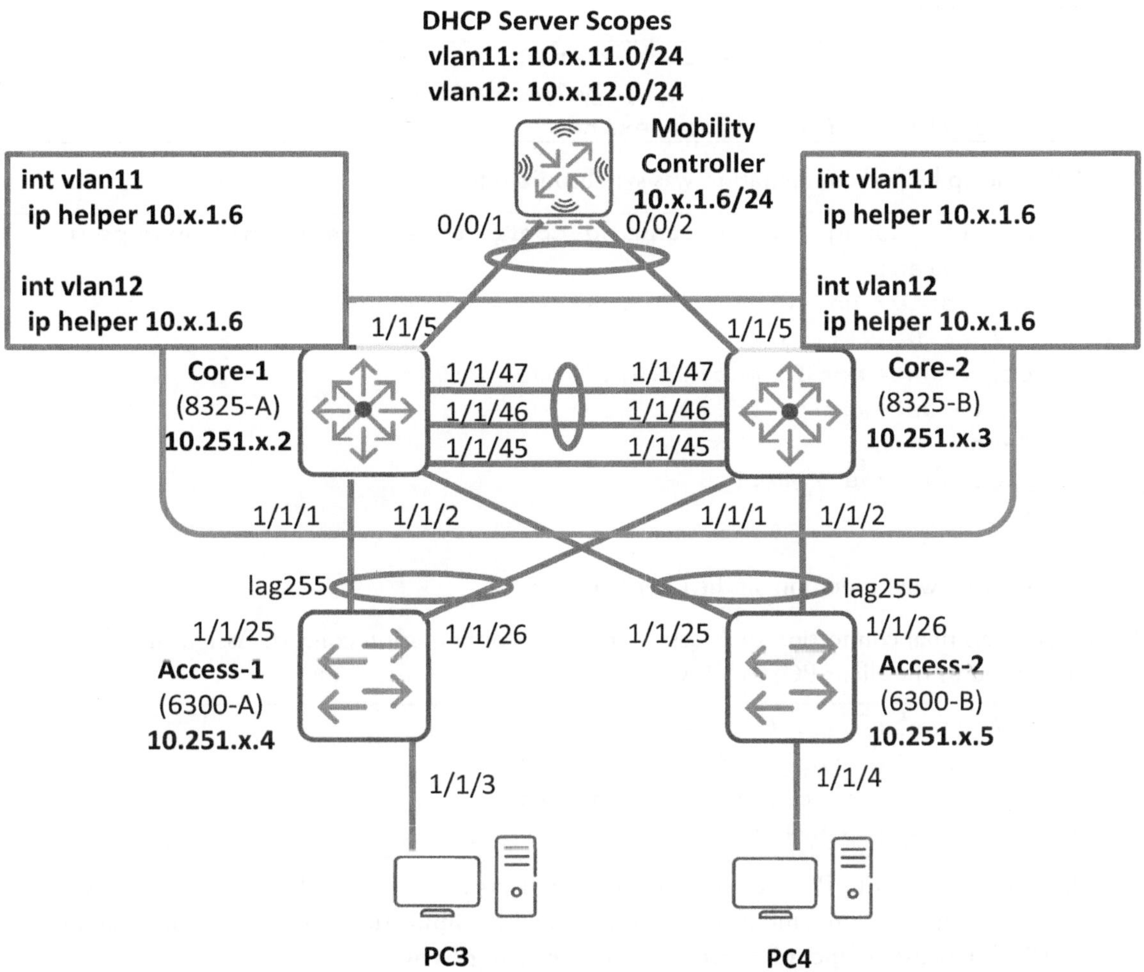

Figure 4-35 Task 4: VSX Layer3—Active-Gateway

1. On the Core1, apply the **'ip helper'** command to VLAN 11. The MC has IP address 10.x.1.6.

```
ICX-Tx-Core1(config)# interface vlan11
ICX-Tx-Core1(config-if-vlan)# ip helper-address 10.x.1.6
ICX-Tx-Core1(config-if-vlan)# exit
```

2. Repeat the configuration for VLAN12.

```
ICX-Tx-Core1(config)# interface vlan12
ICX-Tx-Core1(config-if-vlan)# ip helper-address 10.x.1.6
ICX-Tx-Core1(config-if-vlan)# exit
```

3. Verify the 'ip helper' configuration was synchronized to Core2.

```
ICX-Tx-Core1(config)# show running-config interface vlan11 vsx-peer
interface vlan11
vsx-sync active-gateways policies
ip address 10.12.11.3/24
    active-gateway ip mac 02:02:00:00:12:00
    active-gateway ip 10.12.11.1
    l3-counters
ip helper-address 10.x.1.6
    exit
```

Verify Active-Gateway Operation on the Client PC

1. Open a terminal connection to Access1; enter the configuration context. Assign interface 1/1/3 (connected to the client PC) to VLAN 11.

```
ICX-Tx-Access1(config)# interface 1/1/3
ICX-Tx-Access1(config-if)# vlan access 11
ICX-Tx-Access1(config-if)# no shutdown
ICX-Tx-Access1(config-if)# exit
```

2. Open a connection to PC3 (connected to Access1 port 1/1/3). On the client PC3, renew your IP address. Open a command prompt (cmd.exe) with administrator privileges; release and renew the IP address using "**ipconfig /release**" and "**ipconfig /renew**".

3. On the Access1 console, verify the mac-address table of VLAN 11. The mac-address of the client should now be listed on interface 1/1/3.

   Question: Can you explain the 3 mac-addresses that have been learned on lag255?

   Answer: For both core switches, the system MAC address, and the active-gateway MAC.

```
ICX-Tx-Access1(config)# show mac-address-table vlan 11
MAC age-time              : 300 seconds
Number of MAC addresses : 4

MAC Address           VLAN     Type                     Port
-----------------------------------------------------------------
90:20:c2:bc:97:00     11       dynamic                  lag255
90:20:c2:bc:17:00     11       dynamic                  lag255
00:50:56:b1:7a:37     11       dynamic                  1/1/3
02:02:00:00:12:00     11       dynamic                  lag255
```

4. On the client PC3, verify the system has received an IP address from the VLAN 11 ip range (10.x.11.0/24). In a command prompt (cmd.exe), run **'ipconfig'**.

```
C:\Users\student> ipconfig
Windows IP Configuration
Ethernet adapter Do NOT Touch!:
...
Ethernet adapter Lab NIC:
   Connection-specific DNS Suffix  . :
   IPv4 Address. . . . . . . . . . . : 10.x.11.51
   Subnet Mask . . . . . . . . . . . : 255.255.255.0
   Default Gateway . . . . . . . . . : 10.x.11.1
Ethernet adapter OOBM:
...
C:\Users\student>
```

5. Verify the IP path with a traceroute to the MC (10.x.1.6).

```
C:\Users\student> tracert -d 10.x.1.6
Tracing route to 10.12.1.6 over a maximum of 30 hops
  1    <1 ms<1 ms<1 ms  10.x.11.2
  2    <1 ms<1 ms<1 ms  10.x.1.6
Trace complete.
```

Question: The client PC default gateway is 10.x.11.1, why does the traceroute show 10.x.11.2 or 10.x.11.3?

Answer: The core switch that receives the request (either Core1 or Core2) will respond with its local interface IP address.

6. Verify the ARP entry on the PC3. In a command prompt (cmd.exe), enter **'arp -a'**. The IP address of the default gateway (10.x.11.1) should be listed with the active-gateway MAC address. This confirms that the configured VSX active-gateway MAC is learned by the client's systems.

```
...
Interface: 10.12.11.51 --- 0x10
  Internet Address       Physical Address      Type
10.x.11.1              02-02-00-00-12-00     dynamic
  10.x.11.2              90-20-c2-bc-17-00     dynamic
  10.x.11.3              90-20-c2-bc-97-00     dynamic
  10.x.11.255            ff-ff-ff-ff-ff-ff     static
  224.0.0.22              01-00-5e-00-00-16     static
  224.0.0.251             01-00-5e-00-00-fb     static
  224.0.0.252             01-00-5e-00-00-fc     static
  239.255.255.250         01-00-5e-7f-ff-fa     static
  255.255.255.255         ff-ff-ff-ff-ff-ff     static
...
```

Verify DHCP Relay for PC4—The Client Connected to Access2

1. Open a terminal connection to Access2, enter the configuration context. Assign interface 1/1/4 (connected to the client PC4) to VLAN 12.

```
ICX-Tx-Access2(config)# interface 1/1/4
ICX-Tx-Access2(config-if)# vlan access 12
ICX-Tx-Access2(config-if)# no shutdown
ICX-Tx-Access2(config-if)# exit
```

2. On PC4 (connected to Access2 port 1/1/4), renew your IP address. Open a command prompt (cmd.exe) with administrator privileges; release and renew the IP address using "**ipconfig /release**" and "**ipconfig /renew**" or by **bouncing** the **Lab NIC** network connection (disable/enable).

Task 5: VSX Split-Brain Handling

The ISL between the VSX members should be primarily protected against link failures by using a LAG of multiple member ports, so when a single port between the VSX members fails, this will have no impact on the VSX functionality. Only the link capacity between the VSX members will be reduced.

Split-Brain Problem

However, in case all the members ports of the ISL link would be down, there will be no more VSX state replication between the VSX members, so the primary VSX member may have different MAC/ARP entries compared to the secondary VSX member, and they will not be able to share, for example, the STP state between them.

Solution

This scenario would lead to unpredictable results, so the solution will be to have the secondary node disable its interfaces. The result will be that only the primary node will still be on the network, so the network will operate in a predictable way again.

The secondary node must have a means to detect that the primary node is still active. In case the primary node would have suffered a complete power failure, the ISL link will also be down, but the secondary is supposed to take over complete control. In this case, it is desired to have the secondary active on the network. Only when the primary *and* the secondary node are online at the same time, it is desired to have the secondary disable (shutdown) its interfaces.

How? — Keepalives

This can be achieved by configuring a keepalive between the primary and the secondary node. When the ISL is down, and the secondary still gets a response over the Keepalive, the secondary knows both are still online, and it will disable the VSX LAG interfaces. In case the ISL goes down, and the keepalive does not respond either, the secondary knows the primary is no longer online, so it will keep the VSX LAG interfaces up (Figure 4-36).

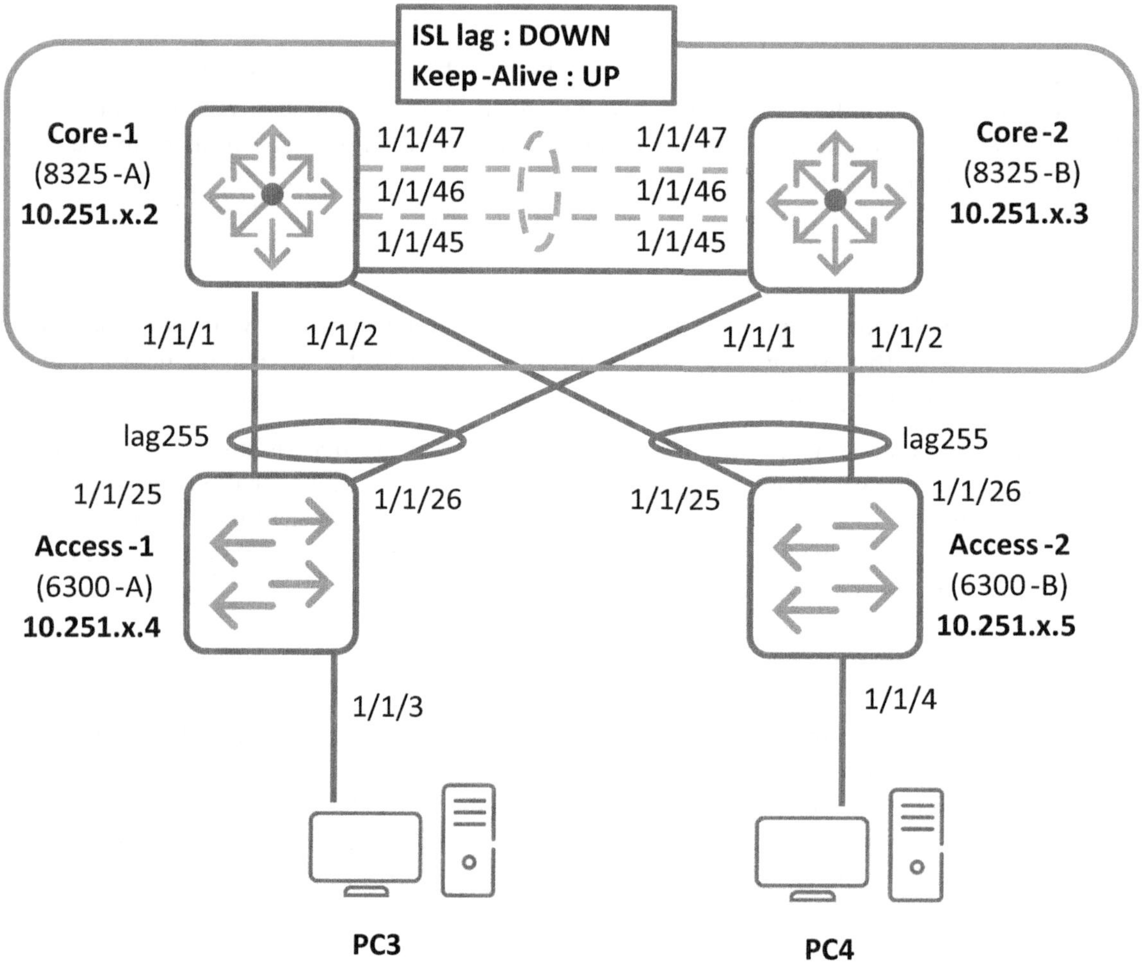

Figure 4-36 Task 5: VSX Split-Brain Handling

Objectives

- Split-brain scenario, review result/output/logs
- Split-brain recovery
- Linkup-delay timer

Steps

The keepalive has been configured as part of the basic VSX configuration task, in these steps, the configuration is reviewed.

1. Open a console connection to Core1.The keepalive is an IP connection between the Core1 and Core2 switches. To make sure this connection is never in conflict or impacted by the normal routing table, a dedicated VRF is typically used. Review the routed port 1/1/45, this is a dedicated link that was used for the VSX keepalive.

```
ICX-Tx-Core1# show running-config interface 1/1/45
interface 1/1/45
    no shutdown
vrf attach KA
ip address 192.168.0.0/31
    exit
```

2. Review the VSX running configuration.

```
ICX-Tx-Core1# show running-config vsx
vsx
    system-mac 02:01:00:00:xx:00
    inter-switch-link lag 256
    role primary
keepalive peer 192.168.0.1 source 192.168.0.0 vrf KA
interface lag 256
   description ISL link
   no shutdown
   no routing
vlan trunk native 1 tag
vlan trunk allowed all
lacp mode active
<output omitted>
```

3. Review the VSX keepalive configuration.

```
ICX-Tx-Core1# show vsx configuration keepalive
Keepalive Interface : 1/1/45
Keepalive VRF       : KA
Source IP Address   : 192.168.0.0
Peer IP Address     : 192.168.0.1
UDP Port            : 7678
Hello Interval      : 1 Seconds
Dead Interval       : 3 Seconds
```

4. Verify the keepalive operational status (Keepalive-Established) and the peer role (on Core1, the peer should be secondary).

```
ICX-Tx-Core1# show vsx status keepalive
Keepalive State               :Keepalive-Established
Last Established              : Mon Dec 23 19:15:09 2019
Last Failed                   : Mon Dec 23 17:56:15 2019
Peer System Id                : 02:01:00:00:xx:00
Peer Device Role              :secondary

Keepalive Counters
Keepalive Packets Tx          : 352151
Keepalive Packets Rx          : 352020
Keepalive Timeouts            : 0
Keepalive Packets Dropped : 0
```

5. Open a console connection to Core2; review the VSX keepalive with the same commands.

```
show running-config interface 1/1/45
show running-config vsx
show vsx configuration keepalive
show vsx status keepalive
```

Force a Split-Brain Condition

6. On Core1, enter configuration mode and disable the LAG 256 (LAG used for the VSX ISL).

```
ICX-Tx-Core1(config)# interface lag 256
ICX-Tx-Core1(config-lag-if)# shutdown
ICX-Tx-Core1(config-lag-if)# exit
```

7. On Core1, review the VSX status.

```
ICX-Tx-Core1(config)# show vsx status
VSX Operational State
---------------------
    ISL channel              : Out-Of-Sync
    ISL mgmt channel         :inter_switch_link_down
    Config Sync Status       : out-of-sync
    NAE                      :peer_unreachable
    HTTPS Server             :peer_unreachable

Attribute           Local               Peer
------------        --------            --------
ISL link            lag256
ISL version         2
System MAC          02:01:00:00:xx:00   02:01:00:00:xx:00
Platform            8325
Software Version    GL.10.04.0030
Device Role         primary
```

8. Review the keepalive status.

```
ICX-Tx-Core1(config)# show vsx status keepalive
Keepalive State            :Keepalive-Established
Last Established           : Fri Dec 27 18:07:37 2019
Last Failed                : Mon Dec 23 17:56:15 2019
Peer System Id             : 02:01:00:00:xx:00
Peer Device Role           :

Keepalive Counters
Keepalive Packets Tx       : 352501
Keepalive Packets Rx       : 352370
Keepalive Timeouts         : 0
Keepalive Packets Dropped : 0
```

Question: Why are there no 'packets dropped' at this point?

Answer: Only the ISL is down at this point, the keepalive operates just fine, so no keepalive packets are dropped.

9. On Core1, notice that the 'vsx-peer' commands are no longer available, since these commands use the ISL link

```
ICX -Tx-Core1(config)# show vsx status keepalive vsx-peer
VSX Peer not reachable
ICX-Tx-Core1(config)#
```

Split-System Detected

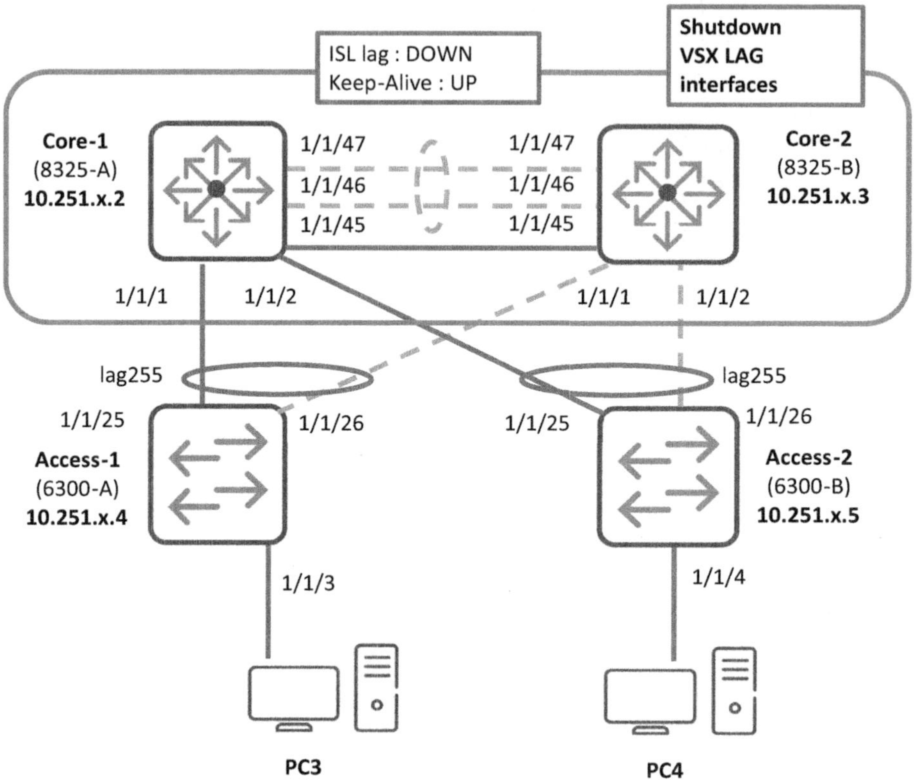

Figure 4-37 Task 5: VSX Split-Brain Handling

1. On Core2, verify that the keepalive has detected that the primary (Core1) is still responding (established) (Figure 4-37).

```
ICX-Tx-Core2# show vsx status keepalive
Keepalive State            : Keepalive-Established
Last Established           : Fri Dec 27 18:08:18 2019
Last Failed                : Mon Dec 23 17:56:56 2019
Peer System Id             : 02:01:00:00:01:00
Peer Device Role           :

Keepalive Counters
Keepalive Packets Tx       : 352481
Keepalive Packets Rx       : 352482
Keepalive Timeouts         : 0
Keepalive Packets Dropped : 0
```

2. Check the log buffer (-r reverse -n number of lines), look for lines containing 'vsx'. This will show an entry that the ISL link is down, but the KeepAlive has been established. This indicates the 'split-system' scenario.

```
ICX-Tx-Core2# show logging -r -n 30 | include vsx
2020-03-02T08:35:36.312254+00:00 ICX-Tx-Core2 hpe-vsxd[2167]:
Event|7014|LOG_INFO|AMM|1/1|VSX 2 state local down, remote down
2020-03-02T08:35:36.306706+00:00 ICX-Tx-Core2 hpe-vsxd[2167]:
Event|7014|LOG_INFO|AMM|1/1|VSX 5 state local down, remote down
2020-03-02T08:35:36.257432+00:00 ICX-Tx-Core2 hpe-vsxd[2167]:
Event|7020|LOG_INFO|AMM|1/1|ISL out-of-sync and keepalive is in established
2020-03-02T08:35:36.254765+00:00 ICX-Tx-Core2 hpe-vsxkad[8376]:
Event|7006|LOG_INFO|AMM|1/1|VSX Keepalive succeeded
2020-03-02T08:35:35.594193+00:00 ICX-Tx-Core2 vsx-syncd[8800]:
Event|7602|LOG_INFO|AMM|-|Configuration sync update : VSX Inter-Switch-Link
is down.
2020-03-02T08:35:35.575153+00:00 ICX-Tx-Core2 hpe-vsxd[2167]:
Event|7011|LOG_INFO|AMM|1/1|VSX 5 state local up, remote down
2020-03-02T08:35:35.570479+00:00 ICX-Tx-Core2 hpe-vsxd[2167]:
Event|7011|LOG_INFO|AMM|1/1|VSX 2 state local up, remote down
2020-03-02T08:35:35.566540+00:00 ICX-Tx-Core2 hpe-vsxd[2167]:
Event|7014|LOG_INFO|AMM|1/1|VSX 1 state local down, remote down
2020-03-02T08:35:35.559596+00:00 ICX-Tx-Core2 hpe-vsxd[2167]:
Event|7004|LOG_ERR|AMM|1/1|VSX ISL port lag256 is Out-Of-Sync with the peer:
link is down
2020-03-02T08:35:35.559336+00:00 ICX-Tx-Core2 hpe-vsxd[2167]:
Event|7015|LOG_INFO|AMM|1/1|VSX ISL sliding window parameters are reset.
2020-03-02T08:35:35.559097+00:00 ICX-Tx-Core2 hpe-vsxd[2167]:
Event|7001|LOG_INFO|AMM|1/1|VSX ISL port lag256 is down
```

3. Due to this condition, Core2 has disabled its local VSX LAG interfaces.

```
ICX-Tx-Core2# show interface brief
----------------------------------------------------------------------------
Port      Native  Mode    Type      Enabled  Status  Reason
Speed
          VLAN
(Mb/s)
----------------------------------------------------------------------------
1/1/1     1       trunk   SFP+DAC1  yes      down    Disabled by VSX
--
1/1/2     1       trunk   SFP+DAC1  yes      down    Disabled by VSX
--
```

```
1/1/3       --       routed  --        no       down        No XCVR installed
--
1/1/4       --       routed  SFP-BT    no       down        Administratively
down  --
1/1/5       1        trunk   SFP-BT    yes      down        Disabled by VSX
--1/1/6       --       routed --        no       down        No XCVR installed
--
<output omitted..>
vlan1       --               --        yes      down        Disabled by VSX
--
vlan11      --               --        yes      down        Disabled by VSX
--
vlan12      --               --        yes      down        Disabled by VSX
--
<output omitted..>
```

4. And the VSX state will show as 'Split-System-Secondary '.

```
ICX-Tx-Core2# show vsx brief
ISL State                              : Out-Of-Sync
Device State                           :Split-System-Secondary
Keepalive State                        : Keepalive-Established
Device Role                            : secondary
Number of Multi-chassis LAG interfaces : 3
```

Split-Brain Recovery—Linkup Delay

When the ISL gets restored, the secondary node will automatically re-enable the disabled interfaces after it has completed the VSX hardware table synchronization. To provide enough time to synchronize all the tables and allow the secondary node time to learn routes from possible OSPF or BGP peers, VSX has a default Linkup-delay timer of 180 seconds (3 minutes).Verify this default behavior in the next steps.

1. On the Core1, enable the LAG256 again.

```
ICX-Tx-Core1(config)# interface lag 256
ICX-Tx-Core1(config-lag-if)# no shut
ICX-Tx-Core1(config-lag-if)# exit
```

2. On Core2, review the VSX and interface status.

```
ICX-Tx-Core2# show vsx brief
ISL State                              : In-Sync
Device State                           : Sync-Secondary-Linkup-Delay
Keepalive State                        : Keepalive-Established
Device Role                            : secondary
Number of Multi-chassis LAG interfaces : 3
```

```
ICX-Tx-Core2# show interface brief
--------------------------------------------------------------------------------
-----------
Port     Native  Mode     Type        Enabled   Status   Reason
Speed
         VLAN
(Mb/s)
--------------------------------------------------------------------------------
1/1/1    1       trunk    SFP+DAC1    yes       down     Disabled by VSX
--
1/1/2    1       trunk    SFP+DAC1    yes       down     Disabled by VSX
--
1/1/3    --      routed   --          no        down     No XCVR installed
--
1/1/4    --      routed   SFP-BT      no        down     Administratively down
--
1/1/5    --      routed   SFP-BT      no        down     Administratively down
--
1/1/6    --      routed   --          no        down     No XCVR installed
--
```

3. It may take up to 3 minutes before the VSX LAG interfaces are enabled again, wait for the interfaces to come up before continuing the lab.

Note

When the two switches have completed the synchronization of the forwarding tables before the timer expires, the interfaces will be enabled again. This is why it will not actually take 3 minutes in the lab, but typically less than a minute.

Note

It is possible for the administrator to manually set the linkup-delay timer. This may be useful for very large deployments when many table entries need to be synchronized between the primary and secondary nodes. Consult the VSX best practice guide for more information.

Task 6: Finalize Configuration for Future Labs

Objectives

In this task, you will complete the IP configuration to reach the ClearPass server. This will be required in future labs. The ClearPass server is reachable via the RouterA device, that is connected to the Core1 port 1/1/7.

In this task, the port 1/1/7 will be enabled, an IP address will be assigned, and a static route will be set for the ClearPass IP subnet.Core2 will be configured with a static route to the ClearPass server via Core1.

The last step will be to save a new checkpoint, so you can revert to this configuration in future labs.

Steps

1. Access a terminal on Core1; enter the configuration mode. Define the uplink connection to RouterA and configured the static route.

```
ICX-Tx-Core1(config)# interface 1/1/7
ICX-Tx-Core1(config-if)# ip address 10.255.101.2/24
ICX-Tx-Core1(config-if)# no shutdown
ICX-Tx-Core1(config-if)# exit
ICX-Tx-Core1(config-)# ip route 10.254.1.0/24 10.255.101.11
```

2. Verify access to the ClearPass server.

```
ICX-Tx-Core1(config)# do ping 10.254.1.23 source vlan1
PING 10.254.1.23 (10.254.1.23) from 10.12.1.2 : 100(128) bytes of data.
108 bytes from 10.254.1.23: icmp_seq=1 ttl=61 time=4.72 ms
108 bytes from 10.254.1.23: icmp_seq=2 ttl=61 time=3.10 ms
...
```

3. Access a terminal on Core2; enter the configuration mode. Configure a static route for the CPPM subnet to next-hop Core1.

```
ICX-Tx-Core2(config)# ip route 10.254.1.0/24 10.x.1.2
```

4. Verify connectivity to the ClearPass host.

```
ICX-Tx-Core2(config)# do ping 10.254.1.23 source vlan1
PING 10.254.1.23 (10.254.1.23) from 10.12.1.3 : 100(128) bytes of data.
108 bytes from 10.254.1.23: icmp_seq=1 ttl=60 time=3.67 ms
108 bytes from 10.254.1.23: icmp_seq=2 ttl=60 time=3.26 ms
...
ICX-Tx-Core2(config)# end
```

Save Configuration Checkpoints for Upcoming Labs

You have now completed the VSX configuration lab.

Important

This configuration will be the base configuration of several future labs, so a checkpoint **MUST** be created to complete the rest of the lab activities in this guide.

1. On all *four* switches (Core1, Core2, Access1, and Access 2), save the current configuration as a checkpoint.

```
Switch(config)# end
Switch# copy run checkpoint icx-lab04-vsx
Configuration changes will take time to process, please be patient.
```

Verify the Checkpoint

1. Verify that the checkpoint exists in the checkpoint list of ***each*** switch.

```
# show checkpoint list | include vsx
icx-lab04-vsx
```

Learning Check

1. With VSX, you can stack two AOS-CX switches to form one single control plane.
   a. True
   b. False
2. Each VSX node buffers and sends its new neighbor ARP/ND entries to the VSX peer every time its buffer is full (64 entries) or when it hits a timeout of 5 minutes.
   a. True
   b. False
3. Match the definition to the term.
   - Definitions
     - Optimizes forwarding for upstream devices
     - Helps prevent split-brain
     - Used for data path traffic forwarding between VSX switches
     - Provides default gateway redundancy
     - Helps avoid traffic drop at VSX LAGs right after a reboot
   - Terms
     - Linkup Delay
     - Active-Gateway
     - Inter-Switch Link
     - Keepalive
     - Active-Forwarding

Summary

Congratulations! VSX has similar benefits as VSF; however, VSX also offers better high availability required in core and data center environments. VSX binds two AOS-CX switches of the same model type to operate as one device for Layer 2. VSX also operates as independent nodes for Layer 3.

You learned about the virtual switching technologies available from different HPE/Aruba switching products. You learned about the benefits and components of AOS-CX VSX, as well as setting up a basic configuration. You should be familiar with how VSX deals with and forwards data traffic and how the VSX cluster deals with a split-brain condition.

5 ACLs

OBJECTIVES

After completing this chapter, you should be able to:

- ✓ Define ACL and identify the criteria by which ACLs select traffic
- ✓ Configure ACLs on AOS-CX switches to select given traffic
- ✓ Apply static ACLs to interfaces to meet the needs of a particular scenario
- ✓ Examine an ACL configuration and determine the action taken on specific packets
- ✓ Leverage object groups to scale an ACL design
- ✓ Understand the rules and restrictions of ACLs
- ✓ Implement traffic policies with classifier policies

Overview

With internal threats so common, you need to secure your network's internal infrastructure and IT resources. In this chapter you will examine one of the basic mechanisms for controlling traffic: access control lists (ACLs).

The chapter begins with an overview of the services that ACLs perform. You will also learn how the various types of ACLs work, and how to configure them and apply them to interfaces on your AOS-CX switches.

ACL Overview

The first section of this chapter introduces ways to use ACLs to secure your network and complete other tasks. You will learn about the components of ACLs and how to apply ACLs to interfaces at a high level.

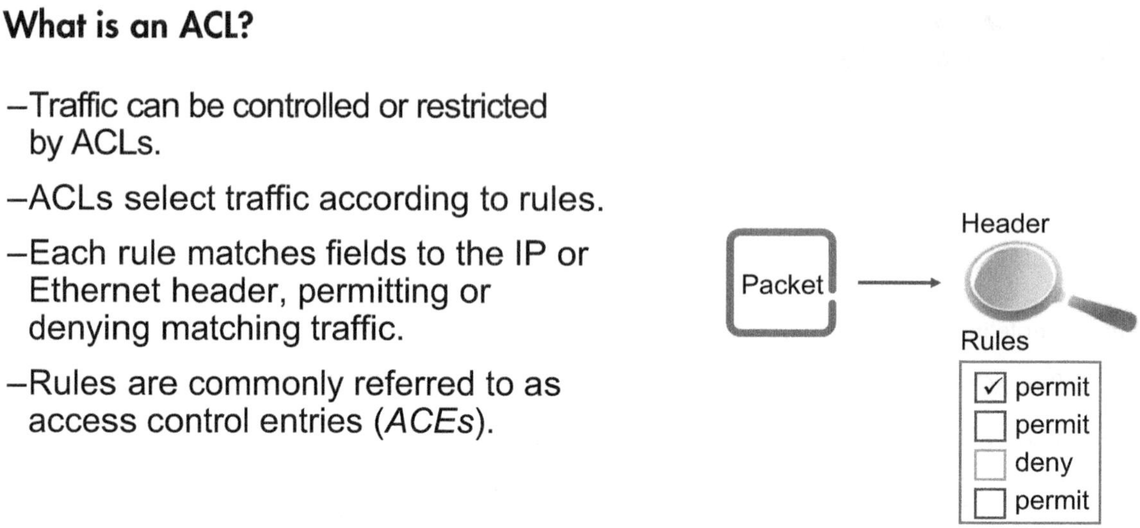

Figure 5-1 What is an ACL?

An ACL is simply a list of rules against which a network infrastructure device, such as a routing switch, checks packet headers. Each rule consists of specific criteria such as source IP address, destination IP address, and TCP or UDP port number. It also consists of an action: permit (select matching packets) or deny (do not select matching packets) (Figure 5-1).

What the routing switch does with selected packets depends on how you apply the ACL. This chapter focuses on packet filtering ACLs—ACLs that are applied to routing switch interfaces to filter incoming and outgoing traffic. For packet filtering ACLs, the permit action allows packets that match the rule, and the deny action discards packets that match the rule.

Note
You might also see rules referred to as *access control entries (ACEs)*.

Reasons to Implement ACLs

Benefit of using ACLs:

–Block unwanted traffic or users

–Identify or classify traffic for QoS features

–Restrict the content of routing updates

–Security to reduce the chance of DoS attacks

–Control management access to switch

–Use with PBR (policy-based routing)

Figure 5-2: Reasons to Implement ACLs

This chapter teaches you specifically about applying ACLs to filter traffic, as shown in Figure 5-2. Without such packet filtering ACLs, each routing switch interface accepts all packets and forwards that traffic based on its forwarding tables. The ACLs enable you to implement more control, improving network performance and enhancing security. As you will see, you can apply packet filtering ACLs to filter traffic to or from an endpoint, a group of endpoints, or entire subnets.

Benefits of using ACLs include:

- Block unwanted traffic or users
- Identify or classify traffic for QoS features
- Restrict the content of routing updates
- Security to reduce the chance of DoS attacks
- Control management access to switch
- Use with PBR (Policy-Based Routing)

You might implement packet filtering ACLs for reasons, such as these:

- At the network edge, ACLs can prevent unwanted IP packets from entering the network infrastructure. You can take restrictive approaches in which you permit the required traffic and deny all other traffic. Or you can take a permissive approach in which you deny specific traffic and permit all other traffic. By combining permit and deny rules, you can create highly flexible policies.
- Implementing ACLs at the network edge can also improve network performance and reduce switch buffer and CPU utilization by reducing the volume of packets that upstream switches and routers handle.

- At the network core and distribution layer, ACLs can similarly improve performance and security. For example, you can use ACLs to ensure various collections of clients only have access to selected destinations. These destinations may be specific hosts, entire subnets, or even particular applications. For example, you may want to ensure that all hosts and servers in a given VLAN are only allowed to communicate within that VLAN or with a limited number of other specific VLANs.
- You can also use ACLs to block IP traffic that has the switch as the destination address. For example, ACLs can deny unauthorized clients attempting to access the switch using functions such as Telnet, Secure Shell (SSH), or a web browser.
- In addition to securing the network infrastructure, you can also use ACLs to control a performance problem quickly by limiting IP traffic generated by a specific device, group of devices, or a subnet. This gives you an opportunity to troubleshoot without sacrificing performance for users outside of the problem area.

Note

The AOS-CX ACL feature implements basic packet filtering. The switches do not support stateful (allowing returning traffic for a permitted connection) or application (payload) inspection functions. If these features are required, then a different product should be used, like Aruba's Mobility Controllers (MCs) or an HPE partner firewall solution.

ACL IDs and Types

ACL type	Extended IP ACLs*	Extended MAC ACLs
Filter traffic based on	Many IP header fields	Many MAC header fields
Valid IDs	Name	Name

Note*: Both IPv4 and IPV6 ACLs extended ACLs are supported

Figure 5-3: ACL IDs and Types

When you create an ACL, you give it a valid ACL identifier (ID) and also determine its type (Figure 5-3).

ACL Types

The two types of ACLs covered in this guide are:

- Extended (IPv4 extended)
- Extended MAC

You can also create IPv6 ACLs; however, this guide covers only IPv4.

MAC ACLs permit or deny traffic according to the MAC header, and IPv4 ACLs select traffic based on the IP header. Standard ACLs of both types (IP and MAC) allow you to create rules based solely on the source address, while extended ACLs allow for a wider range of criteria. Standard ACLs are not currently supported by AOS-CX switches; only extended ACLs are supported.

Note

AOS-CX does ***not*** currently support standard ACLs. (The older AOS switches support standard ACLs—IP and MAC—which allow you to filter on source addresses only.)

ACL IDs

The ACL ID groups together all the rules in the ACL, allowing you to view the ACL, add rules to the ACL, and otherwise edit the ACL. Each ACL must have a unique ID.

Note

You can reuse IDs between IPv4 and IPv6 lists. In other words, an ACL's ID must be unique in IPv4, and its ID must be unique in IPv6, but an IPv4 and IPv6 ACL can use the same ID.

AOS-CX switches use a name to identify an ACL. Assigning a name makes it easier to identify the ACL's intended purpose. The name is a case-sensitive alphanumeric value.

When you create a named IPv4 ACL using this global configuration mode command, you must use the **access-list ip** command and indicate the type:

```
Switch(config)# access-list ip <ACL-name>
Switch(config-acl-ip)#
```

For MAC ACLs, use this command from global configuration mode context:

```
Switch(config)# access-list mac <ACL-name>
Switch(config-acl-mac)#
```

Creating the ACL moves you to configuration context for adding rules and editing the list. You will learn more about creating rules in a moment.

ACL Rule Components

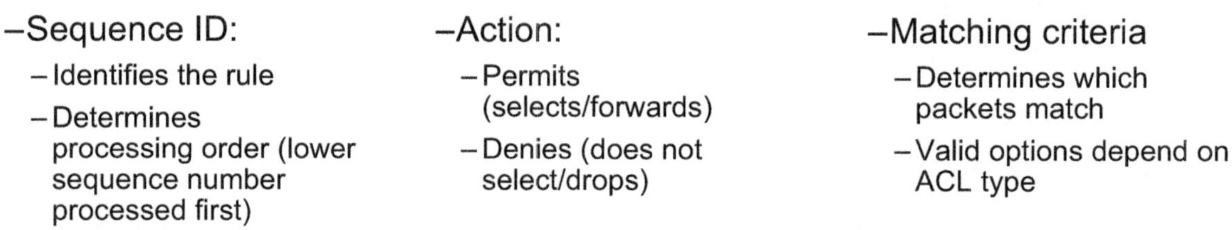

Figure 5-4: ACL Rule Components

An ACL rule consists of three basic components, as shown in Figure 5-4:

- Sequence ID
- Action
- Matching criteria

Sequence ID

The sequence ID identifies the rule within the list, enabling you to identify and, if necessary, remove it. The ID also tells the switch when to process this rule in relation to other rules. The ID with the lowest number is processed first. You will look at the implications of processing order in more detail later. Specifying a sequence ID is optional. If you do not specify the sequence ID, the switch assigns an ID automatically, placing the rule at the end of the list. You will learn more about the automatic sequence IDs a bit later in this chapter.

Action

ACLs have the following actions that are performed on match conditions of the rule:

- Mandatory actions:
  - **permit**—packets matching statements with a permit action will be allowed to progress through the switch.
  - **deny**—packets matching statements with a deny action will be dropped.
- Optional actions:
  - **count**—packets matching statements with a count action will increment hit counts for the specific entry.
  - **log** (available on permit and deny statements depending on platforms) —packets matching statements with a log action will increment hit counts as well for the specified entries (that

is, log performs an implicit count). The first packet that hits any log entry will be copied to the CPU and logged to the operator's specified destination (either console or syslog server). This first packet will start the 5-minute ACL logging timer (the ACL log-timer is configurable from 30s to default: 300s). When the timer expires, the summary of all the hit counts per ACL entry will be sent to the specified logging destination.

A **permit** action tells the ACL to select any packet that matches the criteria. The **deny** action tells the ACL not to select any packet that matches the criteria.

When you are using the ACL to filter packets, permitted packets are forwarded and denied packets are dropped.

Matching Criteria

The switch matches traffic against the rule's matching criteria to determine whether the traffic matches that rule.

Standard (IPv4) ACLs and standard MAC ACLs simply select traffic basic on its source IP or MAC address, so the rules are quite simple. Extended IP and MAC extended ACLs include more matching criteria, giving you more flexibility. In either case, AOS-CX switches currently only support extended ACL.

Example IP ACL Rules

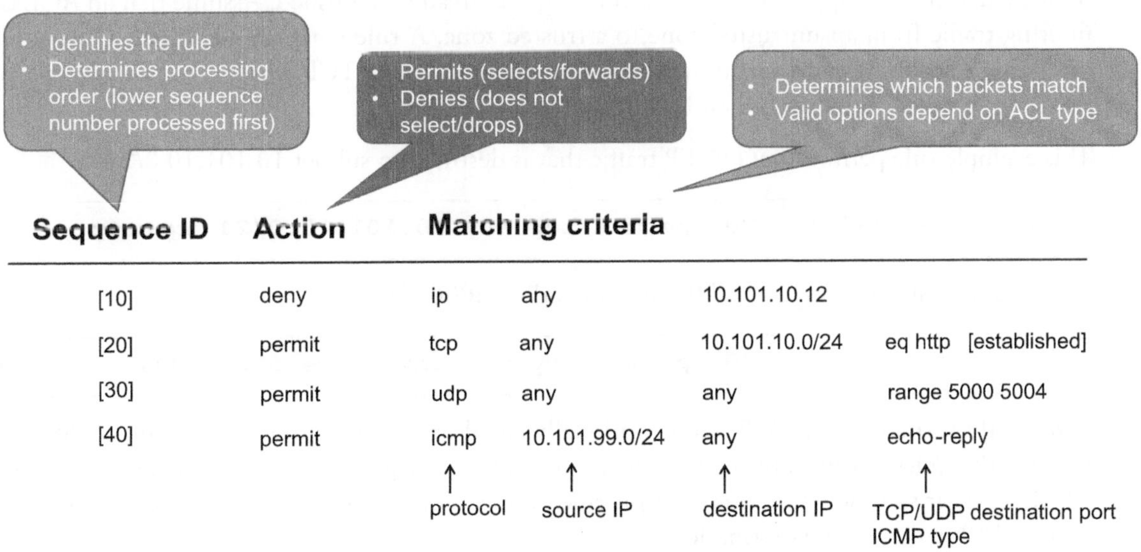

Figure 5-5: Example IP ACL Rules

An IPv4 extended ACL can select packets based on a variety of packet IP header fields (Figure 5-5).

All rules for these types of ACLs include a source and destination IP addresses. You have the same options for specifying the IP addresses as in standard ACLs (any, host <IP address>, or a range specified by prefix length or masking bits). If you care about just the source IP address, or just the destination IP address, specify any for the other.

You can further categorize IPv4 extended ACL rules by the IP protocol type, which is the first option that you specify after **permit** or **deny**:

- **ip**—These rules filter traffic based only on its source IP address, destination IP address, or both. **The IP protocol and other information in the IP header do not matter. This example rule denies all IP traffic to 10.101.10.12 and is placed in the list as sequence number 10:**

```
Switch(config-ext-nacl)# 10 deny ip any 10.101.10.12
```

- **tcp** or **udp**—These rules select particular TCP or UDP applications, typically based on the destination TCP or UDP port or port numbers. You can apply the rule to any IP address or to specific ones. When you specify the port, you must also include a keyword that indicates whether to select that specific port, a range of ports, any port except that port, and other options listed in Table 9-3. Rather than use the port number, you can use the keyword for many well-known ports. For example, if you specify **http**, the switch automatically interprets the port number as 80.

  For TCP only, you can filter traffic based on the TCP flag. For example, you might want to drop TCP RST packets from untrusted IP addresses. You can also include the **established** keyword to indicate that the rule applies only to sessions that are already established. Assume that an ACL is filtering traffic from an untrusted zone to a trusted zone. A rule with the **established** keyword can prevent untrusted endpoints from establishing certain types of TCP sessions, but allow sessions that were established by trusted endpoints to flow.

  This example rule permits any HTTP traffic that is destined to subnet 10.101.10.0/24:

```
Switch(config-acl-ip)# [20] permit tcp any 10.101.10.0/24 eq http
```

  This example allows a range of UDP ports including 5000-5004:

```
Switch(config-acl-ip)# [30] permit udp any any range 5000 5004
```

- **icmp**—These rules filter ICMP traffic, optionally based on its type. For example, you could permit ICMP replies but prohibit ICMP unreachable packets. Again, you can apply the rule to any IP addresses or specific ones. This example rule permits devices in the 10.101.99.0/24 subnet to send ICMP replies to any destination:

```
Switch(config-acl-ip)# [40] permit icmp 10.101.99.0/24 any echo-reply
```

- **igmp**—These rules filter IGMP traffic, optionally based on type and by source and destination address.
- Other protocols—These rules let you permit or deny specific IP protocols such as OSPF. The CLI provides keywords for specifying several protocols, as shown in the job aid. If you do not see a keyword for the protocol that you want to control, use the IP protocol number. Unlike with TCP, UDP, ICMP, and IGMP, you can only specify the IP protocol and the source and destination IP addresses, not other options.

The command syntax depends on the type of protocol in the rule. You saw a few examples above, and the tables below give the full syntax in the order you should enter the components. The parameters indicated in boldface are required while others are optional.

For any of these types of rules, you can specify a QoS mark so that the rule selects only traffic that meets the other criteria and is also marked for a specific priority. (You will learn more about how QoS priorities affect traffic handling later in this guide.) You can specify the traffic's IP precedence value, its Type of Service (ToS) value, or both. As you will learn later in this guide, modern networks often use Differentiated Services code points (DSCPs) to mark traffic for priority handling in its IP header. DSCPs use the same IP header fields as IP precedence and ToS, so you can specify a DSCP by specifying both an IP precedence and ToS value.

Here is the ACE syntax for IP and less common protocols:

```
[<SEQUENCE-NUMBER>] {permit | deny}
{any | ip | ah | gre | esp | igmp | ospf|pim | <IP-PROTOCOL-NUM>}
{any | <SRC-IP-ADDRESS>[/{<PREFIX-LENGTH>|<SUBNET-MASK>}] | <ADDRESS-GROUP>}
{any | <DST-IP-ADDRESS>[/{<PREFIX-LENGTH>|<SUBNET-MASK>}] | <ADDRESS-GROUP>}
[dscp <DSCP-SPECIFIER>] [ecn <ECN-VALUE>]
[ip-precedence <IP-PRECEDENCE-VALUE>] [tos <TOS-VALUE>] [fragment]
[vlan <VLAN-ID>] [ttl <TTL-VALUE>] [count] [log]
```

Here is the ACE syntax for SCTP, TCP, and UDP protocols:

```
[<SEQUENCE-NUMBER>] {permit | deny}
{sctp | tcp | udp}
{any | <SRC-IP-ADDRESS>[/{<PREFIX-LENGTH>|<SUBNET-MASK>}] | <ADDRESS-GROUP>}
[{eq | gt| lt} <PORT> | range<MIN-PORT><MAX-PORT> | group<PORT-GROUP>]
{any | <DST-IP-ADDRESS>[/{<PREFIX-LENGTH>|<SUBNET-MASK>}] |
<ADDRESS-GROUP>}
[{eq | gt |lt} <PORT> | range <MIN-PORT><MAX-PORT> | group <PORT-GROUP>]
[urg] [ack] [psh] [rst] [syn] [fin] [established] [dscp<DSCP-SPECIFIER>]
[ecn <ECN-VALUE>] [ip-precedence <IP-PRECEDENCE-VALUE>]
[tos <TOS-VALUE>] [fragment] [vlan <VLAN-ID>] [ttl <TTL-VALUE>] [count]
[log]
```

Table 5-1 Syntax for UDP or TCP port

Need	Keyword	Example
Specify one port	**eq**	**eq 80** Any traffic with port 80 is selected.
Specify a range of ports	**range**	**range 50000 50100** Any traffic with port 50000-50100 is selected (including 50000 and 50100).
Specify any port with a smaller value than that listed	**lt**	**lt 20** Any traffic with port 1-19 (including 1 and 19) is selected.
Specify the listed port and any port with a greater value	**gt**	**gt 49999** Any traffic with port 50000-65535 (including 50000 and 65535) is selected.

Here is the ACE syntax for the IMCP protocol:

```
[<SEQUENCE-NUMBER>] {permit | deny}
{icmp}
{any | <SRC-IP-ADDRESS>[/{<PREFIX-LENGTH>|<SUBNET-MASK>}] | <ADDRESS-GROUP>}
{any | <DST-IP-ADDRESS>[/{<PREFIX-LENGTH>|<SUBNET-MASK>}] | <ADDRESS-GROUP>}
[icmp-type {echo |echo-reply | <ICMP-TYPE-VALUE>}]
[icmp-code <ICMP-CODE-VALUE>]
[dscp <DSCP-SPECIFIER>] [ecn <ECN-VALUE>]
[ip-precedence <IP-PRECEDENCE-VALUE>] [tos<TOS-VALUE>] [fragment]
[vlan <VLAN-ID>] [ttl <TTL-VALUE>] [count] [log]
```

Note

Please see the *AOS-CX ACLs and Classifier Policies Guide* for a more in-depth coverage of the particular ACE parameters.

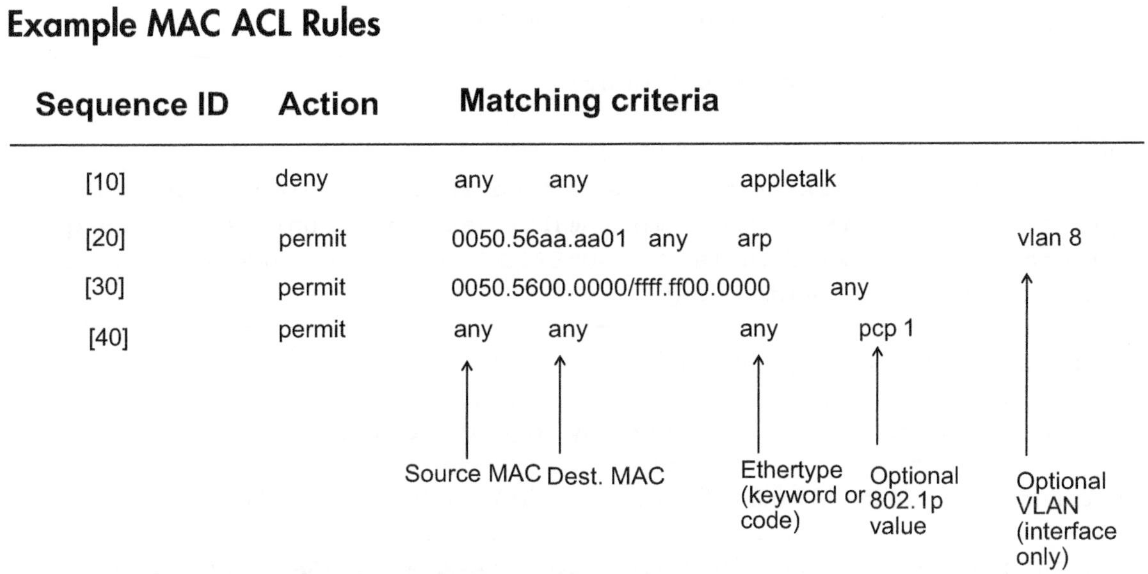

Figure 5-6: Example MAC ACL Rules

When you want to filter traffic based on MAC address, or when you want to filter various types of non-IP traffic, you should use MAC ACLs (Figure 5-6). The match criteria for extended ACLs include:

- Source and/or destination MAC addresses (any, a single address, or a range indicated with masking bits)
- Ethertype—You can specify one of several well-known Ethernet protocols such as IP, IPv6, ARP, FCoE, and so on. You can see a list of these protocols by pressing "?" in the CLI when you reach the portion of the command for specifying the Ethertype. If the protocol that you want to select does not appear in the list, enter the protocol number. You must specify the Ethertype in all rules. If you want the rule to match all Ethernet traffic, specify **any**.
- Optional 802.1Q QoS Priority Code Point (PCP) value

> **Note**
> You will learn more about QoS later in Chapter 13. Often you do not want to deny traffic with a specific PCP (802.1p) value entirely, but instead remove or change the value.

- Optional VLAN number

> **Note**
> The VLAN value is only applicable when the MAC ACL is applied to a port or link aggregation (trunk) interface.

Here is the subcontext syntax for creating a MAC ACE entry:

```
[<SEQUENCE-NUMBER>] {permit | deny}
{any | <SRC-MAC-ADDRESS>[/<ETHERNET-MASK>}]}
{any | <DST-MAC-ADDRESS>[/<ETHERNET-MASK>}]}
{any |aarp |appletalk |arp | fcoe | fcoe-init |ip| ipv6 | ipx-arpa |
ipx-non-arpa | is-is | lldp | mpls-multicast | mpls-unicast | q-in-q |
rbridge | trill | wake-on-lan | <NUMERIC-ETHERTYPE>} [pcp <PCP-VALUE>]
[vlan <VLAN-ID>] [count] [log]
```

This example rule denies all Appletalk traffic:

```
Switch(config-ext-macl)# 10 deny any any appletalk
```

This example rule permits ARP traffic from a specific MAC address in a specific VLAN:

```
Switch(config-ext-macl)# 20 permit host AAAA.AAAA.AAAA any arp vlan 8
```

This example rule denies all traffic with 802.1p value 1:

```
Switch(config-ext-macl)# 30 deny any any any pcp 1
```

Processing Order and Implicit Deny

Processing Order

When applying an ACL, the switch compares a packet against each rule's matching criteria in sequence until it finds a match. By default, AOS-CX switches process ACL rules according to each rule's ID (lowest to highest). When the switch finds a match, it takes the action indicated by the matching rule (deny or permit) and stops processing the ACL.

By combining permit and deny rules, you can create highly flexible policies. For example, you can deny one device within a subnet (such as 10.1.10.10) and permit the complete subnet (10.1.10.0/24). Or, with extended ACLs, you can select traffic associated with a particular application on a particular server; first permit traffic destined to a specific IP address and range of TCP or UDP ports and then deny all other traffic to the IP address.

These scenarios highlight the importance of the order in which the switch processes the rules. For example, in the first scenario, the switch must match packets against the rule that denies a specific device, 10.1.10.10, before the rule that permits the device's subnet, 10.1.10.0/24. If the switch processed the rule that permits the entire subnet first, the switch would permit the packet from 10.1.10.10 and stop processing the ACL. The deny rule would never take effect.

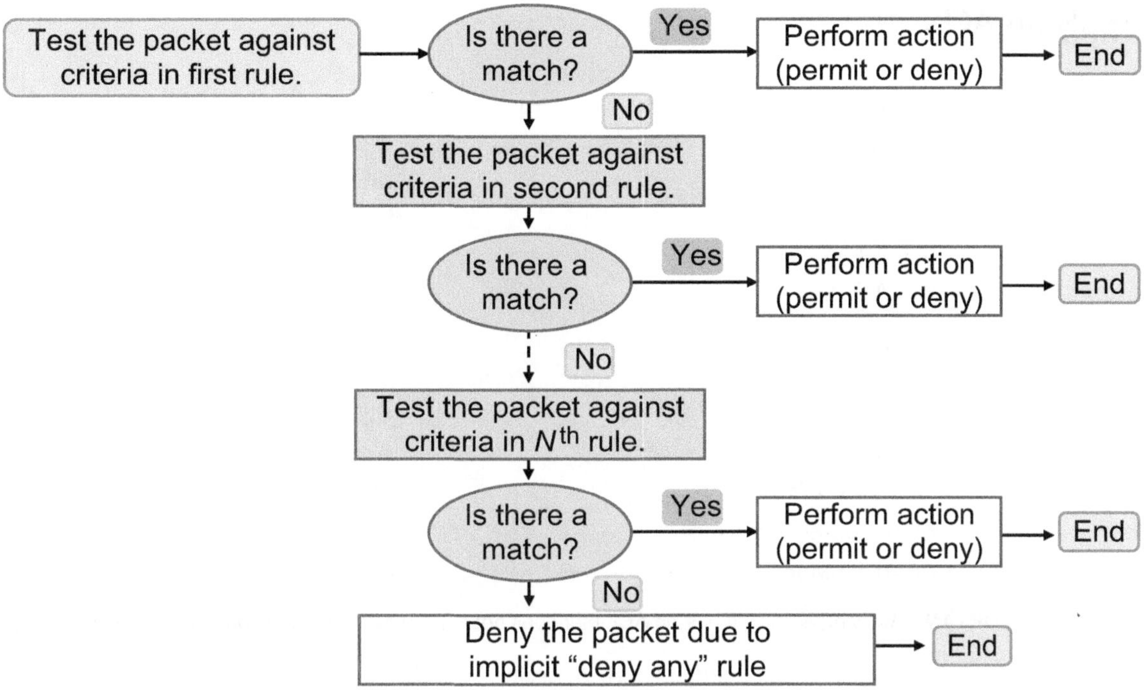

Figure 5-7: Processing Order and Implicit Deny

Implicit Action

You also need to understand how your switch treats packets that do not match any of the rules defined in the ACL. You can then avoid blocking or permitting the wrong traffic (Figure 5-7).

Important!
AOS-CX switches use an implicit deny any at the end of all ACLs.

ACLs on AOS-CX switches have an implicit "*deny any*" at the end. If you apply the ACL to an interface and the switch finds no matches between an inbound packet and the configured criteria in an applicable ACL, the switch drops the packet.

The implicit final rule is not displayed when viewing an ACL. Some administrators like to explicitly define the implicit rule at the end of an ACL to clarify the behavior. If you do so, make sure to assign the rule a very high ID so that you can add as many rules as you want.

If you need to override the implicit deny so that a packet that does not have a match is permitted, then you should create a rule that permits all traffic as the last rule in the ACL. Again, assign this rule a high ID. The table below shows the syntax for a "permit any" rule for each ACL type. It suggests the highest valid sequence number.

Applying ACLs

ACL Type	IPv4		
Direction	IN	OUT	
		6300 6400	832x 8400
L2 interface (port)	Yes	Yes	No
L2 LAG	Yes	Yes	No
L3 interface (port)	Yes	Yes	Yes
L3 LAG	Yes	Yes	Yes
VLAN	Yes	Yes	No
VLAN interface (SVI)	No	No	No
Tunnel interface	No	No	No
Management interface	Yes *	No	No
Control plane	Yes (Per VRF)		

IMPORTANT: Applying an ACL ID for an ACL that does not exist or has no entries permits all traffic.

Figure 5-8: Applying ACLs

After you create an ACL, you can apply it to one or more interfaces or VLANs. Until you actually assign an ACL to a VLAN or physical interface, it is present in the configuration but not used to filter traffic. When you apply an ACL to an interface using a configuration command, the ACL is called a static ACL. Once you apply the static ACL, it remains on the interface permanently until you modify or remove it.

Note

AOS-CX switches can also apply dynamic Port-based ACLs (PACLs) as part of an Authentication, Authorization, and Accounting (AAA) solution. This chapter focuses on static ACLs.

You have three choices as you apply a static ACL. First, you choose the interface (Layer-2 or Layer-3) to which you apply the ACL. Next, you choose the direction for the ACL, which determines whether the ACL filters traffic that arrives on that interface or that is destined out that interface. As you see in Figure 5-8, you can apply both IP and MAC ACLs to VLAN or physical interfaces.

Important!

Currently in AOS-CX 10.04, logical Layer-3 interfaces, like VLAN SVI or GRE tunnel interfaces, are not supported by AOS-CX when applying ACLs.

How you apply the ACL determines which type of ACL the ACL becomes in implementation: a Layer-3 interface ACL (RACL), a VLAN ACL (VACL), or a Port-based ACL (PACL) (applied on a layer-2 interface or a link aggregation or *LAG*). Whether the switch applies the ACL as an RACL, VACL, or PACL in turn determines which packets and frames the switch processes against the ACL:

- RACLs are IP ACLs applied to routed Layer 3 physical interfaces in either the outbound or inbound direction. Inbound RACLs filter traffic that arrives on a VLAN and is routed out another subnet while outbound RACLs filter traffic that is routed out of a VLAN.
- VACLs are applied to a VLAN within the VLAN context. Inbound VACLs filter all traffic that arrives on a VLAN, whether switched or routed. Outbound VACLs filter all traffic that is forwarded out a VLAN, whether the source is within the same subnet (switched) or another subnet (routed). Because both inbound and outbound VACLs filter traffic that arrives on a VLAN and is switched out that VLAN, some of the traffic that they filter overlaps.
- Port-based ACLs (PACLs) are any ACLs applied to Layer-2 physical interfaces. Inbound PACLs filter all traffic that arrives on the interface, whether switched or routed. Outbound PACLs filter all traffic forwarded on the interface, whether switched or routed.

You will explore the different ways these ACLs filter traffic in more detail throughout this chapter.

You should also keep in mind that you can apply an ACL to multiple different interfaces, but each interface supports a maximum of one ACL in each direction. On VLAN interfaces, you are allowed to use the same ACL for both the inbound and outbound directions, but often you should not do so because, of course, the source and destination addresses for your rules might not be valid in both directions.

To apply an ACL to an interface or LAG, use the following configuration:

```
Switch(config)# interface <interface-ID>
Switch(config-if)# apply access-list {ip | mac} <ACL-name> {in | out}
```

To apply an ACL to a VLAN, use the following configuration:

```
Switch(config)# vlan <VLAN-ID>
Switch(config-if)# apply access-list {ip | mac} <ACL-name> {in | out}
```

Note

The extent of ACL support varies among the AOS-CX switch families. Based on the hardware ASIC used by the switch, there might be limitations in how an ACL can be applied. See the table in the slide for the current restrictions in AOS-CX 10.04 and the related switch model to determine which type of ACL can be applied and in which direction.

Tips

Keep the following points in mind when applying ACLs.

- AOS-CX switches allow you to assign a nonexistent ACL name to an interface. When you apply a nonexistent or empty ACL to an interface, the interface permits all traffic until you create an ACL that uses that name *and* add a rule to the ACL. The implicit "deny any" does not take effect until at least one rule is defined. In short, you should be careful to specify the correct ACL name.
- On AOS-CX switches, if you delete an assigned ACL from the switch without subsequently removing the ACL from an interface to which it is assigned, the ACL assignment remains on the interface. The empty ACL does not affect traffic (all traffic is permitted). However, the switch will automatically begin applying any new ACL you create with the same identifier (name). You should clean up your configurations to ensure that ACLs are applied when and where you expect.

Example ACL Configuration

In Figure 5-9 you see a simple example of how you can combine rules into an ACL and apply the ACL to an interface. In this example, you want to strictly control traffic from a device connected on an interface. You configure an IPv4 extended ACL with the two rules shown above and apply it inbound on the interface.

When the device tries to send IP traffic to Server 1, the switch processes the traffic against the ACL. This traffic matches the first rule, which selects all IP traffic destined to Server 1 at 10.101.10.11. The traffic is dropped.

Next the device tries to send IP traffic to Server 2 at 10.101.10.12. Again, the switch processes the traffic against the first rule, but the traffic does not match this rule. The switch then processes the traffic against the second rule, which it does match because 10.101.10.12/30 is within 10.101.10.0/24. The second rule is a permit rule, so the switch forwards the traffic.

Finally, the device tries to send IP traffic to Server 3 at 10.101.30.13. This traffic matches neither rule. Therefore, it is processed by the implicit deny any, and the switch drops it.

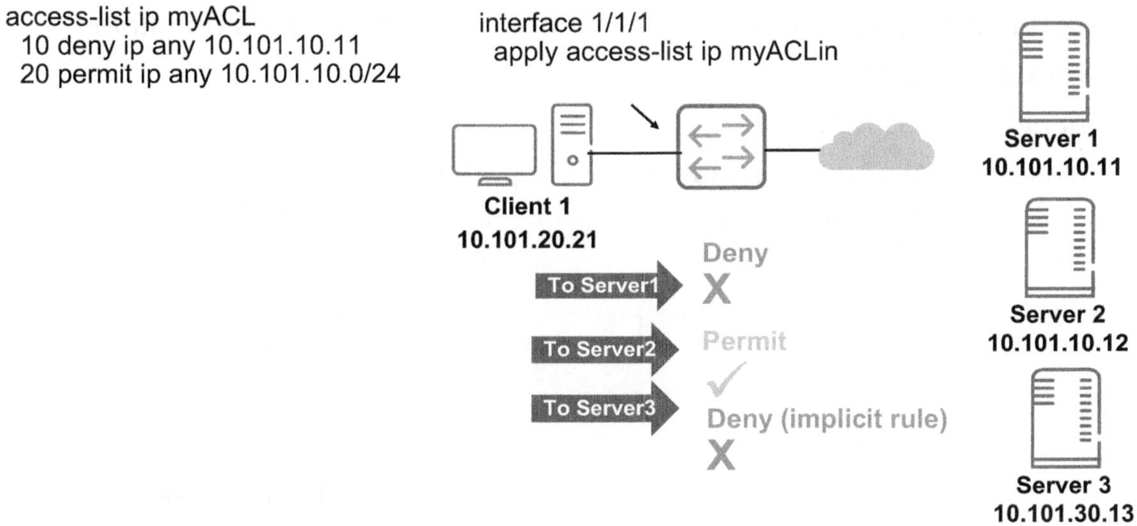

Figure 5-9: Example ACL Configuration

Creating Rules (ACEs)

Now that you have had some practice creating an ACL, you will dive down deeper into the specifics of creating flexible rules, commonly referred to as *access control entries* (ACEs). You will begin by learning strategies for specifying the correct range of addresses. Then you will learn about how to use rule IDs to manage your ACLs and to ensure that traffic is processed in the correct order.

Detailed Look at Source/Destination IP Addresses in ACLs

As you practiced in the lab, you can use a network address and prefix length to define a range of IP addresses in an ACL rule. This option works well when you want to permit or deny an entire subnet. When you looked at the ACL, though, you saw that the range was denoted as shown in Figure 5-10. Instead of 10.101.10.0/24, you saw IP: 10.101.10.0 and Mask: 255.255.255.0. This mask is a subnet mask and you can actually specify the IP address and subnet mask, instead, when you create the rule.

To master both creating and interpreting rules, you need to explore prefix lengths and the relationships between them in more depth.

You can specify source and destination IP address ranges as either:

- Prefix length (/24)
- Subnet address (255.255.255.0)
- Wildcard masks (inverted mask—not supported)

```
Switch# show access-list ip MY_ACL
Type Name
Sequence Comment
         Action                    L3 Protocol
         Source IP Address         Source L4 Port(s)
         Destination IP Address    Destination L4 Port(s)
         Additional Parameters
----------------------------------------------------------
IPv4     MY_ACL
      10 permit                    udp
         any
         172.16.1.0/255.255.255.0
```

Shown as IP with subnet mask

Entered as 172.16.1.0/24

Figure 5-10: Detailed Look at Source/Destination IP Addresses in ACLs

Specifying IP Address Ranges with a Prefix Length

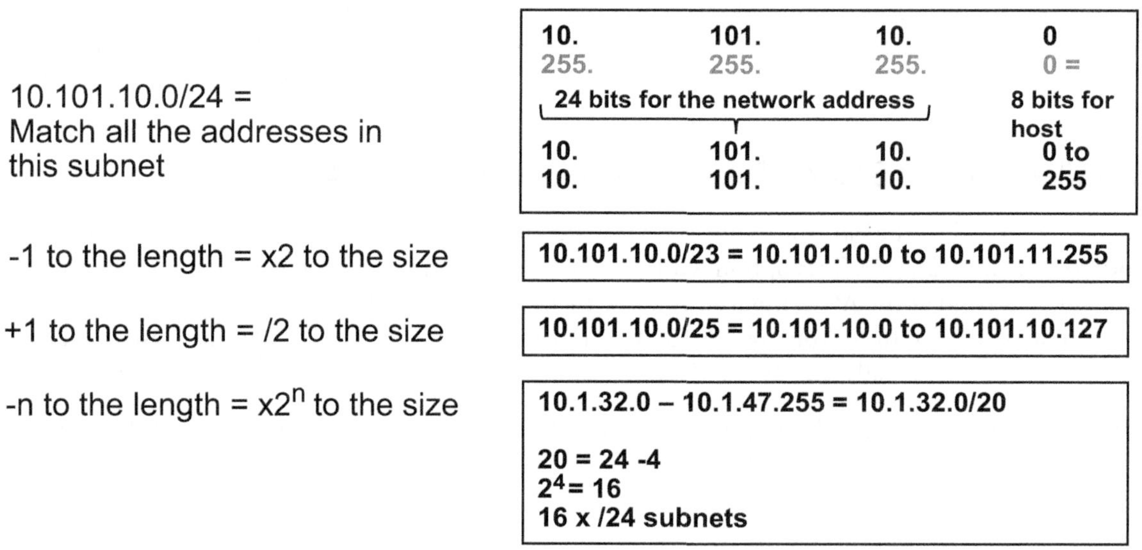

Figure 5-11: Specifying IP Address Ranges with a Prefix Length

When you specify a subnet such as 10.101.10.0/24 in an ACL rule, the rule matches all IP addresses in the subnet from 10.101.10.0 to 10.101.10.255. (Of course, 10.101.10.0 is the subnet address and 10.101.10.255 is the broadcast address, so typical traffic will not use the addresses at either end of the range for the source.)

Subnets with the /24 prefix length are familiar and easy to use. However, you might want to conserve the number of rules within an ACL by specifying larger ranges of IP addresses. Or you might want to specify a subset of a /24 network in one rule rather than several identical rules with different host addresses.

To understand how to specify the desired range of IP addresses, briefly review prefix lengths and their relationship with subnet masks.

Subnet Masks

In common IP addressing, a network (or subnet) mask defines which part of the IP address to use for the network (or subnet) address and which part to use for the hosts on the network:

- The bits set to 1 define the part of the IP address to use for the network address.
- The bits set to 0 define the part of the IP address to use for the host address.

In the example shown in Figure 5-11, the subnet mask is 255.255.255.0, or all 1s within the first three octets. Therefore, 10.1.10.0 is the network address. Valid host numbers in the fourth octet are between 1 and 254. Therefore, valid IP addresses that could be assigned to devices are from 10.1.10.1 through 10.1.10.254. The IP addresses 10.1.10.0 and 10.1.10.255 are reserved for identifying the subnet and broadcast addresses, respectively.

Note

Sometimes the bits are referred to as *wildcard* bits: 1 means to match and 0 can be ignored. For example, a mask of 255.255.0.0 would mean that the first two octets of the packet must match what's in the ACE rule, and the last two octets do not matter.

Prefix Lengths

Classless Inter-Domain Routing (CIDR) notation represents a subnet mask by the prefix length. In other words, the prefix length specifies the number of bits set to 1 in the subnet mask. For example, the subnet mask in the slide has 24 1s and defines a /24 subnet.

Rules of Thumb for Specifying Ranges with Prefix Lengths

You are probably familiar with /8, /16, and /24 subnets. These subnets have their boundaries at the octet border in decimal format, so it is easy to understand the range of addresses included in these subnets.

Sometimes, though, you want to specify ranges of IP addresses of different lengths than these.

As a rule of thumb, you double the size of a subnet when you subtract one from the prefix length. You halve the size when you add one.

For example, 10.101.10.0/23 includes IP addresses in two /24 subnets—IP addresses from 10.101.10.0 to 10.101.11.255. 10.101.10.0/25 includes IP addresses from 10.101.10.0 to 10.101.10.127.

If you want to multiply or divide by more than 2, choose a factor that is a power of 2 such as 4, 8, 16, and so on, and use the related exponent as the number that you add or subtract from the length. For example, you want a rule to select traffic with IP addresses between 10.1.32.0 and 10.1.47.255. This range has 16 /24 subnets, so you subtract 4 from 24 ($2^4 = 16$). You would specify 10.1.32.0/20.

As another example, you want a permit rule to select traffic with source IP addresses between 192.168.4.32 and 192.168.4.39. This range is eight times the size of 192.168.4.32/32, so you would specify 192.168.4.32/29 ($2^3 = 8$).

When you are specifying ranges in this way, you must remember that you are specifying the network address for a subnet. For example, you could not specify 192.168.4.30/29 to select the eight addresses from 192.168.4.30 to 192.168.4.37. This range includes addresses in two different /29 subnets, and 192.168.4.30 is not a valid network address for a /29 subnet. An easy way to check if an IP address is a valid network address for a subnet with a length between /24 and /32 is to determine the subnet's size and make sure that the final octet is divisible by that size. For example, a /29 subnet has 8 IP addresses. 32 is divisible by 8, but 30 is not. You also need to make sure that your range includes a number of addresses that is a power of two (such as 8, 16, 32, and so on).

If you want a range of a different size, you must enter multiple rules. Sometimes it is easier to specify a broader range than you need in the rule and create rules with lower sequence numbers that define exceptions.

You can apply similar logic to larger subnets, paying attention to the most significant octet for that subnet. For example, a /20 subnet includes 16 /24 subnets, so the third octet of the network address must be divisible by 16, and the last octet should be zero.

You can find prefix length calculators on the Internet to help you check your addresses.

Note

AOS-CX switches do *not* support wildcard masks—only prefixes or subnet masks—when creating ACEs.

Specifying MAC Address Ranges

When you want to specify a range of MAC addresses in a MAC ACL rule, you must use wildcard bits. However, these bits use hexadecimal format. Each f indicates that a frame's source or destination MAC address must match the corresponding hexadecimal character in the address in the rule. A 0, on the other hand, tells the switch to ignore the corresponding character in frames' addresses (Figure 5-12).

For example, to match *0050.5600.0000 ffff.ff00.0000*, a frame can have any source MAC address that begins with 0050.56.

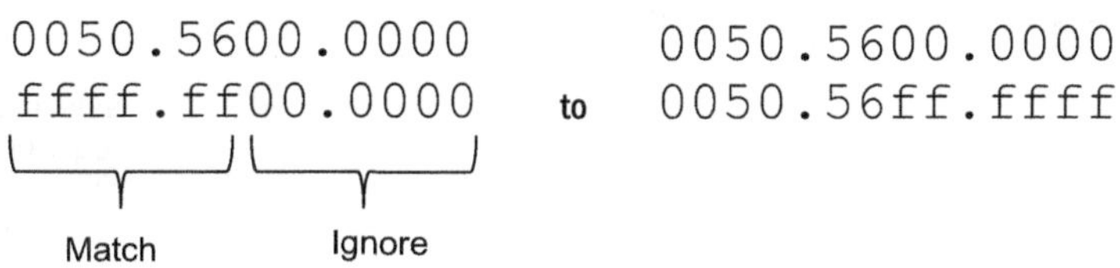

Figure 5-12: Specifying MAC Address Ranges

You can create more complicated rules using different hexadecimal characters in the mask. Determine the exact bits with source or destination MAC addresses that you want the switch to check or ignore. Set checked bits to 0s and ignored bits to 1; then convert to hexadecimal. For example, you enter **0050.5600.0000 ffff.ffff.fffc**. This mask tells the switch to check all bits for all hexadecimal characters until the last character. At that point, the switch checks the first two bits but ignores the last two bits (1100 = hexadecimal c). This rule selects packets with destination MAC addresses 0050.5600.0000 through 0050-5600-0003. As you see, you can use the guideline of subtracting the first address from the last address to obtain the wildcard bits.

However, complicated rules such as these are usually unnecessary.

Managing ACL Rule Sequence

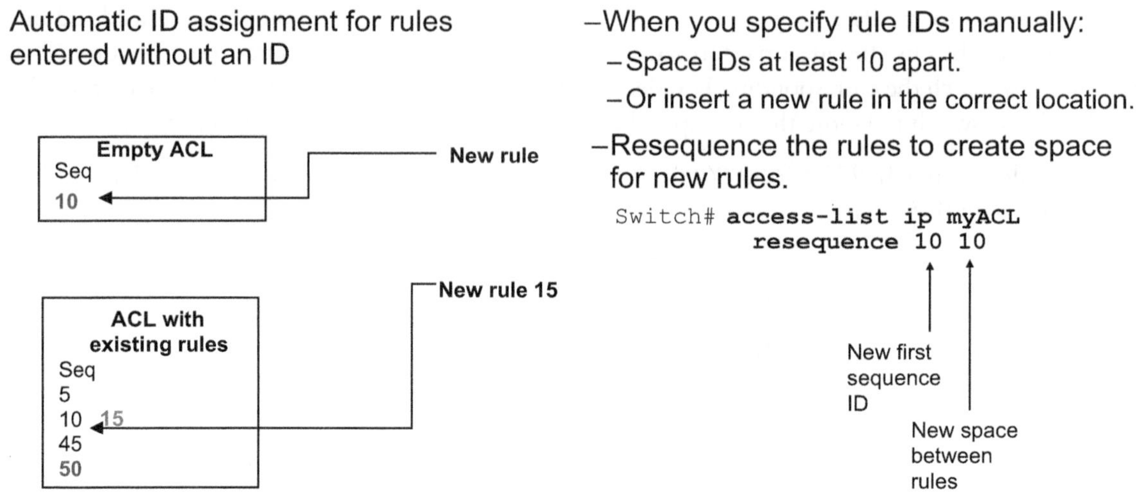

Figure 5-13: Managing ACL Rule Sequence

In the lab, you will see how the AOS-CX switch assigns automatic sequence numbers to the ACL rules when you do not specify a sequence number yourself. You will now examine sequencing issues in more detail. You can specify the rule ID manually, or you can enter the rules in the order in which you want them processed (Figure 5-13).

In any case, you must plan the ACL carefully and configure rules for processing in the correct order, generally entering more specific rules with a lower ID than the ID for less specific rules.

Automatic Numbering

If you do not enter a manual ID, the switch automatically adds rule IDs in order, leaving spaces. New rules are added to the *end* of the list, even if spaces exist earlier in the list.

For example, if the first rule that you enter does not have a manual ID, an AOS-CX switch numbers the rule as 10. Subsequent rules without rule numbers are numbered in increments of 10: 10, 20, 30, and so on. The switch always adds a rule without a manual ID after the *final* explicit rule. If this rule has an ID that is not divisible by 10, such as 45, the switch adds the new rule with the next ID that is divisible by 10, such as 50.

Manual Numbering

When you enter rules manually, it is best practice for you to space rule IDs, preferably by 10s, so that you can insert additional rules at a later point, if necessary. Then, when you do not want to add a rule to the end of the list, you can choose a rule ID between existing rules to insert the rule in the correct location.

Sequence Renumbering

Sometimes, despite your best planning, you need to change rule IDs to place rules in the correct order.

From the ACL context, you can also easily remove a rule using the **no <sequence-number>** command. In addition, you can redefine the sequence numbers of all rules in a given ACL using this command:

```
Switch(config)# access-list {ip | mac} <ACL-name> resequence
<start-sequence> <increment>
```

In these commands, **<start-sequence>** is the sequence number you want to assign to the first rule, and **<increment>** is the incrementing value by which subsequent rules will be numbered. This command leaves the rules in the same relative order. However, with more spaces between the rules, you can remove rules and add them in the appropriate location as necessary.

Logging and Counting ACL Matches

You now have a good sense of how to create rules. In addition to the other options, an ACL rule on an AOS-CX switch can include the **log** or **count** options at the end.

Logging

The **log** option signals the switch to generate an Event Log message when a packet matches a packet. The log is created if the action is "deny" *or* "permit," if there is a match, and if you have enabled ACL logging.

log, depending on platforms, will increment hit counts as well for the specified entries (that is log performs an implicit count). The first packet that hits any log entry will be copied to the CPU and logged to the operator's specified destination (either console or syslog server). This first packet will start the 5-minute ACL logging timer (the ACL log-timer is configurable from 30s to default: 300s). When the timer expires, the summary of all the hit counts per ACL entry will be sent to the specified logging destination. To change the default logging period, use the following command:

```
Switch(config)# access-list log-timer {default | <VALUE>}
```

The timer interval can be from 30 to 300 seconds, where 300 is the default (5 minutes).

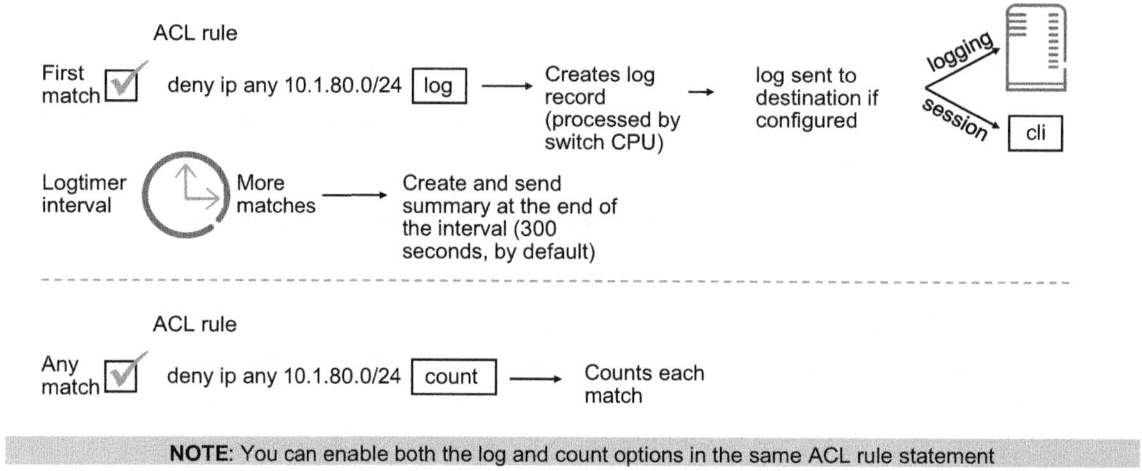

Figure 5-14: Logging and Counting ACL Matches

The first packet that matches an ACE with the log parameter within an ACL log timer window (configured with the **access-list log-timer** command) has its header contents extracted and sent to the configured logging destination, such as the console and syslog server. Each time the ACL log timer expires, a summary of all ACEs with log configured is sent to the logging destination. This capability allows throttling of logging ACL hits (Figure 5-14).

When using multiple ACL types (IPv4, IPv6, or MAC) with logging on the same interface, the first packet that matches an ACE with the log option is logged. Any packets, matching other ACL types, do not create a log until the log-timer wait-period is over. At the end of the wait-period, a summary log is made of all the ACLs that were matched, regardless of type.

Note

You may see a minor discrepancy between the ACL logging statistics and the hit counts statistics due to the time required to record the log message.

To enable ACL logging to a syslog server, you must define a syslog server and a logging level:

```
Switch(config)# logging {<IPV4-ADDR> | <IPV6-ADDR> | <HOSTNAME>}
[udp [<PORT-NUM>] | tcp [<PORT-NUM>] | tls [<PORT-NUM>]]
[include-auditable-events] [severity <LEVEL>] [vrf <VRF-NAME>]
```

The default port for UDP, the most common protocol used for syslog, is 514.

The supported logging levels include the following:

- **alert**: Forwards syslog messages with the severity of alert (6) and emergency (7).
- **crit**: Forwards syslog messages with the severity of critical (5) and above.
- **debug**: Forwards syslog messages with the severity of debug (0) and above.
- **emerg**: Forwards syslog messages with the severity of emergency (7) only.
- **err**: Forwards syslog messages with the severity of err (4) and above
- **info**: Forwards syslog messages with the severity of info (1) and above. Default.
- **notice**: Forwards syslog messages with the severity of notice (2) and above.
- **warning**: Forwards syslog messages with the severity of warning (3) and above.

Certificate and TLS logging are supported. See the *AOS-CX Command-Line Interface Guide* for more information.

Hit Counts

The **count** key word will keep track of each match on an ACE entry. To reset the hit counts for all ACLs, a specific ACL, or a specific interface, use the following command:

```
Switch# clear access-list hitcounts {all | [{ip |ipv6 | mac} <ACL-NAME>]
[interface <IFNAME> | vlan <VLAN-ID>] [in | out]}
```

Note
You can add the **log** and **count** functions in a single ACL rule statement.

Important
Logging information is processed by the CPU of the switch.

Review Activity: Analyzing an ACL

Desired behavior for these sources:

- Permit 10.1.1.1-10.1.1.30
- Permit 10.1.1.40-10.1.1.55
- Deny all others

Sequence	ACL entry
1	deny 10.1.1.31 255.255.255.255 any
2	deny 10.1.1.32 255.255.255.224 any
3	permit 10.1.1.0 255.255.255.192 any
4	permit 10.1.1.40 255.255.255.248 any
5	permit 10.1.1.48 255.255.255.248 any

– What is the current behavior?
– How can you reorder the ACL to use the correct sequence?

Figure 5-15: Review Activity: Analyzing an ACL

Assume that the ACL shown in Table 5-2 has been applied outbound to a VLAN interface, and a switch is now comparing packets being routed out that VLAN against the ACL.

Table 5-2 Extended ACL example

ACL Rule IDs	ACL Rules
Rule ID 1	deny 10.1.1.31 255.255.255.255 any
Rule ID 2	deny 10.1.1.32 255.255.255.224 any
Rule ID 3	permit 10.1.1.0 255.255.255.192 any
Rule ID 4	permit 10.1.1.40 255.255.255.248 any
Rule ID 5	permit 10.1.1.48 255.255.255.248 any

You want the switch to permit only packets with these source IP addresses:

- 10.1.1.1-10.1.1.30

  10.1.1.0 is the network address in this case, so it is okay if the rule permits packets from the address. The switch will not route packets from it in any case.

- 10.1.1.40-10.1.1.55

  1. What is the current behavior?
  2. How can you reorder the ACL to use the correct sequence?

Review Activity: Analyzing an ACL (Hint)

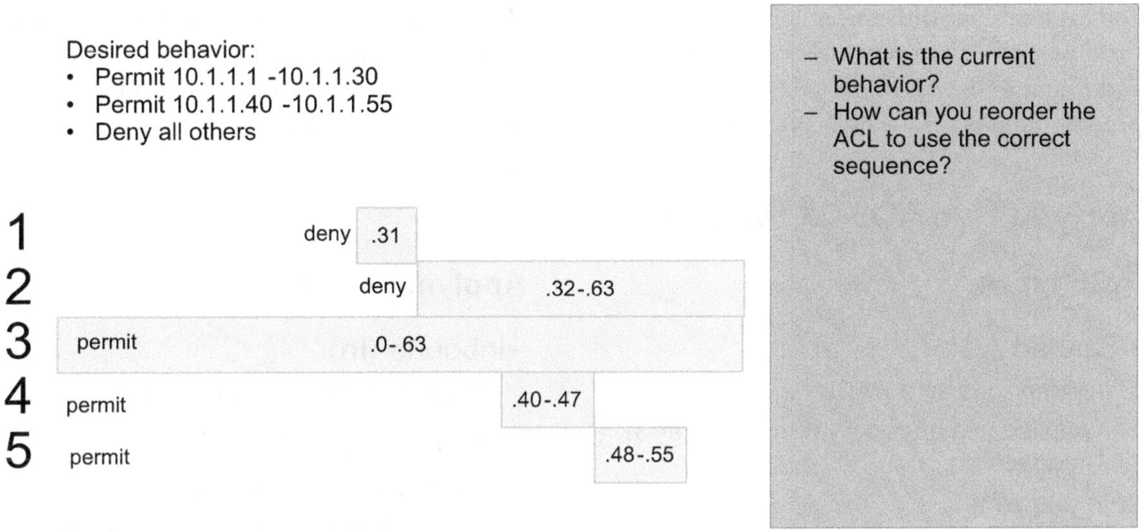

Figure 5-16: Review Activity: Analyzing an ACL (Hint)

Activity Debrief

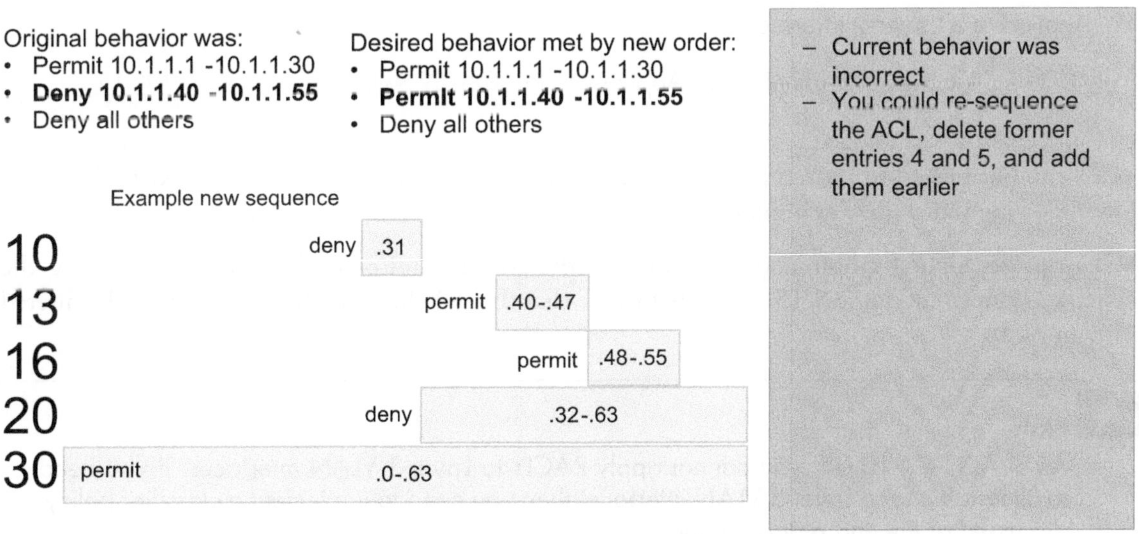

Figure 5 17: Review Activity. Analyzing an ACL (Debrief)

Applying ACLs

You explore some differences between an RACL and VACL in the lab (Figures 5-15–5-17). Some of the differences, however, only become clear in a topology that uses Layer 2 switches at the access layer and routes at the distribution layer or core. In this section, you will dive into more detail about the precise traffic that is—and is not—filtered by RACLs, VACLs, and PACLs.

Apply ACLs to AOS-CX Switches

ACL types

- Routed ACL
  - Referred to as a RACL
  - Applied to a physically routed (Layer-3) interface
- VLAN ACL
  - Referred to as a VACL
  - Applied to a VLAN (Layer-2)
- Port ACL
  - Referred to as a PACL
  - Applied to a Layer-2 interface

Applying ACLs

- Inbound (**in**)
  - Traffic entering the switch
- Outbound (**out**)
  - Traffic leaving the switch
  - Traffic the switch itself generates cannot be filtered with an outbound ACL

Figure 5-18: Apply ACLs to AOS-CX Switches

ACLs can be applied to routed ports (RACLs), VLANs (VACLs), and a Layer-2 ports (PACLs). The following slides show examples to these.

ACLs can be applied inbound (traffic entering the switch) and/or outbound (traffic leaving the switch), as shown in Figure 5-18. Note that traffic that the switch, itself, originates cannot be filtered with an ACL.

Note

As of AOS-CX 10.04, you cannot apply RACLs to Layer-3 VLAN interfaces. If you need to filter traffic for a Layer-3 VLAN interface, then you need to implement a classifier policy, discussed at the end of this chapter.

Inbound RACLs

You should configure an RACL to control traffic at VLAN boundaries and filter *routed* traffic between subnets. RACLs apply to Layer-3 VLAN interfaces, and you should typically apply them on a routing switch that handles routing for that VLAN.

For example, your core routing switch is the default gateway for VLAN 20, which is also configured on several access layer switches. If you want to apply an RACL to control traffic routed to or from VLAN 20, apply the ACL to VLAN 20 on the core routing switch.

RACLs can be either inbound or outbound, and you can apply one RACL per-direction per-physical interface (Layer-2 or Layer-3). On AOS-CX switches, you apply the ACL to the interface in the interface context by specifying the direction (**apply access-list** <ACL-name> **<in | out>**).

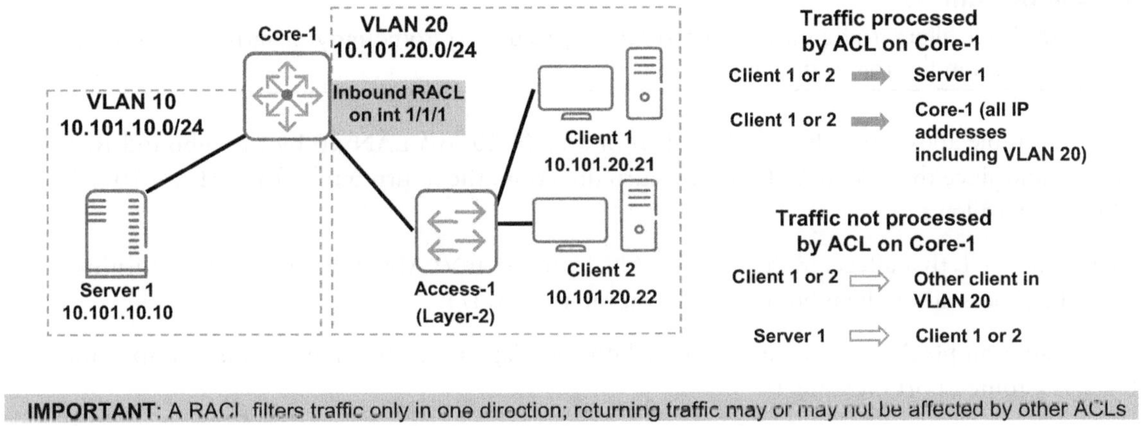

Figure 5-19: Inbound RACLs

An inbound RACL processes the following traffic, as shown in Figure 5-19:

- **Traffic received on this physical interface and routed out another subnet**—For example, you have applied the RACL inbound to the routed interface 1/1/1, which is associated to VLAN 20 and uses the 10.101.20.0/24 subnet. The ACL filters packets that arrive in interface 1/1/1 and are routed to destinations in other subnets. In the example above, this includes traffic from Client 1 or 2 to Server 1. (Note that "arrives in 1/1/1" means that the packet arrives on a port that is untagged for VLAN 20 or with a VLAN tag of 20 on a port that permits such a tag.) Because the ACL applies to traffic that *this* network infrastructure device routes out of this interface, the device must be routing the traffic.
- **Traffic received on this physical interface and destined to this switch**—An RACL does not filter switched IP traffic unless the switch's own IP address on the interface is the destination. For example, as shown above, the ACL processes traffic from Client 1 or 2 to all IP addresses on Core-1, including the VLAN 20 IP address. This helps you to protect access to the switch itself.

Note

The RACL does *not* filter traffic generated on the interface by the switch itself.

In addition, an inbound RACL does not process the following traffic:

- Traffic received on the VLAN and switched on the same subnet (except to the switch itself)
  The inbound ACL does not process traffic between Client 1 and Client 2.
- Traffic received on other VLANs and routed out this VLAN
  The inbound ACL also does not process traffic from Server 1 to either of the clients.

Important

An RACL filters traffic only in one direction; returning traffic may or may not be affected by ACLs in the return direction.

In the example above, if traffic is allowed from VLAN 20 to VLAN 10 by the inbound RACL on Core-1, and since there is no ACL in the return direction, the return traffic from VLAN 10 to VLAN 20 would be allowed.

There is no ACL that affects traffic from VLAN 10 to reach VLAN 20; however, the returning traffic *would* be processed by the inbound RACL on interface 1/1/1.

Here is an example ACL configuration based on the diagram in the slide. In this example, interface 1/1/1 is a routed port on Core-1:

```
Switch(config)# access-list ip example
Switch(config-acl-ip)# permit ip 10.101.20.21/32 any
Switch(config-acl-ip)# exit
Switch(config)# interface 1/1/1
Switch(config-if)# apply access-list example in
```

Based on this example, this traffic would be processed by the ACL and allowed:

- Client1 > Server1
- Client1 > Core1

And this traffic would also be processed by the ACL, but denied:

- Client2 > Server1
- Client2 > Core1

And this traffic is not even processed by the ACL:

- Client1 or Client2 > any other client in VLAN 20
- Server1 > Client1 or Client 2 (but the returning traffic from these clients will be processed by the ACL)

Note
The ACL example is looking at traffic from the source to the destination. Remember that returning traffic might be affected by the ACL, based on the rules and how it is applied.

Outbound RACLs

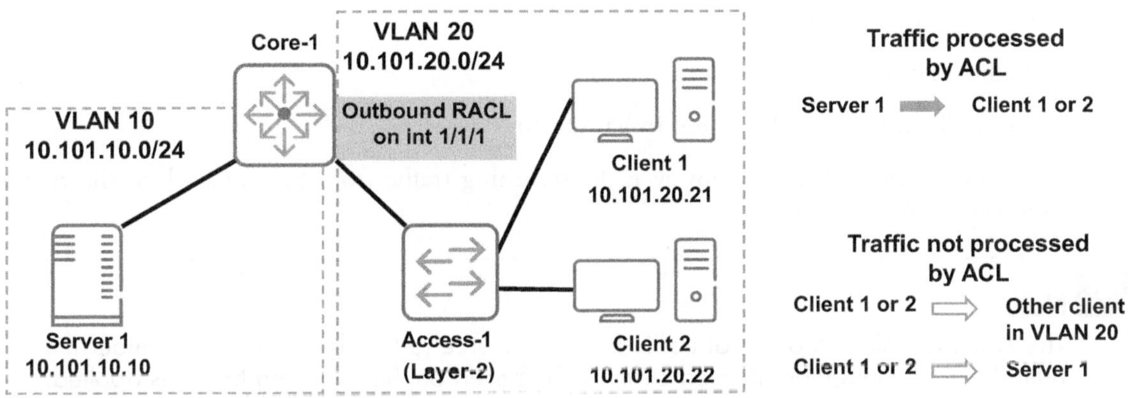

Figure 5-20 Outbound RACLs

An outbound RACL filters traffic received from any subnet and routed to a subnet on this VLAN interface. For example, you have applied an RACL outbound to a switch's 1/1/1 routed interface, which uses the 10.101.20.0/24 subnet. The switch receives a packet from Server 1 on VLAN interface 10, and the packet is destined to Client 1 at 10.101.20.21. This ACL processes that packet because the switch routes the packet to VLAN 20.

An outbound RACL does not process the following traffic:

- Traffic generated by the switch and routed out this VLAN interface
- Traffic received on this VLAN and routed out another subnet
  For example, the ACL shown in Figure 5-20 does not filter traffic from the clients to the server. In other words, the ACL does not process any traffic from the clients.

You can apply only one RACL per-interface to inbound traffic and one RACL per-interface to outbound traffic. Plan the ACL rules accordingly.

Here is an example ACL configuration based on the diagram in the slide. In this example, interface 1/1/1 is a routed port on Core-1:

```
Switch(config)# access-list ip example
Switch(config-acl-ip)# permit ip any 10.101.20.21/32
Switch(config-acl-ip)# exit
Switch(config)# interface 1/1/1
Switch(config-if)# apply access-list example out
```

Based on this example, this traffic would be processed by the ACL and allowed:

- Server1 > Client1

And this traffic would also be processed by the ACL, but denied:

- Server1 > Client2

And this traffic is not even processed by the ACL:

- Client1 or Client2 > any other client in VLAN 20
- Client 1 or Client2 > Server1 (however, the returning traffic from Server1 back to the clients would be processed by the ACL)

Note

The ACL example is looking at traffic from the source to the destination. Remember that returning traffic might be affected by the ACL, based on the rules and how it is applied.

ACL Discussion of Inbound Versus Outbound

So, when should an ACL be applied inbound versus outbound, given that in many instances you could implement your policy with either? The advantage of applying an ACL inbound is that you are dropping the traffic closer to the source, and thus less processing has to be done by the switch. However, if you have many, many interfaces, but only one exit interface, like an uplink, it might be easier to manage the application of the ACL by applying it outbound on the uplink interface. Also, ACLs do consume resources, as discussed toward at the end of the chapter, so for an uplink, applying it outbound on an uplink will consume less resources than applying it inbound on a multitude of ports. These are things you should consider when determining when creating an ACL policy as to whether it is better to use an inbound versus and outbound ACL solution.

Inbound VACLs

As you learned, RACLs applied to VLAN interfaces do not filter traffic that flows within the *same* subnet. When you want to control traffic switched within a subnet, you must apply a different type of ACL.

A PACL (PACL), which you will learn about shortly, filters both routed and switched traffic and meets this need. However, when you want to control all devices in a VLAN in the same way, a VACL is the most efficient mechanism. One VACL applies to all ports that are members of the VLAN. The VACL filters all IP traffic entering a switch on the specific VLAN interface. On a multinetted VLAN (a VLAN with multiple subnets), this includes inbound IP traffic from any subnet.

As you learned earlier, a MAC ACL applied to a VLAN in the inbound direction is always an inbound VACL. For an IP ACL applied to a VLAN, you can apply it inbound or outbound for the 6300 and 6400 switches, but only inbound for the 8400 and 832x switches.

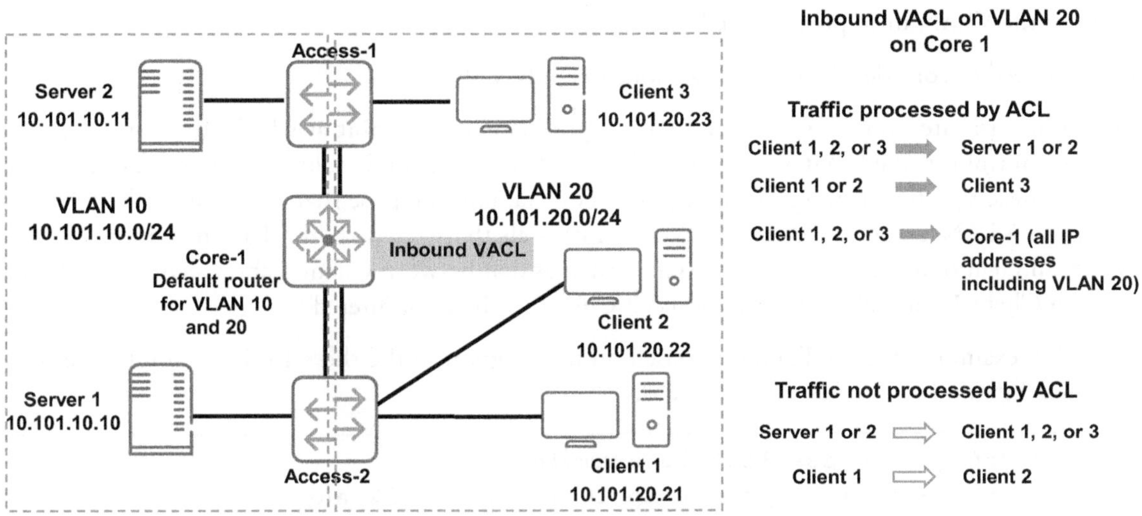

Figure 5-21 Inbound VACLs

The inbound VACL processes routed traffic like an inbound RACL but also filters switched traffic (Figure 5-21). In specific, the VACL processes this traffic:

- Traffic received on this VLAN interface and routed out another subnet
  In the example above, this is traffic from the clients to the servers.
- Traffic received on this VLAN interface and forwarded in the same subnet
  This is traffic between the clients. However, the VACL placement affects which precise traffic is filtered, as discussed below.
- Traffic received on this VLAN interface and destined to this network infrastructure device (on any interface)

The VACL does *not* process:

- Traffic received on another interface and routed to this VLAN interface. (However, the return traffic from a device in this VLAN would be filtered.)

For example, traffic from the servers to the clients is not processed by the ACL.

- Traffic generated by the switch itself using its IP address on this VLAN and routed out another VLAN

Note that, as you will see in the lab, the switch does not require an ACL rule to permit the DHCP traffic that it itself relayed. However, if the ACL were applied to a switch operating at Layer 2 and not implementing DHCP, you would need to permit DHCP (ports 67 and 68) to and from any address.

You can assign the same ACL to multiple VLANs. AOS-CX switches, however, allow you to configure just one inbound VACL per VLAN. (This is in addition to any other ACLs of different types you assign to the VLAN or to ports in the VLAN.)

You also need to consider the correct locations to apply VACLs.

RACLs affect routed traffic, so you naturally apply them at the point at which the traffic that you want to control is routed. But VACLs, both inbound and outbound, control switched traffic, which does not necessary flow through a single point. For example, suppose that you convert the inbound RACL on VLAN 20 to a VACL. The VACL filters all the routed traffic that an inbound RACL would, and it also filters some switched traffic, such as that between Client 1 and Client 3. But traffic between Client 1 and Client 2 does not reach Core-1, so it is not filtered.

Here is an example ACL configuration based on the diagram in the slide. In this example, the ACL is applied inbound for VLAN 20 on Core-1.

```
Switch(config)# access-list ip example
Switch(config-acl-ip)# permit ip 10.101.20.21/32 any
Switch(config-acl-ip)# exit
Switch(config)# vlan 20
Switch(config-if)# apply access-list example in
```

Based on this example, this traffic would be processed by the ACL and allowed:

- Client1 > Server1 or Server2
- Client1 > Client3
- Client1 > Core1

And this traffic would also be processed by the ACL, but denied:

- Client2 and Client3 > Server1 or Server2
- Client3 > Client1
- Client2 > Client3
- Client2 or Client3 > Core1

And this traffic is not even processed by the ACL:

- Client1 > Client2
- Client2 > Client1
- Server1 or Server2 > Client1, Client2, or Client 3 (however, the returning traffic would be processed by the ACL)

Note

The ACL example is looking at traffic from the source to the destination. Remember that returning traffic might be affected by the ACL, based on the rules and how it is applied.

Outbound VACLs

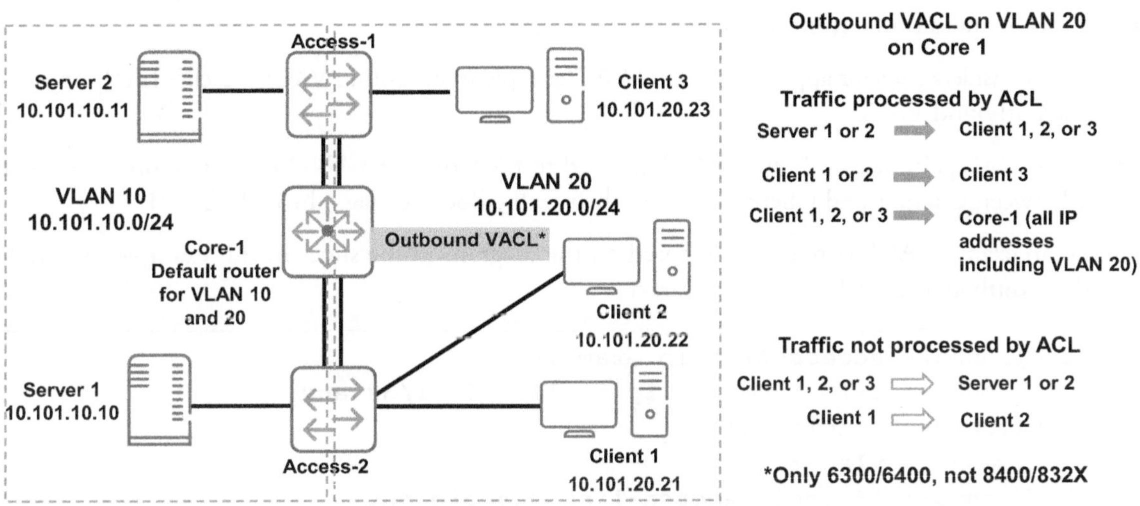

Figure 5-22 Outbound VACLs

In a moment, you will see how VACLs work when applied closer to the edge (Figure 5-22). First, though, you will examine an outbound VACL. IP ACLs must be applied to VLAN context with the **out** option.

Note

Outbound VACLs are currently not supported on the 8400 and 832x switches.

As you see, an outbound VACL filters traffic much like an outbound RACL, but it also filters traffic switched out the VLAN. Because, by definition, switched traffic arrives on and is forwarded in the same VLAN, this means that an outbound VACL also filters some traffic that arrives on the VLAN.

In specific, the outbound VACL processes this traffic:

- Traffic received on another VLAN interface and routed out this VLAN
  In this example, this is traffic from the servers to the clients.
- Traffic received on this VLAN interface and switched out this VLAN
  This is traffic between the clients although, again, traffic between clients connect to the same access switch does not reach the ACL. The ACL also processes traffic from the clients to Core-1's own IP address on VLAN 20.
- If multinetting applies, traffic received on one subnet in this VLAN and routed out another subnet on this VLAN

The VACL does *not* process traffic received on this VLAN interface and routed out another VLAN. Here, this includes traffic from the clients to the servers.

The same considerations for applying inbound VACLs apply to outbound VACLs; each VLAN supports just one outbound VACL.

Also note that, again, the outbound VACL applied to the Core-1 VLAN 20 interface does not filter traffic between Client 1 and Client 2 because their traffic does not pass through Core-1.

Here is an example ACL configuration based on the diagram in the slide. In this example, the ACL is applied outbound for VLAN 20 on Core-1.

```
Switch(config)# access-list ip example
Switch(config-acl-ip)# permit ip 10.101.20.21/32 any
Switch(config-acl-ip)# exit
Switch(config)# vlan 20
Switch(config-if)# apply access-list example out
```

Based on this example, this traffic would be processed by the ACL and allowed:

- Client1 > Server1 or Server2
- Client1 > Client3
- Client1 > Core1
- Server1 or Server2 > Client1 (the returning traffic might be filtered, however)

And this traffic would also be processed by the ACL, but denied:

- Client 2 > Client 3
- Client2 and Client3 > Core-1 (all IP addresses including VLAN 20)

- Client2 > Client3
- Client2 or Client3 > Core1

And this traffic is not even processed by the ACL:

- Client1, Client2, or Client3 > Server1 or Server2
- Client1 > Client2
- Client2 > Client1
- Server1 or Server2 > Client1, Client2, or Client 3 (however, the returning traffic would be processed by the ACL)

Note
The ACL example is looking at traffic from the source to the destination. Remember that returning traffic might be affected by the ACL, based on the rules and how it is applied.

VACLs at the Edge

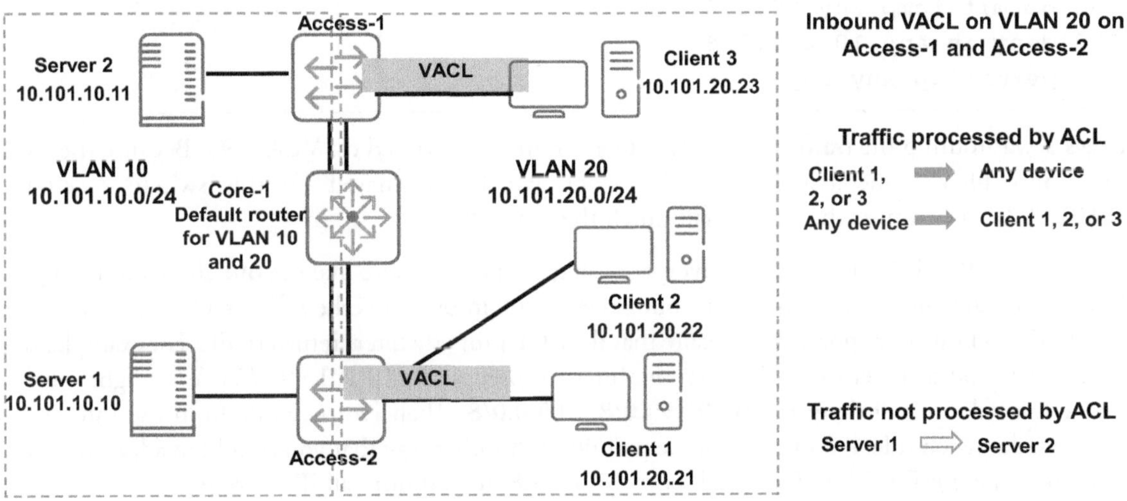

Figure 5-23 VACLs at the Edge

You should typically apply VACLs at the access layer where devices connect to the VLAN in question, as shown in Figure 5-23. You can then be certain to filter all switched traffic, as well as the routed traffic. Note that an Aruba switch can filter routed traffic whether or not it is acting as the default router for the VLAN to which the VACL is applied. It simply processes all of the traffic that arrives in this VLAN.

You do need to be careful, though, to consider what it means for traffic to arrive in the VLAN. On the previous page, you saw that the VACL did not process traffic from the servers to the clients because a VACL applies to traffic that arrives on the VLAN. The traffic from servers arrives on Core-1 in VLAN 10.

However, in this scenario, Core-1 routes the traffic to VLAN 20, and the traffic from servers to clients arrives on Access-1 and Access-2 *in VLAN 20*. That means that the VACLs applied on the access layer switches now process traffic routed by Core-1 into VLAN 20, as well as traffic that arrives on VLAN 20 on the access layer switches. In the example above, the VACL processes traffic from Server 1 to Client 1 and even traffic from Server 2 to Client 1. Even though both Server 2 and Client 1 are connected to Access-2, the traffic from Server 2 passes to Core-1 for routing and then returns to Access-2 in VLAN 20.

If you are planning to apply a VACL to a VLAN on a switch that does not route traffic for that VLAN, be very careful to plan the rules to permit *return traffic* to devices in that VLAN as well as the traffic from the devices.

For example, the FromGuests ACL for guest access might have these rules:

```
50 permit udp any 10.255.0.5/32 eq 67
150 permit udp any 10.255.0.5/32 eq 53
250 permit icmp any 10.255.0.5/32
350 deny ip any 10.0.0.0/8
450 permit ip any any
```

Access-1 was routing the traffic, so it only filtered traffic that arrived on VLAN 99. Because the ACL could only filter traffic assigned to VLAN 99, which terminated on this switch, specifying 10.101.99.0/24 or any as the source had much the same effect.

However, the ACL behavior changes if you are using a topology more like the one shown in the figure above, in which Core-1 routes the traffic, but Access-1 still implements the ACL as a VACL. You would then need to adjust your approach to ensure that the ACL properly filters return traffic. For example, rule 350 above would deny return traffic from the Internet to guests in 10.101.99.0/24. You might want to change this rule to **350 deny ip 10.101.99.0/8 10.0.0.0/8**. Then return traffic from the Internet to guests would match rule 450 instead and be permitted. Another way that you should to adjust the ACL would be to permit DHCP traffic (UDP ports 67 and 68) to and from all IP addresses.

Because, in this example, the access layer switches are not routing VLAN 20 traffic and do not have IP addresses on VLAN 20, applying the ACL as outbound VACL has the same effect as applying it as an inbound VACL. All traffic that arrives in the VLAN is also forwarded in that VLAN.

Note

The ACL example is looking at traffic from the source to the destination. Remember that returning traffic might be affected by the ACL, based on the rules and how it is applied.

PACLs (L2 Interface/LAG)

On an AOS-CX switch, you can apply an IPv4 or MAC ACL to a port or link aggregation to filter traffic inbound or outbound on that physical interface. (Some switches support only inbound PACLs.)

An inbound PACL filters *all* inbound traffic regardless of whether it is routed or switched. The PACL also applies to traffic inbound on the interface with a destination on the switch itself. An outbound PACL filters *all* outbound traffic on the port regardless of whether it is routed or switched.

You apply the PACL with the same command as an RACL. Figure 5-24 shows how a PACL applied to a port on Access-2 filters all traffic to or from the connected client.

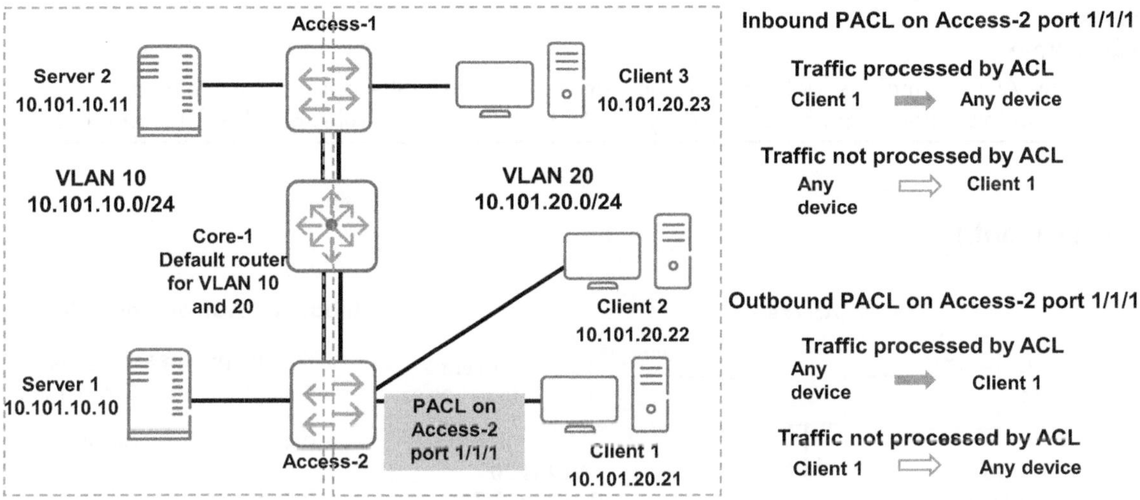

Figure 5-24 PACLs (L2 Interface/LAG)

Here is an example ACL configuration based on the diagram in the slide. In this example, the ACL is applied inbound on port 1/1/1 of Access-2, which is in non-routed mode, but a member of VLAN 20.

```
Switch(config)# access-list ip example
Switch(config-acl-ip)# deny ip 10.101.20.21/32 10.101.20.22/32
Switch(config-acl-ip)# permit ip 10.101.20.21/32 any
Switch(config-acl-ip)# exit
Switch(config)# interface 1/1/1
Switch(config-if)# no routing
Switch(config-if)# apply access-list example in
```

Based on this example, this traffic would be processed by the ACL and allowed:

- Client1 > Client3
- Client1 > Server1 and Server2
- Client1 > Core1

And this traffic would also be processed by the ACL, but denied:

- Client1 > Client2

And this traffic is not even processed by the ACL:

- Any device > Client1

Note

The ACL example is looking at traffic from the source to the destination. Remember that returning traffic might be affected by the ACL, based on the rules and how it is applied.

PACLs (cont.)

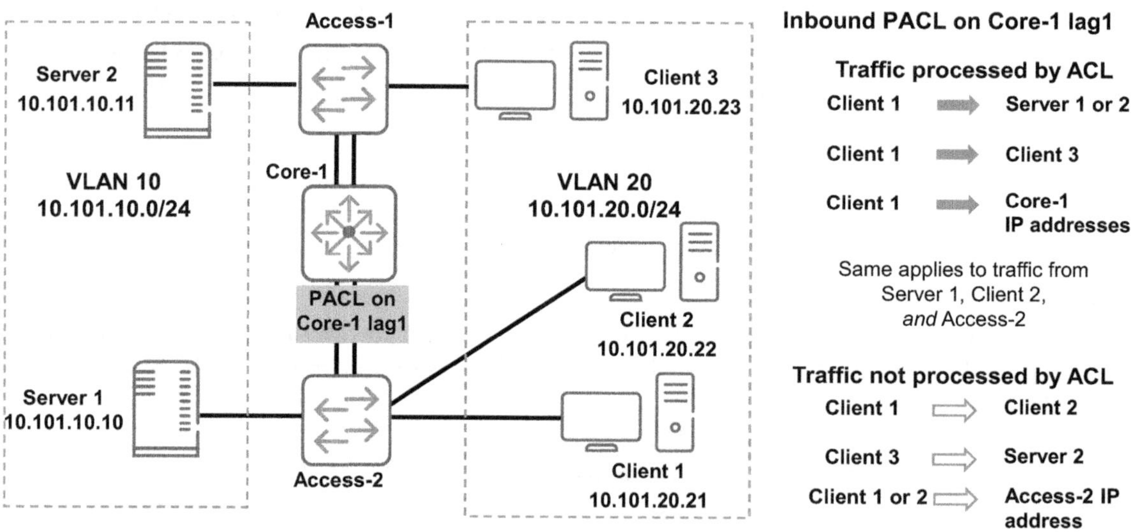

Figure 5-25 PACLs (cont.)

As always, you need to carefully consider where you apply the ACL. For example, if you apply an ACL to a switch-to-switch link, the ACL affects all incoming traffic from that link. Here you see how an ACL applied inbound on the link aggregation between Access-2 and Core-1 filters all traffic from Client 1, Client 2, and Server 1 that passes through Core-1. The filtering even extends to any traffic that Access-2 sends itself—an important implication for you to keep in mind. However, the ACL, of course, cannot filter any communications that do not pass through it. As long as Core-1 is routing the traffic, traffic between Client 1 and Server 1 is filtered, but traffic between Client 1 and Client 2 is not (Figure 5-25).

As this example illustrates, in many cases, when you want to control both routed and switched traffic, you should apply the ACL as close to the edge as possible, as illustrated on the previous page. You can then ensure that all appropriate traffic is filtered. If you only want to control routed traffic, of course, you should apply the ACL as an RACL on the VLAN interface on the VLAN's default router.

This example also illustrates that you can apply PACLs to link aggregations. Keep a few guidelines in mind. You must apply the PACLs to the link aggregation (trunk) rather than to individual ports within the link aggregation. It then automatically applies to the member ports. (Similarly, removing the PACL from the link aggregation, removes it from member ports.) Removing a port from the link aggregation removes the PACL from that port.

Best practice is that you should also remove any ACLs from a port before adding it to a link aggregation.

Note

The ACL example is looking at traffic from the source to the destination. Remember that returning traffic might be affected by the ACL, based on the rules and how it is applied.

Object Groups

This section introduces the concept of object groups, which simplify the implementation on matching on multiple IP addresses and/or subnets and multiple TCP and/or UDP ports.

Object Group Introduction

Figure 5-26 Object Group Introduction

Object groups are useful for defining groups of IP addresses and Layer-4 ports for use exclusively in the ACE rules. Often, common groups of addresses and ports or port ranges are used repeatedly in many ACL definitions (Figure 5-26).

There are two object group types:

- IP addresses
- Layer-4 ports

Without address and port object groups, the same addresses and ports must be repeated in each ACL definition that uses them.

Creating and Using Object Groups

–IP addresses (source or destination):

```
Switch(config)# object-group ip address <object-name>
Switch(config-addrgroup-ip)# [seq-#] any
Switch(config-addrgroup-ip)# [seq-#] <source-ip-address>
Switch(config-addrgroup-ip)# [seq-#] <source-ip-address>/<prefix-length>
Switch(config-addrgroup-ip)# [seq-#] <source-ip-address> <subnet-mask>
```

–Layer-4 ports

```
Switch(config)# object-group port <object-name>
Switch(config-portgroup)# [seq-#] {eq | gt | lt} <port>
Switch(config-portgroup)# [seq-#] {eq | gt | lt} range <min-port> <max-port>
```

–Usage: reference the object group name in the source/destination IP address field or the port field (the latter with the **group** parameter)

Figure 5-27 Creating and Using Object Groups

Creating an object group is done with the object-group command. You can include many objects in a group, but they must be the same type: either addresses and/or networks for an IP address object or a port or ports for a port object (Figure 5-27).

Once they are created, you can reference them in an ACE entry at the appropriate place:

- Source and/or destination IP address
- Source and/or destination Layer-4 port

For example, here's the syntax if you are using object groups for TCP or UDP:

```
Switch(config)# access-list ip <ACL-name>
Switch(config-portgroup)# {permit | deny} {tcp | udp} <source-ip-object-group> [group <source-port-group] <destination-ip-object-group> [group <destination-port-group>]
```

Object Group Example

Object groups are self-documenting. When you are setting up an ACE entry using an IP address or network number, its use may not be obvious. Using object groups with descriptive names makes the use more obvious.

The object group called *Internal-Network* has an obvious use and give you have access to the 172.16.0.0 IP subnet.

The employees in the various VLANs have an ACE entry that allows them access to the internal network that is the 172.16.0.0/16 network. As the network grew, the administrators added the 10.1.0.0/16 subnet. If you did not use an object group then you need to go and update every policy. In this example, you could add the subnet 10.1.0.0/16 to the Internal-Network object group. The sales and admin ACLs are immediately updated. But since the finance ACL does not reference an object group, it is not automatically updated and you must add a new rule manually.

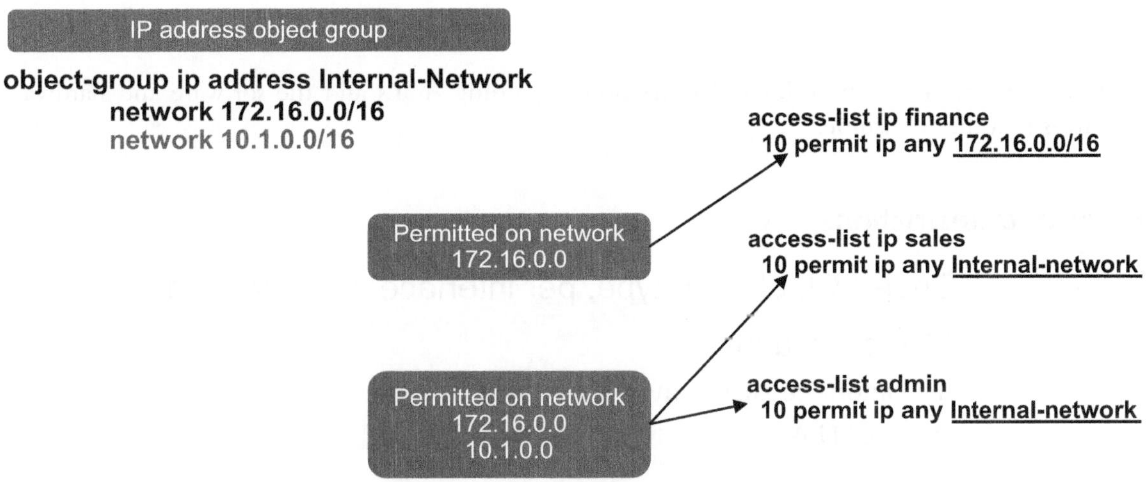

Figure 5-28 Object Group Example

Note

Keep in mind that it is possible to consume many hardware resource entries when using the object group commands (Figure 5-28). For example, in a typical situation, an ACE that uses object groups with 3 source addresses, 3 source Layer-4 ports, 3 destination addresses, and 3 destination Layer-4 ports, a total of 81 hardware entries are consumed (3 * 3 * 3 * 3 = 81). Hardware resources are discussed in the next section.

Here is an example that combines both address and ports:

```
Switch(config)# object-group ip address Internal-Network
Switch(config-addrgroup-ip)# network 172.16.0.0/16
Switch(config-addrgroup-ip)# network 10.1.0.0/16
Switch(config-addrgroup-ip)# exit
Switch(config)# object-group port Web-Servers
Switch(config-addrgroup-ip)# eq 80
Switch(config-addrgroup-ip)# eq 443
Switch(config)# access-list ip Web-Internal
Switch(config-portgroup)# permit tcp any Internal-Network group Web-Servers
```

In this example, anyone could open a web connection (port 80 or 443) to any server with an address in 172.16.0.0/16 or 10.1.0.0/16.

Restrictions and Resources

This section introduces the rules and restrictions regarding ACLs and the software and hardware resources that they consume.

Rules and Restrictions

–Once ACL of each type, per interface, per direction

–ACL precedence:

1. Interface ACL (Layer-2 or Layer-3)
2. VLAN ACL

Figure 5-29 Rules and Restrictions

Only one access-list of each type (IPv4, IPv6, MAC) can be applied on the same interface/VLAN in the same direction (IN or OUT). Any attempt to apply more than one ACL (or policy) on an interface will result in the new list replacing the old one (Figure 5-29).

For the precedence of ACLs, if traffic is to be processed by both an interface (Layer-2 or Layer-3) ACL and a VLAN ACL (based on the VLAN the interface is associated with, the ACLs would be processed in this order:

1. Interface ACL
2. VLAN ACL

Software and Hardware Resources

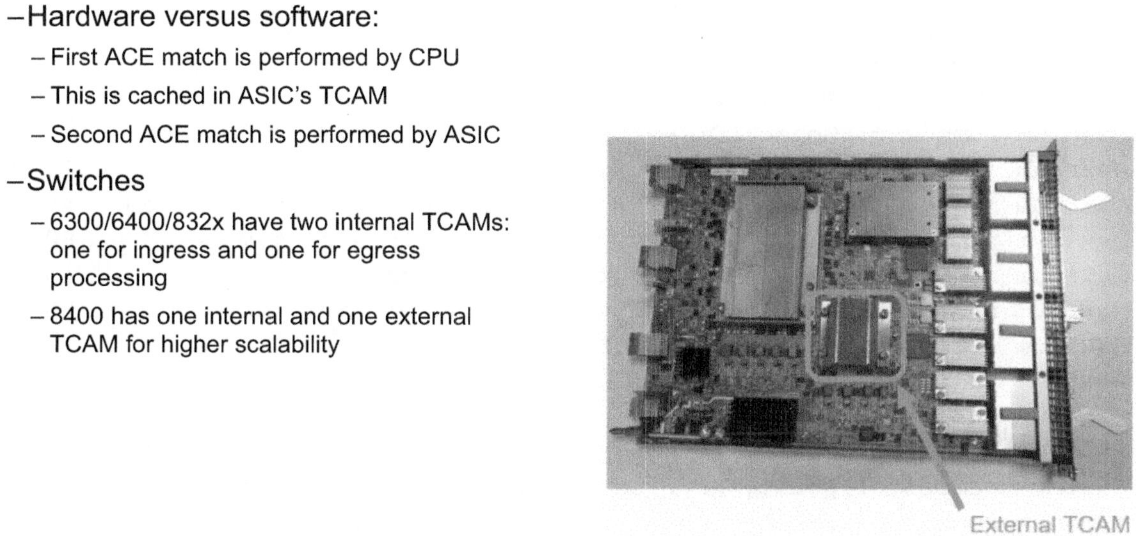

Figure 5-30 Software and Hardware Resources

When applying ACLs or policies, hardware resources are consumed to enforce these rules on the data plane:

- Management Plane Resources: Used when *CREATED*
- ASIC / TCAM (data-plane) Resources: Used when *APPLIED*

Software Resources

AOS-CX allows the administrator to configure more ACLs and policies than those that will be applied with the purpose of providing flexibility (like migrating security from one ACL to another one). ACL, class, and policy definitions consume software-based resources on the management plane. These resources are generally increased along with major AOS-CX releases (Figure 5-30).

The switch capabilities can be seen with the **show capacities** and **show capacities-status** commands. The former command shows the capabilities. Here is an example for a 6300 switch:

```
6300# show capacities classifier
System Capacities: Filter Classifier
Capacities Name Value
-----------------------------------------------------------------------
Maximum number of Access Control Entries configurable in a system64000
Maximum number of Object Group Entries configurable in a system   1000
Maximum number of Object Groups configurable in a system          1000
Maximum number of Access Control Lists configurable in a system   4000
Maximum number of class entries configurable in a system          8000
Maximum number of classes configurable in a system                1000
Maximum number of entries in an Access Control List               8000
Maximum number of entries in a class                              1000
Maximum number of entries in an Object Group                      64
Maximum number of entries in a policy                             128
Maximum number of classifier policies configurable in a system    4000
Maximum number of policy entries configurable in a system         8000
Maximum number of PBR Action Lists configurable in a system        64
Maximum number of PBR Action List entries configurable per PBR Action
List    8
```

Here is an example of the latter command for a 6300 switch:

```
6300# show capacities-status classifier
System Capacities Status: Filter Classifier
Capacities Status Name                    Value       Maximum
-----------------------------------------------------------------------
Number of Access Control Entries currently configured  0        64000
Number of Object Group Entries currently configured    0         1000
Number of Object Groups currently configured           0         1000
Number of Access Control Lists currently configured    0         4000
Number of class entries currently configured           0         8000
Number of classes currently configured                 0         1000
Number of policies currently configured                0         4000
Number of policy entries currently configured          0         8000
Number of PBR Action Lists currently configured        0         64
```

It displays the capabilities and the resources being used on the switch.

Note

Remember that the amount of resources available is dependent on the switch model and will typically vary. Also, available resource limits might increase based on the version of AOS-CX code running on the switch.

Hardware Resources

Switching/routing ASICs have different types of tables where they keep MAC addresses, ARP and ND entries, IPv4 and IPv6 routes, access control lists, and policies. The resource used to perform lookup at hardware speed and to provide index corresponding to a given search-key is called a *TCAM*: Ternary Content Addressable Memory.

All AOS-CX switches have "internal TCAMs" which is responsible for look-ups inside the ASIC of the switch or of the line-card. Aruba 8400 has, in addition, an "external TCAM" —external to the packet-processor ASIC, that gives higher scale capacity (see the picture on the slide).

It may happen that the configured ACL might not be activated due to TCAM resource allocation issue. The **show access-list commands** shows the active configuration of the switch (what is currently being used in RAM and in TCAM). The active configuration is about:

- The ACLs that have been configured and accepted by the system
- The interfaces on which the ACLs have successfully been programmed in the hardware.

The **show access-list commands configuration** shows the ACLs that have been configured. The output of this command may not be the same as what was programmed in the hardware or what is active on the switch. The situation might occur because of one or more of the following:

- Unsupported command parameters might have been configured.
- Unsupported applications might have been specified.
- Applying an ACL might have been unsuccessful due to lack of hardware resources.

To determine if a discrepancy exists between what was configured and what is active, run the show access-list command with the configuration parameter.

If the active ACLs and configured ACLs are not the same, the switch shows a warning message in the output of the **show** command:

```
! access-list ip MY_IP_ACL user configuration does not match active
configuration.
! run 'access-list TYPE NAME reset' to reset access-list to match
active configuration.
```

If the configured ACL is processing, the switch shows an in-progress warning.

```
! access-list ip MY_IP_ACL user configuration currently being
processed
! run 'access-list TYPE NAME reset' to reset access-list to match
active configuration.
```

If the switch shows a warning message or in-progress message, additional changes can be made until the error message is no longer shown in the show command, or you can run this command:

```
Switch(config)# access-list {all |ip <ACL-NAME> | ipv6 <ACL-NAME> | mac
<ACL-NAME>} reset
```

The **access-list reset** command changes the user-specified configuration to match the active configuration. For details, see "Configuring ACLs and Classifier Policies Guide for AOS-CX".

TCAM Resource Consumption

- Using an object group uses the same resources as specific ACE entries
- For 6400, VLAN ACLs, VLAN policies, and Analytics Data Collection (ADC) are applied to all line cards and take associated resources on all line cards, regardless of physical port membership of the VLAN
- VLAN grouping
  - Allows an ACL to be applied to a group of VLANs and to leverage the same HW entries for multiple VLANs (applying the same ACL to multiple VLANs is just a VLAN bitmapping)
  - Only supported on the 6300/6400, not on the 832x/8400
- Port grouping
  - Allows an ACL to be applied to a group of ports and to leverage the same HW entries for multiple ports (applying the same ACL to multiple ports is just a port bitmapping)
  - Only supported on the 6300/6400/8320/8325, not on the 8400

Figure 5-31 TCAM Resource Consumption

Object groups do not reduce resource consumption; as pointed out in the object group section, the switch will expand the ACE entries with the actual values, so the resource consumption would be the same as if you did not use object groups be specified the specific addresses and ports (Figure 5-31). For example, an ACE with groups containing 3 source addresses, 3 destination addresses, 3 source TCP ports, and 3 destination TCP ports will expand to 3x3x3x3 = 81 hardware entries.

Note

Object groups make management of your ACLs easier and more flexible—they do not reduce resource consumption.

When applying Layer-4 port range ACEs that use 'lt', 'gt', 'range', or port groups, they may use more than one hardware entry. When applying an ACL to an interface, each interface to be matched will allocate one extra hardware entry to store the invisible implicit deny rule (ACE) configured to the end of ACL list by default.

Note
There may be additional restrictions or resource consumption based on the switch model.

VLAN and Port Grouping

The VLAN grouping functionality allows an ACL or Policy to be applied to a group of VLANs and to leverage the same HW entries for multiple VLANs (applying the same ACL to multiple VLANs is just a VLAN bitmapping). Such optimization is available only on 6300/6400, not on 832x, 8400.

The port grouping functionality allows an ACL or Policy to be applied to a group of Ports and to leverage the same HW entries for multiple ports (applying the same ACL to multiple ports is just a port bitmapping). Such optimization is possible on 6300/6400/8320/8325, not on 8400.

TCAM Resource Utilization

To verify allocated TCAM resources, two important commands are used:

- From 10.0 to 10.03 release: **diag-dump acl basic**
  To be able to run this command the diagnostics function must be enabled (**diagnostics**).
- From 10.04 release: **show resources**
  This command is a more user-friendly version of the previous command. (no need to enter diagnostics).

Here is an example of the latter command:

```
Switch# show resources
Resource Usage:
Mod Description
Resource                                      Width  Used  Reserved  Free
--------------------------------------------  ----  ----  --------  ----
1/1 Ingress Control Plane Policing
        Ingress TCAM Entries                    3     231    2304
    Egress Control Plane Policing
        Egress TCAM Entries                     2      84     512
    Total
        Policers                                        0    6144
        Ingress TCAM Entries                          231    2304    6912
        Egress TCAM Entries                            84     512    1536
        Ingress L4 Port Ranges                                  0      32
```

Resource data is updated every 10 seconds.

The **show resources** command is a more user-friendly version of the **diag-dump** command. There is no need to enter diagnostics mode and it goes straight to the information. You can use these commands to troubleshoot the installation of ACLs and/or policies.

Because the various AOS-CX switch models have different restrictions and capabilities, here is a list of recommendations from Aruba in regards to ACLs and policy implementation and usage:

- Based on limited TCAM space, 8325 is really not the preferred platform to implement lots of access-list entries or policies.
- 8320 has much better capability than 8325.
- Due to different ASIC structures, 8320 and 8400 will not behave the same on various scenarios.
- New 6300/6400 platforms propose more combinations than 8320, 8325, 8400 which could better fit complex requirements, especially for Egress ACLs or policies.
- For very large scale IPv4 ACL, Ingress Port ACL should be used on the 8400.

For more information about TCAM capabilities and utilization, see the *AOS-CX ACL Policy Resource Consumption White Paper* available on Aruba's site.

Classifier Policies

This section introduces how to use classes and policies to define very specific QoS and other traffic polices for protocols and connections at the global or interface level.

Two Traffic Class-Based Feature Sets

There are basically two feature sets that the AOS-CX switches support in regard to implementing traffic policies: ACLs and classifier policies (Figure 5-32). While the former is primarily used to filter traffic, the latter can be used to implement a multitude of policies, including traffic filtering, rate limiting traffic, changing (re-marking) QoS markings for DSCP or 802.1p, and traffic mirroring.

–ACLs
- –Primarily used to filter traffic
- –Applied to L2 and L3 ports, LAGs, and VLANs

–Classifier policies
- –Used to implement traffic policies, like rate limiting, changing QoS markings, traffic mirroring, and filtering
- –Applied to L2 ports, VLANs, and GRE tunnels

Figure 5-32 Two Traffic Class-Based Feature Sets

Classes

Figure 5-33 shows how to create classes (commonly referred to as "class maps") to identify traffic for which you want to define specific policies. **match** commands specify what you want to include and **ignore** commands which traffic to ignore. The entries are processed in numerical order, so the sequencing of the entries is important. Use the **show class** command to verify your configuration. See the *Command-Line Interface Guide* for a more detailed description of the configuration of classes.

–Match on traffic:

```
Switch(config)# class ip <class-name>
Switch(config-class)# [<seq-#>] match any
Switch(config-class)# [<seq-#>] match tcp <protocol-criteria>
Switch(config-class)# [<seq-#>] match udp <protocol-criteria>
Switch(config-class)# [<seq-#>] match icmp <protocol-criteria>
Switch(config-class)# [<seq-#>] match <protocol-name-or-number>
Switch(config-class)# [<seq-#>] ignore <protocol-information>
Switch(config-class)# [<seq-#>] comment <comment>
```

–Example:

```
switch(config)# class ip MY_IP_CLASS
switch(config-class-ip)# 10 match icmp any any
switch(config-class-ip)# 20 ignore udp any any
switch(config-class-ip)# 30 match tcp 192.168.0.1 192.168.0.2 eq 80
switch(config-class-ip)# exit
```

Figure 5-33 Classes

Policies

– Implement policies:

```
Switch(config)# policy <policy-name>
Switch(config-policy)# [<seq-#>] class ip <class-name> action <action(s)>
```

– Actions:
  - **dscp** <DSCP-code>
  - **local-priority** <802.1P-value>
  - **cir kbs** <bit-rate>
  - **cbs** <burst-size>
  - **exceed** <rate-limit>
  - **drop**
  - **mirror**

– Example:

```
switch(config)# policy MY_Policy
switch(config-policy)# class ip MY_IP_CLASS action dscp EF
```

Figure 5-34 Policies

The above slide shows how to reference classes in a policy and assign a policy action (or multiple actions) to a class. Most commonly, the **dscp** or **local-priority** parameters are used to define the policy. Note that you can specify multiple classes within a policy, and that they are processed numerically based on each entry's sequence number. Use the **show policy** command to verify your configuration. See the *Command-Line Interface Guide* for a more detailed description of the configuration of policies.

Note
If you change the DCSCP value, make sure that the DSCP value is correctly mapped to an appropriate LP value.

An example configuration is shown in a couple of sections that combines the classes and policies (Figure 5-34).

Applying Policies

Policy type Direction	IPv4 In	IPv4 Routed In	IPv4 Out
L2 interface (port)	Yes	-	Yes
L2 LAG	Yes	-	Yes
L3 interface (port)	Yes	Yes	Yes
L3 LAG	Yes	Yes	Yes
VLAN	Yes	-	Yes
VLAN interface	-	Yes (PBR)	-

- Applying them:
  - Globally (inbound only)
  - Interface (in, routed-in, and out)
  - VLAN
- Command: **apply policy** <policy-name> <direction>

Figure 5-35 Applying Policies

The table lists where policies can be applied (Figure 5-35). To apply a policy globally, configure this command:

```
Switch(config)# apply policy <POLICY-NAME> in
```

Globally policies can only be applied inbound. Only one policy can be globally applied at a time. Applying a policy globally again replaces the previous globally applied policy.

Policies can also be applied to a VLAN or an interface. The **apply** command is used, but in the interface or VLAN context.

Policy Example

Let us look at an example:

```
switch(config)# class ip IP_CLASS
switch(config-class)# 10 match udp 172.16.0.0/16 gt 1023 172.16.1.0/24
switch(config-class)# exit
switch(config)# class mac MAC_CLASS
switch(config-class)# 10 match 00-14-22-01-23-45 any arp
switch(config-class)# exit
switch(config)# policy EXAMPLE_POLICY
switch(config-policy)# 10 class ip IP_CLASS action dscp EF
switch(config-policy)# 20 class mac MAC_CLASS action drop
switch(config-policy)# exit
switch(config)# interface 1/1/1
switch(config-if)# apply policy EXAMPLE_POLICY in
switch(config-if)# exit
```

In this example, traffic is possibly affected when it enters inbound on interface 1/1/1. For UDP traffic from 172.16.0.0/16 with a source port greater than 1023 that is destined to 172.16.1.0/24, it will be re-marked (re-classified with a DSCP value of EF). All other traffic will keep its assigned DSCP value, if any. Also, any ARP from 00-14-22-01-23-45 is dropped; but all other ARPs are allowed.


```
switch(config)# class ip IP_CLASS
switch(config-class)# 10 match udp 172.16.0.0/16 gt 1023 172.16.1.0/24
switch(config-class)# exit
switch(config)# class mac MAC_CLASS
switch(config-class)# 10 match 00-14-22-01-23-45 any arp
switch(config-class)# exit
switch(config)# policy EXAMPLE_POLICY
switch(config-policy)# 10 class ip IP_CLASS action dscp EF
switch(config-policy)# 20 class mac MAC_CLASS action drop
switch(config-policy)# exit
switch(config)# interface 1/1/1
switch(config-if)# apply policy EXAMPLE_POLICY in
```


NOTE: There is ***no*** implicit deny in policies. If you want to apply a policy on traffic, it **must match a permit**. Matching on a **deny** statement basically exempts the traffic from the policy.

Figure 5-36 Policy Example

Note

There is *no* implicit deny in policies. If you want to apply a policy on traffic, it must match a **permit**. Matching on a **deny** statement basically exempts the traffic from the policy (Figure 5-36).

Lab 5 ACLs

Lab 5 Overview

In this lab activity, Access-Lists are configured and tested on the switch (Figure 5-37). First, an access-list is defined and then access-list rules are reviewed. Next, the Access-List is applied to a switch port and tested. Then, the object group feature will be demonstrated. This allows the grouping of multiple IP addresses or ports in a logical group, so the Access-List rules can be simplified. The last part of the lab will review the resource utilization of the Access-Lists in the hardware tables.

Lab 5 Diagram

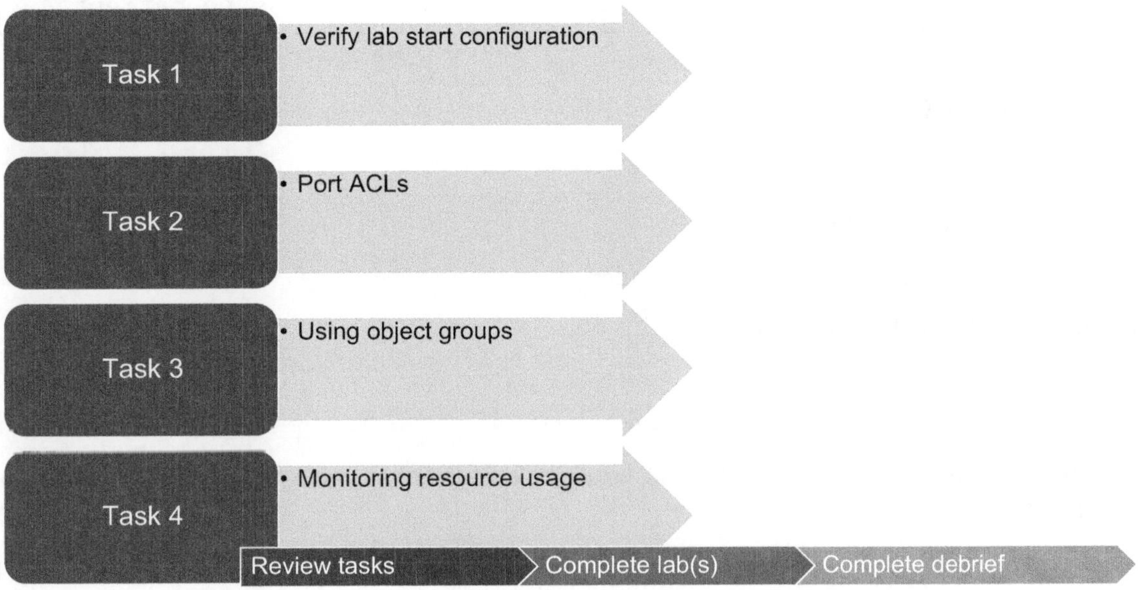

Figure 5-37 Lab 5 Diagram

Objectives

- - Define an Access-List
- - Understand the Access-List rules, remove a rule, and resequence the rules
- - Apply an Access-List on the switch
- - Use object groups for IP addresses and ports
- - Review the hardware resource utilization

Task 1: Verify Lab Start Configuration

Objectives

- If you have just completed Lab 04—VSX, you can skip this task and move to the next task.
- If you have completed any other lab and are performing this lab again, complete these steps to get the base configuration on the devices.

Open a console to ***all four switches*** and load the checkpoint called icx-lab04-vsx:

1. Open a console connection to each switch. Login using **admin/aruba123**.

```
Switch# copy checkpoint icx-lab04-vsx running-config
Configuration changes will take time to process, please be patient.
```

Task 2: Port ACLs

Objectives

- Configure an Access-List
- Understand the Access-List syntax and rules
- Apply an Access-List to an interface

Steps

1. Open a terminal connection to Access2, enter the configuration mode. Enable the port 1/1/4 to the PC4.

```
ICX-TX-Access2(config)# interface 1/1/4
ICX-TX-Access2(config-if)# no shutdown
ICX-TX-Access2(config-if)# exit
```

2. On the PC connected to Access2, verify that a DHCP IP address from the 10.x.12.0/24 subnet was received. (cmd=**ipconfig**)

Define the Access-List

1. On Access2, define a new access-list named '**pc**'.

```
ICX-TX-Access2(config)# access-list ip pc
```

2. Allow DHCP client traffic.

```
ICX-TX-Access2(config-acl-ip)# permit udp any eq 68 any eq 67
```

3. Allow traffic to the local subnet. The wildcard mask is not using inverse bits, but normal subnet mask logic, so '1' to match, '0' to ignore. In this example any destination IP address that has '10' in the first byte, and '11' in the third byte will match the rule (255). The value in the second or fourth byte will be ignored (0). Enable the 'log' and 'count' function as well.

```
ICX-TX-Access2(config-acl-ip)# permit  ip  any  10.0.11.0/255.0.255.0
logcount
```

4. No further lines will be added. Any traffic that is not matching the access-list will be handled by the 'implicit deny' rule, so it will be blocked.

5. Review the access-list. Notice that each line now has a line number, so the order of the lines is important. The line numbers can be used to remove an individual line or to insert a new line between two existing lines.

```
ICX-TX-Access2(config-acl-ip)# show running-config current-context
access-list ip pc
    10 permit udp any eq 68 any eq 67
    20 permit any any 10.0.11.0/255.0.255.0 log count
```

6. Add a new line to match destination 10.0.12.0/255.0.255.0.

```
ICX-TX-Access2(config-acl-ip)# permit ip any 10.0.12.0/255.0.255.0
logcount
```

7. Next verify the configuration again. This shows that entering the same source/destination information does not overwrite the existing line, but simply adds a line to the access-list.

```
ICX-TX-Access2(config-acl-ip)# show running-config current-context
access-list ip pc
    10 permit udp any eq 68 any eq 67
    20 permit any any 10.0.11.0/255.0.255.0 log count
    30 permit any any 10.0.12.0/255.0.255.0 log count
```

8. Next remove line 20 and review the configuration.

```
ICX-TX-Access2(config-acl-ip)# no 20
ICX-TX-Access2(config-acl-ip)# show running-config current-context
access-list ip pc
    10 permit udp any eq 68 any eq 67
    30 permit any any 10.0.12.0/255.0.255.0 log count
```

9. The switch supports resequencing the line numbers; this must be done from the global configuration. There is a start number and an increment number.

```
ICX-TX-Access2(config-acl-ip)# exit
ICX-TX-Access2(config)# access-list ip pc resequence 1000 100
```

10. Review the access-list configuration with the updated line numbers.

```
ICX-TX-Access2(config)# show access-list configuration commands
access-list ip pc
    1000 permit udp any eq 68 any eq 67
    1100 permit any any 10.0.12.0/255.0.255.0 log count
```

Apply the Access-List

1. Enter the interface 1/1/4 context and apply the access-list to the port.

```
ICX-TX-Access2(config)# interface 1/1/4
ICX-TX-Access2(config-if)# apply access-list ip pc in
ICX-TX-Access2(config-if)# exit
```

2. Review the access-list configuration; notice how the access-list commands and the interface commands are combined in the output.

```
ICX-TX-Access2(config)# show access-list configuration commands
access-list ip pc
    1000 permit udp any eq 68 any eq 67
    1100 permit any any 10.0.12.0/255.0.255.0 log count
interface 1/1/4
    apply access-list ip pc in
```

Note

Access-lists *cannot* be applied to an SVI interface (interface VLAN x). If an access-list is required on an SVI interface, a traffic policy can be used on the VLAN interface.

```
ICX-TX-Access2(config)# int vlan 2
ICX-TX-Access2(config-if-vlan)# apply ?
policy  Classifier policy
```

Test the Access-List

1. On PC4, that is connected to Access2 port 1/1/4, open a command prompt with administrator privileges (cmd.exe) and attempt to release and renew the IP address. This should succeed, since this is allowed.

```
C:\Users\student> ipconfig /release
C:\Users\student> ipconfig /renew
```

2. Attempt to ping to 10.x.12.1. This should succeed since this is allowed.

```
C:\Users\student> ping 10.x.12.1

Pinging 10.x.12.1 with 32 bytes of data:
Reply from 10.x.12.1: bytes=32 time<1ms TTL=64
```

3. Attempt to ping to 10.x.11.1. This should fail, due to implicit deny, so when traffic does not match the access-list, it will be rejected.

```
C:\Users\student> ping 10.x.11.1
Pinging 10.12.11.1 with 32 bytes of data:
Request timed out.
```

4. On the Access2, review the access-list hitcount. In the example output, 9 packets have matched the permit rule.

```
ICX-TX-Access2(config)# show access-list hitcounts ip pc
Statistics for ACL pc (ipv4):
Interface 1/1/4* (in):
           Hit Count  Configuration
                -  1000 permit udp any eq 68 any eq 67
9  1100 permit any any 10.0.12.0/255.0.255.0 log count
* access-list statistics are shared among each combination of
  context type (interface, VLAN, VRF) and direction (in, out,
  control-plane).
  Use 'access-list TYPE NAME copy' to create a uniquely named
  access-list.
```

5. Next review the log file on the switch using the command. This shows the log in reverse order, with 10 as the number of lines to display.

```
show logging -r -n 10
```

The log should show two type of entries, one for the line that was matched (event 10002), and one for the actual packet info that matched the line (event 10001).

```
ICX-TX-Access2(config)# show logging -r -n 10
--------------------------------------------------
Event logs from current boot
--------------------------------------------------
2020-02-12T12:45:50.356044+00:00 ICX-TX-Access2 ops-switchd[656]:
Event|10002|LOG_INFO|MSTR|1|pc on 1/1/4 (in):          2 1100
permit any any 10.0.12.0/255.0.255.0 log count
2020-02-12T12:44:02.854143+00:00 ICX-TX-Access2 hpe-restd[726]:
Event|4646|LOG_ERR|AMM|-|Aruba Activate server https://devices-v2.
arubanetworks.com is not reachable through any supported VRF.
2020-02-12T12:40:50.109684+00:00 ICX-TX-Access2 ops-switchd[656]:
Event|10001|LOG_INFO|MSTR|1|List pc, seq# 1100 permitted
icmp 10.x.12.37 ->10.x.12.1 type 8 code 0, on vlan 12, port 1/1/4,
direction in
2020-02-12T12:39:02.854417+00:00 ICX-TX-Access2 hpe-restd[726]:
Event|4646|LOG_ERR|AMM|-|Aruba Activate server https://devices-v2.
arubanetworks.com is not reachable through any supported VRF.
2020-02-12T12:34:02.854338+00:00 ICX-TX-Access2 hpe-restd[726]:
Event|4646|LOG_ERR|AMM|-|Aruba Activate server https://devices-v2.
arubanetworks.com is not reachable through any supported VRF.
2020-02-12T12:32:54.822361+00:00 ICX-TX-Access2 ops-switchd[656]:
Event|10002|LOG_INFO|MSTR|1|pc on 1/1/4 (in):          1 1100
permit any any 10.0.12.0/255.0.255.0 log count
2020-02-12T12:29:02.854213+00:00 ICX-TX-Access2 hpe-restd[726]:
Event|4646|LOG_ERR|AMM|-|Aruba Activate server https://devices-v2.
arubanetworks.com is not reachable through any supported VRF.
2020-02-12T12:27:54.765734+00:00 ICX-TX-Access2 ops-switchd[656]:
Event|10001|LOG_INFO|MSTR|1|List pc, seq# 1100 permitted udp
10.x.12.37(138) -> 10.x.12.255(138) on vlan 12, port 1/1/4, direction in
2020-02-12T12:24:02.854226+00:00 ICX-TX-Access2 hpe-restd[726]:
Event|4646|LOG_ERR|AMM|-|Aruba Activate server https://devices-v2.
arubanetworks.com is not reachable through any supported VRF.
2020-02-12T12:22:54.698250+00:00 ICX-TX-Access2 ops-switchd[656]:
Event|10002|LOG_INFO|MSTR|1|pc on 1/1/4 (in):          1 1100
permit any any 10.0.12.0/255.0.255.0 log count
ICX-TX-Access2(config)#
```

6. To see the last packets that matched an access-list with the 'log' option, use the event ID to filter.

```
ICX-TX-Access2(config)# show logging -r -n 100 | i 10001
2020-02-12T12:40:50.109684+00:00 ICX-TX-Access2 ops-switchd[656]:
Event|10001|LOG_INFO|MSTR|1|List pc, seq# 1100 permitted icmp 10.x.12.37 ->
10.x.12.1 type 8 code 0, on vlan 12, port 1/1/4, direction in
2020-02-12T12:27:54.765734+00:00 ICX-TX-Access2 ops-switchd[656]:
Event|10001|LOG_INFO|MSTR|1|List pc, seq# 1100 permitted udp 10.x.12.37(138) ->
10.x.12.255(138) on vlan 12, port 1/1/4, direction in
2020-02-12T12:17:54.631987+00:00 ICX-TX-Access2 ops-switchd[656]:
Event|10001|LOG_INFO|MSTR|1|List pc, seq# 1100 permitted udp 10.x.12.37(138) ->
10.x.12.255(138) on vlan 12, port 1/1/4, direction in
2020-02-12T12:08:04.493868+00:00 ICX-TX-Access2 ops-switchd[656]:
Event|10001|LOG_INFO|MSTR|1|List pc, seq# 1100 permitted udp 10.x.12.37(138) ->
10.x.12.255(138) on vlan 12, port 1/1/4, direction in
2020-02-12T12:02:54.413634+00:00 ICX-TX-Access2 ops-switchd[656]:
Event|10001|LOG_INFO|MSTR|1|List pc, seq# 20 permitted udp 10.x.12.37(138) ->
10.x.12.255(138) on vlan 12, port 1/1/4, direction in
2020-02-12T11:54:59.289694+00:00 ICX-TX-Access2 ops-switchd[656]:
Event|10001|LOG_INFO|MSTR|1|List pc, seq# 20 permitted icmp 10.x.12.37 ->
10.x.12.1 type 8 code 0, on vlan 12, port 1/1/4, direction in
```

Task 3: Using Object Groups

Objectives

In this task, object groups for access-lists will be introduced. Object groups group objects that would otherwise be used directly in access-lists. For example, suppose a customer has two Web servers and they want to allow TCP port 80 and 443 (http/https) access to these two Web server IP addresses. With a traditional ACL, 4 lines would be required:

- allow tcp 80 to IP1
- allow tcp 80 to IP2
- allow tcp 443 to IP1
- allow tcp 443 to IP2

With object groups, the customer can first assign both IP addresses to an object group (for example, web-servers), and then use this group in the lines:

- allow tcp 80 to web-servers
- allow tcp 443 to web-servers

The administrator can also combine ports into an object group, so both 80 and 443 can be combined into a group (for example, web-ports). The result would be:

- allow web-ports to web-servers

Whenever new ports or new IPs must be added, only the groups need to be updated, the ACL entry remains the same.

Steps

Define group for Core switches IP

1. Open the terminal connection to Access2, enter the configuration mode. Define a new object group 'core-switch'.

```
ICX-TX-Access2(config)# object-group ip address core-switch
```

2. Check the possible object types.

```
ICX-TX-Access2(config-addrgroup-ip)# ?
<1-4294967295>   Object Group sequence number
A.B.C.D          Specify IP host address
  A.B.C.D/M        Specify IP network address with prefix length
  A.B.C.D/W.X.Y.Z  Specify IP network address with network mask
  end              End current mode and change to enable mode.
  exit             Exit current mode and change to previous mode
  list             Print command list
  no               Negate a command or set its defaults
  show             Show running system information
```

Question: What types of addresses can be added to the object group?

Answer: A single IP address, a network address with a prefix mask, a network address with a network mask.

3. Add the two IP addresses of the 2 VSX Core switches in VLAN 12.

```
ICX-TX-Access2(config-addrgroup-ip)# 10.x.12.2
ICX-TX-Access2(config-addrgroup-ip)# 10.x.12.3
```

Note

Do not add 10.x.12.1; this address will be used in a validation test, so it should not belong to the object-group.

4. Review the object group; notice the line numbers that are automatically generated.

```
ICX-TX-Access2(config-addrgroup-ip)# show run cur
object-group ip address core-switch
    10 10.x.12.2
    20 10.x.12.3
ICX-TX-Access2(config-addrgroup-ip)# exit
```

Define Object Group for Port 80 and 443

1. Define a new object group, named 'switch-ports'.

```
ICX-TX-Access2(config)# object-group port switch-ports
```

2. Review the object group options.

```
ICX-TX-Access2(config-portgroup)# ?
<1-4294967295>  Object Group sequence number
  end             End current mode and change to enable mode.
eq              Laycr 4 port equal to
  exit            Exit current mode and change to previous mode
gt              Layer 4 port greater than
  list            Print command list
lt              Layer 4 port less than
  no              Negate a command or set its defaults
range           Layer 4 port range
  show            Show running system information
```

3. Add the ports 80 and 443 to the object group.

```
ICX-TX-Access2(config-portgroup)# eq 80
ICX-TX-Access2(config-portgroup)# eq 443
```

4. Review the current configuration.

```
ICX-TX-Access2(config-portgroup)# show run cur
object-group port switch-ports
    10 eq 80
    20 eq 443
ICX-TX-Access2(config-portgroup)# exit
```

Combine the Object Groups into an Access-List

1. Enter the access-list 'pc' context; review the current settings.

```
ICX-TX-Access2(config)# access-list ip pc
ICX-TX-Access2(config-acl-ip)# show run cur
access-list ip pc
    1000 permit udp any eq 68 any eq 67
    1100 permit any any 10.0.12.0/255.0.255.0 log count
```

2. Overwrite the current line 1100 with the new line based on the object-groups.

```
ICX-TX-Access2(config-acl-ip)# 1100 permit tcp any core-switch
group switch-ports
```

3. Verify the new configuration.

```
ICX-TX-Access2(config-acl-ip)# show run cur
access-list ip pc
     1000 permit udp any eq 68 any eq 67
     1100 permit tcp any core-switch group switch-ports
ICX-TX-Access2(config-acl-ip)# exit
```

Verify the Operation

1. Using PC4, connected to Access2, open a browser and navigate to **https://10.x.12.2**. This should succeed. There is no need to login.
2. Navigate to **https://10.x.12.3**. This should succeed.
3. Attempt to navigate to **https://10.x.12.1**. This should fail.

Task 4: Resource Usage

Objectives

Access-lists and traffic classifiers consume resources in the switch TCAM tables. When large or many access-lists are configured, the administrator can review the current resource utilization of the TCAMs. In this task, the resources will be reviewed, and the impact of object groups will be demonstrated.

Steps

- Review the current resource usage.
- Adjust the object groups, to increase the TCAM use.
- Verify the updated resource usage.

Review the Current Resource Usage

1. On Access2, review the current usage.

```
ICX-TX-Access2(config)# show resources
Resource Usage:
Mod  Description
         Resource                                           Used      Free
----------------------------------------------------------------------------
1/1  Ingress IP Port ACL Lookup
Ingress TCAM Entries                                  6     5107
     Total
         Ingress Lookups                                       1         4
         Egress Lookups                                        0         4
Resource data is updated every 10 seconds.
```

2. Enter the object-group ip address core-switch and add one IP address.

```
ICX-TX-Access2(config)# object-group ip address core-switch
ICX-TX-Access2(config-addrgroup-ip)# 10.x.12.1
```

3. Wait about 10 seconds; then review the resources.

```
ICX-TX-Access2(config-addrgroup-ip)# show resources
Resource Usage:
Mod  Description
         Resource                                           Used      Free
----------------------------------------------------------------------------
1/1  Ingress IP Port ACL Lookup
Ingress TCAM Entries                                  8     5105
     Total
         Ingress Lookups                                       1         4
         Egress Lookups                                        0         4
Resource data is updated every 10 seconds.
```

4. Next add two more IP addresses to the group.

```
ICX-TX-Access2(config-addrgroup-ip)# 10.x.12.4
ICX-TX-Access2(config-addrgroup-ip)# 10.x.12.5
ICX-TX-Access2(config-addrgroup-ip)# exit
```

5. Wait about 10 seconds; then review the resources.

```
ICX-TX-Access2(config)# show resources
Resource Usage:
Mod  Description
         Resource                                  Used      Free
---------------------------------------------------------------------
1/1  Ingress IP Port ACL Lookup
Ingress TCAM Entries                        12      5101
      Total
          Ingress Lookups                              1         4
          Egress Lookups                               0         4
```

6. Enter the port object-group and add a port and port range to the group.

```
ICX-TX-Access2(config)# object-group port switch-ports
ICX-TX-Access2(config-portgroup)# eq 22
ICX-TX-Access2(config-portgroup)# range 1024 2048
ICX-TX-Access2(config-portgroup)# exit
```

7. Wait about 10 seconds, then review the resources. This shows that the object-groups are very convenient for the administrator, but internally they are extracted so they still consume the same hardware resources as if individual lines would have been created.

```
ICX-TX-Access2(config)# show resources
Resource Usage:
Mod  Description
         Resource                                  Used      Free
---------------------------------------------------------------------
1/1  Ingress IP Port ACL Lookup
Ingress TCAM Entries                        27      5086
      Total
          Ingress Lookups                              1         4
          Egress Lookups                               0         4
Resource data is updated every 10 seconds.
```

Learning Check

1. What are the three general components of an ACL rule?
   a. Prefix length, IP or MAC address, and rule action
   b. ACL type, ACL application, and rule
   c. ACL type, subnet mask, and prefix length
   d. Sequence number, action, and matching criteria
2. An administrator wants to configure an IPv4 standard ACL to deny one device within a subnet (10.1.10.10) but permit every other device in the complete subnet (10.1.10.0/24). Which set of ACL entries meets these requirements?
   a. 10 permit 10.1.10.0 255.255.255.0 any
      20 deny 10.1.10.10 255.255.255.255 any
   b. 10 deny 10.1.10.10 255.255.255.255 any
      20 permit 10.1.10.0 255.255.255.0 any
   c. 10 permit 10.1.10.0 255.255.255.255 any
      20 deny 10.1.10.10 255.255.255.255 any
   d. 10 deny 10.1.10.10 255.255.255.255 any
      permit 10.1.10.0 255.255.255.255 any
3. You can apply an ACL to a layer-3 SVI VLAN interface.
   a. True
   b. False
4. Traffic matches an applied port and VLAN ACL. The action in which ACL will take precedence?
   a. Port
   b. VLAN

Summary

Congratulations! You have learned the key concepts you need to understand how to implement ACLs on AOS-CX switches. ACLs are composed of one or more entries called rules and identified by a common ACL ID (a number, a name, or in some cases both). Rules specify the matching criteria the switch applies to determine whether the ACL selects a particular packet.

Once you create an ACL, you can assign it to a switch interface or to another function. Until you assign the ACL, it has no effect on traffic the switch processes. When you assign an ACL to a switch interface, it functions as a packet filter, permitting selected packets and dropping other packets. Depending on the switch model, you can assign an ACL to an interface as an inbound or outbound RACL, to a VLAN as a VACL, or to a physical port as an inbound or outbound PACL. The type of ACL determines which packets are matched against the ACL. Remember that not all switches support all types of ACL applications (*in* versus *out*).

ACLs (and policies) consume resources and understanding the capabilities of the switches helps in designing a correct solution.

Lastly, you learned how to implement classifier policies to restrict traffic on logical interfaces (SVI and GRE).

6 Advanced OSPF

OBJECTIVES

After completing this chapter, you should be able to:

- ✓ Deploy multi-area OSPF within enterprise networks
- ✓ Efficiently use multi-area OSPF for scalability and stability
- ✓ Import external networks in a variety of OSPF environments
- ✓ Achieve fast convergence during failover situations
- ✓ Use virtual links requirement and implementation
- ✓ Implement OSFP authentication

Overview

In this chapter, you will learn how to implement Open Shortest Path First (OSPF) routing in multiple area designs. You will examine several advanced scenarios and learn ways to configure OSPF to meet their needs. In the ACSA Fundamentals course, you learned how to implement OSPF in a small, single-area design. This chapter will quickly review what you learned, but then expand upon this for a large campus design. Design features that you will explore including implementing multiple areas, area types, and redundancy. You will also learn how to import (redistribute) routes from an external network (that is, protocol), into OSPF as well as some additional OSPF features.

Reviewing Basic OSPF

You will begin this chapter by exploring how OSPF works in simple networks. This is primarily a review from the OSPF material covered in the ArubaOS-CX Switching Fundamentals (CXF)-related course.

OSPF Overview

–Dynamic routing protocol for complex, redundant topologies

–IGP designed for use within an organization or autonomous system (AS)

–Link state routing protocol:

- –Advertise links
- –Calculate lowest cost route based on topology
- –Communicate updates and converge quickly
- –Uses Dijkstra algorithm (aka, SPF algorithm)

–Hierarchical, area-based design

Figure 6-1 OSPF Overview

A very simple campus might have a single core switch that routes all traffic for the campus and uses a default route to send traffic out to the Internet. However, many companies have multiple routers and routing switches which need to send traffic across the campus. The routing devices use routes to tell them how to forward traffic to each destination network. Static routes quickly become too time-consuming and error-prone to manage, particularly in a complex or redundant topology. A dynamic routing protocol, on the other hand, enables routers to discover routes automatically and to automatically update the routes when the topology changes.

OSPF, an open standard routing protocol, is the typical choice for enterprise private networks. As an Interior Gateway Protocol (IGP), OSPF facilitates the exchange of routing information among routers under the same organizational control, or in other words within the same autonomous system (AS) (Figure 6-1).

OSPF is a link state protocol. Rather than advertise routes themselves, routers advertise information about their connected Layer 3 interfaces, also called links, and the cost (or metric) associated with that interface. These link state advertisements (LSAs) propagate across participating routers. Routers use the advertisements to construct a topology of the network, consisting of all the known links, the routers connected to the links, and the associated costs. Using the topology, routers calculate their own lowest cost route to each destination subnet.

Link state protocols such as OSPF tend to choose better routing paths and to converge faster than distance vector protocols such as Router Information Protocol (RIP). The algorithm implements the Dijkstra algorithm, also known as the shortest-path first (SPF) algorithm to find the least cost, loop-free paths.

To provide scalability, OSPF supports a two-layer hierarchy based on areas: the backbone and areas connected to the backbone.

Basic OSPF Setup

1. Creating routing process.
2. Optionally define a router ID (recommended).
3. Create an area.
4. Enable OSPF on layer 3 interfaces and place in an area:
   –Enables the switch to find OSPF neighbors on the same subnet
   –Enables the switch to advertise the layer 3's subnet as a link
   –Define interface(s) as passive (optional)

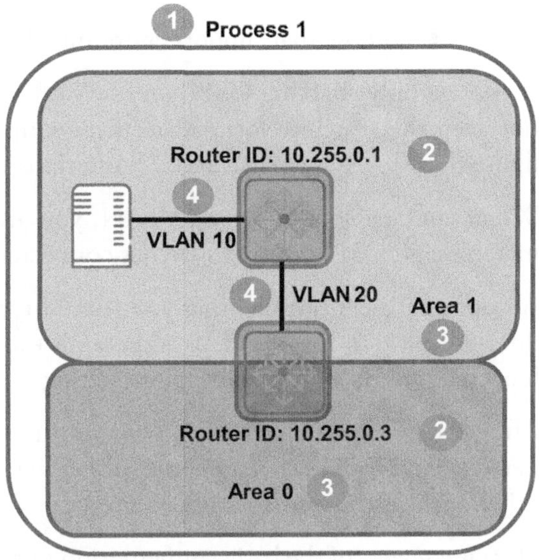

Figure 6-2 Basic OSPF Setup

You will now review the basic steps for setting up OSPF (Figure 6-2). Of course, configuring OSPF to meet your organization's needs has many more nuances—many of which are covered in this chapter. However, these basic steps can get your AOS-CX switches routing traffic across the network:

1. Create an OSPF routing process.
2. Optionally define a router ID (highly recommended).
3. Create an area.
   - OSPF uses areas to segment the network into smaller, more manageable pieces and to enable route aggregation. For the initial configuration, you will simply use one area, area 1. You will then learn about multiple area solutions.
4. Enable OSPF on layer 3 interfaces. For AOS-CX switches, these are either routed or VLAN interfaces. Enabling OSPF on an interface has two effects:
   - The routing switch sends OSPF messages on the interface and can form neighbor relationships with other routers on the same interface. Neighbors that fully exchange their topology information are called fully adjacent.
   - The routing switch advertises this interface in OSPF. For example, if the interface is associated with IP address 10.255.0.1/24, the routing switch advertises that it has a link to 10.255.0.0/24.

- VLANs that need to be advertised in OSPF include:
  - Those that connect routing switches (like VLAN 255 on Access-1 and Core-1)
  - Those that support endpoints (like VLAN 10 on Core-1)

If you are only enabling OSPF on the VLAN because you want to advertise its subnet, and you do not want the switch to form adjacencies with other routers or routing switches on the VLAN, configure the VLAN as a passive OSPF interface.

When you enable OSPF on a VLAN, you also specify the VLAN's OSPF area. The area ID must match on all OSPF routing switches connected on the same VLAN or subnet.

An optional step, but one that you should typically perform, is setting a router ID. The router ID does not have to be a valid IP address on the switch, but you often should use an IP address on a loopback interface. You will explore setting the router ID in the lab.

After you complete these steps, your routing switches will automatically create a topology of your network and learn routes to every subnet within it. If a link fails, the routing switches inform each other of the change and learn new routes.

Here is a review of the basic configuration of the OSPF routing process, covered in the ACSA course:

```
switch(config)# router ospf <process-ID>
switch(config-router)# router-id <router-ID>
switch(config-router)# enable
switch(config-ospf-1)# area <area-ID>
```

By default, OSPF is enabled when you create the routing process the first time. If you disable it with the **disable** command, use the corresponding **enable** command to re-enable it. This allows you to temporarily turn off OSPF without losing your OSPF configuration.

You must then enable OSPF on your required layer 3 (routed, loopback and/or VLAN) interfaces:

```
switch(config)# interface <layer-3-ID>
switch(config-if)# ip ospf <process-ID> area <area-ID>
```

Optionally you can specify the type of connection (defaults to *broadcast*):

```
switch(config)# interface <layer-3-ID>
switch(config-if)# ip ospf network {broadcast | point-to-point}
```

To define an interface as passive, configure the following:

```
switch(config)# interface <layer-3-ID>
switch(config-if)# ip ospf passive
```

Router IDs

At various points, this explanation will refer to a routing switch's OSPF router ID. The router ID identifies the router uniquely within the OSPF system. This ID has the format of an IP address, and it can be an IP address on one of the routing device's interfaces. However, you can also set an ID manually, and this ID does not necessarily need to match an IP address on the router. The figures that follow use a very simple topology in which the routers connect on a single shared subnet, and they each have a router ID that matches their IP address on that subnet. (When you set up a more complex topology in the lab, you will learn how to set the router ID to match a loopback interface ID. This ensures that the associated IP address is always reachable, even if some of the router's links fail.)

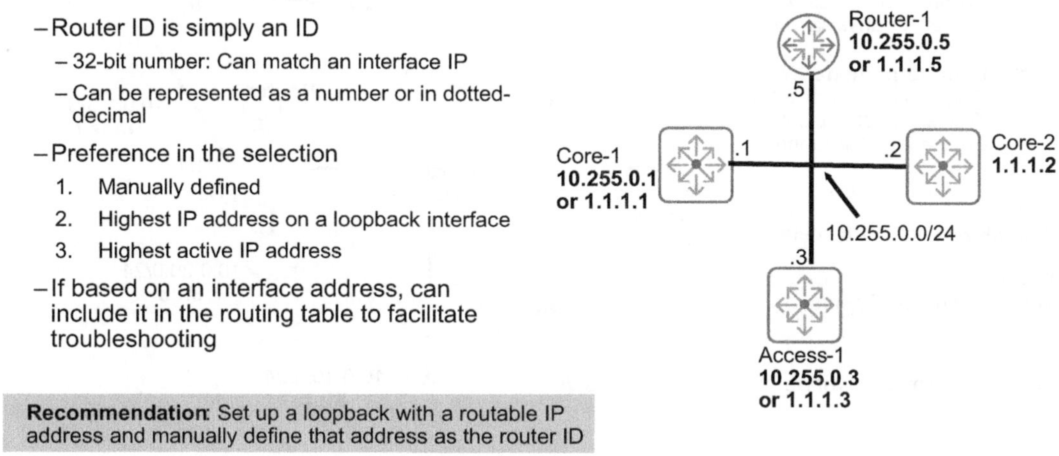

Figure 6-3 Router IDs

Note

It is best practice to set up a loopback interface with the router ID and including the loopback interface in an OSPF area. This ensures that the admin can always ping the address, even if links' statuses change, which greatly facilitates troubleshooting OSPF problems (Figure 6-3).

OSPF Network Types

OSPF routers run the protocol on layer 3 interfaces, or networks. Layer 3 interfaces include VLAN interfaces, physical interfaces set to routed mode, link aggregations set to routed mode, and loopback interfaces. AOS-CX switches support two types of networks: broadcast and point-to-point. Ethernet is a broadcast protocol, and a VLAN is a common example of a broadcast network.

You can connect the OSPF routing switches to the VLAN in some sort of redundant tree topology, directly to each other or through Layer 2 switches.

Here is an example of a Layer 3 connection with a circle on which all of the routing switches have an interface; the Layer 2 connections are not shown. In a broadcast network, a designated router (DR) is elected to establish relationships, called adjacencies, with the other routers and to handle responsibilities such as receiving and flooding link state updates (LSUs). A backup DR (BDR) is also elected to take over if the DR fails. OSPF routers multicast messages to the DR and BDR at 224.0.0.6.

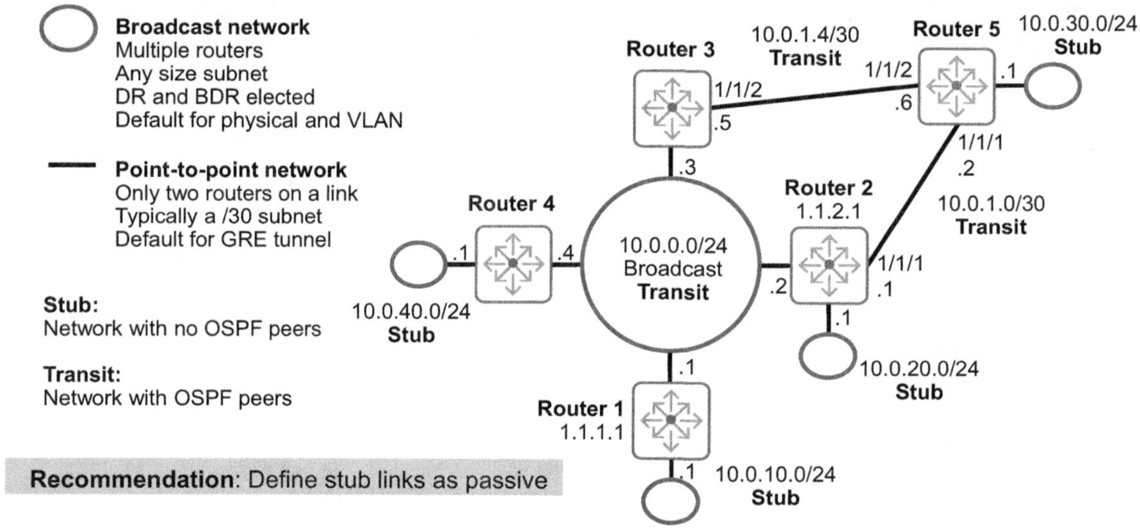

Figure 6-4 OSPF Network Types

When you directly connect two OSPF routing switches, it is generally preferable to set up a point-to-point network. This network is typically associated with a /30 or /31 subnet. On AOS-CX switches, GRE tunnel interfaces are point-to-point by default, and loopback interfaces are a special loopback type. It could also include VLAN interfaces, but only the two routers belong to the associated VLAN. But most interfaces are broadcast networks by default, including physical route-only ports and VLAN interfaces. However, you can set route only ports and link aggregations to point-to-point, assuming that the routed link connects directly to a routed link on another OSPF device. You can even set VLAN interfaces to point-to-point if they follow the rules. (Remember, though, that a VSX LAG between a VSX pair running OSPF and another OSPF router should be a broadcast network because the network has three routers: each VSX switch and the connected router.) Since a point-to-point network has only two routers, it does not require the DR and BDR roles (Figure 6-4).

Note

OSPF point-to-point networks converge faster than OSPF broadcast networks and therefore are more preferred when applicable.

OSPF also distinguishes between transit and stub networks. A transit network is any network on which a router discovers at least one neighbor; it could be a broadcast or point-to-point network. A stub network is any network on which the router does not detect another OSPF device. The reason that the router runs OSPF on the stub network is to advertise the network to other routers in the AS. Often a stub network is a VLAN interface for which the OSPF router is the default gateway.

Note
Two routers (even a VSX core) on the same subnet, with passive interfaces, also result in stub network.

Passive Interfaces

Optionally you can define the interface as *passive* if it will have no OSPF neighbors off of the interface and you do not wish to form adjacencies to anyone connected to the related interface:

```
switch(config)# interface <layer-3-ID>
switch(config-if)# ip ospf passive
```

Neighbors: Partial Adjacency

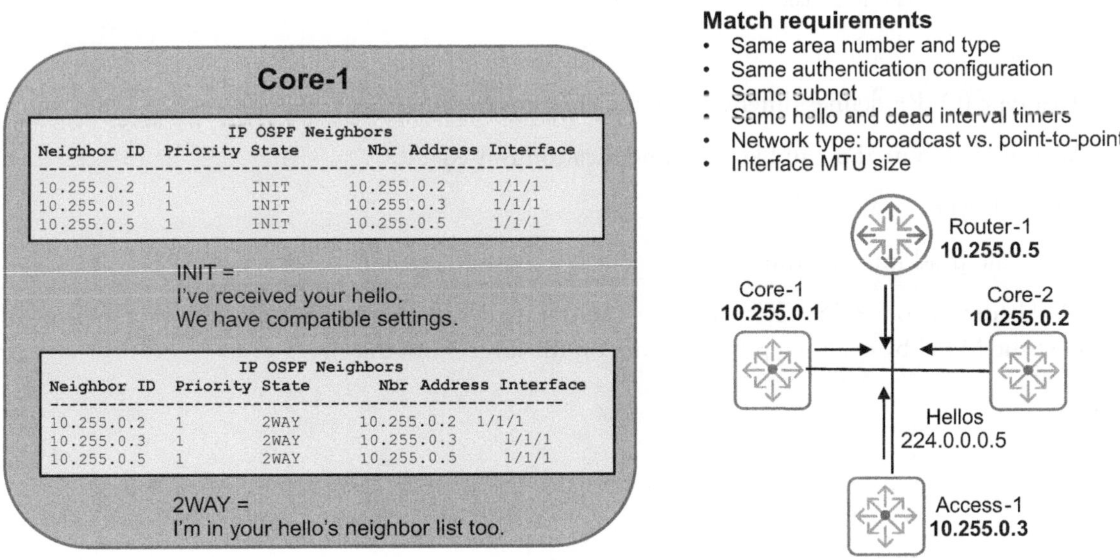

Figure 6-5 Neighbors: Partial Adjacency

Now you will review how an OSPF router discovers its neighbors (Figure 6-5). The router sends out hellos on each OSPF interface. (An OSPF interface is a Layer 3 interface with an IP address on which OSPF is enabled. On AOS-CX switches, the Layer 3 interface is a VLAN.) The hello includes information about the router's OSPF settings on the interface, as well as a list of neighbors discovered on the interface. The neighbor list is empty until the router receives hellos from neighbors. The hellos are destined to a multicast IP address, 224.0.0.5, the standard OSPF multicast address for all routers. Therefore, all other OSPF routers in the same subnet will hear the hello.

A receiving router checks the settings in the hello to make sure that they match its own settings on the interface. Table 6-1 shows the settings that must match for the router to accept the hello. Note that these settings might be mismatched initially, or configuration changes might cause these settings to change after neighbors already have an established relationship. Routers continue to transmit hellos periodically, so the neighbor will receive the hello with the mismatched settings and remove the neighbor relationship. If these do not match, the OSPF routers will fail to form an adjacency and will be stuck in an INIT state.

But assuming that the settings match, the router adds the neighbor that sent the hello as an OSPF neighbor in the INIT state. It also adds the neighbor's router ID in the neighbor list included in its hellos. When an OSPF router receives a hello with its own ID in this list, it knows that it has bidirectional connectivity with the neighbor. It moves the neighbor to 2WAY state.

Settings that must match on OSPF neighbors:

- Network address and mask
- Area ID
- Area type (OSPF defines different types of areas covered in other training)
- Authentication method and key if authentication is used
- Network type
- Hello and dead interfval timer
- MTU (default on AOS-CX switches is the standard Ethernet maximum 1500 bytes. You can raise the MTU by enabling jumbo frames on the layer 3 interface).

Designated and Backup Designated Routers (DR/BDR)

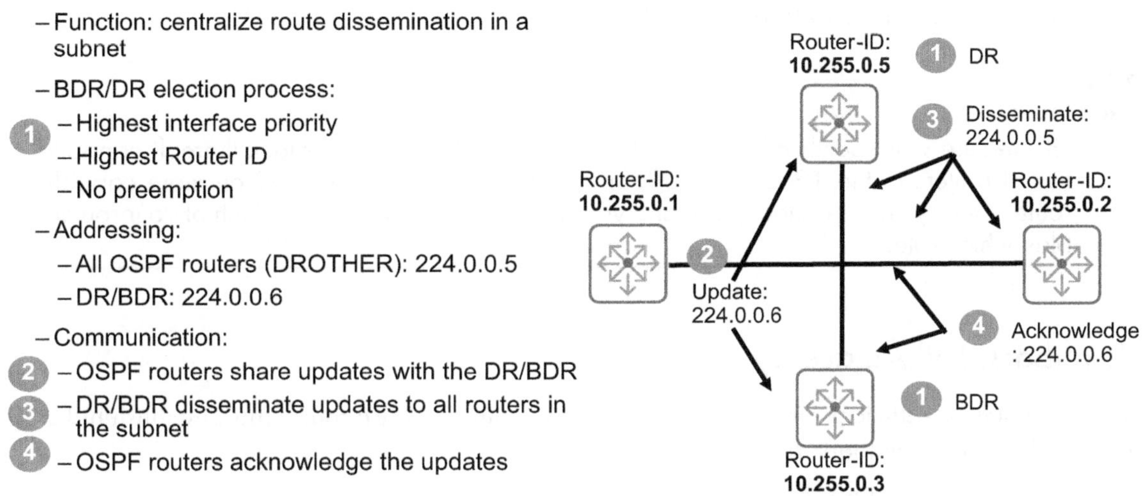

Figure 6-6 Designated and Backup Designated Routers (DR/BDR)

An OSPF router will not form adjacencies to just any router. Instead, a client/server design is implemented in OSPF on each broadcast segment. For each multi-access broadcast segment, such as Ethernet, there is a DR and a BDR as well as other OSPF routers, called DROTHERs (Figure 6-6). As an example, if you have 10 VLANs/subnets in your switched area, you will have 10 DRs and 10 BDRs. The one exception of a segment not having these two routers is on a point-to-point link.

When an OSPF router comes up, it forms adjacencies with the DR and the BDR on each multi-access segment to which it is connected; if it is connected to three segments, it will form three sets of adjacencies. Any exchange of routing information is between these DR/BDR routers and the other OSPF neighbors on a segment (and vice versa). An OSPF router talks to a DR using the IP multicast address of 224.0.0.6. The DR and the BDR talk to all OSPF routers using the 224.0.0.5 multicast IP address.

OSPF routers use link state advertisements (LSAs) to communicate with each other. One type of LSA is a hello, which is used to form neighbor relationships and as a keepalive function. Hellos are generated every 10 seconds. When sharing link information (directly connected routes), links are sent to the DR (224.0.0.6) and the DR disseminates this to everyone else (224.0.0.5) on the segment. On point-to-point links, since no DR/BDR is used, all OSPF packets are addressed to 224.0.0.5.

The OSPF router with the highest priority becomes the DR for the segment. If there is a tie, the router with the highest router ID (not IP address on the segment) will become the DR. By default, all routers have a priority of 1 (priorities can range from 0 to 255—it is an 8-bit value). If the DR fails, the BDR is promoted to DR and another router is elected as the BDR. If a router does not become a DR or BDR, it is referred to as a designated router-other, or commonly *DROTHER*, for short. Please note that there is no preemption of the DR/BDR role. If a DR/BDR exists and a router with a higher router ID joins the segment, it will not preempt the existing DR/BDR. Election only occurs if there is no DR or BDR on a segment.

Note

This feature was specifically designed based on the hardware (or lack thereof) capabilities of routers in the 1980s. The DR/BDR functions would be placed on more capable routers; today, this is a moot point and you should not be concerned which of your routers play which role.

Neighbors: Full Adjacency

The 2WAY state is sufficient for some OSPF neighbors. But an OSPF router must establish full adjacency with certain neighbors: the DR and BDR.

OSPF routers must establish full adjacency with:

- The single neighbor on a point-to-point interface
- The Designated Router (DR) and Backup Designated Router (BDR) of a broadcast or non-broadcast multi-access (NBMA) network
    - The DR for a subnet running OSPF (called an OSPF link) is elected based on the priority advertised in the hello (higher priority value wins) and, in the case of a tie, higher router ID.
    - When a link has many routers, the DR and BDR roles reduce the number of adjacencies on routers and allow routers to listen for LSUs from a single source. If an interface goes down and back up the router can quickly achieve adjacency with just two routers. Although every router on a broadcast link does not necessarily achieve full adjacency, all routers still have identical LSDBs because everyone achieves full adjacency with the DR and BDR.
    - An Ethernet network such as a VLAN is an example of a broadcast network. However, you can design your network such that a VLAN acts more like a point-to-point link (a routed port). When a link has only two routers, which devices take the DR and BDR role do not usually matter.

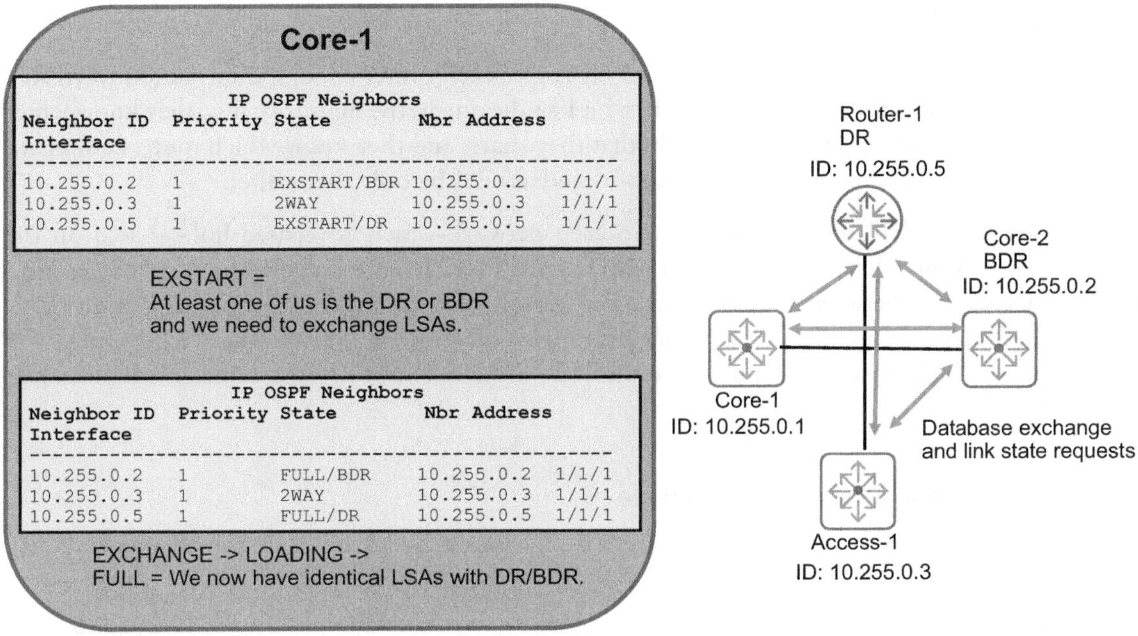

Figure 6-7 Neighbors: Full Adjacency

Periodic hellos (every 10 seconds, by default) maintain the 2WAY or FULL state. If the OSPF router misses for hellos from a neighbor, it moves the neighbor to down. You will learn about how OSPF routers detect that neighbors are down in more detail later.

Table 6-1 Roles for routers on broadcast networks

Role	Description
Designated Router (DR)	Achieves adjacency with all other routers on the network Advertises Type 2 (Network) LSAs Receives Link State Updates (LSUs) from other routers (and sends its own LSUs) Advertises LSUs on the all routers multicast address, 224.0.0.5
Backup Designated Router (BDR)	Achieves adjacency with all other routers on the network Receives LSUs from other routers (and sends its own LSUs to the DR) Takes over other DR roles if the DR fails
Other (DROTHER)	Achieves adjacency with the DR and BDR Has 2WAY relationship with other routers Sends LSUs to 224.0.0.6 (on which the DR and BDR listen)

SPF Algorithm

Within an OSPF area, the Type 1 and Type 2 LSAs give each router enough information to create a topology (sometimes called a directed graph) a bit like the one in the figure. That is, they know which routers connect to other routers by the links that they share, and they know which routers offer gateways to which stub networks, which are networks advertised by only that router.

Each router then calculates the best route to each network—each advertised link—based on this topology. Specifically, they run the shortest path first (SPF), or Dijkstra, algorithm, which determines the lowest cost path between the router and the network. For example, in Figure 6-7, Core-1 has learned that it has a route to 10.100.56.0/30 through next hop 10.255.0.5 (the actual Router-1 IP address on the transit network, not the router ID, although they are the same in this instance) (Figure 6-8).

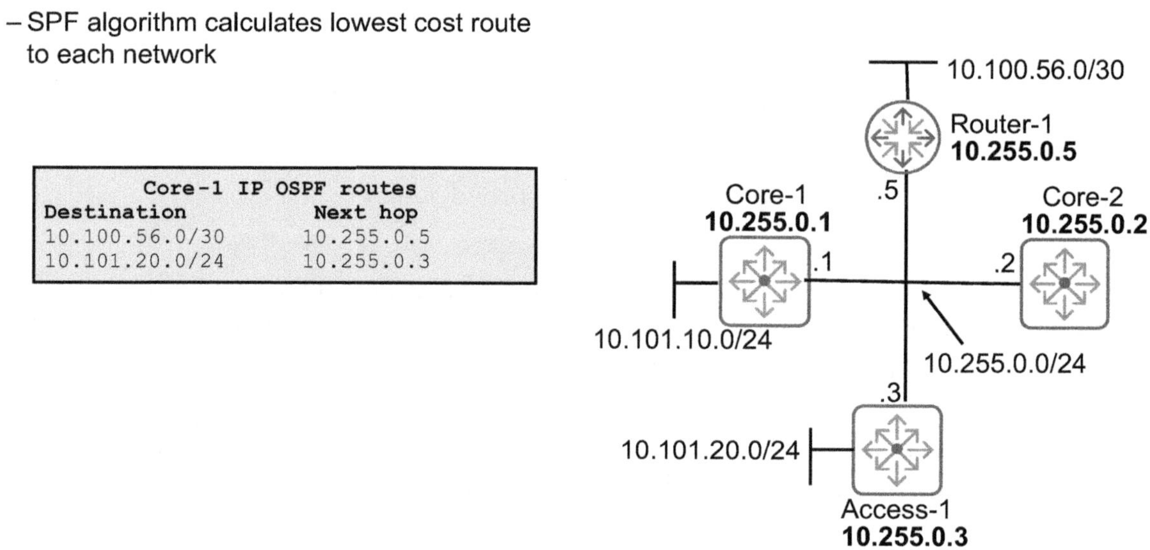

Figure 6-8 SPF Algorithm

LSUs

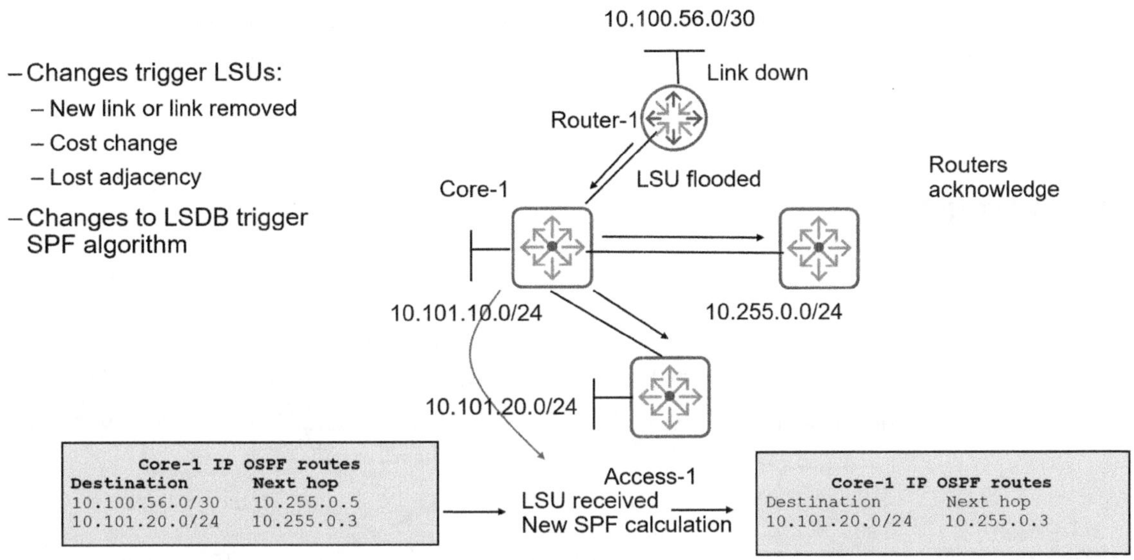

Figure 6-9 LSUs

LSAs have an age, and they age out of the database when the LSA reaches the max age (standard 1800 seconds). Routers periodically re-advertise the LSAs that they have generated to reset the age and maintain them. If a router needs to withdraw one of its LSAs, it can flush it from the system by re-advertising the LSA with an age set to the max age.

But an LSA aging out is not the typical way that routers learn about changes to the topology; this would be far too slow. Instead, if a router needs to change information in one of its LSA, it sends a link state update (LSU) and waits for an acknowledgement. For example, Core-1 adds a new link to 10.101.10.0/24, so it adds that new link to its Type 1 (router) LSA and sends an LSU for that LSA. As you see in Figure 6-9, the DR in a broadcast network is responsible for forwarding the information on the Ethernet network. In a larger system, the routers that receive the LSU would then flood it out on other OSPF interfaces until the LSU floods across the entire system.

If Router-1, the DR, lost adjacency with Access-1, it would update the Network LSA and send an LSU. Then the other routers would know that Access-1 is no longer available on the 10.255.0.0/24 subnet, and they could adjust routes accordingly.

Or in another example, a stub link goes down on Router-1. The router updates its router LSA to indicate that it has fewer links. In this example, the system has a topology with multiple Layer 3 hops. Neighbors still flood the LSU between each other (and send acknowledgments) until the LSU propagates throughout the system. The routers also update the appropriate LSA in their LSDBs.

LSUs and changes to the LSDB trigger the router to re-run the SPF algorithm so that it can calculate new best routes. In the example above, the change to the topology causes Core-1 to remove a route to a destination that is no longer available. In a more complex and redundant topology—such as the ones you will explore later—the router might find a new next hop for the route.

Lab 6.1

Lab 6.1 Diagram

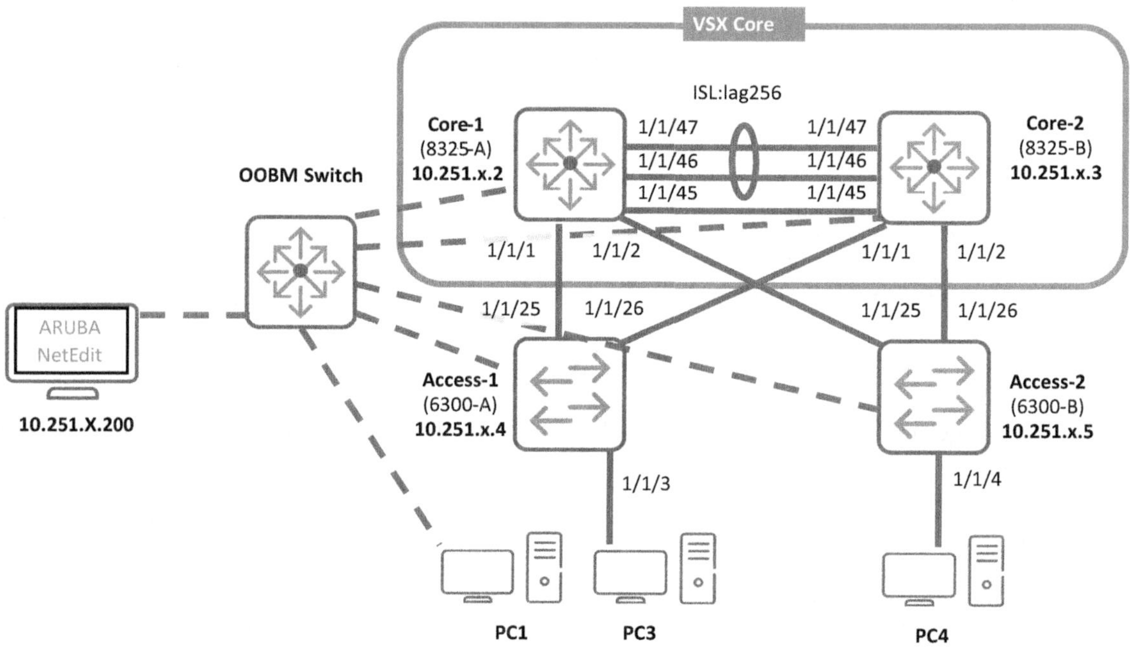

Figure 6-10 Lab 6.1 Diagram

Overview

In this lab activity, as shown in Figure 6-10, OSPF will be configured using a single backbone area (0.0.0.0) on the devices in the lab. In following lab activities, additional areas will be introduced (Figure 6-11).

Objectives

- Use loopback interfaces
- Configure single area OSPF on the AOS-CX switches
- Review OSPF passive interfaces

Task 1: Verify Lab Start Configuration

Objectives

- If you have just completed Lab 04—VSX, you can skip this task and move to the next task.
- If you have completed any other lab and are performing this lab again, complete these steps to get the base configuration on the devices.

Steps

1. Load the "icx-lab04-vsx" checkpoint on all *four* switches using the following command.

```
Switch# copy checkpoint icx-lab04-vsx running-config
Configuration changes will take time to process, please be patient.
```

Task 2: Basic OSPF Setup on Core Area 0

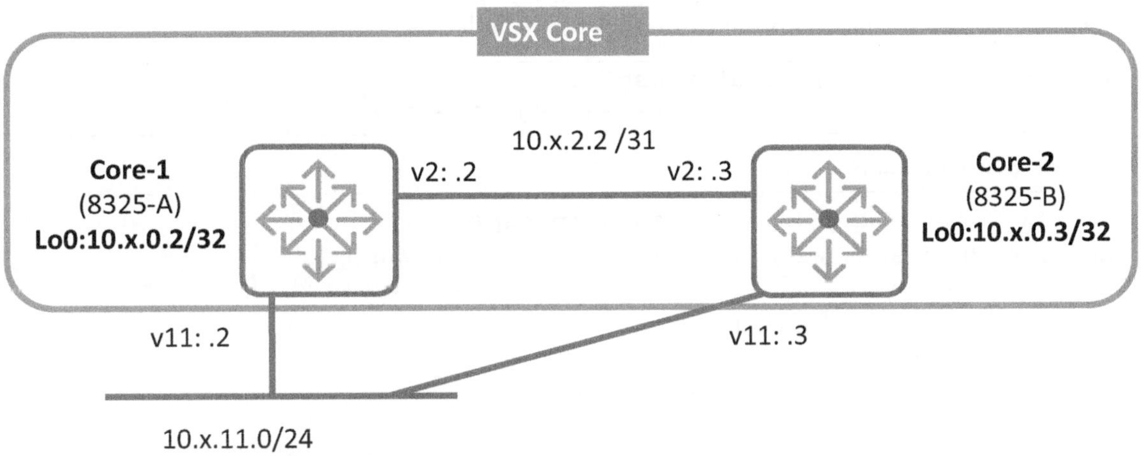

Figure 6-11 Task 2: Basic OSPF Setup on Core Area 0

Objectives

- Use Loopback interfaces
- Refresh the OSPF single area configuration

- Set up OSPF in a VSX cluster
- Use OSPF point-to-point connections
- Use OSPF passive interface feature

Steps

1. Open a terminal connection to Core1; enter configuration mode. Define a new IP Loopback interface and assign the IP address. Replace X with your table number (Figure 6-11).

```
ICX-Tx-Core1(config)# interface loopback 0
ICX-Tx-Core1(config-loopback-if)# ip address 10.x.0.2/32
ICX-Tx-Core1(config-loopback-if)# exit
```

2. Start a new OSPF process with process ID 1. Assign the same IP as the Loopback as the router ID to ensure stability for the router ID.
   - The process ID is locally significant.
   - By default, the process is linked to the VRF ‘default'.

```
ICX-Tx-Core1(config)# router ospf 1
ICX-Tx-Core1(config-ospf-1)# router-id 10.x.0.2
```

3. Review current status.

```
ICX-Tx-Core1(config-ospf-1)# show ip ospf
Routing Process 1 with ID : 10.x.0.2 VRF default
--------------------------------------------------
OSPFv2 Protocol is enabled
Graceful-restart is configured
Restart Interval: 120, State: inactive
Last Graceful Restart Exit Status: none
SPF: Start Time: 200ms, Hold Time: 1000ms, Max Wait Time: 5000ms
Maximum Paths to Destination: 4
Number of external LSAs 0, checksum sum 0
Number of areas is 0, 0 normal, 0 stub, 0 NSSA
Number of active areas is 0, 0 normal, 0 stub, 0 NSSA
BFD is disabled
Reference Bandwidth: 100000 Mbps
```

4. Define area 0.

```
ICX-Tx-Core1(config-ospf-1)# area 0
```

5. Review the current OSPF LSDB. Since no interfaces have been enabled for OSPF, the database does not contain any LSA information yet.

```
ICX-Tx-Core1(config-ospf-1)# show ip ospf lsdb
No OSPF LSAs found on VRF default.
ICX-Tx-Core1(config-ospf-1)# exit
```

6. Enable the loopback interface for OSPF.

```
ICX-Tx-Core1(config)# interface loopback 0
ICX-Tx-Core1(config-loopback-if)# ip ospf 1 area 0
ICX-Tx-Core1(config-loopback-if)# exit
```

Note

The **ip ospf** command allows fine control over which interface is assigned to which OSPF process and in which area.

7. Review the LSDB again.

```
ICX-Tx-Core1(config)# show ip ospf lsdb
OSPF Router with ID (10.x.0.2) (Process ID 1 VRF default)
===========================================================

Router Link State Advertisements (Area 0.0.0.0)
------------------------------------------------

LSID      ADV Router       Age     Seq#          Checksum       Link Count
-----------------------------------------------------------------------------
10.x.0.2        10.x.0.2        27         0x80000001 0x00009773      1
```

Question: What type of LSA has been added into the LSDB?

Answer: A Type 1 LSA, known as a 'router' LSA.

Question: How many links (IP subnets) are announced by this LSA?

Answer: Currently, only the loopback interface is announced in the LSA, so one link.

Dedicated Routed Link Between Core1 and Core2

It is best practice to have a dedicated routed subnet between the VSX members. Dedicated means that there are no other devices on this subnet. This subnet will be used as the transit network for any routes that would exist on only one of the VSX members. While technically any existing subnet could be used for this, it provides a cleaner design to have a dedicated subnet for this purpose, a subnet that cannot be impacted by any other end-point devices.

1. On Core1, define VLAN 2 interface. It will be used as the transit network. Since only Core1 and Core2 will be using this subnet, a /31 mask is used.

Note

It is best practice to use a /31 subnet for point-to-point links when both sides support the /31 mask.

```
ICX-Tx-Core1(config)# vlan 2
ICX-Tx-Core1(config-vlan-2)# vsx-sync
ICX-Tx-Core1(config-vlan-2)# exit
ICX-Tx-Core1(config)# interface vlan 2
ICX-Tx-Core1(config-if-vlan)# ip address 10.x.2.2/31
```

2. Open a terminal connection to Core2; enter configuration mode. Define the VLAN 2 interface.

```
ICX-Tx-Core2(config)# interface vlan 2
ICX-Tx-Core2(config-if-vlan)# ip address 10.x.2.3/31
```

3. Verify connectivity to Core1 with a ping.

```
ICX-Tx-Core2(config-if-vlan)# do ping 10.x.2.2
PING 10.x.2.2 (10.x.2.2) 100(128) bytes of data.
108 bytes from 10.x.2.2: icmp_seq=1 ttl=64 time=14.1 ms
108 bytes from 10.x.2.2: icmp_seq=2 ttl=64 time=0.231 ms
...
ICX-Tx-Core2(config-if-vlan)# exit
```

4. Enable OSPF on interface VLAN 2 for process 1 area 0.

```
ICX-Tx-Core1(config-if-vlan)# ip ospf 1 area 0
```

Note

It is best practice to use the lowest possible cost for this link. By default, the cost is calculated based on the interface bandwidth, using 100Gbps as the reference. This results in a cost 100 by default for the VLAN interfaces. For the VSX transit link, the lowest possible cost will be set, that is, a cost of 1.

---

5. On Core1, apply this cost to the interface VLAN 2.

```
ICX-Tx-Core1(config-if-vlan)# ip ospf cost 1
ICX-Tx-Core1(config)# exit
```

6. Review the LSDB again.

```
ICX-Tx-Core1(config)# show ip ospf lsdb
OSPF Router with ID (10.x.0.2) (Process ID 1 VRF default)
============================================================

Router Link State Advertisements (Area 0.0.0.0)
------------------------------------------------
LSID            ADV Router      Age       Seq#       Checksum      Link Count
-----------------------------------------------------------------------------
10.x.0.2        10.x.0.2        91        0x80000002 0x0000322f     2

Network Link State Advertisements (Area 0.0.0.0)
-------------------------------------------------
LSID            ADV Router      Age       Seq#       Checksum
--------------------------------------------------------------
10.x.2.3        10.x.12.3       45        0x80000003 0x00008f4c
```

Question: How many links are active for the router LSA 10.x.0.2?

Answer: There are 2 links now: loopback and VLAN2.

7. Configure Core2 for OSPF. First review the current OSPF configuration.

```
ICX-Tx-Core2(config)# show running-config ospf
router ospf 1
   area 0.0.0.0
interface vlan2
   ip ospf 1 area 0.0.0.0
   ip ospf cost 1
```

Question: Why is there already an OSPF configuration on Core2?

Answer: VSX-sync is enabled for OSPF, so many OSPF configurations are automatically synchronized to Core2.

8. Configure the loopback and set the router-id.
   - IP Loopback 0 10.x.0.3/32
   - OSPF process 1, router-id 10.x.0.3/32, define area 0

```
ICX-Tx-Core2(config)# interface loopback 0
ICX-Tx-Core2(config-loopback-if)# ip address 10.x.0.3/32
ICX-Tx-Core2(config-loopback-if)# exit
ICX-Tx-Core2(config)# router ospf 1
ICX-Tx-Core2(config-ospf-1)# router-id 10.x.0.3
OSPFv2 protocol will be reset.
Do you want to continue (y/n)? y
ICX-Tx-Core2(config-ospf-1)# exit
```

Note

Changing the OSPF router-id requires the OSPF process to restart. Make sure to confirm the restart with 'y'.

9. On Core2, check the current configuration of the Loopback 0 interface.

```
ICX-Tx-Core2(config)# show run interface loopback 0
```

   Question: Is OSPF enabled on the interface? If so, why?

   Answer: Yes, OSPF is enabled. VSX OSPF configuration sync took care of this.

10. On Core1, review the OSPF LSDB.

```
ICX-Tx-Core1(config)# show ip ospf lsdb
OSPF Router with ID (10.x.0.2) (Process ID 1 VRF default)
===========================================================

Router Link State Advertisements (Area 0.0.0.0)
------------------------------------------------

LSID       ADV Router       Age        Seq#       Checksum     Link Count
-------------------------------------------------------------------------
10.x.0.2       10.x.0.2       601        0x80000005 0x00000c55      2
10.x.0.3       10.x.0.3       602        0x80000002 0x0000263a      2

Network Link State Advertisements (Area 0.0.0.0)
-------------------------------------------------

LSID             ADV Router       Age        Seq#        Checksum
-------------------------------------------------------------------
10.x.2.2       10.x.0.2       606        0x80000001 0x0000688f
```

Question: What are the 2 LSA types in this LSDB?

Answer: Router (Type 1) and Network (Type 2).

Question: What does the network LSA represent?

Answer: A network LSA is representing a multi-access network between two or more OSPF routers. Since the VLAN 2 Ethernet interface is a type 'broadcast' interface, by default OSPF will start the DR/BDR election process and the DR will generate the Network LSA.

11. Review the current OSPF neighbor list.

```
ICX-Tx-Core1(config)# show ip ospf neighbors
OSPF Process ID 1 VRF default
==============================

Total Number of Neighbors: 1

Neighbor ID   Priority  State           Nbr Address       Interface
--------------------------------------------------------------------
10.x.0.3         1         FULL/BDR        10.x.2.3             vlan2

ICX-Tx-Core1(config)#
```

Question: What does the DR/BDR stand for?

Answer: Designated Router and Backup Designated Router are elected on a multi-access network, such as an Ethernet broadcast network. This is the default operation of OSPF.

OSPF Point-to-Point Connection

A network type broadcast means that more than two devices could come online on the subnet, so this is why OSPF prepares itself and elects the DR/BDR for the subnet. This election takes some time during the link setup phase. When the design ensures that only two OSPF routers will ever be online on a subnet that is transported on a broadcast network, the administrator can change the OSPF network type to 'point to point'. For this reason, even when the physical network is still broadcast, such as an ethernet VLAN, this configuration will instruct OSPF to assume that only one peer is available on this subnet. This will effectively skip the DR/BDR election process. This will also eliminate the type 2 Network LSA from the LSDB.

It is best practice to set the OSPF network type to point-to-point for point-to-point links.

1. On the Core1, change the VLAN 2 interface OSPF network type to 'point to point'.

```
ICX-Tx-Core1(config)# interface vlan 2
ICX-Tx-Core1(config-if-vlan)# ip ospf network point-to-point
ICX-Tx-Core1(config-if-vlan)# exit
```

2. Review the configuration changes that were pushed to Core2 by VSX sync.

```
ICX-Tx-Core1(config)# show run int vlan2 vsx-peer
interface vlan2
    ip address 10.x.2.3/31
    ip ospf 1 area 0.0.0.0
    ip ospf cost 1
    ip ospf network point-to-point
    exit
```

3. On Core1, review the OSPF LSDB. The network LSA that was previously present for the broadcast transit network has now been removed.

```
ICX-Tx-Core1(config)# show ip ospf lsdb
OSPF Router with ID (10.x.0.2) (Process ID 1 VRF default)
===========================================================

Router Link State Advertisements (Area 0.0.0.0)
------------------------------------------------

LSID            ADV Router      Age       Seq#        Checksum
----------------------------------------------------------------
10.x.0.2       10.x.0.2        130       0x80000004 0x00007163
10.x.0.3       10.x.0.3        131       0x80000004 0x0000874a
ICX-Tx-Core1(config)#
```

Route Verification

1. Verify there is an OSPF route in the routing table for the peer Core switch loopback interface using the 'show ip route ospf' command.

Note

The 'show ip route' command has many filtering options. In real-world environments with many routes, these filter options can help the administrator to narrow down the output of the command.

```
ICX-Tx-Core1(config)# show ip route ospf
Displaying ipv4 routes selected for forwarding
'[x/y]' denotes [distance/metric]
10.x.0.3/32, vrf default
        via  10.x.2.3,  [110/1],  ospf

ICX-Tx-Core1(config)#
```

2. Verify connectivity between the loopback interfaces with a ping from the local Loopback IP address to the peer switch Loopback IP address.

```
ICX-Tx-Core1(config)# do ping 10.x.0.3 source loopback0
PING 10.x.0.3 (10.x.0.3) from 10.x.0.2 : 100(128) bytes of data.
108 bytes from 10.x.0.3: icmp_seq=1 ttl=64 time=0.179 ms
108 bytes from 10.x.0.3: icmp_seq=2 ttl=64 time=0.174 ms
108 bytes from 10.x.0.3: icmp_seq=3 ttl=64 time=0.186 ms
108 bytes from 10.x.0.3: icmp_seq=4 ttl=64 time=0.205 ms
108 bytes from 10.x.0.3: icmp_seq=5 ttl=64 time=0.248 ms
--- 10.x.0.3 ping statistics ---
5 packets transmitted, 5 received, 0% packet loss, time 4086ms
rtt min/avg/max/mdev = 0.174/0.198/0.248/0.029 ms
ICX-Tx-Core1(config)#
```

Question: Why is the loopback IP address configured as the source IP for this test?

Answer: By default, a router will use the IP address of the outbound interface as the source IP. In this case, that would have been the VLAN 1 interface. If the administrator wants to test if the remote router has an entry in the routing table for the local loopback, the loopback can be set as the source IP.

3. Review the OSPF neighbors.

```
ICX-Tx-Core1(config)# show ip ospf neighbors
OSPF Process ID 1 VRF default
================================

Total Number of Neighbors: 1

Neighbor ID      Priority  State             Nbr Address       Interface
------------------------------------------------------------------------------
10.x.0.3          n/a       FULL              10.x.2.3          vlan2

ICX-Tx-Core1(config)#
```

Review the Detailed OSPF Neighbor State

```
ICX-Tx-Core1(config)# show ip ospf neighbors 10.x.0.3
Neighbor 10.x.0.3, interface address 10.x.2.3
-----------------------------------------------

Process ID 1 VRF default, in area 0.0.0.0 via interface vlan2
Neighbor priority is n/a, State is FULL
Options is 0x42
Dead timer due in 00:00:35
Time since last state change 00h:07m:42s
ICX-Tx-Core1(config)#
```

1. Review the OSPF interfaces; note the 'State' of each interface.

```
ICX-Tx-Core1(config)# show ip ospf interface
Interface loopback0 is up, line protocol is up
-----------------------------------------------
IP address 10.x.0.2/32, Process ID 1 VRF default, area 0.0.0.0
    State Loopback, Status up, Network type Loopback
    Link Speed: NA
    Cost Configured NA, Calculated NA
    Transit delay 1 sec, Router priority 1
    No designated router on this network
    No backup designated router on this network
    Timer Intervals: Hello 10, Dead 40, Retransmit 5
    No authentication
    Number of Link LSAs: 0, checksum sum 0
    BFD is disabled

Interface vlan2 is up, line protocol is up
-------------------------------------------
IP address 10.x.2.2/31, Process ID 1 VRF default, area 0.0.0.0
    State Point-to-point, Status up, Network type Point-to-point
    Link Speed: 1000 Mbps
    Cost Configured 1, Calculated 1
    Transit delay 1 sec, Router priority n/a
    No designated router on this network
    No backup designated router on this network
    Timer Intervals: Hello 10, Dead 40, Retransmit 5
    No authentication
    Number of Link LSAs: 0, checksum sum 0
    BFD is disabled
```

Task 3: OSPF Address Advertisements and Control

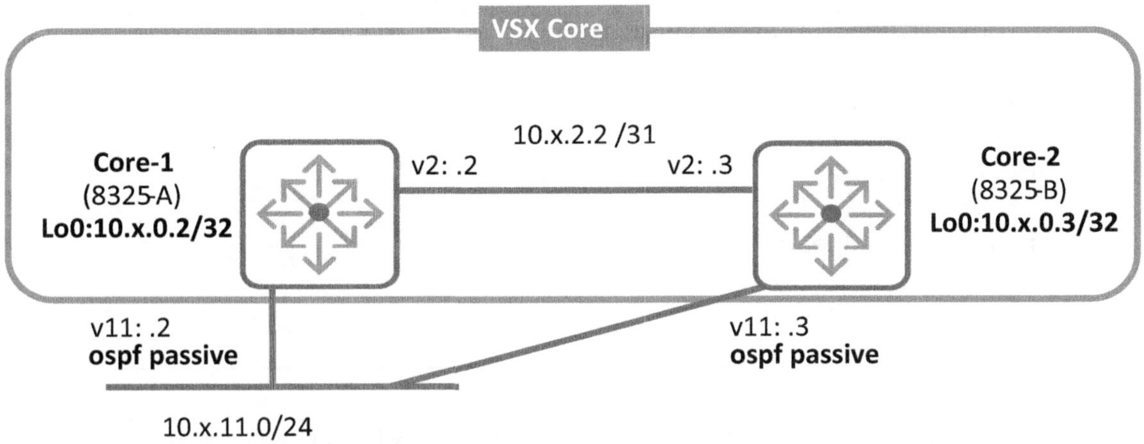

Figure 6-12 Task 3: OSPF Address Advertisements and Control

Objectives

- Enable end-host subnet advertisement into OSPF
- Configure a passive interface
- Use the passive interface default
- Review the administrative distance of OSPF

Steps

1. On Core1, enable the user VLAN 11 for OSPF in area 0 (Figure 6-12).

```
ICX-Tx-Core1(config)# interface vlan11
ICX-Tx-Core1(config-if-vlan)# ip ospf 1 area 0
ICX-Tx-Core1(config-if-vlan)# exit
```

2. Review the running configuration of interface VLAN 11 on both the local device and the VSX peer (Core2).

```
ICX-Tx-Core1(config)# show running interface vlan11
interface vlan11
    vsx-sync active-gateways policies
    ip address 10.x.11.2/24
    active-gateway ip mac 02:02:00:00:12:00
    active-gateway ip 10.x.11.1
    ip helper-address 10.x.1.6
    l3-counters
ip ospf 1 area 0.0.0.0
    exit
```

```
ICX-Tx-Core1(config)# show running interface vlan11 vsx-peer
interface vlan11
    vsx-sync active-gateways policies
    ip address 10.x.11.3/24
    active-gateway ip mac 02:02:00:00:12:00
    active-gateway ip 10.x.11.1
    ip helper-address 10.x.1.6
    l3-counters
ip ospf 1 area 0.0.0.0
    exit
ICX-Tx-Core1(config)#
```

Note

For the VSX OSPF synchronization to work properly, the administrator should use the same physical uplink interface. For instance, if Core1 has a routed uplink port 1/1/45, the Core2 should also use interface 1/1/45 as the routed uplink.

3. Review the OSPF neighbors.

```
ICX-Tx-Core1(config)# show ip ospf neighbors
OSPF Process ID 1 VRF default
==============================
Total Number of Neighbors: 3

Neighbor ID      Priority  State              Nbr Address        Interface
-------------------------------------------------------------------------------
10.x.0.3         1         FULL/DR            10.x.11.3          vlan11
10.x.0.3         n/a       FULL               10.x.2.3           vlan2
```

Question: Why did OSPF establish a neighbor relationship over the user vlan?

Answer: When an interface is enabled for OSPF, it automatically starts sending hello packets.

Question: Is it desired to have OSPF communication over user subnets?

Answer: Typically, OSPF communication is not enabled on user subnets to protect the OSPF protocol against malicious neighbors that may be connected on the user subnets.

Passive Interfaces

Passive interfaces provide a method to have an interface enabled for OSPF, so the subnet will be included in the router LSA announcement. But at the same time, the OSPF protocol will be disabled on this interface, so no OSPF hello packets will be transmitted or received by this interface.

1. Configure the VLAN 11 interface as passive/silent interfaces.

```
ICX-Tx-Core1(config)# interface vlan 11
ICX-Tx-Core1(config-if-vlan)# ip ospf passive
ICX-Tx-Core1(config-if-vlan)# exit
```

2. Verify that only the VLAN2 transit link is now used for the OSPF peering.

```
ICX-Tx-Core1(config)# show ip ospf neighbors
OSPF Process ID 1 VRF default
==============================
Total Number of Neighbors: 1

Neighbor ID       Priority  State             Nbr Address        Interface
--------------------------------------------------------------------------
10.x.0.3          n/a       FULL              10.x.2.3           vlan2
```

Passive Interfaces Default

If a network has many user subnets, it may be more convenient to set new OSPF interfaces to passive by default. This means that only the OSPF uplink interfaces must be configured as 'not passive'. The other advantage is that there is no security risk when adding a new user VLAN, since it will automatically have OSPF disabled.

In the lab setup, the VLANs 1,11,12 can have endpoints connected to them, so they can benefit from the 'passive default' feature. The VLAN 2 interface is a dedicated routed link, so the passive feature should be turned off for this interface.

1. On Core1, enter the OSPF configuration context.

```
ICX-Tx-Core1(config)# router ospf 1
ICX-Tx-Core1(config-ospf-1)# passive-interface default
ICX-Tx-Core1(config-ospf-1)# exit
```

Important

This change will impact the current OSPF adjacencies, so this change should be made during a maintenance window.

2. Enable the VLAN 2 interface again using 'no ip ospf passive'.

```
ICX-Tx-Core1(config)# interface vlan 2
ICX-Tx-Core1(config-if-vlan)# no ip ospf passive
ICX-Tx-Core1(config-if-vlan)# exit
```

3. Add VLAN interfaces 1 and 12 as OSPF enabled interfaces.

```
ICX-Tx-Core1(config)# interface vlan 1,12
ICX-Tx-Core1(config-if-vlan-<1,12>)# ip ospf 1 area 0.0.0.0
ICX-Tx-Core1(config-if-vlan-<1,12>)# exit
```

4. Verify that the new interfaces vlan1 and 12 are now enabled for OSPF.

```
ICX-Tx-Core1(config)# show ip ospf interface brief
OSPF Process ID 1 VRF default
==============================
Total Number of Interfaces: 5

Interface     Area            IP Address/Mask     Cost     State
Status
----------------------------------------------------------------------------------
loopback0     0.0.0.0         10.x.0.2/32         0        Loopback         up
vlan1         0.0.0.0         10.x.1.2/24         100      Dr-other         up
vlan11        0.0.0.0         10.x.11.2/24        100      Dr-other         up
vlan12        0.0.0.0         10.x.12.2/24        100      Dr-other         up
vlan2         0.0.0.0         10.x.2.2/31         1        Point-to-point   up
```

5. But the only OSPF adjacency was formed over VLAN 2.

```
ICX-Tx-Core1(config)# show ip ospf neighbors
OSPF Process ID 1 VRF default
===============================
Total Number of Neighbors: 1

Neighbor ID      Priority  State            Nbr Address       Interface
----------------------------------------------------------------------------
10.x.0.3         n/a       FULL             10.x.2.3          vlan2
```

6. Review the interface statistics of VLAN 11 to confirm that no OSPF packets have been transmitted.

```
ICX-Tx-Core1(config)# show ip ospf statistics interface vlan11 | include Tx
Tx Hello Packets        : 0            Rx Hello Packets       : 0
Tx Hello Bytes          : 0            Rx Hello Bytes         : 0
```

```
Tx DD Packets          : 0          Rx DD Packets          : 0
Tx DD Bytes            : 0          Rx DD Bytes            : 0
Tx LS Request Packets  : 0          Rx LS Request Packets  : 0
Tx LS Request Bytes    : 0          Rx LS Request Bytes    : 0
Tx LS Update Packets   : 0          Rx LS Update Packets   : 0
Tx LS Update Bytes     : 0          Rx LS Update Bytes     : 0
Tx LS Ack Packets      : 0          Rx LS Ack Packets      : 0
Tx LS Ack Bytes        : 0          Rx LS Ack Bytes        : 0
```

Review Administrative Distance

1. First, review the routes learned and calculated by OSPF through the LSDB. These routes will be presented by OSPF to the IP routing table. Notice that routes that are local on Core1 have been learned as 'i' (intra-area) routes based on the Router LSA of Core1.

```
ICX-Tx-Core1(config)# show ip ospf routes
Codes: i - Intra-area route, I - Inter-area route
       E1 - External type-1, E2 - External type-2

OSPF Process ID 1 VRF default, Routing Table
---------------------------------------------
Total Number of Routes : 5

10.x.0.3/32        (i) area: 0.0.0.0
     via 10.x.2.3 interface vlan2, cost 1 distance 110
10.x.1.0/24        (i) area: 0.0.0.0
     directly attached to interface vlan1, cost 100 distance 110
10.x.2.2/31        (i) area: 0.0.0.0
     directly attached to interface vlan2, cost 1 distance 110
<...output omitted...>
```

Question: What is the distance applied to the route 10.x.1.0/24?

Answer: OSPF routes get an administrative distance of 110 by default.

2. Now review the IP routing table.

```
ICX-Tx-Core1(config)# show ip route
Displaying ipv4 routes selected for forwarding

'[x/y]' denotes [distance/metric]

10.x.0.2/32, vrf default
        via  loopback0,  [0/0],  local
10.x.0.3/32, vrf default
via  010.x.2.3,  [110/1],  ospf
```

```
10.x.1.0/24, vrf default
        via  vlan1,   [0/0],   connected
10.x.1.2/32, vrf default
        via  vlan1,   [0/0],   local
<...output omitted...>
```

Question: The output shows that the 10.x.1.0/24 route was not learned by OSPF. What is the source of the 10.x.1.0/24 route?

Answer: The source is 'connected'; this indicates an IP subnet that is locally connected on the router.

Question: Why was this route selected by the routing table over the OSPF route?

Answer: The administrative distance of directly connected routes is 0, so these routes will always win from any routing protocol. OSPF has a default distance of 110.

Task 4: OSPF Peering Using VSX LAG

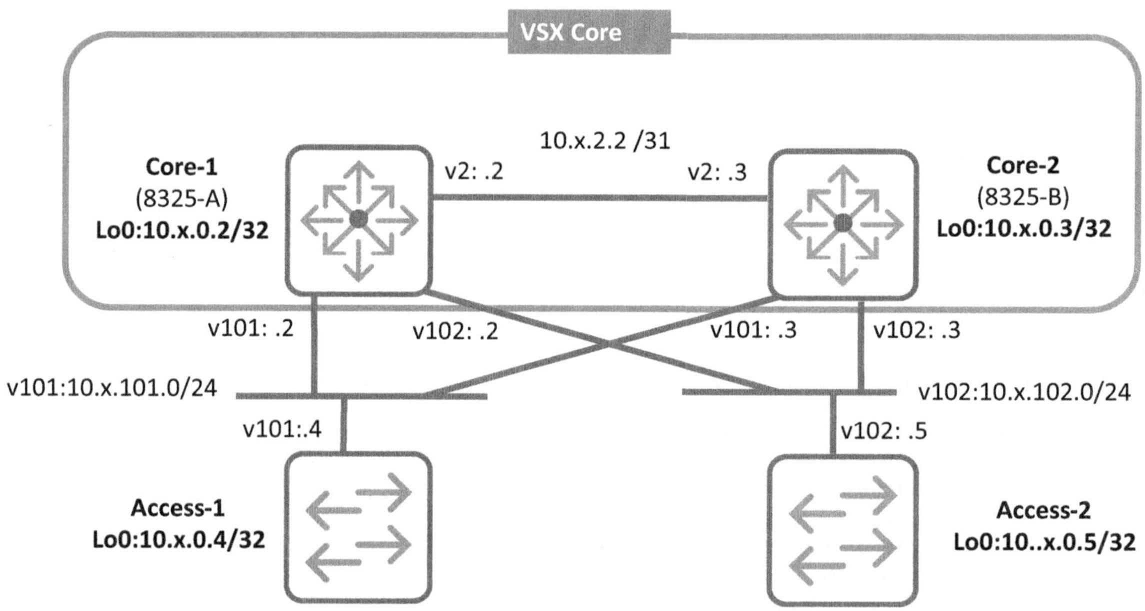

Figure 6-13 Task 4: OSPF Peering Using VSX LAG

Objectives

- Configure VSX LAG with OSPF to neighbor routers
- Understand and configure the Active Forwarding feature

Steps

Define a new routed VLAN between Access and the VSX Core and enable OSPF between Access1 and the Core VSX (Figure 6-13).

Routed VLAN between Access and Core VSX

1. On Core1, define VLAN 101 (to Access1) and 102 (to Access2).

```
ICX-Tx-Core1(config)# vlan 101
ICX-Tx-Core1(config-vlan-101)# vsx-sync
ICX-Tx-Core1(config-vlan-101)# exit

ICX-Tx-Core1(config)# vlan 102
ICX-Tx-Core1(config-vlan-102)# vsx-sync
ICX-Tx-Core1(config-vlan-102)# exit
ICX-Tx-Core1(config)#

ICX-Tx-Core1(config)# interface lag 1
ICX-Tx-Core1(config-lag-if)# vlan trunk allowed 101
ICX-Tx-Core1(config-lag-if)# exit

ICX-Tx-Core1(config)# interface lag 2
ICX-Tx-Core1(config-lag-if)# vlan trunk allowed 102
ICX-Tx-Core1(config-lag-if)# exit
```

2. For VLAN 101, configure the IP address and enable OSPF.

```
ICX-Tx-Core1(config)# interface vlan 101
ICX-Tx-Core1(config-if-vlan)# description L3-access1
ICX-Tx-Core1(config-if-vlan)# ip address 10.x.101.2/24
ICX-Tx-Core1(config-if-vlan)# ip ospf 1 area 0
ICX-Tx-Core1(config-if-vlan)# exit
```

3. VLAN 102 is only prepared with an IP address at this point, it is **not** enabled for OSPF at this point, this will be done in the next lab.

```
ICX-Tx-Core1(config)# interface vlan 102
ICX-Tx-Core1(config-if-vlan)# description L3-Access2
ICX-Tx-Core1(config-if-vlan)# ip address 10.x.102.2/24
ICX-Tx-Core1(config-if-vlan)# exit
```

4. On Core2, define VLAN 101 and 102 IP addresses (L2 VLAN and OSFP are automatically enabled by vsx-sync).

```
ICX-Tx-Core2(config)# int vlan 101
ICX-Tx-Core2(config-if-vlan)# ip address 10.x.101.3/24
ICX-Tx-Core2(config-if-vlan)# description L3-access1
ICX-Tx-Core2(config-if-vlan)# exit
```

```
ICX-Tx-Core2(config)# int vlan 102
ICX-Tx-Core2(config-if-vlan)# ip address 10.x.102.3/24
ICX-Tx-Core2(config-if-vlan)# description L3-access2
ICX-Tx-Core2(config-if-vlan)# exit
```

On Access1, Define the VLAN 101 Uplink Interface

1. Access a terminal session on Access1; enter the configuration mode. Add VLAN 101; define the IP interface.

Note

In the VSX lab activity, the LAG255 was set to allow all VLANs; this is why there is no step to allow the VLAN 101 on the VLAN trunk.

```
ICX-Tx-Access1(config)# vlan 101
ICX-Tx-Access1(config-vlan-101)# exit
ICX-Tx-Access1(config)# interface vlan 101
ICX-Tx-Access1(config-if-vlan)# description L3-core
ICX-Tx-Access1(config-if-vlan)# ip address 10.x.101.4/24
ICX-Tx-Access1(config-if-vlan)# exit
```

2. Verify ping works between the Access1 and Core1/Core2.

```
ICX-Tx-Access1(config)# do ping 10.X.101.2
PING 10.x.101.2 (10.x.101.2) 100(128) bytes of data.
108 bytes from 10.x.101.2: icmp_seq=1 ttl=64 time=16.7 ms
...

ICX-Tx-Access1(config)# do ping 10.X.101.3
PING 10.x.101.3 (10.x.101.3) 100(128) bytes of data.
108 bytes from 10.x.101.3: icmp_seq=1 ttl=64 time=15.4 ms
...
```

3. Configure OSPF on Access1.
    - OSPF router id, area 0
    - Loopback interface with IP 10.x.0.4/32 and enable for OSPF
    - Enable VLAN 101 for OSPF

```
ICX-Tx-Access1(config)# router ospf 1
ICX-Tx-Access1(config-ospf-1)# router-id 10.x.0.4
ICX-Tx-Access1(config-ospf-1)# enable
ICX-Tx-Access1(config-ospf-1)# area 0
ICX-Tx-Access1(config-ospf-1)# exit
ICX-Tx-Access1(config)# interface loopback 0
ICX-Tx-Access1(config-loopback-if)# ip address 10.x.0.4/32
ICX-Tx-Access1(config-loopback-if)# ip ospf 1 area 0
ICX-Tx-Access1(config-loopback-if)# exit
ICX-Tx-Access1(config)# interface vlan 101
ICX-Tx-Access1(config-if-vlan)# ip ospf 1 area 0
ICX-Tx-Access1(config-if-vlan)# exit
```

4. Verify OSPF neighbors; the expectation would be to see Core1 and Core2 in FULL state.

```
ICX-Tx-Access1(config)# show ip ospf neighbors
No OSPF neighbor found on VRF default.
```

Question: What could be wrong with the configuration?

Answer: Try to troubleshoot this using these commands on the Access1 and Core1.

```
show ip ospf neighbors
show ip ospf interface
show ip ospf statistics interface vlan101
```

5. Example output for the statistics:

```
ICX-Tx-Access1(config-ospf-1)# show ip ospf statistics interface
vlan101
OSPF Process ID 1 VRF default, interface vlan101 statistics (cleared
0h4m6s ago)
====================================================================
============

Tx Hello Packets      : 25          Rx Hello Packets      : 0
Tx Hello Bytes        : 1600        Rx Hello Bytes        : 0
Tx DD Packets         : 0           Rx DD Packets         : 0
Tx DD Bytes           : 0           Rx DD Bytes           : 0
Tx LS Request Packets : 0           Rx LS Request Packets : 0
```

```
Tx LS Request Bytes    : 0          Rx LS Request Bytes    : 0
Tx LS Update Packets   : 0          Rx LS Update Packets   : 0
Tx LS Update Bytes     : 0          Rx LS Update Bytes     : 0
Tx LS Ack Packets      : 0          Rx LS Ack Packets      : 0
Tx LS Ack Bytes        : 0          Rx LS Ack Bytes        : 0
```

6. The troubleshooting commands should have shown that there are no Receive statistics for the OSPF interface VLAN 101. This is because the passive-interface default was configured on the VSX Core side, so any new interface on the VSX Core are passive by default.

7. On the Core1, enable the new routed VLAN interface for OSPF.

```
ICX-Tx-Core1(config)# interface vlan 101
ICX-Tx-Core1(config-if-vlan)# no ip ospf passive
ICX-Tx-Core1(config-if-vlan)# exit
```

8. On Access1, check the OSPF neighbors again.

```
ICX-Tx-Access1(config)# show ip ospf neighbors
OSPF Process ID 1 VRF default
==============================
Total Number of Neighbors: 2

Neighbor ID      Priority  State              Nbr Address        Interface
-------------------------------------------------------------------------
10.x.0.2         1         FULL/DR            10.x.101.2         vlan101
10.x.0.3         1         FULL/BDR           10.x.101.3         vlan101
```

Note

The Role (DR/BDR/DROther) may be different in your output, but the state should be FULL.

Implementing Multiple Area OSPF Designs

You will now learn about dividing OSPF autonomous systems into multiple areas. In addition to learning how to establish multiple areas, you will learn *why* you would want to do so. You will explore the differences between intra-area OSPF routes and inter-area OSPF routes, as well as the LSAs that help to propagate routing information across the area boundaries.

OSPF and Scalability

Most of the rest of this chapter will discuss the scalability features, as shown in Figure 6-14, in OSPF, including the following:

- Areas and their components, including Area Border Routers (ABRs) and the type of LSAs they generate between areas (LSA Type 3)
- External routes and their components, including Autonomous System Boundary Routers (ASBRs) and the type of LSAs that are generated (LSA Types 4 and 5)
- Summarization, including how ABRs can summarize and filter routes to reduce the size of the link state database in non-backbone areas
- Area types, including stubby, totally stubby, not-so-stubby (NSSA), and totally NSSA areas to reduce the number of routes in a non-backbone area
- Fast convergence, including features like Bidirectional Forwarding Detection (BFD), VSX operations with OSPF, and OSPF graceful restart

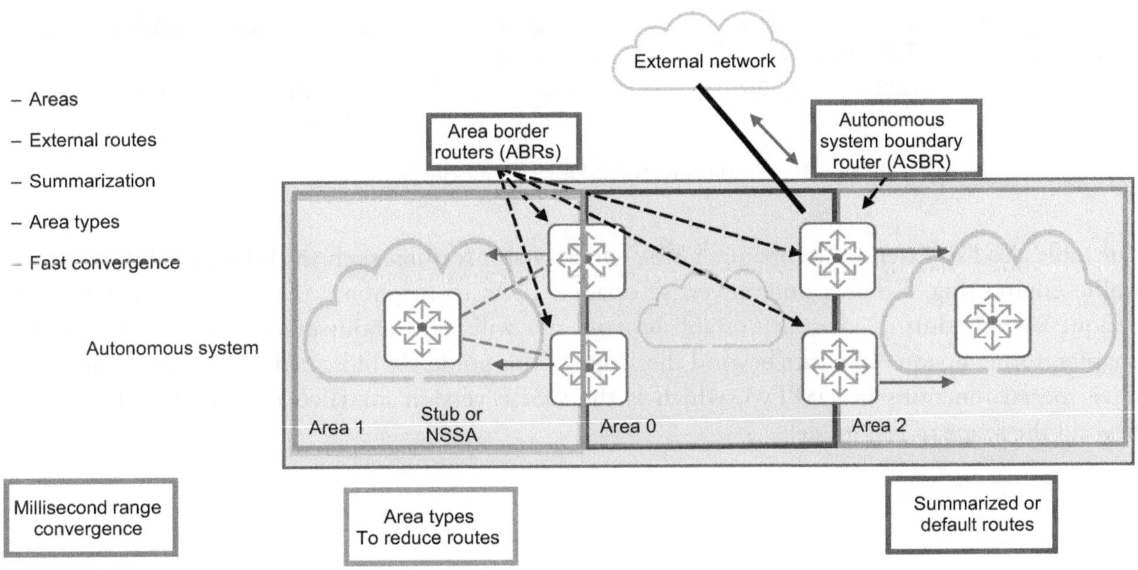

Figure 6-14 OSPF and Scalability

This section will discuss implementing multiple areas in OSPF.

OSPF LSA Introduction

Here is a chart of key information summarizing the various types of LSAs. This table does not show Type 6 LSAs because they advertise multicast groups for Multicast OSPF (MOSPF), a protocol that routers rarely use and that AOS-CX switches do not support (Figure 6-15).

Table 6-2 provides information about LSA types. You already learned about Type 1 and 2 LSAs. You will learn about LSA types 3 to 7 in the rest of this chapter.

	Type	Name	Advertised by	Scope of advertisement	Included information
Internal LSDB	1	Router	All routers	Area	Links (ID, type, and metric)
	2	Network	DRs for broadcast (or non-broadcast multicast) networks	Area	DR IP on the network Network mask IDs of routers attached to the network
	3	Summary	ABRs	Area	Network in another area (network IP, mask, and metric)
External LSDB	4	ASBR	ABRs	Area	ASBR router ID and metric
	5	AS External	ASBRs	All normal areas in the AS	External network, mask, metric, metric type
	7	NSSA External	ASBRs	Area	External network, mask, metric, metric type

Figure 6-15 OSPF LSA Introduction

The table also lists extended or opaque LSAs, which enable features such as OSPF graceful restart and traffic engineering. Routers only advertise opaque LSAs to neighbors that indicate that they are opaque capable during adjacency establishment. You will learn about graceful restart later in this chapter. Other opaque LSAs are beyond the scope of this guide. As indicated in the table, some LSAs have special functions in OSPFv3, which is the OSPF version for IPv6 routing. OSPFv3 is also beyond the scope of this guide.

Table 6-2 LSA Types

Type	Name	Information advertised	Advertised by	Scope
1	Router	The OSPF links on a routing device (transit and stub networks)	Each OSPF routing device	Area
2	Network	The routers on broadcast or NBMA networks	DR for the network	Area
3	Summary	Routes to networks (or aggregated ranges of networks) in another area (copied from or into the backbone area)	ABR	Area
4	ASBR	Route to an ASBR	ABR	All non-stub areas
5	External (or ASE)	Routes imported into OSPF from another routing protocol or method	ASBR	All non-stub areas
6	Multicast group membership (not commonly used)	Multicast groups desired on this router's networks router (Not generally used)	Multicast OSPF capable router (DR in broadcast networks)	Area
7	NSSA	Routes imported into OSPF from another routing protocol or method	ASBR	NSSA
8	Intra-area prefix (OSPFv3 only)	OSPFv3, the network prefixes associated with stub and transit networks in Type 1 and 2 LSAs	Each OSPF routing device (that is capable)	Area (OSPFv3)
9	Opaque link-local	Extensions (such as graceful restart)	Each OSPF routing device (that is capable)	Link
10	Opaque area-local	Extensions (such as traffic engineering)	Each OSPF routing device (that is capable)	Area
11	Opaque AS	Extensions	ASBR (that is capable)	All non-stub areas

OSPF LSA Illustration

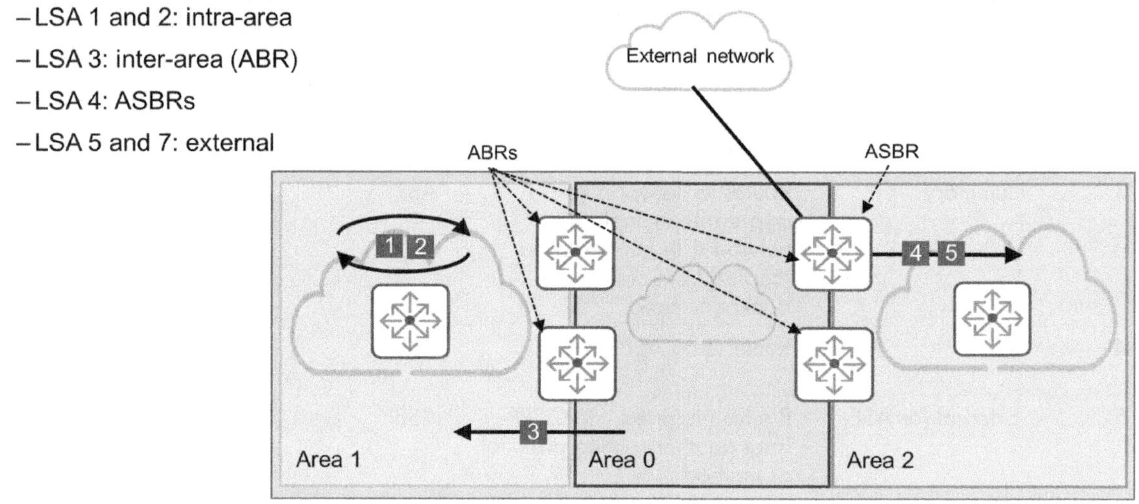

Figure 6-16 OSPF LSA Illustration

Figure 6-16 illustrates where you will find the common LSA types and who advertises them.

OSPF LSA Type 1 and Type 2 Intra-Area Examples

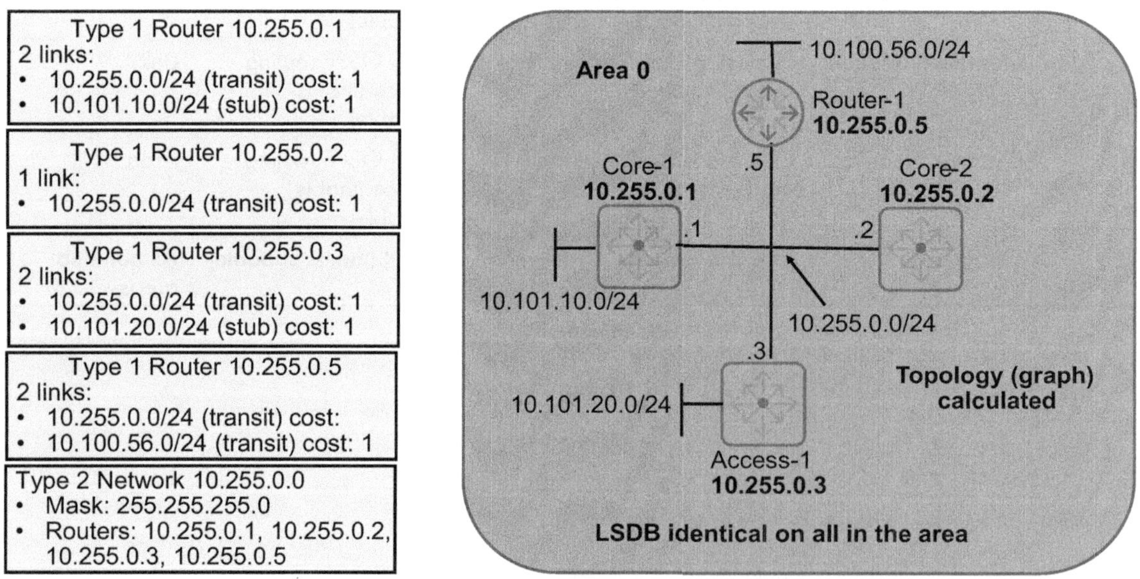

Figure 6-17 OSPF LSA Type 1 and Type 2 Intra-Area Examples

You will next review what is in the LSDB and how routers use that information to create a topology of the OSPF area.

An OSPF router generates a Router link state advertisement (LSA), or Type 1 LSA, with information about its own OSPF networks, or links, and the cost of using those links. The figure gives a summarized view of just some of the critical information in the LSA; the real LSA has many fields.

The DR on a broadcast or NBMA transit network also generates a Network, or Type 2, LSA with information about all the routers on that network. This allows routers throughout the system to determine which routers are available on a network. A stub network, which is a network with just one OSPF router on it, does not require a Type 2 LSA. The Type 1 LSA of the single router on that network is enough to advertise the stub network's location.

The cost in an LSA generally relates to the bandwidth with higher bandwidth links having a lower cost. However, administrators can set the cost as they choose. The router labels itself as the advertising router for these LSAs, using its router ID.

For example, the routers in Figure 6-17 have learned that:

- Core-1 (10.255.0.1) connects to:
    - 10.255.0.0/24 (same network as Router-1, Core-2, and Access-1): This transit link is identified by the IP address of the DR on the link, Router-1 in this example.
    - 10.101.10.0/24: This stub link is identified by Core-1's own IP address on the link.
- Core-2 (10.255.0.2) connects to:
    - 10.255.0.0/24 (same network as Router-1, Core-1, and Access-1)
- Access-1 (10.255.0.3) connects to:
    - 10.255.0.0/24 (same network as Router-1, Core-1, and Core-2)
    - 10.101.20.0/24
- Router-1 (10.255.0.5) connects to:
    - 10.255.0.0/24 (same network as Core-1, Core-2, and Access-2)
    - 10.100.56.0/30

The designated router (DR) in the transit broadcast network has also sent out network LSAs for the network indicating which routers connect to it.

OSPF Multi-Area Overview

Figure 6-18 displays an OSPF network, which consists of two segments, Segment 1 and Segment 2. These segments might be a campus LAN and a data center, a campus LAN and a large branch office, buildings in a large three-tier-campus topology, or any other segments within a larger network. Segment 1 and Segment 2 each represent many routing switches, which ultimately connect to two core routing switches. These core routing switches connect through a network backbone, which might also include more routers and routing switches. The figure only shows two segments for simplicity, but a large enterprise network might have several such segments.

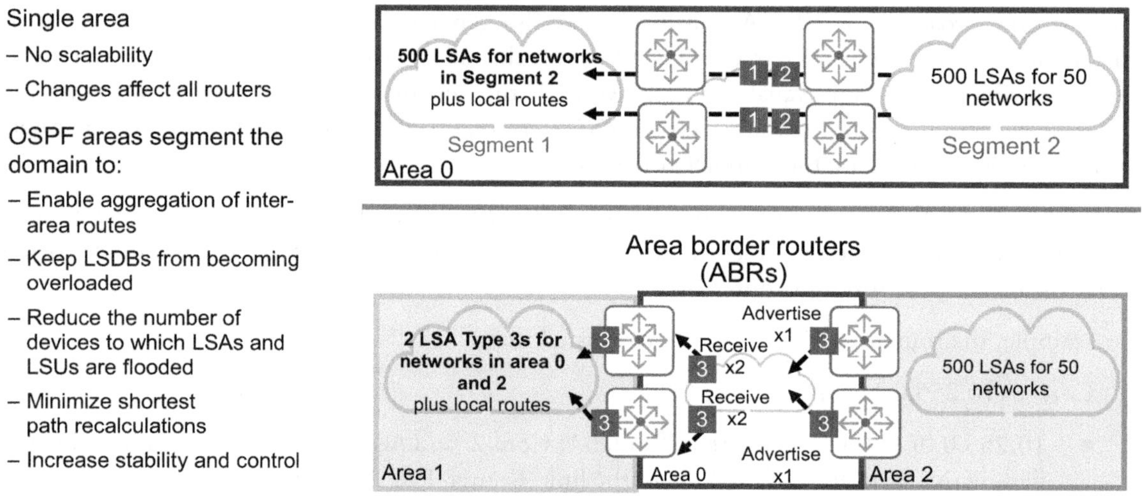

Figure 6-18 OSPF Multi-Area Overview

Every OSPF router in an area must maintain LSAs from every other router in the area in its LSDB. The figure at the top of the page shows how a single area implementation forces each of these Type 1 and 2 LSAs to propagate across the system. In addition, the figure only mentions LSAs associated with Segment 2. Each OSPF routing device would also maintain LSAs for routers and networks in Segment 1 and the backbone.

As a domain grows, the LSDB becomes excessively large and difficult to process. The shortest path algorithm also becomes complicated, and the OSPF routing switch must dedicate valuable processing resources to running it. Often this resource consumption comes with little value. As shown in the figure, networks often feature aggregation such that one segment connects to another through a few core devices. With only two exit points from Segment 1 toward Segment 2, the routing switches in Segment 1 have no reason to maintain so much granular information about networks in Segment 2.

Modern routers and routing switches often do have the power to handle large LSDBs and many calculations. However, there is no reason to burden the devices, network administrators, and support staff with the large, complex LSDBs and routing tables when most of the routes will use the same one or two next hops.

In addition, suppose that two routing switches in Segment 2 provide a connection to the subnet A. One of those switches has a flapping interface. It loses its connection to subnet A and sends an LSU withdrawing that subnet from its list of links. Every routing switch in the network backbone and Segment 1 receives this LSU, adjusts the LSDB, and re-runs the Dijkstra algorithm on the topology. However, these routers still reach subnet A through the same core routing switches. When the flapping interface comes back up, the switch sends another LSU, which propagates throughout the entire network, causing every OSPF router to recalculate shortest paths, again without any significant change.

OSPF areas segment the domain into more stable and manageable pieces. Each OSPF routing device maintains the LSDB and runs the shortest path algorithm only for its own areas. OSPF routers called area border routers (ABRs) forward information necessary for routing between areas. As you see in the figure on the previous page, the ABRs act as bottlenecks for LSAs. Type 1 and Type 2 LSAs do not flow across area boundaries. You will learn about the Type 3 LSAs that do flow between areas over the next pages.

In the simplest configuration, a multi-area design decreases LSDB size dramatically and increases stability—routers do not have to re-run the shortest path algorithm as often—but does not greatly affect the number of routes. OSPF, however, provides options for further optimizing the LSDB and routing table sizes. As you will see, you can aggregate advertisements of networks in between areas, simplifying the routing table. You can also control routes at this boundary, filtering them if you so desire. These benefits still apply even for powerful routers that could support very large areas.

With a single area design, every time that router loses or re-establishes its connection to the subnet, LSUs flood throughout the entire network and every router must re-run the SPF algorithm, even though they might not even change the next hop in their route. With multiple areas, the area 1 and area 0 routers can continue using the same aggregated inter-area route to reach the subnet in question without having to process LSUs or recalculate routes.

In short, a multi-area design increases stability and control. Because every area has its own LSDB, the SPF algorithm only calculates routes within the area. This keeps the routing devices' LSDBs from being overloaded with LSAs and the complexity of the topology. It also minimizes the number of LSUs that routers must process and the SFP calculations that they must run. For example, suppose that OSPF routers in Segment 2 provide a connection to the same subnet. One of those routers has a flapping interface.

ABRs

You learned how each OSPF area defines an isolated region beyond which Type 1 and Type 2 LSAs and shortest path topologies do not extend. However, some routing information must flow between the areas. Area Border Routers (ABRs) are responsible for forwarding this information (Figure 6-19).

When you design a multi-area network, you must understand area 0's special role. This area is also called the backbone area because every other area must connect to it. For example, area 1 reaches area

2 through area 0. Area 0 includes OSPF routers with a special role; these routers are called area border routers (ABRs). Each ABR has interfaces in area 0, which is required, and at least one other area (area 0 can also have internal routers that are only in area 0.)

ABRs have interfaces in at least two areas, one of which is area 0. Area 0 is the backbone area, and OSPF design requires all areas to connect to this backbone (physically or logically).

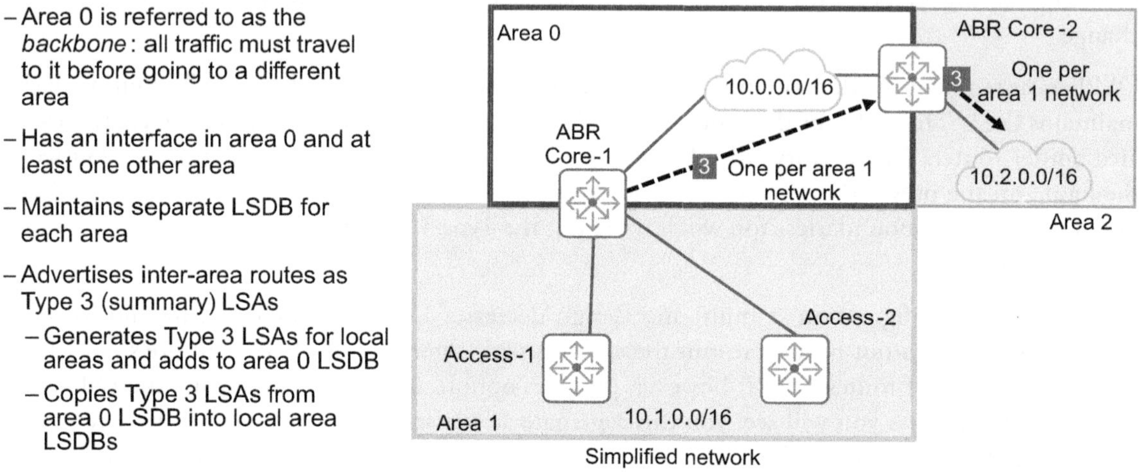

Figure 6-19 ABRs

As a member of multiple areas, the ABR maintains multiple LSDBs, one for each area. In this example, Core-1 is an ABR. It synchronizes Type 1 and Type 2 LSAs with other OSPF routing devices in area 1. The figure shows just two other routing devices, Access-1 and Access-2, for simplicity, but in the real world, the area would usually have many more routing devices. Access-1 and Access-2 reside entirely within area 1 and are called internal routers. Core-1, Access-1, and Access-2 have identical area 1 LSDBs.

The ABR follows the same process in area 0, exchanging Type 1 and Type 2 LSAs and synchronizing its area 0 LSDB with routers such as Router-1 and Core-2.

In each area, the ABR also creates Type 3, or summary LSAs, which advertise routes that it knows in *other* areas. The sections below elaborate on how the ABR conducts this advertisement.

Type 3 LSAs Generated in Area 0

The ABR creates a Type 3, or summary LSA, for each network in *area 1*. It places these Type 3 LSAs in its LSDB for *area 0*. The ABR can then advertise its routes to area 1 networks to other routers in area 0.

For example, Core-1 has an inter-area route to 10.101.20.0/24. It learned about this network from Access-1's Type 1 LSA, contained in its area 1 LSDB. From that LSDB, Core-1 was able to generate an *intra-area* route to 10.101.20.0/24. ABR-A generates a Type 3 LSA for 10.101.20.0/24 and places the Type 3 LSA in its area 0 LSDB. Other area 0 routers, such as Core-2, receive Core-1's Type 3 LSA and add it to their area 0 LSDB. They can then calculate an inter-area route to 10.101.20.0/24.

In addition to the network address, the Type 3 LSA includes a metric, which enables routers to select the best inter-area route when multiple ABRs advertise a Type 3 LSA with the same network ID.

Type 3 LSAs Generated in Non-Backbone Areas

Core-1 also generates Type 3 LSAs to advertise into non-backbone areas. First, just as Core-1 advertised a Type 3 LSA for each area 1 network to routers in area 0, the ABR advertises a Type 3 LSA for each area 0 network to routers in area 1.

The ABR also advertises a Type 3 LSA for each *inter-area* route that it has learned from Type 3 LSAs advertised by other ABRs in area 0. For example, Core-2 has generated Type 3 LSAs for each network in area 2 and advertised them in area 0. Using these LSAs, Core-1 has calculated an inter-area route to each area 2 network. Now Core-1 generates Type 3 LSAs for these routes and advertises them in area 1, using the metric in the routing table. (It does *not* advertise these LSAs in area 0 because the inter-area routes' next hops are in area 0. The original ABR, which always resides in area 0, has already advertised these LSAs in area 0.)

If Core-1 connected to another area, such as area 3, it would place Type 3 LSAs for each area 3 intra-area route in the area 0 LSDB and the area 1 LSDB. In other words, for each area, an ABR creates Type 3 LSAs with routes to *other* areas to which the ABR connects. Remember, though, that the inter-area routes always pass through area 0 even if the same ABR supports multiple non-backbone areas. That is, you cannot configure an OSPF router with area 1 and area 3 and expect the router to advertise area 3 networks in area 1 and area 1 networks in area 3. The router must have interfaces in area 1, area 3, *and* area 0.

The figure shows how internal routing switches Access-1 and Access-2 in area 1 receive the Type 3 LSAs for area 0 and area 2. Note that, although area 1 routers learn routes to area 2, the Type 3 LSAs themselves do not cross area boundaries. Instead Core-2, connected to area 2 and area 0, generates Type 3 LSAs for area 2 in area 0. It is the advertising router for these LSAs. Core-1 receives these LSAs in area 0 and generates *new* Type 3 LSAs for advertising these routes into area 1, and it is the advertising router for these new LSAs.

Need for Route and LSA Aggregation Between Areas

- Routers do not require granular knowledge of other areas:
  - Causes unnecessary disruptions when small changes occur
  - Clutters the LSDB and routing table
- How can you aggregate the Type 3 LSAs?

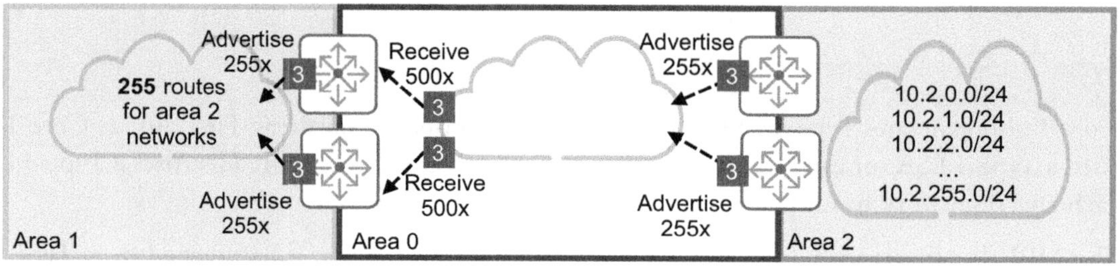

Figure 6-20 Need for Route and LSA Aggregation Between Areas

Simply dividing an AS into multiple areas begins to decrease the size of OSPF routers' LSDBs and to reduce the complexity of SPF calculations. However, to achieve the true benefits of multiple areas, you should further reduce the number of LSAs advertised *between* areas (Figure 6-20).

In this example network, both area 1 and area 2 have only two exits toward the network backbone and other areas. Internal area 1 routers and backbone routers might benefit from some level of detail in the information that they receive about area 2. For example, each ABR's Type 3 LSAs reflect the metrics of reaching the network in question, enabling routers in other areas to select the best ABR for reaching each network in area 2.

However, with only two entry points into area 2, routers (and, in particular, internal area 1 routers) are probably receiving too granular an amount of information about every subnet. This information clutters the routers' LSDB and routing tables.

In addition, small changes in the area 2 topology could flood LSUs through the backbone and area 1, causing routers to re-run the SPF algorithm. For example, network 10.2.40.0/24 in area 2 becomes unavailable. The two area 2 ABRs withdraw their Type 3 LSA for that specific network in area 0, and then the two area 1 ABRs do the same in area 1. However, the area 1 routers have no other path to this network. It might be simpler not to inform routers beyond area 2 of the small change. If they continue to forward traffic for this network, the area 2 ABRs simply drop it.

You need to aggregate the Type 3 LSAs to hide the unnecessary information and to smooth over small changes, thereby gaining the true benefits of a multiple area OSPF configuration.

Note

Although this example focuses on aggregating advertisements for area 2 networks, you would aggregate summaries of area 1 or area 0 networks for similar reasons.

ABR Route Aggregation

You can configure an ABR to aggregate its summary routes. Rather than generate a Type 3 LSA for every network in an area, it generates a few Type 3 LSAs, each of which includes many networks in its range. In other words, the Type 3 LSA advertises a network with a shorter prefix length such as a /20 or a /16 subnet that includes many /24 subnets.

You configure the area summaries on the ABR that connects to the area for which you aggregating the summaries. For example, in the network illustrated in the figure, you configure area summaries for area 2 on the two ABRs on the right.

These ABRs then advertise the summaries to other backbone routers and ABRs in area 0. The other ABRs can then copy them into their own areas. In this example, the aggregated summary 10.102.0.0/16 shows up as a route on ABR A and on internal routing switches in area 1.

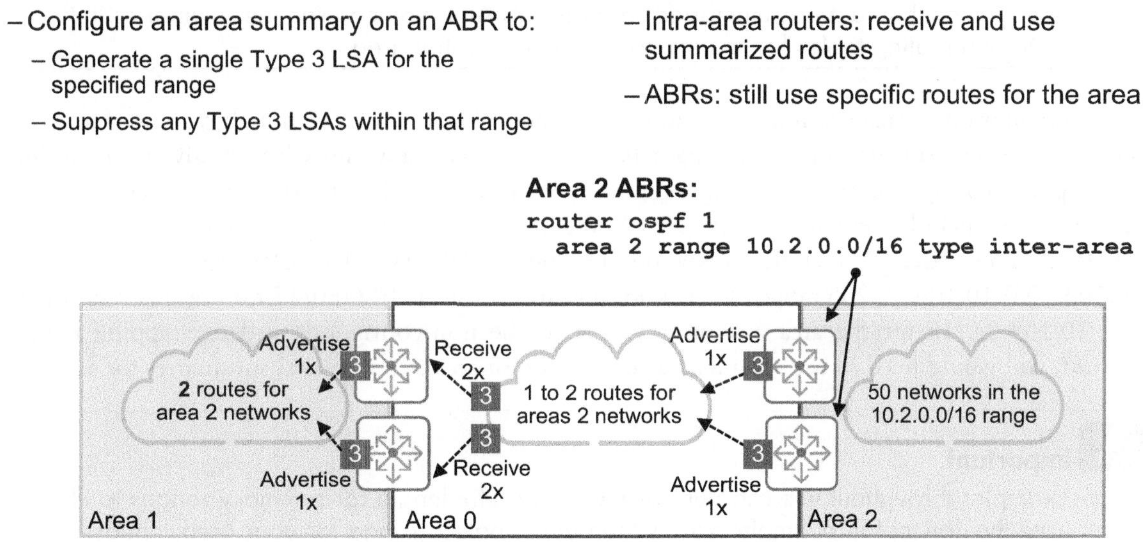

Figure 6-21 ABR Route Aggregation

If you create area summaries for area 1 on the ABRs shown on the left, those summaries aggregate area 1 networks. The area 1 ABRs advertise them into area 0 and other ABRs re-advertise them into area 2.

Figure 6-21 illustrates how area summaries drastically reduce the number of LSAs associated with area 2. In this example, a single summary includes all of the networks in the area.

You enter the AOS-Switch command for creating this area summary in the OSPF configuration mode context:

```
Switch(config)# router ospf 1
Switch(ospf)# area 2 range 10.102.0.0/16 type inter-area
```

When you enter this command, the ABR automatically suppresses the generation of individual Type 3 LSAs for subnets within the specified network. However, it *continues* to advertise individual Type 3 LSAs for networks that do not fall into the range. This is why it is recommended to assign an area contiguous IP addresses within a binary block. Then you can easily aggregate the routes.

Return to the example. The ABRs for area 1 now receive *one* Type 3 LSA with the aggregated summary from *each* of the two ABRs that connect to area 2. Each area 1 ABR selects the best LSA for the summary range and creates an inter-area route to 10.102.0.0/16 through the best next-hop.

Each area 1 ABR then generates an area 1 Type 3 LSA to advertise this inter-area route to routers in area 1. The internal area 1 routers now have two LSAs for all area 2 networks, and they learn routes to only the one aggregated network (up to two routes if the ABRs advertise equal metrics and the internal routers support Equal-Cost Multi-Path [ECMP]).

Note

After you configure area summaries on an area's ABR, you can see the summaries in the LSDB and routing tables for routers *not* connected to that area.

Usually, you want to create as few area summaries as possible. Sometimes, though, you need to create more summaries. For example, areas might have grown organically and without advance planning, creating non-contiguous ranges or ranges that do not fit neatly within a CIDR subnet. For example, area 2 might include networks in the 10.102.0.0-10.102.255.255 range as well as 10.103.20.0-10.103.23.255. Area 3 includes networks in the 10.103.0.0-10.103.19.255 range and the 10.103.30.0-10.103.39.255 range. You cannot use simply use 10.102.0.0/15 for the area 2 summary and 10.103.0.0/16 for the area 3 summary, due to the non-contiguous and overlapping ranges. Instead, you would need to use several area summaries for area 2 and several summaries for area 3.

Important

Examples throughout this chapter use the /16 prefix length for summary ranges to illustrate the concept in a simple way. When you create a range for your area, choose an appropriate range. For example, your area might include 16 /24 subnets, 10.1.0.0/24 to 10.1.15.0/24. This is equal to the 10.1.0.0/20 network, and you should specify that in the **area <ID> range** command.

Filtering Inter-Area Routes

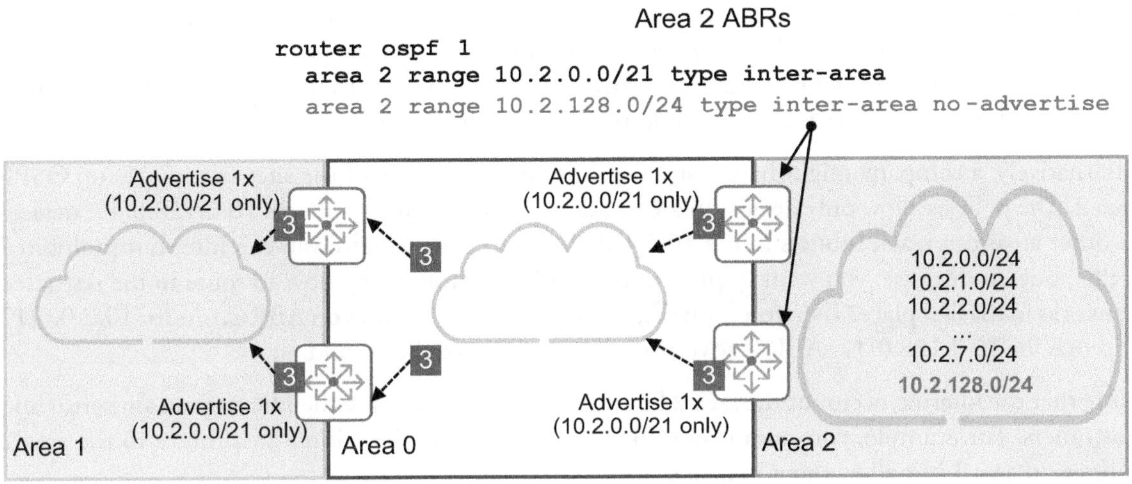

Figure 6-22 Filtering Inter-Area Routes

Remember that failing to configure an area summary for a specific range makes the routing switch continue to advertise the individual routes. If you want to *stop* advertisement of certain routes to certain networks entirely, you must configure a non-advertised area summary on the ABR.

For example, a company has a strict security policy for one of the sites that makes up OSPF area 2. The policies allow only local access to high-security subnets 10.102.128.0/17; devices in other areas can reach subnets 10.102.0.0/17. Of course, a firewall can filter out prohibited traffic, but, in this case, you want to prevent any routing of traffic from other areas to the restricted networks.

Therefore, you configure two area summaries on the area 2 ABRs—one for 10.102.0.0/17 and one for 10.102.128.0/17. ABRs advertise the first but not the second.

Note that the filtering occurs at the area 2 boundary; you cannot apply the filtering to some areas and not others. For example, you *cannot* use this configuration to block inter-area routes to the area 2 subnets in area 1 but allow them in area 0 (Figure 6-22).

The commands for configuring this example are:

```
Core-2(config)# router ospf 1
Core-2(ospf)# area 2 range 10.102.0.0/17 type inter-area no-advertise
```

To enable the advertisement again, configure the same summary but without the no-advertise option:

```
Core-2(ospf)# area 2 range 10.102.0.0/17 type inter-area
```

Simply removing the non-advertised summary would enable the advertisement of individual routes without aggregation.

Remember that failing to configure a range makes the ABR advertise individual networks. If you want to stop advertisement of certain networks entirely, you must configure a non-advertised range on the ABR using the no-advertise option. This is a less common configuration than route aggregation, but a valid one for some scenarios. For example, you may want to use the area 0 networks to only route traffic between area 0 devices, so routers in other areas do not need to know about these networks. You could configure the no-advertise option for the area 0 range on ABR 1 and ABR 2, and internal routers in area 1 and area 2 stop learning the 10.0.0.0/16 route. Traffic destined to other areas can still pass through area 0 to final destinations in other areas.

Alternatively, a company might have a strict security policy for one of the sites that makes up OSPF area 2. The policies allow only devices in area 2 access to high-security subnets 10.2.128.0/17; devices in other areas can reach subnets in the 10.2.128.0/17. Of course, a firewall can filter out prohibited traffic, but, in this case, you want to prevent other areas from learning how to route to the restricted networks in the first place. Therefore, you configure two area summaries on ABR 2, one for 10.2.0.0/17 and one for 10.2.128.0/17. ABR 2 advertises the first but not the second.

Note that the filtering occurs at the area 2 boundary; you cannot apply the filtering to some areas and not others. For example, you cannot use this configuration to block inter-area routes to the area 2 subnets in area 1 but allow them in area 0.

Setting Interface Costs

Link cost provides the basis for route selection within OSPF. To ensure that your routing switches select the best routes, you must remember to assign the VLAN interfaces logical costs, typically based on their bandwidth. By default, a VLAN interface has a cost of 1,000. Because every VLAN interface has the same cost, route selection becomes a matter of hop count, rather than true lowest cost path, if you are using layer 3 VLAN interfaces.

- Default cost for VLAN interface = 1 Gbps (1,000)
  - Route selected based on hop count
- Set cost for layer 3 interface dedicated to router-to-router link based on bandwidth

Bandwidth	Cost
1 Tbps	1
100 Gbps	10
20 Gbps	50
10 Gbps	100
4 Gbps	250
2 Gbps	500
1 Gbps	1000
100 Mbps	10,000

Figure 6-23 AOS-CX: Heart of Aruba's Core, Aggregation, and Access

When you follow the approach of assigning a unique VLAN and subnet to each link between OSPF routing switches, you can correlate the VLAN interface with the bandwidth of that link. Choose a base bandwidth to set to 1, setting this bandwidth well above the maximum bandwidth used in your network for future proofing. Then divide that base bandwidth by the bandwidth of the link or link aggregation associated with the VLAN. Figure 6-23 shows some examples.

Preferably, you want to set the interface costs globally for the OSPF process by changing the bandwidth reference with the following configuration:

```
switch(config)# router ospf <process-id>
switch(config-ospf-1)# reference-bandwidth <Mbps>
```

If the OSPFv2 interface cost is not explicitly set, then the cost of all the OSPFv2 interfaces is recalculated based on the reference bandwidth and link speed of the interface. For VLAN interfaces the link speed value is taken as 1 Gbps (if the OSPFv2 interface cost is not explicitly set). The bandwidth range is 1-4000000 Mbps, where the default is 100000 Mbps.

You can use this command to set the cost on a layer 3 interface, which will override the reference calculation:

```
Switch(config)# interface <interface-ID>
Switch(config-if)# ip ospf cost <cost>
```

Choosing Best Inter-Area Routes

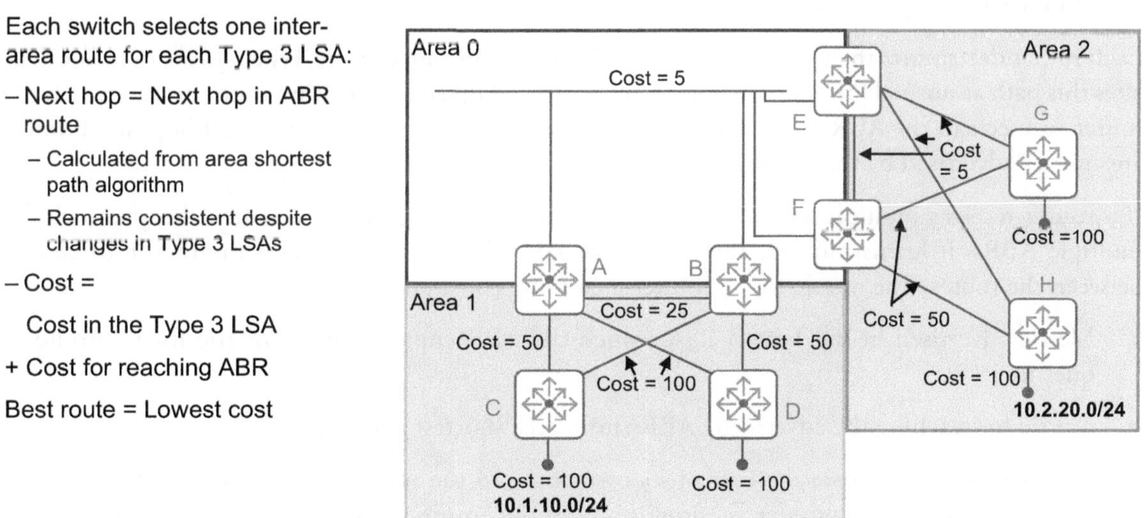

Figure 6-24 Choosing Best Inter-Area Routes

For simplicity, you have been concentrating on OSPF systems that have simple paths. When you are using technologies such as VSF which build redundancy and resiliency into the logical device acting as ABR, a topology such as this might be adequate. Sometimes, though, you need to plan redundant designs more like those in Figure 6-24. There may be times where you will want multiple ABRs for an area, in which case it becomes more important for you to understand how routers calculate inter-area routes. Remember that the SPF algorithm only operates within areas, so routers are not creating a topology of the complete AS and calculating inter-routes from that. Instead, an OSPF router uses the SPF algorithm to calculate a path to each ABR in its area. It considers the ABR as a gateway to the networks that the ABR advertises in Type 3 LSAs.

You have seen how ABRs advertise inter-area routes in Type 3 LSAs. When an area has a single ABR, internal routes send all inter-area traffic to the next hop closest to that ABR. When an area has multiple ABRs and redundant paths, though, you need to understand how routers calculate inter-area routes in more detail.

You will begin at looking at how routers choose the best route for inter-area traffic. This discussion assumes that area 1 and area 2 are normal, stub, or NSSA areas, but not totally stub or totally stub NSSAs. The totally stub areas do not receive Type 3 LSAs, except a default route, so the routers in those areas cannot choose best paths for inter-area traffic based on anything except the cost in the default route.

A Type 3 LSA advertises a *route* to the network. The routers that receive these advertisements do *not* create a topology of the networks in other areas. Instead they treat the ABR as a gateway to all of the networks which the ABR advertises in Type 3 LSAs. That is, those networks are leaves hanging off the ABR in the shortest path tree.

Each router determines the shortest path to the ABR or ABRs advertising Type 3 LSAs to it. It calculates this path as normal for inter-area routes by applying Dijkstra's algorithm to the area in which the router connects to the ABR. The next hop for reaching the ABR becomes the next hop for all inter-area routes advertised by that ABR in Type 3 LSAs.

If a router receives multiple Type 3 LSAs for the same network, as it does when the area includes multiple ABRs, it learns multiple inter-area routes for that network. It uses the metric to choose between the routes. The metric for each inter-area route consists of:

- Metric advertised in the Type 3 LSA, which the ABR copies from its metric for the route in question
- Metric for reaching the advertising ABR (from area shortest path topology)

Because each ABR advertises the cost of its own route to the network, cost increments across the complete system. First consider a situation without route aggregation for the purposes of illustration.

ABR-E advertises 10.2.20.0/24 as a Type 3 LSA with metric 105 in area 0, and ABR-F advertises this route with metric 150. ABR-A adds 5 to each of these metrics because that is its cost for reaching each of the routers. It selects ABR-E as offering the best route and adds an inter-area route with metric 110 to its OSPF table. When ABR-A generates an LSA for 10.2.20.0/24 in area 1, it advertises metric 110. Router C adds its metric for reaching ABR-A to 110, assigning the inter-area route to 10.2.20.0/24 a metric of 160.

Inter-area routing in OSPF combines the best aspects of link-state and distance-vector routing. Router C, for example, uses link-state routing to determine its shortest path to its two ABRs. It can then use those same two paths for all routes to other areas without considering the link states of networks in those areas. Even though Router C only knows a small part of the topology, traffic that it routes toward other areas still receives the benefits of link-state routing across the complete path. For example, Router C sends traffic to 10.2.20.0/24 on its shortest path to ABR-A. ABR-A, in turn, routes the traffic using the shortest path to ABR-E, which it has calculated from its detailed area 0 topology. Finally, ABR-E routes the traffic using the best path calculated by the detailed area 2 topology. In each area, routers maintain just the local segment of the complete path for inter-area traffic.

Also consider how the area boundaries enhance stability. When an OSPF router receives an update for a Type 3 LSA, it does not run the complete shortest path algorithm. Instead it adjusts the networks behind each ABR, as indicated by the update, and adds a new inter-area route, removes an inter-area route, or selects a different inter-area route (due to a cost change), as appropriate. The router *does not,* on the other hand, need to re-calculate the path to the ABR, which is the only segment of the path with which it is concerned.

Some loss of information is introduced by route aggregation at the area boundaries; however, the simplicity is typically worth this loss. For example, in this topology, network administrators might configure an aggregated range of 10.2.0.0/16 for area 2 on ABR-E and ABR-F. They can assign cost 105 to this range on ABR-E, but cost 150 to the range on ABR-F. ABR-A can still choose the route through ABR-E as the lowest cost route. In this example, ABR-A and ABR-B have the same cost to reach ABR-E, so they advertise the same cost for the 10.2.0.0/16 route into area 1. However, ABR-B, for example, had a better cost path to ABR-E, it would advertise a lower cost route, and internal routers in area 1 would direct their area 2 traffic to that ABR.

You could also use multiple area summaries when an area has multiple ABRs, and you want to prefer one ABR for one segment of the area but another ABR for another segment. This approach is more complicated, however. You must also take care to configuring matching summaries on each ABR (although the costs would not match). Otherwise, you can accidentally introduce routing loops.

Lab 6.2

Lab Diagram

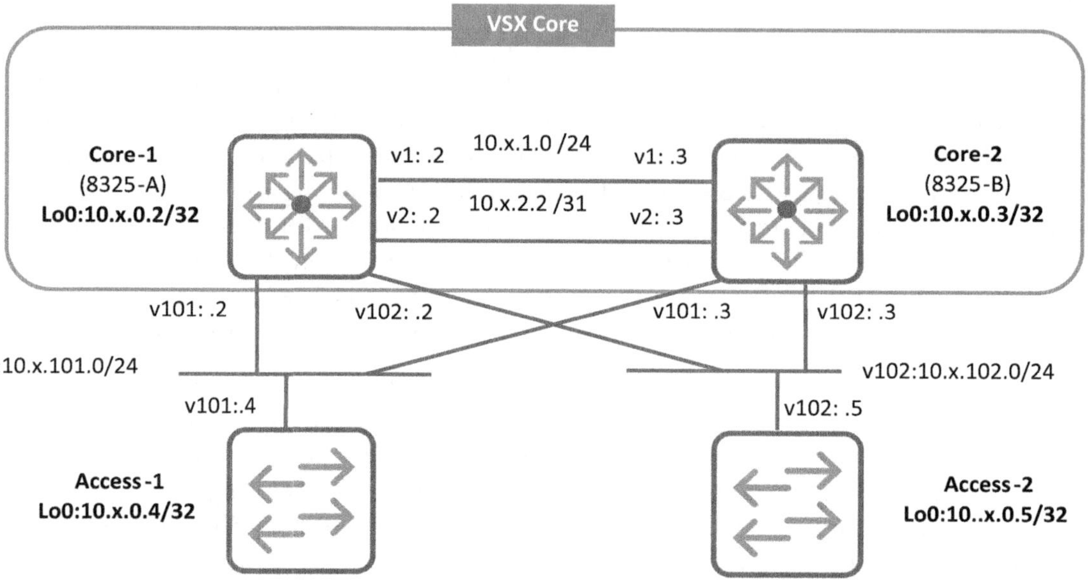

Figure 6-25 Lab Diagram

Overview

This lab activity will introduce multiple areas for OSPF. The lab will demonstrate the benefits of using multiple areas, such as route aggregation and filtering (Figures 6-25).

Objectives

- Learn how to configure an OSPF Area Border Router (ABR)
- Understand how routes from 1 area are announced into other areas
- Understand the need for the backbone area
- Apply route aggregation and route filtering at the ABR

Task 1: Assign Access1 to OSPF Area 1

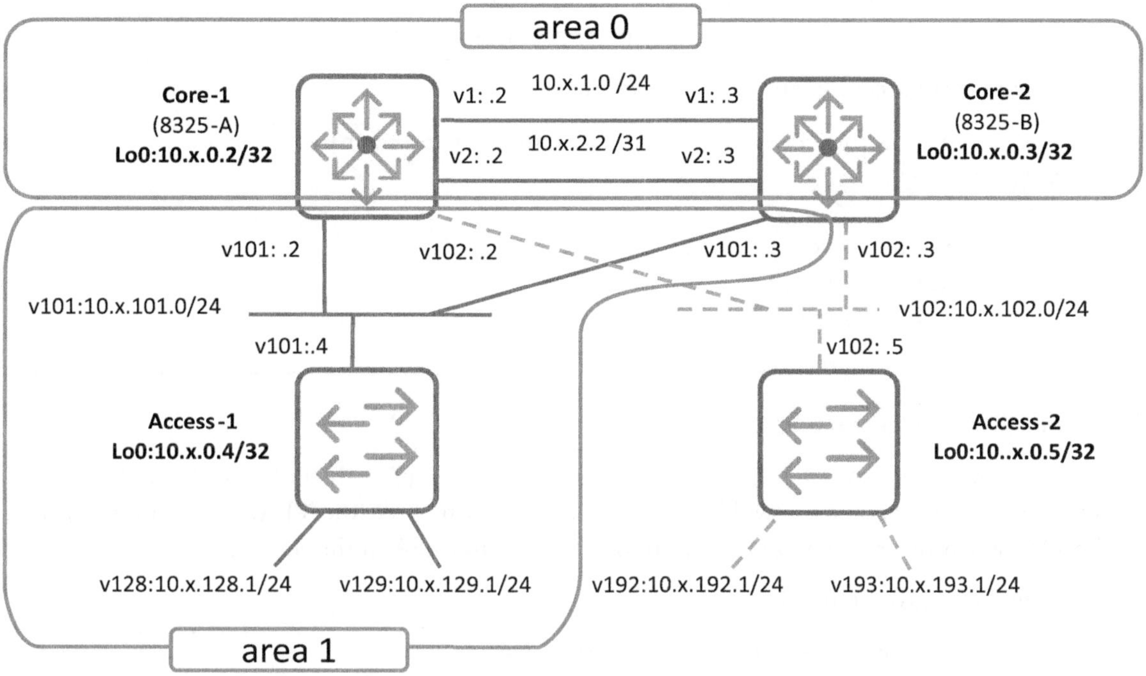

Figure 6-26 Task 1: Assign Access1 to OSPF Area 1

Objectives

- Set up ABR link between Core1 and Access1
- Verify LSA changes
- Set up ABR link between Core2 and Access1

Steps

On Core1, define area 1 and assign interface VLAN 101 to area 1 (Figure 6-26).

On Access1, remove area 0; define area 1. Assign interface VLAN 101 to area 1.

Verify adjacency and operation.

Verify area 1 setup between Access1 and Core2 and verify operation.

1. Open a terminal connection to Core1; enter the configuration mode. Under the **router ospf** context, define a new area with ID of 1.

```
ICX-Tx-Core1(config)# router ospf 1
ICX-Tx-Core1(config-ospf-1)# area 1
ICX-Tx-Core1(config-ospf-1)# exit
```

2. Under the VLAN 101 context, assign area 1 for this interface.

```
ICX-Tx-Core1(config)# interface vlan 101
ICX-Tx-Core1(config-if-vlan)# ip ospf 1 area 1
```

3. Verify the current configuration of this interface.

```
ICX-Tx-Core1(config-if-vlan)# show running current
interface vlan101
    description L3-ccess1
    ip address 10.x.101.2/24
ip ospf 1 area 0.0.0.1
    no ip ospf passive
ICX-Tx-Core1(config-if-vlan)# exit
```

Verify the LSDB Changes on Core1

In each area database, Core1 has inserted a router LSA that contains the links for that area. You will see in the area 1 database, there will be a router LSA with one link (the VLAN 101 interface). Due to the VSX synchronization, Core2 has also inserted a router LSA in this area 1.

1. Review the LSDB for area 1.

```
ICX-Tx-Core1(config)# show ip ospf lsdb area 1
OSPF Router with ID (10.x.0.2) (Process ID 1 VRF default)
============================================================
Router Link State Advertisements (Area 0.0.0.1)
------------------------------------------------


LSID            ADV Router       Age        Seq#        Checksum        Link
Count
-----------------------------------------------------------------------------
10.x.0.2        10.x.0.2        18         0x80000002 0x0000744d     1
10.x.0.3        10.x.0.3        19         0x80000002 0x0000724c     1

Network Link State Advertisements (Area 0.0.0.1)
-------------------------------------------------


LSID            ADV Router       Age        Seq#        Checksum
--------------------------------------------------------------
10.x.101.3      10.x.0.3        24         0x80000001 0x00000c85

Inter-area Summary Link State Advertisements (Area 0.0.0.1)
------------------------------------------------------------
```

```
LSID            ADV Router      Age       Seq#        Checksum
---------------------------------------------------------------
10.x.0.2        10.x.0.2        63        0x80000001 0x00007daf
10.x.0.2        10.x.0.3        63        0x80000001 0x000081a9
10.x.0.3        10.x.0.2        63        0x80000001 0x00007dad
10.x.0.3        10.x.0.3        63        0x80000001 0x00006dbd
10.x.1.0        10.x.0.2        63        0x80000001 0x00007257
10.x.1.0        10.x.0.3        63        0x80000001 0x00006c5c
10.x.2.2        10.x.0.2        63        0x80000001 0x00006bbf
10.x.2.2        10.x.0.3        63        0x80000001 0x000065c4
10.x.11.0       10.x.0.2        63        0x80000001 0x000004bb
10.x.11.0       10.x.0.3        63        0x80000001 0x0000fdc0
10.x.12.0       10.x.0.2        63        0x80000001 0x0000f8c5
10.x.12.0       10.x.0.3        63        0x80000001 0x0000f2ca
```

Question: How many links are there in the router LSA for Core1 inside area 1 (10.x.0.2)?

Answer: The router LSA inside the area 1 only contains the VLAN101 interface, so only one link will be present in the router LSA at this point.

2. The ABR is now responsible to convert the routes that were learned through the Router (Type 1) and Network (Type 2) LSAs between the areas. This means that the VLAN 2,11,12 IP prefixes that are known on the Router LSA in area 0 have been converted into a 'Summary' LSA (Type 3) in area. In the same output, verify that the IP prefixes of area 0 are known as inter-area summary (Type 3) LSAs in area 1.

Note

'Summary' does not indicate route summarization: it only indicates that this LSA is not used for the topology calculation of this area. Only Router and Network LSAs are used to build the topology of an area.

```
ICX-Tx-Core1(config-ospf-1)# show ip ospf lsdb area 1
OSPF Router with ID (10.x.0.2) (Process ID 1 VRF default)
===========================================================
Router Link State Advertisements (Area 0.0.0.1)
-----------------------------------------------


LSID            ADV Router      Age       Seq#        Checksum       Link Count
-------------------------------------------------------------------------------
10.x.0.2        10.x.0.2        18        0x80000002 0x0000744d     1
10.x.0.3        10.x.0.3        19        0x80000002 0x0000724c     1
```

```
Network Link State Advertisements (Area 0.0.0.1)
-------------------------------------------------

LSID            ADV Router      Age       Seq#        Checksum
--------------------------------------------------------------
10.x.101.3      10.x.0.3        24        0x80000001 0x00000c85

Inter-area Summary Link State Advertisements (Area 0.0.0.1)
------------------------------------------------------------

LSID            ADV Router      Age       Seq#        Checksum
--------------------------------------------------------------
10.x.0.2        10.x.0.2        63        0x80000001 0x00007daf
10.x.0.2        10.x.0.3        63        0x80000001 0x000081a9
10.x.0.3        10.x.0.2        63        0x80000001 0x00007dad
10.x.0.3        10.x.0.3        63        0x80000001 0x00006dbd
10.x.1.0        10.x.0.2        63        0x80000001 0x00007257
10.x.1.0        10.x.0.3        63        0x80000001 0x00006c5c
10.x.2.2        10.x.0.2        63        0x80000001 0x00006bbf
10.x.2.2        10.x.0.3        63        0x80000001 0x000065c4
10.x.11.0       10.x.0.2        63        0x80000001 0x000004bb
10.x.11.0       10.x.0.3        63        0x80000001 0x0000fdc0
10.x.12.0       10.x.0.2        63        0x80000001 0x0000f8c5
10.x.12.0       10.x.0.3        63        0x80000001 0x0000f2ca
```

3. Review the LSDB for area 0.

```
ICX-Tx-Core1(config)# show ip ospf lsdb area 0
OSPF Router with ID (10.x.0.2) (Process ID 1 VRF default)
===========================================================
Router Link State Advertisements (Area 0.0.0.0)
------------------------------------------------

LSID            ADV Router      Age       Seq#        Checksum        Link Count
--------------------------------------------------------------------------------
10.x.0.2        10.x.0.2        421       0x80000014 0x0000369c      6
10.x.0.3        10.x.0.3        422       0x80000010 0x0000785b      6
10.x.0.4        10.x.0.4        1069      0x80000003 0x0000eca3      2

Network Link State Advertisements (Area 0.0.0.0)
-------------------------------------------------

LSID            ADV Router      Age       Seq#        Checksum
--------------------------------------------------------------
10.x.101.4      10.x.0.4        1069      0x80000002 0x0000a1ce

Inter-area Summary Link State Advertisements (Area 0.0.0.0)
------------------------------------------------------------
```

```
LSID            ADV Router      Age       Seq#       Checksum
--------------------------------------------------------------
10.x.101.0      10.x.0.2        416       0x80000002 0x00002044
10.x.101.0      10.x.0.3        417       0x80000002 0x00001a49
```

Note

You may still notice the Access1 (10.x.0.4) Router LSA in the area 0 LSDB, even though the link to Access1 was already assigned to area 1. This is because that Router LSA still needs to age-out from the LSDB, so it will disappear automatically after 3600 seconds.

Question: The interface VLAN 101 IP subnet is now active in area 1. Is it known as a 'summary' LSA in area 0?

Answer: Yes, the 10.x.101.0 is listed as a summary LSA.

Area Border routers can be easily found in the LSDB since they are advertising the 'Summary' LSAs. The 'ADV Router' indicates the advertising router ID.

Question: Which routers are currently ABR?

Answer: Both 10.x.0.2 and 10.x.0.3 are currently advertising a summary LSA.

Question: The configuration was only performed on Core1. How is it possible that Core2 (10.x.0.3) is also advertising the 10.x.101.0 Summary LSA?

Answer: Due to the VSX configuration synchronization, area 1 was also defined on Core2, and the interface VLAN 101 was also moved into this area 1. Therefore, without accessing the Core2 configuration, it also became an ABR.

On Access1, Remove Area 0, Define Area 1, and Assign Interface VLAN 101 to Area 1

1. On Access1, enter the configuration mode. Remove area 0 and define area 1.

```
ICX-Tx-Access1(config)# router ospf 1
ICX-Tx-Access1(config-ospf-1)# no area 0
ICX-Tx-Access1(config-ospf-1)# area 1
ICX-Tx-Access1(config-ospf-1)# exit
```

2. Assign interface VLAN 101 to area 1.

```
ICX-Tx-Access1(config)# interface vlan 101
ICX-Tx-Access1(config-if-vlan)# ip ospf 1 area 1
ICX-Tx-Access1(config-if-vlan)# exit
```

3. On Access1, define some local IP subnets. These subnets simulate client subnets and will be used to test routing. The Access1 router will be the only host in these test subnets. The test subnets for area 1 are assigned in the 10.x.128-191 block, so it will be possible to summarize these in a later step.

4. Define the test VLANs. Enable them as VLAN trunk on the port to the client PC. This is only done to ensure the VLAN is 'up'.

Note

If a VLAN does not contain any port in the 'up' state, the Layer3 IP interface remains down as well. As a workaround to bring these VLANs 'UP', these 2 VLANs are enabled on the port to the PC.

```
ICX-Tx-Access1(config)# vlan 128,129
ICX-Tx-Access1(config-vlan-<128,129>)# exit
ICX-Tx-Access1(config)# interface 1/1/3
ICX-Tx-Access1(config-if)# no shutdown
ICX-Tx-Access1(config-if)# vlan trunk allowed 128,129
ICX-Tx-Access1(config-if)# exit
ICX-Tx-Access1(config)#
```

1. Define the test subnets.

```
ICX-Tx-Access1(config)# interface vlan 128
ICX-Tx-Access1(config-if-vlan)# ip address 10.x.128.1/24
ICX-Tx-Access1(config-if-vlan)# ip ospf 1 area 1
ICX-Tx-Access1(config-if-vlan)# exit
ICX-Tx-Access1(config)# interface vlan 129
ICX-Tx-Access1(config-if-vlan)# ip address 10.x.129.1/24
ICX-Tx-Access1(config-if-vlan)# ip ospf 1 area 1
ICX-Tx-Access1(config-if-vlan)# exit
ICX-Tx-Access1(config)#
```

2. On Access1, review the LSDB for area 1; note the link count for the Router LSA of Access1.

```
ICX-Tx-Access1(config)# show ip ospf lsdb area 1
OSPF Router with ID (10.x.0.4) (Process ID 1 VRF default)
=============================================================
Router Link State Advertisements (Area 0.0.0.1)
------------------------------------------------


LSID            ADV Router       Age        Seq#        Checksum        Link
Count
-----------------------------------------------------------------------------
10.x.0.2        10.x.0.2         757        0x80000002 0x0000744d       1
10.x.0.3        10.x.0.3         132        0x80000003 0x0000704d       1
10.x.0.4        10.x.0.4         11         0x80000005 0x00004b57       3

Network Link State Advertisements (Area 0.0.0.1)
-------------------------------------------------
```

```
LSID              ADV Router       Age         Seq#         Checksum
---------------------------------------------------------------
10.x.101.3       10.x.0.3         132        0x80000002 0x0000adc4

Inter-area Summary Link State Advertisements (Area 0.0.0.1)
-------------------------------------------------------------

LSID              ADV Router       Age         Seq#         Checksum
---------------------------------------------------------------
10.x.0.2         10.x.0.2         802        0x80000001 0x00007daf
10.x.0.2         10.x.0.3         802        0x80000001 0x000081a9
10.x.0.3         10.x.0.2         802        0x80000001 0x00007dad
10.x.0.3         10.x.0.3         802        0x80000001 0x00006dbd
10.x.1.0         10.x.0.2         802        0x80000001 0x00007257
10.x.1.0         10.x.0.3         802        0x80000001 0x00006c5c
10.x.2.2         10.x.0.2         802        0x80000001 0x00006bbf
10.x.2.2         10.x.0.3         802        0x80000001 0x000065c4
10.x.11.0        10.x.0.2         802        0x80000001 0x000004bb
10.x.11.0        10.x.0.3         802        0x80000001 0x0000fdc0
10.x.12.0        10.x.0.2         802        0x80000001 0x0000f8c5
10.x.12.0        10.x.0.3         802        0x80000001 0x0000f2ca
```

5. On Core1, verify that the same information is known in the area 1 LSDB. So Core1 also knows about the three links of the Access1 router in the area 1 database.

Note

Remember that an OSPF area LSDB contains the same information on all routers of that area.

```
ICX-Tx-Core1(config)# show ip ospf lsdb area 1
OSPF Router with ID (10.x.0.2) (Process ID 1 VRF default)
=============================================================
Router Link State Advertisements (Area 0.0.0.1)
-----------------------------------------------

LSID         ADV Router      Age      Seq#          Checksum         Link Count
-----------------------------------------------------------------------------
10.x.0.2        10.x.0.2         808        0x80000002 0x0000744d        1
10.x.0.3        10.x.0.3         184        0x80000003 0x0000704d        1
10.x.0.4        10.x.0.4         24         0x80000007 0x00004759        3

Network Link State Advertisements (Area 0.0.0.1)
-----------------------------------------------
```

```
LSID              ADV Router       Age        Seq#        Checksum
---------------------------------------------------------------
10.x.101.3      10.x.0.3        184        0x80000002 0x0000adc4
Inter-area Summary Link State Advertisements (Area 0.0.0.1)
-------------------------------------------------------------
LSID              ADV Router       Age        Seq#        Checksum
---------------------------------------------------------------
<...output omitted...>
```

6. The Core1 Area Border has converted the routes of this Router LSA from area 1 to Summary Routes into area 0. Verify this by reviewing the area 0 database.

```
ICX-Tx-Core1(config)# show ip ospf lsdb area 0
OSPF Router with ID (10.x.0.2) (Process ID 1 VRF default)
===========================================================
Router Link State Advertisements (Area 0.0.0.0)
------------------------------------------------

LSID              ADV Router       Age        Seq#        Checksum        Link
Count
---------------------------------------------------------------------------
10.x.0.2         10.x.0.2         596        0x80000005 0x00000332      6
10.x.0.3         10.x.0.3         151        0x8000000d 0x00006bbd      6
Network Link State Advertisements (Area 0.0.0.0)
------------------------------------------------

LSID              ADV Router       Age        Seq#        Checksum
-------------------------------------------------------------
10.x.102.3       10.x.0.3         600        0x80000002 0x0000fe90
Inter-area Summary Link State Advertisements (Area 0.0.0.0)
-----------------------------------------------------------

LSID              ADV Router       Age        Seq#        Checksum
-------------------------------------------------------------
10.x.101.0       10.x.0.2         641        0x80000002 0x00002044
10.x.101.0       10.x.0.3         150        0x80000003 0x0000184a
10.x.128.0       10.x.0.2         339        0x80000001 0x0000e302
10.x.128.0       10.x.0.3         340        0x80000001 0x0000dd07
10.x.129.0       10.x.0.2         329        0x80000001 0x0000d80c
10.x.129.0       10.x.0.3         329        0x80000001 0x0000d211
```

Note

The Core2 ABR has performed the same action; this is why the 10.x.128.0 and 10.x.129.0 Summary LSAs are listed two times.

7. On Core1, review learned OSPF routes and notice the OSPF route code.

```
ICX-Tx-Core1(config)# show ip ospf routes
Codes: i - Intra-area route, I - Inter-area route
       E1 - External type-1, E2 - External type-2

OSPF Process ID 1 VRF default, Routing Table
---------------------------------------------
Total Number of Routes : 8

10.x.0.3/32        (i) area: 0.0.0.0
     via 10.x.2.3 interface vlan2, cost 1 distance 110
10.x.1.0/24        (i) area: 0.0.0.0
     directly attached to interface vlan1, cost 100 distance 110
10.x.2.2/31        (i) area: 0.0.0.0
     directly attached to interface vlan2, cost 1 distance 110
10.x.11.0/24       (i) area: 0.0.0.0
     directly attached to interface vlan11, cost 100 distance 110
10.x.12.0/24       (i) area: 0.0.0.0
     directly attached to interface vlan12, cost 100 distance 110
10.x.101.0/24      (i) area: 0.0.0.1
     directly attached to interface vlan101, cost 100 distance 110
10.x.128.0/24      (i) area: 0.0.0.1
     via 10.x.101.4 interface vlan101, cost 200 distance 110
10.x.129.0/24      (i) area: 0.0.0.1
     via 10.x.101.4 interface vlan101, cost 200 distance 110
```

Question: Why are all OSPF routes on Core1 listed as (i) > intra-area route?

Answer: In the current state of the lab, Core1 has direct access to both area 0 and area 1, so from the Core1 perspective, all learned routes are intra-area routes.

8. On Core1, review the IP routing table. The 10.x.128.0/24 and 10.x.129.0/24 subnets should be visible.

```
ICX-Tx-Core1(config)# show ip route ospf
Displaying ipv4 routes selected for forwarding
'[x/y]' denotes [distance/metric]

10.x.0.3/32, vrf default
        via  10.x.2.3,  [110/1],  ospf
```

```
10.x.128.0/24, vrf default
        via  10.x.101.4,  [110/200],  ospf
10.x.129.0/24, vrf default
        via  10.x.101.4,  [110/200],  ospf
```

Task 2: Assign Access2 to OSPF Area 2

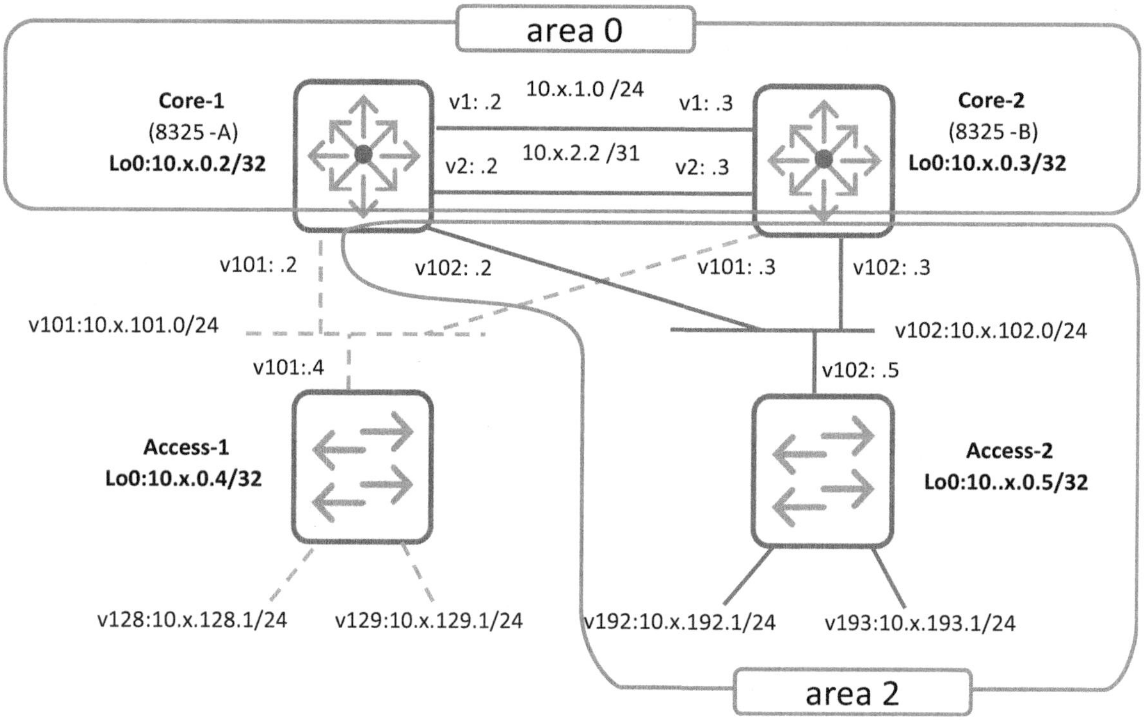

Figure 6-27 Task 2: Assign Access2 to OSPF Area 2

Objectives

- In this task, Access2 will be configured into its own area 2.
- Once the area 2 has been defined, the LSA propagation will be reviewed.
- Set up ABR link
- Verify how the LSA changes when traversing through area 2, to area 0, then into area 1.

Steps

1. On Core1, define area 2; assign interface VLAN 102 to area 2 (Figure 6-27).

```
ICX-Tx-Core1(config)# router ospf 1
ICX-Tx-Core1(config-ospf-1)# area 2
ICX-Tx-Core1(config-ospf-1)# exit

ICX-Tx-Core1(config)# interface vlan 102
ICX-Tx-Core1(config-if-vlan)# ip ospf 1 area 2
ICX-Tx-Core1(config-if-vlan)# no ip ospf passive
ICX-Tx-Core1(config-if-vlan)# exit
```

2. Open a terminal connection to Access2; enter the configuration mode. On Access2, enable OSPF with the Access2 router-id and define area 2.

```
ICX-Tx-Access2(config)# router ospf 1
ICX-Tx-Access2(config-ospf-1)# router-id 10.x.0.5
ICX-Tx-Access2(config-ospf-1)# area 2
ICX-Tx-Access2(config-ospf-1)# exit
```

3. On Access2, define the VLAN 102.

Note
In the VSX lab activity, the LAG255 was set to allow all VLANs; this is why there is no step to allow the VLAN 101 on the VLAN trunk.

```
ICX-Tx-Access2(config)# vlan 102
ICX-Tx-Access2(config-vlan-102)# exit
```

4. Enable IP and verify connectivity to Core1 and Core2.

```
ICX-Tx-Access2(config)# interface vlan 102
ICX-Tx-Access2(config-vlan)# ip address 10.x.102.5/24
ICX-Tx-Access2(config-vlan)# ip ospf 1 area 2
ICX-Tx-Access2(config)# do ping 10.x.102.2
PING 10.x.102.2 (10.x.102.2) 100(128) bytes of data.
108 bytes from 10.x.102.2: icmp_seq=1 ttl=64 time=16.7 ms
108 bytes from 10.x.102.2: icmp_seq=2 ttl=64 time=0.173 ms
<output omitted>
ICX-Tx-Access2(config)# do ping 10.x.102.3
PING 10.x.102.3 (10.x.102.3) 100(128) bytes of data.
108 bytes from 10.x.102.3: icmp_seq=1 ttl=64 time=0.182 ms
108 bytes from 10.x.102.3: icmp_seq=2 ttl=64 time=0.175 ms
```

5. Configure the loopback interface.

```
ICX-Tx-Access2(config)# interface loopback 0
ICX-Tx-Access2(config-loopback-if)# ip address 10.x.0.5/32
ICX-Tx-Access2(config-loopback-if)# ip ospf 1 area 2
ICX-Tx-Access2(config-loopback-if)#exit
```

6. Configure some local test subnets.

```
ICX-Tx-Access2(config)# vlan 192,193
ICX-Tx-Access2(config-vlan-<192,193>)# exit
ICX-Tx-Access2(config)# interface 1/1/4
ICX-Tx-Access2(config-if)# no shutdown
ICX-Tx-Access2(config-if)# vlan trunk allowed 192,193
ICX-Tx-Access2(config-if)# exit
ICX-Tx-Access2(config)#
ICX-Tx-Access2(config)# interface vlan 192
ICX-Tx-Access2(config-if-vlan)# ip address 10.x.192.1/24
ICX-Tx-Access2(config-if-vlan)# ip ospf 1 area 2
ICX-Tx-Access2(config-if-vlan)# exit
ICX-Tx-Access2(config)#
ICX-Tx-Access2(config)# interface vlan 193
ICX-Tx-Access2(config-if-vlan)# ip address 10.x.193.1/24
ICX-Tx-Access2(config-if-vlan)# ip ospf 1 area 2
ICX-Tx-Access2(config-if-vlan)# exit
```

7. Verify the OSPF adjacencies have been established with Core1 and Core2.

```
ICX-Tx-Access2(config)# show ip ospf neighbors
OSPF Process ID 1 VRF default
==============================
Total Number of Neighbors: 2

Neighbor ID      Priority  State              Nbr Address       Interface
---------------------------------------------------------------------------
10.x.0.2         1         FULL/BDR           10.x.102.2        vlan102
10.x.0.3         1         FULL/DR            10.x.102.3        vlan102
```

Verify Route Propagation and LSA Changes from Area 2 to Area 0 to Area 1

In the next steps, the route propagation between the areas will be reviewed. For this example, the route 10.x.192.0/24 will be used. This is the test subnet that was defined on Access2 in area 2. In previous steps, the 'show ip ospf lsdb' command was used to review the LSAs in the LSDB.

In the next steps, the command 'show ip ospf routes' will be used. This command shows the actual routes that have been calculated by OSPF for both intra-area (Router and Network LSA) and inter-area LSAs (Summary LSA).

1. On Access2, verify the 10.x.192.0/24 route is known as an intra-area route.

> **Note**
> The lowercase 'i' is used for intra-area, while the uppercase 'I' is used for inter-area.

```
ICX-Tx-Access2(config)# show ip ospf routes
Codes: i - Intra-area route, I - Inter-area route
       E1 - External type-1, E2 - External type-2
OSPF Process ID 1 VRF default, Routing Table
---------------------------------------------
Total Number of Routes : 19

10.x.0.2/32        (I)
     via 10.x.102.2 interface vlan102, cost 100 distance 110
10.x.0.3/32        (I)
     via 10.x.102.3 interface vlan102, cost 100 distance 110
10.x.1.0/24        (I)
     via 10.x.102.2 interface vlan102, cost 200 distance 110
10.x.1.0/24        (I)
     via 10.x.102.3 interface vlan102, cost 200 distance 110
10.x.2.2/31        (I)
     via 10.x.102.2 interface vlan102, cost 101 distance 110
10.x.2.2/31        (I)
     via 10.x.102.3 interface vlan102, cost 101 distance 110
10.x.11.0/24       (I)
     via 10.x.102.2 interface vlan102, cost 200 distance 110
10.x.11.0/24       (I)
     via 10.x.102.3 interface vlan102, cost 200 distance 110
10.x.12.0/24       (I)
     via 10.x.102.2 interface vlan102, cost 200 distance 110
10.x.12.0/24       (I)
     via 10.x.102.3 interface vlan102, cost 200 distance 110
10.x.101.0/24      (I)
     via 10.x.102.2 interface vlan102, cost 200 distance 110
10.x.101.0/24      (I)
     via 10.x.102.3 interface vlan102, cost 200 distance 110
```

```
10.x.102.0/24      (i) area: 0.0.0.2
     directly attached to interface vlan102, cost 100 distance 110
10.x.128.0/24      (I)
     via 10.x.102.2 interface vlan102, cost 300 distance 110
10.x.128.0/24      (I)
     via 10.x.102.3 interface vlan102, cost 300 distance 110
10.x.129.0/24      (I)
     via 10.x.102.2 interface vlan102, cost 300 distance 110
10.x.129.0/24      (I)
     via 10.x.102.3 interface vlan102, cost 300 distance 110
10.x.192.0/24      (i) area: 0.0.0.2
     directly attached to interface vlan192, cost 100 distance 110
10.x.193.0/24      (i) area: 0.0.0.2
     directly attached to interface vlan193, cost 100 distance 110
```

2. On Core1, review the OSPF routing table; look for the 10.x.192.0/24 subnet.

```
ICX-Tx-Core1(config)# show ip ospf routes
Codes: i - Intra-area route, I - Inter-area route
E1 - External type-1, E2 - External type-2
OSPF Process ID 1 VRF default, Routing Table
---------------------------------------------
Total Number of Routes : 12

10.x.0.3/32        (i) area: 0.0.0.0
     via 10.x.2.3 interface vlan2, cost 1 distance 110
10.x.0.5/32        (i) area: 0.0.0.2
     via 10.x.102.5 interface vlan102, cost 100 distance 110
10.x.1.0/24        (i) area: 0.0.0.0
     directly attached to interface vlan1, cost 100 distance 110
10.x.2.2/31        (i) area: 0.0.0.0
     directly attached to interface vlan2, cost 1 distance 110
10.x.11.0/24       (i) area: 0.0.0.0
     directly attached to interface vlan11, cost 100 distance 110
10.x.12.0/24       (i) area: 0.0.0.0
     directly attached to interface vlan12, cost 100 distance 110
10.x.101.0/24      (i) area: 0.0.0.1
     directly attached to interface vlan101, cost 100 distance 110
10.x.102.0/24      (i) area: 0.0.0.2
     directly attached to interface vlan102, cost 100 distance 110
10.x.128.0/24      (i) area: 0.0.0.1
     via 10.x.101.4 interface vlan101, cost 200 distance 110
```

```
10.x.129.0/24       (i) area: 0.0.0.1
     via 10.x.101.4 interface vlan101, cost 200 distance 110
10.x.192.0/24       (i) area: 0.0.0.2
     via 10.x.102.5 interface vlan102, cost 200 distance 110
10.x.193.0/24       (i) area: 0.0.0.2
     via 10.x.102.5 interface vlan102, cost 200 distance 110
```

Question: Why is the route listed as an intra-area route?

Answer: Core1 has both area 2 and area 0 databases locally. Both the area 2 and area 0 are offering this route to the OSPF routing table. But an intra-area route takes precedence over an inter-area route, so the intra-area route is listed here.

3. Also review the Summary LSAs in the area 0 LSDB.

```
ICX-Tx-Core1(config)# show ip ospf lsdb summary area 0
OSPF Router with ID (10.x.0.2) (Process ID 1 VRF default)
=============================================================
Inter-area Summary Link State Advertisements (Area 0.0.0.0)
-------------------------------------------------------------

LSID             ADV Router        Age        Seq#        Checksum
-------------------------------------------------------------------
10.x.0.5         10.x.0.2          454        0x80000001 0x00004b7a
10.x.0.5         10.x.0.3          455        0x80000001 0x0000457f
10.x.101.0       10.x.0.2          404        0x80000003 0x00001e45
10.x.101.0       10.x.0.3          405        0x80000003 0x0000184a
10.x.102.0       10.x.0.2          743        0x80000002 0x0000154e
10.x.102.0       10.x.0.3          740        0x80000002 0x00000f53
10.x.128.0       10.x.0.2          1437       0x80000001 0x0000e302
10.x.128.0       10.x.0.3          1439       0x80000001 0x0000dd07
10.x.129.0       10.x.0.2          1418       0x80000001 0x0000d80c
10.x.129.0       10.x.0.3          1419       0x80000001 0x0000d211
10.x.192.0       10.x.0.2          414        0x80000001 0x00002184
10.x.192.0       10.x.0.3          415        0x80000001 0x00001b89
10.x.193.0       10.x.0.2          398        0x80000001 0x0000168e
10.x.193.0       10.x.0.3          399        0x80000001 0x00001093
```

Question: Which routers are advertising the Summary LSA for the 10.x.192.0/24 subnet?

Answer: As ABRs, both Core1 and Core2 are advertising this Summary LSA.

4. On Core1, review the area 1 LSDB; look for the 10.x.192.0 Summary LSA. An ABR will convert Router and Network LSAs from non-backbone areas (not area 0.0.0.0) into Summary LSAs in the backbone area. These Summary LSAs will be copied as Summary LSAs into any other areas that exist on the ABR.

```
ICX-Tx-Core1(config)# show ip ospf lsdb summary area 1
OSPF Router with ID (10.x.0.2) (Process ID 1 VRF default)
===========================================================
Inter-area Summary Link State Advertisements (Area 0.0.0.1)
------------------------------------------------------------

LSID            ADV Router       Age       Seq#          Checksum
--------------------------------------------------------------
10.x.0.2        10.x.0.2        459        0x80000002 0x00007bb0
10.x.0.2        10.x.0.3        460        0x80000002 0x00007faa
10.x.0.3        10.x.0.2        459        0x80000002 0x00007bae
10.x.0.3        10.x.0.3        460        0x80000002 0x00006bbe
10.x.0.5        10.x.0.2        504        0x80000001 0x00004b7a
10.x.0.5        10.x.0.3        505        0x80000001 0x0000457f
10.x.1.0        10.x.0.2        459        0x80000002 0x00007058
10.x.1.0        10.x.0.3        460        0x80000002 0x00006a5d
10.x.2.2        10.x.0.2        459        0x80000002 0x000069c0
10.x.2.2        10.x.0.3        460        0x80000002 0x000063c5
10.x.11.0       10.x.0.2        459        0x80000002 0x000002bc
10.x.11.0       10.x.0.3        460        0x80000002 0x0000fbc1
10.x.12.0       10.x.0.2        459        0x80000002 0x0000f6c6
10.x.12.0       10.x.0.3        460        0x80000002 0x0000f0cb
10.x.102.0      10.x.0.2        793        0x80000002 0x0000154e
10.x.102.0      10.x.0.3        789        0x80000003 0x00000d54
10.x.192.0      10.x.0.2        464        0x80000001 0x00002184
10.x.192.0      10.x.0.3        465        0x80000001 0x00001b89
10.x.193.0      10.x.0.2        448        0x80000001 0x0000168e
10.x.193.0      10.x.0.3        449        0x80000001 0x00001093
```

Question: Which routers are advertising the Summary LSA?

Answer: Again, as ABRs, both Core1 and Core2 are advertising this Summary LSA.

5. On Access1, review the OSPF LSDB and the routing table.

```
ICX-Tx-Access1(config)# show ip ospf lsdb summary area 1
OSPF Router with ID (10.x.0.4) (Process ID 1 VRF default)
=============================================================
Inter-area Summary Link State Advertisements (Area 0.0.0.1)
-------------------------------------------------------------

LSID            ADV Router      Age       Seq#        Checksum
--------------------------------------------------------------
10.x.0.2        10.x.0.2        536       0x80000002 0x00007bb0
10.x.0.2        10.x.0.3        535       0x80000002 0x00007faa
10.x.0.3        10.x.0.2        536       0x80000002 0x00007bae
10.x.0.3        10.x.0.3        535       0x80000002 0x00006bbe
10.x.0.5        10.x.0.2        580       0x80000001 0x00004b7a
10.x.0.5        10.x.0.3        580       0x80000001 0x0000457f
10.x.1.0        10.x.0.2        536       0x80000002 0x00007058
10.x.1.0        10.x.0.3        535       0x80000002 0x00006a5d
10.x.2.2        10.x.0.2        536       0x80000002 0x000069c0
10.x.2.2        10.x.0.3        535       0x80000002 0x000063c5
10.x.11.0       10.x.0.2        536       0x80000002 0x000002bc
10.x.11.0       10.x.0.3        535       0x80000002 0x0000fbc1
10.x.12.0       10.x.0.2        536       0x80000002 0x0000f6c6
10.x.12.0       10.x.0.3        535       0x80000002 0x0000f0cb
10.x.102.0      10.x.0.2        870       0x80000002 0x0000154e
10.x.102.0      10.x.0.3        864       0x80000003 0x00000d54
10.x.192.0      10.x.0.2        540       0x80000001 0x00002184
10.x.192.0      10.x.0.3        540       0x80000001 0x00001b89
10.x.193.0      10.x.0.2        524       0x80000001 0x0000168e
10.x.193.0      10.x.0.3        524       0x80000001 0x00001093
```

6. Review the OSPF routes; the route to 10.x.192.0/24 should be listed as an inter-area route. This demonstrates that a route on a Router LSA in area 2 is converted into a Summary LSA by the ABR into the backbone area (0.0.0.0). An ABR will copy any Summary LSA from the backbone area into any other area LSDB.

```
ICX-Tx-Access1(config)# show ip ospf routes 10.x.192.0/24
Codes: i - Intra-area route, I - Inter-area route
       E1 - External type-1, E2 - External type-2
OSPF Process ID 1 VRF default, Routing Table for prefixes 10.x.192.0/24
```

```
--------------------------------------------------------------------------
Total Number of Routes : 2

10.x.192.0/24      (I)
     via 10.x.101.2 interface vlan101, cost 300 distance 110
10.x.192.0/24      (I)
     via 10.x.101.3 interface vlan101, cost 300 distance 110
```

Note

An ABR will only exchange information between an area and the backbone (0.0.0.0) area LSDB databases. It will never exchange information directly between two non-backbone areas, for example between area 1 and area 2 LSDBs.

Task 3: Route Summarization

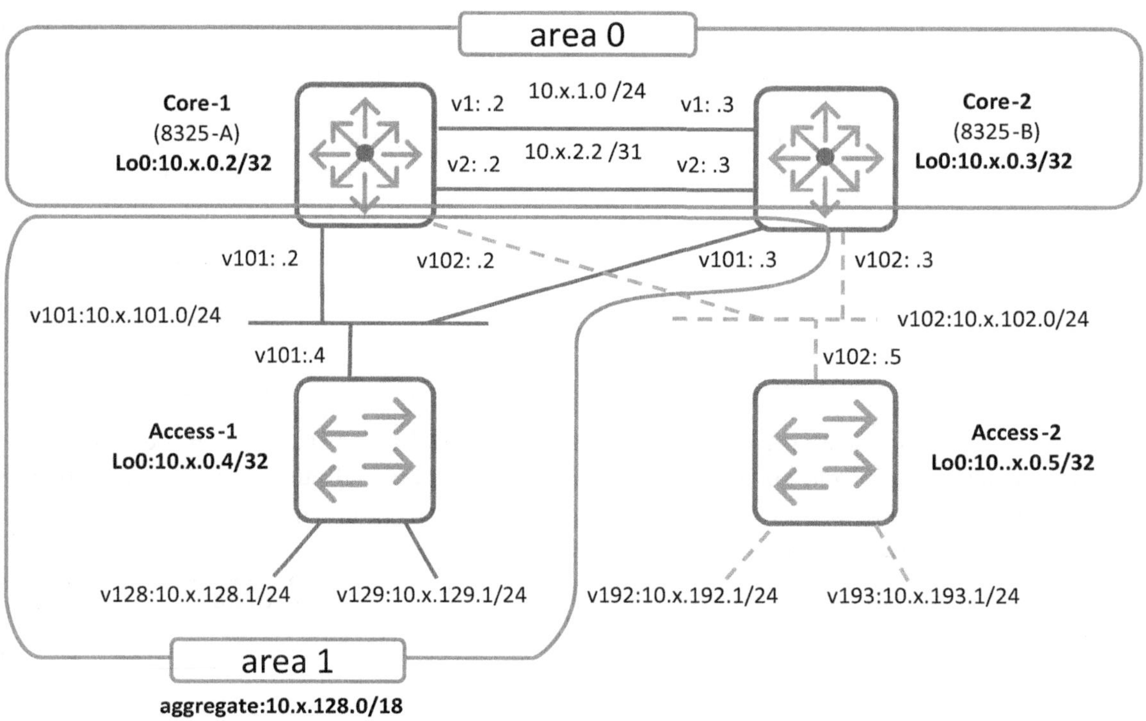

Figure 6-28 Task 3: Route Summarization

Objectives

- Implement route summarization between the areas

Steps

First summarize routes injected by area 1 into area 0 on Core1 (Figure 6-28).

Verify in area 2; verify LSA type and cost.

Summarize area 2 test subnets.

Summarize the Area 1 Test Subnets

In area 1, the test subnets 10.x.128.0/24 and 10.x.129.0/24 can be summarized into a 10.x.128.0/18 prefix.

1. On Core1, configure the summarization rule in the OSPF area 1 context.

```
ICX-Tx-Core1(config)# router ospf 1
ICX-Tx-Core1(config-ospf-1)# area 1 range 10.x.128.0/18 type inter-area
ICX-Tx-Core1(config-ospf-1)# exit
```

Important

The route aggregation must be performed on every ABR that is connected to this area to be effective. An ABR that does not have the aggregation route will still be announcing the more specific routes into the area. As a result, all traffic to these subnets will go via the 'most specific match', meaning the ABR that does not have the aggregate route configured.

In this lab environment, the VSX configuration synchronization is also synchronizing the OSPF commands; the 'range' command is automatically set on the ABR Core2.

2. Review how this affects the area 0 LSDB on Core1. Previously, these subnets were known as unique Summary LSAs; now only the summarized route is listed.

```
ICX-Tx-Core1(config)# show ip ospf lsdb summary area 0
OSPF Router with ID (10.x.0.2) (Process ID 1 VRF default)
============================================================
Inter-area Summary Link State Advertisements (Area 0.0.0.0)
-------------------------------------------------------------

LSID            ADV Router      Age       Seq#        Checksum
---------------------------------------------------------------
10.x.0.5        10.x.0.2        962       0x80000001 0x00004b7a
10.x.0.5        10.x.0.3        963       0x80000001 0x0000457f
10.x.101.0      10.x.0.2        912       0x80000003 0x00001e45
10.x.101.0      10.x.0.3        913       0x80000003 0x0000184a
10.x.102.0      10.x.0.2        1251      0x80000002 0x0000154e
10.x.102.0      10.x.0.3        1248      0x80000002 0x00000f53
10.x.128.0      10.x.0.2        162       0x80000002 0x0000a57e
```

```
10.x.128.0      10.x.0.3       161        0x80000002 0x00009f83
10.x.192.0      10.x.0.2       922        0x80000001 0x00002184
10.x.192.0      10.x.0.3       923        0x80000001 0x00001b89
10.x.193.0      10.x.0.2       906        0x80000001 0x0000168e
10.x.193.0      10.x.0.3       907        0x80000001 0x00001093
```

3. And since the area 0 only contains the summarized entry, the area 2 LSDB will also reflect this. Review Summary LSAs in the LSDB for area 2.

```
ICX-Tx-Core1(config)# show ip ospf lsdb summary area 2
OSPF Router with ID (10.x.0.2) (Process ID 1 VRF default)
===========================================================
Inter-area Summary Link State Advertisements (Area 0.0.0.2)
------------------------------------------------------------

LSID            ADV Router      Age        Seq#        Checksum
--------------------------------------------------------------
10.x.0.2        10.x.0.2        1322       0x80000001 0x00007daf
10.x.0.2        10.x.0.3        1319       0x80000001 0x000081a9
10.x.0.3        10.x.0.2        1322       0x80000001 0x00007dad
10.x.0.3        10.x.0.3        1319       0x80000001 0x00006dbd
10.x.1.0        10.x.0.2        1322       0x80000001 0x00007257
10.x.1.0        10.x.0.3        1319       0x80000001 0x00006c5c
10.x.2.2        10.x.0.2        1322       0x80000001 0x00006bbf
10.x.2.2        10.x.0.3        1319       0x80000001 0x000065c4
10.x.11.0       10.x.0.2        1322       0x80000001 0x000004bb
10.x.11.0       10.x.0.3        1319       0x80000001 0x0000fdc0
10.x.12.0       10.x.0.2        1322       0x80000001 0x0000f8c5
10.x.12.0       10.x.0.3        1319       0x80000001 0x0000f2ca
10.x.101.0      10.x.0.2        1322       0x80000001 0x00002243
10.x.101.0      10.x.0.3        1319       0x80000001 0x00001c48
10.x.128.0      10.x.0.2        233        0x80000002 0x0000a57e
10.x.128.0      10.x.0.3        229        0x80000003 0x00009d84
```

4. On Access2, this is a router that only knows area 2; review the LSDB. Since all the database for an area must be the same on all the routers of an area, this area 2 LSDB will also contain the summarized Summary LSA.

```
ICX-Tx-Access2(config)# show ip ospf lsdb summary area 2
OSPF Router with ID (10.x.0.5) (Process ID 1 VRF default)
===========================================================
Inter-area Summary Link State Advertisements (Area 0.0.0.2)
------------------------------------------------------------
LSID            ADV Router      Age        Seq#        Checksum
--------------------------------------------------------------
10.x.0.2        10.x.0.2        1368       0x80000001 0x00007daf
```

```
10.x.0.2        10.x.0.3        1365      0x80000001 0x000081a9
10.x.0.3        10.x.0.2        1368      0x80000001 0x00007dad
10.x.0.3        10.x.0.3        1365      0x80000001 0x00006dbd
10.x.1.0        10.x.0.2        1368      0x80000001 0x00007257
10.x.1.0        10.x.0.3        1365      0x80000001 0x00006c5c
10.x.2.2        10.x.0.2        1368      0x80000001 0x00006bbf
10.x.2.2        10.x.0.3        1365      0x80000001 0x000065c4
10.x.11.0       10.x.0.2        1368      0x80000001 0x000004bb
10.x.11.0       10.x.0.3        1365      0x80000001 0x0000fdc0
10.x.12.0       10.x.0.2        1368      0x80000001 0x0000f8c5
10.x.12.0       10.x.0.3        1365      0x80000001 0x0000f2ca
10.x.101.0      10.x.0.2        1368      0x80000001 0x00002243
10.x.101.0      10.x.0.3        1365      0x80000001 0x00001c48
10.x.128.0      10.x.0.2        281       0x80000002 0x0000a57e
10.x.128.0      10.x.0.3        275       0x80000003 0x00009d84
```

5. Verify the OSPF routing table; it should only contain the summarized entry **10.x.128.0/18**, so the **10.x.128.0/24** and **10.x.129.0/24** subnets should not appear anymore.

```
ICX-Tx-Access2(config)# show ip ospf routes
Codes: i - Intra-area route, I - Inter-area route
       E1 - External type-1, E2 - External type-2
OSPF Process ID 1 VRF default, Routing Table
---------------------------------------------
Total Number of Routes : 17

10.x.0.2/32        (I)
     via 10.x.102.2 interface vlan102, cost 100 distance 110
10.x.0.3/32        (I)
     via 10.x.102.3 interface vlan102, cost 100 distance 110
10.x.1.0/24        (I)
     via 10.x.102.2 interface vlan102, cost 200 distance 110
10.x.1.0/24        (I)
     via 10.x.102.3 interface vlan102, cost 200 distance 110
10.x.2.2/31        (I)
     via 10.x.102.2 interface vlan102, cost 101 distance 110
10.x.2.2/31        (I)
     via 10.x.102.3 interface vlan102, cost 101 distance 110
10.x.11.0/24       (I)
     via 10.x.102.2 interface vlan102, cost 200 distance 110
10.x.11.0/24       (I)
     via 10.x.102.3 interface vlan102, cost 200 distance 110
10.x.12.0/24       (I)
     via 10.x.102.2 interface vlan102, cost 200 distance 110
```

```
10.x.12.0/24        (I)
     via 10.x.102.3 interface vlan102, cost 200 distance 110
10.x.101.0/24       (I)
     via 10.x.102.2 interface vlan102, cost 200 distance 110
10.x.101.0/24       (I)
     via 10.x.102.3 interface vlan102, cost 200 distance 110
10.x.102.0/24       (i) area: 0.0.0.2
     directly attached to interface vlan102, cost 100 distance 110
10.x.128.0/18       (I)
     via 10.x.102.2 interface vlan102, cost 300 distance 110
10.x.128.0/18       (I)
     via 10.x.102.3 interface vlan102, cost 300 distance 110
10.x.192.0/24       (i) area: 0.0.0.2
     directly attached to interface vlan192, cost 100 distance 110
10.x.193.0/24       (i) area: 0.0.0.2
     directly attached to interface vlan193, cost 100 distance 110
```

Reject Route for the Summarized Route

When an ABR is announcing a summary route to other routers, it introduces the risk that remote systems may send traffic to a subnet that is simply not online or available. In this example, Core1 and Core2 ABRs are announcing the 10.x.128.0/18 summarized route to Area 2. This means that devices connected to Access2 could try to send traffic to, for example, the 10.x.130.0/24 subnet, since this traffic also fits under the 10.x.128.0/18 route.

To prevent this, the ABR router that has the summarized route configured and will automatically get a 'reject' route in its routing table for the summarized route. In this example the 10.x.128.0/18 route is rejected. While this may seem like it would block all the traffic, the ABR still has the more specific routes for the 10.x.128.0/24 and 10.x.129.0/24 in its routing table, so these routes take precedence over the summarized route.

1. On Core1, review the IP routing table. Verify that the summarized route is listed as a 'reject' route, while the more specific routes still exist as normal routes.

```
ICX-Tx-Core1(config)# show ip route
Displaying ipv4 routes selected for forwarding
'[x/y]' denotes [distance/metric]
...
10.x.128.0/18, vrf default
reject route,  [110/0],  static
10.x.128.0/24, vrf default
via  10.x.101.4,  [110/200],  ospf
10.x.129.0/24, vrf default
via  10.x.101.4,  [110/200],  ospf
...
```

2. Therefore, if any traffic would arrive for the non-existing 10.x.130.0/24 subnet, it would be rejected since it only matches the reject route.

```
ICX-Tx-Core1(config)# show ip route 10.x.130.0
Displaying ipv4 routes selected for forwarding
'[x/y]' denotes [distance/metric]

10.x.128.0/18, vrf default
reject route,   [110/0],   static
```

Note

While this reject route is listed as a static route, it will not be visible on the running configuration. OSFP summarized route entries are automatically added to the operational routing table as a static route with the reject option.

Summarize Area 2 Test Subnets

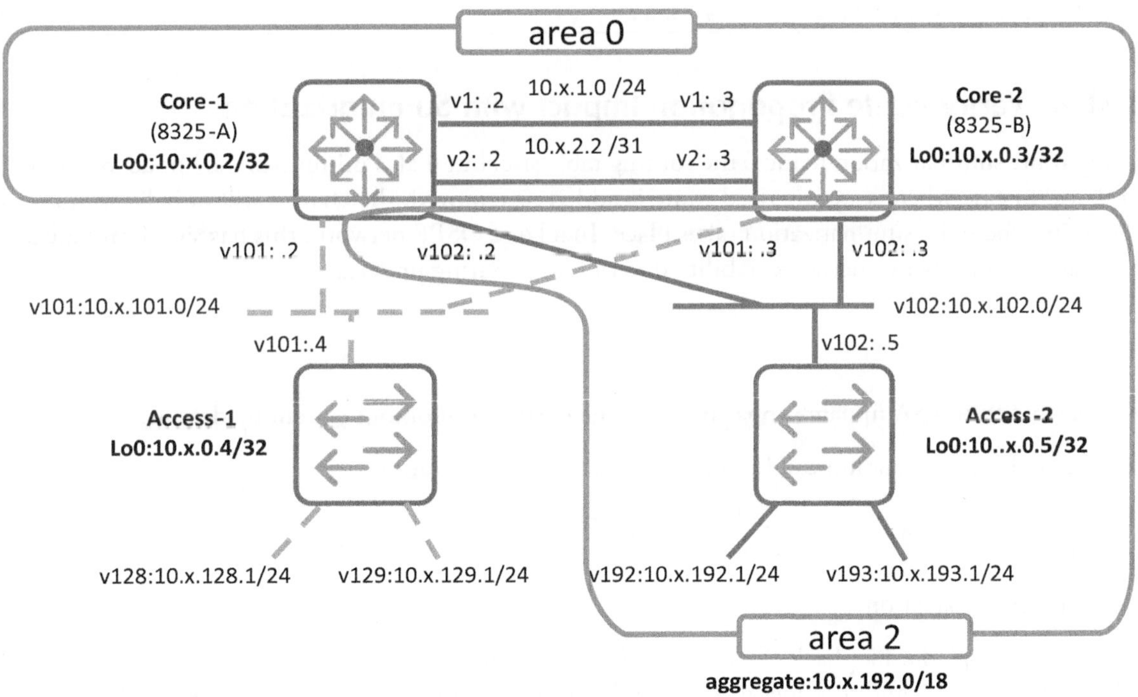

Figure 6-29 Task 3: Route Summarization

1. Now attempt to summarize the area 2 test subnets 10.x.192.0/24 and 10.x.193.0/24 into a 10.x.192.0/18 summary route (Figure 6-29). Try to apply the commands yourself. If you are not sure, the commands can be found in the next steps.
2. Verify on Access1 (area1) that only the summary route is listed.

```
ICX-Tx-Access1(config)# show ip route 10.x.192.0
Displaying ipv4 routes selected for forwarding
'[x/y]' denotes [distance/metric]

10.x.192.0/18, vrf default
via  10.x.101.3,   [110/300],   ospf
via  10.x.101.2,   [110/300],   ospf
```

Solution

1. On Core1, the steps are as follows:

```
ICX-Tx-Core1(config)# router ospf 1
ICX-Tx-Core1(config-ospf-1)# area 2 range 10.x.192.0/18 type inter-area
ICX-Tx-Core1(config-ospf-1)# exit
```

Task 4: Verify Route Propagation Impact with Summarization

Using route summarization reduces the routing table size, but it also minimizes the impact of routing updates. In case where a summarized route is added or removed, the change will only be seen up to the point where the summarization takes place. In a large OSPF network, this has significant advantages and ensures better network stability due to fewer routing updates.

Objectives

- Verify OSPF LSA update propagates over the entire autonomous system by default.
- Verify LSA propagation can be controlled using summarization.

Steps

Default LSA propagation

In the lab setup, the loopback 0 interface of Access2 will be disabled. Since this interface has IP address 10.x.0.5/32, and this does **not** match the summarization rule, the LSA change will propagate over the entire Autonomous System (AS).

These are the high-level steps:

- First check the OSPF SPF count on Access1.
- On Access2, disable the loopback interface to simulate a route change.
- On Access1, check the SPF count again; it should have increased since the LSA is propagated over the entire AS.

1. On Access1, review the OSPF SPF count and routing table.

Note

In each lab, the number of calculations may be different; the output below is just an example.

```
ICX-Tx-Access1(config)# show ip ospf
Routing Process 1 with ID : 10.x.0.4 VRF default
--------------------------------------------------
OSPFv2 Protocol is enabled
Graceful-restart is configured
Restart Interval: 120, State: inactive
Last Graceful Restart Exit Status: none
SPF: Start Time: 200ms, Hold Time: 1000ms, Max Wait Time: 5000ms
Maximum Paths to Destination: 4
Number of external LSAs 0, checksum sum 0
Number of areas is 1, 1 normal, 0 stub, 0 NSSA
Number of active areas is 1, 1 normal, 0 stub, 0 NSSA
BFD is disabled
Reference Bandwidth: 100000 Mbps
Area (0.0.0.1) (Active)
  Interfaces in this Area: 3 Active Interfaces: 3
  Passive Interfaces: 0 Loopback Interfaces: 0
SPF calculation has run 42 times
  Area ranges:
  Number of LSAs: 20, checksum sum 652089
```

2. On Access1, check the OSPF database summary.

```
ICX-Tx-Access1(config)# show ip ospf lsdb database-summary
OSPF Router with ID (10.x.0.4) (Process ID 1 VRF default)
==========================================================
Area 0.0.0.1 database summary
------------------------------

LSA Type             Count
---------------------------
Router               3
Network              1
Inter-area Summary   18
ASBR Summary         0
NSSA External        0
Subtotal             22

Process 1 database summary
---------------------------

LSA Type             Count
---------------------------
Router               3
Network              1
Inter-area Summary   18
ASBR Summary         0
NSSA External        0
AS External          0
Total                22
```

3. On Access2, disable the loopback 0 interface for OSPF.

```
ICX-Tx-Access2(config)# interface loopback 0
ICX-Tx-Access2(config-loopback-if)# ip ospf shutdown
```

4. On Access1, review the SPF count and the LSDB database summary.

```
ICX-Tx-Access1(config)# show ip ospf | include SPF
OSPFv2 Protocol is enabled
SPF: Start Time: 200ms, Hold Time: 1000ms, Max Wait Time: 5000ms
SPF calculation has run 44 times
ICX-Tx-Access1(config)#
ICX-Tx-Access1(config)# show ip ospf lsdb database-summary
```

```
OSPF Router with ID (10.x.0.4) (Process ID 1 VRF default)
===========================================================

Area 0.0.0.1 database summary
------------------------------

LSA Type             Count
---------------------------
Router               3
Network              1
Inter-area Summary   16
ASBR Summary         0
NSSA External        0
Subtotal             20
<...output omitted...>
```

5. On Access2, enable the Loopback 0 for OSPF again. This demonstrates that LSA updates are propagated over the entire AS by default.

```
ICX-Tx-Access2(config-loopback-if)# no ip ospf shutdown
ICX-Tx-Access2(config-loopback-if)# exit
ICX-Tx-Access2(config)#
```

Verify LSA Propagation Can Be Controlled Using Summarization

Now an interface that was summarized will be disabled. This should have no impact on the LSDB and the SPF count in the other areas. For this example, on Access2, the interface VLAN 192 will be disabled. Again, verify the SPF count on Access1 first, then make the change on Access2, and verify the count again on Access1.

1. On Access1, review the current SPF count.

```
ICX-Tx-Access1(config)# show ip ospf | include SPF
OSPFv2 Protocol is enabled
SPF: Start Time: 200ms, Hold Time: 1000ms, Max Wait Time: 5000ms
SPF calculation has run 45 times
```

2. On Access2, disable the VLAN 192 interface. This interface was summarized using the 10.x.192.0/18 range command.

```
ICX-Tx-Access2(config)# interface vlan 192
ICX-Tx-Access2(config-if-vlan)# shutdown
```

3. On Access1, verify the SPF count has not increased. This demonstrates the advantage of route summarization between OSPF areas.

```
ICX-Tx-Access1(config)# show ip ospf | include SPF
OSPFv2 Protocol is enabled
SPF: Start Time: 200ms, Hold Time: 1000ms, Max Wait Time: 5000ms
SPF calculation has run 45 times
```

4. On Access2, enable the VLAN 192 interface again.

```
ICX-Tx-Access2(config)# interface vlan 192
ICX-Tx-Access2(config-if-vlan)# no shutdown
ICX-Tx-Access2(config-if-vlan)# exit
```

Task 5: ABR Route Filtering

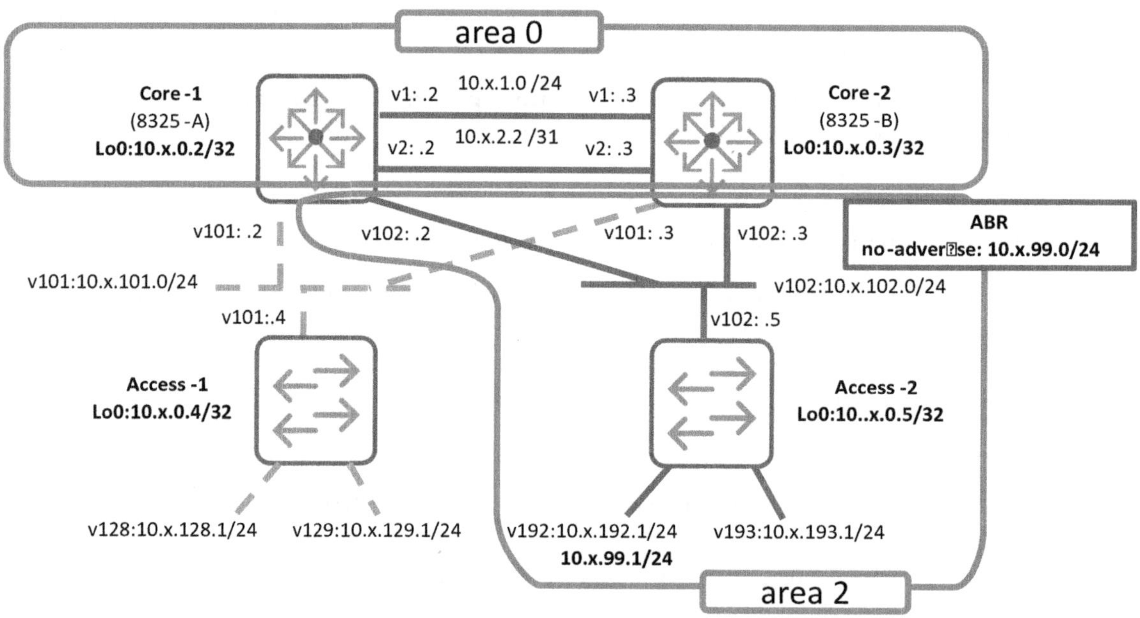

Figure 6-30 Task 5: ABR Route Filtering

On the ABR, the network administrator can also filter routes. This feature is useful in case some routes only need to be known within the local area, but they should not be advertised to the rest of the autonomous system (Figure 6-30).

Objectives

- Understand ABR route filtering
- Configure ABR route filtering

Steps

To demonstrate this, a new IP interface will be enabled on Access2 in area 2. This route will be visible to the Core1 and Core2 routers, since they also belong to area 2. Therefore, the route can be used by all the routers that belong to this area. However, the administrator does not want this route to be visible in the other areas, so a route filter will be used.

- Introduce a new subnet on Access2 in area 2.
- On the ABR, filter the route in the OSPF area 2 LSDB.
- Verify the result on Access1, a route in area 1.

1. On Access2, introduce a new route by adding a secondary IP address on the VLAN 192 interface.

```
ICX-Tx-Access2(config)# interface vlan 192
ICX-Tx-Access2(config-if-vlan)# ip address 10.x.99.1/24 secondary
```

2. On Access1, verify the route is visible in the routing table, since no filtering has been applied yet.

```
ICX-Tx-Access1(config)# show ip route 10.x.99.0
Displaying ipv4 routes selected for forwarding

'[x/y]' denotes [distance/metric]

10.x.99.0/24, vrf default
        via  10.x.101.3,  [110/200],  ospf
        via  10.x.101.2,  [110/200],  ospf
```

3. On Core1, review that the 10.x.99.0 Summary LSA exists in the area 0 database.

```
ICX-Tx-Core1(config)# show ip ospf lsdb summary area 0 | include 99.0
10.x.99.0       10.x.0.2       10          0x80000001 0x0000382f
10.x.99.0       10.x.0.3       9           0x80000001 0x00003234
```

4. Apply the filter for area 2 so the 10.x.99.0/24 subnet is not announced anymore.

```
ICX-Tx-Core1(config)# router ospf 1
ICX-Tx-Core1(config-ospf-1)# area 2 range 10.x.99.0/24 type inter-
area no-advertise
ICX-Tx-Core1(config-ospf-1)# exit
```

5. Verify that the 10.x.99.0/24 summary route is no longer listed in the area 0 database.

```
ICX-Tx-Core1(config)# show ip ospf lsdb summary area 0 | include 99.0
ICX-Tx-Core1(config)#
```

6. As a result, it will also be removed from the area 1 database.

```
ICX-Tx-Core1(config)# show ip ospf lsdb summary area 1 | include 99.0
ICX-Tx-Core1(config)#
```

7. Verify the result on Access1.

```
ICX-Tx-Access1(config)# show ip route 10.x.99.0
No ipv4 routes configured
```

All Devices

8. Save the configurations on all devices using '**write memory**'.

Redistributing External Routes into OSPF

In this section, you learn when an OSPF autonomous system (AS) might require external routes. You learn how to redistribute these routes into the OSPF AS, how the OSPF routers advertise and learn the external routes, and how they choose between external routes to the same destination.

Need for Redistributing External Routes into OSPF

Options for routes redistributed into OSPF	Example use case
Static	The OSPF router needs to advertise its default static route through an ISP router to the OSPF domain.
Another routing protocol	During a migration from RIP to OSPF, OSPF segments need to learn about RIP segments.
Directly connected	You do not want to configure connected stub networks as passive OSPF interfaces.

Figure 6-31 Need for Redistributing External Routes into OSPF

Sometimes the OSPF AS needs to learn routes to networks outside the OSPF AS. As you have learned, OSPF is a link state protocol. OSPF routers advertise network interfaces that run OSPF, and ABRs advertise inter-area routes. But sometimes an OSPF router has other routes in its IP routing table (a static route, for example), and you want the router to advertise those routes to its OSPF neighbors (Figure 6-31).

Examples include:

- A company uses OSPF internally. One or two of the company's routers connect to an ISP. They have static default routes to this ISP and need to communicate the default route to the rest of the OSPF AS.
- You are upgrading a network from RIP to OSPF. During the upgrade, some segments of the network will continue to run RIP. The OSPF AS needs to know about the networks in the RIP segment, just as the devices running RIP need to know about the networks in the OSPF segment.
- Often you make stub networks (networks with just one OSPF router) passive OSPF interfaces. However, you might choose instead to *not* enable OSPF on the stub network interfaces at all. You can redistribute connected routes into OSPF so that the router can advertise routes to these networks.

You can make any of these types of routes available to OSPF by redistributing (or importing) the routes into OSPF. In detail, you can redistribute these routes:

- Static routes
- Any routes discovered by another routing protocol supported on the routing switch, which might include:
    - RIP
    - BGP
    - Connected routes on which OSPF is not enabled

You redistribute routes by type (static, specific routing protocol, or directly connected). By default, the OSPF process receives all routes discovered by the router through the specified mechanism. You can filter the redistributed routes using route maps.

External Routes and ASBRs

The router on which you redistribute the routes is called an Autonomous System Border Router (ASBR) because it communicates routing information between the OSPF AS and other routing processes. A redistributed route becomes an *external* OSPF route, which is sometimes referred to as an AS external route. All of the routes calculated from Type 1, Type 2, and Type 3 LSAs, including both intra-area and inter-area routes, are *internal* OSPF routes.

ASBRs advertise external routes in Type 5 LSAs. The LSA includes the network address for the redistributed route, the router ID of the advertising ASBR, and the metric, which you assign when you redistribute the route into OSPF.

OSPF routers propagate the Type 5 LSA in LSUs throughout the entire AS, making Type 5 LSAs different from Type 1, Type 2, and Type 3 LSAs. (Remember: although Type 3 LSAs advertise inter-area routes, each area has its own set of Type 3 LSAs.)

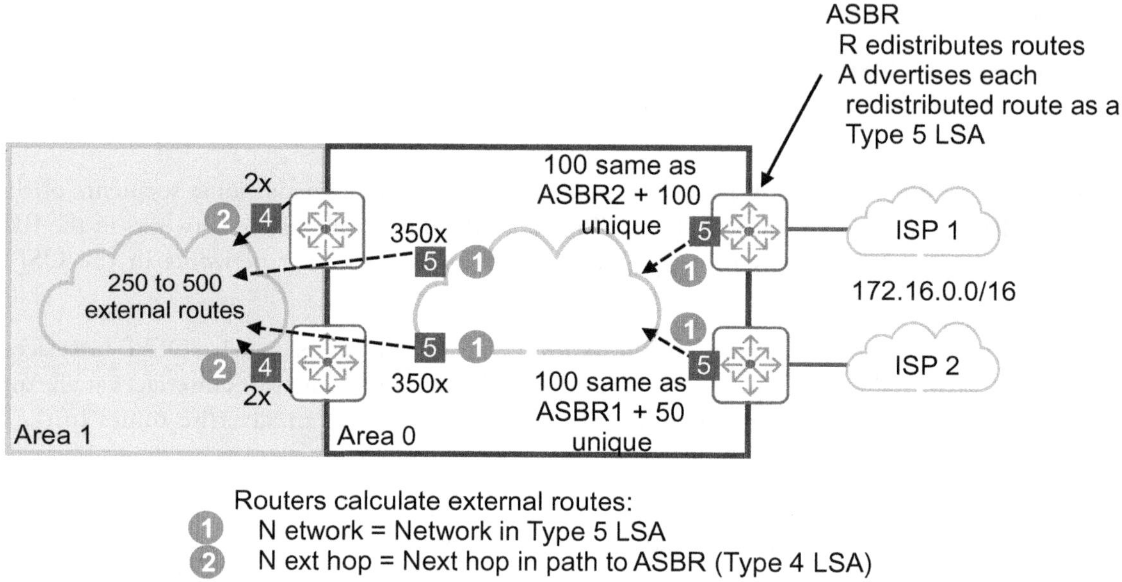

Figure 6-32 External Routes and ASBRs

To calculate an external route from the Type 5 LSA, a router refers to the LSA's advertising ASBR. The router has calculated a shortest path to each ASBR. The forwarding interface and next hop for that path become the forwarding interface and next hop for all external routes advertised by that ASBR.

In other words, routers do *not* add the external networks to the directed graph for the shortest path algorithm. Instead they add them to a list of networks for which the advertising ASBR is the gateway. Therefore, changes to the particular external networks advertised by an ASBR do not affect the area topology (Figure 6-32).

Configuring an ASBR

Configuring an ASBR is as simple as redistributing routes from another source into OSPF, like this:

```
Switch(config)# router ospf <process-id>
Switch(config-router)# redistribute {static | connected | bgp}
[route-map <map-name>]
Switch(config-router)# default-metric <metric-value>
```

By default, all the routes from the route type will be redistributed unless you employ route maps. When you redistribute routes into OSPF, they are assigned a *seed* metric to them: a beginning cost value. If you specify a default metric with the **default-metric** command, that would be applied to redistributed routes; if you want to have different metrics for different external routes, then use a route map to accomplish this task.

Note

Intra-area routes always preferred over inter-area. Inter-area routes are always preferred over external routes. These rules are applied before the cost evaluation.

OSPF Route-Map Example

By default, when you redistribute a certain type of route into OSPF, the AOS-CX switch redistributes all routes of that type. However, you can filter the routes that are redistributed at the ASBR by applying a route map to the **redistribute** command. Here is an example:

```
ip prefix-list Net10 seq 10 permit 172.16.0.0/16
route-map Net10 permit seq 10
  match ip address prefix-list Net10
  set metric-type external type-1
router ospf 1
  router-id 1.1.4.1
  area 0
  redistribute static route-map Net10
```

The route map refers to an IP prefix list that specifies the networks that you want the ASBR to redistribute into OSPF. In this example, the ASBR has several static routes, but only wants to redistribute the route to 10.10.0.0/16 into OSPF. Optionally you can set the metric type to an LSA 5 Type-1, as shown above; omitting this would have the route imported as an LSA 5 Type-2. For more information about route maps, see the Aruba *IP Routing Guide* for AOS-CX.

Here is the routing table on the ASBR:

```
ASBR# show ip route
Displaying ipv4 routes selected for forwarding
'[x/y]' denotes [distance/metric]
10.8.0.0/16, vrf default
via  10.1.100.1,  [1/0],  static
10.9.0.0/16, vrf default
via  10.1.100.1,  [1/0],  static
172.16.0.0/16, vrf default
via  10.1.100.1,  [1/0],  static
```

Notice that the last static route matches the prefix list.

Here is the LSDB entry for the redistributed route:

```
ASBR# show ip ospf lsdb external
OSPF Router with ID (1.1.4.1) (Process ID 1 VRF default)
==========================================================
AS External Link State Advertisements
--------------------------------------
LSID            ADV Router      Age        Seq#       Checksum
-------------------------------------------------------------
172.16.0.0      1.1.4.1         305        0x80000002 0x0000adef
```

Note that on the ASBR, the local static route, because its administrative distance is 1 is placed in its local routing table; however, other adjacent OSPF routers will receive the LSBD redistributed route and place that in their routing table if it happens to have the best distance and metric.

This is just a simple example of a route map.

Summary ASBR Advertisements

When a router receives a Type 5 LSA from an ASBR in the same area, it can use the area's topology to calculate the shortest path to that ASBR, the ASBR route. The next hop in this route becomes the next hop for all external networks for which that ASBR is the gateway.

Routers in different areas from the ASBR also receive the Type 5 LSA, but they need help determining how to reach the ASBR: Type 4 LSAs are used to denote the ASBRs themselves. The Type 5 LSA indicates the advertising ASBR by router ID. You have learned how to make router IDs routable. However, because OSPF does not *require* routable router IDs, it must provide another mechanism for informing routers in other areas how to reach the ASBR (Figure 6-33).

Also, even if OSPF did require routable router IDs, an OSPF router in another area might not want to use its typical inter-area routes to reach the ASBR. In areas with multiple ABRs, the ABR with the lowest cost for the broader area range might not provide the best path to the ASBR within the area.

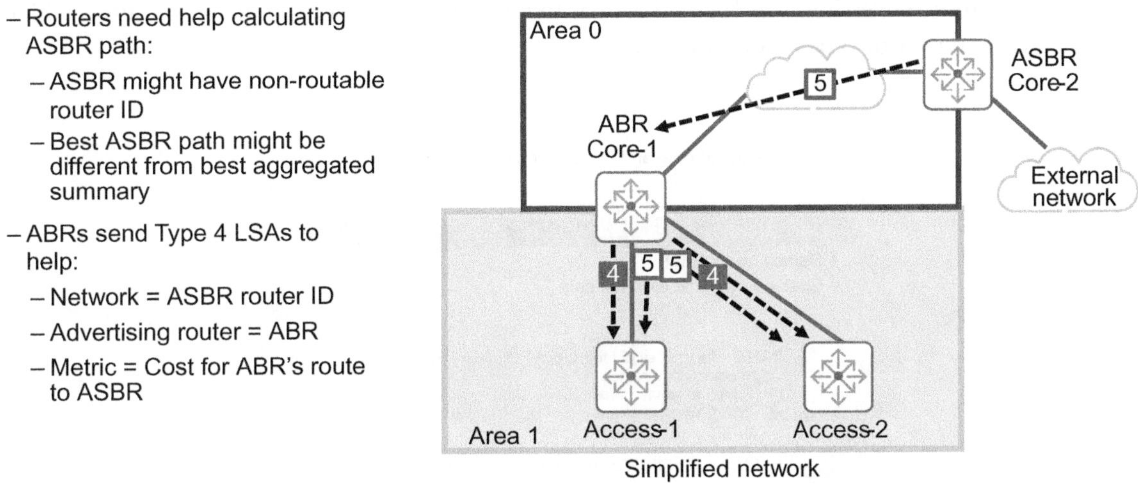

Figure 6-33 Summary ASBR Advertisements

OSPF defines the Type 4 summary LSA so that the routers in other areas can learn the best ABR through which to reach particular ASBRs. For each area, an ABR generates one Type 4 LSA for each ASBR that it can reach in *another* area. As the metric for this LSA, the ABR specifies the cost for its shortest path to the ASBR. For example, in the figure, Core-1 would specify its cost for reaching Core-2.

Internal routers that receive the Type 4 LSAs use them to select the best path to each ASBR in other areas. In this example, the choice is simple because area 1 has only one ABR.

Example OSPF External Routes (ASBR in Another Area)

The sections below provide examples of an external OSPF route learned by an internal area 1 router from the ASBR in area 0.

You can see those Type 4 LSAs in the section below. You can also see the Type 5 LSA in the router's LSDB. Note that the Type 5 LSA matches the one in area 0, and the advertising router remains the ASBR that redistributed the route. Type 5 LSAs extend across the AS. The ABR is the advertising router for the Type 4 LSA, on the other hand.

Options for External Route Metrics

You will next consider how OSPF routers choose the best external route in networks with redundant ASBRs, as well as redundant paths to the ASBRs. Multiple ASBRs might send Type 5 LSAs for the same network. The Type 5 LSA includes a metric and metric type, helping other routers to choose the best ASBR for reaching that network.

Every external route advertised in a Type 5 LSA has two important properties: the metric-type, which is an "external" type 1 or type 2, and the metric.

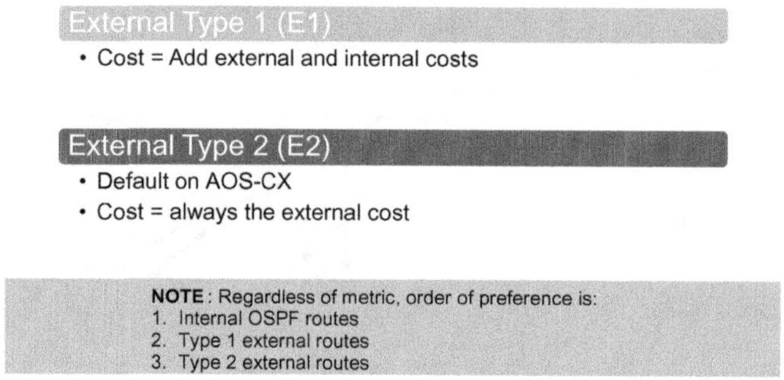

Figure 6-34 Options for External Route Metrics

By default, OSPF prefers routes based on the following order:

1. Internal OSPF routes
2. External type 1 routes
3. External type 2 routes

The ASBR that advertises the Type 5 LSA chooses the metric type and sets the metric. Figure 6-34 shows the AOS-Switch settings that you use to control default metric for all routes redistributed into OSPF on this router:

```
Switch(config)# router ospf <process-ID>
Switch(config-router)# default-metric <cost>
```

Sometimes this is referred to as the seed cost of the external route.

The following pages explain the properties of external type 1 and 2 routes in more detail.

External Type 2

Metric type 2 (external type 2) tells OSPF routers to consider external costs only; internal costs are considered negligible in comparison. In other words, routers use the route calculated from the LSA with the lowest metric regardless of the metric for reaching the ASBR. However, if multiple LSAs tie for the lowest value, the metric for reaching the ASBR is a tie breaker. If a tie occurs again, the router uses ECMP. For example, if OSPF uses metric type 2, what is Internal 1's next hop for the external route? In this case, the external route from ASBR 1's LSA 5 external type 2 has a cost of 1, and from ASBR 2's LSA 5 external type 2 has a cost of 2. Internal 1 chooses ASBR 1. Its lowest cost path to ASBR 1 is through ABR 1, so ABR 1 is the next hop (Figure 6-35).

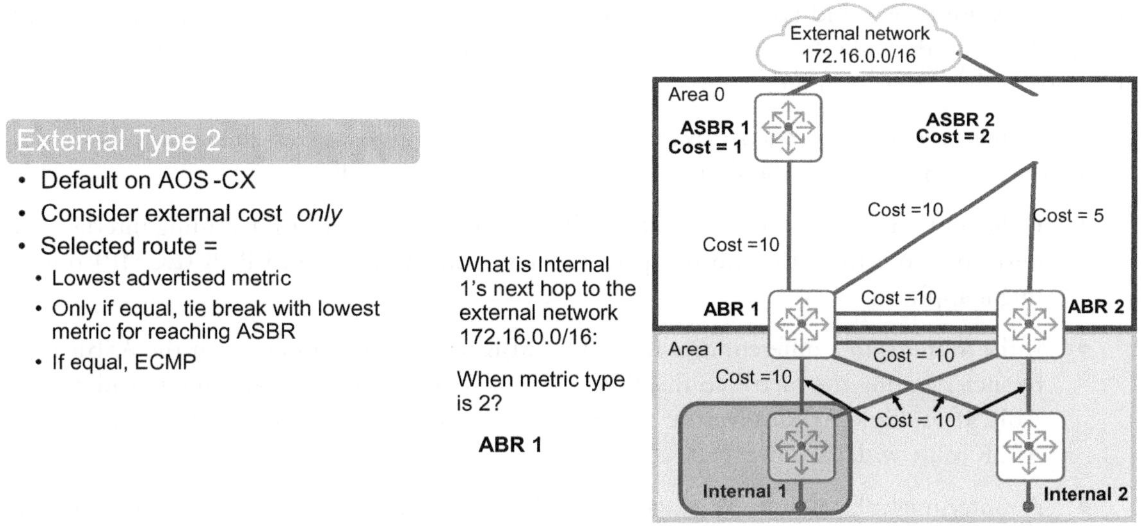

Figure 6-35 External Type 2

Choosing Best External Routes to the Same Network

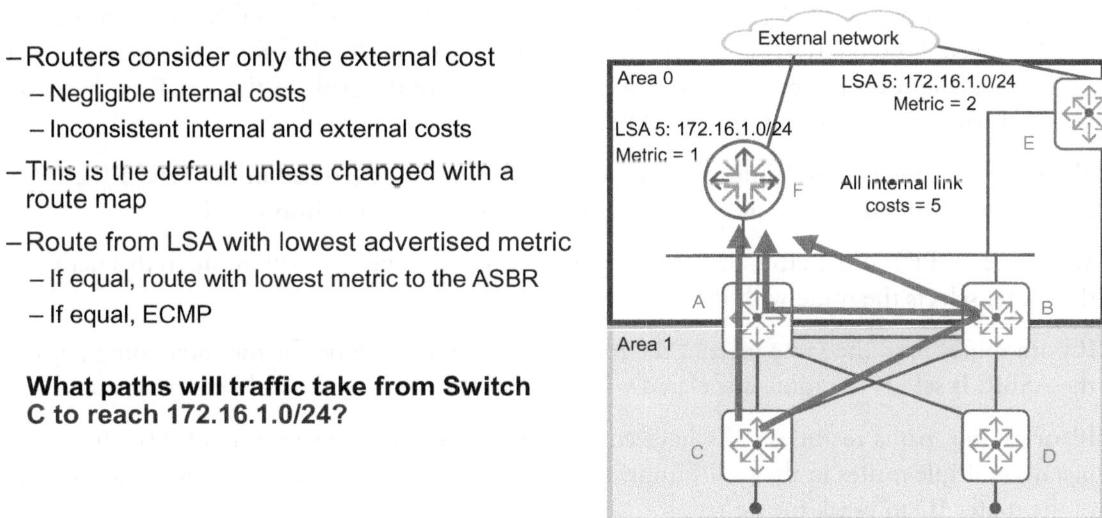

Figure 6-36 Choosing Best External Routes to the Same Network

You will now examine how OSPF routers use the metric to choose which external route to install in the routing table when they receive multiple LSAs for the same external route (see Figure 6-36).

Type 5 LSAs use type 1 and type 2 metrics. When routers examine a type 2 metric, which is the default, they consider only the metric advertised by the ASBR. OSPF follows this high-level process to choose the best external route:

1. The router uses the Type 5 LSA to calculate the external route, setting the correct forwarding interface and next hop for the shortest path to the advertising ASBR.
   - If the router is in the same area as the ASBR, it knows the correct forwarding interface and next hop from the area's shortest path topology. Equal-Cost Multi-Path (ECMP) routing might apply.
   - If the router is in a different area from the ASBR, it calculates a metric for the ASBR route by incrementing the metric in the Type 4 LSA with the metric for reaching the advertising ABR. If multiple ABRs advertise a Type 4 LSA to the same ASBR, the router chooses the ASBR route with the lower *total* cost.
   - A router might have multiple equal cost paths to an ASBR. Multiple ABRs might offer the router an equal-cost path to the ASBR, and the router has a different next hop for each ABR. Or the router might have multiple equal-cost paths to one ABR.
   - The best path might not match the IP route to the ASBR's IP address in the routing table. For example, the ABRs in the figure above advertise the same cost to the ASBRs. However, in Figure 6-26, router A and router B might advertise the same cost for the area 0 summary. However, ABR-B advertises a better Type 4 LSA for ASBR-E. Therefore, the internal area 1 routers will use their best path to router B to calculate the path to the ASBR, rather than load-balance over the link to both ABRs.
2. The router sets the external route's metric equal to the metric advertised in the Type 5 LSA. The advertising ASBR added this metric when it redistributed the route into OSPF.
3. When the OSPF routing table already includes an external (type 2) OSPF route to this network, the router selects the route with the lower metric.
4. If both routes have the same metric, the router examines the metric for the forwarding path to the ASBR. It selects the route associated with the ASBR to which it has a lower cost path.
5. If forwarding paths to the ASBRs have equal costs and the router supports ECMP, the router installs multiple routes in the OSPF routing table. (Otherwise, it uses another mechanism such as the router ID to break the tie.)

When all ASBRs use type 2 metrics, an OSPF router will always select the external route through the ASBR that advertises the lowest metric for it, *even if the router is closer to another ASBR that advertises the same route*. However, if multiple ASBRs advertise the route with the same metric, other routers do take the cost of reaching the ASBR into account.

The reasoning behind this behavior is that the cost of reaching the ASBR through the OSPF AS is often negligible compared to the cost of reaching the external network. In addition, the ASBR might not be assigning metrics to the external routes that correspond to the metrics used in the OSPF AS. In other words, a metric of 10 for the external route might not mean the same thing that a 10 metric on an OSPF link means, in terms of how strongly the company prefers using a particular path.

Note

Figure 6-38 examines the selection process when OSPF is choosing between identical *external* OSPF routes. Usually, a network advertised in a Type 5 LSA should not be associated with an internal OSPF route, but a misconfiguration could cause this situation to occur. In that case, the OSPF always prefers internal (intra-area and then inter-area) routes.

And, of course, the router uses administrative distance to choose between the OSPF route and routes learned through other means.

Discussion Questions

Which ASBR does router C, in area 1, select to reach the external route, 172.16.1.0/24?

What is the next hop in router C's external route to 172.16.1.0/24? (This router supports ECMP.)

What if both F and G advertised the 172.16.1.0/24 network with the some initial (seed) cost, say for example a metric of 1? How would that effect the routing for A, B, C, and D? (Hint: ECMP)

External Type 1

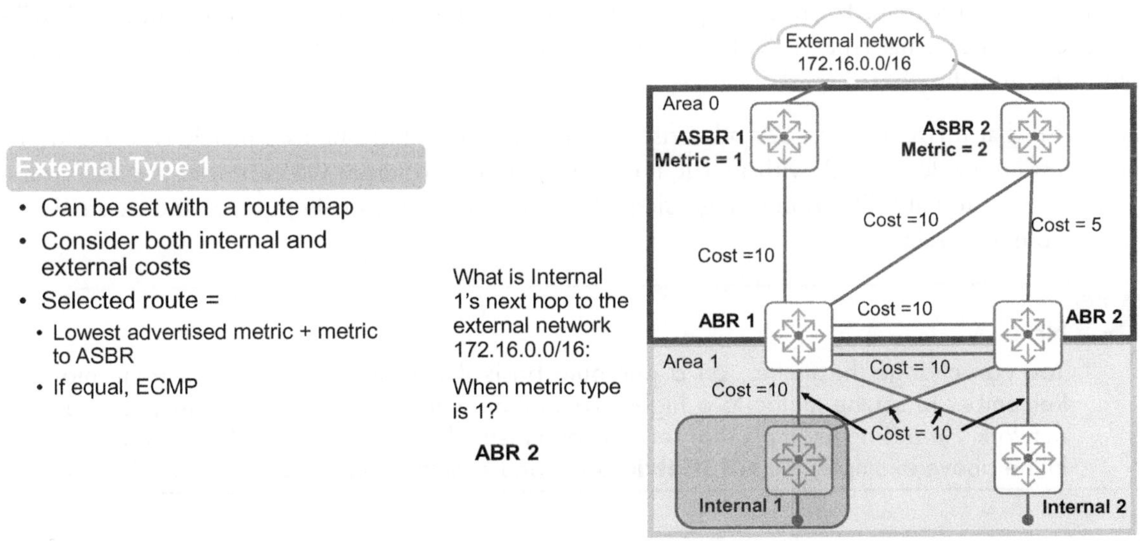

Figure 6-37 External Type 1

To change the LSA metric-type (type 1 or 2), you must use a route map (Figure 6-37). Here is an example of a route map that assigns the metric type a type 1 for 172.16.0.0/16:

```
ip prefix-list router1ext seq 10 permit 172.16.0.0/16
route-map ospf_from_static permit seq 10
  match ip address prefix-list router1ext
  set metric-type external type-1
  set metric 10000
  exit
router ospf 1
  redistribute static route-map ospf_from_static
  exit
```

The prefix list specifies the routes to match. The **type-1** metric in the **set metric-type** command defines a type-1 route. **type-2** is the default. The redistribute command will redistribute the matching route into OSPF if it is static.

Metric type 1 tells routers to consider both internal and external costs when selecting the best ASBR. That is, the router adds the advertised metric in an external LSA to the metric for reaching the advertising ASBR. It selects the external route through the ASBR with the lowest total cost. If a tie occurs, ECMP lets the router add multiple routes. In this example, which route to the external network would Internal 1 select when type 1 metrics area used? ASBR 1 advertises an LSA with metric 1. The cost for Internal-1 to reach ASBR 1 is 20 for a total of 21. ASBR 2 advertises the same route with metric 2. The cost for Internal 1 to reach ASBR 2 is 15 for a total of 17. So Internal 1 chooses a route through ASBR 2, and ABR 2 offers the shortest path to ASBR. ABR 2 is the next hop.

AOS-CX switches require extra setup to use metric type 1. When you redistribute the routes, you must apply a route map. The route map is configured to match the routes that you want to redistribute and to set external type 1. Without this extra configuration, the AOS-CX switches use metric type 2 for all redistributed routes.

Note also that if two Type 5 LSAs advertise the same network, but one uses metric type 1 and one uses metric type 2, the LSA with metric type 1 is preferred. Internal OSPF routes are also always preferred to external OSPF routes, regardless of metric, although usually internal and external networks do not overlap.

Note

You can change the metric, on a per-route basis if necessary, by using a route map. Remember to set the metric to a higher value than what is used internally in your OSPF network. Here is an example that sets the seed metric for 172.16.0.0/16 to a high value. In the above example, the **set metric** command specified an initial metric of 10,000.

Choosing Between External Routes to the Same Network: External Type 1 Example

Sometimes the cost of reaching the ASBR is not negligible. In that case, you might want routers to take the cost of reaching the ASBR into account when selecting the ASBR for a particular external network (as opposed to the path to the already selected ASBR). Use a type 1 metric, which signals routers to add the cost of reaching the ASBR to the metric advertised in the Type 5 LSA. You should also ensure that ASBRs redistribute the external routes with metrics that make sense when compared to costs used within the OSPF process (Figure 6-38).

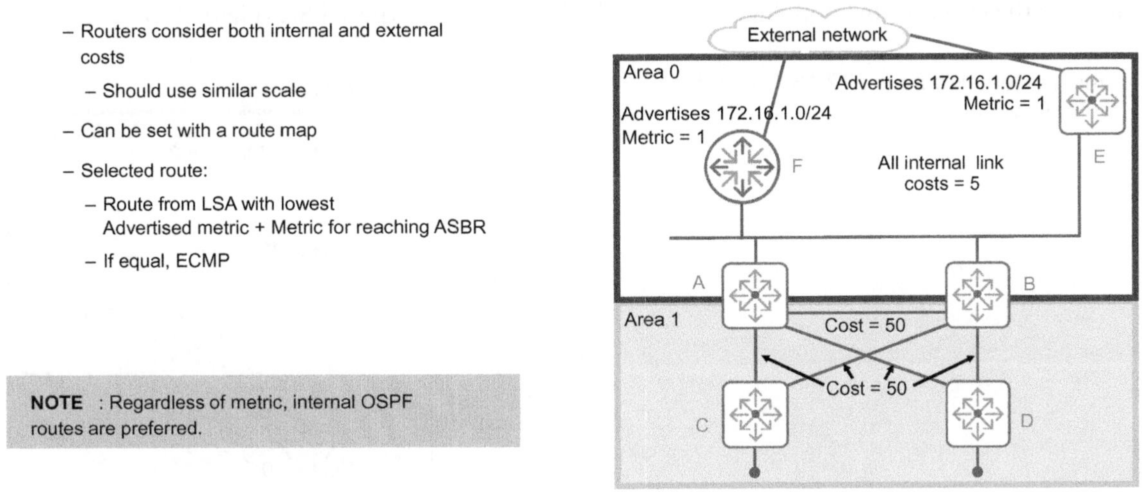

Figure 6-38 Choosing Between External Routes to the Same Network: External Type 1 Example

In more detail, an OSPF router chooses between type 1 external routes to the same network as follows:

1. The router uses the Type 5 LSA to calculate the external route, setting the correct forwarding interface and next hop for the path to the advertising ASBR.
2. The router sets the external route's metric equal to:

   The metric advertised in the Type 5 LSA + the metric for the forwarding path to the advertising ASBR
3. When the OSPF routing table already includes an external (type 2) OSPF route to this network, the router selects the route with the lower metric.
4. If both routes have the same metric, the router installs multiple routes in the OSPF routing table. (Otherwise, it uses a mechanism such as router ID to break the tie.)

Discussion Questions

Which ASBR does router C, in area 1, select to reach the external route, 172.16.1.0/24? Is this choice different from the choice when ASBRs use type 2 metrics?

What is the next hop in router C's external route to 172.16.1.0/24? (This router supports ECMP.)

Choosing Between External Routes to the Same Network: External Type 1 Example (cont.)

Consider the effects of this topology when the ASBRs advertise Type 1 LSA (Figure 6-39).

– Which external route to 172.16.1.0/24 does router C select?

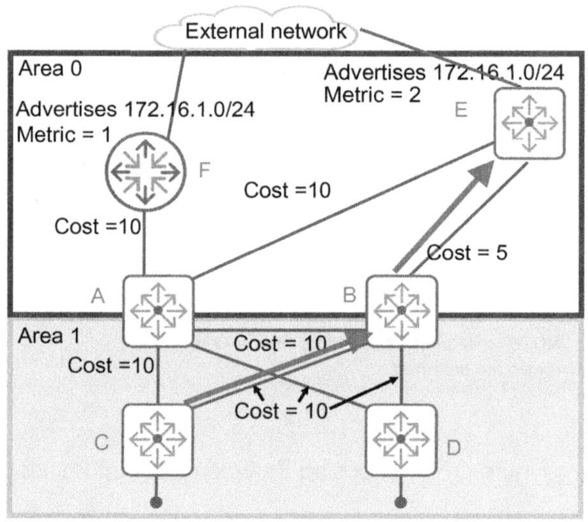

Figure 6-39 Choosing Between External Routes to the Same Network: External Type 1 Example (cont.)

Discussion Questions

Which ASBR does router C, in area 1, select to reach the external route, 172.16.1.0/24? Is this choice different from when the ASBRs use type 2 metrics?

What is the next hop in router C's external route to 172.16.1.0/24? (This router supports ECMP.)

External Type 1 versus External Type 2: Which Would You Use?

–You want to leverage all paths to destinations:

External Type 2 with the same default metric

–You want to use the closest exit point:

External Type 1 with the appropriate seed metric

–You want to have a primary exit with a secondary backup exit:

External Type 2, the primary with a lower default metric than the secondary

–You want to ensure traffic through a firewall is seen in both directions:

External Type 2 with the appropriate seed metric to prefer one primary path

Figure 6-40 External Type 1 versus External Type 2: Which Would You Use?

Figure 6-40 helps determine which LSA 5 external type(s) you should use based on the policy you are trying to implement.

OSPF Area Types

You will now explore the use of area types to more easily deal with external routes in OSPF.

Need for Eliminating Excessive External Routes

The internal routers in some OSPF areas often do not require all of the external routes.

Remember the primary benefit of individual Type 4 and Type 5 LSAs. The Type 5 LSAs help routers choose the best ASBR for reaching a particular external network. If that ASBR is in another area, Type 4 LSAs further help the routers choose the best ABR for reaching that ASBR. (Depending on the external metric type, the Type 4 LSA might also help the routers select the best ASBR.) You should examine each non-backbone area and determine whether routers in the area truly need to choose between paths for particular external networks.

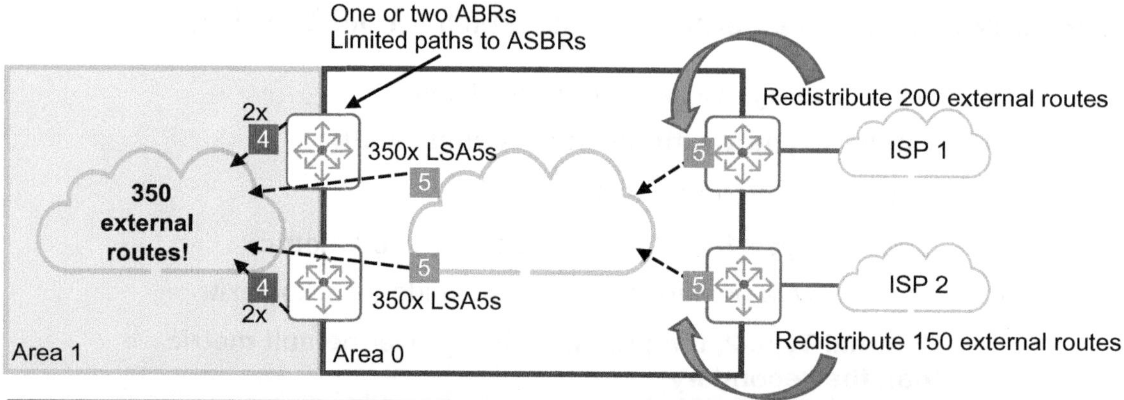

Area type	Intra-area routes	Type 3 LSAs Inter-area routes	Type 5 LSAs External routes
Normal	☑	☑	☑
Stub	☑	☑ + default route	
Totally stub	☑	Default only	

Figure 6-41 Need for Eliminating Excessive External Routes

First, consider whether the area includes any ASBRs. If it does not, then all external traffic must pass through the area's ABRs. The number of ABRs in the area restricts the number of paths for external routes. If the area has only one ABR, the area has only one path for external traffic. A default route through the ABR provides the same benefit as individual external route advertisements much more efficiently (Figure 6-41).

If the area has multiple ABRs, internal routers *might* benefit from choices for external paths. As you learned, these choices extend not just to choosing the best ASBR but also the best ABR for reaching a particular ASBR. You need to assess, however, whether the internal routers truly receive a benefit from this level of detail and choice. In many cases, the ABRs offer roughly equivalent paths to the external networks, so the internal routers can receive the same benefit from a default route advertised by both.

Often internal routers in some OSPF areas do not require all of the Type 5 LSAs and the external routes. Instead, they use a default route to cover all external traffic. The main value in a router's maintaining specific external routes is that the router can choose a different next hop for routes to different external networks, based on factors such as cost. However, an area often has only one or two exit points in the form of ABRs, and the internal routers will be choosing the same next hop or hops for all external routes.

In this case, you might choose to filter the Type 5 LSAs at the area boundary. You do so by configuring the area as a special type: stub and totally stubby. These area types reduce the Type 3, 4, and/or 5 LSAs by only advertising a default route. Stub and totally stubby areas are discussed further in the next few pages.

Using Stub Areas to Eliminate External Routes

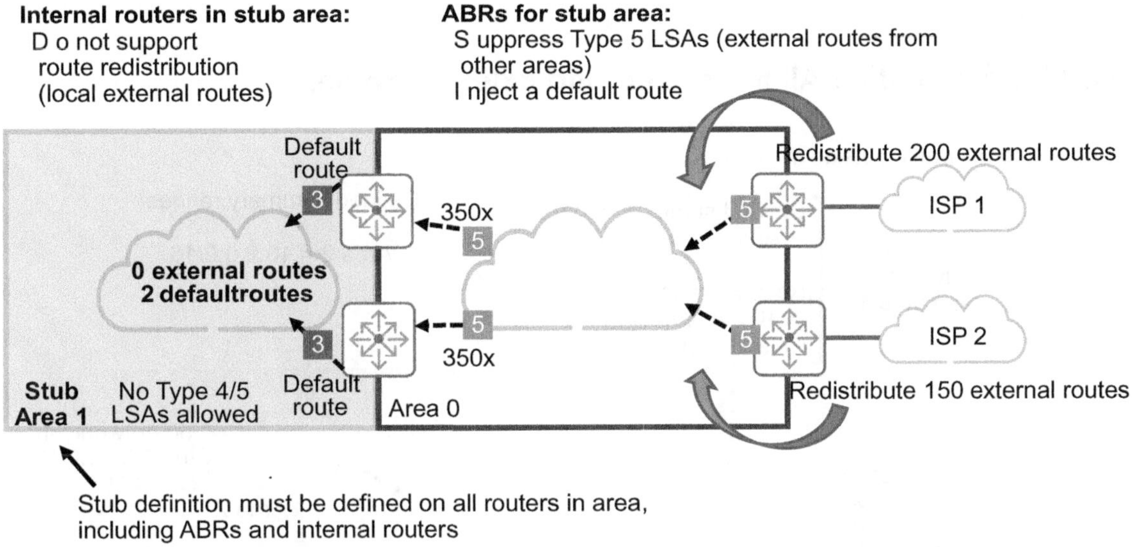

Figure 6-42 Using Stub Areas to Eliminate External Routes

To eliminate external routes and advertisements from an area, define the area as a stub area (Figure 6-42). ABRs for stub areas do not forward Type 4 or Type 5 LSAs into those areas, and internal routers in those areas do not generate or accept them. You must define the stub area setting on each OSPF routing device within the stub area as well as the ABR. Otherwise, the devices cannot become neighbors and establish adjacency.

When you activate this option on the ABR, it automatically generates a default route, which it injects as a Type 3 LSA into the stub area. As usual, the ABR assigns a metric to the default route, and you can manipulate metrics to set up one ABR as a preferred exit for external traffic.

Note that, although Type 3 LSAs for inter-area routes are not shown in this picture, the stub area acts like a normal area in this respect. It receives summary LSAs for other areas through ABRs; the summary LSAs include individual or aggregated routes as configured on the ABRs. Therefore, internal routers in the stub area can continue to select the best path for inter-area traffic, based on the cost of the summary routes advertised by the ABRs.

The OSPF command for configuring a stub area:

```
Switch(config)# router ospf <process-id>
Switch(config-router)# area <area-ID> stub
```

In this case, you might choose to filter the Type 5 LSAs at the area boundary. You do so by configuring the area as a special type. In this example, area 1 is a stub area. The area 1 ABR suppresses all Type 5 LSAs at the boundary. It begins to advertise a default route in a Type 3 LSA and routes from other areas of our OSPF domain (Type 3 LSA). Type 5 LSAs are also suppressed within the area; in other words, internal routers in area 1 cannot redistribute routes. Area 2 is a totally stub area (which is a stub area) but the ABR also suppressed Type 3 LSAs with inter-area networks. It sends only the default route.

Need for Eliminating All Inter-Area and External Routes

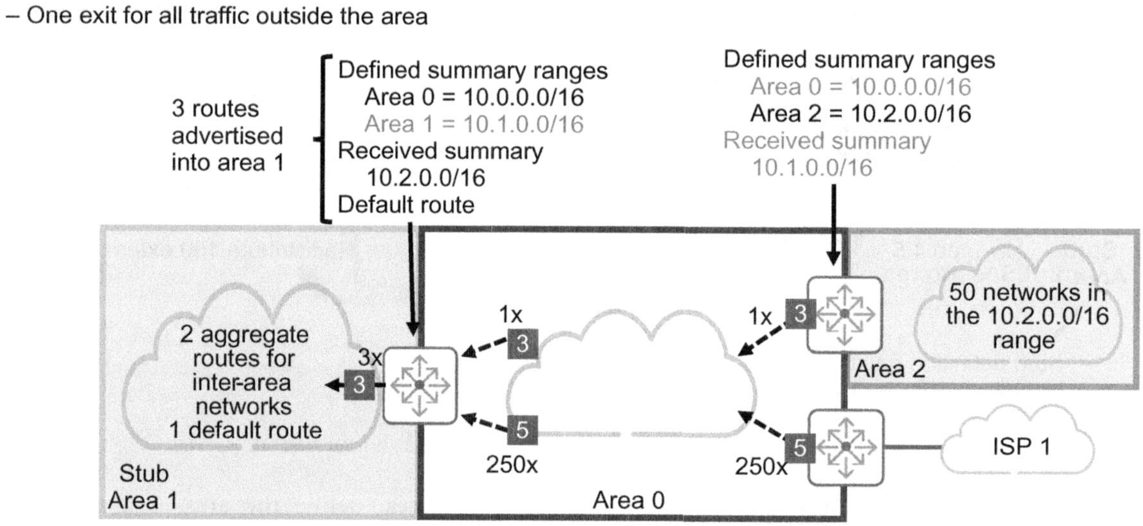

Figure 6-43 Need for Eliminating All Inter-Area and External Routes

In the example network above, area 1 is a stub area. All traffic destined to it terminates there. In addition, the area has only one exit for all non-local traffic, including traffic destined to the backbone, to other OSPF areas, and to the ISP. In such an environment, the internal area 1 routers do not gain a benefit from multiple inter-area routes (Figure 6-43).

You can configure the OSPF system to suppress all inter-area routes in this area in addition to all external routes.

Using Totally Stubby Areas

You define a totally stub area by configuring the ABR or ABRs connected to that area to suppress summaries. You enter this OSPF configuration on all ABRs that connect to the area:

```
Switch(config)# router ospf <process-id>
Switch(config-router)# area <ID> stub no-summary
```

The **no-summary** option is what transforms a stub area to a totally stub area. This command suppresses all external route advertisements as normal for a stub area. It also prevents the ABR from generating non-aggregated summary routes for this area. For example, the ABR in Figure 6-46 would not generate area 1 summary LSAs for the routes that the ABR knows to area 0 and area 2 networks. Instead, the internal routers in area 1 use the default route to reach the other areas.

- Area defined as stub on all routers in the area
- Required on ABRs only: Stub definition has "**no-summary**" option
- ABRs connected to totally stub areas:
  - Suppress summaries (Type 3 LSAs)
  - Suppress external route advertisements (Type 4 and 5 LSAs)
  - Inject a default route only

Figure 6-44 Using Totally Stubby Areas

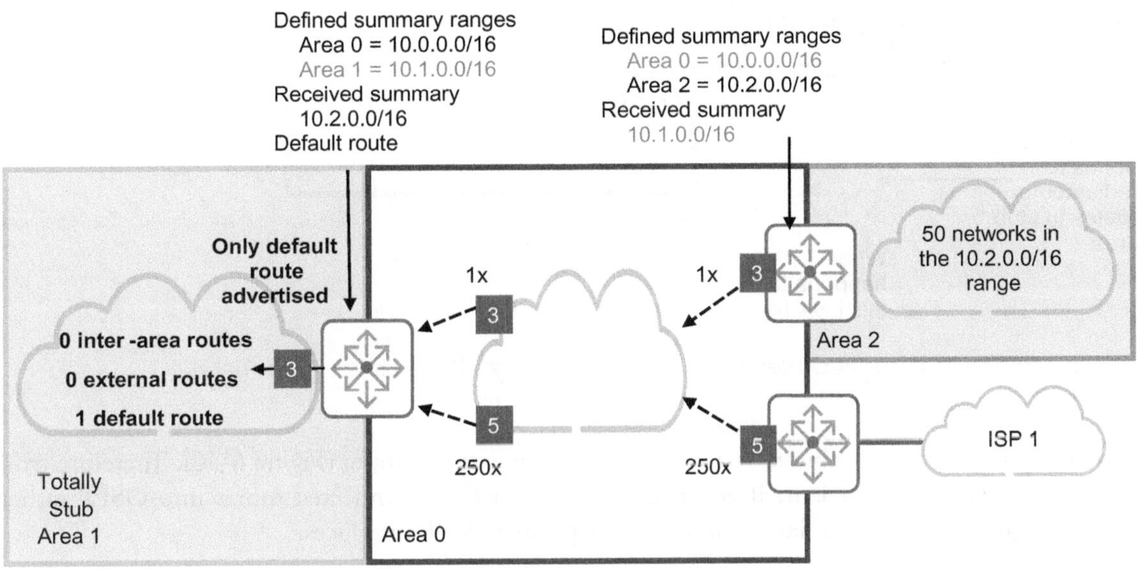

Figure 6-45 Using Totally Stubby Areas (cont.)

Note

Other routers in the area that are non-ABRs only need to be configured as a stub (Figure 6-44 and 6-45).

The ABR can suppress inter-area routes in the NSSA, in which case it advertises only a default route (now as a Type 3 LSA).

Need for Advertising External Routes into a Stub Area

A stub or totally stub area might have its own local connection to an external network. The area would still benefit from a suppression of external routes from other sources. You should define the area such that the internal OSPF routers receive the local external routes but not external routes from other areas.

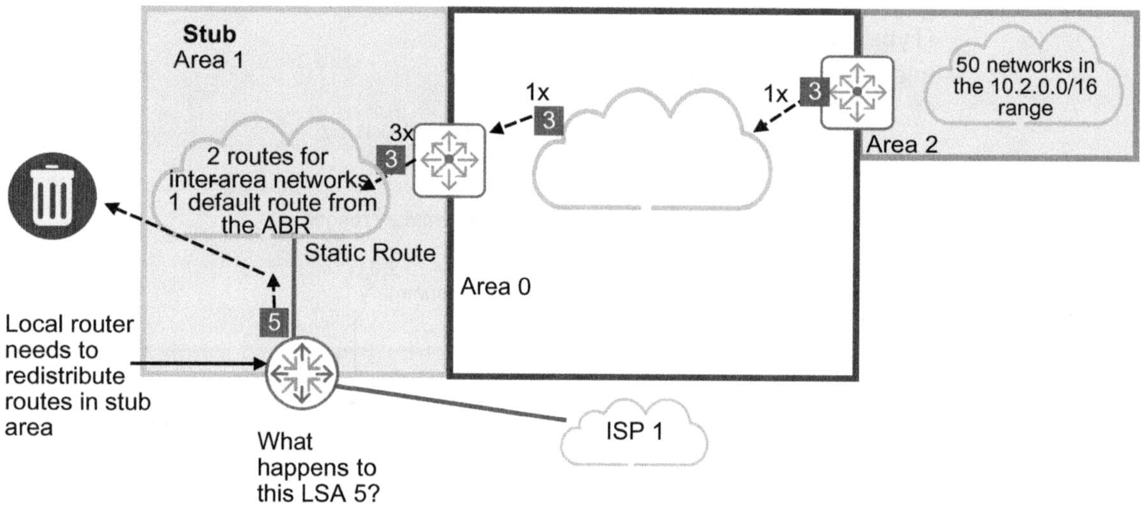

Figure 6-46 Need for Advertising External Routes into a Stub Area

Remember that any redistributed route is defined as an external route (Figure 6-46). Therefore, you would encounter a similar issue if you decided to redistribute connected routes into OSPF rather than configure the associated layer 3 interfaces as passive OSPF interfaces.

Using Not-So-Stubby Areas (NSSAs)

A not-so-stubby area (NSSA), as shown in Figure 6-47, furnishes the solution for this problem. You must define this area type on every OSPF router in the area.

The OSPF configuration is:

```
Switch(config)# router ospf <process-id>
Switch(config-router)# area <ID> nssa
```

An NSSA acts like a stub area. However, the area permits external routes that are advertised in OSPF by a local ASBR. These external routes are carried in Type 7 LSAs.

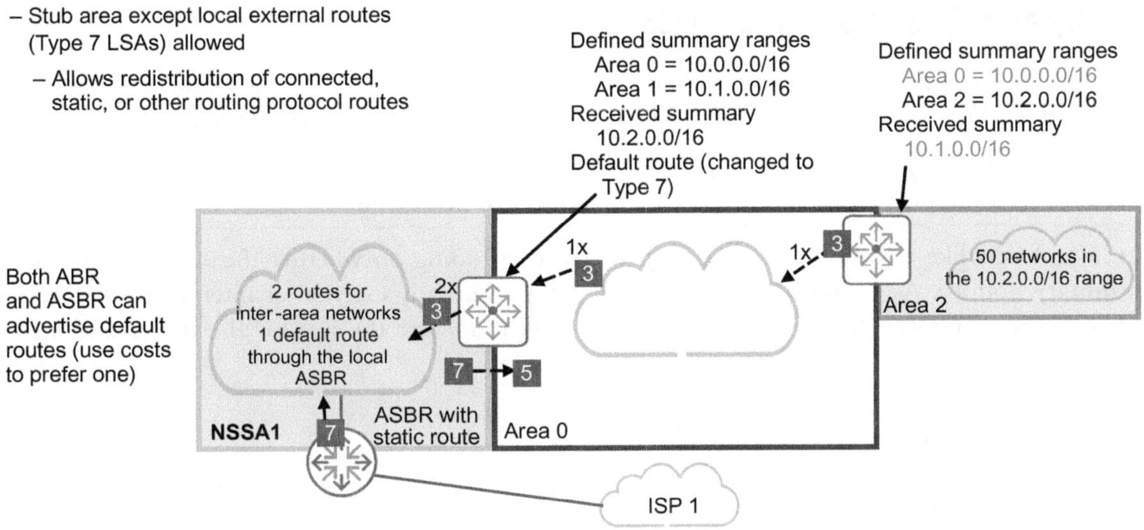

Figure 6-47 Using Not-So-Stubby Areas (NSSAs)

Of course, you must configure the local ASBR to redistribute routes, advertise a default route, or both, as you learned in the section on configuring ASBRs and external routes. Like other ASBRs, the NSSA ASBR assigns a metric (type 1 or type 2) to the external routes that it advertises in OSPF, which you can adjust to influence route selection. For NSSA external routes, these are designated as N1 and N2 respectively and are similar to the E1 (type 1) and E2 (type 2) routes for a normal area.

The ABR translates the Type 7 LSAs (N1 and N2) into area 0 as Type 5 LSAs (E1 and E2) that it appears to originate. The ABR still filters Type 5 LSAs from other areas and does not advertise them in this area. It also continues to advertise a default route in the NSSA, but as a Type 7 LSA rather than a Type 3 one. If the NSSA's ASBR advertises a default route as well, you must adjust metrics such that your routing devices prefer the route that you want them to prefer.

In this example, area 1 is a not so stubby area (NSSA). As for a stub area, the ABR suppresses Type 5 LSAs. However, internal routers in the area can redistribute routes. These special ASBRs use Type 7 LSAs to advertise the external routes within the area. The ABR can translate the Type 7 LSAs to Type 5 LSAs for advertisement in the backbone. The ABR can optionally aggregate the LSAs with a **range** command set to the **nssa** type. You can filter the ranges with the no-advertise option if you want to keep the NSSA external routes local. In software 10.1, AOS-CX ABRs always advertise a default route in NSSAs, although the OSPF standard allows ABRs not to do so. This default route uses a Type 7 LSA rather than a Type 3 LSA. If the local ASBR also advertises a default route, use metrics to make routers prefer the local or backbone route, as you prefer.

Totally Not-So-Stubby Areas (NSSAs)

You can also set up an NSSA area as a totally not-so-stubby area, similar to a totally stubby area (Figure 6-48). You only need to add the **no-summary** option to the area configuration:

```
Switch(config)# router ospf <process-id>
Switch(config-router)# area <ID> nssa no-summary
```

An NSSA acts like a stub area or totally stub area (depending on whether the ABR uses the **no-summary** option). As a totally NSSA, the ABR will prevent any external or inter-area routes from entering the area; instead, the ABR will inject a default route into the area for all external and inter-area routes.

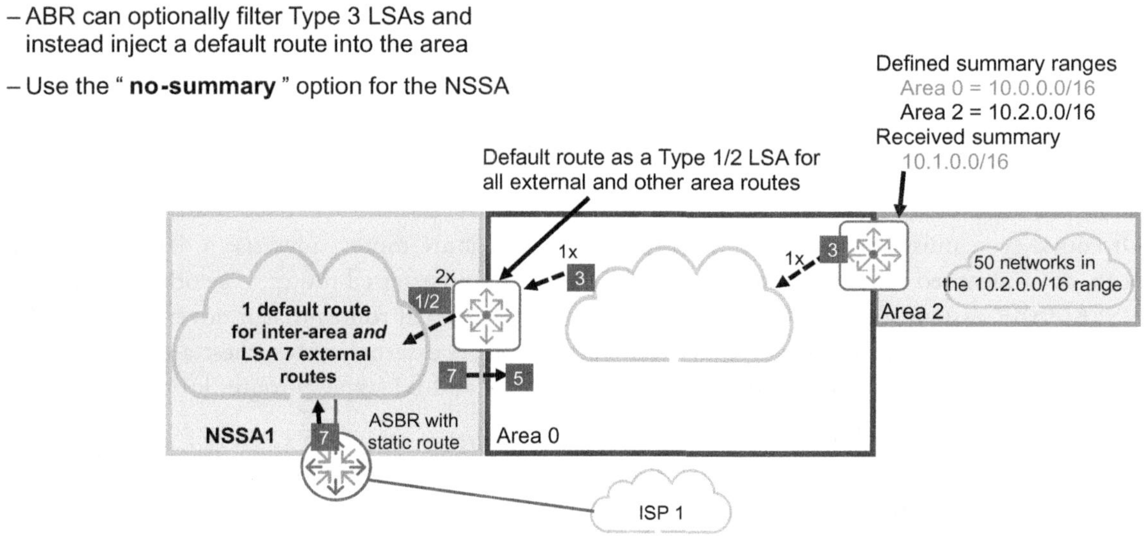

Figure 6-48 Totally Not-So-Stubby Areas (NSSAs)

Review: Factors that Affect OSPF Route Selection

Before moving on, take a moment to review what you have learned (Figure 6-49). Consider Router C, an internal router in area 1, which is a stub area with two ABRs, Router A and Router B. For intra-area routes such as that to 10.1.20.0/24, link costs alone determine the best path and selected next hop. In other words, if the cost of the C-to-B link + the B-to-D link is less than the cost of the C-to-A + the A-to-D link, C will use B as the next hop. If the costs are the same, C will learn two routes and use a hash to assign conversations to each.

Link costs also play a large factor in determining how C forwards inter-area traffic such as that destined to 10.2.20.0/24. Remember, though, that C is using 10.2.0.0/19 route for all traffic destined to area 2 (10.2.0.0 to 10.2.31.255). You need to consider the link costs from C to its ABRs and then from those ABRs to the area 2 ABRs. At that point, you add the cost of the 10.2.0.0/19 summary that the area 2 ABR advertises. In other words, the cost set for the summary range on the area 2 ABR influences the path for the inter-area traffic destined to that area, but a router's cost for reaching that ABR is also taken into account.

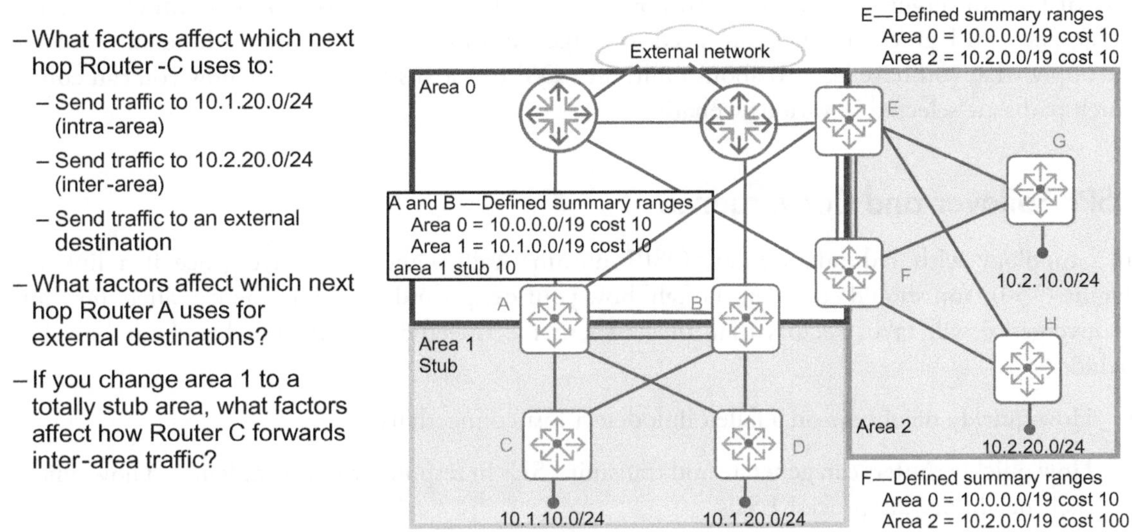

Figure 6-49 Review: Factors that Affect OSPF Route Selection

Because this is a stub area, Router C uses a default route to reach external destinations. It chooses the default route based on the metric advertised by the ABR and the cost for reaching the ABR. The next hop is the next hop in the best path to the advertising ABR. So, the next hop for the default route is affected by link costs within area 1 and the cost set in the **area 1 stub** command on the ABRs.

More factors affect Router A's choice of next hop for routes to external destinations. The metric type (1 or 2) advertised by the ASBRs plays a role, as does the advertised metric itself. Link costs within area 0 can also affect the choice. If ASBRs use Type 1 LSAs, these costs are incremented with the advertised metric when Router A chooses the best of two external LSAs for the same destination. Even if ASBRs use Type 2 LSAs, the area 0 costs will still affect Router A's best path to the ASBR that advertises the best LSA.

As a final review, pretend that you have changed area 0 to a totally stub network. In this case, Router C uses its default route for both inter-area and external OSPF routes. Therefore, the ways to influence how Router C forwards inter-area traffic are to manipulate the link costs within area 1 and the cost in the **area 1 stub** command on the ABRs.

Implementing OSPF Redundancy

You will now explore redundant OSPF networks. You will begin by exploring how to predict and control path selection in complex and redundant networks.

You will then explore how to ensure that OSPF systems with redundant links provide the required level of fast convergence. You will learn how features such as Bidirectional Forwarding Detection (BFD) and OSPF graceful restart can speed convergence. You will also examine redundant topologies and apply what you have learned about multi-area OSPF systems to determine how you can control which paths are selected in various scenarios.

OSPF Failover and Convergence

In a topology with redundant links, OSPF automatically handles reconvergence if a link fails (Figure 6-50). You should consider, though, how your design and configuration can affect how long reconvergence will take. Factors that affect whether connectivity is disrupted and for how long include:

- How quickly neighbors on a failed link detect lost connectivity
- How quickly routers can generate and transmit LSUs in response to the problem and how quickly their neighbors can process LSUs
- How many routers have to re-run the shortest path algorithm and how much of the algorithm they have to run
- How far LSUs withdrawing LSAs need to propagate (the more routers that need to receive and generate updates, the longer it takes for the system to converge)

When a link or a router fails:

- How quickly do neighbors detect lost connectivity?
- How quickly can routers generate, transmit, and receive LSUs
- How far do LSUs need to propagate?
- How many routers have to rerun the shortest path algorithm?

Type of link to neighbor	Time for removing neighbor relationship depends on:	Typical times:
Ethernet dedicated VLAN on direct links	Time for detecting Layer 2 issue and bringing the VLAN interface down	Under a second
Ethernet with indirect links: Multiple routing devices on the network Intervening Layer 1 or Layer 2 devices	Interface OSPF dead timer	40 seconds (default) 1 seconds (minimum)

Figure 6-50 OSPF Failover and Convergence

Set aside the first factor for a moment. (You will look at ways to speed lost neighbor detection as the next topic.) For the next factor, the default timers often provide sufficiently speedy LSU generation and propagation. When very fast convergence is required, you can adjust OSPF timers such as the LSA generation interval. However, in most cases, you should leave the intervals at their defaults; tuning them is beyond the scope of this guide.

For the third and fourth questions, consider how what you have learned about multi-area designs help to stabilize the system and enhance convergence.

Area borders act as boundaries for changes, and often LSUs generated by a change within the area will not prompt LSUs for other areas. In addition, only changes within the OSPF area cause a router to re-run the full shortest path algorithm. Updates to summary, summary-ASBR, and external LSAs require just a partial re-run. The router simply adds a new network to the list of networks reachable behind the ABR, removes a network from the list, or adjusts the cost for reaching the network. The router does not need to re-calculate and run the shortest path algorithm because it cares only about the segment of the inter-area path between itself and the proper ABR for reaching the inter-area network. Those paths have not changed.

For example, assume Router B loses its link to Router C. Routers in area 1 learn this information, and begin Router D and B route all traffic to 10.1.10.0/24 through Router A. However, Router A and Router B still have a route to this network, so they do not withdraw its Type 3 LSA for the subnet. It might need to update the cost, but usually it will not even need to do that because it is aggregating the area 1 summaries anyway. As far as routers in area 0 and area 2 are concerned nothing has changed. As you see, changes and any attendant disruptions are isolated to area 1.

In a well-designed OSPF AS with proper area boundaries, the time to detect failed neighbor relationships often determines how seamlessly OSPF routes fail over.

Here you are examining a situation in which an OSPF router has lost its connection to the next hop in one of its routes. Either a link has failed or the neighbor as a whole has failed. To remove the invalid route and begin using an alternate, the OSPF router must detect the failure of the next hop neighbor in the primary route. Often the detection of the problem makes up the bulk of the time required for routes to failover.

When two neighbors have a point-to-point connection on a direct link, the status of the interface correlates rather well to the status of the neighbor. If the neighbor fails, the interface with the direct connection goes down.

The router can immediately remove any routes through that interface. Similarly, when a VLAN interface is dedicated to a single physical link, the failure of that link brings the VLAN interface down. The routing switch can then remove any routes through that interface.

In either case, the time to detect the link layer problem affects the time for detecting the failed neighbor relationship. This time varies depending on the media and is acceptable for many companies' needs.

However, sometimes the status of an OSPF interface and the status of an OSPF neighbor do not directly correlate. Examples relevant to AOS-CX switches include:

- The neighbors connect on a broadcast network such as a VLAN but the VLAN has multiple links, and possibly multiple neighbors, associated with it.
- The neighbors do not have a direct Layer 2 connection. For example, a non-routing switch intervenes between two OSPF neighbors.
- The neighbors have a direct Layer 2 connection, but problems occur at Layer 3. For example, a misconfiguration has prevented one of the neighbors from implementing OSPF on the network.

In those cases, the OSPF router must rely on the OSPF timers to determine the neighbor status. That is, if the dead time expires without a hello from the neighbor, the router considers the neighbor down and removes routes using that neighbor as a next hop from the routing table. The OSPF dead timer is always four times the hello timer. Because the default hello timer is 10 seconds, the default dead timer is 40 seconds, which is far too long for contemporary networks.

You can adjust the hello and dead timers, but the lowest standard hello timer is 1 second, making the lowest dead timer 4 seconds, still too long for many contemporary networks:

```
switch(config)# interface <interface-ID>
switch(config-if)# ip ospf hello-interval <seconds>
switch(config-if)# ip ospf dead-interval <seconds>
```

Note

Care should be used when setting the dead interval timer. The dead timer, by default, is 4 times the hello timer. Typically, it is not recommended to set the hello and dead interval timer to 1 second each, since this could cause inadvertent missed hellos.

OSPF and Bidirectional Forwarding Detection (BFD)

– OSPF BFD speeds detection of a lost neighbor on a broadcast network

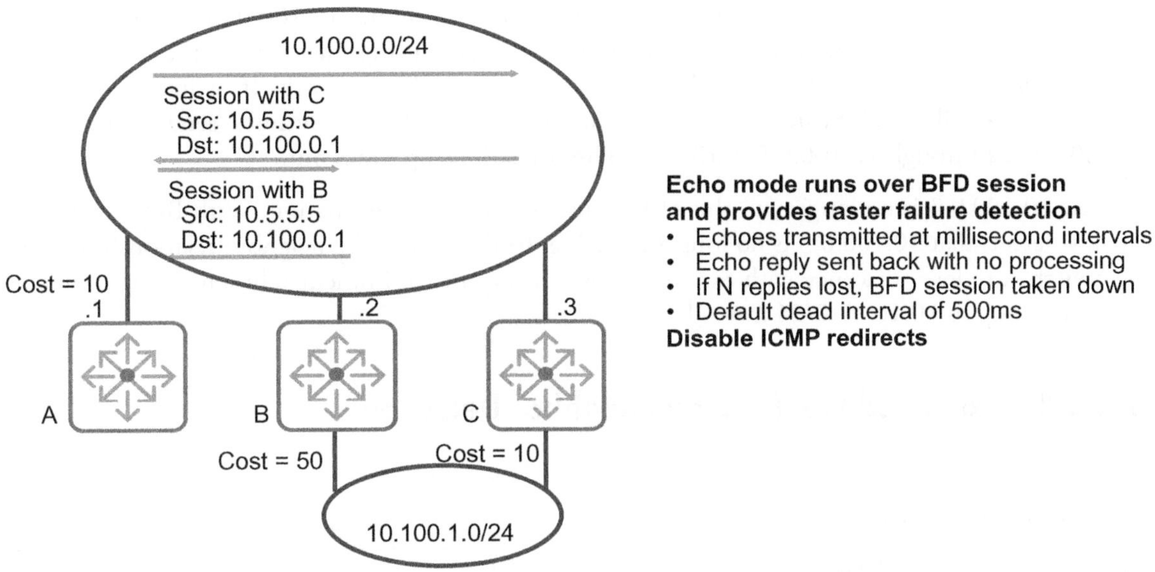

Figure 6-51 OSPF and Bidirectional Forwarding Detection (BFD)

There are several ways you can help OSPF respond quickly and gracefully in the event of topology changes such as failed link.

For point-to-point links on routed ports and link aggregations, link status is directly correlated with Layer 3 interface status. If the physical link between the switches goes down, the Layer 3 interface also goes down, and OSPF immediately knows to remove the neighbor on that interface. But on broadcast networks, an AOS-CX switch could have no change in its own link status but still lose contact with a neighbor.

For example, if router C loses its connection on the 10.100.0.0/24 broadcast network, Router A is still connected to this network. In this situation it would take router A the OSPF dead time to detect that it can no longer reach router C and should stop sending traffic to 10.100.1.0/24 through it. The dead time is 40 seconds by default; you can lower it to 1 second at minimum, but Aruba recommends at least 4 seconds with 1 second hellos.

Bidirectional Forwarding Detection (BFD) provides a standard, reliable mechanism for detecting failed neighbors in any of the cases you examined in Figure 6-50.

BFD tests the connectivity between two IP addresses in a BFD session (see Figure 6-51). BFD reports when connectivity is lost. The router (or routing switch) can then use that information to take the appropriate actions, depending on the functions to which you have tied BFD.

When you enable OSPF BFD on an OSPF layer 3 interface, BFD assumes responsibility for testing connectivity to the neighbor. If the BFD session fails, the switch removes the BFD neighbor relationship, enabling the switch to remove all LSAs through that neighbor and update routing paths. (The interface still sends out OSPF hellos, but BFD will generally detect any problems first).

For example, in Figure 6-53, three routing switches connect on subnet 10.100.0.0/24. Switch B and Switch C also connect to network 10.100.1.0/24. Switch A is using Switch C as the next hop for 10.100.1.0/24 because Switch C has the lower cost link on this network. If Switch C's link on 10.100.0.0/24 fails, and Switch A is not using BFD, Switch A continues sending traffic to 10.100.1.0/24 through 10.100.0.3 until its neighbor relationship times out.

Because 10.100.0.3 is no longer up, this traffic does not reach its destination. With BFD, Switch A quickly detects that 10.100.0.3 is no longer available. BFD removes the neighbor relationship, causing Switch A to lose adjacency with Switch C. Switch A can then immediately start using Switch B as the next hop to 10.100.1.0/24 instead.

Using BFD to Speed OSPF Failed Neighbor Detection

Enabling BFD

Next enable BFD globally.

```
Switch(config)# bfd
```

When you enable BFD, it automatically enables in echo mode. There is a **bfd echo disable** command, which disables echo mode, but this is not *recommended*. Use the **no** form of the command to re-enable.

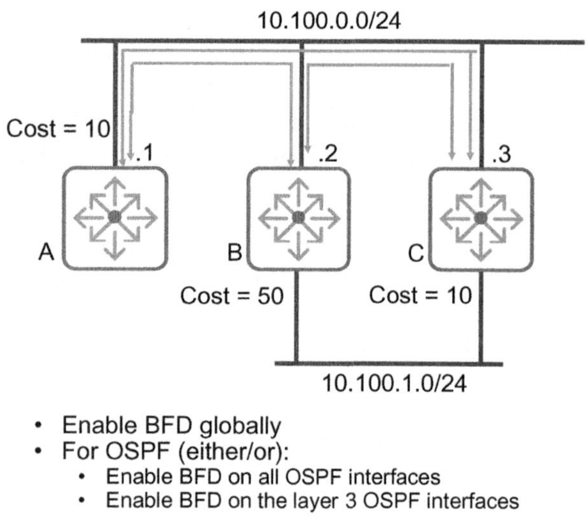

BFD sessions on A

IP source	IP destination
10.100.0.1	10.100.0.2
10.100.0.1	10.100.0.3

BFD sessions on B

IP source	IP destination
10.100.0.2	10.100.0.1
10.100.0.2	10.100.0.3

BFD sessions on C

IP source	IP destination
10.100.0.3	10.100.0.1
10.100.0.3	10.100.0.2

Figure 6-52 Using BFD to Speed OSPF Failed Neighbor Detection

Enabling BFD on OSPF Interfaces

Next you can either enable OSPF BFD on all interfaces in the OSPF context. Or you can enter the desired Layer 3 interface context, and enable BFD on that interface specifically.

```
Switch(config)# router ospf <process-ID>
Switch(config-router)# bfd all-interfaces
```

-Or-

```
Switch(config)# interface <interface-id>
Switch(config-if)# ip ospf bfd
```

Because AOS-CX switches use active mode, the interface automatically attempts to establish a BFD session with each OSPF neighbor on that interface. It transmits a unicast BFD control packets on UDP port 3784 to each neighbor. As you see in Figure 6-52, a BFD session is point-to-point. In this example, the 10.100.0.0/24 network has three OSPF routers, each of which implements OSPF BFD. Each router will attempt to establish a session with each of its two neighbors for six total BFD sessions on the network.

Note

If an OSPF neighbor does not support BFD, the switch continues to try to establish a BFD session with that neighbor. It lists the session as down, but, because the session was never up, the down state does not cause the switch to tear down the neighbor relationship.

To establish a BFD session, the neighbors simply determine that both support BFD and negotiate timers.

BFD Control Messages and Asynchronous Mode

Each neighbor in the session has its own active Tx timer, which determines how often it transmits BFD control packets. You do not configure the active Tx timer manually. Instead this timer derives from the Min Tx and Min Rx timers, which are configurable intervals on each OSPF interface. An interface's active Tx timer in a particular BFD session is the *larger* of two values: its Min Tx timer (the Tx timer that the interface wants to use) and its *neighbor's* Min Rx timer (the smallest interval at which the neighbor can receive control packets).

Each neighbor in the session also has its own detect timer, which determines how long the interface can go without receiving a control packet from the neighbor before taking the session down. When the session goes down, the switch tears down the OSPF neighbor relationship even if the dead timer has not yet expired.

The detect timer derives from the detect multiplier configured on the interface multiplied by the *neighbor's* active Tx timer, which in turn is the larger of the neighbor's Min Tx timer or this interface's

Min Rx timer. You can set the interface's Min Rx timer to 0 if you do not want the switch to track control messages; in this case, the switch will not tear down the session if it fails to receive control messages from the peer.

In short, an interface's Min Tx timer determines how quickly a neighbor can detect a control message timeout. The interface's Min Rx timer determines how quickly *this* interface can detect a neighbor no longer sending control messages. However, the neighbor values will also affect these settings, if they are larger. The detect multiplier also affects how quickly this interface detects failed neighbors; the default is 5, and you can lower it to 4 or 3 if you have a reliable link that loses little traffic. If you set the Min Tx and Min Rx timers to the minimum value (1 second), do not set the detect multiplier lower than 3.

The active Tx timer and detect time on the two neighbors in a BFD session do not have to match. However, they often do.

When the switch uses the control message timeout alone to determine when a session fails, it operates in asynchronous mode. In this mode, BFD does not provide sub-second detection of issues, which is often what you want from BFD. Therefore, you should usually enable OSPF BFD to operate in echo mode.

ICMP Redirects

It is also best practice to disable ICMP redirects on the switches that use BFD in echo mode. Before you enable OSPF BFD, you should disable ICMP redirects on the AOS-CX switch. In some cases, the echo could have a source and destination on the same subnet, which would usually trigger the switch to send an ICMP redirect. The extra processing can cause issues on the switch. Disabling ICMP redirects prevents these issues.

```
Switch(config)# no ip icmp redirect
```

Echo Messages

If you want, you can adjust the BFD timers, but Aruba recommends the default values (see the *AOS-CX Command-Line Interface Guide* for more details on how to do this.

You should set up BFD in the same way on all the OSPF routers connected on the interface.

In echo mode, control messages still maintain the BFD session, but echo messages, which are transmitted at sub-second intervals, allow BFD to respond to issues much more quickly. The interface implementing BFD sends an echo message to the other side of the session. The other side of the session simply echoes the message back without processing it. If the interface does not receive its echo message back, BFD takes down the session and the OSPF neighbor relationship. (The switches still exchange control messages in echo mode, but these become less important for determining when the session has failed.)

Echo Source IP Address

By default, AOS-CX switches support echoing echo messages back to their BFD neighbors at a 500ms interval. However, they will *not* send echo messages themselves until you set a global BFD echo source for the packets, which is *not* set by default on the 8400s. Until you set the address, the BFD session will have echo mode disabled. You should choose a unique "dummy" IP address that is *not* used on this device.

On the 8400 switches, you should next set a global echo mode IP address, which the switch includes as the source IP address for the echo packets in all sessions. Remember that the destination is the switch's own IP address, so the source is just a "dummy" address. It should be an IP address on a subnet you're not using on the switch or the network. You cannot set this address on 8320 or lower switches.

```
Switch(config)# echo-src-ip-address <IPV4-ADDR>
```

This sets the source IPv4 address for BFD echo packets. This address is used in all echo sessions. The source IP address must not be on the same network segment as any switch interface, otherwise a large number of ICMP redirect packets may be sent by the remote device, causing network congestion.

The switch uses this as the source for the echo packets. The destination is the switch's own IP address, which allows the neighbor to send message back without processing it. Setting the source IP address to a different subnet ensures that the neighbor does not have to process the packet and send ICMP redirects.

Using OSPF with VSX

Now that you have learned about OSPF in depth, briefly review how the protocol works with VSX. When a VSX pair runs OSPF, each member of the pair runs the protocol separately. In this example, two aggregation layer switches, Agg-1 and Agg-2, are a VSF pair. They have a VSX link aggregation to a core routing switch, and each switch has its own IP address on the Layer 3 VLAN interface assigned to the LAG. (If you were using multiple VRFs, the LAG would carry multiple VLANs; but in this example, the LAG has just one VLAN.) The core switch learns ECMP routes to the VLAN 10 and 20 subnets through both Agg-1 and Agg-2. Because the ECMP next hop selection algorithm will not necessarily match the link aggregation selection algorithm, the core switch might send traffic through next hop 10.0.0.1 but on the link to Agg-2. The active forwarding, which is set per-VLAN, enables Agg-2 in this situation to route the traffic itself even though the traffic was destined to 10.0.0.1. You should typically enable active forwarding on every OSPF interface that is a transit network.

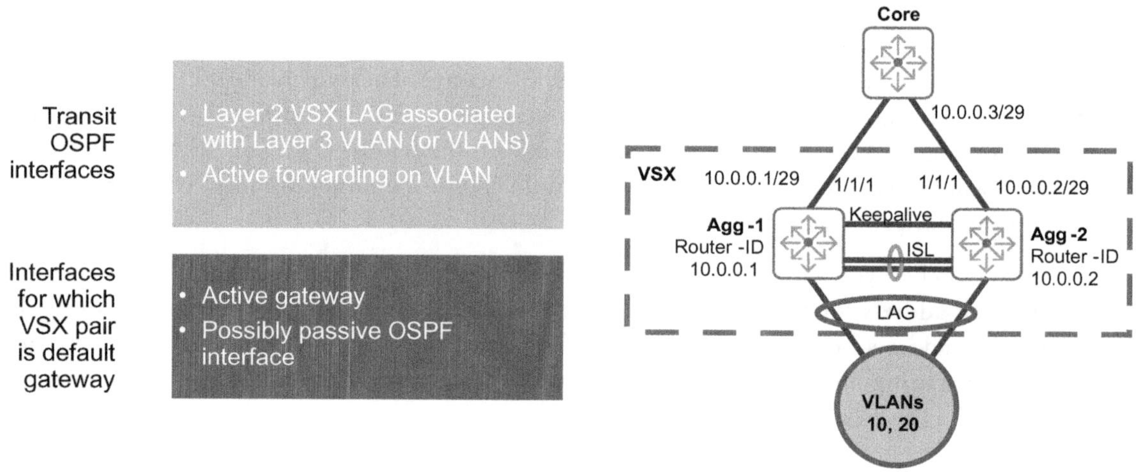

Figure 6-53 Using OSPF with VSX

The VSX pair is probably the default gateway for subnets such as those associated with VLANs 10 and 20. You should typically set up the active gateway feature on those VLANs. As you learned, this feature enables the VSX switches to act as active-active default gateways for a subnet. You might be running OSPF on these subnets, but you could do so in passive mode since the VSX peers do not need to become OSPF neighbors on all of the subnets (Figure 6-53). (Alternatively, you could redistribute connected routes into OSPF.)

Implementing Additional OSPF Features

As a final topic, you will look at several additional features that you might need to implement in various situations.

The Need for Graceful Restart

Next consider situations in which an OSPF system includes routers that also implement other protocols for high availability. You have explored several ways to ensure redundancy of the default router (or routing switch):

- Virtual Switching Framework (VSF) (preferred when possible on the 6300s)
- Virtual Router Redundancy Protocol (VRRP)
- VSX (with chassis-based switches employing dual management cards)

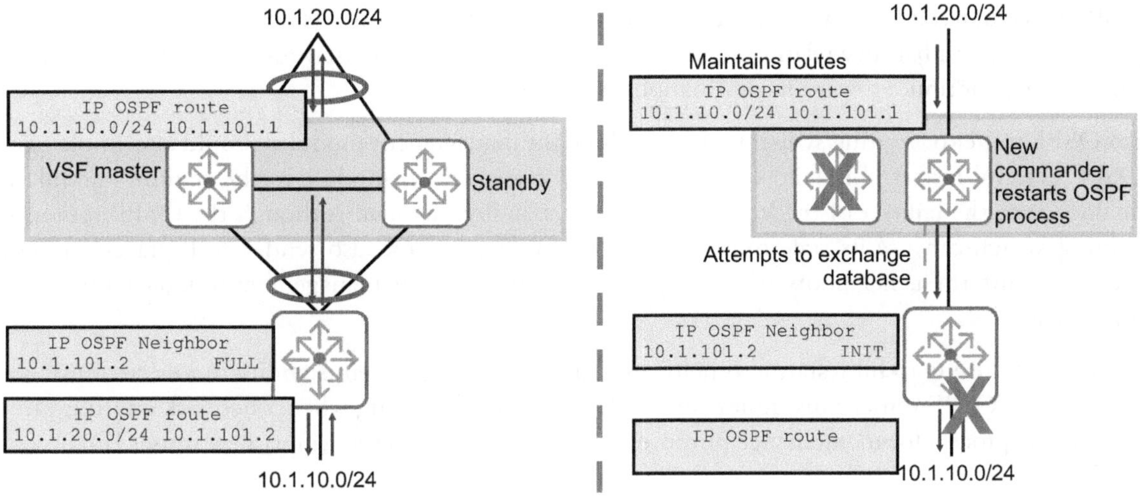

Figure 6-54 The Need for Graceful Restart

However, simply ensuring that the default gateway functions are maintained does not ensure that failure of the VSF master or VRRP master does not disrupt the routing system as a whole. When you use VSF, OSPF graceful restart ensures non-stop routing as the standby member takes over as the master. Figure 6-54 illustrates why graceful restart is necessary.

The master of the VSF fabric maintains routing tables and routing protocol information in its control plane. (In a chassis switch, the master's primary management module maintains this information.) The master proxies this information to other members' control planes, but if the master fails, the routing processes must restart on the new master.

The VSF members have routes proxied to the forwarding information databases (FIBs) in their control planes (or the control planes of their LPUs, in the case of chassis-based switches). They can continue to route traffic with these stale routes until the new master builds the routes in its own control plane—and, when the VSF fabric is using static routes or Routing Information Protocol (RIP) routes, they do seamlessly.

However, standard OSPF does not allow OSPF neighbors to entirely resynchronize the LSDBs without tearing down the old adjacency relationship. Therefore, when the new master tries to re-establish adjacency, the VSF fabric's neighbors take down the neighbor relationship and send out LSUs as if the fabric were no longer available. Routes reconverge away from VSF fabric—even though the fabric is perfectly capable of routing the traffic—causing unnecessary disruption to the traffic flow and possible interruption to service.

OSPF graceful restart, on the other hand, enables the VSF fabric to ask its neighbors to maintain the neighbor and/or adjacency relationship undisturbed while the new master restarts the OSPF process. Thus, traffic continues toward its destination undisturbed.

An OSPF router or routing switch that has redundant management modules should also implement OSPF graceful restart. The failover of the primary management module to the standby module is analogous to the failover of the VSF master to the standby member. Although the OSPF router or routing switch can use its stale routes to forward traffic, it must also send OSPF graceful restart requests to inform its neighbors not to drop its LSAs while the new management module rebuilds the adjacencies.

Note that OSPF graceful restart also helps to maintain routing system stability in *any* circumstance in which an OSPF router must restart its OSPF processes, including when a network administrator restarts the process for maintenance purposes (such as applying configuring a new router ID).

OSPF Graceful Restart Process

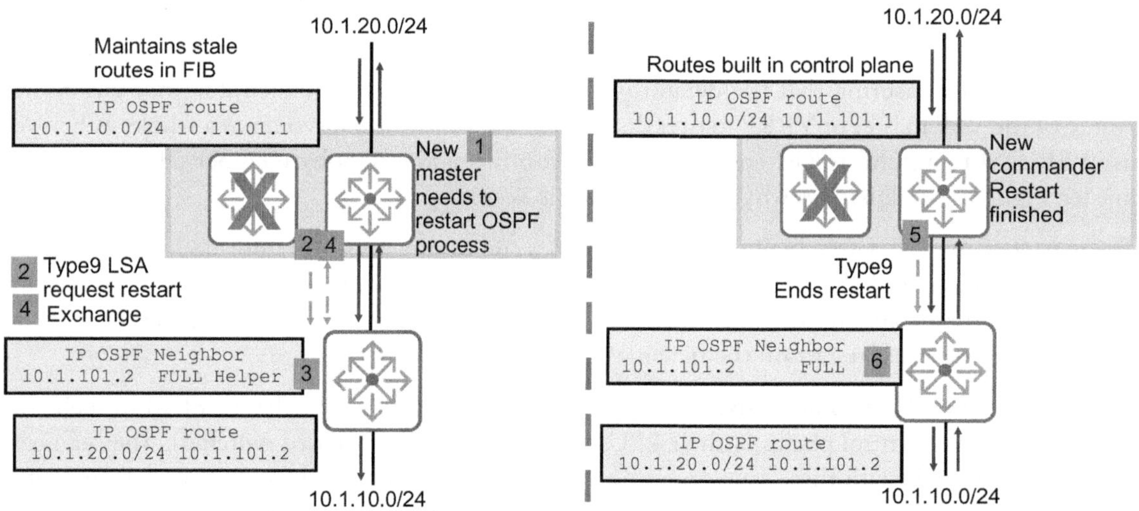

Figure 6-55 OSPF Graceful Restart Process

When an OSPF router restarts the process—for example, because a main management module fails and a redundant one takes over—it must re-establish neighbor relationships. This triggers the router's neighbors to clear the router and its LSAs out of the topology. Routing is disrupted across the network until the router finishes restarting the process. AOS-CX switches support OSPF graceful restart, which lets an OSPF router restart the process without causing disruptions for traffic (Figure 6-55).

Now that you understand when and why graceful restart is required, you can examine the IETF standard graceful restart process:

1. The switch configured to support graceful restart, or the GR Restarter, determines that it needs to restart its OSPF process.
   As you learned, this often occurs when a new VSF member takes over the master role or when a redundant management module takes over.
2. The GR Restarter sends a Type 9 opaque LSA, or grace LSA, to its neighbors, which requests that the neighbor(s) transition to graceful helper mode. The LSA includes:
   - A grace period timer, which specifies how long the neighbors stay in graceful helper mode
   - A graceful restart reason:
     - 0 = Unknown
     - 1 = Software restart
     - 2 = Software upgrade
     - 3 = Failover from an active to a standby management module, or, for VSF, failover from master to standby
   - The GR Restarter's IP address
3. The neighbors, which must be configured as IETF standard GR Helpers, place the GR Restarter in graceful restart mode. In this mode, they behave as if they have full adjacency with the GR Restarter no matter what is actually occurring. Therefore, the GR Helpers continue routing traffic to the GR Restarter and maintain LSAs from it, trusting that the GR Restarter can truly continue to route traffic with its stale routes.
4. During this time, the GR Restarter is establishing neighbor relationships and adjacencies with the GR Helpers. As always during this process, the switch obtains LSAs advertised by OSPF routing devices throughout the area. Some of these LSAs were advertised by itself (or the previous VSF master); the Restarter labels those LSAs as stale.
5. After the GR Restarter has established adjacency with all of its neighbors, it sends a grace LSA, requesting that the Helpers leaver helper mode (the grace period time is set to 0).
6. The GR Helpers leave helper mode. However, because they have achieved adjacency with the GR Restarter, they continue to route traffic to it without interruption.

GR Restarter has continued routing traffic with stale routes. However, it must ensure the truth of what it asked the GR Helpers to trust: it knows the correct routes, and the topology that it advertised before the restart remains accurate. During and after the process of establishing adjacency, the GR Restarter recalculates routes, changes stale routes to active routes, and determines whether any updates are necessary:

- The GR Restarter calculates routes from the LSAs that it received from OSPF neighbors. The new routes replace the stale routes. If any stale routes remain, they are deleted as no longer valid. The GR Restarter now knows that it is routing traffic with the most up-to-date information.
- The GR Restarter generates its own LSAs and compares them to its own stale LSAs, which it received from the Helpers. Unless its connections have changed, the GR Restarter's LSAs will match its stale LSAs. The GR Restarter removes the stale designation from those LSAs and takes no further action (its neighbors already know the LSAs).
- If the GR Restarter has generated any new LSAs, it advertises them to neighbors as normal in an LSU message. Similarly, if any stale LSAs remain (no matching current LSA), the GR Restarter deletes those LSAs and withdraws them in an LSU message.

The GR Restarter and the GR Helpers now know the proper LSAs, network topology, and routes. Throughout the process, all of the OSPF routing switches continued routing traffic with stale routes, only removing the routes if they were demonstrated to be truly invalid. Because the stale routes typically prove to be valid, the routing switches typically transition seamlessly from routing with stale routes to routing with active routes.

Note

The OSPF graceful restart standard dictates that GR Helpers must leave helper mode if the topology changes in a way that would affect the GR Restarter. That is, the GR Helper generates or receives an LSA that it would normally send to the GR Restarter. This provision prevents routing loops.

Implementing OSPF Graceful Restart

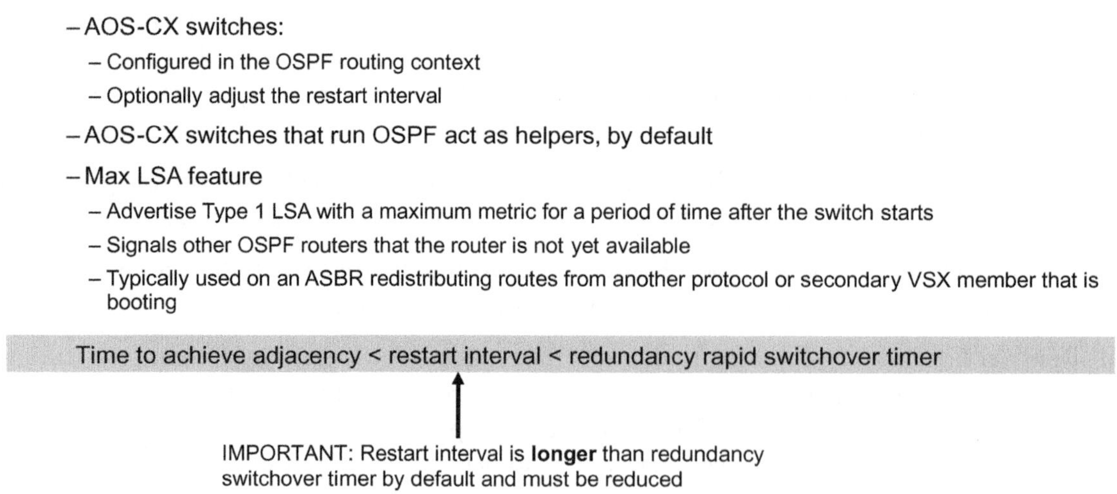

Figure 6-56 Implementing OSPF Graceful Restart

Now that you understand why you need to enable OSPF graceful restart, doing so is simple. Configure VSF fabrics, as well as routing devices that must support non-stop routing during management module failover, as GR Restarters. As a best practice, you could also enable the restarter function on other routing devices that support it, protecting the network in case an administrator accidentally restarts the OSPF process in a live environment (Figure 6-56).

All neighbors of the GR Restarters must act as GR Helpers. As a best practice, you should generally ensure that all OSPF routing devices in the AS support this function.

There are a few steps you need to complete to configure a graceful restart on the AOS-CX switch. Graceful restart itself is *always* enabled and cannot be disabled. Graceful restart helper is *enabled* by default, but can be disabled. However, you can adjust the graceful restart timer (defaults to 120 seconds) and enable or disable the helper function:

```
switch(config)# router ospf <process-ID>
switch(config-ospf)# graceful-restart restart-interval <seconds>
switch(config-ospf)# graceful-restart helper
```

After this timer expires, the switch removes any stale routes—that is, routes not recalculated from the reconstructed LSDB. The restart interval dictates the amount of time that the switch promises its neighbors that it can continue to route traffic while it achieves adjacency and reconstructs the LSDB. Therefore, the rapid switchover time must exceed the restart interval. (For example, exceed the restart interval by 3 seconds.)

Note

All AOS-CX switches automatically have graceful restart enabled (it cannot be disabled). All AOS-CX switches automatically act as GR Helpers.

The max LSA feature is another feature than can smooth OSPF convergence. This feature tells the OSPF router to send out a Type 1 Router LSA with the maximum metric either permanently (until you remove the command) or for a period after the switch starts up. The max metric signals to other OSPF routers that the router is not available. You would typically use this feature on an ASBR that is redistributing routes from another protocol. You want to ensure that other OSPF routers do not start sending any traffic through the ASBR until the ASBR has fully loaded its other protocols. For example, BGP can take longer to load the full table than OSPF. Simply set the max LSA time period to a period a bit longer than you think it will take the ASBR to load all of its routing protocols.

Another example where the MAX LSA feature is useful is when you have a secondary VSX member that is booting up. This feature allows the secondary VSX member to learn upstream routes while the VSX uplink delay is keeping the VSX LAGs down. So, when the VSX LAG(s) comes up, routing table is populated. Later on, the secondary member will reduce the LSA metric, so it can also attract traffic from backbone for the local users.

Here's the configuration for the MAX LSA feature:

```
switch(config)# router ospf <process-id>
switch(config-ospf)# max-metric router-lsa
switch(config-ospf)# max-metric router-lsa on-startup
switch(config-ospf)# max-metric router-lsa on-startup <seconds>
```

The default is a 600 second delay.

Implementing OSPF and VRRP

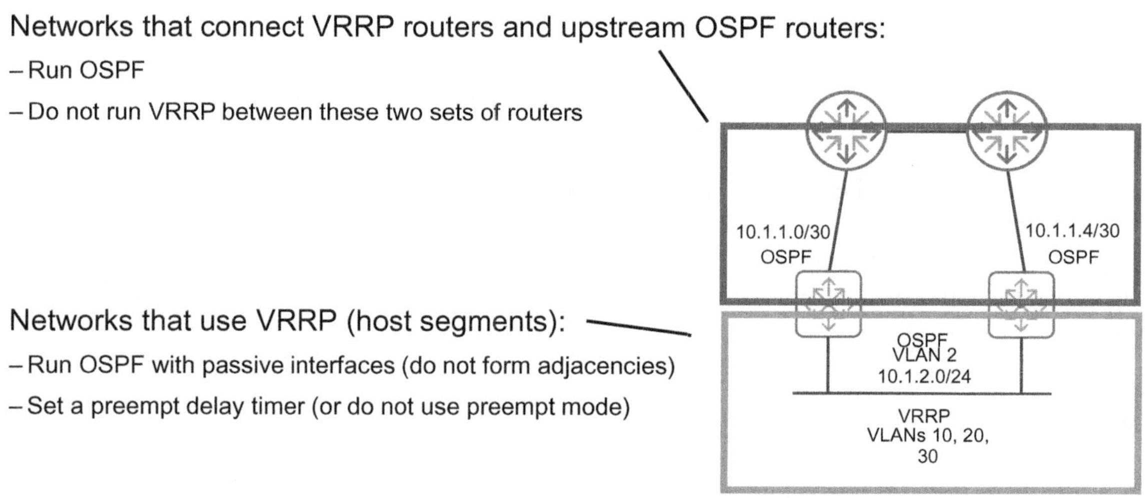

Figure 6-57 Implementing OSPF and VRRP

As you have learned, you should use VSF to provide redundancy for the default router role whenever possible. VSF provides redundancy while allowing the VSF fabric to act as a single entity in the routing protocol, making implementing VSF with OSPF almost as easy as implementing OSPF without redundancy (Figure 6-57). However, sometimes customer requirements might force you to implement OSPF and VRRP. You need to design the solution carefully to ensure that the OSPF and VRRP functions work will together.

When a router implements VRRP and OSPF on the same interface, it uses its actual IP address to run OSPF. However, the protocol interoperations can cause complexities. To minimize these complexities, you should avoid running OSPF and VRRP on the same interfaces.

First, connect VRRP routers to upstream OSPF routers on their own networks and do *not* run VRRP on these networks. This design helps an upstream router to immediately determine when it loses connectivity to a VRRP router.

Second, do not establish OSPF adjacencies on the interfaces that run VRRP (where the hosts reside). Because VRRP provides redundancy for default gateway services, VRRP runs on directly connected networks, which are generally stub networks. You can redistribute the directly connected networks as external networks. (Make sure to set up the area as a normal area or an NSSA.) Aruba recommends that you configure the interfaces as *passive* OSPF interfaces.

Third, choose the VRRP design in which none of the VRRP routers own the virtual IP address. Otherwise, when the VRRP Owner fails and comes back up, it immediately takes over routing on the interfaces for which it owns the VRRP address. However, it has not yet established adjacencies with upstream OSPF routers, disrupting connectivity on those VLANs. By configuring a virtual IP address that none of the VRRP routers owns, you can prevent this problem. Either disable preempt mode or set a preempt mode delay time that is longer than the time required to establish adjacency with all neighbors and calculate the OSPF routes (generally, 2 or 3 minutes).

Example Situations that Require Virtual Links

- Area expands and needs to be segmented, but new segment cannot connect to area 0 (shown below)
- Area requires a redundant link to backbone but no connection to area 0 ABR available
- OSPF rule: all traffic routed between areas must travel to the backbone *first*

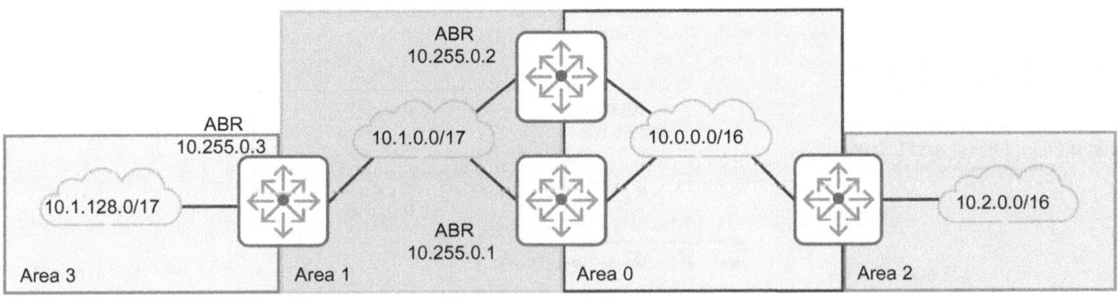

Figure 6-58 Example Situations that Require Virtual Links

Well-designed OSPF systems should ensure that you can always connect new areas directly to the backbone. However, sometimes the company expands in unexpected ways, and you cannot meet this requirement.

For example, in the scenario illustrated in Figure 6-58, the company needs to expand to new sites (10.1.128.0/17). Routers in area 1 are available for connecting to the new routers. However, area 1 has grown so large that you would prefer to establish the new sites in area 3. However, the rules of OSPF prevent you from creating the new area because this area would need to connect directly to routers in area 0, not area 1.

Note

A main rule of OSPF is that if traffic needs to travel between areas, like area 3 to area 1, the travel must travel through the backbone (area 0).

Similar issues can arise when you need to add a redundant link between an area and the backbone area 0. As you have learned, you can create link aggregations between internal area routers and the ABR, which might be one router or, for even better redundancy, two physical routing switches in a VSF fabric. You can also connect internal area routers to two ABRs in area 0. You should choose one of these solutions whenever possible.

In this case, however, a second connection between a particular site and an ABR at the backbone is not available. You must establish the link through a transit site.

Virtual Links

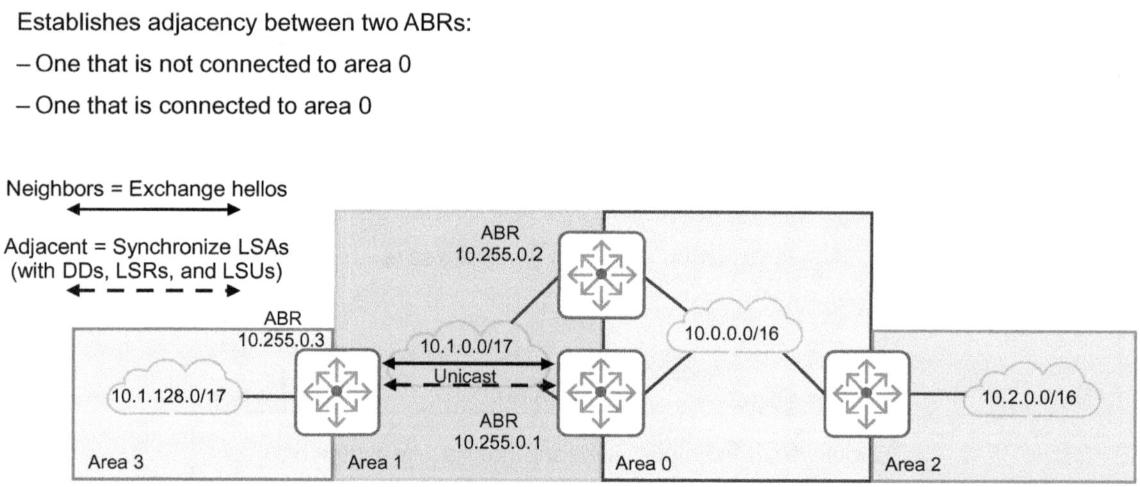

Figure 6-59 Virtual Links

You can use a virtual link to resolve both of these issues. You establish the virtual link across a transit area (area 1, in this example). A routing device on the border between the non-backbone connected area and the transit area uses the virtual link to connect to an ABR between area 0 and the transit area. A virtual link acts like a shared network interface, allowing the two OSPF routing devices to exchange hellos and establish adjacency. Logically, the virtual link acts as a point-to-point OSPF network on which both ABRs have an interface (Figure 6-59). In this example, you would also configure a virtual link between ABR 10.255.0.3 and ABR 10.255.0.2 for redundancy.

Note that you should *not* generally rely on virtual links as part of your design because they introduce complexity. They also negate some of the benefits of multi-area designs by leaking backbone routing information into non-backbone areas. Instead use virtual links as a patch when you have no other way to create the necessary link to the backbone at the current time.

Virtual Link Configuration Process

Figure 6-60 indicates the process for adding the virtual link. Before completing these steps, you should configure the basic OSPF settings on all of the routers involved in the solution. The section below provides more detailed steps.

1. Ensure the transit area is not a stub area.
2. Ensure the routers establishing the virtual link are configured for OSPF and support the correct areas.
3. Add the virtual link to the non-backbone ABR:
   - Router ID of an ABR connected to the transit area and area 0
   - Link established in the transit area
   - Consistent OSPF timers
4. Add the virtual link to the other ABR:
   - Router ID of the non-backbone ABR
   - Link established in the transit area
   - Consistent OSPF timers

Figure 6-60 Virtual Link Configuration Process

1. Make sure that the transit area is not defined as a stub area or NSSA.
2. Configure the virtual link on the ABR that does not connect to area 0.

   As mentioned above, this ABR should have its basic OSPF settings defined:

   - Router ID
   - The area without the direct connection to the backbone (area 3 in the example)
   - The transit area (area 1 in the example)
   - OSPF enabled on the appropriate interfaces in each area
   - Any other settings required for the OSPF solution (such as aggregated area summaries)
3. In the transit area (area 1 in the example), configure a virtual link. Specify the router ID of the device at the other end of the link.

```
NonbackboneABR(config)# router ospf
NonbackboneABR(ospf)# area 1 virtual-link 10.255.0.1
```

4. Configure the virtual link on the ABR that connects to area 0.

   Again, this ABR should have its basic OSPF settings defined:

   - Router ID
   - Area 0
   - The transit area (area 1 in the example)
   - OSPF enabled on the appropriate networks in each area
   - Any other settings required for the OSPF solution

   a. In the transit area, configure a virtual link, specifying the router ID of the device at the other end of the link.

```
BackboneABR(ospf)# area 1 virtual-link 10.255.0.3
```

Note

Note that the OSPF routing devices have connectivity within the transit area. As always, if you want to be able to ping the router ID, use an IP address on loopback interface that runs OSPF.

   b. You must check consistency for the typical settings required for two OSPF routers on a link to achieve adjacency. These settings include the OSPF timers. (The virtual link does not have a network associated with it, so you do not have to check consistency for its type.)

Note

There are other options you can configure for virtual links. See the *AOS-CX IP Routing Guide* for more detail.

OSPF Authentication

- Choose authentication type per-area:
  - Null—Provides no authentication
  - Simple—Protects against misconfigurations
  - Cryptographic—Protects against unauthorized routers
- Simple authentication
  - Password per-interface
  - Must match with neighbors on the same interface

```
Switch-1(config)# interface <interface-ID>
Switch-1(config-if)# ip ospf authentication simple-text
Switch-1(config-if)# ip ospf authentication-key <key>
```

- Cryptographic:
  - Key per-interface
  - Set the MD5 key per-interface
  - Key identifier ID and key secret (password) must match with neighbors on the same interface

```
Switch-1(config)# interface <interface-ID>
Switch-1(config-if)# ip ospf authentication message-digest
Switch-1(config-if)# ip ospf message-digest-key <key-id>
                     md5 simple-text <key>
```

Figure 6-61 OSPF Authentication

You can implement authentication for OSPF processes on particular router or routing switch interfaces. When an OSPF interface implements authentication, it includes authentication data in all OSPF packets that it transmits. It also checks this data in all OSPF packets that it receives and rejects any packets that fail the check. In other words, only OSPF routers configured with the same authentication keys can establish neighbor relationships (Figure 6-61).

A packet's authentication field specifies the type (as the AuthID), so receiving routers know how they are expected to authenticate the packet. They only accept packets that are using the same authentication type configured on their interface. For each OSPF area, you can choose from several authentication options:

- **Null**—The default authentication type, in which OSPF interfaces do not enforce authentication. The OSPF packets have an authentication field, but the field does not include any data. An OSPF interface implementing null authentication does not examine the authentication field but process all valid OSPF packets.
- **Simple**—The OSPF interface places the authentication key in every packet's OSPF header. Other OSPF routers, also implementing this type, examine this field. They only accept OSPF packets for which the field matches their own key.
  Because packets include the key in plaintext, anyone who can collect an OSPF packet transmitted on the network can learn the key. You should use this form of authentication only if you primarily aim to eliminate misconfigurations and routers inadvertently connecting on the wrong networks. You should not use it to secure your OSPF system from unauthorized routers and hackers.

- **Cryptographic (MD5)**—The OSPF interface hashes the OSPF packet data and the key. It then places the hash at the end of the packet. The authentication field includes the key ID, a length for the hash, and a cryptographic sequence number; however, it does not include the key itself, protecting it from eavesdroppers.
  A router receiving the OSPF packet hashes the packet with its secret key, identified by the key ID. If the hash matches, the router knows that the transmitting router has the correct secret key for this key ID, so it accepts the packet.
  The cryptographic sequence number provides a degree of protection against replay attacks. An OSPF interface only accepts packets with a sequence number equal to or higher than the number for the most recent accepted OSPF packet from this neighbor. The sequence number might be a counter, but is usually based on the system clock. In either case, the number is always increasing.
  If a hacker obtains a legitimate OSPF packet and attempts to retransmit it later, the packet's cryptographic sequence number is no longer valid, and the other routers on the network reject it. A hacker could replay a packet in the window before the legitimate neighbor sends a packet with a higher sequence, but this window is quite small.
  Cryptographic authentication provides authenticity, ensuring that only OSPF interfaces configured with the same key can communicate. It does not provide privacy: the contents of the packet are not encrypted.
  All Aruba routers and routing switches support MD5 for the cryptographic hashing algorithm.

To configure authentication, move to the layer 3 interface context. Set the authentication type and then set the authentication key. The slide shows a configuration example for the message digest option.

You can verify if key authentication is enabled for an interface:

```
switch(config-if)# show ip ospf interface 1/1/1
Interface 1/1/1 is up, line protocol is up
------------------------------------------
IP address 10.0.0.1/30, Process ID 1 VRF default, area 0.0.0.0
    State Point-to-point, Status up, Network type Point-to-point
    Link Speed: 1000 Mbps
    Cost Configured NA, Calculated 100
    Transit delay 1 sec, Router priority n/a
    No designated router on this network
    No backup designated router on this network
    Timer Intervals: Hello 10, Dead 40, Retransmit 5
    Md5 authentication
    Number of Link LSAs: 0, checksum sum 0
    BFD is disabled
```

Lab 6.3

Lab 6.3 Diagram

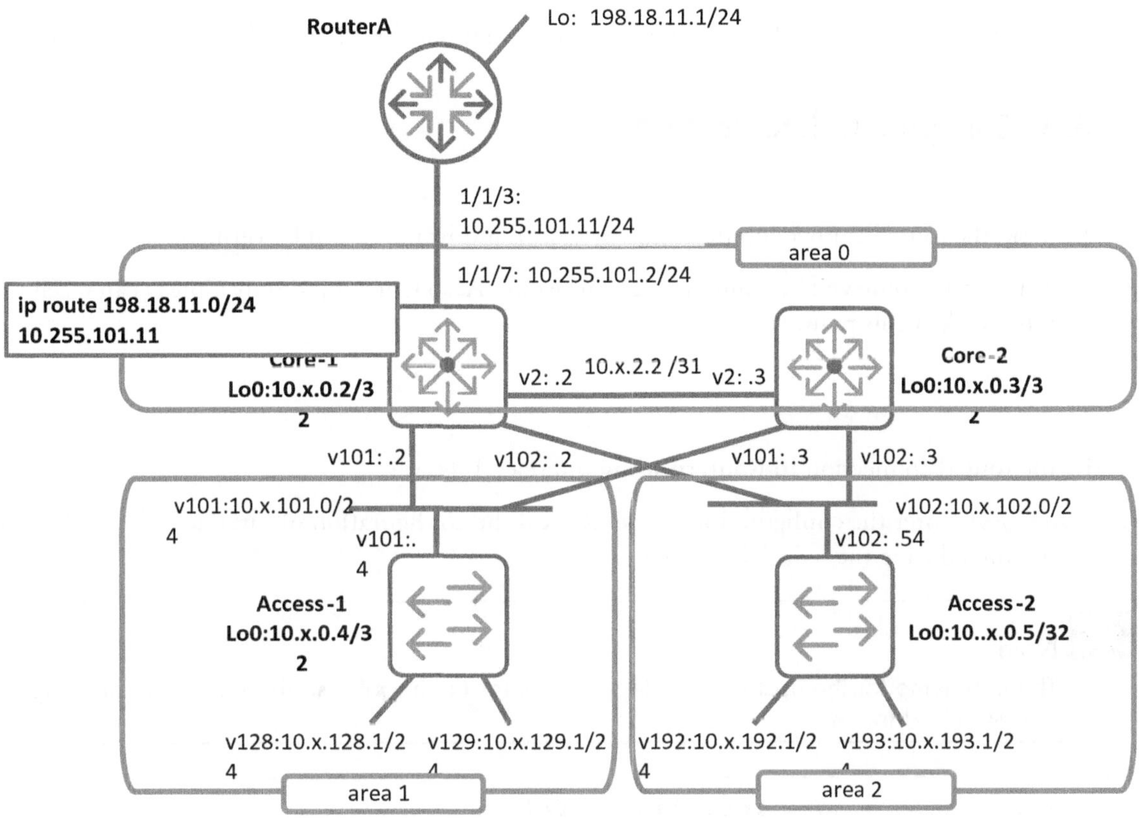

Figure 6-62 Lab 6.3 Diagram

Overview

This lab activity will demonstrate how OSPF can be used to distribute routes to external networks to other OSPF routers in the OSPF Autonomous System (AS) (Figure 6-62). The router that is performing this redistribution is referred to as the Autonomous System Boundary Router (ASBR). This will be demonstrated using Core1 in the backbone and Access2 in area2.

Once the external routes have been exchanged, the lab will show how a route map can be used to control the cost and the list of routes that can be redistributed. The last section of the lab will show how area types can be used to optimize which external and OSPF routes will be announced into an area.

Objectives

- Learn how to configure an ASBR to redistribute routes.
- Configure a route map to control external cost types, such as metric type1 and type2.
- Understand the difference between Stub, Stub no-summary and Not So Stubby Area types.

Task 1: Configure Link to RouterA

Objectives

In this task, the routed connection between the Core1 and RouterA will be verified.

On Core1, a static route will be configured to this RouterA, so Core1 (and only Core1) can reach the external network at this point.

Steps

Verify the routed connection to RouterA using interface 1/1/7.

1. On Core1, enter the configuration mode. Review the configuration of interface 1/1/7. This was configured during the VSX lab activity.

Note

The IP scheme for the upstream routers is local for each table, so there is no 'x' marking in these IP addresses.

```
ICX-Tx-Core1(config)# interface 1/1/7
ICX-Tx-Core1(config-if)# show run current-context
interface 1/1/7
    no shutdown
    ip address 10.255.101.2/24
    exit
ICX-Tx-Core1(config-if)# exit
```

2. Verify connectivity to the RouterA IP.

```
ICX-Tx-Core1(config)# do ping 10.255.101.11
PING 10.255.101.11 (10.255.101.11) 100(128) bytes of data.
108 bytes from 10.255.101.11: icmp_seq=1 ttl=64 time=1.75 ms
...
```

3. Define a static route to the remote subnet. This represents a business partner network outside of this organization OSPF AS.

```
ICX-Tx-Core1(config)# ip route 198.18.11.0/24 10.255.101.11
```

4. Test with a ping to 198.18.11.1; this IP is hosted by the RouterA using a loopback interface.

```
ICX-Tx-Core1(config)# do ping 198.18.11.1
PING 198.18.11.1 (198.18.11.1) 100(128) bytes of data.
108 bytes from 198.18.11.1: icmp_seq=1 ttl=64 time=2.20 ms
...
```

5. Review the IP Routing table on the Core1.At this point, the Core1 can reach the external network, but the rest of the OSPF AS cannot reach this 198.18.11.0/24 network yet. This will be solved with route redistribution in the next task.

```
ICX-Tx-Core1(config)# show ip route static
Displaying ipv4 routes selected for forwarding

'[x/y]' denotes [distance/metric]

10.x.128.0/18, vrf default
      reject route,  [110/0],  static
10.x.192.0/18, vrf default
      reject route,  [110/0],  static
10.254.1.0/24, vrf default
      50198.18.11.0/24, vrf default
via  10.255.101.11,  [1/0],  static
```

Task 2: Redistribute Static Routes into OSPF

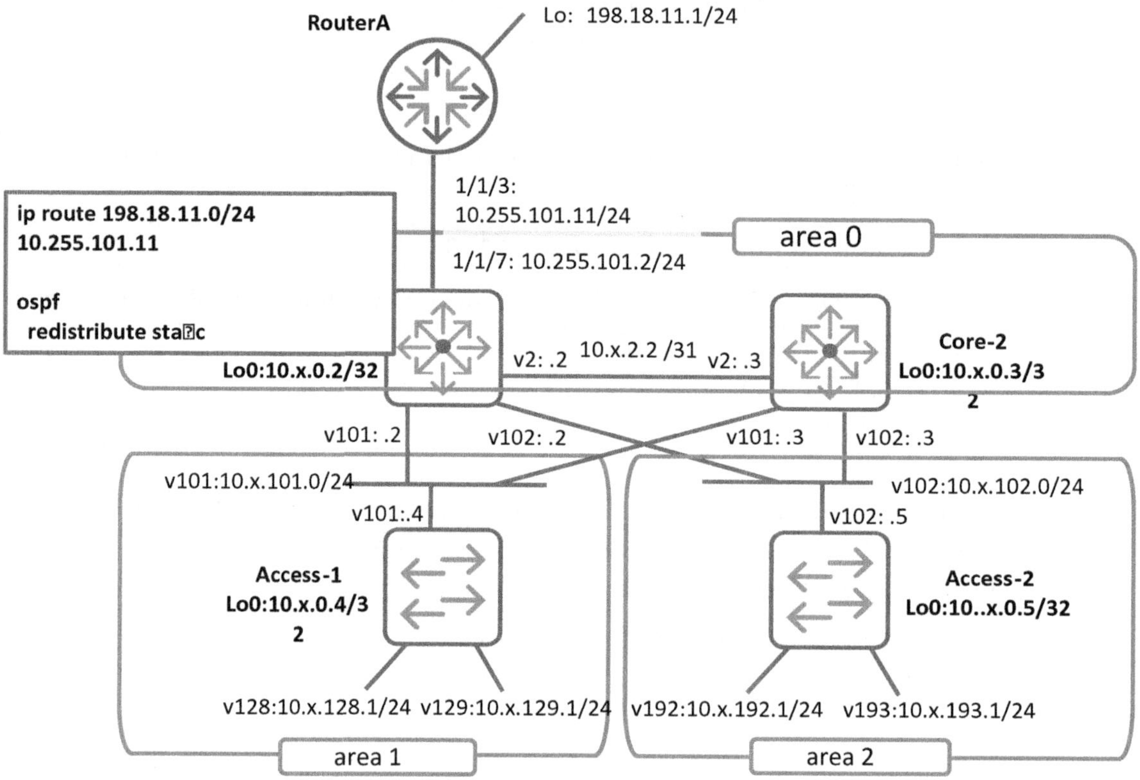

Figure 6-63 Task 2: Redistribute Static Routes into OSPF

Objectives

In this task, the static route that was installed on the Core1 router will now be distributed to the other routers using OSPF route redistribution. The router that is inserting 'external' routes into OSPF is known as the ASBR, the autonomous system boundary router. The ASBR can be a router in the backbone area or a router in another area. Other area types are covered in a later task.

In order to allow other OSPF routers to make a distinction between the routes of the OSPF autonomous system and routes that are injected (so not originated) into the autonomous system (external routes), OSPF uses a different LSA type from the intra-area (Router/Type 1 and Network/Type 2) and the inter-area (Summary/Type 3).

All the routes that are injected by the ASBR are inserted as Type 5 LSAs in the LSDB. Therefore, when a complete AS has two routers that are injecting 100 routes each, the LSDB will contain 200 Type 5 LSAs (2x100 routes) (Figure 6-63).

Steps

Redistribute static routes into OSPF.

Verify the OSPF LSA Type 5 in the backbone and other areas.

1. Open a terminal session to Core1; enter the configuration mode.
2. Review the current OSPF database summary. There are currently no external routes in the database.

```
ICX-Tx-Core1(config)# show ip ospf lsdb database-summary
...
Process 1 database summary
---------------------------

LSA Type             Count
---------------------------
Router               8
Network              2
Inter-area Summary   44
ASBR Summary         0
NSSA External        0
AS External          0
Total                54
```

3. Enter the OSPF router context; enable route redistribution of the static routes. This will instruct the OSPF process to look into the local routing table for routes that match the redistribution condition; in this case, the condition is 'static' routes.

```
ICX-Tx-Core1(config)# router ospf 1
ICX-Tx-Core1(config-ospf-1)# redistribute static
ICX-Tx-Core1(config-ospf-1)# exit
```

4. Verify in the LSDB that a new record was created for this external route.

```
ICX-Tx-Core1(config)# show ip ospf lsdb database-summary
...
Process 1 database summary
---------------------------

LSA Type             Count
---------------------------
Router               8
Network              2
Inter-area Summary   44
```

```
ASBR Summary          0
NSSA External         0
AS External           3
Total                 57

ICX-Tx-Core1(config)# show ip ospf lsdb external
OSPF Router with ID (10.x.0.2) (Process ID 1 VRF default)
===========================================================

AS External Link State Advertisements
--------------------------------------
LSID            ADV Router      Age        Seq#       Checksum
--------------------------------------------------------------
10.254.1.0      10.x.0.2        129       0x80000001 0x00009502
10.254.1.0      10.x.0.3        129       0x80000001 0x00008f07
198.18.11.0     10.x.0.2        129       0x80000001 0x0000ac11
```

Note

The 10.254.1.0/24 static route was added during the VSX lab on both Core1 and Core2. It provides access to the ClearPass server subnet. Due to the VSX OSPF sync, Core2 is now also redistributing its static route to the 10.254.1.0/24 subnet. These routes can be ignored in this lab.

5. Now check the LSDB on Core2 and Access2. Access2 is connected via Core2 to Core1. Review that the external route has arrived in the LSDB.

```
ICX-Tx-Core2(config)# show ip ospf lsdb external
OSPF Router with ID (10.x.0.3) (Process ID 1 VRF default)
===========================================================
AS External Link State Advertisements
--------------------------------------


LSID            ADV Router      Age        Seq#       Checksum
--------------------------------------------------------------
10.254.1.0      10.x.0.2        176       0x80000001 0x00009502
10.254.1.0      10.x.0.3        174       0x80000001 0x00008f07
198.18.11.0     10.x.0.2        176       0x80000001 0x0000ac11
```

```
ICX-Tx-Access2(config)# show ip ospf lsdb external
OSPF Router with ID (10.x.0.5) (Process ID 1 VRF default)
=============================================================
AS External Link State Advertisements
--------------------------------------

LSID            ADV Router       Age        Seq#        Checksum
--------------------------------------------------------------
10.254.1.0      10.x.0.2         200        0x80000001 0x00009502
10.254.1.0      10.x.0.3         199        0x80000001 0x00008f07
198.18.11.0     10.x.0.2         200        0x80000001 0x0000ac11
```

6. On Core1, this route is a static route in the routing table. Now review the IP routing table on Access2.

```
ICX-Tx-Access2(config)# show ip route ospf 198.18.11.0
...
Displaying ipv4 routes selected for forwarding
'[x/y]' denotes [distance/metric]
198.18.11.0/24, vrf default
      via  10.x.102.2,   [110/25],  ospf
```

Question: Which router is the next hop IP of this route?

Answer: This 10.x.102.2 is the Core1 router. It was calculated by OSPF to be the shortest path to the ASBR that is announcing this route (Core1).

7. On Access1, attempt to ping the remote host 198.18.11.1 to validate that all the routers on the path to the ASBR know how to route this traffic. This demonstrates how OSPF can be used to distribute routes in the OSPF Autonomous System that were not originated by the OSPF routers themselves.

```
ICX-Tx-Access1(config)# do ping 198.18.11.1
PING 198.18.11.1 (198.18.11.1) 100(128) bytes of data.
108 bytes from 198.18.11.1: icmp_seq=1 ttl=63 time=2.52 ms
...
```

Note

IP always needs bidirectional communication paths. On the remote router, a static route for 10.0.0.0/8 exists already in the configuration to handle the return traffic.

Access2—External Routes

Autonomous System Boundary Routers (ASBRs) do not have to be in the backbone area. A router in a normal area can also redistribute routes into the OSPF Autonomous System.

In the next steps, Access2 will be configured to inject an external route. For testing purposes, Access2 will be configured with a local static route that will be redistributed into OSPF. To provide a test IP in this subnet, a local loopback interface will be used. Since this test loopback interface is not enabled for OSPF, it will not be known as a native OSPF route. Only the static route will be known to OSPF due to the redistribution (Figure 6-64).

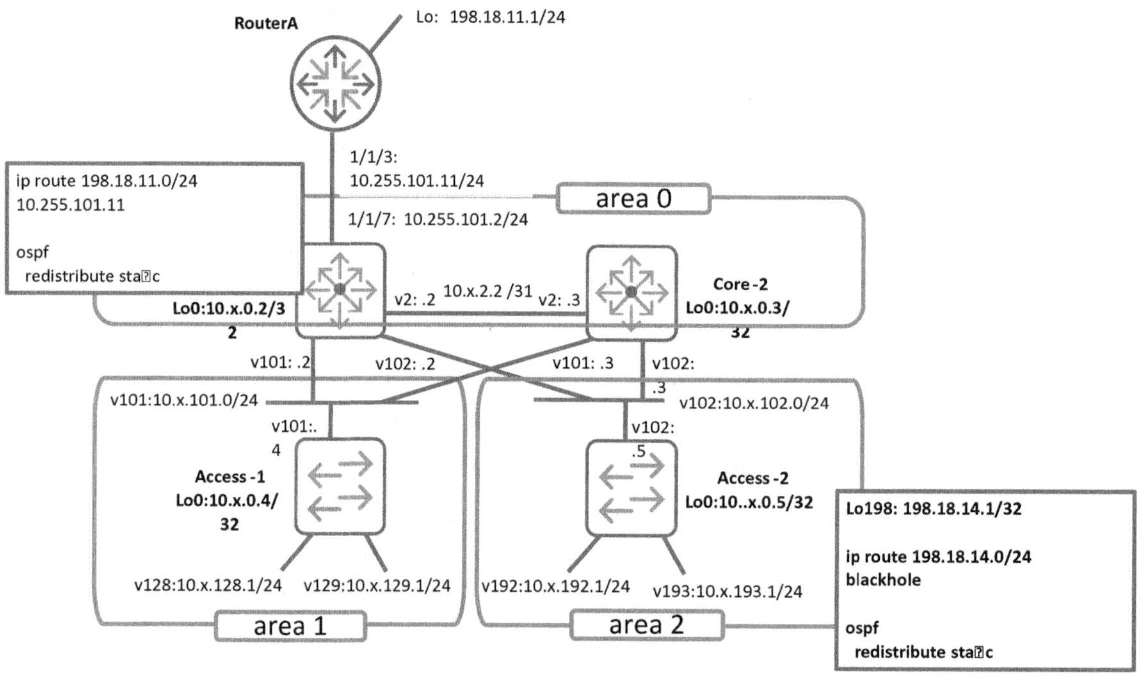

Figure 6-64 Access2—External Routes

1. On Access2 (OSPF area 2), define a new static route. A normal static route would be configured to a real next-hop IP address. Since this is a test subnet, and there is no real next-hop router, the next-hop will be set to 'blackhole'. This means that all traffic arriving for this subnet will be dropped. In order to perform a test ping, a loopback address will be made in this test subnet.

```
ICX-Tx-Access2(config)# ip route 198.18.14.0/24 blackhole
```

2. Define a new loopback interface; this can be used to test access to the 198.18.14.0/24 subnet.

```
ICX-Tx-Access2(config)# interface loopback 198
ICX-Tx-Access2(config-loopback-if)# ip address 198.18.14.1/32
ICX-Tx-Access2(config-loopback-if)# exit
```

3. Redistribute the static route into OSPF.

```
ICX-Tx-Access2(config)# router ospf 1
ICX-Tx-Access2(config-ospf-1)# redistribute static
ICX-Tx-Access2(config-ospf-1)# exit
```

4. Verify in the backbone area that the External route is available.

```
ICX-Tx-Core1(config)# show ip ospf routes 198.18.14.0/24
Codes: i - Intra-area route, I - Inter-area route
       E1 - External type-1, E2 - External type-2
OSPF Process ID 1 VRF default, Routing Table for prefixes
198.18.14.0/24
-----------------------------------------------------------------------
Total Number of Routes : 1
198.18.14.0/24      (E2)
       via 10.x.102.5 interface vlan102, cost 25 distance 110
```

Verify in OSPF Area 1 that the New External Route is Available

1. On Access1, check the IP routing table for the 198.18.14.0 subnet.

```
ICX-Tx-Access1 # show ip route 198.18.14.0
Displaying ipv4 routes selected for forwarding

'[x/y]' denotes [distance/metric]

198.18.14.0/24, vrf default
via  10.x.101.3,  [110/25],  ospf
via  10.x.101.2,  [110/25],  ospf
```

Question: Why are there 2 paths available for this route?
Answer: OSPF calculates the best path to reach the ASBR. In this case, there are 2 equal cost paths to reach the Access2 router, so both paths are entered in the routing table.

2. Perform a traceroute to the test IP in the 198.18.14.0/24 subnet. The path should use either Core1 or Core2 to reach the Access2 router.

```
ICX-Tx-Access1# traceroute 198.18.14.1
traceroute to 198.18.14.1 (198.18.14.1), 1 hops min, 30 hops max, 3
sec. timeout, 3 probes
   1   10.x.101.2  0.202ms  0.099ms  0.504ms
   2   198.18.14.1  0.188ms  0.101ms  0.099ms
ICX-Tx-Access1#
```

Task 3: Control Route Redistribution and Metric Types

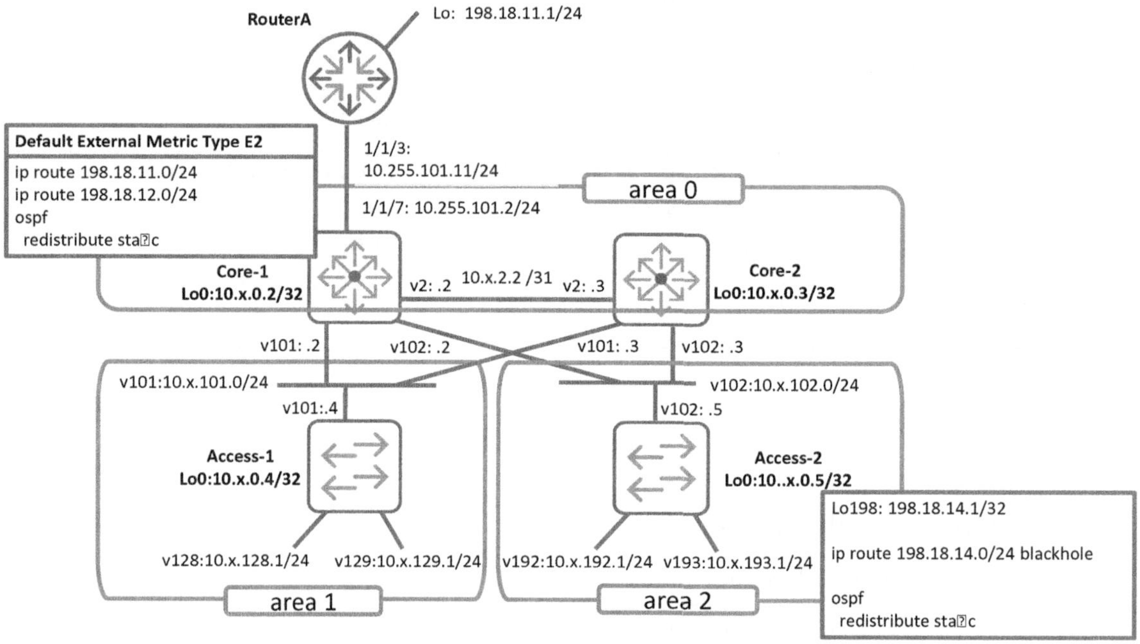

Figure 6-65 Task 3: Control Route Redistribution and Metric Types

Introduction to Metric Types

OSPF has 2 metric types to describe the cost for external routes: External type 1 and External type 2 (default) (Figure 6-65).

External Type 2

In case of External type 2, the external route is entered into the OSPF LSDB with a static cost. This static cost is **not** adjusted as the route is distributed by the OSPF routers. Therefore, a router that is several hops away would still see the route with the same cost that was initially set by the redistributing ASBR.

This is convenient to force the entire network to use a specific ASBR to reach some external network, instead of the 'closest' ASBR. This applies to scenarios where the traffic to the external network must pass a firewall and the customer wants to avoid asynchronous routing.

External Type 1

When there is no need for a 'fixed' ASBR to the external network, OSPF can be configured to use the path to the closest ASBR. This can be achieved by configuring the external route with a metric type 1. In this case, the OSPF path cost to reach the ASBR is added to the initial cost of the external route.

Route Maps

The configuration of the route metric types is done through a route policy. Route policies can also be used to filter routes that should not be redistributed.

Steps

Review the default cost and metric type of OSPF external routes.

Add a static route on Core1 that should not be redistributed using OSPF.

Define a route policy on Core1 to set the OSPF metric-type 2 and set the initial cost to 100.

1. On Core1, add a dummy static route. In the current configuration, every static route will be redistributed by OSPF. This route will be filtered by the route policy in the upcoming step.

```
ICX-Tx-Core1(config)# ip route 198.18.12.0/24 blackhole
```

2. Verify this static route is redistributed in the current configuration.

```
ICX-Tx-Core1(config-ospf-1)# show ip ospf lsdb external
OSPF Router with ID (10.x.0.2) (Process ID 1 VRF default)
==========================================================

AS External Link State Advertisements
-------------------------------------

LSID            ADV Router      Age       Seq#       Checksum
-------------------------------------------------------------
10.254.1.0      10.x.0.2        213       0x80000003 0x00009104
10.254.1.0      10.x.0.3        213       0x80000003 0x00008b09
198.18.11.0     10.x.0.2        213       0x80000003 0x0000a813
198.18.12.0     10.x.0.2        7         0x80000001 0x0000a11b
198.18.14.0     10.x.0.5        1661      0x80000002 0x0000773f
```

3. Review the default cost and metric type. On Access2, review the OSPF routing table; look for the routes **198.18.11.0/24** and **198.18.12.0/24**. Note the (E2) marking:

```
ICX-Tx-Access2# show ip ospf routes 198.18.11.0/24
Codes: i - Intra-area route, I - Inter-area route
       E1 - External type-1, E2 - External type-2
OSPF Process ID 1 VRF default, Routing Table for prefixes
198.18.11.0/24
-------------------------------------------------------------------

Total Number of Routes : 1

198.18.11.0/24      (E2)
  via 10.x.102.2 interface vlan102, cost 25 distance 110
```

```
ICX-Tx-Access2# show ip ospf routes 198.18.12.0/24
Codes: i - Intra-area route, I - Inter-area route
       E1 - External type-1, E2 - External type-2
OSPF Process ID 1 VRF default, Routing Table for prefixes
198.18.12.0/24
------------------------------------------------------------------
Total Number of Routes : 1

198.18.12.0/24      (E2)
    via 10.x.102.2 interface vlan102, cost 25 distance 110
```

Question: What is the default cost for the external route?

Answer: The default cost is 25.

Define Route Map to Control Redistribution

Now a route map will be created on Core1 to change the external route to metric type 1 for the 198.18.11.0/24 prefix. This will also prevent the route 198.18.12.0/24 from being redistributed.

First a prefix list must be defined; this defines which routes need to be controlled by the policy.

1. On Core1, define a prefix list that matches the external route to RouterA. Any name can be used, try to use a descriptive name. A prefix list can contain many prefixes, and the administrator can control whether the entry should be matched (permit) or ignored (deny). This is why the order sequence (seq) is important if permit/deny combinations would be used. In this example, only 1 entry is used.

```
ICX-Tx-Core1(config)# ip prefix-list routerAext seq 10 permit
198.18.11.0/24
```

Define Route Map

1. Next, define a route map that references the prefix list and sets the metric-type to External Type 1. Only routes that are permitted in the route policy are passing the route-map. There is an implicit deny at the end of the route-map. Since the 198.18.12.0.24 does not match the prefix list and does not match any other rule in the route-map, it will not pass the route-map.

```
ICX-Tx-Core1(config)# route-map ospf_from_static permit seq 10
ICX-Tx-Core1(config-route-map-ospf_from_static-10)# match ip address
prefix-list routerAext
ICX-Tx-Core1(config-route-map-ospf_from_static-10)# set metric-type
external type-1
```

2. Review the configuration.

```
ICX-Tx-Core1(config-route-map-ospf_from_static-10)# show run cur
ip prefix-list routerAext seq 10 permit 198.18.11.0/24 ge 24 le 24
!
route-map ospf_from_static permit seq 10
      match ip address prefix-list routerAext
      set metric-type external type-1
```

3. Exit the route-map context.

```
ICX-Tx-Core1(config-route-map-ospf_from_static-10)# exit
```

Activate Route Map for Redistributed Routes

1. Activate the route policy on the OSPF redistribution for static routes.

```
ICX-Tx-Core1(config)# router ospf 1
ICX-Tx-Core1(config-ospf-1)# redistribute static route-map
ospf_from_static
ICX-Tx-Core1(config-ospf-1)# exit
```

2. Verify the result on the Access2 router. The 198.18.11.0/24 route should now be listed as E1, and the cost will reflect the path to reach the Core1 (100) plus the initial cost (25 by default).

```
ICX-Tx-Access2# show ip ospf routes 198.18.11.0/24
Codes: i - Intra-area route, I - Inter-area route
      E1 - External type-1, E2 - External type-2
OSPF Process ID 1 VRF default, Routing Table for prefixes
198.18.11.0/24
---------------------------------------------------------------------------
Total Number of Routes : 1

198.18.11.0/24      (E1)
      via 10.x.102.2 interface vlan102, cost 125 distance 110
```

3. The route to 198.18.12.0/24 should have been removed as well since it does not match the route policy.

```
ICX-Tx-Access2# show ip ospf routes 198.18.12.0/24
Codes: i - Intra-area route, I - Inter-area route
      E1 - External type-1, E2 - External type-2
OSPF Process ID 1 VRF default, Routing Table for prefixes
198.18.12.0/24
---------------------------------------------------------------------------
Total Number of Routes : 0
```

4. Return to Core1, and modify the route policy so the initial cost is now 1000.

```
ICX-Tx-Core1(config)# route-map ospf_from_static permit seq 10
ICX-Tx-Core1(config-route-map-ospf_from_static-10)# set metric 1000
ICX-Tx-Core1(config-route-map-ospf_from_static-10)# exit
```

5. Verify the result on Access2. The cost should now be 1100, that is 1000 initial cost plus cost 100 to reach the Core1. This demonstrates how a route policy can be used to control external routes.

```
ICX-Tx-Access2(config)# show ip ospf routes 198.18.11.0/24
Codes: i - Intra-area route, I - Inter-area route
      E1 - External type-1, E2 - External type-2
OSPF Process ID 1 VRF default, Routing Table for prefixes
198.18.11.0/24
--------------------------------------------------------------------
Total Number of Routes : 1

198.18.11.0/24      (E1)
      via 10.x.102.2 interface vlan102, cost 1100 distance 110
```

Task 4: Filter Routes with Stub and Totally Stub Areas

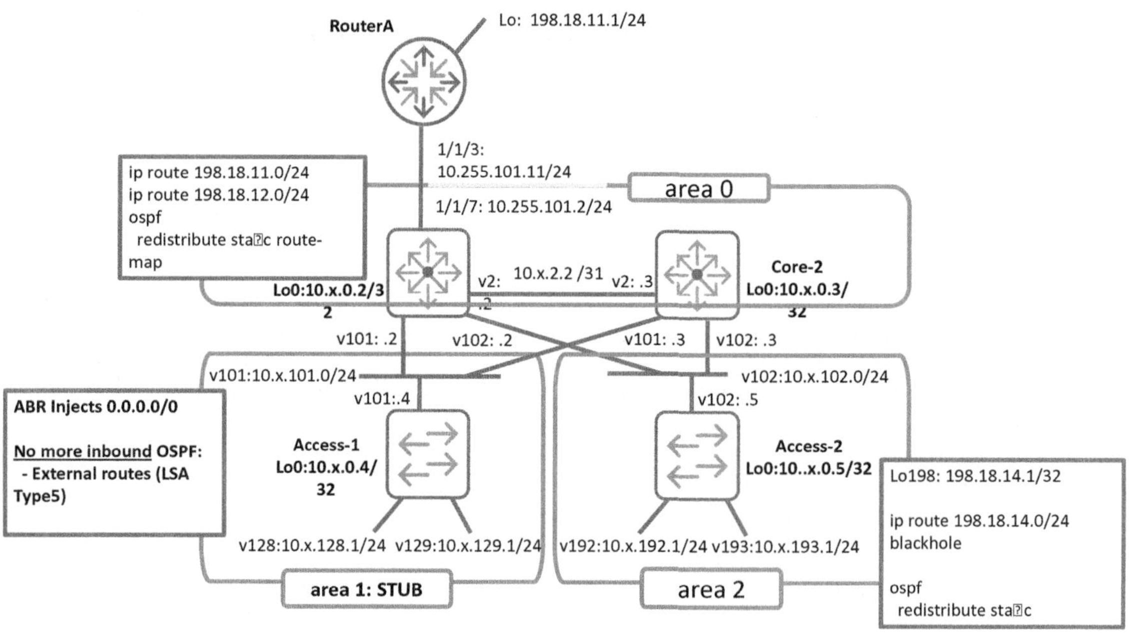

Figure 6-66 Task 4: Filter Routes with Stub and Totally Stub Areas

Objectives

In this task, the stub and totally stubby (sometimes referred to as 'no-summary') area types will be configured (Figure 6-66).

Stub

When an area does not have an ASBR inside the area, this means that all the traffic destined to external networks will need to go through the ABR systems. The logic here is: why distribute all those external routes into the area, if the traffic has to go through the ABR systems anyway?

It would be convenient to 'aggregate' all those external routes using the default route (0.0.0.0/0), that is operating as the ultimate aggregation route. This is exactly what the Stub area feature provides:

- The ABR will not announce the external Type 5 routes from the backbone into the stub area.
- The ABR will announce a default route (0.0.0.0/0) into the area.
- Routers inside the stub area will see the 0.0.0.0/0 route, but they will not see the external routes anymore.
- Routers inside the stub area will still see all the OSPF intra-area and inter-area (OSPF LSA Type 3 Summary).

The stub area feature must be configured on *every* router in the area.

Stub No-Summary

On top of the stub area feature, an administrator can configure the area to be a 'Stub No-summary' area. This extra 'no-summary' feature is only configured on the ABR systems.

Since the routers inside the stub area already have the default route 0.0.0.0/0, this default route could also be used to 'aggregate' all the OSPF inter-area routes (OSPF LSA Type 3 Summary routes). This results in the name 'stub **no-summary**'. This feature is also known as a 'totally stubby area'.

Steps

Make Area 1 an OSPF Stub Area

1. Review that Access1 in area 1 sees all the external routes. On Access1, check the IP routing table. Notice that there is no default route needed at this point, since all external routes are actually known to the router. So there is no 0.0.0.0/0 entry at this moment.

```
ICX-Tx-Access1# show ip route 0.0.0.0
No ipv4 routes configured
```

2. Make area 1 a stub area. This will summarize all the external routes into the default route 0.0.0.0/0. This action is done at the ABR and should be done on **each** ABR. In this lab setup, Core1 and Core2 are part of a VSX setup, to making area 1 a stub area on Core1 will automatically be synchronized to Core2 due to the VSX OSPF synchronization. Open Core1 and make area 1 a stub under the OSPF context.

```
ICX-Tx-Core1(config)# router ospf 1
ICX-Tx-Core1(config-ospf-1)# area 1 stub
```

3. Verify using the **vsx-peer** command that Core2 also has area 1 set as stub.

```
ICX-Tx-Core1(config-ospf-1)# show run ospf vsx-peer
router ospf 1
    router-id 10.x.0.3
    passive-interface default
    redistribute static route-map ospf_from_static
    area 0.0.0.0
area 0.0.0.1 stub
    area 0.0.0.1 range 10.x.128.0/18 type inter-area
    area 0.0.0.2
    area 0.0.0.2 range 10.x.99.0/24 type inter-area no-advertise
    area 0.0.0.2 range 10.x.192.0/18 type inter-area
interface loopback 0
    ip ospf 1 area 0.0.0.0
interface vlan1
    ip ospf 1 area 0.0.0.0
<...output omitted...>
ICX-Tx-Core1(config-ospf-1)# exit
```

4. On Access1 router (router inside area 1), check the ip routing table.

```
ICX-Tx-Access1# show ip route ospf
```

Question: Are there any OSPF routes in the routing table?

Answer: No, there are no more OSPF routes.

Question: Why did the OSPF routes disappear?

Answer: The OSPF stub area option must be enabled on all routers in the area. The stub option is checked using the OSPF hello packets; a mismatch will prevent an OSPF neighbor adjacency.

5. Check the OSPF interface statistics. There should be dropped hello packets due to 'Options mismatch'.

```
ICX-Tx-Access1# show ip ospf statistics interface vlan101
...
Reason                        Packets Dropped
---------------------------------------------
Invalid type                  0
Invalid length                0
Invalid checksum              0
Invalid version               0
Bad or unknown source         8
Area mismatch                 0
Self-originated               0
Duplicate router ID           0
Interface standby             0
Total Hello packets dropped   62
  Network Mask mismatch       0
  Hello interval mismatch     0
  Dead interval mismatch      0
Options mismatch             62
  MTU mismatch                0
```

6. On Access1, change the area 1 type to stub.

```
ICX-Tx-Access1(config)# router ospf 1
ICX-Tx-Access1(config-ospf-1)# area 1 stub
ICX-Tx-Access1(config-ospf-1)# exit
```

7. Review the routing table, the external routes should have been replaced with a default route by the ABR.

Note

It may take a few moments for the OSPF adjacencies to re-establish. Within about 30 seconds the OSPF routes should appear.

```
ICX-Tx-Access1(config)# show ip route 0.0.0.0
Displaying ipv4 routes selected for forwarding
'[x/y]' denotes [distance/metric]

0.0.0.0/0, vrf default
        via  10.x.101.2,  [110/101],  ospf
        via  10.x.101.3,  [110/101],  ospf
<...output omitted...>
```

Question: What is the cost of the default route?

Answer: The cost is 101. This is based on 100 to reach the Core1/Core2; the metric for the default route is 1 by default.

8. On Access1, check which route it would take for the traffic to 198.18.11.0. Since the specific route to 198.18.11.0 is no longer available, the default route is used.

```
ICX-Tx-Access1(config)# show ip route 198.18.11.0
Displaying ipv4 routes selected for forwarding
'[x/y]' denotes [distance/metric]
0.0.0.0/0, vrf default
        via  10.x.101.2,   [110/101],  ospf
        via  10.x.101.3,   [110/101],  ospf
```

9. On Core1, review the routing table; look for the default route 0.0.0.0/0. This demonstrates how the 'stub' area feature of OSPF can automatically summarize all external routes with the default route.

```
ICX-Tx-Core1(config)# show ip route 0.0.0.0
No ipv4 routes configured
```

Question: Is there a default route on the Core1?

Answer: No, the ABR will announce the default route into the stub area, but it does not need the default route by itself, since it knows all the external routes.

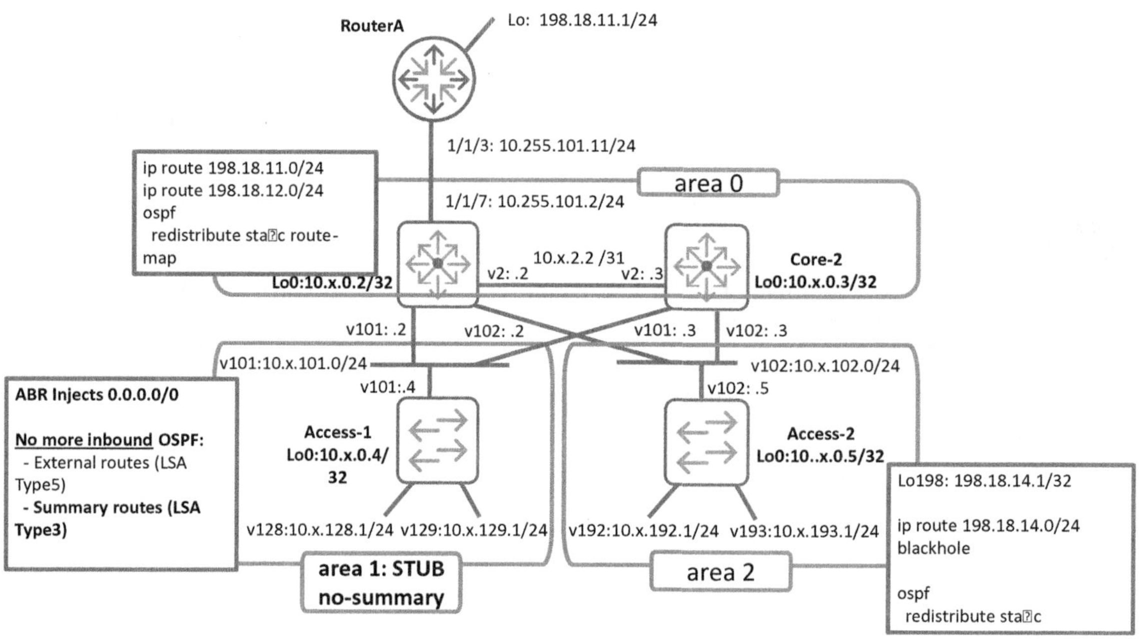

Figure 6-67 Make Area 1 Stub No-Summary Area (Totally Stubby Area)

Make Area 1 Stub No-Summary Area (Totally Stubby Area)

The stub feature in area 1 is summarizing all the external routes for this area into the default route, while it still sees all the detailed OSPF inter-area routes. It is also possible to summarize all the OSPF inter-area routes into this default route, so all the OSPF summary LSAs (Type 3) will be removed as well. Since the OSPF summary LSA is suppressed by this action, this feature is known as 'stub no-summary' (Figure 6-67).

1. First verify on Access1 that the OSPF inter-area routes are still visible. On Access1, review the IP routing table, look for OSPF routes.

```
ICX-Tx-Access1(config)# show ip route ospf
Displaying ipv4 routes selected for forwarding
'[x/y]' denotes [distance/metric]

0.0.0.0/0, vrf default
        via  10.x.101.2,  [110/101],  ospf
        via  10.x.101.3,  [110/101],  ospf
10.x.0.3/32, vrf default
        via  10.x.101.3,  [110/100],  ospf
10.x.0.5/32, vrf default
        via  10.x.101.2,  [110/200],  ospf
        via  10.x.101.3,  [110/200],  ospf
10.x.0.2/32, vrf default
        via  10.x.101.2,  [110/100],  ospf
10.x.1.0/24, vrf default
        via  10.x.101.2,  [110/200],  ospf
        via  10.x.101.3,  [110/200],  ospf
10.x.2.2/31, vrf default
        via  10.x.101.2,  [110/101],  ospf
        via  10.x.101.3,  [110/101],  ospf
10.x.11.0/24, vrf default
        via  10.x.101.2,  [110/200],  ospf
        via  10.x.101.3,  [110/200],  ospf
10.x.12.0/24, vrf default
        via  10.x.101.2,  [110/200],  ospf
        via  10.x.101.3,  [110/200],  ospf
10.x.102.0/24, vrf default
        via  10.x.101.2,  [110/200],  ospf
        via  10.x.101.3,  [110/200],  ospf
10.x.192.0/18, vrf default
        via  10.x.101.2,  [110/300],  ospf
via  10.x.101.3,  [110/300],  ospf
```

2. Now make the area a 'stub no-summary' area. This must only be done on the ABR, since that is the router that will filter the routes.

3. On Core1, change the area 1 to no-summary. This change should be made on every ABR, but due to the VSX synchronization, this is automatically pushed to Core2.

```
ICX-Tx-Core1(config)# router ospf 1
ICX-Tx-Core1(config-ospf-1)# area 1 stub no-summary
ICX-Tx-Core1(config-ospf-1)# exit
```

1. On Access1, verify the impact on the routing table. All OSPF external and inter-area routes have been replaced with the default route.

```
ICX-Tx-Access1(config)# show ip route ospf
Displaying ipv4 routes selected for forwarding
'[x/y]' denotes [distance/metric]

0.0.0.0/0, vrf default
        via  10.x.101.2,  [110/101],  ospf
        via  10.x.101.3,  [110/101],  ospf
```

2. Verify that Access1 can still reach the external network to RouterA and Access2.

```
ICX-Tx-Access1(config)# do ping 198.18.11.1
PING 198.18.11.1 (198.18.11.1) 100(128) bytes of data.
108 bytes from 198.18.11.1: icmp_seq=1 ttl=63 time=2.39 ms
<...output omitted...>

ICX-Tx-Access1(config)# do ping 198.18.14.1
PING 198.18.14.1 (198.18.14.1) 100(128) bytes of data.
108 bytes from 198.18.14.1: icmp_seq=1 ttl=63 time=0.183 ms
<...output omitted...>
```

3. Verify Access1 can still reach the loopback IP on Access2 (an inter-area route).

```
ICX-Tx-Access1(config)# do ping 10.x.0.5
PING 10.x.0.5 (10.x.0.5) 100(128) bytes of data.
108 bytes from 10.x.0.5: icmp_seq=1 ttl=63 time=0.180 ms
<...output omitted...>
```

4. This demonstrates how the routing table of Access1 can benefit from the summarization while it still maintains full connectivity to the rest of the network.

Task 5: Filter Routes with a Not So Stubby Area (NSSA)

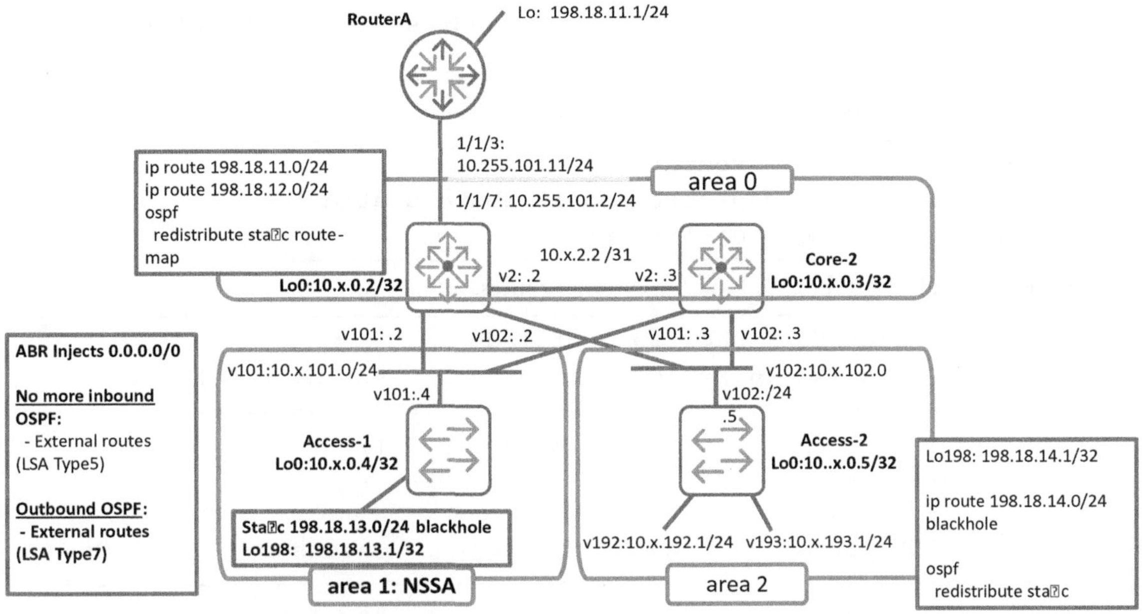

Figure 6-68 Task 5: Filter Routes with a Not So Stubby Area (NSSA)

Objectives

While a stub area benefits from the route summarization that is performed by the ABR, it is also limited now, since it cannot announce any external networks by itself anymore. When the administrator attempts to redistribute a route on a router in a stub area, OSPF will simply not process the request (Figure 6-68).

In these steps, the Access1 will make a connection to an external network and the rest of the OSPF AS needs access to this external network as well. At the same time, Access1 should still be optimized, so it does not get all the external routes from the backbone area.

Steps

Verify the problem.

1. On Access1, introduce a new external network. Since there is no real external network in this lab, it will be simulated using a blackhole static route and a local loopback interface. This is similar to the setup on Access2.

```
ICX-Tx-Access1(config)# ip route 198.18.13.0/24 blackhole
ICX-Tx-Access1(config)# interface loopback 198
ICX-Tx-Access1(config-loopback-if)# ip address 198.18.13.1/32
ICX-Tx-Access1(config-loopback-if)# exit
```

2. Now attempt to redistribute the static route into OSPF.

```
ICX-Tx-Access1(config)# router ospf 1
ICX-Tx-Access1(config-ospf-1)# redistribute static
ICX-Tx-Access1(config-ospf-1)# exit
```

3. Check the local OSPF LSDB, look for external routes.

```
ICX-Tx-Access1(config)# show ip ospf lsdb
OSPF Router with ID (10.x.0.4) (Process ID 1 VRF default)
===========================================================
Router Link State Advertisements (Area 0.0.0.1)
------------------------------------------------


LSID        ADV Router      Age       Seq#        Checksum     Link Count
---------------------------------------------------------------------------
10.x.0.2       10.x.0.2       166        0x80000006 0x00008a35     1
10.x.0.3       10.x.0.3       2          0x80000009 0x00008237     1
10.x.0.4       10.x.0.4       1          0x8000000d 0x00005943     3

Network Link State Advertisements (Area 0.0.0.1)
-------------------------------------------------


LSID             ADV Router      Age       Seq#        Checksum
--------------------------------------------------------------
10.x.101.3     10.x.0.3       2          0x80000002 0x0000cba8

Inter-area Summary Link State Advertisements (Area 0.0.0.1)
-------------------------------------------------------------


LSID             ADV Router      Age       Seq#        Checksum
--------------------------------------------------------------
0.0.0.0          10.x.0.2       1506       0x80000003 0x0000c87b
0.0.0.0          10.x.0.3       1506       0x80000003 0x0000c280
```

Question: Are there any external LSAs in the OSPF LSDB?

Answer: No, since this is a stub area, OSPF does not actually perform the redistribution. This means that the Core1 and Core2 would never be able to learn about this 198.18.13.0/24 route.

4. A filtered view 'external' on the LSDB shows the same result.

```
ICX-Tx-Access1(config)# show ip ospf lsdb external
No OSPF LSAs found on VRF default.
```

Solution: NSSA

The solution for this is to convert the area into an NSSA area type. This will allow external routes to be exchanged via the OSPF LSDB as LSA Type 7 entries (since LSA Type 5 is not allowed by a stub area). The ABR will convert the Type 7 LSAs into the regular Type 5 LSAs in the backbone. Any other areas in the OSPF autonomous system are not aware that this NSSA configuration was used, since they only see the external routes as LSA Type 5.

1. On the Access1, convert the area type to NSSA.

```
ICX-Tx-Access1(config)# router ospf 1
ICX-Tx-Access1(config-ospf-1)# area 1 nssa
ICX-Tx-Access1(config-ospf-1)# exit
```

2. Review the OSPF LSDB. There should be an NSSA external LSA.

```
ICX-Tx-Access1(config)# show ip ospf lsdb
OSPF Router with ID (10.x.0.4) (Process ID 1 VRF default)
===========================================================

Router Link State Advertisements (Area 0.0.0.1)
------------------------------------------------

LSID          ADV Router       Age      Seq#       Checksum      Link Count
---------------------------------------------------------------------------
10.x.0.4        10.x.0.4        30         0x80000001 0x0000928d      3

NSSA External Link State Advertisements (Area 0.0.0.1)
-------------------------------------------------------
LSID               ADV Router       Age         Seq#        Checksum
----------------------------------------------------------------
198.18.13.0      10.x.0.4         30          0x80000001 0x000071c0
```

Question: Why are all the other LSAs gone from the LSDB?

Answer: The NSSA area type is also included in the OSPF hello. Since the Core1 and Core2 still have the stub area type, Access1 no longer has an OSPF adjacency with them. This can be verified using 'show ip ospf neighbors'.

3. Notice that the NSSA external (LSA Type 7) and regular external (LSA Type 5) are shown separately in the LSDB.

```
ICX-Tx-Access1(config)# show ip ospf lsdb external
No OSPF LSAs found on VRF default.

ICX-Tx-Access1(config)# show ip ospf lsdb nssa-external
OSPF Router with ID (10.x.0.4) (Process ID 1 VRF default)
===========================================================

NSSA External Link State Advertisements (Area 0.0.0.1)
-------------------------------------------------------

LSID            ADV Router      Age         Seq#        Checksum
-----------------------------------------------------------------
198.18.13.0     10.x.0.4        10          0x80000001 0x000071c0
```

4. On Core1, change the area 1 area-type to nssa.

```
ICX-Tx-Core1(config)# router ospf 1
ICX-Tx-Core1(config-ospf-1)# area 1 nssa
ICX-Tx-Core1(config-ospf-1)# exit
```

5. Wait a few moments for the Adjacencies to re-established. Verify that NSSA external LSAs are now appearing in the LSDB of area 1.

```
ICX-T12-Core1(config)# show ip ospf lsdb nssa-external area 1
OSPF Router with ID (10.x.0.2) (Process ID 1 VRF default)
===========================================================
NSSA External Link State Advertisements (Area 0.0.0.1)
-------------------------------------------------------

LSID            ADV Router      Age         Seq#        Checksum
-----------------------------------------------------------------
0.0.0.0         10.x.0.2        93          0x80000001 0x00002891
0.0.0.0         10.x.0.3        89          0x80000001 0x00002296
198.18.11.0     10.x.0.2        93          0x80000001 0x00006407
198.18.13.0     10.x.0.4        221         0x80000001 0x000071c0
```

6. Verify the routes in another area, like area 2.Now switch to Access2; verify the routing table. The route to the 198.18.13.0 should now be available. This demonstrates how Area 1 still benefits from the route summarization of the stub area feature, while at the same time it can announce a route to an external network.

```
ICX-Tx-Access2(config)# show ip route 198.18.13.0
Displaying ipv4 routes selected for forwarding

'[x/y]' denotes [distance/metric]

198.18.13.0/24, vrf default
       via  10.x.102.3,  [110/25],  ospf
       via  10.x.102.2,  [110/25],  ospf
```

7. Review the OSPF LSDB of area 2; look for the 'external' and 'nssa-external' entries in the LSDB.

```
ICX-Tx-Access2# show ip ospf lsdb nssa-external
No OSPF LSAs found on VRF default.

ICX-T12-Access2# show ip ospf lsdb external
OSPF Router with ID (10.x.0.5) (Process ID 1 VRF default)
===========================================================

AS External Link State Advertisements
--------------------------------------

LSID            ADV Router       Age        Seq#         Checksum
---------------------------------------------------------------
198.18.11.0     10.x.0.2         1373       0x80000007 0x0000560f
198.18.13.0     10.x.0.3         193        0x80000001 0x0000ed4d
198.18.14.0     10.x.0.5         29         0x80000006 0x00006f43
```

Question: Why is the entry for the 198.18.13.0/24 network not shown as an NSSA-external route?

Answer: The NSSA-external has only meaning ***inside*** the NSSA area. When the ABR receives these NSSA (LSA Type 7) entries, it converts them into regular 'external' routes (LSA Type 5) in the backbone area, so the backbone area and any other areas are not aware of this.

Revert Area 1 to a Normal Area

The area 1 will now be reverted to a normal area.

1. On Core1, remove the NSSA type for area 1.

```
ICX-Tx-Core1(config)# router ospf 1
ICX-Tx-Core1(config-ospf-1)# no area 1 nssa
ICX-Tx-Core1(config-ospf-1)# exit
```

2. On Access1, repeat this step.

```
ICX-Tx-Access1(config)# router ospf 1
ICX-Tx-Access1(config-ospf-1)# no area 1 nssa
ICX-Tx-Access1(config-ospf-1)# exit
```

3. On Access1, verify OSPF adjacency is back to both core switches.

```
ICX-Tx-Access1(config)# show ip ospf neighbors
OSPF Process ID 1 VRF default
==============================
Total Number of Neighbors: 2

Neighbor ID    Priority  State          Nbr Address      Interface
-----------------------------------------------------------------------
10.x.0.2       1         FULL/BDR       10.x.101.2       vlan101
10.x.0.3       1         FULL/DROther   10.x.101.3       vlan101
```

Note

It may take a few moments for the OSPF adjacencies to re-establish. Repeat the command until the '**FULL**' state is shown.

4. Verify that external routes are available again; check, for example, the OSPF route to 198.18.11.0/24 network.

```
ICX-Tx-Access1(config)# show ip route 198.18.11.0
Displaying ipv4 routes selected for forwarding

'[x/y]' denotes [distance/metric]

198.18.11.0/24, vrf default
        via  10.x.101.2,   [110/1100],   ospf
```

5. This concludes the NSSA task. On ***each*** switch, save a checkpoint for the current lab.

```
copy run checkpoint icx-lab63
```

Learning Check

1. What are the advantages of designing an OSPF AS to use multiple areas?
2. Two OSPF routers are on the same network. One defines the dead interval as 1 second and another uses the default?
   A. The router that defines the network as point-to-point becomes DR.
   B. The router that defines the network as broadcast becomes DR.
   C. The routers cannot become successfully become neighbors.
   D. The two routers cannot become fully adjacent neighbors and cannot install each other's LSAs in the LSDB.
3. What is one requirement for an ABR?
   A. It must have interfaces in at least two areas with any IDs.
   B. It must have interfaces in area 0 and at least one other area.
   C. It must have interfaces in every area in the AS.
   D. It must have at least two interfaces in area 0, but do not require another area.
4. Which type of routes should you expect internal routers in a stub area to learn?
   A. Intra-area routes only
   B. Intra-area routes and a default route
   C. Intra-area routes, a default route, and inter-area routes
   D. Intra-area routes, a default route, inter-area routes, and external routes
5. What purpose does configuring OSPF BFD on an AOS-CX switch layer 3 interface fulfill?
   A. The switch can restart OSPF without affecting connectivity during the restart.
   B. The switch detects when it has lost connectivity with an OSPF neighbor more quickly.
   C. The switch avoids connecting to a rogue or unauthorized OSPF device.
   D. The switch detects OSPF configuration errors and automatically mitigates their effects.
6. Match the LSA type with its description.

LSA 1	External network, mask, metric, metric type
LSA 2	ASBR router ID and metric
LSA 3	Network in another area (network IP, mask, and metric)
LSA 4	DR IP on the network, Network mask, IDs of routers attached to the network
LSA 5	Links (ID, type, and metric)
LSA 7	External network, mask, metric, metric type, but must be translated by ABR before sending it to Area 0

Summary

Congratulations! In this chapter, you have learned how to implement more complex OSPF systems. You know why you might need to divide an OSPF AS into multiple areas, how to establish the areas, and how the area borders affect LSA propagation. You understand how OSPF routers use metrics to select inter-areas routes, and you can aggregate and filter routes between areas.

You also know when and how to redistribute external routes into OSPF. You understand how routers calculate external routes using the best path to the ASBR, and external type 1 and type 2 metrics help them choose between identical external routes. You can also aggregate external networks with ASBR summaries, as well as eliminate the external routes from stub areas entirely.

You know which types of areas benefit from being defined as stub areas and from being defined as totally stub areas. You can also set up an NSSA to allow local external routes within a stub area.

You also explored strategies and technologies for enhancing OSPF convergence. In particular, you learned when and how to use BFD to speed the detection of a failed neighbor. You can also use OSPF graceful restart to ensure seamless failover of an OSPF process on a VSF fabric or routing device with redundant management modules.

You examined several situations when a virtual link might be necessary, and you practiced creating such a link.

Finally, you learned how to implement OSPF authentication to minimize misconfigurations as well as to provide some protection against hackers.

7 BGP

OBJECTIVES

After completing this chapter, you should be able to:

- ✓ Establish and monitor BGP sessions between your routers and ISP routers
- ✓ Understand BGP route metrics
- ✓ Advertise an IP block to multiple ISP routers
- ✓ Configure a BGP router to advertise a default route in OSPF
- ✓ Filter routes to prevent transit networks

Overview

This chapter introduces you to Border Gateway Protocol (BGP), a powerful routing protocol designed for Internet Service Providers (ISPs) and very large enterprise networks. BGP is well suited to these use cases because it permits administrators to manipulate and even add attributes to route advertisements. This chapter will also introduce to you BGP route manipulation using BGP metrics.

Border Gateway Protocol (BGP) is a powerful routing protocol designed for Internet Service Providers (ISPs) and large enterprise networks. First, you will learn appropriate ways to incorporate this routing protocol in customer networks and discover some simple strategies for making BGP meet the requirements of specific scenarios. You will learn the basics of BGP, including the most common use cases for BGP within a campus network. You will also learn how to set up BGP neighbors, to advertise routes in BGP, and to ensure that when iBGP neighbors advertise routes to each other the route is valid. Next you learn how to influence route selection using route maps and other techniques. Then, you will learn why using route reflectors to minimize the iBGP sessions is required in larger networks and then complete two lab activities. Last, you will learn how to filter BGP routes to ensure that your company does not become a transit AS.

Introduction to BGP

This section provides a brief introduction to BGP, including use cases of connecting different company or service provider networks together.

BGP Use Case: Multi-Homed ISP Connections

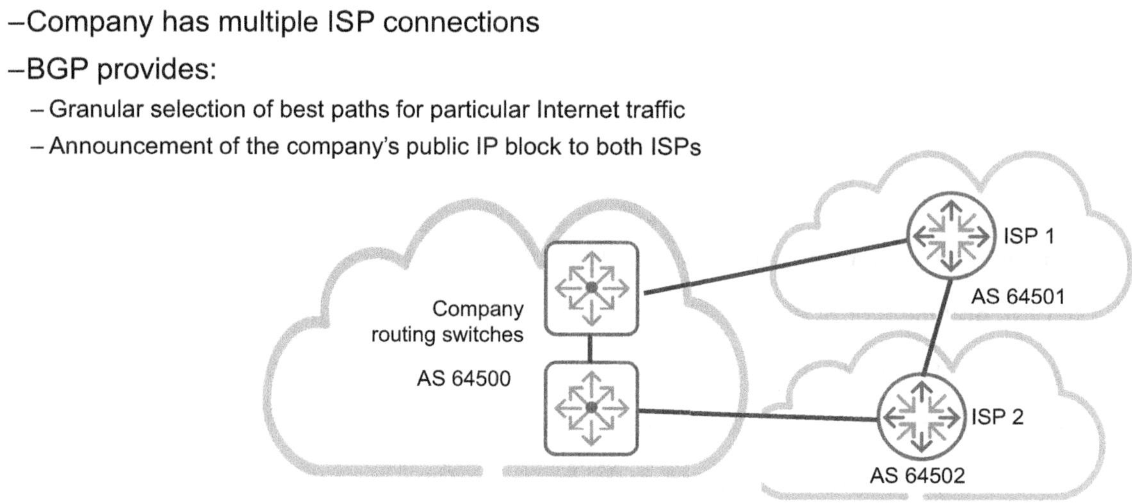

Figure 7-1 BGP Use Case: Multi-Homed ISP Connections

BGP is an exterior gateway protocol (EGP), which means that it communicates routes between different organizations, typically Internet Service Providers (ISPs). The figure illustrates the primary use case that you will examine in this chapter: a company needs to communicate with multiple ISP routers. You must understand when this scenario and similar scenarios call for BGP, as well as when it does not.

You do not need to implement BGP simply to connect to an ISP. You only need to do so when the company specifically needs to communicate routing information with the ISP. Typically, a company with a single connection to an ISP does not require BGP:

- The ISP handles announcing the block of public IP addresses assigned to the company.
- The company's routers use a default route for reaching all public IP addresses.

Note
This refers to "BGP routers" as shorthand for routing AOS-CX switches that support BGP.

When the company has multiple connections to the same ISP, it might benefit from communicating routing information with the ISP:

- The company router can discover more granular information about which connection offers the best route to particular external networks.
- In some special cases, the company might need to advertise different IP blocks over different connections.

The figure shows a case in which BGP might become even more useful: the company router is multi-homed to different ISPs:

- Again, the company router can discover which connection offers the best connection for particular traffic.
- The company router might need to announce the company's public IP address block to the second ISP. That ISP can then propagate this advertisement throughout the Internet, enabling external devices to reach the company over the best path, which might include either ISP. Alternatively, *both* ISPs might be able to handle advertising the block of addresses. The company would need to discuss the proper solution with both ISPs. If the ISPs handle announcing the company's addresses, the company might not need to implement BGP at all. You should assess whether the benefit of selecting the particular connection for particular external routes outweighs the complexities of implementing BGP.

Figure 7-1 shows a design in which a different router connects to each ISP. This design offers better resiliency than a design in which a single router connects to both ISPs; however, it can be slightly more complex because it requires two BGP routers, which communicate with each other as well as the ISP routers.

Unlike OSPF, BGP does not attempt to create a topology. Instead BGP acts as a distance vector protocol in which routers advertise routes that they know to neighbors. Because BGP is designed for use on the Internet, it can handle millions of routes. The protocol also permits a high level of administrative control for each organization. Organizations can aggregate routes, filter routes, and manipulate attributes in routes.

You can alternatively use VSF to combine two physical AOS-CX switches that support BGP, such as 6300 switches. You can then connect to the two ISPs on different physical chassis, but still retain the simplicity of a single (logical) BGP router for both connections.

Other BGP Use Cases

ISPs use BGP to communicate routes:

- Within their domains
- With other ISPs
- With some customers

Companies with large, complicated networks can also use BGP:

- Within their own domain
- With ISPs

Figure 7-2 Other BGP Use Cases

You do not need to implement BGP simply to connect the core routing switches an ISP. In many cases, the company switches can use a default route to the ISP router, and the ISP can handle advertising any public IP addresses assigned to the company in the Internet (Figure 7-2).

However, some companies want connections to multiple ISPs for better redundancy. In this case, the company may need to use BGP to advertise its public IP addresses to the second ISP. That ISP can then propagate this advertisement throughout the Internet, enabling external devices to reach the company over the best path, which may include either ISP. Running BGP on the company routing switches also enables the switches to choose the best paths for particular Internet traffic.

BGP is designed specifically to communicate routes between organizations controlled by different entities and scales to hundreds of thousands of routes. For these reasons, ISPs use BGP to communicate routes with other ISPs, and BGP underlies all Internet routing. ISPs use BGP to communicate routes with other ISPs, and BGP underlies all Internet routing. For the same reasons, large enterprises that have outgrown a routing protocol such as OSPF can implement BGP. The enterprise can segment itself into multiple OSPF autonomous systems and use BGP to communicate routes between these autonomous systems in a scalable manner.

For the same reasons, large enterprises that have outgrown a routing protocol such as OSPF can implement BGP. The enterprise can segment itself into multiple OSPF autonomous systems and use BGP to communicate routes between these autonomous systems in a scalable manner.

Note

Implementing a complete BGP solution for a service provider or ISP or for a large organization that involves confederations is beyond the scope of this guide. This guide focuses on how smaller organizations can connect to a service provider using BGP when static routes are not sufficient or do not meet the company's accessibility policies.

BGP AS

BGP is an external gateway protocol (EGP) used to connect different autonomous systems, between a company and an ISP, multiple ISPs, or even segments within a large private network.

Note

Do not confuse the fact that BGP is an external gateway protocol (EGP) with a deprecated routing protocol, which is also called EGP.

The AS forms the fundamental building block of BGP, and each organization such as a company or ISP generally has its own AS, identified by a unique number (Figure 7-3). Originally, BGP supported only 16-bit AS numbers, ranging between 0 and 65535.

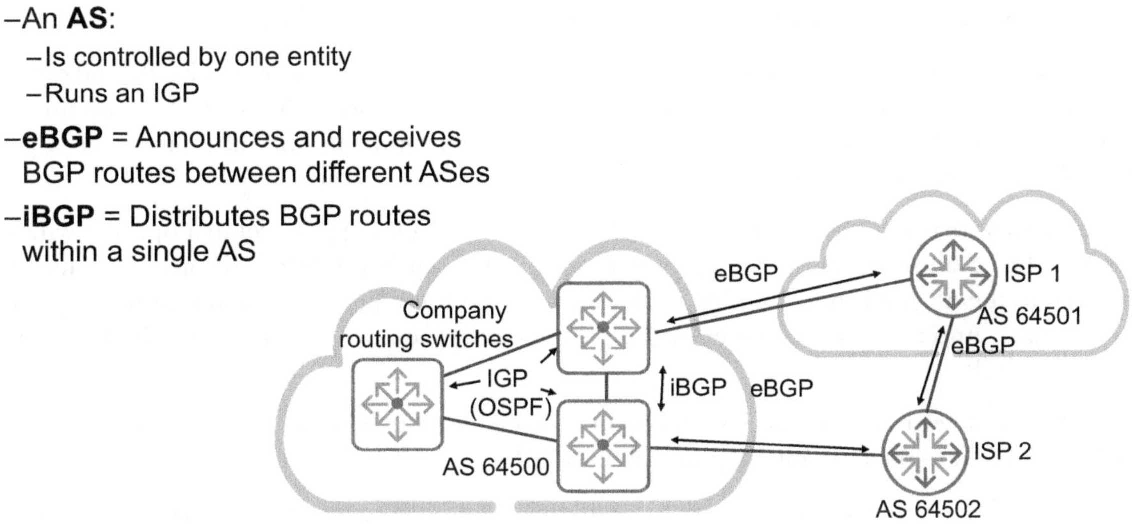

Figure 7-3 BGP AS

Table 7-1 BGP AS 4-byte

Purpose	**AS Numbers**
Reserved	0 and 65535
Public IANA-assigned	1-64495
Documentation and examples	64496-64511
Private	64512-65534

Because 16-bit numbers allow for only 65535 unique numbers, Request for Comments (RFC) 4893 establishes 32-bit AS numbers, increasing the range of AS numbers to 4 billion. AOS-CX switches support 32-bit numbers in one of two formats:

- **1-4294967295**: The autonomous system number (ASN) for the domain
- **0.1-65535.65535**: The autonomous system number (ASN) for the domain in dotted decimal format

When a company determines that it needs to run BGP in a multihomed scenario, it must obtain a valid public AS from the proper regional authority.

BGP operates in one of two forms depending on the autonomous systems to which the communicating neighbors belong:

- Neighbors in different autonomous systems communicate with exterior BGP (*eBGP*).
- Neighbors in the same AS communicate with interior BGP (*iBGP*).

The same router might use eBGP with one neighbor and iBGP with another.

Neighbors in different autonomous systems communicate with the exterior BGP (eBGP), and eBGP is responsible for advertising routes from one AS to another. Neighbors in the same AS communicate with interior BGP (iBGP), and iBGP distributes BGP routes within an AS. The same router might use eBGP with one neighbor and iBGP with another.

It is important that you understand that iBGP is not the only routing protocol that operates within the AS. The AS also runs an interior gateway protocol (IGP) such as OSPF, RIP, or IS-IS, which is localized to the AS and handles routing the local traffic. Typically, just a few routers in the AS—the routers that connect to other autonomous systems and perhaps some core routers—run BGP in addition to the IGP.

Typically, just a few routers in the AS—the routers that connect to other autonomous systems—run BGP in addition to the IGP routing protocol like OSPF.

There are a few commands you can use to enable BGP and configure the basic settings. Start by creating the BGP process and setting the AS number. Remember the company needs to obtain this number from a regional authority. You can create only one process and AS on the switch:

```
Switch(config)# router bgp <autonomous-system-number>
```

Optionally, but highly recommended, you can assign a BGP router-ID to your switch:

```
Switch(config-bgp)# bgp router-id <router-ID>
```

Within the BGP context, you can optionally set the BGP router ID. If you do not set the router ID manually, the AOS-CX switch uses the highest IP address on a loopback interface, or, if no loopback interfaces exist, the highest IP address on any interface. You can also change the administrative distance for BGP, if you want. By default, the switch uses a different administrative distance for routes the eBGP discovers rather than by the iBGP.

Note

In some cases, the ISP might place a company within the ISP's own AS. In this case, however, the company router would use iBGP to communicate with the ISP routers. The company would also need a different AS to connect to another ISP. This guide does not cover these use cases.

Establishing BGP Connections

This section discusses how BGP routers connect to each other using TCP, including the connection types (internal versus external) and the stages of the connection.

BGP TCP Sessions

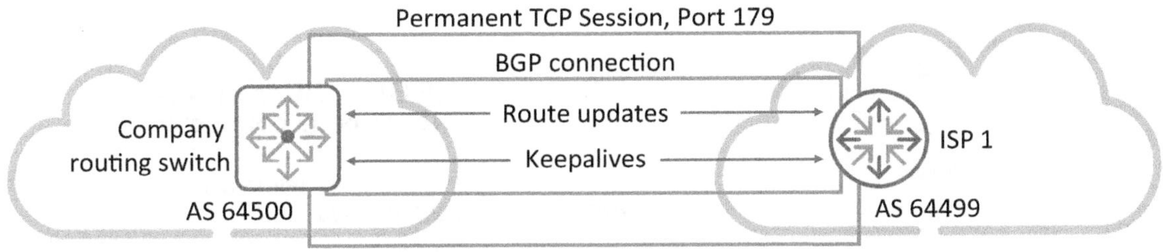

Figure 7-4 BGP TCP Sessions

With OSPF, you enable OSPF on an interface, and it will automatically discover neighbors. BGP takes a different approach. You must manually define each BGP neighbor on your BGP router to enable the router to establish the connection. BGP neighbors establish a TCP session on port 179. They then open a BGP connection within the session. The routers can then exchange their BGP routing tables.

BGP neighbors establish a TCP session on port 179 (Figure 7-4). They then open a BGP connection within the session. This connection carries all messages and routing updates between the neighbors, and the TCP session provides a degree of reliability for the communications. The BGP connection also features keepalives, which helps each router determine its neighbor's reachability.

The BGP connection carries all messages and routing updates between the neighbors, and the TCP session provides a degree of reliability for the communications. The BGP connection also features keepalives, which helps each router determine its neighbor's reachability. On AOS-CX switches, keepalives are sent every 60 seconds by default, and the switches have a hold-down timer of 180 seconds, three times the keepalive interval.

BGP Neighbor Addresses: eBGP

You must manually define each BGP neighbor on your BGP router to enable the router to establish the connection. Use this BGP configuration:

```
Switch(config-bgp)# neighbor <IP-address> remote-as <AS>
Switch(config-bgp)# address-family ipv4 unicast
Switch(config-bgp-ipv4-uc)# neighbor <IP-address> activate
```

The remote AS is the AS to which the neighbor belongs. If this AS is different from the AOS-CX switch's own AS, the neighbor is automatically defined as an eBGP neighbor. If this AS is the same of the AOS-CX switch's AS, the neighbor is automatically defined as an iBGP neighbor.

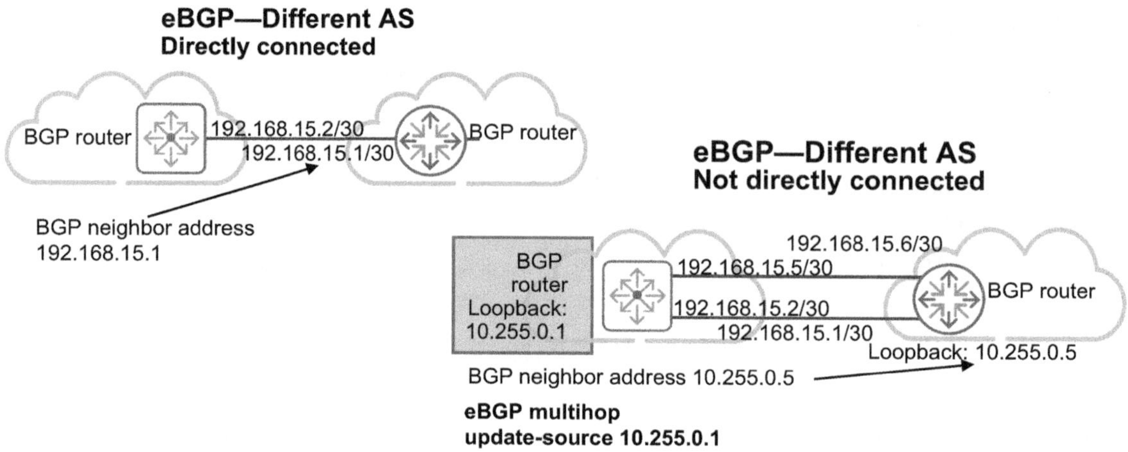

Figure 7-5 BGP Neighbor Addresses: eBGP

Guidelines for specifying the neighbor IP address depend on whether the neighbor is an eBGP neighbor or an iBGP neighbor (Figure 7-5).

eBGP Neighbors

By default, eBGP neighbors must establish the session on a direct Layer 3 connection. In other words, they have IP addresses on the same subnet (a Layer 2 device could intervene without issue.) The eBGP protocol enforces this criterion by checking that the neighbor IP address is on a network connected to the local BGP router and also by using messages with a TTL of 1. In most cases, you should keep this behavior.

However, sometimes you need to configure a session between neighbors on different networks. For example, your router might have two redundant Layer 3 connections to the same router. Each connection has its own IP address, but you want to establish a single connection to the neighbor with a stable IP address. Therefore, you configure the BGP neighbor's loopback interface IP address as the neighbor IP address on your routing switch. Similarly, the neighbor sets the local router's IP address to its loopback interface. You can then set the neighbor's loopback IP address as the neighbor IP address.

Although the loopback IP addresses are on directly connected routers and are technically only one hop apart, they are not on the same link. You must enable eBGP multihop, which disables the directly connected subnet check and optionally sets the TTL (hop count) for the BGP messages higher than 1:

```
Switch(config-bgp)# neighbor <ipv4-addr> ebgp-multihop [2-255]
```

You must also ensure that the routers have routes to each other's loopback interfaces. Create static routes to the neighbor's loopback interface; the next hop for each route is the neighbor's IP address on one of the connected interfaces. Depending on whether you want to load-balance traffic over the redundant links to the ISP router, set the same administrative distance on the routes (load-balance) or different administrative distances (active route has lower distance). In addition, with the 10.2 software release the AOS-CX switches support BGP connections over GRE tunnels.

Similarly, ensure that the neighbor creates routes to your router's loopback interface.

Finally, consider one other issue. By default, each switch uses its IP address on the forwarding interface to the neighbor as the source for its BGP messages. The neighbor expects the message from a neighbor IP address configured on it, so it rejects the messages. You can use this command to make the AOS-CX switch use its loopback IP address as the source for messages to the BGP neighbor instead:

```
Switch(config-bgp)# neighbor <ipv4-addr> update-source
<local-loopback-IP-address>
```

Another use case for eBGP multihop is when you must reach the ISP router that runs BGP through another router or routers. To set up this solution, you must set the eBGP multihop to the correct number (2 if one intermediate router intervenes, three if two routers intervene, and so on). Your router also requires a route to the ISP router's IP address, of course. However, it is not recommended to have intervening routers between eBGP neighbors, and you should avoid this setup whenever possible.

BGP Neighbor Addresses: iBGP

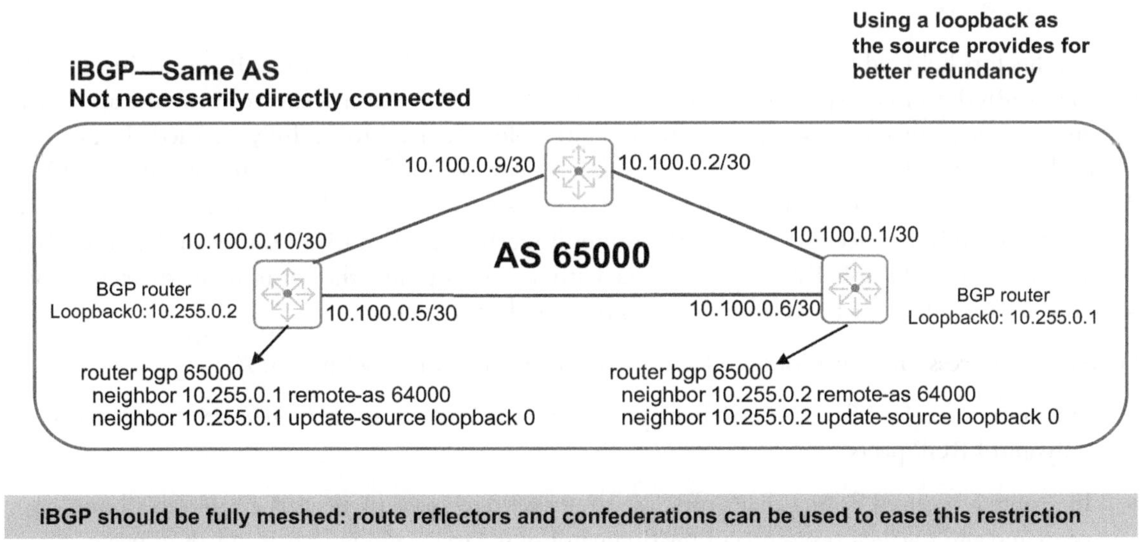

Figure 7-6 BGP Neighbor Addresses: iBGP

iBGP neighbors

Unlike eBGP neighbors, iBGP neighbors do not have to be directly connected (Figure 7-6). Your AS might have many routing devices running an IGP such as OSPF, but only two BGP routers, which might be in different locations. Even if the two BGP routers connect directly, as Core-1 and Core-2 do in your lab topology, you often want them to contact each other's loopback interfaces. The routers can then continue to maintain the BGP session if their direct Layer 3 connection fails and they fail over to an alternative path.

When you plan to connect iBGP neighbors to each other's loopback interfaces, use this command, as in the eBGP scenario:

```
Switch(config-bgp)# neighbor <ipv4-addr> update-source
<local-loopback-IP-address>
```

However, you do not need to enable multihop for iBGP neighbors; iBGP permits multiple hops between neighbors by default.

Note

When you configure the neighbors to contact each other on loopback interfaces, remember that you need to set the *update source* to the local loopback IP address. Also remember to advertise the loopback interfaces in the IGP (usually OSPF) so that the neighbors can find each other.

Route Reflectors

Route reflectors help reduce the number of connections required between iBGP peers within an AS. By default, iBGP routers expect to be fully meshed within an AS: a route reflector provides an alternative method of connectivity where the iBGP routers do not need to be fully meshed. In an AS, a single iBGP router (preferably two for redundancy) can be configured as a route reflector. Other iBGP routers in the AS need only be configured as peers to the route reflector(s). The function of the route reflector(s) is to reflect or "mirror" the routes it receives from an iBGP router to the other iBGP routers in the AS. Multiple iBGP routers peer with a central point, the route reflector (acts a route reflector server). All other IBGP routers act as route reflector clients.

Here is the process on how a route reflector server works for routes within an AS:

- If a route is received from a non-client peer, the route reflector server reflects the route to clients only and EBGP peers.
- If a route is received from a client peer, the router reflector server reflects the route to all non-client peers and also to client peers, except the originator of the route and reflects it to EBGP peers.

The route reflector's purpose is similar to OSPF's designated and backup designated routers (DRs and BDRs) and provides iBGP scalability by reducing the number of peers' connections that need to be established. For example, in an AS of 10 iBGP routers, you would need to define 90 peering statements to implement a fully meshed iBGP solution. However, if you implemented a single route reflector instead, you would only need to implement 18 peering statements. The formula is: (number of routers * 2) / 2. If you wanted to implement a pair of redundant route reflectors, you would only need a total of 36 statements. In either case, your configuration is drastically reduced from a fully meshed iBGP solution.

Clusters

A router reflector(s) and its iBGP clients form a *cluster*. A cluster-ID is associated with every route advertised by the route reflector to its client and/or non-client peers. The cluster-ID is a cumulative, non-transitive BGP attribute and every route reflector *must* prepend its local cluster-ID to the cluster-list in order to avoid routing loops. Route reflectors and confederations both reduce the number of iBGP peerings to each router and thus reduce processing overhead. To provide scalability, clusters can be interconnected.

BGP Confederations

At some point, the use of clusters runs into scalability issues. This is where you can then implement confederations. BGP confederations are sets of autonomous systems. In a typical implementation, only one of the confederation's AS numbers is seen by the Internet. Confederations are used in very large networks where a large AS can be configured to encompass smaller more manageable internal autonomous systems.

Each individual confederated AS within the company has iBGP fully meshed and has connections to other autonomous systems inside the confederation. Even though these internal autonomous systems have eBGP peers to autonomous systems *within* the confederation, the autonomous systems exchange routing as if they used iBGP. By doing this, the confederation preserves next hop, metric, and local preference information. To the outside world, the confederation appears to be a single AS. Within this solution, iBGP transit AS problems can be resolved since iBGP requires a full mesh between all BGP routers.

Confederations can be used in conjunction with route reflectors. Both confederations and route reflectors can be subject to issues unless specific design rules, affecting both BGP and the interior routing protocol, are adhered to. Problems that can occur include:

- Route oscillation
- Sub-optimal routing
- Increase of BGP convergence time

Additionally, route reflectors (and clustering) and BGP confederations were not designed to simplify BGP router configuration. However, these are common tools for experienced BGP network designers and engineers. These tools may be combined, for example, as a hierarchy of route reflectors.

> **Note**
> By default, iBGP routers should be fully meshed. If they cannot be fully meshed, then you need to implement BGP route reflectors. The configuration of route reflectors and confederations is beyond the scope of this book.

MD5 Authentication

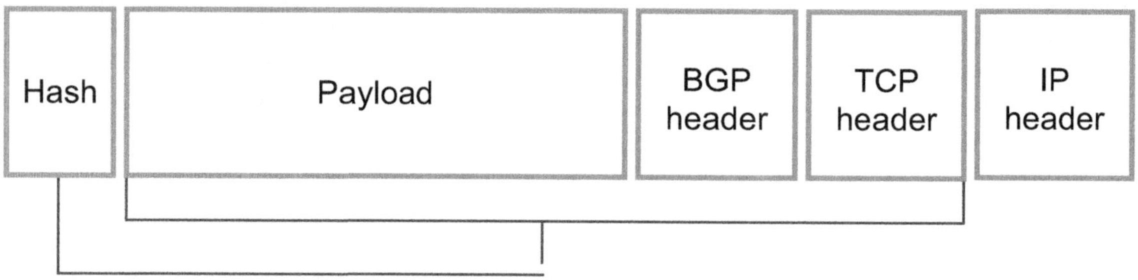

Figure 7-7 MD5 Authentication

The ISP might require your router to authenticate. You simply add a password when you define the neighbor. The BGP neighbors use this password to hash the TCP payload of packets that carry the BGP messages, appending the hash to the packet. If the neighbors' passwords do not match, the TCP session for the BGP connection fails to establish (Figure 7-7).

Because the neighbors add the MD5 hash to each packet sent on the TCP session, MD5 authentication provides data integrity for all BGP messages and for underlying TCP session. In other words, each neighbor knows that the proper neighbor sent the message and that no one has altered the message. However, MD5 does not provide protection against eavesdropping.

To assign the password, use the following command:

```
switch(config-bgp)# neighbor <ipv4-addr> password plaintext <password>
```

BGP Connection States

In the lab, you will see how the BGP neighbors pass into Active state and stayed there when they encountered issues. You will see that a healthy session should have the Established state. Figure 7-8 and the following notes provide more details about the session establishment for your reference.

To establish the BGP connection, the neighbors first open the TCP session on port 179. They then send BGP open messages with a list of parameters for the session and, assuming the parameters match, finally send the first keepalive of the session.

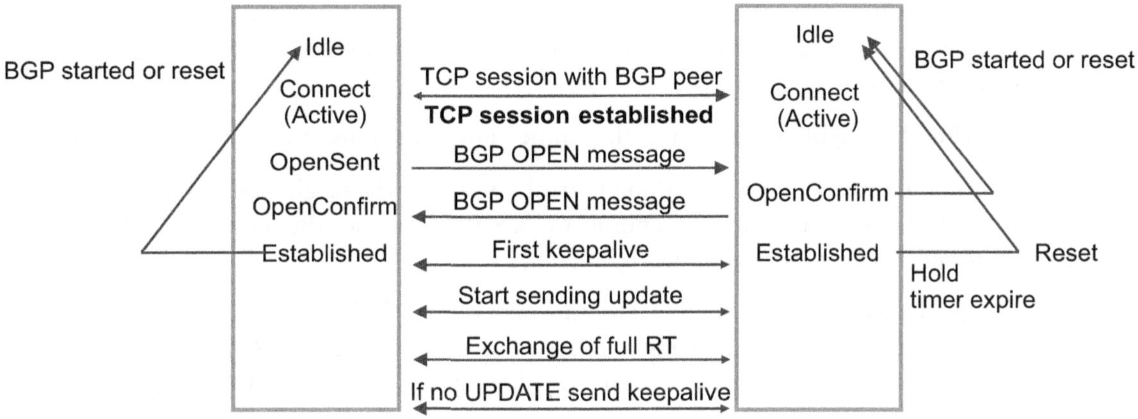

Figure 7-8 BGP Connection States

You can trace the states through which a BGP connection might pass:

- The BGP connection begins in the Idle state and returns to this state when the session establishment times out without success or an error occurs.
- The connection typically transitions immediately to the Connect state, in which the router attempts to contact its neighbor at TCP port 179 and waits for a response.

  If the router is set to Passive TCP mode for this neighbor, the session transitions to Active mode, rather than to Connect mode. In this mode, the router waits for the neighbor to initiate the session.

  The connection also moves to the Active state if the router does not receive a response to its TCP session initiation. In this state, the router waits for the neighbor's response and also, after a timer expires, might try to initiate the connection again. The router might wait in Active state for a significant period of time if the TCP session fails to establish. If you see a router in Active mode after several minutes, the neighbor might be unreachable.
- After the BGP neighbors have established the TCP session, the router sends an open message, either immediately or after a configurable delay. The connection also transitions to the OpenSent state or directly to the OpenConfirm state depending on whether the router has already received the neighbor's open message.
- In the OpenSent state, the router waits for the neighbor's open message. Once it receives that message, it verifies that necessary parameters match (for example, the neighbor's AS matches the remote AS configured on your router). Assuming that the parameters match, the router sends a keepalive and transitions to the OpenConfirm state.

If the parameters do not match, the router sends an error notification and returns to the Idle state. Therefore, if you see a router stuck in the Idle state, you might want to check that you configured the local AS and neighbor AS correctly.

- In the OpenConfirm state, the router waits for neighbor's keepalive message and also sends its own keepalive. It also listens for error notifications such as one indicating that the open message parameters do not match.
- After receiving the neighbor's keepalive, the connection transitions to the Established state.

  The connection remains in this state during normal operation. The neighbors continue to send keepalives. If a BGP router fails to receive a number of keepalives, it ends the connection. Note that the keepalive period is quite long (5 minutes, by default).

New eBGP neighbors exchange their full BGP routing tables. After the eBGP neighbors have exchanged their BGP routing tables, they only exchange updates. For example, a BGP router sends an update if configuration changes affect routing policies or if a topology change has occurred.

Routes remain in the BGP routing table unless an update occurs. A router can also request a route refresh from a neighbor which might be necessary so that the router can apply new policies to routes that it has already received.

BGP Routing Metrics

This section introduces some of the metrics used in BGP route selection.

More Criteria in BGP Best Route Selection

Attribute or criteria	Attributetype	Preferred values
Weight	N/A	Highest
Local preference	Discretionary	Highest
Locally originated	N/A	Prefer the path that was locally originatedwith next hop of 0.0.0.0
AS path length	Mandatory	Local to this AS (learned by IGP or redistributed) Thenshortest path (fewest AS numbers in list)
Origin	Mandatory	IGP < EGP < ? i(< e < ?)
MED	Optional non-transitive	Lowest
eBGP over iBGP	Administrative distance	Prefer the eBGP over iBGP
IGP metric to next hop	N/A	Lowest
ORIGINATOR_ID	Optional, non - transitive	Lowest
CLUSTER_LIST	Optional, non - transitive	Smallest
Router ID	N/A	Lowest
Neighbor's IP address	N/A	Lowest

* See the Learner Guide for more BGP metrics

Figure 7-9 More Criteria in BGP Best Route Selection

When multiple identical BGP routes are valid and have the same administrative distance, BGP uses the criteria shown in the table above to select the best route.

Figure 7-9 shows BGP attributes and the values that are preferred for each attribute. Attributes are listed in the order by which the router examines them when selecting the best route. That is, the router selects the route with the better weight first. Only if those values are equal does the router move on to examine the next attribute, local preference. (Your router can set the weight for specific routes, and that value has meaning only on the router itself. When it sets the local preference, on the other hand, it communicates that value to iBGP neighbors, but not eBGP neighbors.)

Without special manipulation of weight and local preference on your part, your router will tend to prefer routes based on the AS path length. It will accept the route from the ISP that reaches the networks in question through fewer ISPs. Presumably, the shorter AS path indicates a shorter latency; however, this is not necessarily the case.

If the ISP routers advertise routes with the same number of AS IDs in the AS path, the origin might come into play. Routes that were originally injected into BGP are preferred to routes learned from EGP (deprecated) and redistributed routes. However, often the ISPs will have learned the route from a similar ultimate source, so the origin is identical.

The Multi-Exit Discriminator (MED) would take effect only if the ISP routers have explicitly set this attribute. They might do this if they needed to distinguish between multiple paths into your AS (in a scenario in which the multiple connections are to the same ISP). Generally, a router only compares MED values between routes advertised from the same AS. However, in some cases, you can request different ISPs to send routes with different MED values. You must enter this BGP command to permit the AOS-CX switch to compare the MED values between the two ISP routers.

```
switch(config-bgp)# bgp always-compare-med
```

However, without special manipulation such as that, if the AS path is the same length, your router will probably accept the route from the router to which it has a lower cost connection. If the metric to both ISPs is the same, the choice becomes nearly arbitrary. If ECMP is enabled, in fact, the routing AOS-CX switch adds multiple routes with the same next hop cost and load balances over them. If ECMP is disabled, the switch selects the route based on age, then router ID, and then the cluster list—but only if these checks are enabled. The final tie breaker is the advertising router ID.

Similarly, assuming no manipulation of attributes, routers throughout the Internet will tend to route traffic to your company through the ISP to which they are closer.

BGP allows administrators to control several of these attributes, granting both the ISP and you the ability to fine-tune the route selection. Keep in mind that the neighbor router can also manipulate attributes and has ultimate authority over its route selection. Therefore, you can dictate which routes your devices choose, but might not be able to determine the flow for inbound traffic.

Note that the table in the figure on the previous page also indicates the type of attribute. (Rows without an attribute type are not attributes included in the route advertisement, but rather values that the switch determines itself.) It can be helpful to understand the attribute type when you perform more advanced manipulation. Mandatory and discretionary attributes are both well-known attributes that all BGP routers understand; mandatory attributes must be included in every route advertisement, while discretionary attributes are optional. An optional attribute might not be supported by all BGP routers. The "non-transitive" description means that if a BGP router receives this optional attribute and does not support it, it should drop the attribute.

Sometimes customers want to prefer one ISP link over another regardless of the AS path. You can use the default local preference for this situation. The AOS-CX switch assigns the default local preference to all BGP routes that it advertises to iBGP neighbors (unless a set command overrides it in a route map). In this case, you can use the **bgp default local-preference** command. See the IP Routing Guide for more information.

Here are the steps that could be involved to determine which BGP route is preferred:

1. Do not consider route if the next hop is *unreachable*
2. Select the route with the highest *weight*
3. Select the route with the highest *local preference*
4. Select the route *originated by the local* router
5. Select the route with the *shortest AS-PATH*
6. Select the *IGP, EGP, or Incomplete* route in turn, referred to as the "origin" attribute
7. Select the route with the *lowest MED* value
8. Select the route learned from *eBGP, confederation, or iBGP* in turn
9. Select the route with the smallest next hop metric
10. Select the route with the smallest ORIGINATOR_ID
11. Select the route with the shortest CLUSTER_LIST
12. Select the route advertised by the router with the smallest Router ID
13. Select the route advertised by the peer with the lowest IP address

BGP AS Path Length Metric

As you saw on the previous page, BGP has many metrics that you can define to manipulate routing policies. If no metrics are defined (weight or local preference), then the AS path length (number of AS hops to reach the destination network) is used. The AS path attribute is also used by BGP to detect routing loops based on path choices.

Even though a path might be shorter, that does not necessarily mean that it is more preferred: which is why BGP has so many different metrics that you can implement to influence path choice. One option would be to use local preference to influence the exit point to reach a network. Another option is AS path prepending, where you intentionally repeat the next AS number one or more times to make the path less preferable, since the number of hops would be higher. In the above example, if you wanted the traffic to travel 46501 -> 46502 -> 46504, then for the default preferred path, you could do prepending: 46503, 46503, 46503, 46504. In this situation, the path now has more hops than 46501, 46502, 46504 and therefore would be less desirable. (2 versus 3 AS hops)

Note

By default, BGP does not do load sharing: the first "best" path used is what is placed in the routing table unless you enable equal-cost multipath (ECMP) for BGP.

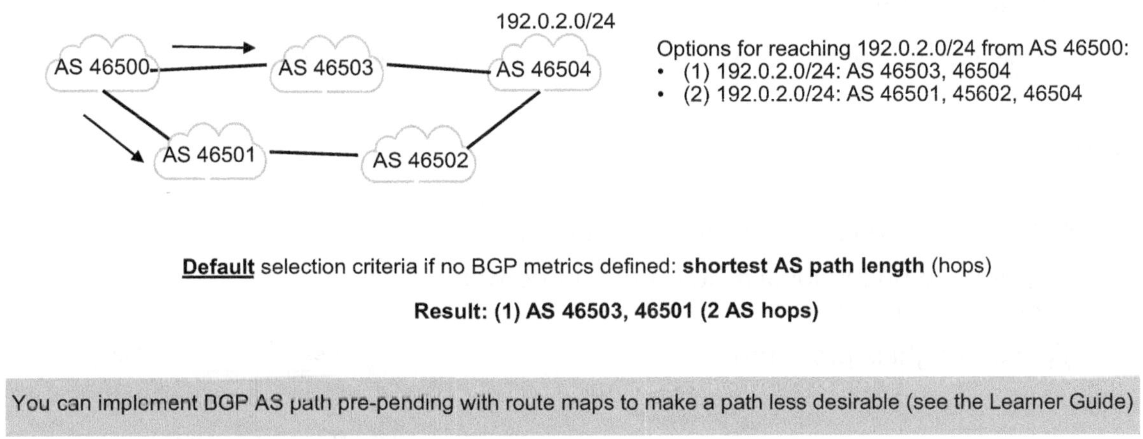

Figure 7-10 BGP AS Path Length Metric

AS Prepending

If for policy reasons you wanted to do use a different path to reach the destination than the one that had the number of shortest hops, you could solve this problem in a few ways. One solution is to implement AS prepending. In Figure 7-10, if you wanted traffic to 192.0.2.0/24 to travel to AS46501 to 46502 to 46504 instead of 46503 to 46504, you could add additional hops to the latter route. This is accomplished using a route map.

Here is an example you would configure on the eBGP router in AS 46500 that connects to its eBGP peer in AS 46503:

```
Switch(config)# ip prefix-list AS46504-routes permit 192.0.2.0/24
Switch(config)# route-map From-AS46503 permit seq 10
Switch(config-route-map)# match ip address prefix-list AS46504-routes
Switch(config-route-map)# set ip as-path prepend 46503 46503
Switch(config-route-map)# exit
Switch(config)# router bgp 46500
Switch(config-bgp)# address-family ipv4 unicast
Switch(config-bgp-ipv4-uc)# neighbor <IP-address-of eBGP-in AS-46503> route-map
From-AS46503 in
```

By doing this, BGP routers in AS 46500 would see two paths:

- (1) AS 46503, 46503, 46503, 46504
- (2) AS 46501, 46502, 46504

Based on the pre pending, the second path would be preferred over the first.

Weight

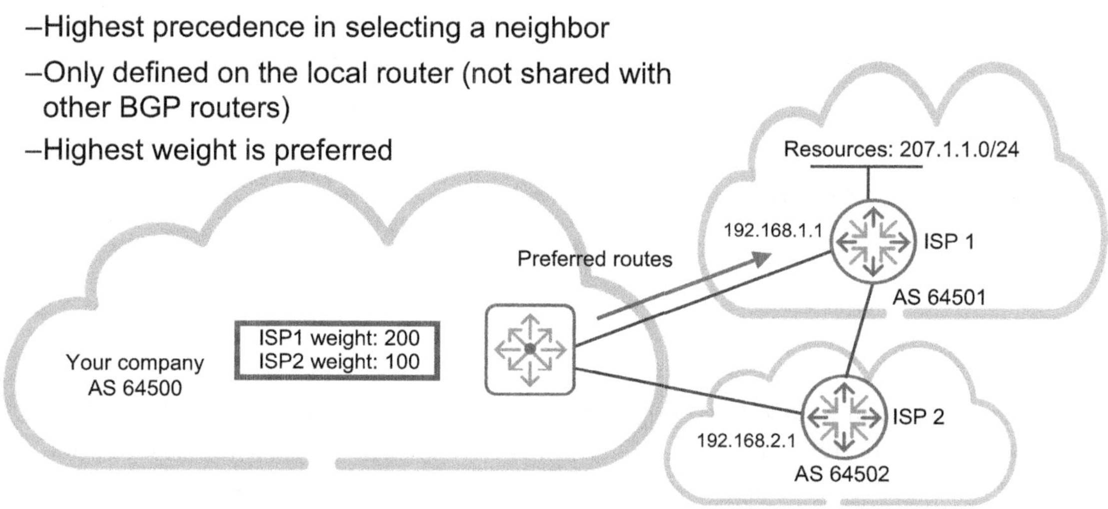

Figure 7-11 Weight

Weight is a metric that is not really part of the BGP standard, since it is not an attribute shared between BGP peers. Instead, the metric allows you to implement a policy on the local router as to which eBGP peer it prefers. The higher the weight, the more preferred the routes from the respective peer (Figure 7-11). To configure weight, use the following configuration:

```
Switch(config)# router bgp <AS-number>
Switch(config-bgp)# neighbor <IP-address> weight <value>
```

Here is an example that would prefer routes from ISP1:

```
Switch(config)# router bgp 64500
Switch(config-bgp)# neighbor 192.168.1.1 weight 200
Switch(config-bgp)# neighbor 192.168.2.1 weight 100
```

Optionally you could implement route maps to weight just a particular route(s) from a neighbor, instead of all the routes of a neighbor, like shown in the above example. If using a route map, you would use the **set weight** command to adjust the weight for matching routes.

Local Preference

Local preference is a metric used in internal BGP to determine the best exit to reach a particular route. The default local preference is 100: the higher the preference, the more preferred the route (Figure 7-12). This value is set with a route map.

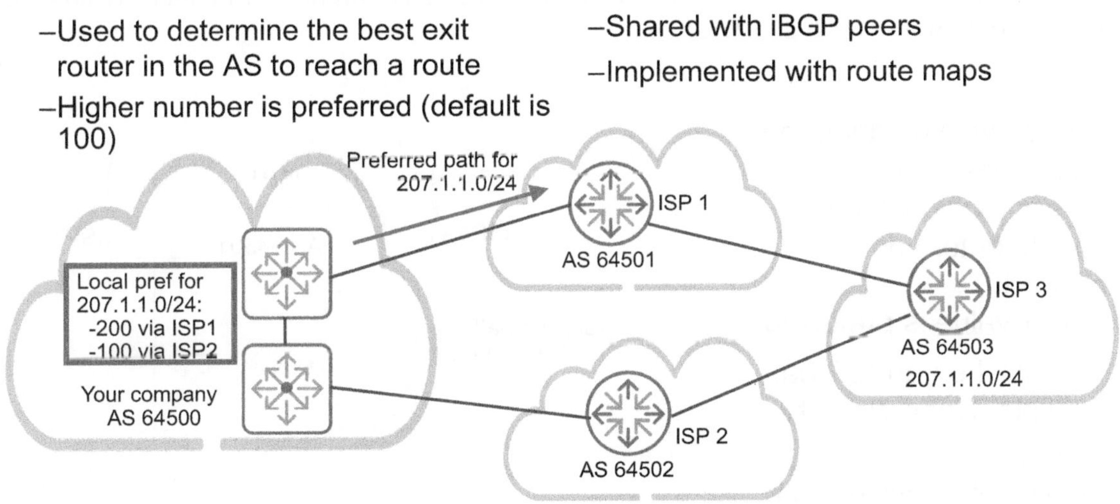

Figure 7-12 Local Preference

Here is an example for the eBGP router in AS 64500 connected to AS 64501:

```
Switch(config)# ip prefix-list AS64501-routes permit 207.1.1.0/24
Switch(config)# route-map From-AS64501 permit seq 10
Switch(config-route-map)# match ip address prefix-list AS64504-routes
Switch(config-route-map)# set local-preference 200
Switch(config-route-map)# exit
Switch(config)# router bgp 64500
Switch(config-bgp)# address-family ipv4 unicast
Switch(config-bgp-ipv4-uc)# neighbor <IP-address-of eBGP-in AS-64501> route-map
From-AS64501 in
```

Multiple Exit Discriminator (MED)

Multiple Exit Discriminator (MED) is an attribute shared with a neighboring ISP (eBGP) to influence how they will enter your network when there are two or more connections between you and the respective ISP.

In the example in Figure 7-13, it makes more sense for traffic destined to 200.1.1.0/24 to enter AS 64500 by choosing the eBGP peer that is closes to that network, in this case Router1. By setting a MED value for the route, via a route map, AS 64500 can advertise this to ISP1 to influence how they will enter AS 64500 to reach 200.1.1.0/24.

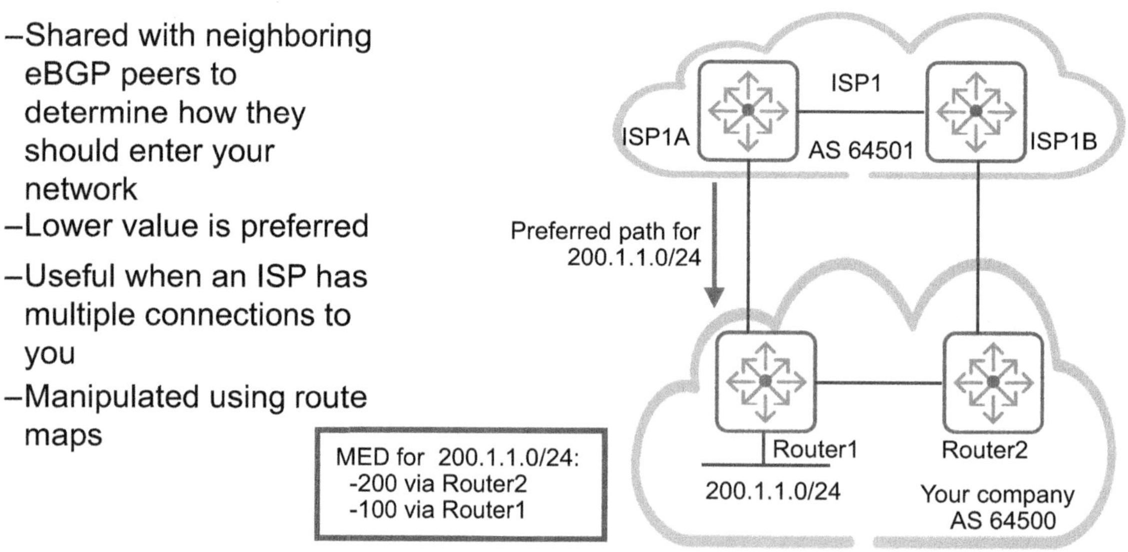

Figure 7-13 Multiple Exit Discriminator (MED)

Here is an example configuration for Router1 and Router2:

```
Router1(config)# ip prefix-list AS64500-routes permit 200.1.1.0/24
Router1(config)# route-map To-AS64501 permit seq 10
Router1(config-route-map)# match ip address prefix-list AS64500-routes
Router1(config-route-map)# set metric 100
Router1(config-route-map)# exit
Router1(config)# router bgp 64500
Router1(config-bgp)# address-family ipv4 unicast
Router1(config-bgp-ipv4-uc)# neighbor <IP-address-of-ISP1A> route-
mapTo-AS64501 out

Router2(config)# ip prefix-list AS64500-routes permit 200.1.1.0/24
Router2(config)# route-map To-AS64501 permit seq 10
Router2(config-route-map)# match ip address prefix-list AS64500-routes
Router2(config-route-map)# set metric 200
Router2(config-route-map)# exit
Router2(config)# router bgp 64500
Router2(config-bgp)# address-family ipv4 unicast
Router2(config-bgp-ipv4-uc)# neighbor <IP-address-of-ISP1B> route-map
To-AS64501 out
```

The only difference between the configurations of Router1 and Router2 is the MED value assigned using the **set metric** command.

Receiving and Advertising Routes

This section introduces viewing routes received from eBGP peers and how to advertise routes to eBGP peers.

BGP Routing Table

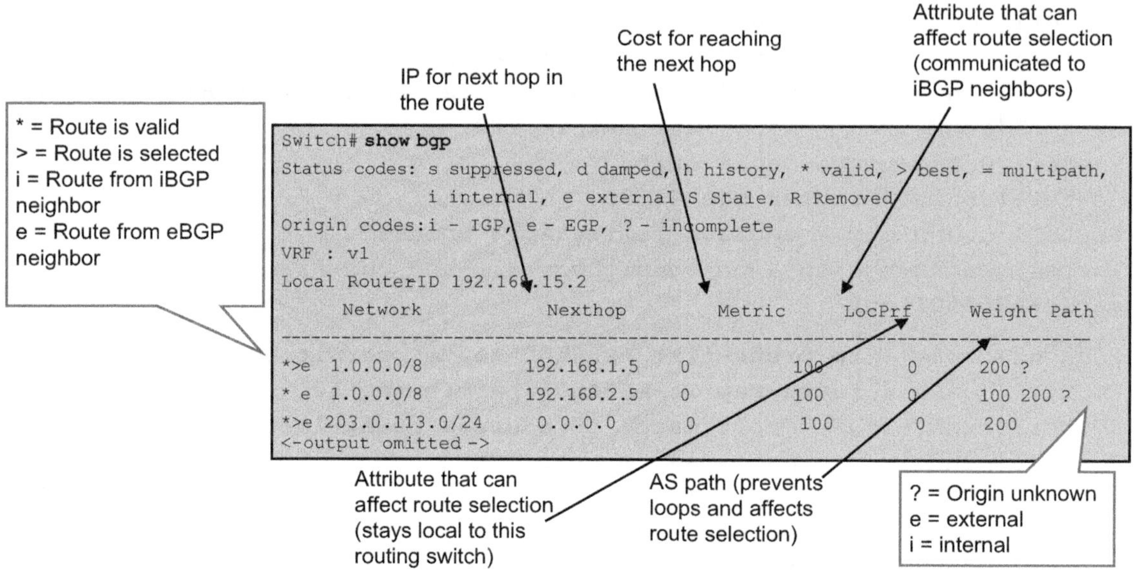

Figure 7-14 BGP Routing Table

After BGP neighbors have established a connection, they exchange their entire BGP routing tables (Figure 7-14). Before you learn more about advertising routes, it can be useful to examine the BGP routing table in more detail.

Each route has several symbols at the beginning. An asterisk (*) indicates that the route is valid, which means that the next hop is reachable. The greater than sign (>) indicates that the router has selected this route as the best one to the network in question. The route's origin is also indicated with i for a route received from an iBGP neighbor and e for a route received from an eBGP neighbor.

The route next indicates the destination network address and the next hop. The metric indicates the cost for reaching the next hop; unlike with OSPF, this metric is not the most important criteria for selecting between routes. *LocPrf* refers to local preference. Both local preference and weight can affect route selection, but local preference is communicated between iBGP routers while weight is locally significant only.

Finally, note the AS path, which is included in every BGP route. When a BGP router first advertises a network in BGP, it puts its AS number in the path. When a BGP router in a different AS receives the route, that BGP router adds its AS to the path, and so on. In this way, the AS path indicates every AS which traffic will traverse to reach the destination.

In this example, the BGP router has two routes to 1.0.0.0/8: one through AS 100 and one through AS 200 and then AS 100. The AS path composes BGP's primary loop elimination technique. If a router receives a route with its own AS in the AS path, it drops the route. The AS path also affects route selection with shorter paths preferred.

Next-Hop Reachability

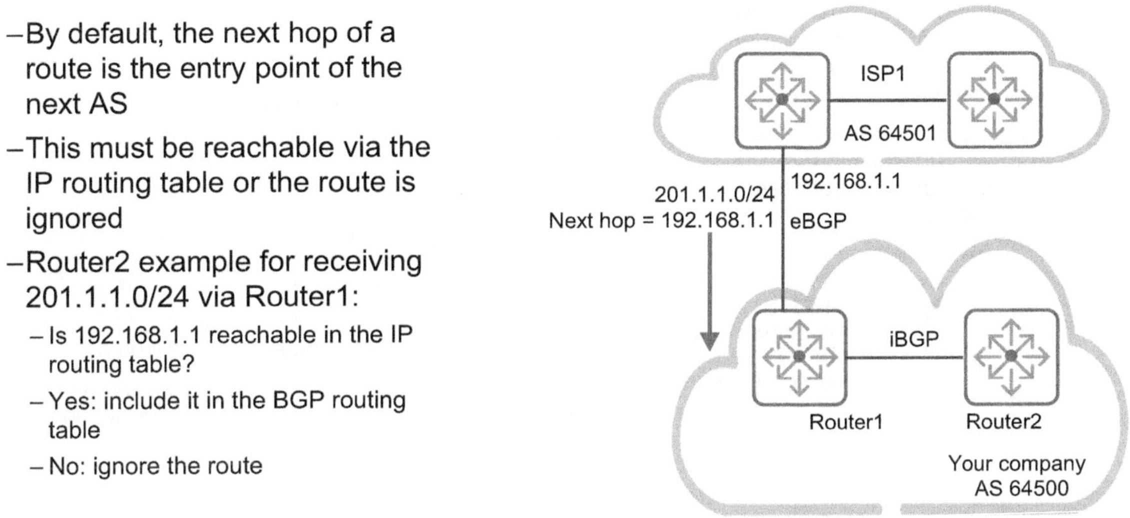

Figure 7-15 Next-Hop Reachability

To accept a route as a potential best route, the router must first determine whether the next hop is valid (Figure 7-15).

In the multi-homing ISP scenarios, your BGP router or routers often receive valid routes to identical networks (same network address *and* prefix length) from multiple neighbors. AOS-CX switches use the administrative distance as the first criteria to choose the best route. Because the default eBGP distance is 20 and the default iBGP distance is 200, by default, your BGP router will prefer all routes received from an eBGP neighbor to all routes received from an iBGP neighbor.

If you keep this behavior, the default routes advertised in OSPF determine to which BGP router various local routing switches send Internet traffic. When the traffic arrives on the BGP router, that router uses its own ISP connection to forward the traffic.

When a router advertises an eBGP route to another eBGP neighbor, it advertises its IP address on the connection with the neighbor as the next hop. However, when a router advertises an eBGP route to an iBGP neighbor, it retains the advertising eBGP neighbor IP address as the next hop. This means that both of your BGP routers must have a route to both of your ISP routers.

Next-Hop Reachability: Next-Hop-Self

Since a BGP router will ignore a route if the next-hop address is unreachable for your neighboring AS's router advertising the route, one option is to make sure the network of the next-hop address is in your local routing table. For the example in the slide, if AS 64500 was running OSPF, make sure 192.168.1.0/24 appears in the IP routing table via OSPF.

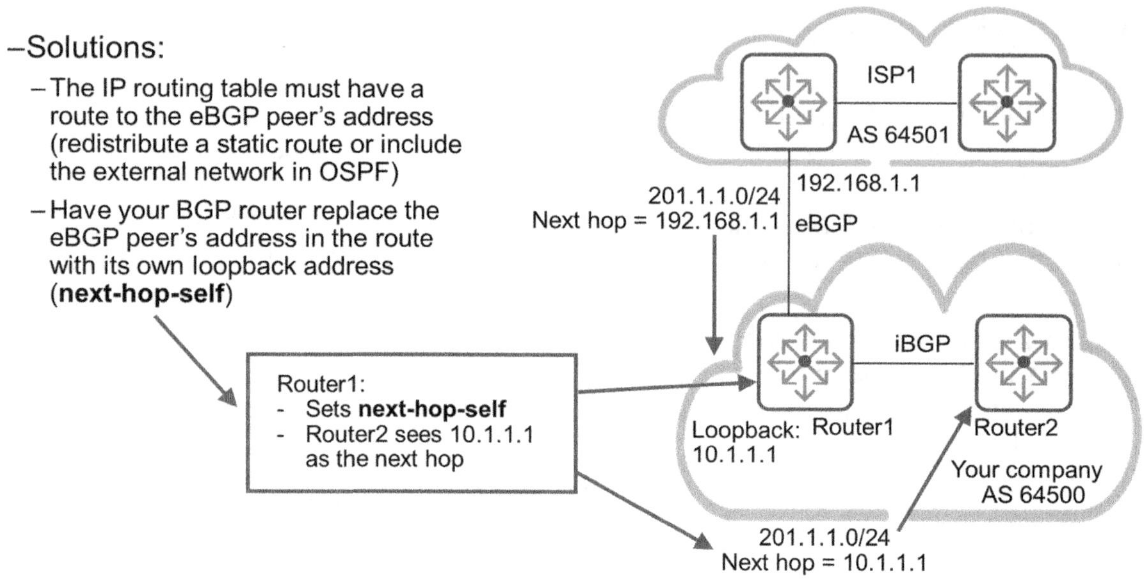

Figure 7-16 Next-Hop Reachability: Next-Hop-Self

Alternatively, you can configure your BGP router to always advertise itself as the next hop with this command:

```
Switch(config-bgp)# neighbor <ipv4-addr> next-hop-self
```

By configuring this command, when you share the routes to your internal iBGP routers, your router's IP address (preferably its loopback) is used in the next-hop address in the BGP routing update. Just ensure the BGP router's next-hop-self address (its loopback) is in the IP routing table (Figure 7-16).

In the above example, you would configure Router1 as the next hop for routes received via the eBGP peer 192.168..1.1, like this:

```
Router1(config)# router bgp 64500
Router1(config-bgp)# neighbor 192.168.1.1 next-hop-self
```

Receiving Routes from BGP Neighbors

After BGP neighbors have established a connection, they exchange their entire BGP routing tables. More specifically, they advertise their best route to each network in the BGP routing table to the neighbor. The best route is indicated by the > character, as shown in the slide. The asterisk (*) indicates that the route is valid—that is, the router has a route to the next hop.

In the example shown in the slide, the company BGP router does not have any routes in its BGP routing table before it establishes a connection with its neighbor. After these connections establish, the neighbors send route advertisements. Figure 7-17 shows just a couple of advertisements as an example. Of course, in the real world, BGP routing tables are very large.

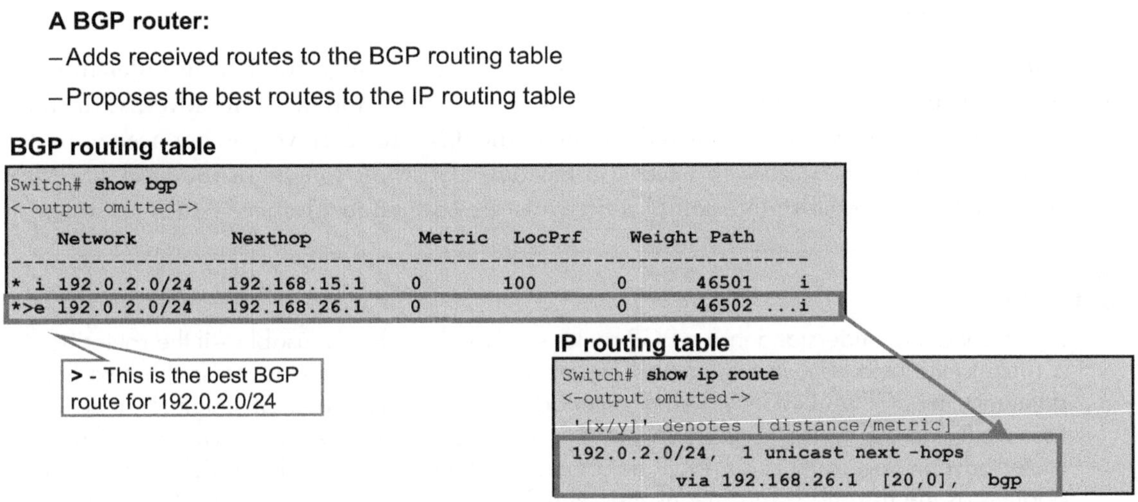

Figure 7-17 Receiving Routes from BGP Neighbors

Your router follows this process when it receives routes from an *eBGP* neighbor:

- The router adds the routes to its BGP routing table.

  The route specifies the eBGP neighbor as the advertiser. By default, other BGP attributes remain intact.

  If the BGP router has received routes to identical networks from multiple neighbors, it must select the best route. You will look at the specific selection process during the lab.

- The router proposes the *best* routes to the global IP routing table.
- The router advertises the best routes to other BGP neighbors.

  The routes received from BGP neighbors are already part of the BGP routing table. You do not need to take additional steps to configure the BGP router to announce these routes to other BGP neighbors.

  Of course, a router never advertises a route that it received from a neighbor back to that neighbor. But it does advertise the route to other neighbors even if those neighbors have advertised an identical, but less preferred route to it.

When a router advertises an eBGP route to another eBGP neighbor, it advertises its IP address on the connection with the neighbor as the next hop. However, when a router advertises an eBGP route to an iBGP neighbor, it retains the advertising eBGP neighbor IP address as the next hop. This means that both of your BGP routers must have a route to both of your ISP routers. Alternatively, you can configure the BGP router to always advertise itself as the next hop with this command:

```
Switch(config-bgp)# neighbor <ipv4-addr> next-hop-self
```

BGP routers handle advertising routes that they have received through iBGP a bit differently. For example, they do not advertise the routes to other iBGP neighbors. And they only advertise the route to eBGP neighbors after they have learned the route in the IGP. However, you do not need to understand these rules in depth because this scenario has only two BGP routers in the local AS. More information and guidelines for more complex networks are covered in advanced Aruba training.

Note

It is important to understand that a BGP route is only valid—that is, usable—if the router has a route to the next hop. You must also understand that BGP routers advertise the next hop differently in eBGP and iBGP. When a router advertises a route to a eBGP neighbor, it advertises its IP address on the connection with the neighbor as the next hop. However, when a router advertises a route to an iBGP neighbor, it retains the advertising eBGP neighbor IP address as the next hop. This means that all BGP routers within your AS must have a route to all of your ISP routers. Make sure that the route is learned in the IGP, not in BGP.

Advertising Routes to BGP Peers

- Must add a route to the IP block in order to advertise it to eBGP neighbors:
  - Inject (preferred)
  - Redistribute (use route maps to restrict routes to advertise)

Figure 7-18 Advertising Routes to BGP Peers

If you want the BGP router to advertise any other routes, such as routes to local networks, you must add those routes to the BGP routing table explicitly. For example, your BGP router needs to advertise the company's IP block to the ISP. You must add a route to that block to the BGP routing table (Figure 7-18).

You add routes from the BGP router's IP routing table, either by injecting the routes or by redistributing them from another protocol, such as OSPF, or from static or connected routes.

The next pages explain the injection method in more detail, as it is the approach that you should typically take.

Although redistributing routes enables you to import many routes into the BGP routing table with a single command, you do not have the same level of control provided by injecting routes. For example, redistributing OSPF routes into BGP adds all of the OSPF routes indiscriminately, including many private routes that you should not advertise to your ISPs. You can apply a route policy with the redistribute command to filter out undesired routes, but this approach is usually more complicated than you require.

Redistribution

To redistribute OSPF or static routes into BGP, perform the following:

```
switch(config-bgp)# redistribute {connected | ospf | static}
[route-map <route-map-name>]
```

Preferably use a route map to control which routes can be propagated into BGP. If you want to aggregate routes, then create a static route that defines the aggregation and redistribute that route into BGP.

Note

BGP applies an origin attribute of "?" for redistributed routes, indicating an unknown origin. Keep in mind that neighbors prefer routes with an "i" origin, so the choice to redistribute rather inject the routes might affect whether neighbors choose to route traffic to this router. The redistribute method is the least preferable of two options to have your BGP router advertise BGP routes.

Preferred Solution: Inject Routes

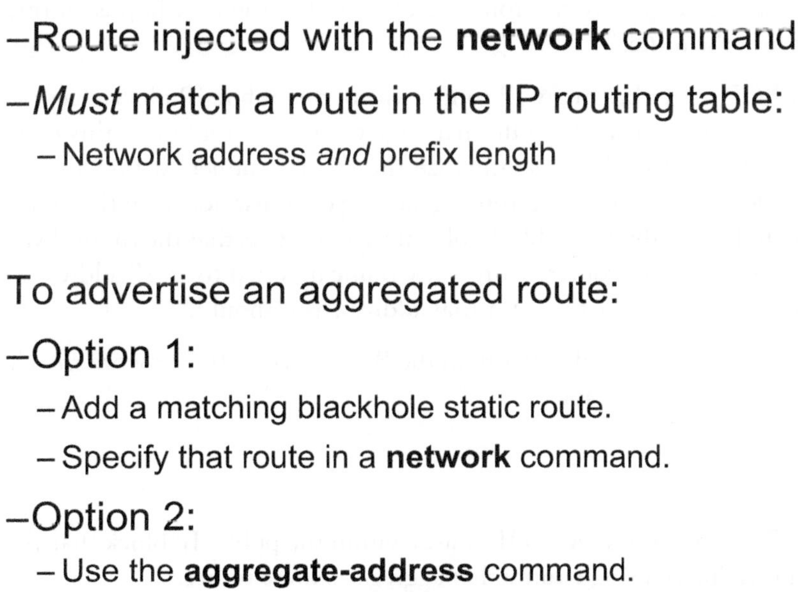

Figure 7-19 Preferred Solution: Inject Routes

If you want the BGP router to advertise routes to local networks, you must explicitly announce the network in BGP. You add routes to BGP from the BGP router's IP routing table, either by injecting the routes or by redistributing them. You can redistribute from another protocol, such as OSPF, or from static or connected routes. Usually you should use the injection method, which lets you control precisely which networks the router announces. Redistributing routes can either redistribute more routes than you desire or require route maps to filter routes. You can inject any route in the IP routing table into the BGP routing table by entering this configuration:

```
switch(config-bgp)# address-family ipv4 unicast
Switch(config-bgp-ipv4-uc)# network <network IP address/prefix length>
```

You must specify a network address and prefix length that matches the route in the routing table exactly. For example, you might want to advertise two ranges to your ISP:

- 203.0.113.0/25
- 203.0.113.128/25

You can enter **network 203.0.113.128/25** on the router with routing table shown above. The network is added to the BGP routing table because the routing table includes this exact route.

You should always view the BGP routing table to check the routes that your router will advertise to its neighbors. Figure 7-19 shows how the 203.0.113.128/25 route appears in the BGP routing table. When you inject the route into the BGP routing table, the BGP routing process adds a number of BGP-specific attributes, including origin and next hop. The origin of the route is i, indicating that the BGP router has learned this route from one of its IGPs. The next hop is empty, indicating that this router advertises the route.

Sometimes your BGP router has many IP routes within the public IP block that you want to advertise, and you want to inject a single route that aggregates these routes. In this example, you might want to advertise 203.0.113.0/25 to summarize the shorter subnets within that range. When the aggregated route does not exist in the routing table, you must add a static route to the network through the blackhole. Specifying the blackhole interface ensures that the route always remains in the routing table. It also allows the router to drop any traffic destined to an IP address within this range, if it does not have a more specific route for that address, as it should.

You can then specify the aggregated network in the BGP process. The network matches the blackhole route, so it is added to the BGP table.

BGP Route Aggregation

Sometimes your BGP router has several IP routes within the public IP block that you want to advertise, and you want to inject a single route that aggregates these routes.

For example, you may want to advertise a single route, 203.0.113.0/24, to summarize the shorter subnets within that range. You can add the **aggregate-address** command and specify the desired aggregated address and range. Then, as long as the BGP routing table has at least one network in that range, the AOS-CX switch will begin to advertise a route to the aggregated network.

The switch also automatically adds a reject route to the aggregated network in the IP routing table. This allows the router to drop any traffic destined to an IP address within this range, if it does not have a more specific route for that address, which is the proper behavior. Use the **summary-only** option with the aggregate-address command to tell the switch to suppress advertisement of the individual networks within the range.

You still need to use the **network** command to inject the individual networks (technically, the **network** command for only one network is required, but you probably want the switch to continue advertising the aggregated address if it has contact with any of the networks.) When you add the **aggregate-address** command, the aggregated route does not show up in the switch's BGP routing table. You will see an "s" at the front of each individual network in the aggregated range because those routes are suppressed. And you can see the switch advertise the aggregated range to neighbors, and the route appears in their tables.

Another approach for aggregating BGP advertisements exists by manually adding a static reject route to the aggregated network address and then injecting that network into BGP with the **network** command instead of the individual networks. However, with this static approach, the BGP router will continue to advertise the aggregated network even if it loses all active routes to the networks within the range. Therefore, the more dynamic **aggregate-address** approach is preferable.

Inject Routes Example

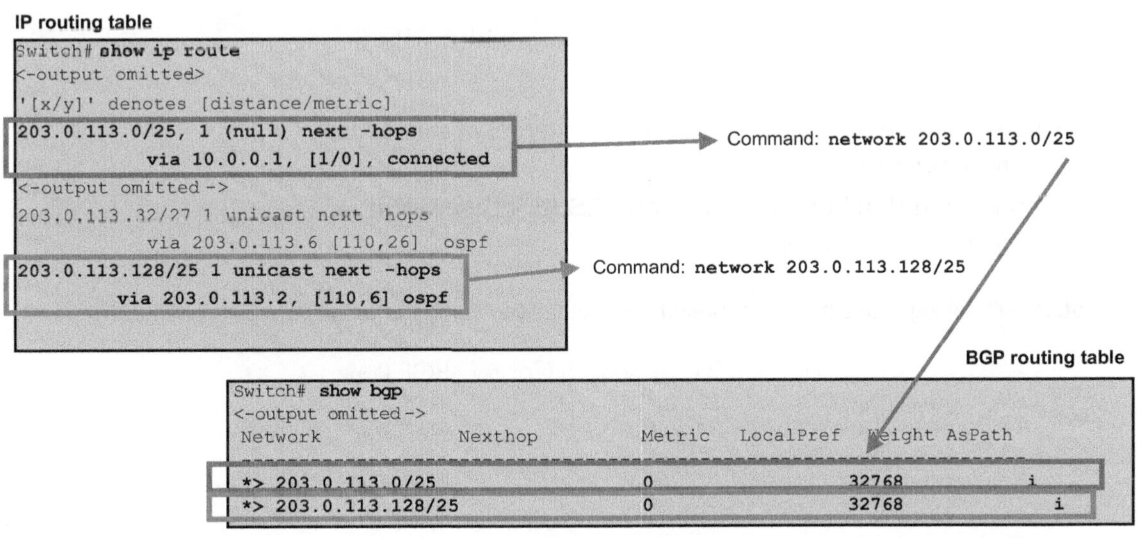

Figure 7-20 Inject Routes Example

In the above IP routing table, as shown in Figure 7-20, two routes are injected into the BGP routing table: 203.0.113.0/25 and 203.113.128/25. You could easily summarize these into one route with the following configuration:

```
Switch(config)# router bgp 65010
Switch(config-bgp)# address-family ipv4 unicast
Switch(config-bgp-ipv4-uc)# network 203.0.113.0/25
Switch(config-bgp-ipv4-uc)# network 203.0.113.128/25
Switch(config-bgp-ipv4-uc)# aggregate-address 203.0.113.0/24 summary-only
```

Note that the two /25 routes must be in the IP routing table, like shown in the slide, in order for them to be injected into the BGP routing table with the **network** or **aggregate-address** commands. In this configuration, a summarized route is advertised to peers instead of the individual routes. Here are the results:

```
Switch# show bgp
<-output omitted->
Network                   Nexthop          Metric LocalPref  WeightAsPath
---------------------------------------------------------------------------
*> 203.0.113.0/24                          0                    32768i
The "i" at the end denotes internal (injected).
```

Route Control

This section introduces the basics of controlling routes with BGP.

- Choose appropriate exit points to reach external destinations:
  - Control routes you receive
- Ensure you don't become a transit AS for other ISPs:
  - Control routes you advertise

Note: Use Looking Glass (free web-based Internet tool) to verify the results of your configuration

Figure 7-21 Reasons to Control eBGP Routes

Reasons to Control eBGP Routes

There are many reasons to control external BGP (eBGP) routes, as shown in Figure 7-21. The two most common are:

- Choose appropriate exit points to reach external destinations
- Ensure you do not become a transit AS for other ISPs

For example, if you have resources in ISP1 that you commonly access, it makes sense to use the connection you have to ISP1 to reach them, versus go through another ISP to reach those resources. Second, you do not want ISPs to use your company's bandwidth in order to connect to other ISPs, which is referred to as a *transit* AS. Based on these two reasons, you will need to implement eBGP route control through prefix or AS path lists to control the external BGP routes you receive and/or advertise.

Note
Use **Looking Glass** (**https://www.us.ntt.net/support/looking-glass/**) to verify the results of your configuration.

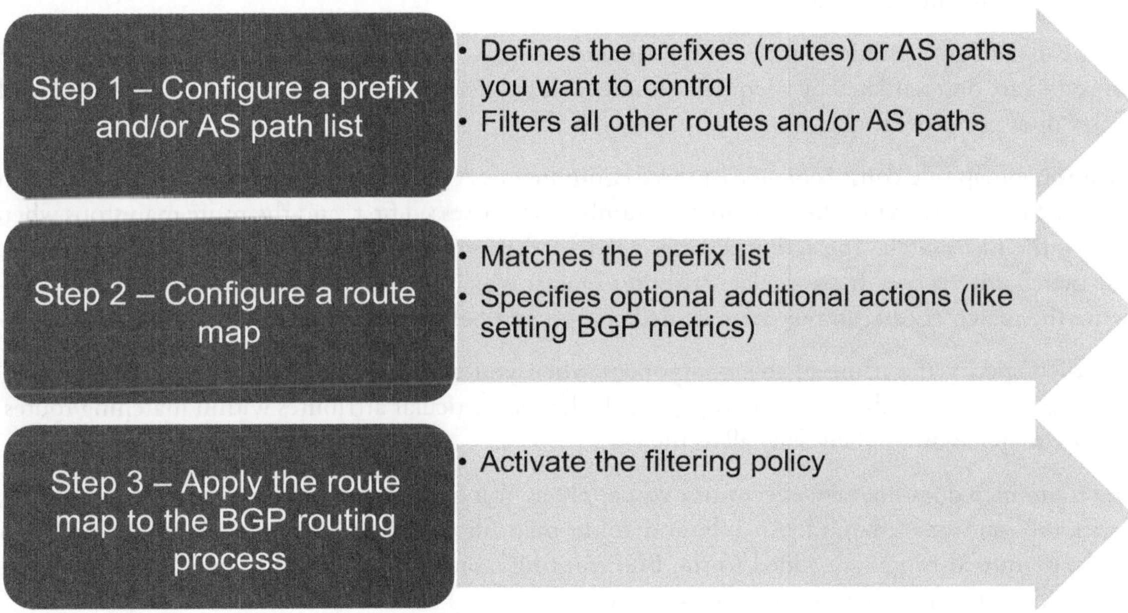

Figure 7-22 Route Control Implementation

Route Control Implementation

To manipulate route preference in more complex ways, you need to understand how to use route maps. Route maps have rules that match route attributes—a little bit like an access control list (ACL) for a route. When the map finds a match, it permits the route and optionally changes its attributes, or it denies the route (Figure 7-22).

Due to the broad range of match criteria and attribute changes that route maps support, you can use route maps for many different use cases. For example, you can use maps to filter inbound and outbound BGP route advertisements. You can also use them to control which BGP routes your AOS-CX switch selects or to influence the choices of other BGP routers. You can also use route maps to select specific routes for redistribution into another protocol.

Route policies control routing paths by filtering and modifying routing information using route maps. Routing policies can filter advertised, received, and redistributed routes. They can also modify attributes for specific routes.

Configuring a route policy is a two-step process:

1. Configure filters based on route attributes, such as destination address and the advertising router address.

2. Create a route map and apply filters to it.

Route maps can be used for route redistribution. Route map entries consist of a list of match and set criteria. Match criteria specify match conditions for incoming routes. Set criteria specify the action taken if match criteria are met.

Users can configure multiple entries in the same route map. These entries contain the same route map name and are differentiated by a sequence number. A sequence number will automatically be assigned if user does not provide one.

Each route map rule consists of at least three components. A sequence number orders the rule within the route map; rules with a lower sequence number are processed first, and the route map stops when it finds the first match. The action dictates whether the route is selected ("permit") or not ("deny"). The match criteria specify particular attributes against which routes are matched. You generally configure the match criteria as a separate named component before you create the route map.

You then specify the name of this component when you configure the map. Finally, for "permit" rules, you can optionally add set changes, which change particular attributes within matching routes. A route map has an implicit deny all at the end.

The route map does not take effect until you apply it. You can apply route maps to BGP neighbors, either inbound or outbound. An inbound route map filters the BGP routes which the neighbor sends; permitted routes are added to the BGP routing table, potentially with attributes changed as indicated in the map; denied routes are dropped.

An outbound route map filters the BGP routing table and sends only permitted routes to that BGP neighbor, again potentially with attributes changed. A route map applied to the redistributed routes—for example, BGP routes redistributed into OSPF—redistributes permitted routes and filters out denied ones.

Creating a Route Map

Create a route map with one or more route map entries arranged by the sequence number under a unique route map name. The route map entry has the following parameters:

- Sequence number
- Permission (permit or deny)
- Match criteria
- Set changes

By default, a route map processes routes starting from the lowest sequence number to the highest. Other filtering mechanisms include Prefix List, AS Path List, and Community List.

Match Criteria

You can use a variety of criteria to match a route in a route map. Some criteria, such as BGP community lists and AS Path Lists, are applicable only to a specific routing protocol. Other criteria, such as the Prefix lists, can be used for any route.

When a routing protocol processes a route through a route map, it compares the route to each of the configured match statements. If the route or packet matches the configured criteria, the routing protocol processes it based on the permit or deny configuration for that match entry in the route map.

The match categories and parameters are as follows:

- **BGP parameters**: Match based on AS Path Lists, Community Lists, or Origin code
- **Prefix lists**: Match based on an address or range of addresses
- **AS path lists**: Match on AS numbers or other information in the AS path list of the route(s)
- **Other parameters**: Match based on an IP next-hop address or metric, as well as many other items

Set Changes

Once a route matches an entry in a route map, the route can be changed based on one or more configured set statements.

Set changes are as follows:

- **BGP parameters**: Change the AS path, community, local preference, origin, or weight attributes.
- **Metrics**: Change the route metric.
- **Other parameters**: Change the forwarding address or the IP next-hop address.

IP Prefix Lists

Use prefix lists to permit or deny an address or range of addresses. Filtering by a prefix list involves matching the prefixes of routes with the prefixes listed in the prefix list. An implicit deny is assumed if a prefix does not match any entries in a prefix list. Prefix lists can be configured for both IPv4 and IPv6 addresses.

Users can configure multiple entries in a prefix list and permit or deny the prefixes that match the entry. Each entry has an associated sequence number.

AS Path Lists for BGP

Use AS path lists to filter inbound or outbound BGP route updates. If the route update contains an AS path attribute that matches an entry in the AS path list, the router processes the route based on the configured permit or deny condition.

Configure multiple AS path entries in an AS path list by using the same AS path list name. The router processes the first matching entry. You can also configure an AS path list to compare the AS numbers against a regular expression.

Community Lists for BGP

Filter BGP route updates based on the BGP community attribute by using community lists in a route map. Match the community attribute based on a community list and set the community attribute using a route map. Community lists are beyond the scope of this guide.

Route Redistribution and Route Maps

Use route maps to control the redistribution of routes between routing domains. Route maps match on the attributes of the routes to redistribute routes that pass the match criteria. The route map can also modify the route attributes using set changes.

The router matches redistributed routes against each route map entry.

- If there are multiple match statements, the route must pass all match criteria.
- If a route passes the match criteria defined in a route map entry, actions defined in the entry are executed.
- If the route does not match the criteria, the router compares the route against subsequent route map entries.

Route processing continues until a match is made or the route is processed by all entries in the route map with no match. If the router processes the route against all entries in a route map with no match, the router accepts the route (inbound route maps) or forwards it (outbound route maps).

BGP Route Policy Configuration

Here are the basic commands match on routes:

```
Switch(config)# ip aspath-list <ASPATH-LIST-NAME> [seq <SEQ>] {permit | deny}
          <REGEXP>
Switch(config)# ip prefix-list <PREFIX-LIST-NAME> [seq <SEQ>] ip
          <IP-PREFIX/MASK> [ge <0-32>] [le <0-32>]
```

The **ip aspath-list** command configures an AS path list to match a specific AS path. AS path lists are named lists of regular expression rules. They are used to match AS path attributes in the routes for inclusion in or exclusion from route policies. The sequence number is optional and is autogenerated whenever it is not explicitly mentioned. All AS path list rules with the same name are grouped together. The configuration of IP AS path lists is beyond the scope of this guide.

The **ip prefix-list** command configures a prefix list to match a set of prefixes. Prefix lists are named lists of route prefixes. They are used to match routes for inclusion in or exclusion from route policies. The sequence number determines the order of matching. The matches are performed starting from the lowest sequence number to the highest sequence number until there is a match. The sequence number is however optional and is autogenerated whenever it is not explicitly mentioned. All prefixes with the same prefix list name are grouped.

Optionally, you can define an AS path list or IP prefix to be used in a **match** command in a route map; however, other match criteria can be used other than these two.

The autogenerated sequence number is derived by adding 10 to the highest sequence number available. This technique makes it possible to insert new prefix list sequence number in between.

The **ge** and **le** parameters are used to combine prefixes with a range of network mask. For example, **172.131.0.0/16 ge 16 le 24** will match all prefixes within the 172.131.0.0/16 network that have a mask greater than or equal to 16 bits and less than or equal to 24 bits in length. For instance, 172.131.1.0/18 would match, because its length is between 16 and 24 but 172.0.0.0/8 or 172.131.1.128/25 would not match.

Your routing information then needs to be referenced in a route map:

```
Switch(config)# route-map <name> {permit | deny} seq <NUMBER>
Switch(config-route-map-name)# match <match-attributes>
Switch(config-route-map-name)# set <set-attributes>
```

The **route-map** command configures a route map entry with the given name and action by taking the CLI in the route map context. All route map entries with the same name belong to the same route map. The route map entry rules are processed in order by sequence number, until a match is found.

match commands specify what is to be matched on. Optionally, **set** commands can be used to modify the attributes of the route, like the metric or local preference (if BGP). Here is a list of some common **match** commands you can use (see the IP Routing Guide for the details of the usage of these commands):

- **match aspath-list**: Matches the AS path attribute of the route with one or more regular expressions in the AS path list you previously created.
- **match interface**: Matches the outgoing interface value of the route with the value configured in the match clause.
- **match ip address prefix-list**: Matches the destination IP address prefix of the routes with one or more addresses in a prefix list you previously created.
- **match ip next-hop**: Matches the next-hop address of the route with the configured address in the match clause.
- **match route-type**: Matches the metric-type value of the OSPF external route (external LSA 5 type-1 or type-2) with the value configured in the match clause.
- **match source protocol**: Matches the source routing protocol value of the route with the value configured in the match clause (BGP, connected, OSPF, or static).

Here is a list of some of the common **set** commands you can use (see the IP Routing Guide for the details of the usage of these commands):

- **set as-path prepend**: Prepends the list of the configured AS numbers to the AS path attribute of the routes.
- **set ip next-hop**: Sets the IP address of the next hop of the route with the value configured in the set clause.
- **set local-preference**: Modifies the BGP local-preference attribute of the route entry with the value configured in the set clause.
- **set metric**: Modifies the metric value of the route with the value configured in the set clause.

Note

You must at least have one **match** command in a route map. A **set** command(s) for a corresponding **match** command is optional.

Last, you need to activate the route map in your BGP routing process for a particular BGP neighbor and direction:

```
router bgp <AS-number>
  address-family ipv4 unicast
  neighbor <neighbor-IP-address> route-map <route-map-name> {in|out}
```

You will see a couple of examples in the next two sections.

Note

For more details in attributes and advanced route manipulation, attend advanced Aruba training.

Avoid Becoming a Transit AS

In the multi-homed ISP scenario, you only want to advertise *your own* public IP addresses to the ISPs. You do *not* want to announce routes that your BGP routers learn from ISP 1 to ISP 2, nor routes learned from ISP 2 to ISP 1. If your routers do so, it is possible that the ISPs will accept these advertised routes as better than the ones that they are currently using. They could start sending Internet traffic through your AS as a transit AS. Your router will quickly become overburdened by external Internet traffic (Figure 7-23).

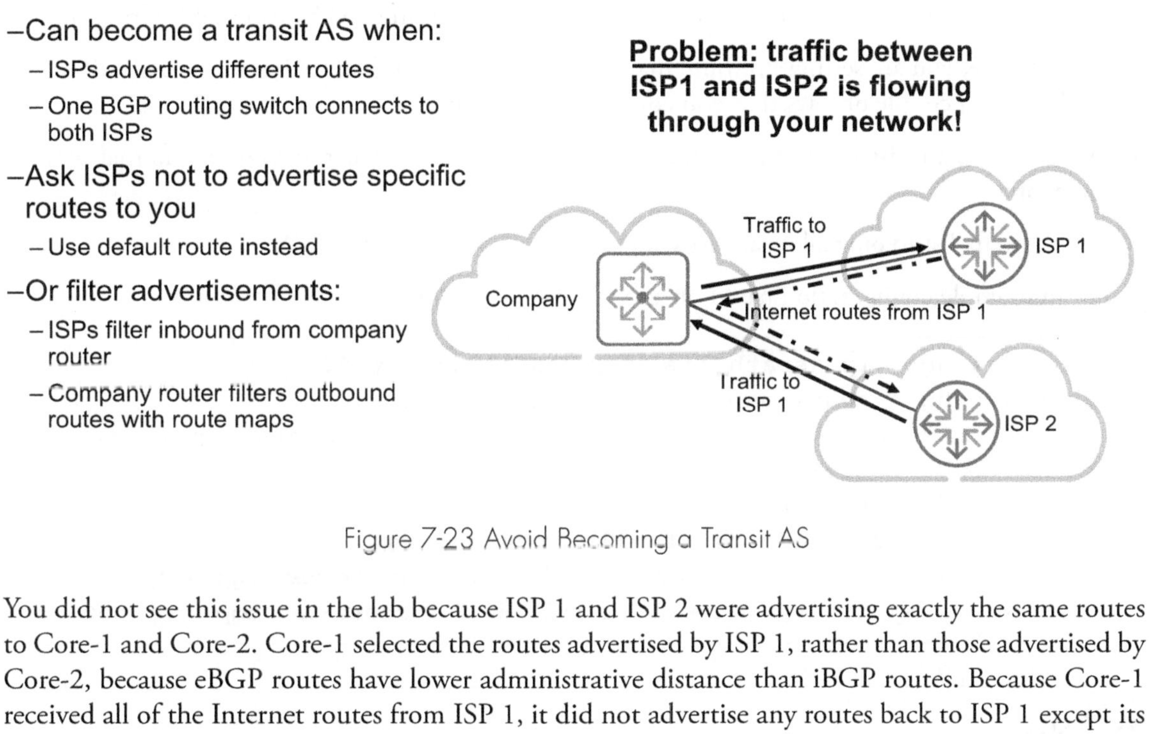

Figure 7-23 Avoid Becoming a Transit AS

You did not see this issue in the lab because ISP 1 and ISP 2 were advertising exactly the same routes to Core-1 and Core-2. Core-1 selected the routes advertised by ISP 1, rather than those advertised by Core-2, because eBGP routes have lower administrative distance than iBGP routes. Because Core-1 received all of the Internet routes from ISP 1, it did not advertise any routes back to ISP 1 except its own local routes. Core-2 did the same with ISP 2.

However, in the real world, several scenarios could lead to your AS becoming a transit AS:

- The ISPs advertise Internet routes differently with different aggregation. Any route that your BGP routers receive from only one ISP, they could begin advertising to the other ISP.
- You connect a single AOS-CX switch or VSF fabric to both ISPs. In this case, the switch has two eBGP neighbors, and it will advertise best routes received from one to the other.

You should communicate with your ISPs to prevent issues in any of these scenarios.

Sometimes you are using BGP primarily to announce your public IP block. For traffic outbound to the Internet, you do not care about finding the best path. You might want to use the connection to one ISP as the primary connection and the other as a standby only if the first fails, or you might want to load balance across both. In cases such as these, you might ask your ISPs not to send any route advertisements to you. You can then create static default routes on the BGP routers. Or in some cases, you might want the ISP to send only a default route in BGP.

If you want to receive routing advertisements from the ISPs, you will need to take care that your router does not pass them on to the other ISP. You can ask the ISP router to filter inbound advertisements from you. But it is best practice to filter outbound advertisements yourself.

In a multi-homed campus scenario, you do not want to announce routes that your BGP routers learn from one ISP to another. If they do, it is possible that the ISPs will accept these advertised routes as better than the ones that they are currently using. They could start sending Internet traffic through your AS as a transit AS. Your routers will quickly become overburdened by external Internet traffic.

In this example, you are setting up route maps to restrict outbound advertisements to eBGP neighbors. There are a couple of ways that you could solve this issue:

- Use an AS path list where the path list is empty, indicating that the route is internal to your network
- Use a prefix list to only allow advertisement of your routes to other ISPs

Here's an example configuration based on an empty AS path list:

```
Company(config)# ip aspath-list bgp-local permit ^$
Company(config)# route-map bgp-ebgp-out permit
Company(config-route-map-bgp-ebgp-out-10)# match aspath bgp-local
Company(config-route-map-bgp-ebgp-out-10)# exit
Company(config)# router bgp 64500
Company(config-bgp)# address-family ipv4 unicast
Company(config-bgp-ipv4-uc)# neighbor 192.168.1.1 route-map bgp-ebgp-out out
Company(config-bgp-ipv4-uc)# neighbor 192.168.2.2 route-map bgp-ebgp-out out
```

Note

See `https://www.regex101.com` for regular expression examples.

These regex values are used:

- '^' indicates 'must begin with'
- '$' indicates 'must end with'

Combined, they result in '^$', which represents an empty string.

All the routes that are originated inside this AS will have an empty AS path attribute, while any route that was received via an external AS (eBGP) will have at least the value of that external AS in the AS path. To check the AS path of a route, a regular expression can be used. Also notice that the route map is applied to both ISP1 and ISP2 peers. This or a similar configuration would need to be performed on your other eBGP peered routing devices.

Control Inbound Routes

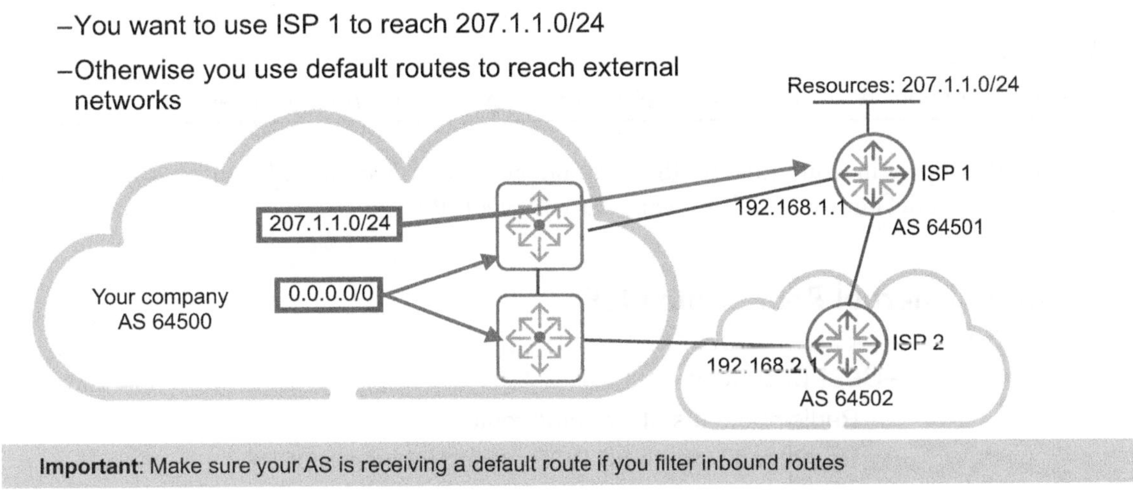

Figure 7-24 Control Inbound Routes

Here is an example route map that filters routes the BGP routers receives from its eBGP neighbor. In this example, you run BGP primarily to announce your public block of IP addresses, and care less about receiving all of the BGP routes in the Internet routing tables. You can filter those down in a few different ways. You may choose to just accept routes for larger ranges less than a specific prefix length. Or you might choose to accept just routes that originate in the eBGP neighbor AS because those are the ones where the company will benefit the most by sending the traffic out this specific router. You could also take a combination of these approaches. In any case, you must ensure that the eBGP neighbor (the ISP) is announcing a default route, which your BGP router can accept and use for all the Internet traffic for which it does not receive a specific route.

In this example shown in the slide, there are resources in ISP1, 207.1.1.0/24, where you want to reach those resources efficiently by using the BGP connection you have directly to ISP1. For other networks, a default route is typically sufficient (Figure 7-24). Here is an example configuration:

```
ip prefix-list ISP1resources seq 10 permit 207.1.1.0/24 eq 24
route-map ISP1 permit seq 10
  match ip address prefix-list ISP1resources
router bgp 64500
  address-family ipv4 unicast
    neighbor 192.168.1.1 route-map ISP1 in
```

The example configuration uses an IP prefix list to select a specific route to learn from ISP1: 207.1.1.0/24. Please note that you might need to perform similar inbound route filtering to make intelligent choices to reaching resources in ISP2 as well.

Important

Make sure your AS is receiving a default route if you filter inbound routes.

What would happen in your link to ISP1 would go down? You would still be able to access 207.1.1.0/24 via a default route to leave your network via ISP2.

Advertising External Routes into OSPF

–Best practice:
- –Redistribute a static *default* route
- –Do *not* redistribute full BGP routing table into OSPF

Figure 7-25 Advertising External Routes into OSPF

You need to consider how much of the routing information that your BGP router receives from the ISP routers available to the company IGP, typically OSPF. Although you can redistribute BGP routes into OSPF, it is not typically recommended. The large BGP routing table might overwhelm the OSPF processes on the local router and on other routers throughout the AS (Figure 7-25).

Often, you can simply have your BGP routers advertise default routes in OSPF. If they are already acting as ABRs for stub areas, they already advertise default routes in those areas. You might need to have the BGP routers advertise default routes in the OSPF backbone, though. A simple approach is to configure a static route through its ISP connection on the BGP router. Then redistribute static routes into OSPF.

Here is the configuration to redistribute routes into OSPF (this is done from the OSPF routing process):

```
Switch(config-ospf)# redistribute {connected | bgp | static}
[route-map <route-map-name>]
```

It is highly recommended that you use a route map, discussed in the next section, to qualify exactly which route(s) you want to redistribute into OSPF.

To inject a default route on an ASBR, use the following configuration:

```
Switch(config)# router ospf <process-ID>
Switch(config-ospf) default-information originate always
```

Note

Your ISP might advertise a default route to your BGP router. In that case, instead of redistributing static routes, you could redistribute just the BGP default route. When you redistribute BGP into OSPF, you apply a route map that permits only that route.

Lab 7

Lab 7 Diagram

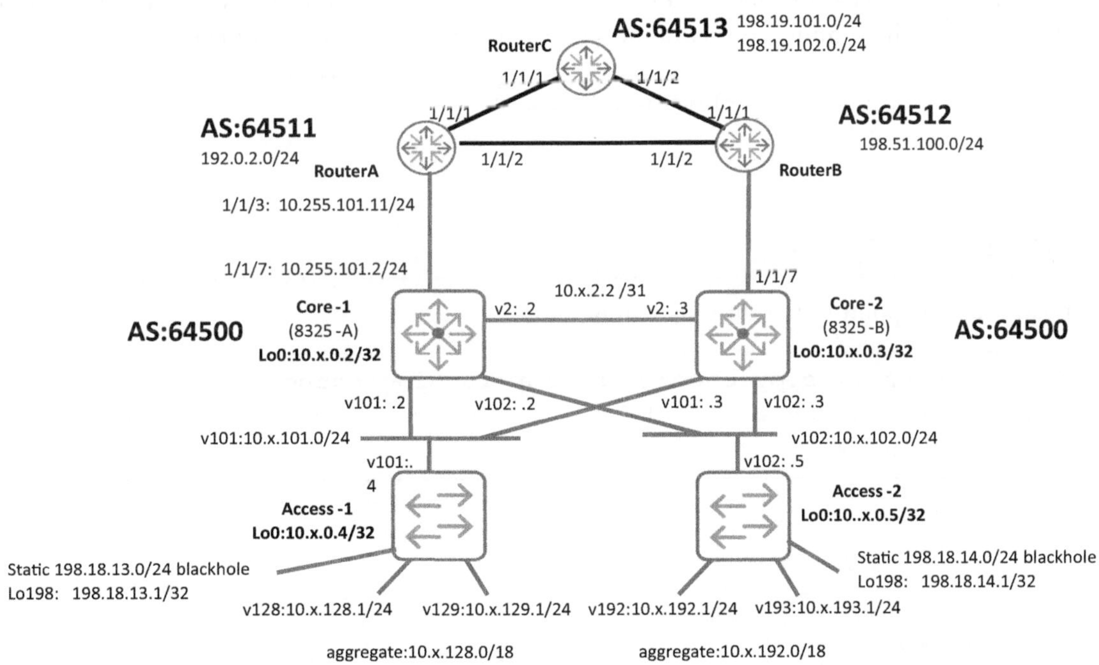

Figure 7-26 Lab 7 Diagram

Overview

In this lab activity, basic BGP peering will be demonstrated. The two core switches will be configured to use iBGP between each other. They will use eBGP to communicate with two different ISPs, one connected to each Core switch (Figures 7-26).

Once the BGP peering has been established, a route advertisement will be configured.

The Core switches will also be configured with a route policy so they do not become a transit AS for traffic between the service providers.

Objectives

- Set up eBGP and iBGP peering
- Advertise routes using BGP
- Configure a route policy to control BGP routing updates

Task 1: Prepare the Lab Setup

This lab requires the completion of the OSPF lab activities (Single area, Multi-area, and External routes). In this task, you will load the checkpoint for the BGP lab on RouterA.

1. Connect to RouterA and login with username **admin**, password **aruba123**. Load the BGP checkpoint to the running configuration. Verify that the 'bgp' checkpoint exists.

```
ICX-RouterA-ospf# show checkpoint list
ospf
bgp
startup-config
<...output omitted...>
```

2. Load the checkpoint to the running configuration.

```
ICX-RouterA-ospf# copy checkpoint bgp running-config
Configuration changes will take time to process, please be patient.
ICX-RouterA-ospf#
```

3. Press 'enter' a few times, until the updated hostname is displayed.

```
ICX-RouterA-ospf# <ENTER>
ICX-RouterA-bgp#
```

Task 2: Core1 eBGP Peering to ISP1

Objectives

In this task, Core1 will be configured to establish an eBGP peering with ISP RouterA. Since the RouterA is running as a VM, there is no direct physical link between the Core1 and RouterA, so it can take more time to detect that the peer is unreachable. This will be handled using BFD, Bidirectional Forward Detection, a simple keepalive protocol.

Steps

1. Open a terminal connection to Core1 and enter configuration mode. In the OSPF lab, a routed link was established to RouterA; verify Core1 can reach the Router.

```
ICX-Tx-Core1(config)# do ping 10.255.101.11
PING 10.255.101.11 (10.255.101.11) 100(128) bytes of data.
108 bytes from 10.255.101.11: icmp_seq=1 ttl=64 time=1.49 ms
108 bytes from 10.255.101.11: icmp_seq=2 ttl=64 time=1.79 ms
```

2. Enable BGP for AS 64500.

```
ICX-Tx-Core1(config)# router bgp 64500
```

3. Define RouterA as a BGP neighbor.

```
ICX-Tx-Core1(config-bgp)# neighbor 10.255.101.11 remote-as 64511
```

4. Enter the IPv4 address-family; enable the peer RouterA for IPv4.

```
ICX-Tx-Core1(config-bgp)# address-family ipv4 unicast
ICX-Tx-Core1(config-bgp-ipv4-uc)# neighbor 10.255.101.11 activate
```

```
ICX-Tx-Core1(config-bgp-ipv4-uc)# exit
ICX-Tx-Core1(config-bgp)# exit
```

5. Verify the status of the BGP session; it should be established. The state may be 'Idle' initially; wait for the state to change to 'Established'.

```
ICX-Tx-Core1(config)# show bgp all summary
VRF : default
BGP Summary
-----------
 Local AS                    : 64500      BGP Router Identifier   : 10.x.0.2
 Peers                       : 1          Log Neighbor Changes    : No
Cfg. Hold Time              : 180        Cfg. Keep Alive         : 60

Address-family : IPv4 Unicast
-----------------------------
 Neighbor        Remote-AS MsgRcvdMsgSent  Up/Down Time  State       Ad-
minStatus
10.255.101.11   64511       10       12      00h:03m:30s   Established Up

Address-family : IPv6 Unicast
-----------------------------

Address-family : L2VPN EVPN
-----------------------------
```

Verify the Impact of the Default BGP Keepalive Interval (60 seconds)

1. On Core1, disable the interface that connects to the RouterA.

```
ICX-Tx-Core1(config)# interface 1/1/7
ICX-Tx-Core1(config-if)# shutdown
ICX-Tx-Core1(config-if)# exit
```

2. Review the status of the BGP neighbor using the command **'show bgp all summary'**.

3. Wait about 30 seconds and review the status again; it should still be 'Established', even when the link is down.

```
ICX-Tx-Core1(config)# show bgp all summary
```

4. There is no need to wait for the status to transition to 'Idle'. This output simply shows what the result would be after about three minutes (3 x 60 seconds).

```
ICX-Tx-Core1(config)# show bgp all summary
VRF : default
BGP Summary
-----------
 Local AS             : 64500        BGP Router Identifier  : 10.x.0.2
 Peers                : 1            Log Neighbor Changes   : No
Cfg. Hold Time       : 180          Cfg. Keep Alive        : 60

Address-family : IPv4 Unicast
-----------------------------
 Neighbor          Remote-AS  MsgRcvdMsgSent   Up/Down Time  State    Ad-
minStatus
 10.255.101.11    64511       12      18      00h:01m:06s  Idle     Up

Address-family : IPv6 Unicast
-----------------------------

Address-family : L2VPN EVPN
-----------------------------
```

5. This demonstrates that, by default, it can take several minutes before BGP detects that a peer is not reachable. In the next section a solution will be configured.

6. Enable the interface to the RouterA again.

```
ICX-Tx-Core1(config)# interface 1/1/7
ICX-Tx-Core1(config-if)# no shutdown
ICX-Tx-Core1(config-if)# exit
```

Use BFD for Faster Peer Keepalive Detection

1. On Core1, enter the BGP context and enable BFD for the RouterA neighbor. On RouterA, this command should also be enabled. In the lab setup, this has been done already.

```
ICX-Tx-Core1(config)# router bgp 64500
ICX-Tx-Core1(config-bgp)# neighbor 10.255.101.11 fall-over bfd
ICX-Tx-Core1(config-bgp)# exit
```

2. Verify the current BFD sessions.

```
ICX-Tx-Core1(config)# show bfd
Admin status: disabled
Statistics:
Total number of control packets transmitted: 0
Total number of control packets received: 0
Total number of control packets dropped: 0
Session  Interface  VRF      Source       Destination IP Echo   State
Application
--------------------------------------------------------------------
1        1/1/7     default  10.255.101.2  10.255.101.11       enabled
admin_down bgp
ICX-Tx-Core1(config)# show bfd session 1
BFD session information - Session 1
VRF: default
Min Tx interval (msec): 3000
Min Rx interval (msec): 3000
Min echo Rx interval (msec): 500
Detect multiplier: 5
Application: bgp
Local discriminator: 13211
Remote discriminator: 366
Echo: enabled
Local diagnostic: administratively_down
Remote diagnostic: no_diagnostic
State flaps: 0
Interface Source IP  Destination IP  State  Pkt Rx  Pkt Tx  Pkt drop
--------- ---------------------------------------------------------
1/1/7     10.255.101.2   10.255.101.11 admin_down 27     26        0
```

Question: Has a BFD session been established to RouterA, and what would be the reason?

Answer: No BFD session is active at the moment, since the BFD process is not enabled at the global level (admin down).

3. Enable BFD globally.

```
ICX-Tx-Core1(config)# bfd
```

4. Review the state. The state will transition from admin_down to down>init> up.

```
ICX-Tx-Core1(config)# show bfd session 1
BFD session information - Session 1
VRF: default
Min Tx interval (msec): 3000
Min Rx interval (msec): 3000
Min echo Rx interval (msec): 500
Detect multiplier: 5
Application: bgp
Local discriminator: 13211
Remote discriminator: 366
Echo: enabled
Local diagnostic: no_diagnostic
Remote diagnostic: no_diagnostic
State flaps: 0
Interface Source IP   Destination IP State   Pkt Rx   Pkt Tx   Pkt drop
------------------------------------------------------------------------
1/1/7     10.255.101.2  10.255.101.11  up     0        0         0
```

Verify the BFD Operation

1. Now repeat the test by bringing down the interface to RouterA.

```
ICX-Tx-Core1(config)# interface 1/1/7
ICX-Tx-Core1(config-if)# shutdown
ICX-Tx-Core1(config-if)# exit
```

2. Check the BGP neighbor state. Within a few seconds, the state should now transition to 'Idle'.

```
ICX-Tx-Core1(config)# show bgp all summary
VRF : default
BGP Summary
-----------
 Local AS               : 64500        BGP Router Identifier    : 10.x.0.2
 Peers                  : 1            Log Neighbor Changes   : No
Cfg. Hold Time         : 180          Cfg. Keep Alive        : 60

Address-family : IPv4 Unicast
-----------------------------
 Neighbor          Remote-AS MsgRcvdMsgSent  Up/Down Time State   Ad-
minStatus
10.255.101.11   64511        30       32      00h:00m:00s  Idle    Up
```

```
Address-family : IPv6 Unicast
-----------------------------

Address-family : L2VPN EVPN
-----------------------------
```

3. Enable the interface to RouterA again.

```
ICX-Tx-Core1(config)# interface 1/1/7
ICX-Tx-Core1(config-if)# no shutdown
ICX-Tx-Core1(config-if)# exit
```

4. This demonstrates how BFD can help with a faster detection of the peer reachability.

Note

For eBGP peers, the switch can also monitor if the link used to reach a directly adjacent peer goes down and then reset the BGP session immediately.
This can be enabled under the 'router bgp' context using the command 'bgp fast-external-fallover'.

```
router bgp <as>
  bgp fast-external-fallover
```

Verify Received Routes via BGP

1. Now review the routes that have been received via BGP on Core1.

```
ICX-Tx-Core1(config)# show bgp all paths
Status codes: s suppressed, d damped, h history, * valid, > best, = multipath,
i internal, e external S Stale, R Removed
VRF : default
Local Router-ID 10.x.0.2

Address-family : IPv4 Unicast
-----------------------------
```

```
    Network              Next Hop          Path
*>e 192.0.2.0/24         10.255.101.11     64511
*>e 198.19.101.0/24      10.255.101.11     64511 64513
*>e 198.19.102.0/24      10.255.101.11     64511 64512 64513
*>e 198.51.100.0/24      10.255.101.11     64511 64512
Total number of entries 4

Address-family : IPv6 Unicast
-----------------------------
    Network              Next Hop          Path
Total number of entries 0
```

Question: Route 192.0.2.0/24 has AS path 64511. What does this mean?

Answer: Since the neighbor 10.255.101.11 belongs to AS 64511, this means that the route 192.0.2.0/24 is originated by this neighbor AS.

Question: Which AS originates the route 198.19.102.0/24?

Answer: The last AS in the AS path indicates the originating AS, so this route is originated by AS 64513; it traverses AS 64512 and then AS 64511.

Question: Both 198.19.101.0/24 and 198.19.102.0/24 originate from AS 64513. Why are they using a different path (different AS path)?

Answer: BGP allows the administrator to control the routing paths. In this case, apparently some route policy was defined on Routers A, B, or C so that the 198.19.101.0/24 and 198.19.102.0/24 are taking a different path to reach their destination. You only see the result of that policy here.

Task 3: Core1 and Core2 iBGP Peering

Objectives

In this task, iBGP peering will be configured between the Core1 and the Core2 devices. The VSX synchronization for BGP will be reviewed and disabled, so each Core switch can have its own BGP configuration. With the iBGP peering in place between the two core switches, the BGP routes and the next hop will be analyzed. This will result in the configuration of the next-hop-self for the iBGP peers.

Steps

Set up iBGP Peering Between Core1 and Core2

1. On Core1, add a new neighbor for Core2; use the same AS, so BGP knows this is iBGP.

```
ICX-Tx-Core1(config)# router bgp 64500
ICX-Tx-Core1(config-bgp)# neighbor 10.x.0.3 remote-as 64500
```

2. For iBGP, the peering is typically configured between the loopback IPs of the routers, instead of the outgoing interface IP. Configure the loopback IP as the source IP for this neighbor.

```
ICX-Tx-Core1(config-bgp)# neighbor 10.x.0.3 update-source loopback 0
```

3. Enable the neighbor for IPv4 unicast.

```
ICX-Tx-Core1(config-bgp)# address-family ipv4 unicast
ICX-Tx-Core1(config-bgp-ipv4-uc)# neighbor 10.x.0.3 activate
ICX-Tx-Core1(config-bgp-ipv4-uc)# exit
ICX-Tx-Core1(config-bgp)# exit
```

4. Switch to Core2; enter the configuration mode if needed; review the current configuration; look for the BGP section.

```
ICX-Tx-Core2(config)# show run bgp
router bgp 64500
    neighbor 10.x.0.3 remote-as 64500
    neighbor 10.x.0.3 update-source loopback 0
    neighbor 10.255.101.11 remote-as 64511
    neighbor 10.255.101.11 fall-over bfd
    address-family ipv4 unicast
        neighbor 10.x.0.3 activate
        neighbor 10.255.101.11 activate
    exit-address-family
```

Question: Why is there already a BGP configuration on Core2?

Answer: Since Core1 and Core2 are in a VSX cluster, and all the VSX synchronization features had been turned on, the BGP commands are automatically replicated.

5. This is very useful in case the VSX cluster is in a datacenter and needs to have the same neighbor peering commands on both Core switches. In this lab environment, the BGP configuration of both Core1 and Core2 will be unique, so the VSX Synchronization will be disabled.

Note

In case only minor differences are needed, it is possible to exclude the neighbor configuration synchronization at the neighbor level in the bgp configuration. An example would be:

```
example(config)# router bgp 64500
example(config-bgp)# neighbor 10.1.1.1 vsx-sync-exclude
```

It is not needed to apply this command in the lab, since the entire BGP synchronization will be disabled.

6. On Core1, disable the VSX synchronization of the BGP feature.

```
ICX-Tx-Core1(config)# vsx
ICX-Tx-Core1(config-vsx)# no vsx-sync bgp
ICX-Tx-Core1(config-vsx)# exit
```

1. On Core2, verify the BGP configuration.

```
ICX-Tx-Core2(config)# show run bgp
```

Question: Is the BGP configuration still in the running configuration?

Answer: Yes, it is still there. Only the VSX synchronization was stopped. Now the administrator can make 'local' changes to the Core2.

7. To cleanup, remove the BGP configuration.

```
ICX-Tx-Core2(config)# no router bgp 64500
This will delete all BGP configurations on this device.
Continue (y/n)? y
```

8. Now try to set up the BGP router by yourself; add the Core1 as an iBGP neighbor; use the loop-back IP as the source IP; verify the peering.
9. The commands are only listed here in case you want to verify your commands.

```
ICX-Tx-Core2(config)# router bgp 64500
ICX-Tx-Core2(config-bgp)# neighbor 10.x.0.2 remote-as 64500
ICX-Tx-Core2(config-bgp)# neighbor 10.x.0.2 update-source loopback 0
ICX-Tx-Core2(config-bgp)# address-family ipv4 unicast
ICX-Tx-Core2(config-bgp-ipv4-uc)# neighbor 10.x.0.2 activate
ICX-Tx-Core2(config-bgp-ipv4-uc)# exit-address-family
```

10. The result should be an 'Established' iBGP session.

```
ICX-Tx-Core2(config-bgp)# show bgp all summary
VRF : default
BGP Summary
-----------
 Local AS            : 64500       BGP Router Identifier   : 10.x.0.3
 Peers               : 1           Log Neighbor Changes    : No
Cfg. Hold Time     : 180          Cfg. Keep Alive        : 60

Address-family : IPv4 Unicast
-----------------------------
 Neighbor     Remote-AS  MsgRcvdMsgSent   Up/Down Time  State       Ad-
minStatus
10.x.0.     64500         7       3       00h:00m:37s   Established Up

Address-family : IPv6 Unicast
-----------------------------

Address-family : L2VPN EVPN
-----------------------------
```

Verify Received Routes

1. Now review the received BGP routes on Core2.

```
ICX-Tx-Core2(config-bgp)# show bgp all path
Status codes: s suppressed, d damped, h history, * valid, > best, =
multipath,
i internal, e external S Stale, R Removed
VRF : default
Local Router-ID 10.x.0.3

Address-family : IPv4 Unicast
-----------------------------
    Network            Next Hop         Path
* i 192.0.2.0/24       10.255.101.11    64511
* i 198.19.101.0/24    10.255.101.11    64511 64513
* i 198.19.102.0/24    10.255.101.11    64511 64512 64513
* i 198.51.100.0/24    10.255.101.11    64511 64512

Total number of entries 4

Address-family : IPv6 Unicast
-----------------------------
    Network            Next Hop         Path
Total number of entries 0
```

Question: Do you notice a difference in the flags compared to the output on Core1?

Answer: There is no 'best' route on Core2, so the '>' flag is missing. In the next steps this will be investigated.

2. Review the IP routing table on Core2. Is there a route to the 198.19.101.0/24 network?

```
ICX-Tx-Core2(config-bgp)# show ip route 198.19.101.0
No ipv4 routes configured
```

Question: What would be the reason that this route that is visible in the BGP routing table is not inserted into the IP routing table?

Answer: BGP always checks if the next-hop IP address of a route is reachable. In this case, the Core1 announces the external next-hop IP 10.255.101.11. This IP address is not reachable for Core2, so it cannot inject these routes into the IP routing table.

```
ICX-Tx-Core2(config-bgp)# show ip route 10.255.101.11
No ipv4 routes configured
```

Solution: iBGP next-hop-self

The behavior seen in the previous section occurs because, by default, iBGP keeps the next hop of the eBGP peer. In many cases, this is not desired, so the internal iBGP IP should be used as the next hop for the announced IP routes. This will now be configured on both Core1 and on Core2 on the neighbor definitions to each other.

1. Open Core1, enter the IPv4 address-family under the BGP router context, and enable the 'next-hop-self' for the Core2 neighbor.

```
ICX-Tx-Core1(config)# router bgp 64500
ICX-Tx-Core1(config-bgp)# address-family ipv4 unicast
ICX-Tx-Core1(config-bgp-ipv4-uc)# neighbor 10.x.0.3 next-hop-self
ICX-Tx-Core1(config-bgp-ipv4-uc)# exit
```

2. Review the configuration.

```
ICX-Tx-Core1(config-bgp)# show running-config current-context
router bgp 64500
    neighbor 10.x.0.3 remote-as 64500
    neighbor 10.x.0.3 update-source loopback 0
    neighbor 10.255.101.11 remote-as 64511
    neighbor 10.255.101.11 fall-over bfd
    address-family ipv4 unicast
        neighbor 10.x.0.3 activate
neighbor 10.x.0.3 next-hop-self
        neighbor 10.255.101.11 activate
    exit-address-family
```

3. On Core2, repeat this for the neighbor Core1.

```
ICX-Tx-Core2(config-bgp)# address-family ipv4 unicast
ICX-Tx-Core2(config-bgp-ipv4-uc)# neighbor 10.x.0.2 next-hop-self
ICX-Tx-Core2(config-bgp-ipv4-uc)# exit
```

4. On Core2, review the BGP routing table; check the next-hop IP for the routes.

```
ICX-Tx-Core2(config-bgp)# show bgp all path
Status codes: s suppressed, d damped, h history, * valid, > best, =
multipath,
i internal, e external S Stale, R Removed
VRF : default
Local Router-ID 10.x.0.3

Address-family : IPv4 Unicast
-----------------------------
    Network             Next Hop          Path
* i 192.0.2.0/24        10.255.101.11     64511
* i 198.19.101.0/24     10.255.101.11     64511 64513
* i 198.19.102.0/24     10.255.101.11     64511 64512 64513
* i 198.51.100.0/24     10.255.101.11     64511 64512
Total number of entries 4
```

Question: Did the next hop change for the routes?

Answer: No, this change is only effective for the next update, so the session must be refreshed for these changes to be visible.

5. On Core2, clear the BGP session with Core1.

```
ICX-Tx-Core2(config-bgp)# do clear bgp 10.x.0.2
```

6. Review the BGP routing table; the next hop should now be the loopback IP of the Core1. Also notice that the '>' best flag is now shown again for the routes.

```
ICX-Tx-Core2(config-bgp)# show bgp all path
Status codes: s suppressed, d damped, h history, * valid, > best, =
multipath,
i internal, e external S Stale, R Removed
VRF : default
Local Router-ID 10.x.0.3

Address-family : IPv4 Unicast
-----------------------------
    Network              Next Hop        Path
*>i 192.0.2.0/24         10.x.0.2        64511
*>i 198.19.101.0/24      10.x.0.2        64511 64513
*>i 198.19.102.0/24      10.x.0.2        64511 64512 64513
*>i 198.51.100.0/24      10.x.0.2        64511 64512
```

7. Review the IP routing table; are the routes visible now?

```
ICX-Tx-Core2(config-bgp)# show ip route 198.19.101.0
Displaying ipv4 routes selected for forwarding
'[x/y]' denotes [distance/metric]

198.19.101.0/24, vrf default
via  10.x.2.2,  [200/0],  bgp
```

8. This demonstrates the need for next-hop-self between iBGP peers.

Note

Do not attempt to ping the remote hosts. The Core1 and Core2 are receiving the routes from the ISP, but they are not announcing any routes themselves, so there is no return path to make a connection possible at this point in the lab.

Task 4: Core2 eBGP Peering to ISP2

Objectives

In this task, Core2 will be configured with an eBGP peering session to RouterB (another ISP). Once the peering is established, the routes will be reviewed. This will also reveal that the customer now has become a transit AS, so traffic between RouterA and RouterB could be using the path via the customer network. A solution using a route map will be configured to prevent this transit AS behavior.

Steps

1. On Core2, configure the routed uplink to RouterB.

```
ICX-Tx-Core2(config)# interface 1/1/7
ICX-Tx-Core2(config-if)# ip address 10.255.102.3/24
ICX-Tx-Core2(config-if)# no shutdown
ICX-Tx-Core2(config-if)# exit
```

2. Verify Core2 can reach RouterB on the new link.

```
ICX-Tx-Core2(config)# do ping 10.255.102.12
PING 10.255.102.12 (10.255.102.12) 100(128) bytes of data.
108 bytes from 10.255.102.12: icmp_seq=1 ttl=64 time=1.43 ms
108 bytes from 10.255.102.12: icmp_seq=2 ttl=64 time=1.23 ms
```

3. On Core2, attempt to configure RouterB (**10.255.102.12**) as a BGP neighbor for **AS 64512** by yourself. Only use the commands below in case you want to verify your commands.

```
ICX-Tx-Core2(config)# bfd
ICX-Tx-Core2(config)# router bgp 64500
ICX-Tx-Core2(config-bgp)# neighbor 10.255.102.12 remote-as 64512
ICX-Tx-Core2(config-bgp)# neighbor 10.255.102.12 fall-over bfd
ICX-Tx-Core2(config-bgp)# address-family ipv4 unicast
ICX-Tx-Core2(config-bgp-ipv4-uc)# neighbor 10.255.102.12 activate
ICX-Tx-Core2(config-bgp-ipv4-uc)# exit
```

Verify the Received Routes from the eBGP Peer

1. On Core2, verify the status of the eBGP peering. The state with 10.255.102.12 should be 'Established'.

```
ICX-Tx-Core2(config-bgp)# show bgp all summary
VRF : default
BGP Summary
-----------
 Local AS              : 64500     BGP Router Identifier   : 10.x.0.3
 Peers                 : 2         Log Neighbor Changes    : No
Cfg. Hold Time         : 180      Cfg. Keep Alive         : 60

Address-family : IPv4 Unicast
-----------------------------
 Neighbor      Remote-AS MsgRcvdMsgSent  Up/Down Time State       Ad-
minStatus
 10.x.0.2      64500       30      27     00h:19m:53s  Established Up
10.255.102.12 6451        16      18     00h:00m:30s  Established Up

Address-family : IPv6 Unicast
-----------------------------

Address-family : L2VPN EVPN
-----------------------------
```

2. Review that routes have been received from this eBGP peer.

```
ICX-Tx-Core2(config-bgp)# show bgp all paths
Status codes: s suppressed, d damped, h history, * valid, > best, =
multipath,
i internal, e external S Stale, R Removed
VRF : default
Local Router-ID 10.x.0.3

Address-family : IPv4 Unicast
-----------------------------
    Network              Next Hop          Path
*>i 192.0.2.0/24         10.x.0.2          64511
* e 192.0.2.0/24         10.255.102.12     64512 64511
*>i 198.19.101.0/24      10.x.0.2          64511 64513
* e 198.19.101.0/24      10.255.102.12     64512 64511 64513
*>e 198.19.102.0/24      10.255.102.12     64512 64513
```

```
*>e 198.51.100.0/24     10.255.102.12     64512

Total number of entries 6

Address-family : IPv6 Unicast
-----------------------------
    Network              Next Hop          Path
Total number of entries 0
```

Transit AS Problem: Verify the Routes That Are Advertised to the eBGP Peer

By default, BGP will advertise all routes that it has received from other BGP peers. The risk for a customer with BGP peering to two different ISPs is that it becomes a transit AS between these ISPs. It is best practice to apply a route filter to the eBGP peers to ensure that only locally originated routes can be announced to them. First, review that Core2 is indeed advertising routes to RouterB.

1. On Core2, no configuration has been performed to announce routes to the eBGP system. Check if any routes are being advertised to the eBGP peer.

```
ICX-Tx-Core2(config-bgp)# show bgp ipv4 unicast neighbors
10.255.102.12advertised-routes
Status codes: s suppressed, d damped, h history, * valid, > best, = multipath,
i internal, e external S Stale, R Removed
Origin codes: i - IGP, e - EGP, ? - incomplete

VRF : default
Local Router-ID 10.x.0.3

    Network            Nexthop         Metric   LocPrf   Weight   Path
*>e 192.0.2.0/2        10.255.102.3    0        0        0        64500 64511 i
*>e 198.19.101.0/24    10.255.102.3    0        0        0        64500 64511 64513 i
Total number of entries 2
```

2. This shows that the 2 routes that were received by RouterA (via Core1) are being advertised by Core2 to RouterB.

3. On Core1, the issue can also be verified. It is currently advertising routes that it received via Core2 from RouterB.

```
ICX-Tx-Core1(config-bgp)# show bgp ipv4 unicast neighbors
10.255.101.11 advertised-routes
Status codes: s suppressed, d damped, h history, * valid, > best, = multipath,
i internal, e external S Stale, R Removed
Origin codes: i - IGP, e - EGP, ? - incomplete

VRF : default
Local Router-ID 10.x.0.2

    Network           Nexthop        Metric  LocPrf  Weight  Path
*>e 198.19.102.0/24  10.255.101.2  0       0       0        64500
64512 64513 i
*>e 198.51.100.0/24  10.255.101.2  0       0       0        64500
64512 i
Total number of entries 2
```

Solution: Route Policy for Locally Originated Networks

In the next section, a route policy will be created to ensure that only routes that have originated in the local AS can be advertised to the eBGP peers. This will be achieved by checking the AS path attribute. All the routes that are originated inside this AS will have an empty AS path attribute, while any route that was received via an external AS (eBGP) will have at least the value of that external AS in the AS path.

To check the AS path of a route, a regular expression can be used. See https://www.regex101.com for regular expression examples. These regex values are used:

- '^' indicates 'must begin with'
- '$' indicates 'must end with'

Combined, they result in '^$', which represents an empty string.

Since the outbound route filter will be used by both Core1 and Core2, the configuration will be performed on Core1, so the route map will by synchronized by VSX (**'route-map'** is a separate synchronization feature of VSX).

1. On Core1, define a new AS path list that only allows an 'empty' AS path value.

```
ICX-Tx-Core1(config)# ip aspath-list bgp-local permit ^$
```

2. Define a new route map to select routes matching the new AS path list.

```
ICX-Tx-Core1(config)# route-map bgp-ebgp-out permit
ICX-Tx-Core1(config-route-map-bgp-ebgp-out-10)# match aspath bgp-local
ICX-Tx-Core1(config-route-map-bgp-ebgp-out-10)# exit
```

3. The outbound policy must be defined on each Core separately. On Core1, apply the policy to the neighbor definition to RouterA.

```
ICX-Tx-Core1(config)# router bgp 64500
ICX-Tx-Core1(config-bgp)# address-family ipv4 unicast
ICX-Tx-Core1(config-bgp-ipv4-uc)# neighbor 10.255.101.11 route-map
bgp-ebgp-out out
ICX-Tx-Core1(config-bgp-ipv4-uc)# exit
```

4. On Core2, the route map was synchronized by VSX. Verify that the route map exists in the configuration.

```
ICX-Tx-Core2(config-bgp)# show route-map
Route-map: bgp-ebgp-out
   Seq 10, permit,
Match :
aspath-list                   :bgp-local
Set :

Route-map: ospf_from_static
   Seq 10, permit,
Match :
ip prefix-list                :routerAext
Set :
       metric                        : 1000
       metric-type                   : external_type1
```

5. On Core2, apply the policy to the neighbor definition to Router B. The switch should still be in the 'router bgp 64500' context.

```
ICX-Tx-Core2(config-bgp)# address-family ipv4 unicast
ICX-Tx-Core2(config-bgp-ipv4-uc)# neighbor 10.255.102.12 route-map
bgp-ebgp-out out
ICX-Tx-Core2(config-bgp-ipv4-uc)# exit
```

6. The update in the policy will be effective after the BGP sessions are restarted. Reset the eBGP session on Core1.

```
ICX-Tx-Core1(config-bgp)# do clear bgp 10.255.101.11
```

7. Reset the eBGP session on Core2.

```
ICX-Tx-Core2(config-bgp)# do clear bgp 10.255.102.12
```

8. Wait a few moments so the eBGP session can be re-established. Now the route policy should be effective. On Core1, check the outbound routes.

```
ICX-Tx-Core1(config-bgp)# show bgp ipv4 unicast neighbors 10.255.101.11
advertised-routes
Status codes: s suppressed, d damped, h history, * valid, > best, =
multipath, i internal, e external S Stale, R Removed
Origin codes: i - IGP, e - EGP, ? - incomplete

VRF : default
Local Router-ID 10.x.0.2

    Network              Nexthop      Metric     LocPrf      Weight Path
Total number of entries 0
ICX-Tx-Core1(config-bgp)# exit
```

9. Verify this on Core2 as well.

```
ICX-Tx-Core2(config-bgp)# show bgp ipv4 unicast neighbors 10.255.102.12
advertised-routes
Status codes: s suppressed, d damped, h history, * valid, > best, =
multipath,
i internal, e external S Stale, R Removed
Origin codes: i - IGP, e - EGP, ? - incomplete

VRF : default
Local Router-ID 10.x.0.3

    Network          Nexthop         Metric     LocPrf     Weight Path
Total number of entries 0
ICX-Tx-Core2(config-bgp)# exit
```

10. This demonstrates how a route policy can prevent the customer from becoming a transit AS for other BGP autonomous systems.

Task 5: Announce Routes to eBGP Peers

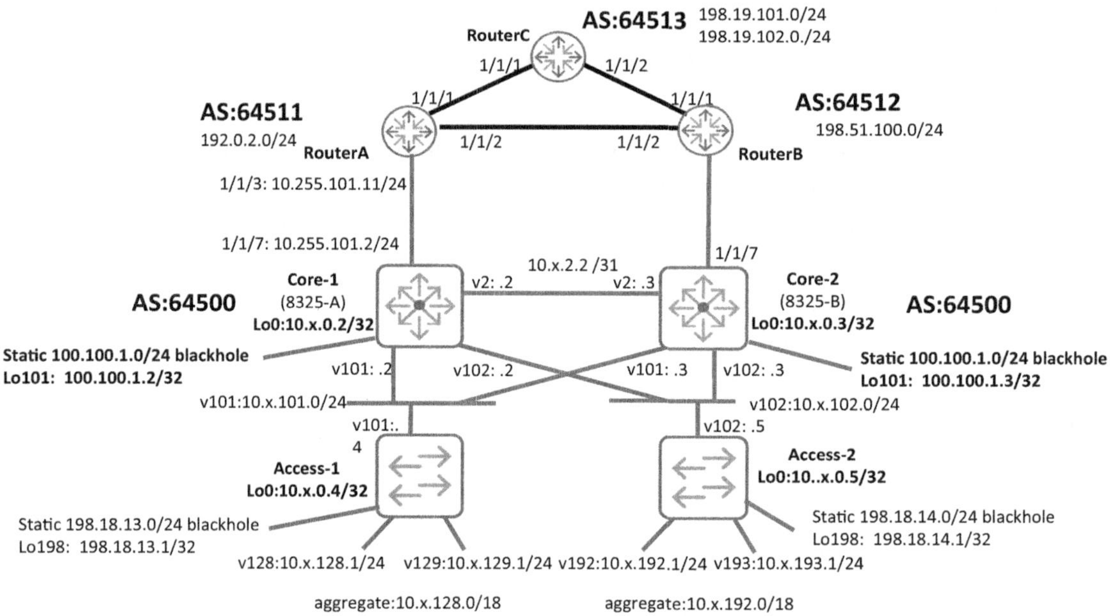

Figure 7-28 Task 5: Announce Routes to eBGP Peers

Objectives

In this task, the customer would like to advertise its local, 'public' subnet to the 2 ISPs (Figure 7-28). First, a 'public' subnet will be defined on the Core1 and Core2 systems. Next, Core1 will be configured to announce this subnet using eBGP to RouterA (ISP 64511) and the advertisement will be verified using RouterC. The last step will be to repeat this configuration on Core2; the route is also advertised to RouterB (ISP 64512).

Steps

Define the Subnet on Core1 and Core2 for External Use

The Core1 and Core2 BGP AS 64500 will be hosting the **100.100.1.0/24** network. Each Core switch will be configured with a loopback interface in this subnet for testing purposes. This loopback will be included in the OSPF topology so Core1 and Core2 can reach each other's 100.100.1.0/24 interface and also forward data to the peer switch.

1. On Core1, define the new loopback with the public test IP.

```
ICX-Tx-Core1(config)# interface loopback 101
ICX-Tx-Core1(config-loopback-if)# ip address 100.100.1.2/32
ICX-Tx-Core1(config-loopback-if)# ip ospf 1 area 0
ICX-Tx-Core1(config-loopback-if)# exit
```

2. On Core2, define the new loopback IP as well.

```
ICX-Tx-Core2(config)# interface loopback 101
ICX-Tx-Core2(config-loopback-if)# ip address 100.100.1.3/32
ICX-Tx-Core2(config-loopback-if)# ip ospf 1 area 0
ICX-Tx-Core2(config-loopback-if)# exit
```

3. On Core2, verify the new loopback IP on Core1 can be reached via OSPF, while using the local loopback as source IP.

```
ICX-Tx-Core2(config)# do ping 100.100.1.2 source 100.100.1.3
PING 100.100.1.2 (100.100.1.2) from 100.100.1.3 : 100(128) bytes of data.
108 bytes from 100.100.1.2: icmp_seq=1 ttl=64 time=0.197 ms
108 bytes from 100.100.1.2: icmp_seq=2 ttl=64 time=0.169 ms
```

eBGP on Core1: Announce Local Subnet to RouterA

In these steps, Core1 will announce the 100.100.1.0/24 prefix to the RouterA.

1. On Core1, enter the BGP router context.

```
ICX-Tx-Core1(config)# router bgp 64500
ICX-Tx-Core1(config-bgp)# address-family ipv4 unicast
```

2. Use the 'network' command to inject the 100.100.1.0/24 route into the IPv4 BGP table.

```
ICX-Tx-Core1(config-bgp-ipv4-uc)# network 100.100.1.0/24
ICX-Tx-Core1(config-bgp-ipv4-uc)# exit
ICX-Tx-Core1(config-bgp)# exit
```

3. Verify if the new network is part of the IPv4 unicast routing table.

```
ICX-Tx-Core1(config)# show bgp ipv4 unicast paths
Status codes: s suppressed, d damped, h history, * valid, > best, =
multipath, i internal, e external S Stale, R Removed
VRF : default
Local Router-ID 10.x.0.2

    Network              Next Hop          Path
*>e 192.0.2.0/24         10.255.101.11     64511
*>e 198.19.101.0/24      10.255.101.11     64511 64513
*>i 198.19.102.0/24      10.x.0.3         64512 64513
* e 198.19.102.0/24      10.255.101.11     64511 64512 64513
*>i 198.51.100.0/24      10.x.0.3         64512
* e 198.51.100.0/24      10.255.101.11     64511 64512
Total number of entries 6
```

Question: Is the new route visible?

Answer: No, the new route is not injected yet. BGP requires the route to exist in the local routing table before it can be announced to BGP peers.

4. Since the local routing table only contains the /32 loopback routes, but not the /24 route, BGP rejects the route. To solve this, a dummy static route can be created. This should only be done in case more specific subnets are still available in the routing table, such as the /32 subnets in this lab. Define the dummy static route.

```
ICX-Tx-Core1(config)# ip route 100.100.1.0/24 blackhole
```

5. Next, verify if the route appears in the local BGP routing table.

```
ICX-Tx-Core1(config)# show bgp ipv4 unicast paths
Status codes: s suppressed, d damped, h history, * valid, > best, =
multipath,
i internal, e external S Stale, R Removed
VRF : default
Local Router-ID 10.x.0.2

    Network              Next Hop          Path
*>  100.100.1.0/24       0.0.0.0
*>e 192.0.2.0/24         10.255.101.11     64511
*>e 198.19.101.0/24      10.255.101.11     64511 64513
*>i 198.19.102.0/24      10.x.0.3         64512 64513
* e 198.19.102.0/24      10.255.101.11     64511 64512 64513
```

```
*>i 198.51.100.0/24     10.x.0.3         64512
* e 198.51.100.0/24     10.255.101.11     64511 64512
Total number of entries 7
```

6. Verify if the route passes the outbound route map to the RouterA.

```
ICX-Tx-Core1(config)# show bgp ipv4 unicast neighbors 10.255.101.11
advertised-routes
Status codes: s suppressed, d damped, h history, * valid, > best, =
multipath,
i internal, e external S Stale, R Removed
Origin codes: i - IGP, e - EGP, ? - incomplete
VRF : default
Local Router-ID 10.x.0.2

    Network            Nexthop        Metric    LocPrf    Weight   Path
*>e 100.100.1.0/24    10.255.101.2  0         0         0        64500 i
Total number of entries 1
```

7. Verify connectivity using this IP to the RouterC (this router is connected behind RouterA and RouterB). If this router can be reached using a ping, it means RouterC knows about the 100.100.1.0/24 subnet as well. RouterC has several loopback test IP addresses; one of them is 198.19.101.50.

```
ICX-Tx-Core1(config)# do ping 198.19.101.50 source 100.100.1.2
PING 198.19.101.50 (198.19.101.50) from 100.100.1.2 : 100(128) bytes
of data.
108 bytes from 198.19.101.50: icmp_seq=1 ttl=62 time=3.82 ms
108 bytes from 198.19.101.50: icmp_seq=2 ttl=62 time=3.55 ms
108 bytes from 198.19.101.50: icmp_seq=3 ttl=62 time=3.37 ms
```

8. On Core2, verify RouterC (198.19.101.50) can be reached when using the local public IP as the source IP (100.100.1.3). The reply confirms that all the hosts on the 100.100.1.0/24 subnet can be reached from the ISPs using a path via Core1.

```
ICX-Tx-Core2(config)# do ping 198.19.101.50 source 100.100.1.3
PING 198.19.101.50 (198.19.101.50) from 100.100.1.3 : 100(128) bytes
of data.
108 bytes from 198.19.101.50: icmp_seq=1 ttl=62 time=3.67 ms
108 bytes from 198.19.101.50: icmp_seq=2 ttl=62 time=3.82 ms
108 bytes from 198.19.101.50: icmp_seq=3 ttl=62 time=3.46 ms
```

9. Now repeat the configuration of the route advertisement on Core2.

```
ICX-Tx-Core2(config)# ip route 100.100.1.0/24 blackhole
ICX-Tx-Core2(config)# router bgp 64500
ICX-Tx-Core2(config-bgp)# address-family ipv4 unicast
ICX-Tx-Core2(config-bgp-ipv4-uc)# network 100.100.1.0/24
ICX-Tx-Core2(config-bgp-ipv4-uc)# exit
ICX-Tx-Core2(config-bgp)# exit
```

Route Validation on RouterC

1. Open a connection to RouterC (**admin/aruba123**). On RouterC, verify that there are now 2 paths for the 100.100.1.0/24 subnet.

```
ICX-RouterC-bgp# show bgp ipv4 unicast
Status codes: s suppressed, d damped, h history, * valid, > best, =
multipath,
i internal, e external S Stale, R Removed
Origin codes: i - IGP, e - EGP, ? - incomplete

VRF : default
Local Router-ID 203.0.113.50

     Network            Nexthop          Metric LocPrf  Weight   Path
*>e 100.100.1.0/24   10.255.104.11   0       100      0   64511 64500 i
* e 100.100.1.0/24   10.255.105.12   0       100      0   64512 64500 i
*>e 192.0.2.0/24     10.255.104.11   0       100      0   64511 i
* e 192.0.2.0/24     10.255.105.12   0       100      0   64512 64511 i
*>  198.19.101.0/24 0.0.0.0          0       100      0         i
*>  198.19.102.0/24 0.0.0.0          0       100      0         i
* e 198.51.100.0/24 10.255.104.11   0       100      0   64511 64512 i
*>e 198.51.100.0/24  10.255.105.12   0       100      0         64512 i
*>  203.0.113.0/24   0.0.0.0          0       100      0         i
Total number of entries 9
```

Question: What is the AS path for each of the routes?

Answer: There should be 1 entry with as path '64511 64500' and another entry with '64512 64500'.

Question: Why is only 1 route selected as the best path ('>')?

Answer: BGP default path selection will only select 1 best path when the AS path length is the same for multiple paths.

2. Review the IP routing table for the 100.100.1.0/24 route. Notice that the next hop is in line with the BGP routing table shown in the previous step.

```
ICX-RouterC-bgp# show ip route 100.100.1.0
Displaying ipv4 routes selected for forwarding

'[x/y]' denotes [distance/metric]

100.100.1.0/24, vrf default
via  10.255.104.11,  [20/0],  bgp
```

Learning Check

1. Compare OSPF and BGP.

	OSPF	BGP
Type of routing protocol (IGP or EGP)		
Designed for routing tables of what size		
How neighbor relationships are established		
What neighbors advertise to each other		

2. What determines whether your AOS-CX switch forms an eBGP relationship versus an iBGP relationship with a neighbor?
   a. Whether the "exterior" or "interior" option is appended to the neighbor configuration
   b. Whether the neighbor uses a loopback interface for its address or not
   c. Whether the neighbor has the same AS number as the AOS-CX switch router or not
   d. Whether the AOS-CX switch is running BGP in exterior or interior mode
3. An administrator enters **network 192.0.2.0/24** in the BGP context on an AOS-CX switch. What is required for the switch to add this network to its BGP routing table?
   a. It has a route to any subnet within this range in its IP routing table.
   b. It has this exact route in its IP routing table, learned from any source.
   c. It has learned a route to any subnet within this range using OSPF.
   d. It has learned this exact route using OSPF.

Summary

Congratulations! You have completed the BGP chapter. This chapter introduced you to BGP, focusing on how eBGP neighbors use the protocol to exchange routing information between different autonomous systems in a stable, highly manageable manner.

You can establish and monitor eBGP connections between a company router and an ISP router. You can also add routes from your router's global IP routing table to the BGP routing table so that your router advertises the correct networks. Specifically, you have learned how to configure a BGP solution for a company router that connects to two ISP routers. You can also influence route selection in a variety of ways. You learned about route maps and explored several examples of ways to use route maps to achieve common goal.

8 IGMP

OBJECTIVES

After completing this chapter, you will be able to:

- ✓ Understand multicast addressing
- ✓ Understand the components and messages used by IGMP
- ✓ Use IGMP to optimize forwarding of multicast traffic within VLANs
- ✓ Describe the differences between IGMP and IGMP snooping

Overview

Enterprises need networks that can deliver a variety of multicast services to the right destinations. In this chapter, you learn about multicast traffic and how to use Internet Group Management Protocol (IGMP) to control it.

This chapter covers two sections: an introduction to multicasting and its uses followed by an introduction to the IGMP protocol. First, you will begin by learning how multicasts work. Later, you will learn about routing multicast traffic across a layer-3 network.

Multicast Introduction

This section introduces multicasting and multicast addressing.

Multicast Overview

You are familiar with unicast traffic, which is directed to a unique destination device, and with broadcast traffic, which every device in a subnet/VLAN (broadcast domain) receives and processes. IPv4 defines a third type of traffic, multicast traffic, which flows from one source to multiple destinations. In other words, multicast addressing allows one-to-many or many-to-many communication among hosts on a network (Figure 8-1).

The multicast source includes the multicast address as the destination IP address for the packet. Because multiple receivers can listen for the same address, switches might need to flood the packet on multiple interfaces. Any source that is listening for that address processes the packet. Because multiple IPv4 nodes listen for the same multicast address, this address is often referred to as a *group address*.

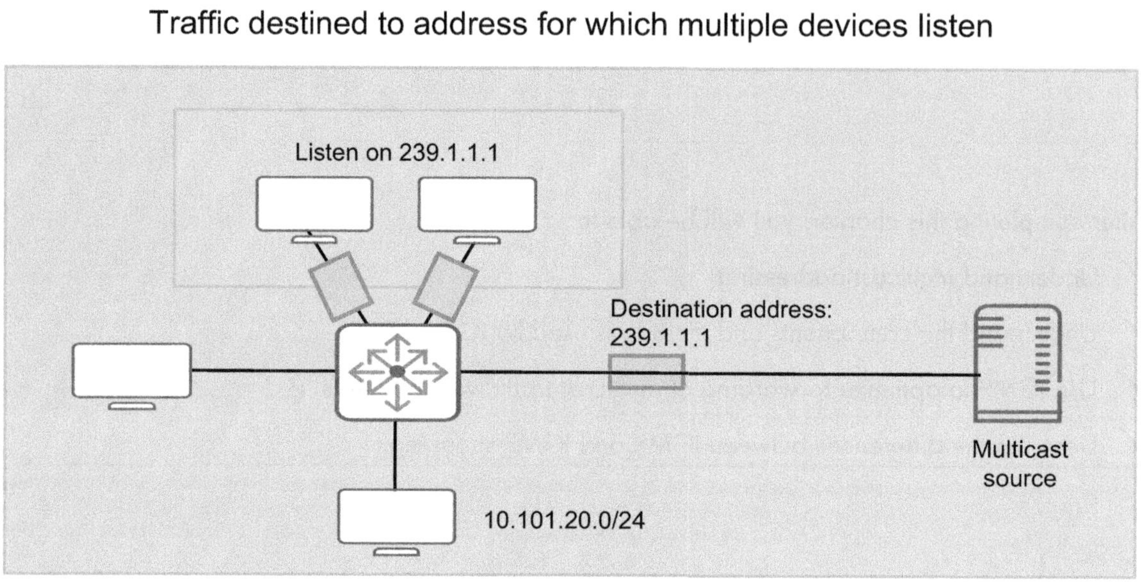

Figure 8-1 Multicast Overview

Note

The term *stream* is commonly used in multicast to denote traffic associated with a particular multicast destination address.

As a review, there are three general types of destination addresses:

- **Unicast**: Traffic is forwarded to just one destination
- **Broadcast**: Traffic is flooded throughout the VLAN/subnet (everyone will see it)
- **Multicast**:
    - Traffic is destined to 0 or more (or all) destinations in a VLAN/subnet
    - Traffic is flooded, by default, throughout the VLAN/subnet

Multicast Uses: Examples

Latest generation network applications often feature more collaborative components, making them well suited for multicast traffic (Figure 8-2). Applications that often rely on multicasting include:

- Unified communications and collaboration applications such as:
  - IP voice conference calling
  - Music or audio streaming
  - Video and desktop conferencing and collaboration
  - Telepresence
  - Video streaming applications
  - Virtual classroom applications
  - Stock ticker tape streaming applications
  - Network management protocols, like the Network Time Protocol (NTP) and the Aruba Discovery Protocol (ADP), used by Aruba campus APs to find and connect to an Aruba Mobility Controller
- IT administrators might also assign servers or endpoints to multicast groups so that they can deliver patches, software updates, and other controls to a targeted group.

Figure 8-2 Multicast Uses: Examples

Multicasting presents two primary challenges to network administrators:

- Multicast traffic for sophisticated applications, particularly multimedia applications, can consume a great deal of bandwidth, particularly when it is copied for distribution to multiple locations. In fact, even copying multicasts can consume processing power on network infrastructure devices. To maintain a high-performing network environment, administrators must implement multicast control technologies properly to minimize unnecessary flooding and duplication. Not only do administrators need to preserve bandwidth, they also need to protect endpoint functionality. An endpoint NIC must process the multicasts that it receives, even if it is not listening for that multicast, which can consume CPU cycles.
- Users and devices that require specific multicast traffic often connect in a variety of locations. Network administrators might need to route the traffic across multiple VLANs and even campus LAN sites.

You will learn about meeting this first challenge in this chapter. Then, in the next chapter, you will build on that knowledge and learn about multicast routing.

Multicast Addressing: IP (Layer-3)

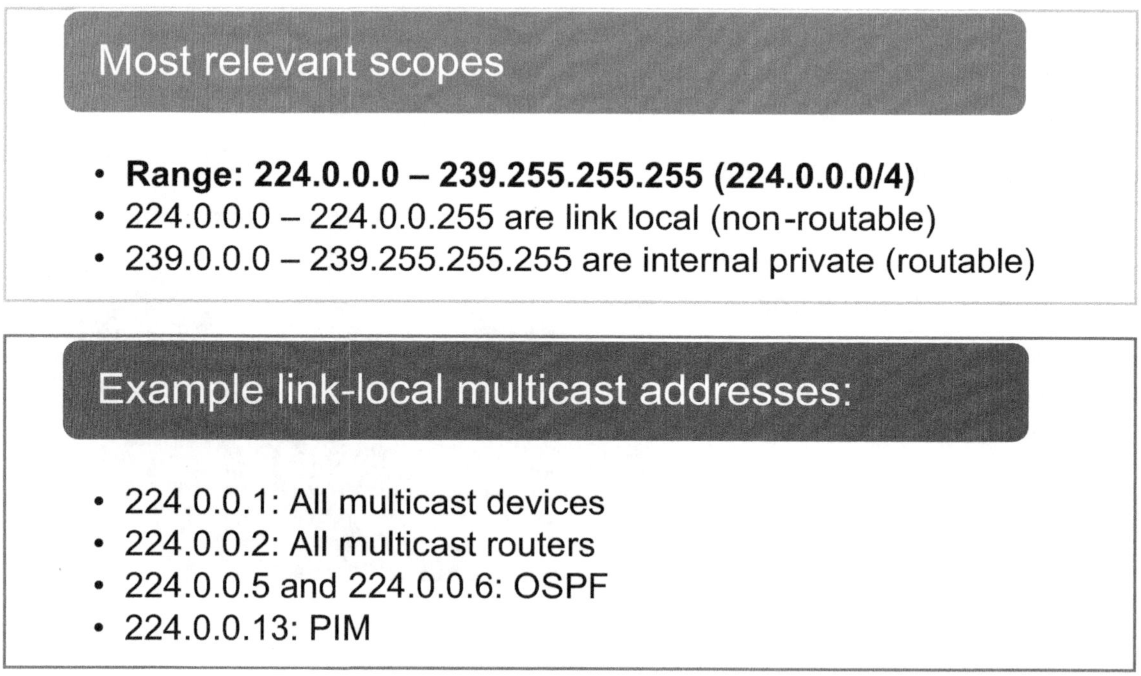

Figure 8-3 Multicast Addressing: IP (Layer-3)

Multicast addresses fall within the 224.0.0.0/4 range (224.0.0.0 to 239.255.255.255), as shown in Figure 8-3. Internet Assigned Numbers Authority (IANA) has assigned specific multicast addresses to some protocols. For example, Open Shortest Path First (OSPF) routers communicate with each other on multicast address 224.0.0.5 and 224.0.0.6. As shown in the table, IANA has assigned other addresses to specific organizations. Some applications, such as applications that use Session Announcement Protocol (SAP), can dynamically select multicast addresses from a certain range. Finally, individual organizations can define administratively scoped multicast addresses in the 239.0.0.0/8 range as they want; these multicasts should not leave the administrative domain.

Table 8-1 summarizes the Layer-3 multicast addresses:

Table 8-1 IP Multicast Addresses

IP Multicast Address Range	Description	Routable
Local subnetwork	Local subnetwork	No
224.0.1.0 to 224.0.1.255	Internetwork control	Yes
224.0.2.0 to 224.0.255.255	AD-HOC block 1	Yes
224.3.0.0 to 224.4.255.255	AD-HOC block 2	Yes
232.0.0.0 to 232.255.255.255	Source-specific multicast	Yes
233.0.0.0 to 233.251.255.255	GLOP addressing	Yes
233.252.0.0 to 233.255.255.255	AD-HOC block 3	Yes
234.0.0.0 to 234.255.255.255	Unicast-prefix-based	Yes
239.0.0.0 to 239.255.255.255	Administratively scoped (private addresses)	Yes

Depending on the type of application, the multicast source and multicast receivers might be statically configured to stream to, and listen for, a specific multicast address. Or they might negotiate the address dynamically. Determining the multicast address to use is the application's responsibility; the network infrastructure must simply ensure that the traffic reaches its destination. Here are some examples of multicast addresses that are used by common protocols:

- 224.0.0.1: all multicast-capable devices
- 224.0.0.2: all multicast routers
- 224.0.0.5 and 224.0.0.6: OSPF
- 224.0.0.13: PIM
- 224.0.0.251: Multicast DNS (MDNS)

Note

The last range of addresses can be used in Table 8.1 and routed in a private network.

You can refer to IANA for the latest assignments: **https://www.iana.org/assignments/multicast-addresses/multicast-addresses.xhtml**.

Multicast Addressing: MAC (Layer-2)

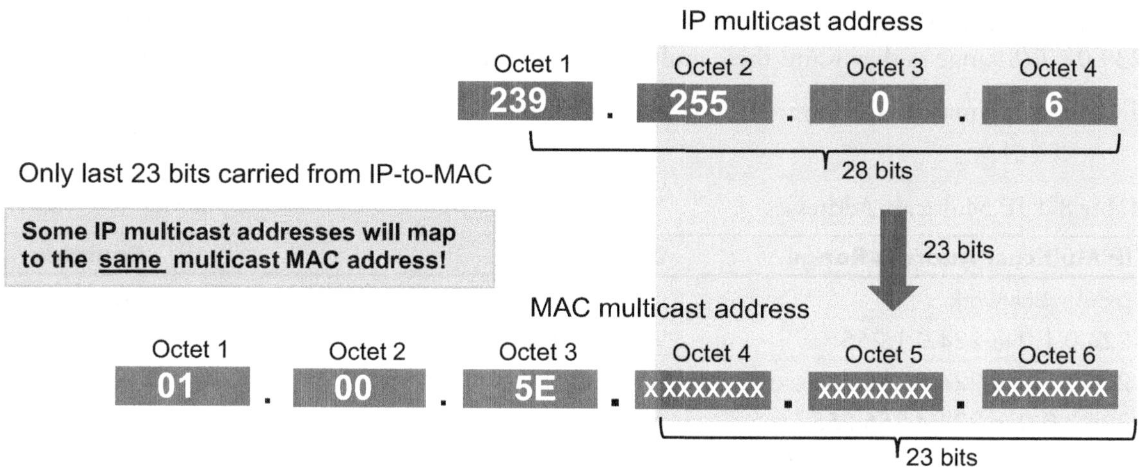

Figure 8-4 Multicast Addressing: MAC (Layer-2)

Multicast addressing is also denoted in Ethernet MAC addresses (Figure 8-4). Ethernet frames with a value of 1 in the least-significant bit of the first octet (xxxxxxx1) of the destination MAC address are identified as multicast frames. These are flooded to all points on the VLAN/subnet. While frames with ones in all bits of the destination address (*FF-FF-FF-FF-FF-FF*) are sometimes referred to as broadcasts. Layer-2 multicast addresses begin with 01:00:5E:xx:xx:xx. Basically, from a HEX perspective, all multicast addresses begin like this: 00000001.00000000:01011110:0. Notice that the highest-ordered bit in the last 24 bits is a 0 (1 is reserved). For the last 24 bits, the highest bit 0xxxxxxx:xxxxxxxx:xxxxxxxx; meaning that there are only 23 available bits for multicast addresses. Basically, the range of multicast address at Layer 2 is 0100.5E00.0000 to 0100.5E7F.FFFF.

Layer-3 multicast addresses are mapped to Layer-2 MAC addresses. IP addresses are 32 bits in length, where the first five bits are used to identify the multicast address range and the last 28 bits the specific multicast addresses. The problem this poses is that at Layer-2, you have 23 bits (see the last paragraph), but at Layer-3 you have 28 bits. The lower 23 bits of the IP multicast MAC address is mapped to the available 23 bits in the Ethernet MAC address. However, since not all 28 bits are mapped from IP-to-MAC, some Layer-3 IP multicast addresses are mapped to the *same* Layer-2 multicast address (actually there are 32 Layer-3 multicast addresses mapped to each single Layer-2 multicast address).

The IEEE has allocated the address block *01-80-C2-00-00-00* to *01-80-C2-FF-FF-FF* for group addresses for use by standard protocols implementing multicast at Layer-2. Of these, the MAC group addresses in the range from *01-80-C2-00-00-00* to *01-80-C2-00-00-0F* are not relayed by switches conforming to 802.1D; that is, they are not flooded. Examples of these would include LACP, STP BPDUs, LLDP, CDP, and others.

Important

With a broadcast, all devices in a subnet receive it. Their respective NICs then have the local device's CPU process it. With a multicast, the NIC can make an intelligent decision as to whether the CPU should process the frame or if the NIC should drop the frame based on if the multicast MAC address is in use by a multicast-based application on the device. Therefore, the NIC can conserve CPU cycles based on what multicast addresses need to be seen by a running multicast application on the device, making multicast a much better solution to deliver information to a broad range of devices than broadcasts.

Multicast Addressing: Overlapping Address Issues

- Some multicast Layer-3 addresses, when converted to Layer-2, will overlap
- Overlapping example: 224.0.0.0/24 and 239.0.0.0/24
  - Because 224.0.0.0/24 are link-local, IGMP snooping would never filter them
  - Thus IGMP snooping would see both 224.0.0/24 and 239.0.0/24 as the same MAC address, which could create problems
- Recommendation: Don't use x.0.0.x or x.128.0.x multicast addresses

Layer-3 multicast address	Corresponding Layer-2 multicast address	Address use
224.0.0.1	01.00.5E.00.00.01	Link-local Not forwarded from local segment (not routable)
239.0.0.1	01.00.5E0.0.00.01	Internal private, but overlaps with 224.0.0.1 Treated as a link-local

Figure 8-5 Multicast Addressing: Overlapping Address Issues

Because only 23 bits of the 28-bit address are carried from the Layer-3 to the Layer-2 multicast address, you will over some Layer-3 multicast address share the same Layer-2 multicast address. You should ***avoid*** this situation (Figure 8-5).

Basically, multicast addresses that include x.0.0.x and x.128.0.x will overlap. Multicast addresses in the 224.0.0.0/24 range are link local multicast addresses. They are used for protocol discovery and are flooded to every port. For example, OSPF uses 224.0.0.5 and 224.0.0.6 for neighbor and DR discovery. For a switch that is doing IGMP snooping, these are ***not*** added to the snooping list and thus are not filtered. Therefore, if you would use an IP address like 239.0.0.1, IGMP snooping would not filter its corresponding Layer-2 multicast address, thinking that this was an IGMP-related message.

Multicast Flooding within VLANs

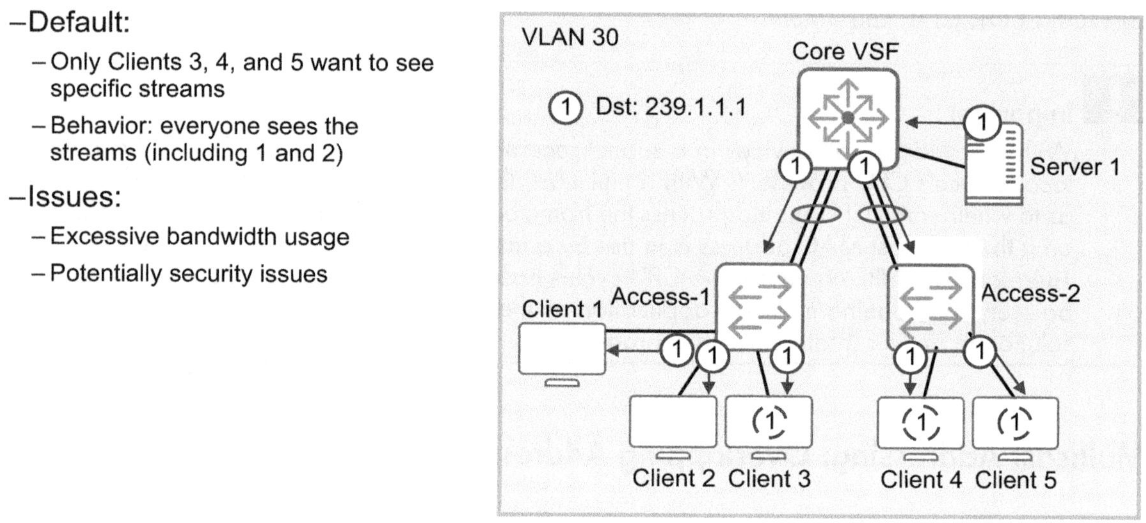

Figure 8-6 Multicast Flooding within VLANs

By default, in an Ethernet network, switches flood multicasts on all ports in a VLAN, or broadcast domain (Figure 8-6). Thus, although multicasts should target only the specific devices that require them, they act like *broadcasts*, creating congestion for an entire subnet. Contemporary unified communications and collaboration applications, such as video-conferencing applications, often involve high bandwidth streams of multicast traffic. If all edge ports must carry traffic for all multicast groups within the VLAN, overall performance quickly suffers.

In addition, broadcasting multicast packets can introduce security issues because every endpoint in a subnet receives traffic that is actually meant for a particular group. For example, even if most users would not know how to eavesdrop on the multicast traffic from a neighboring meeting room's video conference that shows up unnecessarily on their ports, some users might—which could violate privacy regulations. Finally, service providers that provide for-pay services must limit multicast traffic to the properly registered receivers so that they can track who actually uses the services.

In summary, to deploy multicasting applications effectively, you must enable the switches to suppress specific multicasts on ports that do not require them.

Applications and Processing

Applications are defined to use Layer-3 IP multicast addresses, but the actual hardware, like NICs or switches, are processing the Layer-2 addresses. By default, devices treat multicasts like broadcasts (with few exceptions). However, once multicasting support is enabled, devices can typically and intelligently process the multicast traffic. For example, if a device did not have multicast enabled, the NIC would treat it as a broadcast and forward it up the protocol stack for the CPU to process. However, with multicasting enable, like shown in the slide, the NIC will listen for the multicast addresses for which applications have an interest in, and thus can make an intelligent decision as to which traffic the NIC should process or drop.

The second problem is that switches flood multicast traffic. In the example shown in the slide, Clients 1 and 2 are receiving the multicast streams, even though they are not running a multicast application. This wastes CPU cycles on these clients to basically process and drop the multicast traffic. The switches need an intelligent method of forwarding/filtering multicasts instead of treating them as a broadcast (Figure 8-7).

Roles of IGMP and Multicast Routing (PIM)

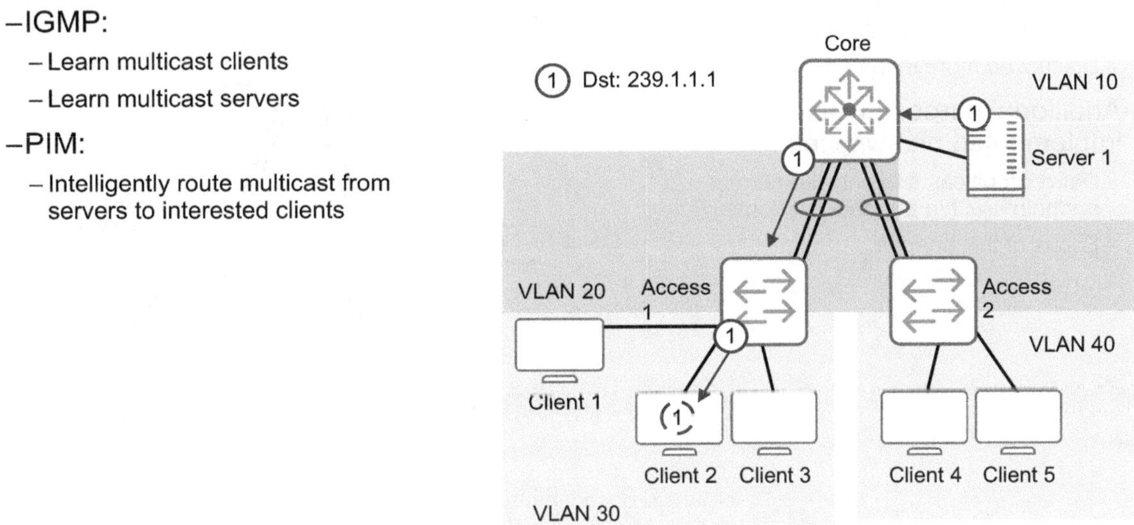

Figure 8-7 Roles of IGMP and Multicast Routing (PIM)

There are two protocols responsible for intelligently delivering multicast streams to interested clients.

- IGMP
- PIM

IGMP learns where the interested clients and servers are. PIM intelligently routes traffic between the two. IGMP is covered in this chapter while PIM is covered in the next chapter.

IGMP

This section introduces the IGMP protocol.

IGMP Use Cases

In a network where IP multicast traffic is transmitted for various multimedia applications, you can use the switch to reduce unnecessary bandwidth usage on a per-port basis by configuring IGMP (Internet Group Management Protocol). IGMPv3 (RFC 3376) and IGMPv2 (RFC 2236) are the current RFCs for IGMP.

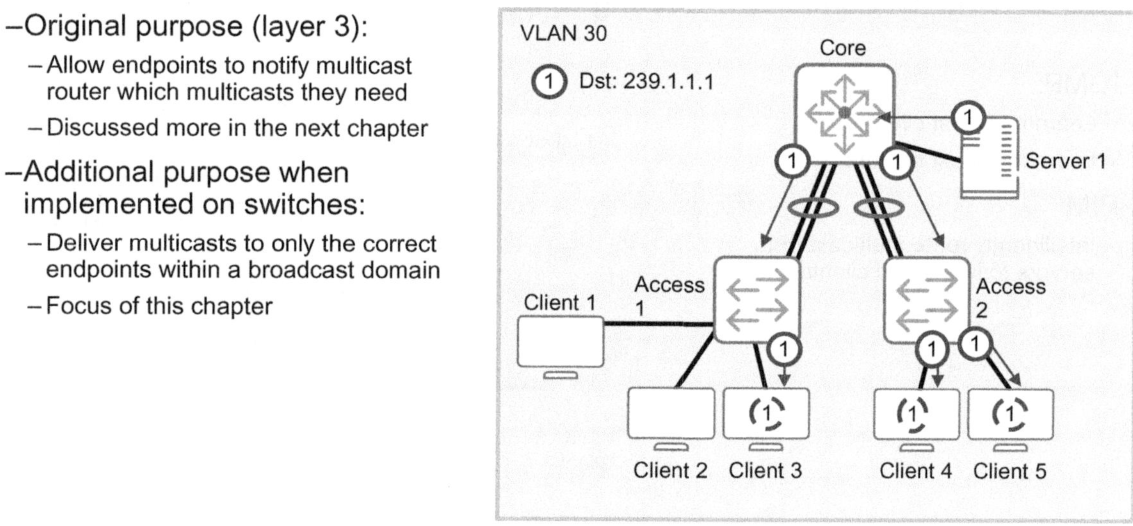

Figure 8-8 IGMP Use Cases

IGMP is a Layer-3 protocol, originally developed to allow hosts to inform their multicast router which multicasts the router should forward into the subnet. For this use case, the router only cares whether any host requires multicasts in a particular group; it does not care how many hosts require the multicasts or where within the Layer-2 topology the hosts are located.

When a switch or routing switch implements IGMP, IGMP can also act at Layer 2 to fulfill another purpose, which is the focus for this chapter. The switch can discover which specific hosts within the VLAN require multicasts for various multicast groups and, therefore, which physical interfaces must forward the traffic. Figure 8-8 shows the traffic flow for multicasts with IGMP (or IGMP snooping) is operating on all of your switches. Server 1 is transmitting multicasts to 239.1.1.1 in VLAN 20. These multicasts flow to Core-1, Access1, and Client 3, the only device that wants them in this VLAN. Similarly, the multicasts to 239.2.2.2 only flow to the client listening for them, Client 2. The same process occurs in VLAN 30; multicasts only flow on the path toward clients that need them. Unnecessary multicasts are removed, reducing congestion.

Note

The IGMP functions fulfilled by switches are sometimes called IGMP snooping because switches traditionally did not generate IGMP messages, but only listened for the ones sent by routers and hosts.

Routing AOS-CX switches, though, can fulfill all the IGMP functions of both a multicast router and a switch. You enable IGMP on a routed interface (Layer 3), while you enable IGMP snooping on a VLAN (Layer 2). However, whether the VLAN has an IP address *does* affect the functionality, as you will learn in this chapter.

IGMP Components

–Devices

Device	Description
Querier	Determines what receivers exist in a VLAN
Receiver	Wish to receive a multicast stream

–Message types

Message	Description
Query	Sent by the querier to determine existing receivers in a VLAN
Report	Sent by a receiver to identify steam(s) to receive
Join	Initiated by a receiver to identify stream(s) to receive
Leave	Initiated by a receiver to identify stream(s) to stop receiving

Figure 8-9 IGMP Components

There are two kinds of devices, as shown in Figure 8-9, in a subnet that requires multicasting:

- Querier
- Receiver

A querier is a Layer-3 switch that implements the IGMP protocol. It sends periodic queries, asking hosts in the subnet for which multicast groups that they wish to receive. A multicast group is commonly referred to as a multicast *stream*: the application information, like a video stream. A multicast receiver is a host that wishes to receive a particular multicast stream or streams, like a video conference unit or a user's desktop.

IGMP manages multicast group memberships based on a query and response mechanism. The multicast group uses four fundamental types of messages to communicate:

- **Query**: A message sent from the querier (multicast router or switch) asking for a response from each host belonging to the multicast group. If a multicast router supporting IGMP is not present, the switch must assume this function to elicit group membership information from the hosts on the network.
- **Join**: A message sent by a host to the querier to indicate that the host wants to be or is a member of a given group indicated in the join message.
- **Leave**: A message sent by a host to the querier to indicate that the host has ceased to be a member of a specific multicast group.
- **Report**: A message sent by a host, in response to a multicast router query, identifying the particular multicast stream or streams the host wishes to receive.

IGMP Queriers

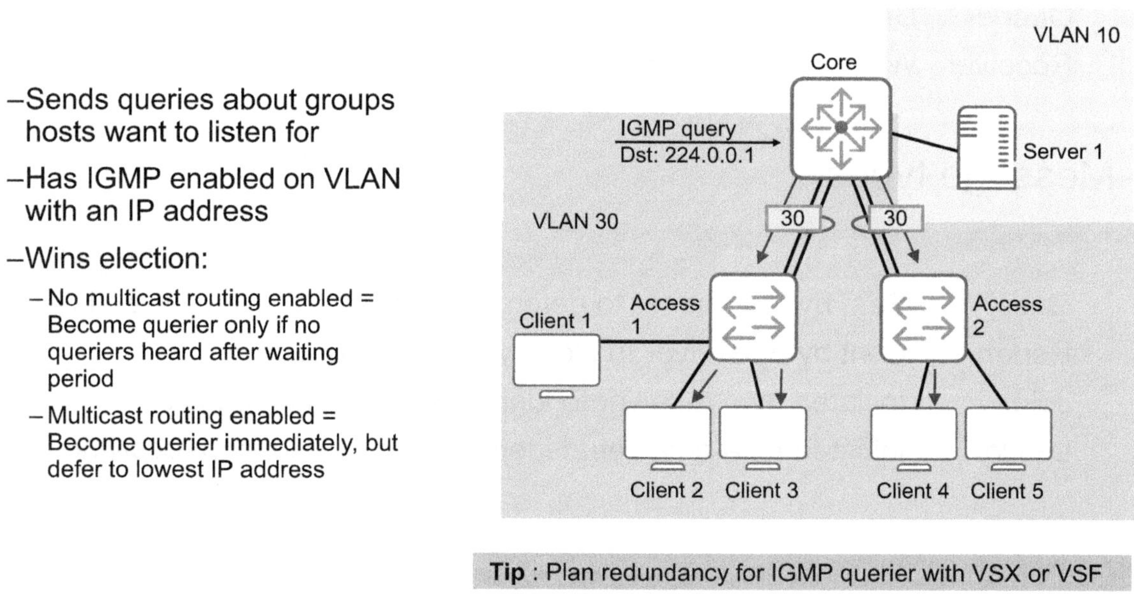

Figure 8-10 IGMP Queriers

A routing switch that implements IGMP, called an IGMP querier, sends periodic queries, asking hosts for which multicast groups they want to listen. In the above slide the Core is a routing switch acting as the IGMP querier (Access1 and 2 are Layer-2 switches). The queries are directed to multicast address 224.0.0.1, and all IGMP-capable devices listen on this address. The next slide illustrates how they respond with the groups for which they want to receive traffic.

Generally, the default router for a VLAN should act as the IGMP querier.

Enabling IGMP

You enable IGMP on a per VLAN basis. In Figure 8-10, the Core is running IGMP in VLAN 20 only. If you want the benefits of IGMP in VLAN 30, you must enable it on the routed interface for VLAN 30.

Enter this configuration to enable IGMP on a Layer-3 VLAN interface:

```
Switch(config)# interface vlan <ID>
Switch(config-if-vlan)# ip igmp enable
```

Enter this configuration to enable IGMP on a Layer-3 VLAN interface:

```
Switch(config)# interface <X/Y/Z>
Switch(config-if-vlan)# ip igmp enable
```

Once you enable IGMP on a Layer-3 interface, by default, IGMPv3 is the default implementation. Use the **disable** parameter to disable IGMP on a Layer-3 interface. Note that if you disable IGMP on an interface and then later re-enable IGMP on that VLAN, the switch restores the last-saved IGMP configuration for that interface. Use the **no ip igmp** command to completely remove it from an interface.

Tip

You should plan redundancy for the IGMP querier role by implementing either VSX or VSF on your AOS-CX switches.

Verifying IGMP Enablement

The following command shows IGMP configuration information and status, or shows information by VRF:

```
Switch# show ip igmp [vrf <VRF-NAME> | all-vrfs] [vsx-peer]
```

Here is an example showing an IGMP configuration and status:

```
switch# show ip igmp
VRF Name : default
Interface : vlan2
IGMP Configured Version : 3
IGMP Operating Version : 3
Querier State : Querier
Querier IP [this switch] : 20.1.1.1
Querier Uptime : 1m 4s
Querier Expiration Time : 0m 1s
IGMP Snoop Enabled on VLAN : True
```

The following command shows IGMP joined group information for the specified group, or shows joined group source and display information by VRF.

```
Switch# show ip igmp group <GROUP-IP> [source <SOURCE-IP>] [vrf
<VRF-NAME> | all-vrfs] [vsx-peer]
```

Here is an example showing IGMP joined group details for group 239.1.1.10:

```
switch# show ip igmp group 239.1.1.10
IGMP group information for group 239.1.1.10
Interface Name: vlan2
VRF Name: default
Group Address: 239.1.1.10
Last Reporter: 100.1.1.10
                                V1        V2        Sources   Sources
Vers Mode Uptime    Expires     Timer     Timer     Forwarded Blocked
---- ---- --------- --------- --------- --------- --------- --------
3    EXC   16m 34s  2m 27s
```

You can also use the **show ip igmp groups** command, which will list all IGMP groups the querier knows about.

The following command shows the IGMP configuration information and operation for interface VLAN 2:

```
switch# show ip igmp interface vlan <ID>
IGMP Configured Version : 3
IGMP Operating Version : 3
Querier State : Querier
Querier IP [this switch] : 20.1.1.1
Querier Uptime : 1m 46s
Querier Expiration Time : 0m 1s
Snoop Enabled on VLAN : True
```

Many other **show** commands are available to verify the operation of IGMP.

Multiple IGMP Queriers and Elections

Just as you need to consider redundancy for the default gateway, you should consider how you will provide redundancy for the IGMP querier role. In the example shown above, the core is a VSF fabric, which has built-in redundancy.

If you are using a protocol such as Virtual Router Redundancy Protocol (VRRP), you should usually implement a backup IGMP querier. Simply enable the querier function on both VRRP devices. Even if you do not have redundancy for routing within the VLAN, though, you can still create a backup IGMP querier. Just add an IP address on the VLAN to one of the non-routing switches and enable IGMP.

Only one device acts as the IGMP querier within the VLAN. Other querier-capable switches become IGMP listeners. As you will see, a listener continues to use IGMP to learn the multicast traffic that endpoints desire in the interface, just like the querier. It simply refrains from sending queries itself. The listener also takes over as querier if it fails to hear a query within two times the querier interval.

The AOS-Switch behavior in determining whether to act as IGMP querier or listener differs based on whether the switch is also implementing a multicast routing protocol such as PIM. You will learn about PIM in the next chapter, but the behavior with PIM enabled is described below for your reference.

Behavior Without PIM Enabled

When you enable IGMP on a switch VLAN with an IP address, the querier capability is enabled by default. However, based on the presumption that a multicast router will act as IGMP querier, the switch does not attempt to become querier immediately. Instead it listens for IGMP queries for a waiting period equal to twice the IGMP querier interval. If it hears any queries in this period, it becomes an IGMP listener. If it does not, it becomes the querier. However, if the switch later hears a query from another device, it disables the querier function and defers to that device.

If you enable IGMP on two AOS-Switches that are not running PIM, the first switch on which you enable IGMP becomes the querier.

Behavior with PIM Enabled

When an AOS-Switch has PIM and IGMP enabled on a VLAN, it uses the IGMPv2 rules for its querier functions. As soon as IGMP is enabled, the switch begins to send IGMP queries at the designated interval. If it ever hears a query from another querier with a lower IP address, it stops sending queries and becomes an IGMP listener. In other words, the switch running IGMP and PIM with the lowest IP address becomes querier, possibly pre-empting the role from another switch.

IGMP operates separately from Virtual Router Redundancy Protocol (VRRP). That is, if two routing switches implement VRRP and IGMP in VLAN 20, either the VRRP backup or the VRRP master could be elected as the IGMP querier regardless of its VRRP role. This is because the switches use their actual IP addresses for the election (the VRRP master does not use its virtual address).

Building Membership Tables with IGMP Reports

–Clients respond with report messages:

(1) IGMP report with 239.1.1.1 (sent to 224.0.0.2 or 239.1.1.1)

(2) IGMP report with 239.2.2.2 (sent to 224.0.0.2 or 239.2.2.2)

–Core:

- Add interfaces that receive reports
- Remove interfaces that time out (or receive leaves if using fast-leave)
- VLAN 30 multicast forwarding table:

Group	Interface
239.1.1.1	To Access-1
239.2.2.2	To Access-2

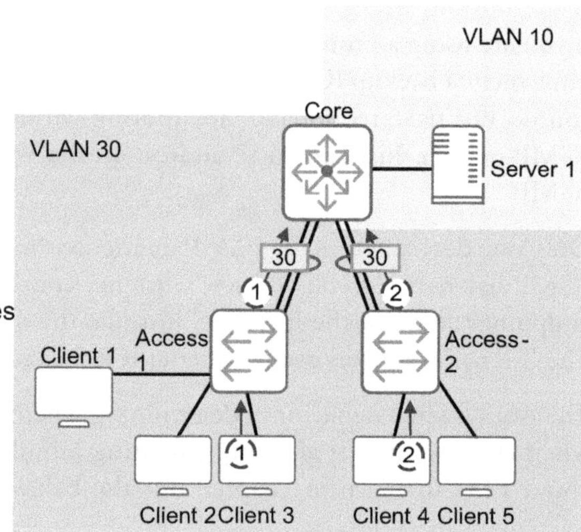

Figure 8-11 Building Membership Tables with IGMP Reports

When an IGMP host such as a computer receives an IGMP query, it sends an IGMP membership report that lists the multicast groups for which it wants to receive traffic (Figure 8-11). This report is multicast to 224.0.0.2. Note also that multicast receivers do not need to wait for an IGMP query to send a report. They can send a report for a group as soon as they want to join it—for example, as soon as a user starts the multicast application. This group-specific report is destined to the multicast address in question. For example, if the application wants to listen for 239.1.1.1, the endpoint sends the IGMP report to 239.1.1.1.

Any network infrastructure device that implements IGMP, whether or not it is the active querier, uses both of these types of reports to construct multicast forwarding tables.

When the switch receives the first report for a particular multicast group on a VLAN interface, it adds a table for that group to the VLAN. Each VLAN that implements IGMP has its own forwarding tables. Because the switch implements IGMP at Layer 2, as well as Layer 3, the physical interface on which the switch received the report becomes a forwarding interface for that group. If the switch receives another membership report on a different physical interface, it adds that interface to the forwarding table as well.

The group membership entries do not persist indefinitely. Instead the switch also sets a timer for the group membership, which it resets every time that its query produces another report. If the timer expires, the switch removes the group membership from the interface.

However, IGMPv2 defines a faster way for an interface to leave a group. When a host no longer requires multicast traffic in a particular group, it can send an IGMP leave group message. The IGMP querier instantly sends one or more queries for the multicast group in question. This allows another IGMP host connected to the same interface to send a membership report indicating that it still wants to receive the multicasts.

Supplemental Information on how AOS-CX Switches Handle Reports

In the example above, only one IGMP host in VLAN 20 wants to join the 239.1.1.1 group, and, as you see, the core VSF fabric receives only one membership report. Even if multiple hosts on Access1 wanted to join this group, though, they would all receive the membership report from the first host to submit the report because this report is a multicast. Those hosts would then suppress their own reports, and a single report still flows to the core. (This behavior is a bit different when Access1 also implements IGMP, as you will see later.)

IGMP defines this behavior because it was originally designed to inform multicast routers if at least one host in the subnet requires multicasts in the subnet. How many hosts required the multicasts does not really matter. Because routing AOS-CX switches also implement IGMP at Layer 2, and need to discover on which physical interfaces to forward traffic, they alter this behavior a bit. The core VSF switch, which implements IGMP, suppresses the membership reports that it receives on each physical interface and does not forward them on other physical interfaces in the VLAN. This behavior prevents hosts on Access2 from hearing the membership reports from hosts on Access1. In this way, the core fabric can receive a report on the Access2 link—for example, if any hosts connected to that switch wanted to listen on 239.1.1.1.

Query and Report Issue

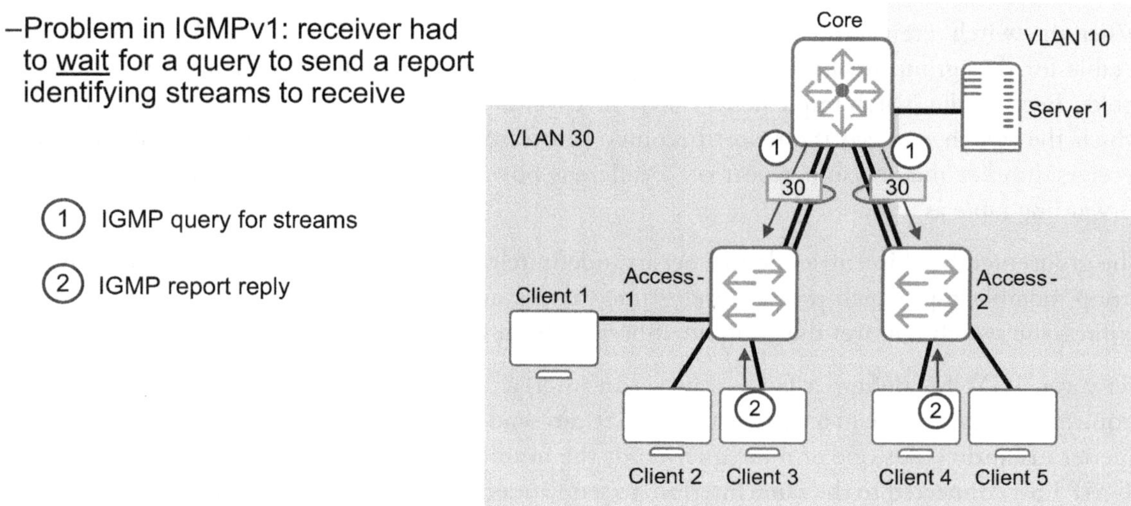

Figure 8-12 Query and Report Issue

The original implementation of IGMP, IGMPv1 only supported two message types: queries and reports (Figure 8-12).

Join and Leave Messages

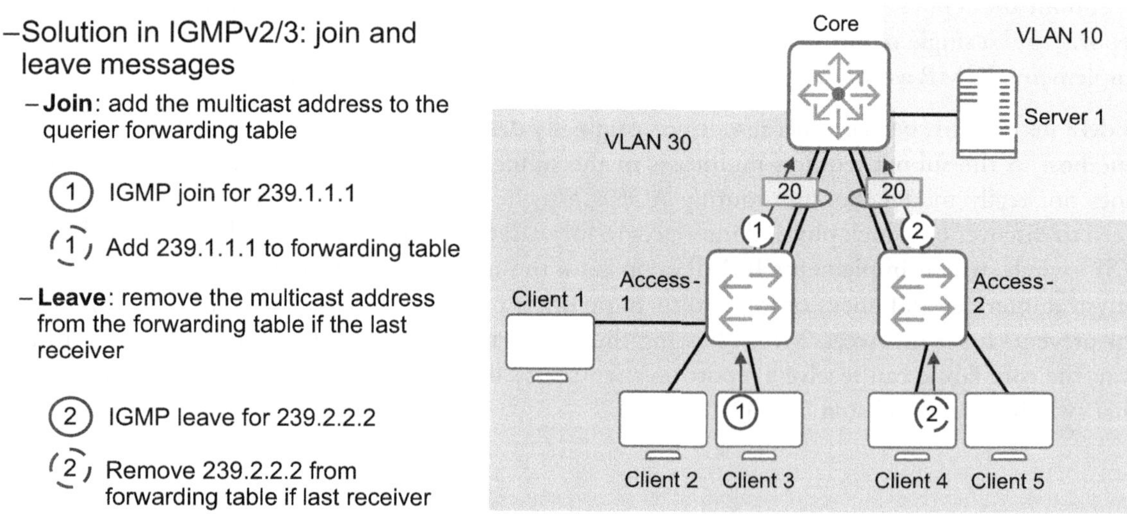

Figure 8-13 Join and Leave Messages

There are two problems with the original implementation and these message types:

- The host has to wait for a query before sending a report; this slows down access to the stream in which the user is interested.
- When a user is done with the multicast application, the host would still receive the stream until a corresponding query would resolve the issue, wasting bandwidth.

The current versions of IGMP (IGMPv2 and v3) introduce two new message types: joins and leaves (Figure 8-13). A join message allows a multicast host to immediately signal a querier of a multicast group that the host needs to receive, expediting the receipt of the stream. And a leave message allows a host to immediately notify a querier when the host no longer needs the stream for the multicast group.

Forwarding Traffic Based on Membership Tables

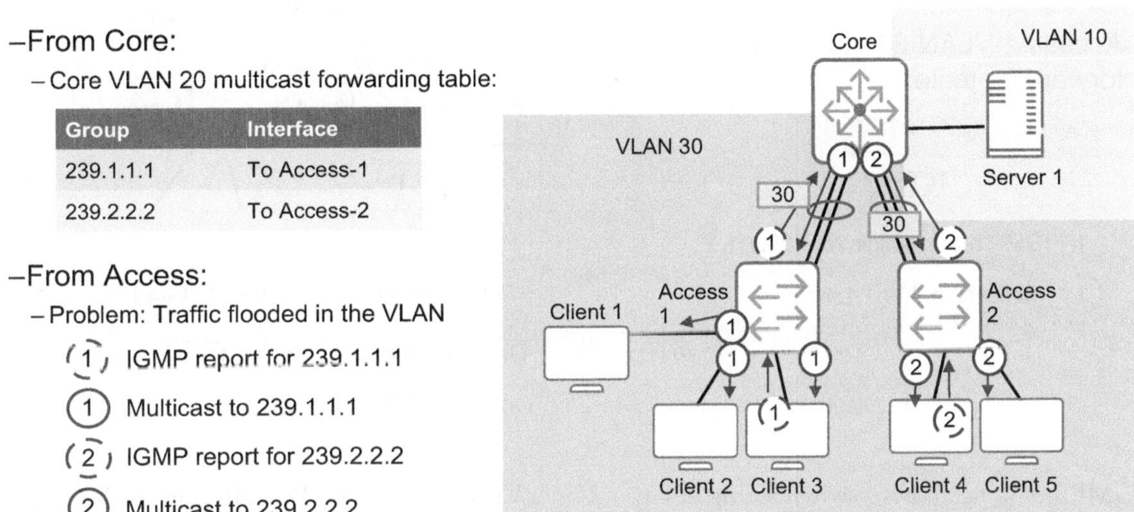

Figure 8-14 Forwarding Traffic Based on Membership Tables

The multicast group table filters traffic for multicasts destined to that address. Rather than forward these multicasts on all ports, the switch forwards multicasts only on ports listed in the table.

In this example, the core is the only switch running IGMP, and it is the IGMP querier. Based on the membership reports that it has received in VLAN 20, it has created two forwarding tables, one for 239.1.1.1 and one for 239.2.2.2.

You also see that the table controls how the switches forward the multicasts. Now the core VSF sends multicasts for 239.1.1.1 only to Access1, which supports a host in that group. And it sends multicasts for 239.2.2.2 only to Access2, which has a host in that group.

Figure 8-14 shows one issue for a design that uses Layer-3 switches at the core (or distribution layer) and Layer-2 switches at the access layer. The core is filtering multicasts, but the access layer switches are not. Access1, for example, sends a multicast to Client 2, which is not listening for this group.

Intelligent Layer-2 Forwarding: IGMP Snooping

IGMP snooping solves this issue. IGMP snooping runs on a Layer-2 device as a multicast constraining mechanism to improve multicast forwarding efficiency. It creates Layer-2 multicast forwarding entries from IGMP packets that are exchanged between the hosts and the router (querier).

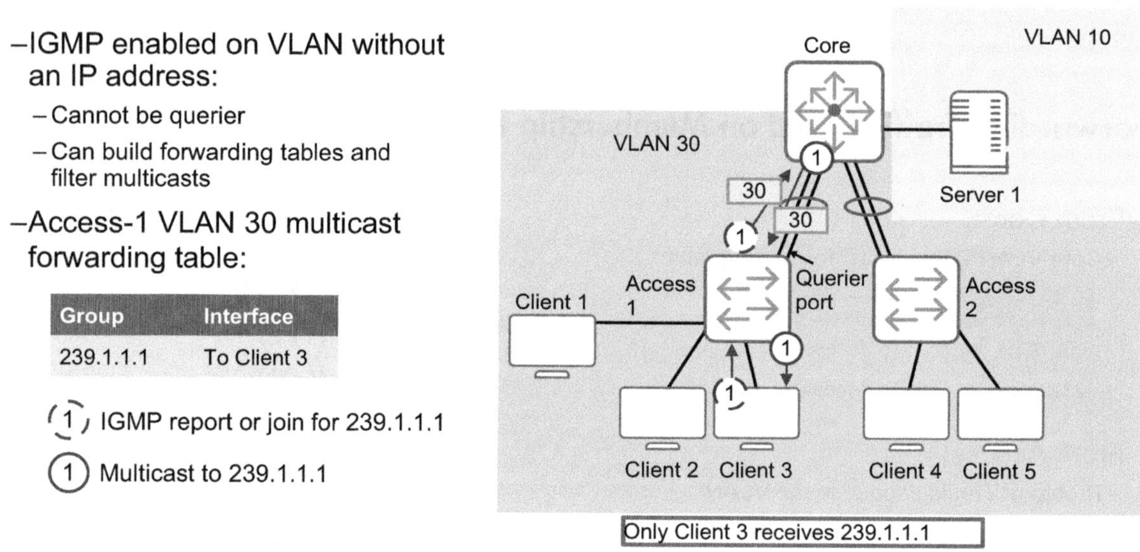

Figure 8-15 Intelligent Layer-2 Forwarding: IGMP Snooping

IGMP snooping allows a switch acting at Layer 2 on a VLAN—it has no IP address in the VLAN—to partially implement IGMP. These switches do not act as IGMP queriers or backup queriers, but they can still use hosts' IGMP messages to create efficient multicast forwarding tables.

The IGMP snooping switch eavesdrops on IGMP traffic (reports, joins, and leaves), using what it learns to determine which ports require specific multicast traffic. It stores this information in a table, creating one table for each VLAN interface on which IGMP snooping is enabled.

To create the table, the switch follows these basic rules, which allow it to discover necessary information about group memberships without disturbing IGMP communications between multicast receivers and their default routers:

1. The switch tracks the ports that receive IGMP general queries.
   - AOS-CX switches call these ports, querier ports.
   - The switch needs to identify router or querier ports so that it knows on which ports to forward IGMP reports and so that it can forward all received multicasts out this port. In Figure 8-15, the link aggregation to the core VSF is the querier port.
2. When the switch receives a multicast receiver's IGMP report, it maps the incoming port to the group in the report in the appropriate VLAN IGMP snooping table. Or, if the port is already mapped to that group, the switch resets the dynamic port member aging timer for that port and group.
   - When hosts hear IGMP reports from other hosts in the same group, they typically suppress their own reports to minimize floods or reports. However, the IGMP snooping switch requires more granular information about the receivers on each port. Therefore, the switch only forwards IGMP reports on router or querier ports. Other hosts, not hearing the report, send their own reports, and the switch can learn their group memberships.
   - The snooping switch minimizes floods of reports to the IGMP querier by forwarding a report only when it creates the initial entry for a multicast group in its IGMP snooping table (rather than every time it adds a new port to the entry).
3. Inactive group memberships time out. How the switch handles leave messages depends on the fast-leave setting, which you will examine in a moment.

Following these rules, the IGMP snooping switch builds up a table such as the one in the figure. When the switch receives multicast packets for a particular group on a router port, it forwards them only on the ports mapped to the group.

Note

The switch updates its forwarding table based on the Layer-2 multicast MAC addresses (01:00:5e:xx:xx:xx) and makes forwarding decisions based on what it learned via snooping. The querier role remains unchanged (the Core switch in the topology. What is different is that the Layer-2 switches (Access1 and 2) spy on the query, report, join, and leave messages to learn where the multicast sources and destinations reside and therefore where the multicast stream (239.1.1.1) needs forwarded.

Configuring IGMP Snooping

IGMP snooping is disabled by default. The default behavior is to flood multicast traffic in the VLAN. Use the following to enable IGMP snooping. Unlike the IGMP protocol, which is enabled on a Layer-3 interface, IGMP snooping is enabled on a Layer-2 interface (VLAN) with the following configuration:

```
switch(config)# vlan <VLAN-ID>
switch(config-vlan)# ip igmp snooping enable
```

How AOS-CX Switches Handle Unknown Multicast Destinations

- The multicast source is directly connected to this switch, and it starts streaming before any clients join the group.
- A multicast source is streaming, and another switch in the path between the source and this switch does not support IGMP.
- The switch has removed a multicast group filtering table because the last member left the group. However, a multicast router forwarding the traffic has not yet received the leave, so it continues to forward the multicasts.

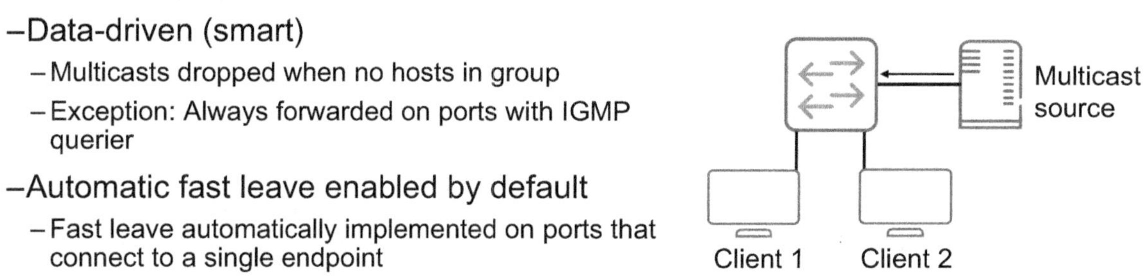

Figure 8-16 How AOS-CX Switches Handle Unknown Multicast Destinations

Sometimes an IGMP or IGMP snooping switch receives a multicast for a group for which the switch does not have a filtering table (Figure 8-16). Called "unknown multicasts," these multicasts can occur when:

AOS-CX switches operate data-driven (or smart) mode. They filter all multicasts for which they do not have a multicast table. If no host has joined the group, but the switch receives multicasts, the switch drops them.

One exception applies: an IGMP snooping switch does forward both unknown and known multicasts on any port on which it has heard IGMP queries. (This behavior is required so that a multicast stream can reach the multicast router.) In fact, by default, the switch forwards unknown multicasts that arrive on one VLAN on any port on which it has heard queries in *any* VLAN.

If you want to change this behavior and restrict the forwarding to the querier ports for that specific VLAN, you must enter this command:

```
Switch(config)# ip igmp snooping drop-unknown vlan-exclusive
```

The default mode is **vlan-shared**. It is important that you understand that the **igmp filter-unknown-mcast** command has no effect on how the data-driven switch behaves with non-querier ports. The switch always filters unknown multicasts on these ports.

Data-Driven Mode and Fast Learn

Configuring fast learn on a port enables faster response to topology change notifications. When spanning tree changes the port state from blocked to forwarding, the device acting as querier will immediately send a general query on the fast learn enabled port. Then the device acting as a non-querier will replay the joins. This will help in faster convergence of multicast flows.

```
Switch(config)# vlan <ID>
Switch(config-vlan)# ip igmp snooping fastlearn <port_ID_list>
```

AOS-CX Considerations

Configuration task	Context	Default
IGMP querier	Layer-3 interface	Disabled
IGMP snooping	Layer-2 VLAN	Disabled

Figure 8-17 AOS-CX Considerations

With the factory default setting, multicast data transmitted from the sources will be flooded on all ports in the VLAN. Configuring IGMP snooping avoids flooding and causes the switch to forward data only to the receivers.

IGMP configuration considerations include the following:

- For IGMP to be operational, the interface has to be administratively up. For interface VLANs, the L2 VLAN has to be up and one of the ports in the VLAN has to be up.
- The IP address must be assigned for the interface to become querier. Without an IP address, the device will remain in a non-querier state.
- A querier is required for proper IGMP operation. For this reason, you must enable IGMP on the L3 Interface. If the querier functionality is not configured or disabled, you must ensure that there is an IGMP querier in the same VLAN.

- For IGMP snooping to be operational on a VLAN, the VLAN has to be administratively up and at least one port in the VLAN has to be up.
- If the switch becomes the querier for a particular interface, then subsequently detects queries transmitted from another device on the same VLAN, the switch ceases to operate as the querier for that interface.
- The switch automatically ceases querier operation in an IGMP-enabled interface if it detects another querier on the interface. You can also use the switch CLI to disable the querier capability.

Each of the AOS-CX switches has different capabilities in regard to the number of multicast steams supported by the switch (Figure 8-17). Here is a summary:

- 8400 switches: AOS-CX supports 16K IPv4 multicast groups.
- 8320/8325 switches: AOS-CX supports 4K IPv4 multicast groups.
- 6400/6300 switches: AOS-CX supports 4K IPv4 multicast groups.

Important

By default, though, switches will treat multicasts as "broadcasts" and flood them in a VLAN unless IGMP snooping is enabled. This wastes bandwidth on segments in a VLAN. Thus, any time multicast is implemented, IGMP snooping should be enabled for VLANs on AOS-CX switches.

VSX and Multicasting: IGMP

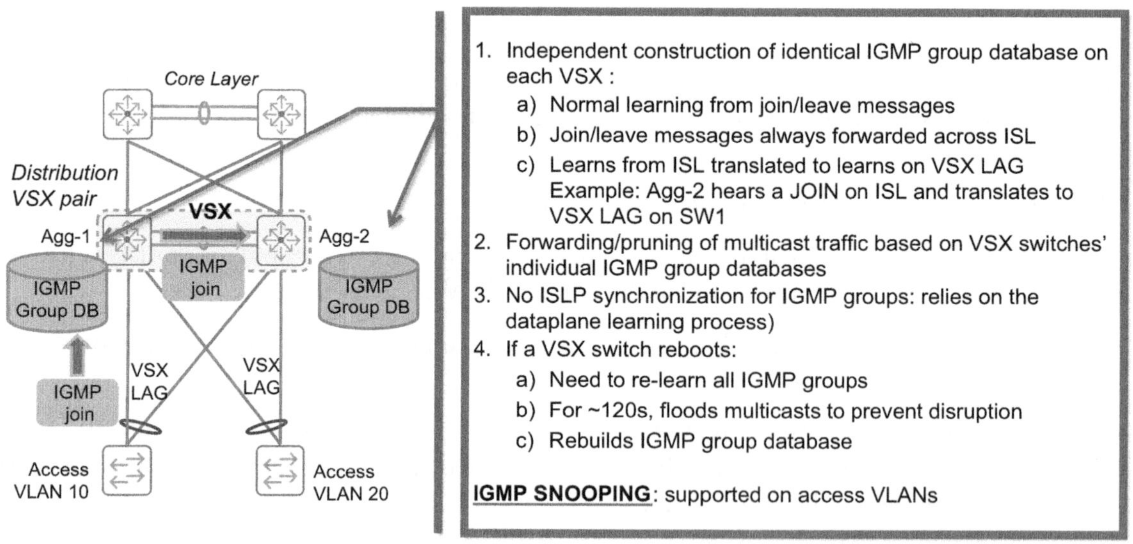

Figure 8-18 VSX and Multicasting: IGMP

You should also understand how VSX affects the forwarding of multicast traffic (Figure 8-18). Each VSX switch constructs its own IGMP group database, which is identical to its peer's IGMP group database. Both switches hear JOIN/LEAVE messages they receive from the downstream VSX LAGs because the ISL is always included as a forwarding port for IGMP. For example, SW1 has a VSX LAG to the aggregation switches.

In this example, it chooses the link to Agg-1 for forwarding the IGMP JOIN, and Agg-1 learns the group on the VSX LAG. The IGMP JOIN crosses the ISL to Agg-2. The VSX IGMP process translates the IGMP JOIN learned on the ISL into an IGMP JOIN message learned on the VSX LAG, just as if the JOIN had arrived on the link from SW1. Therefore, Agg-2 also learns the group on the VSX LAG to SW1.

In this way, each VSX switch can determine on which interfaces to forward or prune multicast traffic for particular IGMP groups, based on its own IGMP group database. Because the IGMP database construction relies on this data plane-based process, ISLP does synchronize IGMP groups between VSX peers. If a VSX switch reboots, it needs to re-learn all of the IGMP groups. For about 120 seconds after rebooting, the VSX switch floods multicast traffic within VLANs that have active, forwarding physical ports, which prevents disruption of multicast forwarding during the learning process. The VSX switch also sends an All Hosts Query (AHQ) message. Clients send JOIN messages in response, so the VSX switch can re-learn the groups and re-create the IGMP group database.

You can configure IGMP snooping on access VLANs. It enables VSX switches operating at Layer 2 on the VLAN to similarly construct identical IGMP group databases.

Lab 8

Lab 8 Diagram

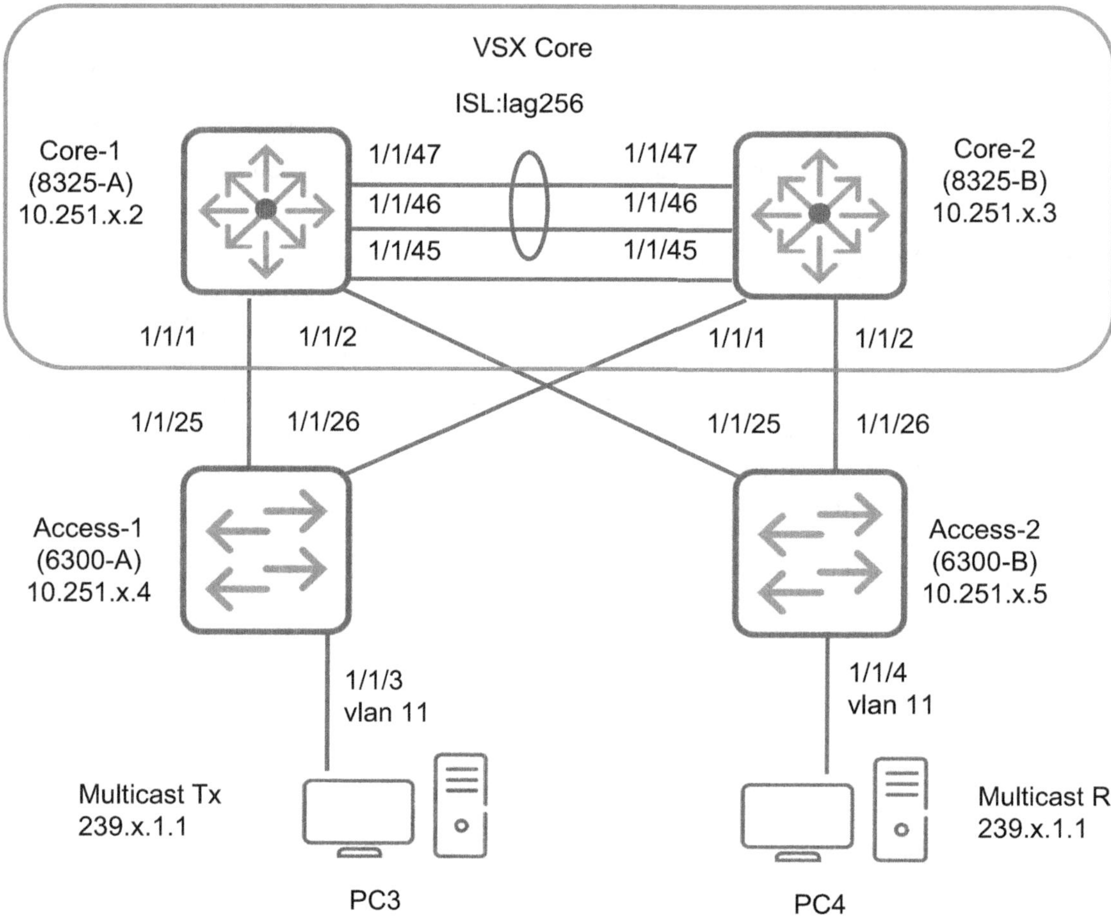

Figure 8-19 Lab 8 Diagram

Overview

In this lab activity, as shown in Figure 8-19, IGMP Querier and IGMP snooping will be configured and demonstrated. The Core VSX will be configured to perform the IGMP Querier function, since the core has the IP interface in the user VLAN.

The Access switches will be configured with IGMP snooping. This will ensure that the multicast traffic is only delivered to the ports with active subscribers.

The PC3, connected to Access1, will be transmitting some test multicasts, the PC4, connected to Access2, will be configured to register and listen for the test multicast traffic.

Objectives

- Configure IGMP Querier on the VSX system
- Configure IGMP Snooping on the Access switches
- Understand the need for IGMP configuration
- Verify the IGMP operation

Task 1: Prepare the Lab Start Configuration

Objectives

- This lab is built on the base VSX topology.
- Make sure to complete these steps to get the base VSX checkpoint configuration on the devices.

Steps

1. Open a console connection to all ***four*** switches (Access1, Access2, Core1, and Core2. Log in using admin/aruba123. Restore the 'icx-lab04-vsx' checkpoint to the running-config.

```
Switch# copy checkpoint icx-lab04-vsx running-config
Configuration changes will take time to process, please be patient.
```

2. On Access1, enter configuration mode; assign port 1/1/3 (connected to PC3) as access port to VLAN11 and enable the port.

```
ICX-Tx-Access1(config)# interface 1/1/3
ICX-Tx-Access1(config-if)# vlan access 11
ICX-Tx-Access1(config-if)# no shutdown
ICX-Tx-Access1(config-if)# exit
```

3. Open a connection to PC3; reset the Lab NIC (disable/enable).Verify the PC3 has an IP address from VLAN11 (10.x.11.0/24).

4. On Access2, enter configuration mode; assign port 1/1/4 (connected to PC4) as access port to VLAN11 and enable the port.

```
ICX-Tx-Access2(config)# interface 1/1/4
ICX-Tx-Access2(config-if)# vlan access 11
ICX-Tx-Access2(config-if)# no shutdown
ICX-Tx-Access2(config-if)# exit
```

5. Open a connection to PC4; reset the Lab NIC (disable/enable).Verify the PC4 has an IP address from VLAN11 (10.x.11.0/24).

Task 2: Set up the Multicast Sender and Receiver

Objectives

In this task, the default behavior of the switches will be demonstrated for intra-VLAN IP multicast traffic. The PC3 (connected to Access1 1/1/3) will be transmitting test multicast traffic. On the PC4 (connected to Access2 1/1/4), Wireshark will be used to verify that the traffic is flooded to all the ports on the network, even without any IGMP joins.

Steps

1. Open the PC3 (connected to Access1). Start the UDP Multicast test tool from the desktop.
2. Under the 'Sender' section (top half of the screen), configure:
   - **Local** Interface **address**: Enter your local Lab NIC *IP* (in 10.x.11.0/24 subnet). Do not confuse this with 'Local Multicast Interface Address'.

Note

You may also drag and drop your 10.x.11.y IP from the 'Local interfaces' list to the 'Local Interface' field. See the screenshot below.

- Destination multicast address: **239.x.1.1**
- Click the '**Start Sender**' button to start.

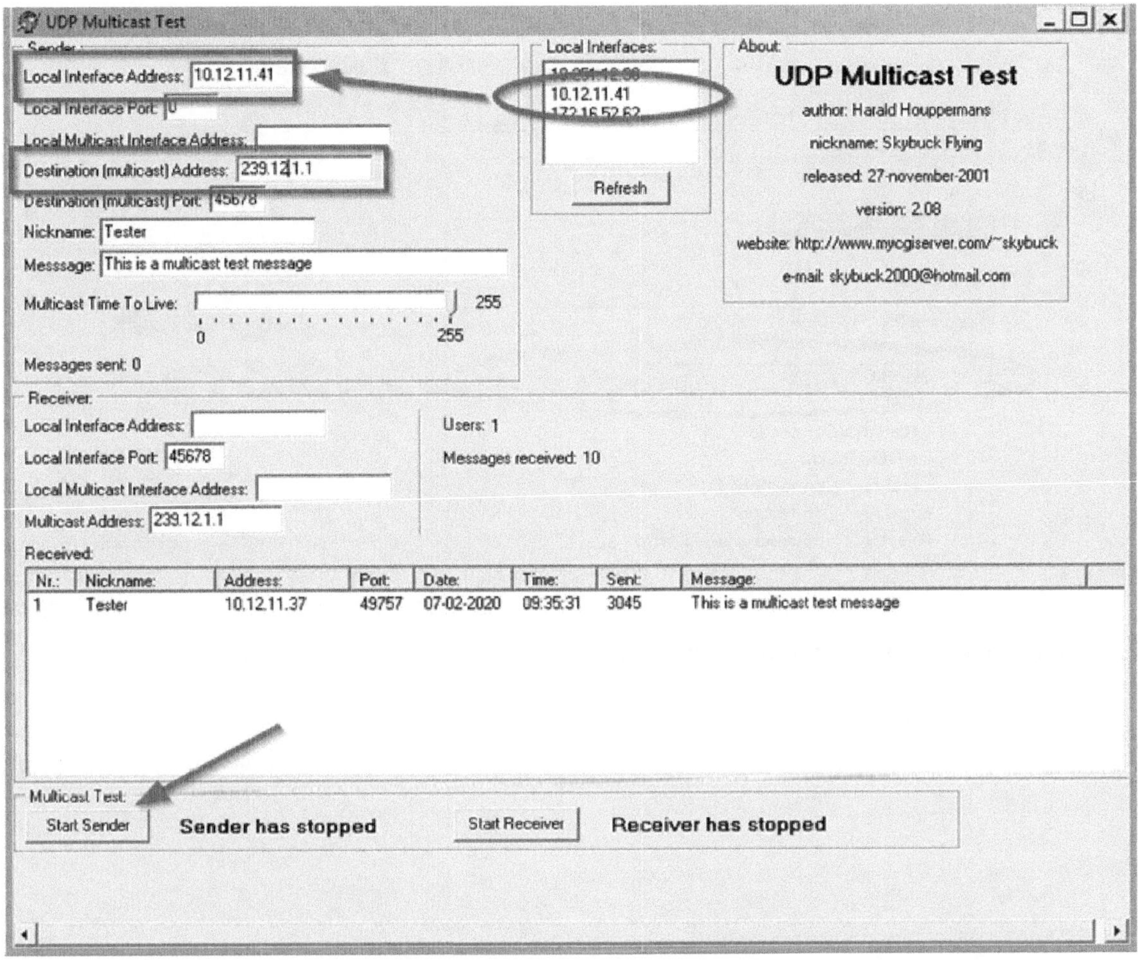

On PC3, Locally Verify the Transmitted Multicast Traffic

1. On PC3, open Wireshark and select the 'Lab NIC' and start the capture (double-click).

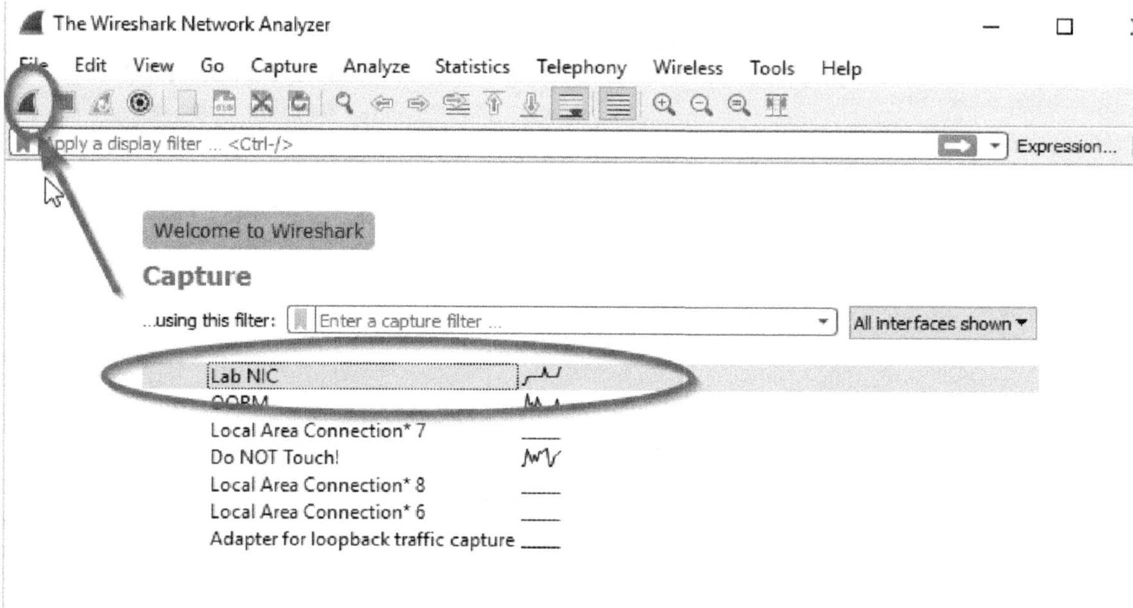

2. After about 5 seconds, stop the capture again.

3. Verify that packets are transmitted to the 239.x.1.1 multicast IP address.

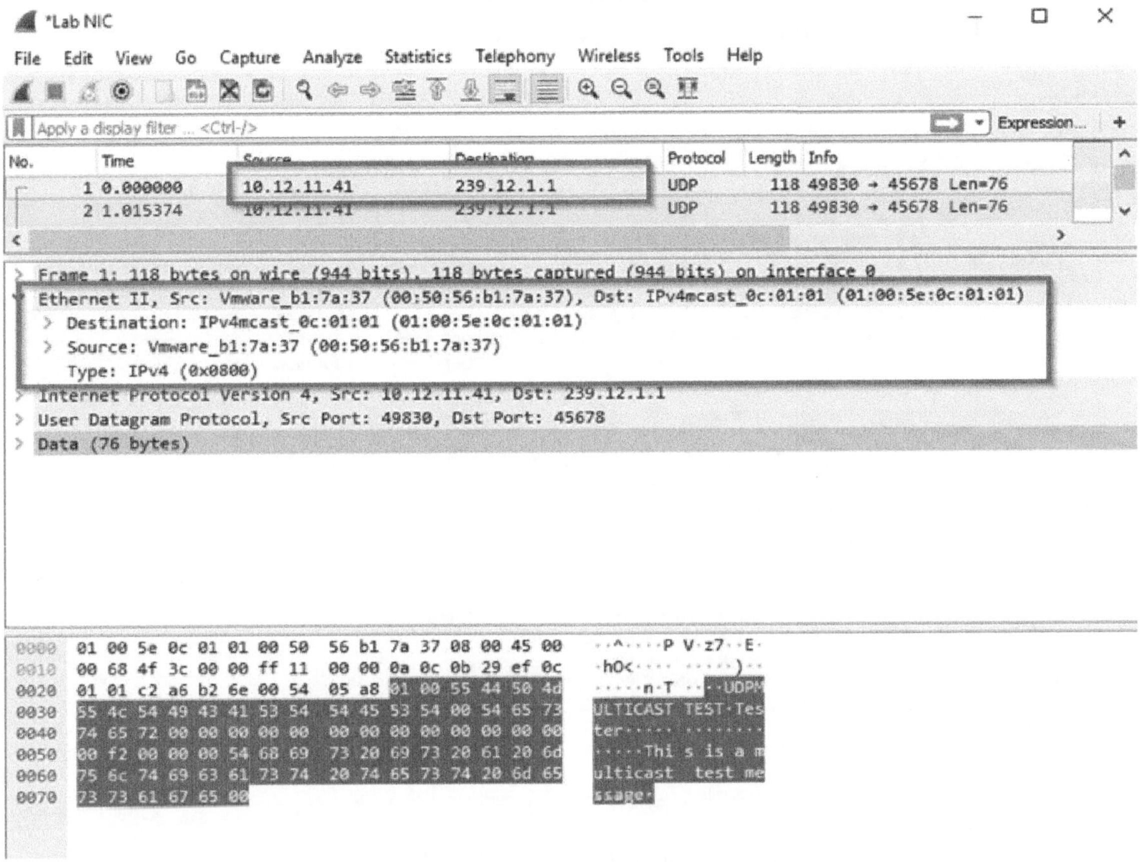

4. Open PC4 (connected to Access2); start Wireshark, and perform a packet capture on the ‘Lab NIC’ for about 5 seconds.

5. Verify that the multicast traffic is received on the 'Lab NIC'. If there is too much other traffic, apply this display filter to limit the display to IP multicast traffic.
   - **ip.addr == 224.0.0.0/4**

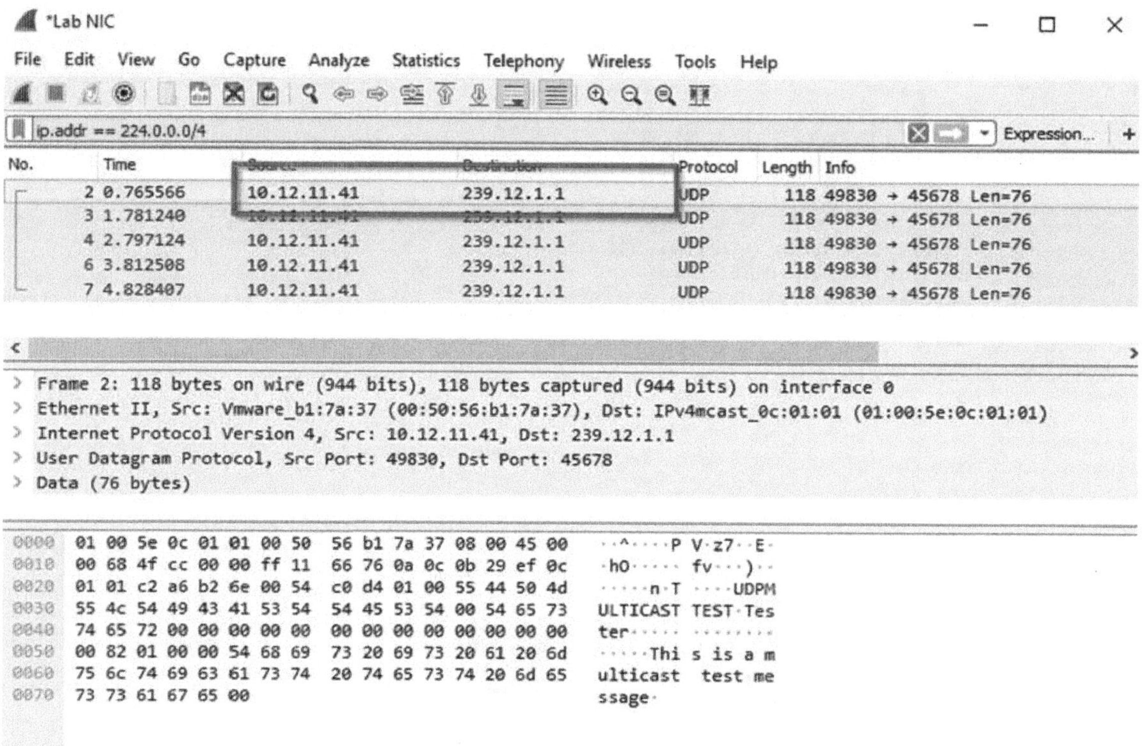

6. This demonstrates that multicast traffic is flooded by default.
7. On PC3, stop the multicast transmission, so you can start the next task without multicast traffic.

Task 3: Enable IGMP Querier and Snooping

Objectives

In this task, the network switches will be configured with IP IGMP snooping. IP IGMP snooping will look for IP IGMP joins that are sent by the multicast listener devices. To operate correctly, there should be an IP IGMP querier on the network. This function will be configured on the VSX Core devices.

Steps

Core1—IGMP Querier and Snooping

1. Open a terminal connection to Core1; enter the configuration mode. Review the default IP IGMP querier state.

```
ICX-Tx-Core1(config)# show ip igmp interface vlan11
IGMP is not enabled
```

2. Enable the querier function for VLAN11 and VLAN12.

```
ICX-Tx-Core1(config)# interface vlan11
ICX-Tx-Core1(config-if-vlan)# ip igmp enable
ICX-Tx-Core1(config-if-vlan)# exit
```

Note

The 'ip igmp querier' role is default on the Layer3 VLAN SVI interface, so it is only required to enable IGMP on the VLAN interface.

3. Repeat this for VLAN12.

```
ICX-Tx-Core1(config)# interface vlan12
ICX-Tx-Core1(config-if-vlan)# ip igmp enable
ICX-Tx-Core1(config-if-vlan)# exit
```

4. Verify that IP IGMP querier is now in the 'initial wait' state.

```
ICX-Tx-Core1(config)# show ip igmp interface vlan11
IGMP Configured Version  : 3
IGMP Operating Version   : 3
Querier State             :Initial Wait
Querier IP                :
Querier Uptime            :
Querier Expiration Time   :
IGMP Snoop Enabled on VLAN :False
```

Question: Based on this output, what is the default IGMP snooping status on the VLAN?

Answer: By default, IGMP snooping is disabled on the VLAN. Therefore, the IGMP querier and snooping functions are enabled separately. The IGMP Querier is enabled on the L3 VLAN Interface (interface vlan x), while the IGMP snooping is configured on the L2 VLAN context (vlan x).

5. Enable IGMP snooping on VLANs 11 and 12.

```
ICX-Tx-Core1(config)# vlan 11,12
ICX-Tx-Core1(config-vlan-<11,12>)# ip igmp snooping enable
ICX-Tx-Core1(config-vlan-<11,12>)# exit
```

6. Verify the updated state.

```
ICX-Tx-Core1(config)# show ip igmp interface vlan11
IGMP Configured Version  : 3
IGMP Operating Version   : 3
Querier State               : Initial Wait
Querier IP                  :
Querier Uptime              :
Querier Expiration Time     :
IGMP Snoop Enabled on VLAN : True

Active Group Address   Vers Mode Uptime    Expires
---------------------- ---- ---- --------- ---------
239.255.255.250        3    EXC  2m 55s    1m 25s
```

Note

The multicast group 239.255.255.250 may be observed at this point. This depends on the Windows client that may or may not have used this address already at this point.

Core2—IGMP Querier and Snooping

1. Open a terminal connection to Core2; enter the configuration mode. Enable the querier function for VLAN11 and VLAN12.

```
ICX-Tx-Core2(config)# interface vlan11
ICX-Tx-Core2(config-if-vlan)# ip igmp enable
ICX-Tx-Core2(config-if-vlan)# exit
ICX-Tx-Core2(config)# interface vlan12
ICX-Tx-Core2(config-if-vlan)# ip igmp enable
ICX-Tx-Core2(config-if-vlan)# exit
```

2. Enable IGMP snooping on the Layer-2 VLANs 11 and 12.

```
ICX-Tx-Core2(config)# vlan11,12
ICX-Tx-Core2(config-vlan-<11,12>)# ip igmp snooping enable
ICX-Tx-Core2(config-vlan-<11,12>)# exit
```

3. Review the status of IGMP.

```
ICX-Tx-Core2(config)# show ip igmp interface vlan11
IGMP Configured Version   : 3
IGMP Operating Version    : 3
Querier State                : Initial Wait
Querier IP                   :
Querier Uptime               :
Querier Expiration Time      :
IGMP Snoop Enabled on VLAN   : True

Active Group Address    Vers Mode Uptime    Expires
---------------------- ---- ---- --------- ---------
239.255.255.250         3    EXC  2m 45s    1m 35s
```

Note

Depending on your lab pace, the switches may already have transitioned from 'Initial Wait' to 'Querier' or 'Non-Querier' at this point.

Enable IP IGMP Snooping on Access1 and Access2

1. Open a terminal connection to Access1; enter the configuration mode. Enable IGMP snooping for VLAN11 and VLAN12.

```
ICX-Tx-Access1(config)# vlan 11,12
ICX-Tx-Access1(config-vlan-<11,12>)# ip igmp snooping enable
ICX-Tx-Access1(config-vlan-<11,12>)# exit
```

2. Verify the configuration status of IGMP snooping.

```
ICX-Tx-Access1(config)# show ip igmp snooping vlan11
IGMP Snooping Protocol Info
Total VLANs with IGMP enabled                : 2
Current count of multicast groups joined     : 0

IGMP Drop Unknown Multicast                  : Global
VLAN ID : 11
VLAN Name : VLAN11
IGMP Configured Version    : 3
IGMP Operating Version : 3
Querier Address :
Querier Port :
Querier UpTime :
Querier Expiration Time :
```

3. Open a terminal connection to Access2; enter the configuration mode. Enable IGMP snooping for VLAN11 and VLAN12.

```
ICX-Tx-Access2(config)# vlan 11,12
ICX-Tx-Access2(config-vlan-<11,12>)# ip igmp snooping enable
ICX-Tx-Access2(config-vlan-<11,12>)# exit
```

Verify the IGMP Querier Status on the Core1

It may take a few minutes before Core1 transitions to the IP Querier state. Make sure to wait in the lab until this has occurred.

1. On Core1, verify the state until the 'initial wait' has changed to 'querier'.

```
ICX-Tx-Core1(config)# show ip igmp interface vlan11
IGMP Configured Version   : 3
IGMP Operating Version    : 3
Querier State              :Querier
Querier IP [this switch]   : 10.x.11.2
Querier Uptime             : 7m 17s
Querier Expiration Time    : 0m 5s
IGMP Snoop Enabled on VLAN : True
```

2. Repeat this on Core2; verify it has transitioned to 'Non-Querier'.

```
ICX-Tx-Core2(config)# show ip igmp interface vlan11
IGMP Configured Version   : 3
IGMP Operating Version    : 3
Querier State              :Non-Querier
Querier IP                 : 10.x.11.2
Querier Uptime             : 9m 17s
Querier Expiration Time    : 2m 20s
IGMP Snoop Enabled on VLAN : True
```

3. Now that the Core switch is sending out regular queries for IGMP membership, the Access switches IGMP snooping should be able to detect the 'querier' port.

4. On Access1, verify that the upstream IGMP querier was detected on the lag255 (this is the LAG to the VSX core).

```
ICX-Tx-Access1(config)# show ip igmp snooping vlan11
IGMP Snooping Protocol Info
Total VLANs with IGMP enabled                : 2
Current count of multicast groups joined     : 1

IGMP Drop Unknown Multicast                  : Global
VLAN ID : 11
VLAN Name : VLAN11
IGMP Configured Version  : 3
IGMP Operating Version : 3
Querier Address :10.x.11.2
Querier Port : lag255
Querier UpTime :5m 33s
Querier Expiration Time :2m 54s
```

5. Repeat this verification on Access2.

```
ICX-Tx-Access2(config)# show ip igmp snooping vlan11
IGMP Snooping Protocol Info
Total VLANs with IGMP enabled                : 2
Current count of multicast groups joined     : 1

IGMP Drop Unknown Multicast                  : Global
VLAN ID : 11
VLAN Name : VLAN11
IGMP Configured Version  : 3
IGMP Operating Version : 3
Querier Address :10.x.11.2
Querier Port : lag255
Querier UpTime :6m 40s
Querier Expiration Time :3m 53s
```

Task 4: Verify the IGMP Snooping Operation

Objectives

In this task, the multicast test traffic will be used again, but this time, the multicast traffic should be filtered by default due to the IGMP snooping configuration. Once the lab has demonstrated that the traffic was filtered, the client device will send an IGMP join, using the multicast test application, and the multicast traffic should be forwarded to the port. Any other ports that have not sent an IGMP join should not receive the multicast traffic for the test group.

Steps

Verify Multicast Traffic Is No Longer Flooded

1. Open PC3 (connected to Access1) and start the multicast test traffic again by clicking the '**Start Sender**' button. You may optionally re-start the Wireshark packet capture for a few seconds to confirm traffic is sent out.
2. Open PC4 (connected to Access2) and start the Wireshark packet capture for a few seconds and then stop again. Confirm that **no** multicast test traffic was received.

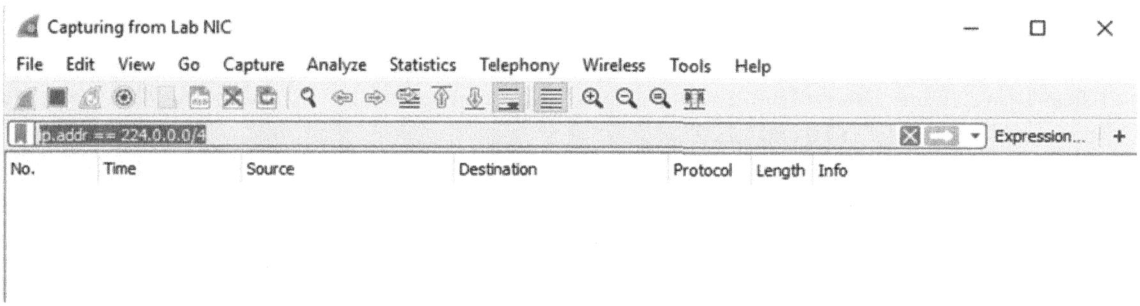

Note
Some IGMP traffic may be observed since the Core IGMP querier will send regular membership query reports.

Verify Multicast Traffic Is Still Delivered When Requested

1. On the PC4, connected to Access2, start the Wireshark capture again. Start the UDP Multicast test tool from the desktop. Configure the **Receiver** section (bottom half of the screen).
   - **Local Multicast Interface address**: Enter the PC4 Lab NIC IP address

Note
Do not confuse this with the 'Local Interface Address' field.

   - Multicast address: **239.x.1.1**
   - Click the Start Receiver button

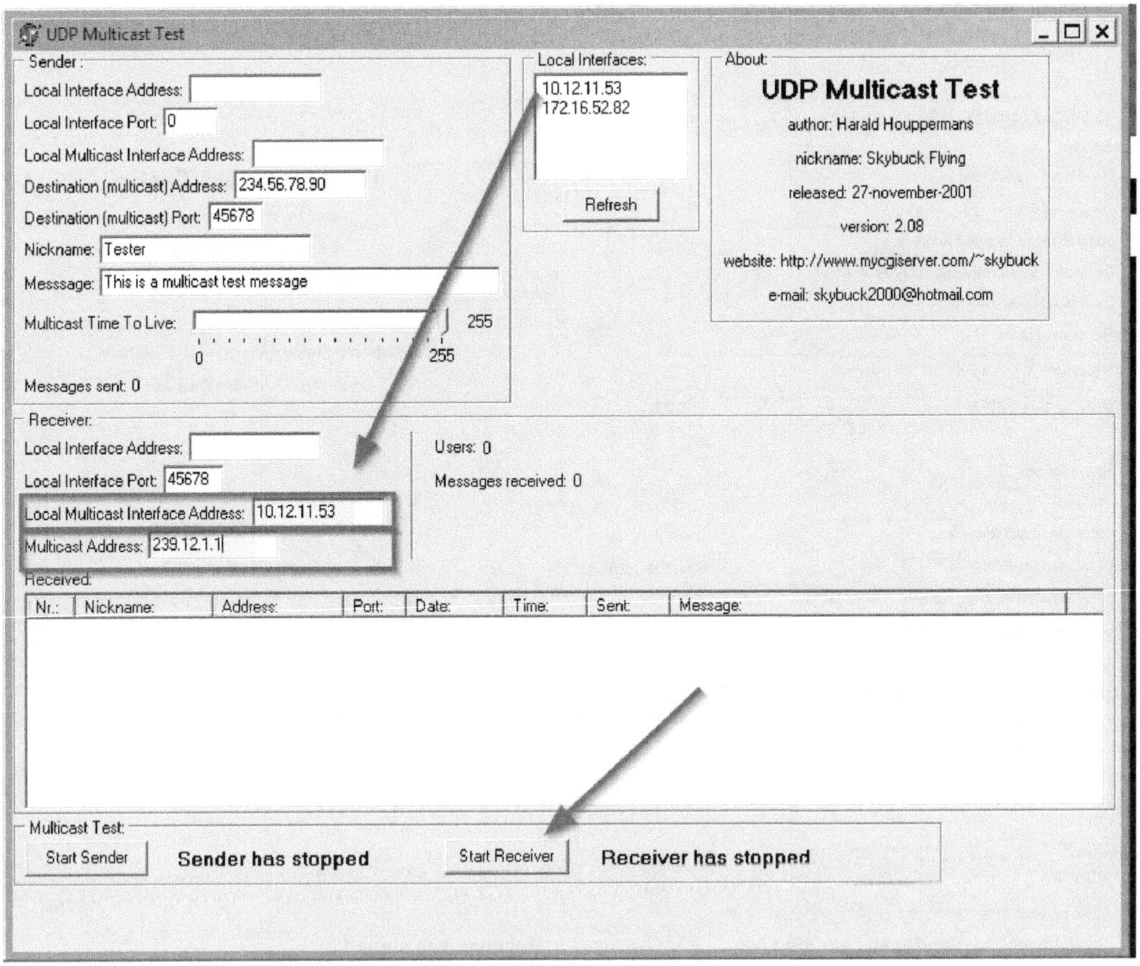
UDP Multicast Test
Sender:
Local Interface Address:
Local Interface Port: 0
Local Multicast Interface Address:
Destination (multicast) Address: 234.56.78.90
Destination (multicast) Port: 45678
Nickname: Tester
Messsage: This is a multicast test message
Multicast Time To Live: 255
0
255
Messages sent: 0
Local Interfaces:
10.12.11.53
172.16.52.82
Refresh
About:
UDP Multicast Test
author: Harald Houppermans
nickname: Skybuck Flying
released: 27-november-2001
version: 2.08
website: http://www.mycgiserver.com/~skybuck
e-mail: skybuck2000@hotmail.com
Receiver:
Local Interface Address:
Local Interface Port: 45678
Local Multicast Interface Address: 10.12.11.53
Multicast Address: 239.12.1.1
Users: 0
Messages received: 0
Received:
Nr.: Nickname: Address: Port: Date: Time: Sent: Message:
Multicast Test:
Start Sender
Sender has stopped
Start Receiver
Receiver has stopped

2. In the UDP Multicast test application, the **Received** section should now show the incoming test message.

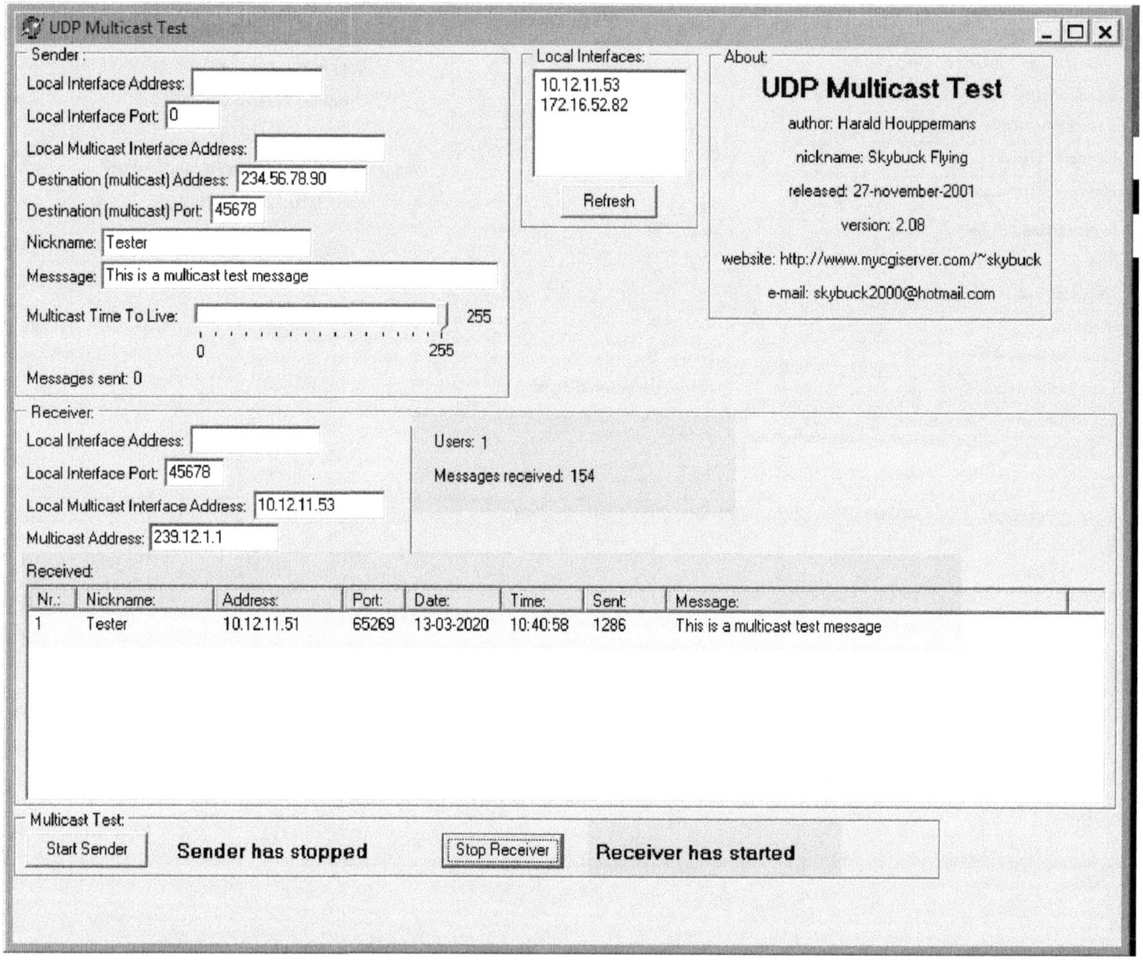

3. Stop the Wireshark trace and scroll back to the start of the trace. The trace should show that at the moment the multicast test client application starts the receiver, the IGMP join is sent by the PC. Following the join message, the actual multicast traffic will now be received by this switch port.

⚠ Tip

It may be easier to apply display filter '**ip.addr == 224.0.0.0/4**' (**not /24 !**) to see only the multicast traffic.

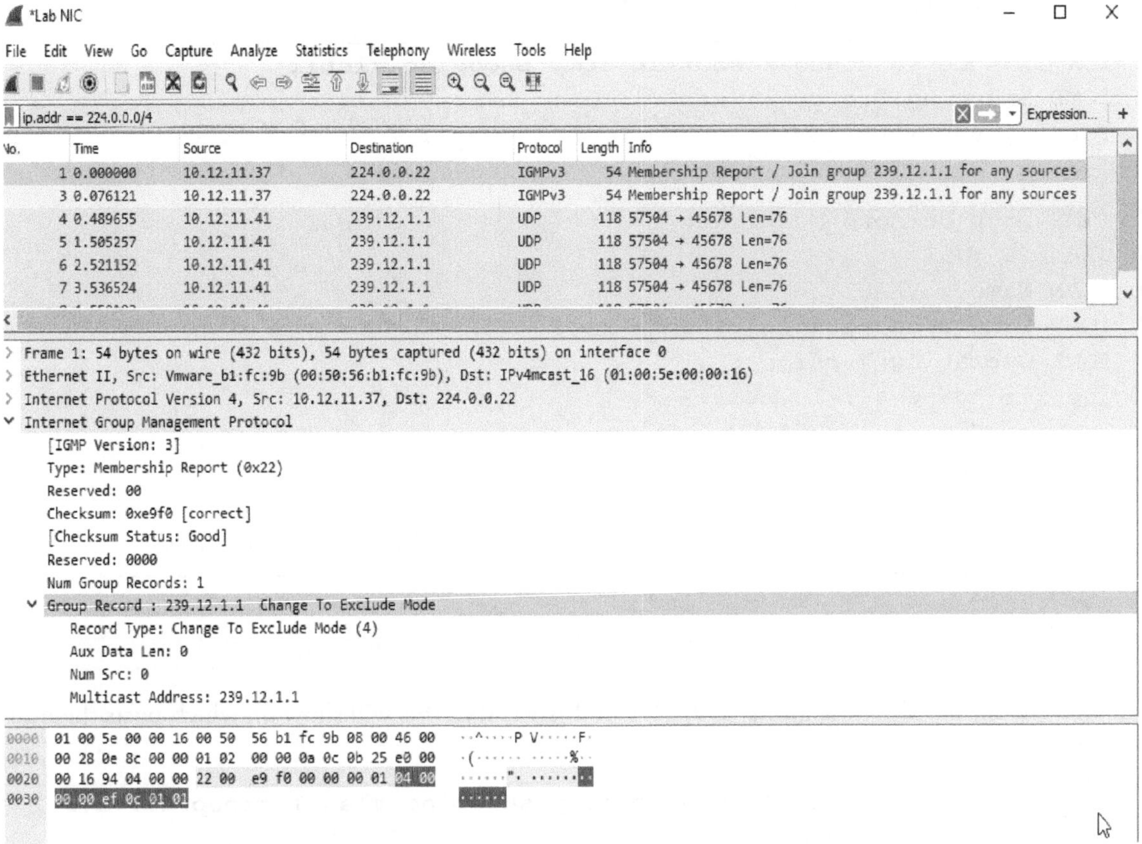

Verify the IGMP Snooping Status on the Switches

1. On Access2, review all the IGMP snooping groups.

```
ICX-Tx-Access2(config)# show ip igmp snooping groups
IGMP Group Address Information

VLAN ID Group Address   Expires   UpTime    Last Reporter  Type
------- --------------- --------- --------- -------------- ------
11      239.x.1.1       3m 34s    48m 32s   10.x.11.37     Filter
11      239.255.255.250 3m 36s    1h 16m    10.x.11.37     Filter
```

2. Next, review the IGMP group tables for VLAN11.

```
ICX-Tx-Access2(config)# show ip igmp snooping vlan11
IGMP Snooping Protocol Info
Total VLANs with IGMP enabled                  : 2
Current count of multicast groups joined       : 2

IGMP Drop Unknown Multicast                    : Global
VLAN ID : 11
VLAN Name : VLAN11
IGMP Configured Version     : 3
IGMP Operating Version : 3
Querier Address : 10.x.11.2
Querier Port : lag256
Querier UpTime :23m 15s
Querier Expiration Time :4m 6s
Active Group Address   Tracking  Vers Mode Uptime    Expires
-------------------- ---------- ---- ---- --------- ----------
239.x.1.1             Filter     3    EXC  5m 46s    4m 16s
239.255.255.250        Filter     3    EXC  23m 11s   4m 18s
```

3. Review the details of the group 239.x.1.1 in this VLAN. This will show on which ports the multicast was requested.

```
ICX-Tx-Access2(config)# show ip igmp snooping vlan11 group 239.x.1.1
IGMP ports and group information for group 239.12.1.1

VLAN ID   : 11
VLAN Name : VLAN11

Group Address : 239.x.1.1
Last Reporter : 10.x.11.37
Group Type    : Filter

                                           V1     V2      Sources
Sources
Port   Vers Mode  Uptime   Expires  Timer  Timer   Forwarded  Blocked
----   ---- ----  ------   -------  -----  -----   ---------  -------
1/1/4  3    EXC   5m 58s   4m 4s                   0          0
```

4. On the Core1 and Core2, review the IGMP group table 239.x.1.1. Both systems should show a joined client on the lag2. This is the LAG to the Access2 switch where the receiver is connected.

```
ICX-Tx-Core2(config)# show ip igmp snooping vlan11 group 239.x.1.1
IGMP ports and group information for group 239.x.1.1

VLAN ID   : 11
VLAN Name : VLAN11
```

```
Group Address : 239.x.1.1
Last Reporter : 10.x.11.37
Group Type    : Filter

                                        V1     V2      Sources
Sources
Port   Vers Mode  Uptime   Expires  Timer  Timer   Forwarded  Blocked
----   ---- ----  ------   -------  -----  -----   ---------  -------
lag2   3    EXC   8m 21s   3m 51s                  0          0
ICX-Tx-Core2(config)# show ip igmp snooping vlan11 group 239.x.1.1
IGMP ports and group information for group 239.12.1.1

VLAN ID   : 11
VLAN Name : VLAN11

Group Address : 239.x.1.1
Last Reporter :10.x.11.37
Group Type    : Filter

                                        V1     V2      Sources
Sources
Port   Vers Mode  Uptime   Expires  Timer  Timer   Forwarded  Blocked
----   ---- ----  ------   -------  -----  -----   ---------  -------
lag2   3    EXC   8m 52s   3m 19s                  0          0
```

5. On the Access1, review the IGMP group tables.

```
ICX-Tx-Access1(config)# show ip igmp snooping vlan11
IGMP Snooping Protocol Info
Total VLANs with IGMP enabled               : 2
Current count of multicast groups joined    : 1

IGMP Drop Unknown Multicast                 : Global
VLAN ID : 11
VLAN Name : VLAN11
IGMP Configured Version   : 3
IGMP Operating Version : 3
Querier Address : 10.x.11.2
Querier Port : lag255
Querier UpTime :28m 17s
Querier Expiration Time :3m 50s

Active Group Address   Tracking  Vers Mode Uptime    Expires
--------------------   --------  ---- ---- -------   -------
239.255.255.250        Filter    3    EXC  28m 14s   3m 28s
```

Question: Why is the 239.x.1.1 group address not listed here?

Answer: Multicast traffic is always forwarded to the IGMP querier port, so there is no need to filter the traffic on this port.

6. This demonstrates the filtering and forwarding of the multicast traffic.

Learning Check

1. How do AOS-CX switches treat multicast traffic at the factory default settings?
   a. They forward the multicasts on interfaces that connect to other switches, but drop them on edge ports.
   b. They drop the multicasts.
   c. They forward the multicasts only on interfaces that have received IGMP reports for destination group.
   d. They flood traffic throughout the VLAN in the same manner as a broadcast.
2. A network administrator wants to ensure that multicasts in VLAN 4 are only forwarded to devices listening for those multicasts. Layer-2 access switches support VLAN 4, and a core switch routes traffic for VLAN 4. On which devices should the administrator enable IGMP?
   a. On the core switch only
   b. On the core switch and all access switches
   c. On the core switch and just one of the access switches
   d. On the access switches only
3. By default, IGMP snooping is enabled.
   a. True
   b. False
4. For an IGMP querier, IGMP is enabled on a Layer-3 interface.
   a. True
   b. False

Summary

Congratulations! Now you have the essential knowledge and skills to implement the IGMP protocol and IGMP snooping on AOS-CX switches. This chapter introduced you to IGMP, a technology that enables a network infrastructure to better support the multicast traffic that is becoming more and more ubiquitous. You can implement IGMP and IGMP snooping to reduce excessive multicasts.

9 Multicast Routing

OBJECTIVES

After completing this chapter, you will be able to:

✓ Distinguish between PIM-DM and PIM-SM

✓ Implement PIM-DM and PIM-SM to route multicast traffic

Overview

In this chapter, you will be introduced to Protocol Independent Multicast (PIM), which allows switches to determine which interfaces should receive multicast traffic in a Layer-3 network, like a campus.

In the previous chapter, you learned about how AOS-CX switches can learn where the multicast source (typically a server) and the multicast receivers (typically a user devices) reside. The problem in a larger campus network is that the multicast source and destinations are commonly on different subnets, which requires a routing function. Unicast routing protocols like OSPF will not route multicast traffic. Multicast routing protocol is needed. This chapter has three main sections that address multicast routing: an introduction to the PIM routing protocol and the two modes of PIM: dense mode and sparse mode.

PIM Introduction

This section introduces the Protocol Independent Multicast (PIM) routing protocol for multicast traffic. The AOS-CX switches also support static multicast routing; but for scalable networks, you will want to implement PIM.

Multicast Routing Use Cases

In a network, IP multicast traffic transmitted for multimedia applications is blocked at routed interface boundaries unless a multicast routing protocol is running. Protocol Independent Multicast (PIM) is a family of routing protocols. It forms multicast trees to forward traffic from multicast sources to subnets which use protocols such as IGMP and MLD to request the traffic. IGMP is used in IPv4 and MLD is used in IPv6.

–Need to multicast across Layer-3 boundaries

–Need to send multicasts from a single source into multiple subnets

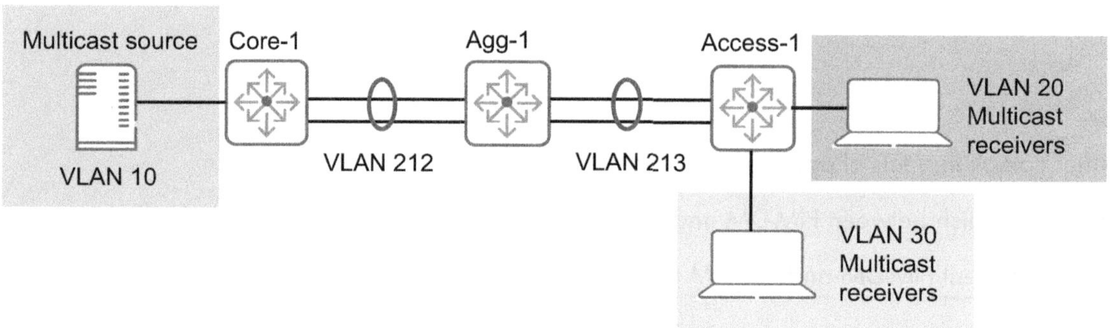

Figure 9-1 Multicast Routing Use Cases

In the last chapter, you have seen how only devices in VLAN 10 receive multicasts from a source in VLAN 10. If you want hosts in VLAN 20 to receive multicasts in the same group, you must add another multicast source to VLAN 20. Sometimes companies want to isolate multicasts within a VLAN, but sometimes it would be more efficient to allow a single multicast source to transmit to devices in multiple VLANs. Multicast routing enables a source in one VLAN to stream to receivers in multiple VLANs.

Multicast routing is also useful when the multicast source is in a different location from the multicast receivers, as shown in Figure 9-1.

Note

If you want to route multicast traffic into a VLAN, it is recommended that you avoid multi-netting on that VLAN (configuring more than one subnet).

Multicast Routing

You have seen how unicast routes direct traffic for a specific destination to a next hop. Due to the nature of multicasting, multicast routes function a bit differently.

Instead of a unicast destination network such as 10.101.20.0/24, the multicast route is directed toward a multicast group such as 239.1.1.1.

Instead of a next hop, the multicast route has downstream interfaces. Many endpoints across many subnets might need to receive multicasts; therefore, the forwarding path takes the shape of a tree with many leaves (endpoints), all of which require the traffic. In keeping with that tree shape, the multicast routing table entry can feature multiple downstream interfaces rather than a single forwarding interface to a next hop.

	Traffic from:	And destined to:	Is forwarded on:
Unicast route	Any	Destination network	Forwarding interface to next hop
Multicast route	**Source (S)** (received on correct upstream interface)	**Multicast group address (G)**	Downstream interfaces

```
Switch# show ip mroute brief
VRF: default
Total number of entries : 1
Group Address Source Address Neighbor     Interface
------------- -------------- --------     ---------
239.1.1.1     10.101.10.10   10.101.121.1 vlan1213
```

Standard multicast route notation: (S,G) -- (10.101.10.10, 239.1.1.1)

Figure 9-2 Multicast Routing

In addition, unlike for most unicast routes, the source matters for multicast routes. A multicast route must track the upstream interface that is closest to the source so that the router can verify that the multicasts are arriving on the correct interface. It can then drop multicasts that arrive on the wrong interface, preventing multicasts from looping through the network. An active multicast route is called an (S, G) route because it includes both the source IP address (S) and the destination multicast group address (G). Multicast routing devices create an (S, G) route after they receive a multicast from a source to a group. For example, the (10.101.10.10, 239.1.1.1) route refers to traffic from 10.101.10.10 to 239.1.1.1 (Figure 9-2).

You will learn more about (S, G) routes and another type of route called a (*, G) route as you see multicast routing in action during the lab.

Discovering Multicast Routes

Now that you understand the anatomy of a multicast route, consider how the route is created.

Forwarding paths can change because destinations that require multicasts frequently change. For example, a user might close the application that receives a multicast video stream, causing the endpoint to leave the multicast group. Routers and routing switches require a way to discover which destination devices require which multicast traffic. Unicast routing protocols such as OSPF enable routers to discover the next hop for unicast routes dynamically. Routers dynamically discover the downstream interfaces for multicast routes with two protocols, working together:

- **IGMP**—You learned in the previous chapter about how endpoints use IGMP to inform infrastructure devices that they want to listen for specific multicast groups. In that chapter you focused on IGMP and IGMP snooping's filtering functions, but IGMP also informs a subnet's multicast router which multicasts the router must forward into the subnet. The router can then make sure that the corresponding interface (VLAN on AOS-CX switches) is listed as a downstream interface in any multicast routes for the group in question.

- **PIM**—On its own, IGMP allows multicast routers to discover downstream interfaces attached to multicast receivers, but not downstream interfaces attached to other multicast routers that need the traffic. For example, Access-1 can learn VLAN 20 as a downstream interface for multicast group 239.1.1.1, but Core-1 cannot use IGMP to learn that it should forward these multicasts to Access-1. PIM allows multicast routers to communicate with each other about which multicast traffic they need. The system of multicast routing switches, each with a multicast route for a particular group, together compose the shortest path tree (SPT) for a particular multicast stream, as identified by source and group.

–**IGMP** = Discover downstream interfaces attached to multicast receivers

–**PIM** = Build shortest path tree (SPT) for a multicast stream across multiple routing switches

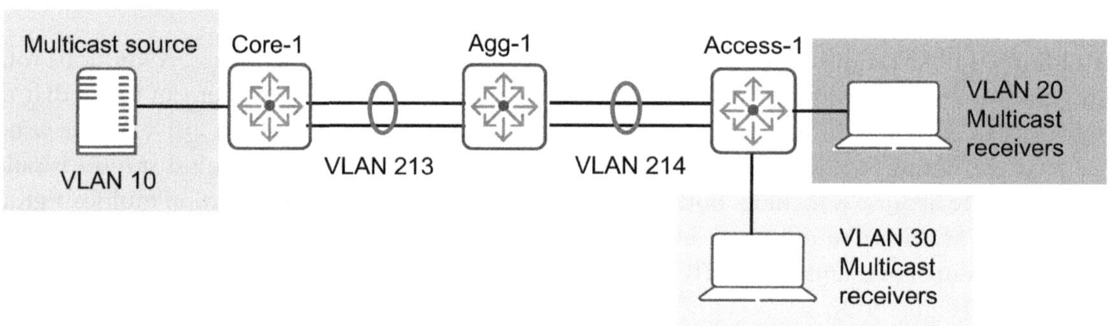

Figure 9-3 Discovering Multicast Routes

It is important that you understand that IGMP alone is never enough to provide multicast routing even if the multicast source and multicast receivers are connected to VLANs on the same multicast routing switch. This switch must still have multicast routing enabled and run PIM on the VLAN interfaces to route multicast traffic from one subnet to another.

PIM also relies on the *unicast* routing tables to identify the path back to a multicast source. This routing method is known as reverse path forwarding (RPF). The unicast routing protocols create the unicast routing tables. With this information, PIM sets up the distribution tree for the multicast traffic (Figure 9-3).

PIM-DM versus PIM-SM

The routing switches can construct the multicast routing tree in one of two modes:

- **PIM-Dense Mode (DM)**—PIM-DM dynamically creates the multicast routing tree when a source begins streaming traffic for a multicast group. VLAN interfaces on which PIM-DM is enabled flood multicasts to all neighbors until the neighbors indicate that they do not need them by sending a prune. Prune is the term that PIM uses for a leave message. In addition, the upstream neighbor sets a timer for the pruned interface. When the timer expires, the interface reverts to the default behavior—forwarding multicasts until explicitly requested not to. (However, as you will learn later, PIM-DM has measures for preventing the timer from expiring.)
  - This mode works best in environments with high bandwidth and high tolerance for congestion, such as a high-speed Ethernet network. Because the PIM-DM routers automatically create the multicast routing tree for a particular stream when that stream begins, PIM-DM is quite simple to set up.
- **PIM Sparse Mode (SM)**—PIM-SM builds the multicast routing tree for a group in advance and then forwards multicasts on that tree when a source begins to stream to that group. PIM-SM-enabled routing interfaces must specifically indicate that they want to receive multicast traffic in a particular group by sending a join for the tree. The interface must then periodically refresh its join. If its upstream neighbor does not receive joins, it reverts to its default behavior: not forwarding traffic (Figure 9-4).
  - Because PIM-SM establishes efficient forwarding paths, it is well suited for a lower-bandwidth environment, such as one built on WAN links. PIM-SM also gives you more control over which multicast groups are routed.

PIM-DM (dense mode):

–*Push* concept

–Forwards multicasts unless requested not to by a prune message

–Reverts to forwarding when prune state times out

–Used on high-bandwidth routed connections

PIM-SM (sparse mode):

–*Pull* concept

–Does not forward multicasts unless requested to by a join message

–Periodic joins required to maintain the tree

–Used on lower bandwidth routed connections such as a WAN

IMPORTANT: PIM-DM and PIM-SM cannot run together in the same VRF: the same mode is required throughout a VRF.

Figure 9-4 PIM-DM versus PIM-SM

The best way of comparing the two protocols is *push* (PIM-DM) versus *pull* (PIM-SM).

PIM-SM has more configuration options and tends to be more complex to set up.

PIM-DM operates at the router level to direct traffic for a particular multicast group along the most efficient path to the network which has hosts that have joined that group. A unicast source address and a multicast group address comprise a given source/group (S/G) pair. Multicast traffic moving from a source to a multicast group address creates a flow to one or more areas of the network requiring the traffic. The flow destination is the multicast group address and not a specific host or VLAN. A single multicast flow has one source and one multicast group address (destination), but may reach many hosts in different subnets, depending on which hosts have issued joins for the same multicast group.

Your AOS-CX switch supports both PIM-DM and PIM-SM; however, it can run only one mode concurrently (within a VRF). All multicast routing switches in the network (in their respective VRF) must also agree and run the same type of PIM.

PIM routes the multicast traffic for a particular S/G pair on paths between the source unicast address and to the interfaces where it is requested (by joins from hosts connected to those subnets). Physical destinations for a particular multicast group can be hosts in different networks. Individual hosts use IGMP/MLD configured per-subnet to send joins requesting membership in a particular multicast group. All hosts that have joined a given multicast group (defined by a multicast address) remain in that group as long as they continue to issue periodic joins.

PIM-DM interoperates with IGMP/MLD and the switch's routing protocols. PIM operates independently of the routing protocol that is chosen to run on the switches. So, PIM-DM can be used with RIP, OSPF, BGP, or static routes configured. PIM-DM uses a unicast routing table to find the path to the originator of the multicast traffic and sets up multicast trees for distributing multicast traffic.

AOS-CX Defaults and Restrictions

- PIM is disabled, by default
- Either PIM-DM or PIM-SM can be configured within a VRF at a time
  - All interfaces within the VRF must run the same mode
- Enabled on layer 3 interfaces (routed and SVI)
  - Maximum of 1,000 interfaces, with 128 per VRF
- Fully interoperable with VRRP for quick transition of routes in a failover
- PIM-SM: 8 static RPs per VRF
- PIM-DM:
  - Not currently supported with VxLAN, 6in4, 6in6, and GRE interfaces
  - Active-active functionality is not available with VSX deployments

Figure 9-5 AOS-CX Defaults and Restrictions

PIM (DM or SM) is disabled by default (Figure 9-5). Either PIM-SM or PIM-DM can be configured within a VRF at a time. All the interfaces within the VRF must run with same mode.

PIM uses unicast routing information from any of the routing protocols that are running on the system, such as OSPFv2, OSPFv3, BGP. Static routes are also supported with next-hop IP addresses.

PIM can be enabled on an ROP (routed port) and SVI (**interface vlan**) interfaces. PIM can be enabled across all VRFs on a maximum of 1,000 interfaces with an upper limit of 128 per VRF.

Note

Although up to 128 PIM DM enabled interfaces can be configured, when configuring trunk interfaces with multiple Dense enabled SVIs, the trunk interfaces must have sufficient bandwidth or have only the required number of trunks it can support. This ensures that the link utilization is not exceeded due to the initial flooding nature of the protocol.

PIM-DM is compatible with IGMP version 2 and version 3, MLD version 1 and version 2, and is fully interoperable with IGMP/MLD for determining multicast flows. PIM-DM is fully interoperable with VRRP to quickly transition multicast routes in a failover. PIM-DM can run on multiple VRF instances in parallel. It is supported on all VRFs supported in the system.

PIM-DM currently does not support the following:

- VxLAN, 6in4, 6in6, and GRE interfaces
- PIM-DM can be enabled on VSX deployments; however active-active functionality is not available.

Note

Since active-active is not supported a slightly higher traffic recovery time can be expected compared to sparse mode, in the event of failovers. Hence, it is recommended to use PIM-SM on VSX. Ensure that the ISL is not oversubscribed while using PIM-DM with VSX. In case of numerous PIM enabled SVIs, ensure that ISL is configured to handle the flooding on all VLANs since ISL is member of all SVIs.

If BFD is enabled globally, it will be enabled by default on all PIM interfaces as well. The only exception is when it is disabled specifically on an interface using the **ip pim-dense bfd disable** interface command. If BFD is disabled globally, it will be disabled by default on all interfaces. The only exception is when it is enabled specifically on an interface using the **ip pim-dense bfd** interface command.

PIM-DM

This section introduces the PIM-DM (dense mode) routing protocol implementation.

PIM-DM Operation: Flooding and Pruning

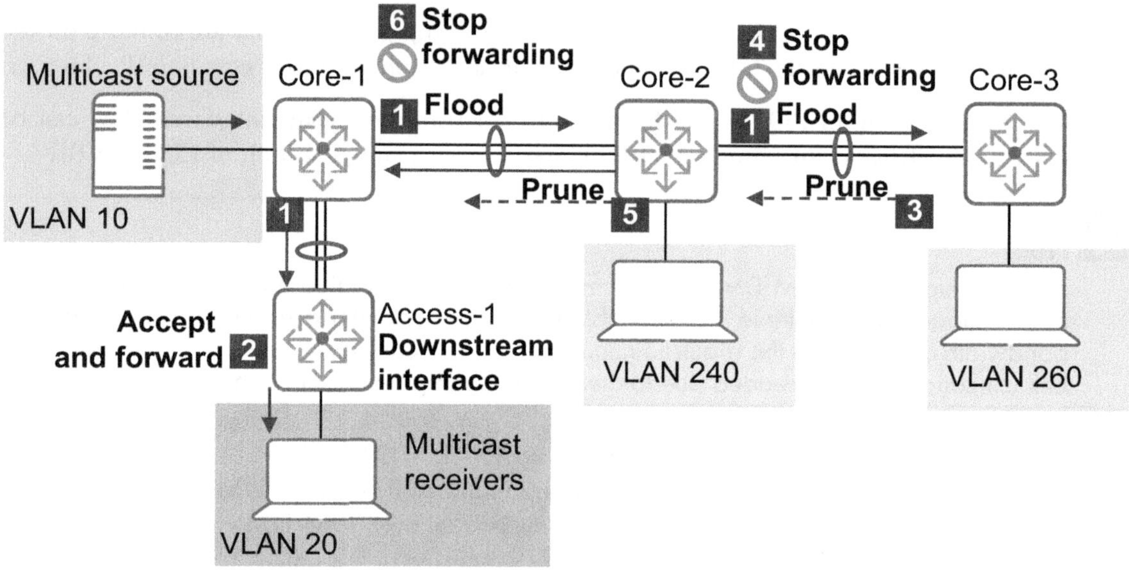

Figure 9-6 PIM-DM Operation: Flooding and Pruning

When a multicast source begins to transmit, the source's default router receives the multicasts. The VLAN interface on which the multicasts arrive should be enabled for PIM-DM. The router then floods the multicasts on every PIM-DM interface, including:

- Interfaces that connect to PIM-DM neighbors; in this example, these neighbors are Core-2 and Access-1
- Interfaces that connect to receivers that have requested the multicast using IGMP; in this example, Core-1 does not have any interfaces with directly attached multicast receivers

The downstream multicast routers follow the same steps to flood the multicast. In this simple network, Access-1 and Core-2 do not have any neighbors except Core-1. Access-1 has learned that VLAN 20 is a downstream interface for this group from IGMP. Core-3, though, does not have any multicast receivers for this group on VLAN 260, its only other PIM-DM interface; this is also true of Core-2 with VLAN 240. With Core-3 and Core-2, since there are no multicast receivers for the multicast stream, they send prune messages in the upstream direction to stop the flow of the multicast stream to them (Figure 9-6).

Note

When a router running PIM-DM receives a new multicast flow, it initially floods the traffic to all downstream multicast routers. Branches that do not have members send Prune messages toward the source to prune off the unwanted/unnecessary traffic.

Because Access-1 has one downstream interface, it continues to accept the traffic from Core-1. Because Core-2 has no downstream interfaces, it prunes itself (from the tree by sending a prune (leave) message on the upstream interface. The upstream neighbor removes the interface on which it receives the message from the downstream interfaces for this route.

Note that Core-2 still maintains the multicast route [the (S, G) entry], which it can use to receive multicasts later, if necessary.

Note

For a multicast group "X" on a given interface, when the last host belonging to group "X" leaves the group, PIM places that interface in a prune state. Multicast traffic from group "X" is now blocked to that interface. The prune state remains until a host on the same interface issues a join for group "X", in which case the router cancels the prune state and changes the flow to the forwarding state.

PIM-DM Operation: Grafts

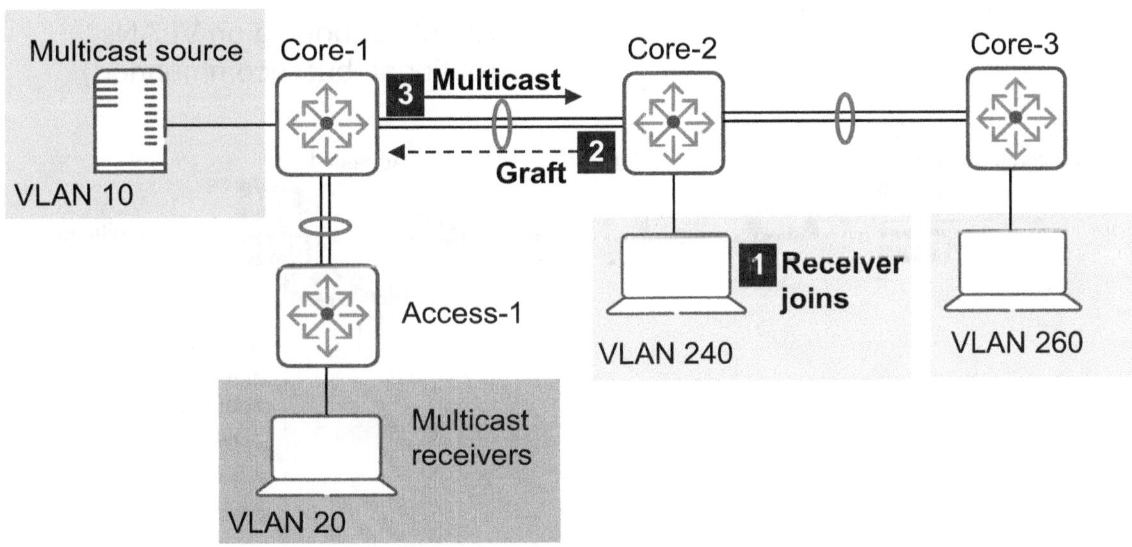

Figure 9-7 PIM-DM Operation: Grafts

After pruning, Core-1 is forwarding multicast traffic to Access-1 only, which forwards the traffic to receivers in VLAN 20.

Because group memberships change all the time, the SPT can change as well. First, PIM-DM operates on preferring forwarding unnecessary multicast traffic over failing to forward necessary traffic. Therefore, prune messages expire, and the routing switch that had received the prune message begins forwarding multicast traffic again.

In addition, group members leave groups. For example, if all of the multicast receivers in VLAN 20 left the group, then Access-1 would send a prune message to Core-1, stopping the flow of traffic.

Figure 9-7 illustrates another change in the situation: a multicast receiver for this group becomes active in VLAN 40 connected to Core-2. (Perhaps a user starts a multicast video streaming application.) The host sends an IGMP report for this group, and Core-2 adds VLAN 40 as a downstream interface for its (S, G) multicast route for this multicast stream. Eventually, the prune message would expire, and Core-2 would receive traffic again. However, PIM-DM provides a faster method of pulling the multicast traffic down. Core-2 sends a graft message on the upstream interface, requesting to be added to the tree.

Core-1 adds the interface that connects to Core-1 back to the (S, G) multicast route's list of downstream interfaces. Core-2 begins to receive the traffic again, and it forwards it to the receiver.

Enabling PIM-DM

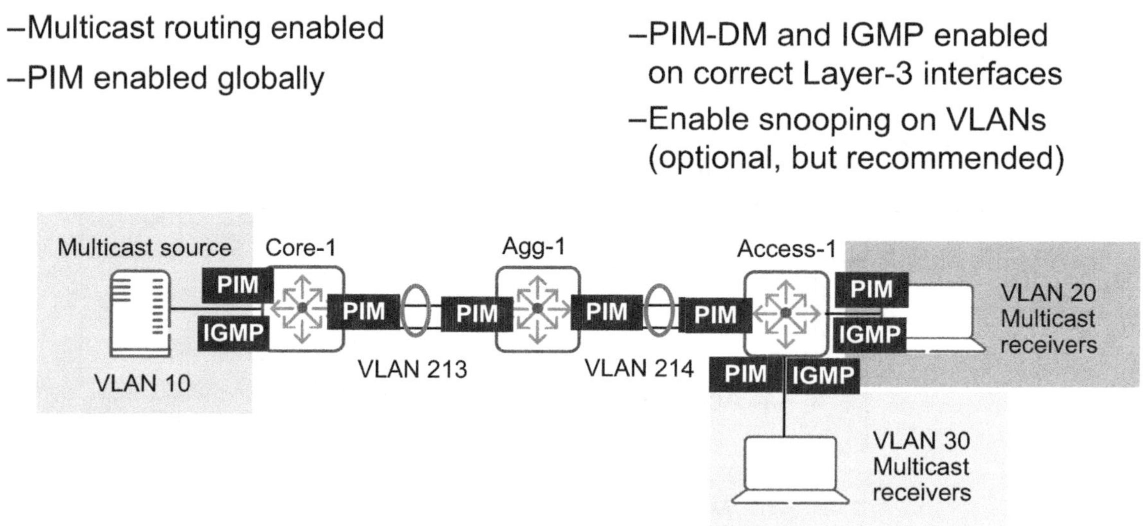

Figure 9-8 Enabling PIM-DM

PIM-DM must be enabled on all VLAN interfaces between the multicast sources and the multicast receivers:

- Interfaces on which multicast sources reside
- Interfaces on which multicast receivers reside (IGMP-enabled interfaces)
- Interfaces between all routers and routing switches that connect sources and receivers

Figure 9-8 indicates the interfaces on which you would enable PIM-DM, as well as the interfaces on which you must enable IGMP, in an example network. Note that you should also enable IGMP on the server VLAN; although IGMP is not strictly required in the source VLAN, it enables Core-1 to filter multicasts within that VLAN.

You should begin by ensuring that unicast routing is in place. You must then enable both multicast routing and PIM-DM globally. Finally, you can enable PIM-DM on the VLAN interface, as shown below.

```
Switch(config)# router pim [vrf <name>]
Switch(config-pim)# enable
Switch(config)# interface <ID>
Switch(config-if/if-vlan/lag-if)# ip pim-dense {enable | disable}
```

PIM-DM interfaces automatically discover neighbors on the same subnet by transmitting and listening for hellos. PIM-DM routers communicate on multicast address 224.0.0.13.

Note

MLD and PM-DM are not currently supported for IPv6 in AOS-CX; however, MLD and PIM-SM are.

Enabling PIM and IGMP in a Larger System

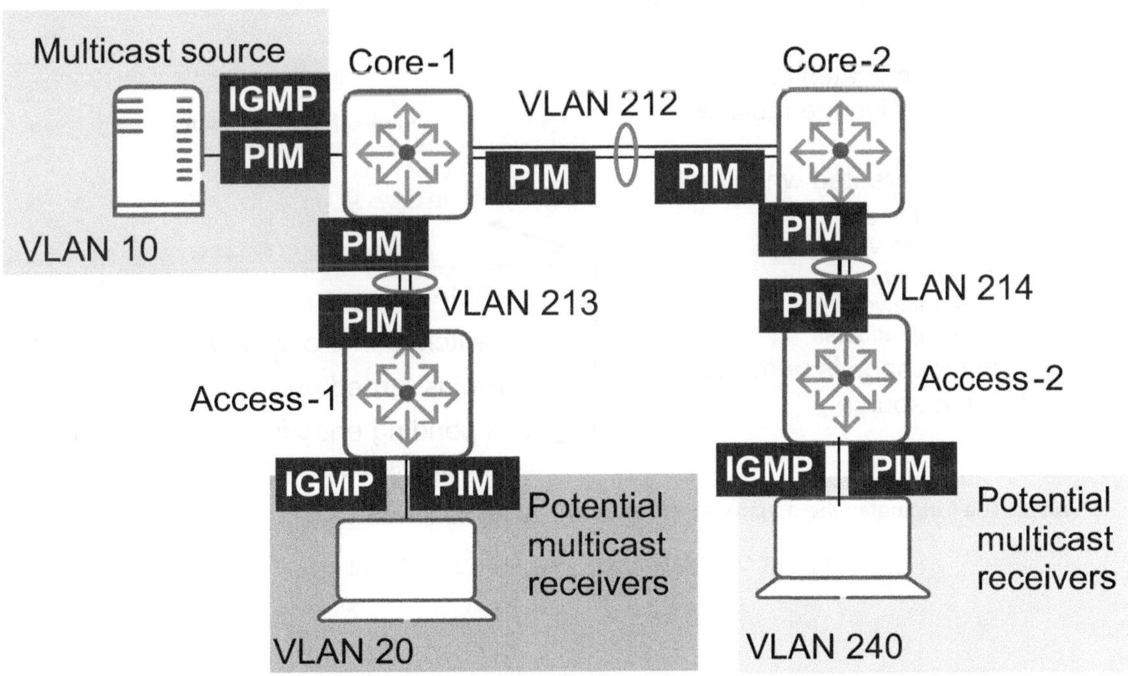

Figure 9-9 Enabling PIM and IGMP in a Larger System

Figure 9-9 illustrates a more complex system. Note that Core-2 must support PIM even though it does not directly connect to any subnets with multicast sources or receivers.

A routing switch uses hello packets to inform neighbor routers of its presence. The following configures the frequency at which the router transmits PIM hello messages on the current interface:

```
Switch(config)# interface <ID>
Switch(config-if/if-vlan/lag-if)# ip pim-dense hello-interval <interval>
```

The default is 30 seconds and the range is 5-300 seconds. The routing switch also uses this setting to compute the hello hold-time, which is included in hello packets sent to neighbor routers. The hello hold-time tells neighbor routers how long to wait for the next hello packet from the routing switch. If another packet does not arrive within that time, the router removes the neighbor adjacency on that interface from the PIM adjacency table, which removes any flows running on that interface. Shortening the hello interval reduces the hello hold-time. If they do not receive a new hello packet when expected, it changes how quickly other routers stop sending traffic to the routing switch.

Note

BFD can be used to speed up the convergence of PIM. If BFD is globally enabled, BFD is automatically enabled for PIM on interfaces where PIM is also enabled. BFD was previously covered in the OSPF chapter.

Interpreting PIM-DM (*, G) Entries

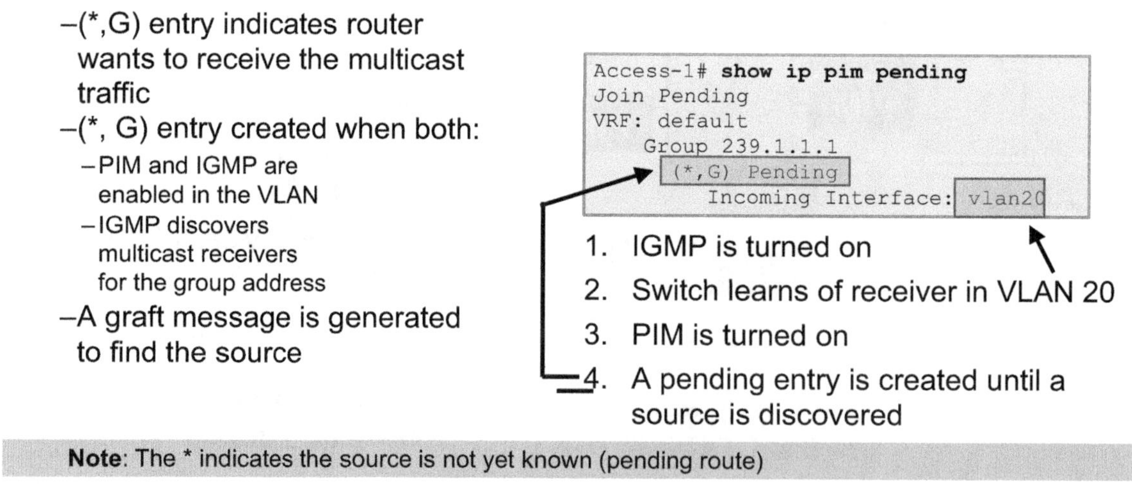

Figure 9-10 Interpreting PIM-DM (*, G) Entries

When you are monitoring and troubleshooting a multicast routing solution, you do not have an illustration tracing multicasts for you. It can be helpful for you to understand more about the multicast route entries, how to interpret them, and how the routing switch uses them to forward traffic.

Begin with (*, G) entries.

As soon as PIM-DM is enabled on a switch VLAN interface, the switch creates a (*, G) entry for each group membership discovered by IGMP on that VLAN. This entry specifies the downstream interfaces from which a tree can be formed when multicasts begin to arrive from a particular source.

When you use PIM-DM, the (*, G) entry essentially acts as a placeholder, listing the downstream interfaces that require multicasts in this group, as discovered by IGMP. The framework of the tree that delivers these multicasts is not filled in. For example, no upstream interface is specified (the routing switch does not know where multicasts will arrive).

The (*, G) entry exists only as a pending route; it is not an active route forwarding multicasts. The (*, G) entry remains in the PIM routing table for as long as an IGMP membership for the group exists on at least one interface. This signals to the routing switch that it should stay part of the multicast routing tree for any multicast stream to this group, regardless of whether it needs to forward the traffic to any downstream PIM-DM neighbors.

Typically you will see (*, G) entries when there has been a purge. Now a client wants to receive a stream, but the switch is not receiving the stream because of a previous purge. The switch generates a graft message and sends it to its upstream neighbors to find the source so that traffic can begin to be flooded back to the switch. The other situation where you will see (*, G) entries if there is a network issue where the source is no longer reachable and thus no multicast stream is being received, yet the switch still has clients locally or downstream that desire to receive the stream.

To view (*, G) routes, enter the **show ip pim pending** command. To view information about IGMP groups, enter **show ip igmp groups** or **show ip igmp group** command, qualifying it with a specific multicast address.

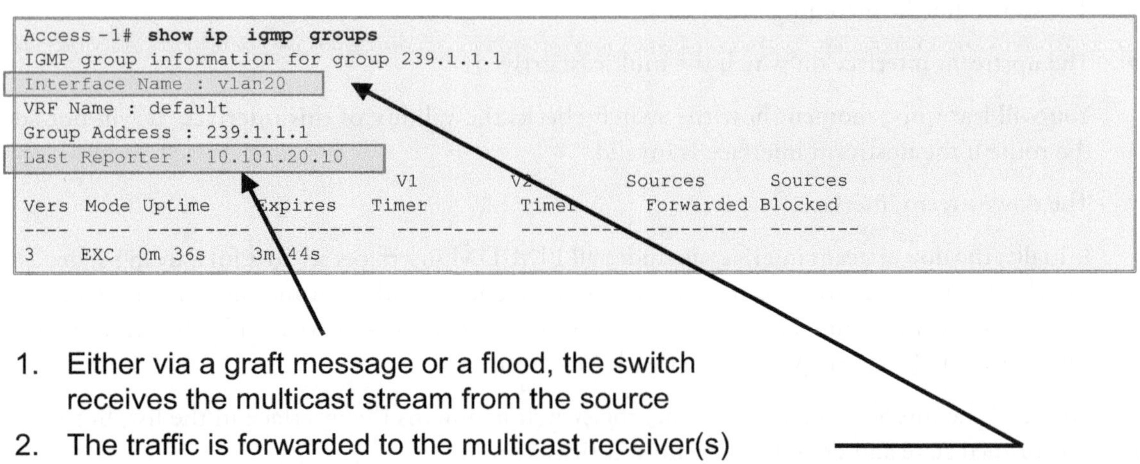

Figure 9-11 Interpreting PIM-DM (*, G) Entries

To view (*, G) routes, enter the **show ip pim pending** command. To view information about IGMP groups, enter **show ip igmp groups** or **show ip igmp group** command, qualifying it with a specific multicast address (Figures 9-10 and 9-11).

Interpreting PIM-DM (S, G) Entries

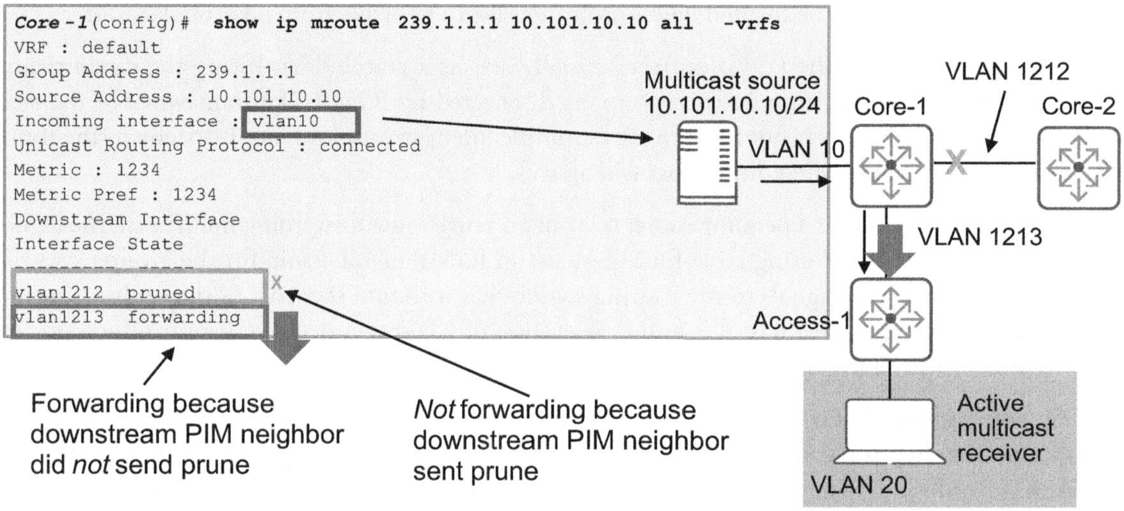

Figure 9-12 Interpreting PIM-DM (S, G) Entries

When the switch receives a multicast on the proper upstream interface for the source, it creates an (S, G) entry. It uses this entry to route the multicast traffic on the correct interface or interfaces.

The (S, G) entry includes:

- The source for the incoming multicasts
- The upstream interface on which the multicast arrived

  You will learn in a moment how the switch checks the validity of this interface. It will not add the route if the upstream interface is invalid.
- The downstream interfaces

  Initially, the downstream interface includes all PIM-DM interfaces set to a forwarding state. The switch maintains the forwarding state unless a neighbor sends a prune on that interface. The switch also always maintains the forwarding state for interfaces discovered by IGMP as long as they are in the (*, G) entry associated with this group.

As you see, if the interface receives a prune, the switch maintains the interface in the list, but places it in the pruned state and does not forward multicasts on it.

If the (S, G) entry has downstream interfaces or if it the source is connected directly to the routing switch, the routing switch adds the (S, G) entry to its active multicast routing table. The routing switch then uses the (S, G) entry to forward multicasts (Figures 9-12 and 9-13).

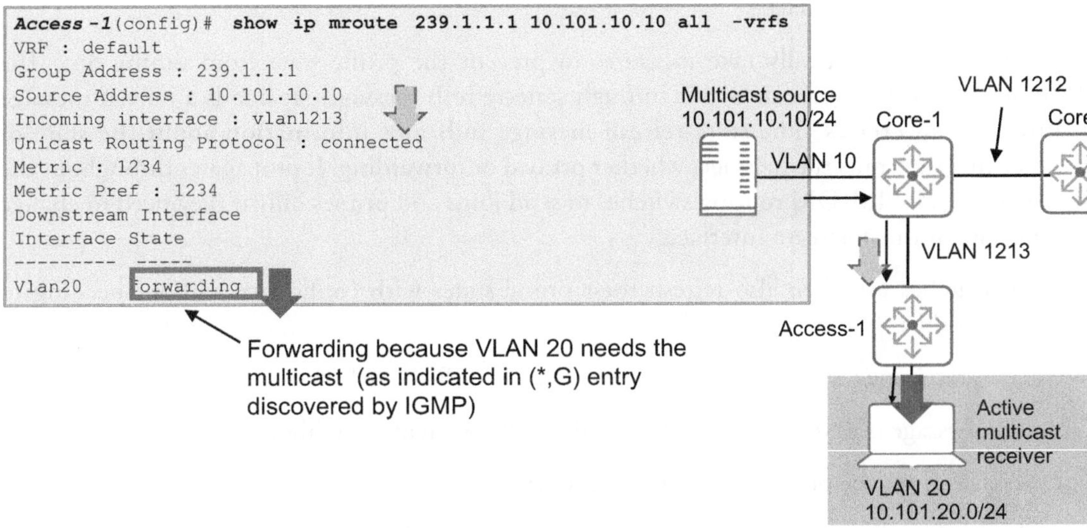

Figure 9-13 Interpreting PIM-DM (S, G) Entries (cont.)

Using State Refreshes to Minimize Flooding

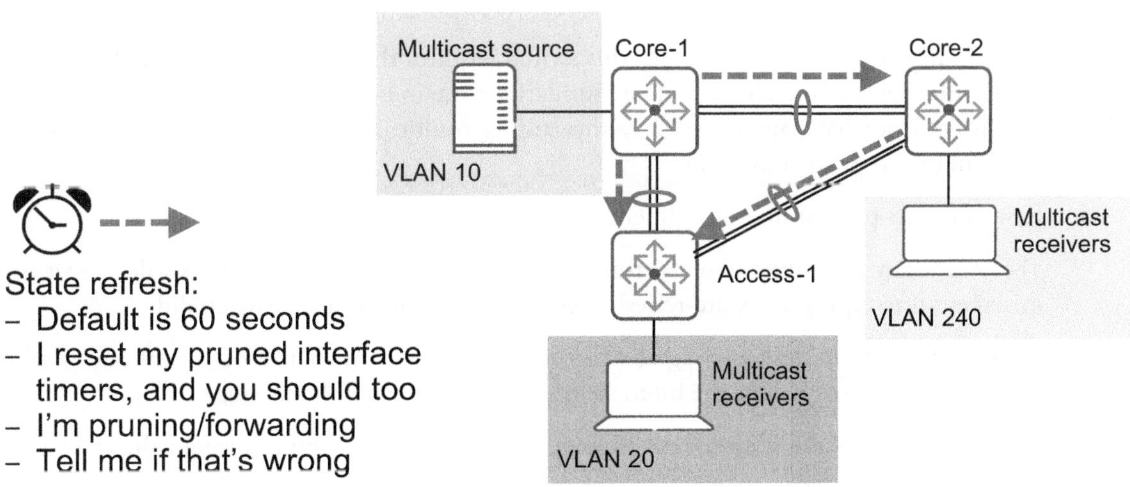

Figure 9-14 Using State Refreshes to Minimize Flooding

As mentioned earlier, prunes periodically time out, causing PIM-DM-enabled interfaces to begin again to flood multicasts to neighbors that had sent prune messages. If the neighbor still does not require the traffic, it must send another prune message. These bursts of unnecessary traffic can contribute to congestion restarting the sending of a multicast stream when there still might not be any receivers off of a pruned interface.

AOS-CX switches automatically take measures to prevent the prune state from timing out. The switch connected to the source does this through state-refresh messages. It floods a refresh message on all PIM-DM interfaces. The state-refresh message indicates information about the state of the interface that transmits the message, whether pruned or forwarding. It propagates throughout the system, triggering all PIM-DM routing switches to send joins and prunes only if they need to change the current state of the upstream interface.

The routing switches can then also refresh their prune states with confidence without needing to flood multicast traffic.

In more detail, receiving a state-refresh message triggers the PIM-DM interface to take these actions:

- Drop the message unless it has arrived from the RPF upstream neighbor.
- For messages from the proper upstream neighbor:
    - Check the indicated state of the upstream interface and determine whether it matches this routing switch's requirements.
    - If the indicated state is pruned and this routing switch has no downstream interfaces for the (S, G) entry, the indicated state is correct. Similarly, if the indicated state is forwarding and this routing switch does have downstream interfaces on which it must forward traffic, the state is correct.
    - If the indicated state is pruned, and this switch requires the multicasts, the switch sends an (S, G) join upstream to alter the state. Similarly, if the indicated state is forwarding, but this switch does not have an active entry forwarding multicast traffic downstream, the switch sends an (S, G) prune upstream.
    - Reset all of its pruned interface timers.

      The switch can safely reset all of the timers because its downstream neighbors will correct any mistakes on receipt of the state-refresh message, just as this routing switch did.
    - Forward the state-refresh message (with one less value in the TTL) on all interfaces with PIM-DM neighbors except the interface on which it received the message.

      The TTL prevents the state-refresh message from endlessly looping through the PIM-DM domain.

AOS-CX switches automatically support state-refresh messages, but only the routing switch connected directly to the unicast source initiates state-refresh messages. All other PIM routers in the network only propagate these state-refresh messages.

You can configure the interval in seconds (10 to 100) between successive state-refresh messages. The default setting is 60 seconds. You should keep the interval below the PIM-DM prune expiry time to prevent periodic unnecessary floods of traffic (Figure 9-14).

```
Switch(config)# router pim
Switch(config-pim)# state-refresh [10-100]
```

Understanding Reverse Path Forwarding (RPF)

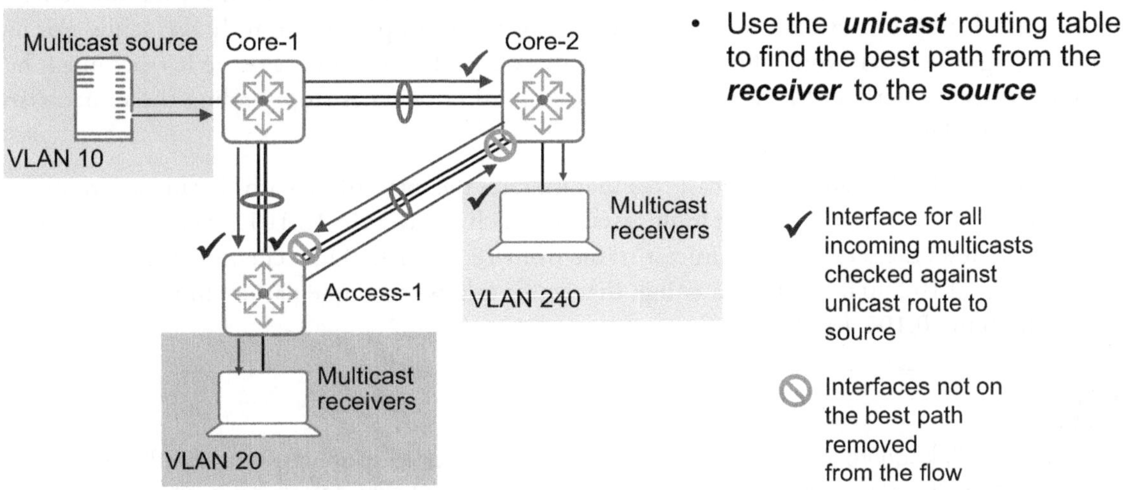

Figure 9-15 Understanding Reverse Path Forwarding (RPF)

Up until now you have examined a simple network with just one path for multicasts. However, networks often feature redundant links and loops like the ones shown in Figure 9-15. Because PIM-DM routing switches flood multicasts on all PIM-DM interfaces except the one on which the multicasts arrived, they run the risk of looping multicasts. PIM-DM automatically deals with this situation, so you can use the protocol in redundant network designs without worry. PIM-DM prunes the forwarding paths into a loop-free tree, rooted at the multicast source with the lowest cost path to each receiver subnet. (Note that you are looking at redundant Layer-3 links; loops at Layer 2 must be eliminated by a protocol such as spanning tree, as you have learned earlier.)

Although PIM operates independently from unicast routing protocols, it uses the unicast routing table for this purpose. This process occurs as follows:

1. The multicast source's default router sends the multicasts to all PIM neighbors. In this example, Core-1 sends multicasts to Access-1 and Core-2.

2. The PIM neighbors run a reverse path forwarding (RPF) check on the traffic, which verifies that the upstream interface on which the traffic arrives is the forwarding interface for the unicast route to the source.

3. If the multicast passes the RPF check, the routing switch accepts it and sets the RPF flag for the (S, G) entry with that upstream interface. This flag allows the switch to accept future multicasts on this interface without the processing overhead of running the RPF check again.
4. The routing switch then forwards the multicast on all PIM-DM interfaces.

As you see, this means that Core-2 sends multicasts to Access-1, and Access-1 sends multicasts to Core-2. However, the routing switches do not accept these multicasts because they do not pass the RPF check. They also exchange assert messages, which enable them to choose which routing switch has a better path to the source. The switch that loses removes this interface from its downstream interface list. It now knows that, for this source, its neighbor is upstream to it. It also sends a prune to the routing switch that won, telling that switch to stop sending the multicasts to it—because it has a better upstream interface. In short—the multicast routing switches stop sending the unnecessary traffic to each other.

In this way, PIM-DM creates a multicast tree that imitates the forwarding paths for unicast traffic. In other words, 10.101.10.10 is sending multicasts, for which receivers in 10.101.20.0/24 are listening. This traffic follows the same path as unicast traffic from 10.101.10.10 to a client in 10.101.20.0/24. If receivers in 10.102.40.0/24 start listening, that traffic follows the same path as unicast traffic from 10.101.10.10 to 10.102.40.0/24.

Note

And if a link failure would occur in the topology, similar to spanning tree, the PIM routers would quickly discover the issue and rectify the issue quickly determining an alternative, loop-free path.

If you ever have an issue in which multicasts are not following the path that you expect, you should remember to check the unicast routing table, as well as that PIM-DM is enabled on the correct interfaces.

You should also understand that the PIM-DM router must receive the multicasts on the forwarding interface for the unicast route to the source. If PIM-DM is not enabled on that interface, the router does *not* accept the traffic on the second-best route. For example, you enable PIM-DM on the link between Core-1 and Core-2, as well as the link between Core-2 and Access-1. But you do not enable PIM-DM on the link between Core-1 and Access-1. However, Access-1's route to the multicast source's subnet is through the link to Core-1. Access-1 will drop all multicasts because they are arriving on the wrong interface, and multicast receivers will fail to receive the traffic.

This is also why you needed to enable PIM-DM on VLAN 1212 between Core-1 and Core-2. Core-2 can reach 10.101.10.0/24 through VLAN 1212 or 212, but VLAN 1212 offers the better route. If the multicasts arrived on VLAN 212, but not VLAN 1212, Core-2 would have dropped them. You could enable PIM-DM on VLAN 212 for additional redundancy, which would also add to the bursts of bandwidth consumption. Remember that PIM-SM, covered in other Aruba training, helps to minimize bandwidth usage for multicast routing.

In short, be careful to enable PIM-DM on the correct interfaces.

Understanding How a Multicast Forwarder Is Elected

In Figure 9-16, you see a slightly different scenario: the company has two switches performing routing for VLAN 20. It has chosen this solution rather than a VSF fabric, which is typically recommended. The switches run VRRP and also PIM-DM. Just as only one of the redundant switches can act as the active VRRP master, only one of the switches can forward multicasts. Otherwise, endpoints could receive duplicate copies of the multicasts, causing errors.

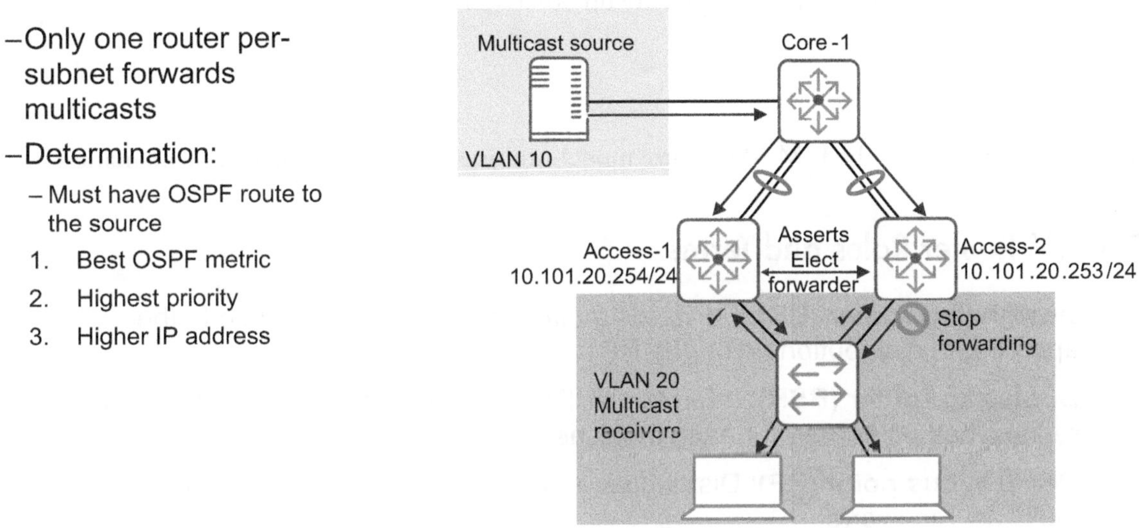

Figure 9-16 Understanding How a Multicast Forwarder Is Elected

When Access-1 and Access-2 receive multicasts from Core-2, they flood the multicasts to each other. As you saw on the previous page, the RPF fails, and the switches send an assert. You will now look at that assert in more detail.

The PIM routing switches examine each other's asserts to elect a multicast forwarder for the interface. The assert includes the (S, G) entry under dispute and information about the PIM routing switch's unicast path to the source. The routing switch with the more favorable path becomes the multicast forwarder, as determined first by administrative distance (preference) and then, if the administrative distance ties, by metric or cost. If the metric ties as well, the routing interface with the higher IP address is elected.

In this example, both switches have OSPF routes (preference 10) to the multicast source and both have the same cost for the route. However, Access-2 has the higher IP address. Therefore, Access-2 is elected multicast forwarder for VLAN 20.

Access-1 removes this VLAN from its list of downstream interfaces in its (S, G) entry. It also sends a prune to Access-2. Access-2 continues to forward multicasts in VLAN 20 because multicast receivers connect in this VLAN. However, the prune would be important if this VLAN did not include receivers; as you saw, on the previous page, it would stop routing switches from looping traffic across redundant paths.

If you are using a design such as this, you might want to pay attention to the actual IP addresses that you assign to the routing switches. To load balance the Master and multicast forwarder role on different VLANs, assign one switch a higher IP address and VRRP priority on some VLANs and the other switch a higher IP address and VRRP priority on other VLANs.

PIM-SM

This section introduces the PIM-SM (sparse mode) multicast routing protocol implementation.

PIM-SM Router Roles and Terms

- **Designated router (DR)**: Forwards multicast traffic from a source to the appropriate distribution point (the RP)
- **Bootstrap router (BSR)**: Informs all PIM-SM routers of the currently assigned rendezvous point (RP) for each multicast group
- **Rendezvous point (RP)**: Distributes a multicast stream from a source to a multicast receiver(s)
  - **Static RP**: This option forwards traffic in the same way as an RP, but requires manual configuration on all routers in the domain to be effective.
  - **Candidate RP (C-RP)**: Sends advertisement messages to the BSR, which collects RP-set information for the RP election of a multicast stream
  - **RP Tree (RPT)**: The tree structure a PIM router builds to connect multicast sources and receivers to the RP
  - **Shortest Path Tree (SPT)**: Using the RPT, finding the best path to the RP using the underlying unicast routing protocol

Figure 9-17 PIM-SM Router Roles and Terms

DR

In a LAN segment populated by one or more routers running PIM-SM, one such router is elected the DR for that LAN segment (Figure 9-17). When the DR receives a Join request from a multicast receiver on that LAN segment, it forwards the join toward the router operating as the RP for the requested multicast group.

Where multiple PIM-SM routers exist in a LAN segment, the following criteria are used to elect a DR:

1. The router configured with the highest DR priority in the LAN segment is elected.
2. If multiple routers in the LAN segment are configured with the same DR priority, the router having the highest IP address is elected.

In a given domain, each LAN segment capable of receiving multicast traffic from a unicast source should have at least one DR. (Enabling PIM-SM on a LAN segment automatically enables the router as a DR for that LAN segment.) Because there is an election process for DR on each LAN segment, all routers on a LAN segment must be enabled for DR. Where it is important to ensure that a particular router is elected as the DR for a given LAN segment, you can increase the DR priority on that LAN segment configuration for that router. By default the DR priority is 1.

If it is necessary to prevent a router from operating as a DR on a given LAN segment, disable DR operation by configuring the DR priority as zero (0).

BSR

Before a DR can forward encapsulated packets for a specific multicast group to an RP, it must know which router in the domain is the elected RP for that multicast group. The BSR function enables this operation by doing the following:

1. Learns the group-to-RP mappings on the C-RPs in the domain by reading the periodic advertisements each one sends to the BSR.
2. Distributes the aggregate Candidate-RP (C-RP) information as an RP-set to the PIM-SM routers in the domain. This is followed by an election to assign a specific multicast group or range of groups to the C-RPs in the domain. The software supports assignment of up to four multicast addresses and/or ranges of multicast addresses to a Candidate Rendezvous Point.

The BSR periodically sends bootstrap messages to the other PIM-SM routers in the domain to maintain and update the RP-set data throughout the domain, and to maintain its status as the elected BSR.

RP

Instead of flooding multicast traffic as is done with PIM-DM, PIM-SM uses a set of multiple routers to operate as RPs. Each RP controls multicast traffic forwarding for one or more multicast groups as follows:

- Receives traffic from multicast sources (S) through a DR.
- Receives multicast joins from routers requesting multicast traffic.
- Forwards the requested multicast traffic to the requesting routers.

The routers requesting multicast traffic are either edge routers or intermediate routers. Edge routers are directly connected to specific multicast receivers using IGMP/MLD to request traffic. Intermediate routers are on the path between edge routers and the RP. This is known as an RP Tree (RPT) where only the multicast address appears in the routing table. For example:

- (*, G), where:
    - * = a variable (wildcard) representing the IP address of any multicast source
    - G = a particular multicast group address.

C-RP

Within a PIM-SM domain, different RPs support different multicast addresses or ranges of multicast addresses. That is, a given PIM-SM multicast group or a range of groups is supported by only one active RP, although other C-RPs can also be configured with overlapping or identical support.

A C-RP's group-prefix configuration identifies the multicast groups the RP is enabled to support. If multiple C-RPs have group-prefixes configured so that any of these RPs can support a given multicast group, then the following criteria are used to select the RP to support the group:

1. The C-RP configured with the longest group-prefix mask applicable to the multicast group is selected to support the group. Step 2 of this procedure applies if multiple RP candidates meet this criterion.
2. The C-RP configured with the highest priority is selected. Step 3 of this procedure applies if multiple RP candidates meet this criterion
3. A hash function (using the configured **bsr-candidate hash-mask-length** value) generates a series of mask length values that are individually assigned to the set of eligible C-RPs. If the hash function matches a single RP candidate to a longer mask length than the other candidates, that candidate is selected to support the group. Apply step 4 of this procedure if the hash function matches the longest mask length to multiple RP candidates.

4. The C-RP having the highest IP address is selected to support the group.

Also, within a PIM-SM domain, a router can be configured as a C-RP available for a given multicast group or range of groups and as the static RP for a given multicast group or range of groups. The recommended practice is to use C-RPs for all multicast groups unless there is a need to ensure that a specific group or a range of group is always supported by the same routing switch.

Loopback, Route Only Port (ROP), and Switched Virtual Interface (SVI) are interfaces that can be configured as RPs. Anycast RP is also supported with the help of MSDP mesh groups.

Static RP

Like C-RPs, static RPs control multicast forwarding of specific multicast groups or ranges of contiguous groups. However, static RPs are not dynamically learned, and increase the configuration and monitoring effort to maintain them. As a result, static RPs are not recommended for use except where one of the following conditions applies:

- It is desirable to designate a specific router interface as a backup RP for specific groups.
- Specific multicast groups are expected, and a static RP would help to avoid overloading a given RP with a high volume of multicast traffic.
- A C-RP for the same groups is less reliable than another RP that would not normally be elected to support the groups.
- Tighter traffic control or a higher priority is desired for specific multicast groups.

RP Tree (RPT)

In phase one, a multicast receiver expresses its interest in receiving traffic destined for a multicast group. It does this using IGMP. One of the receiver's local routers is elected as the Designated Router (DR) for that subnet. On receiving the receiver's expression of interest, the DR then sends a PIM Join message toward the RP for that multicast group. This Join message is known as a (*, G) Join because it joins group G for all sources to that group. The (*, G) Join travels hop-by-hop toward the RP for the group, and in each router it passes through, multicast tree state for group G is instantiated. Eventually, the (*, G) Join either reaches the RP or reaches a router that already has (*, G) Join state for that group.

When many receivers join the group, their Join messages converge on the RP and form a distribution tree for group G that is rooted at the RP. This is known as the RP Tree (RPT), and is also known as the shared tree because it is shared by all sources sending to that group. Join messages are resent periodically so long as the receiver remains in the group. When all receivers on a leaf-network leave the group, the DR will send a PIM (*, G) Prune message toward the RP for that multicast group. However, if the Prune message is not sent for any reason, the state will eventually time out.

A multicast data sender just starts sending data destined for a multicast group. The sender's local router (DR) takes those data packets, unicast-encapsulates them, and sends them directly to the RP. The RP receives these encapsulated data packets, decapsulates them, and forwards them onto the shared tree. The packets then follow the (*, G) multicast tree state in the routers on the RP Tree, being replicated wherever the RP Tree branches, and eventually reaching all the receivers for that multicast group. The process of encapsulating data packets to the RP is called registering, and the encapsulation packets are known as PIM Register packets. At the end of phase one, multicast traffic is flowing encapsulated to the RP, and then natively over the RP tree to the multicast receivers.

Note

The RPT is built by using an underlying IP unicast routing protocol, like OSPF. Multicast traffic from a source and to a destination is always sent via the RP and an RPT is built, using a unicast IP protocol to determine the best path to use from the source to the RP and the RP to the receivers (destination).

Shortest Path Tree (SPT)

Although having the RP join back toward the source removes the encapsulation overhead, it does not completely optimize the forwarding paths. For many receivers, the route via the RP may involve a significant detour when compared with the shortest path from the source to the receiver.

To obtain lower latencies or more efficient bandwidth utilization, a router on the receiver's LAN, typically the DR, may optionally initiate a transfer from the shared tree to a source-specific shortest path tree (SPT). To do this, it issues an (S,G) join toward S. This instantiates state in the routers along the path to S. Eventually, this join either reaches S's subnet or reaches a router that already has (S,G) state. When this happens, data packets from S start to flow following the (S,G) state until they reach the receiver.

At this point, the receiver (or a router upstream of the receiver) will be receiving two copies of the data: one from the SPT and one from the RPT. When the first traffic starts to arrive from the SPT, the DR or upstream router starts to drop the packets for G from S that arrive via the RP tree. In addition, it sends an (S,G) Prune message toward the RP. This is known as an (S,G,rpt) Prune. The Prune message travels hop-by-hop, instantiating state along the path toward the RP indicating that traffic from S for G should NOT be forwarded in this direction. The prune is propagated until it reaches the RP or a router that still needs the traffic from S for other receivers.

By now, the receiver will be receiving traffic from S along the shortest path tree between the receiver and S. In addition, the RP is receiving the traffic from S, but this traffic is no longer reaching the receiver along the RP tree. As far as the receiver is concerned, this is the final distribution tree.

Note

If just RPT would be used, then all traffic would flow through the RP, which would be sub-optimal in certain cases. To alleviate this, SPT allows PIM-SM to set up an efficient routing path (using the underlying IP unicast routing protocol) directly between the multicast source (S) and the multicast receiver(s).

PIM-SM Overview

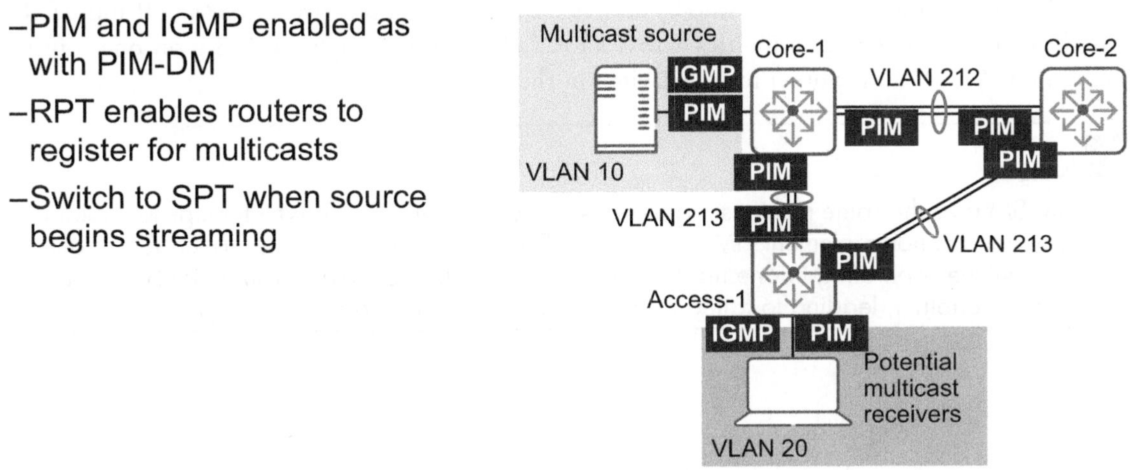

Figure 9-18 PIM-SM Overview

PIM-SM involves a little more setup than PIM-DM because PIM-SM routing switches cannot assume that they are part of the initial multicast routing tree for all traffic. Instead, PIM-SM routing switches must explicitly join that tree, and you must configure them to do so (Figure 9-18).

Note

PIM-SM assumes that most hosts do not want to receive multicast traffic. It uses a non-flooding multicast model to direct traffic from the source to the interface when there are multicast receivers in the group. As a result, this model sends traffic only to the routers that specifically request it.

PIM-SM can be configured on physical ports, VLAN interfaces, LAG interfaces, and loopback interfaces.

Configuring PIM-SM is similar to configuring PIM-DM in some ways. For example, you must enable PIM-SM on every interface between multicast sources and receivers, including:

1. Layer-3 interfaces on which multicast sources reside
2. Layer-3 interfaces on which multicast receivers reside (IGMP-enabled interfaces)
3. Layer-3 interfaces between all routers and routing switches that connect sources and receivers

As with PIM-DM, PIM SM-enabled interfaces exchange hellos on 224.0.0.13. In addition to establishing neighbor relationships, PIM interfaces in broadcast or multi-access networks elect a designated router (DR). The DR is responsible for forwarding multicasts and is selected according to priority (higher priority is preferred) and by address. The same best practice as for MSTP and VRRP apply: load balance DR responsibilities across VLANs by setting a higher priority on one routing switch in one VLAN and another routing switch in the other.

Note

PIM-SM uses the same multicast address as PIM-DM, 224.0.0.13, which helps to explain why you cannot implement PIM-SM and PIM-DM in the same domain. PIM-enabled routing switches operating in one mode would expect certain behavior from neighbors operating in another, leading to failed establishment of the multicast forwarding tree.

RPT

PIM-SM routers must explicitly join multicast forwarding trees for traffic that receivers on their subnets require. However, with no knowledge of the source address, the routing switches have no way of knowing where to direct their joins. Similarly, the DR for the source would not know where to direct the multicast traffic. Without these joins, the DR has no way of discovering which PIM-SM routing switches require the traffic.

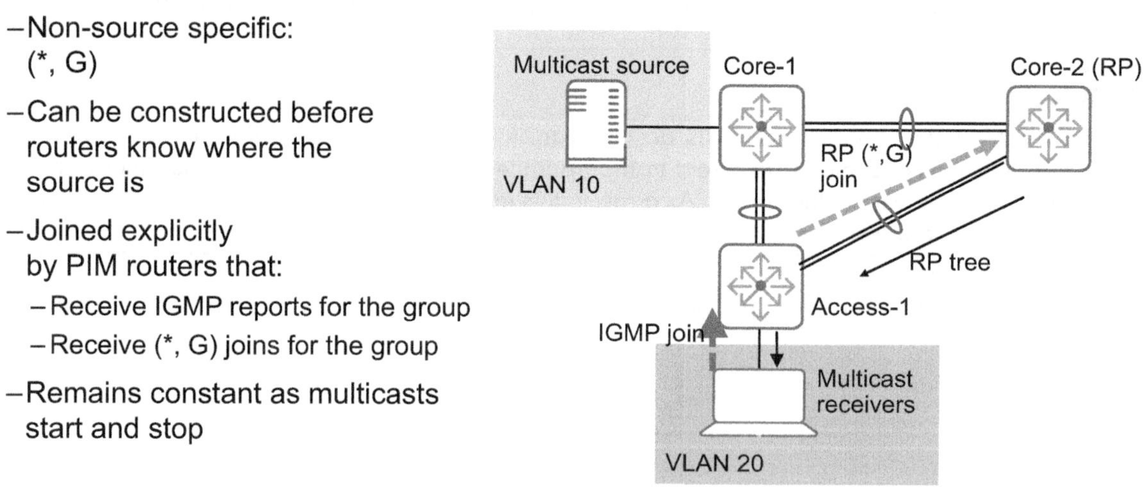

Figure 9-19 RPT

Note

PIM-SM assumes that most hosts do not want to receive multicast traffic. It uses a non-flooding multicast model to direct traffic from the source to the interface when there are multicast receivers in the group. As a result, this model sends traffic only to the routers that specifically request it. In a given PIM-SM domain, routers identified as DRs, RPs, and a BSR participate in delivering multicast traffic to the IP multicast receivers that request it. This approach avoids the flooding method of distributing multicast traffic (employed by PIM-DM) and is best suited for lower bandwidth situations.

To avoid this problem, the routing switches that are interested in a particular multicast group direct their joins to a router selected as the rendezvous point (RP) and establish an RP tree (RPT) rooted at that device. The source's DR also directs multicast traffic to the RP (you will see exactly how a bit later). Thus, the RPT connects the multicast traffic to the devices that need it. Depending on where the source resides, the RP might not provide the *best* root for tree, but what is most important is that it provides a well-known root. (You will see later how PIM-SM enables devices to establish more efficient paths after traffic starts to flow.)

As you see in Figure 9-19, interested multicast receivers begin the process of establishing the RPT by sending IGMP reports for the group in question. The IGMP join triggers the DR to join the RPT, sending a (*, G) join toward the RP.

As with PIM-DM, the (*, G) entry is called a pending PIM route on the AOS-CX switches. A PIM routing device such as Access-1 creates a (*, G) entry for the groups that IGMP informs it clients want. However, unlike the PIM-DM (*, G) entry, this (*, G) entry has an upstream interface, which enables the PIM routing switch to explicitly join the tree. The switch discovers the upstream interface by looking up the forwarding interface in the unicast route to the RP.

The PIM-SM upstream interface transmits a join message, asking the upstream neighbor to add this interface as a downstream interface in the RPT tree. The upstream neighbor adds the interface in the (*, G) entry in question. It then discovers the upstream interface and sends a join message out that interface. The join messages travel up the tree in this manner until they reach the RP.

The RPT, which will forward multicasts, follows the reverse flow of the RPT joins.

Behavior as Source Begins Forwarding

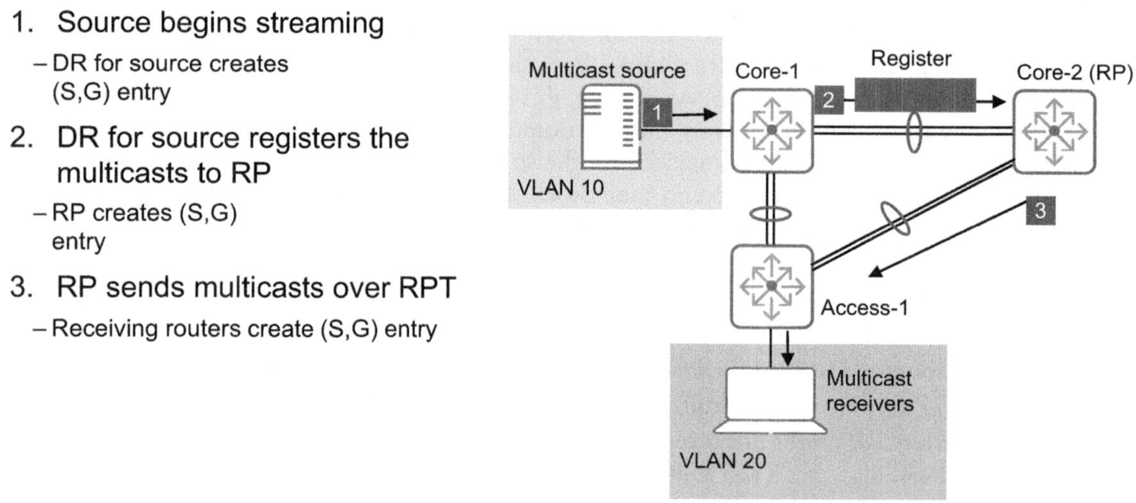

Figure 9-20 Behavior as Source Begins Forwarding

Figure 9-20 shows an RPT that is ready to deliver multicast traffic from the RP to all PIM routing switches connected to receivers for the group. The RP simply needs to receive the traffic.

When a source begins to forward multicast traffic for this group, this process occurs:

1. The default router for the source's subnet receives the traffic. This router is called the DR. (If more than one PIM router exists on the subnet, the DR is elected as you learned with PIM-DM.)
2. The DR registers with the RP. The unicast register messages encapsulate the multicast traffic.
3. The RP decapsulates the multicast traffic and forwards it on the RPT multicast tree.

A designated router (DR) is required on both the source-side network and receiver-side network. A source-side DR acts on behalf of the multicast source to send register messages to the RP. The receiver-side DR acts on behalf of the multicast receivers to send join messages to the RP.

The DR election process is as follows:

1. The routers on the shared-media LAN send hello messages to one another. The hello messages contain the DR priority for DR election. The router with the highest DR priority is elected as the DR.
2. The router with the highest IP address wins the DR election under one of following conditions:
   - All the routers have the same DR election priority.
   - A router does not support carrying the DR priority in hello messages.

If the DR fails, its PIM neighbor lifetime expires and the other routers will initiate to elect a new DR.

3. To forward this traffic, the DR, the RP, and any other routing switches in the path use (S, G) entries, which specify the active source and the multicast destination. Each router creates the (S, G) entry as soon as it receives multicast traffic on the RPT, copying the downstream interfaces from the (*, G) entry into the new entry. The DR also includes the tunnel on which it sends register messages as downstream interfaces.

The upstream interface depends on whether the routing switch uses the RPT or the shortest path tree (SPT). The RPT initially forwards the traffic as shown in the figure above, and the (S, G) routes used for this forwarding have an RPT bit, indicating that the RPT is being used. However, you will almost never see an (S, G) entry with the RPT bit because the PIM-SIM routing switch quickly transitions to a more efficient tree.

Consider this point. A more efficient traffic flow would have the DR as the root of the multicast forwarding tree. For example, in this network, multicasts flow from the source to Core-1 (the DR), which tunnels them in unicast messages to Core-2 (the RP). Core-2 then forwards the multicasts to Access-1. If Core-1 could forward the traffic directly to Access-1, the multicast stream would consume less bandwidth. Core-1 and Core-2 would also not need to encapsulate and decapsulate the multicasts, which would impose less of a burden on the DR and RP.

Switching to SPT

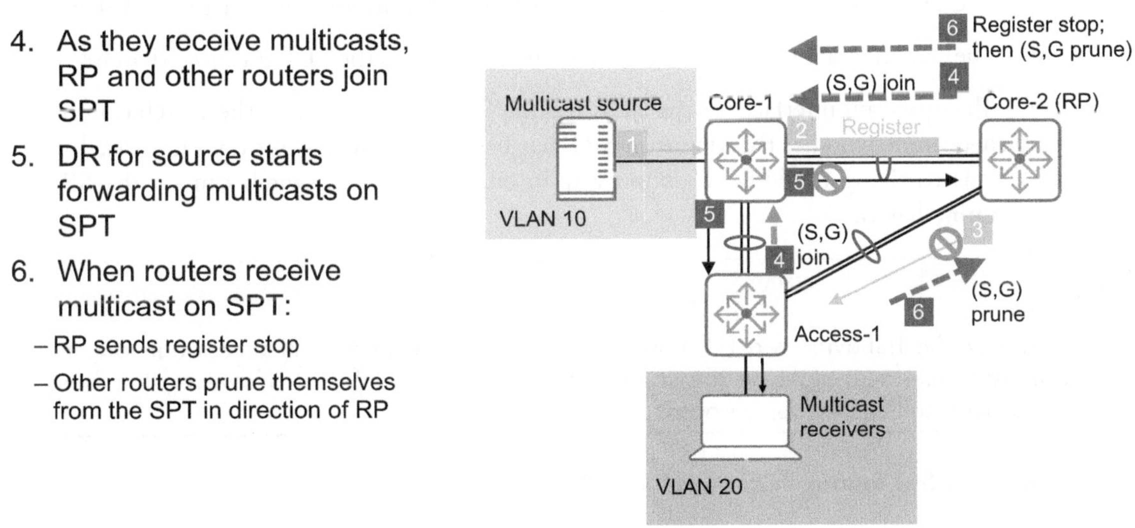

Figure 9-21 Switching to SPT

PIM-SM allows routing devices to transition from the RPT to the SPT with the DR at the root.

The arrival of the first multicast packet in a group triggers a switch from the RPT to the SPT on the DR, RP, and any PIM-SM routing device that forwards traffic into a VLAN for IGMP hosts.

To switch to the SPT, the PIM-SM routing devices perform these tasks (numbering below matches Figure 9-21, which continues from the previous page):

4. The PIM-SM router determines the upstream interface for the SPT, using RPF to discover the forwarding interface for the shortest path to the source. It then sends an (S, G) join on this interface.

5. At this point, to ensure that traffic flow continues uninterrupted, the switch continues to accept traffic on the upstream interface for the RPT.

6. The DR receives the (S, G) joins and adds the receiving interfaces to the downstream interface list for its (S, G) entry. Now it starts forwarding multicasts on the SPT. It continues sending multicasts in register packets too in case some devices have not yet joined the SPT.

7. The RP and DRs for receivers monitor the incoming interface for multicast traffic to determine when they can set the SPT bit.

    - The SPT bit prevents the routing switch from accepting multicasts on any interface except the correct upstream for the SPT, preventing duplication of multicast streams. Routing switches can set this bit when they are certain that the SPT has been established above them—that is, they can receive traffic on the correct interface for this tree.
    - Routing switches can determine that the upstream SPT has been established in a few different ways, which include:
        - The switch receives a multicast on the correct upstream interface for the (S, G) entry.
        - The switch is the DR so, as the root of the SPT, it sets the SPT bit immediately.
        - The upstream interface for the RPT and the SPT are the same, so the switch cannot ever determine whether the upstream SPT has been established—but does not care because it is receiving traffic in the same way in either case. This switch can set the SPT bit immediately.

Note

In reality, the behavior is a bit more nuanced because, in a multi-access network, the upstream interface might be the same but the neighbor different. However, this basic description suffices for our purposes.

8. When a PIM-SM routing device sets the SPT bit:

    - A non-RP routing switch sends an RPT (S, G) prune on the upstream interface for the RPT (unless that is the same as for the SPT). It no longer needs multicasts on this path. Note that the PIM-SM routing switch does not prune itself from the RPT; it maintains its (*, G) entry and its place in the RPT so that it can continue to receive multicasts in this group from other sources. Rather this prune removes the routing switch from the RPT *for the specific source.*

- The RP sends register stop messages. These messages request that the DR to stop sending the encapsulated multicast messages because it can receive the multicasts on the SPT more efficiently. In the example in the figure, the RP also prunes itself from the SPT because it no longer has downstream interfaces in this tree after Access-1 pruned itself. But the RP could remain part of the SPT, depending on the topology.

Thus, PIM routing switches always ensure that the SPT has been established upstream of them before they prune themselves from the RPT. This process ensures that the multicast stream is never interrupted.

This process can occur very quickly. Once the SPT is established, it resembles the PIM-DM tree. Traffic flows from the source to the destination following the best path, as calculated by the unicast routing table.

You can disable and enable the switch to the SPT with this command:

```
Switch(config)# router pim
Switch(config-pim)# spt-threshold
```

However, it is generally recommended that you leave the default behavior of enabled.

Note

SPTs are especially useful in high data-rate applications where reducing unnecessary traffic concentrations and throughput delays are significant. In the default PIM-SM configuration, SPT operation is automatically enabled.

Reverse Path Forward

Reverse Path Forward (RPF) checking is a core multicast routing mechanism that ensures that multicast traffic received arrived on the expected router interface before it is considered for further processing. If the RPF check fails for a multicast packet, the packet is discarded.

For traffic arriving on the SPT, the expected incoming interface for a given source/group multicast flow is the interface toward the source address of the traffic (as determined by the unicast routing system). For traffic arriving on the RP tree, the expected incoming interface is the interface toward the RP. PIM must be enabled on all paths where the unicast route points an ECMP path to the source.

RPF override is a feature that allows the override of the normal RPF lookup mechanism and indicates to the router that it may accept multicast traffic on an interface other than that which would be normally selected by the RPF lookup mechanism. This includes accepting traffic from a source directly connected to the router when the source IP address is invalid for the subnet or VLAN to which it is connected. Traffic may also be accepted from a valid PIM neighbor that is not on the reverse path toward the source of the received multicast traffic.

RPF checking is applied to all multicast traffic and is significant in preventing network loops. Up to eight manual RPF overrides can be specified.

Specifying the RP

- Choose RP that can handle load
  - Typically a core device
- RP must match on every PIM router
- Set the RP
  - Static
    - Only one allowed per range
    - Takes priority over bootstrap if override option set
  - Dynamic bootstrap mechanism
    - Selected from RP set sent by bootstrap router
    - Recommended for redundancy and load-balancing

Figure 9-22 Specifying the RP

You now have a basic idea of how PIM-SM routers join an RPT in order to receive initial multicasts and then switch to an SPT for more efficient traffic flow (Figure 9-22). Besides enabling PIM-SM on the proper interfaces, the most important step for configuring the system is specifying the RP or RPs.

A PIM-SM router must have the correct RP address for every multicast address for which it needs to forwards traffic. Otherwise, the router cannot receive the stream. And every PIM-SM router in the domain must always select the same RP for the same multicast addresses. Clearly, if some routers that need a particular type of multicast traffic established an RPT to one RP, and the DR then registers to another RP, the traffic will go astray.

It is recommended that you select core routers for RPs, which encourages devices to establish the RPT over backbone links. Traffic would need to flow over these links in any case, so placing the RP there does not redirect the traffic to an area that might not otherwise have to support it. For example, in this scenario, Core-1 or Core-2 is the natural choice for the RP because all other PIM-SM devices connect directly to it.

In addition, because RPs might need to store many multicast route entries and handle a great deal of multicast traffic, you should also select high-performance routing switches capable of meeting the needs.

When the PIM-SM routing switches meet these criteria, you should also try to place them as near multicast sources as possible, which makes the transition to the SPT more efficient.

You can either specify a single RP for all multicast groups. Or you can configure the bootstrap mechanism, which enables the PIM-SM domain to elect an RP for each group dynamically.

Static

When you set the RP address manually, you must set the same, single RP on every device. Because the domain will have only one RP, you should generally select the PIM-SM routing device that is the fewest hops from most other routers or has the highest bandwidth and throughput capabilities. If you have a relatively small core and you know that multicast traffic will be originating from a specific location, you could alternatively set the DR for that location as the RP.

Enter this PIM command to specify the static RP:

```
Switch(config)# router pim
Switch(config-pim)# rp-address <IP-address> [group-address/group-mask]
[override]
```

You must enter the command on *every* PIM-SM router and routing switch in the domain; PIM neighbors do *not* advertise static RPs to each other. The group address and group mask settings are optional. Specify these to limit the RP to supporting the multicast addresses included in that range. For example, if you specify 239.0.0.0/8, the RP can only support multicasts between 239.0.0.0 and 239.255.255.255.

You can only define one manual RP address on each AOS-CX switch per range, which makes the manual option less conducive to redundancy than the bootstrap option. The **override** option dictates whether the manual RP address takes precedence over one sent by bootstrap.

Dynamic Bootstrap

The bootstrap mechanism is typically recommended over a manual configuration. Not only is it simpler to set up, it enables more than one RP to operate in the system. Each RP supports different multicast groups. Therefore, the burden of the role is load balanced. The system also has greater redundancy because, if one RP fails, another RP can be selected to support the multicast groups that the failed RP used to support.

To determine how many PIM-SM devices to configure as C-RPs, you should consider the size of your network and the number of multicast receivers. In an environment with thousands of receivers, you should configure several RPs, which load balance groups between them.

Finally, keep in mind that, if you configure an RP address on a PIM-DM routing device manually, and the routing device also receives RP addresses through the bootstrap mechanism, the manual configuration overrides the bootstrap message. For consistency, you should *not* configure an address manually if you plan to use bootstrap.

The next pages explain the bootstrap mechanism in more detail.

Bootstrap Mechanism

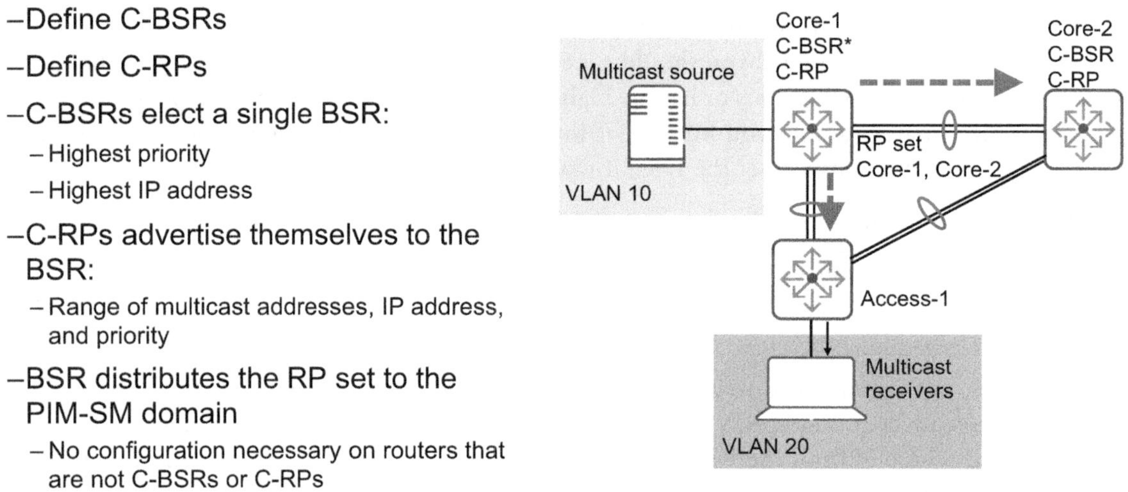

Figure 9-23 Bootstrap Mechanism

Instead of specifying an RP on all PIM-SM devices, you can set up the bootstrap mechanism (Figure 9-23). With this approach, you configure each device with its role and make no configurations at all on devices that do not require a role:

- Candidate RPs (C-RPs) are PIM-SM devices that can act as RPs. In the pool of C-RPs, only one is elected the RP for a particular group. However, multiple RPs can be active at once, each supporting a different group.
- A Bootstrap Router (BSR) is a PIM-SM device that distributes information about RPs to other PIM-SM devices in the domain. You can configure a pool of Candidate BSRs (C-BSRs). Only one BSR is active while the others function as backups.

In more detail, C-BSRs use their bootstrap messages, which they begin to send as soon as they are configured with the role, to elect the active BSR. That is, when a C-BSR receives a bootstrap message with a higher priority than its own, it suppresses its messages. If the priority is the same, the C-BSR defers to the C-BSR with a higher IP address. Thus, after all C-BSRs have heard each other's messages, only the C-BSR with the highest priority, or tied highest priority and highest IP address, remains active.

Note

The C-BSR uses the IP address of the interface that you specify with the C-BSR command. PIM-SM must be enabled on this interface, or the BSR cannot send messages.

The C-BSRs continue to listen for the BSR's periodic messages. If the hold-time expires without a message, the C-BSRs become active again, electing a new BSR.

C-RPs send C-RP advertisements to the active BSR. The advertisements include the RP's IP address, the range of multicast addresses that it supports, and its priority for each range. The BSR compiles the information as an RP set, which it advertises to all PIM-SM routing devices in the domain.

For example, you have configured both Core-1 and Core-2 as C-BSRs. You have also configured both Core-1 and Core-2 as C-RPs. Example commands are:

```
Core-1(config)# router pim
Core-1(config-pim)# bsr-candidate source-ip-interface vlan1212
Core-1(config-pim)# bsr-candidate priority 250
Core-1(config-pim)# rp-candidate source-ip-interface vlan1212
```

```
Core-2(config)# router pim
Core-2(config-pim)# bsr-candidate source-ip-vlan vlan1212
Core-2(config-pim)# rp-candidate source-ip-vlan vlan1212
```

For the source VLAN in these commands, you must choose a VLAN has PIM-SM enabled on it. You should choose a VLAN that offers as much redundancy as possible (for example, it is carried on a link aggregation).

In this example, Core-1 is elected as BSR because it has the higher priority. It is also a C-RP. Core-2 is also a C-RP, and it advertises itself as such to Core-1. Both C-RPs are configured with priority 100, and neither is limited in the groups that it supports. Core-1 would send bootstrap messages with this RP set:

- Core-1's C-RP IP address for 224.0.0.0/4 priority 100
- Core-2's C-RP IP address for 224.0.0.0/4 priority 100

Remember that you only need to enter the **rp-candidate** command on the routers that you actually want to act as C-RPs, not on the C-BSRs. The C-RPs automatically advertise themselves to the BSR. In this example, you entered the **rp-candidate** command on the C-BSRs because you wanted your core switches to be able to perform both the BSR and RP roles.

Selecting the RP from the RP Set

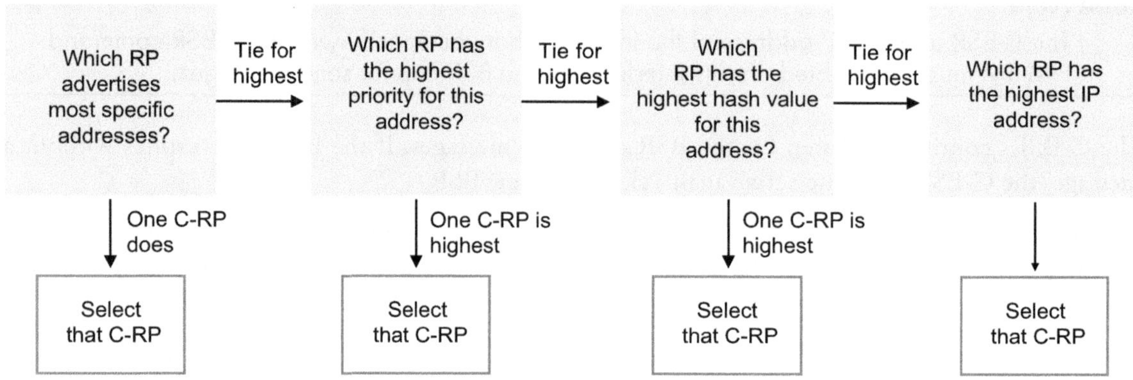

Figure 9-24 Selecting the RP from the RP Set

To view the RPs that are manually configured on the AOS-CX switch, as well as the ones received from the BSR, enter this command (Figure 9-24). Example output is provided.

```
Switch# show ip pim rp-set all-vrfs
VRF: default

Status and Counters - PIM-SM Static RP-Set Information
Group Address    Group Mask       RP Address       Override
---------------  ---------------  ---------------  --------
233.100.128.255  255.255.255.255  100.10.10.1      Yes
238.100.128.255  255.255.255.255  100.10.10.3      Yes

Status and Counters - PIM-SM Learned RP-Set Information
Group Address Group Mask RP Address Hold Time Expire Time
--------------- --------------- --------------- --------- -----------
223.2.2.34 255.0.0.0 9.0.0.25 12 0
<-output omitted->
```

PIM-SM routing devices that have identical RP sets—which they should—always select the same RP for the same multicast address, following these rules:

1. Select the RP that advertises the most specific range of multicast addresses that includes the desired address.
2. If more than one C-RP advertises a range of the same specificity, select the C-RP configured with the highest priority.
3. If more than one C-RP is configured with the highest priority, a hash function generates a series of mask length values that are individually assigned to the set of eligible C-RPs. If the hash function matches a single RP candidate to a longer mask length than the other candidates, that candidate is selected to support the group.
4. If the hash function matches the longest mask length to multiple RP candidates, the C-RP that has the highest IP address is selected to support the group.

The PIM-SM devices store the RP set, but only calculate an RP when they need to join an RPT for a group (when a connected IGMP host sends a report for the address or when a downstream neighbor sends a (*, G) join. This behavior preserves memory and processing power.

Now that you understand how PIM-SM routing devices select the RP, you can consider ways to affect the selection by adding options to the candidate RP configuration.

Group Prefixes

Perhaps one of your PIM-DM routers is closer to the multicast sources for a specific multicast address or range of addresses, so you want other routers to prefer it as the RP for those addresses. Tell the RP to advertise that specific address or range with this PIM configuration command:

```
Switch(config)# route pim
Switch(config-pim)# rp-candidate group-prefix <group-address/prefix>
```

For example, enter:

```
Switch(config-pim)# rp-candidate group-prefix 239.255.0.0/16
```

As long as other candidate RPs are advertising a less specific range, this switch is the preferred RP for multicast groups in the 239.255.0.0/16 range, regardless of priority.

You can enter the command multiple times to advertise multiple ranges.

You should keep in mind that the **source-ip-vlan<*ID*>** option is required the first time that you enter the **rp-candidate** command. If you specify a group-prefix option the first time that you enter the command, the switch *only* supports the specified range.

But if you first enter the **rp-candidate source-ip-vlan<ID>** command without any group-prefix range, the switch automatically supports all multicast groups (224.0.0.0/4). For example, you enter this command:

```
Switch(pim)# rp-candidate source-ip-vlan 1212
```

You will see this in the running-config:

```
router pim
rp-candidate source-ip-interface vlan1212
rp-candidate group-prefix 224.0.0.0 240.0.0.0
```

Later you might enter a specific range such as the following:

```
Switch(config-pim)# rp-candidate group-prefix 239.255.0.0/16
```

Then the switch advertises *both* ranges. This lets you create scenarios in which various RPs are preferred for different specific ranges, but they can all support any group if the preferred RP for that group goes down.

Priority

As indicated above, when no RP advertises a more specific range into which the multicast group falls, priority comes into play. You can set the priority with this command:

```
Switch(config)# route pim
Switch(config-pim)# rp-candidate priority <0-255>
```

A single priority applies to all ranges advertised by the RP.

Load Balancing

If you want to load balance the role roughly evenly over multiple active RPs, you should explicitly set the same priority on each C-RP because different models of switches use different default priorities. After you set up each C-RP in this way, the hash algorithm will automatically allocate multicast addresses among the various C-RPs in a more or less equal fashion.

Consider this statement in more detail.

As you just learned, the hash algorithm assigns each RP a value for a block of multicast addresses. The length of the range of addresses that produce the same value for the same RP depends on the length of the mask that is advertised by the BSR. When PIM-SM devices use the hash algorithm to select an RP for a particular multicast address, they apply an AND function on the multicast address and the mask (much as an IP address is combined with a mask to produce a network address). Therefore, a 32-bit mask would result in a different value for each multicast address. With a 31-bit mask, the hash would produce the same value for two addresses in a row (because the 31-bit mask reduces two addresses to the same value), and a 24-bit mask would produce the same result for 256 addresses.

You can set the hash length on the BSR to control the size of the blocks of addresses that are always assigned to the same RP. The smaller the size (the longer the hash length), the more likely it is that multicast addresses will be distributed equally among the C-RPs. If the BSR advertises a shorter hash that produces large blocks of addresses, the same RP might happen to be selected for a preponderance of the multicast addresses—particularly, if server administrators select multicast addresses in a row.

The default mask length is 30, which produces the same hash for blocks of four addresses. In other words, the PIM-SM domain will elect the same RP for multicast group 239.255.0.0, 239.255.0.1, 239.255.0.2, and 239.255.0.3. A different hash is produced for 239.255.0.4-239.255.0.7, so a different RP can be elected. The more multicast addresses that are used, the higher the likelihood that they will be distributed more or less equally.

To configure the hash algorithm on the C-BSRs, use this PIM configuration command:

```
Switch(config)# route pim
Switch(config-pim)# bsr-candidate hash-mask-length <1-32>
```

VSX and Multicasting: PIM-SM

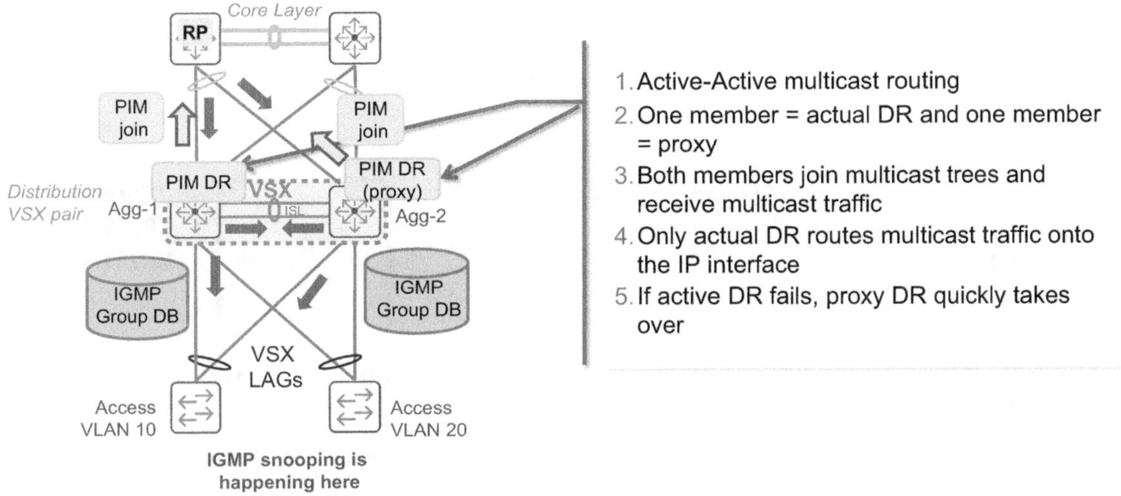

Figure 9-25 VSX and Multicasting: PIM-SM

As of software 10.02, AOS-CX supports dual designated router (DR) functionality for VSX. One VSX member is elected the actual DR for each IP interface that runs PIM, using the typical PIM election process. The other VSX member becomes a proxy DR. Both the actual DR and proxy DR send PIM joins to join the rendezvous point (RP) tree for any multicast group learned on the IP interface. And when a multicast stream begins, both members receive the multicast traffic and remain part of the shortest path tree (SPT). However, only the actual DR routes the received multicast traffic onto the IP interface, which prevents duplication of the multicast stream (Figure 9-25).

In this example, Agg-1 is the actual DR for VLAN 10 and the proxy DR for VLAN 20. Agg-2 is the actual DR for VLAN 20 and the proxy DR for VLAN 10. Both Agg-1 and Agg-2 receive multicast traffic for all groups learned on VLAN 10 and VLAN 20; however, only Agg-1 routes the multicasts onto VLAN 10, and only Agg-2 routes the multicasts onto VLAN 20.

If the actual DR fails, the proxy DR can take over almost immediately. If the actual DR comes back up, it comes up as a proxy DR rather than tries to preempt the role.

Note

You can implement load balancing so that for each VSX pair, one switch can be the DR for half the VLANs and the other switch the DR for the other half of the VLANs. Also, IGMP snooping should be implemented on the VLANs at the access switches that are operating in Layer-2 mode.

Lab 9

Lab Diagram

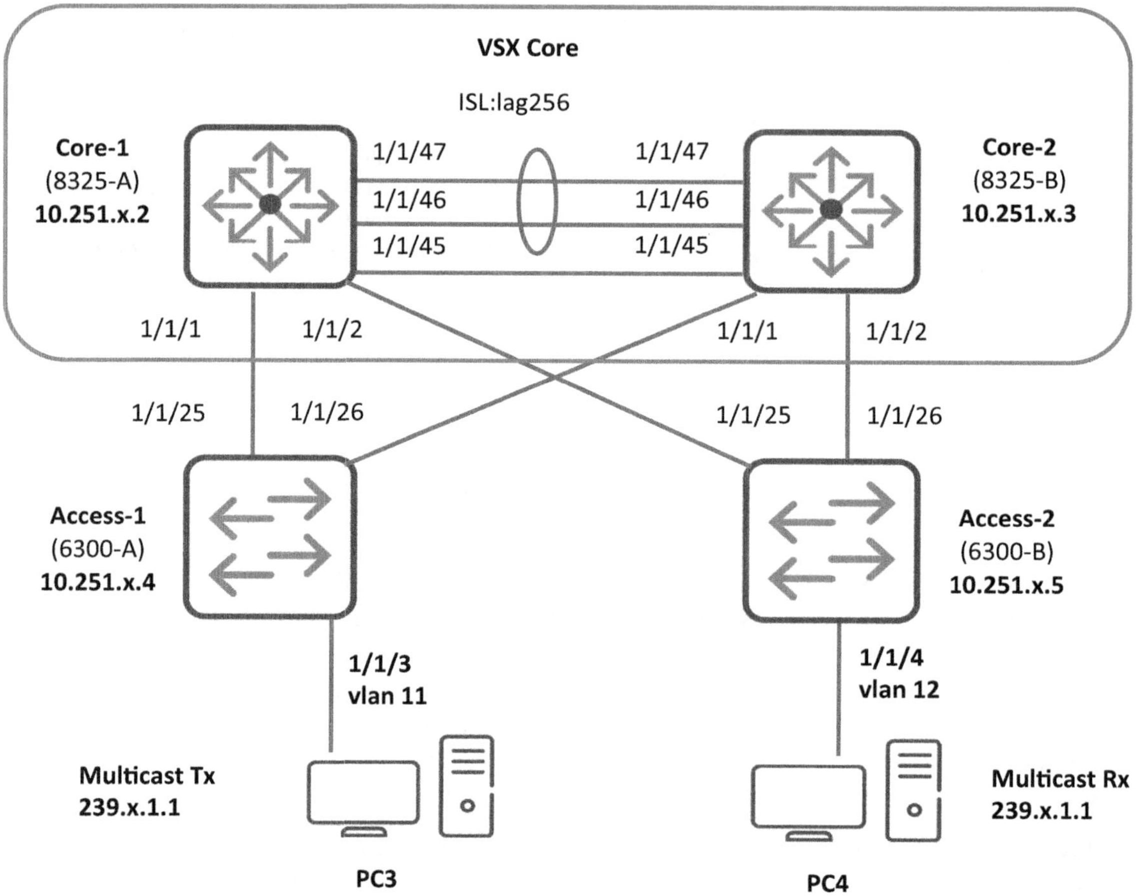

Figure 9-26 Lab Diagram

Overview

In this lab activity (Figures 9-26), multicast routing will be configured using PIM Sparse Mode on the VSX Core. Multicast routing also requires an IGMP Querier; this function has been enabled in the previous lab activity (Configuring IGMP). The result will be that the multicast that is transmitted by PC3 in VLAN 11 can be received by PC4 in VLAN 12.

Objectives

- - Understand multicast routing
- - Apply PIM Sparse Mode global and interface level configuration
- - Verify the multicast routing table

Task 1: Prepare and Review the Lab Setup

Objectives

This lab requires the completion of the 'Configuring IGMP' lab activity.PC3 should be in VLAN 11, in this task; PC4 will be moved to VLAN 12.

Steps

1. Access the terminal of Access2 and enter configuration mode. Assign the port of PC4 to VLAN 12.

```
ICX-Tx-Access2(config)# interface 1/1/4
ICX-Tx-Access2(config-if)# vlan access 12
ICX-Tx-Access2(config-if)# exit
```

2. Open PC4 (connected to Access2). Renew the IP address by bouncing (disable/enable) the 'Lab NIC' port.

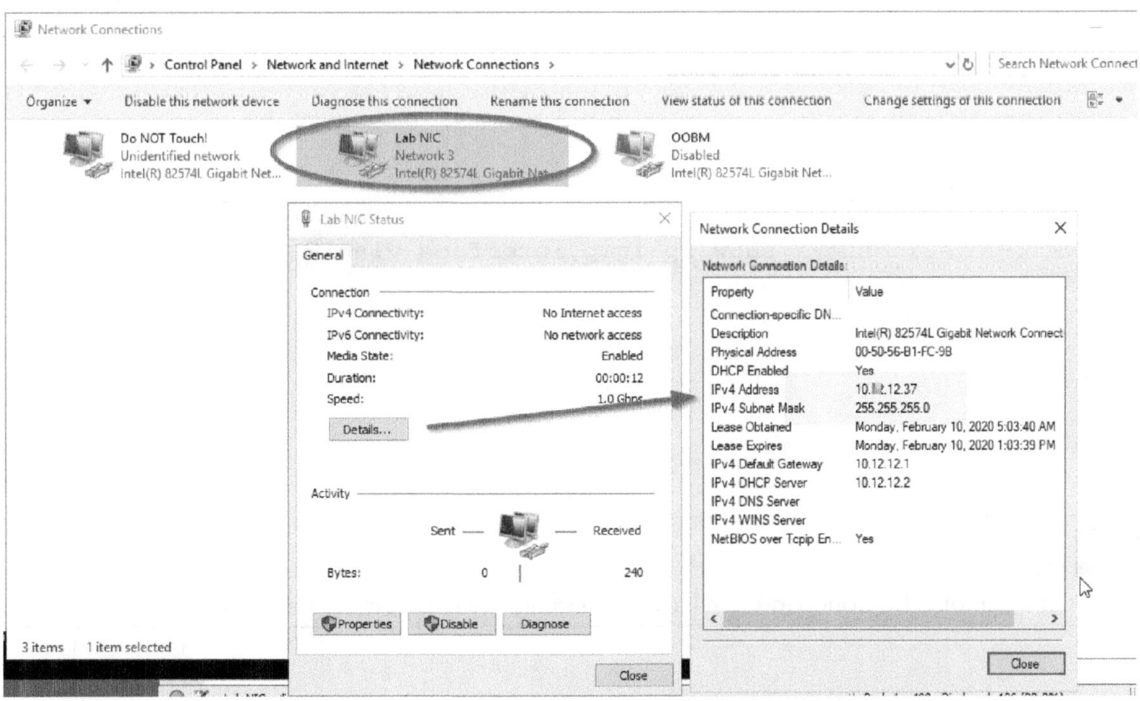

3. The client should now have an IP address from the VLAN 12 range.

Verify IP IGMP Querier on the Core Switches

PIM multicast routing relies on IGMP join packets from the client devices to learn which multicasts are requested by the clients. Therefore, IP IGMP querier function must be enabled and functional on the receiving client interfaces before PIM routing can operate.

1. On Core1, verify the IP IGMP Querier status for VLAN 11 and VLAN 12 interfaces.

```
ICX-Tx-Core1(config)# show ip igmp interface vlan11
IGMP Configured Version    : 3
IGMP Operating Version     : 3
Querier State               :Querier
Querier IP [this switch]    : 10.x.11.2
Querier Uptime              : 3h 38m
...
ICX-Tx-Core1(config)# show ip igmp interface vlan12
IGMP Configured Version    : 3
IGMP Operating Version     : 3
Querier State               :Querier
Querier IP [this switch]    : 10.x.12.2
Querier Uptime              : 5m 24s
Querier Expiration Time     : 1m 58s
```

2. Repeat the verification on Core2.

```
ICX-Tx-Core2(config)# show ip igmp interface vlan11
IGMP Configured Version    : 3
IGMP Operating Version     : 3
Querier State               :Non-Querier
Querier IP                  : 10.x.11.2
Querier Uptime              : 26m 30s
Querier Expiration Time     : 2m 57s
```

```
ICX-Tx-Core2(config)# show ip igmp interface vlan12
IGMP Configured Version    : 3
IGMP Operating Version     : 3
Querier State               :Non-Querier
Querier IP                  : 10.x.12.2
Querier Uptime              : 5m 27s
Querier Expiration Time     : 3m 32s
```

Note

This can also be done via Core1 by appending **'vsx-peer'** to the commands.

Task 2: Configure PIM Sparse

Objectives

In this task, the PIM Sparse Mode (PIM-SM) Candidate Bootstrap Router (C-BSR) is configured. Once the BSR has been elected, the Candidate Rendezvous points (RP) will be elected and distributed by the BSR. On the RP, the administrator can specify that the RP should be the handling point for a specific range of multicast addresses.

Steps

Core1 PIM-SM Configuration

1. Open a terminal to Core1; enter the configuration mode. Access the router PIM context.

```
ICX-Tx-Core1(config)# router pim
```

2. For multicast on a VSX cluster, the best practice is to configure PIM Dual-DR under the PIM router command. With the 'active-active' command, the proxy-DR will also learn the multicast routes and this will allow fast recovery time if the actual DR fails.

```
ICX-Tx-Core1(config-pim)# active-active
```

Note

In a VSX cluster, the VSX member with the highest IP address will be the forwarder of the multicast traffic. In this lab setup, the Core2 will become the forwarder. Do not configure PIM interface level DR priority when active-active is enabled, since the active-active feature will over-rule the manually configured interface priority.

3. Attempt to enable the C-BSR function using the VLAN 1 interface as the source address.

Note

In a typical deployment, a loopback interface would be used for this function. This lab uses the VLAN 1 IP interface since it is already configured. If a loopback interface is used, make sure it is routable in the network.

```
ICX-Tx-Core1(config-pim)# bsr-candidate source-ip-interface vlan1
PIM SM should be configured on one or more interface.
```

Question: Why did the switch return an error?

Answer: While the VLAN 1 IP interface exists, the PIM protocol must first be enabled on the interface before it can be used in the PIM election process.

4. Enable PIM on the VLAN 1 interface.

```
ICX-Tx-Core1(config-pim)# exit
ICX-Tx-Core1(config)# interface vlan1
ICX-Tx-Core1(config-if-vlan)# ip pim-sparse enable
ICX-Tx-Core1(config-if-vlan)# exit
```

5. Re-try to enable the C-BSR function using the loopback interface and enable the PIM routing protocol.

```
ICX-Tx-Core1(config)# router pim
ICX-Tx-Core1(config-pim)# bsr-candidate source-ip-interface vlan1
ICX-Tx-Core1(config-pim)# enable
```

6. Assign the Core1 BSR priority 250.

```
ICX-Tx-Core1(config-pim)# bsr-candidate priority 250
ICX-Tx-Core1(config-pim)# exit
```

7. Review the local BSR candidate information.

```
ICX-Tx-Core1(config)# show ip pimbsr local
Status and Counters - PIM-SM Local Candidate-BSR Information

VRF                          : default
C-BSR Admin Status           :This system is a Candidate-BSR
C-BSR Address                : 10.x.1.2
C-BSR Priority               : 250
C-BSR Hash Mask Length       : 30
C-BSR Message Interval       : vlan1
```

8. Enable PIM SM on interfaces VLAN 11 and VLAN 12.

```
ICX-Tx-Core1(config)# interface vlan11
ICX-Tx-Core1(config-if-vlan)# ip pim-sparse enable
ICX-Tx-Core1(config-if-vlan)# exit
ICX-Tx-Core1(config)# interface vlan12
ICX-Tx-Core1(config-if-vlan)# ip pim-sparse enable
ICX-Tx-Core1(config-if-vlan)# exit
```

Core2 PIM-SM Configuration

1. On Core2, configure PIM-SM on the interfaces and make it C-BSR.

```
ICX-Tx-Core2(config)# interface vlan1
ICX-Tx-Core2(config-if-vlan)# ip pim-sparse enable
ICX-Tx-Core2(config-if-vlan)# exit
ICX-Tx-Core2(config)# interface vlan11
ICX-Tx-Core2(config-if-vlan)# ip pim-sparse enable
```

```
ICX-Tx-Core2(config-if-vlan)# exit
ICX-Tx-Core2(config)# interface vlan12
ICX-Tx-Core2(config-if-vlan)# ip pim-sparse enable
ICX-Tx-Core2(config-if-vlan)# exit
ICX-Tx-Core2(config)# router pim
ICX-Tx-Core2(config-pim)# active-active
ICX-Tx-Core2(config-pim)# bsr-candidate source-ip-interface vlan1
ICX-Tx-Core2(config-pim)# enable
ICX-Tx-Core2(config-pim)# exit
```

Verify the BSR Election

1. On the Core1, review the elected BSR information.

```
ICX-Tx-Core1(config)# show ip pimbsr elected
Status and Counters - PIM-SM Elected Bootstrap Router Information

VRF                          : default
E-BSR Address                : 10.x.1.2
E-BSR Priority               : 250
E-BSR Hash Mask Length       : 30
E-BSR Up Time                : 1 mins 57 secs
Next Bootstrap Message       : 13 secs
```

2. On Core2, review the elected BSR information.

```
ICX-Tx-Core2(config)# show ip pim bsr elected
Status and Counters - PIM-SM Elected Bootstrap Router Information

VRF                          : default
E-BSR Address                : 10.x.1.2
E-BSR Priority               : 250
E-BSR Hash Mask Length       : 30
E-BSR Up Time                : 2 mins 40 secs
Next Bootstrap Message       : 1 mins 40 secs
```

Note

It may take up to 2 minutes before Core2 shows 10.x.1.2 as the E-BSR address.

PIM-SM Rendezvous Point (RP)

1. On the Core1, review the default RP candidate information and active RP sets. This shows that there is no default RP on the system.

```
ICX-Tx-Core1(config)# show ip pim rp-candidate
ICX-Tx-Core1(config)# show ip pim rp-set
```

2. Make the Core1 a candidate RP.

```
ICX-Tx-Core1(config)# router pim
ICX-Tx-Core1(config-pim)# rp-candidate source-ip-interface vlan1
```

3. Make Core2 a candidate RP.

```
ICX-Tx-Core2(config)# router pim
ICX-Tx-Core2(config-pim)# rp-candidate source-ip-interface vlan1
```

Core1—Verify the RP Set

1. On Core1, review the RP set.

```
ICX-Tx-Core1(config-pim)# show ip pim rp-set
VRF: default
Status and Counters - PIM-SM Learned RP-Set Information
Group Address    Group Mask       RP Address       Hold Time  Expire
                                                               Time
--------------- --------------- --------------- --------- -----------
224.0.0.0        240.0.0.0        10.x.1.3         150        149
224.0.0.0        240.0.0.0        10.x.1.2         150        149
```

Note

It may take a minute for the Core2 (10.x.1.3) to appear in the list. You do not need to wait for it.

RP for Multicast Subset Group

By default, an RP will be RP for all possible multicast entries (224.0.0.0/4). In a large network with multiple sites or regions, the administrator may want to have a regional RP for the local multicast traffic. In this case, the administrator should use structural IP Addressing for the multicast applications.

In this lab, each table will be assumed a 'region', so the local RPs will be configured to be the preferred RPs for the local multicast ranges (239.x.0.0/16).

1. On Core1, configure the 239.x.0.0/16 group-prefix for the RP.

```
ICX-Tx-Core1(config-pim)# rp-candidate group-prefix 239.x.0.0/16
ICX-Tx-Core1(config-pim)# exit
```

2. Repeat this on Core2.

```
ICX-Tx-Core2(config-pim)# rp-candidate group-prefix 239.x.0.0/16
ICX-Tx-Core2(config-pim)# exit
```

3. On Core2, review the resulting local candidate RP information.

```
ICX-Tx-Core2(config)# show ip pim rp-candidate
Status and Counters- PIM-SM Candidate-RP Information

VRF                          : default
C-RP Admin Status            : This system is a Candidate-RP
C-RP Address                 : 10.x.1.3
C-RP Hold Time               : 150
C-RP Advertise Period        : 60
C-RP Priority                : 192
C-RP Source IP Interface     : vlan1

Group Address    Group Mask
---------------  ---------------
224.0.0.0        240.0.0.0
Group Address    Group Mask
---------------  ---------------
239.12.0.0       255.255.0.0
```

Verify RP Set and Group Prefixes

1. Verify that both Core1 (10.x.12.2) and Core2 (10.x.12.3) are now listed in the RP set for the 239.x.0.0/16 group-prefix.

```
ICX-Tx-Core2(config)# show ip pim rp-set
VRF: default

Status and Counters - PIM-SM Learned RP-Set Information
Group Address    Group Mask      RP Address      Hold Time   Expire Time
---------------  -------------   -------------   ---------   -----------
224.0.0.0        240.0.0.0       10.x.1.3        150         131
224.0.0.0        240.0.0.0       10.x.1.2        150         131
239.12.0.0       255.255.0.0     10.x.1.2        150         131
239.12.0.0       255.255.0.0     10.x.1.3        150         131
```

Note

It may take up to a minute before the updated RP SET is available.

Task 3: Verify Multicast Forwarding

Objectives

In this task, the multicast routing will be tested between the hosts in VLAN 11 and VLAN 12.

- PC3 (connected to Access1) belongs to VLAN 11 and will be transmitting the multicast test traffic.
- PC4 (connected to Access2) belongs to VLAN 12 and will request the test multicast traffic.

Once the multicast traffic arrives the status of the multicast group information will be reviewed on the Core switches.

Steps

Test Multicast Transmitter and Registration

1. On PC3 (connected to Access1), configure the UDP Multicast Test tool as '**Sender**'. (The tool can be found on the desktop.)
    - Local Interface Address: **10.x.11.y** (Your PC as shown in 'Local Interfaces' list)
    - Destination multicast address: **239.x.1.1**
2. Click on '**Start Sender**' to make the multicast Sender is active. It will now start to send traffic to the 239.x.1.1 destination address, using the local interface 10.x.11.y.

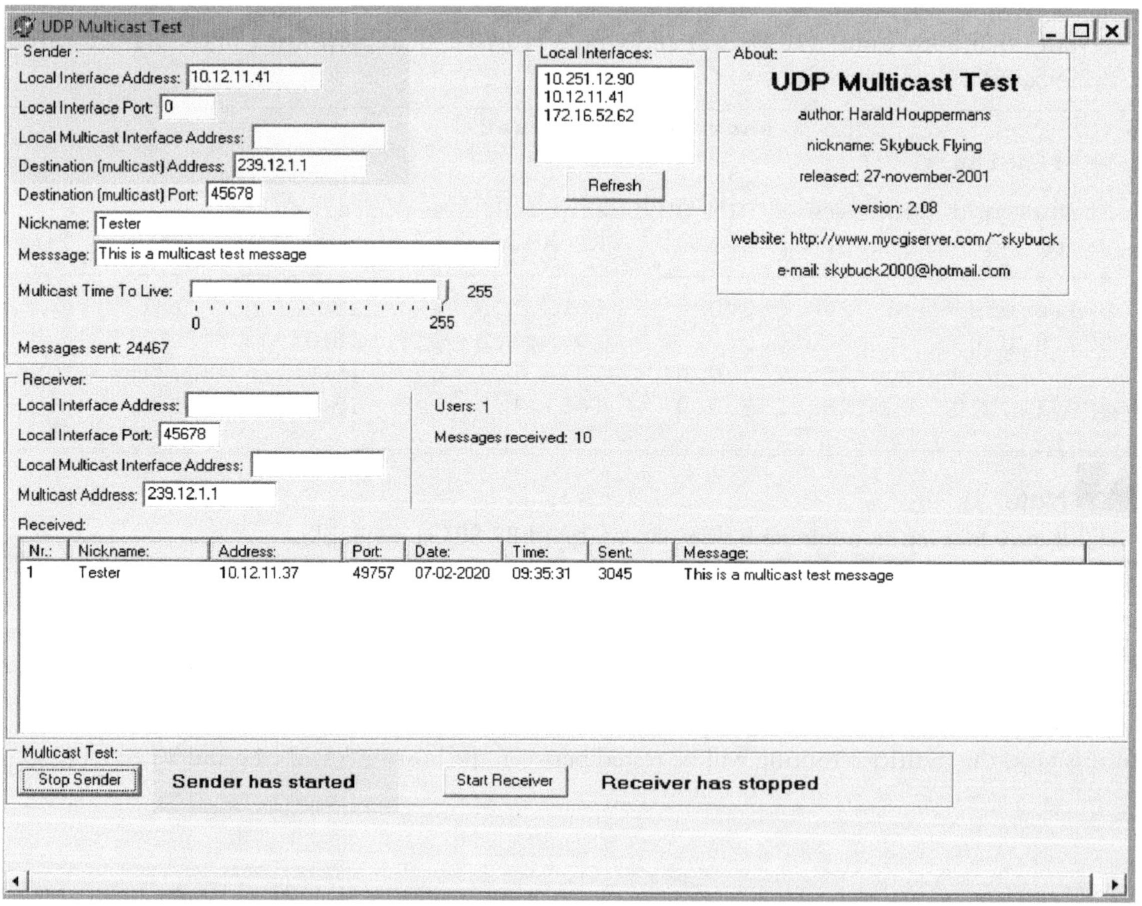

3. On the Core1, review the brief output of the current multicast routing table. The 239.x.1.1 multicast should have been learned by the data-plane on VLAN 11. This also shows the source address of the transmitter (10.x.11.y).

```
ICX-Tx-Core1(config)# show ip mroute brief
IP Multicast Route Entries

VRF : default
Total number of entries : 1

Group Address        Source Address       Neighbor             Interface
-------------        --------------       --------             ---------
239.12.1.1           10.x.11.y            10.x.11.3           vlan11
```

4. Review the details of the 239.x.1.1 route. This will show that the multicast was registered with the PIM-SM protocol.

```
ICX-Tx-Core1(config)# show ip mroute 239.x.1.1
IP Multicast Route Entries

VRF : default

Group Address                  : 239.12.1.1
Source Address                 : 10.x.11.y
Neighbor                       : 10.x.11.3
Incoming interface             : vlan11
Multicast Routing Protocol     : PIM-SM
Unicast Routing Protocol       : connected
Metric                         : 0
Metric  Pref                   : 0
```

Question: What is the Incoming interface?

Answer: The multicast traffic is received by the Core switch on the VLAN 11 interface.

Question: Are there any outgoing interfaces listed?

Answer: Since there are no registered subscribers, there are no outgoing interfaces at this moment.

Test the Multicast Routing Forwarding

1. On PC4 (connected to Access2), start a Wireshark trace on the 'Lab NIC'.
2. Next enable the UDP Multicast test tool as **'Receiver'**(lower).
   - Local Multicast interface address: 10.x.12.yMake sure this is the updated VLAN12 ip address; you can click on 'Refresh' button to see the updated 'Local Interfaces'.
   - Multicast address: 239.x.1.1
3. Scroll down and click on **'Start Receiver'**. Verify that the test messages are received in the tool.

4. Return to the Wireshark, stop the trace. The test tool has sent the IGMP join request. The Core switch has received the IGMP join and has initiated the multicast routing forwarding process.

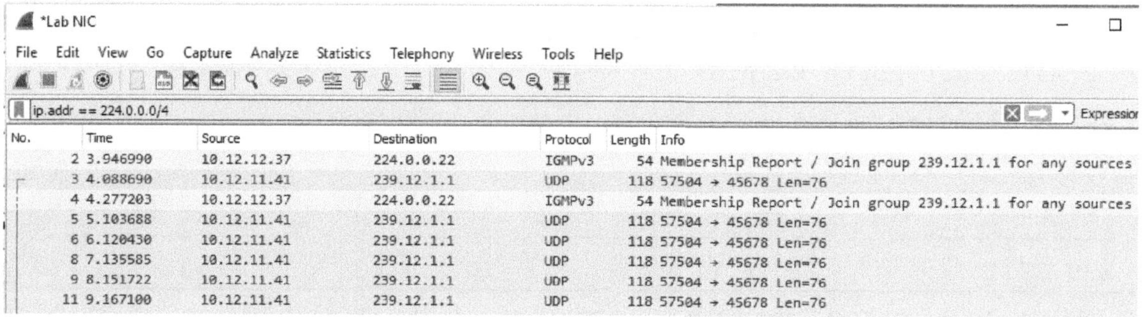

No.	Time	Source	Destination	Protocol	Length	Info
2	3.946990	10.12.12.37	224.0.0.22	IGMPv3	54	Membership Report / Join group 239.12.1.1 for any sources
3	4.088690	10.12.11.41	239.12.1.1	UDP	118	57504 → 45678 Len=76
4	4.277203	10.12.12.37	224.0.0.22	IGMPv3	54	Membership Report / Join group 239.12.1.1 for any sources
5	5.103688	10.12.11.41	239.12.1.1	UDP	118	57504 → 45678 Len=76
6	6.120430	10.12.11.41	239.12.1.1	UDP	118	57504 → 45678 Len=76
8	7.135585	10.12.11.41	239.12.1.1	UDP	118	57504 → 45678 Len=76
9	8.151722	10.12.11.41	239.12.1.1	UDP	118	57504 → 45678 Len=76
11	9.167100	10.12.11.41	239.12.1.1	UDP	118	57504 → 45678 Len=76

5. On Core1, review that the host in VLAN 12 has joined using IGMP.

```
ICX-Tx-Core1(config)# show ip igmp group 239.x.1.1
IGMP group information for group 239.12.1.1

Interface Name    : vlan12
VRF Name          : default

Group Address     : 239.12.1.1
Last Reporter     : 10.x.12.y

                                  V1        V2        Sources   Sources
Vers Mode Uptime    Expires   Timer     Timer     Forwarded Blocked
---- ---- --------- --------- --------- --------- --------- --------
3    EXC  4m 13s    3m 7s
```

6. On the Core1, review the multicast routing table. Notice the downstream interface; this was initiated based on the IGMP join. The Proxy DR is used by VSX to synchronize the active multicast routes between the two VSX nodes.

```
ICX-Tx-Core1(config)# show ip mroute 239.x.1.1
IP Multicast Route Entries

VRF : default

Group Address                 : 239.12.1.1
Source Address                : 10.x.11.y
Neighbor                      : 10.x.11.3
Incoming interface            : vlan11
Multicast Routing Protocol    : PIM-SM
Unicast Routing Protocol      : connected
Metric                        : 0
Metric  Pref                  : 0
Downstream Interface
Interface      State              By_Proxy_Dr
---------      -----              -----------
vlan12         forwarding         false
```

7. And check the VSX-peer as well (output from Core2).

```
ICX-Tx-Core1(config)# show ip mroute 239.x.1.1 vsx-peer
IP Multicast Route Entries

VRF : default

Group Address                  : 239.12.1.1
Source Address                 : 10.x.11.y
Neighbor                       : 10.x.11.2
Incoming interface             : vlan11
Multicast Routing Protocol     : PIM-SM
Unicast Routing Protocol       : connected
Metric                         : 0
Metric  Pref                   : 0
Downstream Interface
Interface       State                By_Proxy_Dr
---------       -----                -----------
vlan12          forwarding           true

Group Address                  : 239.12.1.1
Source Address                 : 10.x.11.y
Neighbor                       : 10.x.12.2
Incoming interface             : vlan12
Multicast Routing Protocol     : PIM-SM
Unicast Routing Protocol       : connected
Metric                         : 0
Metric  Pref                   : 0
```

Learning Check

1. What is one advantage of PIM-DM as compared to PIM-SM?
   a. PIM-DM uses bandwidth more conservatively.
   b. PIM-DM tends to be simpler to set up.
   c. PIM-DM is designed for routing across WAN links.
   d. PIM-DM does not require the use of IGMP.
2. A network administrator is configuring a multicast routing solution. Potential multicast receivers are a VLAN 5. What must the administrator enable on this VLAN?
   a. PIM-DM only
   b. PIM-DM and IGMP
   c. IGMP only
   d. PIM-DM and PIM-SM

Summary

Congratulations! You are now familiar with Protocol Independent Multicast (PIM), which allows switches to determine which interfaces should receive multicast traffic in a Layer-3 network, like a campus. Where IGMP learns what devices are or need to be using a particular multicast stream, PIM routes the multicast stream across a Layer-3 network. In this chapter, you learned about the two modes of PIM—dense mode and sparse mode—and their advantages and disadvantages.

10 802.1X Authentication

OBJECTIVES

By the time that you have completed this chapter, you should be able to:

✓ Implement 802.1X on AOS-CX switch ports

✓ Integrate AOS-CX switches with an Aruba ClearPass solution, which might apply dynamic VLAN assignments, ACLs, quality of service (QoS) priorities, and rate limits

✓ Understand when to use local user roles and downloadable user roles

Overview

This chapter introduces you to port-based authentication and teaches you how to implement 802.1X authentication technology on AOS-CX switches. You will learn of a very scalable, flexible, and easy-to-use feature to apply policies: local user roles and downloadable user roles.

Introduction to User Authentication

You will first be introduced to the topic of authentication of user devices connecting to a network.

Port-Based Authentication

Port-based authentication works within the Authentication, Authorization, and Accounting (AAA) model. AAA provides a framework for implementing centralized policies to control access to particular services. For port-based authentication, network access is the service in question, and the AAA server is usually a RADIUS server (Figure 10-1). In detail, AAA defines:

- **Authentication**—A user must prove his or her identity in some way to the authentication server. As you will see, for port-based authentication, the user usually submits a username and password. The user might alternatively submit a digital certificate that includes a valid username and is signed by a trusted certificate authority (CA).
- **Authorization**—The authenticated user is authorized by a RADIUS server policy to obtain network access. The policy might authorize the user for particular port settings (such as VLAN and rate limit), which the switch port applies dynamically.
- **Accounting**—The switch submits information about the user's connection to the RADIUS accounting server, supporting user tracking and auditing functions.

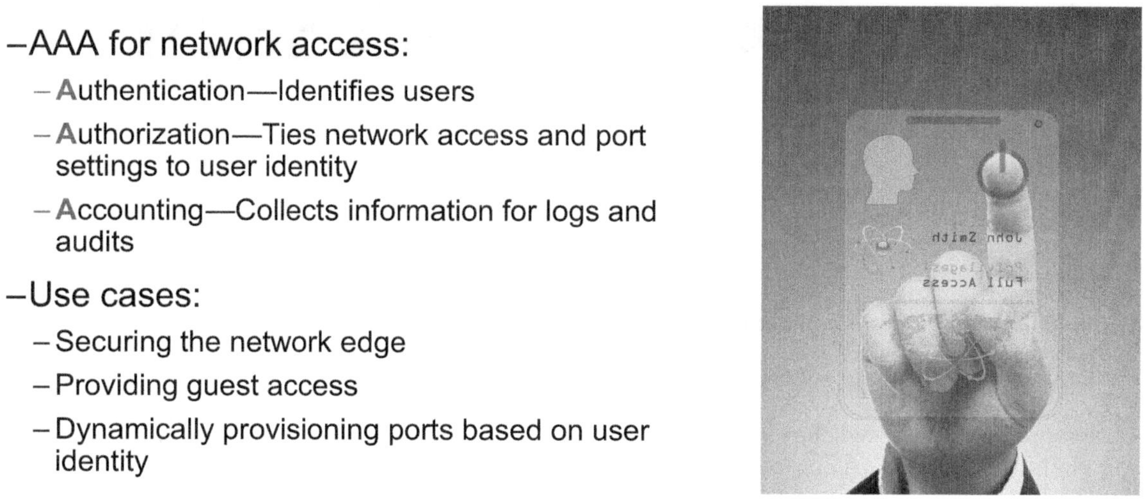

Figure 10-1 Port-Based Authentication

Companies typically implement port-based authentication for one or more of these reasons:

- They need to prevent unauthorized users from connecting to open ports. This security may be required to comply with their own security policies, which may include compliance with government regulations.
- They want to provide guest access, ensuring that guests are placed in the proper guest VLAN and also forcing guests to log in for legal and tracking purposes.
- They have user groups with different access rights and want to ensure the correct port settings for each group. Users might connect to any port, so the IT staff would struggle to keep up. In addition, companies may want to ensure users are given consistent access no matter how they log in—from a wired or a mobile connection. The authorization component of port-based authentication enables the port to adjust to the user dynamically.

For example, a school district might have a faculty/administrators VLAN and a student VLAN. Port-based authentication enables any user to connect to any port. Users submit their identity to the centralized authentication server, which directs the switch port to grant the user access in the correct VLAN.

As you will learn, port-based authentication can also dynamically provision ports with ACLs, rate limits, and other settings.

Note

This chapter focuses on employee authentication.

Controlling Network Access

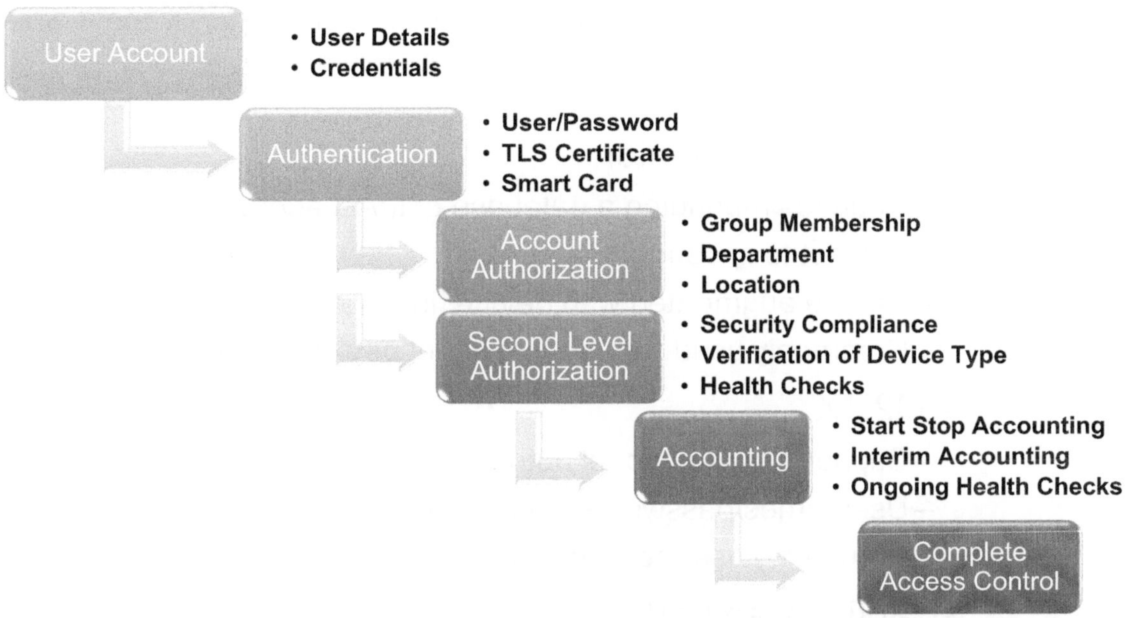

Figure 10-2 Controlling Network Access

All of the functionality in the health club example exists on your network. When the user joins the organization, they are given an account that has details about their relationship to the organization and they are issued some form of credentials to reference back to the account.

During authentication, the network checks the user's credentials for validity. Typically, this is done via an AAA server like ClearPass.

Then network authorizes the user's account details and client device. The network may grant or deny access based on a complete picture of the client.

If network gives the client access to the network, the system will continue to monitor the client's activity. This is done through start/stop and interim accounting messages and ongoing compliance checks.

By leveraging all of the available information and implementing sound access rules, the network, utilizing an AAA tool like ClearPass, becomes a complete access control system (Figure 10-2).

Common Methods of Authentication

Authentication is the process of identifying and determining the identity or a user or device on the WLAN. In most cases you want to ensure that you only allow authorized users with proper network credentials to use the network. This is similar to checking a driver's license credential to verify someone's identity (Figure 10-3).

A MAC address, passphrase, password, or certificate all serve to authenticate a user. The credential is pre-configured on the network for the user. The user successfully authenticates after presenting a credential that matches the network's credential. If the credential that the user presents does not match the stored credential, then the user will not receive network access.

- MAC authentication
  - Requires managing a database of MAC addresses
  - Subject to spoofing
  - Can be augmented with device fingerprinting
  - Commonly used for non-intelligent devices, like IoT
- 802.1X
  - Supports bi-directional authentication
  - Usernames/passwords and/or certificates
  - Commonly used for employees
- Captive/web portal
  - Commonly used in guest networks
  - User device uses a web browser to authenticate
  - Commonly used for guests

Figure 10-3 Common Methods of Authentication

MAC authentication is a rudimentary form of authentication whereby the controller validates a WLAN client radio MAC address against a list of valid MAC addresses. The network access device (NAD) reads the client MAC address from the physical hardware NIC and then stores it in the software registry in Windows or other OS, making it susceptible to MAC spoofing. Additionally, the MAC address is not encrypted, including wireless, so it is easy to capture it and spoof to gain access to the WLAN. A common strategy for WLAN clients that do not support advanced enterprise class authentication such as EAP is to use MAC filtering in conjunction with another method of access control or device fingerprinting. Device fingerprinting is examining protocol information from a device, like DHCP and HTTP payload information, and using this information to identify additional information about the device, like the product, operating system, and other information.

The Extensible Authentication Protocol (EAP) is a common way of authenticating WLAN users to the network using a RADIUS server such as Active Directory or ClearPass. There are many flavors of EAP, including PEAP, EAP-TLS, EAP-TTLS, and others. These EAP types are primarily intended for use with open media such as wireless. EAP uses 802.1X to transport the user credentials between the user device and the NAD. 802.1X happens at Layer 2 where users will be authenticated before an IP address is assigned. This is independent of the Layer-3 protocol. Most NAD solutions will then forward the EAP information onward to a centralized AAA server using the RADIUS protocol.

Some WLANs also use Layer-3 authentication such as Captive Portal web authentication or VPN software. Captive portal is commonly used in guest networks to register and restrict their access. Captive portal is web based and thus only requires a web browser on the user device. Given that web is based on the HTTP protocol, minimal layer-3 access needs to be allowed: DHCP, DNS, and restricted HTTP to perform the captive portal process.

Aruba's dynamic segmentation feature, which is unique in the industry, automatically enforces consistent policies across wired and wireless networks to keep traffic for any user or device separate and secure, regardless of the application or service. The Aruba switch (AOS or AOS-CX) performs the authentication function and tunnels the user traffic to an Aruba Mobility Controller, which will then provide the authorization function via firewall, bandwidth, and other security policies. This feature allows you to extend the user role, application deep packet inspection, and device profiling features on the Aruba Mobility Controllers for both wireless and wired access, simplifying and centralizing your authorization policy decisions. Dynamic segmentation still uses MAC-Auth, 802.1X, or captive portal authentication; what's unique about dynamic segmentation is:

- Applying user roles (authorization policies)
- Locally switching the traffic or tunneling it to a mobility controller

Basic 802.1X

You will first examine 802.1X, an open standard technology for controlling users' network access based on their identity.

802.1X Overview

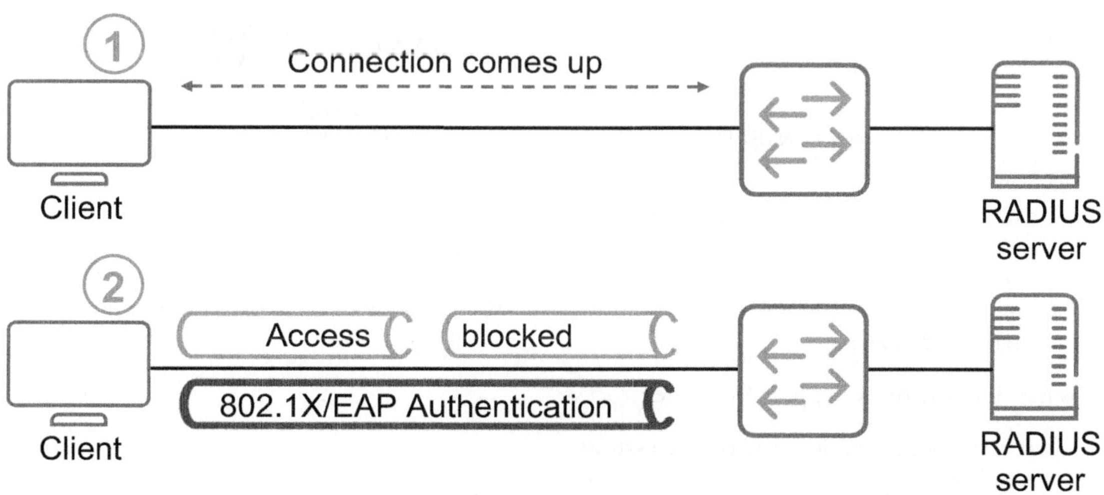

Figure 10-4 802.1X Overview

802.1X forces users to authenticate as soon as the connection between the switch port and the client comes up (Figure 10-4). To restrict an unauthenticated user so that client can send only authentication messages, 802.1X divides the port into two logical ports.

Controlled Port

The controlled port allows all types of traffic, but it can be disabled. Both sides of the connection control the port based on their assessment of the authentication state. In other words, no unauthorized traffic flows across the link.

Uncontrolled Port

The uncontrolled port is always active, but it can carry only the Extensible Authentication Protocol (EAP) packets used for authentication.

Without the uncontrolled port, this high level of security would shut out all traffic from users, preventing even authorized users from proving that they are authorized.

Note, however, that the uncontrolled port does not carry DHCP messages, DNS messages, and so on. You will see how 802.1X allows the client to authenticate without an IP address.

802.1X Device Roles

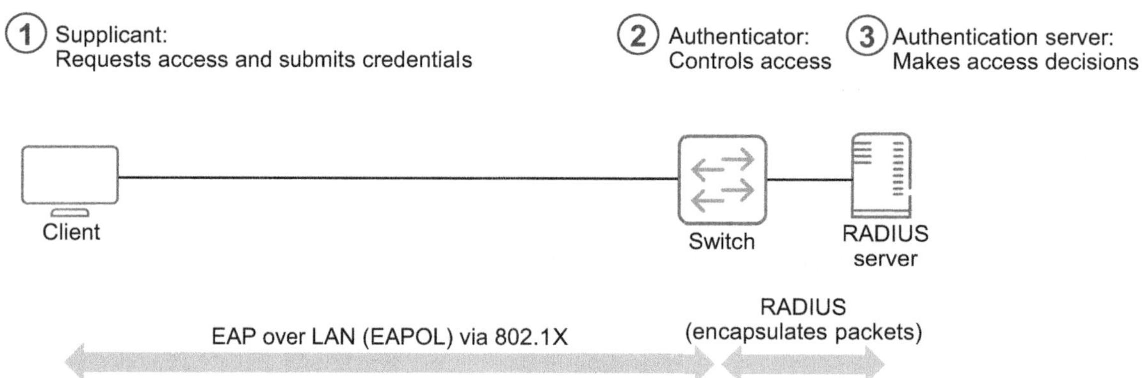

Figure 10-5 802.1X Device Roles

To understand 802.1X authentication, you must understand the devices involved in the process and the role each device plays:

- What does the device expect from the process?
- What responsibilities does the device assume?
- What protocols does the device use to communicate?

Keep these questions in mind as you learn about the three devices involved in the 802.1X authentication process:

- Supplicant
- Authenticator
- Authentication server

Supplicant

The supplicant is the 802.1X component that runs on the endpoint attempting to connect to the network.

The supplicant requests access to the network and proves that it deserves this access by authenticating—typically in response to a challenge from the far end of the connection (for example, the switch port).

In addition to responding to a challenge, the supplicant may also initiate the authentication process on its own behalf by transmitting an EAP-Start packet. This mechanism protects supplicants that receive the challenge before the station has entirely booted, causing authentication to time out before the user can submit his or her credentials.

Authenticator

The authenticator is the 802.1X component on the other side of the supplicant's connection. In this guide, the authenticator is the AOS-CX switch. The authenticator controls network access, forcing a supplicant to authenticate before it can send any non-EAP traffic over the connection. The authenticator initiates the authentication process but then relays authentication messages between the supplicant and the authentication server.

After the authentication is completed, the authenticator decides how to control the connection. If the authentication server has accepted the user's request, the authenticator opens the controlled port, allowing traffic to flow. In other words, the station is now completely connected to the network. If the authentication server rejects the user's request, the authenticator enforces this denial and keeps the port closed.

Authentication Server

The authentication server makes decisions about whether or not users can access the network. These decisions are based on criteria such as whether the user:

- Can prove his or her identity (the users' credentials are correct)
- Is connecting in the proper time and location

For example, even legitimate guests might be prohibited from accessing the network after regular work hours.

The server also submits its own credentials to the supplicant. In essence, the supplicant and the server authenticate each other, although the authenticator always acts as a proxy in this process.

The authentication server is a RADIUS server, and the authenticator and authentication server use RADIUS messages to communicate. The authenticator encapsulates the supplicant's EAP messages in this protocol (Figure 10-5).

802.1X Requirements

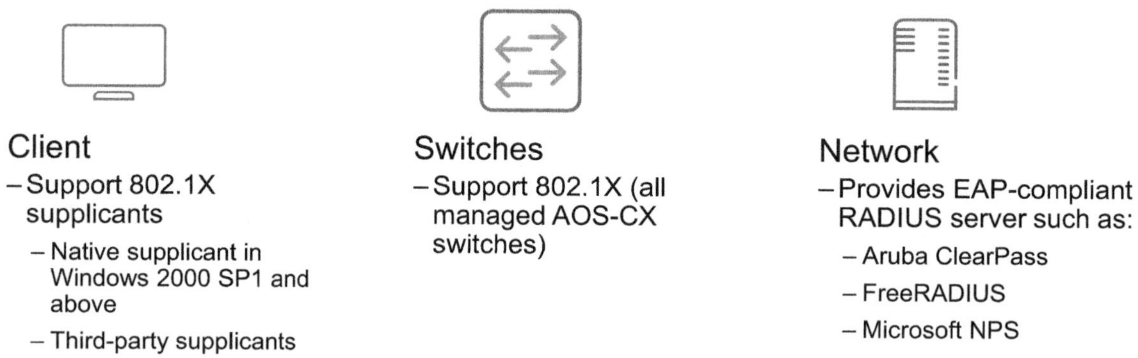

Figure 10-6 802.1X Requirements

802.1X requires particular capabilities on clients, network servers, and switches (Figure 10-6).

First, the switch must support this authentication standard, which AOS-CX switches do.

Next, your network also requires a RADIUS server:

- Aruba ClearPass provides a RADIUS server, as well as other capabilities for monitoring and managing user access.
- You can alternatively use a third-party RADIUS server such as Microsoft Network Policy Server (NPS) or an open source server such as FreeRADIUS.

In addition, any device that needs an Ethernet connection must include an 802.1X supplicant. Windows and Mac operating systems provide native supplicants, which you can use. You can also choose from a number of third-party supplicants, including freely available ones.

EAP and RADIUS Together

EAP Framework

Now that you have seen the 802.1X authentication process in action, you will examine how it works in more detail. Understanding this process can help you to pinpoint and troubleshoot issues.

EAP, the protocol 802.1X uses for authentication, defines a flexible framework into which you can fit authentication methods that meet the needs of your environment and security policies. The illustration above shows this general framework. As you follow the process, remember that the authenticator (switch) relays all messages from the client to the RADIUS server, encapsulating them with RADIUS as necessary. The vertical line underneath the switch shows the point at which the authenticator encapsulates the messages (Figure 10-7).

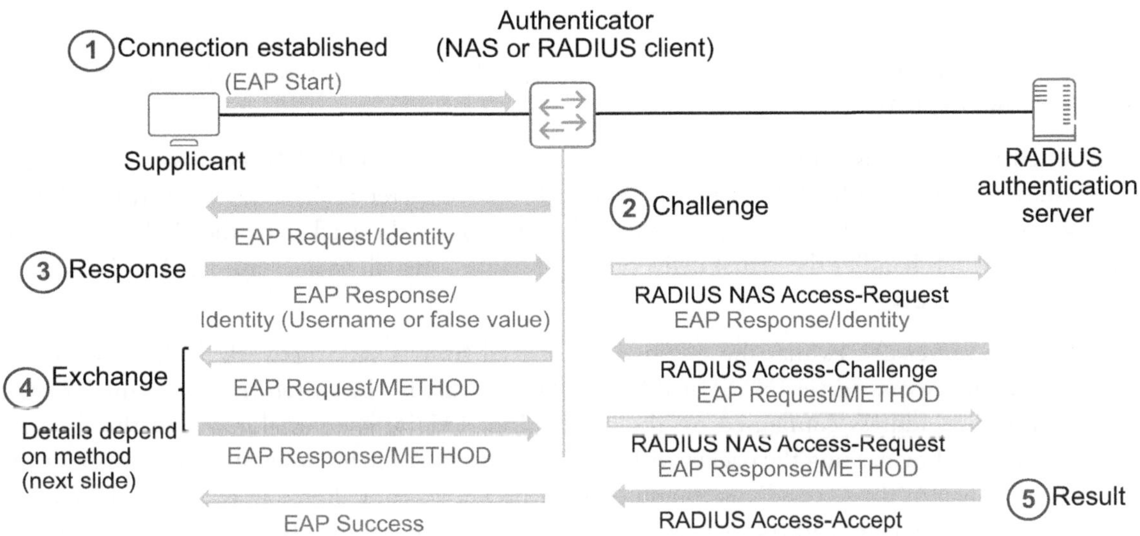

Figure 10-7 EAP and RADIUS Together

1. The client and switch port establish an Ethernet connection.
2. The switch keeps the controlled port shut, blocking all traffic except EAP, and issues a challenge. The challenge is an EAP Request/Identity packet. Basically, this frame initiates the authentication process and asks the client to identify itself but not to send any other information.
3. The client responds with an EAP Response/Identity packet, which typically includes a username. The authenticator includes the user's identity in all future frames so that the server can keep track of which EAP messages belong to which user. The user's identity also marks any accounting frames for the connection—which are important for companies with rigorous auditing requirements. Depending on the EAP method, though, the username submitted at this point might not

be the actual username. Some methods have the supplicant submit a false name at this point and the true name later in the process after a secure and encrypted session has been established. This protects the username from hackers.

4. The RADIUS server receives the EAP Response/Identity (forwarded in RADIUS by the switch). The server initiates an EAP method for exchanging credentials. The particular messages and type of authentication credentials exchanged by the client and server depend on the EAP method.

5. Based on information received in step 4, the authentication server determines whether or not the client has authenticated successfully and informs the switch. The switch then either activates the connection and transmits an EAP-Success or leaves the connection deactivated and transmits an EAP-Failure.

EAP and RADIUS Together

Now let us look at how the authenticator (switch) actually relays the messages between the client supplicant and the RADIUS server.

The authenticator encapsulates a supplicant's EAP message in a RADIUS Access-Request packet. It also hashes the packet with MD5, using the RADIUS shared secret as the key. It adds the hash to a message authenticator field. The authenticator then transmits the packet to the RADIUS server. Because the switch handles the actual delivery of the frames, the client does not need an IP address or any network access.

The RADIUS server checks that the message has arrived from a valid network device (sometimes called a Network Access Server [NAS] or RADIUS client); that is, the switch IP address must match a network device address configured on the server. The RADIUS server also checks the message authenticator field by hashing the packet with its shared secret. If the hashes match, it knows that the valid client truly sent the Access Request and that the packet was not altered in transit. If the request is not from a known network device with a correct shared secret, the RADIUS server does not respond to the message.

If the switch is known and uses a correct secret, though, the server decapsulates the EAP messages and formulates the appropriate responses, which it encapsulates in RADIUS Challenge messages. These messages are also authenticated with the message authenticator field.

At the end of the process, the RADIUS server sends either:

- An Access-Accept message—Two requirements are met:
  - The client has successfully authenticated.
  - The policy that applies to this access request allows access.

- An Access-Reject message—One of these situations occurred:
  - The client could not complete authentication, whether because the RADIUS server does not trust the authenticator, because the client and server do not support compatible EAP methods, or some other problem.
  - The client does not trust the RADIUS server's certificate, so the server failed authentication.
  - The client failed authentication.
  - The policy that applies to this access request does not allow access.
  - No policy applies to this access request.

To ensure that the switch can participate in this process, you must set the correct RADIUS server address or addresses and the correct RADIUS secret. You need to make sure that the switch uses the same RADIUS authentication port as the RADIUS server. You also need to ensure that the switch sends the RADIUS messages with the source IP address specified as a valid NAS or RADIUS client on the server.

Choosing an EAP Method

–Consider:

- Supported methods on client and RADIUS server
- Security needs
- Ease of implementation

EAP method	RADIUS server certificate	Supplicant certificate
EAP-TLS	Yes	Yes
PEAP MS-CHAPv2	Yes	No

Figure 10-8 Choosing an EAP Method

When choosing an EAP method, you must always consider if both the supplicant and the server support the method. EAP-TTLS tends to be less widely supported (Figure 10-8). For example, Microsoft Windows does not support TTLS natively; you must install additional software to provide this support.

The AOS-CX switch, as the authenticator, simply encapsulates and decapsulates the EAP messages, which it can do for any valid method.

Note

You can configure local authentication for 802.1X and have the switch act as the authentication server. In this case, you would need to consider the EAP methods that the switch supports. However, this guide does not cover this use case. Check the *Security Guide* documentation for more details.

You should also keep in mind the level of security that you require. EAP-TLS tends to be the most secure choice because users authenticate with secure digital certificates. On the other hand, many enterprises prefer PEAP or EAP-TTLS because usernames and passwords provide enough security for their purposes. They value the easier implementation of PEAP or EAP-TTLS with an inner method such as MS-CHAPv2.

Note that, although some EAP methods do not require client certificates, EAP-TLS, EAP-TTLS, and PEAP all require a certificate on the RADIUS server. The server uses this certificate to authenticate to the clients and generate key material for the secure TLS tunnel. System administrators should make sure to install a valid certificate, signed by a trusted CA, on the RADIUS server. If they choose to use a self-signed certificate on the RADIUS server, they should install that certificate as trusted on client. Or they could configure the clients to prompt users to validate an untrusted certificate on the first connection.

Note

EAP-TTLS and PEAP could use TLS as an inner method, which would require a supplicant certificate. However, this is not a typical implementation.

Common EAP Methods: EAP-TLS

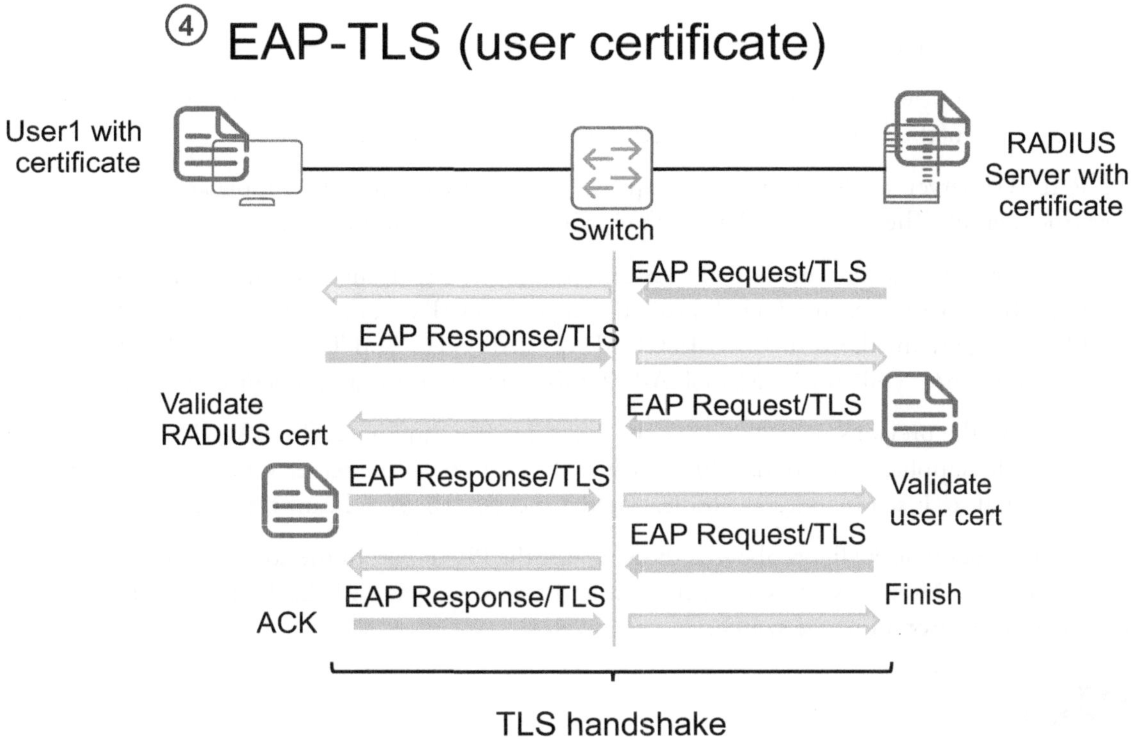

Figure 10-9 Common EAP Methods: EAP-TLS

PEAP and EAP-Tunneled TLS (TTLS)

Protected EAP (PEAP) was developed to provide much of the security of EAP-TLS without forcing stations to have digital certificates—drastically reducing implementation costs. For this reason, it is among the most commonly used EAP methods (Figure 10-9).

Tunneled Transport Layer Security (TTLS) is a similar, but less commonly used, method. (TTLS was developed by Funk Software and Certicom; PEAP was developed by Microsoft, Cisco Systems, and RSA Security.)

TTLS and PEAP function in very similar ways. Both methods involve a two-step authentication process; in the first step, the outer method creates a secure tunnel in which the second step takes place.

Step 1—Outer Method

Like EAP-TLS, TTLS and PEAP use a TLS handshake to generate encryption keys and negotiate a tunnel secured by those keys. Only the server authenticates itself with a digital certificate during this exchange, but you must ensure that the clients trust the CA that signed the server certificate. The encryption keys for the tunnel are derived from the public key in this certificate.

Step 2—Inner Method

The client authenticates itself in the second step; it uses a weaker—and so more easily implemented—authentication method, protected by the secure tunnel in which it takes place.

The RADIUS server sends a new EAP Request/Identity packet and the supplicant responds with their true identity. The server then begins the inner authentication method.

For the inner authentication method, TTLS can use a weaker EAP method, such as EAP-GTC, or a legacy RADIUS method, such as CHAP, PAP, or Microsoft CHAP variants (MS-CHAP v1 or MS-CHAP v2). PEAP supports methods such as MS-CHAP v2, EAP-GTC, and TLS. Because Windows native supplicants support PEAPv0 with MS-CHAP v2, this is by far the most prevalent EAP method.

The figure on the previous page illustrates the MS-CHAP v2 method. The RADIUS server sends a challenge. The supplicant responds with a hash of the password. The server validates that the hash is correct, and, if so, it sends a message indicating the success. The supplicant responds.

Again, remember that the figure above is showing just the PEAP part of the complete 802.1X authentication process. After these messages, the tunnel is taken down, and the RADIUS server sends a RADIUS Access-Accept to the switch.

Note

For 802.1X on wireless connections, whether implemented through EAP-TLS, EAP-TTLS, or PEAP, the authentication server sends the authenticator the encryption material. The wireless client and authenticator continue to use encryption to secure the connection. On Ethernet connections, however, the client and switch port do not encrypt traffic in this way.

Advantages

Like EAP-TLS, EAP-TTLS and PEAP provide strong, mutual authentication. Because TTLS and PEAP use encrypted tunnels to secure usernames and passwords (rather than require digital certificates on stations), you can implement these methods more easily than you can TLS.

TTLS has one unique benefit: it always protects the username. Depending on how PEAP is implemented, the username might be transmitted in plain text in the initial EAP/Response Identity packet, allowing a hacker to detect the user's identity and possibly lock the user out of his or her account.

Disadvantages

As compared to EAP-TLS, EAP-TTLS and PEAP have the disadvantage of a weaker authentication method.

Configuring 802.1X

Configuring 802.1X typically involves two components: defining one or more RADIUS servers and setting up 802.1X locally on the switch. This section introduces both configuration components.

Specifying the RADIUS Server

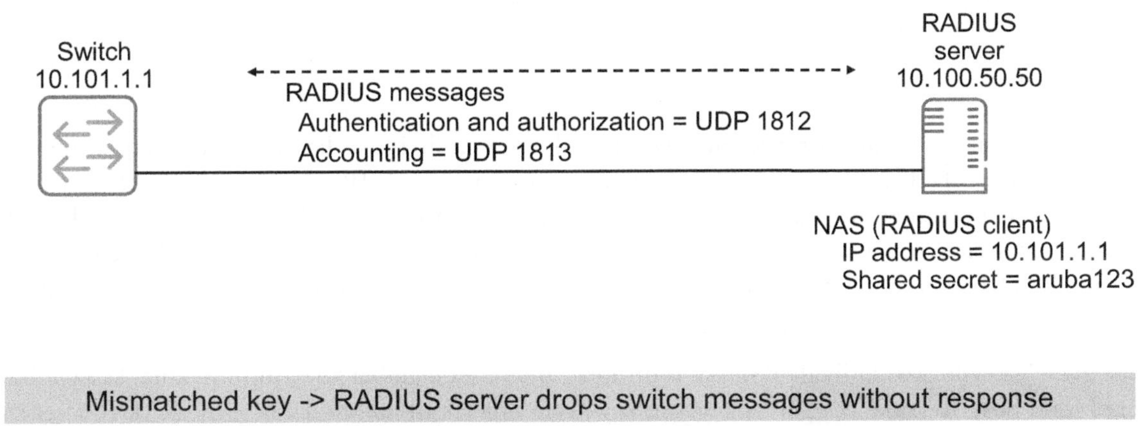

Figure 10-10 Specifying the RADIUS Server

Before you enable 802.1X on a switch, you must set up the authentication server that the switch will use. Define the RADIUS server that with this command:

```
Switch(config)# radius-server host <IP-address-or-FQDK>
       key plaintext <secret-key> [port <port-number>] [timeout <seconds>]
       [auth-type {pap | chap}] [acct-port <ACCT-PORT>]
       [retries <RETRY-COUNT>] [vrf <VRF-name>]
```

The switch will then send a RADIUS Access-Request to this IP address whenever it needs to complete any form of authentication that uses RADIUS as its type. By default, the switch uses the RADIUS standard UDP port 1812 for the authentication messages. After the RADIUS server has authorized a user for access, the switch can continue to communicate information about the user session in accounting packets sent to port 1813 (Figure 10-10).

If you define an FQDN name for the RADIUS server, you will have to define a DNS server to resolve the name to an IP address:

```
Switch(config)# ip dns server-address <IP-ADDR> [vrf <VRF-NAME>]
```

Without this command, using an FQDN for the RADIUS server host address will fail.

You will learn how to configure the switch to use RADIUS for authenticating and accounting 802.1X users in a moment.

Note

You can also include the option **auth-port** and **acct-port** options in the **radius-server host** command to change the authentication and accounting ports. You can add a number of other options, which are documented in the switch *Security* guide.

Global Key or Shared Secret

The key option in the **radius-server host** command sets an individual shared secret for communicating with the RADIUS server. The RADIUS server has the switch IP address configured on it as a RADIUS client (sometimes called Network Access Server (NAS) or, on ClearPass, a network device). The shared secret configured for the switch on the RADIUS server must match the key configured for the RADIUS server on the switch. Otherwise, the RADIUS server will not respond to the switch's messages.

Setting the key for the individual server is optional if you set a global key. An individual key configured for a host overrides the global key, but if you do not set an individual key, the RADIUS server uses the global key. You might choose to use the global key if you have multiple RADIUS servers that use the same shared secret. The command for setting a global key is:

```
Switch(config)# radius-server key plaintext <secret-key>
```

Defining a RADIUS host with a key will override the global key setting.

Note

RADSEC (RADIUS with TLS) is supported by AOS-CX switch in version 10.05. To configure this, see the *Security* guide.

Need for Changing Authorization Information for Devices Dynamically

The two examples shown in Figure 10-11 illustrate situations where a user has authenticated, but their authorization information needs to change based on what is happening in the network. In the first example, the user authenticates and is assigned their normal VLAN. However, once the user's session times out, they should be placed in a restricted VLAN until they re-authenticated. Or in the second example, a company originally deployed PEAP for 802.1X, but is migrating to certificates. If a user connects and uses PEAP, they should be placed in a restricted VLAN that allows them to perform onboarding. Once the user is onboarded and has downloaded a root and a new identity certificate, they should re-authenticate using EAP-TLS and be placed in their normal VLAN.

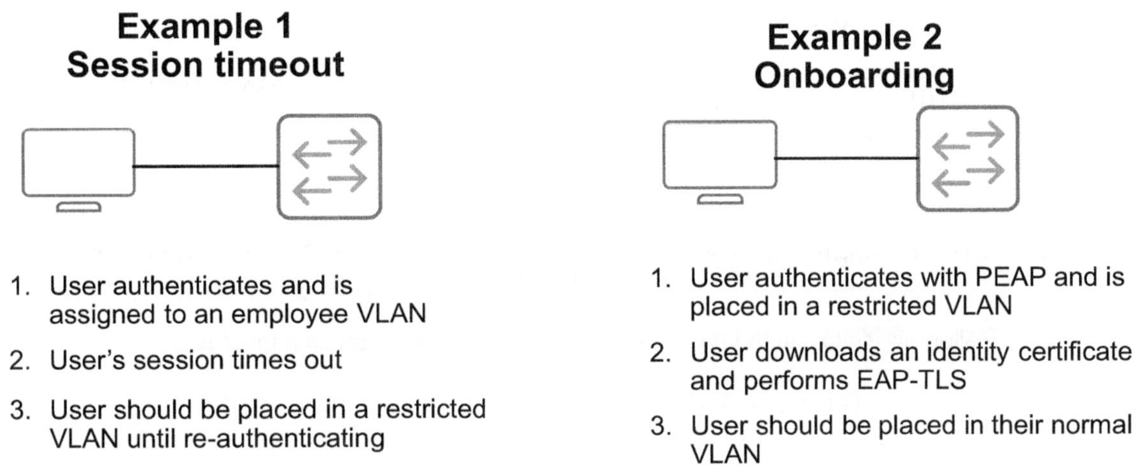

Figure 10-11 Need for Changing Authorization Information for Devices Dynamically

There are many examples where a company needs to change authorization information based on what devices are doing in the network: using the authorization information originally assigned to the user when they authenticated can create problems based on these network changes. RADIUS supports a Change of Authorization (CoA) that allows a RADIUS server to push new authorization information to a network device and have it use for a user's session.

Important
Most networking devices ignore RADIUS CoA messages from an AAA server unless you explicitly enable it. This is true of both ArubaOS and AOS-CX switches.

Dynamic Authorization Configuration

When you use Aruba ClearPass as the RADIUS server, it is recommended that you add a few settings to ensure that the AOS-CX switch interoperates with the ClearPass RADIUS server correctly (Figure 10-12).

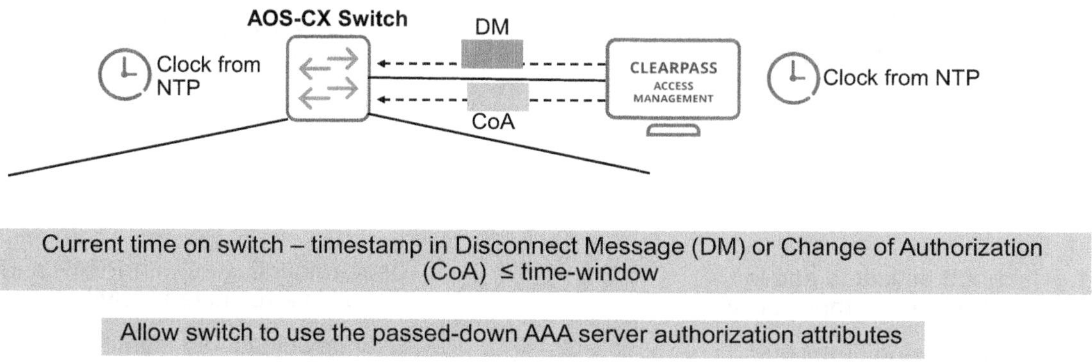

Figure 10-12 Dynamic Authorization Configuration

Enabling Acceptance of Change of Authorization (CoA) Messages

Aruba ClearPass can assess endpoints on an ongoing basis and change an endpoint's authentication status or settings. To make these changes, ClearPass sends disconnect messages (DMs) and CoA messages. For the switch to accept these messages, you must enable dynamic authorization for the RADIUS globally on the switch:

```
Switch(config)# radius-server dyn-authorization enable
```

If you do not include this option, some components of the solution might work, but others will fail.

If **dyn-authorization** is enabled, the switch accepts these messages on the default UDP port 3799, which is also the default port on ClearPass. You can change that setting, if necessary, in your environment:

```
Switch(config)# radius-server dyn-authorization port <number>
```

If you are using a different RADIUS server from ClearPass, you should check whether the server needs to send DMs (disconnect messages) and change of authorization (CoA) messages.

You can use the **show radius dyn-authorization** command to verify the configuration and operation of CoA for all servers, and restrict the view to one server with the **show radius dyn-authorization client** command.

Setting the Time Window

Even when an AOS-CX switch is configured to allow CoA and DM messages, it checks these messages to determine if they are current. The message should include a timestamp for the event that caused the RADIUS server to change the user status. The switch only accepts the message if the time between the timestamp and the current time on the switch falls within its RADIUS time window.

The default time window is 300 seconds. You can adjust the time window with this command:

```
Switch(config)# radius dyn-authorization client <IP-address-or-FQDN>
                time-window <1-65535> [vrf <VRF-name>]
```

To ensure that the switch can accept the CoA and DM messages, make sure that the switch has the correct time. It is best practice to configure NTP on the switch and the RADIUS server and have them take their time from the same clock.

You must also determine whether the RADIUS server always includes a timestamp with its DM and CoA messages. ClearPass does not.

Unlike the older ArubaOS switches, you cannot disable the time window check. Instead set up NTP. Here is an example configuration to specify an NTP server (10.250.1.3) in the mgmt VRF.

```
PX-6300-A(config)# ntp server 10.250.1.3 iburst
PX-6300-A(config)# ntp vrf mgmt
PX-6300-A(config)# ntp enable
PX-6300-A(config)# ntp authentication
PX-6300-A(config)# ntp authentication-key 1 sha1 aruba123 trusted
```

For the explanation of these commands, see the *Fundamentals Guide*.

Enabling 802.1X

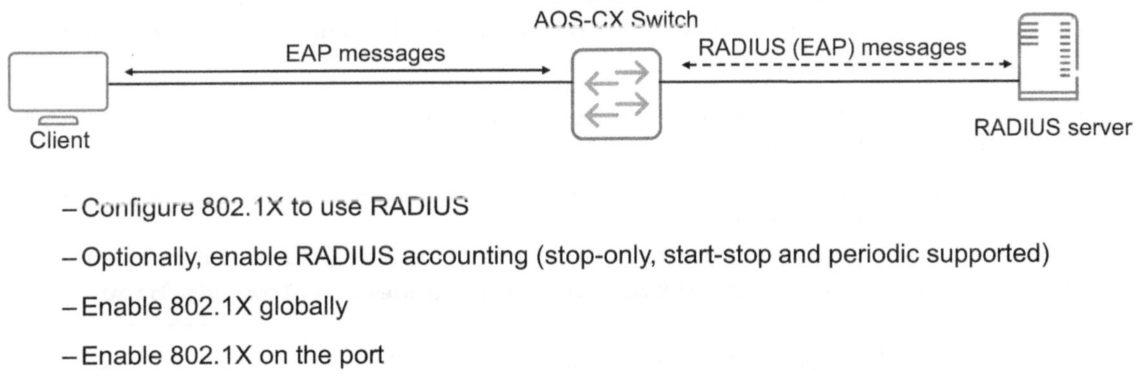

Figure 10-13 Enabling 802.1X

After you have specified the RADIUS server, you can enable 802.1X (Figure 10-13). First, specify that you want to use RADIUS authentication with 802.1X using this command:

```
Switch(config)# aaa authentication port-access dot1x
                    authenticator auth-method eap-radius
```

To specify that any RADIUS server can be used on the switch, you must configure the following command:

```
Switch(config)# aaa authentication port-access dot1x
                    authenticator radius server-group radius
```

The first server defined with the **radius-server host** command will be used, by default. A bit later you will see how you can restrict the use of a particular RADIUS server(s) by creating a group.

However, the switch does not actually enforce 802.1X on the specified interfaces until you also enable 802.1X globally:

```
Switch(config)# aaa authentication port-access dot1x authenticator
enable
```

Last, you enable 802.1X on a per-interface basis with this command:

```
Switch(config)# interface <interface-id>
Switch(config-if)# aaa authentication port-access dot1x authenticator
Switch(config-if-dot1x-auth)# enable
```

Now the switch will act as described earlier. It will keep the port closed to all non-EAP traffic and send EAP messages to trigger an 802.1X supplicant on the connected device to authenticate. If the user succeeds in authenticating to the RADIUS server, the switch opens the port for normal traffic. If the user fails, the port remains closed.

If you need to allow LLDP/CDP or BPDU packets on a secure port, you will need to configure the following on the respective interface:

```
switch(config)# interface <interface-ID>
switch(config-if)# aaa authentication port-access allow-lldp-bpdu
switch(config-if)# aaa authentication port-access allow-cdp-bpdu
```

This configuration might be necessary for devices like a phone or camera where LLDP (or Cisco's CDP) must be exchanged for the device to operate correctly prior to authentication occurring on the port.

RADIUS accounting

If you want to enable RADIUS accounting for 802.1X, enter this command:

```
Switch(config)# aaa accounting port-access start-stop
                    group {radius | <GROUP-NAME>}
```

RADIUS accounting takes effect after a user successfully authenticates. The switch then creates a session for the user, defining the network access that the user is provided. If you selected start-stop, the switch sends a start accounting message to the RADIUS server when the session begins. With either stop-only or start-stop, the switch sends a message when the session ends (because the user disconnects or the session times out, for example). These messages include a number of standard RADIUS attributes that describe the user's identity (User-Name), location (NAS-IP-Address and NAS-Port), and bandwidth consumption (Acct-Output-Packets and Acct-Input-Packets), as well as other information.

For more detailed session tracking, you can configure the switch to send periodic accounting messages during the session:

```
Switch(config)# aaa accounting port-access start-stop interim <minutes>
                    {radius | <GROUP-NAME>}
```

The default interval is 60 minutes—in most cases you will want to make this a smaller interval for more frequent updates to your statistics. Refer to your AOS-CX switch manual's list of network accounting attributes for a complete list of the RADIUS accounting attributes that it supports for 802.1X.

Managing Multiple RADIUS Servers using RADIUS Groups

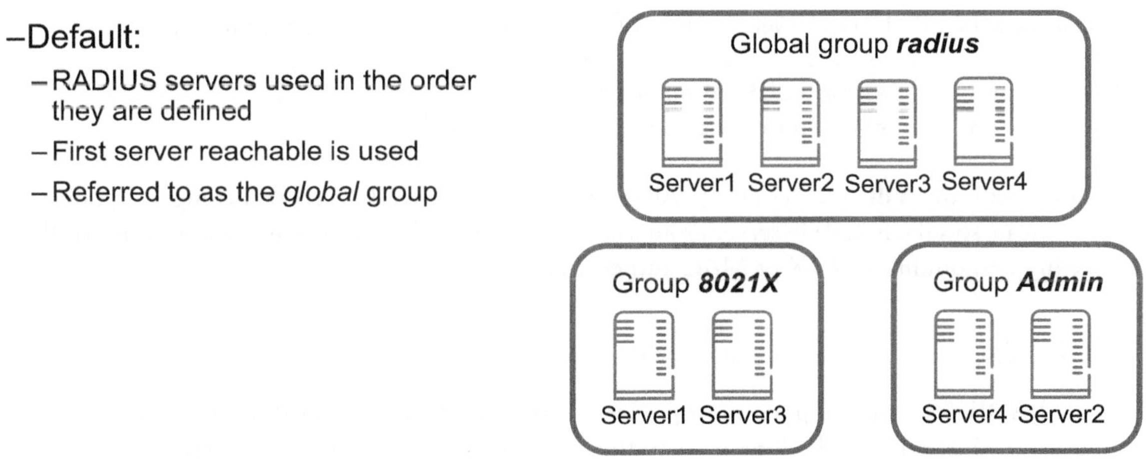

Figure 10-14 Managing Multiple RADIUS Servers using RADIUS Groups

Companies deploy multiple RADIUS servers to provide redundancy. The servers that you add are automatically added to the global RADIUS server group, which is called **radius**. The switch uses this group, by default, for all types of authentication for which you have enabled RADIUS.

For example, you enter this command to enable authentication for 802.1X:

```
Switch(config)# aaa authentication port-access dot1x
                  authenticator radius server-group radius
```

Now the switch uses the global **radius** group to authenticate users who connect to ports with 802.1X enabled on them.

You might want to use only a subset of servers for a particular task, instead of all the globally defined ones. You can do this by creating RADIUS groups (you are restricted to 28 groups per switch).

```
Switch(config)# aaa group server radius <group-name>
Switch(config-sg)# server <IP-address-or-FQDN> vrf <VRF-instance-name>
```

To use a specific group for the 802.1X, in the aaa authentication port-access command, you specify the group name. Here is an example:

```
Switch(config)# aaa group server radius clearpass
Switch(config-sg)# server 10.254.10.10 vrf mgmt
Switch(config-sg)# exit
Switch(config)# aaa authentication port-access dot1x authenticator radius
                  server-group clearpass
```

You can see which RADIUS servers are part of the **radius** group with these commands:

```
Switch(config)# show radius-server
Switch(config)# show aaa server-group radius
```

You cannot edit the **radius** server group. All globally defined RADIUS servers belong to it; however, you can create specific RADIUS server groups and include only the servers you want for the RADIUS service in question, like 802.1X or MAC authentication, for example.

How the Switch Handles Requests to Groups with Multiple Servers

When a RADIUS server group has multiple servers, the switch does *not* load balance requests to different servers. Instead it sends all requests to the first server in the group that it successfully accesses. It uses the other servers as backups in case it cannot reach the first server.

For this reason, you should prepare before adding RADIUS servers to your switch and enable 802.1X. Ensure that the switch has connectivity to the RADIUS servers, and the RADIUS servers are configured to accept messages from it. You should then add the RADIUS servers in the order in which you want the switch to use them.

You can see the order in which the switch will attempt to access RADIUS servers in a particular group by entering the **show server-group radius *<name>*** command. The order is generally based on the order in which you specify the servers; you can specify different servers first on different switches for rudimentary load sharing of requests on a switch-wide basis. The switch first attempts to access the server at the top of the list. If the first server does not respond after a certain timeout and number of retransmit attempts, the switch will try to contact the next RADIUS server.

For example, the default timeout is 5 seconds and the default retransmit setting is 3. After 20 seconds, the switch determines that the RADIUS server is not available. The switch then tries to reach the next RADIUS server in the list. If the switch cannot reach that RADIUS server either, after 20 seconds, it tries the next server on the list. If the switch cannot reach any of the servers, it tries the first server in the list again.

However, you can configure the switch to wait a set period after the last failed retransmit to a particular server before attempting to communicate with that server again. You might do this to prevent a switch from endlessly attempting to send RADIUS packets during a network outage. This period is called the dead time.

These are global settings that apply to all RADIUS servers and groups. You can adjust the timeout (in seconds—5 is the default) and the number of retransmits (1 is the default), and the dead time (in minutes) with these commands:

```
Switch(config)# radius-server timeout <1-60>
Switch(config)# radius-server retries <0-5> fail-through
```

By default, if a RADIUS server is reachable and the user fails authentication, the switch uses this result. However, if the user is a visitor from a different location, like a neighboring campus, and their credentials are not stored on the local campus server, but the remote campus server, the user would be denied access by default.

You can enable the fail-through feature, so that if the first RADIUS server is reachable and returns a "failed" result, the switch can proceed and try other RADIUS servers in the list or group. This feature is disabled by default, but can be enabled with this command:

```
Switch(config)# aaa authentication allow-fail-through
```

Other RADIUS Server Groups

This chapter in the guide focuses on 802.1X authentication. However, as you will learn in other chapters, AOS-CX switches can use RADIUS with other types of authentication such as captive portal and the authentication of Telnet, SSH, or web UI managers.

When you want to use different RADIUS servers for different types of authentication, you need to place those servers in different RADIUS server groups.

You must first define the RADIUS server. You can then add it to a group. There is no command for creating a group. Instead the first time that you add a server to a group with a new name, the switch creates the group and adds the specified server to it.

The command for adding a RADIUS server to a new or existing server group is:

```
Switch(config)# aaa server-group radius <group name> host <IP address>
```

Use the **no** form of the command to delete the server from the group. Each group can have up to three RADIUS servers.

A RADIUS server can be part of more than one group. If, for example, you add a server that is part of the **radius** server group to a new group, the server remains part of the **radius** group, as well. Therefore, you should define the servers that you want to use for the global group *before* adding the servers for the other groups. Otherwise, the servers that you intend for other groups will take up the slots in the global **radius** group.

To use the new RADIUS server group, you must choose the type of authentication to which it applies. Use this command to specify a server group for 802.1X authentication:

```
Switch(config)# aaa authentication port-access eap-radius
                    server-group <group name>
```

RADIUS Group Example

In Figure 10-14, the top part of the picture shows the global group, referred to as *radius* in the CLI configuration. When you define an AAA feature, like 802.1X or restricting administrative access, and reference the global group, the servers RADIUS servers are accessed, in the order you defined them, with the global **radius-server host** commands. However, you can create specific RADIUS groups, like 8021X and Admin, as shown above, and reference these for a specific AAA function. For example, Serverl and Server3 are placed in the AAA server group called *8021X* and this group is then referenced for use in 802.1X AAA functions. The group called *Admin* is referenced in the AAA function that handles administrative access and control on the AAA switches. With the AAA group feature, you can control which servers are used and the order that they are used, outside of how they were originally defined globally with the **radius-server host** commands.

RADIUS Attributes

You will now examine some of the more advanced scenarios for 802.1X authentication.

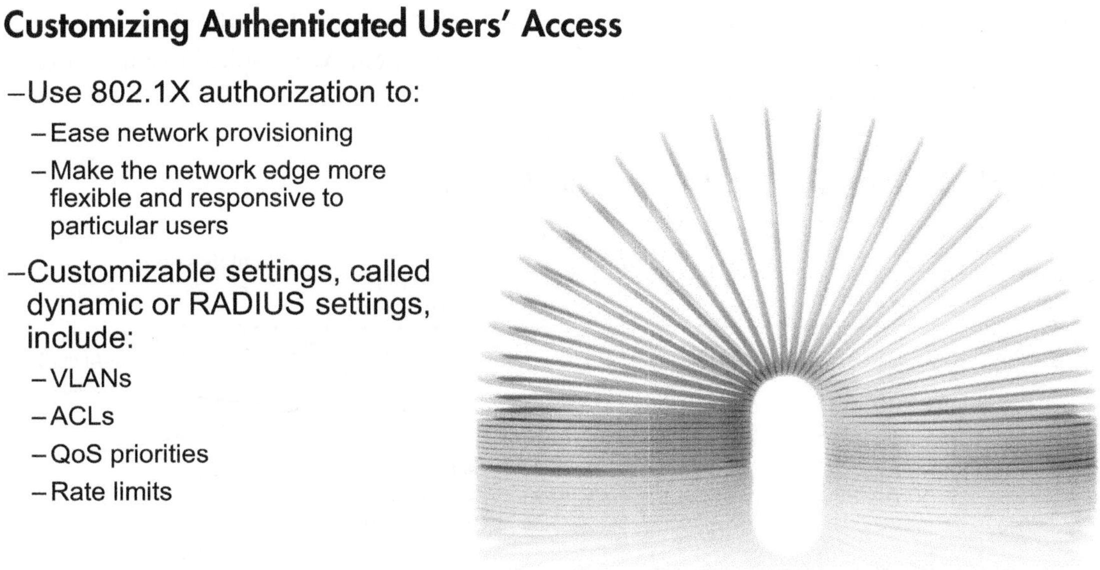

Figure 10-15 Customizing Authenticated Users' Access

Beyond the security benefits, port-based authentication such as 802.1X helps network administrators to provision the network edge more quickly. Traditionally, administrators had to configure each port with the appropriate settings for the user who connected to that port. If a user moved, the user might not receive the correct settings without a great deal of effort on the administrator's part (Figure 10-15).

With 802.1X, the RADIUS server, together with the switch acting as the NAS, have already determined the user's identity as well as other characteristics of the connection, such as the time and location. A RADIUS server policy can use this information to choose the appropriate settings for the connection. The network edge as a whole becomes more flexible and adaptable.

Examples of customized settings include:

- VLAN
- ACL
- Class of Service (CoS), or 802.1p, priority value
- Rate limits (inbound and outbound)

A CoS value tells the switch to give packets from the user a specific priority in forwarding. Generally, the higher the priority value, the higher the priority. However, 802.1p values 1 and 2 have a lower priority than 0, which is used for normal traffic. Rate limits restrict the amount of bandwidth that the user is allowed to send (inbound) or receive (outbound).

Because the switch applies these settings to a user session automatically, as dictated by the RADIUS server, these settings are sometimes called RADIUS settings or dynamic settings. For example, a dynamic VLAN assignment is the VLAN assigned to a user session by the RADIUS server when the user authenticates to the network. A dynamic ACL is the (port-based) ACL applied to a user session by the RADIUS server when the user authenticates, and so on.

How the RADIUS Server Sends Dynamic Settings

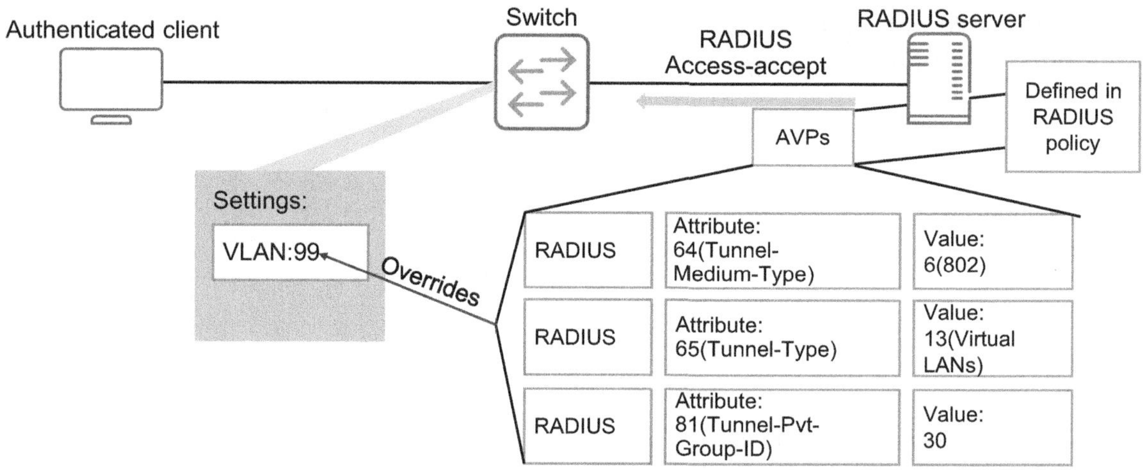

Figure 10-16 How the RADIUS Server Sends Dynamic Settings

A RADIUS server such as ClearPass has policies that define the dynamic settings that apply to certain users based on those users' identities and other conditions. The server communicates the dynamic settings to the switch acting as the NAS in Attribute Value Pairs (AVPs) within the RADIUS-Accept message. These AVPs defined by the IETF RFC standards are vendor-specific attributes. The switch then applies the AVPs as settings to control the user's traffic.

Note

Figure 10-16 shows the dynamic VLAN overriding the static untagged VLAN (native VLAN) on the port, which is a good approximation of the behavior when a single device connects to the port. You will learn about exactly how the switch applies the VLAN in more detail later.

Even if you are not in charge of setting up the RADIUS server, it can be useful for you to understand the AVPs behind the settings so that you can coordinate with those who are.

Refer to Table 10-1 on the next page to find the attribute name or code for the parameter that you want to set. (This table shows the AVPs supported by AOS-CX switches as of the publication of this guide; however, you should double-check the guide for your own switches.)

AVPs fall in several general categories: standard RADIUS, extended RADIUS, and vendor specific. When possible, you should use standard RADIUS attributes because they are supported across many vendors. Depending on the software version, AOS-CX switches might support multiple attributes for some settings. Generally, earlier software used vendor-specific attributes while the more up-to-date software added standard RADIUS attributes for applying the same setting. Aruba recommends that you typically use the standard RADIUS setting, and only use the vendor-specific one if you need to accommodate a legacy solution.

As you see, RADIUS defines two ways to specify a dynamic VLAN. Typically, RADIUS servers send the dynamic native VLAN assignment with the Tunnel-Type, Tunnel-Medium-Type, and Tunnel-Private-Group-ID AVPs. Egress-VLANID and Egress-VLAN-Name AVPs are usually used for tagged traffic.

Determine the appropriate value for the AVP to set the parameter as required in your environment. The final column provides guidelines. For example, this column for the ACL parameter indicates the proper syntax for an ACL.

Keep a few guidelines in mind when coordinating the value for a dynamic VLAN with ClearPass administrators. The Tunnel-Private-Group-ID can be a VLAN ID or a name. You might use the name option to simplify policies in a large or multi-site network. For example, switches in one building might name VLAN 10 "Students" while switches in another building name VLAN 11 the same name. The RADIUS server could use a single policy to assign students to the "Students" VLAN with the Egress-VLAN-Name AVP. The switch through which the individual student authenticated would then assign the student's untagged traffic (native VLAN) to the correct VLAN ID associated with the "Students" name on that switch.

Be very careful, though, that the name in the attribute matches the name of a VLAN on the switch; names are case sensitive. Similarly, a VLAN ID must match a VLAN on the switch. If the RADIUS server sends a VLAN name or ID that does not exist on the switch, the switch does *not* apply the port's static VLAN to the user session. Instead, the authentication fails—much as it would if the user entered an incorrect password.

The switch should also have the dynamic VLAN setup, either already statically tagged on its uplinks or configured with IP settings. Otherwise, the switch cannot forward the user traffic to the rest of the network.

Provide the AVPs to the RADIUS administrator. For each AVP, include the attribute name (or code) and value.

Make sure that the RADIUS server supports these AVPs. Also make sure that the administrators know to define the vendor-specific AVPs, when required.

Table 10-1 RADIUS Attributes

Setting	AVP Types	Attribute Name and Code	Value
VLAN (untagged/native VLAN	Standard RADIUS	Tunnel-Medium-Type (64)	802 (6)
		Tunnel-Type (65)	Virtual LANs (13)
		Tunnel-Private-Group-ID (81)	*VLAN ID or name string*
VLAN (untagged or tagged)	Standard RADIUS	Egress-VLAN ID (56)	*VLAN ID string*
VLAN (untagged or tagged)	Standard RADIUS	Egress-VLAN-Name (58)	*VLAN name string*
Inbound PACL (IPv4 and IPv6)	Standard RADIUS	NAS-Filter-Rule (92)	**<permit** | **deny> in <ip** | *protocol_number>* **from** <any | *IP_address* | *IP_address/PrefixLength>* **to <any** | *IP_address* | *IP_address/PrefixLength>* *[TCP/UDP port list* | *ICMPtype]* **[cnt]**
Inbound PACL (IPv4 only or IPv4 and IPv6) Vendor specific	HP = 11 (Legacy attribute not typically recommended)	NAS-Filter-Rule (61)	**<permit** | **deny> in** < **ip** | *protocol_number>* **from** <any | *IP_address* | *IP_address/PrefixLength>* **to <any** | *IP_address* | *IP_address/PrefixLength>* *[TCP/UDP port list* | *ICMPtype]* **[cnt]**
	HP = 11 (Legacy attribute not typically recommended)	NAS-Filter-Rule (63)	1 | 2 1 = ACL defined with AVP 61 applies to IPv4 and IPv6 traffic 2 = ACL defined with AVP 61 applies only to IPv4 traffic
Class of service (CoS) priority (802.1p)	Standard RADIUS	User-Priority-Table (59)	X0X1X2X3X4X5X6X7, in which Xn = priority to which traffic with n priority is mapped. For example, this setting configures the switch to apply priority 5 to all user traffic: 55555555. Enter the same value for every space
CoS priority (802.1p) Vendor specific	HP = 11 (Legacy attribute not typically recommended)	40	X0X1X2X3X4X5X6X7, in which Xn = priority to which traffic with n priority is mapped.
Ingress rate limit Vendor specific	HP = 11	46	HP-Bandwidth-Max-Egress=<Kbps>
Egress rate limit (most recent assignment applies to the port as a whole) Vendor specific	HP = 11	48	HP-RATE-LIMIT=< Kbps>

Device-Based Mode

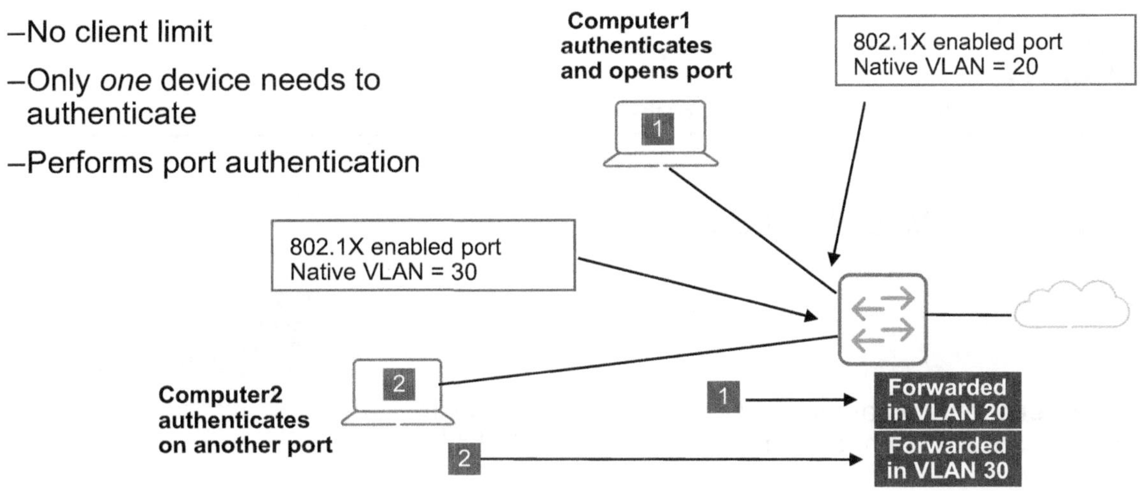

Figure 10-17 Device-Based Mode

You will now learn more about why the switch behaved as you observed in the lab. Precisely how the switch applies the settings depends on whether the port is operating in port-based or user-based mode for 802.1X. The mode also determines how the port establishes authentication sessions.

With device-based/port-based control, the switch establishes a *single* session for all traffic sent and received on the port. As long as any one user passes authentication, the switch permits *all* traffic without referring to the source or destination MAC address. Untagged traffic (native VLAN), regardless of source MAC, is forwarded in the native VLAN assigned to the port (either statically or through RADIUS, as you have learned).

Often, only a single device connects to the switch port, so all traffic does originate from a single source MAC address. The example above illustrates this situation (Figure 10-17), where Computer1 and Computer2 are connected to two different switch ports and are assigned different VLANs based on their 802.1X credentials.

To configure the port mode, configure the following:

```
switch(config)# interface <interface-ID>
switch(config-if)# aaa authentication port-access auth-mode
                    [client-mode | device-mode]
```

client-mode specifies the authentication mode for the port as client-mode. In this mode, all clients connecting to the port will be sent for authentication. The maximum number of clients allowed to connect to the port is limited by the client limit value configured by using the client-limit command.

device-mode specifies the authentication mode for the port as device-mode. In this mode, only the first client connecting to the port will be sent for authentication. Once this client is authenticated, the port is considered as open and all subsequent clients trying to connect on that port are not sent for authentication.

Note

Client mode is the default mode of the port.

Device-Based Mode Use Case

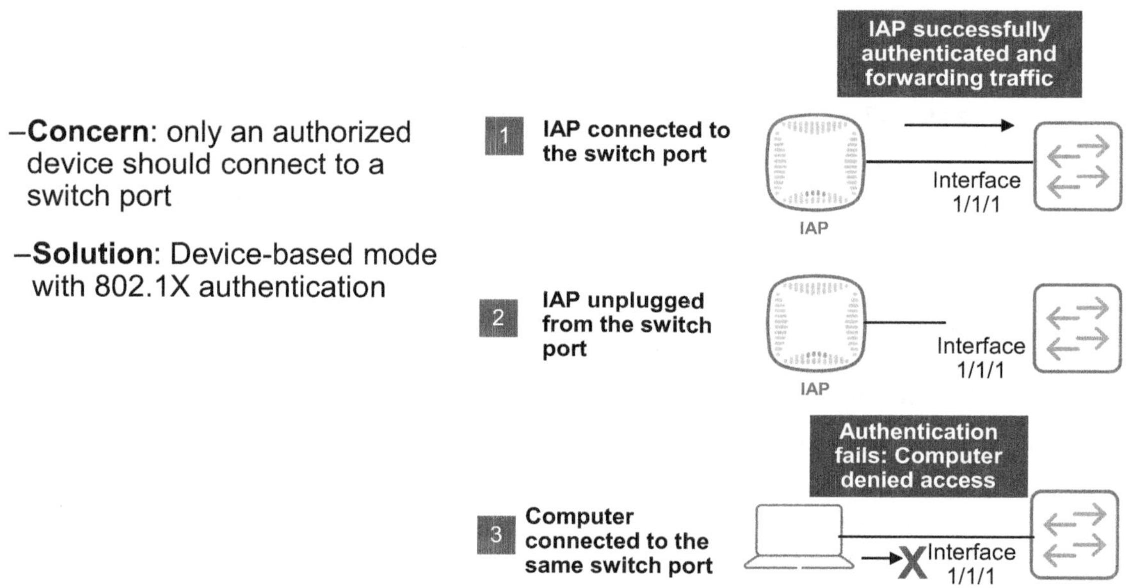

Figure 10-18 Device-Based Mode Use Case

The concern with some customers is that the access switch might be in an environment that is not secure. So, for example, if company statically defined policy settings for a switch port for Instant APs (IAPs), for example, and someone unplugged an IAP and plugged in an unauthorized device, the unauthorized device would have the same policy settings applied as the IAP (Figure 10-18).

To mitigate this problem, you could implement device-based mode authentication. If someone unplugged the IAP and plugged in an authorized device in this situation, the unauthorized device would be denied access to the network unless it successfully authenticated.

Note

Device-based mode is useful when you know that you will only have one device connected to a port, you need to authenticate access on the port, and desire to apply policies dynamically to the port based on authentication credentials (and possibly other information, like fingerprinting).

Issues with Device-Based Mode

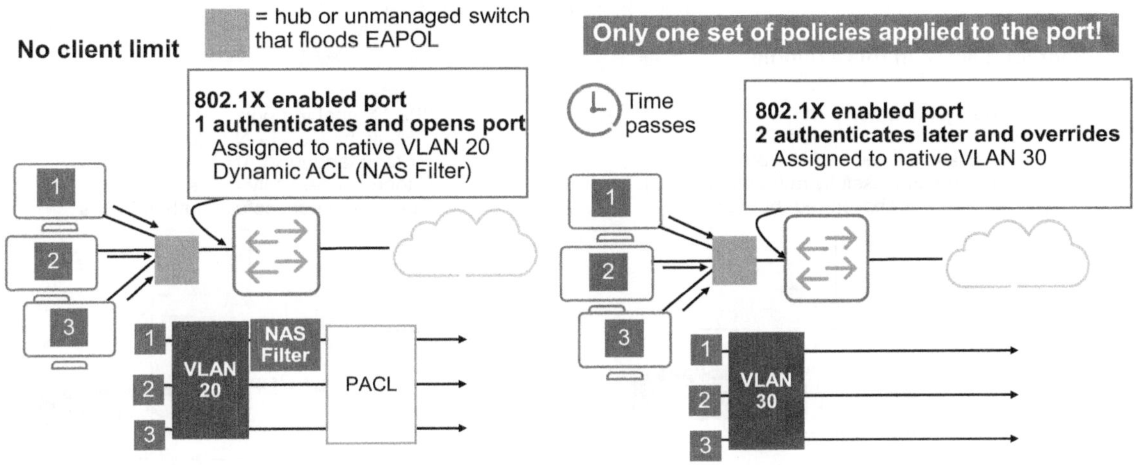

Figure 10-19 Issues with Device-Based Mode

An 802.1X-enabled interface might also connect to multiple devices if it connects to a hub or perhaps to a switch that does not know how to process EAPOL frames and simply floods them. Figure 10-19 illustrates how the port-based mode interface handles the traffic.

The interface has a single untagged VLAN (native VLAN) assignment, which is the static VLAN or the dynamic VLAN sent by the RADIUS server when the most recently authorized user authenticated. As you see in the example above, user 1 has authenticated and been assigned to VLAN 20. Users 2 and 3 have not authenticated, but they can also send traffic in VLAN 20.

On the other hand, AOS-CX switches automatically bind a dynamic ACL to a user's MAC address, even when 802.1X operates in port-based mode on the interface. Therefore, unauthenticated devices can receive access, and their traffic is not filtered by the dynamic ACL. Any static port ACL (PACL) on the port applies to both the authenticated client and the unauthenticated ones—as do in VACLs or RACLs that would normally filter the devices' traffic.

Also keep in mind that, if one of the unauthenticated devices authenticates, and the RADIUS server sends new dynamic settings, those new settings override the ones from the first device. This can cause connectivity issues, as the devices are moved to a new VLAN.

If only one device connects to the port at once, port-based mode can work well. But sometimes multiple devices connect to the same port. In these cases, port-based control introduces these potential issues:

- Unauthorized users gaining access to the network by "piggybacking" on the same connection as an authorized device
- Inconsistent dynamic settings
- Dynamic ACLs not controlling all incoming traffic

Client-Based Mode

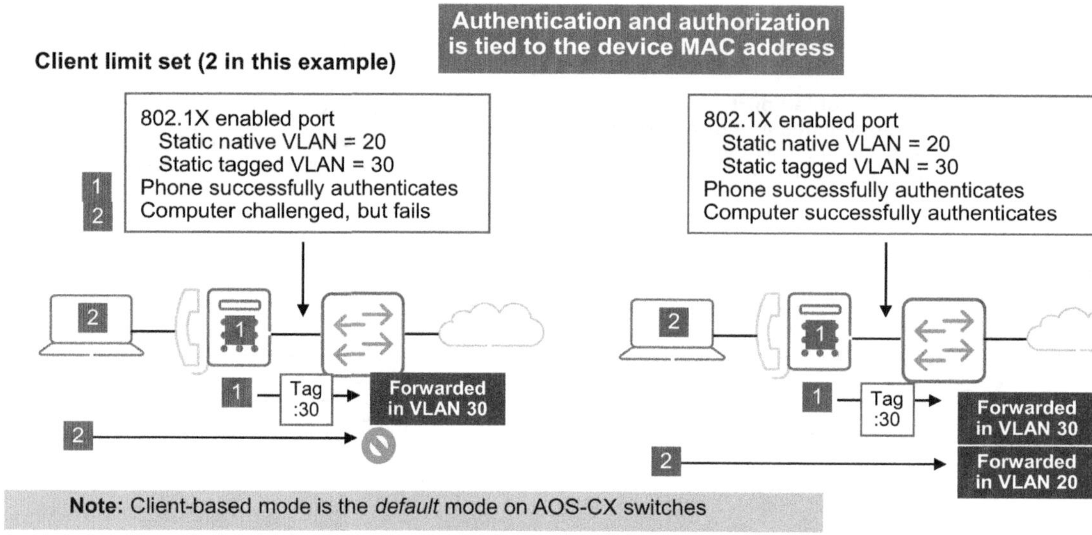

Figure 10-20 Client-Based Mode

Client-based mode is recommended for scenarios in which you want the switch port itself to authenticate and control multiple clients (Figure 10-20). In particular, it is recommended for cases in which the RADIUS server might implement different dynamic settings for different clients. But you should also often enable user-based control even when the port should only connect to a single device to prevent unauthorized devices from "piggybacking" on the port.

In user-based mode the port authenticates *each* downstream device, as identified by source MAC address. You enable this mode when you set the client limit on the port to any value *including 1.*

If you are configured client-mode, the default number of allowed clients is 1.

```
switch(config)# interface <interface-ID>
switch(config-if)# aaa authentication port-access auth-mode client-mode
switch(config-if)# aaa authentication port-access
                    client-limit <CLIENT-LIMIT>
```

The default value is 1 if you do not specify a limit with the latter command.

The port now creates a separate session for each device, and each session has its own authorized status. In other words, the switch permits ingress traffic with a particular source MAC address only if that MAC address's session is authorized. Conversely, it permits egress traffic based on the destination MAC address's authorization status. The limit value indicates how many devices can be authorized.

After you set the limit, the port begins tracking MAC addresses and defines the authorization status and settings for each separately. For example, in the scenario with the computer and VoIP phone, the switch port sends an EAP Request/Identity to each separate MAC address detected on the port. If the VoIP phone authenticates successfully, but the computer fails, the computer traffic is blocked.

Example of How Client-Based Mode Operates

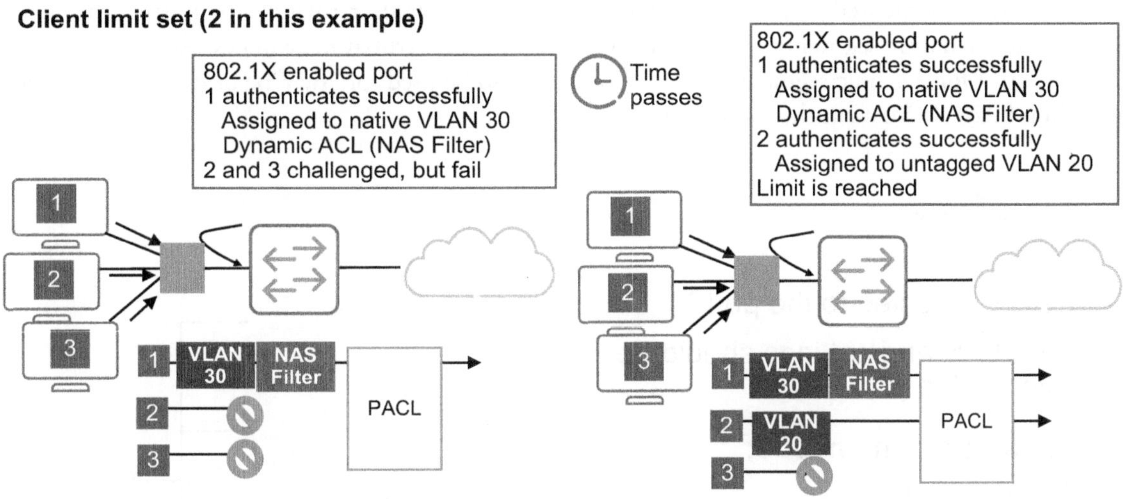

Figure 10-21 Example of How Client-Based Mode Operates

Here you see how client-based mode works in the second scenario, which has a client limit of two also for the sake of illustration (Figure 10-21). Initially, only user 1 has authenticated, so the switch drops user 2's and user 3's traffic. Then user 2 authenticates successfully, so the switch forwards that user's traffic. Now the limit is reached, so user 3 cannot authenticate until another user disconnects.

The examples above also illustrate how port-based mode allows each session to have its own dynamic attributes, such as VLAN and ACL.

In user-based mode, the dynamic VLAN applies to the user's device only. The switch forwards any untagged traffic (native VLAN) sent by the user device in the dynamic VLAN. And when it needs to forward traffic to the device, it forwards the traffic without a tag. If the port supports multiple users, the users can have different native VLAN assignments. If any users do not receive a dynamic assignment, the static native VLAN applies to their traffic.

In the example above both user 1 and user 2 have authenticated and been assigned to different VLANs. The switch recognizes which user is sending traffic based on source MAC address and forwards the traffic in the correct VLAN.

Note that the switch must flood native VLAN traffic in all VLANs out of the port. This means that devices will receive broadcasts and multicasts for all untagged VLANs (native VLANs) applied to the port. Keep this in mind when you plan multi-client scenarios.

User Roles

This section introduces a feature that was copied from the Aruba Mobility Controllers, called user roles, and is implemented in AOS-CX switches, referred to as user roles. Initially this feature was designed for dynamic segmentation and was first seen on the ArubaOS switches. AOS-CX switches also support it for dynamic segmentation, but roles can also be used for any type of user authentication, including 802.1X, MAC auth, and captive portal.

Colorless Ports

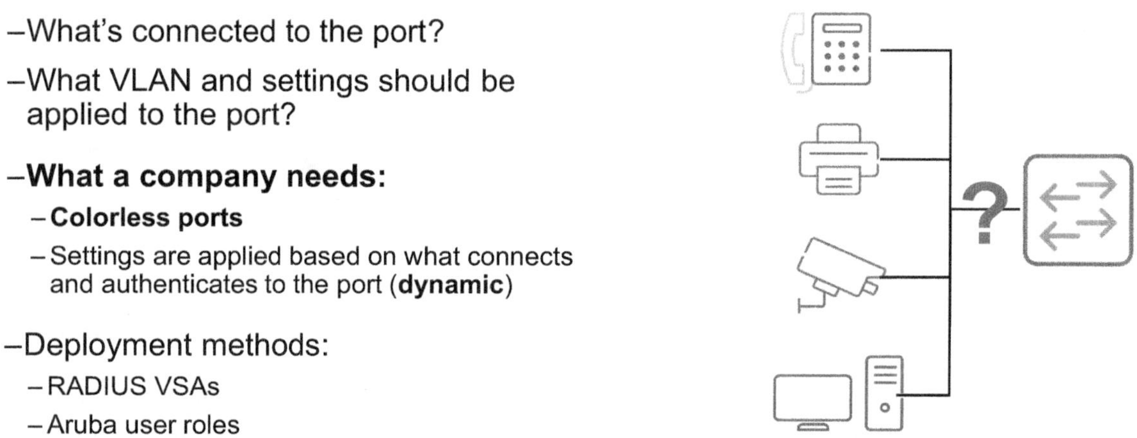

Figure 10-22 Colorless Ports

Historically, the problem with not understanding what is connected to a port hindered movement of devices in a network, since most ports were configured with static policy settings, like VLAN, QoS, and other policy information.

The concept of a *colorless port* is that these settings can be dynamically assigned based on a user authenticating to a port (Figure 10-22). Historically, this was done with RADIUS VSA attributes. However, Aruba supports a feature called user roles that can be used instead. User roles are supported on Aruba Mobility Controllers and AOS-CX and AOS switches. User roles allow for a single process configuration that can be used for user devices that can connect both to wired switch ports and wirelessly, providing these advantages:

- Simplifying the definition of policies
- Providing scalability
- Centralized management of policies

If using PEAP authentication, and the administrator is not sure of what device the user is connecting to the network when the user enters their user credentials, the administrator can leverage the profiling capabilities of a product like ClearPass, which can perform fingerprinting to determine the type of device and operating system it is running. For example, when a user connects their corporate laptop to the network, they should be assigned their normal policies. However, what if the user connected a personal laptop to the network and entered the *same* credentials as they used on their laptop? Fingerprinting information can then be used to determine the policies that should be assigned to the port based on the actual device that is connecting.

Important

Using EAP-TLS with certificates gives you much more control over what is connecting to the network, since as an administrator, you control which devices get certificates. Using PEAP for authentication gives you less control, since you do not know what devices the user is using when connecting, but the user can still use their same credentials. Therefore, if using PEAP, you should complement your 802.1X authentication with a fingerprinting feature like that supported by ClearPass, which can help identify the hardware (like a security camera versus an Apple iPhone) and/or operating system used by the device.

Note

The switches in most companies will have the switch locally switch the traffic. The Dynamic Segmentation chapter, covered later, will discuss a tunneling solution to tunnel traffic from the switch to an Aruba Mobility Controller and have the Mobility Controller process the user's traffic. This is also a policy decision that can be applied to a colorless port.

User Roles Overview

Roles can be configured locally on the switch using a Local User Role (LUR) or on a ClearPass server, using a downloadable user role (DUR). Roles that are configured locally can be assigned via any RADIUS server, using the *Aruba-User-Role* VSA. When using DUR, the ClearPass HPE-CPPM-Role VSA is used in combination with HTTPS to transfer the role to the switch (Figure 10-23).

The benefits of assigning "roles" to users and/or devices is well known within the Aruba wireless world. This has simply been adapted to the wired switch port. Just as with Aruba Wireless, there is now the ability to simplify the burden of configuration, grouping policies into a "role" that can be referenced by many device or user types. Additionally, when ClearPass is incorporated, context can be added (time of day, type of machine, device profiling) when deciding if a user/device will be allowed on the network, and what access rights will be granted or denied.

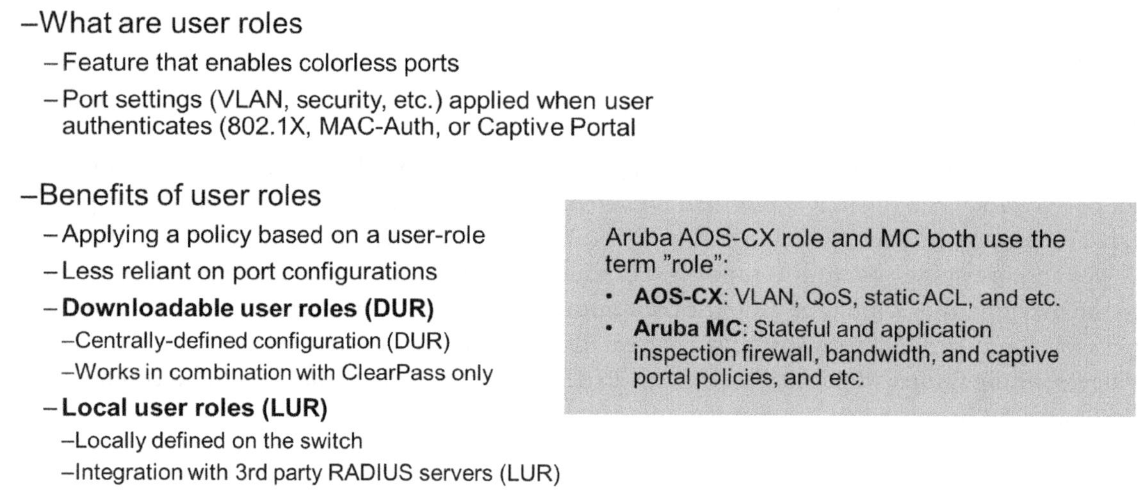

Figure 10-23 User Roles Overview

A role is a role—A role at a minimum will dictate what VLAN is to be assigned (tagged or untagged) and if the traffic is locally switched, or if tunneled back to AOS Mobility Controller. Optionally a role can also assign a policy (ACL/QOS), reauthentication timers, and a captive portal redirect. The same syntax is used if it is pre-defined on a switch (local-roles) or downloaded from ClearPass, it must exist on the switch before it can be applied to a device/user.

Important

The term "role" is used with both the Aruba Mobility Controllers (MCs) and the AOS-CX switches. The two should not be confused, since a role on an MC pertains to firewall, bandwidth, and captive portal policies, while a role on an AOS-CX switch pertains to VLAN, QoS, ACL, and other policies. In other words, roles on both devices apply policies, but the types of policies differ.

Role Assignment: LUR

There are two user role implementations that the switch can use:

- **Local User Role (LUR)**: LUR allows us to use a third-party AAA server. Local user Roles are defined on the switch. When a device connects and authenticates successfully, a User-Role name (VSA) is passed to the switch, then the switch will apply that User-Role to the device.

- **Downloadable User Role (DUR)**: The switch does not need the User-Role defined on the switch. Downloadable user Roles only work with ClearPass Server, not third-party authentication server. When a device connects and authenticates successfully, the switch will download the User-Role to the switch and the switch will apply it to the device (Figure 10-24).

Note

In the current release (10.04), Aruba does not support role download for a gateway (controller) or secondary role to the mobility controller when implementing dynamic segmentation. In other words, the switch cannot download the controller's role information directly.

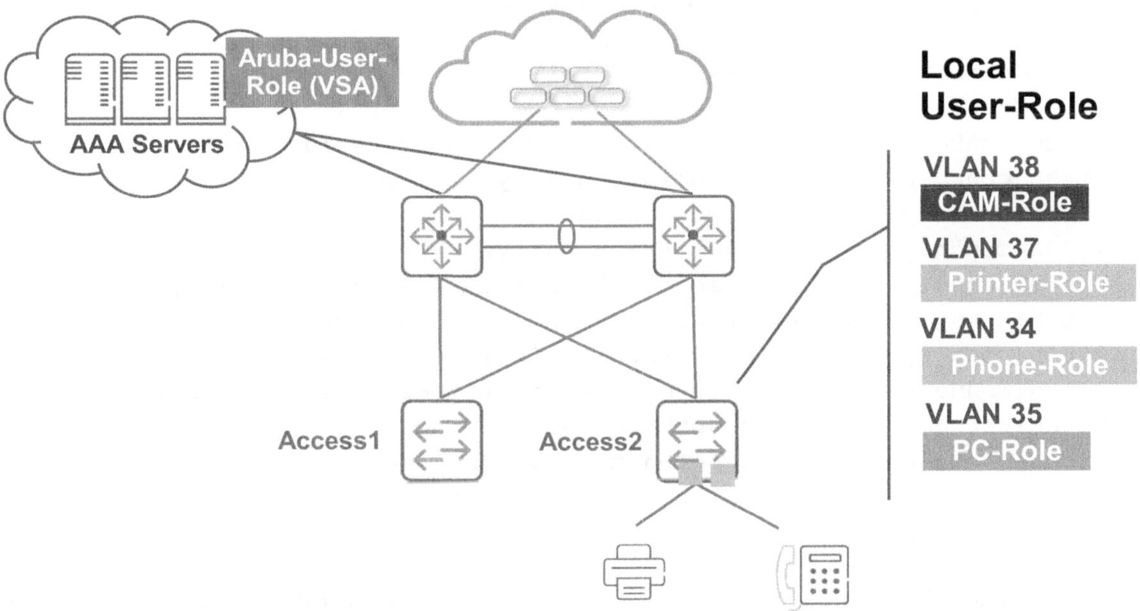

Figure 10-24 Role Assignment: LUR

Local User-Roles

A user role consists of the following optional parameters:

- **ingress user policy**: L3 (IPv4 and/or IPv6) ordered list of classes with actions.
- **captive-portal-profile**: Assigns a captive portal profile for this role.
- **inactivity-timeout**: The inactivity timeout period in seconds with a range of 300 to 4294967295 for the authenticated client for an implicit logoff.
- **reauth-period**: Sets the reauthentication period in seconds or 0 to disable.

- **vlan access**: Sets the untagged VLAN ID (native VLAN).
- **vlan-id-tagged**: Sets the tagged VLAN ID.
- **auth-mode**: Sets the configuration in user role to either device-mode or port-mode (client-mode). The following are the attributes:
- **poe-priority**: Specifies the PoE priority for the interface.
- **mtu**: Configures the MTU support for the client.
- **tagged-vlan**: Specifies the list of tagged VLANs configured for the interface.
- **trust-mode**: Configures the QoS trust mode for the client.

To create a local user role, use the following configuration:

```
Switch(config)# port-access role <role-name>
Switch(config-pa-role)# description <description>
Switch(config-pa-role)# associate captive-port-profile <profile-name>
Switch(config-pa-role)# associate policy <policy-name>
Switch(config-pa-role)# vlan access <VLAN-ID>
Switch(config-pa-role)# vlan trunk native <VLAN-ID>
Switch(config-pa-role)# vlan trunk allowed {<VLAN-ID> | all}
Switch(config-pa-role)# trust-mode {dscp | cos | none}
Switch(config-pa-role)# poe-priority {critical | high | low}
Switch(config-pa-role)# auth-mode {client-mode | device-mode}
Switch(config-pa-role)# reauth-period <seconds>
Switch(config-pa-role)# session-timeout <seconds>
Switch(config-pa-role)# client-inactivity time <seconds>
Switch(config-pa-role)# mtu <byte-size>
```

Please note that role names are *case-sensitive*! Use the **show port-access role** command to verify your local role's configuration.

Important

Role names are case-sensitive!

See the AOS-CX *Security Guide* for more information to configure the various role properties.

Role Assignment: DUR

Downloadable user-role enables AOS-CX switches to download user-roles, policy, and class information from the ClearPass Policy Manager server instead of locally configuring the roles on the switches. The download facilitates the setup of policies and attributes for a specific user-role which can then be stored on the switch. New users can be configured and assigned the same stored version of the user-role in ClearPass, saving the administrator time reconfiguring each user individually (Figure 10-25).

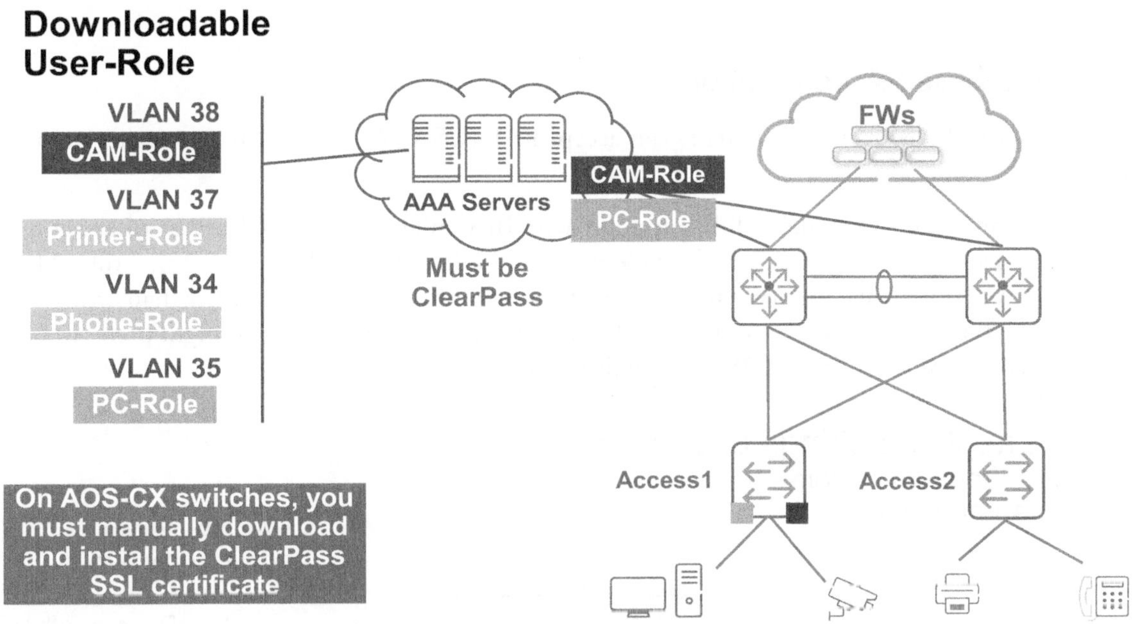

Figure 10-25 Role Assignment: DUR

The **radius-server host** command should only be used if the entire user role configuration is going to be downloaded from the ClearPass Policy Manager server:

```
Switch(config)# radius-server host <IP-address-or-FQDN>
                 clearpass-username <account-name>
                 plaintext clearpass-password <password>
```

Note

Because the login process from the AOS-CX switch uses HTTPS, the switch will have to validate the certificate of the ClearPass server. On the older AOS switches, they would automatically download and install the ClearPass certificate. Unfortunately, in AOS-CX 10.04, this process is not automatic. You will need to access the ClearPass server, download its SSL certificate, and install it on the AOS-CX switch. This process is described in Chapter 12.

User Role-Based Authorization

You have learned how AOS-CX switches can accept RADIUS VSAs to customize access for authenticated devices.

Some companies prefer to take a different approach. They might be using ClearPass to apply user roles to authenticated users based on their identities and other criteria (Figure 10-26). Aruba MCs, acting as RADIUS clients, use these roles to decide how to filter user traffic. Rather than create new profiles with the RADIUS VSAs for dynamic VLANs and ACLs, administrators might prefer to have ClearPass simply send a role to AOS-CX switches too.

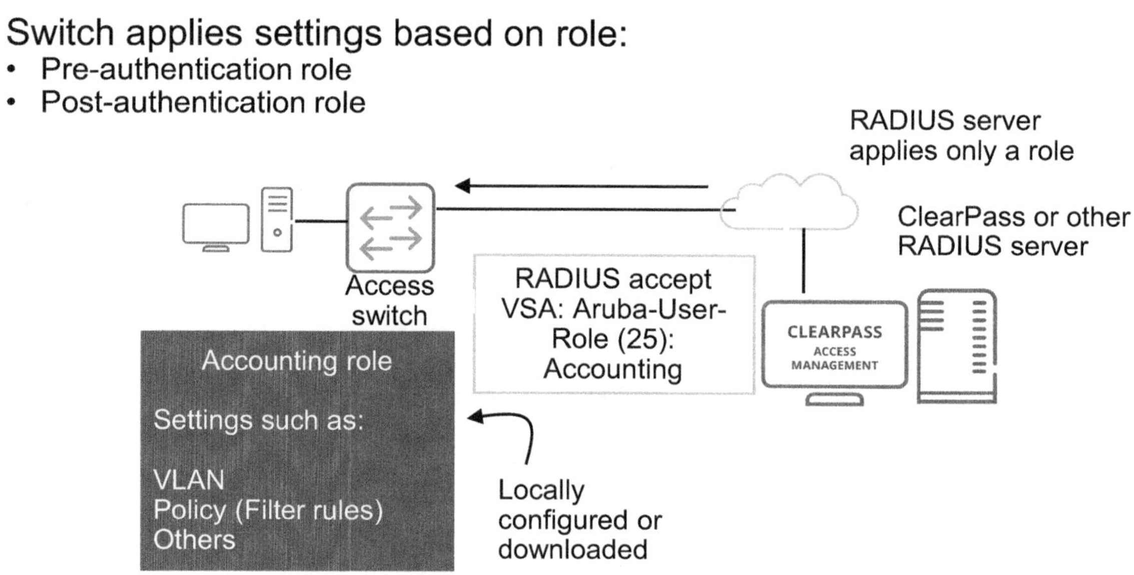

Figure 10-26 User Role-Based Authorization

Every client is associated with a role. Roles associate with a set of attributes for authenticated clients (clients with authentication configuration) and unauthenticated clients, applied to each user session. Roles are always enabled, by default, on a switch.

Examples of user roles are:

- Employee—All access
- Contractor—Limited access to resources. Each user role determines the client network privileges
- Frequency of reauthentication, applicable bandwidth contracts, and other permissions
- Guest—Browse Internet

The VSA that AOS-CX switches accept from RADIUS servers like ClearPass has these properties:

- Type: RADIUS vendor specific for Aruba
- Name: Aruba-User-Role
- ID: 25
- Value: <*role name*>

Note

The role name is case-sensitive!

You can define the user role locally. This approach moves the control over customizing settings from RADIUS server administrators to infrastructure administrators, which some companies might prefer. The User Derived Role is applied when the roles are enabled. UDR will have the same precedence order as the authentication type (802.1x, MAC authentication). UDRs are locally configured on the switch using the port-access role command. The configuration of UDRs is beyond the scope of this guide. See the *Security Guide* for more information to configure the **port-access role** profile locally.

Local Authorization Role Options

Figure 10-27 lists the different kinds of roles (and their respective policies) that can be assigned to a user connecting to a switch port.

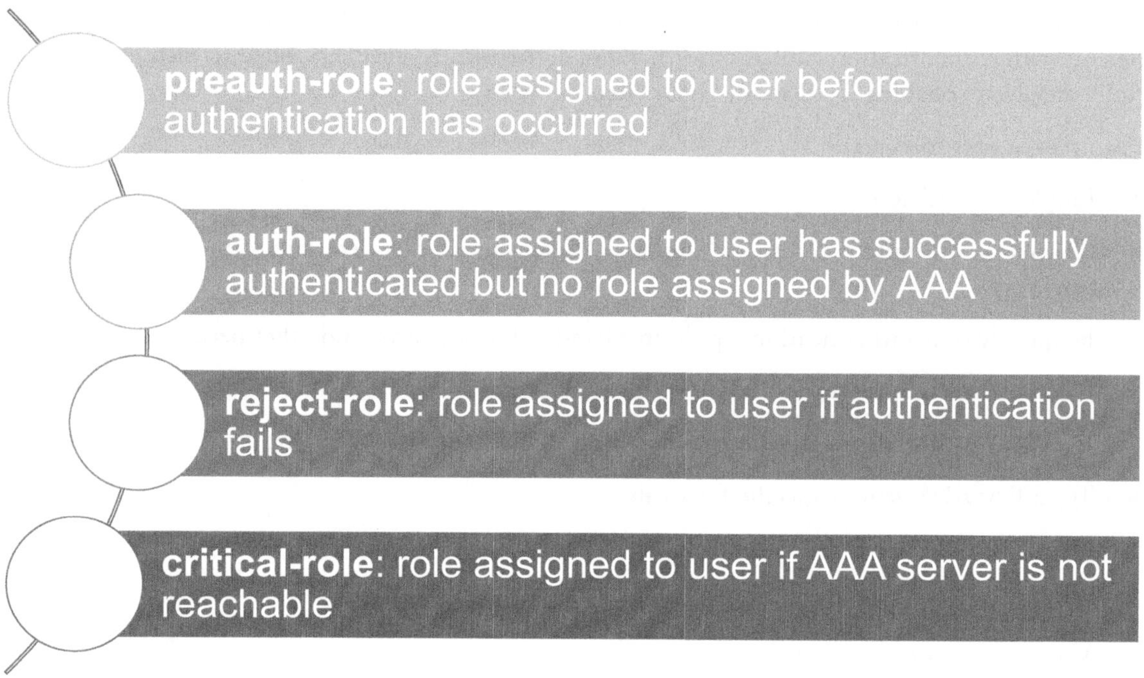

Figure 10-27 Local Authorization Role Options

Pre-Authentication Role

The pre-authentication (pre-auth) role allows a device, such as an IP Phone, to have network access before the device is authenticated. The pre-auth role can also be used to allow DHCP, DNS, and the web redirect for captive portal authentications.

The pre-auth role is triggered when a MAC-based client is connected to an Aruba switch before being authenticated by the RADIUS server. To provide network connectivity for devices, they must be assigned a VLAN. Two new VLANs are created for pre-auth role functionality, one for voice traffic and one for data traffic. Pre-auth role VLANs can be configured on the switch individually or within a user-role. Devices that can be connected to the switch without authentication are divided into two categories:

- Devices that send voice traffic
- Devices that send data traffic

Note

Either one of pre-auth role VLAN (voice and/or data) or a pre-auth role can be configured for a port. However, both a VLAN and role cannot coexist for an interface. Initial traffic on the port is restricted only by ACLs configured for the port or for VLANs or ACLs in the role.

To define a pre-authentication role, configure the following:

```
Switch(config)# interface <interface-ID>
Switch(config-if)# aaa authentication port-access preauth-role <role-name>
```

Impacts of pre-auth role on existing features include the following:

- Unauthenticated devices: Configuring pre-auth role VLAN will change the behavior of unauthenticated devices. Normally, authentication-enabled ports will not provide unauthenticated client any network access until the device is authenticated by the RADIUS server. With pre-auth role VLAN configured, the client will be assigned to the pre-auth role VLAN until the RADIUS server authenticates the device. Unauthenticated clients will be placed into the VLAN specified in the pre-auth role. After authentication by the RADIUS server, the client will be placed into the VLAN specified by the RADIUS authentication command string or as specified in the RADIUS authentication accept string.
- LLDP-Bypass: When LLDP-bypass is enabled on the switch, Aruba APs are not authenticated. Therefore, the pre-auth role VLAN is not applicable.
- Bypass using device-identity: Pre-auth role VLAN is not applicable to VoIP devices because they do not need authentication. It is applicable to PCs which need authentication.
- ACLs applied on an Interface: If an ACL rule is applied on an interface which is part of a pre-auth role VLAN, traffic coming through that interface will be affected. Traffic will be affected based on the rule in the ACL.
- ACLs applied on a VLAN: If an ACL rule is applied on a pre-auth role VLAN, traffic entering that VLAN will be affected. Traffic will be affected based on the rule in the ACL.
- Rate-limiting on an interface: If the traffic is rate-limited on an interface as part of a pre-auth role VLAN, the traffic will be impacted. The traffic will be affected based on the rule in the rate-limiting configuration command.
- Authenticated or rejected clients: Clients which are either authenticated or rejected by the RADIUS server are given different VLANs. These clients are moved from pre-auth role to new VLANs based on authentication by the RADIUS server.
- MAC pinning: Clients whose MAC addresses are pinned and have undergone authentication will always be treated as authenticated. Pre-auth role VLAN is not applicable in this scenario.

- Effect of RADIUS tracking on pre-auth role: If RADIUS tracking is enabled and no RADIUS server is available for authentication, the port will be changed from a pre-auth role VLAN to a critical VLAN. The time taken to move from pre-auth role VLAN to critical VLAN depends on the time it takes for RADIUS tracker to inform the subsystem.

Default Role

When implementing AAA, an AAA server will authenticate the user. If the AAA server does not reply with a role name, or the role name sent in the AAA request does not exist on the switch (case-sensitive), then a default role can be assigned to the user if the following has been configured.

To define a pre-authentication role, configure the following:

```
Switch(config)# interface <interface-ID>
Switch(config-if)# aaa authentication port-access auth-role <role-name>
```

Critical Role

A critical role can be assigned to a user when the switch sends an AAA request(s) to an AAA server(s), but no response is received, perhaps because there is a network issue preventing communication between the two sets of devices. By default, the authentication would fail and the user would be denied access. However, you can override this behavior by defining a critical role for the interface, like this:

```
Switch(config)# interface <interface-ID>
Switch(config-if)# aaa authentication port-access critical-role <role-name>
```

If the AAA server(s) is not reachable, then the critical role is applied. This allows important devices, like VoIP phones, for example, to stay connected to the network at all times.

Once an AAA server is reachable, however, the device(s) connected to the interface must be authenticated, at which point the critical role is not used.

Reject Role

Normally, if a user fails authentication, they will have no access beyond the switch port. Optionally, you can assign a reject (failed authentication) role to the user that would give them minimal network access, perhaps to download software to become compliant in order to connect to the network, like an 802.1X supplicant. To define a reject role, configure the following:

```
Switch(config)# interface <interface-ID>
Switch(config-if)# aaa authentication port-access reject-role <role-name>
```

Lab 10

Lab 10 Diagram

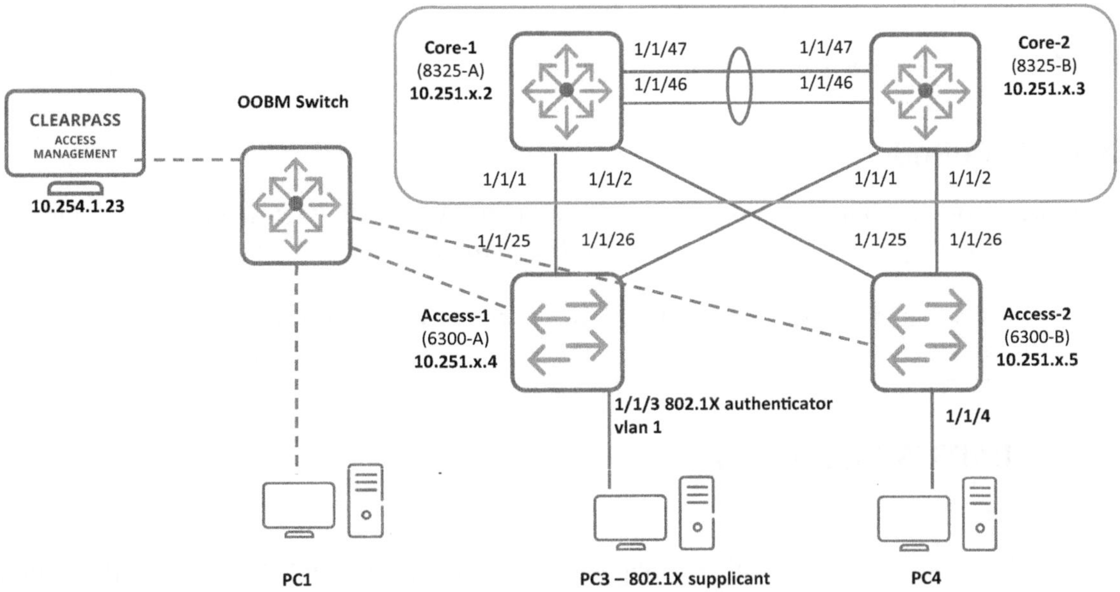

Figure 10-28 Lab 10 Diagram

Overview

In this lab activity, 802.1X will be configured on an access switch (Figures 10-28). This will require the configuration of a RADIUS server and will include RADIUS change of authorization (CoA) support. For the first 802.1X authentication part of the lab, the RADIUS server will provide standard IETF attribute value pairs (AVP) to assign the user to a VLAN. Next, the lab will introduce Aruba user-roles; therefore, the access instructions will be stored in the switch configuration and the RADIUS server will use the Aruba Vendor-Specific Attribute (VSA) called *Aruba-User-Role.*

Objectives

- Configure RADIUS server, authentication groups, and dynamic authorization (CoA)
- Configure RADIUS tracking
- Configure 802.1X on a switch port
- Configure user roles with policies and classes

Task 1: Prepare the Lab Start Configuration

Objectives

- This lab is built on the base VSX topology.
- Make sure to complete these steps to get the base VSX checkpoint configuration on the devices.

Steps (Required)

1. Open a console connection to all four switches (6300A, 6300B, 8325A, and 8325B) and load the VSX checkpoint. This must be done on ***ALL four*** switches.

```
ICX-Tx-Access1# copy checkpoint icx-lab04-vsx running-config
Configuration changes will take time to process, please be patient.
```

Task 2: RADIUS Server Setup

Objectives

In this task, the Access1 switch will be configured to use the ClearPass RADIUS server. The training lab is using the OOBM network to access the RADIUS server since that is readily available. In real deployments, the RADIUS server would typically be reachable over the in-band network.

AOS-CX supports the use of server groups. RADIUS accounting and interim accounting will be enabled. CoA (RFC3576 support) will be enabled and verified. RADIUS server tracking will be enabled to verify that the RADIUS server is operational.

Steps

1. Open a session to Access1 and enter the configuration mode.

   In a later lab, the ClearPass Downloadable User Roles will be configured. Since this feature will require an HTTPS connection between the switch and the ClearPass host, this HTTPS connection will be validated by the switch; therefore, the CPPM HTTPS certification subject name must match with the DNS name.

   To prepare for this later activity, the RADIUS server will be defined based on the hostname and not based on an IP address. If the customer has an entry for the ClearPass host in the DNS system, that can be used as well.

   In this lab setup, the hostname will be locally defined on the switch, similar to the 'hosts' file on many Operating Systems.

2. Define a new hostname for the cppm.arubatraining.com in the mgmt VRF.

```
ICX-Tx-Access1(config)# ip dns host cppm.arubatraining.com 10.254.1.23
vrf mgmt
```

3. Verify that the new entry works with a test ping.

```
ICX-Tx-Access1(config)# do ping cppm.arubatraining.com vrf mgmt
PING cppm.arubatraining.com (10.253.1.23) 100(128) bytes of data.
108 bytes from 10.253.1.23: icmp_seq=1 ttl=63 time=0.727 ms

...
```

4. Define a new RADIUS host for the ClearPass server.

Note
Make sure to use the correct VRF commands, otherwise the RADIUS server will be defined in the default VRF, but it will not be reachable. Typically, the RADIUS would be configured in an in-band VRF, such as the 'default' VRF. The 'mgmt' VRF is convenient in the training lab environment.

Note
Make sure to verify the key when entering the command.

```
ICX-Tx-Access1(config)# radius-server host cppm.arubatraining.com key
plaintext aruba123 vrf mgmt
```

5. Define a new server group; add the previously defined CPPM host. Again, make sure to enter the correct VRF.

```
ICX-Tx-Access1(config)# aaa group server radius cppm
ICX-Tx-Access1(config-sg)# server cppm.arubatraining.com vrf mgmt
ICX-Tx-Access1(config-sg)# exit
```

6. Enable RADIUS accounting to this server group, enable interim accounting, and set the interim accounting to 5 minutes. This will ensure that the switch updates the radius server about the connected devices every 5 minutes and will ensure that ClearPass has a view over the currently connected devices in the network.

```
ICX-Tx-Access1(config)# aaa accounting port-access start-stop interim
5 group cppm
```

7. Enable the Change of Authorization (CoA) processing on the switch. This is also known as RFC 3576 support or dynamic authorization. This allows the RADIUS server (ClearPass) to send a message to the switch to request an update in the authorization or a re-authentication. Basically, ClearPass can have a 'triggered' re-authentication based on authentication events. This could be required in a later lab when using the Captive Portal authentication.

```
ICX-Tx-Access1(config)# radius dyn-authorization client cppm.arubatraining.com
secret-key plaintext aruba123 vrf mgmt replay-protection disable
ICX-Tx-Access1(config)# radius dyn-authorization enable
```

Note

Replay protection disable indicates that the timestamp of the CoA packet will not be inspected by the switch. In a real deployment, the replay protection should be enabled. The default allowed time difference between the RADIUS host and the switch is 300 seconds. Since in the lab, the time of the switch and CPPM may not be in sync, the replay-protection is disabled.

Note

Since ClearPass will send a RADIUS CoA message to the switch, it is important that the switch is configured to accept these RADIUS messages. Typically, it is the switch that sends the RADIUS Request packets to the RADIUS server, and the RADIUS server responds to these request packets. In case of the CoA, it is the RADIUS server that initiates the packet, so it is considered to be the CoA client, while the switch receives the CoA packet, so it is considered to be the CoA server.

8. Enable RADIUS tracking credentials. RADIUS tracking is a feature that allows the switch to send radius test requests on a regular basis, so it can detect if the RADIUS server is still responding. For this feature, dedicated credentials and ClearPass service can be configured, so it does not interfere with any regular production credentials or ClearPass services. The tracking test is performed every 5 minutes by default; this can also be changed if needed.

```
ICX-Tx-Access1(config)# radius-server tracking user-name icx-radius-
track password plaintext aruba123
```

9. The tracking must be enabled per radius-server host.

Note

Make sure to enter the correct hostname and VRF context, otherwise a new radius-server is defined in the configuration.

```
ICX-Tx-Access1(config)# radius-server host cppm.arubatraining.com vrf
mgm tracking enable
```

10. Access PC1 and open a web browser connection to the ClearPass host (https://10.254.1.23/tips). Log in with these credentials:

- Username: **icx-adminX** (replace X with your table number)

For example, icx-admin12 for Table 12, icx-admin1 for Table1

- Password: **aruba123**

11. Navigate to **Monitoring > Live Monitoring > Access Tracker**. At the right-top, select **'Edit'** to change the columns.

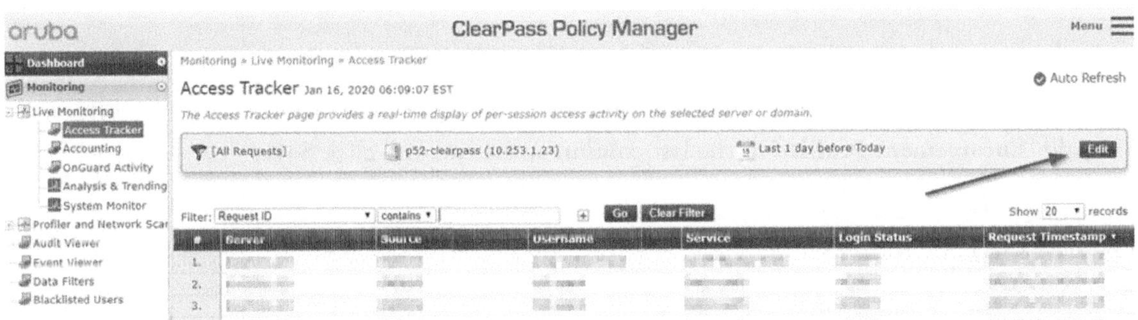

12. Add the **'NAS IP Address'** and the **'Host MAC Address'** columns to the View and arrange them in a logical order (see image for an example).

Note

In some remote lab environments, these column settings may have been applied previously. If the columns **'NAS IP Address'** and **'Host MAC Address'** have been configured already, move to the next step.

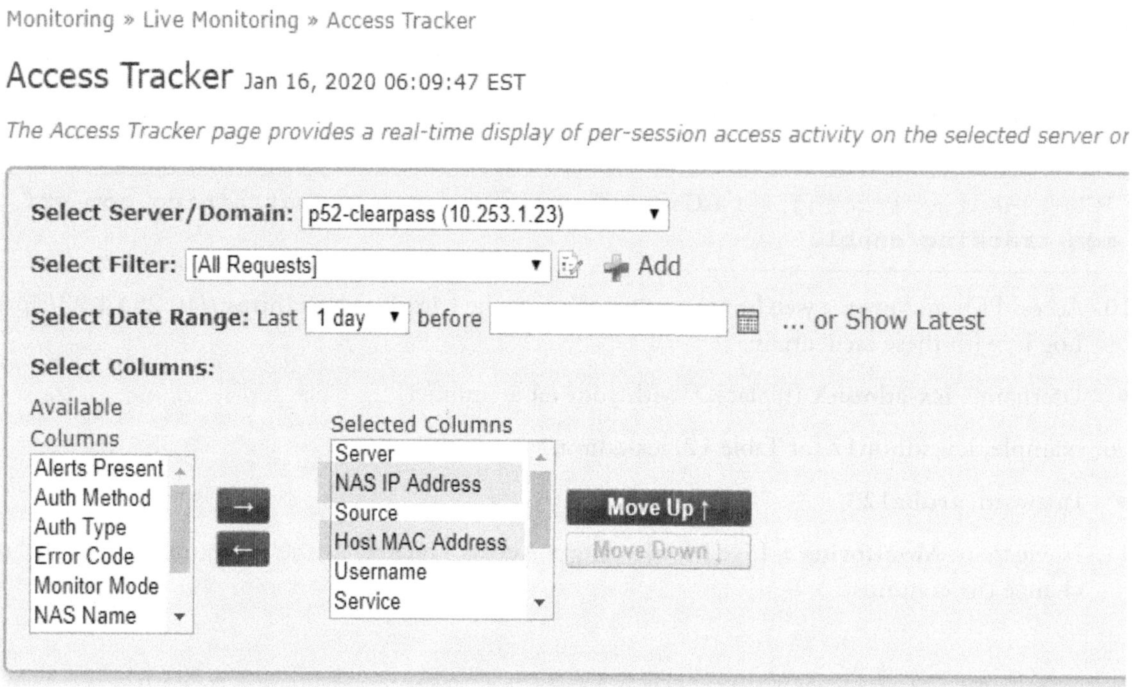

13. Add **'Enforcement Profiles'** as the last column at the end and click **Save**.

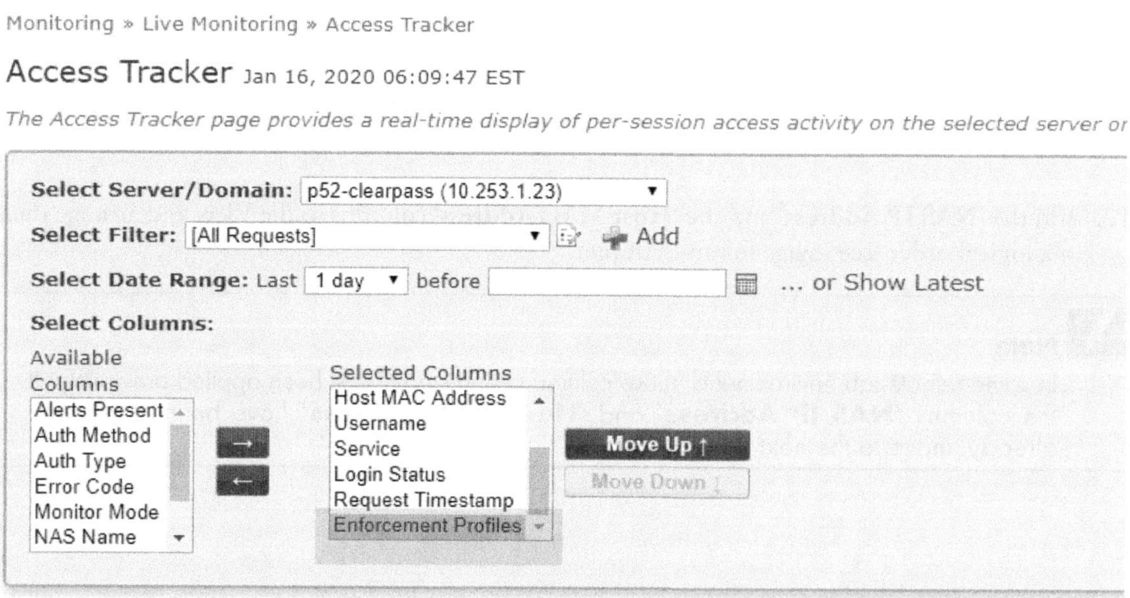

14. The switch from your table can be recognized based on the NAS IP Address in the view now (10.251.X.4). There should be an 'ACCEPT' message displayed for your Access1 switch.

Filter Access Tracker

1. To make sure you only see the authentication requests of your own table, you can apply a display filter based on your NAS-IP of your table (so 10.251.x (replace x with your table #) is sufficient to differentiate from the other tables).

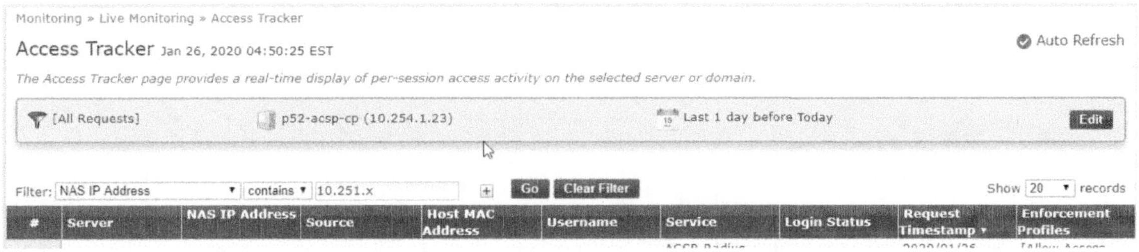

- If there is no request from your switch, apply these troubleshooting steps:
  - Verify the IP DNS entry on the switch.
  - Verify the RADIUS server entry on the switch is using the correct name.
  - Verify on the switch if a ping to this name works.
  - Verify the RADIUS secret on the switch.
- If there is a Reject message, apply these troubleshooting steps:
  - Verify the RADIUS tracking username and password on the switch.

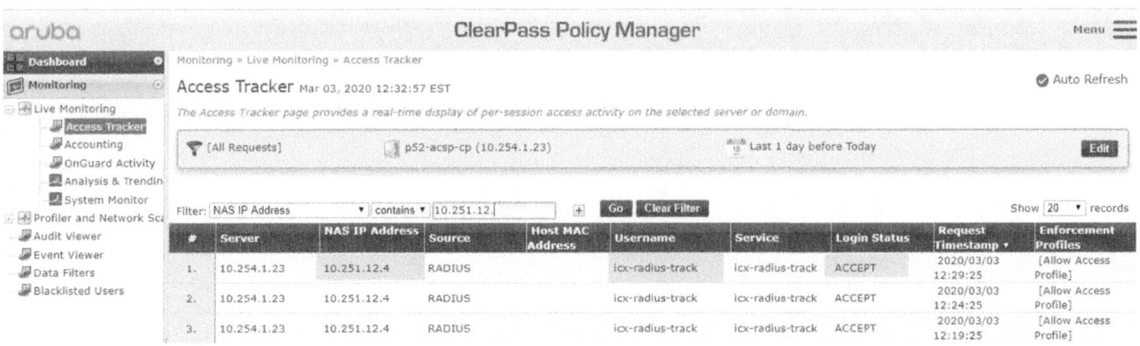

2. Click on your switch's entry in ClearPass and review the 'Input' and 'Output' tabs

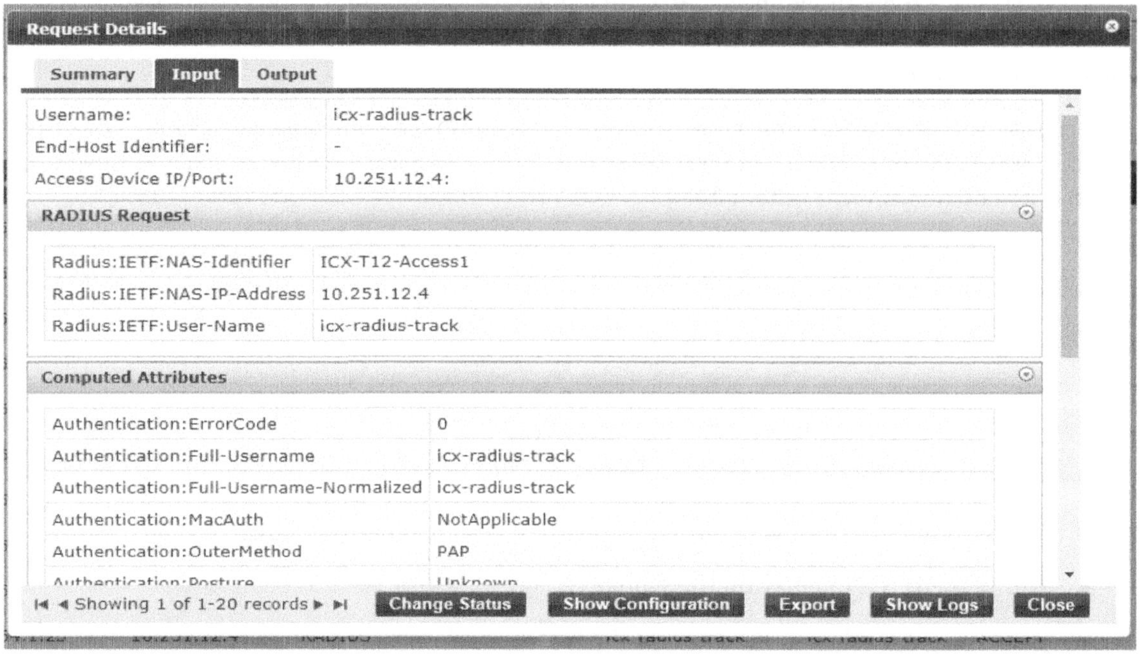

3. On the Access1 switch, check the RADIUS tracking status.

```
ICX-Tx-Access1(config)# show radius-server detail
******* Global RADIUS Configuration *******
Shared-Secret: None
Timeout: 5
Auth-Type: pap
Retries: 1
Tracking Time Interval (seconds): 300
Tracking Retries: 1
Tracking User-name: icx-radius-track
Tracking Password:
AQBapUmeqwuSjUoetq4KWXbTnUyBILPjxzok4qzRZeSXsBIzCQAAACMxHv6lEnY7jA==
Number of Servers: 1

****** RADIUS Server Information ******
Server-Name                  : cppm.arubatraining.com
Auth-Port                    : 1812
Accounting-Port              : 1813
VRF                          :mgmt
Shared-Secret                : AQBapVWcNJavUClNBQenFa-
JwwRrR+nWcJUvsQlHUbuaiOvlDCAAAAMCnYwT2Ful+
Timeout (default)            : 5
Retries (default)            : 1
Auth-Type (default)          : pap
Server-Group                 :cppm
Group-Priority               : 1
Tracking                     : enabled
Reachability-Status          : reachable
ClearPass-Username           :
ClearPass-Password           : None
```

4. Review the RADIUS server statistics.

```
ICX-Tx-Access1(config)# show radius-server statistics authentication
  Server Name      : cppm.arubatraining.com
  Auth-Port        : 1812
  Accounting-Port  : 1813
  VRF              :mgmt
```

```
  Authentication Statistics
  -------------------------
     Round Trip Time              : 3
     Pending Requests             : 0
     Timeouts                     : 0
     Bad Authenticators           : 0
     Packets Dropped              : 0
     Access Requests              : 3
     Access challenge             : 0
     Access Accepts               : 3
     Access Rejects               : 0
     Access Response Malformed    : 0
     Access Retransmits           : 0
Tracking Requests             : 3
Tracking Responses            : 3
     Unknown Response Code        : 0
```

5. In case that the switch does not receive a RADIUS response from the RADIUS server, the switch will consider it 'unreachable' and it will use another RADIUS server, if defined.

Note

The switch does not need a RADIUS Accept packet for the tracking to be successful. Any RADIUS response, both Accept and Reject, results in the tracking feature to mark the RADIUS server as reachable.

6. Here is an example output for failed tracking; this is for reference only. In this example, the switch did not receive any response from the RADIUS server.

```
ICX-Tx-Access1(config)# show radius-server statistics authentication
Server Name       : cppm.arubatraining.com
Auth-Port         : 1812
Accounting-Port : 1813
VRF               :mgmt

  Authentication Statistics
  -------------------------
     Round Trip Time            : 0
     Pending Requests           : 0
     Timeouts                   : 4
     Bad Authenticators         : 0
     Packets Dropped            : 0
```

```
     Access Requests              : 10
     Access challenge             : 0
     Access Accepts               : 4
     Access Rejects               : 2
     Access Response Malformed : 0
     Access Retransmits           : 3
Tracking Requests               : 7
     Tracking Responses           : 6
     Unknown Response Code        : 0
```

```
ICX-Tx-Access1(config)# show radius-server detail
******* Global RADIUS Configuration *******

Shared-Secret: None
Timeout: 5
Auth-Type: pap
Retries: 1
Tracking Time Interval (seconds): 300
Tracking Retries: 1
Tracking User-name: icx-radius-track
Tracking Password: AQBapdsoTpeGwAuE0Yi7Kbh7A+z2T0kIGViZ+ESpcz43A1ApCw
AAAL77YGoIkfiI9BIC
Number of Servers: 1
****** RADIUS Server Information ******
Server-Name              : cppm.arubatraining.com
Auth-Port                : 1812
Accounting-Port          : 1813
VRF                      :mgmt
Shared-Secret                                                              :
AQBapRkC49b8TnigvMULoSuIJ2ndGHK9Tnn6RCU6I0bG3Ft3AwAAAPOclQ==
Timeout (default)        : 5
Retries (default)        : 1
Auth-Type (default)      : pap
Server-Group             :cppm
Group-Priority           : 1
Tracking                 : enabled
Reachability-Status      : unreachable
ClearPass-Username       :
ClearPass-Password       : None
```

Task 3: Basic 802.1X Authentication with a Single User

Objectives

In this task, the PC3 (connected to Access1) will be performing 802.1X authentication.

The purpose of this lab is to demonstrate the basic 802.1X authentication process and some of the RADIUS attributes that a RADIUS server can return to an AOS-CX switch in order to control the client sessions. This task will not be using the role-based configuration yet; that will be done in an upcoming task.

In order for ClearPass to process this authentication request differently from the upcoming authentication with the user-roles, the hostname of the switch will be changed. The hostname of the switch is included in the RADIUS request to the RADIUS server as the 'NAS Identifier'. A service on the ClearPass server has been pre-configured to look for the string 'avp' in the 'NAS Identifier'.

For this task, the ClearPass server will need to return some standard RADIUS Attribute Value Pairs (AVP); therefore, the hostname should also contain the string 'avp' to match this service.

Steps

1. Change the hostname of the Access1 switch for this lab task. Replace x with your table number. Example for table 12: ICX-T12-Access1-avp, for table1: ICX-T1-Access1-avp

> **Note**
> Make sure the string '**avp**' is present in your hostname.

```
ICX-Tx-Access1(config)# hostname ICX-Tx-Access1-avp
```

> **Note**
> The hostname is used as the NAS-identifier in the access-request to ClearPass. ClearPass has been pre-configured to look for the value '**avp**' in the NAS-identifier to return standard IETF **Attribute Value Pairs** with VLAN instructions. This lab depends on these instructions.

2. Enable 802.1X authentication on the switch and ensure it is using the previously defined RADIUS server group.

```
ICX-Tx-Access1-avp(config)# aaa authentication port-access dot1x
authenticator radius server-group cppm
ICX-Tx-Access1-avp(config)# aaa authentication port-access dot1x
authenticator enable
```

3. Assign port 1/1/3 to VLAN 1. In this lab, it is simply used as the base landing VLAN in case the RADIUS server does not assign a VLAN. There is no DHCP server or no other resources in this VLAN in this example.

```
ICX-Tx-Access1-avp(config)# interface 1/1/3
ICX-Tx-Access1-avp(config-if)# vlan access 1
```

4. Enter the 802.1X authenticator context and enable 802.1X on the port.

```
ICX-Tx-Access1-avp(config-if)# aaa authentication port-access dot1x
authenticator
ICX-Tx-Access1-avp(config-if-dot1x-auth)# enable
ICX-Tx-Access1-avp(config-if-dot1x-auth)# exit
ICX-Tx-Access1-avp(config-if)# exit
```

Configure the Wired 'Lab NIC' with 802.1X Authentication

1. On PC3 (connected to the Access1 port 1/1/3), ensure that the Windows Service '**Wired AutoConfig**' is started. This service is not started by default. Open a command prompt with administrator rights; enter '**net start dot3svc**'
2. Open Network Connections (Click **Start** > **Settings** > **Network & Internet** > **Ethernet** > **Change adapter options**).
3. Under network connections, open the Properties of the '**Lab NIC**'. Click the '**Authentication**' tab and select '**Enable IEEE 802.1X authentication**'.

Note

The **'Authentication'** tab is not available; the 'Wired AutoConfig' service has not been started on the client PC. Check the previous steps to ensure the service is started.

---

4. Open **'Settings'** for the 'PEAP' method and **uncheck** 'Verify the server certificate'.

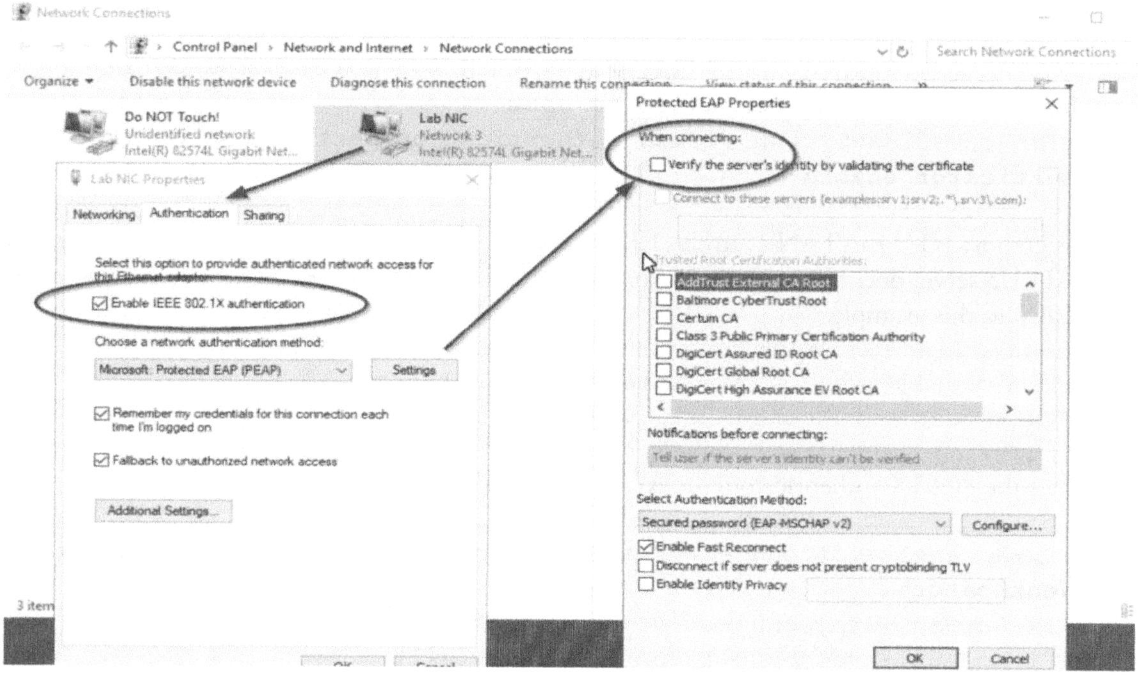

5. Click **'Configure'** next to the 'EAP-MSCHAP v2' method. Make sure the option 'Automatically use my Windows logon name' is **unchecked**. Click **'OK'** to close the window.

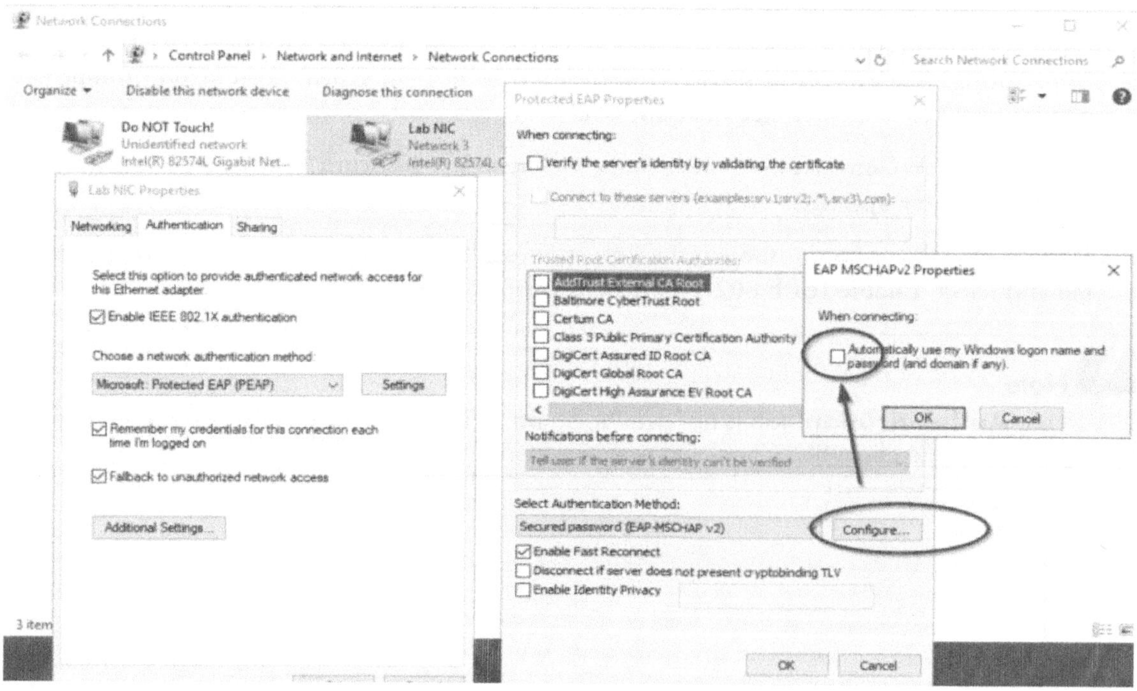

6. Click **'OK'** to close the 'Protected EAP Properties'.
7. Click 'Additional Settings', check 'Specify authentication mode', and select 'User authentication'.
8. Click **'Save credentials'** to enter the credentials.
   - username:**icx-avp1**
   - password: **aruba123**

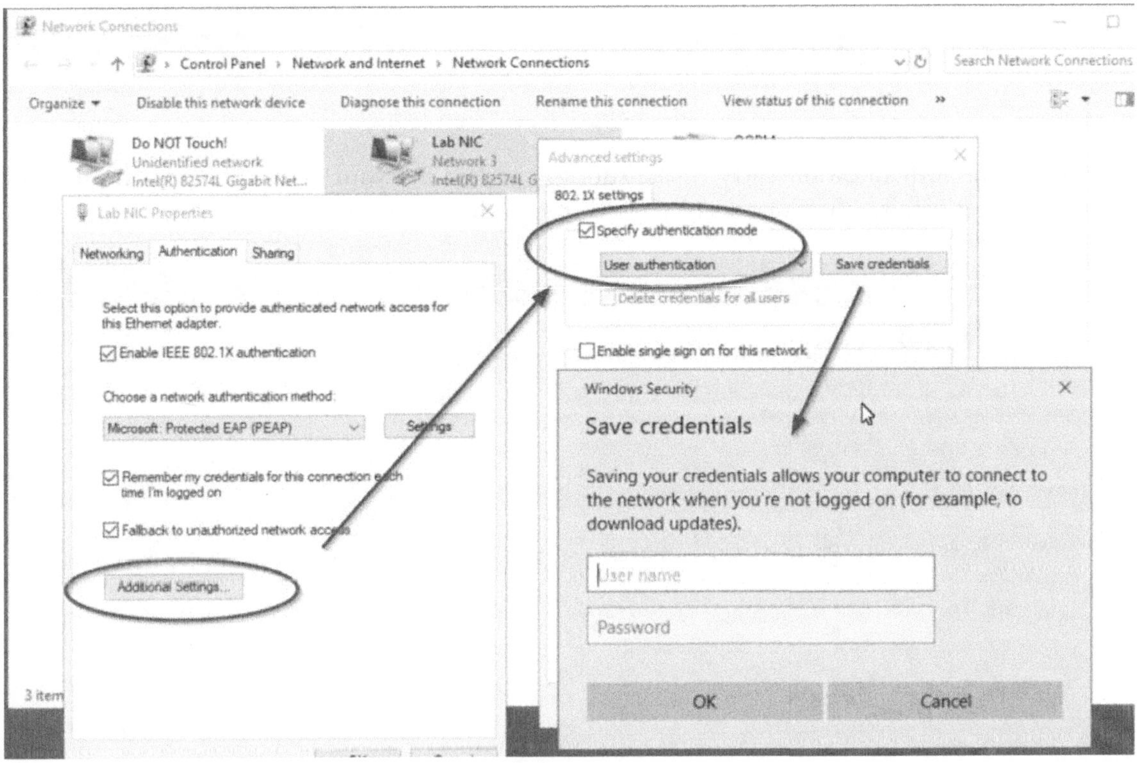

9. Click **'OK'** to save the credentials. Click **'OK'** to close the 'Advanced settings'. Click **'OK'** to close the 'Lab NIC Properties'.

10. Using PC1 (the OOBM mgmt PC), check Access Tracker in ClearPass.

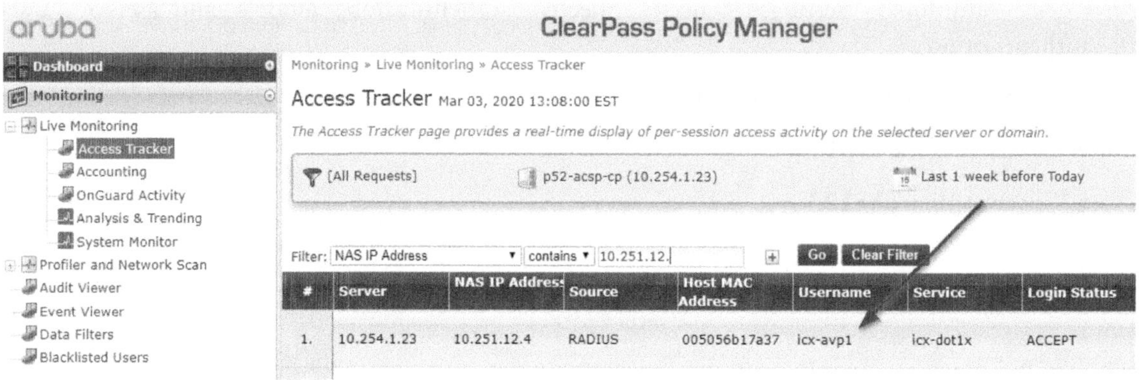

11. Open your authentication entry (make sure to check it has your NAS IP), click **'Input'**, and review the attributes that were sent by the switch in the access-request.

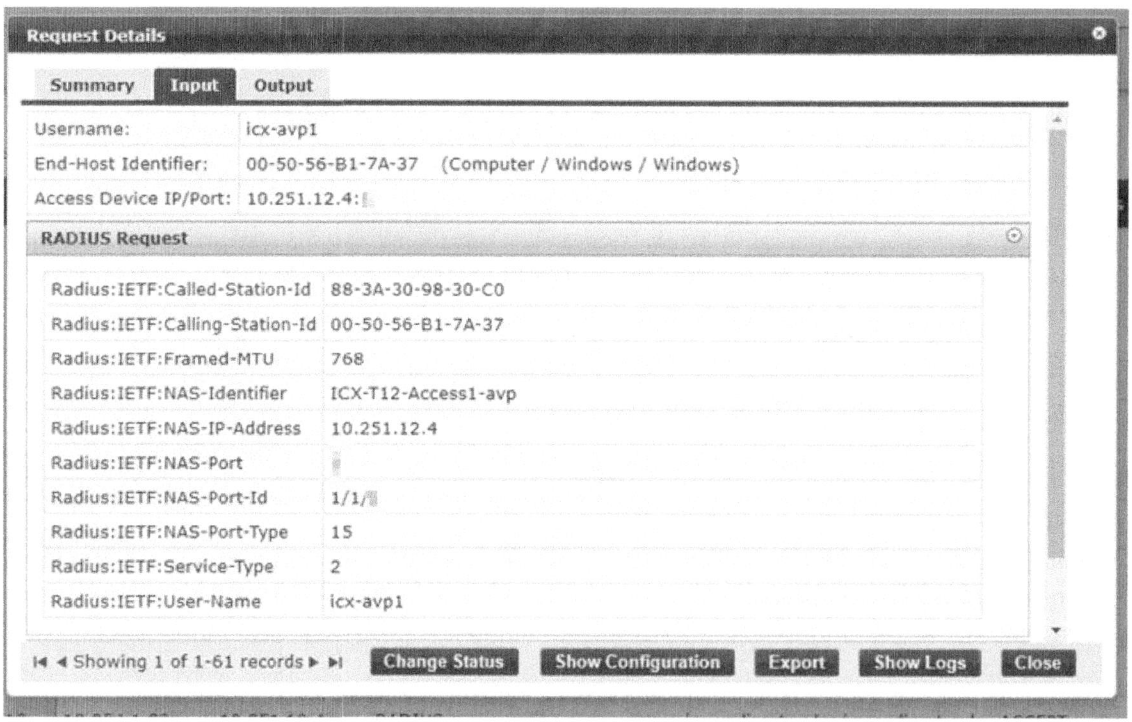

12. Next review the **'Output'** tab. This shows that ClearPass is returning the IETF VLAN attributes and a session timeout of 180 seconds to the switch.

> **Note**
> The value of 180 seconds was used in the lab environment to demonstrate the re-authentication. In a real deployment this value would be controlled by the customer security policy, this may be several hours.

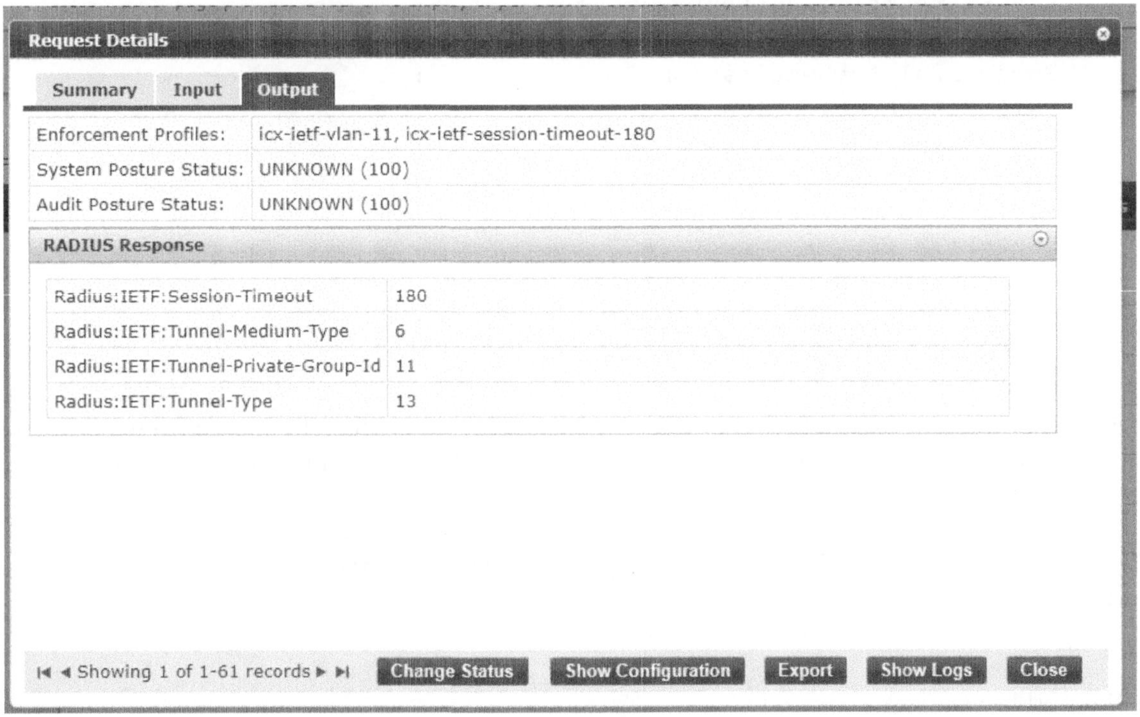

13. On the switch, check the authenticated clients. Take note of the MAC address of the authenticated client.

```
ICX-Tx-Access1-avp(config)# show aaa authentication port-access dot1x au-
thenticator interface all client-status
Client 00:50:56:b1:7a:37, icx-avp1, 1/1/3
==========================================

  Authentication Details
  ----------------------
    Status                              : Authenticated
    Type                                : Pass-Through
```

```
    EAP-Method                      : PEAP
    Auth Failure reason             :
    Time Since Last State Change    : 66s

  Authentication Statistics
  -------------------------
    Authentication                           : 9
    Authentication Timeout                   : 0
    EAP-Start While Authenticating           : 2
    EAP-Logoff While Authenticating          : 0
    Successful Authentication                : 1
    Failed Authentication                    : 7
    Re-Authentication                        : 0
    Successful Re-Authentication             : 0
    Failed Re-Authentication                 : 0
    EAP-Start When Authenticated             : 0
    EAP-Logoff When Authenticated            : 0
    Re-Auths When Authenticated              : 0
    Cached Re-Authentication                 : 0
```

14. Review the mac-address table. The client MAC address should have been assigned to VLAN 11 by port-access-security. Remember that the default VLAN of the interface 1/1/3 has been set to VLAN 1.

```
ICX-Tx-Access1-avp(config)# show mac-address-table
MAC age-time              : 300 seconds
Number of MAC addresses : 10

MAC Address          VLAN     Type                        Port
--------------------------------------------------------------
20:4c:03:5f:98:02    1        dynamic                     lag256
88:3a:30:97:b6:00    1        dynamic                     lag256
00:50:56:b1:7a:37    11       port-access-security        1/1/3
02:02:00:00:12:00    11       dynamic                     lag256
90:20:c2:bc:17:00    11       dynamic                     lag256
90:20:c2:bc:97:00    11       dynamic                     lag256
90:20:c2:bc:97:00    12       dynamic                     lag256
02:02:00:00:12:00    12       dynamic                     lag256
88:3a:30:97:b6:00    12       dynamic                     lag256
90:20:c2:bc:17:00    12       dynamic                     lag256
```

15. Review the switch log for entries of the **'port-accessd'** process. After a few minutes (180seconds), the user will be re-authenticated based on the RADIUS session-timeout. These are the options used:

- **-r**: show log in reverse order
- **-n 4**: last 4 lines of the log
- **-d**: filter on daemon (process)

```
ICX-Tx-Access1-avp(config)# show logging -r -n 4 -d port-accessd
---------------------------------------------------
Event logs from current boot
---------------------------------------------------
2020-03-03T18:01:27.948757+00:00 ICX-T12-Access1-avp port-accessd[2929]:
Event|10503|LOG_INFO|MSTR|1|Port 1/1/3 is unblocked by port-access
2020-03-03T18:01:27.775739+00:00 ICX-T12-Access1-avp port-accessd[2929]:
Event|10502|LOG_INFO|MSTR|1|Port 1/1/3 is blocked by port-access
2020-03-03T17:58:28.654705+00:00 ICX-T12-Access1-avp port-accessd[2929]:
Event|10503|LOG_INFO|MSTR|1|Port 1/1/3 is unblocked by port-access
2020-03-03T17:44:29.107796+00:00 ICX-T12-Access1-avp port-accessd[2929]:
Event|10502|LOG_INFO|MSTR|1|Port 1/1/3 is blocked by
```

16. Review the client accounting information. Notice that the session time will never exceed 180 seconds due to the re-authentication interval.

```
ICX-Tx-Access1-avp(config)# show aaa accounting port-access interface all
client-status
Port Access Client Status Details

Client 00:50:56:b1:7a:37, icx-avp1
============================
  Session Details
  ---------------
    Port                    : 1/1/3
Session Time            : 45s
```

```
Accounting Details
----------------------
  Accounting Session ID  : 1579185236543
  Input Packets          : 1197
  Input Octets           : 186098
  Output Packets         : 809
  Output Octets          : 82067
  Input Gigaword  : 0
  Output Gigaword  : 0
```

AOS-CX Internal User Roles

AOS-CX will internally always apply the authorization settings as a role. This is a significant change compared with the ArubaOS-Switch devices, where the switch was either in 'radius' mode **or** in 'user-role' mode. With those switches it was not possible to have some devices authenticated and authorized with RADIUS attributes, while other devices would be using a user-role.

In AOS-CX, this is solved by converting any RADIUS authorization attributes into a temporary user role of type 'radius'. Therefore, this role can coexist with any local defined roles or with any ClearPass downloadable user roles.

1. On the Access1 switch, review the port-access roles; note the type of the role. This shows which radius attributes were returned and converted into this temporary user role.

```
ICX-Tx-Access1-avp(config)# show port-access role
Role Information:
Name  : RADIUS_496422333
Type  : radius
----------------------------------------------
    Reauthentication Period              :
    Authentication Mode                  :
Session Timeout                      : 180 secs
    Client Inactivity Timeout            :
    Description                          :
    Gateway Zone                         :
    UBT Gateway Role                     :
Access VLAN                          : 11
    Native VLAN                          :
    Allowed Trunk VLANs                  :
    MTU                                  :
    QOS Trust Mode                       :
    PoE Priority                         :
    Captive Portal Profile               :
    Policy                               :
```

2. Next review the authenticated users on the interfaces. Notice the difference with the previous command client-status:

- To show 802.1X authenticated clients: **show aaa authentication port-access dot1x authenticator interface all client-status**
- To show the role authorization: **show aaa authentication port-access interface all client-status**

```
ICX-Tx-Access1-avp(config)# show aaa authentication port-access
interface all client-status
Port Access Client Status Details
Client 00:50:56:b1:7a:37, icx-avp1
============================
  Session Details
  ---------------
    Port         : 1/1/3
    Session Time : 123s

  Authentication Details
  ----------------------
    Status          : dot1x Authenticated
    Auth Precedence : dot1x - Authenticated, mac-auth - Not attempted

Authorization Details
----------------------
    Role    : RADIUS_496422333
Status : Applied
```

Task 4: Change of Authorization Verification

Objectives

Verify that a disconnect message from the ClearPass RADIUS host is processed correctly by the switch. This allows the ClearPass server to dynamically trigger re-authentication on the access device when the access security policy or the access conditions would have changed.

Steps

1. First review the current online time of the 802.1X authenticated user. When the CoA disconnect message is sent in the next steps, you should see that this timer will be reset, since the CoA will trigger a new authentication.

```
ICX-Tx-Access1-avp(config-if)# show aaa authentication port-access
interface all client-status
Port Access Client Status Details
Client 00:50:56:b1:7a:37, icx-avp1
=============================
  Session Details
  ---------------
    Port         : 1/1/3
Session Time :136s

  Authentication Details
  ----------------------
    Status          : dot1x Authenticated
    Auth Precedence : dot1x - Authenticated, mac-auth - Not attempted

  Authorization Details
  ----------------------
    Role    : RADIUS_496422333
Status : Applied
```

2. On the ClearPass system, navigate to **Monitoring > Live Access > Access Tracker**.
3. Open the latest authentication event from your own Access switch (use the NAS IP to find your own authentication session).
4. On the **'Summary'** page, use the **'Change Status'** to get access to the CoA options.

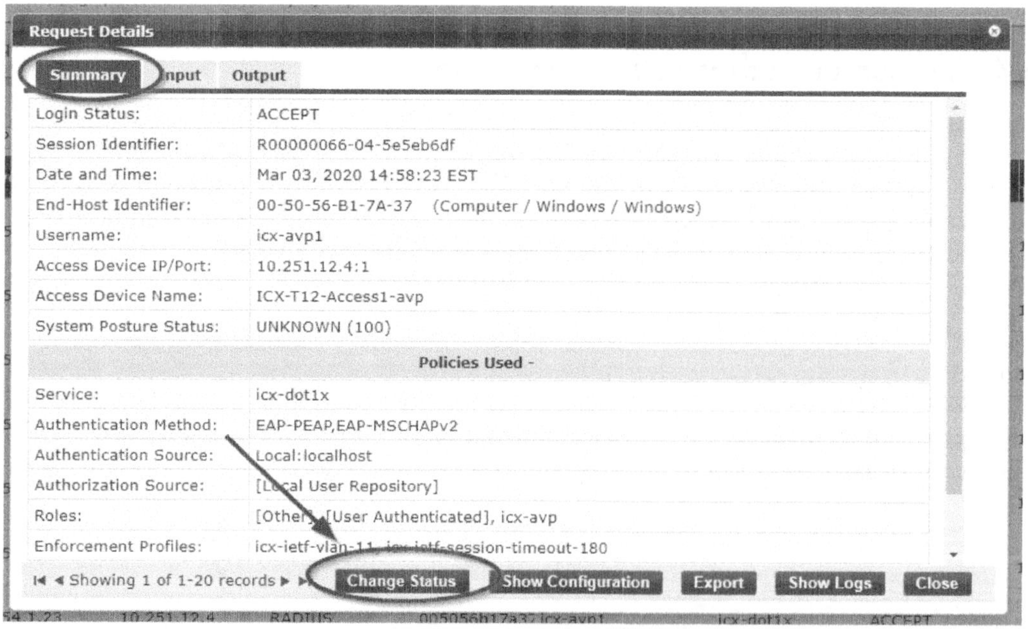

5. Use **'Submit'** to test the CoA.

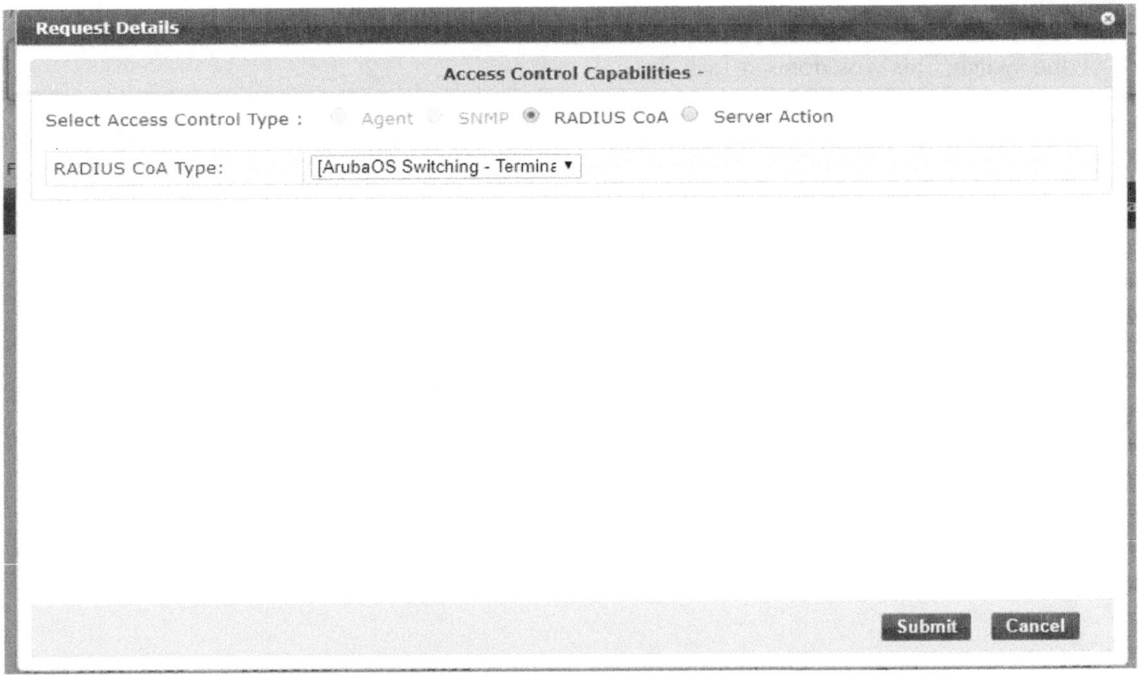

6. After a few seconds, a 'successful' message should be displayed.

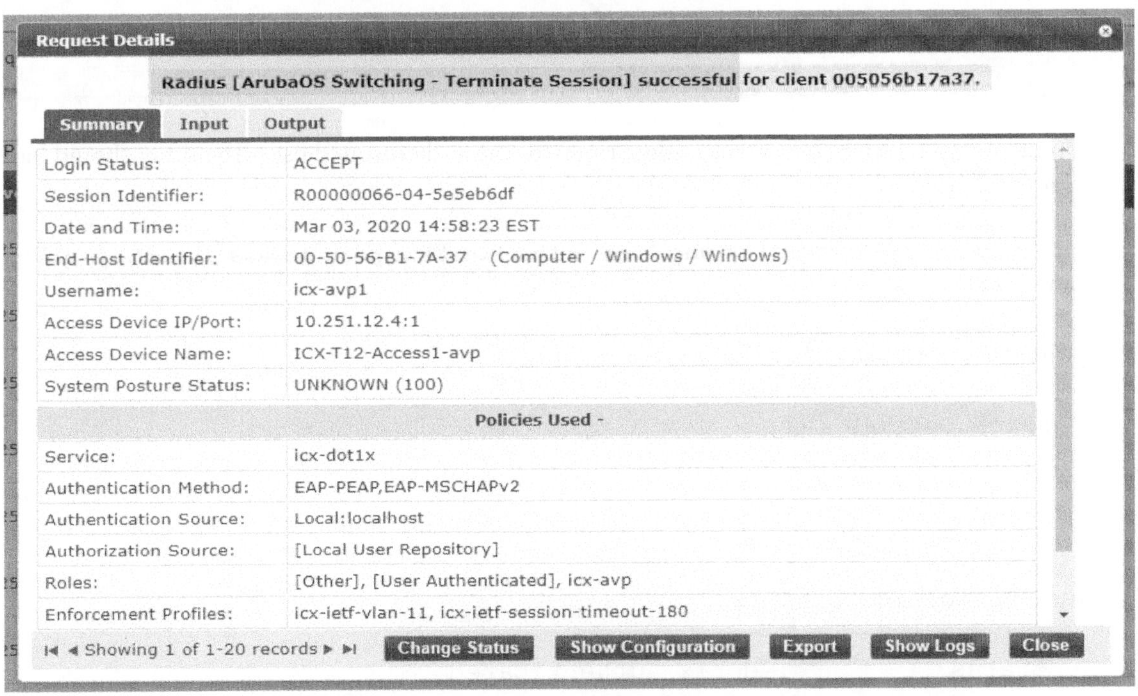

Note

If the CoA is not successful, you should check the dynamic authorization configuration on the switch. This was done in Task 2.

7. In the Access tracker list, a new authentication entry should show up a few seconds later.

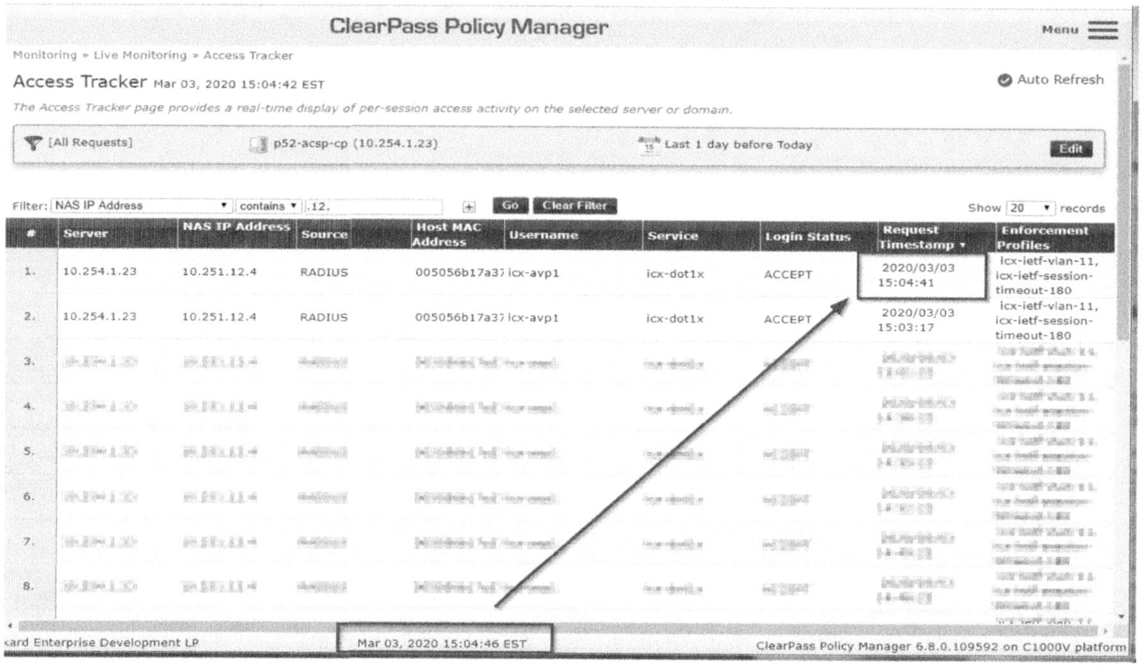

8. On the Access1 switch, review the 'online time' for the authenticated user. The timer should have been reset.

```
ICX-Tx-Access1-avp(config-if)# show aaa authentication port-access interface all
client-status
Port Access Client Status Details
Client 00:50:56:b1:7a:37, icx-avp1
==============================
   Session Details
   ---------------
      Port           : 1/1/3
Session Time : 10s

   Authentication Details
   ----------------------
      Status           : dot1x Authenticated
      Auth Precedence  : dot1x - Authenticated, mac-auth - Not attempted
```

```
   Authorization Details
   ----------------------
     Role    : RADIUS_496422333
Status : Applied
```

9. Review the statistics of 'dynamic authorization'.

```
ICX-Tx-Access1-avp(config)# show radius dyn-authorization
Status and Counters - RADIUS Dynamic Authorization Information

  RADIUS Dynamic Authorization                    : Enabled
  RADIUS Dynamic Authorization UDP Port           : 3799
  Invalid Client Addresses in CoA Requests        : 0
  Invalid Client Addresses in Disconnect Requests: 0

Dynamic Authorization Client Information
=========================================

IP Address           : cppm.arubatraining.com
VRF                  :mgmt
Replay Protection    : Disabled
Time Window          : 300
Disconnect Requests : 1
Disconnect ACKs      : 1
Disconnect NAKs      : 0
CoA Requests         : 0
CoA ACKs             : 0
CoA NAKs             : 0
Shared-Secret        : AQBapVWcNJavUClNBQenFa-
JwwRrR+nWcJUvsQlHUbuaiOvlDCAAAAMCnYwT2Ful+
ICX-Tx-Access1-avp(config)#
```

10. And the details for the CPPM client.

```
ICX-Tx-Access1-avp(config)# show radius dyn-authorization client cppm.
arubatraining.com vrf mgmt
Status and Counters - RADIUS Dynamic Authorization Client Information

  VRF Name                :mgmt
  Authorization Client    : cppm.arubatraining.com
  Unknown Packets         : 0
```

```
   Message-Type                             Disconnect         CoA
   ----------------------------------------------------------------
Total Requests                           1                0
   Authorize Only Requests                 0                0
   Malformed Requests                      0                0
   Bad Authenticator Requests              0                0
   Dropped Requests                        0                0
   Total ACK Responses                     2                0
   Total NAK Responses                     0                0
   Session Not Found Responses             0                0
User Sessions Modified                  1                0
ICX-Tx-Access1-avp(config)#
```

Task 5: Aruba User Role-Based Access

Objectives

In this task, you will explore how Aruba User Roles will simplify how settings can be assigned to an authenticated user or device. On the switch, user roles will be defined for an employee and contractor, each role will have different network access.

The ClearPass server will return this role to the switch when the users complete successful authentication. In order for ClearPass to return the correct Aruba VSA (Vendor-Specific-Attribute) 'Aruba-User-Role', you.will change the hostname of the switch, so a different policy will be applied by the ClearPass server for this task.

To define the roles, you will first define classes and policies. These can control the access to the network.

- The role employee will be assigned to VLAN 11, with an unrestricted ACL.
- The role contractor will be assigned to the same VLAN 11, but with a restricted ACL.

Steps

Define Traffic Classes

Each user role will be configured with unique access restrictions to the network. To control the network access, the administrator first needs to describe the traffic classes.

These are global objects that can be used in multiple policies.

1. Open a terminal session to Access1 and enter the configuration mode. Define a new class for 'any' traffic.

```
ICX-Tx-Access1-avp(config)# class ip any
ICX-Tx-Access1-avp(config-class-ip)# match any any any
ICX-Tx-Access1-avp(config-class-ip)# exit
```

2. Define a new class for 'servers'. This is for lab purpose only, so two IP addresses of the Core switches are used. The class is using the /255.0.255.255 to handle the unique Table x in each table IP address.

```
ICX-Tx-Access1-avp(config)# class ip servers
ICX-Tx-Access1-avp(config-class-ip)# match any any 10.0.1.2/255.0.255.255
ICX-Tx-Access1-avp(config-class-ip)# match any any 10.0.1.3/255.0.255.255
```

3. Notice how the system automatically adds line numbers for each entered line.

```
ICX-Tx-Access1-avp(config-class-ip)# show running  current-context
class ip servers
10 match any any 10.0.1.2/255.0.255.255
   20 match any any 10.0.1.3/255.0.255.255
```

4. The sequencing makes it easy to remove a single line, or to insert a line between two existing lines. Remove the second line again and verify 1 server is listed.

```
ICX-Tx-Access1-avp(config-class-ip)# no 20
ICX-Tx-Access1-avp(config-class-ip)# show running current-context
class ip servers
10 match any any 10.0.1.2/255.0.255.255
ICX-Tx-Access1-avp(config-class-ip)# exit
```

Define Policy for Employee

These are not the actual roles yet. A policy assigns an action to a traffic class.

1. Define the employee policy. Employees are granted full access to the network.

```
ICX-Tx-Access1-avp(config)# port-access policy employee
ICX-Tx-Access1-avp(config-pa-policy)# class ip any
```

2. By default, when a class is added to a policy, it gets an action 'permit', but many more actions are possible, such as QOS actions. Review the available actions using the '?' option, but no action must be configured in this step (due to the default 'permit').

```
ICX-Tx-Access1-avp(config-pa-policy)# class ip any action ?
cir               Specify the committed information rate
drop              Drop all traffic
dscp              Specify a Differentiated Services Code Point value
ip-precedence     Specify the IP precedence
local-priority    Specify a local priority value
```

```
pcp                 Specify the Priority Code Point (PCP) value
redirect            Specify a redirect destination
<cr>
ICX-Tx-Access1-avp(config-pa-policy)# exit
```

3. Define the contractor policy. Contractors will not be allowed access to the class 'servers', so this action is set to 'drop'. Any other traffic is permitted. The order of the policy is important for the traffic processing. Just like with the classes, the policy object will automatically add line numbers for each entry.

```
ICX-Tx-Access1-avp(config)# port-access policy contractor
ICX-Tx-Access1-avp(config-pa-policy)# class ip servers action drop
ICX-Tx-Access1-avp(config-pa-policy)# class ip any
```

4. Review the current context configuration.

```
ICX-Tx-Access1-avp(config-pa-policy)# show run current-context
port-access policy contractor
   10 class ip servers action drop
   20 class ip any
ICX-Tx-Access1-avp(config-pa-policy)#
```

5. The policy also allows the administrator to add a comment to each line.

```
ICX-Tx-Access1-avp(config-pa-policy)# 10 comment No server access
forContractors
ICX-Tx-Access1-avp(config-pa-policy)# show run cur
port-access policy contractor
   10 class ip servers action drop
10 comment No server access for Contractors
   20 class ip any
ICX-Tx-Access1-avp(config-pa-policy)# exit
```

6. Review the policy that was just created for the contractor.

```
ICX-Tx-Access1-avp(config)# show port-access policy contractor
Access Policy Details:
======================
Policy Name   : contractor
Policy Type   : Local
Policy Status : Applied
```

```
SEQUENCE    CLASS                           TYPE ACTION
----------- ----------------------------- ----
----------------------------------
10          servers                         ipv4 drop
20          any                             ipv4 permit
```

Define the User Roles for Employee

1. Define the user role for employee. In this step, the previously defined access policy will be bound to the role. The role also contains the L2 VLAN assignment.

```
ICX-Tx-Access1-avp(config)# port-access role employee
ICX-Tx-Access1-avp(config-pa-role)# associate policy employee
ICX-Tx-Access1-avp(config-pa-role)# vlan access 11
ICX-Tx-Access1-avp(config-pa-role)# exit
```

2. Define the user role for contractor.

```
ICX-Tx-Access1-avp(config)# port-access role contractor
ICX-Tx-Access1-avp(config-pa-role)# associate policy contractor
ICX-Tx-Access1-avp(config-pa-role)# vlan access 11
ICX-Tx-Access1-avp(config-pa-role)# exit
ICX-Tx-Access1-avp(config)#
```

3. Review the defined objects. Notice that these roles are 'local' roles, while in the previous section, the **'radius'** role was automatically defined based on the RADIUS attributes. In a later lab, role definitions will be downloaded from ClearPass; these are not **'local'** roles, but will be **'clearpass'** roles.

```
ICX-Tx-Access1-avp(config)# show port-access role
Role Information:
Name  : RADIUS_496422333
Type  : radius
----------------------------------------------
    Reauthentication Period              :
    Authentication Mode                  :
    Session Timeout                      : 180 secs
    Client Inactivity Timeout            :
    Description                          :
    Gateway Zone                         :
    UBT Gateway Role                     :
    Access VLAN                          : 11
    Native VLAN                          :
    Allowed Trunk VLANs                  :
```

```
     MTU                                   :
     QOS Trust Mode                        :
     PoE Priority                          :
     Captive Portal Profile                :
     Policy                                :

Name  : contractor
Type  : local
----------------------------------------------
     Reauthentication Period               :
     Authentication Mode                   :
     Session Timeout                       :
     Client Inactivity Timeout             :
     Description                           :
     Gateway Zone                          :
     UBT Gateway Role                      :
     Access VLAN                           : 11
     Native VLAN                           :
     Allowed Trunk VLANs                   :
     MTU                                   :
     QOS Trust Mode                        :
     PoE Priority                          :
     Captive Portal Profile                :
     Policy                                : contractor

Name  : employee
Type  : local
----------------------------------------------
     Reauthentication Period               :
     Authentication Mode                   :
     Session Timeout                       :
     Client Inactivity Timeout             :
     Description                           :
     Gateway Zone                          :
     UBT Gateway Role                      :
     Access VLAN                           : 11
     Native VLAN                           :
     Allowed Trunk VLANs                   :
     MTU                                   :
     QOS Trust Mode                        :
     PoE Priority                          :
     Captive Portal Profile                :
     Policy                                : employee
```

Test Access for User-Role Employee

1. Change hostname string from **'avp'** to **'vsa'**. Also, replace **Tx** with your table information; for example, T1 would be Table 1 and T12 would be Table 12.

```
ICX-Tx-Access1-avp(config)# hostname ICX-Tx-Access1-vsa
ICX-Tx-Access1-vsa(config)#
```

> **Note**
> The hostname is used as the NAS-identifier. ClearPass has been pre-configured to look for the value '**vsa**' in the NAS-identifier to return the **Aruba-User-Role** VSA attributes that are needed for this lab.

2. On PC3 (connected to Access1 port 1/1/3), change the 802.1X authentication credentials to:
   - Username: **icx-employee**
   - Password: **aruba123**

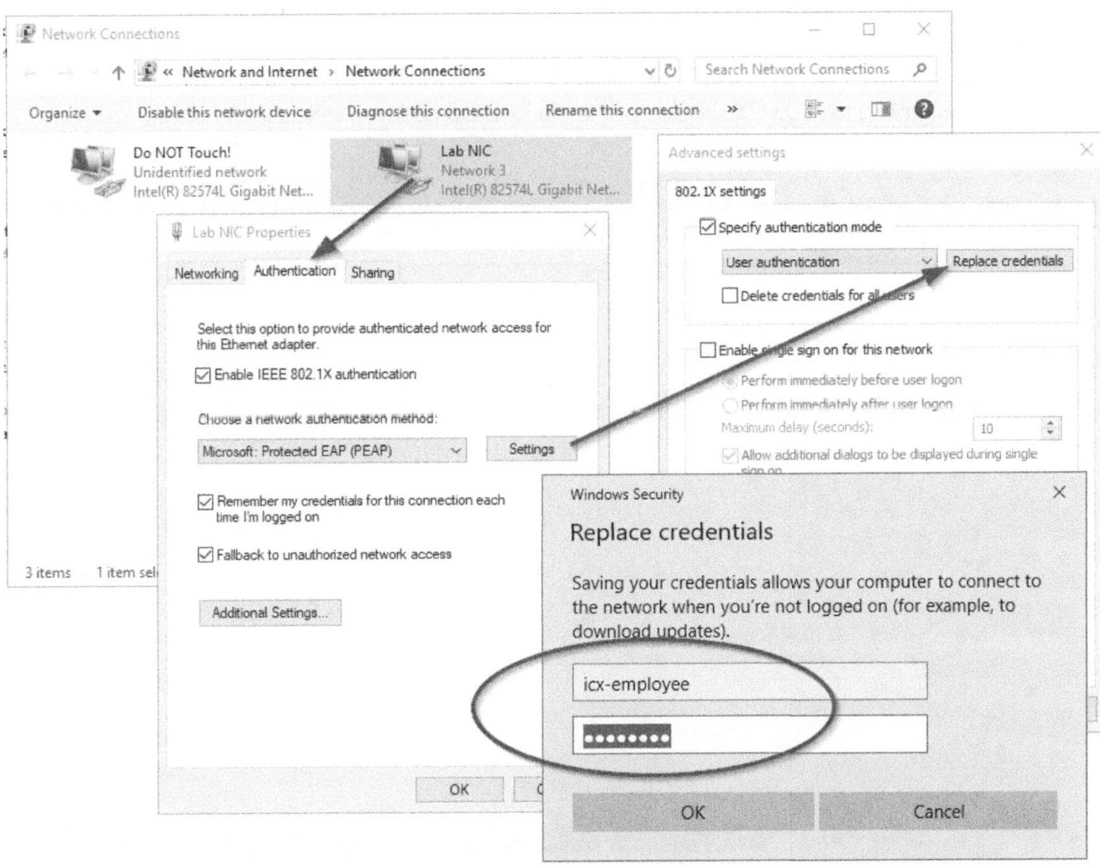

3. On the ClearPass system, navigate to Access tracker. Open your most recent authentication entry (it should have a username of 'icx-employee'. Make sure to check the NAS-IP so you are not looking at the entry of another table. Apply the filter 'NAS IP Address' contains '10.251.x' if you only want to see your own authentication events.

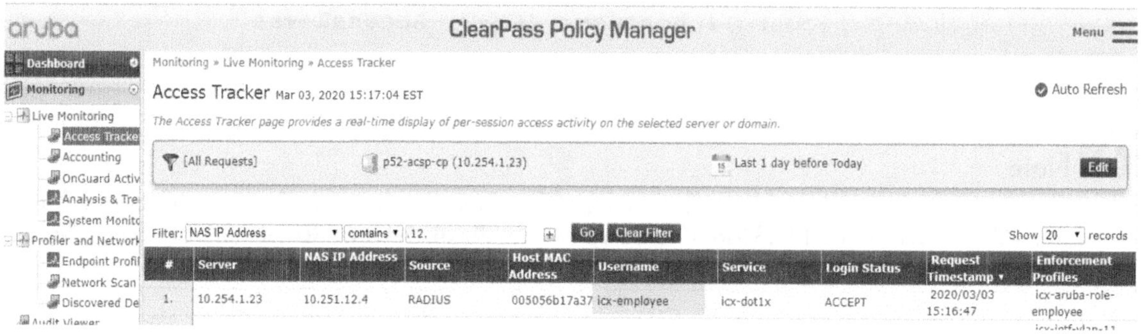

4. Check the '**Output**' of the entry and expand the "**RADIUS Response**" section. Notice that AOS-CX is now also using the Aruba RADIUS dictionary, so to push a user role, the 'Aruba-User-Role' attribute is used, just like the Aruba Mobility Controller.

Note

The ArubaOS-Switch platform was using the 'Hewlett-Packard-Enterprise' RADIUS dictionary, so customers migrating to AOS-CX should update the RADIUS policy to reflect this change.

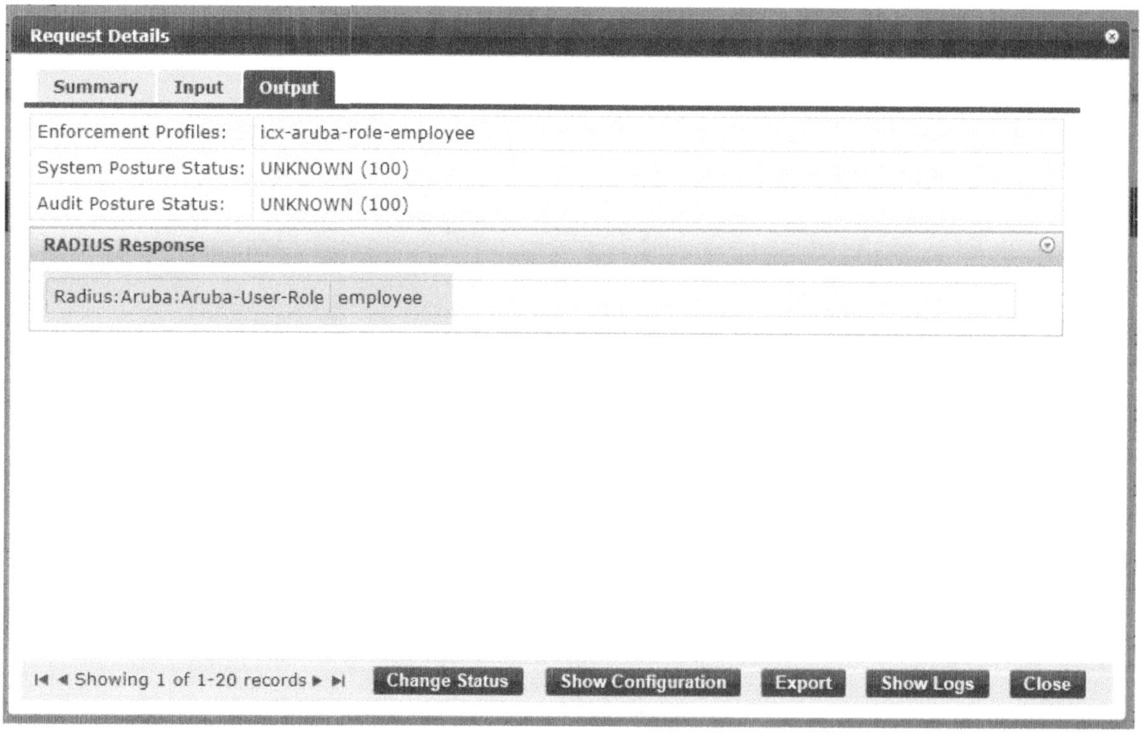

5. On the switch review the authenticated 802.1X users.

```
ICX-Tx-Access1-vsa(config)# show aaa authentication port-access
dot1x authenticator interface all client-status

Client 00:50:56:b1:7a:37, icx-employee, 1/1/3
============================================

  Authentication Details
  ----------------------
    Status                          : Authenticated
    Type                            : Pass-Through
    EAP-Method                      : PEAP
    Auth Failure reason             :
    Time Since Last State Change    : 906s
```

6. Review the user role authorization; the user should have been assigned the role 'employee' based on the RADIUS Aruba-User-Role assignment by ClearPass.

```
ICX-Tx-Access1-avp(config)# show aaa authentication port-access interface
all client-status
Port Access Client Status Details

Client 00:50:56:b1:7a:37, icx-employee
==============================
  Session Details
  ---------------
    Port         : 1/1/3
    Session Time : 1073s

  Authentication Details
  ----------------------
    Status          : dot1x Authenticated
    Auth Precedence : dot1x - Authenticated, mac-auth - Not attempted

  Authorization Details
  ----------------------
    Role    : employee
  Status : Applied
```

7. On PC3, verify that the employee role can access the 'server' host. Ping should be successful.

```
ping 10.x.1.2
```

Test Access for User-Role Contractor

You may test the contractor access, but these are optional steps.

1. On PC3 (connected to Access1 1/1/3), change the 802.1X credentials to:
   - Username: **icx-contractor**
   - Password: **aruba123**
2. ClearPass has been configured to return the Aruba-User-Role **'contractor'** for this user. Check the Output tab's RADIUS Response for the Access Tracker record.
3. On the switch, review the authentication result.

```
ICX-Tx-Access1-avp(config)# show aaa authentication port-access dot1x
authenticator interface all client-status
Client 00:50:56:b1:7a:37, icx-contractor, 1/1/3
=========================================

  Authentication Details
  ----------------------
    Status                          : Authenticated
    Type                            : Pass-Through
    EAP-Method                      : PEAP
    Auth Failure reason             :
    Time Since Last State Change    : 6s
```

4. Review the role authorization.

```
ICX-Tx-Access1-avp(config)# show aaa authentication port-access interface all
client-status
Port Access Client Status Details

Client 00:50:56:b1:7a:37, icx-contractor
============================
  Session Details
  ---------------
    Port         : 1/1/3
    Session Time : 1340s
```

```
   Authentication Details
   ----------------------
      Status           : dot1x Authenticated
      Auth Precedence : dot1x - Authenticated, mac-auth - Not attempted

Authorization Details
----------------------
      Role    : contractor
Status : Applied
```

5. On the client PC, verify the contractor role cannot access the 'server' host. Ping should **not** be successful.

```
ping 10.x.1.2
```

Task 6: Unknown Role Assignment

Objectives

Test result of configuration inconsistency between the RADIUS host and the switch configuration. From PC3, you will log in with user **'icx-badrole'** and verify the switch status.

Steps

On PC3, log in with a user that has an incorrect role assignment.

1. On the PC3, change the 802.1X authentication credentials to:
   - Username: **icx-badrole**
   - Password: **aruba123**
2. Verify the result on the switch. On the Access1 switch, verify the user has authenticated successfully.

```
ICX-Tx-Access1-avp(config)# show aaa authentication port-access dot1x
authenticator interface all client-status
Client 00:50:56:b1:7a:37, icx-badrole, 1/1/3
==========================================

   Authentication Details
   ----------------------
Status                          : Authenticated
      Type                        : Pass-Through
      EAP-Method                  : PEAP
      Auth Failure reason         :
      Time Since Last State Change : 39s
```

3. Review the role assignment.

```
ICX-Tx-Access1-avp(config)# show aaa authentication port-access interface all
client-status
Port Access Client Status Details

Client 00:50:56:b1:7a:37, icx-badrole
============================
  Session Details
  ---------------
    Port         : 1/1/3
    Session Time : 1887s

  Authentication Details
  ----------------------
    Status          : dot1x Authenticated
    Auth Precedence : dot1x - Authenticated, mac-auth - Not attempted

Authorization Details
----------------------
    Role :
Status : Invalid
```

4. Disable port 1/1/3 so that it does not interfere with the next lab.

```
ICX-Tx-Access1-avp(config)# interface 1/1/3
ICX-Tx-Access1-avp(config-if)# shutdown
ICX-Tx-Access1-avp(config-if)# exit
```

Learning Check

1. A company plans to use ClearPass to authenticate employees with 802.1X. Which role do AOS-CX switches at the access layer play in 802.1X authentication?
   a. supplicants
   b. authenticators
   c. authentication servers
   d. authentication aggregators
2. A network administrator is specifying ClearPass as a RADIUS server on an AOS-CX switch. What should the administrator configure to prevent issues of accepting and using VSAs?
   a. radius-server dyn-authorization enable
   b. radius-server dyn-authorization port set 1812
   c. time window set to 0
   d. enable NTP

Summary

Congratulations! In this chapter, you learned how to enforce 802.1X on an AOS-CX switch using on external RADIUS server such as Aruba ClearPass. You know how to set up the basic 802.1X authentication and authorization solution, and you can also integrate your switches with more advanced features that customize user access dynamically. These features include standards-based IETF VSAs as well as Aruba's switch roles, local and downloadable.

11 MAC Authentication

OBJECTIVES

By the time that you have completed this chapter, you should be able to:

✓ Implement RADIUS-based MAC Authentication (MAC-Auth) on AOS-CX switch ports

✓ Implement device profiles to provision devices by dynamically assigning the switch port settings based on LLDP or CDP information

Overview

This chapter teaches you how to implement MAC Authentication (MAC-Auth) technology on AOS-CX switches. Typically, MAC authentication is used when devices do not support other methods of authentication, as a second form of authentication, and in combination with captive portal. In this chapter you will learn how to implement MAC authentication and how to configure a port where both 802.1X and MAC-Auth are supported on a switch port.

RADIUS MAC-Auth

You will first learn how to implement MAC-Auth with RADIUS-based authentication.

MAC-Auth Use Cases

- Access control for clients with limited authentication capabilities:
  - Based on client source MAC address
  - No requirements on the client side
- Second form of authentication for access control
- Captive portal with MAC-Auth
- Minimal security (easily spoofed)
- Simplified provisioning (VLAN assignment) for devices such as printers and IoT devices

Figure 11-1 MAC-Auth Use Cases

MAC-Auth allows companies to impose network access control for devices with limited capabilities.

Essentially, the switch uses a client's MAC address to authenticate the client. Because Ethernet clients always include their MAC address as the source of their Ethernet frames, the client does not need to be configured to submit credentials. Therefore, this authentication method provides an option for devices that do not have a user interface or support for 802.1X.

When you need rigorous security, you should use 802.1X, whenever possible, since it supports username/password and digital certificate authentication at layer-2. Often it is trivial for a hacker to discover MAC addresses used in your system, whether by eavesdropping or accessing a legitimate device. The hacker can then easily spoof an authorized MAC address. MAC authentication might also be more difficult to manage than other forms of authentication, requiring directory or domain administrators to create accounts for each MAC address on each device, whereas 802.1X can use the user accounts already in the directory or domain.

Rather than a security measure, MAC-Auth is perhaps most useful for simplifying the provisioning for devices such as printers, Internet of Things (IoT) devices, IP phones, and security cameras. In addition to permitting a device network access based on its group, the authentication server can assign the dynamic settings, such as a VLAN ID and QoS priority, to device's session.

MAC authentication relies on a RADIUS server to authenticate network access. This simplifies access security management by allowing the control of access from a master database in a single server. Up to three RADIUS servers can be used for backup in case access to the primary server fails. It also means the same credentials can be used for authentication, regardless of which switch or switch port is the current access point into the LAN.

On a port configured for MAC authentication, the switch operates as a port-access authenticator using a RADIUS server, and the CHAP and PAP protocols. Inbound traffic is processed by the switch alone, until authentication occurs. Some traffic from the switch to an unauthorized client is supported (for example, broadcast or unknown destination packets) before authentication occurs (Figure 11-1).

RADIUS-Based MAC-Auth

1. The switch prohibits traffic to and from unauthenticated MAC addresses.
2. The switch submits the unauthenticated MAC address to the RADIUS server.
3. If the switch receives a RADIUS accept, the switch allows the traffic.

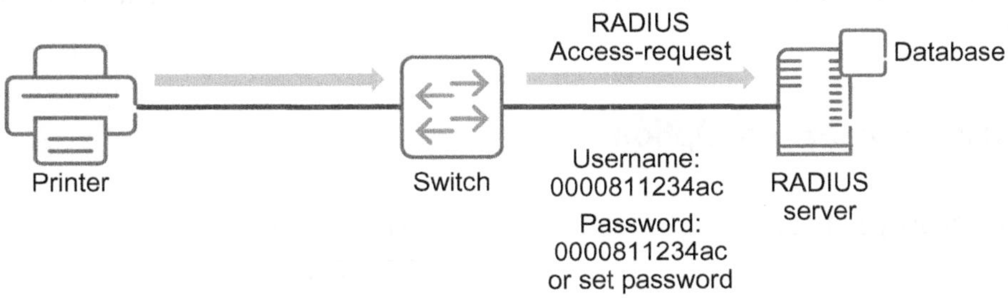

Figure 11-2 RADIUS-Based MAC-Auth

You can enable RADIUS-based MAC-Auth on individual switch ports (Figure 11-2). This basic process occurs when a client connects to an AOS-CX switch port that enforces RADIUS MAC-Auth:

1. The client is initially unauthenticated. The switch does not transmit traffic on the line. Authentication is not triggered until the client begins to send traffic on its own. This traffic is initially dropped while the switch completes the next steps.
2. The switch submits credentials to a RADIUS server on the client's behalf.

   Often these credentials consist of the client's MAC address as the username and password. However, the password can be different from the MAC address.
3. The RADIUS server authenticates the MAC address against a user account. Only the switch and the server are involved in the exchange of authentication messages, unlike with other port-based authentication methods. The RADIUS server uses its user database—which should have an account for the client's MAC address—and policies to determine whether to grant access. It communicates its decision to the switch in a RADIUS Accept-Access or Reject-Access message.
4. The switch handles the client according to the RADIUS server's decision.

If the server accepted access, the switch allows all traffic to and from the client with that MAC address.

If the server rejected access, the client remains in the unauthenticated state, and the switch handles its traffic as indicated in step 1.

The switch continues to examine incoming frames. If a new client connects, the switch will authenticate that client. The switch also attempts to authenticate the client for which authentication failed again. By default, the switch suppresses authentication requests for such clients over the quiet period—by default, 60 seconds. It then sends another authentication request.

Before gaining access to the network, a client first presents authentication credentials to the switch. The switch then verifies the credentials with a RADIUS authentication server. Successfully authenticated clients receive access to the network, as defined by the system administrator. Clients who fail to authenticate successfully receive no network access or limited network access as defined by the system administrator.

RADIUS-Based MAC-Auth Options

- Authentication protocol :
  - PAP
  - CHAP
- Credentials:
  - Default:
    - Username = MAC address
    - Password = MAC address
- Option:
  - Username = MAC address
  - Password = Global (fixed) password
- MAC address format

Figure 11-3 RADIUS-Based MAC-Auth Options

You need to make several choices related to RADIUS MAC-Auth. The sections below describe each of these choices (Figure 11-3).

Authentication Protocol

You have two choices for the protocol that the switch uses to send the credentials to the RADIUS server:

- Password Authentication Protocol (PAP)
- Challenge Handshake Authentication Protocol (CHAP)

You learned about how RADIUS works with EAP in 802.1X. AOS-CX switches can use PAP or CHAP for MAC-Auth. In this case, the switch acts as the authentication client rather than the client itself, generating the PAP request messages. Note that PAP sends passwords in clear-text, which can pose a security threat.

Alternatively, on the AOS-CX switches, you can choose CHAP for the authentication protocol. RADIUS has specific messages for CHAP authentication and most RADIUS servers support this option. You should be aware that the mechanisms of CHAP require passwords to be stored with reversible encryption, which poses a potential security hazard and is not typical for most directories and domains. This limitation would mean, for example, that the directory, domain, or RADIUS administrator who creates the accounts for the clients would have to take special measures to store the passwords with reversible encryption. (For a Microsoft Windows domain, the administrators can edit the group policy object (GPO) and enable reversal encryption in the computer policies for account settings.)

The command for setting the protocol is:

```
Switch(config)# aaa authentication port-access mac-auth
Switch(config-macauth)# auth-method <chap | pap>
```

Credentials

You need to decide the precise credentials that switches will send so that the RADIUS, directory, or domain administrator can set up the accounts accordingly.

By default, AOS-CX switches send the MAC address for both the username and password. You can set up a global password, which the switch uses for the password instead of the device's MAC address. The switch itself places the password in the authentication request. No configuration is required on the client. The switch continues to use the client's MAC address for the username, so every client requires a user account on the RADIUS server (or background directory).

The password option is intended to add a bit of security to the solution. However, keep in mind. Hackers can still spoof an authorized MAC address, connect to the switch, and gain access to the network because the switch adds the password on its end. Remember: MAC-Auth provides basic security; you should use 802.1X when you require more rigorous security.

To specify a global password for all MAC addresses, use the following configuration:

```
Switch(config)# aaa authentication port-access mac-auth
Switch(config-macauth)# password plaintext <password>
```

MAC Address Format

When you are using MAC addresses for the username, password, or both, you must ensure that the switch sends the credentials with the same format used in the user accounts. The table below shows the options and the syntax for configuring a specific format for AOS-CX switches.

Use this configuration for specifying the address format:

```
Switch(config)# aaa authentication port-access mac-auth
Switch(config-macauth)# addr-format <delimiter-format>
```

Use Table 11-1 for the parameters. The default is **no-delimiter**.

Note

Accounts in Microsoft Active Directory (AD) domains cannot use colons, so choose a format that does not include colons if you use AD.

Table 11-1 MAC Address Formats

Format	AOS-CX Switch Parameter
aabbccddeeff	**no-delimiter**
aabbcc-ddeeff	**single-dash**
aa-bb-cc-dd-ee-ff	**multi-dash**
aa:bb:cc:dd:ee:ff	**multi-colon**
AABBCCDDEEFF	**no-delimiter-uppercase**
AABBCC-DDEEFF	**single-dash-uppercase**
AA-BB-CC-DD-EE-FF	**multi-dash-uppercase**
AA:BB:CC:DD:EE:FF	**multi-colon-uppercase**

MAC-Auth and Provisioning with ClearPass

Aruba ClearPass can fulfill the role of RADIUS server for MAC-Auth as well as for 802.1X.

ClearPass provides MAC-Auth-specific service templates that make it easy for administrators to set up ClearPass to act as the RADIUS server for your MAC-Auth solution. The service can specify profiles to apply to clients based on their MAC addresses and other capabilities. In this way, ClearPass can communicate the correct settings for the connected device, which the switch applies to the port in much the same way as it applies settings with 802.1X. For example, if you are using MAC-Auth to authenticate IP phones, ClearPass policies could assign the correct voice VLAN and QoS priority for the phones' traffic.

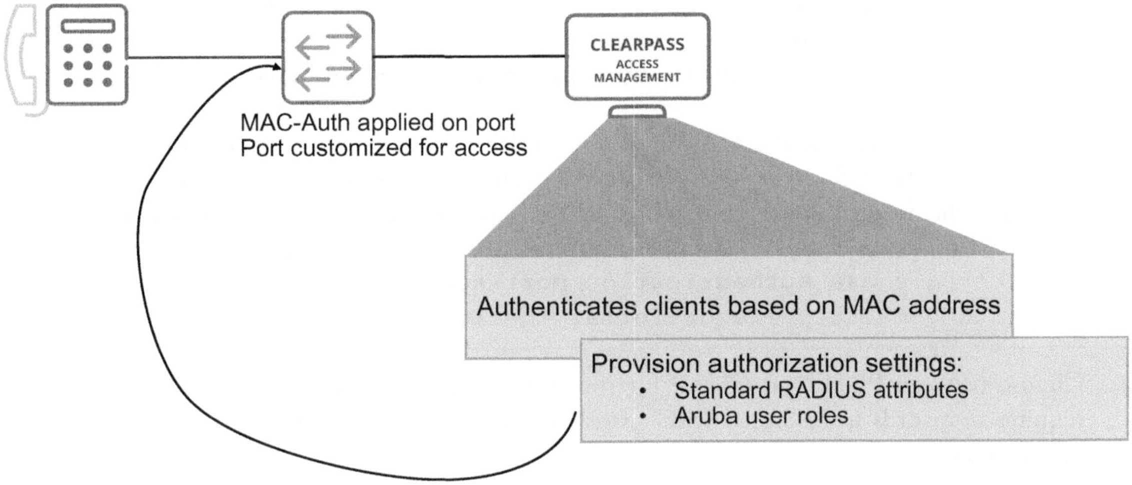

Figure 11-4 MAC-Auth and Provisioning with ClearPass

You can provision authorization settings using standard RADIUS attributes, like a VLAN, ACL, or QoS settings, or using Aruba user roles (Figure 11-4).

RADIUS-Based MAC-Auth Configuration Process

1. Specify RADIUS server IP addresses and keys (global key or per-server).
2. Configure the MAC-Auth credential format.
3. Select the authentication protocol.
4. Specify the RADIUS server(s)/group.
5. Enable MAC-Auth globally.
6. Enable MAC-Auth on individual ports.

Figure 11-5 RADIUS-Based MAC-Auth Configuration Process

Here are the steps to implement MAC-Auth:

1. Specify your RADIUS server (Figure 11-5). In this example, you are using only the global group. These commands specify the server and set the proper options for ClearPass. Remember to set the key to match the secret configured for this switch on ClearPass. These commands, as well as others, are used for a RADIUS server(s) configuration:

```
Switch(config)# radius-server host <IP-address-or-FQDN>
                key plaintext <secret-key>
Switch(config)# radius-server dyn-authorization enable
```

2. Configure the format for the MAC-Auth credentials so that they match the credentials configured on the RADIUS server (or its backend directory). See Table 11-1 for formats. (ClearPass often uses the no-delimiter option, which is also the default option on AOS-CX switches.)

```
Switch(config)# aaa authentication port-access mac-auth
Switch(config-macauth)# addr-format <delimiter-format>
```

3. Choose between PEAP and CHAP for the authentication protocol. (Remember that CHAP requires passwords to be stored with reversible encryption, which is not the default for many directories.)

```
Switch(config)# aaa authentication port-access mac-auth
Switch(config-macauth)# auth-method <chap | pap>
```

4. Specify the RADIUS server group:

```
Switch(config)# aaa authentication port-access mac-auth
switch(config-macauth)# radius server-group {radius | <group-name>}
```

5. Enable MAC-Auth globally.

```
switch(config)# aaa authentication port-access mac-auth
switch(config-macauth)# enable
```

6. Enable MAC-Auth on the individual ports that you want to enforce this type of authentication.

```
switch(config)# interface <interface-ID>
switch(config-if)# aaa authentication port-access mac-auth
switch(config-if-macauth)# enable
```

Verification

You can use the following commands to verify the configuration and operation of MAC-Auth:

- **show aaa authentication port-access mac-auth interface [interface name] | all port-statistics**: Displays information related to MAC authentication ports on the switch.
- **show aaa authentication port-access mac-auth interface all client-status**: This command displays MAC authentication clients' status on the interface.

- **clear mac-auth statistics [interface]**: Clear the MAC authentication statistics associated with the port and all the MAC authentication state machines attached to this port.
- **show tech mac-auth [local-file]**: Displays output of the following commands:
  - **show aaa authentication port-access mac-auth interface all port-statistics**
  - **show aaa authentication port-access mac-auth interface all client-status**
  - **show aaa authentication port-access interface all client-status**
  - **diag-dump mac-auth basic**

Optional Configuration Steps

1. Define the MAC address format
2. Set a MAC-Auth password.
3. Adjust other settings such as quiet and reauthentication periods.
4. Allow LLDP on the individual ports.

Figure 11-6 Optional Configuration Steps

Here are some optional steps, as shown in Figure 11-6, for MAC-Auth:

1. Configure the format for the MAC-Auth credentials so that they match the credentials configured on the RADIUS server (or its backend directory). See Table 11-1 for formats. (ClearPass often uses the no-delimiter option, which is also the default option on AOS-CX switches.)

```
Switch(config)# aaa authentication port-access mac-auth
Switch(config-macauth)# addr-format <delimiter-format>
```

2. If you want the switch to send a password, rather than MAC address in the password field, specify the global (fixed) password.

```
Switch(config)# aaa authentication port-access mac-auth
Switch(config-macauth)# password plaintext <password>
```

3. Optionally, you can adjust other settings such as the timers for the quiet period and re-authenticating clients. (If you set the reauth period to 0, the switch does not enforce reauthentication.) All of these timers are set in seconds. You can refer to your switch's *Access Security Guide* to learn about more MAC-Auth-related options.

```
Switch(config)# aaa authentication port-access mac-auth
Switch(config-macauth)# quiet-period <1-65535>
Switch(config-macauth)# reauth
Switch(config-macauth)# reauth-period <0-65535>
```

4. Optionally allow LLDP on the port.

```
Switch(config)# interface <interface-ID>
Switch(config-if)# aaa authentication port-access allow-lldp-bpdu
```

Multiple Client and Authentication Method Scenarios

Next you will look at some more complex scenarios. You will also explore authentication in scenarios in which multiple devices can connect to a single switch. You will learn how to enforce MAC-Auth and 802.1X on the same port.

Combining MAC-Auth and 802.1X

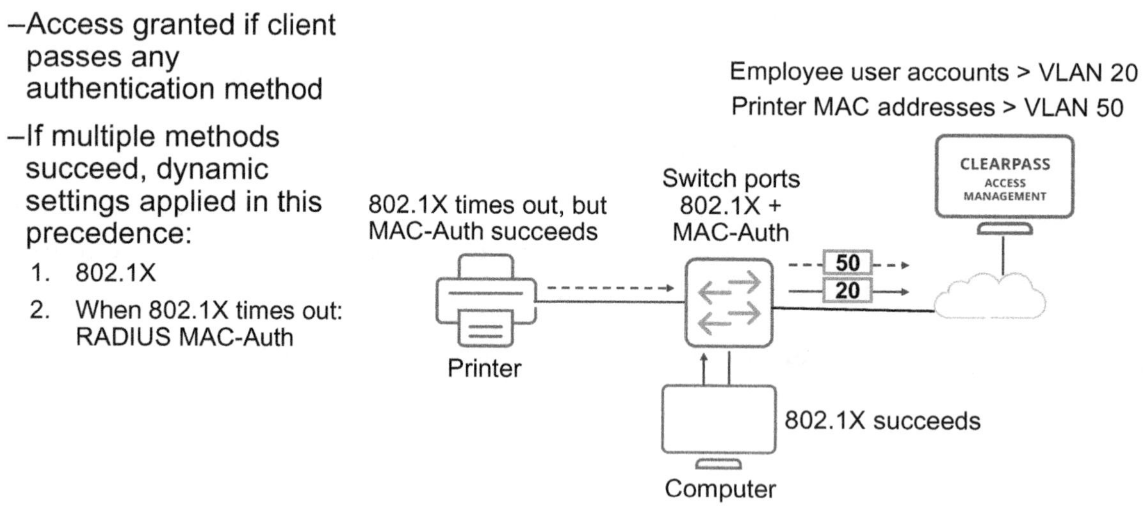

Figure 11-7 Combining MAC-Auth and 802.1X

Implementing MAC-Auth on Ports with Multiple Clients

You have assumed until now that you are implementing authentication on edge ports that support one endpoint at a time, which is true in many environments. However, you often apply LMA and RADIUS MAC-Auth to IP phones. And often a computer connects to the IP phone, and the IP phone then connects to the switch port on a second port. In another scenario, a company might have a hub, an unmanaged switch, or an unmanaged AP to which multiple devices connect (Figure 11-7).

For these scenarios, set up LMA or RADIUS MAC-Auth as you learned how to do earlier. By default, the switch allows only one MAC address to authenticate on the port at the same time. After a connected client passes authentication, the switch drops traffic received from any other MAC address even if that address would otherwise pass authentication. You need to raise the MAC address limit with one of these commands, depending on whether you are using RADIUS MAC-Auth or LMA:

```
Switch(config)# interface <interface-ID>
Switch(config-if)# aaa authentication port-access client-limit <1-256>
```

The default value is 1. You typically assign tagged VLANs to IP phones and untagged VLANs to computers. If you want to enforce authentication for the computers, you can assign the untagged VLAN through the RADIUS profile, or you can have computers use the port's static VLAN.

Note

802.1X port access and MAC authentication can be configured at the same time on a port. A total of 256 clients can be configured per port and 16,384 clients on the entire switch, irrespective of the authentication method. After the limit of 16,384 clients is reached, no additional authentication clients are allowed on any port for any method. The default is one client.

MAC authentication, MAC lockout, and port security are mutually exclusive on a given port. If you configure any of these authentication methods on a port, you must disable LACP on the port.

Combining MAC-Auth and 802.1X

A port can support multiple authentication methods, enabling it to authenticate different types of devices and users. For example, you have devices that are capable of completing 802.1X authentication, but also some devices (such as IP phones and printers) that are not.

Important

By default, 802.1X is performed first (unless changed). If 802.1X times out, the switch assumes that the device does not support it. If MAC-Auth is also enabled on the port, then the switch will authenticate the device with MAC-Auth.

First you will look at a scenario in which a port supports one device at a time, but you are not sure which type of device will connect to a specific port. You want to make sure that any type of device can pass authentication and receive the correct customized access.

You want to make sure that each port supports RADIUS MAC-Auth and 802.1X authentication.

Because the use of 802.1X implies that you have a RADIUS infrastructure, you might choose to combine RADIUS MAC-Auth and 802.1X.

A port that implements RADIUS MAC-Auth with 802.1X immediately uses the device's MAC address to submit an access request, just as it would if MAC-Auth were the only authentication method:

- If RADIUS MAC-Auth succeeds, the device is authorized for network access with the settings returned by the RADIUS server profile.
- If RADIUS MAC-Auth fails, the user still has the option to pass 802.1X authentication. If the user succeeds, the device is authorized for network access with the settings returned by the RADIUS server.
- If both types of authentication fail, the device is prohibited access.
- Even if RADIUS MAC-Auth succeeds, the user device might initiate 802.1X. (However, the switch itself will not.) If the user then authenticates successfully with 802.1X, the settings returned at the end of the 802.1X process take precedence over any settings applied by RADIUS MAC-Auth.

Keep in mind the following guidelines when enabling MAC-Auth or LMA and 802.1X on the same port:

- Ensure that the port operates in user-based mode for 802.1X. Set a client limit with this command, even if that client limit is 1:

```
Switch(config)# interface <interface-ID>
Switch(config-if)# aaa authentication port-access client-limit <1-256>
```

- Ensure that each type of device and user receives the correct VLAN assignment. For example, you might have the RADIUS server profile assign MAC-Auth clients to different VLANs from 802.1X users.

- MAC-Auth remains vulnerable to spoofing. If you are concerned about untrusted users accessing the port, you should take appropriate measures to filter traffic in the VLANs assigned to MAC-Auth clients.
- If you are using MAC-Auth, make sure that the RADIUS server has the correct policies and accounts for providing MAC-Auth only for the headless devices that require it. Similarly, if you are using LMA, only set up MAC groups and profiles for the headless devices. MAC-Auth is the weakest link in the security system, so you want clients capable of 802.1X to fail initial authentication and perform 802.1X authentication instead. Note also that, although 802.1X settings take precedence, it can interfere with a client's connection to be first placed in a VLAN by MAC-Auth and then be placed in another VLAN after 802.1X authentication. Also, a client that has successfully received access with MAC-Auth sometimes might not initiate 802.1X.

By default, 802.1X will be tried by the switch first. If no 802.1X response is received by the supplicant, the switch will then try MAC-Auth. You can change the order, per-interface, with this configuration:

```
Switch(config)# interface <interface-ID>
Switch(config-if)# aaa authentication port-access auth-precedence
                    [dot1x mac-auth | mac-auth dot1x}
```

Combining MAC-Auth and 802.1X in Multiple Client Scenarios

Here you are looking at multiple client scenarios similar to the ones that you examined a moment earlier. Now, however, the switch enforces 802.1X authentication for some devices such as computers, rather than MAC authentication or no authentication (Figure 11-8).

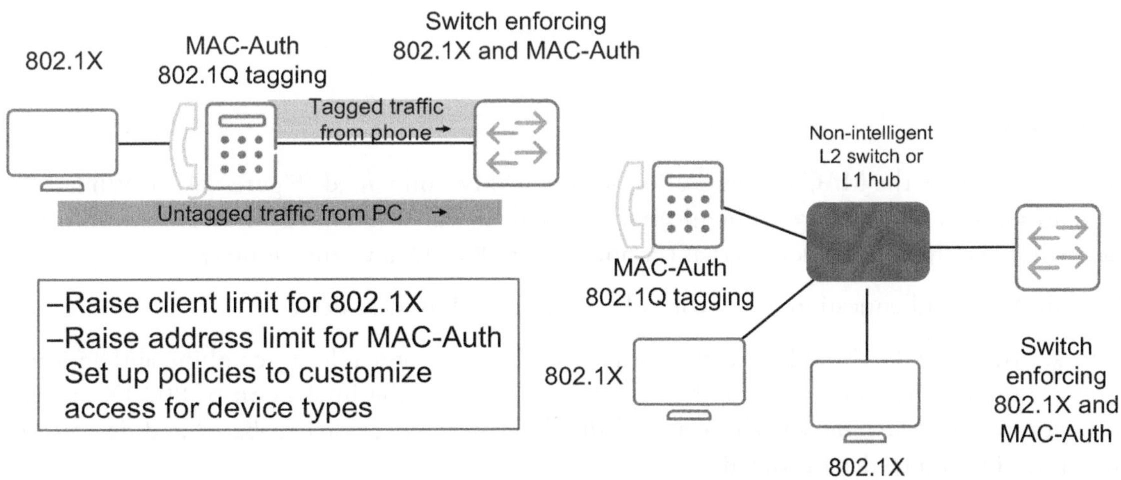

Figure 11-8 Combining MAC-Auth and 802.1X in Multiple Client Scenarios

To support this scenario, enable both 802.1X and RADIUS MAC-Auth on the same port. Then make sure that you raise *both* the client limit for 802.1X and the address limit for RADIUS MAC-Auth to accommodate the number of devices that the port should support. The switch counts the 802.1X limit separately from the RADIUS MAC-Auth limit, but clients might be able to succeed multiple forms of authentication, or you might not know which forms of authentication clients will use. Set up policies to customize access for the different types of devices.

Lab 11

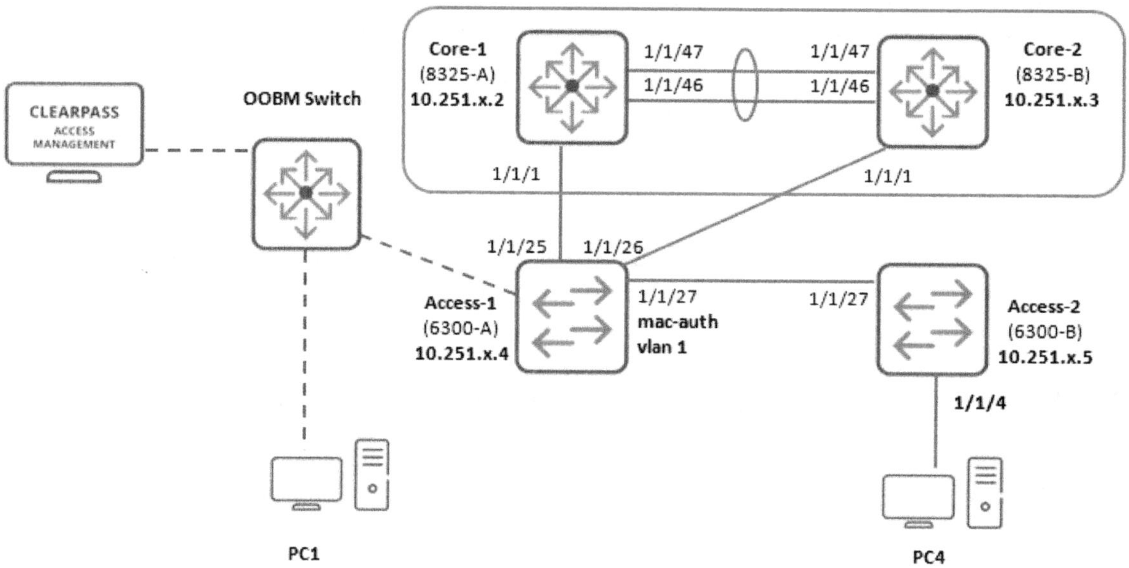

Figure 11-9 Lab 11

Overview

In this lab activity, the MAC authentication feature will be configured (Figures 11-9). While MAC authentication is not a secure authentication method, it will be required in most networks, since there will typically be some devices that cannot perform 802.1X authentication.

By using MAC authentication, some control can be applied to these devices.

Just like with the 802.1X authentication, it is possible to use user roles to combine authentication settings into a logical object group. The lab will also explore the interaction of 802.1X and mac authentication on the same switch port, and the difference between client-based and device-based authentication will be demonstrated.

The last part of the lab will show how LLDP device profiles can be used to push the correct configuration to a switch port when, for instance, an Aruba AP is connected. While this is technically not MAC authentication, the device-profile feature is also based on information received by a peer device via LLDP.

Objectives

- Configure MAC authentication and review single and multiple users on a port
- Configure user roles with MAC authentication
- Review the interaction between 802.1X and MAC authentication on the same port
- Understand client-mode and device-mode authentication
- Understand the LLDP device-profile feature

Task 1: MAC Authentication with a Single Device on a Port

Objectives

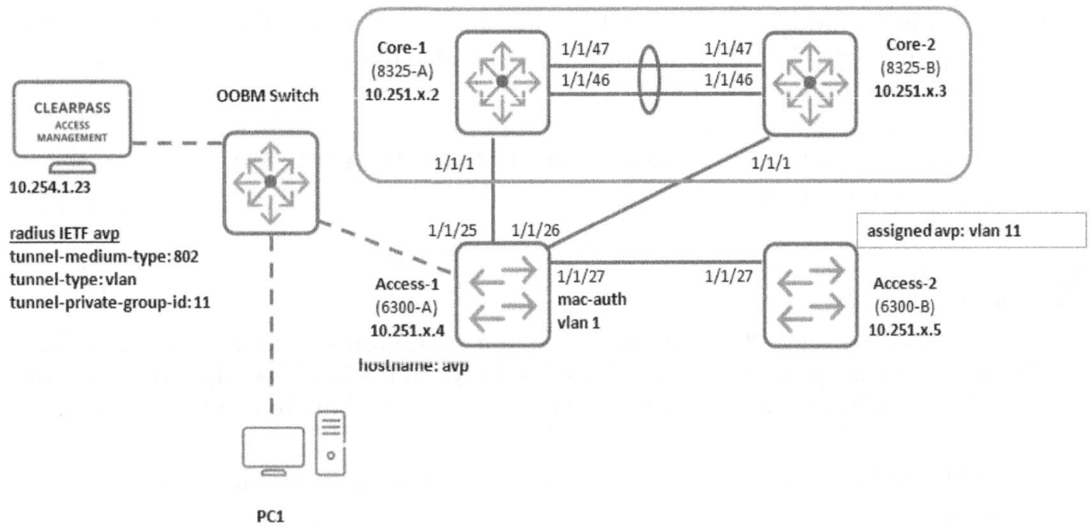

Figure 11-11 Task 1: MAC Authentication with a Single Device on a Port

Set up MAC authentication on the port connected to **Access2**. This will allow you to use Access2 as a 'connected device', and by using the PC that is connected to Access2, it will be possible to verify the operation with multiple clients on the same physical port (Figure 11-11).

Steps

Disconnect the Access2 switch from the VSX Core

1. Open a terminal session to Access2. This switch will act as an endpoint during the authentication labs. On Access2, disable the uplink ports to the VSX Core1 and Core2.

```
ICX-Tx-Access2# configure terminal
ICX-Tx-Access2(config)# interface 1/1/25,1/1/26
ICX-Tx-Access2(config-if-<1/1/25,1/1/26>)# shutdown
ICX-Tx-Access2(config-if-<1/1/25,1/1/26>)# exit
```

2. On Access2, enable the port 1/1/27 that connects to Access1. This port is still at its default configuration state: it is an access port in VLAN 1.

```
ICX-Tx-Access2(config)# interface 1/1/27
ICX-Tx-Access2(config-if)# no shutdown
ICX-Tx-Access2(config-if)# exit
```

Enable MAC Authentication on Access1

1. Open a terminal session to Access1 and enter configuration mode. Change the hostname to include 'avp'. Change "Tx" to "T" followed by your table number; for example, Table 1 would be "T1" and Table 12 would be T12.

```
ICX-Tx-Access1-vsa(config)# hostname ICX-Tx-Access1-avp
ICX-Tx-Access1-avp(config)#
```

Note

The hostname is used as the NAS-identifier in the access-request to ClearPass. ClearPass has been pre-configured to look for the value '**avp**' in the NAS-identifier to return standard IETF **Attribute Value Pairs** with VLAN instructions that are needed for this lab.

2. Enable MAC authentication on the switch and ensure it is using the previously defined RADIUS server group.

```
ICX-Tx-Access1-avp(config)# aaa authentication port-access mac-auth radius
server-group cppm
ICX-Tx-Access1-avp(config)# aaa authentication port-access mac-auth enable
```

3. Assign port 1/1/27 to VLAN 1. In this lab, it is simply used as the base landing VLAN in case the RADIUS server does not assign a VLAN. There is no DHCP server or no other resources in this VLAN in this example.

```
ICX-Tx-Access1-avp(config)# interface 1/1/27
ICX-Tx-Access1-avp(config-if)# vlan access 1
```

4. Enter the MAC-Auth context and enable MAC-Auth on the port.

```
ICX-Tx-Access1-avp(config-if)# aaa authentication port-access mac-auth
ICX-Tx-Access1-avp(config-if-macauth)# enable
ICX-Tx-Access1-avp(config-if-macauth)# exit
```

5. Enable the port.

```
ICX-Tx-Access1-avp(config-if)# no shutdown
ICX-Tx-Access1-avp(config-if)# exit
```

6. Verify that the MAC address of the Access2 switch is now authenticated. The ClearPass system has been configured to assign the MAC OUI range of the Aruba Switch to VLAN 11.

Note

It may take a few moments for Access2 to generate some traffic, repeat below command until the authentication shows up. This should occur within about 30 seconds.

```
ICX-Tx-Access1-avp(config)# show aaa authentication port-access mac-auth
interface 1/1/27 client-status
Port Access Client Status Details

Client  88:3a:30:97:b6:00, 883a3097b600, 1/1/27
========================================

  Authentication Details
  ----------------------
Status                                         : Authenticated
    Auth-Method                                    : chap
    Auth Failure reason                            :
    Time Since Last State Change                   : 23s

  Authentication Statistics
  -------------------------
    Authentication                    : 1
    Authentication Timeout            : 0
    Successful Authentication         : 1
    Failed Authentication             : 0
    Re-Authentication                 : 0
    Successful Re-Authentication      : 0
    Failed Re-Authentication          : 0
    Re-Auths When Authenticated       : 0
    Cached Re-Authentication          : 0
```

7. Confirm the MAC-address on the port is now dynamically learned on VLAN 11 by reviewing the mac-address-table.

```
ICX-Tx-Access1-avp(config)# show mac-address-table
MAC age-time               : 300 seconds
Number of MAC addresses : 9

MAC Address           VLAN      Type                      Port
--------------------------------------------------------------
20:4c:03:5f:98:02     1         dynamic                   lag256
88:3a:30:97:b6:00     11        port-access-security      1/1/27
02:02:00:00:12:00     11        dynamic                   lag256
90:20:c2:bc:17:00     11        dynamic                   lag256
90:20:c2:bc:97:00     11        dynamic                   lag256
<...output omitted...>
```

8. For this initial MAC authentication lab, ClearPass returns standard RADIUS IETF VLAN assignment attributes. These are dynamically assigned into a role on the switch. Review the authorization of this MAC address:

```
ICX-Tx-Access1-avp(config)# show aaa authentication port-access inter-
face 1/1/27 client-status
Port Access Client Status Details
Client 88:3a:30:97:b6:00, 883a3097b600
============================
  Session Details
  ---------------
    Port         : 1/1/27
    Session Time : 7s

  Authentication Details
  ----------------------
    Status          : mac-auth Authenticated
    Auth Precedence : dot1x - Not attempted, mac-auth - Authenticated

 Authorization Details
  ----------------------
    Role    : RADIUS_1881452276
Status : Applied
```

9. Review the role details to discover the assigned RADIUS attributes.

```
ICX-Tx-Access1-avp(config)# show port-access role radius
Role Information:
Name   : RADIUS_1881452276
```

```
Type  : radius
---------------------------------------------
   Reauthentication Period                :
   Authentication Mode                    :
   Session Timeout                        :
   Client Inactivity Timeout              :
   Description                            :
   Gateway Zone                           :
   UBT Gateway Role                       :
Access VLAN                            : 11
   Native VLAN                            :
   Allowed Trunk VLANs                    :
   MTU                                    :
   QOS Trust Mode                         :
   PoE Priority                           :
   Captive Portal Profile                 :
   Policy                                 :
```

Task 2: Verify Access with Two Devices Connected on the Same Port

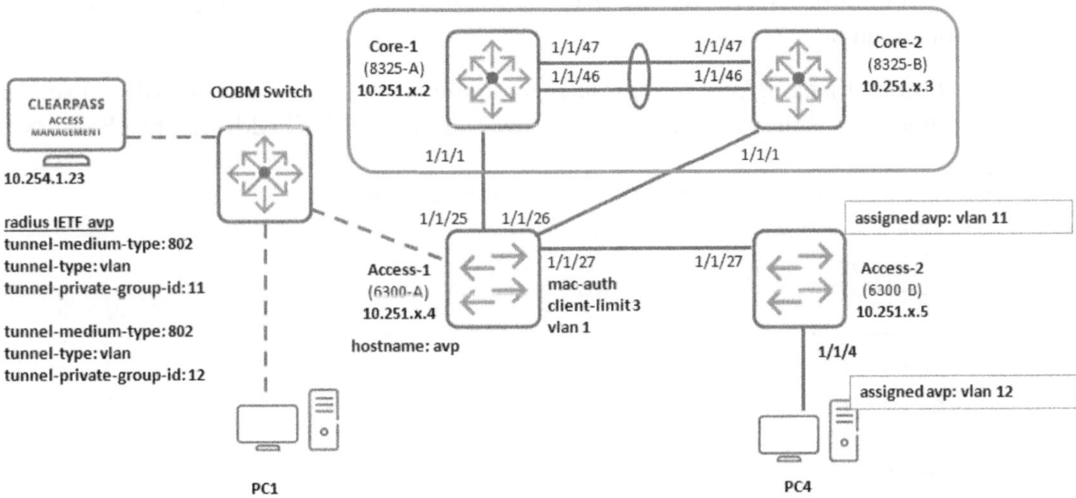

Figure 11-12 Task 2: Verify Access with Two Devices Connected on the Same Port

Objectives

In this task, the PC that is connected to Access2 will be authenticated as well (Figure 11-12). This will result in two untagged devices that are authenticated on the same physical port, but they are still assigned to different VLANs. This is also known as MAC-based VLAN (MBV), since the switch assigns the traffic to the correct VLAN based on the authenticated client MAC address.

Initially two clients (PC4 and Access2) will be connected to the same port 1/1/27 on Access1. Only one of these two clients will be able to come online, since there is a default client limit of *one*. Next, this client limit will be increased so both clients can come online at the same time.

Steps

1. On the Access2 switch, enable port 1/1/4 and assign it to VLAN 1. This is the port that connects to PC4.

```
ICX-Tx-Access2(config)# int 1/1/4
ICX-Tx-Access2(config-if)# vlan access 1
ICX-Tx-Access2(config-if)# no shutdown
ICX-Tx-Access2(config-if)# exit
```

2. Open a connection to **PC4** connected to Access2. Open the Network Connections; look for the 'Lab NIC'. Bounce the **'Lab NIC'** interface (disable/enable). This will trigger the DHCP client to send out a request.
3. Verify on Access2 that a MAC address is learned on the port 1/1/4. The MAC will probably start with **00:50:56**, that is the range used by VMware to generate MAC addresses for the VMs.

```
ICX-Tx-Access2(config)# show mac-address-table
MAC age-time              : 300 seconds
Number of MAC addresses : 5
MAC Address          VLAN     Type                    Port
--------------------------------------------------------------
90:20:c2:bc:97:00    1        dynamic                 1/1/27
90:20:c2:bc:17:00    1        dynamic                 1/1/27
88:3a:30:98:30:c0    1        dynamic                 1/1/27
00:50:56:b1:fc:9b    1        dynamic                 1/1/4
02:02:00:00:12:00    1        dynamic                 1/1/27
```

4. Review the active clients on the port 1/1/27.

Note

In the output below, it may be either the MAC address of PC4 or the Access2 that is authenticated on the port.

```
ICX-Tx-Access1-avp(config)# show aaa authentication port-access
interface 1/1/27 client-status
Port Access Client Status Details
Client 88:3a:30:97:b6:00, 883a3097b600
============================
  Session Details
  ---------------
    Port          : 1/1/27
    Session Time  : 50s

  Authentication Details
  ----------------------
    Status          : mac-auth Authenticated
    Auth Precedence : dot1x - Not attempted, mac-auth - Authenticated

  Authorization Details
  ----------------------
    Role    : RADIUS_242871489
Status: Applied
```

Question: How many authenticated clients are there on the interface?

Answer: Only one client is authenticated, even though two clients (the Access2 switch and the client PC4) are connected to the port.

5. Review the mac-address table on Access1 using the **'detail'** option word. Look for the **'Denied'** column. This reveals that the mac-address of the client has been seen on the port but is not allowed to become active.

Note

In the output below, it can be either the PC4 or the Access2 MAC address that is 'denied' on the port 1/1/27. This depends on which MAC address was authenticated on the port, the other MAC address will be denied.

```
ICX-Tx-Access1-avp(config)# show mac-address-table detail
MAC age-time               : 300 seconds
Number of MAC addresses : 11

MAC Address        VLAN  Type                   Port    Age  Denied nev-er_ageout
----------------------------------------------------------------------------------
88:3a:30:97:b6:00  1     port-access-security   1/1/27  300  true   false
00:50:56:b1:fc:9b  1     port-access-security   1/1/27  300  true   false
...
88:3a:30:97:b6:00 12     port-access-security   1/1/27 300  false false
...
```

6. This is because the switch applies a default client limit of one client on each switch port.
7. Now increase the client limit, to ensure multiple clients can be authenticated on the same switch port. On Access1, enter the interface 1/1/27 context and increase the client limit to three. Reset the interface to trigger the Access2 switch to send some packets.

```
ICX-Tx-Access1-avp(config)# interface 1/1/27
ICX-Tx-Access1-avp(config-if)# aaa authentication port-access client-limit 3
ICX-Tx-Access1-avp(config-if)# shutdown
ICX-Tx-Access1-avp(config-if)# no shutdown
```

8. On PC4, disable and enable the 'Lab NIC' again.
9. On Access1, there should now be two clients authenticated on the same port.

```
ICX-Tx-Access1-avp(config-if)# show aaa authentication port-access interface
1/1/27 client-status
Port Access Client Status Details

Client 88:3a:30:97:b6:00, 883a3097b600
============================
  Session Details
  ---------------
    Port         : 1/1/27
    Session Time : 255s

  Authentication Details
  ----------------------
    Status          : mac-auth Authenticated
    Auth Precedence : dot1x - Not attempted, mac-auth - Authenticated

  Authorization Details
  ----------------------
    Role    : RADIUS_242871489
Status : Applied

Client 00:50:56:b1:fc:9b, 005056b1fc9b
============================
  Session Details
  ---------------
    Port         : 1/1/27
    Session Time : 19s

  Authentication Details
  ----------------------
    Status          : mac-auth Authenticated
    Auth Precedence : dot1x - Not attempted, mac-auth - Authenticated
```

```
   Authorization Details
   ----------------------
    Role    : RADIUS_242871489
Status : Applied
```

10. Review the RADIUS attributes that were pushed to for the client PC MAC-Auth by checking the radius roles.

```
ICX-Tx-Access1-avp(config-if)# show port-access role radius
Role Information:
Name  : RADIUS_1881452276
Type  : radius
----------------------------------------------
   Reauthentication Period                 :
   Authentication Mode                     :
   Session Timeout                         :
   Client Inactivity Timeout               :
   Description                             :
   Gateway Zone                            :
   UBT Gateway Role                        :
Access VLAN                           : 11
   Native VLAN                             :
   Allowed Trunk VLANs                     :
   MTU                                     :
   QOS Trust Mode                          :
   PoE Priority                            :
   Captive Portal Profile                  :
   Policy                                  :

Name  : RADIUS_242871489
Type  : radius
----------------------------------------------
   Reauthentication Period                 :
   Authentication Mode                     :
   Session Timeout                         :
   Client Inactivity Timeout               :
   Description                             :
   Gateway Zone                            :
   UBT Gateway Role                        :
Access VLAN                           : 12
   Native VLAN                             :
   Allowed Trunk VLANs                     :
   MTU                                     :
```

```
    QOS Trust Mode                          :
    PoE Priority                            :
    Captive Portal Profile                  :
    Policy                                  :
```

11. Review the updated MAC address table on port 1/1/27. Notice how both MAC addresses of the Access2 and the PC4 are now active, but each has been assigned to its own VLAN, based on the instructions of the RADIUS server.

```
ICX-Tx-Access1-avp(config-if)# show mac-address-table port 1/1/27
MAC age-time                : 300 seconds
Number of MAC addresses : 2
MAC Address             VLAN      Type                      Port
--------------------------------------------------------------
88:3a:30:97:b6:00       11        port-access-security      1/1/27
00:50:56:b1:fc:9b       12        port-access-security      1/1/27
```

This demonstrates that multiple untagged devices can be concurrently active on the same physical port, each with their own network access security settings applied to them.

Review the Authentication and Attributes on the ClearPass System

1. On the ClearPass access tracker, use Access Tracker to verify that two authentications were processed.

2. Open the MAC-Auth entry for MAC **005056** (the PC4 VM); click on the **'Input'** to review the attributes that are used for MAC authentication.

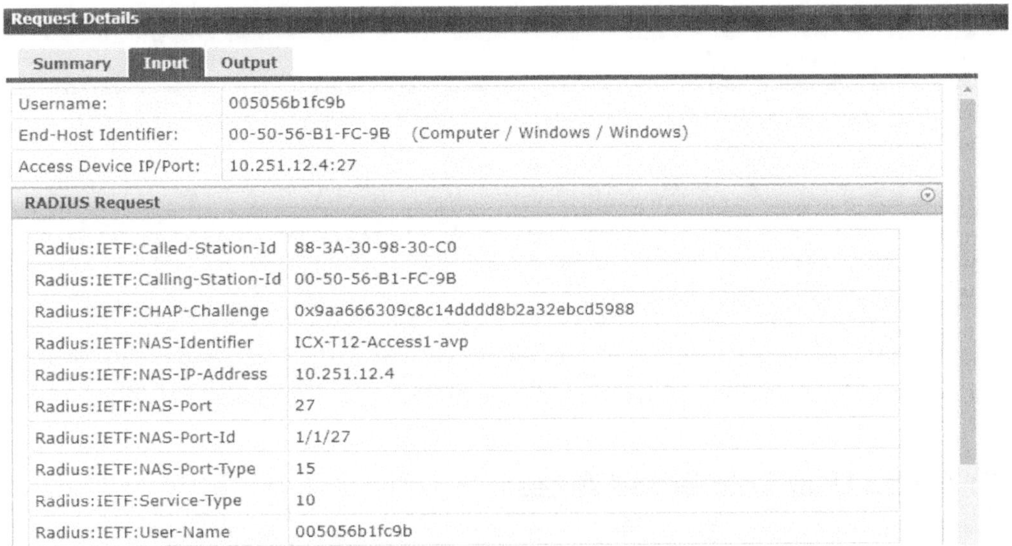

3. Check the **'Output'** tab; click on 'RADIUS response' to see the VLAN that was returned to the switch. **Close** the 'Request details'.

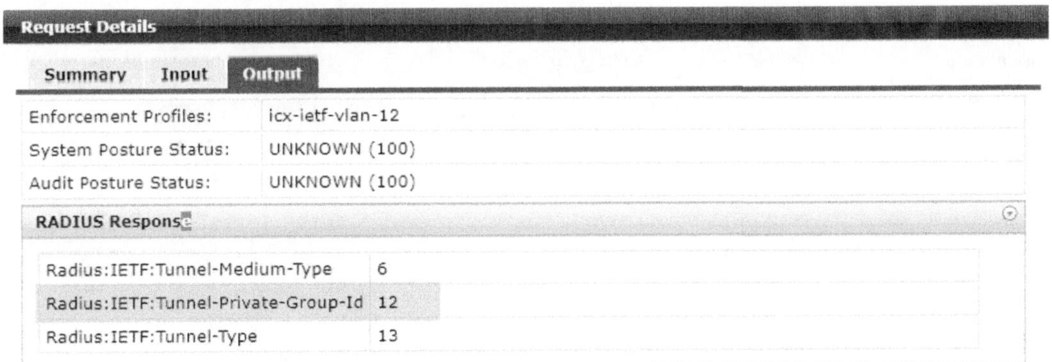

4. Open the second MAC authentication entry (for the Access2 switch) and review the **'Output'** settings. Example for the Switch (assigned to VLAN 11):

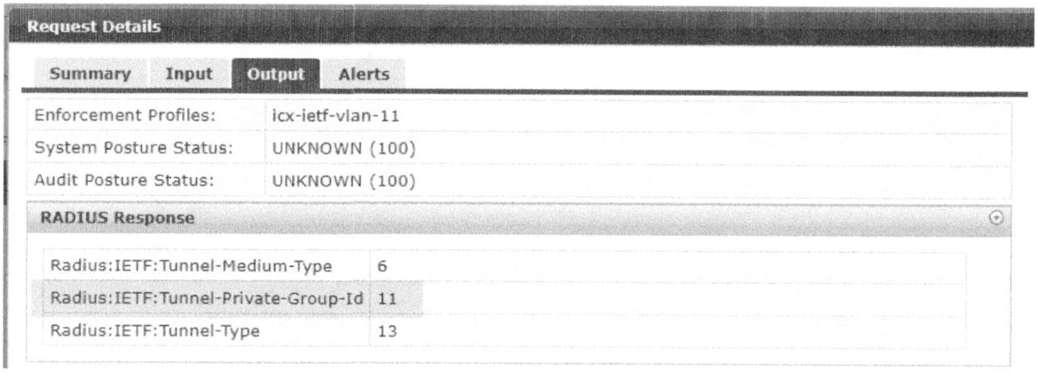

Task 3: Aruba User Role-Based Access

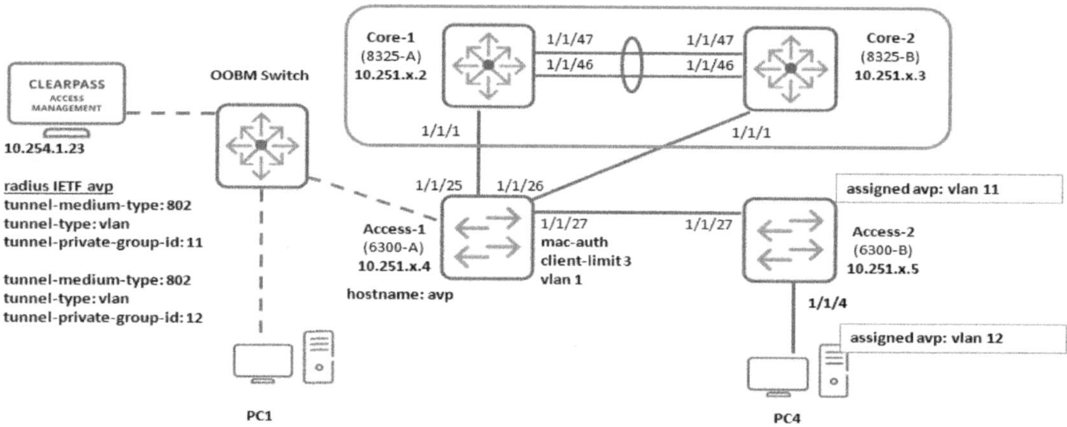

Figure 11-13 Task 3: Aruba User Role-Based Access

Objectives

Similar to the 802.1X authentication, MAC authentication also supports the use of user roles that are defined on the switch. User roles on the switch have the advantage of grouping all the relevant access settings (VLAN, ACL, QOS, POE priority) into a single logical object. This simplifies the RADIUS server configuration, since the RADIUS server only needs to assign the role to the switch, while the switch knows the configuration of that role.

In this lab, the Access2 switch will be assigned the role **'dev-switch'**, while the PC connected to the Access2 switch will be assigned the role **'employee'** (Figure 11-13).

In the previous Lab (Configuring 802.1X) the 'employee' role was already defined, so these steps are not included here. This task will define the new user role for the Access2 switch and show that the role can also be used to control both tagged and untagged access for the user role.

Steps

1. Open a terminal connection to Access1; enter the configuration mode. Define a new port-access user-role named **'dev-switch'**. Provide the role a VLAN trunk with native VLAN 11, and allowed VLANs 11,12,13.

```
ICX-Tx-Access1-avp(config)# port-access role dev-switch
ICX-Tx-Access1-avp(config-pa-role)# vlan trunk native 11
ICX-Tx-Access1-avp(config-pa-role)# vlan trunk allowed 11,12,13
ICX-Tx-Access1-avp(config-pa-role)# exit
ICX-Tx-Access1-avp(config)#
```

2. Change the hostname to get the Aruba VSA Aruba-User-Role ClearPass rule set. On Access1, change the hostname; replace the **'avp'** hostname with **'vsa'**. Change "Tx" to "T" followed by your table number; for example, Table 1 would be "T1" and Table 12 would be T12.

```
ICX-Tx-Access1-avp(config)# hostname ICX-Tx-Access1-vsa
ICX-Tx-Access1-vsa(config)#
```

Note

The hostname is used as the NAS-identifier. ClearPass has been pre-configured to look for the value '**vsa**' in the NAS-identifier to return the **Aruba-User-Role** VSA attributes that are needed for this lab.

Test Role Assignment

1. On the Access1 switch, disable and enable the port 1/1/27.

```
ICX-Tx-Access1-vsa(config)# interface 1/1/27
ICX-Tx-Access1-vsa(config-if)# shutdown
ICX-Tx-Access1-vsa(config-if)# no shutdown
ICX-Tx-Access1-vsa(config-if)# exit
```

2. You may need to generate some traffic to trigger the MAC-Auth on the 'clients': That is, the Access2 switch and the PC connected to it.

3. On the Access2, disable and enable the VLAN 1 IP interface; this will send out a DHCP request.

```
ICX-Tx-Access2(config)# interface vlan 1
ICX-Tx-Access2(config-if-vlan)# shutdown
ICX-Tx-Access2(config-if-vlan)# no shutdown
ICX-Tx-Access2(config-if-vlan)# exit
```

On the PC4 connected to Access2, disable and enable the 'Lab NIC'.

Note

This is important, since the PC4 may be assigned to a different VLAN, so it needs to renew its IP address.

Verify the Results

1. On the Access1 switch, review the authenticated clients and the role that was assigned to the clients.

```
ICX-Tx-Access1-vsa(config)# show aaa authentication port-access interface
1/1/27 client-status
Port Access Client Status Details
Client 00:50:56:b1:fc:9b, 005056b1fc9b
============================
  Session Details
  ---------------
    Port         : 1/1/27
    Session Time : 4s
  Authentication Details
  ----------------------
    Status          : mac-auth Authenticated
    Auth Precedence : dot1x - Not attempted, mac-auth - Authenticated
Authorization Details
  ----------------------
    Role   : employee
Status : Applied

Client 88:3a:30:97:b6:00, 883a3097b600
============================
  Session Details
  ---------------
    Port         : 1/1/27
    Session Time : 179s
```

```
   Authentication Details
   ----------------------
     Status            : mac-auth Authenticated
     Auth Precedence : dot1x - Not attempted, mac-auth - Authenticated

Authorization Details
   ----------------------
      Role    : dev-switch
Status : Applied
```

2. Review the VLAN port status of the port 1/1/27.

```
ICX-Tx-Access1-vsa(config)# show vlan port 1/1/27
--------------------------------------------------------------------------
VLAN  Name                                  Mode             Mapping
--------------------------------------------------------------------------
1     DEFAULT_VLAN_1                        native-untagged port
11    VLAN11                                trunk            port-access,mbv
12    VLAN12                                trunk            port-access
13    VLAN13                                trunk            port-access
```

Question: What is the listed method for the tagged VLAN, for example VLAN 12, assignment mapping?

Answer: The VLAN 12 is assigned by the 'port-access' module, while a manual VLAN trunk would be listed as mapped by the 'port' configuration, as can be seen for VLAN 1.

3. Using the PC1 Management PC, access ClearPass, open Access Tracker, and review the output of both authentication events. This demonstrates that the Aruba VSA User-Role was used for the assignment.

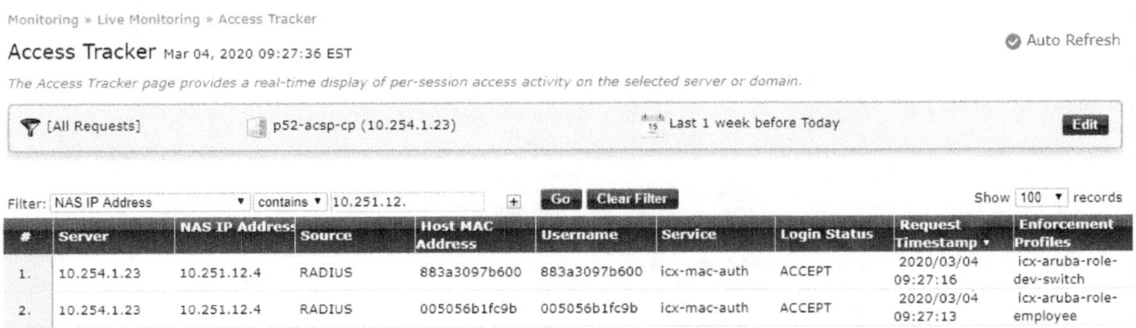

4. Review each entry; check that the VSA Aruba-User-Role was now assigned to Access1 instead of the IETF VLAN assignment.

   - For the PC4:

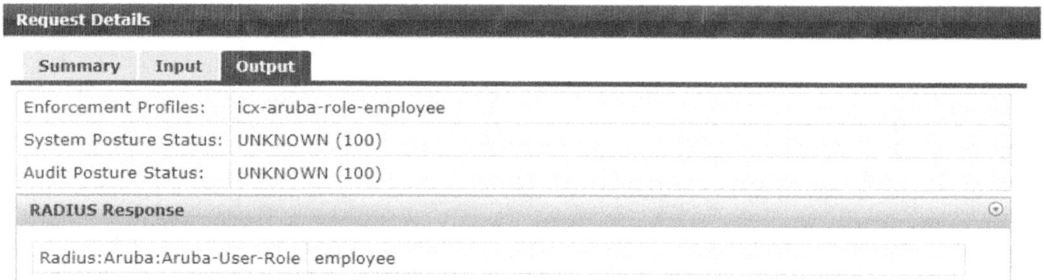

   - For the Switch Access2:

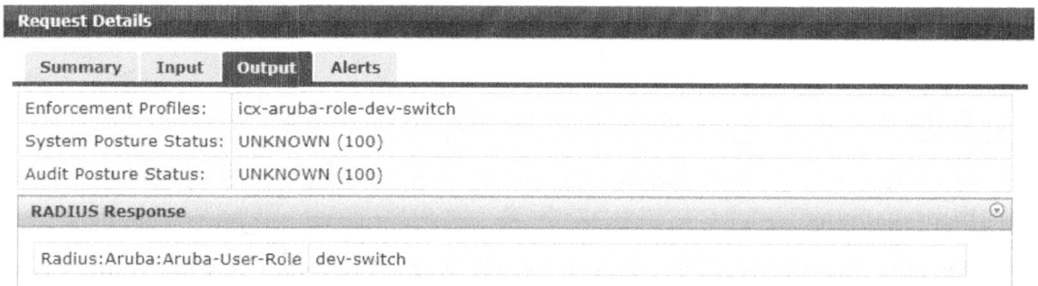

Task 4: Client-Mode versus Device-Mode Port Authentication

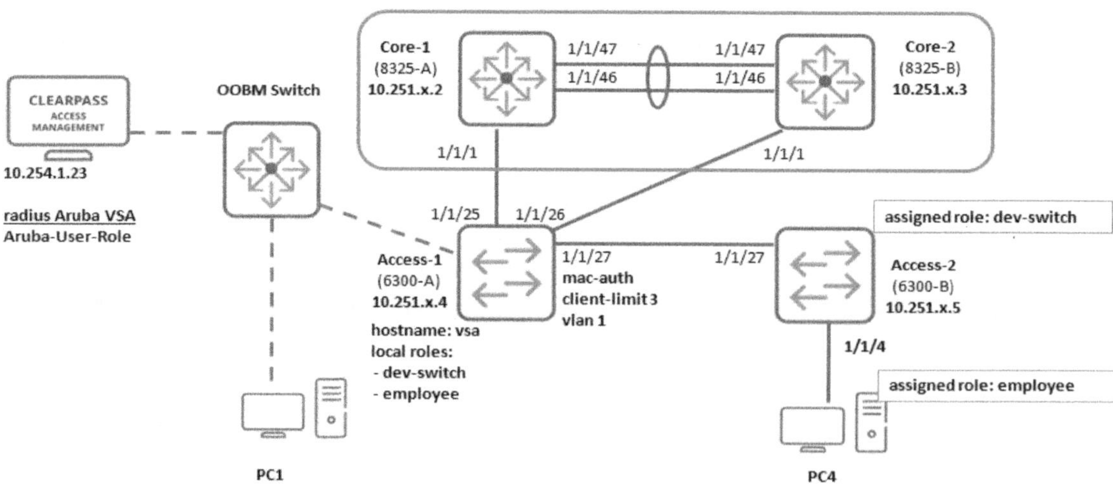

Figure 11-14 Task 4: Client-Mode versus Device-Mode Port Authentication

Objectives

In the previous task, it was demonstrated that multiple devices can be connected to the same switch port, and each device can be assigned its own network access policy by using Aruba user roles. However, sometimes it may not be desired to authenticate each device on the port, for example, if the connected device itself is responsible to perform authentication.

This would apply, for example, to Aruba Instant APs that are connected to a switch port. With an Instant AP, the wireless traffic will be forwarded by the AP as either tagged or untagged traffic to the switch port. This is also referred to as local breakout at the AP or bridging at the AP level. The result is that the switch port will actually see all the MAC addresses that are connected to the IAP device.

The IAP itself is responsible to handle the authentication, so it would perform 802.1X authentication with the wireless clients. But then the traffic is forwarded as regular traffic on the switch port, so the switch would also attempt to perform authentication of this client. Since the 802.1X traffic of the client is terminated at the IAP, the switch would attempt to perform MAC authentication for the client MAC address.

This is unnecessary and confusing, since ClearPass would see the same MAC address as 802.1X authenticated on the IAP, and MAC-authenticated on the switch port.

For this scenario, the switch can be set to 'port-based' authentication; that is, device mode. When a specific device (such as an IAP or an access switch in a meeting room) is connected to the switch port, the switch will open the port for <u>**all**</u> traffic, so it will not perform MAC authentication for the other MAC addresses seen off of the port anymore.

In this task, you will change the user-role of the Access2 switch 'dev-switch' to become a role that operates as **'device-mode'**. When the switch completes its authentication, any device connected to the switch will automatically be allowed access to the network as well. In this lab, the Access2 is not actually performing any authentication itself for PC4, but it simply demonstrates the concept of the **'device-mode'** authentication (Figure 11-14).

Steps

1. Open Access2; disable the port to the PC. This is done to ensure that the Access2 switch's MAC address will be guaranteed to be the first seen MAC address on the port.

```
ICX-Tx-Access2(config)# interface 1/1/4
ICX-Tx-Access2(config-if)# shutdown
```

2. On Access1, modify the user-role for 'dev-switch'.

```
ICX-Tx-Access1-vsa(config)# port-access role dev-switch
ICX-Tx-Access1-vsa(config-pa-role)# auth-mode device-mode
ICX-Tx-Access1-vsa(config-pa-role)# exit
```

3. Reset the port 1/1/27.

```
ICX-Tx-Access1-vsa(config)# interface 1/1/27
ICX-Tx-Access1-vsa(config-if)# shutdown
ICX-Tx-Access1-vsa(config-if)# no shutdown
ICX-Tx-Access1-vsa(config-if)# exit
```

4. Verify the connected switch has authenticated.

```
ICX-Tx-Access1-vsa(config)# show aaa authentication port-access interface
1/1/27 client-status
Port Access Client Status Details
Client 88:3a:30:97:b6:00, 883a3097b600
============================
  Session Details
  ---------------
    Port         : 1/1/27
    Session Time : 131s

  Authentication Details
  ----------------------
    Status          : mac-auth Authenticated
    Auth Precedence : dot1x - Not attempted, mac-auth - Authenticated

  Authorization Details
  ----------------------
    Role   : dev-switch
Status : Applied
```

5. On Access2, enable the PC port to verify it passes network access without authentication.On Access2, enable the port 1/1/4 of the PC again.

```
ICX-Tx-Access2(config-if)# no shutdown
```

6. On the PC4, disable and enable the 'Lab Nic' interface.

7. On the Access1, verify the MAC address table shows 2 MAC addresses on the interface 1/1/27, and the 'Denied' status is **'false'**. This means these MAC addresses have access to the network.

```
ICX-Tx-Access1-vsa(config)# show mac-address-table detail
MAC age-time            : 300 seconds
Number of MAC addresses : 10
```

```
MAC Address        VLAN Type                  Port    Age  Denied never_
                                                                   ageout
---------------------------------------------------------------------------
20:4c:03:5f:98:02 1    dynamic                lag256  300  false  false
88:3a:30:97:b6:00 11   port-access-security 1/1/27  300  false  false
00:50:56:b1:fc:9b 11   port-access-security 1/1/27  300  false  false
02:02:00:00:12:00 11   dynamic                lag256  300  false  false
90:20:c2:bc:17:00 11   dynamic                lag256  300  false  false
<...output omitted...>
```

8. Navigate to ClearPass's Access Tracker from PC1.

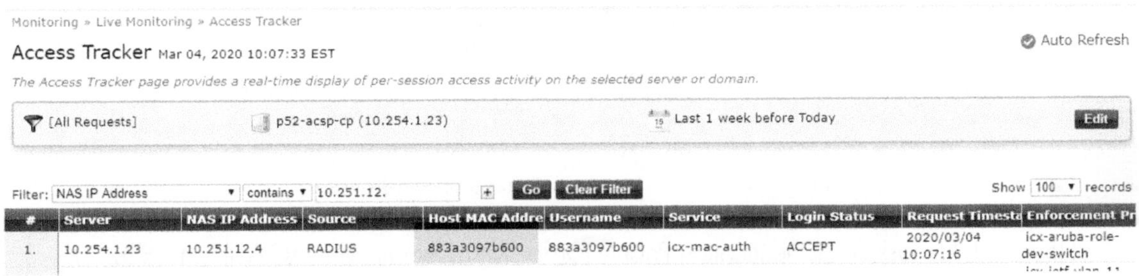

Question: How many authentication events are there for the last test?

Answer: Only one authentication was done by the switch. The role that was assigned contains the **'auth-mode: device-mode'**: device' option, so no other authentications are needed on this port.

Revert Configuration

1. On Access1, change the 'dev-switch' role back to client based and disable the port.

```
ICX-Tx-Access1-vsa(config)# port-access role dev-switch
ICX-Tx-Access1-vsa(config-pa-role)# auth-mode client-mode
ICX-Tx-Access1-vsa(config-pa-role)# exit
ICX-Tx-Access1-vsa(config)# interface 1/1/27
ICX-Tx-Access1-vsa(config-if)# shutdown
ICX-Tx-Access1-vsa(config-if)# exit
```

2. On Access2, disable the port 1/1/4 to PC4.

```
ICX-Tx-Access2(config-if)# shutdown
ICX-Tx-Access2(config-if)# exit
```

Task 5: Authentication Priority Order with Combined MAC-Auth and 802.1X

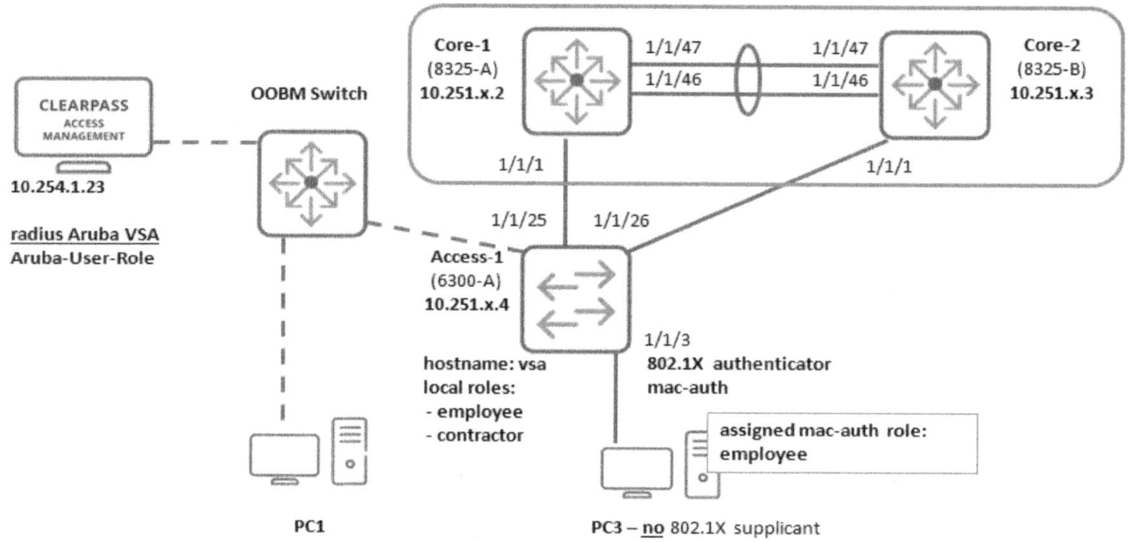

Figure 11-15 Task 5: Authentication Priority Order with Combined MAC-Auth and 802.1X

Objectives

This task will show how a port that combines 802.1X and MAC authentication will handle the combined authentication of a device (Figure 11-15).

For each MAC address that connects to the switch, only one authentication method can be active to control the network access. When a MAC address comes online, the switch will either apply the role that was received for the MAC authentication *or* the role that was received for the 802.1X authentication, but never both at the same time.

Since 802.1X is a more secure authentication method than MAC-Auth, the switch will, by default, give the 802.1X role precedence over the MAC-Auth role.

In a real-world deployment, the administrator should realize that a PC with an 802.1X configuration will only start the 802.1X process when it has booted. During the boot process, the PC may already send some frames that may trigger MAC authentication on the switch port. A few seconds later, the 802.1X process would also succeed and the 802.1X role would overrule the MAC-Auth role.

In this task, this behavior will be observed by enabling MAC-Auth on the port 1/1/3 of Access1. The PC that performs 802.1X will first be authenticated using MAC-Auth. Then the 802.1X supplicant will be enabled, so the 802.1X role will overrule the MAC-Auth role.

Steps

Disable the 802.1X Supplicant on PC3

1. Open a session to the PC3. Get the properties for the '**Lab NIC' > Authentication**' and **uncheck** the 'Enable IEEE 802.1X authentication' checkbox. Confirm the message that saved credentials will be deleted, if prompted.

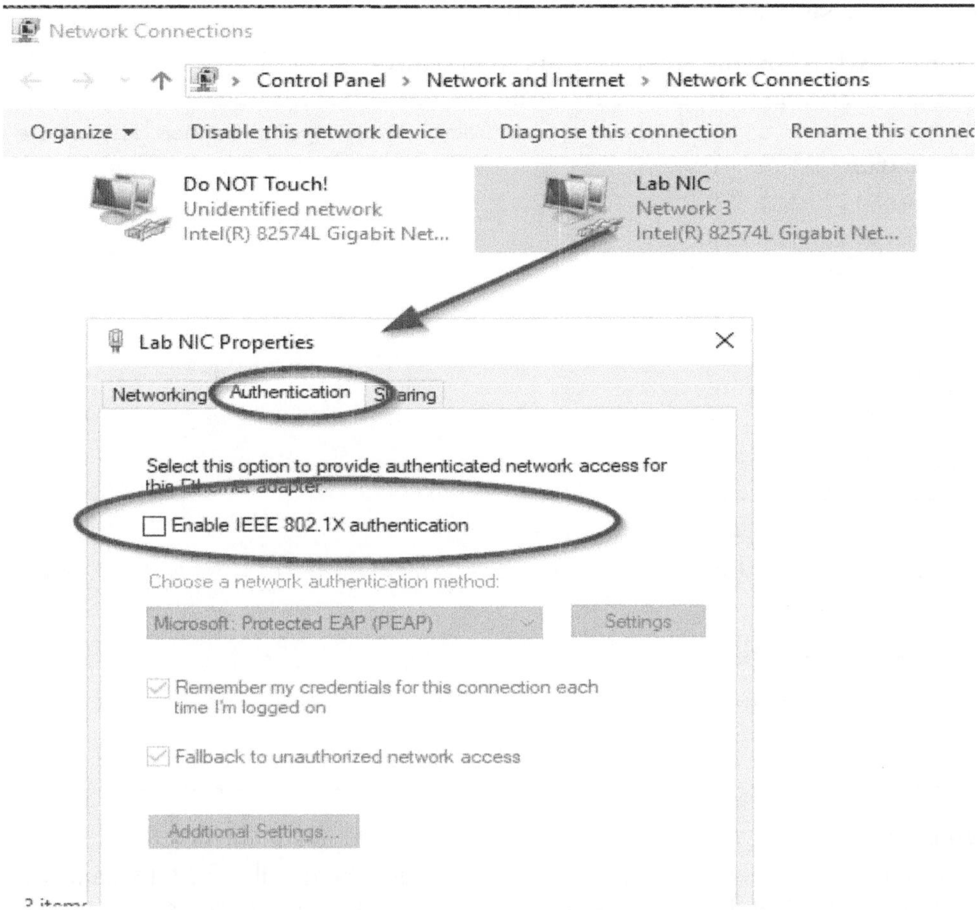

Enable MAC-Auth on the Access1

1. On Access1, configure port 1/1/3 for MAC-Auth.

```
ICX-Tx-Access1-vsa(config)# interface 1/1/3
ICX-Tx-Access1-vsa(config-if)# aaa authentication port-access mac-auth enable
```

2. Reset the port.

```
ICX-Tx-Access1-vsa(config-if)# shutdown
ICX-Tx-Access1-vsa(config-if)# no shutdown
ICX-Tx-Access1-vsa(config-if)# exit
```

3. On the PC3, disable and enable the 'Lab NIC'.
4. On the Access1, follow the client authentication status.

```
ICX-Tx-Access1-vsa(config)# show aaa authentication port-access interface 1/1/3
client-status
Port Access Client Status Details
Client 00:50:56:b1:7a:37
============================
  Session Details
  ---------------
    Port         : 1/1/3
    Session Time : 15s
  Authentication Details
  ----------------------
Status           : Authenticating
Auth Precedence  : dot1x - Authenticating, mac-auth - Not attempted
  Authorization Details
  ----------------------
     Role    :
Status :
```

Note

With the default timers, it may take several minutes before the 802.1X times out and performs the MAC-Auth. During testing, about 3 minutes were observed.

5. Eventually, the switch will consider that 802.1X has failed and it will perform MAC-Auth.

```
ICX-Tx-Access1-vsa(config)# show aaa authentication port-access interface 1/1/3
client-status
Port Access Client Status Details
```

```
Client 00:50:56:b1:7a:37, 005056b17a37
==============================
   Session Details
   ---------------
     Port          : 1/1/3
 Session Time : 208s

   Authentication Details
   ----------------------
 Status            : mac-auth Authenticated
 Auth Precedence   : dot1x - Unauthenticated, mac-auth - Authenticated

   Authorization Details
   ----------------------
      Role    : employee
Status : Applied
```

Adjust the Timers to Achieve Faster MAC authentication

1. Configure updated timers for the 802.1X authenticator on the port 1/1/3.

```
ICX-Tx-Access1-vsa(config)# interface 1/1/3
ICX-Tx-Access1-vsa(config-if)# aaa authentication port-access dot1x
authenticator
ICX-Tx-Access1-vsa(config-if-dot1x-auth)# eapol-timeout 30
ICX-Tx-Access1-vsa(config-if-dot1x-auth)# max-eapol-requests 1
ICX-Tx-Access1-vsa(config-if-dot1x-auth)# max-retries 1
ICX-Tx-Access1-vsa(config-if-dot1x-auth)# exit
```

Note

These are the validated timers when the labs were developed, adjust these timers based on the requirements of the deployment.

2. Review the resulting port configuration.

```
ICX-Tx-Access1-vsa(config-if)# show running-config current-context
interface 1/1/3
     no shutdown
     no routing
vlan access 1
aaa authentication port-access dot1x authenticator
```

```
eapol-timeout 30
max-eapol-requests 1
max-retries 1
        enable
aaa authentication port-access mac-auth
        enable
    exit
```

3. Disable and enable the port.

```
ICX-Tx-Access1-vsa(config-if)# shutdown
ICX-Tx-Access1-vsa(config-if)# no shutdown
```

4. Verify the authentication status. It may help to disable/enable the 'Lab Nic' on the client PC to generate some client traffic.
5. On the Access1, repeat the 'show aaa authentication port-access interface 1/1/3 client-status' command to follow the state transitions.

Note

If you use the 'repeat' command on the switch, the repeat loop can be stopped using the **<CTRL>-c** key combination.

- Before any traffic was received on the port:

```
ICX-Tx-Access1-vsa(config-if)# show aaa authentication port-access interface
1/1/3 client-status
Port Access Client Status Details

ICX-Tx-Access1-vsa(config-if)# do repeat delay 5
```

- Once the first frame from the client was received:

```
ICX-Tx-Access1-vsa(config-if)# show aaa authentication port-access interface
1/1/3 client-status

Port Access Client Status Details

Client 00:50:56:b1:7a:37
============================
   Session Details
   ---------------
     Port          : 1/1/3
Session Time : 1s
```

```
   Authentication Details
   ----------------------
     Status           : Authenticating
Auth Precedence : dot1x - Initialized, mac-auth - Not attempted
```

- While the 802.1X is re-trying:

```
ICX-Tx-Access1-vsa(config-if)# show aaa authentication port-access interface
1/1/3 client-status
Port Access Client Status Details
Client 00:50:56:b1:7a:37
============================
   Session Details
   ---------------
     Port          : 1/1/3
Session Time : 3s
   Authentication Details
   ----------------------
     Status           : Authenticating
     Auth Precedence : dot1x - Authenticating, mac-auth - Not attempted
```

- Once the 802.1X authentication is considered 'failed', it will take about 60 seconds with the configured timers for MAC-Auth to be performed.

```
ICX-Tx-Access1-vsa(config-if)# show aaa authentication port-access interface
1/1/3 client-status
Port Access Client Status Details
Client 00:50:56:b1:7a:37, 005056b17a37
============================
   Session Details
   ---------------
     Port          : 1/1/3
Session Time : 63s
   Authentication Details
   ----------------------
Status           : mac-auth Authenticated
Auth Precedence : dot1x - Unauthenticated, mac-auth - Authenticated
```

```
    Authorization Details
    ----------------------
      Role    : employee
 Status : Applied
```

6. If you used the 'repeat' command, use <CTRL>-C to stop the output. This ensures that any device that is not 802.1X capable, such as IOT devices, will still be able to access the network using MAC-Auth. Notice that the current role of the device is 'employee': this was assigned by the MAC-Auth authentication process.

Verify 802.1X Authentication Precedence over MAC-Auth

In the next steps, the 802.1X default precedence over MAC-Auth will be demonstrated. This means that in case if both MAC-Auth and 802.1X would succeed, the 802.1X authentication method will control the final access for the client device.

1. On PC3, enable 802.1X again; make sure to enter the credentials again.
   - Username: **icx-contractor**
   - Password: **aruba123**

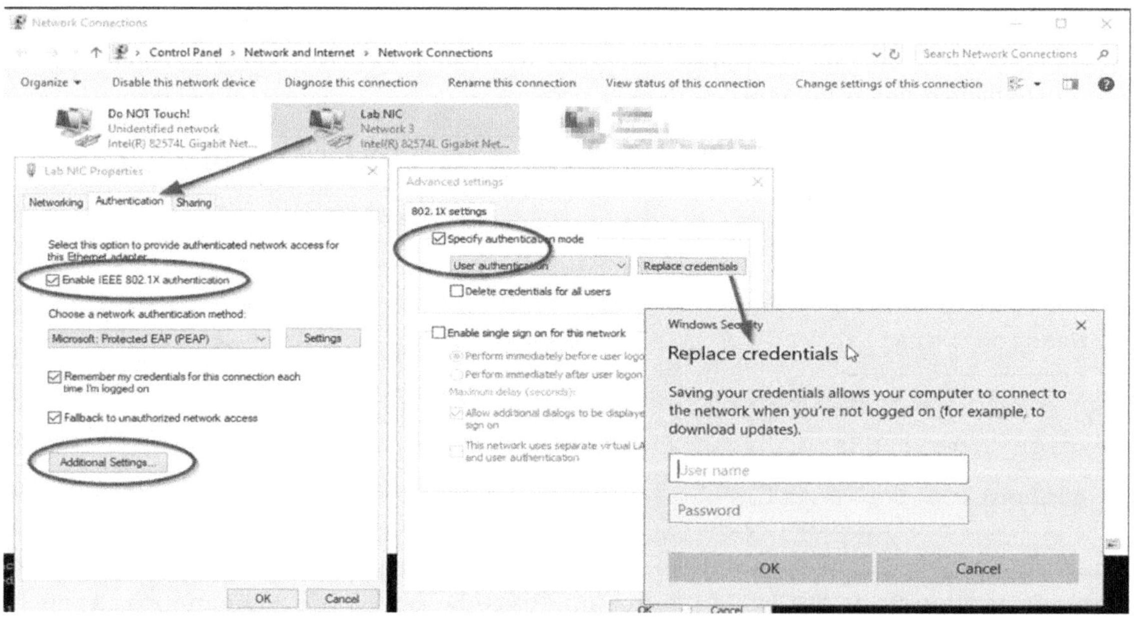

2. On the Access1, check the authenticated client status.

```
ICX-Tx-Access1-vsa(config-if)# show aaa authentication port-access
interface 1/1/3 client-status
Port Access Client Status Details
Client 00:50:56:b1:7a:37, icx-contractor
=============================
  Session Details
  ---------------
    Port         : 1/1/3
    Session Time : 295s

  Authentication Details
  ----------------------
Status          : dot1x Authenticated
    Auth Precedence : dot1x - Authenticated, mac-auth - Not attempted

  Authorization Details
  ----------------------
Role   : contractor
Status : Applied
```

Question: What is the role that was applied to the client?

Answer: The role is 'contractor'. This is based on the 802.1X authentication since 802.1X authentication has precedence over a successful MAC authentication.

Verify Combination of Failed 802.1X and Successful MAC-Auth

In the next steps (optional), you will see that in case a device fails 802.1X authentication, it can still succeed MAC-Auth and get controlled network access based on MAC-Auth.

1. On the PC3, update the 802.1X credentials on the 'Lab Nic' to incorrect credentials:
   - Username: **icx-contractor**
   - Password: **bad**

2. On Access1, verify the result.

```
ICX-Tx-Access1-vsa(config-if)# show aaa authentication port-access interface
1/1/3 client-status
Port Access Client Status Details
Client 00:50:56:b1:7a:37, 005056b17a37
============================
  Session Details
  ---------------
    Port         : 1/1/3
    Session Time : 452s

  Authentication Details
  ----------------------
    Status          : mac-auth Authenticated
    Auth Precedence :dot1x - Held, mac-auth - Authenticated

  Authorization Details
  ----------------------
    Role   :employee
Status : Applied
```

3. And a few moments later, once the 802.1X authentication has failed:

```
ICX-Tx-Access1-vsa(config-if)# show aaa authentication port-access interface
1/1/3 client-status

Port Access Client Status Details

Client 00:50:56:b1:7a:37, 005056b17a37
============================
  Session Details
  ---------------
    Port         : 1/1/3
    Session Time : 35s

  Authentication Details
  ----------------------
Status          : mac-auth Authenticated
    Auth Precedence : dot1x - Unauthenticated, mac-auth
 - Authenticated

  Authorization Details
  ----------------------
    Role   : employee
Status : Applied
ICX-Tx-Access1-vsa(config-if)# exit
```

Task 6: Device Profiles with LLDP

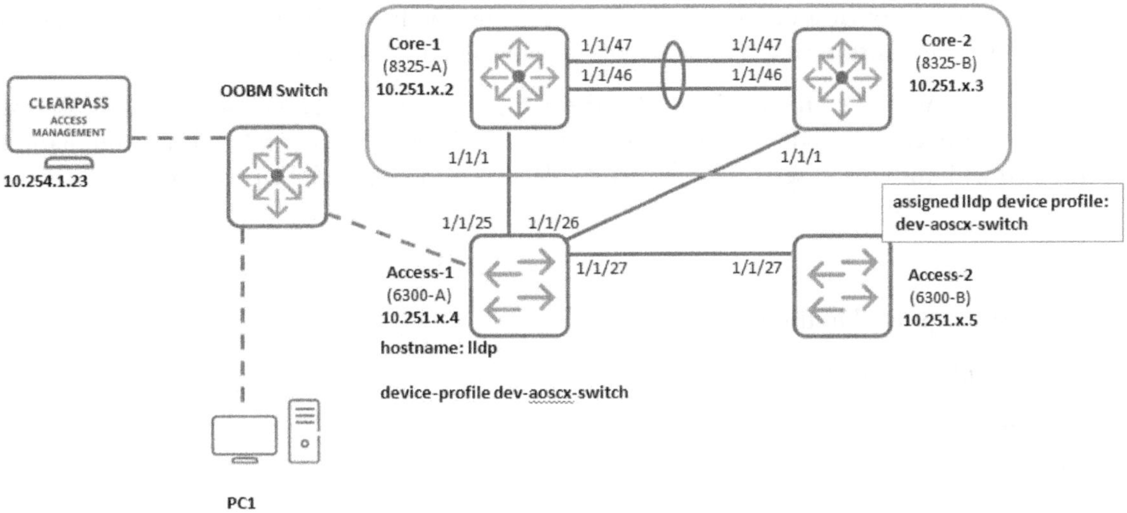

Figure 11-16 Task 6: Device Profiles with LLDP

Objectives

In this task, the AOS-CX device profiles will be demonstrated. This is not a security feature, but a convenience feature, similar to MAC-Auth (Figure 11-16).

In this case, instead of using the client MAC address for authentication, like MAC-Auth, it is possible to configure a switch port based on the incoming LLDP or CDP messages. Since many network devices support LLDP or CDP, this means that the switch port of those devices can be easily provisioned based on the received LLDP communication from these network devices.

LLDP is more difficult to spoof compared to a client MAC address, but it should still be understood that there is no actual authentication happening; so with a more advanced toolset, the LLDP messages can still be spoofed. This is why the Aruba device-profiles feature is considered a 'convenience' feature.

Some examples for real-world deployment:

- Aruba AP is connected to any switch port. The switch assigns a device profile with the correct VLAN untagged and tagged states.
- Any vendor AP that supports LLDP or CDP is connected to any switch port. The switch assigns a device profile with the correct VLAN untagged and tagged states.
- Any vendor media device, such as a conference room controller, that supports LLDP or CDP, can now automatically be assigned to the correct VLAN.

All of these examples are handled by the switch itself; they do not require a RADIUS server or other authentication infrastructure. While it is possible to have the same results with 802.1X or MAC-Auth, not every customer may be willing to set up the RADIUS infrastructure. In that case, device profiles can assist to simplify the life of the network administrator.

In this task, the Access2 switch will be used as the 'test LLDP' device that is connected to the Access1. Based on the Access2 LLDP communication, the switch port on Access1 will be automatically configured with the correct settings based on the device profile that will be prepared.

Steps

These are the steps used in this task:

- Collect information of the peer LLDP device
- Prepare the device profile
- Associate the device profile to LLDP settings
- Prepare the test > hostname
- Verify the configuration

Collect Information of the Peer LLDP Device

1. Open a terminal session on Access1 and enter the configuration mode. Change the hostname to get the Aruba VSA Aruba-User-Role ClearPass rule set. Change the hostname, replace the **'vsa'** hostname with **'lldp'**. Change "Tx" to "T" followed by your table number; for example, Table 1 would be "T1" and Table 12 would be T12.

```
ICX-Tx-Access1-vsa(config)# hostname ICX-Tx-Access1-lldp
ICX-Tx-Access1-lldp(config)#
```

Note

The hostname is used as the NAS-identifier. ClearPass has been pre-configured to look for the value **'lldp'** in the NAS-identifier; in this case it will return an **access-reject** for the MAC authentication. This is required for this lab, since the local device profile will be used to assign the user-role instead of the RADIUS server.

2. Enable port 1/1/27; this is the port connected to Access2.

```
ICX-Tx-Access1-lldp(config)# interface 1/1/27
ICX-Tx-Access1-lldp(config-if)# no shutdown
ICX-Tx-Access1-lldp(config-if)# exit
```

3. Review the current LLDP neighbors.

```
ICX-Tx-Access1-lldp(config)# show lldp neighbor-info
LLDP Neighbor Information
=========================

Total Neighbor Entries          : 2
Total Neighbor Entries Deleted  : 5
Total Neighbor Entries Dropped  : 0
Total Neighbor Entries Aged-Out : 3

LOCAL-PORT  CHASSIS-ID         PORT-ID  PORT-DESC    TTL    SYS-NAME
--------------------------------------------------------------------
1/1/25      90:20:c2:bc:17:00  1/1/1    1/1/1        120    CX-T12-C...
1/1/26      90:20:c2:bc:97:00  1/1/1    1/1/1        120    CX-T12-C...
```

Question: Is Access2 switch listed as an LLDP neighbor?

Answer: No, on ports with port-access authentication enabled, LLDP packets are disabled by default. LLDP would start to operate once a device has been successfully authenticated.

4. Enable LLDP packets on the port-access protected interface. Review the port-access options; next enable LLDP BPDUs.

```
ICX-Tx-Access1-lldp(config)# interface 1/1/27
ICX-Tx-Access1-lldp(config-if)# aaa authentication port-access allow-?
  allow-cdp-bpdu    Allow or block cdpbpdu.
  allow-lldp-bpdu   Allow or block lldpbpdu.
ICX-Tx-Access1-lldp(config-if)# aaa authentication port-access allow-lldp-bpdu
ICX-Tx-Access1-lldp(config-if)# exit
```

5. Wait up to 30 seconds; then review the LLDP neighbors. On port 1/1/27 there should be an LLDP neighbor now.

```
ICX-Tx-Access1-lldp(config)# show lldp neighbor-info

LLDP Neighbor Information
=========================

Total Neighbor Entries          : 3
Total Neighbor Entries Deleted  : 5
Total Neighbor Entries Dropped  : 0
Total Neighbor Entries Aged-Out : 3
```

```
LOCAL-PORT  CHASSIS-ID         PORT-ID   PORT-DESC  TTL   SYS-NAME
--------------------------------------------------------------------
1/1/25      90:20:c2:bc:17:00  1/1/1     1/1/1      120   ACSP-P52-...
1/1/26      90:20:c2:bc:97:00  1/1/1     1/1/1      120   ACSP-P52-...
1/1/27      88:3a:30:97:b6:00  1/1/27    1/1/27     120   ACSP-P52-...
```

6. Review the details for the neighbor on interface 1/1/27. The device profile can be applied to the **chassis-name** and the **chassis-description** information. It is also possible to assign the device profile based on a vendor-specific LLDP TLV, but that feature is less frequently implemented. The Aruba APs, AOS-Switch, and AOS-CX switches do report a specific Vendor OUI, so it is possible to apply the vendor OUI filter for those devices. In this lab, the assignment will be done based on the LLDP system description. The Access2 switch is a specific switch model, and the AOS-CX switches report their model code (JXXXX) in the LLDP system description. Take note of the Jxxxx code in the system description in this lab guide: it is JL668A.

Note

The lab assumes that the Core switches are using a different model number than the Access switches. If your lab would be using the same model number, it is possible to use the system name (access) instead of the model number.

```
ICX-Tx-Access1-lldp(config)# show lldp neighbor-info 1/1/27
Port                              : 1/1/27
Neighbor Entries                  : 1
Neighbor Entries Deleted          : 0
Neighbor Entries Dropped          : 0
Neighbor Entries Aged-Out         : 0
Neighbor Chassis-Name             : ICX-Tx-Access2
Neighbor Chassis-Description      : Aruba JL668A  FL.10.04.0030
Neighbor Chassis-ID               : 88:3a:30:97:b6:00
Neighbor Management-Address       : 10.251.x.5
Chassis Capabilities Available    : Bridge, Router
Chassis Capabilities Enabled      : Bridge, Router
Neighbor Port-ID                  : 1/1/27
Neighbor Port-Desc                : 1/1/27
Neighbor Port VLAN ID             : 1
TTL                               : 120

Neighbor Mac-Phy details
Neighbor Auto-neg Supported       : true
Neighbor Auto-Neg Enabled         : false
Neighbor Auto-Neg Advertised      :
Neighbor MAU type                 : 10 GIGBASEER
```

7. Define a new role that will be used in this task. The device-profile feature also uses the same port-access roles that are used by the 802.1X and MAC-Auth modules. For the purpose of this lab a dedicated role with be defined.

Note

For this lab demo device-mode authentication is enabled. This means that the port will be '**open**' for any mac-address after this device profile has been applied. This would apply to Aruba Instant APs, for example, since the AP will be performing the wireless user authentication.

```
ICX-Tx-Access1-lldp(config)# port-access role demo-lldp-switch
ICX-Tx-Access1-lldp(config-pa-role)# auth-mode device-mode
ICX-Tx-Access1-lldp(config-pa-role)# vlan trunk native 11
ICX-Tx-Access1-lldp(config-pa-role)# vlan trunk allowed 11,12
ICX-Tx-Access1-lldp(config-pa-role)# exit
ICX-Tx-Access1-lldp(config)#
```

Define an LLDP Group to Match the Peer LLDP Device

1. With an LLDP group, the administrator can assign LLDP devices based on the reported System Description, System Name, or a Vendor OUI TLV in the LLDP frame. In this lab, the assignment will be done based on the LLDP system description. The Access2 switch is a specific switch model, and the AOS-CX switches report their model code (JXXXX) in the LLDP system description.

2. Define a new LLDP group profile. This LLDP group will match on the LLDP system description of the neighbor LLDP switch.

```
ICX-Tx-Access1-lldp(config)# port-access lldp-group demo-switch
```

3. Review the selection criteria of the match command.

```
ICX-Tx-Access1-lldp(config-lldp-group)# match ?
  sys-desc    Configure LLDP system description.
sysnameConfigure LLDP system name.
  vendor-oui  Configure LLDP vendor OUI.
<cr>
```

4. Define a new match criteria based on the LLDP neighbor system description.

```
ICX-Tx-Access1-lldp(config-lldp-group)# match sys-desc JL668A
```

5. Review the current configuration of the LLDP group and exit the group context.

```
ICX-Tx-Access1-lldp(config-lldp-group)# show running-config current-context
port-access lldp-group demo-switch
     seq 10 match sys-desc JL668A
ICX-Tx-Access1-lldp(config-lldp-group)# exit
```

Define a Device Profile to Bind the LLDP Group to a User-role

1. Define a new port-access device profile.

```
ICX-Tx-Access1-lldp(config)# port-access device-profile dev-aoscx-switch
```

2. Bind the LLDP group and the user-role to this device profile and enable it.

```
ICX-Tx-Access1-lldp(config-device-profile)# associate role demo-lldp-switch
ICX-Tx-Access1-lldp(config-device-profile)# associate lldp-group demo-switch
ICX-Tx-Access1-lldp(config-device-profile)# enable
ICX-Tx-Access1-lldp(config-device-profile)# exit
```

3. Review the current device-profile configuration.

```
ICX-Tx-Access1-lldp(config)# show port-access device-profile
     Profile Name             : dev-aoscx-switch
     LLDP Groups              : demo-switch
     CDP Groups               :
     Role                     : demo-lldp-switch
     State                    : Enabled
```

4. Reset the port connected to Access2.

```
ICX-Tx-Access1-lldp(config)# int 1/1/27
ICX-Tx-Access1-lldp(config-if)# shutdown
ICX-Tx-Access1-lldp(config-if)# no shutdown
ICX-Tx-Access1-lldp(config-if)# exit
```

5. Review the device-profile status for all interfaces.

```
ICX-Tx-Access1-lldp(config)# show port-access device-profile interface all
  Port 1/1/27, Neighbor-Mac  88:3a:30:97:b6:00
    Profile Name:              : dev-aoscx-switch
    LLDP Group:                : demo-switch
    CDP Group:                 :
    Role:                      : demo-lldp-switch
    State:                     :applied
    Failure Reason:            :
```

6. Review that no other successful authentication device is online on this port.

```
ICX-Tx-Access1-lldp(config)# show aaa authentication port-access interface
1/1/27 client-status
Port Access Client Status Details
```

7. Review that the port VLAN status is now active based on the VLAN settings of the device-profile user-role. This method can be used to auto-provision the port and VLAN settings for many LLDP device types.

```
ICX-Tx-Access1-lldp(config)# show vlan port 1/1/27
------------------------------------------------------------------------------
VLAN  Name                                Mode             Mapping
------------------------------------------------------------------------------
11    VLAN11                              native-untagged  port-access
12    VLAN12                              trunk            port-access

Overridden VLAN list: 1
```

8. Disable the device-profile feature.

```
ICX-Tx-Access1-lldp(config)# port-access device-profile dev-aoscx-switch
ICX-Tx-Access1-lldp(config-device-profile)# disable
ICX-Tx-Access1-lldp(config-device-profile)# exit
```

9. Verify that the VLAN configuration of the port 1/1/27 has been reverted.

```
ICX-Tx-Access1-lldp(config)# show vlan port 1/1/27
-----------------------------------------------------------------------------
VLAN  Name                             Mode              Mapping
-----------------------------------------------------------------------------
1     DEFAULT_VLAN_1                   access            port
```

10. Remove the 'allow-lldp-bpdu' feature on the port 1/1/27.

```
ICX-Tx-Access1(config)# interface 1/1/27
ICX-Tx-Access1(config-if)# no aaa authentication port-access allow-lldp-bpdu
ICX-Tx-Access1(config-if)# exit
```

Task 7: Save checkpoint configuration

This task is required; upcoming lab activities are based on this configuration.

Steps

1. On Access1, change the hostname back to the default lab hostname. Change "Tx" to "T" followed by your table number; for example, Table 1 would be "T1" and Table 12 would be T12.

```
ICX-Tx-Access1(config)# hostname ICX-Tx-Access1
```

2. Save checkpoint **'icx-lab11-mac'**.

```
ICX-Tx-Access1(config)# end

ICX-Tx-Access1# copy run checkpoint icx-lab11-mac
Configuration changes will take time to process, please be patient.
```

3. Save checkpoint **'icx-lab11-mac'**.

```
ICX-Tx-Access2(config)# end
ICX-Tx-Access2# copy run checkpoint icx-lab11-mac
Configuration changes will take time to process, please be patient.
```

Learning Check

1. A network administrator sets up both 802.1X and RADIUS-based MAC-Auth on a port. For which clients does the RADIUS server need accounts with their MAC addresses?
   a. All clients
   b. Clients that do not support 802.1X
   c. Clients that support 802.1X
   d. Clients that support CHAP
2. An administrator enables both 802.1X and MAC-Auth on a switch port. By default, which method will the switch implement first?
   a. MAC-Auth
   b. 802.1X

Summary

Congratulations! In this chapter, you have explored appropriate situations for implementing MAC-Auth solutions. You now know when and how to set up the basic solutions, and you can also create solutions that combine 802.1X and MAC-Auth.

12 Dynamic Segmentation

OBJECTIVES

After completing this chapter, you should be able to:

- ✓ Understanding the operation of user-based tunneling
- ✓ Configure dynamic segmentation on AOS-CX switches
- ✓ Describe when and how to configure PAPI-enhanced security, high availability, and fallback switching for tunneled-node

Overview

This book focuses on AOS-CX switches, but switches and Aruba Mobility Controllers (MCs) and APs will likely only be part of your solution in an Aruba Mobility First Network. In addition to Aruba Central or AirWave (for network management) and Aruba ClearPass (for user access control), you may also have Aruba APs connected to Mobility Controllers (MCs). You might want to leverage the access control, firewall, and packet inspection capabilities of the MCs that currently secure your wireless devices to secure your wired endpoints as well.

In this chapter, you will learn how to use the dynamic segmentation feature, including tunneled-node, for this purpose.

Dynamic Segmentation Overview

You will now examine the use cases for tunneled-node. You will learn when to use tunneled-node, how the switch tunnels traffic to the control, and the modes in which tunneled-node can operate.

Colorless Ports

The greatest impact/benefit of colorless ports is that we no longer have to statically pre-configure access ports to any VLANs. Colorless ports signify traditional, legacy networks where the ports were assigned a "color" physically on the switch so that specific policy is assigned to that port. Specific devices were assigned a color and could only be plugged into the corresponding ports (Figure 12-1).

–Use 802.1X whenever possible

–Fallback to MAC authentication for non-802.1X capable devices

–Leverages ClearPass profiling for wired/wireless (IoT, laptops, mobile phones)

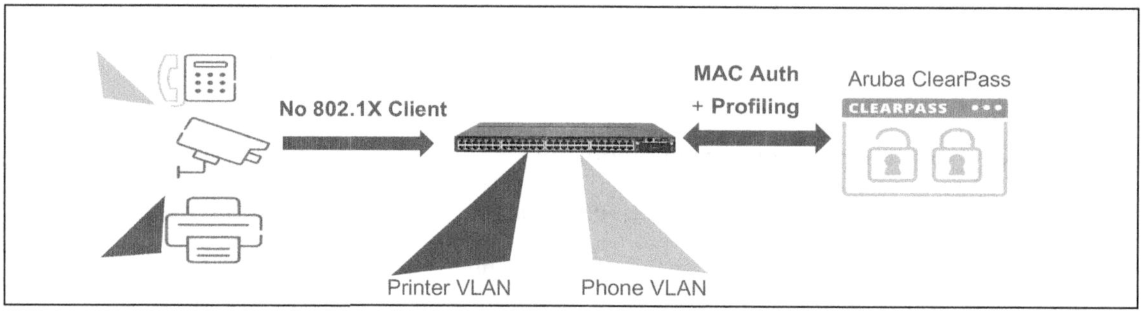

Figure 12-1 Colorless Ports

By using colorless ports, IT operating cycles are significantly reduced, leading to efficient planning for initial deployment or ongoing configuration changes which will accommodate future additions, moves, or changes. Colorless Ports demonstrate that switched access ports can automatically apply a role/policy required to support the connected device in real time.

Colorless Ports at the most basic level can be demonstrated with a single standalone switch using local user roles or device profiling with LLDP. Without using external RADIUS or tunneling, a customer can observe how the same port takes on different policies (QoS/ACL/VLANs) depending on *what* device connects to the port.

Note

ClearPass supports a feature called device profiling, which will learn the hardware (Apple iPhone versus a Linksys security camera) and/or operating system of the device connected to the network. This information can then be used in your policy decision process. Note that this feature requires ClearPass and allows you implement more granular policies and restrictions based on user account and device information.

Benefits of Tunneled-Node

Tunneled-node offers many benefits (Figure 12-2). Tunnel-node simplifies your wiring closet switch configuration. There is no need to configure 30-40 VLANs on the closet switch and allow those VLANs on the uplink trunks ports, as well as other policy configurations. Instead, traffic from the switch is tunneled to an Aruba Mobility Controller (MC) and the MC is responsible to handling VLAN and policy functions.

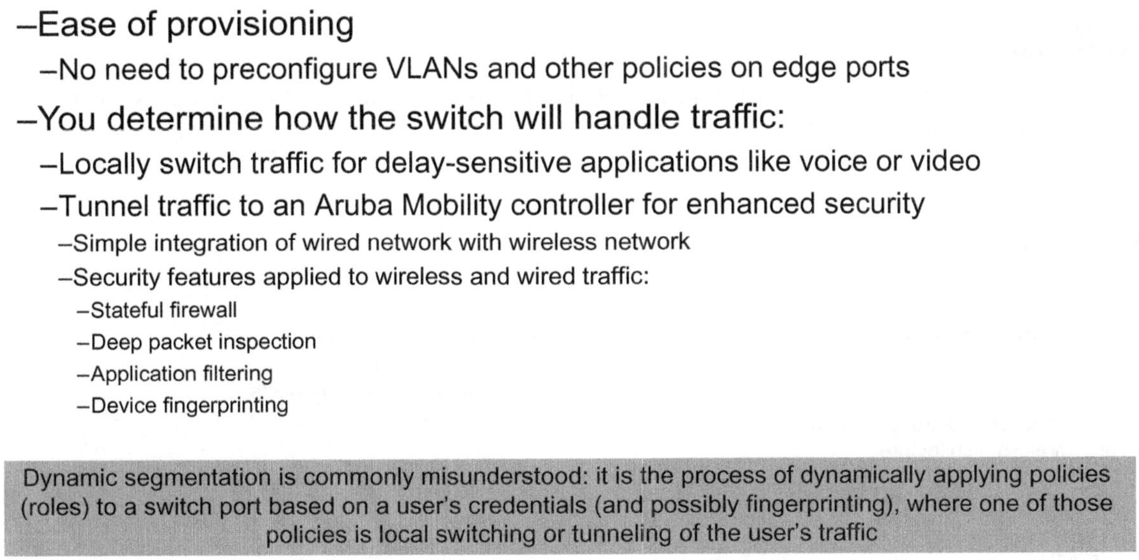

Figure 12-2 Benefits of Tunneled-Node

As another example, the company might have vulnerable devices that require extra filtering for their traffic. Surveillance cameras, payment card readers, and some IoT devices can be easily hacked or blocked by DoS attacks because they do not have an internal firewall. By having the switch tunnel all the client's traffic to the MC—just like an AP tunnels all traffic to the MC using GRE—you can take advantage of the controller's security features to protect both the vulnerable device and the network. These security features include a stateful firewall, deep packet inspection (DPI), and finger printing.

Aruba ClearPass and port-based authentication implemented on switches provide one method for unifying access policies. Both the MCs and AOS-CX switches can enforce 802.1X authentication to users and apply the policies returned by ClearPass. However, ClearPass cannot simply send the same settings to both MCs and switches. For example, ClearPass often simply sends the role assigned to a user to an MC, and the MC has firewall rules associated with that role configured on it. On the other hand, ClearPass would need to send a policy with dynamic ACLs to apply similar controls to an AOS-CX switch.

Tunneled-node provides tighter and simpler unification of wired and wireless access. Switches simply tunnel traffic to the MC, which handles the traffic much as it would handle traffic tunneled from an AP. An employee can connect through their desktop, log in, be assigned a role, and receive customized access. Later the employee can connect wirelessly using a laptop in a meeting room, log in, be assigned the same role, and receive the same access.

Do keep in mind that tunneling the wired devices' traffic to the MC, of course, increases the demands on that device. Architects will need to plan the Aruba solution's capacity and licensing accordingly. A list of general guidelines is provided later in this chapter.

> **Note**
> Dynamic segmentation, including tunneled-node, is supported on both Aruba switching products: AOS-CX and AOS switches.

Use Cases

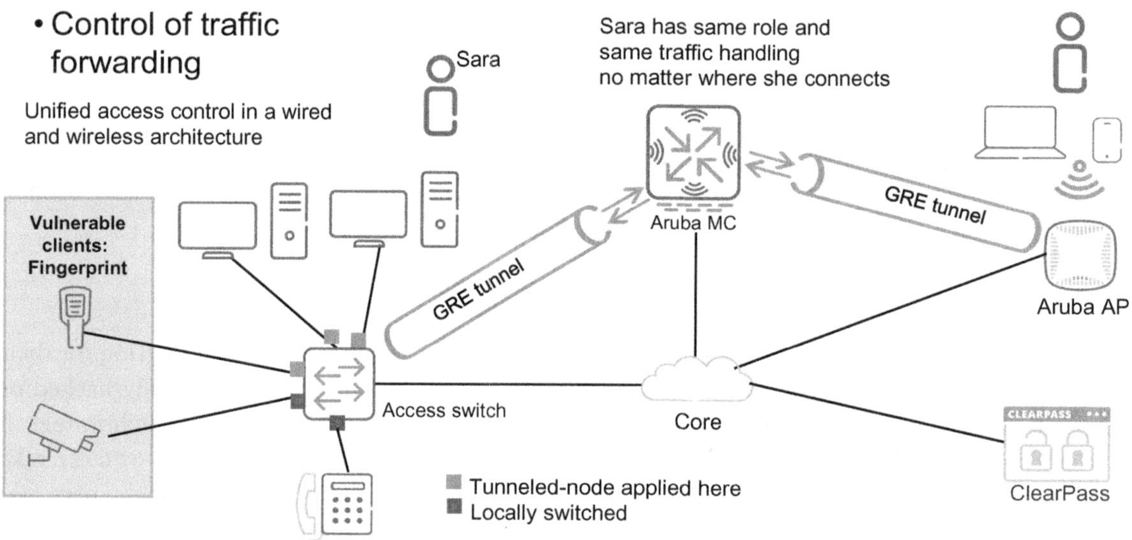

Figure 12-3 Use Cases

You should use the tunneled-node feature whenever you want to apply the same traffic control capabilities that an Aruba controller-based solution traditionally provides for wireless traffic to wired traffic as well. The tunneled-node feature can also play a role in unifying access control for users, so that the same policies apply regardless of whether they have a wired or wireless connection (Figure 12-3).

Switch and Mobility Controller (MC) Communications

The switch uses two protocols to connect to an Aruba Mobility Controller (MC): PAPI (control plane) and GRE (data plane). PAPI is the same protocol used by AP-to-MC communications. However, where APs use IPSec to protect the PAPI connection between the AP and MC, AOS-CX switches do not support this protection. Instead, you can optionally implement an MD5 HMAC function to protect PAPI between the AOS-CX switches and MCs (Figure 12-4).

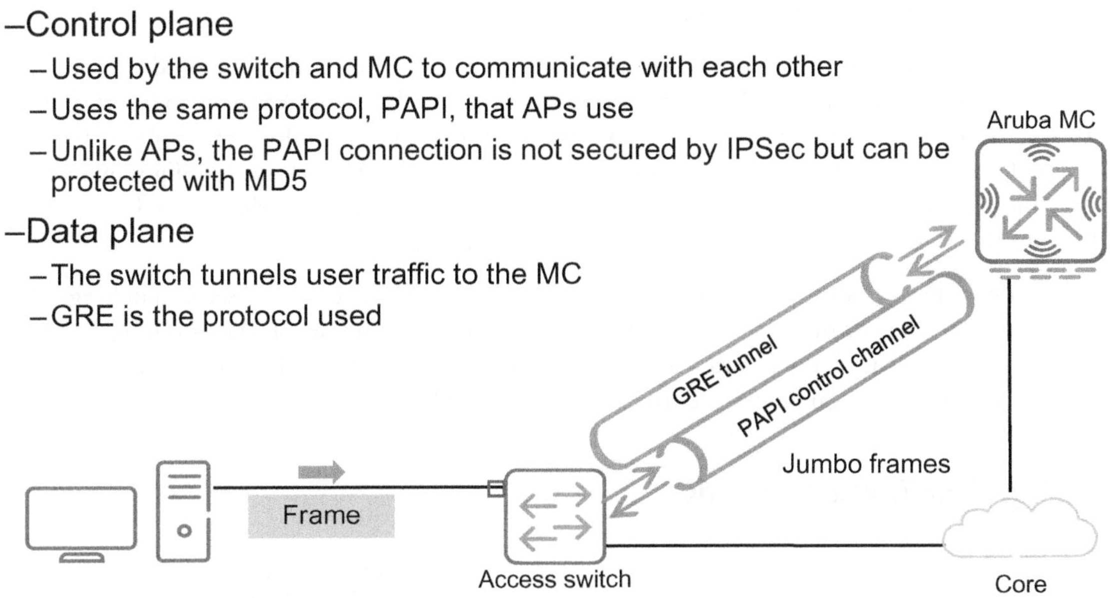

Figure 12-4 Switch and Mobility Controller (MC) Communications

Enhanced PAPI Security

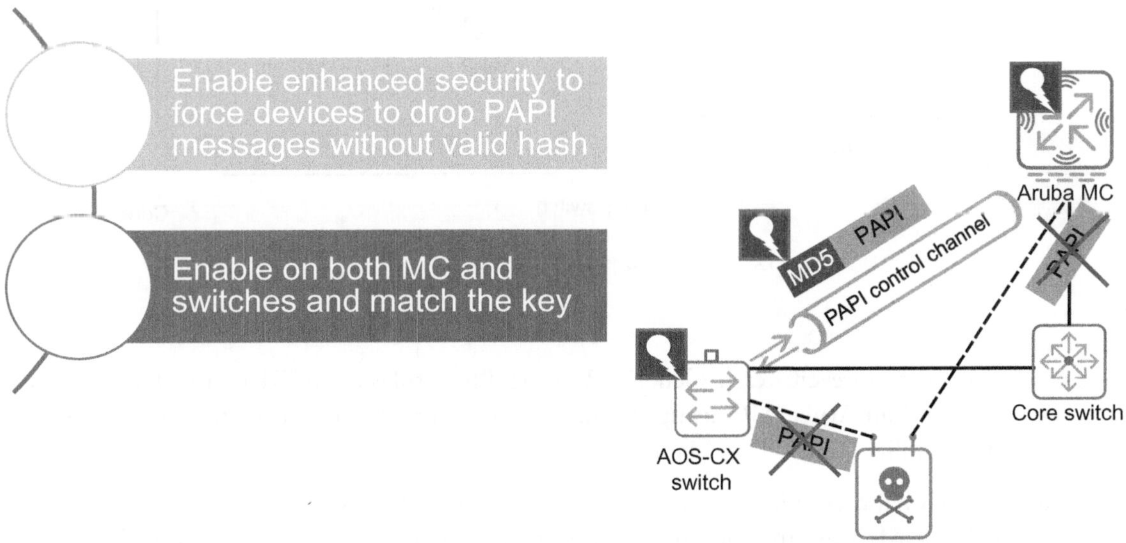

Figure 12-5 Enhanced PAPI Security

Switches use PAPI to communicate with the MC.

This communication creates a potential security risk (Figure 12-5). Rogue devices could start sending PAPI messages to the APs and switches and disrupt functionality. They could also try to insert spoofed PAPI messages on the controller to disrupt communications or obtain information about the network. PAPI-enhanced security minimizes this risk by using an MD5 and user-configurable key to hash the message. If a rogue device tries to spoof or tamper with a message, the hash will not check out because the rogue does not know the correct key to create the hash.

If administrators have enabled PAPI-enhanced security on the MC, you must set a matching PAPI key on the switch. The key must be between 10 and 64 characters. The switch then no longer accepts PAPI messages unless they have a valid hash created with this key. It is also able to send its PAPI messages with the correct key. Enhanced security mode is disabled by default.

Tunneling User Traffic to an MC

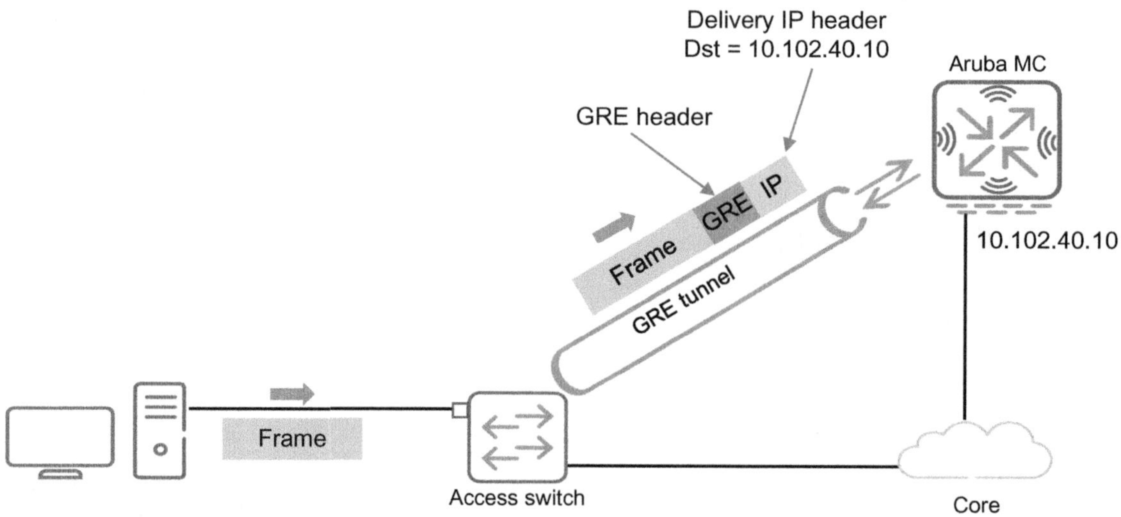

Figure 12-6 Tunneling User Traffic to an MC

The tunneled-node feature creates a Generic Routing Encapsulation (GRE) tunnel between the AOS-CX switch and an Aruba MC using the same technology that encapsulates packets between Aruba APs and Mobility Controllers (Figure 12-6).

The switch and MC also establish a control channel that uses Provisioning API (PAPI), the same Aruba protocol that MCs use to send configs and other important messages to APs. PAPI traffic is always carried outside of the GRE tunnels in a separate PAPI control channel.

How the MC Handles Tunneled-Node Traffic

From its side, the MC divides the arriving tunneled traffic into one tunnel per tunneled-node port. It decapsulates the traffic and applies various controls to it. While learning how to configure the MC to control tunneled-node traffic is beyond the scope of this guide, you should understand how the configuration on the switch plays into the MC's decisions.

The switch communicates the untagged VLAN configured on a tunneled-node port to the MC. The MC must have this VLAN configured on it. It then handles the tunneled traffic based on the settings in the wired AAA profile assigned to that VLAN. For example, the MC might apply MAC Auth or 802.1X—or some combination. After the successful authentication, the controller applies a role to the traffic. Then based on that role, it controls the traffic with firewall policies or performs other policy actions. Finally, it forwards the packet toward its destination.

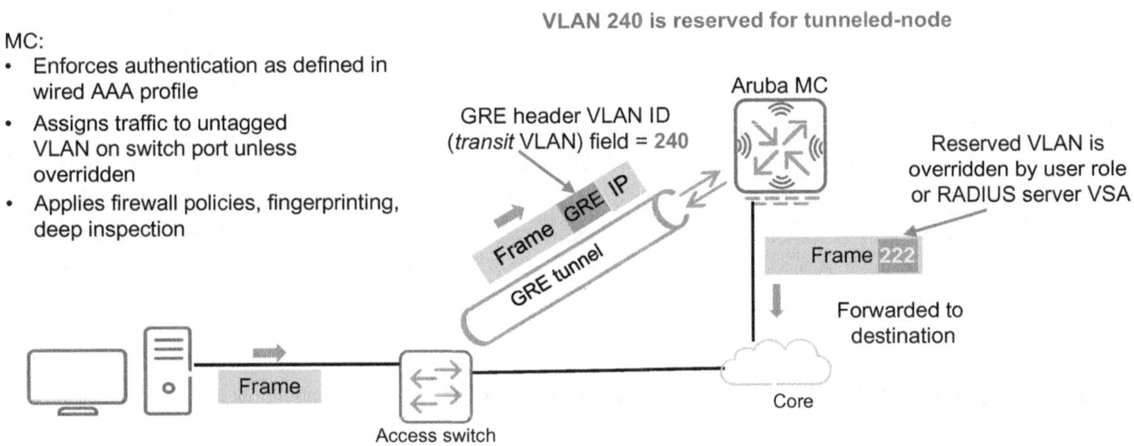

Figure 12-7 How the MC Handles Tunneled-Node Traffic

You must also set up the MC to forward the traffic in the tunneled-node ports' untagged VLAN at Layer 2 or Layer 3, as desired. In Figure 12-7, the MC is using Layer-2 forwarding. It forwards the frame tagged for VLAN 240. If the MC were using Layer-3 forwarding, it would have an IP address on VLAN 240 and route traffic out of this VLAN.

You can configure different VLANs on different tunneled-node ports to inform the controller to assign those nodes to different VLANs. However, the MC is also capable of applying different firewall rules to different devices in the same VLAN, again based on dynamic settings applied during authentication. For example, the MC could enforce MAC-Auth and use the devices' MAC addresses to assign different roles to different devices. You should coordinate with the MC administrators and make sure to match the switch configuration with their desired configuration.

Keep in mind that the switch is simply using the untagged VLAN on the tunneled-node port to communicate the desired default VLAN to the controller. It is *not* switching the tunneled-nodes' traffic in this VLAN, so you do not need to tag it on the switches' uplinks as you normally would. (The use of fallback switching mode makes an exception as you will learn later.) Instead the VLAN exists on the MC at the distribution or core. In keeping with this design, the switch is restricted from implementing many normal features—such as an IP address—on any untagged VLAN on a tunneled-node port. Aruba recommends reserving the tunneled-node VLANs for tunneled-node ports only.

You should also understand that the MC can override the default VLAN assignment after it authenticates the device. For example, it might apply 802.1X authentication to tunneled-nodes and receive a dynamic VLAN assignment from Aruba ClearPass. The MC would then forward the tunneled-node device traffic in this VLAN, rather than the untagged VLAN configured on the switch port. Even if you plan to apply dynamic VLANs for some devices, though, the MC must support the untagged VLAN on tunneled-node ports; the VLAN defines the wired AAA profile.

Finally, note that the figure above shows a single tunneled-node port on the AOS-Switch for simplicity. When tunneled-node is applied to multiple ports, the MC sees one tunnel *per port*.

As to terms, the use of term *transit* or *reserved* VLAN is the number placed in the GRE header in the Key field. This helps the MC determine the WLAN profile policies that should be used, by default, if nothing else is received, like the security policies and VLAN that should be applied to the user. In this example, the AAA server did not send a VLAN attribute, so what was used in the VLAN header is the final VLAN for the user on the MC. Note that this VLAN must be pre-configured on the MC. If the AAA server had passed down a specific VLAN attribute, like VLAN 888, then this would have become the user's final VLAN number and what the MC would use to tag the user's traffic before forwarding it onward.

Guidelines for the Path Between Switch and MC

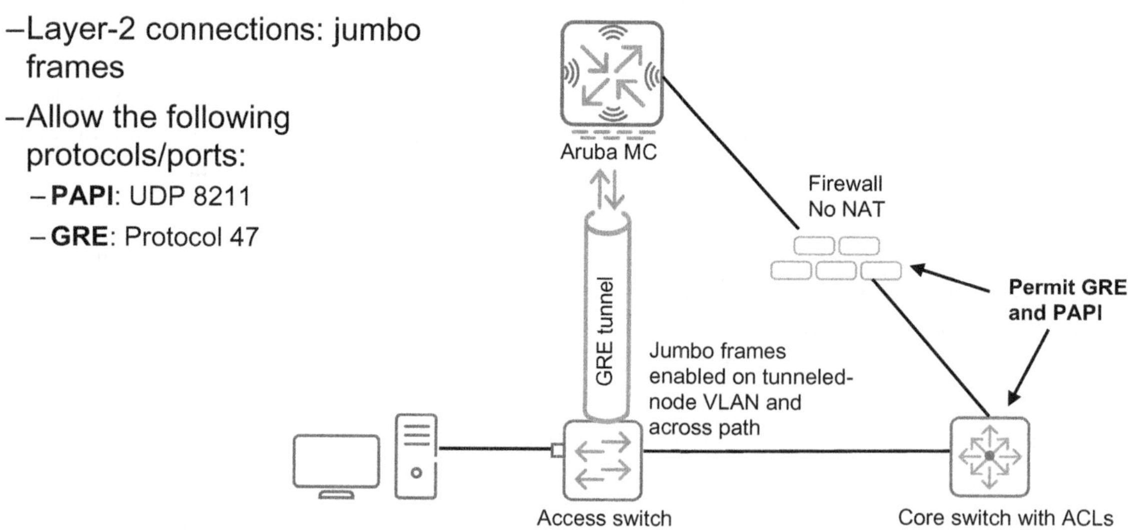

Figure 12-8 Guidelines for the Path Between Switch and MC

You should check the network infrastructure between the AOS-CX switches that implement tunneled-node and the MCs. Make sure that the infrastructure will not interfere with communications in any way (Figure 12-8).

If any firewalls or network infrastructure devices with ACLs are in the path, they must allow GRE and PAPI traffic. Enable GRE on IP protocol 47 and PAPI on UDP port 8211.

You must also understand that NAT cannot be applied in the path between the switch and the controller. It is best if you can direct the tunneled-node switch to a local MC.

Also keep in mind that encapsulating frames can cause them to exceed the MTU. However, tunneled-node ports do not support the features typically used to prevent MTU violations, including fragmentation, PMTU detection, or reassembly. Aruba recommends that you enable jumbo frames across the path from the switch to the MC. On AOS-CX switches, you enable jumbo frames on a VLAN basis. Make sure that every VLAN that carries traffic between the switch and the MC supports jumbo frames.

Make sure that you know the IP address that your AOS-CX switches will use to establish the tunnel with the MC. Typically, the switch acts at Layer 2 and has a single IP address and a default gateway for reaching all other subnets. But if your switch has multiple IP addresses, it uses the IP address on the forwarding VLAN for its route to the MC. Make sure that the MC can also reach this IP address (through its own route or its default gateway).

Important

Because the original user Ethernet frame is tunneled by adding a GRE, IP, and a second Ethernet header, you will need to make sure you have jumbo frames enabled in the network infrastructure between the access switches and the MCs, minimally.

What is User-Based Tunneling (UBT)?

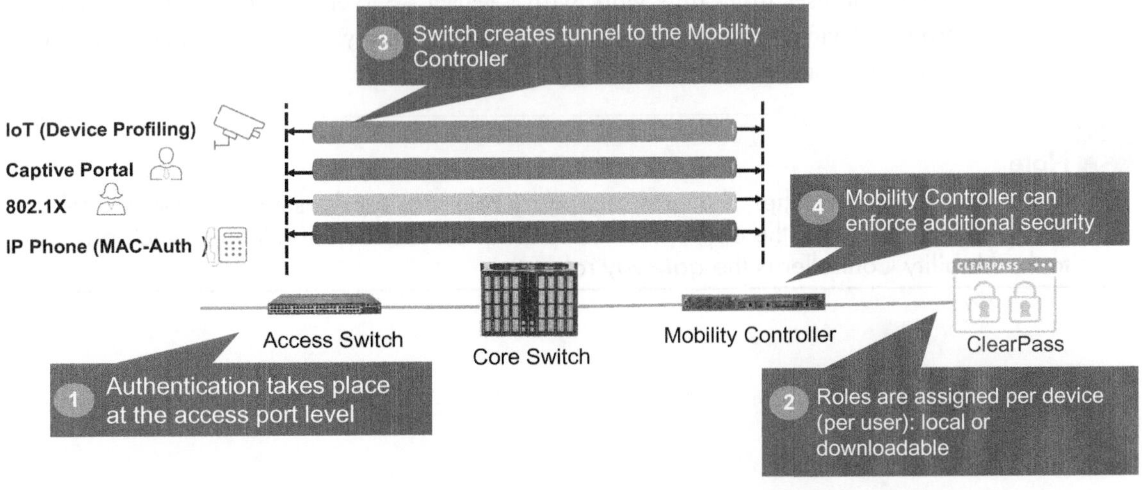

Figure 12-9 What is User-Based Tunneling (UBT)?

UBT uses the concept of a colorless access port. It does not matter what you connect to the port; roles and policies are assigned per device (Figure 12-9).

Authentication takes place at the access port level; Successful authentication enforces VLAN and ACL assignments can create a user or device-based tunnel to the Mobility Controller. Mobility Controller can enforce additional security.

UBT provides these features:

- Secured and flexible control of access layer: With ClearPass or switch configuration, only traffic from a specific user/device role is sent to the Mobility Controller Policies (for example, QoS, ACL, rate-limit can be enforced at tunneled ports or at the controller).
- Access to Controller's applications: Users can access Controller's applications such as stateful firewall and AppRF
- Policy enforcement is achieved by local user roles or downloadable user roles
- Local user roles are configured on the switch
- Downloadable user roles are configured on ClearPass and pushed to the switch
- High availability and scalability
- Load balance to multiple controllers for high scalability
- Stateful failover to standby mobility controller

There are two user roles that the switch can use:

- **Local User Role (LUR)**: LUR allows us to use a third-party AAA server. Local user Roles are defined on the switch. When a device connects and authenticates successfully, a User-Role name (VSA) is passed to the switch, then the switch will apply that User-Role to the device.
- **Downloadable User Role (DUR)**: The switch does not need the User-Role defined on the switch. Downloadable user Roles only work with ClearPass Server, not third-party authentication server. When a device connects and authenticates successfully, the switch will download the User-Role to the switch and the switch will apply it to the device.

Note

On the older AOS switches, the term *secondary* role was used instead of *gateway* role. With AOS-CX switches, the appropriate term used to describe the role the switch passes to the Mobility Controller is the *gateway* role.

Note

In the current release (10.04), Aruba does not support role download for a gateway (controller) or secondary role to the mobility controller, which either a) the role will need to pre-exist on the MC or b) the MC will have to download the controller from ClearPass directly.

Local Switching versus UBT

The table in Figure 12-10 compares the two approaches of switching traffic: local switching and UBT. Local switching is typically used when delay-sensitive traffic is involved between access-layer devices, like voice or video communications (VoIP phones, for example) or a third-party firewall already exists in the network and the company wants to continue using the policy function of that firewall. However, the main detractor to local switching is that less security is available on access switches. For example, if you wanted to filter traffic, you would be limited to ACLs with no stateful or application inspection features. In many cases, companies use only VLANs for security at the access layer, where devices in a VLAN can free interact with each other: their traffic is only processed by the firewall if it leaves the subnet. Allowing this type of promiscuous behavior can lead to many security issues (user devices can attack other user devices in the same subnet).

	Local Switching	UBT
How it works	Switch locally switches traffic	Switch tunnels traffic to an Aruba MC, which processes the traffic
When to use it	• Delay-sensitive traffic, like voice or video communications • Third-party firewall already installed	• Wired and wireless traffic should have the same (or similar) policies applied to them • Aruba MCs are part of the existing network or new design
Advantages	• Less delay when user or network devices need to communicate at the access layer	• **More secure since Aruba MCs support stateful firewall, application inspection, and many other security features** • **Traffic is controlled before a device can communicate with another device**
Disadvantages	• **Allows user -to-user connections unless filtered by ACLs (less secure)** • **Access layer switches do not support stateful firewall or application inspection features**	• Requires possible additional MCs for Ethernet bandwidth needs • Switches consume AP licenses • Requires AOS-CX or AOS switches only

Figure 12-10 Local Switching versus UBT

UBT, on the other hand, has the switch authenticate the user, but then tunnel the user's traffic to an Aruba MC where its traffic will be processed by security policies. The main and big advantages that UBT has over local switching include:

- Centralized security policies for both wired and wireless traffic: For example, a user in Human resources would have the very similar, if not the same security policies applied to them whether they connected via wireless or an Ethernet switch port.
- A user device's traffic must be processed by the Aruba MC before it can be forwarded to any other device. This allows the MC to apply stateful and application inspection policies, as well as other security features, to better secure the traffic, greatly limiting user-to-user threats in the same VLAN.
- Easier to scale: scalability is provided by the Aruba MCs, where the 7280 MC supports a theoretical stateful firewall throughput of 100 Gbps.
- Easier to implement security policies, because only one product is primarily used for the user traffic: Aruba Mobility Controllers. The problem with a company that has Aruba MCs for wireless and a third-party firewall is that it becomes very difficult to ensure that policies are consistent between the third-party firewall and the Aruba MCs.

Local Switching or UBT Process

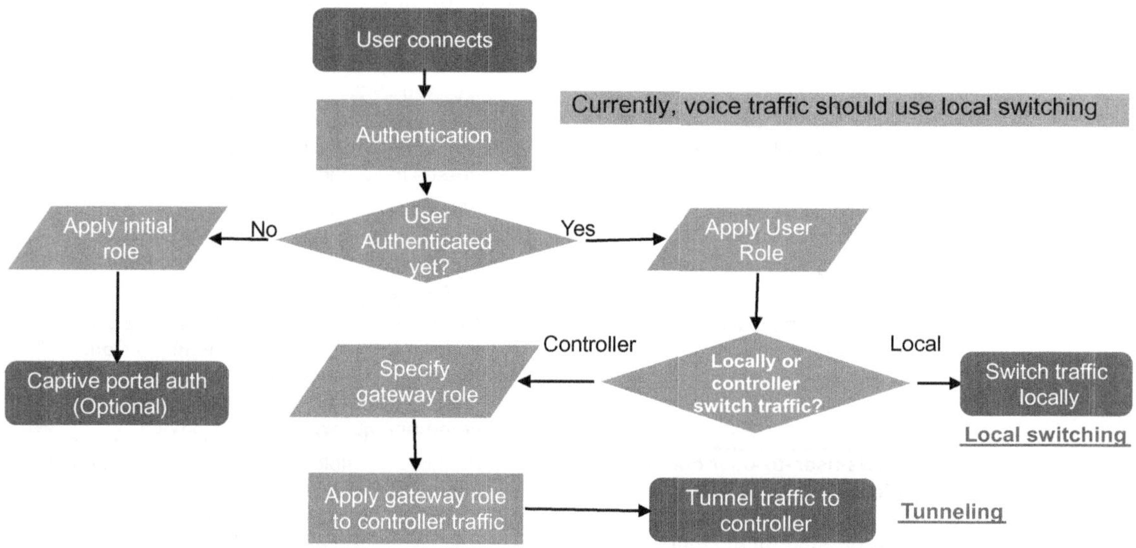

Figure 12-11 Local Switching or UBT Process

By identifying if the *redirect* parameter exists, the switch can easily decide that the client traffic is tunneled to the Mobility Controller or is locally switched (Figure 12-11).

Important

Currently, voice traffic must use local switching.

Policy Source and Enforcement for Different Scenarios

The table in Figure 12-12 summarizes where the policy is obtained and used and where the enforcement is done based on the scenario.

Note

Port-based tunnel mode is currently not supported in AOS-CX (it is supported in AOS). Only UBT is currently supported. The older ArubaOS switches support both modes: port-based and user/role-based.

Scenario	Data path & Policy Enforcement	Switch mode	Policy decision	Policy/role Content
Colorless portswith RADIUS VSA control	Local switch	Standard	ClearPass	ClearPass
Colorless ports with role based access	Local switch	Role-based access	ClearPass (fallback local)	Local switch
User-based tunnel	Switch (local) / Controller (tunneled)	Role-based access	ClearPass (fallback local)	Switch (local) / Controller (tunneled)

Figure 12-12 Policy Source and Enforcement For Different Scenarios

There are two user roles that the switch can use:

- **Local User Role (LUR)**: LUR allows us to use a third-party AAA server. Local user Roles are defined on the switch. When a device connects and authenticates successfully, a User-Role name (VSA) is passed to the switch, then the switch will apply that User-Role to the device.
- **Downloadable User Role (DUR)**: The switch does not need the User-Role defined on the switch. Downloadable user Roles only work with ClearPass Server, not third-party authentication server. When a device connects and authenticates successfully, the switch will download the User-Role to the switch and the switch will apply it to the device.

License Requirements

Initially, Aruba did not require any licensing to implement dynamic segmentation. Starting with AOS 8.4 on the MCs, the switch is not treated as an AP and will consume licenses as an AP. Note that if you set up a virtual switch (VSF) that is comprised of multiple physical AOS-CX switches, only the virtual switch will consume licenses (Figure 12-13).

A standalone MC (or centralized MM-based solution) needs one AP license for each switch that is running dynamic segmentation. If the solution is using firewall functionality, it also needs one Policy Enforcement Firewall (PEF) license for each switch implementing dynamic segmentation.

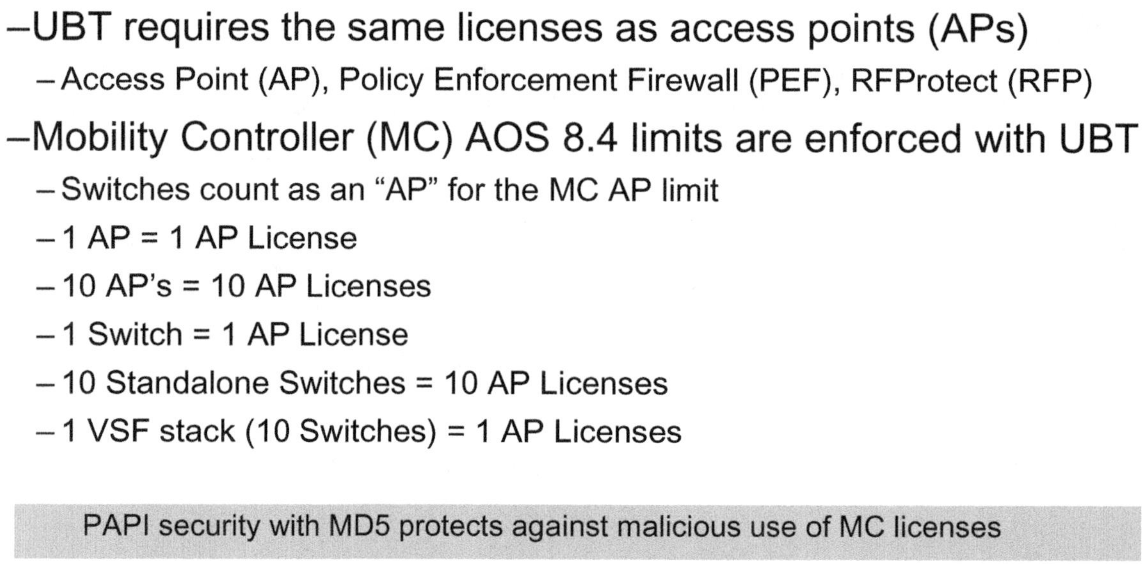

Figure 12-13 License Requirements

If the MC is using the RF Protect features, it should have one RFP license for each dynamic segmentation switch as well. The RFP license is not strictly required. However, licensing works such that, when RF Protect is enabled, the MC should have the same number of AP, PEF, and RFP licenses; if it has fewer RFP licenses, it disables the excess AP and PEF licenses until it has the same count. The company might choose to deploy Aruba MCs dedicated to supporting the wired tunneled-nodes. In this case, the MC would not use RF Protect, and the RFP licenses would not be required.

If the MC is part of an MM-based solution, an MM license is also required for the dynamic segmentation switch, just as it would be for an AP.

To conserve licenses, you may choose to consolidate the dynamic segmentation feature to one or just a few switches.

Important

You should always implement PAPI MD5 security to protect communications between the controller and switch, as well as protecting against malicious misuses of licenses, since each switch request consumes a license(s) on the MC.

UBT Scalability

The table in Figure 12-14 shows the number of supported tunnels for both the MCs and the AOS-CX switches. Typically, the number of tunnels required to implement dynamic segmentation is not a concern if you are implementing one tunnel per port on a switch. However, if you are implementing multiple tunnels on a port, because there are multiple downstream devices (perhaps another switch or a blade server with many VMs in a data center), then care must be taken that no more than 256 tunnels are created per port.

Controller	Maximum Supported Tunnels
7280	32768
7240 /7240XM	32768
7220	16384
7210	8192
7205	4096
7030	1024
7024	512
7010	512
7008	256
7005	256

Switch Series	Maximum Supported Tunnels
6300 – Per Switch/Stack	1000 tunnels
6300 – Per Port	256 tunnels
6400–Per Switch/per system	1000 tunnels
6400 – Per Port	256 tunnels

Figure 12-14 UBT Scalability

As mentioned earlier, architects should consider the dynamic segmentation feature as they plan. In addition to the licensing requirements, they should keep in mind tunneling requirements. The MC treats each user as a separate tunnel. Architects should also remember that a single tunneled-node port could connect to multiple devices (if, for example, the port connects to an unmanaged switch), which could raise the user count. The MC will need to support these additional tunnels.

Finally, architects should consider the effects of the wired traffic on the firewall throughput and whether the controller can support the bandwidth; and if not, an additional controller(s) will need to be purchased.

Of course, administrators will also need to implement the policies for controlling wired traffic. However, configuring the MC to control and forward the traffic is beyond the scope of this guide and should be handled by an experienced Aruba controller administrator.

Note

Also make sure that your MCs are running up-to-date software. Minimally, ArubaOS 8.4 is required on your MCs to support user-based mode on the AOS-CX switches.

Lab 12.1

Lab 12.1 Diagram

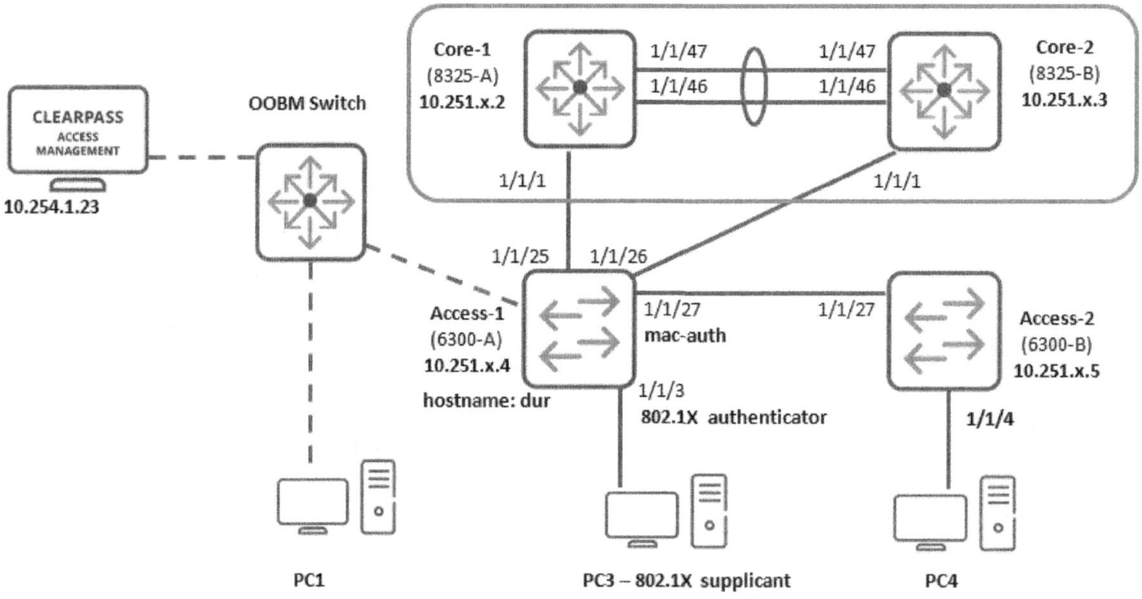

Figure 12-15 Lab 12.1 Diagram

Overview

This lab requires the completion of the 802.1X (Lab10) and MAC authentication (Lab11) lab activities (Figure 12-15).

This lab activity will demonstrate how ClearPass downloadable user roles can be used to simplify the deployment of the authentication user roles to the switches. The roles are only defined on the ClearPass host and they will be downloaded on the fly, as needed, by the access switches.

This means that the administrator still needs to understand the concept of roles. But it is not necessary anymore to check that all the switches have the latest configuration/policy version of all these user roles in their configuration, since this will be done automatically for the administrator. This will also reduce the operational configuration file of the access switches, since these roles are not saved in the configuration file.

The switch will download the definition from ClearPass as part of the authentication process using the REST API; therefore, credentials must be configured on the switch to access the ClearPass host to download the role configuration.

Objectives

- Define secure HTTPS access between the switch and ClearPass by importing the Trust Anchor certificate
- Define the credentials to access the ClearPass REST API
- Verify the operation of the downloadable user roles

Task 1: CPPM REST API Communication

Objectives

Review the requirements on the switch to validate the CPPM certificate: check NTP, and the name resolution for the certificate subject name

Verify CPPM has been configured with a read-only admin user account.

On the Access switch, install the CPPM CA certificate as a 'trust anchor'. This will enable the switch to validate the CPPM server certificate. This procedure can be done using the CLI or using NetEdit.

On the Access switch, configure the (read-only) admin account that the switch should use to access the CPPM REST API when downloading user-roles.

Steps

Verify Requirements for Certificate Validation

The AOS-CX switch should be able to verify the validity of the ClearPass server certificate. This requires a valid time to be set on the switch and the switch should have a valid certificate chain (Trust Anchor) to validate the certificate on the ClearPass server. In the next steps, these requirements will be configured and verified.

Review Time is Synchronized Correctly

1. Open a terminal session on Access1; enter the configuration mode. Verify the time.

```
ICX-Tx-Access1(config)# show clock
Mon Jan 27 18:14:35 EDT 2020
System is configured for timezone : US/Eastern
```

2. Verify the NTP status.

```
ICX-Tx-Access1(config)# show ntp status
NTP Status Information
NTP                           : Enabled
NTP Authentication            : Disabled
NTP Server Connections        : Using the mgmt VRF

System time                   : Mon Jan 27 18:14:31 EDT 2020
NTP uptime                    : 6 hours, 31 minutes, 39 seconds
```

Trust Anchor (TA) Installation

This installation can be done using the CLI or using NetEdit. The lab guide provides instructions for the CLI only.

1. Review the default Trust Anchor configuration. There should be no root CAs installed by default.

```
ICX-Tx-Access1(config)# show crypto pki ta-profile
TA Profile Name                  TA Certificate     Revocation Check
-------------------------------- ------------------ ----------------
```

2. Define a new TA profile **'cppm'**.

```
ICX-Tx-Access1(config)# crypto pki ta-profile cppm
```

3. Run the **'import'** command.

```
ICX-Tx-Access1(config-ta-cppm)# ta-certificate import
Paste the certificate in PEM format below, then hit enter and ctrl-D:
```

4. On PC1, open the **ICX-Files** folder on the desktop. Open the cert file: "**lab 12.1 - clearpass - root - ca.txt**"; copy the contents and paste the content in the CLI.

Note

The file can manually be downloaded from ClearPass on this 'well-known' URL: **http://<cppm-ip>/.well-known/aruba/clearpass/https-root.pem**. For the lab this would be: **http://10.254.1.23/.well-known/aruba/clearpass/https-root.pem**.

5. Here is the example output:

```
ICX-T12-Access1(config-ta-cert)# -----BEGIN CERTIFICATE-----
MIIEGTCCAwGgAwIBAgIBEjANBgkqhkiG9w0BAQ0FADCBkzELMAkGA1UEBhMCVVMx
ICX-T12-Access1(config-ta-cert)# MIIEGTCCAwGgAwIBAgIBEjANBgkqhkiG
9w0BAQ0FADCBkzELMAkGA1UEBhMCVVMx
ICX-T12-Access1(config-ta-cert)# EzARBgNVBAgMCkNhbGlmb3JuaWExEjAQBg
NVBAcMCVN1bm55dmFsZTEYMBYGA1UE
ICX-T12-Access1(config-ta-cert)# CgwPQXJ1YmEgRWR1Y2F0aW9uMQwwCgYDVQ
QLDANFZHUxEDAOBgNVBAMMB0FDU1Ag
ICX-T12-Access1(config-ta-cert)# Q0ExITAfBgkqhkiG9w0BCQEWEmFjc3AtY2
FAYWNzcC5sb2NhbDAeFw0yMDAxMjcx
ICX-T12-Access1(config-ta-cert)# ODE5NDRaFw0zMDAxMjcxODQ5NDRaMIGTMQ
swCQYDVQQGEwJVUzETMBEGA1UECAwK
ICX-T12-Access1(config-ta-cert)# Q2FsaWZvcm5pYTESMBAGA1UEBwwJU3Vubn
l2YWxlMRgwFgYDVQQKDA9BcnViYSBF
ICX-T12-Access1(config-ta-cert)# ZHVjYXRpb24xDDAKBgNVBAsMA0VkdTEQMA
4GA1UEAwwHQUNTUCBDQTEhMB8GCSqG
ICX-T12-Access1(config-ta-cert)# SIb3DQEJARYSYWNzcC1jYUBhY3NwLmxvY2
FsMIIBIjANBgkqhkiG9w0DAQEFAAOC
ICX-T12-Access1(config-ta-cert)# AQ8AMIIBCgKCAQEAwwpyOsCEii0f8eSNjHI6
WcEQ+EOKHYMoNROGWy2YmhFqcAEf
ICX-T12-Access1(config-ta-cert)# V0Df9Mto0tPIJGth3CmQcZELBz+8WpSdaJvl
lqj9QbNJZNklT44al5Sbv59pOyUM
ICX-T12-Access1(config-ta-cert)# XsnJj+KwUmLWL/SUvxM8R81pAK36wRAyAeNr+
plVj1RpIxUl2xHsQv8qMTypShkw
ICX-T12-Access1(config-ta-cert)# YfEs+mCl/VKZ8iWtoupRX+iuWUhBXj39+8gM
7c+8sSiImWYmkLlqQfXzxN9TQ4hj
ICX-T12-Access1(config-ta-cert)# Xc6Hk4ovxUri2YzO1ZXtx5zJYKz/AqlZ1gfU
dBKyNFZwRPRt4F0mLKMsQnyG19Cg
ICX-T12-Access1(config-ta-cert)# j10sClvzysqjfXk7KbrJU+XE0z4meiNxWmem
mQIDAQABo3YwdDAdBgNVHQ4EFgQU
ICX-T12-Access1(config-ta-cert)# XYYnMTUJlJxEmOqT8QoA1pYb8KEwDwYDVR0
PAQH/BAUDAweGADAPBgNVHRMBAf8E
ICX-T12-Access1(config-ta-cert)# BTADAQH/MDEGA1UdJQQqMCgGCCsGAQUFBwM
JBggrBgEFBQcDAgYIKwYBBQUHAwEG
```

```
ICX-T12-Access1(config-ta-cert)#
CCsGAQUFBwMDMA0GCSqGSIb3DQEBDQUAA4IBAQAjLKEREPA/QGVdP5xi1tcMe7LI
ICX-T12-Access1(config-ta-cert)# jaG987qoFmCwi9ocDhfMMggNnOny9m0uW4GN
sHeBSPIcTgN+JYjjBuN4+V5Iz74Z
ICX-T12-Access1(config-ta-cert)#
LUqHP2YwZFqwIWtNr3agBEievCj0AQNSdFNwKU7BS6B0BaT2RBWyy6x5U7ljBKAl
ICX-T12-Access1(config-ta-cert)# OQH5xzcNyRpetbTIdf0q5Aa0kC7QmbYYGxBa
mwbzS5luU+akQy2HD9vr2bi+X5Aq
ICX-T12-Access1(config-ta-cert)# jVBKTUkTPuFPQhQroXp2VI3ldIPJYaWz1Gk5
NTAQkv/9bImdr5f4NfJrMI/kubjy
ICX-T12-Access1(config-ta-cert)# bdXTI+LyPtiLpkbF2dDCN8GBKovNQFvhlXtG
T4b/umOzSS2AzHcVj/SldVw6
ICX-T12-Access1(config-ta-cert)# -----END CERTIFICATE-----
ICX-T12-Access1(config-ta-cert)#
```

6. When the paste is complete, enter the '**<CTRL>D**' key combination from a blank line. This will instruct the switch to parse the pasted cert and show the subject name. Now confirm that this cert is ok.

```
ICX-Tx-Access1(config-ta-cert)#
The certificate you are importing has the following attributes:
Subject: C = US, ST = California, L = Sunnyvale, O = Aruba Education, OU = Edu,
CN = ACSP CA, emailAddress = acsp-ca@acsp.local
Issuer:  C = US, ST = California, L = Sunnyvale, O = Aruba Education, OU = Edu,
CN = ACSP CA, emailAddress = acsp-ca@acsp.local
Serial Number: 0x12
TA certificate import is allowed only once for a TA profile
Do you want to accept this certificate (y/n)? y
ICX-Tx-Access1(config-ta-cppm)#
```

7. Exit the context and verify that the TA profile is installed.

Important

The actual import will be done when the TA-import context is closed, so make sure to use **'exit'** before checking the CA cert import status.

```
ICX-Tx-Access1(config-ta-cppm)# show crypto pki ta-profile
TA Profile Name                  TA Certificate      Revocation Check
-------------------------------- ------------------- -----------------

ICX-Tx-Access1(config-ta-cppm)# exit
ICX-Tx-Access1(config)# show crypto pki ta-profile
```

```
TA Profile Name                   TA Certificate        Revocation Check
--------------------------------- -------------------- ----------------
cppm                              Installed, valid     disabled
```

CPPM REST API Read-Only User Account

A read-only administrator has been defined on ClearPass. In the next steps, you will verify that this administrator has been defined.

1. Using the PC1 management station, open a connection to ClearPass on https://10.254.1.23/tips
   - Username: **icx-adminX** (replace X with your table number). Examples: icx-admin1 for table1, icx-admin12 for table12
   - Password: **aruba123**
2. Navigate to **Administration > Users and Privileges > Admin Users**. Verify that an admin account has been created named **'duradmin'** (**downloadable user role** admin), with read-only privileges.

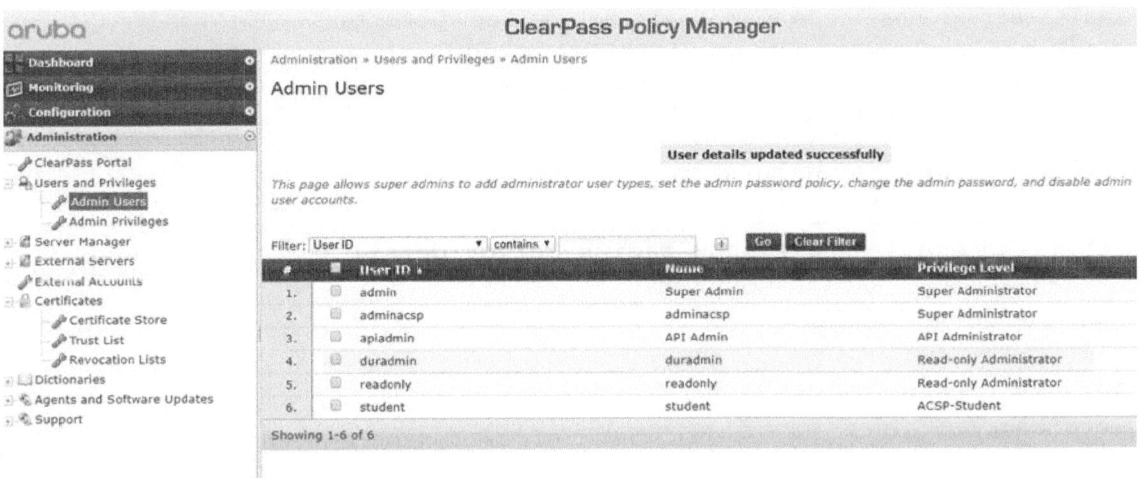

Note

In this lab environment, a Read-only Administrator is used. ClearPass also provides a more restrictive admin privilege **Aruba User Role Download** that can be assigned to the download account. This role can only access ClearPass using the REST API and it can only read the enforcement profiles.

Switch: Define the ClearPass Credentials to Access the REST API

1. On the Access1 switch, define the REST API credentials on the ClearPass RADIUS server object with the name '**cppm.arubatraining.com**'.

Note

Pay attention to define the correct **hostname** and VRF **mgmt**.

```
ICX-Tx-Access1(config)# radius-server host cppm.arubatraining.com vrf
mgmt clear pass-username duradmin clearpass-password plaintext aruba123
```

2. Verify the running configuration for RADIUS server lines; there should be only one RADIUS server.

```
ICX-Tx-Access1(config)# show run | include radius-server
radius-server tracking user-name icx-radius-track password ciphertext
AQBapUmeqwuSjUoetq4KWXbTnUyBILPjxzok4qzRZeSXsBIzCQAAACMxHv6lEnY7jA==

radius-server host cppm.arubatraining.com key ciphertext AQBapVWcNJavUClN-
BQenFaJwwRrR+nWcJUvsQlHUbuaiOvlDCAAAAMCnYwT2Ful+ tracking enable
clearpass-username duradmin clearpass-password ciphertext
AQBapUmeqwuSjUoetq4KWXbTnUyBILPjxzok4qzRZeSXsBIzCQAAACMxHv6lEnY7jA== vrf mgmt
```

3. You can also review the RADIUS list in a different format.

```
ICX-Tx-Access1(config)# show radius-server detail
******* Global RADIUS Configuration *******
Shared-Secret: None
Timeout: 5
Auth-Type: pap
Retries: 1
Tracking Time Interval (seconds): 300
Tracking Retries: 1
Tracking User-name: icx-radius-track
Tracking Password:
AQBapUmeqwuSjUoetq4KWXbTnUyBILPjxzok4qzRZeSXsBIzCQAAACMxHv6lEnY7jA==
Number of Servers: 1

****** RADIUS Server Information ******
Server-Name                 : cppm.arubatraining.com
Auth-Port                   : 1812
Accounting-Port             : 1813
VRF                         : mgmt
```

```
Shared-Secret                 : AQBapVWcNJavUClNBQenFaJwwRrR+nWcJUvsQlHUbu
aiOvlDCAAAAMCnYwT2Ful+
Timeout (default)             : 5
Retries (default)             : 1
Auth-Type (default)           : pap
Server-Group                  : cppm
Group-Priority                : 1
Tracking                      : enabled
Reachability-Status           : reachable
ClearPass-Username            : duradmin
ClearPass-Password
:AQBapUmeqwuSjUoetq4KWXbTnUyBILPjxzok4qzRZeSXsBIzCQAAACMxHv6lEnY7jA==
```

Task 2: CPPM User Role Definitions

Objectives

There are no configuration steps in this task. You will review the user role configuration that has been prepared on the ClearPass Policy Manager. Downloadable user roles have been pre-defined for:

- employee
- contractor

Steps

Review the ClearPass Enforcement Profile Configuration

1. Use PC1 to open a session to the ClearPass server. Navigate to **Configuration > Enforcement > Profiles**. Enter **'dur'** in the 'Name' filter and select **'Go'**.

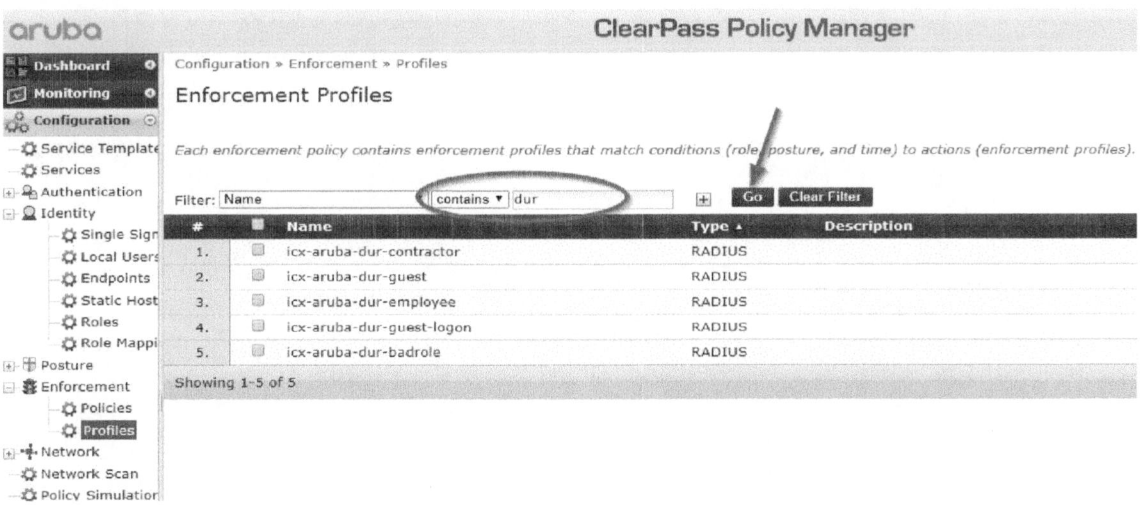

2. Open the **'icx-aruba-dur-employee'**. The RADIUS VSA attribute used here is *Aruba-CPPM-Role*. The data contains the CLI commands that define the complete user role.

Note

In the enforcement profile, the user-role name is not important; in the example 'dur' is used. When the profile is downloaded by the switch, the switch will put the provided configuration under a role name that will be based on the Enforcement Policy name, that is "**icx-aruba-dur-employee**" in this example.

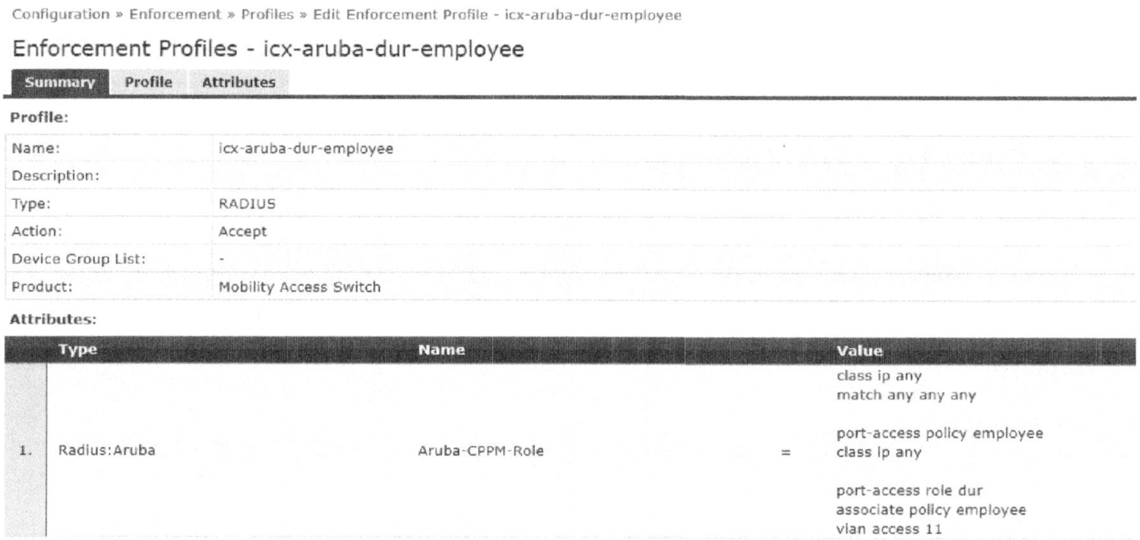

3. Click **Cancel** to close the Employee profile.

4. Click the **icx-aruba-dur-contractor** profile to see the configuration.

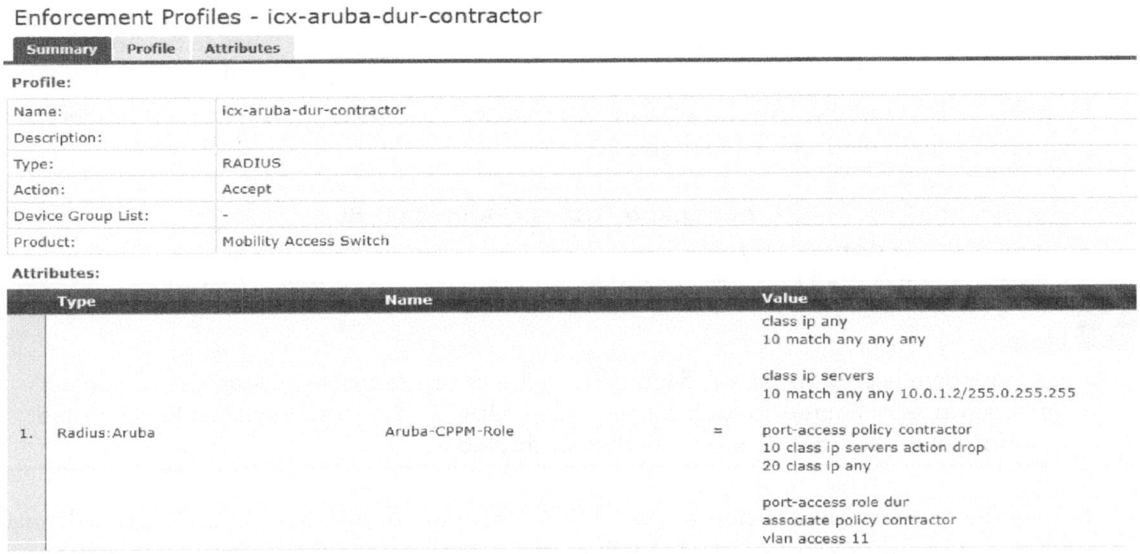

Note

The 'port-access role' name is again **'dur'**, but as stated before, this name will not be used in the operational status in the switch, since every downloadable role will have its unique name based on the ClearPass enforcement profile name. For this example, it would be "**icx-aruba-dur-contractor**".

5. Click **Cancel** to close the Contractor profile.

Task 3: Testing 802.1X DUR with Employee and Contractor

Objectives

In this task, the downloadable user role will be tested using the 802.1X client PC (PC3). Once the user has authenticated, ClearPass will return the name of the downloadable user role and the switch will dynamically collect the details of the role using a REST API connection over HTTPS to ClearPass.

In the lab setup, ClearPass must be made aware that it needs to return the Aruba-CPPM-role, so the hostname on the switch must be updated to include '**dur**' (this is based on the Services that were predefined on the Lab CPPM server).

Steps

Testing Employee Access

1. Open a terminal session to Access1 and enter the configuration mode. Change the hostname to include the string **'dur'**. This will ensure the correct ClearPass policy rules are used for the Downloadable User Roles. Also, make sure you change "Tx", where "x" is your table number; for example, T1 for Table 1 or T12 for Table 12.

```
ICX-Tx-Access1(config)# hostname ICX-Tx-Access1-dur
ICX-Tx-Access1-dur(config)#
```

Note

The hostname is used as the NAS-identifier in the access-request to ClearPass. ClearPass has been pre-configured to look for the value '**dur**' in the NAS-identifier to return the downloadable user roles that are needed for this lab.

2. Review the current configuration of port 1/1/3. This port should have 802.1X enabled (mac authentication can also be enabled, but will not be tested on this port).

```
ICX-Tx-Access1-dur(config)# show run int 1/1/3
interface 1/1/3
    no shutdown
    no routing
    vlan access 1
    aaa authentication port-access dot1x authenticator
        eapol-timeout 30
        max-eapol-requests 1
        max-retries 1
        enable
    aaa authentication port-access mac-auth
        enable
    exit
```

3. On the PC3, connected to Access1 port 1/1/3, enable 802.1X on the 'Lab NIC' and configure the employee credentials (refer to the 802.1X lab for instructions on how to do this):

   - Username: **icx-employee**
   - Password: **aruba123**

   Troubleshooting steps in case the authentication would fail:

   - Verify the TA cert import
   - Verify the hostname

- Verify the user credentials
- Verify the switch log (show logging -r -n 20) for any errors

4. Review the authenticated users on port 1/1/3.

```
ICX-Tx-Access1-dur(config)# show aaa authentication port-access inter-
face 1/1/3 client-status
Port Access Client Status Details

Client 00:50:56:b1:7a:37, icx-employee
============================
  Session Details
  ---------------
    Port         : 1/1/3
    Session Time : 31273s

  Authentication Details
  ----------------------
    Status          : dot1x Authenticated
    Auth Precedence : dot1x - Authenticated, mac-auth - Not attempted

  Authorization Details
  ----------------------
Role    : icx_aruba_dur_employee-3044-7
    Status : Applied
```

1. Next review the current roles on the switch. Notice how the 'local', 'radius', and 'clearpass' (DUR) roles all co-exist on the same switch.

```
ICX-Tx-Access1-dur(config)# show port-access role
```

2. Next review just the ClearPass downloaded roles.

```
ICX-Tx-Access1-dur(config)# show port-access role clearpass
Role Information:
Name  : icx_aruba_dur_employee-3044-2
Type  : clearpass
Status: Completed
----------------------------------------------
    Reauthentication Period             :
    Authentication Mode                 :
    Session Timeout                     :
    Client Inactivity Timeout           :
    Description                         :
```

```
    Gateway Zone                              :
    UBT Gateway Role                          :
    Access VLAN                               : 11
    Native VLAN                               :
    Allowed Trunk VLANs                       :
    MTU                                       :
    QOS Trust Mode                            :
    PoE Priority                              :
    Captive Portal Profile                    :
    Policy                                    : employ-
ee_icx_aruba_dur_employee-3044-7
```

Question: What is the VLAN assigned to this role?

Answer: VLAN access 11

5. Next review the port-access policies. Between the locally defined policies, there should also be one downloaded policy.

```
ICX-Tx-Access1-dur(config)# show port-access policy
Access Policy Details:
======================
<...>
Policy Name   : employee_icx_aruba_dur_employee-3044-7
Policy Type   : Downloaded
Policy Status : Applied

SEQUENCE    CLASS                        TYPE ACTION
----------- ---------------------------- --------------------------
10          any_icx_aruba_dur_employ... ipv4 permit
<...>
```

Question: What is the name of the traffic class in this policy?

Answer: The IP class name begins with 'any_icx_aruba_dur_employee'.

6. Next review the IP classes in the system.

```
ICX-Tx-Access1-dur(config)# show class ip
Type           Name
               Additional Class Parameters
  Sequence Comment
               Action                          L3 Protocol
               Source IP Address               Source L4 Port(s)
               Destination IP Address          Destination L4 Port(s)
               Additional Entry Parameters
```

7. In the output, there should be a downloaded IP Class.

```
--------------------------------------------------------------------------------
IPv4        any_icx_aruba_dur_employee-3044-7
        10
           match                              any
           any
           any
```

8. This demonstrates that the downloaded user roles and their member objects are added to the operational configuration of the switch.

9. Review the running configuration; look for any user roles, policies, or classes with 'dur' in the name.

```
ICX-Tx-Access1-dur(config)# show run | include dur
```

Question: Are there any *user-roles* in the configuration?

Answer: No, the ClearPass Downloadable User Roles are always downloaded on the fly and are not stored in the switch's configuration. This demonstrates that the downloaded user roles and their member objects are added to the operational configuration of the switch, but they are not added to the running or startup configuration of the switch.

Verify the Contractor DUR

1. On PC3, change the 802.1X credentials to the contractor account:
   - Username: **icx-contractor**
   - Password: **aruba123**
2. On the switch, review the authenticated clients on port 1/1/3.

```
ICX-Tx-Access1-dur(config)# show aaa authentication port-access interface 1/1/3
client-status
Port Access Client Status Details
Client 00:50:56:b1:7a:37, icx-contractor
==============================
  Session Details
  ---------------
    Port         : 1/1/3
    Session Time : 32275s
```

```
   Authentication Details
   ----------------------
     Status          : dot1x Authenticated
     Auth Precedence : dot1x - Authenticated, mac-auth - Not attempted

   Authorization Details
   ----------------------
Role    : icx_aruba_dur_contractor-3042-8
Status : Applied
```

3. Review the downloaded roles.

```
ICX-Tx-Access1-dur(config)# show port-access role clearpass
Role Information:
Name  :icx_aruba_dur_contractor-3042-8
Type  :clearpass
Status: Completed
----------------------------------------------
    Reauthentication Period                   :
    Authentication Mode                       :
    Session Timeout                           :
    Client Inactivity Timeout                 :
    Description                               :
    Gateway Zone                              :
    UBT Gateway Role                          :
    Access VLAN                               : 11
    Native VLAN                               :
    Allowed Trunk VLANs                       :
    MTU                                       :
    QOS Trust Mode                            :
    PoE Priority                              :
    Captive Portal Profile                    :
    Policy                                    : contractor_
icx_aruba_dur_contractor-3042-8
```

Question: Is the employee DUR still available in the role list?

Answer: No, when the last online user with a downloadable user role goes offline, the role is no longer maintained in the switch memory.

3. Review the policy list.

```
ICX-Tx-Access1-dur(config)# show port-access policy
```

The output should contain:

```
Policy Name   : contractor_icx_aruba_dur_contractor-3042-6
Policy Type   : Downloaded
Policy Status : Applied
SEQUENCE    CLASS                          TYPE  ACTION
----------- ------------------------------ ----- -----------------------
10          servers_icx_aruba_dur_co...   ipv4  drop
20          any_icx_aruba_dur_contra...   ipv4  permit
```

4. This demonstrates how the complete user-role definition can be downloaded on the fly from the ClearPass Policy Manager server.

Task 4: ClearPass DUR Configuration and Troubleshooting

When defining the user-role on ClearPass, the administrator should note that:

- The downloadable user role fully 'self-contained'. In the role it can have its own classes, policies, and captive profile objects.
- The downloadable user role cannot use any classes, policies, or captive portal profiles that are locally defined in the switch. This means that any referenced object in a DUR must be defined within the ClearPass enforcement profile.
- ClearPass will automatically generate a name for the downloadable user role; this is based on:
  - The name of the "Enforcement Profile"
  - The ClearPass internal enforcement object ID (3xxx)
  - The version number of the "Enforcement Profile". Every time the enforcement profile is saved on the ClearPass server, the version number will increment with 1.
- In the object names within the downloadable user role, any <space> or hyphen (-) is automatically replaced with an underscore (_).
- It is not allowed to have 'comment' lines in the downloadable user role.
- For classes and policies, it is not required to include line numbers; in that case, the line order will be used.
- It is important to order the objects correctly in the ClearPass Enforcement Profile:

  - Classes should be defined before the policy.
  - Policy and Captive Portal profile should be defined before the actual user-role.
- The downloadable user role can refer to a 'ubt' zone. This is covered in the Mobility Controller lab activity.
- The downloadable user role cannot be used to create a ubt zone. That must be done in the switch configuration.

Config Version Information

Every time the enforcement profile is saved in ClearPass, the internal enforcement profile version number is increased. At the next authentication, ClearPass will return the new version number in the DUR name to the switch. This ensures both previous and current version of the same enforcement profile can be online at the same time on the switch.

Migration to the new version occurs based on the reauthentication configuration, allowing for a smooth transition of any ClearPass changes to the actual authenticated devices. When all the devices that were online on the previous version of the DUR have reauthenticated, the old version of the DUR will automatically disappear from the switch.

Steps

Detailed Operation of Downloadable User Roles

1. Using PC1, open a session to ClearPass; navigate to **Configuration > Enforcement >Profiles**. Open the '**icx-aruba-dur-contractor**' profile.

Enforcement Profiles - icx-aruba-dur-contractor

Summary | Profile | Attributes

Profile:

Name:	icx-aruba-dur-contractor
Description:	
Type:	RADIUS
Action:	Accept
Device Group List:	-
Product:	Mobility Access Switch

Attributes:

	Type	Name		Value
1.	Radius:Aruba	Aruba-CPPM-Role	=	class ip any 10 match any any any class ip servers 10 match any any 10.0.1.2/255.0.255.255 port-access policy contractor 10 class ip servers action drop 20 class ip any port-access role dur associate policy contractor vlan access 11

Question: What is the name of the enforcement profile?

Answer: In this lab, the enforcement profile name is '**icx-aruba-dur-contractor**'.

Question: Why is this name relevant to the switch?

Answer: The name of the downloadable user role on the switch will be based on the enforcement profile name. Using a meaningful enforcement profile name helps when troubleshooting on the switch.

2. Navigate to **Monitoring > Live Monitoring > Access Tracker** and open the latest authentication for user '**icx-contractor**'. Check the 'output' tab.

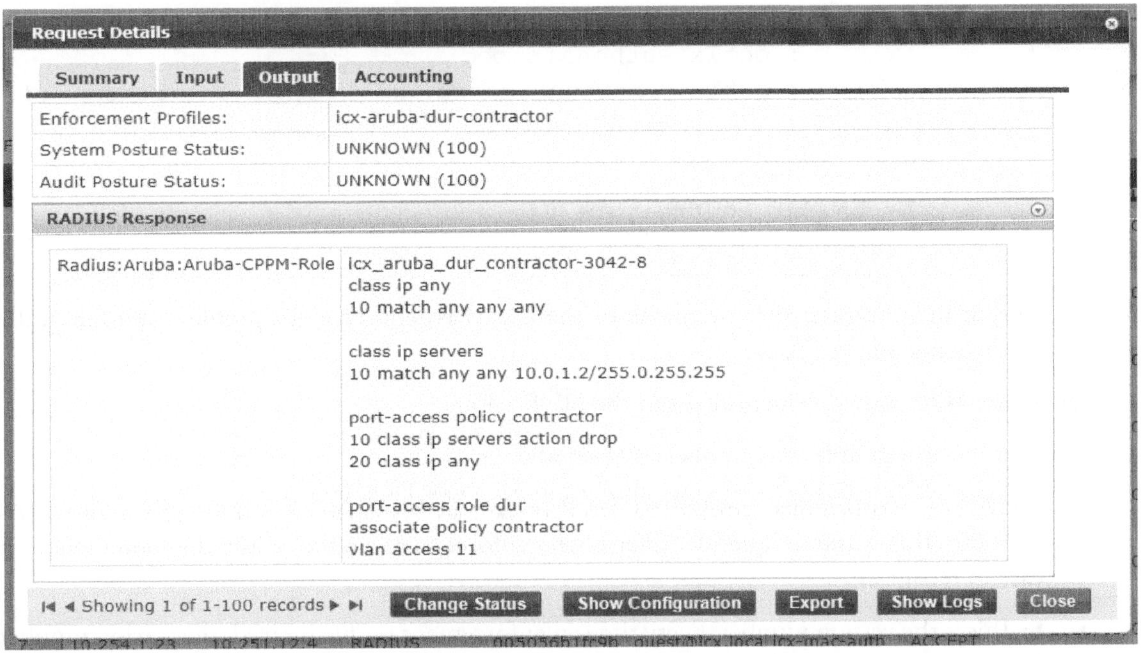

3. This seems to suggest that the contents of the DUR are sent to the switch as part of the RADIUS Access-Accept.

4. On the Access1, review the name of the role on port 1/1/3.

```
ICX-Tx-Access1-dur(config)# show aaa authentication port-access
interface 1/1/3 client-status
Port Access Client Status Details
Client 00:50:56:b1:7a:37, icx-contractor
============================
  Session Details
  ---------------
    Port         : 1/1/3
    Session Time : 71574s

  Authentication Details
  ----------------------
    Status          : dot1x Authenticated
    Auth Precedence : dot1x - Authenticated, mac-auth - Not attempted

  Authorization Details
  ----------------------
Role    : icx_aruba_dur_contractor-3042-8
    Status : Applied
```

5. The output demonstrates that the name of the ClearPass enforcement profile is automatically part of the name of the DUR.

   Question: What other elements exist in the DUR name?

   Answer: In this example, the numbers 3042 and 4.

   - **3042**: Every enforcement profile in ClearPass has an internal object number; the range starts at 3000. This is the unique identifier of the enforcement profile, while the name makes it easy to recognize.
   - **8**: This is the version number. Every time an enforcement profile is saved, the version number is incremented with 1.

   The complete DUR consists of:

   - Enforcement Profile name
   - Enforcement Profile internal object number
   - Enforcement Profile version number

   When a ClearPass receives an authentication request that has an Aruba-CPPM-Role in the result, it will not send the detailed commands in the RADIUS request, but only a reference name to the current enforcement profile.

6. Example RADIUS trace of the Access-Accept sent by ClearPass:

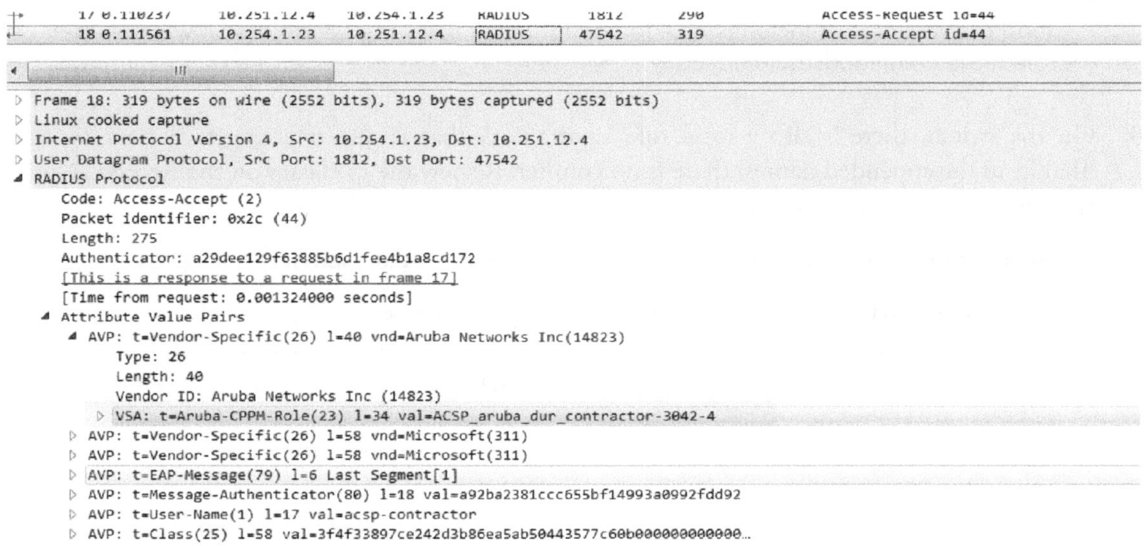

7. Next, the switch will access the REST API of ClearPass over HTTPS (this required the TA profile installation) and download these enforcement profile contents. The contents are then installed as a 'clearpass role' in the port-access module. Any names of referenced objects (classes, policies, or captive portal names) are automatically appended with this generated enforcement-profile DUR name. This ensures no conflicts can occur between roles or even locally defined roles. This is an *example* of the cli configuration of the Role Contractor:

```
class ip any
 10 match any any any

class ip servers
 10 match any any 10.255.0.200

port-access policy contractor
 10 class ip servers action drop
 20 class ip any

port-access role dur
 associate policy contractor
 vlan access 11
```

Note

ClearPass version 6.9 includes a UI to configure the role. The ClearPass UI will then generate these commands automatically.

8. On the switch, there is also a local role 'contractor', that is also referring to a class 'servers'. Thanks to the appended names, there is no conflict. Review the ip classes on the Access1. Notice that there are two server classes:

   - **servers:** locally define on the switch during the 802.1X Lab Activity
   - **servers_icx_aruba_...:** part of the downloadable user role

```
ICX-Tx-Access1-dur(config)# show class ip
<...output omitted...>
---------------------------------------------------------------------------
IPv4        servers
       10
          match                                 any
          any
          10.0.1.2/255.0.255.255
---------------------------------------------------------------------------
IPv4        servers_icx_aruba_dur_contractor-3042-8
       10
          match                                 any
          any
          10.0.1.2/255.0.255.255
```

9. This demonstrates that objects in DUR roles will not interfere with each other or with locally defined roles or objects.

Example of Invalid DUR configuration on ClearPass

In the next steps, a DUR that contains an error will be returned to the switch, to demonstrate to effect in the switch. A **'badrole'** DUR has been prepared on the ClearPass system. It will be returned when the 'icx-badrole' user account connects to the network using 802.1X on the PC3 (connected to Access1).

1. On the PC3, connected to Access1, change the 802.1X credentials to:

   - Username: **icx-badrole**
   - Password: **aruba123**

2. After the authentication completes, check the authentication status on the Access1 switch port 1/1/3.

```
ICX-Tx-Access1-dur(config)# show aaa authentication port-access
interface 1/1/3 client-status
Port Access Client Status Details
Client 00:50:56:b1:7a:37, icx-badrole
============================
  Session Details
  ---------------
    Port         : 1/1/3
    Session Time : 73386s

  Authentication Details
  ----------------------
    Status          : dot1x Authenticated
    Auth Precedence : dot1x - Authenticated, mac-auth - Not
    attempted

  Authorization Details
  ----------------------
    Role   :
Status : Not Ready
```

Question: What is the status of the role?

Answer: The status is reported as 'Not Ready'; this indicates some error with the role processing.

3. Use PC1 to open ClearPass Access Tracker, check the 'icx-badrole' authentication entry, and open the **'output'** tab to see the details of the role.

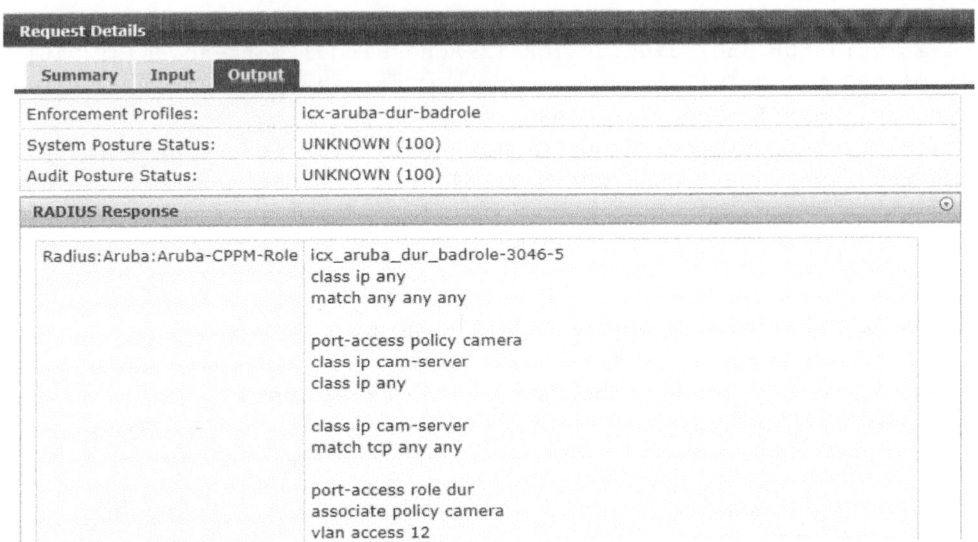

4. This is the configuration of the role:

```
icx_aruba_dur_badrole-3046-5
class ip any
match any any any

port-access policy camera
class ip cam-server
class ip any

class ip cam-server
match tcp any any

port-access role dur
associate policy camera
vlan access 12
```

Question: What is wrong with this example role?

Answer: The order of the objects is incorrect. The policy references the class 'cam-server' before it is defined.

5. On the Access1 switch, check the log file. There should be LOG_ERR line that states that the class does not exist.

```
ICX-Tx-Access1-dur(config)# show logging -r -n 10
---------------------------------------------------
Event logs from current boot
---------------------------------------------------

2020-01-28T08:44:06.851047+00:00 ICX-Tx-Access1-dur port-accessed[2956]:
Event|9301|LOG_ERR|MSTR|1|Failed to apply ClearPass role -
icx_aruba_dur_badrole-3046-5 - Error at Line 4 - class ip cam-ser
2020-01-28T08:44:06.850753+00:00 ICX-Tx-Access1-dur port-accessd[2956]:
Event|9301|LOG_ERR|MSTR|1|Failed to apply ClearPass role -
icx_aruba_dur_badrole-3046-5 - Class does not exi
2020-01-28T08:44:06.514464+00:00 ICX-Tx-Access1-dur port-accessd[2956]:
Event|Unknown Event Name CERT_CHAIN_VERIFIED
```

Lab Cleanup

1. Revert the Access1 switch hostname to the base hostname.

```
ICX-Tx-Access1-dur(config)# hostname ICX-Tx-Access1
ICX-Tx-Access1(config)#
```

UBT Configuration

This section introduces you to the configuration of UBT using local user roles (LUR) and downloadable user roles (DUR).

User Role Review

- LUR
  - Used with ClearPass or third-party AAA servers
  - Disadvantages:
    - More difficult to manage: requires replication of configuration policies on access switches
    - Doesn't scale well
- DUR
  - Supported by ClearPass *only*
  - Advantage:
    - Easier to manage: centralizes the policies and their configuration on ClearPass
    - Scales to very large sizes

Figure 12-16 User Role Review

A Local User Role (LUR) is where the role is defined locally on the switch, and DUR is where the role is defined on the ClearPass server and downloaded to the switch (the role does not pre-exist on the switch) (Figure 12-16).

With a Downloadable User Role (DUR), instead of having the user role configured on the edge switch, however, the user role is configured on ClearPass and downloaded to the edge switch after successful authentication. The method for sending the user role is through REST API using an SSL connection. This means that an HTTPS certificate has to be installed on the edge switch. In addition, a username/password has to be configured to authenticate the switch with ClearPass.

Let us have a look at how this is done:

1. First, ensure that ClearPass has obtained a valid HTTPS certificate
2. Automatically download the certificate from ClearPass (ClearPass 6.7.8+ or a later version is required)
3. On ClearPass, create a read-only admin user that will be used by the switch for authentication in order to download the actual role information
4. On the switch, create the user entry for the read-only user and enable downloadable user roles and configure the downloadable user roles profiles
5. Assign the profiles to a policy and the policy to a service on the ClearPass server

In the above example, a cluster of controllers are used; however, you could easily have used a stand-alone controller.

Note

Because the login process from the AOS-CX switch uses HTTPS, the switch will have to validate the certificate of the ClearPass server. On the older AOS switches, they would automatically download and install the ClearPass certificate. Unfortunately, in AOS-CX 10.04, this process is not automatic. You will need to access the ClearPass server, download its SSL certificate, and install it on the AOS-CX switch. You will see this as part of the lab when implementing dynamic segmentation later in this chapter.

Important

UBT/local switching and user roles are two different, but related concepts. They are both used to implement dynamic segmentation. With Aruba AOS-CX switches, some devices could be locally switched with a pre-defined local role, perhaps for VoIP phones; but for other devices, their role information could be downloaded from ClearPass and the traffic tunneled to an Aruba MC. It is flexible in how you want to set it up. However, Aruba recommends that if you are using ClearPass and have either AOS-CX or the older AOS switches, that you implement DUR because of the scalability and ease of centralized policy management that it provides.

UBT: LUR Configuration

1. Enable MAC/802.1X authentication on the switch
2. Configure AAA server to send Aruba-User-Role (VSA) to switch
3. Configure zone:
   –Define the controller
   –Enable MD5 security for PAPI
4. Define the transit VLAN
5. Configure gateway role:
   –Role name needs to match what the AAA server sends in the Aruba-User-Role VSA
   –Define the zone to which the controller belongs
   –Define the name of the role that should be used on the controller (gateway role)

Recommended if you have **third-party** AAA servers

Figure 12-17 UBT: LUR Configuration

First, you must configure 802.1X, MAC-Auth, and/or captive portal on your AOS-CX switch, along with connectivity to an AAA server, like ClearPass (Figure 12-17). (The configuration for these security solutions is not listed here.)

Defining a Zone

To set up UBT LUR, you first need to define a zone:

```
switch(config)# ubt zone <zone-name> vrf <VRF-name>
switch(config-ubt-zone)# primary-controller ip <IP-address>
switch(config-ubt-zone)# backup-controller ip <IP-address>
switch(config-ubt-zone)# papi-security-key <key>
switch(config-ubt-zone)# enable
switch(config)# ip source-interface ubt {interface <IFNAME> | <IPV4-ADDR>}
                 [vrf <VRF-NAME>]
```

First you create the zone and define the VRF instance that will be used. Next, you define the primary, and optionally, backup IP address of the controller(s). Unlike the APs, the switches currently do not support Control Plane Security (CPSec). Instead, you can optionally protect the PAPI control messages using MD5 signatures. They key that you specify must match what the MC(s) have configured. Last, you need to enable the zone. Optionally you can define which IP address the switch should use when tunneling the GRE packets (by default this is based on the local routing table).

Note
In AOS-CX 10.04, currently only one zone is supported per switch.

To verify your configuration, there are various **show** commands that you can use:

```
switch# show ubt
Zone Name : my-zone
Primary Controller : 10.116.51.10
Backup Controller : 10.116.51.11
SAC HeartBeat Interval : 1
UAC KeepAlive Interval : 60
Reserved VLAN Identifier : 4094
VRF Name : my-vrf
Admin State : ENABLED
PAPI Security Key : AQBapdxySvGPvdTlkYn1/naKX4O3jKHrm28xLYfO6mLOK-
499BwAAAHdJp/bL4FE=
```

```
switch# show ubt information
SAC Information
Active : 10.116.51.12
Standby : 10.116.51.13
Node List Information
Cluster Name : my-cluster
Node List
10.1.1.1
10.1.1.2
10.1.1.3
Bucket Map Information
Bucket Map Active : [0...255]
Bucket ID A-UAC     S-UAC     Connectivity
--------------------------------------------------------------
0         10.1.1.1  10.1.1.2  L2
1         10.1.1.2  10.1.1.3  L2
2         10.1.1.3  10.1.1.1  L2
```

Define the Transit VLAN

To define the transit VLAN, use the following configuration:

```
Switch(config)# vlan<VLAN-ID>
Switch(config-vlan)# exit
Switch(config)# ubt-client-vlan <VLAN-ID>
```

Remember that the transit VLAN is what the switch will use when tunneling the user traffic to an MC (if the switch is not performing switching of the traffic).

Configuring a Gateway Role

Next, you need to define the role names locally on the switch:

```
switch(config)# port-access role <role-name>
switch(config-pa-role)# gateway-zone zone <zone-name> gateway-role
<controller-role-name>
```

The role name in the port-access role command must exactly match the Aruba-User-Role VSA that the AAA server, like ClearPass, will pass back to the switch. In the role configuration, you must define the zone that this is used for (currently only one zone is supported) and then the role name that is passed to the MC. Note that the switch role name and the MC role name could be the same, or different, names. The controller role name is also case-sensitive. See the Security Guide for other configuration options for the role. For example, you could define a policy to define a pre-authentication VLAN, ACL, QoS, and other parameters that should be used before the user is authenticated.

Enable User Authentication

After you have configured the role information, you then need to set up user authentication, like MAC or 802.1X (captive portal is also supported). Here is an example with 802.1X:

```
Switch(config)# aaa authentication port-access dot1x authenticator
auth-method eap-radius
Switch(config)# aaa authentication port-access dot1x authenticator
radius server-group radius
Switch(config)# aaa authentication port-access dot1x authenticator
enable
Switch(config)# interface <interface-id>
Switch(config-if)# aaa authentication port-access dot1x authenticator
Switch(config-if-dot1x-auth)# enable
Switch(config-if-dot1x-auth)# exit
```

Optionally, you can define a pre-authentication role on the interface—this is applied to the user's traffic prior to authentication:

```
Switch(config-if)# aaa authentication port-access preauth-role <role-name>
```

Also, if you need to exempt LLDP, CDP, and/or BPDU traffic, use the following two commands:

```
switch(config-if)# aaa authentication port-access allow-lldp-bpdu
switch(config-if)# aaa authentication port-access allow-cdp-bpdu
```

This configuration might be necessary for devices like a phone or camera where LLDP (or Cisco's CDP) must be exchanged for the device to operate correctly prior to authentication occurring on the port.

Configure your AAA Server Role Policy

Last, you need to define a policy on your AAA server to return the respective role name for the user. This is done using an Aruba VSA called *Aruba-User-Role*. Remember that the role names are case-sensitive!

You can also see a list of the users and the roles assigned to them when verifying the operation of LUR:

```
switch# show ubt users all
Downloaded user roles are preceded by *
Port   Mac Address       Tunnel Status  Secondary UserRole  Failure Reason
----------------------------------------------------------------------------
1/1/1 00:00:00:11:12:03 activated      authenticated       ---/---
```

UBT: DUR Configuration Tasks

1. Steps 1-4 of LUR are performed here as well
2. Configure ClearPass with the downloadable user role information
3. Define the ClearPass RADIUS server and key
   - Set up DNS on the switch
   - Use the FQDN of the hostname of the ClearPass server that is on server's SSL certificate
4. Validate the ClearPass server certificate
   - Verify that both ClearPass and the switch use the same NTP time source
   - Manually download and import the root or self-signed ClearPass certificate on the switch
5. Define the REST API Access credentials
   - Create an administrator account on ClearPass with the appropriate privilege level
   - Specify the administrator credentials on the switch

Recommended if you have **ClearPass** servers

Figure 12-18 UBT: DUR Configuration Tasks

Steps 1-4 of the LUR configuration task, as shown in Figure 12-18, are performed here as well (shown here):

- Enable MAC/802.1X authentication on the switch
- Configure the ClearPass server to send Aruba-User-Role (VSA) to switch
- Configure the zone on the switch:
  - Define the controller
  - Enable MD5 security for PAPI
- Define the transit VLAN on the switch and the Mobility Controller

Once this is done, you need to perform the steps 2-5 listed in the above slide. These steps are covered in the next pages.

ClearPass Configuration

The process for DUR is very much the same as LUR. Instead of having the user role configured on the edge switch, however, the user role is configured on ClearPass and sent to the edge switch after successful authentication. The method for sending the user role is through REST API using an SSL connection. This means that an HTTPS certificate has to be installed on the edge switch. In addition, a username/password has to be configured to authenticate the switch with ClearPass.

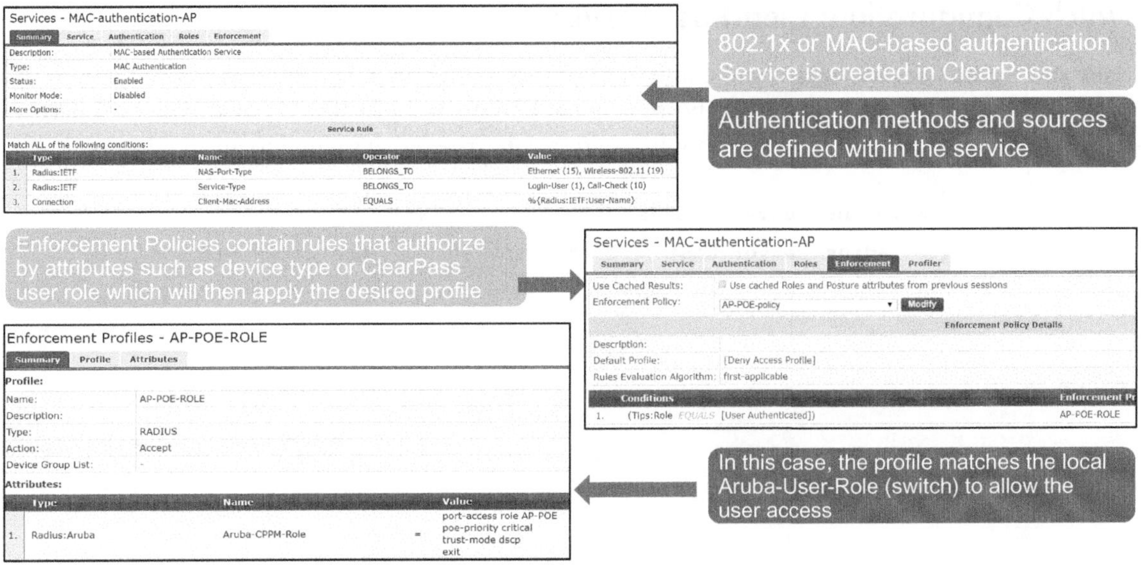

Figure 12-19 ClearPass Configuration

Let us have a look at how this is done:

1. First, ensure that ClearPass has obtained a valid HTTPS certificate
2. Automatically download the certificate from ClearPass (ClearPass 6.7.8+ or a later version is required)
3. On ClearPass, create a read-only admin user that will be used by the switch for authentication in order to download the actual role information
4. On the switch, create the user entry for the read-only user and enable downloadable user roles and configure the downloadable user roles profiles
5. Assign the profiles to a policy and the policy to a service on the ClearPass server

Note
LUR should be used if you have a generic AAA server product. Either LUR or DUR can be used if you have ClearPass.

Figure 12-19 lists the authentication service/enforcement policy and profile configuration on ClearPass. Please see the ClearPass documentation for more information on configure services, enforcement policies, and enforcement profiles.

Switch Configuration: ClearPass Server

Make sure **radius-server host** name configured on the switch matches the Common Name (CN) field of ClearPass HTTPS server certificate (Figure 12-20). If an FQDN is used, you will need to specify a DNS server that the switch should use to resolve the server's name to an IP address.

```
switch(config )# ip dns server-address <IP-address> vrf <VRF-name>
switch(config)#  radius-server host dev-cppm.tmelab.net key <key> vrf <VRF-name>
```

Figure 12-20 Switch Configuration: ClearPass Server

Switch Configuration: Certificate Validation

ClearPass will send a user role to the edge switch after successful authentication. The method for sending the user role is through the REST API using an SSL connection. This means that a valid HTTPS certificate has to be installed on the edge switch: one from a trusted Certificate Authority (CA) of both the switch and the ClearPass server.

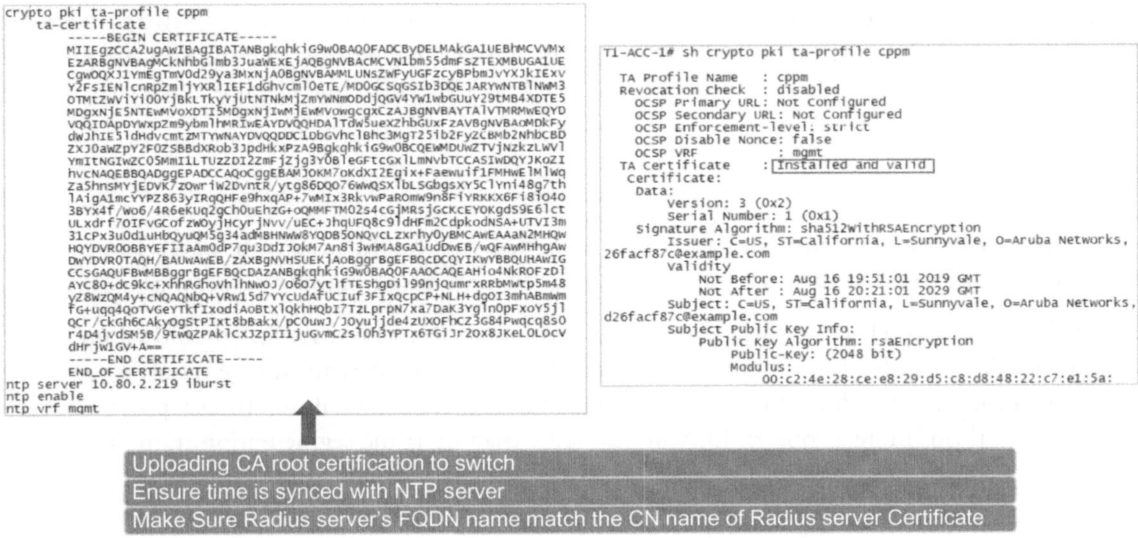

Figure 12-21 Switch Configuration: Certificate Validation

You will also need to configure NTP to ensure the certificate for switch is valid based on the current date and time and the time range defined on the certificate. If the switch's time falls outside the range of the time on the certificate, the certificate is automatically invalidated (Figure 12-21).

Switch Configuration: ClearPass Account

```
switch(config)# radius-server host dev-cppm.tmelab.net key <key>
                clearpass-username duradmin clearpass-password <password>
                vrf <VRF-name>
```

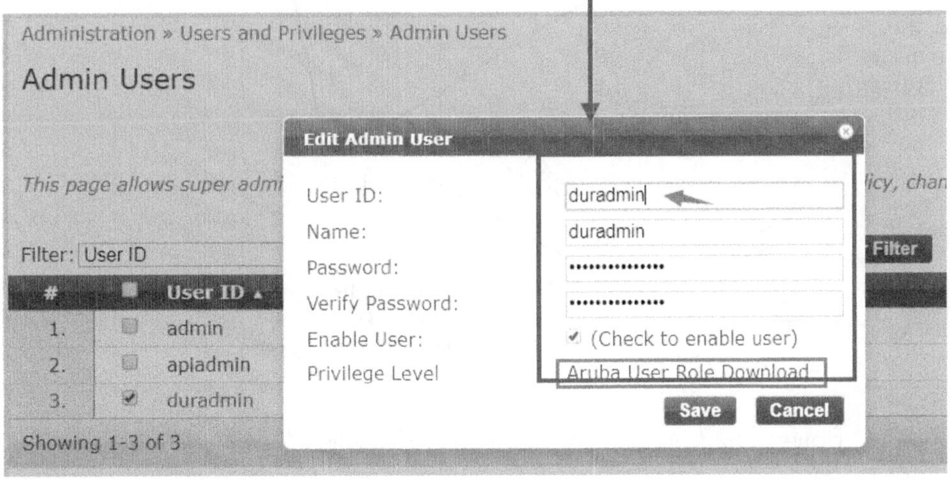

Figure 12-22 Switch Configuration: ClearPass Account

In addition, a username and password have to be configured to authenticate the switch with the ClearPass server. This is defined on the ClearPass server, but referenced on the switch. The privilege level can be "Aruba User Role Download" or "Read-Only Administrator" (Figure 12-22).

High Availability

To ensure uninterrupted connectivity for tunneled-nodes, you should work with the MC administrators to design the solution such that the AOS-CX switch can tunnel traffic to at least two MCs.

When the primary and backup MCs are in the same subnet, MC administrators should set up VRRP between the MCs. Preferably, the MCs should also form a cluster. As you will see in more detail in a moment, clustering provides better load balancing and more seamless failover. (It also provides better roaming, but this is more a concern for wireless traffic than dynamic segmentation traffic.)

You must also ensure that the Aruba MC software supports the feature for tunneled-node switches; your MCs must use software 8.4 or higher.

You can configure a backup controller on the switch either instead of, or in addition to, the VRRP or cluster-based redundancy.

You will now look at each of these options in more detail.

Supporting High Availability with Clustering

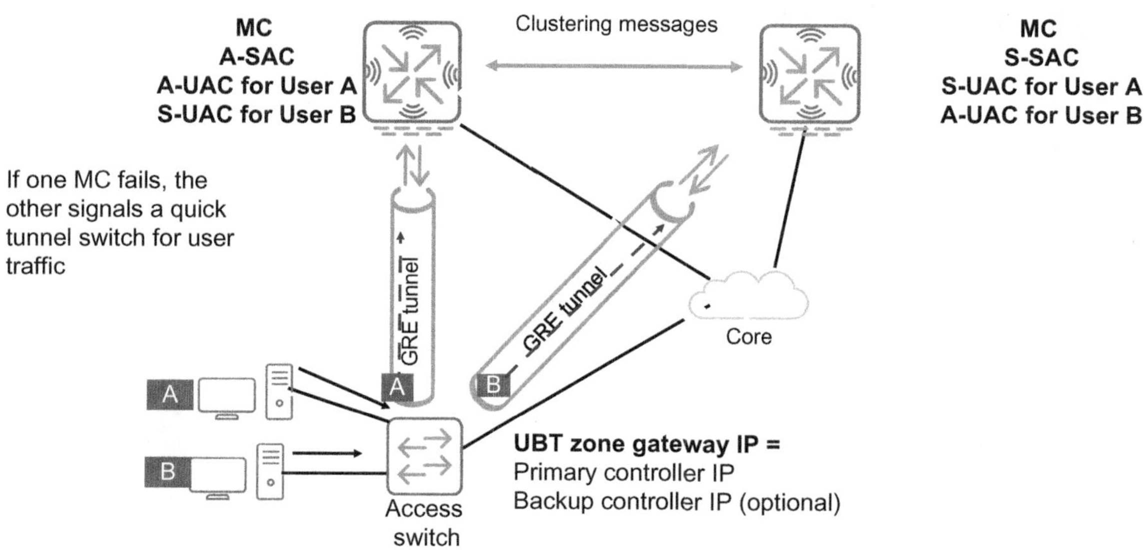

Figure 12-23 Supporting High Availability with Clustering

When the switch uses role-based tunneled-node, it can tunnel traffic to clustered MCs. Typically the switches will be connecting to a cluster of MCs. Clustering enables load balancing and failover capabilities over other redundancy solutions (Figure 12-23).

With this method, again, you only need to set a single tunnel node server (controller) IP address on the AOS-CX switch. At least define one IP address of a cluster member, and optionally a secondary address as a backup. When the switch contacts a member of the cluster, it receives assignments with the actual IP addresses of two MCs. One is the switch's active Switch Anchor Controller (A-SAC), and the other is the switch's standby SAC (S-SAC). The switch establishes PAPI tunnels with both controllers.

In addition, the switch receives a bucket map. When the switch starts tunneling a new device's traffic, the switch hashes information about the session. It looks up the hash in the bucket map to determine the correct active User Anchor Controller (A-UAC) and standby UAC (S-UAC) for that device. The switch tunnels the device's traffic to the A-UAC, but the state for the session is synchronized between the A-UAC and the S-UAC, enabling more seamless failover. (The degree of synchronized information depends on the device's needs.) In addition, because the cluster dictates where the switch tunnels each user's traffic, load balancing is improved.

If the switch's A-SAC or any of its A-UACs fail, the cluster can detect that failure very quickly and signal to the switch to failover to the appropriate standby tunnel, rather than the switch having to wait for its heartbeats to time out.

In the above example, notice that user A and B's active and standby tunnels are not on the same controller. User A's active tunnel is on the left controller while User B's active tunnel is on the right controller.

As you have seen, the AOS-CX switch can participate in high availability solutions with a *single* controller IP address specified in its tunneled-node server profile. For additional redundancy, the primary and secondary addresses can be controllers in two *different* clusters. The zone profile can also include a backup controller, though, specified with the following configuration.

```
switch(config)# ubt zone <zone-name> vrf <VRF-name>
switch(config-ubt-zone)# primary-controller ip <cluster1-IP-address>
switch(config-ubt-zone)# backup-controller ip <cluster2-IP-address>
```

Supporting High Availability with a Backup Controller

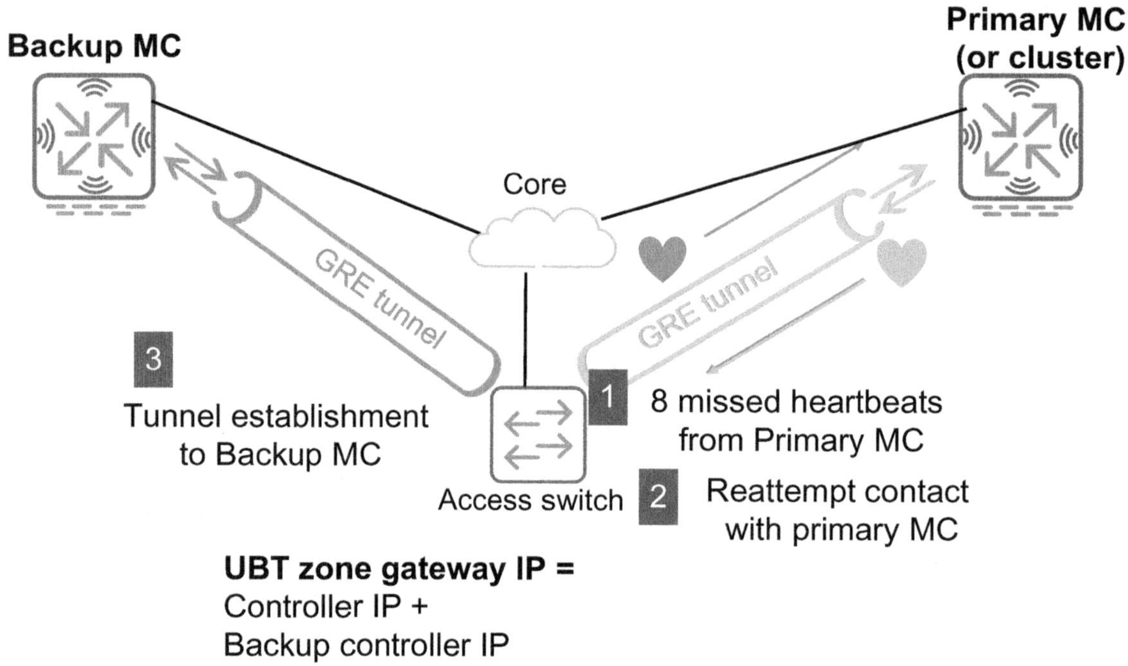

Figure 12-24 Supporting High Availability with a Backup Controller

As you have seen, the AOS-CX switch can participate in high availability solutions with a *single* controller IP address (not part of a cluster) specified in its tunneled-node server profile (Figure 12-24). This profile can also include a backup controller, though, specified with this command:

```
switch(config)# ubt zone <zone-name> vrf <VRF-name>
switch(config-ubt-zone)# primary-controller ip <IP-address>
switch(config-ubt-zone)# backup-controller ip <IP-address>
```

These commands were discussed previously. The backup controller allows the switch to failover to an MC (or cluster) in a different subnet from its primary MC (or cluster).

As discussed earlier, the switch and its MC—or any of its SACs and UACs when clustering is used—send each other keepalives over the GRE tunnel every second to assess the tunnel's health. If the switch fails to hear keepalives over the keepalive timeout period, it attempts to re-establish communications with the *primary* controller. In this scenario, though, the company has a standalone MC at a different location. After failing to connect to the primary MC (or cluster), the switch establishes a tunnel with the backup controller at the different location.

After switching over to the backup controller, the switch continues to check whether the primary controller is available every 30 seconds. If it re-establishes communication with the primary controller, it moves its tunnel back to that controller.

Again, MC administrators might choose an active-standby or active-active deployment. Communicate with them to determine whether all switches will use the same primary controller IP and backup controller IP (active-standby) or whether you should alternate these roles on different switches (active-active). Often, the MCs are deployed in different locations, and each switch uses the local MC as its primary MC and the remote MC as its backup.

Verification

This last section examines some commands you can use to verify the configuration and operation of dynamic segmentation on your AOS-CX switch.

AAA Client Status

```
T1-ACC-1# sh aaa authentication port-access interface  all  client-status

Port Access Client Status Details

Client 40:e3:d6:c4:30:1a
============================
  Session Details
  ---------------
    Port         : 1/1/1
    Session Time : 132s

  Authentication Details
  ----------------------
    Status          : Authentication Failed, Server-Timeout
    Auth Precedence : dot1x - Not attempted, mac-auth - Unauthenticated

  Authorization Details
  ---------------------
    Role   :
    Status :
```

Authenticated failed or server not reachable

Figure 12-25 AAA Client Status

```
T1-ACC-1# sh aaa authentication port-access interface  all  client-status

Port Access Client Status Details

Client 40:e3:d6:c4:30:1a, 40e3d6c4301a
============================
  Session Details
  ---------------
    Port         : 1/1/1
    Session Time : 9s

  Authentication Details
  ----------------------
    Status          : mac-auth Authenticated
    Auth Precedence : dot1x - Not attempted, mac-auth - Authenticated

  Authorization Details
  ----------------------
    Role   :
    Status : Not Ready
```

Authenticated but no downloadable user role

Figure 12-26 AAA Client Status (cont. 1)

The **show aaa authentication port-access interface all client-status** command allows you to see the status of a client(s) on a port(s), including their authentication status and assigned user role in any. This example (Figure 12-25) shows an issue contacting the ClearPass server. Mostly commonly, certificate errors and the ClearPass username and password being misconfigured cause this issue.

This example (Figure 12-26) shows a status of "Not Ready". In this example, ClearPass passed down the user role called "Authenticated", but this does not exist in a **port-access role** command.

```
T1-ACC-1# sh aaa authentication port-access interface all client-status

Port Access Client Status Details

Client 40:e3:d6:c4:30:1a, 40e3d6c4301a
============================
  Session Details
  ---------------
    Port         : 1/1/1
    Session Time : 5s

  Authentication Details
  ----------------------
    Status          : mac-auth Authenticated
    Auth Precedence : dot1x - Not attempted, mac-auth - Authenticated

  Authorization Details
  ----------------------
    Role   : AP_POE_ROLE-3009-5
    Status : Applied
```

Authenticating and downloading role are all successful

Figure 12-27 AAA Client Status (cont. 2)

This example (Figure 12-27) shows a Status of "Applied", indicating that everything is working normal and that the Authenticated user role is applied to the client connected to port 1/1/1.

Applying the profile makes the port function like a controlled Aruba AP. The switch no longer forwards traffic that arrives on the ports locally as it normally would. Instead it uses the GRE tunnel to send all the traffic to the IP address that you configured in the tunnel server profile. The tunnel acts at Layer 2. It encapsulates not just the IP payload but also the MAC header, and it forwards all traffic including broadcasts and multicasts.

The main difference between the tunneled-node and AP-based tunnels is that tunneled-node encapsulates 802.3 instead of 802.11 frames. Note also that often wireless traffic is encrypted; however, wired traffic is not encrypted, and GRE does not provide encryption either. However, the wired network infrastructure is typically trusted, so encryption is not required.

Note that the switch continues to function as normal for all traffic that arrives on the non-tunneled-node ports.

Important

Tunneled-node ports are intended for wired endpoints. You should avoid plugging controlled Aruba APs into wired tunneled ports because these APs are already fulfilling similar functions on their own. You would be causing the network to encapsulate wireless clients' traffic twice. Lab tests show that the tunneled-node will still operate properly, but the double encapsulation can create performance and resource issues.

Port Access Role

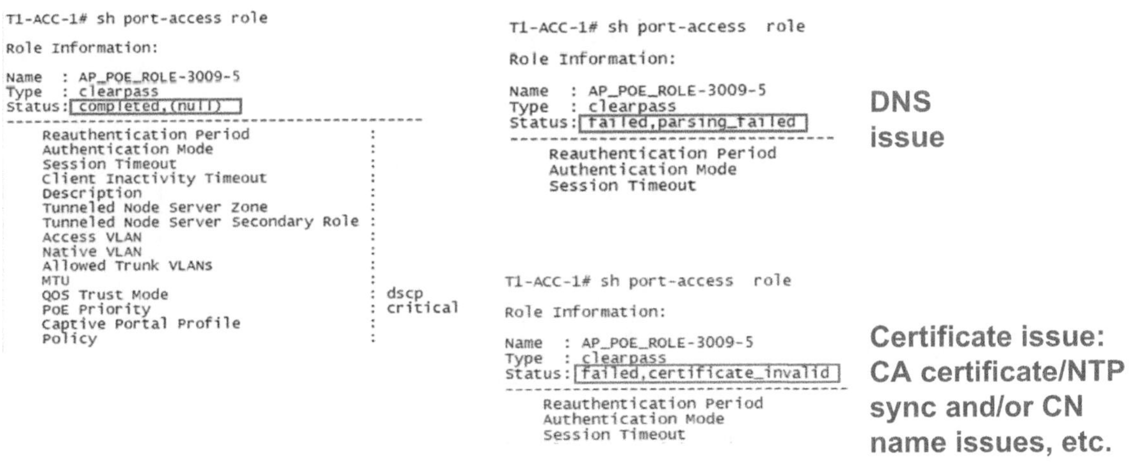

Figure 12-28 Port Access Role

The **show port-access role** command can be used to verify the connectivity to the ClearPass server when using DUR. The left-hand example shows a successful connection and inter-operation with the ClearPass server: the Status is *completed.* The top-right example shows a *parsing_failed* status, typically indicative of either a DNS or network connectivity issue (Figure 12-28). The bottom-right example shows a certificate error, which could be caused by a number of things:

- Time issue (use NTP to ensure the correct time)
- The CN name of the ClearPass certificate is not defined on the switch correctly (or at all)
- The certificate has expired

Controller Commands

To verify the connectivity from the controller side, use the **show tunneled-node-mgr tunneled-nodes** command.

To see the users that are being tunneled from the switch, on the MC use the **show tunneled-node-mgr-tunneled-users** command.

To see the log messages related to tunneled-node on the MCs, use the **show tunneled-node-mgr trace-buf** command.

To see the tunneled connections in the MC's state table, use the **show datapath** command.

Lab 12.2

Lab Diagram

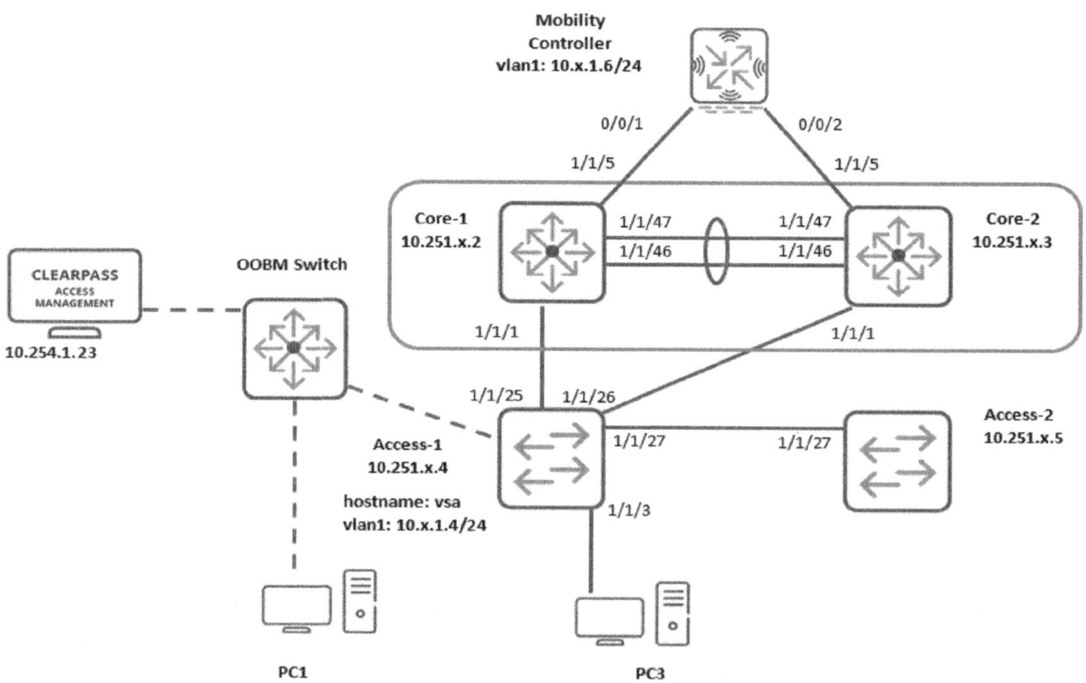

Figure 12-29 Lab Diagram

Overview

If you just completed Lab 12.1, the switch configurations are valid and you can start with this lab activity. This lab activity requires at least the completion of Lab11 (MAC Auth).

In this lab activity, the AOS-CX switch will be integrated with the Aruba Mobility Controller. The controller licensing and firewall user-roles will be reviewed.

On the switch, the connection to the controller will be defined using a gateway zone.

Next, the switch user-roles will be updated. The user-role will now point to the MC as the 'gateway zone' and a firewall user-role instruction will be included. Once the user has authenticated, the user and session information will be reviewed on the MC (Figure 12-29).

Objectives

- Define a connection to the MC for the User-Based Tunneling
- Define user-roles that use the UBT feature
- Verify the state and operation of the tunnels on the Switch
- Verify the state and operation of the tunnels on the Mobility Controller

Task 1: Prepare the Lab Devices

Introduction

This lab requires the completion of the 'Integration with CPPM' lab activity. In this task, the MC licenses and firewall visibility are verified and adjusted as needed.

Steps

Prepare the MC Licensing and Firewall

1. Open a terminal connection to the MC:
    - Username: **admin**
    - Password: **aruba123**

2. Review that Access Point (AP) and Policy Enforcement Firewall (PEF) licenses have been installed.

```
(ICX-Tx-MC) [mynode] # show license
License Table
-------------
Key   Installed  Expires(Grace period expiry)      Flags      Service Type
---   ---------  ----------------------------      -----      ------------
uoX+qhM0-rJrBIco4-C8I6V8+1-68KaOfcy-9p081sXP-ork 2019-11-18 15:56:42 Never
E     Access Points: 16
1SQ0Oeuv-hmGIDCLc-tdoNhcLN-vjB0LzVG-nuGwp4d7-G94 2019-11-18 15:56:44 Never
E     Next Generation Policy Enforcement Firewall Module: 16

License Entries: 2

Flags: A - auto-generated; E - enabled; S - Subscription; R - reboot required
to activate; D - Not enabled on license client

Note: Time under 'Installed' for Subscription licenses is the license generation
time.
```

3. Verify if the PEF license feature has been enabled. This command must be executed at the /mm context level. In the lab setup, it is expected that this feature has been enabled.

```
(ICX-Tx-MC) [mynode] # cd /mm
(ICX-Tx-MC) [mm] # show license-pool-profile-root
License root(/) pool profile
----------------------------
Parameter              Value
---------              -----
enable PEFNG feature   Enabled
enable RFP feature     Disabled
enable ACR feature     Disabled
enable WebCC feature   Disabled
```

4. Enable the Deep Packet Inspection (DPI) and the application visibility.

```
(ICX-Tx-MC) [mm] # configure terminal
(ICX-Tx-MC) [mm] (config)# firewall
(ICX-Tx-MC) ^[mm] (config-submode)# dpi
Warning: Application visibility/control is enabled, this change
would take effect after reloading the controller(s) in "/mm"
(ICX-Tx-MC) ^ [mm] (config-submode)# exit
```

```
(ICX-Tx-MC) ^ [mm] (config)# firewall-visibility
(ICX-Tx-MC) ^ [mm] (config)# end
(ICX-Tx-MC) ^ [mm] # write memory
Saving Configuration...
```

5. Reload the MC to activate the DPI engine.

```
(ICX-Tx-MC) [mm] # reload
Do you really want to restart the system(y/n): y
```

Task 2: Aruba MC Integration

Objectives

In this task, the MC will be configured with the transit VLAN for the user tunnel. In an earlier version of the user-based tunneling, the final VLAN that the wired user would be assigned to on the MC had to exist on the switch as well.

To simplify the VLAN administration, the current version only needs a single VLAN to transport wired users via the GRE tunnel to the MC. Once the wired user traffic arrives at the MC, the MC will map the traffic to the final VLAN, so the MC will do a VLAN re-write of the transit VLAN to the final user VLAN.

The switch will be configured with the IP address of the MC as the tunneled-node server. In the switch configuration, this is defined as a 'user-based-tunnel' (ubt) zone.

Steps

Configure Tunnel VLAN on MC

1. Open a terminal connection to the MC; enter the configuration mode. At the /mm level, define the VLAN 4000; this is used as the transport VLAN between the switch and the controller.

Note

This is the transport VLAN inside the IP GRE tunnel between the switch and the MC, so this VLAN does not need to exist on the intermediate network between the switch and the MC.

```
(ICX-Tx-MC) [mynode] (config)# cd /mm
(ICX-Tx-MC) [mm] (config)# vlan 4000
(ICX-Tx-MC) ^[mm] (config-submode)# write memory

Saving Configuration...

Configuration Saved.
(ICX-Tx-MC) [mm] (config-submode)# end
(ICX-Tx-MC) [mm] #
```

Note

It is not strictly required to define the transport VLAN on the Mobility Controller, if all authenticated devices are assigned controller firewall user-roles that include a VLAN instruction (This is the method used in this lab activity). However, if a device is assigned to a firewall user-role without VLAN instruction, then the device would still be in the assigned transport VLAN. In this case, the transport VLAN should be defined on the MC and it should be allowed on the Mobility Controller uplink VLAN trunk port(s) to the upstream switch.

Access1 UBT Zone Configuration

Define the gateway zone and set the MC IP.

1. On Access1, define an in-band IP on VLAN 1.

```
ICX-Tx-Access1(config)# interface vlan1
ICX-Tx-Access1(config-if-vlan)# no ip dhcp
ICX-Tx-Access1(config-if-vlan)# ip address 10.x.1.4/24
ICX-Tx-Access1(config-if-vlan)# exit
```

2. Verify connectivity to the MC with a ping to 10.x.1.6 (MC IP).

```
ICX-Tx-Access1(config)# do ping 10.x.1.6
PING 10.x.1.6 (10.x.1.6) 100(128) bytes of data.
108 bytes from 10.x.1.6: icmp_seq=1 ttl=64 time=25.8 ms
108 bytes from 10.x.1.6: icmp_seq=2 ttl=64 time=0.357 ms
108 bytes from 10.x.1.6: icmp_seq=3 ttl=64 time=0.362 ms
108 bytes from 10.x.1.6: icmp_seq=4 ttl=64 time=0.333 ms
108 bytes from 10.x.1.6: icmp_seq=5 ttl=64 time=0.350 ms
--- 10.x.1.6 ping statistics ---
5 packets transmitted, 5 received, 0% packet loss, time 4052ms
rtt min/avg/max/mdev = 0.333/5.442/25.808/10.183 ms
```

3. Set the IP source interface for UBT packets to this VLAN 1 interface.

```
ICX-Tx-Access1(config)# ip source-interface ubt interface vlan1
```

4. Define the UBT zone for the MC. In the current release, only one UBT zone is supported. Make sure to enable the zone.

   - Zone name: **mc**
   - Controller IP: **10.x.1.6**

```
ICX-Tx-Access1(config)# ubt zone mc vrf default
ICX-Tx-Access1(config-ubt-mc)# primary-controller ip 10.x.1.6
ICX-Tx-Access1(config-ubt-mc)# enable
ICX-Tx-Access1(config-ubt-mc)# exit
```

5. Verify the UBT zone configuration.

```
ICX-Tx-Access1(config)# show ubt
Zone Name                : mc
Primary Controller       : 10.x.1.6
Backup Controller        : ---/---
SAC HeartBeat Interval   : 1
UAC KeepAlive Interval   : 60
VLAN Identifier          : ---/---
VRF Name                 : default
Admin State              : Enabled
PAPI Security Key        : Disabled
```

Question: What information seems to be incomplete in the given UBT zone configuration?

Answer: The switch has not been configured to use a transport VLAN yet for the user tunneled traffic.

6. Define VLAN 4000 as the UBT transport VLAN.

```
ICX-Tx-Access1(config)# vlan 4000
ICX-Tx-Access1(config-vlan-4000)# exit
ICX-Tx-Access1(config)# ubt-client-vlan 4000
```

7. Review the UBT configuration.

```
ICX-Tx-Access1(config)# show ubt
Zone Name                : mc
Primary Controller       : 10.x.1.6
Backup Controller        : ---/---
SAC HeartBeat Interval : 1
UAC KeepAlive Interval : 60
VLAN Identifier          : 4000
VRF Name                 : default
Admin State              : Enabled
PAPI Security Key        : Disabled
```

Verify State on MC

1. On Access1, verify that the switch has registered with the MC.

```
ICX-Tx-Access1(config)# show ubt state
Local Master Server (LMS) State:
LMS Type       IP Address     State
-----------------------------------------------------
Primary      : 10.x.1.6   ready_for_bootstrap

Switch Anchor Controller (SAC) State:

               IP Address       MAC Address           State
-------------------------------------------------------------------
Active       : 10.x.1.6       20:4c:03:5f:98:02    Registered
```

2. On the MC, verify that the switch is listed as a tunneled-node.

```
(ICX-Tx-MC) [mynode] # show tunneled-node-mgr tunneled-nodes
Tunneled Node Table Entries
---------------------------
Flags: A - Active  Switch Anchor Controller(A-SAC),
       S - Standby Switch Anchor Controller(S-SAC),
       U - Active  User   Anchor Controller(A-UAC),
       X - Standby User   Anchor Controller(S-UAC),
       C - Convert BC & MC into Unicast,

Name Tunneled    Node  Mac IP Address    Age(d:h:m)  Key Tunnel
---- --------    ----  --- ----------    ---------   --- ------
Index  SAC IP Address S-SAC IP Address   A-Users S-Users Flags
-----  --- -- ------- ----- -- -------   ------- ------- -----
ICX-Tx-Access1    88:3a:30:98:30:c0 10.x.1.4     00:00:23    deed
tunnel9     10.x.1.6     0.0.0.0      0      0      AC
(ICX-Tx-MC) [mynode] #
```

3. On the MC, verify the license usage. The output shows that the switch consumes a license on the controller like an AP.

Note
Only the first columns are displayed on this example output.

```
(ICX-Tx-MC) [mynode] # show license-usage
License Clients License Usage for pool /
----------------------------------------
Hostname    IP Address   Mac addr     AP    PEF   RF Protect  ACR
--------    ----------   --------     ----  ----  ----------  ----
ICX-Tx-MC   10.x.1.6     20:4c:03:5f:98:02 1    1     0     0     0
TOTAL       1     1     0     0     0
Total no. of clients: 1
(ICX-Tx-MC) [mynode] #
```

4. Review the current datapath tunnels.

```
(ICX-Tx-MC) [mm] (config)# show datapath tunnel
...
Datapath Tunnel Table Entries
-----------------------------
Flags: E - Ether encap, I - Wi-Fi encap, R - Wired tunnel, F - IP fragment
OK
       W - WEP,  K - TKIP,  A - AESCCM,  G - AESGCM,  M - no mcast src filtering
       S - Single encrypt, U - Untagged, X - Tunneled node, 1(cert-id) -
802.1X Term-PEAP
       2(cert-id) - 802.1X Term-TLS, T - Trusted, L - No looping, d - Drop
Bcast/Unknown Mcast,
       D - Decrypt tunnel, a - Reduce ARP packets in the air, e - EAPOL only
       C - Prohibit new calls, P - Permanent, m - Convert multicast, B - Bgw peer
uplink tunnel
       n - Convert RAs to unicast(VLAN Pooling/L3 Mobility enabled), s - Split
tunnel
       V - enforce user vlan(open clients only), x - Striping IP, z - Datazone
       H - Standby (HA-Lite), u - Cluster UAC tunnel, b - Active AAC tunnel, t
- Cluster s-AAC tunnel
```

```
       c - IP Compression, g - PAN GlobalProtect Tunnel, w - Tunneled Node
Heartbeat
       B - Cluster A-SAC Mcast, G - Cluster S-SAC Mcast, l - Tunneled Node user
tunnel
       f - Static GRE Tunnels, k- keepalive enabled, Y - Convert BC/MC to Unicast
# Source     Destination   Prt    Type   MTU    VLAN   Acls   BSSID  Decaps
--------     -----------   ---    ----   ---    ----   ----   -----  ------
Encaps       Heartbeats Flags     EncapKBytes   DecapKBytes
------       ---------- -----     -----------   -----------
9     10.x.1.6      10.x.1.4      47     deed   1500   0      0      0      0
0     0       88:3a:30:98:30:c0   1854   0      1854 TESw
```

Question: Why is there already a tunnel if there are no clients active? Check the '**w**' flag.

Answer: This is the keepalive check GRE tunnel. Thanks to this tunnel, all the other tunnels will not have to perform their own keepalive checks. This concept is similar to the Aruba AP GRE data tunnels and keepalive tunnel.

Task 3: User-Role Configuration on the Switch and the MC

Objectives

In this task, the 'employee 'user-role on the switch will be configured to forward the traffic of the authenticated user to the Aruba Mobility Controller. First, you will disable the Access1 switch ports 1/1/3 and 1/1/27 so no devices are authenticated. The hostname will be updated to match the correct ClearPass policies. On the Aruba Mobility Controller, a new firewall user-role will be defined. In this lab, the role will have 'full access' to the network, but this will still demonstrate that the client traffic visibility is in the firewall.

Steps

Access1: Disable Ports 1/1/3 and 1/1/27, Remove VLAN 11

1. Access the Access1 switch. Change the hostname. Add "**vsa**" at the end. Make sure you change "Tx" to your table information, like T1 for Table 1 and T12 for Table 12.

```
ICX-Tx-Access1(config)# hostname ICX-Tx-Access1-vsa
ICX-Tx-Access1-vsa(config)#
```

Note

The hostname is used as the NAS-identifier in the access-request to ClearPass. ClearPass has been pre-configured to look for the value '**vsa**' in the NAS-identifier to return the Aruba VSA Aruba-User-Role attributes that are needed for this lab.

2. Disable the two ports that currently may have active client authentications. These are the ports connected to PC3 (802.1X on 1/1/3) and PC4 (mac-auth via Access2 on 1/1/27).

```
ICX-Tx-Access1-vsa(config)# interface 1/1/3,1/1/27
ICX-Tx-Access1-vsa(config-if-<1/1/3,1/1/27>)# shutdown
ICX-Tx-Access1-vsa(config-if-<1/1/3,1/1/27>)# exit
```

3. Remove VLAN 11. The clients will be transported via the VLAN 4000 to the MC, and the MC will assign them to VLAN 11, so the VLAN 11 does not need to exist on the access switch.

```
ICX-Tx-Access1-vsa(config)# no vlan 11
```

MC: Define a Role for the Employee

4. Open a terminal session on the MC; enter the configuration mode. Define VLAN 11 at the /mm level.

```
(ICX-Tx-MC) [mynode] # cd /mm
(ICX-Tx-MC) [mm] # configure t
Enter Configuration commands, one per line. End with CNTL/Z

(ICX-Tx-MC) [mm] (config)# vlan 11
(ICX-Tx-MC) ^[mm] (config-submode)# exit
```

5. Define a new user-role that will be used for employee. This role has full access to the network. By sending the traffic through the Aruba MC firewall, all traffic can still be inspected and traffic analysis is available.

Note

The user roles on the Aruba Mobility Controller are different from the user roles on the Aruba switches, since they support firewall features. They could have the same name as on the switch, but in this lab setup, the name is kept different to make it easier to differentiate the different roles.

```
(ICX-Tx-MC) ^[mm] (config)# user-role mc-employee
(ICX-Tx-MC) ^[mm] (config-submode)# access-list session allowall
(ICX-Tx-MC) ^[mm] (config-submode)# vlan 11
(ICX-Tx-MC) ^[mm] (config-submode)# exit
(ICX-Tx-MC) ^[mm] (config)# write mem
```

Access1: Update Role Employee to Redirect Traffic to MC Using Secondary Role

1. On the Access1 switch, update the employee role, so traffic is sent to the gateway-zone 'mc' with the secondary role mc-employee.

```
ICX-Tx-Access1-vsa(config)# port-access role employee
ICX-Tx-Access1-vsa(config-pa-role)# gateway-zone zone mc gateway-role
mc-employee
ICX-Tx-Access1-vsa(config-pa-role)# exit
```

Task 4: Test Aruba MC Integration

Objectives

In this task, the integration will be tested using the PC3 (connected to Access1 port 1/1/3) with 802.1X authentication.

Steps

1. On Access1, enable port 1/1/3.

```
ICX-Tx-Access1-vsa(config)# interface 1/1/3
ICX-Tx-Access1-vsa(config-if)# no shutdown
ICX-Tx-Access1-vsa(config-if)# exit
```

2. On PC3, connected to Access1 port 1/1/3, configure the 802.1X authentication with these credentials:

   - Username: **icx-employee**
   - Password: **aruba123**

Verification Status on the Switch

1. Verify that the user authentication and role are successfully applied.

```
ICX-Tx-Access1-vsa(config)# show aaa authentication port-access
interface1/1/3 client-status
Port Access Client Status Details
Client 00:50:56:b1:7a:37, icx-employee
============================
  Session Details
  ---------------
    Port         : 1/1/3
    Session Time : 100s

  Authentication Details
  ----------------------
    Status          : dot1x Authenticated
    Auth Precedence : dot1x - Authenticated, mac-auth - Not
    attempted

  Authorization Details
  ----------------------
Role    : employee
    Status : Applied
```

2. Review all the UBT users. This shows the mac and secondary role (mc-employee) that will be sent to the MC via the PAPI protocol.

```
ICX-Tx-Access1-vsa(config)# show ubt users all
Displaying All UBT Users for Zone: mc
Downloaded user roles are preceded by *
Port    Mac-Address        Tunnel Status  Secondary-UserRole  Failure
                                                              Reason
---------------------------------------------------------------------
1/1/3   00:50:56:b1:7a:37  activated      mc-employee         ---/---
```

3. Review the UBT state.

```
ICX-Tx-Access1-vsa(config)# show ubt state
Local Master Server (LMS) State:
LMS Type      IP Address    State
-----------------------------------------------------
Primary     : 10.x.1.6   ready_for_bootstrap
```

```
Switch Anchor Controller (SAC) State:
                IP Address        MAC Address      State
----------------------------------------------------------------
Active          : 10.x.1.6  20:4c:03:5f:98:02    Registered

User Anchor Controller(UAC): 10.x.1.6

User                  Port     State                  Bucket ID   Gre Key
----------------------------------------------------------------------
00:50:56:b1:7a:37  1/1/3    registered             252         3
```

Note

The bucket map is used in an AOS cluster to distribute clients over the cluster controllers. Each client MAC address is hashed and mapped to a bucket ID based on this hash.

Question: What is the GRE Key for this user?

Answer: 3; this is based on the switch port ID.

Verification Steps on the MC

1. Review the user-tunnel table. This shows the active (GRE) tunnels and the number of users that are active on the tunnel.

```
(ICX-Tx-MC) [mm] (config)# show tunneled-node-mgr user-tunnel-table
Tunnel Info Table Entries
-------------------------
u - Untagged VLAN
Tunnel Id  Tunneled Node   BCMC TO UCast  Key   MTU  Curr Users  VLANs
---------  -------------   -------------  ----  ---- ----------  -----
tunnel 11  10.x.1.4        1              3     1500 1           11
```

Question: What is the Key ID?

Answer: Key ID is 3; this is the same GRE key ID that was observed on the switch, based on the switch port id.

2. The tunneled-user output shows the active tunneled users.

Note

Notice that this output includes the username, client MAC address, the switch (tunneled-node mac), and the VLAN mapping for the user. The tunnel # may be different in your setup.

```
(ICX-Tx-MC) [mm] (config)# show tunneled-node-mgr tunneled-users
Tunneled User Table Entries
---------------------------
Flags: U - User Anchor Controller(UAC),
       S - Standby User Anchor Controller(S-UAC),
       T - Tagged VLAN,
       A - Authenticated on Tunneled Node,
       C - Convert BC & MC into Unicast,

User Tunneled     User Mac     Tunneled Node Mac Vlan   UAC IP Address
---- --------     ---- ---     -------- ---- --- ----   --- -- -------
Key  Tunnel       Index Flags
---- --------     ----- -----
icx-employee      00:50:56:b1:7a:37 88:3a:30:98:30:c0 4000(11)
10.x.1.6   3      tunnel 11    UAC
```

Question: What is the meaning of the value **4000(11)** in the VLAN column?

Answer: The first VLAN, VLAN 4000, is the transport VLAN (inside the GRE tunnel), while the second VLAN is the actual user VLAN on the MC wired uplink port to the core switch.

3. Review the active datapath tunnels.

```
(ICX-Tx-MC) [mm] (config)# show datapath tunnel
...
#  Source    Destination Prt   Type   MTU   VLAN  Acls    BSSID
-  ------    ----------- ---   ----   ---   ----  ----    -----
Decaps Encaps            Heartbeats Flags EncapKBytes DecapKBytes
-- --- ------            ---------- ----- ----------- -----------
9  10.x.1.6 10.x.1.4     47    deed   1500 0      0       0     0      0
0  88:3a:30:98:30:c0     1769  0      1769 TESw
11 10.x.1.6 10.x.1.4     47    3 1500 0    0      0       0     0      0
88:3a:30:98:30:c0        4309  387    0 EUPRlY
(ICX-Tx-MC) [mm] (config)#
```

Question: How many tunnels are active now?

Answer: There are 2 GRE (Protocol 47) tunnels now:

- 1 keepalive tunnel, type **'deed'**
- 1 user data tunnel, type **'3'** (this was based on the switch port id)

4. Finally, review the regular user table on the MC. This is the user table that would show both wireless and wired (tunneled-node) clients.

```
(ICX-Tx-MC) [mm] (config)# show user
This operation can take a while depending on number of users. Please
be patient ....
Users
-----
IP   MAC    Name  Role  Age(d:h:m)  Auth  VPN link    AP name
--   ---    ----  ----  ----------  ----  --- ----    -- ----
Roaming     Essid/Bssid/Phy    Profile      Forward mode       Type
-------     ---------------    -------      ------- ----       ----
Host Name   User Type
---- ----   ---- ----
10.x.11.41 00:50:56:b1:7a:37 icx-employee      mc-employee 00:00:00
Tunneled-User-802.1X    10.x.1.4  Tunneled      tunnel
11/88:3a:30:98:30:c0/1/1/3   default-tunneled-user  tunnel Win 10
TUNNELED USER

User Entries: 1/1
   Curr/Cum Alloc:1/14 Free:0/13 Dyn:1 AllocErr:0 FreeErr:0
```

Application Visibility on MC

Since the wired traffic is now passing through the MC, the network administrator now has visibility in those traffic streams. In the next steps, some traffic will be generated with the wired client PC3 and the resulting analysis will be shown on the MC.

1. On PC3, connected to Access1 port 1/1/3, open a browser and navigate to 10.X.1.1 (the VSX Core switch). Log in using **admin/aruba123**.

2. Using the same PC3, open a new browser tab and navigate to 10.X.1.6 (the MC). Log in using **admin/aruba123**. Navigate to the **'Dashboard>Traffic Analysis'** screen; review the active hosts.

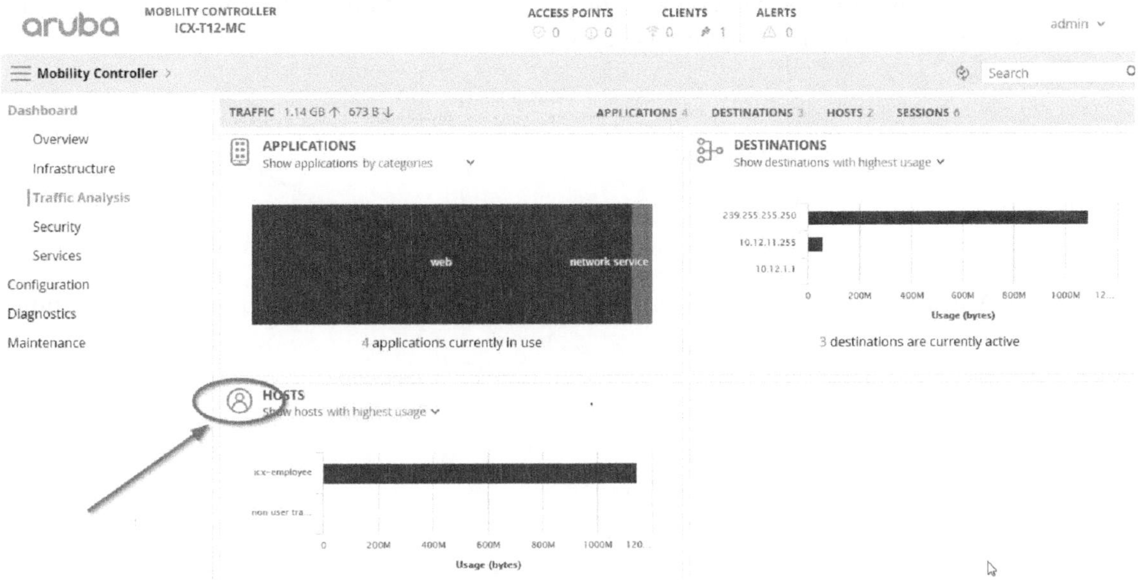

3. Select the **'icx-employee'** host.

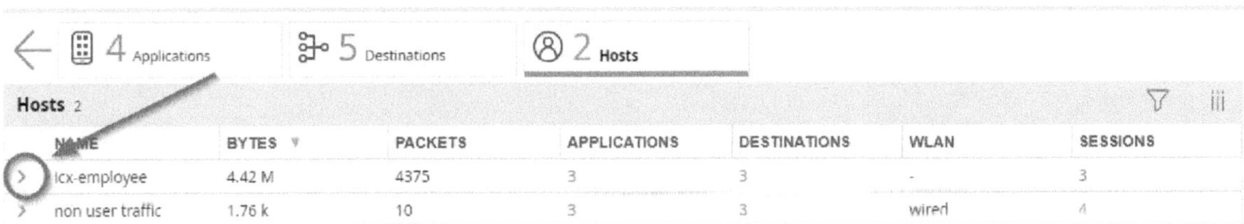

4. Review the details of the traffic sent by this device.

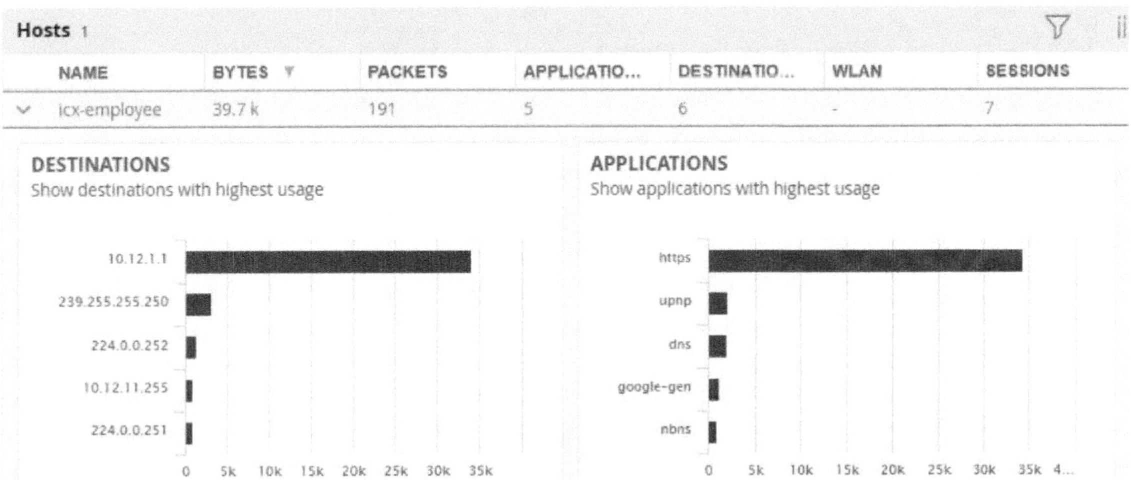

5. In the top bar, click on the 'wired' link under 'clients'. The administrator can clearly see the difference between the wireless and wired clients here.

6. On the Aruba MC, more information about the clients can be shown by enabling additional columns.

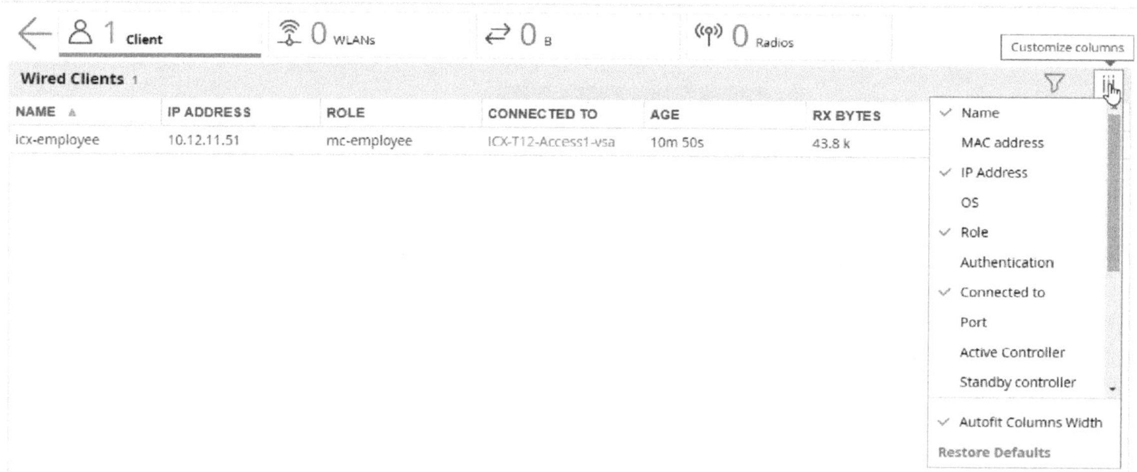

7. This example shows the output with the MAC Address, OS, Authentication, and Port enabled. Take note of the IP address of the client device; this will be used in the next step: __________.

Detailed Firewall Sessions for the Wired Client MC

1. Switch to the terminal of the MC. Review the firewall sessions for the client by using the client IP address as a filter. Replace <client-ip> with the previously noted IP of the client. In the output, the TCP sessions to the core switch (10.X.1.1 with TCP 443) and the MC (10.x.1.6 with TCP 4343) should be listed.

```
(ICX-T12-MC) [mm] (config)# show user ip <client-ip>
This operation can take a while depending on number of users. Please
be patient ....

Datapath Session Table Entries
------------------------------

Flags: F - fast age, S - src NAT, N - dest NAT
       D - deny, R - redirect, Y - no syn
       H - high prio, P - set prio, T - set ToS
       C - client, M - mirror, V - VOIP
       Q - Real-Time Quality analysis
       u - Upstream Real-Time Quality analysis
       I - Deep inspect, U - Locally destined
E - Media Deep Inspect, G - media signal
r - Route Nexthop, h - High Value
       A - Application Firewall Inspect
       J - SDWAN Default Probe stats used as fallback
       B - Permanent, O - Openflow
       L - Log, o - Openflow config revision mismatched

Source IP or MAC Destination IP  Prot SPort DPort Cntr Prio ToS Age
------ -- -- --- ----------- --  ---- ----- ----- ---- ---- --- ---
Destination TAge Packets    Bytes     Flags                  CPU ID
----------- ---- -------    -----     -----                  --- --
10.x.1.1         10.x.11.51      6   443   9640   0/0      0   0  0
tunnel 10   3c   58          64657     F                       7
10.x.11.51       10.x.1.6        6   9672  4343   1/4101   0   0  0
tunnel 10   38   66          19464     FC                      6
10.x.11.51       239.255.255.250 17  51322 1900   0/0      0   0  1
tunnel 10   18   5           1010      FC                      7
10.x.11.51       10.x.1.6        6   9659  4343   1/4101   0   0  1
tunnel 10   c    2           80        FC                      6
10.x.1.1         10.x.11.51      6   443   9643   0/0      0   0  1
tunnel 10   3c   103         135147                            7
10.x.1.1         10.x.11.51      6   443   9645   0/0      0   0  0
tunnel 10   3c   11          3975      F                       7
10.x.1.6         10.x.11.51      6   4343  9672   0/0      0   0  1
tunnel 10   38   108         106310    F                       6
```

```
10.x.11.51        10.x.1.1        6     9645   443      0/0       0     0     0
tunnel 10    3c   10           1969      C                              7
10.x.1.6          10.x.11.51      6     4343   9675     0/0       0     0     1
tunnel 10    37   30           9246      F                              6
<...output omitted...>
```

2. This demonstrates how the MC can be used to get deep visibility into the traffic of the wired devices.

Task 5: MAC Authentication Example Role for IOT

Objectives

In this task, an example IoT use case will be shown. This assumes that a customer wants to assign multiple types of IoT devices to the same VLAN. Since these IoT devices may come from different vendors, the customer is concerned about the security between these IoT devices and would like to apply micro-segmentation. This means that all the traffic, even the intra-VLAN traffic, needs to be firewalled and controlled.

In this lab setup, the PC3 and Access2 will be assigned to the MC in the same VLAN. Initially they will be able to reach each other.

After the Aruba controller firewall user-role is updated, the intra-VLAN traffic will be blocked by the firewall.

To simulate IoT devices, this activity will use MAC-auth.

Steps

PC3: Convert the Lab Setup to MAC-auth

1. On PC3, connected to Access1 port 1/1/3, disable 802.1X on the Lab interface.

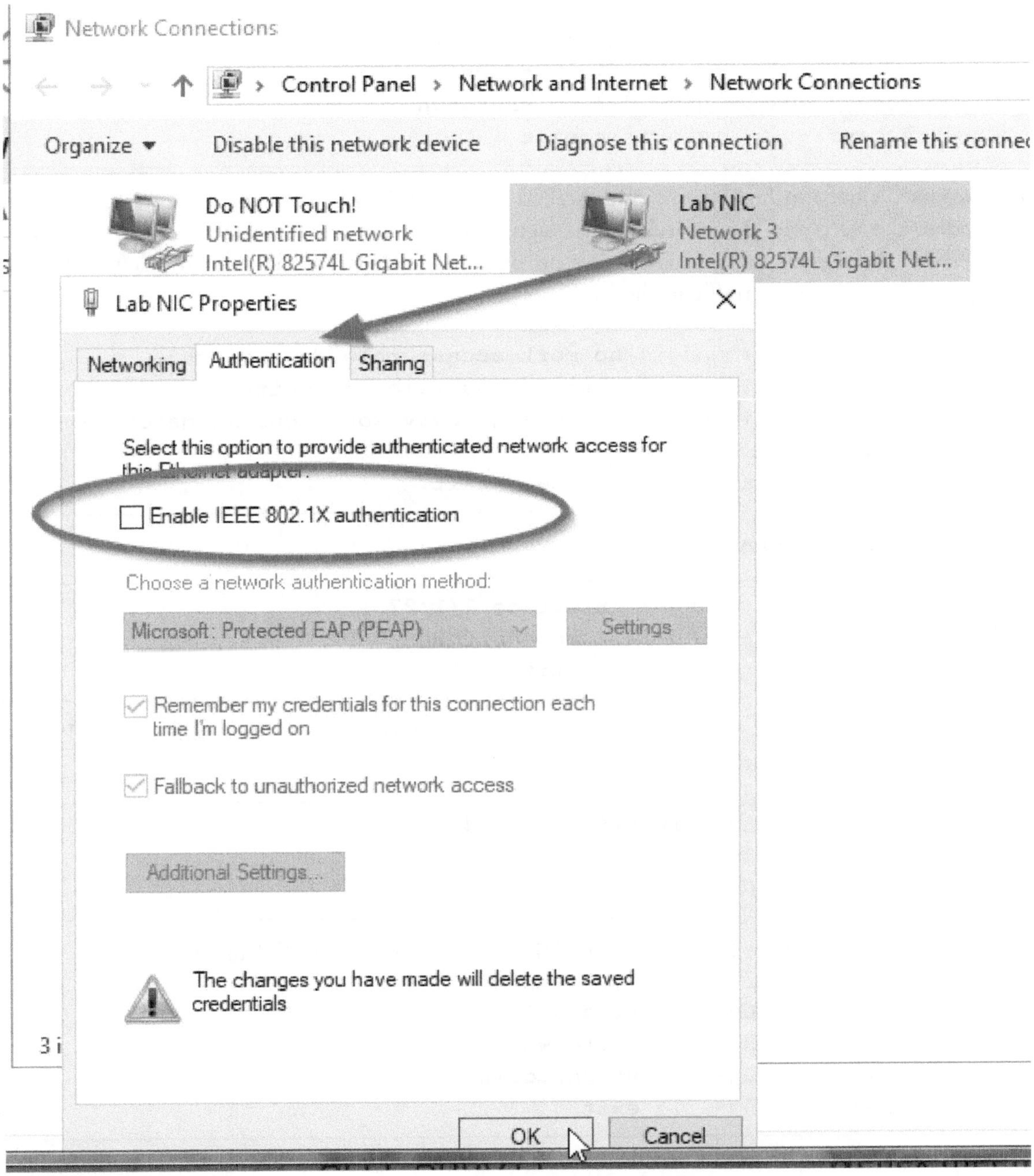

2. On PC3, disable and enable the Lab NIC interface.
3. On Access1, bounce the switch port 1/1/3 to restart the authentication process. Since the PC does not have 802.1X configured, mac-auth will be performed after about one minute. There is no need to wait for the mac-auth at this moment.

```
ICX-Tx-Access1-vsa(config)# interface1/1/3
ICX-Tx-Access1-vsa(config-if)# shutdown
ICX-Tx-Access1-vsa(config-if)# no shutdown
ICX-Tx-Access1-vsa(config-if)# exit
```

4. Prepare connection for Access2. On Access1, the port 1/1/27 connects to Access2. You will update the user-role **'dev-switch'** and assign it also to the **'mc-employee'** role on the MC. Remove the previous role (this ensures no previous settings are maintained), define the role again, and redirect the traffic to the MC.

```
ICX-Tx-Access1-vsa(config)# no port-access role dev-switch
ICX-Tx-Access1-vsa(config)# port-access role dev-switch
ICX-Tx-Access1-vsa(config-pa-role)# gateway-zone zone mc gateway-role
mc-employee
ICX-T12-Access1-vsa(config-pa-role)# exit
```

5. Enable port 1/1/27 to Access2 again.

```
ICX-Tx-Access1-vsa(config)# interface 1/1/27
ICX-Tx-Access1-vsa(config-if)# no shutdown
ICX-Tx-Access1-vsa(config-if)# exit
```

6. Access the terminal of Access2 and enter the configuration mode. Disable the port to PC4 to prevent unnecessary authentications.

```
ICX-Tx-Access2(config)# interface 1/1/4
ICX-Tx-Access2(config-if)# shut
ICX-Tx-Access2(config-if)# exit
```

7. Bounce the uplink port 1/1/27 to trigger VLAN 1 to request a DHCP address

```
ICX-Tx-Access2(config)# interface 1/1/27
ICX-Tx-Access2(config-if)# shutdown
ICX-Tx-Access2(config-if)# no shutdown
ICX-Tx-Access2(config-if)# exit
```

8. After about 30 seconds, the Access2 should have received a DHCP address on its VLAN 1 interface. The assigned IP address may be different in your setup. Take note of this DHCP IP address: __________.

```
ICX-Tx-Access2(config)# show ip interface brief
Interface           IP Address                Interface Status
                                                link/admin
vlan1               10.x.11.52/24             up/up
```

9. Ping to the Core switch to generate some traffic.

```
ICX-Tx-Access2(config)# do ping 10.x.1.1
PING 10.x.1.1 (10.x.1.1) 100(128) bytes of data.
108 bytes from 10.x.1.1: icmp_seq=1 ttl=64 time=0.277 ms
108 bytes from 10.x.1.1: icmp_seq=2 ttl=64 time=0.280 ms
108 bytes from 10.x.1.1: icmp_seq=3 ttl=64 time=0.327 ms
108 bytes from 10.x.1.1: icmp_seq=4 ttl=64 time=0.270 ms
108 bytes from 10.x.1.1: icmp_seq=5 ttl=64 time=0.222 ms
--- 10.x.1.1 ping statistics ---
5 packets transmitted, 5 received, 0% packet loss, time 4100ms
rtt min/avg/max/mdev = 0.222/0.275/0.327/0.034 ms
```

Verify MAC-Auth

1. Verify the authentication status of port 1/1/27 (to Access2). The ClearPass RADIUS server returns the Aruba VSA User-role '**dev-switch**' for the mac-authentication for the switch.

```
ICX-Tx-Access1-vsa(config)# show aaa authentication port-access inter-
face 1/1/27 client-status
Port Access Client Status Details
Client 88:3a:30:97:b6:00, 883a3097b600
============================
  Session Details
  ---------------
    Port          : 1/1/27
    Session Time : 113s
  Authentication Details
  ----------------------
    Status           : mac-auth Authenticated
    Auth Precedence : dot1x - Not attempted, mac-auth - Authenticated
```

```
   Authorization Details
   ----------------------
Role    : dev-switch
     Status : Applied
```

2. About one minute should have passed by now, verify the authentication status of port 1/1/3 (PC3); it should have received the **'employee'** role.

```
ICX-Tx-Access1-vsa(config)# show aaa authentication port-access inter-
face 1/1/3 client-status
Port Access Client Status Details
Client 00:50:56:b1:7a:37, 005056b17a37
============================
   Session Details
   ---------------
     Port         : 1/1/3
     Session Time : 16s
   Authentication Details
   ----------------------
Status                 : mac-auth Authenticated
     Auth Precedence : dot1x - Unauthenticated, mac-auth - Authenticated
   Authorization Details
   ----------------------
Role    : employee
     Status : Applied
```

Note

Both user-roles have been configured to redirect traffic to the MC using the same '**mc-employee**' gateway role, so they are using the same firewall policy.

3. On the MC, review the active users and their IP address. One of the listed IP should match the IP of Access2 (MAC starts with 88:3a:30).

Note

Although both clients are using mac-auth at this moment, the MC may still report the original 802.1X client as 'Tunneled-User-802.1X' at this point.

```
(ICX-Tx-MC) [mynode] # show user
This operation can take a while depending on number of users. Please
be patient ....
Users
-----
IP MAC       Name  Role  Age(d:h:m)  Auth  VPN link    AP name
-- ---       ----  ----  ----------  ----  --- ----    -- ----
Roaming      Essid/Bssid/Phy   Profile      Forward mode      Type
-------      ---------------   ------       ------- ----      ----
Host Name    User Type
---------    ---- ----
10.x.11.51  00:50:56:b1:7a:37 00:50:56:b1:7a:37  mc-employee
00:01:20    Tunneled-User-802.1X           10.x.1.4  Tunneled  tunnel
10/88:3a:30:98:30:c0/1/1/1   default-tunneled-user  tunnel
Win 10              TUNNELED USER

10.x.11.52  88:3a:30:97:b6:00 88:3a:30:97:b6:00  mc-employee
00:00:23    Tunneled-User-MAC              10.x.1.4  Tunneled  tunnel
11/88:3a:30:98:30:c0/1/1/27  default-tunneled-user  tunnel
TUNNELED USER

User Entries: 2/2
  Curr/Cum Alloc:2/25 Free:1/23 Dyn:3 AllocErr:0 FreeErr:0
```

4. On PC3, attempt to ping to this IP. This should succeed, since the mc-employee firewall role has an 'allowall' policy. Example screenshot from Table 12. Make sure to use your own lab IP.

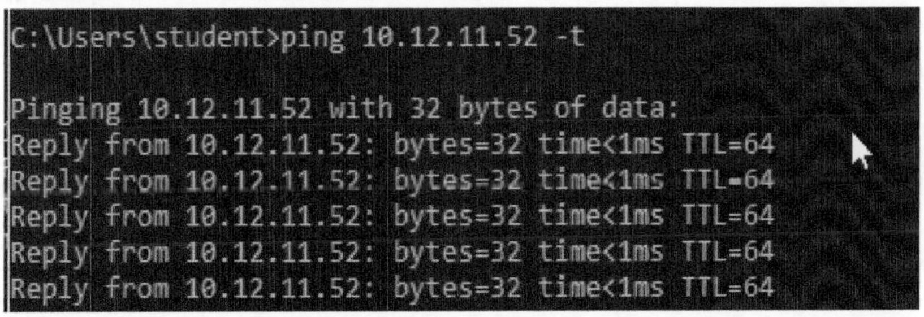

Disable Intra-VLAN Traffic in the Firewall Role

1. On the MC, define a new session policy that denies ICMP traffic to the local VLAN 11.

```
(ICX-Tx-MC) [mynode] # cd /mm
(ICX-Tx-MC) [mm] # configure terminal
Enter Configuration commands, one per line. End with CNTL/Z
(ICX-Tx-MC) [mm] (config)# ip access-list session no-iot-intravlan
(ICX-Tx-MC) ^[mm] (config-submode)# user network 10.x.11.0
255.255.255.0 icmp echo deny
(ICX-Tx-MC) ^[mm] (config-submode)# exit
```

2. Review the current mc-employee role. The 'allowall' access-list is currently in position 3.

```
(ICX-Tx-MC) ^[mm] (config)# show rights mc-employee
...
access-list List
----------------
Position  Name                     Type     Location
--------  ----                     ----     --------
1         global-sacl              session
2         apprf-mc-employee-sacl   session
3         allowall                 session
```

3. Add the "**no-iot-intravlan**" access-list to the firewall role mc-employee.

Note

Make sure to use 'position 3' in the command; it will insert the access-list before the 'allowall'.

```
(ICX-Tx-MC) ^[mm] (config)# user-role mc-employee
(ICX-Tx-MC) ^[mm] (config-submode)# access-list session no-iot-intra-
vlan position3
(ICX-Tx-MC) ^[mm] (config-submode)# exit
```

4. Save the configuration to make it effective.

```
(ICX-Tx-MC) ^[mm] (config)# write mem
Saving Configuration...
Configuration Saved.
```

5. Review the updated mc-employee role. The '**no-iot-intravlan**' access-list is now in position 3.

```
(ICX-Tx-MC) [mm] (config)# show rights mc-employee
...
access-list List
----------------
Position  Name                     Type     Location
--------  ----                     ----     --------
1         global-sacl              session
2         apprf-mc-employee-sacl   session
3         no-iot-intravlan         session
4         allowall                 session
```

6. On the client PC3, the ping will no longer be possible to Access2.

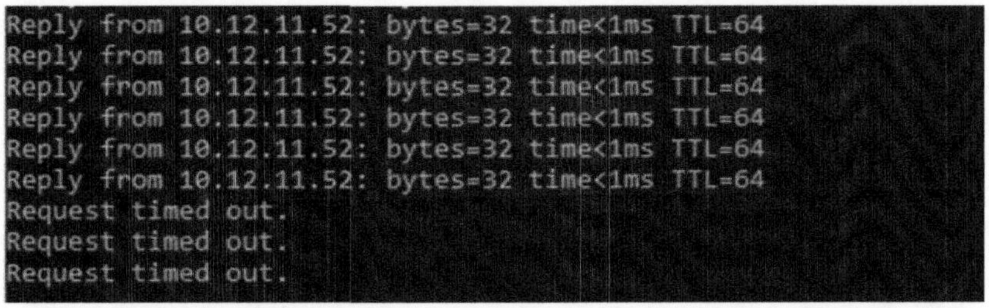

```
Reply from 10.12.11.52: bytes=32 time<1ms TTL=64
Reply from 10.12.11.52: bytes=32 time<1ms TTL=64
Reply from 10.12.11.52: bytes=32 time<1ms TTL=64
Reply from 10.12.11.52: bytes=32 time<1ms TTL=64
Reply from 10.12.11.52: bytes=32 time<1ms TTL=64
Reply from 10.12.11.52: bytes=32 time<1ms TTL=64
Request timed out.
Request timed out.
Request timed out.
```

7. This demonstrates how the Aruba dynamic segmentation solution can offer complete network control, even for intra-VLAN traffic.

Learning Check

1. When deploying dynamic segmentation v2.0, how many AP licenses are needed for one VSF stack which are formed by four 6300 switches?
    a. 4
    b. 5
    c. 1
    d. 2
2. ClearPass can pass down user roles directly to Mobility Controllers when implementing dynamic segmentation.
    a. True
    b. False
3. AOS-CX switches support both user-based/role-based and port-based modes for dynamic segmentation.
    a. True
    b. False

Summary

Congratulations! In this chapter, you learned how dynamic segmentation provides access control and forwarding services on an AOS-CX switch. You were introduced to the option for integrating AOS-CX switches with an Aruba Mobility Controller solution, were you can use tunneled-node to increase security for vulnerable devices or to unify policy enforcement in a wired and wireless architecture.

You can now configure tunneled-node with PAPI-enhanced security, high availability, and failover options. You now know how to implement tunneled-node on the switch and controller, including which settings and licenses you need.

13 Quality of Service (QoS)

OBJECTIVES

After completing this chapter, you should be able to:

- ✓ Determine how an AOS-CX switch will prioritize traffic based on incoming priority value and QoS trust settings
- ✓ Implement rate limiting
- ✓ Use classifier-based policies to assign traffic a new priority based on customer requirements
- ✓ Customize CoS maps, DSCP maps, and queue profiles
- ✓ Understand how scheduling mechanisms differ and select an appropriate scheduling profile

Overview

In the contemporary enterprise network, from the branch office to the campus LAN through the network core, a complex mixture of network applications share links. AOS-CX switches, as key components of Aruba Mobile First Networks, can respond to the needs of heterogeneous traffic flows.

In this chapter you will learn how to implement Quality of Service (QoS) mechanisms that improve the experience of users running a variety of network applications from traditional ones to voice and video applications. The chapter teaches you how to implement the many sophisticated QoS features on AOS-CX switches. To implement these features successfully, however, you must first understand their goal. In the contemporary enterprise network, a complex mixture of network applications share links. AOS-CX switches can intelligently classify heterogeneous traffic flows so that each application receives the handling that it requires, and users' experience of the network improves whether they are running voice, video, or other types of applications.

You will begin by learning about the purpose that QoS serves and how AOS-CX switches use a variety of QoS protocols and mechanisms to determine how to classify traffic into different forwarding queues and how to service those queues.

You will then dive into each of those mechanisms in more detail. You will look at rate limiting on the ingress port. You will then explore how AOS-CX switches use QoS trust settings and port-based DSCP values to assign incoming traffic a priority. You will also examine how queue and schedule profiles translate traffic priorities into actual prioritization as traffic egresses a port. You will learn how to configure and apply your own profiles. Finally, you will practice implementing QoS in a lab. The next section briefly introduces you to some of the problems that these QoS features attempt to solve.

QoS Overview

This chapter will start with an introduction to why quality of service (QoS) is needed in today's networks, where you have a mixture of services and applications with different needs.

Dealing with Congestion

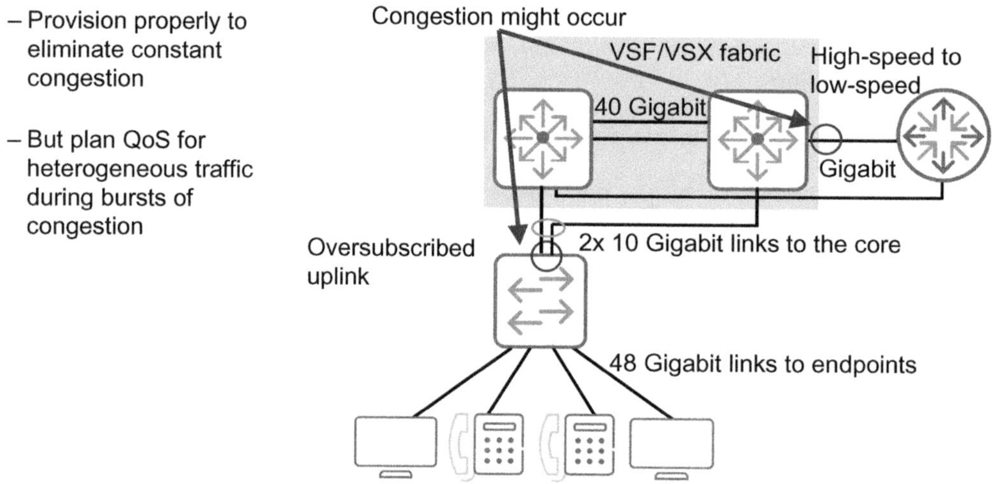

Figure 13-1 Dealing with Congestion

In many environments, switch-to-switch links are oversubscribed; that is, they provide less bandwidth for outgoing traffic than the total amount of traffic that could be incoming from other devices—often many times less. Usually, endpoints need to send and receive only a small fraction of their bandwidth, so oversubscription makes sense. However, on a moment-to-moment basis, fluctuating traffic patterns and bursts of traffic can cause congestion. The lower-bandwidth link acts as a bottleneck, and if traffic continues to arrive more quickly than the port can forward it, the port's buffers fill, and it drops traffic.

A properly designed network architecture can help to eliminate common sources of congestion. For example, a flattened architecture, when appropriate, can reduce latency by eliminating the distribution layer. Architects should properly provision uplinks based on user and device needs. Nonetheless, even a well-designed network features oversubscription and the possibility of momentary bursts of congestion, which can cause great damage for time-sensitive solutions. Network infrastructure devices must implement QoS mechanisms to protect this sensitive traffic and ensure that users have a positive experience running all necessary applications (Figure 13-1).

QoS mechanisms also help companies to enforce business policies that prioritize certain applications or segments of the network. QoS enables network administrators to customize how different types of traffic are serviced on a network, taking into account the unique characteristics of each traffic type and its importance within an organization's infrastructure. QoS ensures uniform and efficient traffic handling, keeping the most important traffic moving at an acceptable speed, regardless of current bandwidth usage. It also provides methods for administrators to control the priority settings of inbound traffic arriving at each network device.

TCP and UDP Response to Congestion

TCP

Tolerates and reduces congestion:

–Acknowledgement and flow-control mechanisms

–Lost packets retransmitted

–Back-off procedure during congestion

UDP

More susceptible to congestion and does not help reduce it:

–No acknowledgement or flow control in protocol (applications might provide)

–No back off, potential to monopolize bandwidth

Figure 13-2 TCP and UDP Response to Congestion

In general, "best-effort" delivery is satisfactory for data traffic. TCP applications are not usually disrupted by packet loss because TCP provides acknowledgement and flow-control mechanisms that ensure dropped packets will be retransmitted. Each segment of a TCP/IP message includes sequence numbers that inform receivers of the proper order and number of packets in the transmission. The receiver in a TCP transmission acknowledges packets by returning messages that include the highest sequence number it has received. TCP applications include a "window" parameter that determines how many bytes can be outstanding and unacknowledged by the receiver at any given moment. This parameter limits the number of packets that can be acknowledged by a single control packet. Delay in delivery of packets or excessive packet loss prompts the sender and receiver to establish a smaller window size. Furthermore, TCP applications back off when network congestion is detected, enabling applications to share bandwidth.

UDP, on the other hand, does not provide acknowledgements or flow control, which enables UDP applications to generate less overhead than TCP applications. Some UDP applications include their own error-checking procedures. However, in most cases, UDP applications are designed to minimize the need for retransmission and use UDP as a transport mechanism precisely because of its lower overhead and network efficiency. UDP also does not provide any back-off procedures.

Because UDP applications do not respond to congestion in any way, they can continue to contribute to congestion, which can also have drastic effects on time-sensitive real-time traffic such as voice and video (Figure 13-2).

Impact of Congestion on Real-Time Traffic

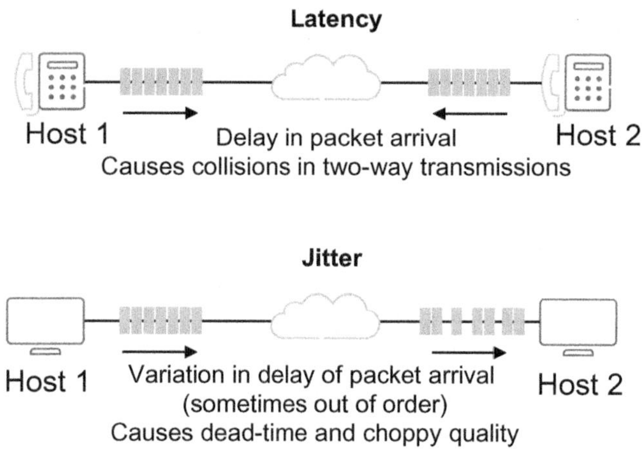

Type of traffic	Needs
Voice (two-way)	Low jitter, Low latency
Video (one-way)	Low jitter

Figure 13-3 Impact of Congestion on Real-Time Traffic

Voice traffic is sensitive to delay, sometimes called latency, which is the amount of time that passes between the sending of a transmission and its arrival at the receiving station.

In Figure 13-3, the rectangles represent packets traveling from sender to receiver. In both examples, the packets are sent at a consistent rate.

In the delay example, latency within the network cloud inevitably causes some elapsed time between transmission and reception. In the case of unidirectional traffic (as video traffic often is), this predictable, measurable period of time is usually tolerable, regardless of its length. However, because multidirectional voice traffic is nearly always interactive, excessive delay can result in conversation collisions. For example, in the diagram, Host 1 begins transmitting in the belief that Host 2 is not transmitting. However, because Host 2 is still transmitting, bits from Host 2 begin arriving before Host 1 concludes its transmission. The conversations overlap.

Voice traffic is also sensitive to jitter, which is the variation in intervals between the arrivals of packets or, in other words, the difference between when a packet is expected and when it actually arrives. Video is also sensitive to jitter.

The figure shows how Host 1 sends data at a constant rate to Host 2. However, devices within the cloud that represents the network experience varying levels of congestion that result in some packets being delayed. The outcome is a variation in the interval between packet arrival, which results in a choppy voice or video stream.

Jitter can have significant effect on real-time applications even if they require very small data streams. For instance, an IP telephone sends a very small packet every 20-30 milliseconds (ms). In order for the receiver to properly interpret the stream, the packets must arrive at the same rate. If the interval between packets grows to 50ms, for instance, the transmission will be unsatisfactory for many users.

Here are some basic implications in regard to QoS:

- All traffic does not require the same handling to receive an appropriate level of service. For example, many TCP applications can tolerate a degree of degradation of service because TCP provides for retransmission of packets and otherwise handles congestion well. In particular, applications such as file transfer applications can experience momentary periods of poor service because the user cares only about the end result.
- Time-sensitive traffic requires prioritization over other traffic so that it is transmitted immediately. This prioritization ensures that traffic transmitted at a constant rate by an endpoint such as an IP phone continues to be transmitted at a constant rate throughout the network, minimizing jitter.
- Less important UDP traffic must be prevented from monopolizing a link because the application will not back off on its own.
- In general, an enterprise might wish to enforce rate limits that ensure certain classes of traffic use only their fair share of bandwidth.
- Congestion can cause widespread degradation of service as all packets are suddenly dropped. Both TCP and UDP traffic is subject to being dropped, but TCP traffic can often tolerate packet loss better because it has built in recovery mechanisms. UDP applications such as those for streaming voice and video cannot recover lost packets. In any case, the lost packets would have little value if recovered due to the real-time nature of the application. Instead the application must attempt to move on without the packet. However, if too many packets are lost at once, user experience suffers. Users have a better experience when the network infrastructure responds to congestion gracefully by dropping less important or sensitive traffic.

Supplemental Information: Delay Over Various Media

Delay is the interval between the time that a message leaves the sender's mouth and the time that it reaches the receiver's ear. Some delay is inevitable, especially in transmissions over significant distances. While the speed of light in a vacuum is 186,000 miles per second (267,000 km per second), signals move through fiber or copper cable at approximately 125,000 miles per second (200,000 km per second). Consequently, a fiber network stretching halfway around the Earth introduces a delay of approximately 70 milliseconds under the best of circumstances with additional delay introduced by the physical transport medium. During periods of congestion, the delay can be much longer.

The effects of delay upon application performance depend heavily upon the expectations of users. The International Telecommunications Union (ITU) recommends no more than 150ms end-to-end delay for voice traffic. Greater delay can cause conversation collisions when each party begins to speak because the line appears quiet. Most users will find this situation to be unacceptable.

QoS Use Case

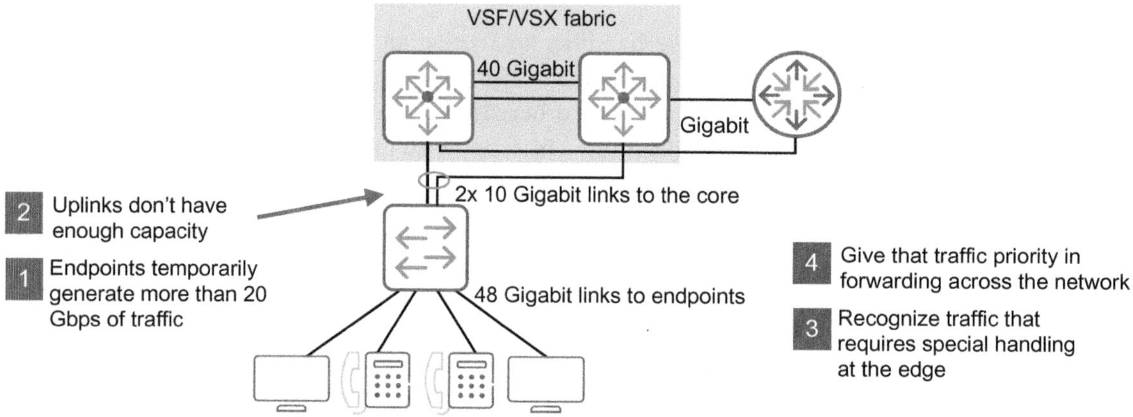

Figure 13-4 QoS Use Case

QoS can help to provide sensitive applications such as voice and video the handling that they need. Sometimes it is just a matter of prioritizing traffic to minimize delay and jitter issues. Other times, it is a temporary congestion issue, like that shown in Figure 13-4, that can have an effect on many different types of applications.

As you will learn throughout the rest of this chapter, AOS-CX switches provide high QoS by recognizing traffic that requires special handling at the edge. They can then give that traffic the high priority that it requires as they forward it across the network.

Classifying Traffic and Applying Policies

This section introduces classifying traffic and applying policies.

QoS Classification and Markings

Now that you understand how AOS-CX switches can queue traffic and deliver service to different queues based on their priority, you need to learn how the switch decides which traffic belongs to which queue.

To communicate the desired priority for traffic between network infrastructure devices, the devices use Class of Service (CoS) marks. These mechanisms define specific values, which request specific priorities for traffic marked with that value. As you will see, AOS-CX switches can take these values into account when determining how to queue traffic.

The QoS settings on each network device must be aligned to achieve the desired end-to-end QoS behavior for a network. Four service types can be used to categorize and prioritize network traffic in most campus networks:

- Best Effort Service
- Ethernet Class of Service (CoS)
- Internet Differentiated Services (DiffServ)
- IP Precedence

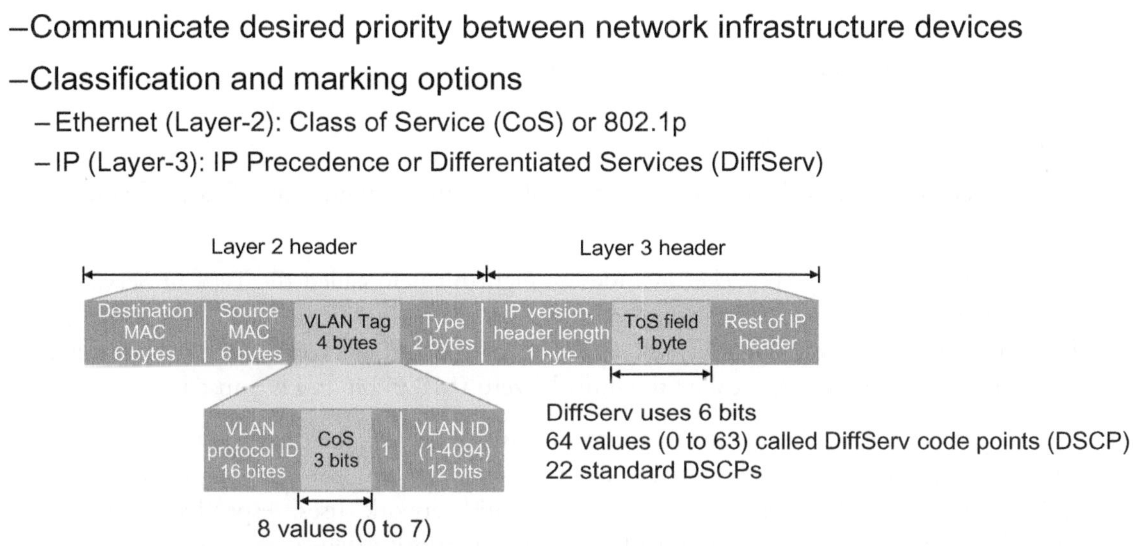

Figure 13-5 QoS Classification and Markings

For a network as a whole, it is best to select one service type to use as the primary end-to-end behavior, and then use the other two service types as needed.

To communicate the desired priority for traffic between network infrastructure devices, devices use standard QoS marks (Figure 13-5). The values reside within frames or packet headers and devices can be passed on with the traffic from device to device. Ethernet LANs carrying IP traffic typically support two types of QoS marks: Class of Service (CoS) (sometimes called 802.1p) and Differentiated Services Code Points (DSCPs).

Best Effort Service

This is the simplest service type. All traffic is treated equally in a first-come, first-served manner. If the traffic load is low in relation to the capacity of the network links, then there is no need for the administrative complexity and costs of maintaining a more complex end-to-end policy. This is sometimes called over-provisioning, as all link speeds are much higher than peak loads on the network.

802.1p or CoS

CoS uses a three-bit field in the 802.1Q VLAN tag to indicate priority. It defines eight values between 0 and 7. Note that because the VLAN tag carries the priority value, native VLAN traffic cannot contain a CoS value. Although this example shows an Ethernet frame that encapsulates an IP packet, an Ethernet frame with an 802.1p field can encapsulate any Layer-3 protocol an Ethernet supports.

Layer-3 Protocols

This section covers QoS marks that apply at Layer 3.

ToS and IP Precedence Bits (no longer used)

ToS is not often used currently, but it can be helpful to understand what ToS is if you hear it referenced.

As the figure illustrates, every IP packet includes an eight-bit field called the Type of Service (ToS) field. As originally defined, the ToS field contained two subfields—a three-bit IP precedence field used for relative prioritization and a four-bit subfield for the specific ToS desired by an individual packet. The remaining bit, bit 7, is called the must be zero (MBZ) bit and is unused.

The three IP precedence bits in the most significant position were to be used to provide eight levels of precedence or priority. The levels are labeled 0 to 7, with 7 being the highest priority and 0 the lowest. The values 6 and 7 are reserved for "Internet" and "network" uses, respectively. This enables routing updates and other critical traffic to have a higher priority than user-generated traffic. The highest user-defined value is 5, which represents "critical" priority.

The four ToS bits were designed to allow applications to instruct routers to choose routing paths with one of the following four characteristics: minimized delay, maximized throughput, maximized reliability, and minimized cost. Only one of the four bits could be "turned on," that is, set to 1.

DiffServ (Current)

Differentiated Services (DiffServ), defined in RFC 2474, supersedes a legacy IP QoS protocol called a type of Service (ToS). In DiffServ, the first six bits of the eight bit ToS field define 64 DiffServ "code points" (DSCPs). Instead of only defining priority relative to each other, the 64 DSCPs are also intended to define distinct forwarding behaviors, or Per Hop Behaviors (PHBs).

The next pages will cover the other latter two types of services.

Layer-3 and Layer-2 Classification

Layer-2 Prioritization: Class of Service (CoS)/802.1p

CoS values request up to eight different priority levels for different types of traffic. The 3-bit Priority Code Point (PCP) field within the 16-bit Ethernet VLAN tag is used to mark the CoS. The standard recommends which types of traffic you should assign to each priority value. The standard recommendation differs based on whether the traffic type is 802.1Q or 802.1D.

For 802.1Q traffic, you should use the most up-to-date recommendations in the IEEE 802.1Q-2014 standard. This standard recommends that you reserve the two highest values (7 and 6) for network control and internetwork control traffic. Network control traffic includes frames for layer-2 control protocols such as spanning tree BPDUs while internetwork control includes layer-3 control frames such as OSPF hellos and LSUs (Figure 13-6).

DSCP Layer 3	CoS/802.1P Layer 2	Traffic Type (802.1Q)
56-63	7	Network control
48-55	6	Internetwork control
40-47	5	Voice (<10ms latency)
32-39	4	Video (<100ms latency
24-31	3	Critical applications
16-23	2	Excellent effort
8-15	0	Best effort
0-7	1	Background

Figure 13-6 Layer-3 and Layer-2 Classification

AOS-CX switches will automatically mark their control traffic for high priority. Voice, value 5, and video, value 4, are given the next highest priority. These recommendations are based on their low latency requirements. Mission-critical applications receive the next highest priority, value 3. The standard recommends assigning Value 2 to traffic that requires excellent effort. It is up to customers to define what they consider critical or excellent effort applications. Next the switch gives its best effort to traffic with the default priority, which is 0. Finally, 802.1p value 1 is assigned to background traffic, which is less important or can tolerate delay. CoS 1 is deliberately set as the lowest CoS. This enables a traffic service level below the default (best effort) traffic level to be specified.

802.1D recommendations are based on the original standard that defines CoS. Some network infrastructures still use these recommendations so it is important for you to be aware of them. In this scheme, network control traffic has just one value, 7 which shifts voice and video traffic up one priority level. Controlled load (rather than critical) has the next highest level and then excellent effort. But again, companies can choose themselves what applications fit in these categories. One of the most crucial differences in the 802.1D standard is that it assigns value 2 to "spare" traffic and is intended for traffic with a priority less than best effort. It is crucial that you understand whether other devices in the network consider value 2 as higher than 0 or less than 0.

Layer-3 Prioritization: DSCP

Differentiated services (DiffServ) is a method for classifying network traffic at layer 3 by marking packets with one of 64 different service classes. Services classes are identified by the Differentiated services Code Point (DSCP) value. There are several standard definitions for DSCPs. RFC 2597 defines 12 Assured Forwarding (AF) DSCPs. These 12 DSCPs break down into four classes indicated by the first three bits (class 1 has the lowest priority and class 4 the highest). Each class includes three DSCPs, indicated by the second three bits, which request a drop precedence.

The table below recommends the type of applications that you might assign to each AF class. For example, you could assign multimedia conferencing applications to AF class 4. These applications are interactive, so they need very low latency. You could assign multimedia streaming, which can use buffering and has a bit less strict latency requirements to AF class 3. You can assign AF class 2 to applications that require low latency, but less than multimedia. For example, interactive network management applications such as SSH could use this class. Finally, AF class 1 is for bulk data that can tolerate delays—it has priority less than 0.

The DSCPs that are divisible by 8 are called Class Selector (CS) and correlate to legacy IP precedence values. For example, DSCP 8 is called CS1. RFC 2598 defines an Expedited Forwarding (EF) DSCP that is intended to produce the lowest levels of jitter and delay. RFC 3246 defines an Expedited Forwarding (EF) DSCP 46, which is intended to produce the lowest levels of jitter and delay. Aruba often recommends this DSCP for voice over IP (VoIP) traffic.

Class Selector (CS) DSCPs are DSCPs that are divisible by 8 and, based on RFC 2472, were designed to correlate to legacy IP precedence values. The table again suggests the types of applications that you could assign to each of these values. Administrators are free to use the remaining 51 DSCPs in any way they choose.

Under the original DiffServ definition, two bits of the eight-bit ToS field were initially allocated as "unused." In 2001, however, RFC 3168 redefined the two unused bits as Congestion Experienced (CE) bits, meaning that routers can use them to signal other devices when they experience congestion. If the CE bits are not in use, a router that experiences significant congestion that causes buffer overflows will drop newer packets rather than place them in its queues. This signals end stations that they should use a smaller TCP window.

DSCP Compatibility with IP Precedence

DSCP and IP precedence can exist in parallel because DiffServ intentionally preserves the three high-order bits for traffic class.

If some applications look for only the three high-order bits, they will recognize the IP Precedence value. An application or device that is using the DiffServ interpretation will interpret those same three bits from its own perspective. Applications and devices will arrive at the same relative priority, although the actual values are different.

QoS Basics

Figure 13-7 illustrates the basic steps that traffic experiences when you implement a QoS solution:

1. A device sends a frame, with or without classification markings.
2. Upon receiving the frame, the switch places the frames in the ingress queue.
3. First, is the traffic marked? And if so, does the switch trust the markings. If the switch does not trust the markings or if there are no markings and you need to define them, you will need to create a classification policy that correctly classifies (marks) the traffic appropriately. If you trust traffic on the interface, then the switch can use the device-defined markings in the traffic. And if there are both types of markings (DSCP and 802.1P), which should you trust? You need to define this policy. Likewise, if there is an ingress rate limiting policy applied on the port, the switch would implement this for the inbound traffic.
4. The switch then uses the classification information and Virtual Output Queuing (VOQ) to determine when the ingress port is allowed to move the frame to the egress queue.
5. The switch then implements the egress queuing policy, based on the traffic classification, to determine when the frame is sent out the port, along with applying any outbound rate limiting policy, if it exists.

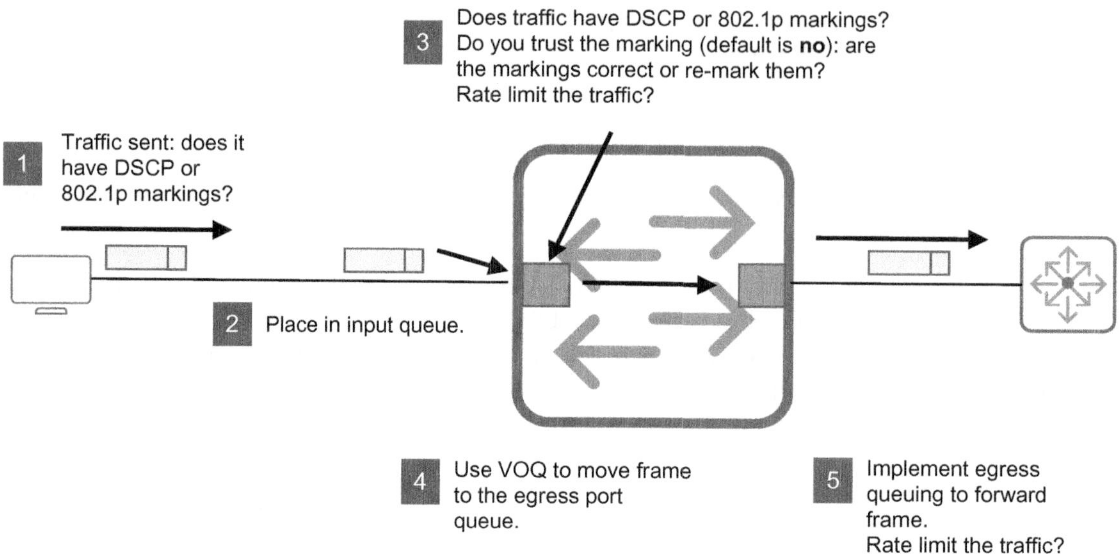

Figure 13-7 QoS Basics

QoS Processing on AOS-CX Switches

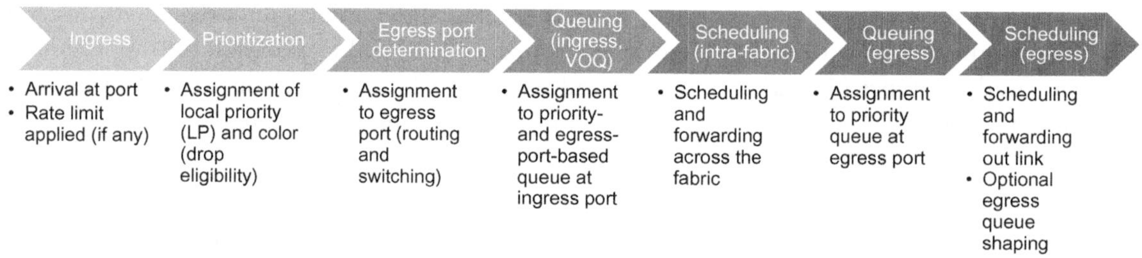

Figure 13-8 QoS Processing on AOS-CX Switches

With this brief review of QoS protocols, you will explore how AOS-CX switches apply QoS from when traffic arrives on a port to when it forwards the traffic (Figure 13-8).

When a frame arrives on a port, the switch applies inbound rate limits, if any. It then determines the correct priority for the traffic and assigns it two values: local priority (LP) and color. LP helps to determine the correct egress priority queue for the traffic while color determines the traffic's drop eligibility if queues become congested to the point that it must drop traffic.

Next the switch uses its switching and routing mechanisms to decide the correct egress port for the switch. The switch then queues the traffic at the ingress port for transmission across the switch fabric to that port. Because AOS-CX switches support virtual output queuing (VOQ), an ingress port maintains separate queues for traffic destined to each egress port. In fact, the ingress port has eight priority queues for each egress port. The switch assigns a frame to one of these queues based on its assigned LP and egress port. It then schedules the packet for forwarding across the fabric. There, a similar queuing and scheduling process occurs. Each egress port has eight queues, one for each priority queue, and traffic is assigned to the appropriate one based on its LP. The switch uses a configurable scheduling mechanism to schedule and forward the frame.

As of software 10.2, you can also apply egress queue shaping in conjunction with strict priority scheduling. This feature sets a rate limit for traffic transmitted per output queue.

Trust Settings

This section discusses what global value you might want to define for trusting the markings for incoming frames and packets.

Trusting Traffic Markings

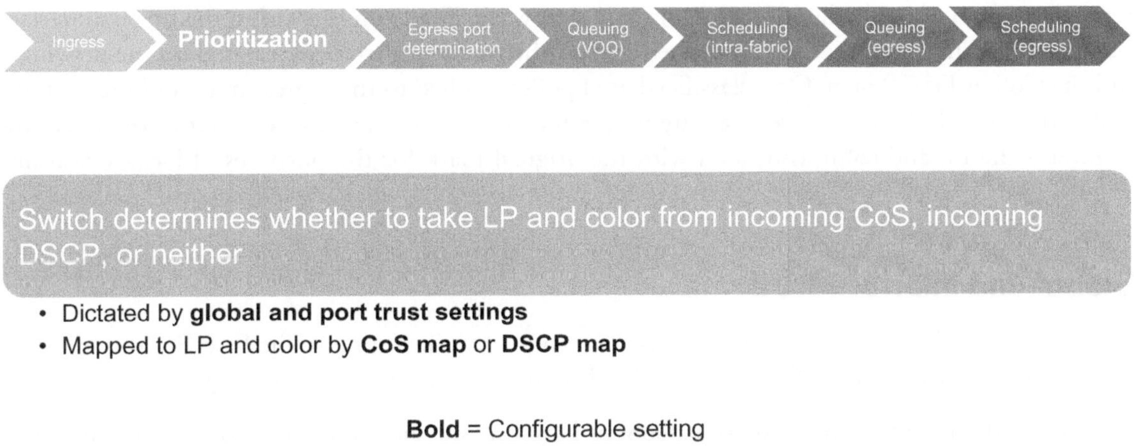

Figure 13-9 Trusting Traffic Markings

You will now examine in more detail how the switch assigns an incoming frame its LP and color. First the switch decides whether to take the LP and color from incoming QoS marks. It can base the LP and color on the incoming DSCP, incoming CoS value, or on neither, depending on the configuration of the global and port trust settings. If the port does trust one of those values, the switch maps the value to the LP and color using a configurable CoS map or DSCP map (Figure 13-9).

Re-marking Traffic

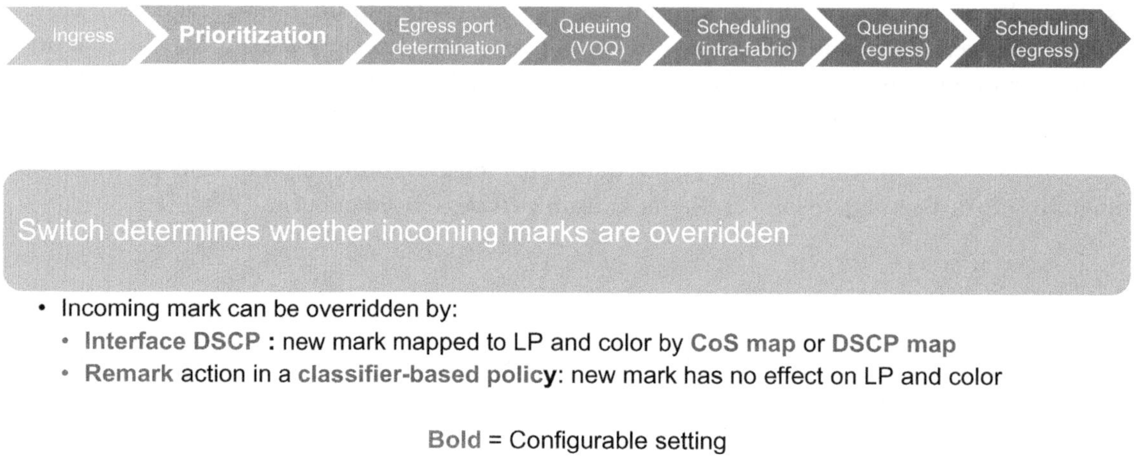

Figure 13-10 Re-marking Traffic

Second, you can override the incoming mark in two ways. First, you can assign the ingress interface a DSCP value. In that case, the switch then derives the traffic's LP and color based on the new mark and the CoS or DSCP map. Or a classifier-based policy applied to the ingress port could remark the DSCP or CoS value. In that case, the outgoing traffic header uses the new value. However, the traffic maintains the LP and color associated with the original mark for the purposes of local forwarding (Figure 13-10).

Global and Interface Trust

Now you will look at how the global and trust settings affect incoming traffic first. For this example, assume that ports are not configured with DSCP values or policies that remark QoS.

Globally, you can set QoS trust to none, CoS, or DSCP. None means that the port ignores incoming values and they have no effect on the priority. Trusting DSCP or CoS means that the port uses that incoming value to set the LP and color (Figure 13-11).

On each individual port, you can either not set the trust or set to none, CoS, or DSCP. It is important that you understand that a port not having a trust configuration is different from the port having a configuration of "none."

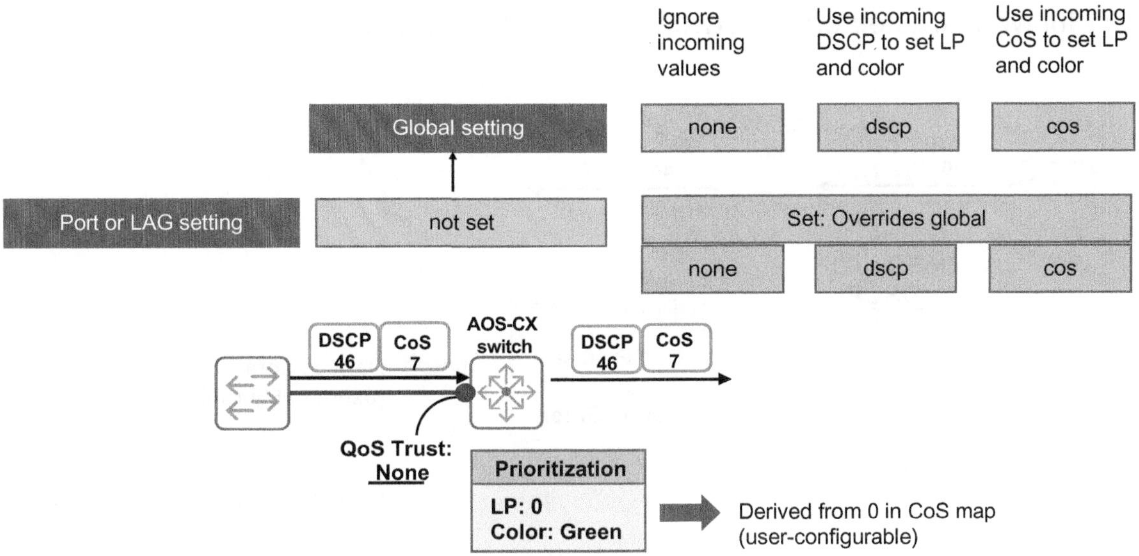

Figure 13-11 Global and Interface Trust

If a port has no setting, the port takes its setting from the global setting. Otherwise, the port setting, including "none," overrides the global setting. In this way, you could globally not trust incoming marks, but trust DSCP on certain ports. You could globally trust DSCP, but use CoS instead on certain ports, and so on.

By default, the global setting is "none," and all ports have no trust setting. This means that all ports use the global setting of "none." A "none" trust setting tells the switch to ignore any incoming values in the traffic headers and to assign all traffic the LP and color associated with CoS 0 in the CoS map. By default, this is an LP of 0 and the color green. The switch preserves any incoming DSCP when it forwards the traffic, as well as an incoming CoS value if the forwarded traffic is tagged. However, these values have no effect on how the switch queues the traffic.

Trust Set to DSCP

Many networks classify traffic at the edge, so it can be useful for the AOS-CX switch to use the already applied classifications to determine the correct priority for the traffic. If other network infrastructure devices are using DSCP to classify traffic, set the global or port trust mode to **dscp**. When a port has a **dscp** trust setting, whether that is set on the port or taken from the global setting, the switch looks at the incoming DSCP in traffic's IP headers and uses its DSCP map to assign the traffic an LP and color (Figure 13-12).

Table 13-1 shows the default DSCP map, which follows the standards and works in most circumstances.

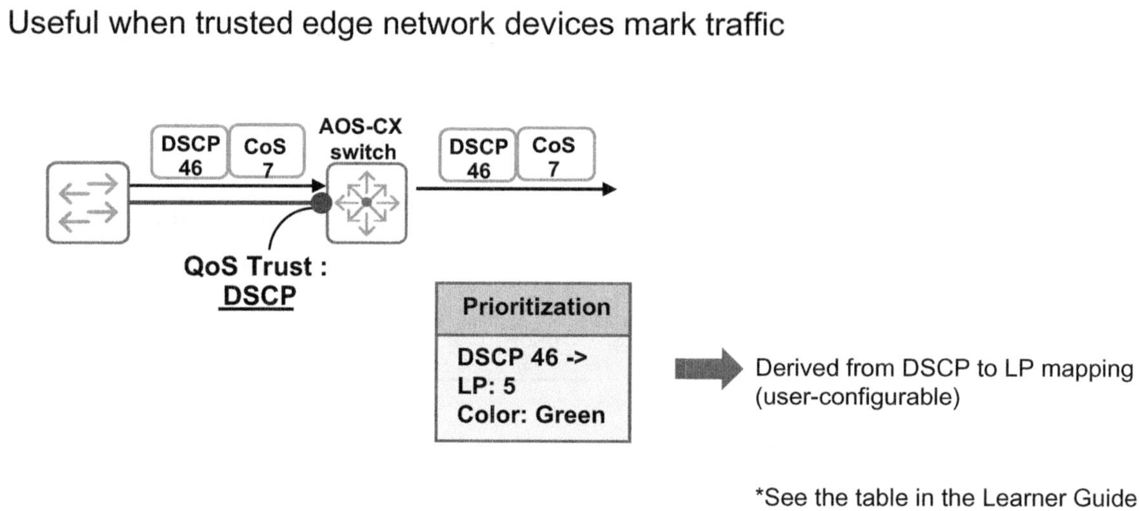

Figure 13-12 Trust Set to DSCP

Table 13-1 DSCP default settings.

DSCP	LP	Color	Name
0	1	Green	CS0
1-7	1	Green	
8	0	Green	CS1
9	0	Green	
10	0	Green	AF11
11	0	Green	
12	0	Yellow	AF12
13	0	Green	
14	0	Red	AF13
15	0	Green	
16	2	Green	CS2
17	2	Green	
18	2	Green	AF21
19	2	Green	
20	2	Yellow	AF22
21	2	Green	
22	2	Red	AF23
23	2	Green	

Table 13-1 DSCP default settings.—cont'd

DSCP	LP	Color	Name
24	3	Green	CS3
25	3	Green	
26	3	Green	AF31
27	3	Green	
30	3	Red	AF33
31	3	Green	
32	4	Green	CS4
33	4	Green	
34	4	Green	AF41
35	4	Green	
36	4	Yellow	AF42
37	4	Green	
38	4	Red	AF43
39	4	Green	
40	5	Green	CS5
41-45	5	Green	
46	5	Green	EF
47	5	Green	
48	6	Green	CS6
49-55	6	Green	
57	7	Green	CS7
58-63	7	Green	

In this example, the map has an entry for DSCP 46, which assigns the incoming traffic LP 5 and color green. However, you can customize this map, setting your own local priority, color, and name for each DSCP. Your goal in customizing the map should be to match the system the devices use from where the switch is receiving the incoming traffic. For example, you may want to change DSCP 46, used for VoIP traffic, to LP 7 if the company wants to give this traffic highest priority.

Note that, if the incoming traffic has a CoS value as well as a DSCP, the switch preserves this value in the outgoing frame, if tagged. However, the CoS value and map have no effect on the traffic's LP and color. Those derive from the DCSP only.

Trust Set to CoS

–Requires traffic to be received with tag

–Useful for non-IP traffic (or networks that don't use DSCP)

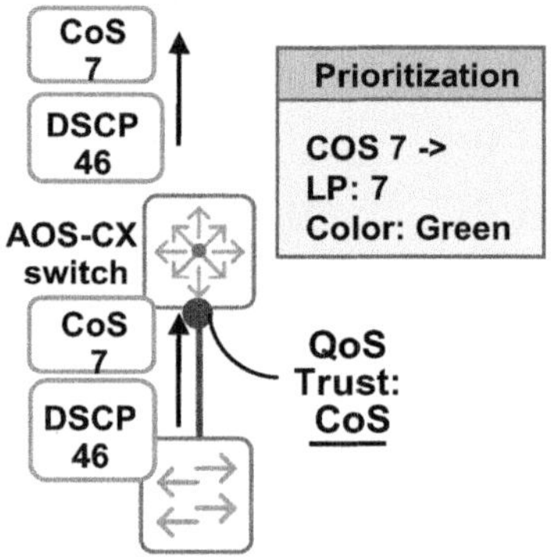

CoS	LP	Color	Name
0	1	green	Best_Effort
1	0	green	Background
2	2	green	Excellent_Effort
3	3	green	Critical_Application
4	4	green	Video
5	5	green	Voice
6	6	green	Internetwork_Control
7	7	green	Network_Control

Figure 13-13 Trust Set to CoS

Instead of using DSCP to assign the LP and color, you can use the CoS value by configuring ports to trust to **cos**. You can set the trust globally and leave ports without individual trust settings, or you can set the trust setting on individual ports. Keep in mind that the CoS is carried in the VLAN tag, so you should not use this setting for ports that receive native VLAN traffic or operate in route-only mode. All traffic that arrives without a VLAN tag is considered as having CoS value 0. In general, you might use the **cos** trust setting if port(s) receive non-IP traffic or if the rest of the network uses CoS in preference to DSCP (Figure 13-13).

This is an example of the default CoS map with the LP and color values associated with each CoS value.

This table provides the traffic LP 7 and color green. AOS-CX switches use the 802.1Q-2014 recommendations in which CoS 1 has the lowest priority, LP 0 and CoS 0 has the next lowest, LP 1. The rest of the CoS values are mapped to an LP with the same value. Again, you can adjust the map to assign each CoS value the LP and color that you desire.

When a port trusts CoS, whether based on the global or port setting, incoming DSCP has no effect on the traffic's LP and color. However, the switch does preserve this DSCP in forwarding the traffic.

Configuring QoS Trust

In global config context

Step	Command	Range / values	Default	Notes
Configure trust mode globally	qos trust	• None • CoS • DSCP	**None**	Applies to all physical interfaces and LAGs with no QoS setting

In physical or LAG interface context

Step	Command	Range / values	Default	Notes
Configure trust mode (per interface)	qos trust	• None • CoS • DSCP	no setting	

```
qos trust dscp
interface 1/1/1
    qos trust cos
interface lag 100
    qos trust none
```

What is the trust for interface 1/1/1? **CoS**

What is the trust for LAG 100? **None**

What is the trust for everything else? **DSCP**

Figure 13-14 Configuring QoS Trust

These are commands for configuring the trust settings. If you want to change the global trust mode, do so from the config context. You set the port trust mode on the physical interface or LAG. If an interface belongs to a LAG, you cannot configure a QoS trust setting on it; instead, this interface derives its trust setting from the configuration done on the LAG itself (Figure 13-14).

Modifying CoS and DSCP Mappings

In config context

Step	Command	Range / values	Default
Map CoS to local priority and color	**qos cos-map** <cos> **local-priority** <lp> [color <color>] [**name** <name>]	cos: 0-7 lp: 0-7 color: green | yellow | red	Refer to earlier slide
Map DSCP to local priority and color	**qos dscp-map** <dscp> **local-priority** <lp> [**color** <color>] [**name** <name>]	dscp: 0-63 lp: 0-7 color: green | yellow | red	Refer to earlier slide

```
qos cos-map 0 local-priority 4
qos dscp-map 20 local-priority 3
```

Figure 13-15 Modifying CoS and DSCP Mappings

You can use these commands if you want to adjust the CoS map or DSCP map. The command changes one row in the map, specifying the desired LP, color, and name to associate with a specific CoS value or DSCP. Specifying the LP is mandatory, but the color and name are optional. If you do not specify a color, the color is set to green. If you do not specify a name, the row in the map has no name (Figure 13-15).

RFC 2697 defines the use of colors with DSCP codes. A Single Rate Three Color Marker (srTCM) meters an IP packet stream and marks its packets either green, yellow, or red. Marking is based on a Committed Information Rate (CIR) and two associated burst sizes, a Committed Burst Size (CBS) and an Excess Burst Size (EBS). A packet is marked green if it does not exceed the CBS, yellow if it does exceed the CBS, but not the EBS, and red otherwise. The srTCM is useful, for example, for ingress policing of a service, where only the length, not the peak rate, of the burst determines service eligibility. See RFC 2697 for more information: https://www.ietf.org/rfc/rfc2697.txt. The use of colors is optional.

Using Interface DSCP to Remark QoS Values

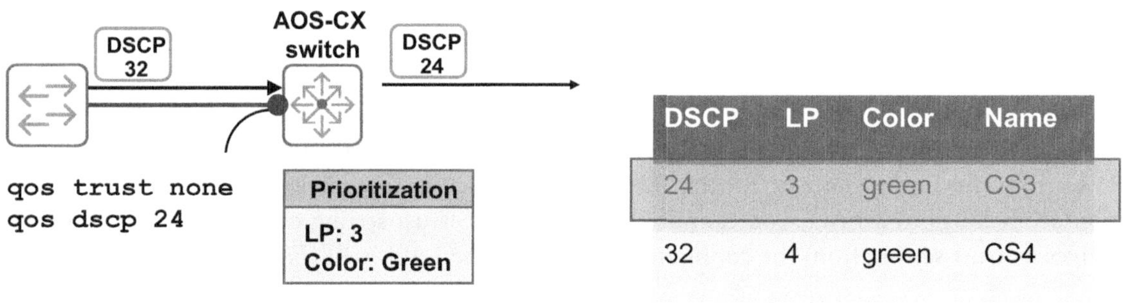

Figure 13-16 Using Interface DSCP to Remark QoS Values

Rather than use the incoming priority to assign the LP, AOS-CX switches can also classify traffic on their own. You should use this approach when connected devices are not capable of or not trusted to assign the correct values. The simplest approach is to assign a DSCP value to the Ethernet interface or LAG. When you use this approach, the trust setting on the interface *must* be none. Then the port overwrites any incoming DSCP with the specified DSCP value on all traffic that arrives on the port. The switch uses that new value and the DSCP map to assign the traffic its LP and color (Figure 13-16).

This does not affect the CoS, and also does not affect the prioritization. In this example, traffic is untagged (native VLAN) and has no CoS.

Queuing and Scheduling

This section introduces queuing and scheduling solutions for the AOS-CX switches.

Queuing and Scheduling Introduction

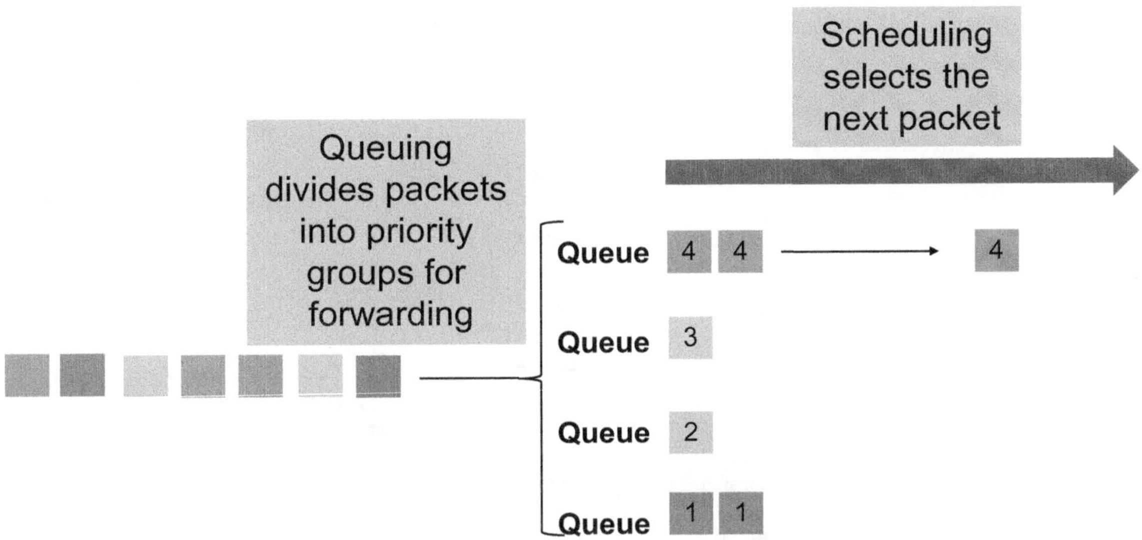

Figure 13-17 Queuing and Scheduling Introduction

As a switch prepares to transmit traffic, it places the traffic in an egress queue for the egress port (Figure 13-17). The buffer size determines how much traffic the switch can buffer, and you can find the specifications for your switch in its documentation.

A switch port that does not implement QoS places all packets in the same egress queue in the order in which they arrive. It follows a simple mechanism, called First-In/First-Out (FIFO), to schedule the packets for transmission. It forwards the first packet that arrived, then the next, and so forth.

However, some packets need priority service. For example, voice packets, transmitted at a constant rate by the endpoint, must be delivered as soon as they arrive to maintain that constant rate (avoiding jitter). To prioritize particular traffic, the switch implements priority queuing, in which it sorts various packets into multiple queues. AOS-CX switches support up to eight egress queues per port.

Once a switch has queued traffic in multiple, priority-based queues, the port's scheduling mechanism selects the next packet for forwarding. Scheduling works in tandem with queuing, ensuring that packets in high-priority queues are transmitted more promptly than packets in other queues. AOS-CX switches support strict priority (SP) queuing and Weighted Fair Queuing (WFQ) or Deficit Weighted Round Robin (DWRR) queuing. You will examine these scheduling mechanisms later in the chapter.

Class-Based QoS

Without any QoS mechanisms, switches schedule traffic on a first in first out (FIFO) basis. A frame arrives on an interface. The switch determines the egress port for the frame based on its switching and routing tables. The switch places the frame at the end of the queue for forwarding on that port. The port forwards traffic strictly based on the order in which it was received: first in is first out (FIFO) (Figure 13-18).

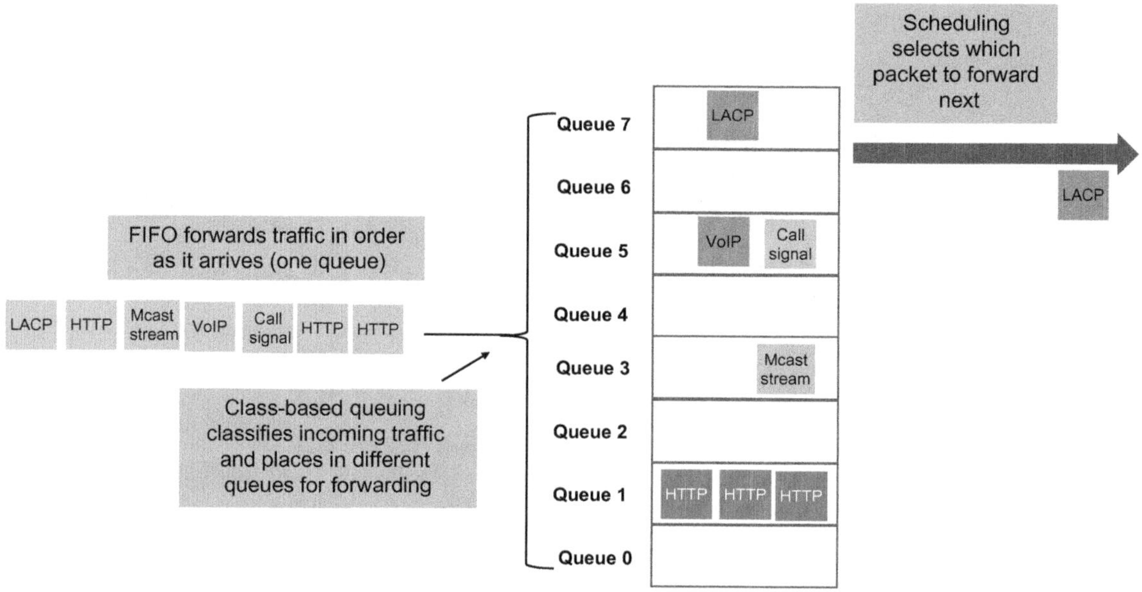

Figure 13-18 Class-Based QoS

However, AOS-CX switches support QoS, and with QoS, every port has eight egress queues, numbered 0 to 7. The switch classifies each piece of incoming traffic with a priority based on a variety of customizable factors. That priority then determines the correct queue for the traffic. This process is called queuing.

QoS relies on scheduling. Scheduling determines how the switch selects which queue forwards traffic at any given moment in a port's service cycle. For example, the scheduling mechanism might forward the frames in queue 7 and then in queue 5 and so on.

Factors that Affect Queuing and Scheduling

The traffic now has the correct LP and color, and the switch has determined the correct egress port for forwarding the traffic. Now the switch must decide how to queue and schedule the traffic. AOS-CX switches use queue and schedule profiles for making these decisions. The queue profile is global, while you can apply schedule profiles globally or to individual ports (Figure 13-19).

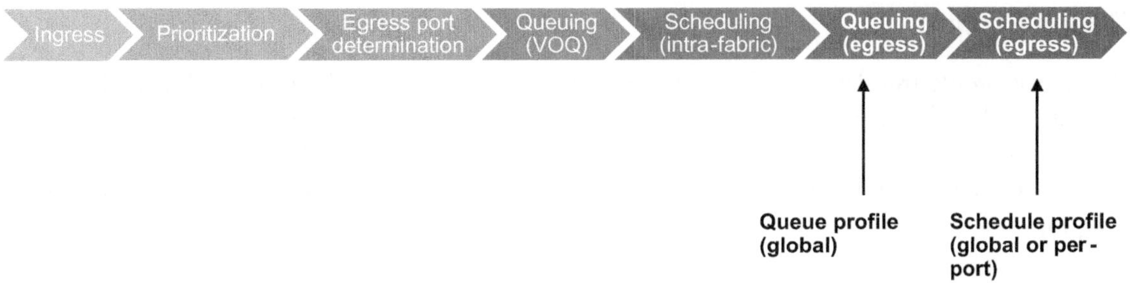

Figure 13-19 Factors that Affect Queuing and Scheduling

Virtual Queuing

The switch uses a virtual output queue (VOQ) architecture where most packet buffering occurs on the ingress line module. Traffic destined for one port (unicast) uses different buffering and scheduling than traffic destined for multiple ports (flood). The relative priority and the amount of packet transmission for these two types of traffic differ.

For unicast traffic, each line module contains eight VOQs for every destination port in the chassis (one per local priority). The queue profile determines which VOQ is used to buffer a local priority. The schedule profile determines the order of VOQ servicing. Unicast packets wait in VOQs until the scheduler selects them to cross the fabric. Each destination port has a shallow egress transmit queue that buffers unicast packets.

Broadcast, multicast, and unknown-unicast packets, collectively called flooded traffic, use a separate path to the destination ports. Each line module contains eight VOQs per destination line module (including itself) to buffer traffic to be flooded (one VOQ per local priority). A copy of the packet to be flooded is buffered in VOQs for each destination line module. The queue profile determines which VOQ is used for each local priority.

Flooded traffic VOQs use a fixed strict schedule profile to determine the order of VOQ servicing. Flooded packets wait in VOQs until the scheduler selects them to cross the fabric. On the destination line module, they are replicated to one or more destination ports. Each destination port has a second shallow egress queue for replicated packets buffered for transmit.

A WFQ scheduler is used to select packets for transmission from the unicast and replicated traffic egress queues. When selecting packets between two non-empty queues, WFQ uses a fixed data weight of four for unicast traffic, and a weight of one for replicated traffic. As long as both queues are non-empty, replicated (flooded) packets comprise approximately 20% of the transmitted traffic, independent of the unicast scheduled percentages.

Queue Profile

The queue profile translates the LP to the priority queue in which the traffic will actually be forwarded. By default, each LP is mapped to a queue with the same numerical value. Usually you can keep this profile since you can make any adjustments that you want for how QoS marks map to LP in the CoS and DSCP maps. However, you can also create a new profile with customized mappings.

Default profile works in most situations

Possibly change to:

- Reduce the number of queues in use by assigning multiple LPs to the same queue
- Not recommended by Aruba

Queue number	LP	Name
0	0	Scavenger_data
1	1	
2	2	
3	3	
4	4	
5	5	
6	6	
7	7	

Figure 13-20 Queue Profile

For example, you may want to reduce the number of queues in use, which can simplify when your network is not classifying traffic granularly and some LPs are unused. You can assign more than one LP to the same queue to ensure that even LPs that you do not think you will use map to a queue (Figure 13-20).

Schedule Profiles

Now that traffic is in the correct queue, the port schedules it for forwarding. The exact method that port uses to determine the order in which to serve priority queues depends on the settings in the port's schedule profile. You can apply a schedule profile to each individual port or LAG. Members of LAGs always take their schedule profile setting from the LAG; you cannot apply a profile to a port in a LAG. If you do not apply a schedule profile to a port or LAG, it takes its schedule profile from the global profile (Figure 13-21).

The schedule profile must include an entry for every queue that you define in the queue profile you have applied globally. The factory default profile has eight queues, numbered 0-7. For each queue, you specify a scheduling algorithm and settings associated with that algorithm. All the AOS-CX switch models support strict priority (SP) for the algorithm. In addition, the 8325, 8320, 6400, and 6300 support deficit weighted round robin (DWRR) while the 8400 supports weighted fair queuing (WFQ).

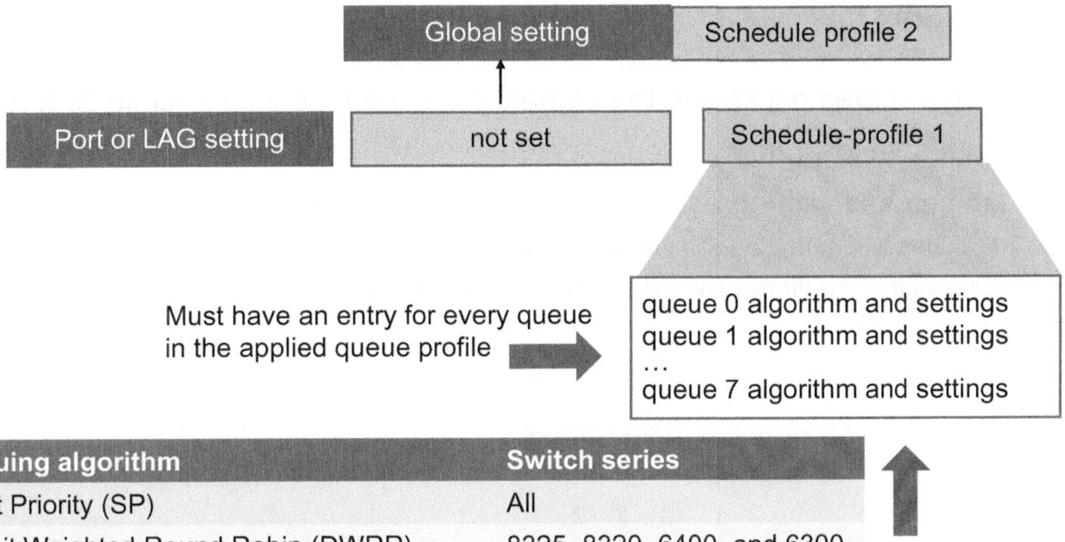

Queuing algorithm	Switch series
Strict Priority (SP)	All
Deficit Weighted Round Robin (DWRR)	8325, 8320, 6400, and 6300
Weighted Fair Queuing (WFQ)	8400

Figure 13-21 Schedule Profiles

Note

Every queue in the profile must use the same algorithm with one exception: the highest priority queue can use SP while the other queues use DWRR or WFQ.

Strict Priority (SP)

- Always serves packets in the highest priority queue with packets to forward
- Can starve low priority queues entirely
- Can be used with egress queue shaping to prevent starvation
  - Max bandwidth and burst size set per priority queue
  - Excess traffic buffered and transmitted at desired rate

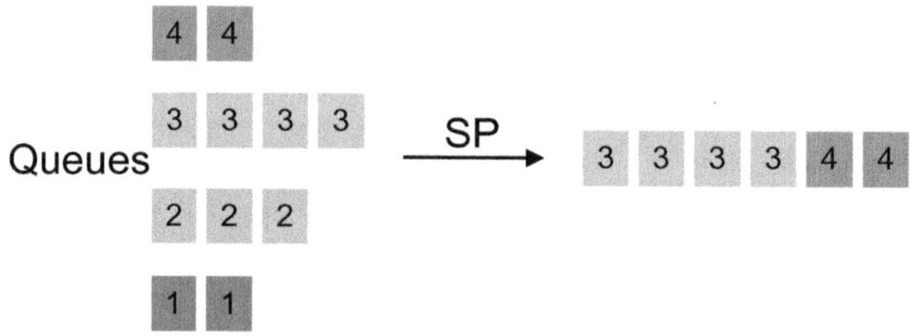

Figure 13-22 Strict Priority (SP)

SP scheduling always forwards the highest priority traffic first. That is, the port forwards all packets in queue 7. When that queue empties, the port forwards all packets in queue 6. If that queue does not include any packets, the port forwards all packets in queue 5, and so forth (Figure 13-22).

Under SP, the port will never forward a packet in a lower priority queue as long as a higher priority queue includes even one packet. If a high-priority queue experiences a spike in traffic—for example, if queue 7 receives more packets before queue 4 has a chance to be served–the lower priority traffic is starved out entirely. Therefore, SP works best when the network assigns only a few applications, which take a relatively low amount of bandwidth, to the higher priority queues—network control traffic and voice over IP (VoIP). The switch then forwards this traffic immediately when it arrives, but still has bandwidth left over for the majority of traffic in the best effort queue.

If you want to use SP alone, you could apply egress queue shaping to the high-priority queues to prevent starvation of low priority queues. Egress queue shaping allows you to apply a maximum bandwidth to a priority queue, as well as a burst size. The port buffers excess traffic up to the burst size and sends the buffered traffic at the max rate, smoothing out bursts while also preventing the high-priority queue from exceeding its maximum rate and starving out lower priority queues.

DWRR and WFQ

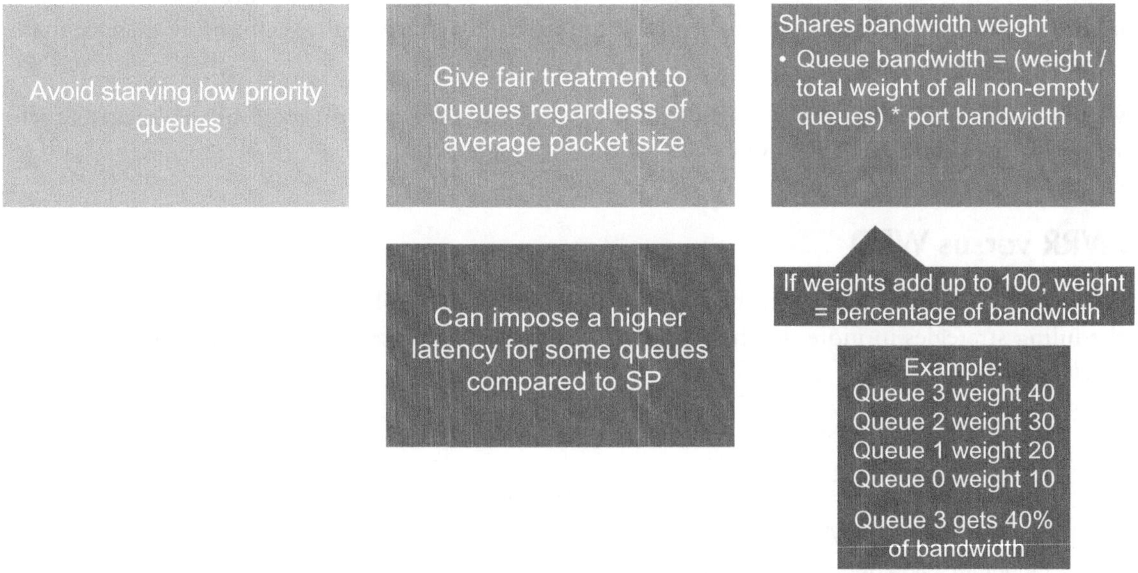

Figure 13-23 DWRR and WFQ

DWRR and WFQ both attempt to avoid the shortcomings of SP and ensure that even low priority queues receive a level of service (Figure 13-23). A simple way to give preferential service to high-priority queues, but also service to low priority queues, is weighted round robin (WRR). This scheme calls for forwarding a varying number of packets from each queue—for example, 10 packets from queue 7, 8 packets from queue 6, and so on. However, because WRR operates at a packet level, it gives more bandwidth to queues with large packets. For example, if queue 7's average packet is a third the size of queue 6's packets, queue 7 actually receives less bandwidth than queue 6.

DWRR and WFQ both attempt to deal with this problem by making the scheduling algorithm work at the bit level, although in different ways. They aim to give fair treatment to every queue regardless of its average packet size. This principle is important for reducing jitter for small packets and can be crucial for applications such as VoIP.

In both algorithms, each queue receives a predictable share of the bandwidth based on the queue's relative priority, or weight. You can calculate the queue's bandwidth by taking the queue weight and dividing it by the total weight of all non-empty queues and then multiplying that by the port bandwidth.

Using weights that add up to 100 makes it easy to estimate the bandwidth: the weight converts to a percentage of the bandwidth. Pay attention to the "non-empty" part of the formula.

For example, a port has four queues with weights 40, 30, 20, and 10. If all queues are contending for bandwidth, the queue with weight 40 is guaranteed up to 40% of the bandwidth. If a queue empties and does not need its full share of the bandwidth, that bandwidth is available for other queues, shared out according to their weight.

While DWRR and WFQ provide all of these advantages, they can impose a bit higher latency for high-priority queues than SP would.

DWRR versus WFQ

Figure 13-24 briefly summarizes the two scheduling strategies. The following slides cover the two scheduling strategies in more depth. See the note for scheduling restrictions based on the AOS-CX switch model.

- DWRR
  - Uses a deficit counter to track number of bytes allowed to send
  - Adds a number of bytes (quantum) to the deficit counter of every non-empty queue
  - Quantum value depends on the queue weight: the larger the weight the more bytes added
  - IE, higher weight queues deficit counters fill up more quickly
- WFQ
  - FQ attempts to imitate bit-by-bit round robin by calculating a virtual finish time for each packet in each queue if the packets were forwarded using bit-by-bit round robin forwarding
  - "Virtual" time is used because it simplifies computations and provides consistency as new packets arrive in queues.
  - Smaller packets have a shorter virtual finish time versus larger packets because they typically finish first in bit-by-bit round robin scheme

Figure 13-24 DWRR versus WFQ

DWRR

To make it bit-aware, DWRR uses a deficit counter to track how many bytes each queue is allowed to send in a scheduling round. At the beginning of a scheduling round, the port scheduler adds a number of bytes, called a quantum, to the deficit counter of every non-empty queue. The queue's quantum depends on its weight relative to other queues' weight. This means higher weight queues' deficit counters fill up more quickly. For example, queue 7 has a weight of 20 and all queues' total weight is 100. Queue 7 receives a quantum that is 20% of the number of bytes available in the scheduling round, which is 1500 in this simplified example. Therefore queue 7's quantum is 300, and all other deficit counters are filled the same way.

The port scheduler examines each non-empty queue in turn, beginning with the highest priority queue. It compares the deficit counter against the packet size of the packet at the front of that queue.

If the packet is smaller than the counter, it forwards the packet and deducts the packet size from the counter.

As long as the packet currently at the front of the queue is smaller than the deficit counter, the port continues to forward packets in that queue. When it reaches a packet that is too big for the remaining counter, the port scheduler moves on to the next queue. In this example, queue 7 can forward both of its small frames.

The scheduler serves other queues in the same way. In this example, many of the lower priority queues do not get to forward traffic in the first round because their deficit counter is smaller than their first packet size.

When the next round begins, the packet scheduler increments the current deficit counter for every non-empty queue with the queue's quantum. If a queue empties, its deficit counter is reset to zero, and it does not receive its quantum until a new packet arrives. Instead the queue's quantum is shared among other queues, based on their weight. The port schedule runs through the same process as before. Eventually, the counter for low priority queues builds up enough that they can forward traffic, although at a slower rate than high-priority queues

WFQ

WFQ is based on fair queuing (FQ), which is designed to achieve fair sharing of bandwidth among queues regardless of packet size. A theoretical way to achieve completely fair transmission for queues with packets of different sizes would be to use bit by bit round robin forwarding rather than packet by packet round robin forwarding. One bit from one queue is forwarded, then one bit from the next queue, and so on. However, this mechanism is not actually achievable in the real world because packets need to be transmitted as whole components, not interspliced bits.

FQ attempts to imitate bit-by-bit round robin by calculating a virtual finish time for each packet in each queue if the packets were forwarded using bit-by-bit round robin forwarding. "Virtual" time is used because it simplifies computations and provides consistency as new packets arrive in queues.

Smaller packets have a shorter virtual finish time then larger packets because they typically finish first in bit-by-bit round robin scheme. The scheduler forwards the packet with the smallest virtual finish time first, so small packets are scheduled preferentially.

WFQ modifies FQ by bringing queue weight into the calculation of the virtual finish time. You can approximate how this process works by thinking of each queue as having its own bandwidth, which is its share of the port bandwidth relative to its weight. Based on this weighted bandwidth, queues with higher weight will have relatively sooner finish times for their packets than queues with lower weights.

Combining SP with DWRR or WFQ

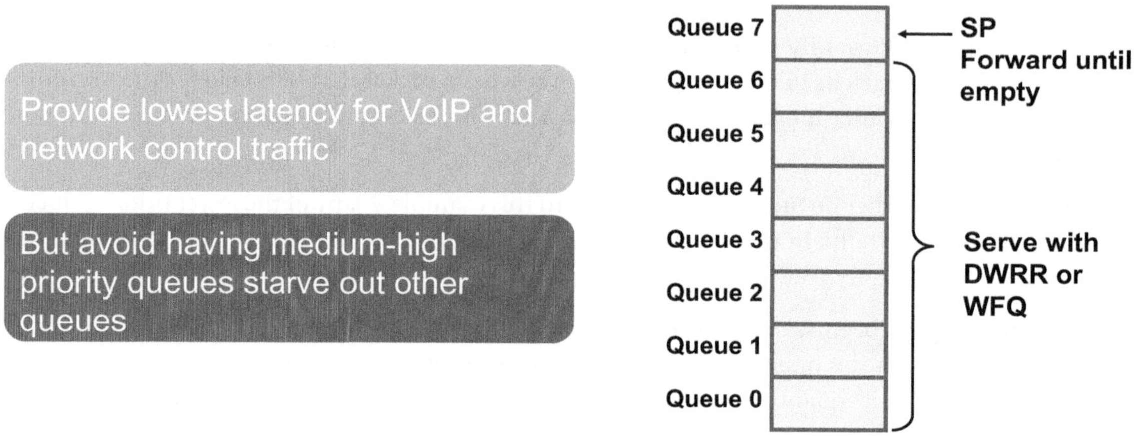

Figure 13-25 Combining SP with DWRR or WFQ

If the network has traffic than requires very low latency and jitter, such as VoIP traffic, you may want to use SP for that traffic because SP does give high-priority traffic the lowest latency and jitter. However, you may not want to use SP for medium high-priority queues due to the risk of starving out other traffic.

AOS-CX switches let you achieve the best of both worlds. You can create a schedule profile that combines either DWRR or WFQ, depending on the switch model, with SP. In a hybrid profile, only the highest priority queue can use SP. This is queue 7 if the profile uses all queues or the highest queue used if the profile does not. You should assign traffic like VoIP to this queue; network control traffic is also automatically assigned to it. The switch forwards traffic from this queue as long as the queue has traffic. When the queue is empty, the port uses the remaining bandwidth to serve other queues. It allocates this remaining bandwidth using DWRR or WFQ. Because VoIP and network control traffic typically have low bandwidth requirements, the risk of starving the other traffic is minimal (Figure 13-25).

Configuring a Schedule Profile

"factory -default" schedule (8320/6400/6300):
All queues = DWRR with weight 1

"factory-default" schedule (8400):
All queues = WFQ with weight 1

In config context

Step	Command	Notes
Create a non-default schedule profile	**qos schedule-profile** <name>	Enters schedule profile context

In schedule profile context

Step	Command	Notes
Assign a queue to use SP.	**strict queue** <queue> [max-bandwidth <kbps> [**burst** <kbps>]]	Algorithm must match for all queues in the profile. Exception: strict can be used for the highest priority queue and another algorithm for the rest. For strict priority queues, use max-band width and burst options to configure egress queue shaping.
Assign a queue to use DWRR or WFQ	[**dwrr** | **wfq**] **queue** <queue> **weight** <weight>	

Figure 13-26 Configuring a Schedule Profile

The 832X, 6400, and 6300 AOS-CX switches default scheduling profile uses DWRR for all queues with all DWRR queue weights the same. The 8400 AOS-CX switches default scheduling profile uses WFQ with all queue weights the same. Clearly you will need to create your own profile or profiles to give the higher priority queues the preference that you desire (Figure 13-26).

Note

Currently, only the AOS-CX 8400 switches support WFQ; the other AOS-CX switches support DWRR.

Activating a Queue Profile

You will apply the global schedule profile when you apply the queue profile. You need to apply the queue and schedule profile together. The queue and schedule profile must use exactly the same queues (Figure 13-27).

If you want, you can keep the factory-default queue profile and apply a new schedule profile with this command: **apply qos queue-profile factory-default schedule-profile <your-profile-name>**.

If you want to override the global schedule profile on a particular physical interface or LAG, access its context and enter the **apply qos schedule-profile** command. Remember that the global schedule profile *and* individual interface schedule profiles must use exactly the same queues that you used in the queue profile. For the factory-default queue profile, there are eight queues from 0 to 7.

In global config context

Step	Command	Default	Notes
Applies the queue profile to all interfaces and LAGs.	**apply qos queue-profile** <queue-name> **schedule-profile** <schedule-name>	Factory-default profile	Schedule profile must be applied at the same time. The queue and schedule profile must use exactly the same queues.

In Ethernet or LAG interface context

Step	Command	Notes
Override the global schedule profile on this interface.	**apply qos schedule-profile** <schedule-name>	The per -interface schedule profile must also use exactly the same queues as the global queue profile.

Figure 13-27 Activating a Queue Profile

Example

Here is an example configuration for a custom queue and schedule profile that works with that queue profile. Notice that only four (4) queues are being used (0, 2, 4, and 6). Based on the schedule profile, DWRR is being used and the queue and schedule profile are applied globally.

```
qos queue-profile 4queues
  map queue 0 local-priority 1
  map queue 0 local-priority 2
  map queue 2 local-priority 0
  map queue 2 local-priority 3
  map queue 4 local-priority 4
  map queue 4 local-priority 5
  map queue 6 local-priority 6
  map queue 6 local-priority 7
  exit
qos schedule-profile 4qDwrrStrict
dwrr queue 0 weight 10
dwrr queue 2 weight 35
dwrr queue 4 weight 55
  strict queue 6
  exit
apply qos queue-profile 4queues schedule-profile 4qDwrrStrict
```

Verification

Use the **show interface** command to display the number of packets and bytes queued for transmission (Figure 13-28). Here is a description of each of the column output for the queues:

- **Tx Bytes**: Total bytes transmitted. The byte count may include packet headers and internal metadata that are removed before the packet is transmitted. Packet headers added when the packet is transmitted may not be included.
- **Tx Packets**: Total packets transmitted.
- **Tx Errors**: Shows the amount of traffic dropped on an egress interface before it was sent. When traffic cannot be forwarded out an egress interface, it backs up on ingress. The more servicing assigned to a queue by a schedule profile, the less likely traffic destined for that queue will back up and be dropped. Tx Errors shows the sum of packets that were dropped across all line modules (due to insufficient capacity) by the ingress Virtual Output Queues (VOQs) destined for the egress port. As the counts are read separately from each line module, the sum is not an instantaneous snapshot.
- **Tx Byte Depth**: Largest byte depth (or high watermark) found on any ingress line module VOQ destined for the egress port.

```
switch# show interface 1/1/5 queues
Interface 1/1/5 is up
 Admin state is up
               Tx Bytes        Tx Packets          Tx Errors           Tx Byte Depth
 Q0          157113373520      1890863919                  0                    1362
 Q1          233312143017      2808451320                 18                   65550
 Q2          156814056423      1887257650                  0                    1392
 Q3          157441358980      1894815504                  0                    1374
 Q4          157700809294      1897941370                  0                    1362
 Q5          157872849381      1900014146                  0                    1392
 Q6          183486049854      2208268429                  0                    4398
 Q7          231607534141      2787913734                  0                   65544
```

Figure 13-28 Verification

Rate Limiting

This section introduces how you can configure rate limiting on AOS-CX switches.

Interface Rate Limiting

Port rate limiting helps control undesirable traffic. Its purpose is to allow enough broadcast, multicast, and unknown-unicast traffic for the network to function properly, while preventing flooding and traffic storms. A certain amount of each type of traffic is required for normal network operation. Broadcast packets may include ARP and DHCP traffic, for instance. Video streams, and certain types of network protocol packets, are multicasts. Unknown-unicast packets may be intended for devices whose addresses have temporarily aged out of network-forwarding caches. Configuring rate limits can help provide the balance between necessary and flooded traffic (Figure 13-29).

On AOS-CX switches, port-based rate limiting applies only to flooded traffic—that is, broadcasts, multicasts, and unknown-unicasts. The goal of this rate limiting is to mitigate the effects of broadcast storms or improper network usage while still permitting enough bandwidth to these types of traffic to support their legitimate use. If you want to rate limit unicast traffic, you should set up traffic policing with a classifier-based policy.

The rate limits apply to inbound traffic and are set in terms of *packets* per second, not bits per second. You set rate limits on physical ports or LAGs. A rate limit on a LAG applies to traffic received across all links in that LAG. You cannot configure an individual rate limit on a physical port.

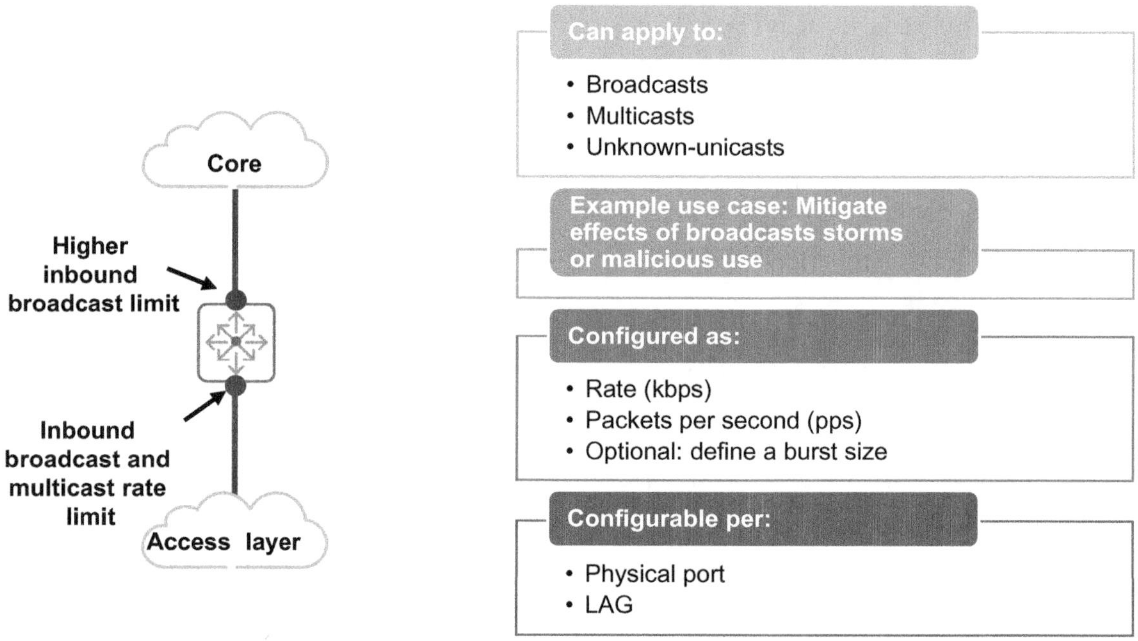

Figure 13-29 Interface Rate Limiting

You can configure different rate limits per-port in order to customize the rules as appropriate for the connected devices. For example, multicasts in your network might flow from upstream devices to downstream devices. You could implement a multicast rate limit on the downstream interfaces but not the upstream ones. You could also give the more trusted upstream network a more general broadcast and unknown-unicast rate limit.

Interface Rate Limiting Configuration

In Ethernet port or LAG context

Step	Command	Range / values	Default
Apply a broadcast rate-limit	**rate-limit broadcast** <pps>	<64-209090910>	No limit
Apply a multicast rate limit	**rate-limit multicast** <pps>	<64-209090910>	No limit
Apply an unknown - unicast rate limit	**rate-limit unknown unicast** <pps>	<64-209090910>	No limit

Figure 13-30 Interface Rate Limiting Configuration

Here you see the commands for configuring rate limits on an Ethernet port or LAG (Figure 13-30). You can set separate limits for broadcasts, multicasts, and unknown-unicasts. You can also choose to set one type of rate limit and not another.

Egress Queue Shaping/Rate Limiting

1. Create a schedule profile
   - Define maximum bandwidth
   - Define burst allowed above average rate
2. Apply profile to an interface

```
switch(config)# qos schedule-profile EQSExample
switch(config-schedule)# strict queue 0
switch(config-schedule)# strict queue 1 max-bandwidth 10000000 burst 120
switch(config-schedule)# strict queue 2
switch(config-schedule)# strict queue 3
switch(config-schedule)# strict queue 4 max-bandwidth 20000000
switch(config-schedule)# strict queue 5
switch(config-schedule)# strict queue 6
switch(config-schedule)# strict queue 7 max-bandwidth 30000000 burst 120
switch(config-schedule)# exit
switch(config)# interface 1/1/1
switch(config-if)# apply qos schedule-profile EQSExample
```

Figure 13-31 Egress Queue Shaping/Rate Limiting

Egress queue shaping limits the amount of traffic transmitted per output queue. The buffer associated with each egress queue stores excess traffic to absorb bursts and smooths the output rate. For example, an administrator might limit strict-priority queue traffic to prevent low priority queue starvation in the event that a device inappropriately sends too many higher priority packets.

Egress queue shaping can be configured on an Ethernet port or on a link aggregation group (LAG). To configure egress queue shaping, define a schedule profile with the strict priority algorithm assigned to each queue (Figure 13-31).

The above example creates a schedule profile named EQS Example, which services all seven queues using strict priority. This profile configures queues 1, 4, and 7 with a bandwidth limit of 10 Gbps, 20 Gbps, and 30 Gbps respectively. Also, queues 1 and 7 are configured with a burst of 120 KB. The profile is then applied to interface 1/1/1. (The actual burst and bandwidth configured on the interface can be found by using the **show interface** <IFNAME>**qos** command.)

LLDP-MED and Device Profiles

You have learned how to classify, prioritize, and apply policies to traffic. You will now learn how to support Voice over IP (VoIP) phones using LLDP-MED. This section introduces the topic of using LLDP to support voice (and other) devices to correctly apply QoS and other important device settings a device might need when it boots up. These devices commonly include VoIP appliances, cameras, and APs.

LLDP and LLDP-MED

- LLDP
  - Provides device discovery information
  - Used for verifying Layer-2 connectivity
- LLDP-MED
  - Assigning LAN policies like VLAN, 802.1P/CoS, DSCP, and other settings based on connected devices
  - Extended and automated power management for PoE devices
  - Location information for device tracking
  - Inventory management

Figure 13-32 LLDP and LLDP-MED

The Link Layer Discovery Protocol (LLDP) is an open-standard link layer protocol used by network devices for advertising their identity, capabilities, and neighbors on a local area network based on IEEE 802 technology, primarily Ethernet. It can be used to verify Layer-2 connectivity between devices as well as learning basic information about directly connected devices (Figure 13-32).

The Media Endpoint Discovery (MED) is an enhancement of LLDP, known as LLDP-MED, that provides the following features:

- Auto-discovery of LAN policies, such as VLAN, Layer-2 Priority (802.1p) and Differentiated Services (DSCP) settings, which can be used to enable plug-and-play networking.
- Device location discovery which allows the creation of location databases (for example, Voice over Internet Protocol (VoIP) and Enhanced 911 services).
- Extended and automated power management of Power-over-Ethernet (PoE) end devices.
- Inventory management, allowing network administrators to track their network devices, and determine device-specific (manufacturer, software and hardware versions, serial or asset number).

LLDP-MED is commonly used to provision devices, like determine the correct power settings for a connected VoIP phone or AP, or automatically assigning the correct VLAN and QoS settings for a connected device.

LLDP-MED Use Case

You have learned how to set up a switch port to connect to a VoIP phone or a VoIP phone and computer. You have learned that you should typically place VoIP phones in their own VLAN and configure a high priority for that VLAN. You have also learned to set up the port to support the voice VLAN as a tagged VLAN and the user or data VLAN as a native (untagged) VLAN.

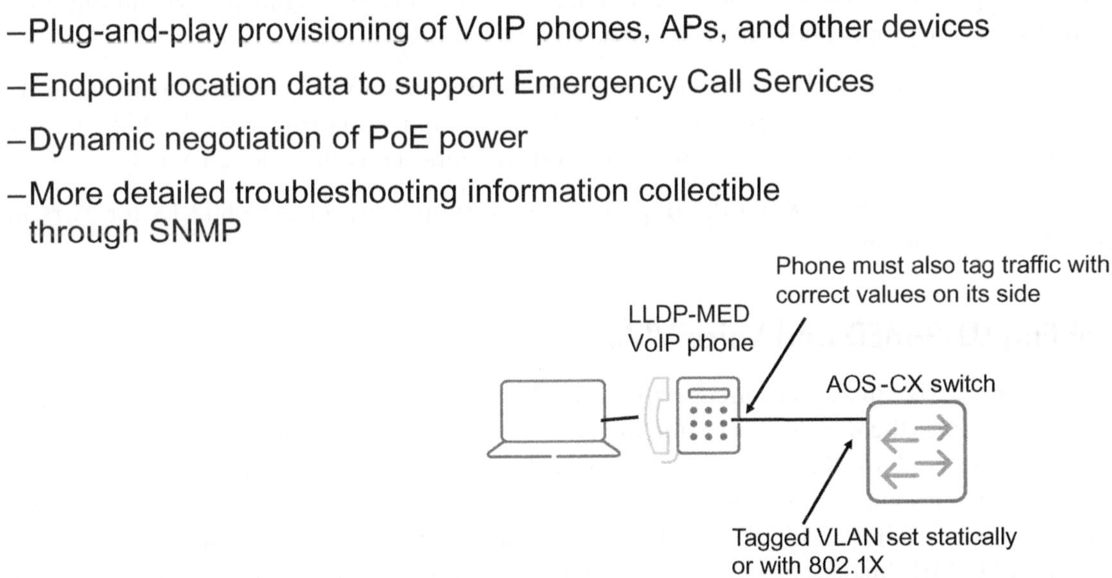

Figure 13-33 LLDP-MED Use Case

However, setting up the switch port to receive the tagged traffic is not enough. The phone also needs to know the VLAN ID that it is supposed to include in the tag. Administrators can program this individually on each phone, but doing so takes time. LLDP-MED enables the switch to dynamically inform a connecting phone of the correct VLAN ID, as well as the correct 802.1p and DSCP settings. In this way, LLDP-MED provides automatic, plug-and-play provisioning for LLDP-MED capable VoIP phones (Figure 13-33).

The switch can also communicate other information to the phone, including its physical location. This information can help to support Emergency Call Services (ECS).

When phones receive Power over Ethernet (PoE) from the switch, LLDP-MED can help the switch allocate and deliver exactly the power that the phone needs.

LLDP-MED can also help in tracking and troubleshooting VoIP phones through a central management platform. SNMP servers can read detailed VoIP endpoint data inventory, PoE status, and information to help troubleshoot the IP telephony network and call quality issues.

Review Interoperation with Authentication

You have learned that you can use authentication to dynamically set the VLAN assignment for a VoIP phone when the phone connects. This sets the VLAN automatically on the *switch* side. LLDP-MED is still required to make the configuration automatic on the *VoIP phone's* side.

You can certainly use 802.1X with LLDP-MED, though. Simply set up 802.1X on the port. Make sure that IP phones support 802.1X and that the RADIUS server has policies and accounts for authenticating them. If you want the server to send the tagged VLAN assignment dynamically, make sure that it has the proper policies for doing so.

For this scenario, you probably want the computer and IP phone to authenticate separately so that an unauthorized user cannot piggyback on the IP phone's session. Make sure to set the 802.1X client-limit to 2 so that the port operates in user-mode and authenticates each device separately.

If you want to enforce 802.1X but the IP phones do not support it, combine 802.1X for users and MAC-Auth for IP phones.

Enabling LLDP-MED and Voice VLANs

The IEEE 802.1AB Link Layer Discovery Protocol (LLDP) provides a standards-based method for network devices to discover each other and exchange information about their capabilities. An LLDP device advertises itself to adjacent (neighbor) devices by transmitting LLDP data packets on all interfaces on which outbound LLDP is enabled, and reading LLDP advertisements from neighbor devices on ports on which inbound LLDP is enabled. Inbound packets from neighbor devices are stored in a special LLDP MIB (management information base). This information can then be queried by other devices through SNMP. LLDP information is used by network management tools to create accurate physical network topologies by determining which devices are neighbors and through which interfaces they connect. LLDP operates at layer 2 and requires an LLDP agent to be active on each interface that sends and receives LLDP advertisements (Figure 13-34).

LLDP advertisements can contain a variable number of TLV (type, length, value) information elements. Each TLV describes a single attribute of a device such as: system capabilities, management IP address, device ID, port ID.

- LLDP
  - LLDP enabled globally (default)
  - LLDP enabled on the interface (default)
  - LLDP-MED TLVs enabled on interface (check)
- Voice VLANs
  - Identify the VLAN with the **voice** parameter

```
Switch# show lldp configuration 1/1/1
LLDP Global Configuration
=========================
LLDP Enabled : Yes
LLDP Transmit Interval : 8
LLDP Hold Time Multiplier : 4
LLDP Transmit Delay Interval : 2
LLDP  Reinit  Time Interval : 2
LLDP Port Configuration
========================
PORT TX -ENABLED RX -ENABLED
---------------------------------------------
1/1/1 Yes  Yes
```

```
switch# show lldp tlv
TLVs Advertised
===============
Management Address
Port Description
Port VLAN -ID
System Capabilities
System Description
System Name
```

Figure 13-34 Enabling LLDP-MED and Voice VLANs

Packet Boundaries

When multiple LLDP devices are directly connected, an outbound LLDP packet travels only to the next LLDP device. An LLDP-capable device does not forward LLDP packets to any other devices, regardless of whether they are LLDP-enabled.

An intervening hub or repeater forwards the LLDP packets it receives in the same manner as any other multicast packets it receives. Therefore, two LLDP switches joined by a hub or repeater handle LLDP traffic in the same way that they would if directly connected.

Any intervening 802.1D device or Layer-3 device that is either LLDP-unaware or has disabled LLDP operation drops the packet.

LLDP-MED

LLDP-MED in the switches uses the standard LLDP commands described earlier in this section, with some extensions, and also introduces new commands unique to LLDP-MED operation. The show commands described elsewhere in this section are applicable to both LLDP and LLDP-MED operation. LLDP-MED enables:

- Configure Voice VLAN and advertise it to connected MED endpoint devices.
- Power over Ethernet (PoE) status and troubleshooting support via SNMP.

LLDP-MED interoperates with directly connected IP telephony (endpoint) clients and provides the following features:

- Advertisement of the voice VLAN configured on the interface which is used by connected IP telephony (endpoint) clients.
- Advertisement of the configured location on the switch that can be used by the connected endpoint.
- Support for the fast-start capability.

Configuring LLDP

To support LLDP-MED, an AOS-Switch must have LLDP enabled globally, which it is by default. If you need to re-enable LLDP, enter this command:

```
Switch(config)# lldp
```

The switch port that connects to the VoIP phone must also be enabled to send and receive LLDP messages. Again, this support is enabled by default. If necessary, you can re-enable it with this command:

```
Switch(config)# interface <interface-ID>
Switch(config-if)# lldp receive
```

You should check whether the switch port is transmitting the LLDP-MED TLVs with this command:

```
Switch# show lldp configuration <interface-ID>
```

Here is an example:

```
Switch# show lldp configuration 1/1/1
LLDP Global Configuration
=========================
LLDP Enabled                 : Yes
LLDP Transmit Interval       : 30
LLDP Hold Time Multiplier    : 4
LLDP Transmit Delay Interval : 2
LLDP Reinit Time Interval    : 2
```

```
LLDP Port Configuration
=======================
Med Priority Override : No

PORT            TX-ENABLED           RX-ENABLED
-----------------------------------------------
1/1/1           Yes                  Yes

TLVs Advertised
===============
Management Address
Port Description
Port VLAN-ID
System Capabilities
System Description
System Name
OUI
Dot3 Power
Dot3 Macphy
Med Capability
Med Network Policy
Med Power
```

The figure above shows the three LLDP-MED TLVs that you should look for:

- MED Capability: The capabilities TLV enables the switch to detect LLDP-MED capable end-points, their class, and their capabilities.
- MED Network Policy: The switch communicates the proper VLAN ID and QoS settings in this TLV. You will learn how to configure those on the next page.
- MED Power (PoE): The switch advertises its capabilities as a power sourcing equipment (PSE). The VoIP phone can also use this TLV to request a specific amount of power after it first powers up or dynamically throughout the connection. Note that PoE+ defines its own LLDP TLV for negotiating the power (a dot3 TLV called poeplus_config), and the phone might use this TLV instead. In either case, the switch will allocate the requested amount of power and reserve it for this port even if the phone is not drawing the full power at the moment.

If you need to enable any of these TLVs, use these commands:

```
Switch(config)# interface <interface-ID>
Switch(config-if)# lldp med capability
Switch(config-if)# lldp med network-policy
Switch(config-if)# lldp med poe [priority-overide]
```

capability specifies advertisement of supported LLDP MED TLVs. The capability TLV is always sent with other MED TLVs; therefore it cannot be disabled when other MED TLVs are enabled. Default: enabled.

network-policy lets endpoints and network devices advertise their VLAN IDs, and IEEE 802.1p (PCP and DSCP) values for voice applications. This TLV is only sent when a voice VLAN policy is present. It is enabled, by default.

The **priority-override** option overrides user-configured port priority for Power over Ethernet. When both **lldp dot3 poe** and **lldp med poe** are enabled, the **lldp dot3 poe3** setting takes precedence.

Use the **lldp select-tlv** command to change what TLVs the switch will send and receive. See the Fundamentals Guide for more information on this command. The **show lldptlv** command shows the LLDP TLVs that are configured for send and receive:

```
Switch# show lldptlv
TLVs Advertised
===============
Management Address
Port Description
Port VLAN-ID
System Capabilities
System Description
System Name
OUI
```

MED Location TLV

It is best practice to populate the location ID TLV for each switch port that might connect to a VoIP phone with the correct location information. For example, the command for specifying the civic address of a media endpoint such as a phone is:

```
Switch(config)# interface <interface-ID>
Switch(config-if)# lldp med-location civic-addr <country-code>
<CA type> <CA value> [<CA type> <CA value>]
```

A CA type specifies the type of location being indicated, such as 3 for a city. You can specify many CA types and values in order to program the city, street, address, and building, for example. For a list of CA types, see your switch Management and Configuration Guide.

You can alternatively specify an Emergency Line Identification Number (ELIN), which is used in North America, if such numbers have been assigned to your phones:

```
Switch(config)# interface <interface-ID>
Switch(config-if)# lldp med-location <octet>
```

Voice VLANs

To create a voice VLAN, configure the **voice** command in the VLAN context, like this:

```
Switch(config)# vlan <VLAN-ID>
Switch(config-vlan)# voice
```

LLDP-MED extensions support voice VLANs.

Device Profiles

AOS-CX supports device profiles to make it even simpler to deploy Aruba APs, such as the IAPs, as well as other devices, where you are not sure what port they might be connected to on a switch. Typically, you have a standard configuration that you want to apply to all ports that connect to APs. This configuration would include the native (untagged) VLAN in which the IAPs have their IP addresses, the tagged VLAN assignments for static (and dynamic) VLANs assigned to WLANs for Aruba IAPs, the PoE settings such as a critical PoE priority, and so on.

A device profile lets you define these settings once on a switch in advance of connecting the APs. You can match on a variety of criteria, but the most common is the device type field in LLDP. You associate the device profile with the Aruba IAPs system description, for example, in its LLDP message. Installers can then connect the IAPs to any switch port without coordinating in advance. The switch detects the Aruba IAP type in an AP's LLDP messages and automatically applies the settings in the device profile (that is, the user role associated with the device profile).

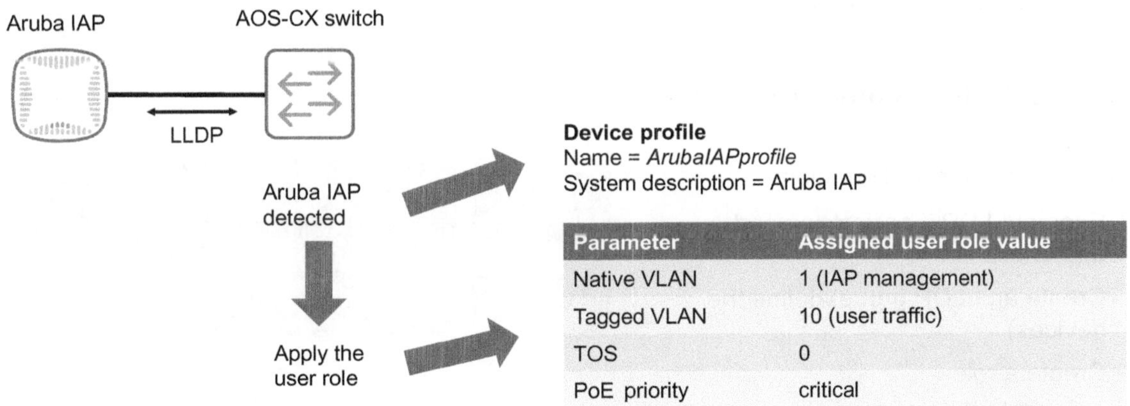

Figure 13-35 Device Profiles

The switch provides support for LLDP and CDP to enable automatic discovery and configuration of other devices on the network.

Device profiles enable predefined configuration settings to be applied to an interface based on the type of devices that are connected to the interface. When a device of a configured type is connected to an interface, the switch automatically applies the corresponding device profile. Connected devices are identified using LLDP. When the LLDP information on the interface ages out, the profile/role is revoked from the interface. Only devices directly connected to the switch are detected and processed for device profile application.

The following interface setting can be applied on the detection of a matching device type:

- **Native (untagged) VLANs**: The VLAN on which untagged frames (normal Ethernet frames) are classified. The process for applying the setting depends on how the VLAN interface is configured. See VLAN interfaces.
- **Tagged VLANs**: The list of allowed tagged VLANs on the interface.
- **Policies**: The policy associated with a role. This mode is set by the **policy** command.
- **PoE priority**: The PoE priority applied to the interface. Supported values are **high**, **low**, and **critical**.
- **QoS Trust**: QoS Trust mode applied to the interface. Supported values are **dscp**, **tos**, and **none**. This mode is set by the **qos trust** command.
- **Jumbo frames**: Enable or disable jumbo frame support for the interface. This mode is set by the **mtu** command.

Figure 13-35 lists the settings defined in a device profile, which is associated with the system description that contains "Aruba IAP". Use the **show lldp neighbor-info** command of an associated device connected to the switch in order to determine what you should actually match on and include in your device profile matching parameter(s).

Device Profiles with LLDP-MED

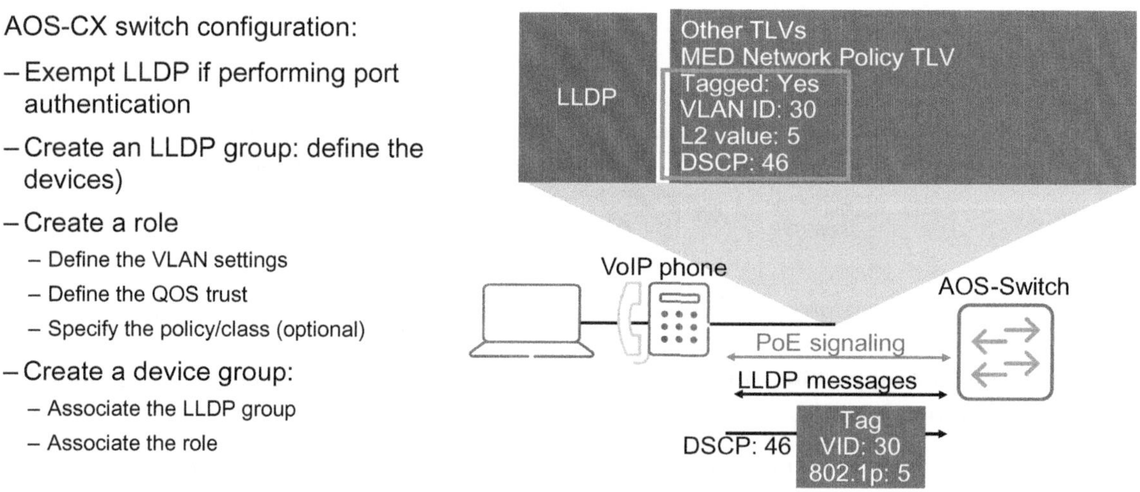

Figure 13-36 Device Profiles with LLDP-MED

Now assume that a phone that also supports LLDP-MED boots up and connects to an AOS-CX switch port with the LLDP-MED TLVs enabled. The phone completes a handshake with the switch port, negotiating PoE (if required). The AOS-CX switch and the phone also exchange LLDP messages (Figure 13-36). The switch's LLDP message includes many TLVs, including the ones that you observed on the previous page.

If you are implementing authentication on the port, like 802.1X, MAC authentication, or captive portal, remember to allow LLDP:

```
switch(config)# interface <interface-ID>
switch(config-if)# aaa authentication port-access allow-lldp-bpdu
```

Creating an LLDP Group

The LLDP group defines the devices to which you want to assign dynamic settings. To create an LLDP group, perform the following:

```
switch(config)# port-access lldp-group <LLDP-group-name>
switch(config-lldp-group)# match <parameter> <parameter-value>
switch(config-lldp-group)# ignore <parameter> <parameter-value>
```

The full **match** command syntax is as follows:

```
switch(config-lldp-group)# match sys-desc <description>
switch(config-lldp-group)# match sysname <system-name>
switch(config-lldp-group)# match vendo-oui <OUI-MAC-address>
switch(config-lldp-group)# match type <OUI-sub-type-key>
switch(config-lldp-group)# match value <OUI-sub-type-number>
```

This creates an LLDP group or modifies an existing LLDP group. An LLDP group is used to classify connected devices based on the LLDP type-length-values (TLVs) advertised by the device. A maximum of 32 LLDP groups can be configured on the switch. Each group accepts 64 match/ignore commands.

You can easily use the **show lldp neighbor-info** command to see what information a device is sending and thus what you should be matching. For example, to match on an Aruba IAP, the system description contains something like this: "ArubaOS (MODEL: 325), Version Aruba IAP". So a corresponding match command to match on this would look like this:

```
switch(config-lldp-group)# match sys-desc "Aruba IAP"
```

match and **ignore** commands are processed in sequence. Once a device matches on a **match** or **ignore** command, other commands in the device group are ignored. If you omit the sequence number, the command is added at the bottom of the LLDP group.

Note

CDP groups are also supported. See the Fundamentals Guide for configuring and using CDP groups.

Local User Roles (LURs)

The role defines the policies to use. To create a local role, perform the following:

```
switch(config)# port-access role <role-name>
switch(config-pa-role)# vlan access <VLAN-ID>
switch(config-pa-role)# vlan trunk native <VLAN-ID>
switch(config-pa-role)# vlan trunk allow <VLAN-ID-range>
switch(config-pa-role)# trust-mode <cos | dscp | none>
switch(config-pa-role)# associate policy <policy-name>
```

Creating a Device Profile

Next, you need to create a device profile and associate the LLDP group to it.

```
switch(config)# port-access device-profile <device-profile-name>
switch(config-device-profile)# associate lldp-group <name>
switch(config-device-profile)# associate role <name>
switch(config-device-profile)# enable
```

The role must be a local user role (downloadable user roles are not supported for this feature). Use the **show port-access device-profile** command to verify your configuration. The device profile is disabled by default, and must be enabled with the **enable** command. You can also disable it with the **disable** command.

As you can see, you can specify VLAN and QoS polices. To define specific policy, you need to create class and policy configurations. A class specifies what to match on, and the policy map specifies the action(s) for the class map. The policy map is then referenced in the role with the **associate policy** command.

Lab 13

Lab 13 Diagram

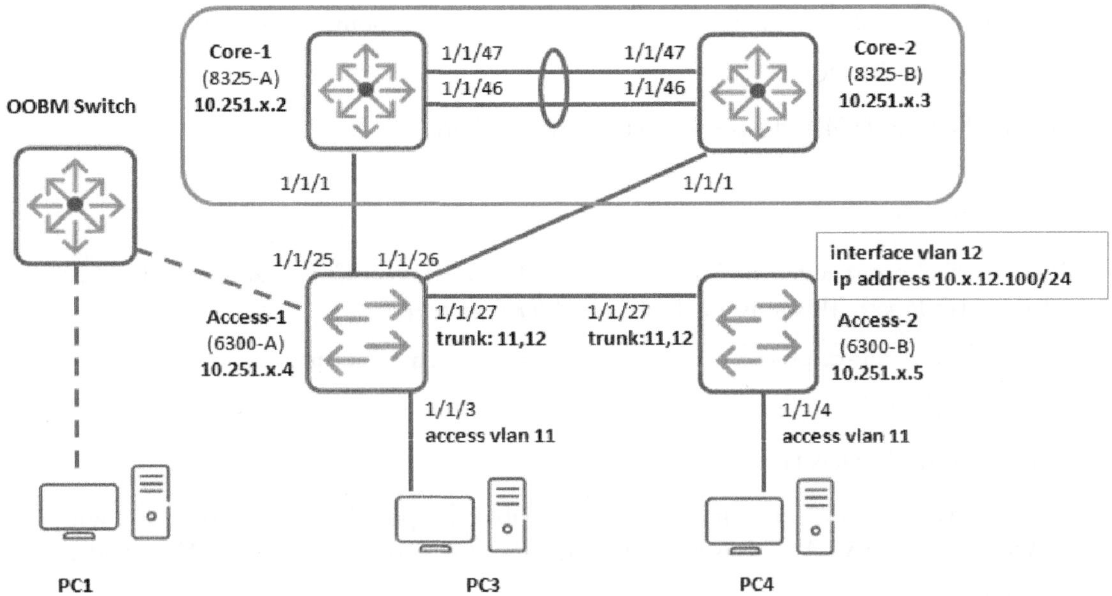

Figure 13-37 Lab 13 Diagram

Overview

In this lab activity, as shown in Figure 13-37, the QOS trust and policy configuration will be explained. The first part of the lab will cover the port and global trust options. Next, the LLDP device profile-based trust will be demonstrated. The second part of the lab will explain how classifiers, policies and actions can be used to mark and prioritize specific traffic. The lab will also show options for the Queue configuration and how to configure an LLDP-MED voice VLAN.

Objectives

- Configure and understand QOS trust modes on the switch
- Understand device profiles
- Configure QOS classifiers
- Understand queue configuration options
- Apply a voice VLAN configuration for LLDP-MED

Task 1: Prepare the Lab Start Configuration

Objectives

- This lab is built on the base VSX topology.
- Make sure to complete these steps to get the base VSX checkpoint configuration on the devices.
- Adjust topology for QOS.
- Force traffic from PC4 and Access2 over Access1 to Core.

Steps (Required)

1. Open a console connection to Access-1, Access-2, Core-1, and Core-2 and load the checkpoint called icx-lab04-vsx. This must be done on ***all four switches***.

```
Switch# copy checkpoint icx-lab04-vsx running-config
Configuration changes will take time to process, please be patient.
```

Adjust Topology for the QOS Lab

1. On Access1, enter the configuration mode. Enable the peer link to Access2, configure it as VLAN trunk using VLAN 11 as native (untagged) VLAN id, and allow VLAN 11 and 12.
   - VLAN 11 can be used to simulate PC/data traffic.
   - VLAN 12 is used to simulate Voice traffic (tagged).

```
ICX-Tx-Access1(config)# interface 1/1/27
ICX-Tx-Access1(config-if)# vlan trunk native 11
ICX-Tx-Access1(config-if)# vlan trunk allowed 11,12
ICX-Tx-Access1(config-if)# no shutdown
ICX-Tx-Access1(config-if)# exit
```

2. Open a terminal to Access2; enter the configuration mode.Disable the uplinks to VSX Core1 and Core2.

```
ICX-Tx-Access2(config)# interface 1/1/25,1/1/26
ICX-Tx-Access2(config-if-<1/1/25,1/1/26>)# shutdown
ICX-Tx-Access2(config-if-<1/1/25,1/1/26>)# exit
```

3. Enable the peer link to Access1, configure it as VLAN trunk, and define an IP on the voice VLAN 12.

```
ICX-Tx-Access2(config)# interface 1/1/27
ICX-Tx-Access2(config-if)# no shutdown
ICX-Tx-Access2(config-if)# vlan trunk native 11
ICX-Tx-Access2(config-if)# vlan trunk allowed 11,12
ICX-Tx-Access2(config-if)# exit
```

4. Define IP address 10.x.12.100 on VLAN 12 and set the default route.

```
ICX-Tx-Access2(config)# interface vlan 12
ICX-Tx-Access2(config-if-vlan)# ip address 10.x.12.100/24
ICX-Tx-Access2(config-if-vlan)# exit
ICX-Tx-Access2(config)# ip route 0.0.0.0/0 10.x.12.1
```

5. Verify the IP and default route with a ping to a VLAN 11 ip address.

```
ICX-Tx-Access2(config)# do ping 10.x.11.1
PING 10.x.11.1 (10.x.11.1) 100(128) bytes of data.
108 bytes from 10.x.11.1: icmp_seq=1 ttl=64 time=0.207 ms
...
```

6. Enable the port to PC4 connected on Access2. Make it a member of VLAN 11 so that PC4 simulates a PC connected to a phone (simulated by Access2) (untagged VLAN 11 PC traffic passing Access2 to Access1).

```
ICX-Tx-Access2(config)# int 1/1/4
ICX-Tx-Access2(config-if)# vlan access 11
ICX-Tx-Access2(config-if)# no shutdown
ICX-Tx-Access2(config-if)# exit
```

7. On PC4, bounce the **'Lab NIC'** to refresh the IP address.

Task 2: Port Classification—Trust Configuration

Objectives

- Access2 is used as a test device to send DSCP marked traffic
- Access1 is where the QOS configuration is applied to deal with the incoming marks
- Review the default QOS trust mode on Access1
- Adjust the default global trust mode and verify the result

Steps

Send normal and marked packets from Access2 to PC3 and verify these using Wireshark.

Default QOS Behavior with Marked Traffic

1. On Access1, enter the configuration mode and clear the interface statistics on ports 1/1/3 (PC) and LAG256 (uplink to the VSX core).

```
ICX-Tx-Access1(config)# do clear interface statistics
```

Note

The lab is using this generic clear interface statistics for simplicity, a more selective clear is available per interface, for example: *do clear interface 1/1/3 statistics*.

Note

In the AOS-CX release used in the lab, the **'clear interface statistics'** command may need to be executed again to be effective.

2. On Core1, enter the configuration mode and clear the interface statistics.

```
ICX-Tx-Core1(config)# do clear interface statistics
```

3. Repeat this on Core2.

```
ICX-Tx-Core2(config)# do clear interface statistics
```

4. Review the current Queue statistics on, for example port 1/1/3, this is the port connected to PC3. Most queues should have statistics that are close to 0.

```
ICX-Tx-Access1(config)# show interface 1/1/3 queues
Interface 1/1/3 is up
 Admin state is up
                Tx Bytes       Tx Packets        Tx Errors
 Q0                    0                0                0
 Q1                    0                0                0
 Q2                    0                0                0
 Q3                    0                0                0
 Q4                    0                0                0
 Q5                    0                0                0
 Q6                    0                0                0
 Q7                  123                1                0
```

Note

If the statistics are not close to 0, you should repeat the 'clear interface statistics' command and verify the queue counters again.

Note

Clearing the queue statistics makes it easier to troubleshoot and understand what traffic is sent via which queue. Feel free to repeat the clear statistics command in case tests need to be repeated.

Note

The switch will automatically send L2 control protocols via Q7; normal user frames will be sent on Q1 by default.

5. Open a connection to PC3 (connected to Access1 port 1/1/3). Check and take note of the IP address (it should have an IP address in VLAN 11); you will need this IP address in the next steps on PC-Access2. IP address of PC3: ____________.

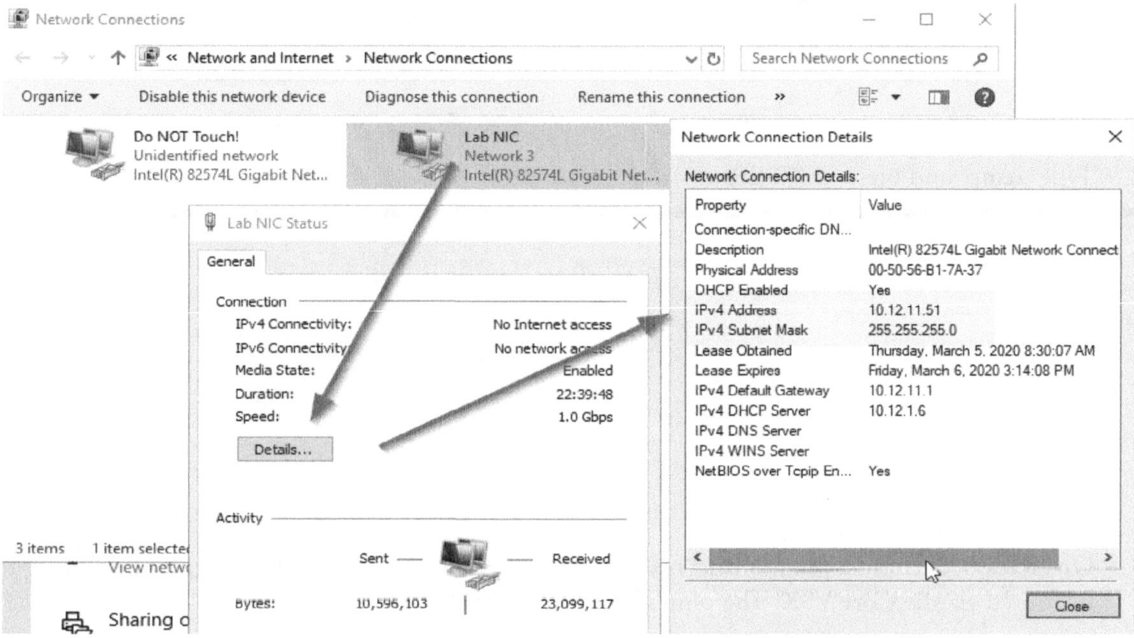

6. Start Wireshark.

7. Double-click the '**Lab NIC**' interface to start a new trace.

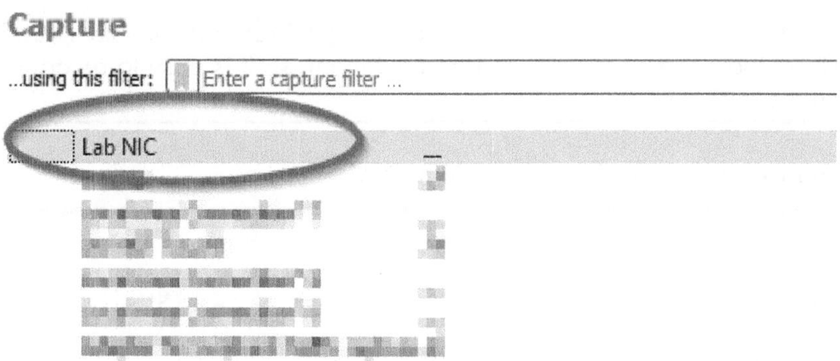

Apply a Display Filter for ICMP Traffic

1. Click in the 'Apply display filter' field.

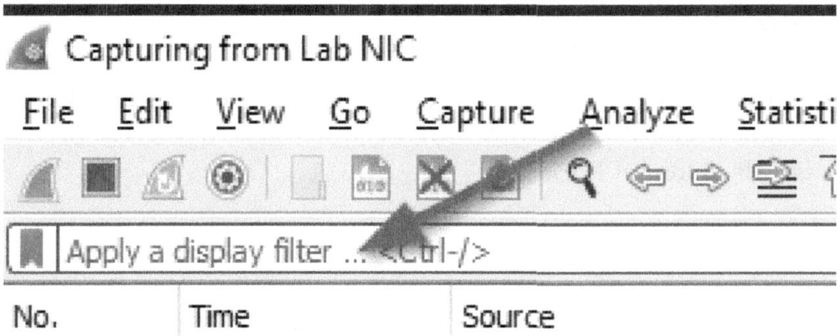

2. Type **'icmp'** and press <**ENTER**>.

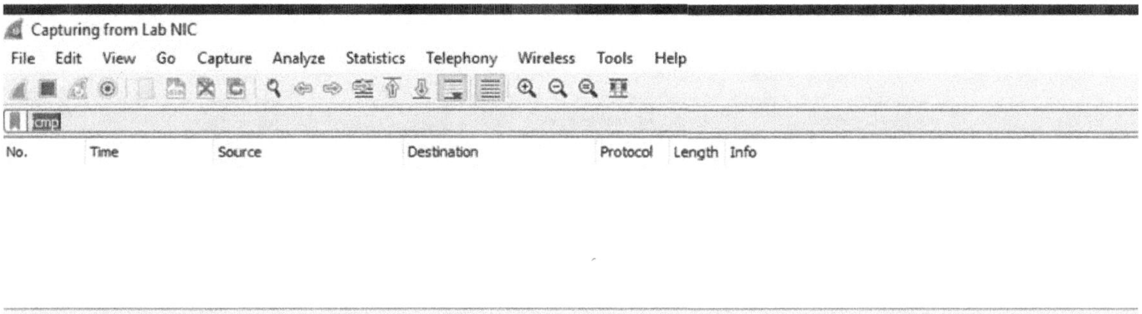

3. On Access2, perform a ping to PC3 on Access1. Access2 has an IP in VLAN12, so this ping will be routed via the Core VSX. The ping should be successful.

```
ICX-Tx-Access2(config)# do ping 10.x.11.y datagram-size 14000 repetitions 10
```

Note

Any ping is fine for this lab, the above ping, using 10 requests of size 14000 generates about 100 outbound packets (due to fragmentation), so it is easy to recognize these test packets in the statistics.

4. On PC3 (connected to Access1), stop the Wireshark capture.

5. Click on packet with source IP of the Access2 (10.x.12.100); open the **'Internet Protocol'** and **'Differentiated Services Codepoint'** sections. Check the DSCP value. Since no configuration was done, this should be Default (0) at this point.

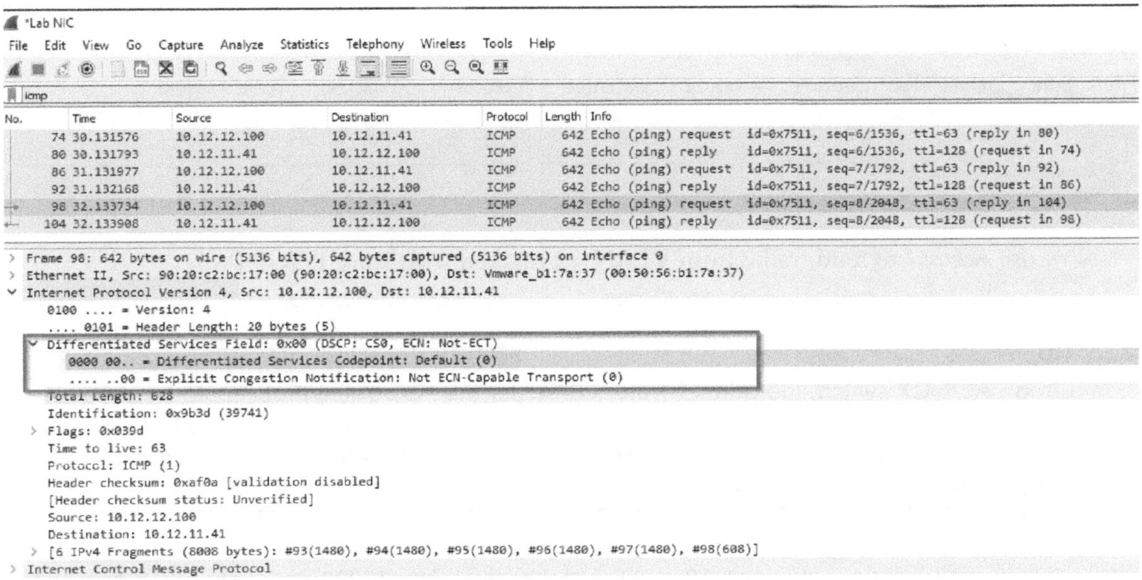

6. On Access1, review the interface 1/1/3 statistics; this traffic should have been sent out using the 'normal' queue. There should be about 100 packets in the Q1 at this moment.

```
ICX-Tx-Access1(config)# show interface 1/1/3 queues
Interface 1/1/3 is up
 Admin state is up
                    Tx Bytes       Tx Packets       Tx Errors
 Q0                        0                0               0
Q1                   144420             106              0
 Q2                        0                0               0
 Q3                        0                0               0
 Q4                        0                0               0
 Q5                        0                0               0
 Q6                        0                0               0
 Q7                     1599               13               0
```

Note

The PC may be generating some other traffic, so the statistics will typically have some variation.

Marked Voice Traffic

1. On PC3 (connected to Access1), start the Wireshark trace. Click **'Continue without saving'** to start the trace.

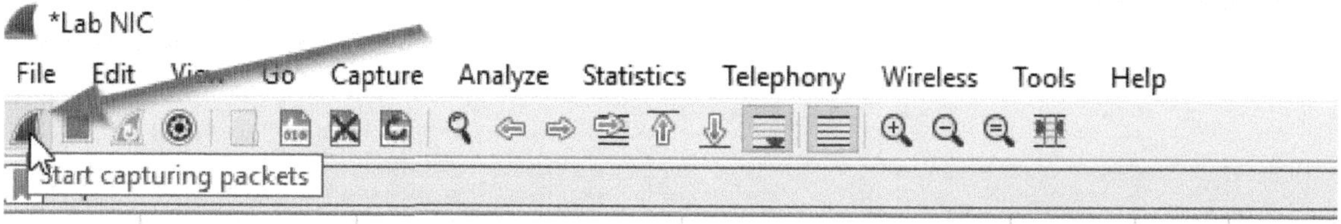

2. Now use Access2 to send traffic from VLAN 12 marked with voice DSCP (46).

Tip

On an AOS-CX switch, the administrator can enter the TOS value that should be used for the outgoing ICMP packets.The binary value for DSCP 46 is '101110'. The IP TOS field has 2 extra bits at the end, so the complete value is '**101110**00'. Converted into decimal, this results in value 184.

```
ICX-Tx-Access2(config)# do ping 10.x.11.y datagram-size 17000 repetitions 8 tos 184
```

3. On the receiving PC, verify the received marked traffic. In Wireshark, stop the trace and verify the incoming DSCP value of the ICMP request (make sure to select a request, not the reply).

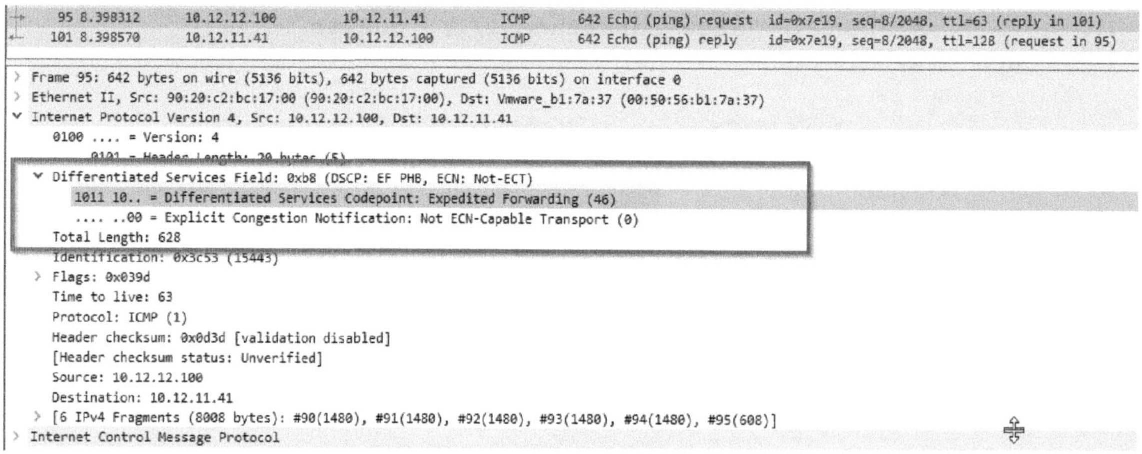

4. On Access1, review statistics on the queues; it should still be normal traffic, even when marked with the DSCP value for voice.

```
ICX-Tx-Access1(config)# show interface 1/1/3 queues
Interface 1/1/3 is up
 Admin state is up
                  Tx Bytes      Tx Packets       Tx Errors
 Q0                      0               0               0
Q1                  283510             238               0
 Q2                      0               0               0
 Q3                      0               0               0
 Q4                      0               0               0
 Q5                      0               0               0
 Q6                      0               0               0
 Q7                   1860              14               0
```

Enable Global DSCP Trust

In the next steps, QOS trust mode on the switches will be set to globally trust the incoming DSCP value. This will ensure that the switch will inspect every incoming packet for a DSCP value, and apply it to the correct local-mapping based on the DSCP map.

1. On Access1, enable the global DSCP trust option.

```
ICX-Tx-Access1(config)# qos trust dscp
```

2. Clear the port counters on Access1.

```
ICX-Tx-Access1(config)# do clear interface statistics
```

3. On Access2, repeat the ping (use the up arrow to get the previous command).

```
do ping 10.x.11.y datagram-size 14000 repetitions 10 tos 184
```

4. Once the ping has completed, review the queue statistics on the Access1 switch.

```
ICX-Tx-Access1(config)# show interface 1/1/3 queues
Interface 1/1/3 is up
 Admin state is up
                  Tx Bytes      Tx Packets       Tx Errors
 Q0                      0               0               0
 Q1                    476               7               0
 Q2                      0               0               0
 Q3                      0               0               0
 Q4                      0               0               0
 Q5                 144280             100               0
 Q6                      0               0               0
 Q7                   2475              20               0
```

5. The DSCP marking of the traffic did not change, but now the switch is using this mark in the incoming packet to assign them to the correct local-priority, which is assigned to queue 5.

Trust End-to-End

The Core VSX also needs to trust DSCP to ensure packets are assigned to the correct queue. It is a best practice to enable global **qos trust dscp** for VSX on Core 1 and Core2 and review the traffic assignment.

1. Enable the global trust on Core1.

```
ICX-Tx-Core1(config)# qos trust dscp
```

2. Repeat this step on Core2.

```
ICX-Tx-Core2(config)# qos trust dscp
```

3. On Access2, repeat the ping (use the up arrow to get the previous command).

```
do ping 10.x.11.y datagram-size 14000 repetitions 10 tos 184
```

4. Review the lag1 (LAG to Access1) queue statistics. You should see that some traffic was sent into Queue 5.

```
ICX-Tx-Core1# show interface lag1 queues
 Aggregate-name lag1
 Aggregated-interfaces :
 1/1/1
 Speed 10000 Mb/s
                     Tx Bytes          Tx Packets          Tx Errors
 Q0                         0                   0                  0
 Q1                     84480                 331                  0
 Q2                         0                   0                  0
 Q3                         0                   0                  0
 Q4                         0                   0                  0
 Q5                    132160                 100                  0
 Q6                       992                   8                  0
 Q7                      3670                  29                  0
```

5. In case there is no traffic stats in queue5, check the command for the peer VSX system, since the link-aggregation on Access1 may have sent the traffic to Core2.

```
ICX-Tx-Core1# show interface lag1 queues vsx-peer
 Aggregate-name lag1
 Aggregated-interfaces :
 1/1/1
 Speed 10000 Mb/s
                  Tx Bytes        Tx Packets        Tx Errors
 Q0                      0                 0                0
 Q1                4566671             29284                0
 Q2                      0                 0                0
 Q3                      0                 0                0
 Q4                      0                 0                0
 Q5                 132160               100                0
 Q6                  89836              1266                0
 Q7                1318752             10425                0
```

Task 3: LLDP Device Profile for QOS Trust

Objectives

Some customers may prefer to control the DSCP and queue assignment using classifiers and policies, so they may not want to enable the global QoS trust DSCP on the access switches.

However, an Aruba controlled AP (this is an AP connected to a Mobility Controller [MC]) can use this DSCP mark as well. It will send wireless traffic over an IP GRE tunnel to the MC and, based on the configuration, the wireless QOS may be copied into the IP DSCP mark. This ensures a high-priority wireless packet can also be recognized as a high-priority packet on the path between the AP and the MC. In this case, the switch should trust the DSCP mark if the traffic comes from a port with an Aruba AP connected.

AOS-CX switches support this scenario using LLDP-based device profiles. The LLDP device trust allows the administrator to leave the global trust level to 'none', since the switch will automatically set the port trust to DSCP when a matching LLDP device is discovered on a switch port.

Steps

Configure a device profile with LLDP trust settings. Use the Access2 Switch to simulate an LLDP device profile to test the device profile.

1. On Access1, remove the global trust DSCP.

```
ICX-Tx-Access1(config)# qos trust none
```

2. Clear statistics and verify incoming marked DSCP traffic is not trusted anymore. Ping test from Access2 should arrive in normal queue (Q1) again.

```
ICX-Tx-Access1(config)# do clear interface statistics
```

3. Repeat the test ping on Access2.

```
do ping 10.x.11.y datagram-size 14000 repetitions 10 tos 184
```

4. Verify on Access1 that the traffic is handled in the normal queue again.

```
ICX-Tx-Access1(config)# show interface lag255 queues
Aggregate-name lag255
 Aggregated-interfaces :
 1/1/25  1/1/26
 Speed 20000 Mb/s
                   Tx Bytes      Tx Packets        Tx Errors
 Q0                       0               0                0
 Q1                  317172             223                0
 Q2                       0               0                0
 Q3                       0               0                0
 Q4                       0               0                0
 Q5                       0               0                0
 Q6                       0               0                0
 Q7                    1240              10                0
```

5. Review the default port trust mode.

```
ICX-Tx-Access1(config)# show interface 1/1/27
Interface 1/1/27 is up
 Admin state is up
 Link transitions: 5
 Description:
 Hardware: Ethernet, MAC Address: 88:3a:30:98:30:ce
 MTU 1500
 Type SFP+DAC1
 Full-duplex
qos trust none
 Speed 10000 Mb/s
 Auto-negotiation is off
 Flow-control: off
```

Configure the Device Profile

6. On Access1, configure the LLDP device profile role with DSCP trust.

```
ICX-Tx-Access1(config)# port-access role demo-lldp-switch
ICX-Tx-Access1(config-pa-role)# trust-mode dscp
ICX-Tx-Access1(config-pa-role)# exit
```

7. Configure the LLDP device profile with an LLDP group for Aruba OS-CX switches. In a real deployment, this would be an Aruba AP, but the Access2 switch is used to simulate the behavior.

```
ICX-Tx-Access1(config)# port-access lldp-group demo-switch
ICX-Tx-Access1(config-lldp-group)# match sys-desc JL668A
ICX-Tx-Access1(config-lldp-group)# exit
ICX-Tx-Access1(config)# port-access device-profile dev-aoscx-switch
ICX-Tx-Access1(config-device-profile)# associate role demo-lldp-switch
ICX-Tx-Access1(config-device-profile)# associate lldp-group demo-switch
ICX-Tx-Access1(config-device-profile)# enable
ICX-Tx-Access1(config-device-profile)# exit
```

8. Verify the LLDP profile has been applied to the port 1/1/27.

```
ICX-Tx-Access1(config)# show port-access device-profile interface all
Port 1/1/27, Neighbor-Mac  88:3a:30:97:b6:00
    Profile Name:             : dev-aoscx-switch
    LLDP Group:               : demo-switch
    CDP Group:                :
    Role:                     : demo-lldp-switch
    State:                    : applied
    Failure Reason:           :
```

9. Verify the changed port QOS trust mode.

```
ICX-Tx-Access1(config)# show interface 1/1/27
Interface 1/1/27 is up
 Admin state is up
 Link transitions: 1
 Description:
 Hardware: Ethernet, MAC Address: 88:3a:30:98:30:ce
 MTU 1500
 Type SFP+DAC1
 Full-duplex
qos trust dscp
 Speed 10000 Mb/s
 Auto-negotiation is off
 Flow-control: off
 Error-control: off
 VLAN Mode: native-untagged
 Native VLAN: 11
 Allowed VLAN List: 11-12
```

10. Repeat the test ping on Access2.

```
do ping 10.x.11.y datagram-size 14000 repetitions 10 tos 184
```

11. Check queue statistics of interface lag255 on Access1; the traffic should now appear in Queue 5 again.

```
ICX-Tx-Access1(config)# show interface lag255 queues
 Aggregate-name lag256
 Aggregated-interfaces :
 1/1/25  1/1/26
 Speed 20000 Mb/s
                       Tx Bytes       Tx Packets        Tx Errors
 Q0                           0                0                0
 Q1                      201464              165                0
 Q2                           0                0                0
 Q3                           0                0                0
 Q4                           0                0                0
 Q5                      144280              100                0
 Q6                           0                0                0
 Q7                        2680               20                0
```

12. This demonstrates how the AOS-CX switch can dynamically enable QOS DSCP trust based on the LLDP neighbor, such as an Aruba AP.

13. Lab cleanup: Disable the LLDP profile.

```
ICX-Tx-Access1(config)# port-access device-profile dev-aoscx-switch
ICX-Tx-Access1(config-device-profile)# disable
ICX-Tx-Access1(config-device-profile)# exit
```

Task 4: QOS Classification

Objectives

In this task, the classifier-based QOS will be demonstrated. The purpose of the classifier is to provide the administrator a mechanism to remark and classify traffic in case the endpoint cannot perform the marking by itself, or the endpoint is not trusted to perform the marking.

In this task, traffic from the Voice VLAN 12 will be changed for these two scenarios:

- **Voice to Voice**: Traffic coming from the simulated voice VLAN 12 to other VLAN 12 hosts will be re-marked as DSCP 46, so even when an unmarked ping is done, the traffic will be marked with value 46.

- **Voice to other**: Traffic coming from the simulated voice VLAN 12 to any other destination will be re-marked as DSCP AF41. This is just an example mark to demonstrate the feature.

Steps

To use the classifier-based QOS, the administrator should complete these steps:

- Define the classes
- Assign the classes into a policy and set actions
- Bind the policy to an interface or VLAN

Define the Classes

1. On Access1, define a new class for the voice to voice traffic; set the count option as well to get class statistics on matched traffic. The 'VLAN' keyword applies the given VLAN ID as additional condition. In the IP class definition, wildcard masks are supported. On some platforms, wildcard masks are inversed bits. For AOC-CX, the wildcard mask is using the same logic as a ***normal*** subnet mask, so a 1 bit to match, 0 bit to ignore the value.Therefore, 10.0.12.0/0.255.0.255 means traffic:
   - matching '10' in first byte
   - with any value in second byte
   - matching '12' in the third byte
   - with any value in the fourth byte

```
ICX-Tx-Access1(config)# class ip voice-dst-voice
ICX-Tx-Access1(config-class-ip)# 10 match any any 10.0.12.0/255.0.255.0
vlan 12 count
ICX-Tx-Access1(config-class-ip)# exit
```

2. Define a new class for the voice to any traffic with the count option.

```
ICX-Tx-Access1(config)# class ip voice-dst-any
ICX-Tx-Access1(config-class-ip)# 10 match any any any vlan 12 count
ICX-Tx-Access1(config-class-ip)# exit
```

Define the Policy and Assign Actions to the Classes

Now combine the traffic classes into a policy with actions. For the voice to voice traffic, a remark action of DSCP value 46 (EF) will be set.For the voice to any traffic, a remark action of DSCP value 34 (AF41) will be set.

1. Define the policy.

```
ICX-Tx-Access1(config)# policy access
ICX-Tx-Access1(config-policy)# 10 class ip voice-dst-voice action dscp EF
ICX-Tx-Access1(config-policy)# 20 class ip voice-dst-any action dscp AF41
ICX-Tx-Access1(config-policy)# exit
```

Apply the Policy

A policy can be applied at various levels (global/VLAN/interface). In this lab, the policy will be applied at the interface level.

1. On the port connected to the Access2, apply the QOS policy on the inbound traffic.

```
ICX-Tx-Access1(config)# interface 1/1/27
ICX-Tx-Access1(config-if)# apply policy access in
ICX-Tx-Access1(config-if)# exit
```

2. Review the applied policy on port 1/1/27.

```
ICX-Tx-Access1(config)# show policy interface 1/1/27
Direction
           Name
           Additional Policy Parameters
  Sequence Comment
           Class Type
                    action
--------------------------------------------------------------------
Inbound
           access
       10
           voice-dst-voice ipv4
dscp EF
       20
           voice-dst-any ipv4
dscp AF41
```

Verify Marking and Queuing for Voice to Data Scenario

In the next steps, the result of the configuration will be verified.

1. Prepare the test:
    - On the PC3, connected to Access1, start a Wireshark trace
    - On Access1, clear the interface statistics (run the command twice)

```
do clear interface statistics
```

2. On the Access2, run the ping to this PC (voice to any) without marking the traffic (so **no tos** in the command). The unmarked traffic should be remarked by the policy.

```
ICX-Tx-Access2(config)# do ping 10.x.11.y datagram-size 14000 repetition 10
```

3. On Access1, verify that the traffic has matched the policy by checking the hit counts of the policy. The number **100** in this example output is the number of packets that have matched the class in the policy.

```
ICX-Tx-Access1(config)# show policy hit counts access
Statistics for Policy access:
Interface 1/1/27* (in):
           Hit Count  Configuration
10 class ip voice-dst-voice action dscp EF
0  10 match any any 10.0.12.0/0.255.0.255 vlan 12 count
20 class ip voice-dst-any action dscp AF41
100  10 match any anyanyvlan 12 count
* policy statistics are shared among each context type (interface, VLAN).
  For routed ingress, they are only shared within the same VRF.
  Use 'policy NAME copy' to create a new policy for separate statistics.
```

4. On the PC, stop the Wireshark trace and check the inbound DSCP value. This should be AF41.

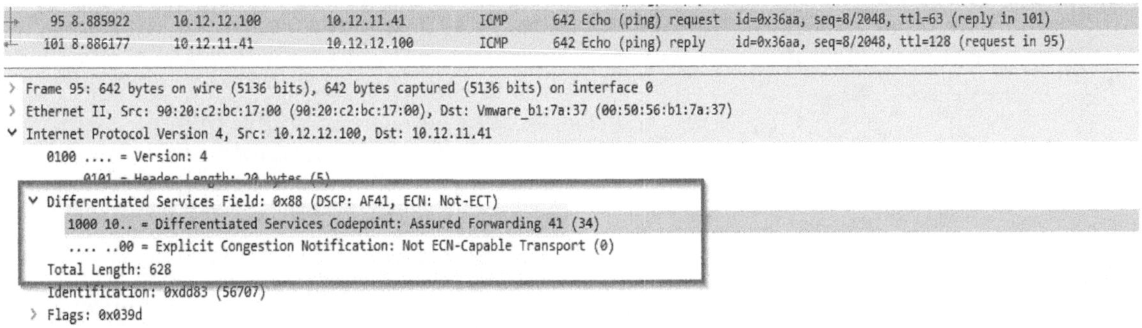

5. Now verify if the traffic was handled by the correct Queue on Access1.

```
ICX-Tx-Access1(config)# show interface 1/1/3 queues
Interface 1/1/3 is up
 Admin state is up
                 Tx Bytes      Tx Packets      Tx Errors
 Q0                     0               0              0
 Q1                144824             108              0
 Q2                     0               0              0
 Q3                     0               0              0
 Q4                     0               0              0
 Q5                     0               0              0
 Q6                     0               0              0
 Q7                  3966              32              0
```

Question: Why is the traffic sent out in the 'normal' queue (Q1), instead of Q4 (the expected Queue for AF41 traffic).

Answer: Check the global QOS trust setting.

6. Review the global trust option.

```
ICX-Tx-Access1(config)# show qos trust
qos trust none
```

7. Adjust the global trust to DSCP.

```
ICX-Tx-Access1(config)# qos trust dscp
ICX-Tx-Access1(config)# show qos trust
qos trust dscp
```

8. Repeat the ping test from Access2 to the PC.
9. On Access1, the traffic should now be visible in Q4.

```
ICX-Tx-Access1(config)# show interface 1/1/3 queues
Interface 1/1/3 is up
Admin state is up
                      Tx Bytes        Tx Packets          Tx Errors
 Q0                          0                 0                  0
 Q1                     160626               332                  0
 Q2                          0                 0                  0
 Q3                          0                 0                  0
 Q4                     144280               100                  0
 Q5                          0                 0                  0
 Q6                          0                 0                  0
 Q7                     122144               988                  0
```

Verify Marking and Queuing for Voice to Voice Scenario

In the next section, traffic from voice to voice will be verified. This will be tested with a basic ping to the default gateway in the voice VLAN (10.x.12.1).

1. Prepare the test: on Access1, clear the interface statistics.

```
ICX-Tx-Access1(config)# do clear interface statistics
```

2. On Access2, ping to the voice default gateway (10.x.12.1) without marking the traffic.

```
ICX-Tx-Access2(config)# do ping 10.x.12.1 datagram-size 8000 repetitions 8
```

3. On Access1, verify the traffic matched by checking the hit counts of the policy.

```
ICX-Tx-Access1(config)# show policy hit counts access
Statistics for Policy access:
Interface 1/1/27* (in):
           Hit Count  Configuration
10 class ip voice-dst-voice action dscp EF
100  10 match any any 10.0.12.0/255.0.255.0 vlan 12 count
20 class ip voice-dst-any action dscp AF41
100  10 match any anyanyvlan 12 count
* policy statistics are shared among each context type (interface, VLAN).
  For routed ingress, they are only shared within the same VRF.
  Use 'policy NAME copy' to create a new policy for separate statistics.
```

4. Now verify that the traffic was assigned to the correct queue on the uplink interface.

```
ICX-Tx-Access1(config)# show interface lag255 queues
 Aggregate-name lag255
 Aggregated-interfaces :
 1/1/25  1/1/26
 Speed 20000 Mb/s
                 Tx Bytes      Tx Packets       Tx Errors
 Q0                     0               0               0
 Q1                335639             305               0
 Q2                     0               0               0
 Q3                     0               0               0
 Q4                     0               0               0
 Q5                     0               0               0
 Q6                     0               0               0
 Q7                  6432              48               0
```

Question: Why would the traffic be assigned to the normal queue?

Answer: In the previous section, the QOS global trust was enabled, however, that does not seem to affect the current setup. This is because any traffic that matches a policy will not be considered to be trusted, so it is not automatically assigned to a queue based on the trust map.

In the previous section, the trust did work, since the traffic was first sent to the VSX core (to be routed between the voice and data VLAN), so when the traffic was sent back from the Core to the Access1 switch, the global 'qos trust dscp' ensured that the incoming DSCP mark was used to assign the packet to the correct queue.

In the current example, the incoming traffic on 1/1/27 matches a policy, the policy remarks the DSCP, but the policy did not apply a local priority to the traffic. Therefore, although the DSCP remark was done, the packet was still considered 'normal' inside the switch.

In the next section, the policy will be adjusted to apply both the DSCP mark and the local priority.

1. To summarize: Any match on an entry in a policy overrules the trust, so the administrator should assign a local priority as well.

Note

This also applied to the previous section, if the uplink LAG255 statistics would have been checked, it would have showed that the traffic was sent in the normal queue, even with the **'qos trust dscp'** enabled.

Adjust the policy to mark and local policy

1. Enter the policy context, review the current configuration.

```
ICX-Tx-Access1(config)# policy access
ICX-Tx-Access1(config-policy)# show running-config current-context
policy access
    10 class ip voice-dst-voice action dscp EF
    20 class ip voice-dst-any action dscp AF41
```

2. Update the policy to include the local-priority action. Make sure to use the line numbers (10 and 20) in the commands. Otherwise, additional configuration lines would be added and the traffic would still match the original first line.

```
ICX-Tx-Access1(config-policy)# 10 class ip voice-dst-voice action
dscp EF action local-priority 5
ICX-Tx-Access1(config-policy)#  20 class ip voice-dst-any action dscp
AF41 action local-priority 4
```

3. Review the updated configuration. Make sure there are only.

```
ICX-Tx-Access1(config-policy)# show running-config current-context
policy access
    10 class ip voice-dst-voice action local-priority 5 action dscp EF
    20 class ip voice-dst-any action local-priority 4 action dscp AF41
ICX-Tx-Access1(config-policy)# exit
```

Note

If you would have added additional lines, these can be removed using 'no' + the line number. Example:

```
ICX-Tx-Access1(config-policy)# no 30
```

---

4. On Access1, check the LAG255 queue statistics.

```
ICX-Tx-Access1(config)# show interface lag255 queues
 Aggregate-name lag255
 Aggregated-interfaces :
 1/1/25  1/1/26
 Speed 20000 Mb/s
                  Tx Bytes       Tx Packets        Tx Errors
 Q0                      0                0                0
 Q1                 146504              197                0
 Q2                      0                0                0
 Q3                      0                0                0
 Q4                    384                4                0
 Q5                      0                0                0
 Q6                      0                0                0
 Q7                  23584              176                0
```

5. And repeat the command. The output will now automatically repeat every 2 seconds.

```
ICX-Tx-Access1(config)# do repeat
```

6. On Access2, repeat the verification test with a ping without mark to the default gateway.

```
ICX-Tx-Access2(config)# do ping 10.x.12.1 datagram-size 8000 repetitions 8
```

7. On Access1, check the LAG255 queue statistics; traffic should pass over Q5 now.

```
****************************************
Iteration : 6 Command : show interface lag256 queues
****************************************
 Aggregate-name lag256
 Aggregated-interfaces :
 1/1/25  1/1/26
 Speed 20000 Mb/s
                  Tx Bytes       Tx Packets        Tx Errors
 Q0                      0                0                0
 Q1                 149021              211                0
 Q2                      0                0                0
 Q3                      0                0                0
 Q4                    384                4                0
 Q5                 144280              100                0
 Q6                      0                0                0
 Q7                  27336              204                0
```

8. Use <CTRL>-C to stop the repeat. This demonstrates the use of classifiers, policies, and actions.

Task 5: Queue configuration

Objectives

In this task, the queue configuration and priority mappings will be reviewed. The priority mapping tables allow the administrator to customize the trust maps:

- DSCP to COS mapping
- COS to local-priority mapping

With the queue configuration, the administrator can control to which queue each of the local-priority values will be mapped.

With a schedule profile, the administrator can control the relative bandwidth of each of the queues and the type of scheduling, such as strict priority or DWRR.

Steps

- Review default statistics
- Change queue profile
- Apply queue profile
- Change schedule profile
- Apply schedule profile

Review default DSCP to local-priority mapping

1. On Access1, review the default QOS DSCP map. Notice how each DSCP code point is mapped to a local priority on the switch. This local priority will be used to assign the packet to a queue. This map is used for any incoming traffic on ports with '**qos trust dscp**' (based on interface, global or dynamic with LLDP or port-access).

```
ICX-Tx-Access1(config)# show qos dscp-map
DSCP     code_pointlocal_priority cos color   name
-------- ---------- ------------- --- ------- ----
000000   0          1                 green   CS0
000001   1          1                 green
000010   2          1                 green
000011   3          1                 green
000100   4          1                 green
000101   5          1                 green
000110   6          1                 green
000111   7          1                 green
001000   8          0                 green   CS1
```

001001	9	0	green	
001010	10	0	green	AF11
001011	11	0	green	
001100	12	0	yellow	AF12
001101	13	0	green	
001110	14	0	yellow	AF13
001111	15	0	green	
010000	16	2	green	CS2
010001	17	2	green	
010010	18	2	green	AF21
010011	19	2	green	
010100	20	2	yellow	AF22
010101	21	2	green	
010110	22	2	yellow	AF23
010111	23	2	green	
011000	24	3	green	CS3
011001	25	3	green	
011010	26	3	green	AF31
011011	27	3	green	
011100	28	3	yellow	AF32
011101	29	3	green	
011110	30	3	yellow	AF33
011111	31	3	green	
100000	32	4	green	CS4
100001	33	4	green	
100010	34	4	green	AF41
100011	35	4	green	
100100	36	4	yellow	AF42
100101	37	4	green	
100110	38	4	yellow	AF43
100111	39	4	green	
101000	40	5	green	CS5
101001	41	5	green	
101010	42	5	green	
101011	43	5	green	
101100	44	5	green	
101101	45	5	green	
101110	46	5	green	EF
101111	47	5	green	
110000	48	6	green	CS6
110001	49	6	green	
110010	50	6	green	
110011	51	6	green	
110100	52	6	green	
110101	53	6	green	

```
110110    54         6                  green
110111    55         6                  green
111000    56         7                  green    CS7
111001    57         7                  green
111010    58         7                  green
111011    59         7                  green
111100    60         7                  green
111101    61         7                  green
111110    62         7                  green
111111    63         7                  green
```

Question: What is the local priority that would be assigned to traffic marked with DSCP 46 (EF), typically used for voice?

Answer: DSCP 46 will be mapped to local-priority 5.

Question: What is the local priority that would be assigned to traffic without DSCP mark (0)?

Answer: DSCP CS0 will be mapped to local-priority 1.

Note

The DSCP map also shows the drop precedence level option as color code (green/yellow); however, this is beyond the scope of this book.

2. Review the default COS to local-priority map. This map would be used for ports that have the '**qos trust cos**' command. Most deployments will opt for the DSCP trust instead.

```
ICX-Tx-Access1(config)# show qos cos-map
code_pointlocal_priority color   name
---------- -------------- ------- ----
0          1              green   Best_Effort
1          0              green   Background
2          2              green   Excellent_Effort
3          3              green   Critical_Applications
4          4              green   Video
5          5              green   Voice
6          6              green   Internetwork_Control
7          7              green   Network_Control
```

Question: What is the local priority that would be assigned to traffic without COS mark (0)?

Answer: COS 0 will be mapped to local-priority 1.

Review the Queue Configuration

1. Review the available queue-profiles. Only 1 queue profile can be applied on the switch; this is a switch global option.

```
ICX-Tx-Access1(config)# show qos queue-profile
profile_statusprofile_name
-------------- ------------
applied        factory-default
```

2. Check the details of this queue profile.

```
ICX-Tx-Access1(config)# show qos queue-profile factory-default
queue_numlocal_priorities name
--------- ---------------- ----
0         0                Scavenger_and_backup_data
1         1
2         2
3         3
4         4
5         5
6         6
7         7
```

Question: To which queue will default traffic (local-priority 1) be assigned?

Answer: Default (Best effort) traffic is assigned to queue1 based on this table. This is consistent with the queue statistics that were observed in previous tasks.

Review the Scheduling Profile

In the next steps, the scheduling of the queues will be reviewed. The scheduling profile controls how each queue will be able to send out traffic, relative to other traffic in the queues.

1. Review the current scheduling profiles.

```
ICX-Tx-Access1(config)# show qos schedule-profile
profile_statusprofile_name
-------------- ------------
applied        factory-default
complete       strict
```

2. Check the details of the 'factory-default' profile.

```
ICX-Tx-Access1(config)# show qos schedule-profile factory-default
queue_num algorithm weight max-bandwidth_kbps
--------- --------- ------ ------------------
0         dwrr      1
1         dwrr      1
2         dwrr      1
3         dwrr      1
4         dwrr      1
5         dwrr      1
6         dwrr      1
7         dwrr      1
```

Question: What does the weight indicate?

Answer: The weight is used to measure the 'weight' of the queue when multiple queues need to deliver traffic. For example, when there is only traffic waiting in Q1 and Q5, the total weight at that moment is 1+1, so both Q1 and Q5 would have 1 out of 2, so up to 50% each. In case only Q1 has traffic waiting, the total weight at that moment is 1, so Q1 would have 1 out of 1, so up to 100% of the bandwidth. The result is that each Q has an equal share of the potential bandwidth when required. In case the administrator wants to ensure that a queue needs more (or less) than this equal share, the weight can be adjusted.

Example: Adjustment of the Queue Profile

In this example the schedule profile will be adjusted, so in case of traffic in various queues, these will be the minimum share values of the bandwidth. To make the calculation easy, use a total of 100 for all the queues; this is not a requirement however (Table 13-2). Each individual queue weight can have a value between 1 and 1023. This means: If there is guest traffic (assuming this is assigned to queue 0) with weight 1, and normal traffic, with weight 39, guest would get 1 out of 40 (39+1), so 2.5%.

Table 13-2 Queues and weights.

Queue	Weight
0	1
1	39
2	10
3	10
4	10
5	10
6	10
7	10

1. Define the new profile; assign each queue a value.

```
ICX-Tx-Access1(config)# qos schedule-profile icx
ICX-Tx-Access1(config-schedule)# dwrr queue 0 weight 1
ICX-Tx-Access1(config-schedule)# dwrr queue 1 weight 39
ICX-Tx-Access1(config-schedule)# dwrr queue 2 weight 10
ICX-Tx-Access1(config-schedule)# dwrr queue 3 weight 10
ICX-Tx-Access1(config-schedule)# dwrr queue 4 weight 10
ICX-Tx-Access1(config-schedule)# dwrr queue 5 weight 10
ICX-Tx-Access1(config-schedule)# dwrr queue 6 weight 10
ICX-Tx-Access1(config-schedule)# dwrr queue 7 weight 10
```

2. Review the configuration.

```
ICX-Tx-Access1(config-schedule)# show running-config current-context
qos schedule-profile icx
dwrr queue 0 weight 1
dwrr queue 1 weight 39
dwrr queue 2 weight 10
dwrr queue 3 weight 10
dwrr queue 4 weight 10
dwrr queue 5 weight 10
dwrr queue 6 weight 10
dwrr queue 7 weight 10
```

3. Apply the new schedule profile to queue 1/1/27.

```
ICX-Tx-Access1(config)# interface 1/1/27
ICX-Tx-Access1(config-if)# apply qos schedule-profile icx
ICX-Tx-Access1(config-if)# exit
```

4. Review the schedule profile list.

```
ICX-Tx-Access1(config-if)# show qos schedule-profile
profile_statusprofile_name
-------------- ------------
applied        icx
applied        factory-default
complete       strict
```

Task 6: LLDP-MED and Voice VLAN configuration

Objectives

When phones are connected to the switch that support LLDP-MED, the switch should be configured with the correct voice VLAN. This will ensure that the switch announces this voice VLAN ID using LLDP-MED to the phone, so the phone will automatically send its own traffic with the voice VLAN tag.

The switch can also be configured to control which LLDP TLV (type/length/value) information is sent out. This may be required for security purposes, so the access ports cannot see the firmware version of the device.

Steps

Configure a Voice VLAN

1. On Access1, configure VLAN 12 as the voice VLAN.

```
ICX-Tx-Access1(config)# vlan 12
ICX-Tx-Access1(config-vlan-12)# voice
ICX-Tx-Access1(config-vlan-12)# exit
```

2. Review the active voice VLAN.

```
ICX-Tx-Access1(config)# show vlan voice
---------------------------------------------------------------------
VLAN   Name      Status    Reason    Type      Interfaces
---------------------------------------------------------------------
12     VLAN12    up        ok        static    1/1/27,lag255
```

3. No further configuration is required. The LLDP-MED TLVs are automatically enabled on all interfaces. When an LLDP-MED capable device would come online, the switch will announce the VLAN ID 12 as the voice VLAN.

Review the Advertised TLV Information

1. Review the advertised TLVs.

```
ICX-Tx-Access1(config)# show lldptlv
TLVs Advertised
===============
Management Address
Port Description
Port VLAN-ID
System Capabilities
System Description
System Name
OUI
```

2. On Access2, review the details of the LLDP neighbor on port 1/1/27 (Access1).

```
ICX-Tx-Access2(config)# show lldp neighbor-info 1/1/27
Port                           : 1/1/27
Neighbor Entries               : 1
Neighbor Entries Deleted       : 0
Neighbor Entries Dropped       : 0
Neighbor Entries Aged-Out      : 0
Neighbor Chassis-Name          : ICX-Tx-Access1
Neighbor Chassis-Description   : Aruba JL668A  FL.10.04.0030
Neighbor Chassis-ID            : 88:3a:30:98:30:c0
Neighbor Management-Address    : 10.251.x.4
Chassis Capabilities Available : Bridge, Router
Chassis Capabilities Enabled   : Bridge, Router
Neighbor Port-ID               : 1/1/27
Neighbor Port-Desc             : 1/1/27
Neighbor Port VLAN ID          : 11
TTL                            : 120

Neighbor Mac-Phy details
Neighbor Auto-neg Supported    : true
Neighbor Auto-Neg Enabled      : false
Neighbor Auto-Neg Advertised   : Other
Neighbor MAU type              : 10 GIGBASEER
```

Question: What is the firmware version of the peer switch?

Answer: Based on the output, the version is FL.10.04.0030.

Question: What is the management IP address?

Answer: Based on the output, the management IP is 10.251.x.4.

3. On Access1, change the LLDP configuration, so the Description and management IP are no longer advertised.

```
ICX-Tx-Access1(config)# no lldp select-tlv system-description
ICX-Tx-Access1(config)# no lldp select-tlv management-address
```

4. Wait up to *30* seconds; then check the LLDP neighbors again on Access2.

```
ICX-Tx-Access2(config)# show lldp neighbor-info 1/1/27
Port                           : 1/1/27
Neighbor Entries               : 1
Neighbor Entries Deleted       : 0
Neighbor Entries Dropped       : 0
Neighbor Entries Aged-Out      : 0
Neighbor Chassis-Name          : ICX-Tx-Access1
Neighbor Chassis-Description   :
Neighbor Chassis-ID            : 88:3a:30:98:30:c0
```

```
Neighbor Management-Address     :
Chassis Capabilities Available : Bridge, Router
Chassis Capabilities Enabled   : Bridge, Router
Neighbor Port-ID               : 1/1/27
Neighbor Port-Desc             : 1/1/27
Neighbor Port VLAN ID          : 11
TTL                            : 120

Neighbor Mac-Phy details
Neighbor Auto-neg Supported    : true
Neighbor Auto-Neg Enabled      : false
Neighbor Auto-Neg Advertised   : Other
Neighbor MAU type              : 10 GIGBASEER
```

Learning Check

1. Which classification assigns traffic a QoS mark in the VLAN tag?
   a. DiffServ
   b. ToS
   c. IP precedence
   d. CoS or 802.1p
2. The global QoS trust setting is defined as DSCP, and a port has no trust setting configured on it. How does the port derive the LP and color for incoming traffic?
   a. It looks at the incoming DSCP and maps it to an LP and color with the DSCP map.
   b. It ignores the incoming DSCP and uses LP 0 and color green.
   c. It ignores the incoming DSCP and uses the incoming CoS and CoS map to derive an LP and color.
   d. It looks at the incoming DSCP, maps it to a CoS value with the DSCP map, and then uses the CoS map to assign an LP and color.
3. Which type of scheduling provides very low latency and jitter for high-priority queues but can starve lower priority queues?
   a. DWRR
   b. WRR
   c. WFQ
   d. SP

Summary

Congratulations! Now you have the essential knowledge and skills to implement QoS features on AOS-CX switches. This chapter has presented the need for switches to handle each traffic flow appropriately, depending on the network application, the traffic's business importance, and other, minutely adjustable, criteria. You can now configure AOS-CX switches to prioritize incoming traffic and assign it to the appropriate queue for transmission. And you can mark outgoing traffic with the appropriate QoS value in order to implement a consistent QoS strategy (rate limiting and/or queuing/scheduling) throughout the network. You also learned of the cutting-edge VOQ technology that can effectively be used to alleviate HOL blocking issues in busy campus networks.

14 Additional Routing Technologies

OBJECTIVES

After completing this chapter, you should be able to:

✓ Implement VRF to isolate routed traffic

✓ Manipulate routing with policy-based routing (PBR)

Overview

This chapter introduces two additional layer-3 routing topics. First, you will be introduced to virtual routing forwarding (VRF), which allows a company to logically separate their routing. This is a common practice by service providers, and allows duplicate addressing across the different VRFs. However, a company network sometimes needs this feature, commonly for security purposes.

You will then be introduced to policy-based routing (PBR). PBR allows you to override the path in the routing table based on policy needs dictated by your company.

Virtual Routing and Forwarding (VRF)

In this first section, you will learn how to segregate your routing traffic using VRF. Sometimes this is referred to as "VRF-lite", where other more scalable and complex solutions are available, like EVPN with multi-protocol BGP (MP-BGP), which also provides "VRF" capabilities. This section introduces VRF-lite (EVPN/MP-BGP is beyond the scope of this guide).

Introduction to VRF

Virtual Routing and Forwarding (VRF) is a Layer-3 level isolation to achieve Virtual Private Network (VPN). VRF provides overlapping IPs to present and also isolate the routing table from other VPN in the system (Figure 14-1).

- Creating separate layer-3 networks on the same routing hardware
  - Similar to a virtual private network (VPN)
- Allows different networks (VRFs) to use the same addressing space
- Accomplished using:
  - Assigning interfaces and/or VLANs to separate VRFs
  - Logically separating the routing tables
- Common uses:
  - Creating a separate management plane (out-of-band management)
  - Separating multiple companies' addressing and routing in service provider networks
  - Providing security in data center networks for back-end resources

Figure 14-1 Introduction to VRF

Virtual routing and forwarding (VRF) is a technology that allows multiple instances of a routing table to co-exist within the same router. Because the routing instances are independent, the same or overlapping IP addresses can be used without conflicting with each other. Network functionality is improved because network paths can be segmented without requiring multiple routers.

Common examples where VRF is typically deployed include:

- Separating network management and user campus traffic
- Separating different companies' traffic in a service provider network
- Separating data center traffic for security purposes (for example, back-end storage or database resources from user or Internet traffic)

Different routing protocols can be used to provide logical separation between users and resources. For example, network management can be assigned to one VRF while the rest of the network can be assigned to a separate VRF. In this instance, routes from the management network are unknown to the rest of the network, providing a logical separation between the two; thus, enhancing security. VRFs can be implemented by service providers to logically separate multiple companies' routes within the service provider's network. This allows the provider to support multiple companies while allowing those companies to use the IP addressing scheme that meets their need, even if it would "overlap" with another company's addressing. The overlapping is a non-issue since the addressing is logically separated into different VRFs and thus different routing tables. Likewise, VRFs can be applied to data center networks to logically separate resources for enhanced security. For example, public services could be defined in one VRF and private or internal services defined in a separate VRF. Even though the both sets of services are in the same data center, they are logically separated since their routes are in different routing tables, thus enhancing security.

VRF Management Example

In this example, the network management traffic is being logically separated (from a routing perspective) from the rest of the campus traffic. No additional switches are needed. Two separate VRF instances are used to accomplish this, each with their own, separate routing table. In this example, this logically separates the management and data plane functions for the campus. In the campus VRF, since they cannot "see" the mgmt VRF routes, they cannot reach them: thus, providing a layer of security (Figure 14-2).

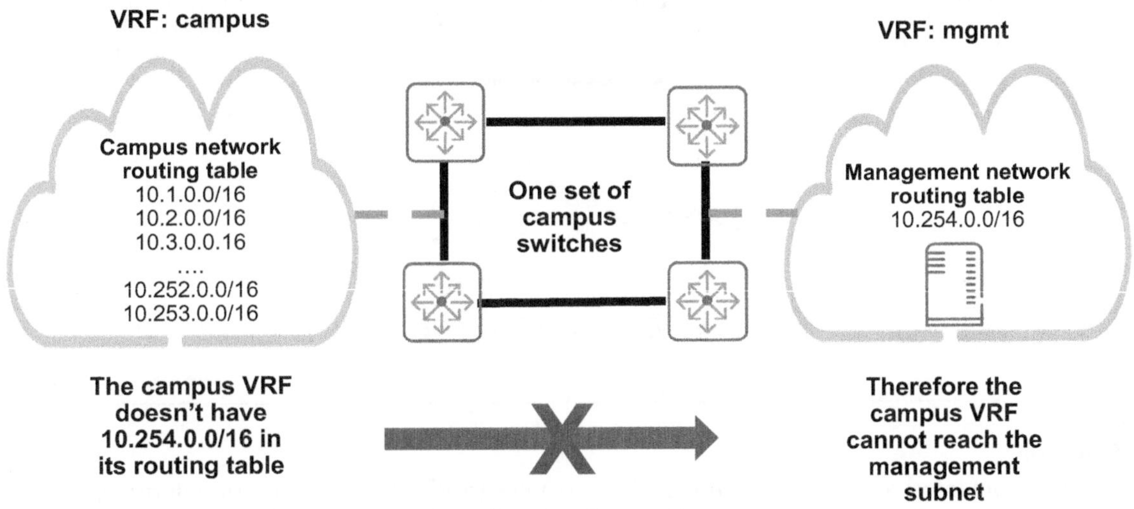

Figure 14-2 VRF Management Example

Note

The reverse is also true: the mgmt VRF does not have the campus routes in its routing table and thus addresses in the mgmt VRF could not reach resources in the campus VRF.

VRF Service Provider Example

In this example, a service provider is using AOS-CX switches and VRF to logically separate two companies, C1 and C2 (Figure 14-3). Notice that even though both companies have an overlapping route, the VRF implementation logically separates the two companies so that they cannot directly interact with each other. By default, the two companies would have to go through an intermediate device, typically a firewall, in order to interact with each other. In the above example, address translation would be required to deal with the overlapping address space. For a service provider, the two companies would have their own public address space and thus would translate their internal address space to a unique public address space in order to interact with other resources in the data center or on the Internet.

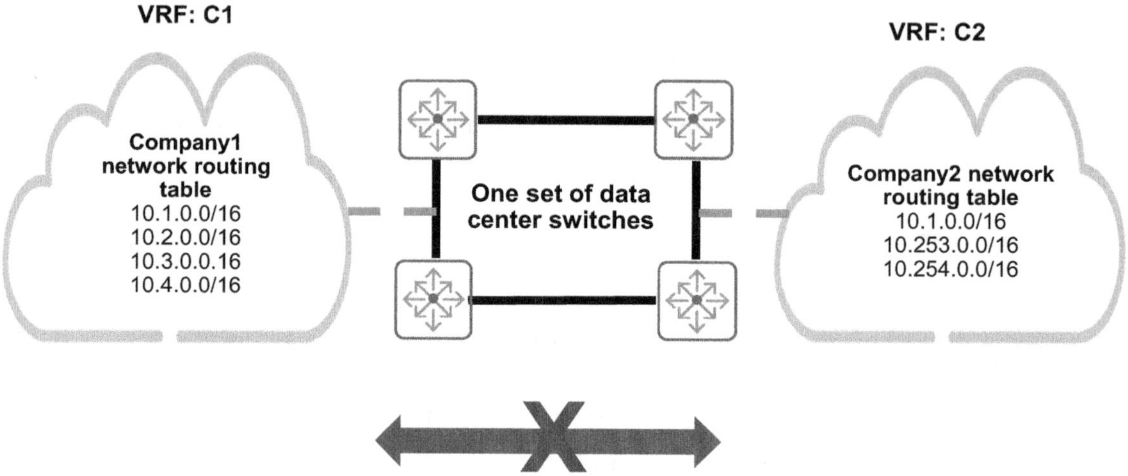

Figure 14-3 VRF Service Provider Example

Note

Different interfaces must be used for the two VRFs (a VRF cannot share an interface).

Creating VRFs

–Create a VRF instance:

```
Switch(config)# vrf <vrf-name>
```

–Assign interfaces to the VRF:

–VLAN:

```
Switch(config)# vlan <VLAN-ID>
Switch(config-vlan)# vrf attach <vrf-name>
```

–Layer-3 interface:

```
Switch(config)# interface <interface-ID>
Switch(config-if)# vrf attach <vrf-name>
```

Figure 14-4 Creating VRFs

To create a VRF, as shown in Figure 14-4, use the following command:

```
Switch(config)# vrf <vrf-name>
```

The VRF name can be up to 32 alphanumeric characters. You are allowed a total of 65 VRFs on your routing switch. By default, two exist on the switch:

- **default**: this is what the routing switch uses if you do not specify a VRF with a configuration command
- **mgmt**: this can be used for out-of-band management (OBBM)

Which means that you can create an additional 63 VRFs.

To attach a port to a VRF, enter the following command in the required context. For a VLAN:

```
Switch(config)# vlan <VLAN-ID>
Switch(config-vlan)# vrf attach <vrf-name>
```

For a layer-3 (routed) interface:

```
Switch(config)# interface <interface-ID>
Switch(config-if)# vrf attach <vrf-name>
```

Note

An interface can only belong to one VRF.

Implementing Routing with VRFs

Many routing switch commands allow you to specify the VRF name that the command should be used with. In the slide (Figure 14-5), you can see that this can be done with static or OSPF routing,

–Assign routing to a VRF instance:

– Static:

```
Switch(config)# ip route <network-ID>/<0-32>
                    <next-hop-IP-address> vrf <vrf-name>
```

– OSPF:

```
Switch(config)# router ospf <OSPF-instance> vrf <vrf-name>
```

Figure 14-5 Implementing Routing with VRFs

but there are many, many other commands that allow you to reference a VRF name and thus compartmentalize your routing functions. The same applies to **show** commands.

> **Note**
>
> If a switch command allows the optional VRF name reference, and you do not configure it, then the command applies to the VRF name called *default*.

Policy-Based Routing (PBR)

In this second section, you will learn how to implement simple PBR policies to override the routing information found in the routing table.

Introduction to PBR

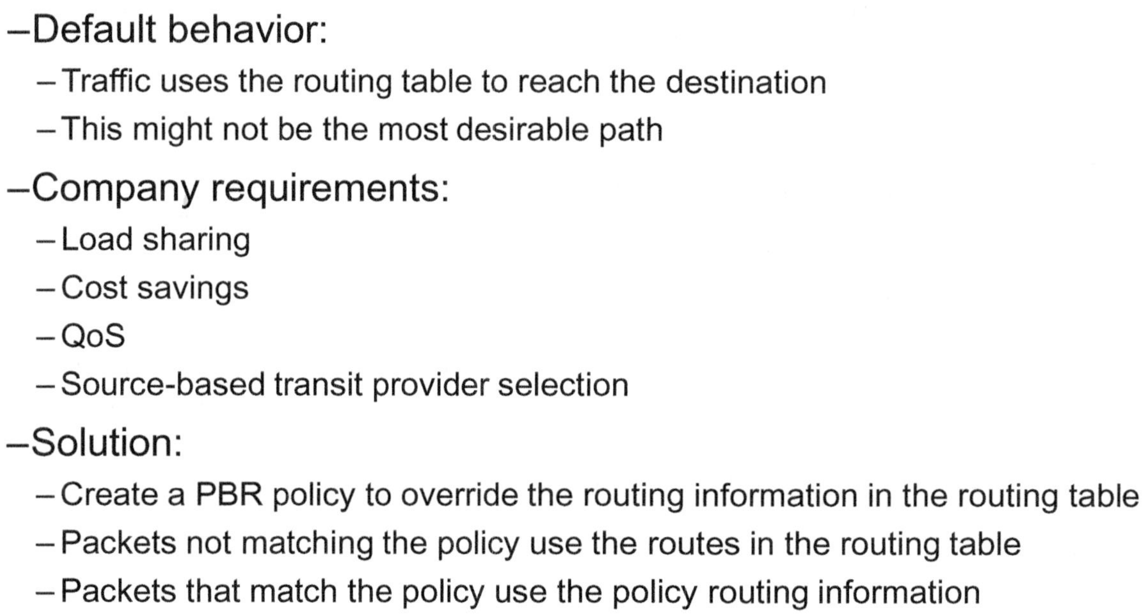

Figure 14-6 Introduction to PBR

By default, a routing device uses its routing table to determine which path to take when reaching a destination (Figure 14-6). There are times, though, where a company needs to override the default routing behavior based on the traffic and, possibly, the network conditions:

- For example, imagine that you have two links for redundancy for a network using OSPF, but one link has a better cost. The worse cost link is available, but is not used, unless the better cost link fails. A company might want to use the secondary link for certain traffic and thus implement a limited form of load balancing.
- A second scenario is when a company might have two Internet connections via two different providers: one (ISP1) where the company is charged a flat rate and a second (ISP2) where the company is allowed a certain amount of bandwidth before the service provider starts charging them for each gigabyte sent or received. In this scenario, the company wants to ensure that even if the ISP2 has better metric routes, that ISP is not used unless ISP1 is unreachable.
- As a third example, dual same-metric connections might exist for an uplink. For one link, a company might want to transmit delay- and/or jitter-sensitive traffic on link, while using the other link for the remaining traffic. The company would still have redundancy but, by logically separating the traffic, could easily meet the company's QoS needs (note that QoS policies for marking and queue scheduling would still need to be implemented in this scenario).
- Fourth, based on the source of the traffic, you might want to ensure it travels a different link than the default. For example, imagine a service provider that has two types of services in their data center: normal and premium. The backbone has two sets of connections: 10 Gbps and 100 Gbps. The service provider wants to ensure that traffic sourced from the premium-tier customers gets more bandwidth and thus is transmitted across the 100 Gbps connections, while normal customers' traffic traverses the 10 Gbps connections.

Policy-Based routing (PBR) lets you manipulate the path of a packet based on the various attributes of the packet, including source and destination IP addresses, as well as other packet fields. Packets that can be manipulated by PBR are packets that are already routing through the system at Layer 3, with a destination IP address that is on a network other than the packet ingress Layer-3 interface.

PBR is an extension of the existing classifier policy system where traffic to be manipulated is matched by a classifier class, and policy actions to be executed on the matching traffic. Matching traffic with the same destination can be routed over different paths so that different types of traffic, such as VoIP or traffic with special security requirements, can be better managed.

Note

PBR's ability to influence a packet path is limited to the current router in that the next router to which the traffic is redirected makes an independent decision on where to forward traffic to next, if anywhere. Packets not matched by a PBR policy entry are not affected and take routes specified in the system route table. In other words, PBR only affects the local router's routing decision. You might have to implement the PBR policy on multiple routing devices in order to achieve the desired outcome if multiple hops exist between a source and destination.

Policy Actions

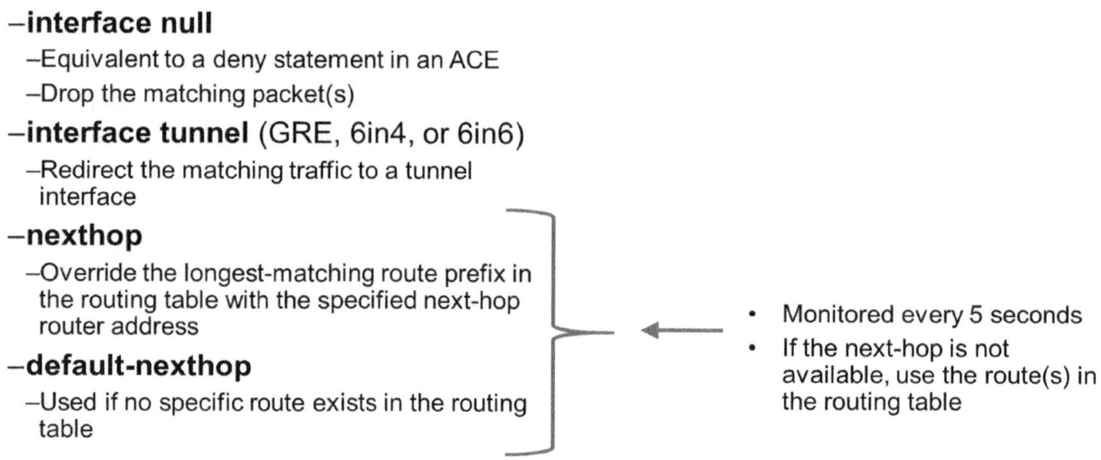

Figure 14-7 Policy Actions

PBR can alter a packet path, as shown in Figure 14-7, through the following PBR actions:

- **interface null**: equivalent to the policy *drop* policing action. Any packets matching the class criteria for that policy entry will be dropped and not routed any further.
- **interface tunnel**: allows for specifying a GRE, 6in4, or 6in6 tunnel as the outbound interface for all matching packets. The tunnel must exist before configuring. Packets sent into the tunnel interface egress at the router at the endpoint of the tunnel. If the tunnel is misconfigured or down the traffic may be lost.
- **nexthop**: allows for overriding the routing table's longest prefix match next-hop router for matching packets. If no such routing table entry exists for matching packets (default or not) this action still affects matching packets.
- **default-nexthop**: allows for specifying a next-hop router for matching packets when there is no longest prefix match for those packets in the routing table. Such a default-nexthop overrides a system default route if already configured and also applies if there is no system default route.

Note

next-hop and **default-nexthop** facilitate routing matching packets where they otherwise might not be, due to the absence of routing table entries. Unlike **next-hop**, **default-nexthop** only applies if there is no destination lookup match in the main routing table for matching packets. If the next-hop address for either command is not available, then the normal routing table entry/entries are used.

PBR and Next-Hop Router Reachability

When a policy with PBR actions is applied to an interface, all **next-hop** and **default-nexthop** entries in the associated action list are continuously monitored for reachability. Probing occurs every 5 seconds for each such entry and guarantees that the reaction to the loss of reachability, or detection of the new reachability of any such entry will be approximately 5 seconds.

For example, if there are two reachable next-hops in an applied action list and the active next-hop (highest priority by lowest sequence number) entry becomes unreachable (loss of link or next-hop power event for example), the switch over to the lower priority next-hop will occur within approximately 5 seconds. If there is only one **next-hop/default-nexthop** entry and no entries of any other type in the action list, routing decisions will return to the system routing table.

Conversely if an applied action list with a single unreachable next-hop becomes reachable, the switch back to routing to that next-hop will occur when reachability of the next-hop on the network is achieved. On an action list with multiple next-hops (where the active next-hop is not the highest priority entry); once the next-hop with the higher priority becomes available, the now reachable next-hop will promote to active once new reachability on the network is achieved.

PBR and ASIC versus CPU Processing

Traffic to be routed that cannot be handled by the switching ASIC (for example, IPv4 packets with IP options) is handled by the switch operating system kernel routing software.

The characteristics of network usage determine the proportion of traffic handled by software path PBR relative to the hardware path. Under normal conditions, software path PBR is likely to range from a fraction of a percent of all traffic to almost none.

Packets with IP options are sent to the hardware ASIC as well as the CPU. Since the software path PBR actions are applied to the packets in the CPU, a default entry is programmed in the hardware to take no action on those packets. This hardware entry count can be seen in diagnostics with the command **diag-dump policy basic**.

Default-Nexthop and ASIC versus CPU Processing

When a policy containing an entry with PBR is applied to an interface and the active action for that entry action list is **'default-nexthop'**, packets that match the class criteria and have no explicit route table hit (that is, no destination address longest prefix match, a.k.a 'route-miss'), they are forwarded to the specified active PBR **default-nexthop**. This is true for packets that follow the hardware and software paths through the switch.

There is a difference between PBR hardware and software path behavior when a route table hit occurs for class-matched packets (when the policy entry is a PBR **default-nexthop**).

Hardware path match criteria for a PBR policy entry with **default-nexthop** is extended to include the route table miss along with the class qualifiers, resulting in a policy entry hit for that policy entry. Conversely when there is a route table hit, the result is a policy entry miss in hardware path. When a policy entry miss occurs, policy processing moves on to the next entry in the policy and takes whatever action is specified, if any exist. This can include a different PBR routing action including interface null or no PBR action at all, for example.

In software path, the class match criteria is the only criteria required to achieve a policy entry hit. When that occurs, policy processing will stop. When there is a class match and a route table hit (with PBR action **default-nexthop**), the packet is forwarded according to that route table entry, not the PBR **default-nexthop** entry, nor is it influenced by any subsequent policy entries.

This difference in behavior is due to a limitation in the software path matching and routing engine, relative to hardware.

Table 14-1 **default-nexthop** and ASIC versus CPU Processing.

Routing packet	System route miss	System route hit
Hardware (ASIC)	Take PBR **default-nexthop** route.	Policy entry miss, continue policy processing with next entry, if present. No further matches result in system default route being used, if present.
Software (CPU)	Take PBR **default-nexthop** route.	Policy entry hit is overridden by system route hit. System route entry used, policy processing stops.

Software Path and System Default Route

AOS-CX default behavior (for packets with destination networks that lack entries in the system route table with a reachable next-hop address) sends packets to the system CPU for special handling, if any are specified (for example, sending an ICMP unreachable reply message).

A side effect of this CPU routing is that it has higher priority than an applied PBR next-hop action. Even though a policy is applied with an entry that matches the traffic and specifies a PBR next-hop action which is reachable, the traffic will still be routed to the system CPU (due to the absence of a reachable next-hop in the system route table), and not through the desired PBR hardware path. With traffic routing to the system CPU, it will be properly routed by PBR software path, but it will also be rate limited by the control plane policing feature. Loss can occur at higher traffic rates.

Important

The workaround for this issue is to create a default next-hop route in the system with a reachable next-hop router/host. This will result in a route hit, or reachable next-hop detected for the traffic with no further need to route traffic to the CPU. The PBR hardware path **next-hop** action will then occur, as desired.

PBR and VRFs

A given physical router can be partitioned into multiple virtual routers. All front-plane ports and logical interfaces are initially in the default VRF. Any subset of front-plane ports or logical interfaces can be selectively moved into a user configured VRF, to establish a routing topology that is different from the default VRF.

Policies with PBR actions can be applied to interfaces in any VRF, and PBR action lists can be used in different policies across different VRFs. The effect of applying the same Policies/PBR action lists across different VRFs depends on the IP networks and interfaces configured in the different VRFs. For example, an action list that specifies actions of 'nexthop 1.1.1.10' and 'interface tunnel gre_10' could be used as the PBR action parameter for an entry in policy_1 and also in policy_2. If policy_1 is applied to an interface in VRF 'red', which has an interface in subnet 1.1.1.0/24 but no GRE tunnel named 'gre_10', then only the 'nexthop' action will be relevant to VRF 'red'. If policy_2 (which contains the same action list) is applied to an interface in VRF 'blue' (which lacks the 1.1.1.0/24 subnet configured but does have a tunnel named 'gre_10'), then *only* that interface tunnel action will apply in that VRF.

Note

It is possible to configure the same subnet in different VRFs; however named tunnel interfaces can only exist in *one*, so in the example of a common action list, the 'next-hop' action could be relevant to both VRFs, but the 'interface tunnel' action may only be relevant to one. If VRFs are part of the router configuration, be mindful of them when creating and applying policies with PBR action lists and their entries. VRF Route Leaking is not supported in the current release of PBR (10.04).

PBR Software Path, VSX, and VRRP

Due to the dynamic nature of the VSX and VRRP protocols, applying a policy with PBR to VSX or VRRP Layer-3 kernel interfaces and then making further changes to those protocols may not result in expected behavior.

Apply policies with PBR to VSX and VRRP Layer-3 interfaces after all changes have been made. If further changes are necessary the policy should be *removed* first and *reapplied* when configuration updates are complete.

Guest Example

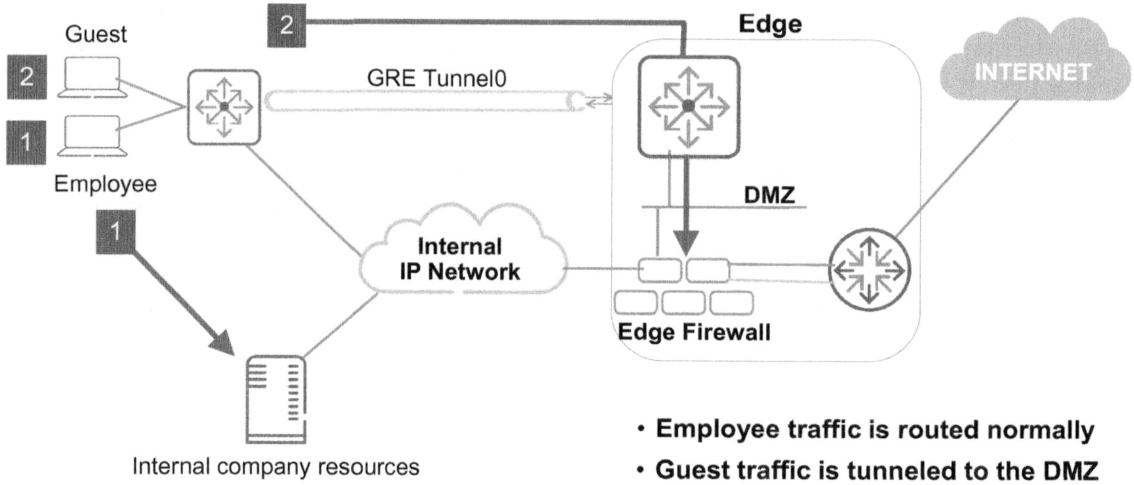

Figure 14-8 Guest Example

In this example (Figure 14-8), because of security concerns, a company does not want guest traffic to natively traverse the campus network. For example, employee traffic is routed normally and can reach internal and external destinations using the campus routing tables on the routing switches; however, because of security concerns, the guest traffic should not be able to directly access internal sources. To solve this problem the company implements PBR for the guest VLANs, redirecting the guest traffic (based on their source addresses) to GRE tunnels that terminate in the DMZ. Once the traffic reaches the DMZ, it is the responsibility of the DMZ security devices to deal with it, which would include any restrictions to both the Internet and internal resources.

Note

Since GRE is a standard protocol, the destination could be any device (firewall or router) that supports the GRE protocol.

Implementing a PBR Policy

1. Create a class to match the traffic to re-route
2. Create a PBR action list with the re-routing instruction(s)
3. Assign the class map and PBR action list to a policy
4. Assign the policy *inbound* to an interface (must be a routed interface)

Example:

```
(1) Switch(config)# class ip guest-traffic
    Switch(config-class-ip)# match ip 192.168.0.0/16 any

(2) Switch(config)# pbr-action-list reroute-GRE
    Switch(config-prb-action-list)# interface tunnel0

(3) Switch(config)# policy guest-policy
    Switch(config-policy)# class ip guest-traffic action pbr reroute-GRE

(4) Switch(config)# interface vlan 999
    Switch(config-if)# apply policy guest-policy routed-in
```

Figure 14-9 Implementing a PBR Policy

Create a Class Map

A class specifies traffic to match on. In the above example (Figure 14-9), the traffic matched on includes traffic sourced from 192.168.0.0/16 where the destination is anywhere.

Create a PBR Action List

Entries in a policy use a class to specify the criteria on what packets to match and a set of one or more policy actions to take on the matching packets such as **dscp** or **mirror**.

PBR is configured for use as another such policy action in a policy entry by using the **pbr** keyword followed by the name of a user configured PBR action list. This list may contain up to eight PBR action entries which are listed according to priority by sequence number. The PBR actions section lists the different action entry choices.

In a given action list applied to an interface, zero entries may be available (that is, reachable). Of the entries that are available, only one can be active for that action list in a given VRF. Due to real-time changes in the network operating environment, list entry availability can change at any moment. At any given time, the highest priority available entry in the list is selected as the active PBR action for that list. If the active entry becomes unavailable, the next highest available entry is automatically selected and replaces that now-unavailable entry as the active entry. If a higher priority entry (other than the current active entry) becomes available, this entry is selected and replaces the current active entry, as the new active entry (even though that current entry is still available). If no entries are available or the only available entry becomes unavailable, routing occurs based on the routing table and is not influenced by PBR.

Note

The **interface null** action is always considered available. If there are no higher priority PBR actions available, it will be selected as the active entry when configured in a PBR action list, and applied to an interface.

Likewise, if multiple entries are in a list, they are processed in order (you can resort them if they are incorrectly ordered). When a policy with PBR actions is applied to an interface, the highest priority action from the action list is applied to matching traffic on that interface and overrides any static, ECMP, or dynamically installed routes in the system.

There is a limit of eight entries per action list and a limit of 512 unique entries across the entire system. This value restricts the sum of all unique next-hops, default-nexthops, tunnel interfaces, and null interfaces applied to all Layer-3 interfaces across all VRFs. A given set of entries that are unique in one VRF count against this limit if the set is applied in another VRF.

For example, a given next-hop specified in an action list applied to an interface counts against the limit once.

If that same next-hop address is entered in a different action list and applied to another interface in the same VRF, this next-hop is not unique in the VRF and does not affect the limit further. If one of those action lists (that specify the address) is applied to an interface in a different VRF, the entry will affect the limit since addresses are unique to each VRF.

Another example is if two PBR action lists with eight unique next-hop entries (for a total of 16 unique next-hops) are configured as PBR actions in a policy. If that policy is applied to 32 route-only ports (each of which is in a different VRF), the entry supply will be exhausted.

To create an action list, use this configuration:

```
Switch(config)# pbr-action-list <PBR-action-list-name>
Switch(config-prb-action-list)# interface null0
Switch(config-prb-action-list)# interface tunnel <number>
Switch(config-prb-action-list)# nexthop <IP-address>
Switch(config-prb-action-list)# default-nexthop <IP-address>
```

Note

PBR does not support remote routers as next-hop or default-nexthop routers (a.k.a recursive). PBR only supports routers that are on a directly connected network.

You can close the PBR action list with the **pbr-action-list copy** command. You can also resequence the list with the **pbr-action-list resequence** command.

Use the **show pbr-action-list** command to verify your configuration:

Assign the Class Map and PBR Action List to a Policy

Once you have defined your class(es) of traffic and your PBR action list(s), you must then associate the two to a policy. Here is the syntax:

```
Switch(config)# policy <policy-name>
Switch(config-policy)# class ip <class-name> action pbr <PBR-action-
list-name>
```

Assign the Policy to an Interface

Last, you need to assign the policy to an interface:

```
Switch(config)# interface <routed-interface-ID>
Switch(config-if)# apply policy <policy-name> routed-in
```

Only layer-3 interfaces such as Route-only ports (ROP), LAGs, or VLAN interfaces (VSI) are valid for PBR policy application, and only in the routed inbound direction.

Note

PBR policies can only be applied *inbound* and only to routed interfaces.

If a policy with an 'interface tunnel' PBR action is applied on a Layer-3 interface in VRF 'A', and that interface tunnel is a member of VRF 'B', the interface tunnel is considered down/unavailable in this policy application in VRF 'A'.

Use the **show pbr** command to verify your configuration:

```
switch# show pbr summary
VRF         Port    Policy        PBR     Seq     TypeNexthop
-------------------------------------------------------------------
default     1/1/1  policy_1    pbr_1 10   nexthop  1.1.1.1(active)
            1/1/2  policy_2    pbr_2 20   nexthop  5.5.5.5(active)
-------------------------------------------------------------------
```

Lab 14

Lab 14 Diagram

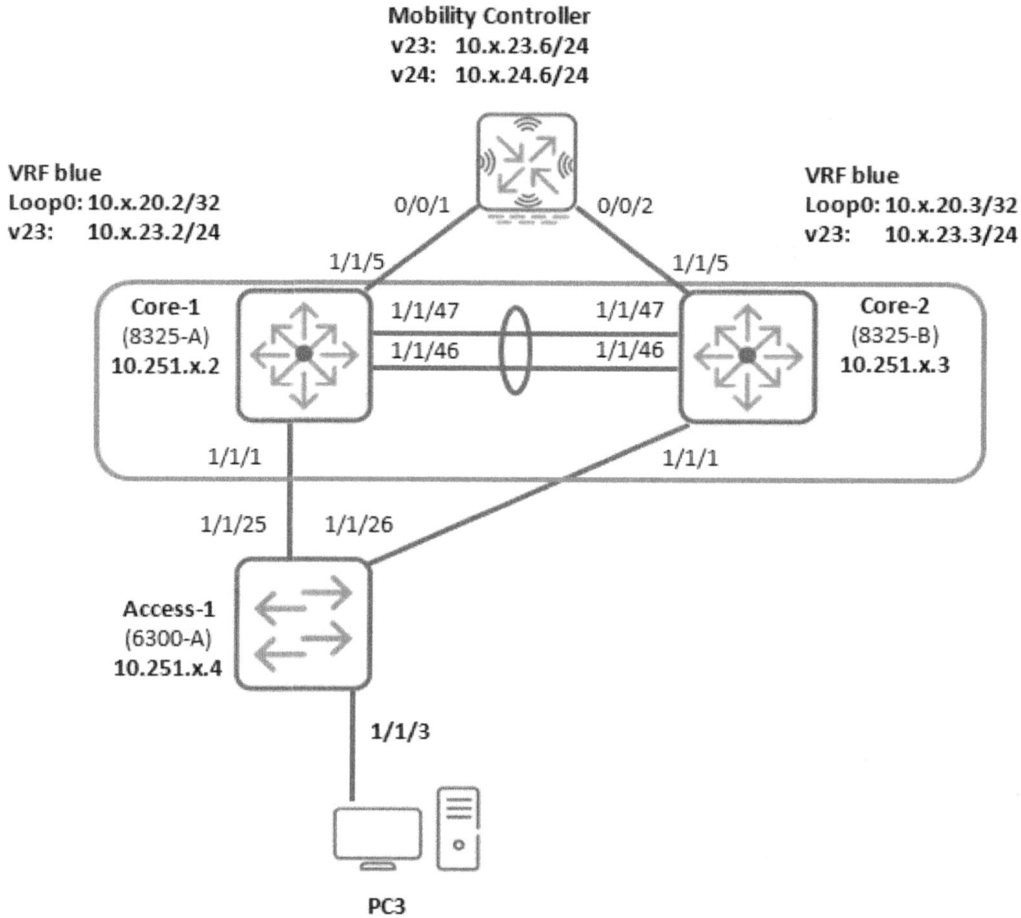

Figure 14-10 Lab 14 Diagram

Overview

In this lab activity (Figure 14-10), the VRF feature will be explored. A new routing table will be defined on the VSX Core switches for an example customer 'blue'. After defining a new routing context, the lab will show how L3 interfaces can be attached to a VRF; this will be done with Loopback and VLAN interfaces. The lab then shows how a static route can be defined within the VRF context, how user subnets in the VRF can be configured and DHCP helper can be enabled. The last section will show how a routing protocol, such as OSPF, can be enabled and bound to a VRF context.

Objectives

- Define a new VRF
- Attach L3 interfaces to a VRF
- Define static routes in a VRF
- Configure OSPF in a VRF context

Task 1: Prepare the lab start configuration

This lab is built on the base VSX topology. Make sure to complete these steps to get the base VSX checkpoint configuration on the devices.

Steps (Required)

1. Perform this step on ***all four*** switches (Access1, Access2, Core1, and Core2).

```
Switch# copy checkpoint icx-lab04-vsx running-config
Configuration changes will take time to process, please be patient.
```

Task 2: Add a New Routing VRF

Objectives

In this task, a new VRF will be defined for a customer 'blue'. Next, L3 IP interfaces, such as Loopback and VLAN interfaces, will be attached to this VRF. On the VSX Core, a routed VLAN with a VSX active-gateway will be defined to the upstream Aruba MC, that will be operating as the upstream firewall in this setup. With this routed connection in place, an example static route will be configured. The next step will be to define a user subnet in the customer VRF and verify the PC has access to the customer resources.

Steps

Review Existing VRFs

1. Open a terminal connection to Core1; enter the configuration mode. Review the currently defined VRFs on the system.

```
ICX-Tx-Core1(config)# show vrf
```

Question: What are the names of the VRFs shown in this output?

Answer: **default** and **KA** (the keep-alive VRF for VSX)

Question: Which VRF is not shown in this output?

Answer: The VRF 'mgmt' is a default, built-in VRF for the management interface.

2. Review the VRF mgmt and the mgmt interface.

```
ICX-Tx-Core1(config)# show vrf mgmt
```

```
VRF Configuration:
------------------
VRF Name    :mgmt
use "show interface mgmt" for mgmt interfaces

ICX-Tx-Core1(config)# show interface mgmt
  Address Mode                  : static
  Admin State                   : up
  Mac Address                   : 90:20:c2:bc:17:01
  IPv4 address/subnet-mask      : 10.251.12.2/24
  Default gateway IPv4          : 10.251.12.254
...
```

Create a New VRF

1. Define a new VRF named 'blue'.

```
ICX-Tx-Core1(config)# vrf blue
ICX-Tx-Core1(config-vrf)# exit
```

2. Define a new loopback interface with id '20' and assign it IP address 10.x.20.2/32.

```
ICX-Tx-Core1(config)# interface loopback 20
ICX-Tx-Core1(config-loopback-if)# ip address 10.x.20.2/32
```

3. Use the 'show vrf' command to review the interfaces and the VRF assignment.

```
ICX-Tx-Core1(config-loopback-if)# show vrf
VRF Configuration:
------------------
VRF Name    : default
        Interfaces              Status
        ------------------------------
        1/1/3                     down
...
loopback20              up
        vlan11                    up
        vlan12                    up
VRF Name    : KA
        Interfaces              Status
        ------------------------------
        1/1/45                    up
VRF Name    : blue
        Interfaces              Status
        ------------------------------
```

Question: To which VRF is an L3 IP interface attached by default?

Answer: The VRF named 'default'; this is the switch global routing table.

4. Review the current configuration on the Loopback 20 interface.

```
ICX-Tx-Core1(config-loopback-if)# show run interface loopback 20
interface loopback 20
ip address 10.x.20.2/32
    exit
```

5. Attach the Loopback 20 interface to the VRF blue. This will automatically remove the interface from the 'default' routing table.

```
ICX-Tx-Core1(config-loopback-if)# vrf attach blue
```

6. Review the current configuration on the Loopback 20 interface again.

```
ICX-Tx-Core1(config-loopback-if)# show run interface loopback 20
interface loopback 20
vrf attach blue
     exit
```

Question: What happens to the existing IP configuration when an interface is moved to a different VRF?

Answer: The existing L3 IP configuration is removed. This is how the switch prevents the IP configuration of one customer to not be accidently inserted into another customer or security environment.

7. Assign the IP address again to the Loopback 20 interface (use the up arrow to get the previous commands).

```
ICX-Tx-Core1(config-loopback-if)# ip address 10.x.20.2/32
ICX-Tx-Core1(config-loopback-if)# exit
```

Review the Default Routing Table versus the VRF Blue Routing Table

1. Review the global routing table using **'show ip route'**.

```
ICX-Tx-Core1(config)# show ip route
Displaying ipv4 routes selected for forwarding
'[x/y]' denotes [distance/metric]

10.x.3.0/24, vrf default
via  1/1/7,  [0/0],  connected
10.x.3.2/32, vrf default
via  1/1/7,  [0/0],  local
10.x.11.0/24, vrf default
        via  vlan11,  [0/0],  connected
10.x.11.2/32, vrf default
        via  vlan11,  [0/0],  local
10.x.12.0/24, vrf default
        via  vlan12,  [0/0],  connected
10.x.12.2/32, vrf default
        via  vlan12,  [0/0],  local
10.255.101.0/24, vrf default
via  1/1/7,  [0/0],  connected
10.255.101.2/32, vrf default
via  1/1/7,  [0/0],  local
```

Question: Is the 10.x.20.2/32 route available in the global routing table?

Answer: No, a VRF provides complete L3 routing isolation.

2. Review the VRF blue routing table using 'show ip route vrf blue' command. Notice that none of the routes of the default routing table are available here.

```
ICX-Tx-Core1(config)# show ip route vrf blue
Displaying ipv4 routes selected for forwarding
'[x/y]' denotes [distance/metric]

10.x.20.2/32, vrf blue
via  loopback20,  [0/0],  local
```

Configure a VLAN in VRF Blue

In the next steps, a VLAN will be defined to make a routed connection to an upstream firewall. In this lab environment, the Aruba MC has the role of the upstream firewall; it will also operate as the DHCP server for hosts in the VRF blue. The VSX core already has a VSX LAG (LAG5) to the MC, so only an extra VLAN and VLAN interface is required for this communication. This will be the routed connection between the VSX Core and the Aruba MC. VLAN 23 will be used for this purpose.

1. Define VLAN 23 and use **vsx-sync** to have it created on Core2 as well.

```
ICX-Tx-Core1(config)# vlan 23
ICX-Tx-Core1(config-vlan-23)# vsx-sync
ICX-Tx-Core1(config-vlan-23)# exit
```

2. Configure the L3 interface and configure the IP settings for the new VLAN. Replace "Tx" with your table number, where Table 1 would be "01" and Table 12 would be "12".

```
ICX-Tx-Core1(config)# interface vlan23
ICX-Tx-Core1(config-if-vlan)# vsx-sync active-gateways
ICX-Tx-Core1(config-if-vlan)# vrf attach blue
ICX-Tx-Core1(config-if-vlan)# ip address 10.x.23.2/24
ICX-Tx-Core1(config-if-vlan)# active-gateway ip mac 02:02:00:00:Tx:00
ICX-Tx-Core1(config-if-vlan)# active-gateway ip 10.x.23.1
ICX-Tx-Core1(config-if-vlan)# exit
```

Configure Core2 to Support the VRF blue

The previous steps were only executed on Core1. In the next steps, Core2 will be configured to support the VRF blue as well.

1. Open a terminal connection to Core2; enter the configuration mode. Define the VRF blue and the Loopback interface 20.

```
ICX-Tx-Core2(config)# vrf blue
ICX-Tx-Core2(config-vrf)# exit
ICX-Tx-Core2(config)# interface loopback 20
ICX-Tx-Core2(config-loopback-if)# vrf attach blue
ICX-Tx-Core2(config-loopback-if)# ip address 10.x.20.3/32
ICX-Tx-Core2(config-loopback-if)# exit
```

2. Define the VLAN 23 L3 interface and verify the VSX active-gateway configuration was synchronized.

```
ICX-Tx-Core2(config)# interface vlan23
ICX-Tx-Core2(config-if-vlan)# vrf attach blue
ICX-Tx-Core2(config-if-vlan)# ip address 10.x.23.3/24
ICX-Tx-Core2(config-if-vlan)# show run current
interface vlan23
vsx-sync active-gateways
vrf attach blue
ip address 10.x.23.3/24
    active-gateway ip mac 02:02:00:00:12:00
    active-gateway ip 10.x.23.1
ICX-Tx-Core2(config-if-vlan)# exit
```

3. On Core1, verify connectivity to the upstream MC with a ping from within the VRF 'blue' context.

```
ICX-Tx-Core1(config)# do ping 10.x.23.6 vrf blue
PING 10.x.23.6 (10.x.23.6) 100(128) bytes of data.
108 bytes from 10.x.23.6: icmp_seq=1 ttl=64 time=7.71 ms
108 bytes from 10.x.23.6: icmp_seq=2 ttl=64 time=0.335 ms
...
```

4. Review the ARP table on Core1.

```
ICX-Tx-Core1(config)# show arp
```

Question: Do you see an ARP entry for the 10.x.23.6 IP address? Why?

Answer: ARP is also processed per VRF, since a VRF may have overlapping IP addresses with another VRF, so isolation is required.

5. Review the ARP table of the VRF blue. Verify that the 10.x.23.6 address is listed in this ARP table.

```
ICX-Tx-Core1(config)# show arp vrf blue
IPv4 Address     MAC               Port   Physical Port    State      VRF
---------------------------------------------------------------------------
10.x.23.6    20:4c:03:5f:a0:c2  vlan23 lag5               reachable  blue
Total Number Of ARP Entries Listed- 1.
```

Configure Static Route in a VRF Context

A VRF is just like a regular routing table, so it can be configured with static routes and dynamic routing protocols. In the next steps, a static route will be added and verified in the VRF blue. The VSX Core currently has a direct link to the MC on the VLAN23. On the MC, there is an additional IP subnet 10.x.24.0/24, where the MC has IP 10.x.24.6. Currently, the VSX Core switches cannot reach the 10.x.24.0/24 subnet. By adding a static route to this subnet on the Core switches, the core switches will be able to reach this IP 10.x.24.6.

1. On the Core1, review the current routing table of the VRF blue.

```
ICX-Tx-Core1(config)# show ip route vrf blue
Displaying ipv4 routes selected for forwarding
'[x/y]' denotes [distance/metric]

10.x.20.2/32, vrf blue
via  loopback20,  [0/0],  local
10.x.23.0/24, vrf blue
via  vlan23,  [0/0],  connected
10.x.23.2/32, vrf blue
via  vlan23,  [0/0],  local
```

2. Add a static route for the 10.x.24.0/24 subnet to the MC IP.

```
ICX-Tx-Core1(config)# ip route 10.x.24.0/24 10.x.23.6 vrf blue
```

3. Verify the routing table again.

```
ICX-Tx-Core1(config)# show ip route vrf blue
Displaying ipv4 routes selected for forwarding
'[x/y]' denotes [distance/metric]

10.x.20.2/32, vrf blue
via  loopback20,  [0/0],  local
10.x.23.0/24, vrf blue
via  vlan23,  [0/0],  connected
10.x.23.2/32, vrf blue
via  vlan23,  [0/0],  local
10.x.24.0/24, vrf blue
via  10.x.23.6,  [1/0],  static
```

4. On Core2, add the static route as well.

```
ICX-Tx-Core2(config)# ip route 10.x.24.0/24 10.x.23.6 vrf blue
```

Note

It is also possible to enable the **'vsx-sync static-routes'** under the VSX context on Core1. In this case the VSX synchronization would define the static route on Core2.

5. Verify that the routing table in the VRF blue now lists a route to the 10.x.24.0 subnet.

```
ICX-Tx-Core2(config)# show ip route 10.x.24.0 vrf blue
Displaying ipv4 routes selected for forwarding
'[x/y]' denotes [distance/metric]

10.10.24.0/24, vrf blue
via  10.10.23.6,  [1/0],  static
```

Test the Static Route

The MC has been pre-configured with IP 10.x.24.6 in the lab. Attempt to ping this IP; this should succeed from both Core1 and Core2.

1. Verify the ping to 10.x.24.6 on Core1.

```
ICX-Tx-Core1(config)# do ping 10.x.24.6 vrf blue
PING 10.x.24.6 (10.x.24.6) 100(128) bytes of data.
108 bytes from 10.x.24.6: icmp_seq=1 ttl=64 time=0.468 ms
108 bytes from 10.x.24.6: icmp_seq=2 ttl=64 time=0.373 ms
...
```

2. Verify the ping to 10.x.24.6 on Core2.

```
ICX-Tx-Core2(config)# do ping 10.x.24.6 vrf blue
PING 10.x.24.6 (10.x.24.6) 100(128) bytes of data.
108 bytes from 10.x.24.6: icmp_seq=1 ttl=64 time=0.468 ms
108 bytes from 10.x.24.6: icmp_seq=2 ttl=64 time=0.373 ms
...
```

3. This demonstrates how a static route can be defined within a VRF context.

Configure User Subnet in the VRF Blue

In these steps, a new user VLAN will be defined in the VRF blue for the PC connected to Access1. The VSX Core will be the default gateway for this subnet in the VRF blue, so active-gateway and DHCP relay will be configured. The new user VLAN is VLAN 21.

1. On Core1, define the new VLAN and IP interface.

```
ICX-Tx-Core1(config)# vlan 21
ICX-Tx-Core1(config-vlan-21)# vsx-sync
ICX-Tx-Core1(config-vlan-21)# exit
```

2. Define the IP Interface. Replace "Tx" with your table number, where Table 1 would be "01" and Table 12 would be "12".

```
ICX-Tx-Core1(config)# interface vlan21
ICX-Tx-Core1(config-if-vlan)# vrf attach blue
ICX-Tx-Core1(config-if-vlan)# ip address 10.x.21.2/24
ICX-Tx-Core1(config-if-vlan)# vsx-sync active-gateways
ICX-Tx-Core1(config-if-vlan)# active-gateway ip mac 02:02:00:00:Tx:00
ICX-Tx-Core1(config-if-vlan)# active-gateway ip 10.x.21.1
```

3. Configure DHCP relay on the VLAN; use the MC as the DHCP server.

```
ICX-Tx-Core1(config-if-vlan)# ip helper-address 10.x.23.6
ICX-Tx-Core1(config-if-vlan)# exit
```

4. Allow the VLAN 21 on the LAG1 to Access1 and verify the configuration.

```
ICX-Tx-Core1(config)# interface lag 1
ICX-Tx-Core1(config-lag-if)# vlan trunk allowed 21
ICX-Tx-Core1(config-lag-if)# show run current
interface lag 1 multi-chassis
    no shutdown
    description access1
    no routing
vlan trunk native 1
vlan trunk allowed 1,11-13,21
lacp mode active
ICX-Tx-Core1(config-lag-if)# exit
```

5. On Core2, several settings have already been synchronized by VSX:

- L2 VLAN
- L2 LAG allowed VLAN list
- L3 VLAN Active-gateway settings
- L3 IP helper

The only remaining configuration steps are:

- Define the L3 interface
- Attach it to VRF
- Assign the interface an IP address

6. Define the L3 interface, attach it to the VRF blue, and set the IP address.

```
ICX-Tx-Core2(config)# interface vlan 21
ICX-Tx-Core2(config-if-vlan)# vrf attach blue
ICX-Tx-Core2(config-if-vlan)# ip address 10.x.21.3/24
```

7. Verify the VSX active-gateway settings have been synchronized correctly.

```
ICX-Tx-Core2(config-if-vlan)# show running-config current-context
interface vlan21
vsx-sync active-gateways
vrf attach blue
ip address 10.x.21.3/24
active-gateway ip mac 02:02:00:00:XX:00
    active-gateway ip10.x.21.1
ip helper-address 10.x.23.6
ICX-Tx-Core2(config-if-vlan)# exit
```

8. Verify VLAN 21 exists and is allowed on LAG1 (to Access1).

```
ICX-Tx-Core2(config)# show vlan 21
--------------------------------------------------------------------------------
VLAN  Name               Status  Reason          Type      Interfaces
--------------------------------------------------------------------------------
21    VLAN21             up      ok              static    lag1,lag5,lag256
```

9. Open a terminal connection on Access1 and enter configuration mode. Define VLAN 21; verify it is allowed on the uplink.

```
ICX-TxAccess1(config)# vlan 21
ICX-TxAccess1(config-vlan-21)# exit
ICX-TxAccess1(config)# show vlan 21
--------------------------------------------------------------------
VLAN  Name          Status  Reason         Type     Interfaces
--------------------------------------------------------------------
21    VLAN21        up      ok             static   lag255
```

10. Assign the port connected to PC3 (1/1/3) as access port in VLAN 21.

```
ICX-TxAccess1(config)# interface 1/1/3
ICX-TxAccess1(config-if)# vlan access 21
ICX-TxAccess1(config-if)# exit
```

11. On PC3, connected to Access1 port 1/1/3, reset (disable/enable) the 'Lab NIC' interface and verify the IP address received via DHCP. This should be in the 10.x.21.0/24 range.

12. On PC3, run a ping and traceroute to 10.x.24.6 (the MC) to test the routing and the static route.

```
C:\Users\student> ping 10.x.24.6
Pinging 10.x.24.6 with 32 bytes of data:
Reply from 10.x.24.6: bytes=32 time<1ms TTL=63
...
Ping statistics for 10.x.24.6:
   Packets: Sent = 5, Received = 5, Lost = 0 (0% loss),
Approximate round trip times in milli-seconds:
   Minimum = 0ms, Maximum = 0ms, Average = 0ms
C:\Users\student> tracert -d 10.x.24.6
Tracing route to 10.x.24.6 over a maximum of 30 hops
1    <1 ms<1 ms<1 ms10.x.21.3
2    <1 ms<1 ms<1 ms10.x.24.6
Trace complete.
```

Note

The traffic of PC3 can be hashed to either Core1 or Core2, so the first response in the traceroute could come from either Core1 (10.x.21.2) or Core2 (10.x.21.3).

13. Close the command prompt using the 'exit' command. This demonstrates how customer devices and subnets can be configured in an isolated routing context.

Task 3: OSPF Routing Protocols Inside the VRF

Objectives

In this task, OSPF routing will be configured inside the VRF blue. The only main difference will be to bind the OSPF process to the VRF. The other steps, such as the configuration of router-id, areas, and interfaces, are the same as the OSPF of the default routing table.

Steps

1. On Core1, define a new OSPF process for VRF blue. Typically, OSPF process id '1' would be used for OSPF in the default routing table, so process id '2' is used here.

> **Note**
> Without the **'vrf blue'** command option, the OSPF process would operate in the default routing table.

```
ICX-Tx-Core1(config)# router ospf 2 vrf blue
```

2. Configure the loopback IP that was defined in the VRF blue as the router-id.

```
ICX-Tx-Core1(config-ospf-2)# router-id 10.x.20.2
```

3. Define OSPF area 0.

```
ICX-Tx-Core1(config-ospf-2)# area 0
ICX-Tx-Core1(config-ospf-2)# exit
```

4. Enable OSPF on the Loopback and upstream routed VLAN 23. Notice that the 'ip ospf' command requires the OSPF process number. Typically, that would be '1' for the OSPF process that is running in the global routing table. In this example, OSPF process id 2 was bound to the VRF blue. This is how the administrator can control to which OSPF process the interface belongs.

> **Note**
> This is different from the VRF attach command, since a single routing table (VRF) may contain multiple OSPF processes!

```
ICX-Tx-Core1(config)# interface loopback 20
ICX-Tx-Core1(config-loopback-if)# ip ospf 2 area 0
ICX-Tx-Core1(config-loopback-if)# exit
ICX-Tx-Core1(config)# interface vlan 23
ICX-Tx-Core1(config-if-vlan)# ip ospf 2 area 0
ICX-Tx-Core1(config-if-vlan)# exit
```

Verify OSPF Operation

1. Review the OSPF settings.

```
ICX-Tx-Core1(config)# show ip ospf
OSPF Process is not running on VRF default.
```

Question: Why is there no information shown about OSPF?

Answer: The default "show ip ospf" command will look for an OSPF process that is bound to the 'default' VRF, but there is no OSPF in the 'default' routing context.

2. Repeat the command, but now use the 'vrf' command option; now the expected OSPF status should be displayed.

```
ICX-Tx-Core1(config)# show ip ospf vrf blue
Routing Process 2 with ID : 10.x.20.2 VRF blue
-----------------------------------------------
OSPFv2 Protocol is enabled
Graceful-restart is configured
Restart Interval: 120, State: inactive
Last Graceful Restart Exit Status: none
SPF: Start Time: 200ms, Hold Time: 1000ms, Max Wait Time: 5000ms
Maximum Paths to Destination: 4
Number of external LSAs 0, checksum sum 0
Number of areas is 1, 1 normal, 0 stub, 0 NSSA
Number of active areas is 1, 1 normal, 0 stub, 0 NSSA
BFD is disabled
Reference Bandwidth: 100000 Mbps
Area (0.0.0.0) (Active)
  Interfaces in this Area: 2 Active Interfaces: 2
  Passive Interfaces: 0 Loopback Interfaces: 1
  SPF calculation has run 8 times
  Area ranges:
  Number of LSAs: 3, checksum sum 75629
```

3. On Core2, VSX synchronization should have completed most of the configuration. Review the OSPF configuration.

```
ICX-Tx-Core2(config)# show run ospf
router ospf 2 vrf blue
    area 0.0.0.0
interface loopback 20
ip ospf 2 area 0.0.0.0
interface vlan23
ip ospf 2 area 0.0.0.0
```

Note

The only missing configuration command is the 'router-id', but an existing IP will be selected by default.

4. Review the OSPF status; notice the router ID 10.x.20.3 was automatically selected.

```
ICX-Tx-Core2(config)# show ip ospf vrf blue
Routing Process 2 with ID :10.x.20.3 VRF blue
------------------------------------------------
OSPFv2 Protocol is enabled
Graceful-restart is configured
Restart Interval: 120, State: inactive
Last Graceful Restart Exit Status: none
SPF: Start Time: 200ms, Hold Time: 1000ms, Max Wait Time: 5000ms
Maximum Paths to Destination: 4
Number of external LSAs 0, checksum sum 0
Number of areas is 1, 1 normal, 0 stub, 0 NSSA
Number of active areas is 1, 1 normal, 0 stub, 0 NSSA
BFD is disabled
Reference Bandwidth: 100000 Mbps
Area (0.0.0.0) (Active)
  Interfaces in this Area: 2 Active Interfaces: 2
  Passive Interfaces: 0 Loopback Interfaces: 1
  SPF calculation has run 8 times
  Area ranges:
  Number of LSAs: 3, checksum sum 75629
```

5. Review the OSPF neighbors; this should be Core1.

```
ICX-Tx-Core2(config)# show ip ospf neighbors vrf blue
OSPF Process ID 2 VRF blue
===========================
Total Number of Neighbors: 1
Neighbor ID      Priority  StateNbr Address       Interface
-------------------------------------------------------------------------------
10.x.20.2        1         FULL/BDR  10.x.23.2          vlan23
```

6. Review the IP routing table of the VRF blue; this should show an OSPF route to the loopback IP of the Core1 switch.

```
ICX-Tx-Core2(config)# show ip route vrf blue
Displaying ipv4 routes selected for forwarding

'[x/y]' denotes [distance/metric]

10.x.20.3/32, vrf blue
via  loopback20,  [0/0],  local
10.x.20.2/32, vrf blue
via  10.x.23.2,  [110/100],  ospf
10.x.21.0/24, vrf blue
via  vlan21,  [0/0],  connected
```

```
10.x.21.3/32, vrf blue
via  vlan21,  [0/0],  local
10.x.23.0/24, vrf blue
via  vlan23,  [0/0],  connected
10.x.23.3/32, vrf blue
via  vlan23,  [0/0],  local
10.x.24.0/24, vrf blue
via  10.x.23.6,  [1/0],  static
```

7. Attempt to ping this remote loopback IP, using the Core2 loopback IP as the source. This should succeed, since Core1 should also have a route to the Core2 loopback IP.

```
ICX-Tx-Core2(config)# do ping 10.x.20.2 source 10.x.20.3 vrf blue
PING 10.x.20.2 (10.x.20.2) from 10.x.20.3 : 100(128) bytes of data.
108 bytes from 10.x.20.2: icmp_seq=1 ttl=64 time=0.233 ms
...
--- 10.x.20.2 ping statistics ---
5 packets transmitted, 5 received, 0% packet loss, time 4092ms
rtt min/avg/max/mdev = 0.131/0.175/0.233/0.040 ms
```

8. This demonstrates how OSPF can be configured to operate within a VRF context.

Learning Check

1. A PBR policy applied to a GRE tunnel can affect two different VRF instances.
   a. True
   b. False
2. When defining a static route, if you do not define the VRF instance name, it defaults to the name ______________.
3. A PBR policy can be applied to what type of interface?
   a. Layer 2 only
   b. Layer 3 only
   c. Layer 2 or layer 3

Summary

Congratulations! You have completed the introduction to additional layer-3 routing technologies: VRF and PRB. VRF allows you to logically separate addressing and/or routing in your network. This is commonly done for user versus network management traffic if a true OOBM solution is not available. VRF allows you to accomplish an OOBM solution logically. PBR can be used to override the routing table entries to implement specific route polices. This can be used to make a specific policy decision, like tunneling guest traffic to the DMZ instead of routing it natively in a campus network.

15 Captive Portal Authentication

OBJECTIVES

By the time that you have completed this chapter, you should be able to:

- ✓ Understand the process AOS-CX switches use for captive portal authentication
- ✓ Configure captive portal authentication on AOS-CX switches to integrate them with an Aruba ClearPass guest and BYOD solution

Overview

There are situations where a company wants to control access to a network, for example, guest access, but using 802.1X or MAC-Auth is not practical. This chapter teaches you how to set up AOS-CX switches to participate in guest and BYOD access solutions by implementing a captive portal solution. Captive portal is where a user uses the web browser on their device to authenticate to the network. Sometimes this is referred to as a *clientless* solution.

Guest Introduction

Today, network services, such as access to email and the Internet, are expected to be readily available and always on. If companies do not provide these network services to them, their competition will. And most networks today typically provide guest access to the Internet. This section introduces guest access.

Guest Access Considerations

Different companies have different expectations and needs for their guest access solution. Some companies might allow guests limited access without any authentication. However, most companies want guests to log in through a Web portal of some kind. Even if they do not care whether the guests authenticate, they want the guests to accept an agreement for legal purposes (Figure 15-1).

- Does the company want guests to:
  - Authenticate in a Web portal?
  - Accept an agreement in a Web portal?
  - Receive limited access without passing through a portal?
- What does the switch need to do:
  - Simply place users in guest VLAN?
  - Participate in a Web or portal based authentication solution?

Figure 15-1 Guest Access Considerations

The company's expectations will dictate whether you need to configure AOS-CX switches at the access layer to enforce or participate in a Web-based authentication solution, or whether you can simply place guests in a guest VLAN. You will focus on the Web-based authentication—also called portal authentication—solutions for most of this chapter. At the end, however, you will learn how you can enforce authentication for employees, but allow limited access to guests without forcing the guests to log in.

Web-Based Authentication

- Authenticates users without requiring:
  - 802.1X supplicant
  - Special configuration on the client
- Generally used for:
  - Guest access
  - Some small-to-medium organizations

Figure 15-2 Web-Based Authentication

Web-based authentication was developed to provide an easier way for users to log in to a network without special requirements on the part of their devices, nor expertise on the part of the users (Figure 15-2). Users simply open a Web browser and are directed to a login page, in which they can enter credentials or sometimes simply accept an agreement to log in.

Due to the simplicity from the user standpoint, but also the relatively lower security, companies often use web-based authentication to provide guest access. However, some SMBs also use web-based authentication for employees.

Advantages of Web-Auth

Security solutions such as 802.1X require specific capabilities, but any client can authenticate to a switch that uses Web-Auth as long as the user has a legitimate username and password and a web browser.

Web-Auth also lets companies control what users see before they receive network access. The company can present a customizable webpage that shows the guest information about the company providing the complimentary access. The company can also force the user to consent to terms and conditions, which can be a legal requirement in many regions.

Environments with external users who may benefit from Web-Auth include:

- Hospitals
- Universities
- Libraries, hotels, and other businesses that provide courtesy Ethernet access

Disadvantages of Web-Auth

Web-Auth does not provide as rigorous security as 802.1X. Users have a degree of network access before they authenticate. The credentials and authentication protocol might not be as secure as with 802.1X; however, you can improve the security by using HTTPS rather than HTTP.

Because Web-Auth requires interaction with the user, you cannot use it to authenticate devices without a user interface.

You should also note that the local Web-Auth features are quite limited. However, the switches can integrate with Aruba ClearPass, which is a sophisticated guest and BYOD solution.

AOS-CX Support for Web-Based Authentication Solutions

In the past, Web-based authentication was as simple as a login page and perhaps a backend authentication server. However, these solutions have evolved. A solution such as ClearPass provides a Web portal as part of its complete user access management solution. Such a solution helps users log in more easily with features such as self-registration. It also helps companies track and monitor users, and it controls their access in sophisticated ways (Figure 15-3).

AOS-CX switches currently support one method of web-based authentication that provides flexibility and scalability to meet the needs of any company:

- **Captive portal**—For companies who want the benefits of a full guest and BYOD access management solution, AOS-CX switches can use captive portal authentication to integrate with Aruba ClearPass. Aruba ClearPass provides the RADIUS server and portal server; the Policy Manager and Guest components are required for this solution. ClearPass OnGuard is required if companies want the endpoint integrity features. Note that AOS-CX switches can also integrate with other third-party AAA guest solutions available in the market place.

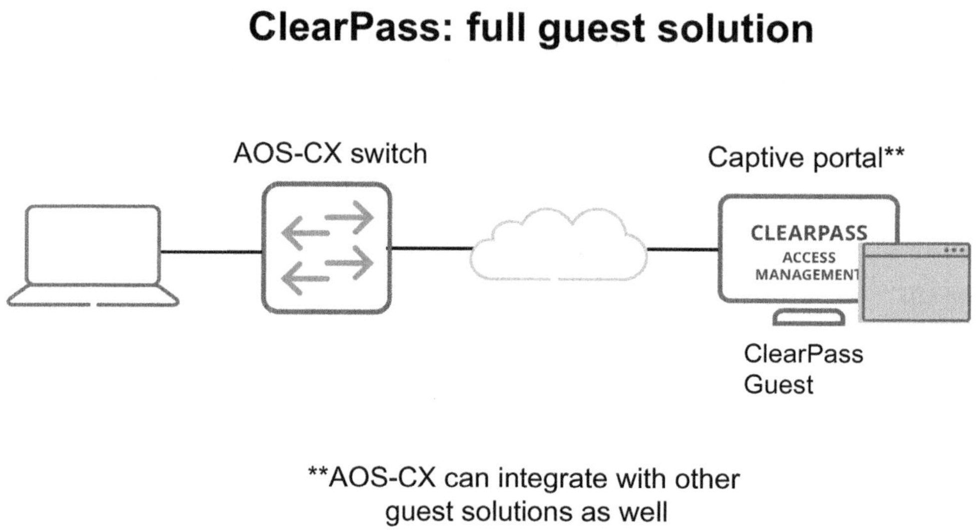

Figure 15-3 AOS-CX Support for Web-Based Authentication Solutions

Currently AOS-CX switches do *not* support a local web authentication (Web-Auth) method, where the switches provide the web server and authentication component locally on the switch.

Note

AOS-CX switches can also integrate with HPE IMC's BYOD solution using the BYOD redirect feature. Or it can use MAC Auth with Failure Redirect (MAFR) to redirect users who fail MAC authentication to register with a server that then adds their MAC address to the authorized list. These features are intended for similar use cases as the captive portal feature, and the use of each feature is mutually exclusive. BYOD redirect and MAFR are not covered in this book.

Captive Portal Authentication

You will now learn how the captive portal process works with AOS-CX switches.

What Users Experience

The captive portal authentication feature requires close teamwork between the AOS-CX switch and Aruba ClearPass. You can better understand how to set up the feature and how the feature works if you first look at the user experience that the feature is intended to deliver.

A user connects a new device to a free Ethernet jack connected to an AOS-CX switch port, or associates with an Aruba access point (AP). The user powers on the device and opens the Web browser. The user sees a portal page, which provides options for logging in as an employee or a guest. At this point, the user device is locked down, so the user cannot browse to other pages or receive access to other network services (Figure 15-4).

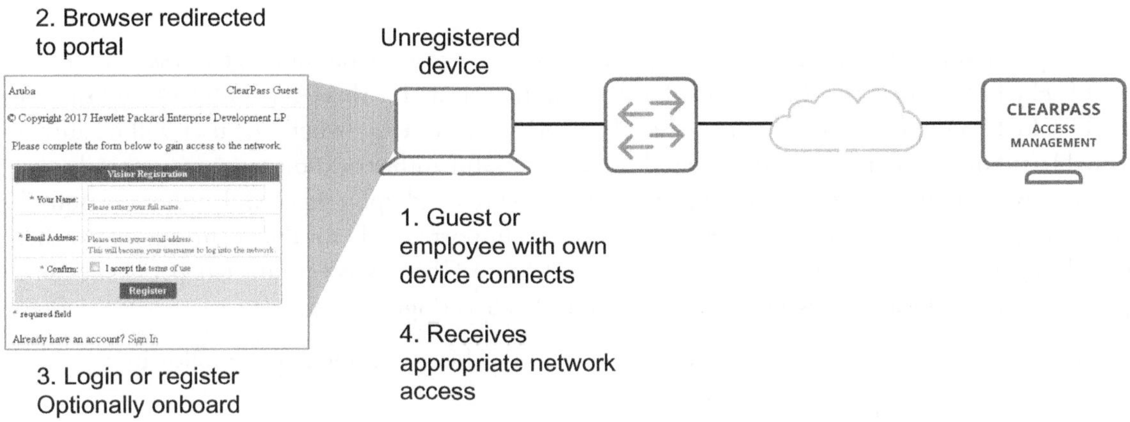

Figure 15-4 What Users Experience

For an employee login, the user would need to enter valid employee credentials such as those stored in on Windows Active Directory. Guests would sign in with credentials created for guests, or they might be allowed to create their own account and log in with that. The options are controlled by the ClearPass Guest solution, and you will observe some of them during the lab.

After logging in or registering for an account, the user is permitted network access, customized based on their identity and possibly other factors such as the health of their device. For example, an employee might receive different access rights than a guest. And a device that complies with security policies will receive fuller access than a potentially insecure device.

If the user connects with the same device later or in a different location, the device is provided the same access rights transparently.

AOS-CX Captive Portal Solution

–Process:

1. The client will first get authenticated with MAC or 802.1X firstly.
2. An HTTP/HTTPS request will be redirected to captive portal server where the user will be authenticated based on username/password.
3. After successful authentication on captive portal server, the client will go through MAC authentication on the switch.
4. Upon successful authentication, the client will get access to internet
5. The redirect parameters per client can be applied through a user role or RADIUS VSA.

–Authenticates users *without* requiring:

–802.1X supplicant

–Special configuration on the client

Figure 15-5 AOS-CX Captive Portal Solution

Captive portal solution is a way of providing access to the users for wider internet access based on the HTTP/HTTPS redirection. The client will first get authenticated with MAC or 802.1X and then the HTTP/HTTPS request will be redirected to the captive portal server where the user will be authenticated based on the username and password. After successful authentication on captive portal server, the client will go through MAC authentication on the switch and upon successful authentication, the client will get the access to the internet. This feature is supported only for the clients getting authenticated through RADIUS server. This feature is client based. The redirect parameters per client can be applied user-roles (local or downloadable) or RADIUS VSAs (Figure 15-5).

If you are implementing LUR, the configuration steps on the switch include the following:

- Configure the captive portal profile.
- Configure the URL and hash key (optional) in the captive portal profile.
- Configure user-role and associate the earlier configured captive portal profile.

When using RADIUS VSA, the "**Aruba-User-Role**" attribute will be sent from RADIUS server in the authentication response packet. The role will be the one that has already been configured on the switch with captive portal profile name. If the role is not present in the switch, the authentication fails. The following Aruba VSAs will be in the authentication response for a client from RADIUS server:

- **Aruba-Captive-Portal-URL**: This will have the captive portal profile URL information. A default role will be considered on the switch and gets applied to the client when this VSA is sent.
  - Length: 1024 characters
  - Type: string
  - Aruba vendor ID: 14823
  - Aruba attribute type: 43

When implementing DUR, the captive portal profile and URL can be configured through the DUR for a client, along with the policies, and the entire role is pushed down to the switch. Through this process, the role does not need to exist on the switch: instead, it is centrally maintained on the ClearPass server.

Authentication Enforced on the AOS-CX Switch

You will now look at how the captive portal solution delivers this experience. First, you must implement RADIUS-based MAC-Auth on any AOS-CX switch port to which users might connect their devices. The switch can then submit access requests for all devices to ClearPass so that ClearPass can decide how to control the devices' access (Figure 15-6).

You can optionally add 802.1X in port-based mode if you want registered devices to eventually authenticate with 802.1X. In this case, ClearPass Onboard would deploy the correct configuration settings and certificates for supporting 802.1X to devices connected to the captive portal. Companies usually use this option for employee BYOD devices, which require more security than guest devices. This chapter focuses more on the guest access option, though.

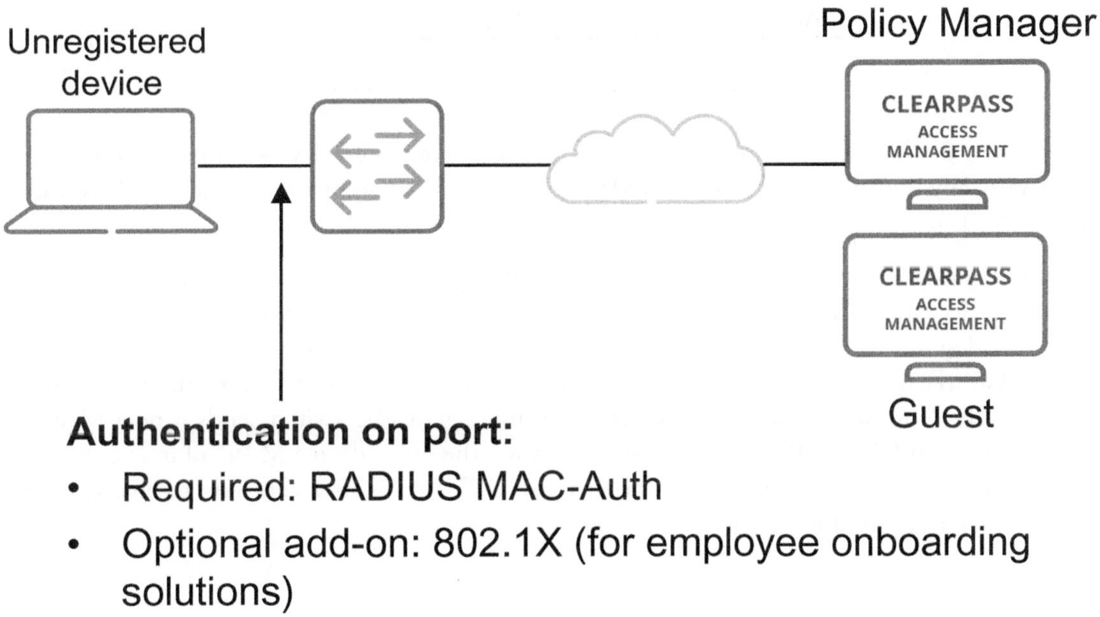

Figure 15-6 Authentication Enforced on the AOS-CX Switch

High-Level Authentication Process

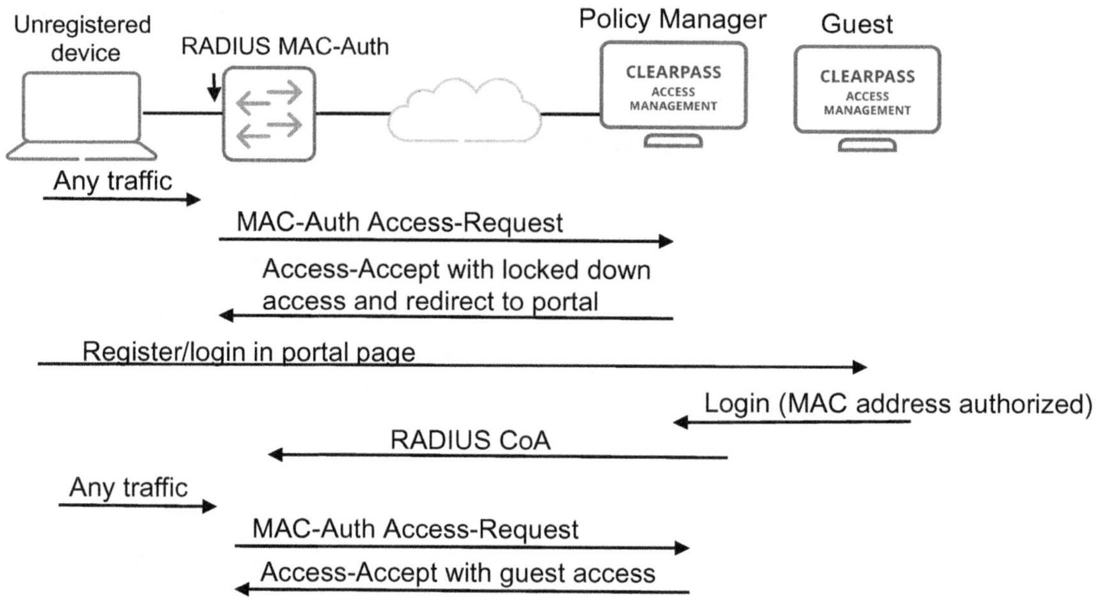

Figure 15-7 High-Level Authentication Process

Here you see at a high level what occurs when an unregistered guest device connects. As soon as the device sends any traffic, the switch sends a MAC-Auth Access-Request with the device's MAC address (Figure 15-7).

Because the device is unknown, ClearPass sends an Accept-Accept with various dynamic settings to limit the device's access and redirect the device to the portal page on ClearPass Guest. The guest uses this page to log in or to register and then log in. At the end of this process, ClearPass Guest logs the user into ClearPass Policy Manager (CPPM). Policy Manager sends a change of authorization (CoA) to the switch. Now when the device sends any traffic again, the switch sends a new MAC-Auth Access-Request to CPPM. Policy Manager now knows the guest device MAC address and sends an Access-Accept with the proper settings for this guest. The guest user can now receive appropriate access such as access to the Internet.

Detailed Look at the Redirection to the Captive Portal

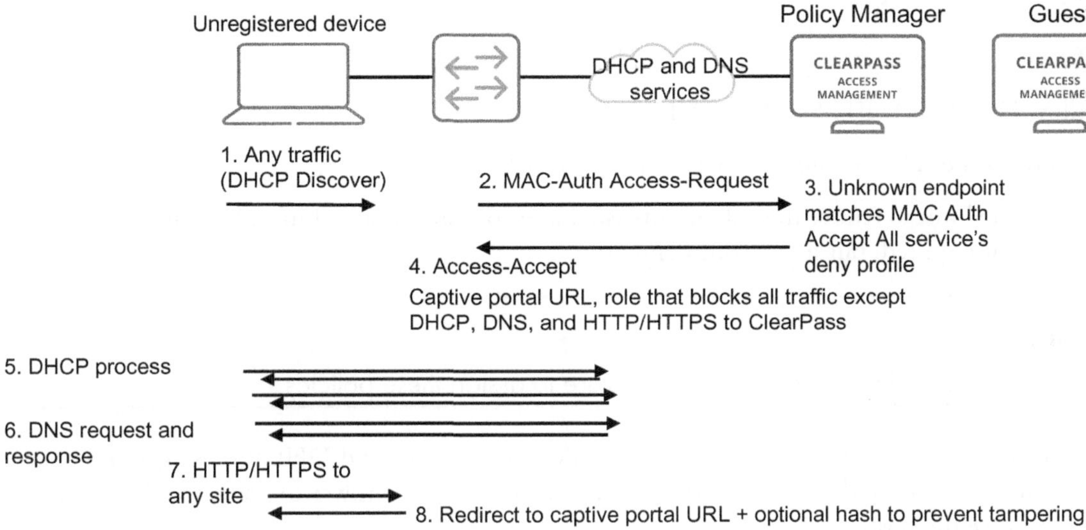

Figure 15-8 Detailed Look at the Redirection to the Captive Portal

You will now look at this process in more detail so that you can better understand what is required on the switch and what you should expect to occur during a successful process (Figure 15-8).

1. The process begins when the unregistered guest device sends any traffic, typically a DHCP discover.
2. The switch port enforces RADIUS MAC-Auth, so it sends an Access-Request to ClearPass Policy Manager, which must be defined as its RADIUS server.
3. At this point ClearPass Policy Manager does not know the guest device MAC address. Typically, when a device cannot authenticate, the RADIUS server sends a RADIUS Reject message, and the switch port denies access. However, for a captive portal solution, ClearPass, as the RADIUS server, behaves differently. It uses a service with a special type of MAC-Auth (called Allow All MAC-Auth). When a device fails authentication, this service matches the device to a "deny any" profile rather than simply rejects the access. The profile defines various RADIUS attributes and VSAs to apply to the device's session.
4. ClearPass sends a RADIUS Access-Accept with these attributes to apply to the device's session. These attributes include:

   A captive portal URL, which indicates the URL of the ClearPass portal in which users will log in or register

   The URL must use standard format such as: **https://clearpass.example.com**. If administrators plan to redirect clients to an HTTPS URL, they must ensure that ClearPass has a certificate that is signed by a well-known trusted certificate authority.

A dynamic ACL with IP filter rules to:

5. Permit DHCP traffic
6. Permit DNS traffic to resolve names to addresses for URLs.
7. Allow HTTP or HTTPS traffic to ClearPass, but…
8. Redirect other HTTP and HTTPS to the redirect URL
    - A rate limit to reduce the risk of untrusted users or devices launching a DoS attack (this VSA is not required, but it is recommended).

Note
You will typically use the Aruba role feature to assign these policies.

Although the device is blocked from most network access, it can send DHCP messages and receive an IP address. And when the user opens a browser and attempts to browse to a site, the device can use DNS to resolve the hostname.

The device then sends an HTTP or HTTPS request to the IP address. The AOS-CX switch intercepts that request and sends a response, posing as that address and redirecting the browser to the captive portal URL. The switch actually appends some information to the URL in a query string. This information includes the device's MAC address and IP address, a timestamp, and the originally requested URL. Hackers could try to obtain inappropriate access by altering the ACL. To prevent this from occurring, the ClearPass portal can require a hash appended to any requests, created by hashing the URL with a secret key. It only responds to requests that have the correct hash and drops other requests. If this security feature is enabled on ClearPass, you must configure a key on your AOS-CX switches that matches the key on ClearPass.

Detailed Look at the Login Process

9. The unregistered device now accesses the ClearPass guest portal page. As you see, traffic flows between the client and the ClearPass Guest portal without any proxying by the switch.
10. The guest might be able to register for an account based on how the portal page is set up. The ClearPass portal's appearance and functionality is highly customizable. Depending on how administrators have set up and customized the portal, guests might log in with an account that has been provided to them or self-register for an account through the portal. The portal might grant all self-registering users immediate access, force them to activate the account through a text message, or force them to receive sponsor approval. ClearPass transparently adds a newly registered account to the guest repository.

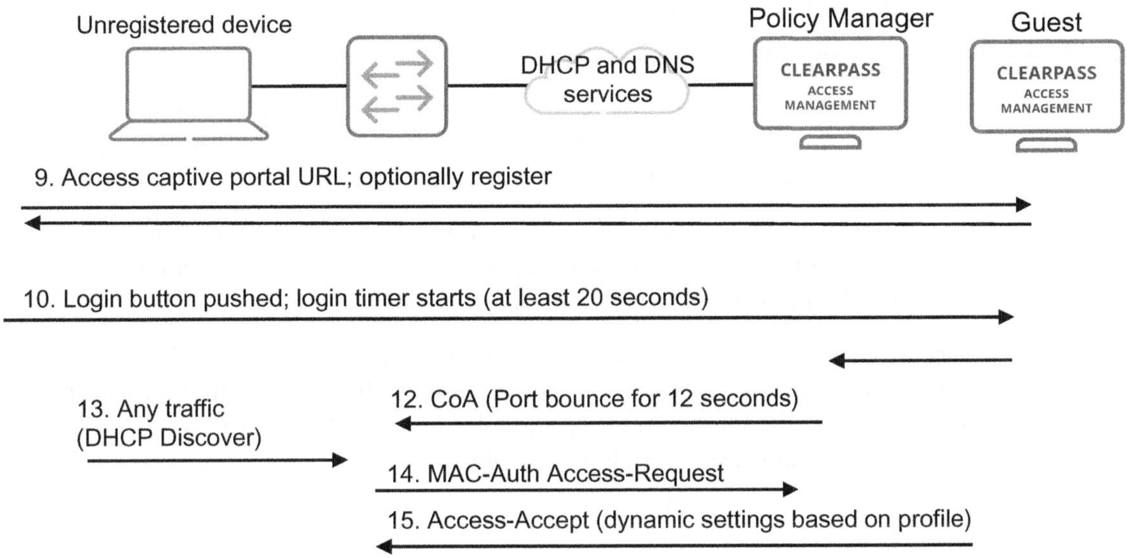

Figure 15-9 Detailed Look at the Login Process

11. When the user clicks a login button, ClearPass Guest transparently logs the guest in to the Policy Manager. Because the wired solution will use MAC-Auth to authenticate the registered devices, ClearPass Guest also makes sure that the guest device's MAC address (submitted in the URL) becomes authorized. The portal page begins a login countdown—recommended at about 20 seconds for a solution that uses AOS-CX switches.

    How the MAC address is authorized depends on the solution. ClearPass might add the guest device to special guest endpoint repository and pair the device with the guest account. Or ClearPass Guest might tell ClearPass Policy Manager to change the guest device, automatically discovered in ClearPass's global Endpoint Repository, to a known device. In any case, ClearPass Policy Manager will now be able to recognize the device MAC address as a known address associated with the known guest.

12. The successful guest login also triggers ClearPass to send a "port bounce" Change of Authorization (CoA) message to the switch. This message causes the switch to de-authenticate the device and hold the port closed for a certain period of time—12 seconds is recommended. Note that ClearPass can be configured to use either a Disconnect Message (DM) or CoA for this purpose, but you should tell ClearPass administrators to use a port bounce CoA for AOS-CX switches.

    It is important that the switch is set up to accept this message. You must enable dynamic authorization when you specify ClearPass as the RADIUS server, and you must make sure that the port is correct. The default dynamic authorization port on both AOS-CX switches and ClearPass is 3799. (If the switch does not accept the CoA message, the client will not re-authenticate, as explained in steps 13 and 14, and the client will continue to be redirected to the portal.)

13. When the port opens again, the device starts to send traffic (probably a DHCP Discover).
14. The switch port enforces MAC-Auth for the device again.
15. Now ClearPass finds the MAC address as a known endpoint, so it authorizes the device for access, assigning it to a profile based on policy settings. For example, it might apply a guest profile that assigns the device to a guest VLAN using the same RADIUS VSA (Figure 15-9).

Because the login counter on the portal page is several seconds longer than the port bounce time, the authentication process is complete before the countdown ends. The guest is now connected to the network and can receive the appropriate services, based on the settings applied by ClearPass.

The next time that the guest connects the device, the MAC-Auth process occurs in the background, and the guest once again receives guest-level access without having to pass through the portal. (ClearPass administrators can also choose to set up the solution such that ClearPass forces the guest to log in through the portal again after a certain period of time.)

BYOD Onboarding

If the company is using the captive portal for BYOD, ClearPass administrators will have set up the portal a bit differently. Employees typically log in to a device provisioning page on the portal with their existing domain or LDAP credentials. They then click a few buttons to accept a configuration that prepares their devices for 802.1X by configuring EAP settings and deploying certificates.

After this process, ClearPass sends a port bounce message to the AOS-CX switch port, forcing the port to close for several seconds. The device then automatically authenticates through 802.1X using the settings deployed during the provisioning process. ClearPass uses the 802.1X service to authenticate the user. The port is now open to the user with optional customization based on the ClearPass policies and profiles.

Because the switch port still enforces MAC-Auth, the switch might also submit a MAC-Auth request for the device, and the device could fail that check. However, the 802.1X authentication settings take precedence, so the device will receive the correct access and will not be redirected to the portal.

Companies could also choose to combine guest and BYOD solutions by adding a link to the device provisioning page on the guest login or registration page.

Optional VLAN for Unregistered Devices

As mentioned earlier, when ClearPass sends the settings to redirect unknown devices to the captive portal, it can also send a dynamic VLAN assignment. This VLAN isolates unregistered devices in their own VLAN. Such isolation is not strictly required for security because the dynamic ACL locks down the unregistered devices' network access. However, you might prefer to place unauthenticated devices in their own VLAN for several reasons:

- So unauthenticated users cannot gain information about your IP addressing scheme.
- When examining traffic, you can distinguish between unauthenticated and authenticated clients.
- Unauthenticated devices cannot use up IP addresses that authenticated clients require. Otherwise, hackers could attempt to obtain a lot of IP addresses to lock out legitimate users.
- You can direct unauthenticated devices to different DHCP and DNS servers than authenticated users. This can help to prevent hackers from launching DoS attacks on these services (Figure 15-10).

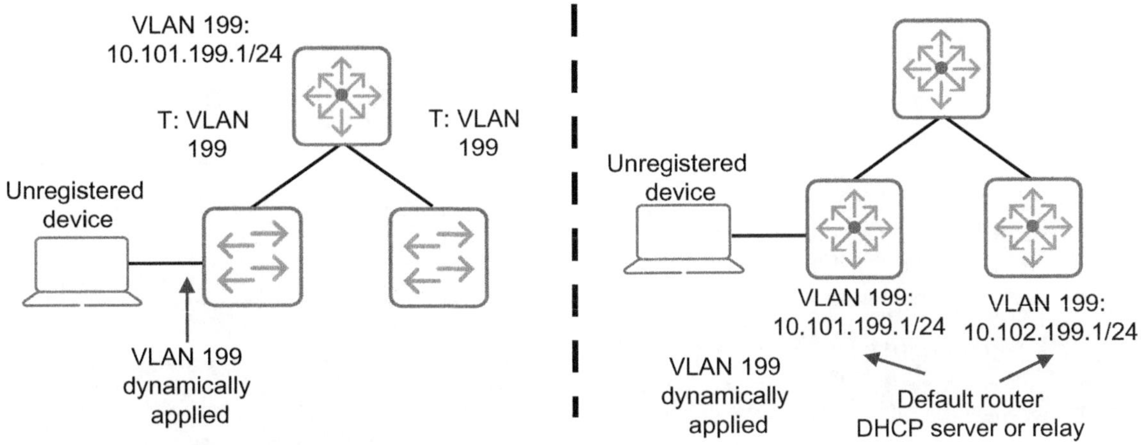

Figure 15-10 Optional VLAN for Unregistered Devices

If ClearPass sends a VLAN assignment for unregistered devices, remember that you must add this VLAN to your network.

When routing occurs at the core layer, tag the VLAN on the access switch uplinks and configure the VLAN and default router IP address on the core switch (or VSF fabric). When routing occurs at the access layer, each access layer switch is the default router for the unregistered VLAN. Every switch uses the same VLAN ID, but must associate that ID with a different subnet. The same principle applies if you are routing at the distribution layer in a three-tier topology.

Remember to configure DHCP services on the switch or switches acting as default router. The switch can either act as the DHCP server or implement DHCP relay to a network DHCP server.

Also set up routing as appropriate to allow communication between the unregistered VLAN and the ClearPass guest server. For example, you might need to enable OSPF, preferably in passive mode, on the VLAN.

Captive Portal Configuration

You will now learn how to implement the captive portal authentication solution, as the solution preferred by most companies seeking a full guest or BYOD access solution.

Basic Web-Auth Setup with User-Roles

There are six basic steps in setting up captive portal with user-roles on AOS-CX switches. The following two slides cover these steps with the associated commands (Figure 15-11).

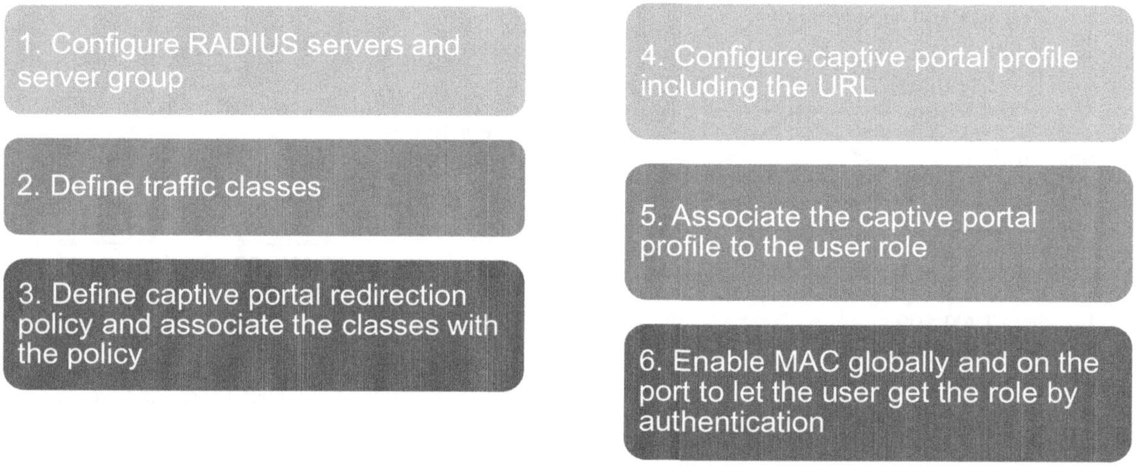

Figure 15-11 Basic Web-Auth Setup with User-Roles

Basic Web-Auth Setup with User-Roles (Steps 1-3)

You now understand how the captive portal solution works (Figure 15-12). Configuring an AOS-CX switch to participate in the solution is simple because ClearPass handles most of the functionality. You need to configure the following:

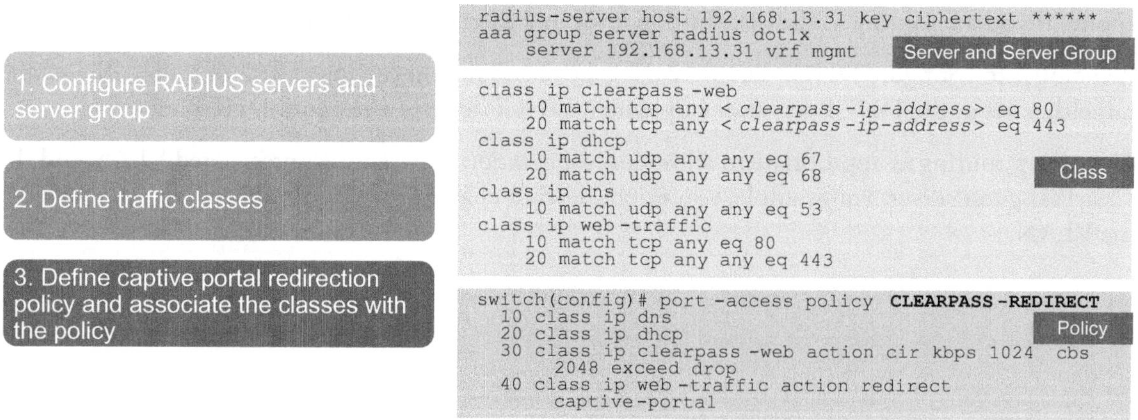

Figure 15-12 Basic Web-Auth Setup with User-Roles (Steps 1-3)

1. Configure RADIUS servers (ClearPass) and a Server Group

As part of the authentication setup, make sure to specify ClearPass as the RADIUS server. Configure the correct shared secret and enable dynamic authorization. Also configure NTP as you learned how to do in previous chapters.

Also make sure that you understand whether ClearPass is deployed as a high availability cluster. The cluster provides shared configuration and databases, but not a virtual IP address. Therefore, you must make sure to specify all ClearPass servers as RADIUS servers on the switch. As you learned in a previous chapter, AOS-CX switches do not load balance requests between RADIUS servers. Instead, they send all requests to the first defined server unless the request to that server times out and all retries expire. If you want, you can configure one RADIUS server IP address first on half of the switches, and a different server IP address first on the other half of the switches. (You cannot define a hostname for the RADIUS server, so a DNS-based load balancer will not work.)

2. Define Traffic Classes

Traffic classes define what to match on for the policy. Traffic classes are covered in more depth in *Chapter 15, "Quality of Service"*.

Note that the clearpass-web class map needs to specify the destination address of the ClearPass (or RADIUS) server that will be handling the web authentication.

3. Define Captive Portal Redirection Policy and Associate the Classes with the Policy

Here you reference the traffic class(es) from Step 2. You also specify the redirect action for web traffic. Optionally you can rate limit traffic. Note that minimally you must allow DHCP and DNS, or the captive portal process will break. The redirect action in the example will redirect all web traffic.

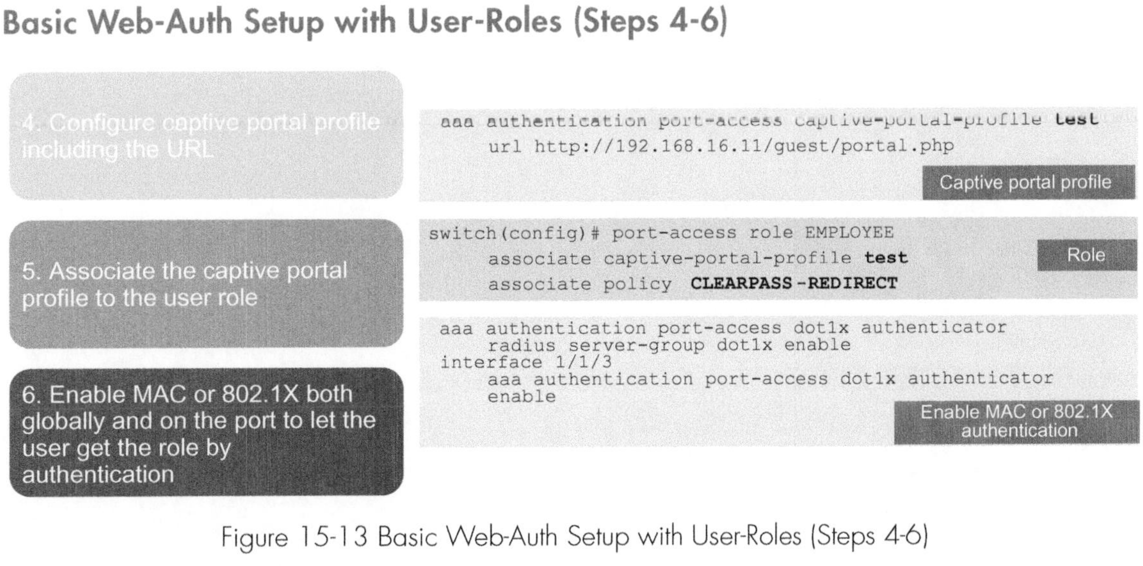

Figure 15-13 Basic Web-Auth Setup with User-Roles (Steps 4-6)

4. Configure Captive Portal Profile including the URL

In this example, the redirect URL is a ClearPass guest portal page. Optionally, you can define a hash key for protection with the **url-hash-key plaintext** command in the captive portal configuration context.

5. Associate the Captive Portal Profile to the User-Role

The role ties together the captive portal profile (the redirect URL) and the previously configured policy.

6. Enable MAC or 802.1X both Globally and on the Port to Let the User Get the Role by Authentication

Since captive portal is implemented with MAC authentication and RADIUS CoA on the AOS-CX switches, only MAC authentication needs to be enabled on the port. Optionally, you can enable both 802.1X and MAC-Auth if you are not sure what type of authentication will be necessary on a switch port (Figure 15-13).

Captive Portal Troubleshooting

The **diag-dump captive-portal basic** command displays the detailed diagnostic information related to the session, client, and port to help troubleshoot captive portal issues, including redirects (Figure 15-14).

The **show port-access captive-portal profile** command displays the configuration information for all captive portal profiles. Here is an example:

```
switch# show port-access captive-portal-profile
Captive Portal Profile Configuration
Name : employee
Type : local
URL : http://1.1.1.1/employee/captiveportal.php
URL Hash Key : SWNGWyMeYubHPDgVIirpEUwNK5Uf+r1vmhBIncQPw1Y=
```

The **show tech captive-portal** command captures the output from the two previous commands.

- **diag-dump captive-portal basic**
  - Displays the diagnostic information related to session, client and port
- **show port-access captive-portal-profile**
  - Displays the configuration information for all captive portal profiles: user role, URL, and the URL hash key
- **show tech captive-portal**
  - Displays output of the following commands:
    - **diag-dump captive-portal basic**
    - **show port-access captive-portal-profile**

Figure 15-14 Captive Portal Troubleshooting

Lab 15

Lab 15 Diagram

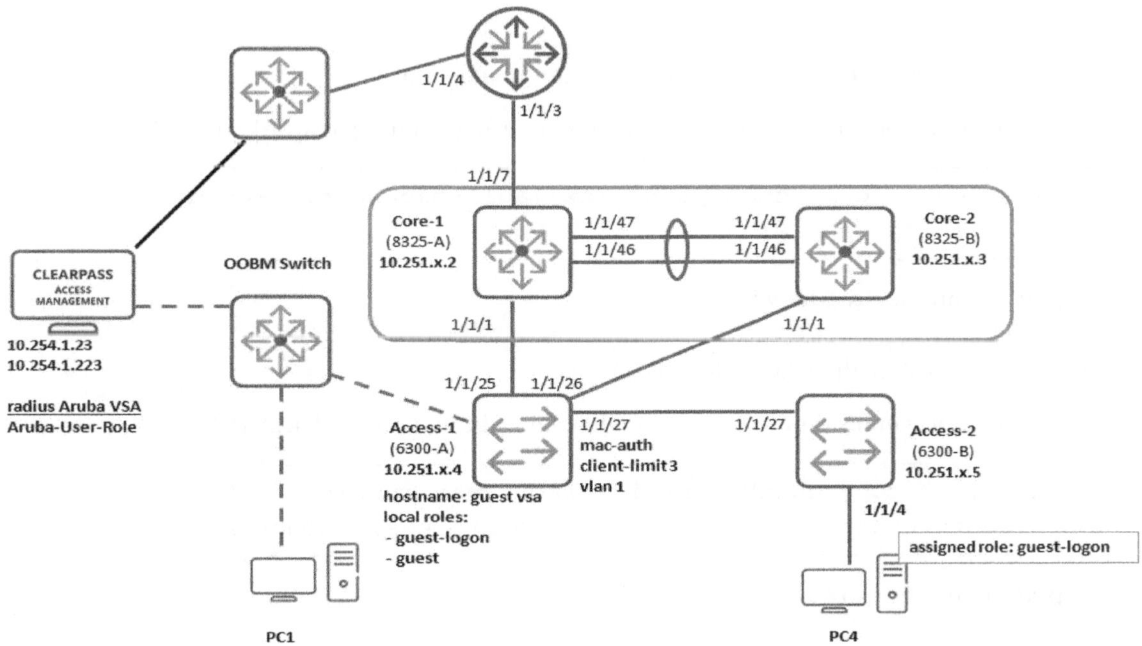

Figure 15-15 Lab 15 Diagram

Overview

In this lab activity, as shown in Figure 15-15, the captive portal function will be configured on the on the Access1 switch. Captive portal authentication relies on MAC-authentication, which was previously configured on the port 1/1/27 of the Access1.

First, the actual captive portal (HTTP intercept) function will be configured using the 'guest-logon' user-role. Once this process has been configured, the lab guest account will connect to the network and the final 'guest' user-role will be assigned. During this process, the RADIUS server will send a Change of Authorization (CoA) request to the switch to trigger the re-authentication with the resulting 'guest' user-role.

Task 1: Prepare the lab start configuration

Overview

- This lab is built on the MAC Authentication topology. This checkpoint was only saved on the Access1 and Access2 switches. The Core switches will be loaded with the VSX checkpoint configuration.
- Make sure to complete these steps to get the required configuration on the devices.

Steps (Required)

Access1 and Access2: Restore the MAC Authentication checkpoint

1. Open a console connection to the Access1. Log in using admin, password aruba123.

```
ICX-Tx-Access1# copy checkpoint icx-lab11-mac running-config
Configuration changes will take time to process, please be patient.
```

2. Repeat this on the ***Access2*** switch.

Core1 and Core2: Restore the VSX configuration checkpoint

1. Open a console connection to Core1. Log in using admin, password aruba123.

```
ICX-Tx-Core1# copy checkpoint icx-lab04-vsx running-config
Configuration changes will take time to process, please be patient.
```

2. Repeat this on the ***Core2*** switch.

Task 2: Define Captive Portal Role

Objectives

In this task, the guest-logon user-role will be defined and tested. This role will allow limited access to the network, so the user can get an IP address through DHCP and perform name resolution through DNS.

Traffic sent to HTTP TCP port 80 will be handled by the switch captive portal process and it will be redirected to the captive portal page on the ClearPass server. Any other traffic will be dropped for this role.

Steps

1. Open a terminal connection to Access1; enter the configuration mode. For this lab, the ClearPass radius server has a number of lab-specific rules that are triggered based on the hostname of the switch. Rename the hostname of the Access1 to include the words '**guest-vsa**'. Replace "Tx" with your table information; for example, Table 1 would be "T1" and Table 12 would be "T12".

Note

The hostname is used as the NAS-identifier in the access-request to ClearPass. ClearPass has been pre-configured to look for the values '**guest** and' '**vsa**' in the NAS-identifier and to return various Aruba Vendor-Specific Attributes (**VSA**) based on the **Aruba-User-Roles** that are needed for this lab.

```
ICX-Tx-Access1(config)# hostname ICX-Tx-Access1-guest-vsa
ICX-Tx-Access1-guest-vsa(config)#
```

Prepare Objects for Captive Portal Role

1. Define IP Class for web access to ClearPass.

```
ICX-Tx-Access1-guest-vsa(config)# class ip cppm-web
ICX-Tx-Access1-guest-vsa(config-class-ip)# match tcp any 10.254.1.23/32
eq 80
ICX-Tx-Access1-guest-vsa(config-class-ip)# match tcp any 10.254.1.23/32
eq 443
ICX-Tx-Access1-guest-vsa(config-class-ip)# exit
```

2. Define IP Class for control protocols, such as DHCP, DNS, and ICMP.

```
ICX-Tx-Access1-guest-vsa(config)# class ip dhcp-dns-icmp
ICX-Tx-Access1-guest-vsa(config-class-ip)# match udp any any eq 67
ICX-Tx-Access1-guest-vsa(config-class-ip)# match udp any any eq 68
ICX-Tx-Access1-guest-vsa(config-class-ip)# match udp any any eq 53
ICX-Tx-Access1-guest-vsa(config-class-ip)# match icmp any any
ICX-Tx-Access1-guest-vsa(config-class-ip)# exit
```

3. Define IP Class for all web traffic.

```
ICX-Tx-Access1-guest-vsa(config)# class ip any-web
ICX-Tx-Access1-guest-vsa(config-class-ip)# match tcp any any eq 80
ICX-Tx-Access1-guest-vsa(config-class-ip)# match tcp any any eq 443
ICX-Tx-Access1-guest-vsa(config-class-ip)# exit
```

Combine the IP Classes into a Port-Access Policy

1. Define a new port-access policy. The logic for the policy is:
   - Allow the client device to get an IP address (DHCP), send DNS queries, and ping (ICMP).
   - Allow access to the ClearPass host on port 80 and 443,but apply a rate limit to ensure the client cannot overload the ClearPass host.
   - Send all other web traffic to the local redirect process on the switch (CPU).

```
ICX-Tx-Access1-guest-vsa(config)# port-access policy cppm-redirect
ICX-Tx-Access1-guest-vsa(config-pa-policy)# class ip dhcp-dns-icmp
ICX-Tx-Access1-guest-vsa(config-pa-policy)# class ip cppm-web action
cir kbps 1024 cbs 2048 exceed drop
ICX-Tx-Access1-guest-vsa(config-pa-policy)# class ip any-web action
redirect captive-portal
ICX-Tx-Access1-guest-vsa(config-pa-policy)# exit
```

Define Captive Portal Profile with URL to ClearPass

1. Define captive portal profile to the ClearPass guest logon page. This will be used by the local redirect process of the switch.

   When the current client sends traffic on port 80, the port-access policy will apply the 'redirect captive-portal' action, so the traffic is delivered to the local redirect process. This redirect process will use the 'Captive Portal profile' to find out to what destination URL the client should be redirected. This URL can be unique for each captive portal role.

First, the global captive portal profile must be defined with the URL; this profile will be linked in the user-role in the next step. This same URL profile could be used by multiple user-roles.

- Profile name: **cppm-guest**
- URL: **http://10.254.1.23/guest/guest-cx.php**

```
ICX-Tx-Access1-guest-vsa(config)# aaa authentication port-access
captive-portal-profile cppm-guest
ICX-Tx-Access1-guest-vsa(config-captive-portal)# url
http://10.254.1.23/guest/guest-cx.php
ICX-Tx-Access1-guest-vsa(config-captive-portal)# exit
```

Define New User-role: Associate the Policy and Captive Portal Profile

1. A new user-role 'guest-logon' is now defined. It represents the access the user will need in order to complete the captive portal logon to the network.

```
ICX-Tx-Access1-guest-vsa(config)# port-access role guest-logon
ICX-Tx-Access1-guest-vsa(config-pa-role)# associate captive-portal-profile
cppm-guest
ICX-Tx-Access1-guest-vsa(config-pa-role)# associate policy cppm-redirect
ICX-Tx-Access1-guest-vsa(config-pa-role)# vlan access 11
ICX-Tx-Access1-guest-vsa(config-pa-role)# exit
```

Test Redirect Role with PC4 (Connected to Access2)

Guest captive portal is using mac-authentication to push the final network access to the switch. Since the current lab setup is using the PC4 on Access2 with mac-authentication, the guest lab will use this PC4 as well for the Captive Portal demonstration.

1. On the Access1 switch, verify the port configuration (no changes were made).The switch port is still configured with mac-authentication, so any 'new' MAC Address will be sent to ClearPass for mac-authentication. Since ClearPass is now configured to return the 'guest-logon' Aruba VSA User-role for any MAC address that is not previously authenticated, the client should come online with this role.

```
ICX-Tx-Access1-guest-vsa(config)# show run int 1/1/27
interface 1/1/27
   no shutdown
   no routing
   vlan access 1
   aaa authentication port-access client-limit 3
```

```
    aaa authentication port-access mac-auth
        enable
    exit
```

2. Bounce the port on Access1 to clear any previously active authentications.

```
ICX-Tx-Access1-guest-vsa(config)# interface 1/1/27
ICX-Tx-Access1-guest-vsa(config-if)# shutdown
ICX-Tx-Access1-guest-vsa(config-if)# no shutdown
ICX-Tx-Access1-guest-vsa(config-if)# exit
```

3. Open a terminal connection to Access2 and enter the configuration mode. Enable port 1/1/4 (connected to PC4).

```
ICX-Tx-Access2(config)# interface 1/1/4
ICX-Tx-Access2(config-if)# no shutdown
ICX-Tx-Access2(config-if)# exit
```

4. On PC4, reset the '**Lab NIC**' network interface to trigger a DHCP request (disable/enable).
5. Verify the result of the initial mac-auth.

```
ICX-Tx-Access1-guest-vsa(config)# show aaa authentication port-access
interface 1/1/27 client-status
Port Access Client Status Details
Client 00:50:56:b1:fc:9b, 005056b1fc9b
============================
   Session Details
   ---------------
     Port         : 1/1/27
     Session Time : 69s

   Authentication Details
   ----------------------
     Status           : mac-auth Authenticated
     Auth Precedence : dot1x - Not attempted, mac-auth - Authenticated

   Authorization Details
   ----------------------
     Role   : guest-logon
     Status : Applied
```

Note

It is possible that the MAC Address of the Access2 switch is also shown in the output. Since the Access2 switch cannot perform actual guest captive portal logon, the training guide is not showing it in the output and only shows the PC4 MAC Address.

6. Use PC1 (Management PC) to open a session to ClearPass and review your authentication entry in Access Tracker. You may see two mac-auth entries, one for the Access2 switch and one for the PC4. In this lab you will only use the PC4.

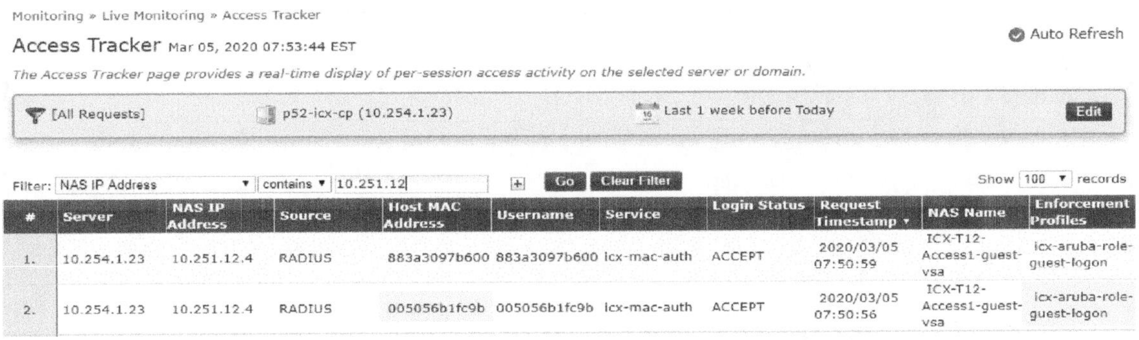

7. Open the entry for your PC4 (should start with MAC address **005056**). Review the '**Output**' tab; it should show the '**guest-logon**' Aruba VSA Aruba-User-Role.

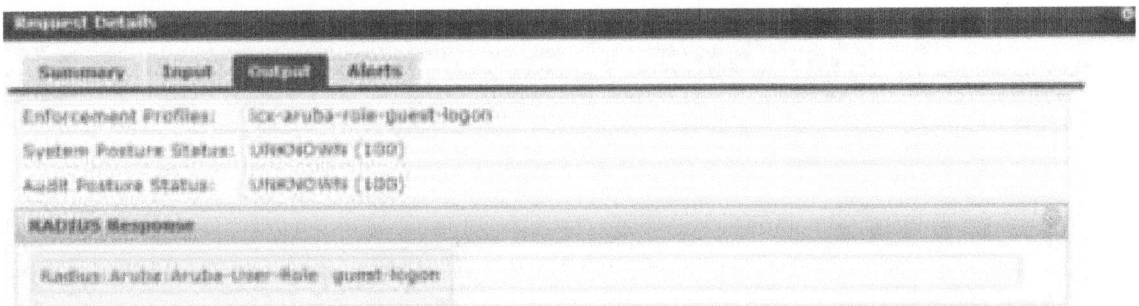

Test CoA

The Change of Authorization or Disconnect Message is critical in the Captive portal process. Once the guest user has entered credentials on the ClearPass web page, ClearPass will mark the MAC address of this client as 'authenticated'. But that information will only be processed during the next authentication request.

After valid credentials have been entered on the Web page, the ClearPass server will send a CoA/DM to the switch to trigger the switch to perform re-authentication. The guest user will see a 'please wait' page with a timer, so the re-authentication can take place at that moment.

In this lab, the 'guest' role and the 'guest-logon' role are in the same VLAN, so the guest user does not need to get a new IP Address, only a new access policy (different access rules in the 'guest-logon' and the 'guest' role). In case they would be assigned to different VLANs, the count-down timer should be large enough to handle a DHCP renew on the client side.

First, test the Disconnect Message for the client.

1. Click 'Change Status'.

2. Click '**Submit**' to send the CoA.

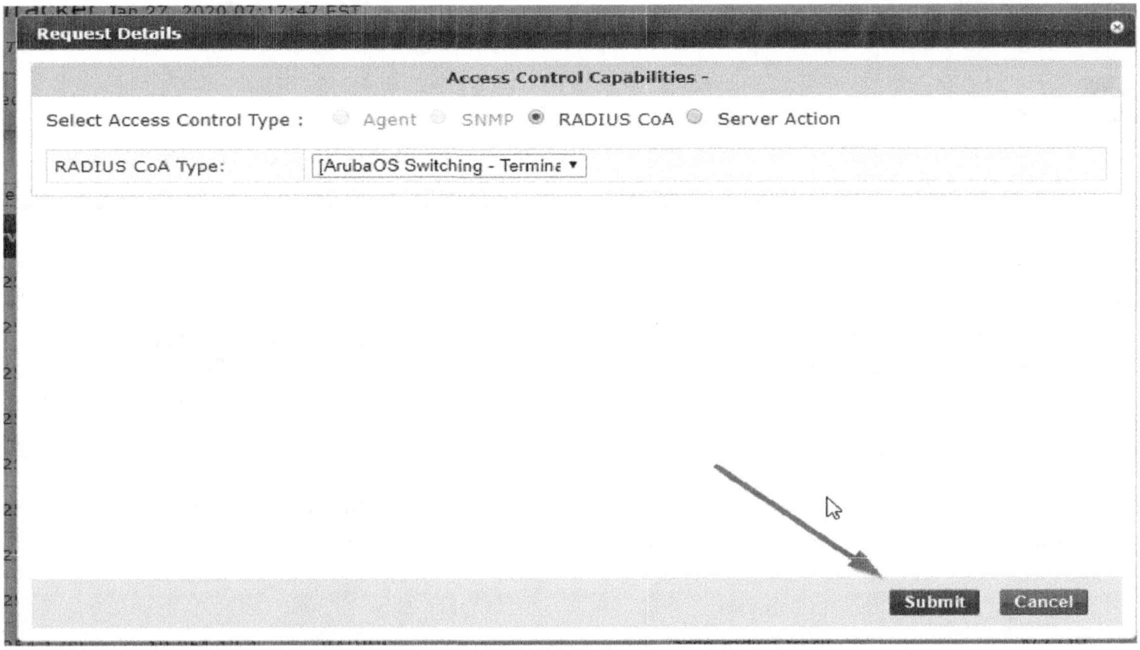

3. Make sure the CoA is 'successful'; then click '**Close**' to close the window.

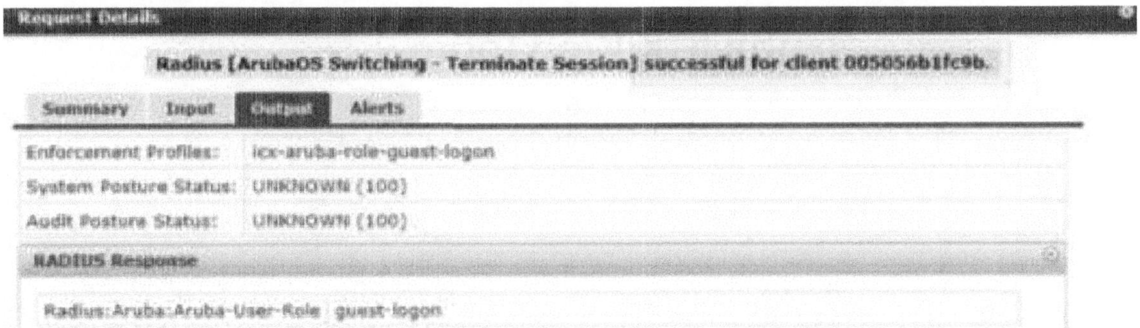

4. Take note of the last two characters of the client MAC address; you can use this in some ClearPass filters in the rest of this lab.

Test the Client

1. Open the PC4, start Firefox, and attempt to navigate to http://10.254.1.223/.

> **Note**
> The lab may not be connected to the full internet, so internet DNS may or may not work. This is why the initial connection is made to an IP address.

> **Note**
> Since there may not be a real internet host, the IP 10.254.1.223 is used to simulate a host on the internet. In reality, this is just a secondary address on the ClearPass server, but since this IP is not allowed by the guest-logon policy, it works fine for the captive portal redirect.

2. You should get redirected by the switch to the ClearPass guest logon page. Do not attempt to logon at this point.

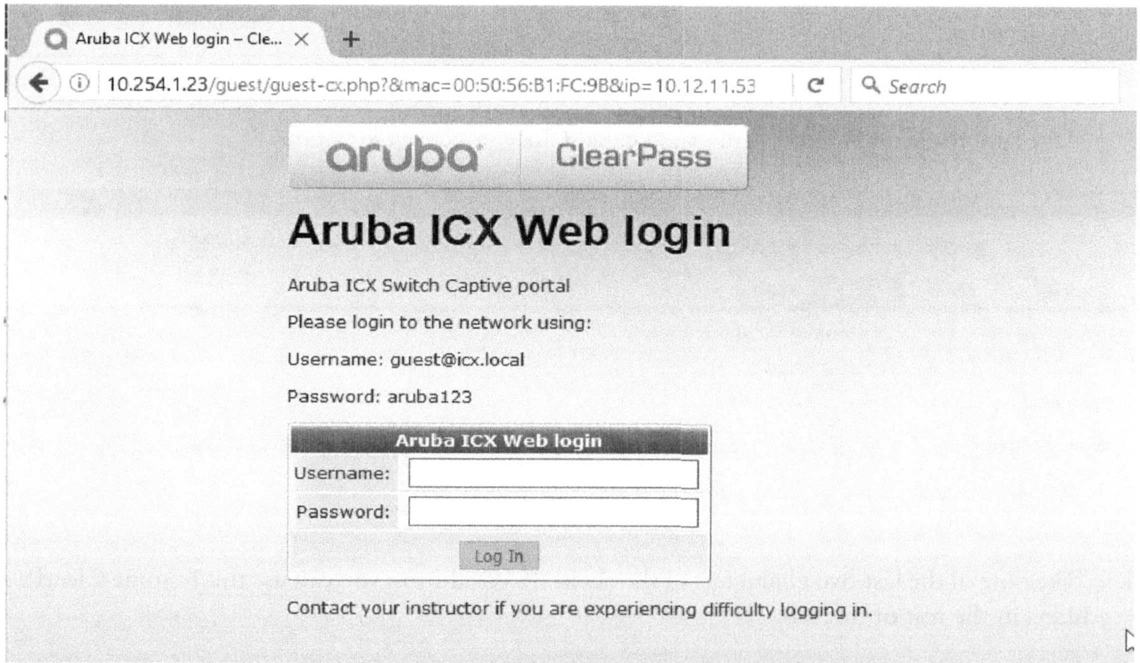

3. Verify that this 'guest-logon' role does not have access to the simulated 'internal' network. Open another tab in the browser and attempt to open a web page to the Core CX switch on http://10.X.11.1. This should also be redirected to the ClearPass captive portal.

Task 3: Define the Guest Role

Objectives

In this task, the user-role that will be assigned to authenticated guests will be defined.

In the lab, it is simulated that an authenticated guest cannot access the internal resources and has full http/https access to the internet. In a real deployment, these rules should be adjusted based on the customer requirements. Since the lab may not have real internet access for the test clients, the host 10.254.1.223 is used to verify access.

The 'internal resources' are defined as '10.0.0.0/8', except for the 10.254.1.0/24 range (since that range is used to test 'internet' access).

Steps

1. On the Access1 switch, define new class to describe the internal network.

```
ICX-Tx-Access1-guest-vsa(config)# class ip internal-networks
ICX-Tx-Access1-guest-vsa(config-class-ip)# ignore any
any10.254.1.0/255.255.255.0
ICX-Tx-Access1-guest-vsa(config-class-ip)# match any any
10.0.0.0/255.0.0.0
```

2. Review the configuration.

```
ICX-Tx-Access1-guest-vsa(config-class-ip)# show run cur
class ip internal-networks
   10 ignore any any 10.254.1.0/255.255.255.0
   20 match any any 10.0.0.0/255.0.0.0
ICX-Tx-Access1-guest-vsa(config-class-ip)# exit
```

3. Define a new policy using the new class and some of the previously defined classes.

```
ICX-Tx-Access1-guest-vsa(config)# port-access policy guest
ICX-Tx-Access1-guest-vsa(config-pa-policy)# class ip dhcp-dns-icmp
ICX-Tx-Access1-guest-vsa(config-pa-policy)# class ip cppm-web action
cir kbps1024 cbs 2048 exceed drop
ICX-Tx-Access1-guest-vsa(config-pa-policy)# class ip internal-networks
actiondrop
ICX-Tx-Access1-guest-vsa(config-pa-policy)# class ip any-web
```

4. Review the configuration.

```
ICX-Tx-Access1-guest-vsa(config-pa-policy)# show run cur
port-access policy guest
   10 class ip dhcp-dns-icmp
   20 class ip cppm-web action cir kbps 1025 cbs 2048 exceed drop
   30 class ip internal-networks action drop
   40 class ip any-web
ICX-Tx-Access1-guest-vsa(config-pa-policy)# exit
```

5. Define a new user-role; associate the policy to the user-role. Set the re-authentication period to 5 min (300 seconds).

Note

In a real deployment, this timer would be much higher, based on the customer requirements. In this lab, the guest authentication is only valid for 5 minutes to be able to demonstrate the logon/logoff process and repeat the task if required.

```
ICX-Tx-Access1-guest-vsa(config)# port-access role guest
ICX-Tx-Access1-guest-vsa(config-pa-role)# associate policy guest
ICX-Tx-Access1-guest-vsa(config-pa-role)# vlan access 11
ICX-Tx-Access1-guest-vsa(config-pa-role)# reauth-period 300
ICX-Tx-Access1-guest-vsa(config-pa-role)# exit
```

6. On the client PC4, enter the credentials on the guest login page:
    - Username: **guest@icx.local**
    - Password: **aruba123**

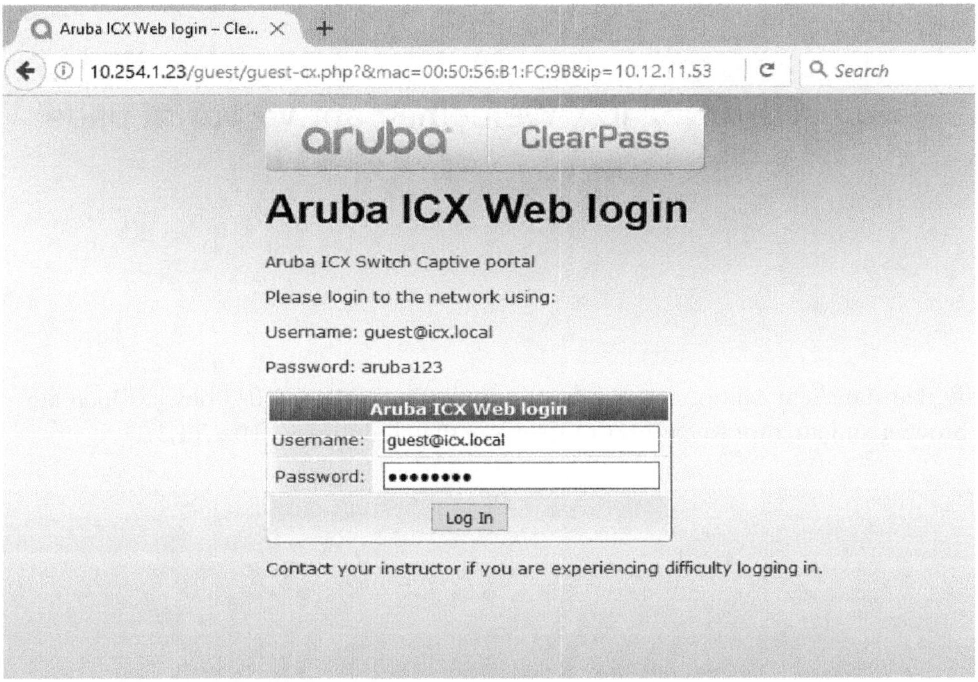

7. ClearPass has been configured to show a logon timer to the 'guest' user. This gives the network some time to complete the CoA and the re-authentication with the 'guest' role.

8. After the timer expires, ClearPass will redirect the client browser to a forced welcome page.

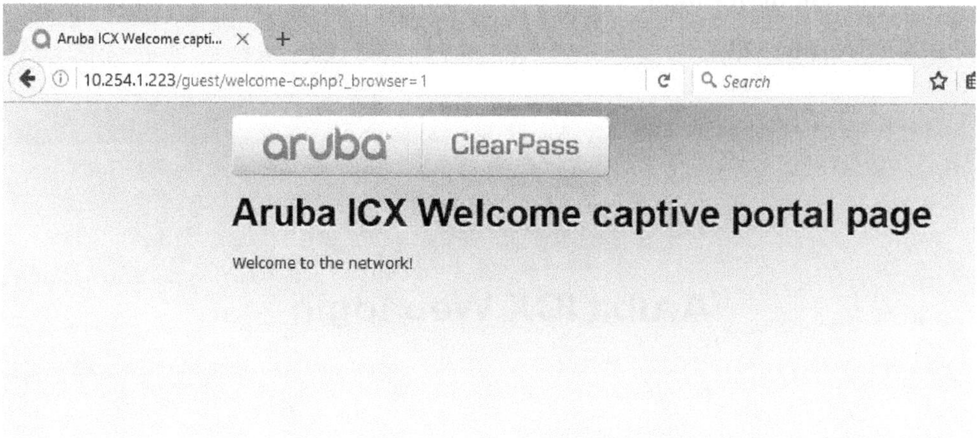

9. Verify that the client cannot access other resources in the 10.0.0.0/8 block. Open a new tab in the browser and attempt to connect to the Core switch on http://10.x.11.1/.

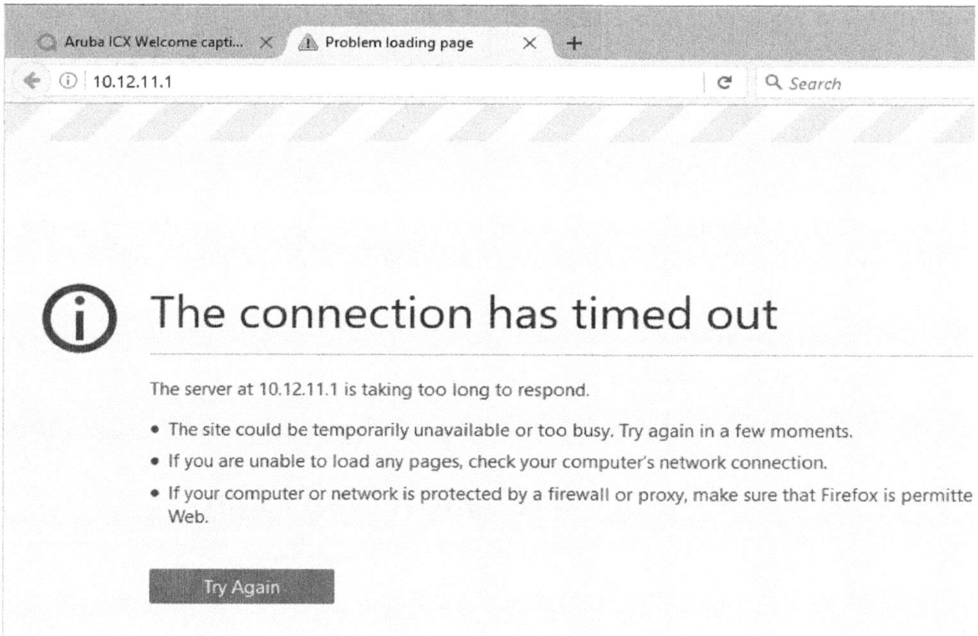

10. On the Access1 switch, review the authenticated devices on port 1/1/27.

```
ICX-Tx-Access1-guest-vsa(config)# show aaa authentication port-access
interface 1/1/27 client-status
Port Access Client Status Details
Client 00:50:56:b1:fc:9b, guest@icx.local
============================
   Session Details
   ---------------
      Port         : 1/1/27
      Session Time : 149s

   Authentication Details
   ----------------------
      Status          : mac-auth Authenticated
      Auth Precedence : dot1x - Not attempted, mac-auth - Authenticated

   Authorization Details
   ----------------------
      Role   : guest
      Status : Applied
```

Question: The switch is using mac-authentication on this port 1/1/27; how is it possible to see the username guest@icx.local in the authentication details?

Answer: While mac-auth is using the mac address as the authentication username sent from the switch to ClearPass, in the response from ClearPass, there is a 'user-name' AVP in the access-accept to the switch, so the switch has a meaningful username for the mac-auth. By default, this would just be the mac address.

11. Check ClearPass Access Tracker. Use the Host MAC address filter and apply the last 2 characters of your client MAC address. First, there is the WEBAUTH by the user, then the guest credentials are submitted to ClearPass. On success authentication, ClearPass updates the endpoint with the correct attributes to mark the MAC address as 'valid'. The success authentication also includes a CoA instruction to trigger re-authentication on the switch.

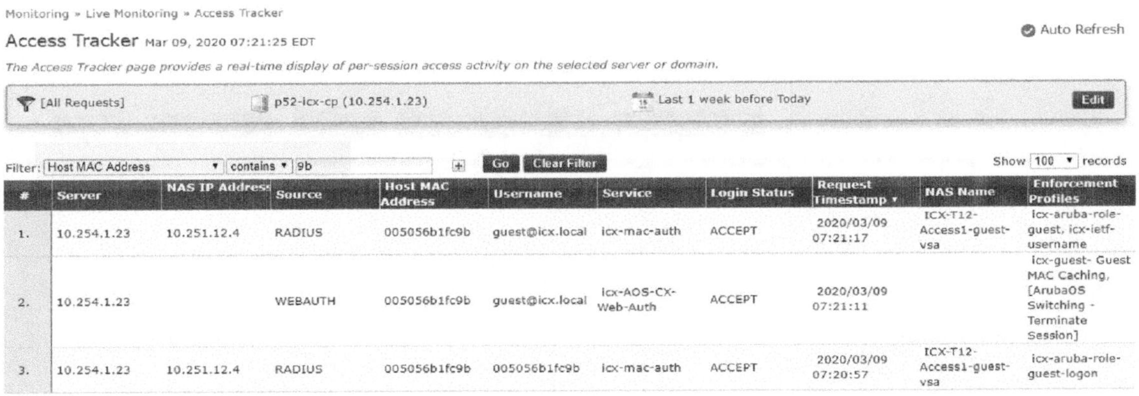

#	Server	NAS IP Address	Source	Host MAC Address	Username	Service	Login Status	Request Timestamp	NAS Name	Enforcement Profiles
1.	10.254.1.23	10.251.12.4	RADIUS	005056b1fc9b	guest@icx.local	icx-mac-auth	ACCEPT	2020/03/09 07:21:17	ICX-T12-Access1-guest-vsa	icx-aruba-role-guest, icx-ietf-username
2.	10.254.1.23		WEBAUTH	005056b1fc9b	guest@icx.local	icx-AOS-CX-Web-Auth	ACCEPT	2020/03/09 07:21:11		icx-guest- Guest MAC Caching, [ArubaOS Switching - Terminate Session]
3.	10.254.1.23	10.251.12.4	RADIUS	005056b1fc9b	005056b1fc9b	icx-mac-auth	ACCEPT	2020/03/09 07:20:57	ICX-T12-Access1-guest-vsa	icx-aruba-role-guest-logon

12. Open this 'WEBAUTH' entry.

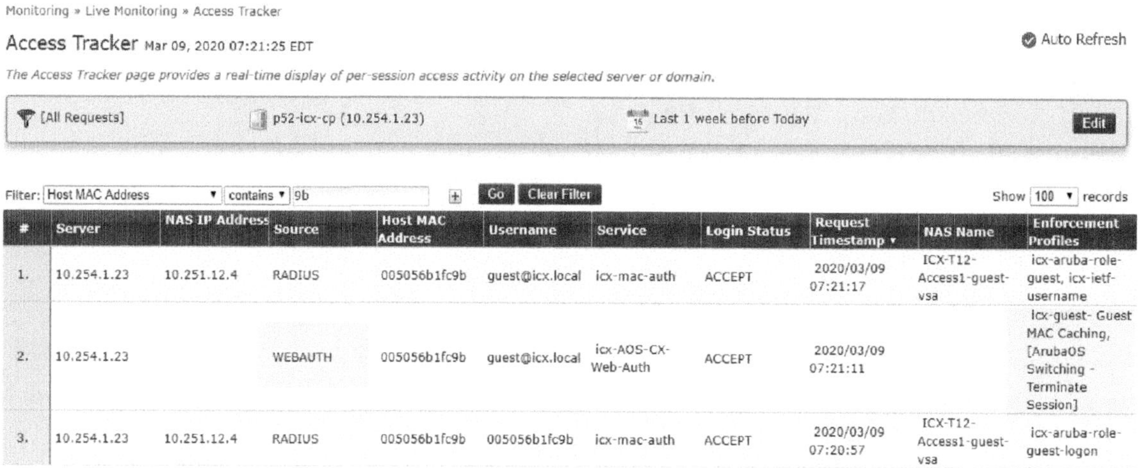

13. Click '**Output**' and verify it shows attributes that have been written on the endpoint. Close the entry.

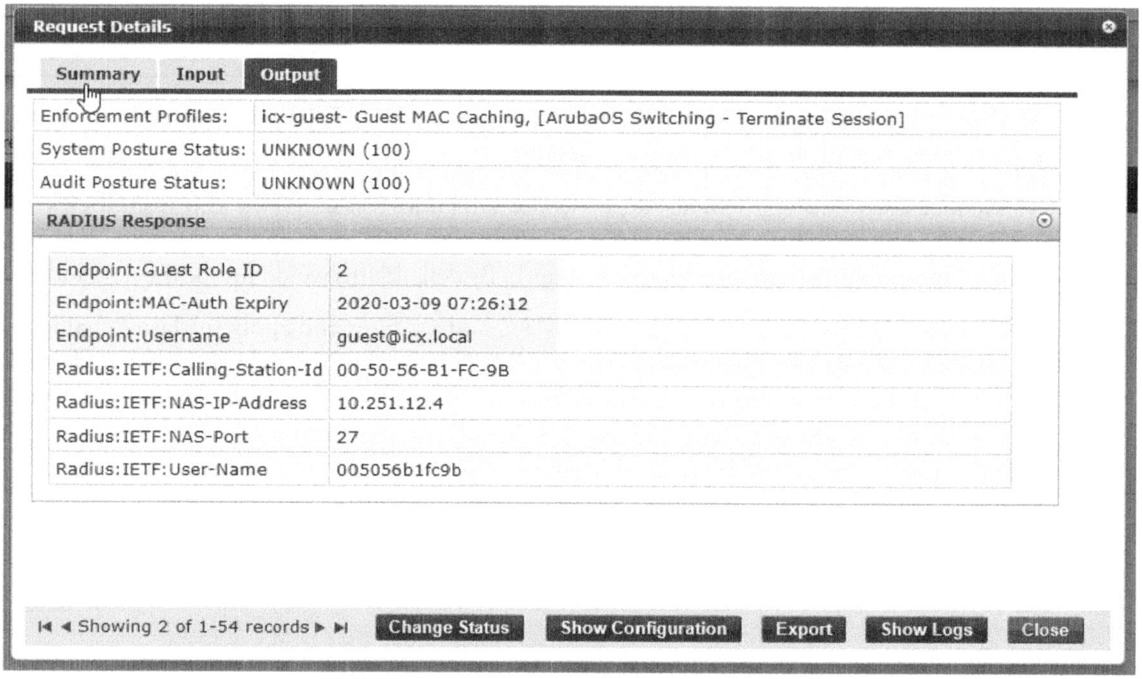

14. A few seconds later, a new RADIUS authentication request will be sent by the switch. This time, the mac-auth will be able to verify the attributes on the endpoint, and the '**guest**' role will be returned.

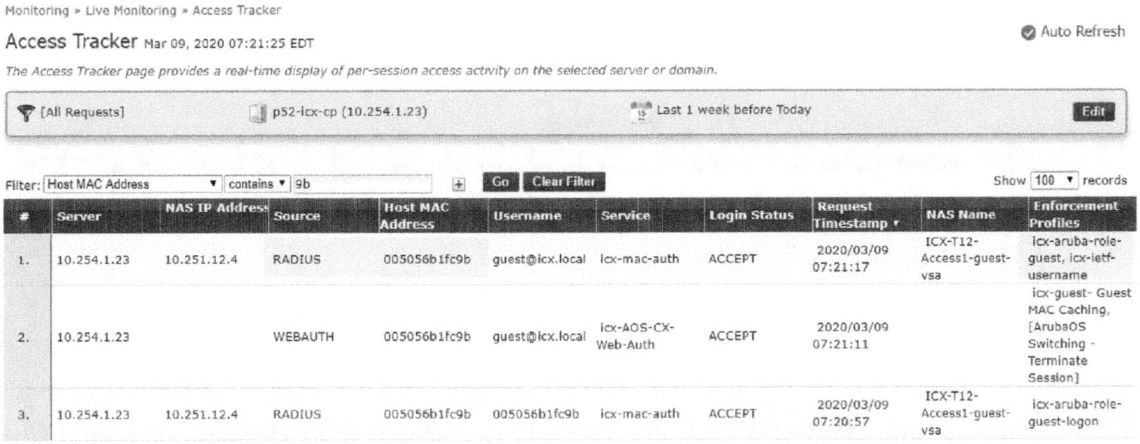

15. Open the entry; verify in the '**Output**' that the RADIUS access-accept contains the Aruba user-role '**guest**' and the **user-name** attribute. It is based on this attribute that the switch is able to show a 'username' for the mac-authenticated devices. Close the entry.

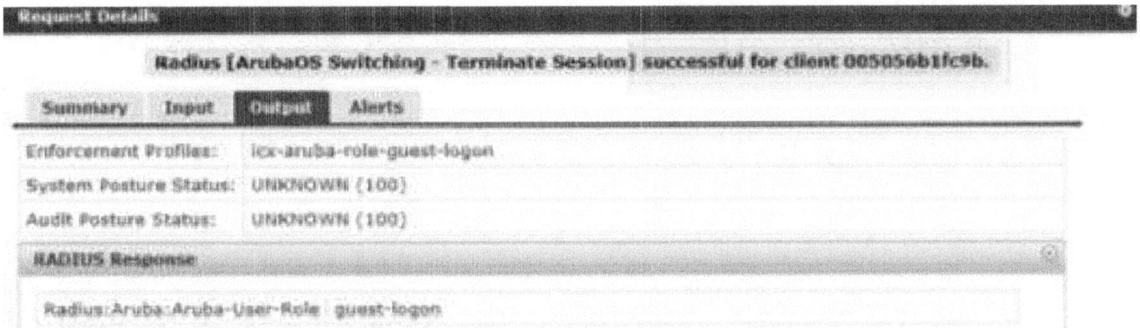

16. Open the *previous* RADIUS session; this is the session that returned the 'guest-logon' for the mac-authentication.

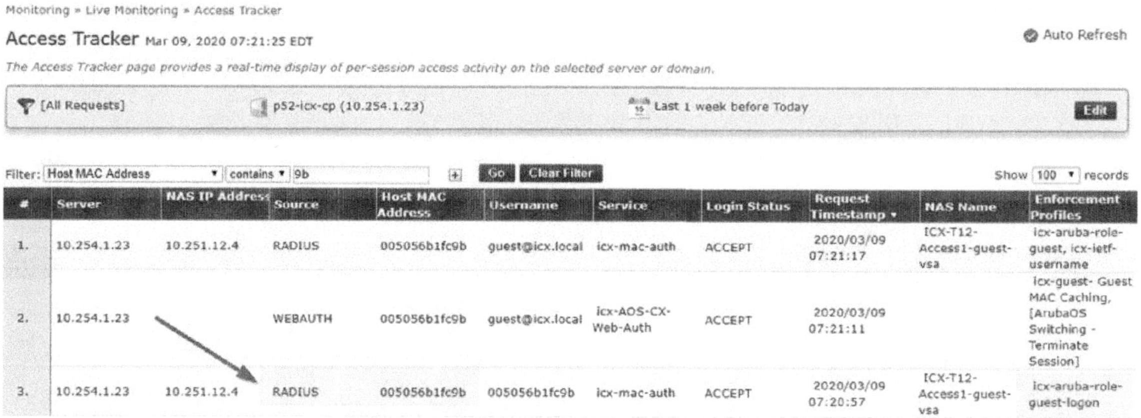

17. This should show a '**RADIUS CoA**' tab. Click on this tab and verify there is a **successful** CoA performed for that session.

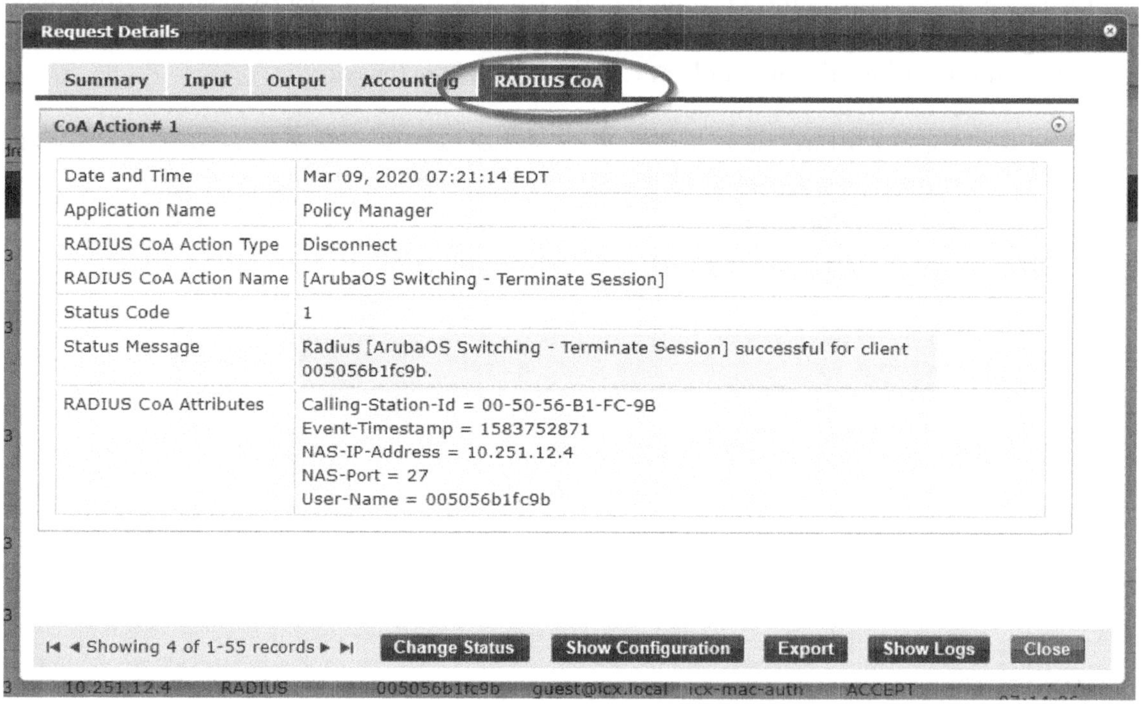

18. Wait about 5 minutes since the guest user has successfully logged in.

Note

In this lab environment, the mac-caching timer has been configured to 5 minutes only, to demonstrate the guest expiration feature as well. In a real deployment, the MAC-caching timer will be much longer.

---

19. On the client PC4, navigate to **http://10.254.1.223** again (You may just 'refresh' the Welcome page if that is still open). Since the authentication has expired, the client has now to be authenticated again as 'guest-logon', so the captive portal page will be shown again.

20. This demonstrates the captive portal configuration process.

Lab Cleanup

1. Change the hostname of the switch to the default hostname, so remove the 'guest' and 'vsa' strings from the hostname.

```
ICX-Tx-Access1-guest-vsa(config)# hostname ICX-Tx-Access1
ICX-Tx-Access1(config)#
```

Learning Check

1. How does the AOS-CX switch know that a user has successfully authenticated on captive portal hosted by a ClearPass server?
    a. MAC authentication
    b. RADIUS CoA
    c. RADIUS authentication
    d. Web authentication
2. What is one benefit of an Aruba ClearPass Guest solution?
    a. It automatically activates the proper authentication settings on AOS-CX switch ports.
    b. It enables companies to develop mobile engagement services for their guests.
    c. It provides self-registration through a captive portal for guests.
    d. It provides load balancing through a virtual IP address.

Summary

Congratulations! In this chapter, you have explored appropriate situations for implementing various guest and BYOD solutions. You can now implement captive portal authentication to integrate AOS-CX switches with an Aruba ClearPass Guest or Onboarding solution.

16 HPE6-A73 Practice Test

OBJECTIVES

✓ Reinforce the material you have learned.

✓ Become familiar with the type and style of questions found on the ACSP exam.

Overview

This chapter provides sample test questions and answers based on the style and difficulty you would find on the real HPE6-A73 exam for the Aruba Certified Switch Professional (ACSP) certification exam.

Exam Information

The ACSP exam validates you have an intermediate level knowledge of Aruba AOS-CX switches and can implement them in a campus design. Candidate should know how to read a customer request and extract the information needed for a large switched campus network. Candidate should know how to implement key technologies like VSX, NetEdit, and NAE, as well as understanding and implementing key networking technologies like advanced routing, security, QoS, and management features.

The exam tests the skills necessary to implement and operate enterprise-level Aruba campus switching solutions. It tests skills of configuring and managing modern, open standards-based networking solutions using ArubaOS-CX routing and switching technologies in medium to large enterprise network solutions.

Ideal Candidate for This Exam

Typical candidates for the ACSP exam are networking IT professionals who have advanced-level implementation experience with ArubaOS-CX wired switching solutions. This candidate has a minimum of four to five years of general networking experience and two years of experience focused on interpreting network architectures and customer requirements to install and configure Aruba solutions. It is suggested all candidates take the course for this exam.

Exam Contents

The ACSP exam has 60 questions. Here are types of questions to expect:

- Multiple choice (multiple responses)
- Multiple choice (single response)

Advice to Help You Take the Exam

Complete the training and review all course materials and documents before you take the exam. Use additional reference materials such as HPE Press study guides, self-directed labs, and practice tests. Exam items are based on expected knowledge acquired from job experience, an expected level of industry standard knowledge, or other prerequisites (events, supplemental materials, etcetera). Successful completion of the course (*Implementing ArubaOS-CX Switching, Rev. 20.21*) or study materials alone does not ensure you will pass the exam.

HPE6-A73 Exam Objectives

Table 16-1 breaks down the objectives covered on the exam.

Table 16-1 HPE6-A73 Exam Objectives

Percentage of Exam	Sections/Objectives
15%	Plan the wired network solution. • Given a scenario with a design and/or a set of customer requirements, determine an appropriate implementation plan.
43%	Install and configure the wired network solution. • Install and Configure NetEdit. • Given an implementation plan, explain how to physically configure the switches. • Given the implementation plan, explain how to configure Layer-2 technologies. • Given an implementation plan, explain how to configure and validate Layer-3 interfaces, services, routing protocols, and overlays. • Explain multicast features and configuration concepts. • Explain Aruba Switch security features and configuration concepts. • Explain QoS Aruba Switch features and configuration concepts. • Explain Aruba solutions integration and configuration concepts.

Table 16-1 HPE6-A73 Exam Objectives—cont'd

Percentage of Exam	Sections/Objectives
22%	Troubleshoot the wired network solution. • Given a scenario, identify a network failure (IP mismatch, VLAN mismatch, hardware configuration or failure, port configuration). • Given an action plan to remediate an issue, determine the implications to the network state. • Given a scenario, determine the cause of the performance problem (QoS issue, configuration issue HW and software, end-node issue).
20%	Manage, maintain, optimize, and monitor the wired network solution. • Given a scenario, determine a strategy to implement configuration management (maintenance, auditing, backup, archiving). • Analyze data that represents the operational state of a network and determine the appropriate action.

Exam Information

Table 16-2 summarizes the information for the exam to register for this exam. You need an HPE Learner ID and a Pearson VUE login and password. No reference material is allowed at the testing site. This exam may contain beta test items for experimental purposes. During the exam, you can make comments about the exam items. HPE/Aruba welcomes these comments as part of our continuous improvement process. To register for the exam, visit http://www.pearsonvue.com/hpe.

Table 16-2 Exam Information

Exam ID	HPE6-A73
Exam type	Proctored
Exam duration	90 minutes
Passing score	71%
Delivery languages	English

Note

More and current information concerning the HPE6-A73 exam can be found here: https://certification-learning.hpe.com/TR/datacard/Exam/HPE6-A73.

Practice Test Questions

The questions listed below are similar to the types of questions you would find on the HPE6-A66 exam. There are three questions each from Chapters 1 through 15, totaling 30 questions. Good luck!

1. To which two databases in the NAE does a Python programmer have access?

   a. Time-series

   b. API

   c. Audit

   d. Configuration

2. Which AOS-CX feature do all AOS-CX switches support to alleviate head-of-line (HOL) blocking?

   a. VOQ

   b. SP

   c. WFQ

   d. DWRR

3. What protocol must be enabled on AOS-CX switches to allow NetEdit to fully manage them?

   a. LLDP

   b. HTTPS

   c. CDP

   d. SNMP

4. A network administrator is managing a network of AOS-CX and third-party vendor switches. The administrator installed NetEdit to fully manage the AOS-CX switches. When accessing the topology window, the administrator is not seeing the third-party devices. Which protocol should be configured on the third-party devices to allow NetEdit to see and monitor them?

   a. HTTPS

   b. SSH

   c. SNMP

   d. ADP

5. A network administrator is interested in monitoring the delay for voice traffic and creating an alarm when the delay exceeds a threshold. Which AOS-CX feature should the administrator implement to solve this problem?

   a. NetEdit

   b. QoS

   c. NAE

   d. VSX

6. A network administrator notices that after performing a firmware upgrade of 6400 campus core switches, some of the ASE NAE scripts stopped working. What should the administrator do to fix this issue?

   a. Download updated scripts from Aruba.

   b. Reboot the affected AOS-CX switches.

   c. Re-install the scripts.

   d. Restart the scripts.

7. An administrator is implementing an AOS-CX VSX switch stack. The administrator defines the following:

   switch(config)# **interface lag 1**

   switch(config-lag-if)# **no shutdown**

   switch(config-lag-if)# **no routing**

   switch(config-lag-if)# **vlan trunk native 1**

   switch(config-lag-if)# **vlan trunk allowed all**

   switch(config-lag-if)# **lacp mode active**

   The administrator then attempts to enable active-active gateway on VLAN 11's SVI interface, but is unsuccessful in getting the feature to work for devices in VLAN 11. What should the administer do to fix this issue?

   a. Enable keepalives on LAG 1.

   b. Enable active-active gateway in the VSX context.

   c. Enable VRRP on the SVI interface.

   d. Define LAG 1 as multi-chassis.

8. Which of the following is considered an Aruba best practice when implementing a VSX stack?
   a. Use a direct layer-2 connection for the keepalives.
   b. Use at least a single 40GbE connection for the ISL link.
   c. Change the default system-defined MAC addressing.
   d. Lower the default timers.
9. Which is true regarding the use of ACLs on AOS-CX switches?
   a. Applying an ACL that has no entries permits all traffic.
   b. A packet that matches no ACE rule is permitted, by default.
   c. An inverse wildcard mask is used to match on a range of addresses.
   d. An ACL cannot be applied to tunnel and layer-3 LAG interfaces.
10. Object groups provide what benefit for AOS-CX switches?
   a. They reduce the number of entries in the TCAM tables.
   b. They make management of addresses and ports easier.
   c. They reduce the number of actual statements used to filter traffic by the OS.
   d. They can be used to implement stateful filtering functions.
11. An administrator implements a totally stubby solution for Area 1 on AOS-CX switches with the following criteria:

   * Area 0 has 20 routes

   * Area 1 has 10 routes

   * Area 2 has 25 routes

   * An ASBR in area 1 is advertising 2 routes

   * Currently area 1 only has one ABR.

   How many OSPF routes will Area 1 routers, with the exception of the ABR, have in their routing table?
   a. 10
   b. 11
   c. 13
   d. 46

12. Which of the following is true regarding LSA types and OSPF?
    a. An LSA 5 external type 2 should be used to select the closest exit point.
    b. An LSA 5 external type 1 should be used to ensure traffic through a firewall is seen in both directions.
    c. An LSA 5 external type 2 should be used to define a primary exit with a secondary backup exit.
    d. An LSA 5 external type 1 should be used to leverage all paths to destinations.
13. Place the BGP metrics in the order that AOS-CX switches use them when evaluating the best path to use for a route.
    a. Local preference
    b. Locally originated
    c. Weight
    d. AS path length
14. What configuration should an administrator implement on AOS-CX switches to define a local preference policy for specific routes from a service provider?
    a. AS path list
    b. Route map
    c. ACL
    d. Policy-based routing
15. An administrator is using a protocol analyzer to examine multicast traffic using an IP address of 239.0.0.1. What MAC address would this traffic be using?
    a. 01.00.5F.00.00.01
    b. 01.00.5E.39.00.01
    c. 01.00.5F.39.00.01
    d. 01.00.5E.00.00.01
16. When implementing a multicast solution in an access-layer VLAN where the switches are configured in a layer-3 VSX stack, how will the network operate?
    a. The IGMP group databases are automatically synchronized.
    b. IGMP synchronization of the group databases must be enabled.
    c. Join and leave messages are synchronized across the VSX ISL LAG.
    d. IGMP should be enabled at the distribution/aggregation layer.

17. Which of the following is correct regarding PIM and AOS-CX switches?
    a. PIM is not supported on GRE tunnels and VXLAN interfaces.
    b. PIM-DM and PIM-SM can be used in the same VRF.
    c. Active-active forwarding is supported with PIM-DM and PIM-SM.
    d. PIM is enabled on layer-2 and layer-3 interfaces.
18. A network of AOS-CX switches is running PIM-DM. Traffic is currently pruned from some uplinks. A new receiver needs to see traffic that is currently pruned. What message type will the AOS-CX switch send to its upstream neighbor to start the forwarding of the requested multicast stream?
    a. Join
    b. Graft
    c. Elect
    d. Unpause
19. Which of the following is true regarding 802.1X user authentication on AOS-CX switches?
    a. 802.1X must be enabled both globally and per port.
    b. Interim accounting is automatically enabled when start-stop is enabled.
    c. Change of authorization is automatically enabled.
    d. A RADIUS group must be defined.
20. Which of the following solutions allows you to implement user roles and/or open-standard RADIUS VSA attributes with an 802.1X server where the company has implemented a free RADIUS server?
    a. Downloadable user roles and open-standard RADIUS VSAs
    b. Downloadable local user roles and open-standard RADIUS VSAs
    c. Local user roles and open-standard RADIUS VSAs
    d. Downloadable local user roles
21. Which of the following is true regarding MAC-Auth and AOS-CX switches?
    a. By default, MAC-Auth is performed before 802.1X on a port.
    b. By default, device mode is implemented when MAC-Auth is enabled.
    c. By default, MAC-Auth must use a different RADIUS server group than 802.1X.
    d. By default, client mode has a default limit of one MAC address.

22. An administrator connects a Windows 10 desktop into the data port of a phone, and the phone's LAN port into a port on an AOS-CX 6300 switch. The Windows 10 desktop is configured for 802.1X, but the phone is not. The switch interface has both 802.1X and MAC-Auth configured and these are enabled globally; all other settings on the interface are factory-default. Which of the following is true regarding authentication of devices on this port?

    a. The first device authenticated is the only device allowed on the port.

    b. The phone will fail authentication since it does not have 802.1X configured.

    c. The first device authenticated on the port opens the port for both devices.

    d. The desktop is authenticated with 802.1X and the phone with MAC-Auth, where their respective policies are applied to each device's MAC address.

23. A large building has an access layer comprised of eight 6405 series switches that connect to a large number of user desktops and laptops, IoT devices, security cameras, and printers. Because of security issues, management requires that all devices go through some type of access control, where Aruba Mobility Controllers, via user-based tunneling, can perform stateful and application inspection. The 6405 switches are configured for VSX. How many Mobility Master (MM) licenses are required for these switches to interface with an MM?

    a. 1

    b. 2

    c. 4

    d. 8

24. When implementing LUR with user-based tunneling, which of the following is true regarding the switch configuration and/or operation?

    a. An SSL server certificate must be manually installed on the switch.

    b. The server's username and password must be defined on the switch.

    c. A transit VLAN must be defined on the switch.

    d. MD5 security must be enabled for PAPI.

25. Which type of queuing tracks the number of bits sent for each packet stream on the egress port?

    a. SP

    b. VoQ

    c. DWRR

    d. WFQ

26. Which of the following is true regarding QoS on AOS-CX switches?
    a. CoS trust has precedence over DSCP trust.
    b. CoS trust is enabled by default.
    c. DSCP trust is enabled by default.
    d. Trust is disabled by default.
27. When implementing policy-based routing (PBR), which of the following is true in regard to AOS-CX switches?
    a. A hop list can be defined that specifies the exact layer-3 hops a packet should take from the source router.
    b. Traffic can be dropped by referencing an ACL in the PBR policy.
    c. If the nexthop and default-nexthop are not reachable, the routing table routes are used to route the packets.
    d. The nexthop and default-nexthop are monitored every 60 seconds.
28. A company has an AOS-CX access switch solution, which performs access control on the edge. Employee and guest access are controlled through 802.1X and captive portal authentication, respectively. Currently, a large number of IoT devices, used for building management, also connected to the switches; however, these devices only support MAC authentication. These devices are managed by a server in the data center. The administrator is concerned about the security of these devices and wants to ensure that their traffic is not intermixed with either the employee or guest traffic as it is forwarded to the server in the data center. What solution should the company implement so that the traffic is tunneled to the server in the data center?
    a. Policy-based routing
    b. User-based tunneling
    c. PAPI tunneling
    d. Port-based tunneling
29. When performing captive portal, what method is used to denote that the user has successfully authenticated to the network, where the network is comprised of AOS-CX switches and AAA servers?
    a. HTTPS
    b. RADIUS dynamic authorization
    c. RADIUS MAC-Auth
    d. Restful API

30. What is true regarding VSX and VSF.

    a. VSF requires active-active gateway for actively forwarding edge device traffic.

    b. Both have the ports disabled, by default.

    c. VSX supports different versions of code on the switches.

    d. Both support dual-control planes on the AOS-CX switches.

Practice Test Answers

This section contains the answers to the Practice Test questions. Besides listing the correct answer, the wrong answers have explanations as to why they are wrong.

1. ☑ **A and D**. An NAE agent monitors the current state of one or more attributes in the Configuration and State Database and then writes the state to a Time-Series Database for an ongoing record. **Reference: Chapter 1**.

   ☒ **B and C** are incorrect because these databases do not exist on AOS-CX switches.

2. ☑ **A**. AOS-CX switching platforms utilize VOQ where the majority of the buffering within the switch is on the ingress port. While the physical buffer is on the input, it represents packets queued on the output side (hence the name virtual output queuing). VOQ is a technique that allows buffers to be balanced across sources contending for a congested output port. To prevent head-of-line blocking. **Reference: Chapter 1**.

   ☒ **B** is incorrect because even though all AOS-CX switches support strict priority queuing, it cannot prevent head-of-line blocking, especially on modular switches. **C and D** are incorrect because not all AOS-CX switches support these queuing solutions, nor can they prevent head-of-line locking, especially on modular switches.

3. ☑ **B**. The REST API interface is disabled by default, and like the HTTPS protocol, must be enabled. The RESTful API uses HTTPS as a transport. Likewise, access requires a switch account with administrative access—thus SSH must also be enabled and a full administrative account username and password must be configured. **Reference: Chapter 2**.

   ☒ **A and C** are incorrect because LLDP is only used in the discovery (not management) process and CDP is not used at all. **D** is incorrect because SNMP is only required for third-party devices.

4. ☑ **C**. SNMP is used to monitor third-party devices in NetEdit. **Reference: Chapter 2**.

   ☒ **A and B** are incorrect because these protocols are used by NetEdit to fully manage AOS-CX switches. **D** is incorrect because ADP is not supported.

5. ☑ **C**. The Aruba NAE is a first-of-its-kind, built-in framework for network assurance and remediation. Combining the full automation and deep visibility capabilities of the AOS-CX operating system, this unique framework enables monitoring, collecting network data, evaluating conditions, and taking corrective actions through simple scripting agents. **Reference: Chapter 3**.

   ☒ **A** is incorrect because NetEdit is used for network management. **B** is incorrect because QoS is used to prevent service issues, not generate alarms when thresholds are reached. **D** is incorrect because VSX is used to provide a highly resilient dual-control plane switching solution.

6. ☑ **A**. An AOS-CX software update might require updates to scripts as well. **Reference: Chapter 3**.

   ☒ **B, C, and D** are incorrect because these answers will not fix this issue.

7. ☑ **D**. A LAG must be defined as "multi-chassis" in order to take advantage of VSX features like active-active gateway. Without this enabled, active forwarding is available, but not active-active gateway. **Reference: Chapter 4**.

   ☒ **A** is incorrect because keepalives is a feature used to prevent a split-brain condition in a VSX stack. **B** is incorrect because active-active gateway is defined on an SVI on a multi-chassis LAG. **C** is incorrect because active-active gateway provides a better redundant solution for the active gateway than VRRP.

8. ☑ **C**. Define the VSX system-MAC addresses and do ***not*** let it default to the built-in system-MAC addresses. **Reference: Chapter 4**.

   ☒ **A** is incorrect because you should use a direct Layer-3 connection for the keepalive connection. **B** is incorrect because the ISL LAG should use at ***least*** 2x40G or faster links. **D** is incorrect because you should leave the timers at their default value.

9. ☑ **A**. Applying an ACL ID for an ACL that does not exist or has no entries permits all traffic. **Reference: Chapter 5**.

   ☒ **B** is incorrect because of the implicit deny rule. **C** is incorrect because a subnet mask or a "/" nomenclature is used to match on a range of packets. **D** is incorrect because an ACL can be applied to layer-3 LAG interfaces.

10. ☑ **B**. Object groups are useful for defining groups of IP addresses and Layer-4 ports for use exclusively in the ACE rules. Often, common groups of addresses and ports or port ranges are used repeatedly in many ACL definitions. Without address and port object groups, the same addresses and ports must be repeated in each ACL definition that uses them. **Reference: Chapter 5**.

    ☒ **A and C** are incorrect because the OS must expand the object entries into separate statements to implement the filtering policies. **D** is incorrect because stateful firewall functions are not currently supported by AOS-CX.

11. ☑ **B**. Since Area 1 is a totally stubby area, it will only see intra-area routes and a default route from the ABR—any external routes (even if the ASBR is in Area 1) will not appear in their routing tables. **Reference: Chapter 6**.

    ☒ **A** is incorrect because it is missing the default route for all other routes outside of area 1. **C** is incorrect because external routes are ignored inside the area. **D** is incorrect because it includes routes from other areas.

12. ☑ **C**. You want to have a primary exit with a secondary backup exit: External Type 2, the primary with a lower default metric than the secondary. **Reference: Chapter 6**.

    ☒ **A** is incorrect because an external type 1 is recommended. **B** is incorrect because an external type 2 is recommended. **D** is incorrect because an external type 2 is recommended.

13. ☑ **C. Weight, local preference, locally originated, and AS path length**, in that order. **Reference: Chapter 7**.

    ☒ **A**, **B**, and **D** are incorrect because weight has the highest preference for BGP metrics.

14. ☑ **B**. Local preference is a metric used in internal BGP to determine the best exit to reach a particular route. A prefix-list and route-map are used to define a preference for specific routes. **Reference: Chapter 7**.

    ☒ **A** is incorrect because an AS path list would match on all routes for an AS(es). **C** is incorrect because ACLs cannot be used with route maps. **D** is incorrect because PBR cannot be used to define BGP metrics.

15. ☑ **D**. An IP address of 293.0.0.1 would have a layer-2 MAC address of 01.00.5E.00.00.01. **Reference: Chapter 8**.

    ☒ **A and C** are incorrect because multicast MAC addresses begin with 01.00.5E. **B** is incorrect because only the lower 23 bits are carried from the IP to MAC and thus the fourth set of hexadecimal digits would be 0, not 39.

16. ☑ **C**. Join/leave messages always forwarded across the ISL link. **Reference: Chapter 8**.

    ☒ **A and B** are incorrect because the switches must build their own group databases: they are never synched between the two switches. **D** is incorrect because the access layer is layer 3; in this situation, PIM would be used between access and aggregation, not IGMP.

17. ☑ **A**. PIM is not currently supported on GRE and VXLAN interfaces. **Reference: Chapter 9**.

    ☒ **B** is incorrect because both cannot be run in the same VRF at the same time, but can be run in different VRFs. **C** is incorrect because active-active forwarding is not supported for PIM-DM. **D** is incorrect because PIM is enabled on layer-3 interfaces.

18. ☑ **B**. Graft messages are used on pruned links to restart the forwarding of a particular multicast stream. **Reference: Chapter 9**.

☒ **A** is incorrect because this is an IGMP message. **C and D** are incorrect because these are non-existent message types.

19. ☑ **A**. You must enable 802.1X both globally and per port. **Reference: Chapter 10**.

☒ **B** is incorrect because interim account must be individually enabled. **C** is incorrect because dynamic authorization must be manually enabled. **D** is incorrect because when a RADIUS server is defined on the switch, it is automatically added to the default RADIUS group called "radius".

20. ☑ **C**. When interfacing with a third-party AAA server solution, local user roles with Aruba's VSA and open-standard RADIUS VSAs can be implemented. **Reference: Chapter 10**.

☒ **A, B, and D** are incorrect because downloadable user roles is only supported with a ClearPass AAA solution.

21. ☑ **D**. The default mode on a port when either 802.1X or MAC-Auth is enabled on the port is client mode, where the default limit is one MAC address. **Reference: Chapter 11**.

☒ **A** is incorrect because 802.1X is performed first, by default. **B** is incorrect because client mode is the default. **C** is incorrect because there is no restriction as to what resource an AAA group can be used by.

22. ☑ **A**. Because the default mode is client mode with a limit of one MAC address, the first device that authenticates is the only device allowed on the port. **Reference: Chapter 11**.

☒ **B** is incorrect because MAC-Auth is enabled on the port. **C** is incorrect because client mode is the default operation. **D** is incorrect because client mode is the default operation, with a limit of one MAC address (client).

23. ☑ **D**. Each switch would need to be licensed separately when using VSX, and thus 8 MM licenses would need to be purchased. **Reference: Chapter 12**.

☒ **A** is incorrect because one license would only be correct for a stack of eight VSF, not VSX, switches. **B** is incorrect because two licenses would only be correct for two stacks of four VSF, not VSX, switches. **C** is incorrect because four licenses would only be correct for four stacks of two VSF, not VSX, switches.

24. ☑ **C**. When implementing UBT, a transit VLAN must be defined and referenced on the switch. **Reference: Chapter 12**.

☒ **A and B** are incorrect because these apply to downloadable, not local, user roles. **D** is incorrect because MD5 security for PAPI is for the control connection and is optional.

25. ☑ **D**. WFQ is based on fair queuing (FQ), which is designed to achieve fair sharing of bandwidth among queues regardless of packet size. A theoretical way to achieve completely fair transmission for queues with packets of different sizes would be to use bit by bit round robin forwarding rather than packet by packet round robin forwarding. One bit from one queue is forwarded, then one bit from the next queue, and so on. However, this

mechanism is not actually achievable in the real world because packets need to be transmitted as whole components, not interspliced bits. **Reference: Chapter 13**.

☒ **A** is incorrect because the strict priority queue has the highest priority and the queuing's methods bandwidth percentage will determine how much traffic is processed at a time. **B** is incorrect because VoQ affects traffic traveling between the ingress and egress ports. **D** is incorrect because DWRR looks at the number of bytes, and not bits, that are transmitted.

26. ☑ **D**. By default, the global setting is "none," and all ports have no trust setting. **Reference: Chapter 13**.

☒ **A** is incorrect depending on what is configured for the port or globally. **B and C** are incorrect because these are not enabled, by default.

27. ☑ **C**. If the **nexthop/default-nexthop** entry/entries are not reachable in the action list, routing decisions will return to the system routing table. **Reference: Chapter 14**.

☒ **A** is incorrect because only the next-hop can be specified. **B** is incorrect because to drop traffic in a PBR, a null interface must be referenced. **D** is incorrect because these are monitored every 5 seconds.

28. ☑ **A**. policy-based routing allows the switch to route traffic, via a GRE tunnel, to a specific destination. **Reference: Chapter 14**.

☒ **B** is incorrect because the destination must be an Aruba Mobility Controller (MC). **C** is incorrect because PAPI is used as the control plane connection between an AOS-CX switch and an MC when performing UBT. **D** is incorrect because the destination would have to be an Aruba MC and in 10.4, port-based tunneling is not currently supported.

29. ☑ **B**. Once the user authenticates to the web portal, the AAA server uses RADIUS dynamic authorization (change of authorization, or CoA) to notify the switch of the user's successful authentication. **Reference: Chapter 15**.

☒ **A and D** are incorrect because this is used for DUR. **C** is incorrect because this is what the switch initially performs, which fails for the user's first access and causes the user to be redirected to the captive portal page.

30. ☑ **C**. Aruba has designed VSX to deliver high availability during software upgrades. The upgrade occurs with near zero downtime and with continuous packet forwarding, where each switch can be upgraded separately. **Reference: Chapter 4**.

☒ **A** is incorrect because this is true of only VSX switches. **B** is incorrect because this is only true for VSF. **D** is incorrect because this is true of only VSX.

Appendix A Learning Check Answers

Overview

This appendix contains the answers to all the Learning Checks found in the previous chapters.

Chapter 1: Introduction to Aruba Switching

This section contains the learning check answers for Chapter 1.

1. ☑ **A**
2. ☑ **C**
3. ☑ **C**

Chapter 2: NetEdit

This section contains the learning check answers for Chapter 2.

1. ☑ **B**
2. ☑ **A and B**
3. ☑ **A**
4. ☑ **A, B, C, F, and G**

Chapter 3: Network Analytics Engine (NAE)

This section contains the learning check answers for Chapter 3.

1. ☑ **B**
2. ☑ **C**
3. ☑ **A**

Chapter 4: VSX

This section contains the learning check answers for Chapter 4.

1. ☑ **B**
2. ☑ **B**
3. ☑ **Link-up delay: Helps avoid traffic drop at VSX LAGs right after a reboot; Active-Gateway: Provides default gateway redundancy; Inter-Switch Link: Used for data path traffic forwarding between VSX switches; Keepalive: Helps prevent split-brain; Active-Forwarding: Optimizes forwarding for upstream devices.**

Chapter 5: ACLs

This section contains the learning check answers for Chapter 5.

1. ☑ **D**
2. ☑ **B**
3. ☑ **B**
4. ☑ **A**

Chapter 6: Advanced OSPF

This section contains the learning check answers for Chapter 6.

1. ☑ **OSPF areas segment the domain into more stable and manageable pieces. Each OSPF routing device maintains the LSDB and runs the shortest path algorithm only for its own areas. A multi-area design decreases LSDB size and increases stability—routers do not have to re-run the SPF algorithm as often. It also lets you aggregate advertisements of networks in between areas, simplifying the routing table and further increasing stability. You can also control routes at this boundary, filtering them if you want. These benefits still apply even for powerful routers that could support very large areas.**
2. ☑ **C**
3. ☑ **B**
4. ☑ **C**
5. ☑ **B**

6. ☑ **LSA 1: Links (ID, type, and metric); LSA 2: DR IP on the network, network mask, IDs of routers attached to the network; LSA 3: Network in another area (network IP, mask, and metric); LSA 4: ASBR router ID and metric; LSA 5: External network, mask, metric, metric type; LSA 7: External network, mask, metric, metric type, but must be translated by ABR before sending it to Area 0.**

Chapter 7: BGP

This section contains the learning check answers for Chapter 7.

1. ☑

	OSPF	BGP
Type of routing protocol (IGP or EGP)	**IGP (a single AS)**	**EGP (between ASes)**
Designed for routing tables of what size	**Thousands of routes**	**Hundreds of thousands or even millions of routes**
How neighbor relationships are established	**Neighbors automatically discovered on OSPF networks**	**Connections established in TCP sessions only with manually configured neighbors**
What neighbors advertise to each other	**Link states (within an area)** **Routes (between areas)**	**Routes**

2. ☑ **C**
3. ☑ **B**

Chapter 8: IGMP

This section contains the learning check answers for Chapter 8.

1. ☑ **D**
2. ☑ **B**
3. ☑ **False**
4. ☑ **False**

Chapter 9: Multicast Routing

This section contains the learning check answers for Chapter 9.

1. ☑ **B**
2. ☑ **B**

Chapter 10: 802.1X Authentication

This section contains the learning check answers for Chapter 10.

1. ☑ **B**
2. ☑ **A and D**

Chapter 11: MAC Authentication

This section contains the learning check answers for Chapter 11.

1. ☑ **B**
2. ☑ **B**

This section contains the learning check answers for Chapter 12.

1. ☑ **C**
2. ☑ **B**
3. ☑ **B**

Chapter 13: Quality of Service

This section contains the learning check answers for Chapter 13.

1. ☑ **D**
2. ☑ **A**
3. ☑ **D**

Chapter 14: Additional Routing Technologies

This section contains the learning check answers for Chapter 14.

1. ☑ **B**
2. ☑ **default**
3. ☑ **B**

Chapter 15: Captive Portal Authentication

This section contains the learning check answers for Chapter 15.

1. ☑ **B**
2. ☑ **C**